The Works of Tho

By Thomas Watson

Contents

The Art of Divine Contentment

I have learned to be content in whatever circumstances I am. I know both how to have a little, and I know how to have a lot. In any and all circumstances I have learned the secret of being content — whether well-fed or hungry, whether in abundance or in need. I am able to do all things through Him who strengthens me.

Philippians 4:11-13

'Man is born unto trouble, as the sparks fly upward'; therefore we all need to learn the same lesson as Paul. 'I have learned,' he said 'in whatever state I am, therewith to be content,' Philippians 4:11. Believers especially wish to attain to a holy composure in their tribulations and under the stresses caused by our increasingly secular society.

The Introduction to the Text

These words are brought in to anticipate and prevent an objection. The apostle had, in the former verse, laid down many grave and heavenly exhortations: among the rest, 'to be anxious for nothing.'

Not to exclude: 1. A prudential care; for, he who provides not for his own house, 'has denied the faith, and is worse than an infidel.' (1 Ti. 5:8)

Nor, 2. A religious care; for we must give all 'diligence to make our calling and election sure.' (2 Pe. 1:10) But,

3. To exclude all anxious worry about the outcomes and events of things; 'do not be anxious about your life—what you shall eat.' (Mat. 6:25) And in this sense it should be a Christian's care not to be anxious. The in the Greek signifies 'to cut the heart in pieces,' a soul-dividing worry; take heed of this. We are bid to 'commit our way unto the Lord;' (Psalm 37:5) the Hebrew word is, 'roll your way upon the Lord.' It is our work to cast away anxiety; (1 Pe 5:7) and it is God's work to take care.

By our immoderate worry, we take his work out of his hand. Worry, when it is extreme, either distrustful or distracting, is very dishonorable to God; it takes away his providence, as if he sat in heaven and did not mind the things here below; like a man who makes a clock, and then leaves it to run by itself. Immoderate worry takes the heart off from better things; and usually while we are thinking how we shall live—we forget how to die. Worry is a spiritual canker which wastes and dispirits; we may sooner by our worry add a furlong to our grief than a cubit to our comfort. God does threaten it as a curse, 'they shall eat their bread with worry.' (Ez. 12:1) Better to fast—than eat of that bread. 'Be anxious for nothing.'

Now, lest anyone should say, 'Yes, Paul you preach that to us which you have scarce learned yourself; have you learned not to be anxious?' The apostle seemed tacitly to answer that, in the words of the text; 'I have learned, in whatever state I am, therewith to be content,' a speech worthy to be engraved upon our hearts, and to be written in letters of gold upon the crowns and diadems of princes.

The text does branch itself into these two general parts.

I. The scholar, Paul; 'I have learned.'

II. The lesson; 'in every state to be content.'

The First Branch of the Text

The Scholar, with the First Proposition.

I begin with the first: the scholar, and his proficiency: 'I have learned.' Out of which I shall observe two things by way of explanation.

1. The apostle does not say, 'I have heard, that in every estate I should be content,' but, 'I have learned.' Whence our first doctrine, that it is not enough for Christians to hear their duty — but they must learn their duty. It is one thing to hear and another thing to learn; as it is one thing to eat and another thing to cook. Paul was a practitioner. Christians hear much — but it is to be feared, learn little. There were four kinds of soils in the parable, (Lu. 8:5) and but one good ground. This is an emblem of this truth — many hearers — but few learners.

There are two things which keep us from learning.

1. Slighting what we hear. Christ is the pearl of great price; when we disesteem this pearl, we shall never learn either its value, or its virtue. The gospel is a rare mystery. In one place, (Ac. 20:24) it is called 'the gospel of grace;' in another, (1 Cor. 4:4) 'the gospel of glory;' because in it, as in a transparent glass, the glory of God is resplendent. But he who has despises this mystery, will hardly ever learn to obey it. He who looks upon the things of heaven as unimportant things; and perhaps the driving of a trade, or carrying on some politic design to be of greater importance, this man is in the high road to damnation, and will hardly ever learn of things concerning his salvation. Who will learn that which he thinks is scarcely worth learning?

2. Forgetting what we hear. If a scholar has his rules laid before him, and he forgets them as fast as he reads them, he will never learn. (Ja. 1:25) Aristotle calls the memory the scribe of the soul; and Bernard calls it the stomach of the soul, because it has a retentive faculty, and turns heavenly food into nutrition. We have great memories in other things, we remember that which is vain. Cyrus could remember the name of every soldier in his huge army. We remember injuries; his is to fill a precious cabinet of the mind, with dung. But as Hierom says, how soon do we forget the sacred truths of God!

We are apt to forget three things: our faults, our friends, our instructions. Many Christians are like sieves; put a sieve into the water, and it is full; but take it forth of the water, and all runs out. Just so, while they are hearing a sermon, they remember something: but like the sieve out of the water — as soon as they are gone out of the church, all is forgotten. 'Let these sayings, (says Christ) sink down into your ears;' (Lu. 9:44) in the original it is, 'put these sayings into your ears,' as a man that would hide the jewel from being stolen, locks it up safe in his chest. Let them sink in. The Word must not fall only as dew that wets the leaf — but as rain which soaks to the root of the tree, and makes it fructify. O, how often does Satan, that fowl of the air, pick up the good seed that is sown!

USE. Let me put you upon a serious trial. Some of you have heard much — you have lived forty, fifty, sixty years under the blessed trumpet of the gospel — what have you learned? You may have heard a thousand sermons, and yet not learned one. Search your consciences.

1. You have heard much against sin. Are you hearers — or are you learners? How many sermons have you heard against covetousness, that it is the root, on which pride and idolatry grow? One calls it a metropolitan sin; it is a complex evil, it does twist a great many sins in with it. There is hardly any sin — but covetousness is a main ingredient of it. And yet are you like the two daughters of the horse-leech, which cries, 'Give! Give!' How much have you heard against rash anger? That is a temporary insanity; that it rests in the bosom of fools? And upon the least occasion do your spirits begin to take fire? How much have you heard against swearing. It is Christ's express mandate, 'swear not at all.' (Mat. 5:34) This sin of all others may be termed the unfruitful work of darkness. It is neither sweetened with pleasure, nor enriched with profit — the usual colors with which Satan paints sin. While the swearer shoots his oaths, like flying arrows at God to pierce his glory — God shoots 'a flying scroll' of curses against him. And do you make your tongue a racket by which you toss oaths as tennis balls? Do you sport

yourselves with oaths, as the Philistines did with Samson, which will at last pull the house down on you? Alas! How have they learned what sin is, who have not learned to leave sin! Does he know what a viper sin is — who will play with it?

2. You have heard much of Christ. Have you learned Christ? The Jews, as Jerome says, carried Christ in their Bibles — but not in their heart. The sound 'went into all the earth; (Ro. 10:18) the prophets and apostles were as trumpets, whose sound went abroad into the world. Yet many thousands who heard the noise of these trumpets, had not learned Christ, 'they have not all obeyed.' (Ro. 10:16)

(1.) A man may know much of Christ — and yet not learn Christ. The devils knew Christ. (Mat. 1:24)

(2.) A man may preach Christ, and yet not learn Christ — as Judas and the false apostles. (Ph. 4:15)

(3.) A man may profess Christ, and yet not learn Christ. There are many professors in the world, who Christ will profess against. (Mat. 7:22, 23)

Question. What it is then to learn Christ?

1. To learn Christ is to be made like Christ, to have the divine character of his holiness engraved upon our hearts. 'We all with open face, beholding as in a glass the glory of the Lord, are changed into the same image.' (2 Cor. 3:18) There is a metamorphosis made; a sinner, viewing Christ's image in the looking-glass of the gospel, is transformed into that image. Never did any man look upon Christ with a spiritual eye — but he went away quite changed. A true saint is a divine landscape picture, where all the rare beauties of Christ are lively portrayed and drawn forth — he has the same spirit, the same judgment, the same will — with Jesus Christ.

2. To learn Christ, is to believe in him — 'my Lord, and my God,' (John 20:28) when we do not only believe God — but in God, which is the actual application of Christ to ourselves, and as it were — the spreading of the sacred medicine of his blood upon our souls. You have heard much of Christ, and yet cannot with a humble adherence say, 'my Jesus;' do not be offended if I tell you — the devil can say his creed as well as you!

3. To learn Christ, is to love Christ. When we have Bible-lives, our lives like rich diamonds cast a sparkling luster in the church of God, and are, in some sense, parallel with the life of Christ, as the transcript with the original. So much for the first notion of the word.

The Second Branch of the Text

This word, 'I have learned,' is a word which imports difficulty. It shows how hard the apostle came by contentment of mind; it was not bred in nature. Paul did not come naturally by it — but he had learned it. It cost him many a prayer and tear, it was taught him by the Spirit. Whence our second doctrine — that good things are hard to come by. The business of true religion is not so easy as most imagine. 'I have learned,' says Paul. Indeed — you need not teach a man to sin; this is natural, (Psalm 58:3) and therefore easy. It comes as water out of a spring. It is an easy thing to be wicked; hell will be taken without storm; but matters of piety must be learned. The trade of sin needs not to be learned — but the art of divine contentment is not achieved without holy industry. 'I have learned.'

There are two pregnant reasons why there must be so much study and exertion:

1. Because spiritual things are against nature. Everything in piety is opposite to nature. There are two things in true religion, and both are against nature.

(1.) Matters of faith. As, for men to be justified by the righteousness of another, to become a fool that he may be wise, to save all by losing all — this is against nature.

(2.) Matters of practice. As, self-denial. As for a man to deny his own wisdom, and see himself blind. As to have his own will, and have it melted into the will of God. As to be plucking out the right eye, beheading and crucifying that sin which is the favorite, and lies nearest to the heart. As for a man to be dead to the world, and in the midst of need to abound. As for him to take up the cross, and follow Christ, not only in golden — but in bloody paths. As to embrace religion, when it is dressed in rags, and all the jewels of honor and preferment are pulled off. All this is against nature — and therefore must be learned.

Likewise with self-examination; for a man to take his heart, as a watch, all in pieces; to set up a spiritual inquisition, and traverse things in his own soul; to take David's candle and lantern, (Psalm 119:105) and search for sin; nay, as judge, to pass the sentence upon himself! (2 Sa. 34:17) This is against nature and will not easily be attained to without learning.

Likewise with self-reformation; to see a man, as Caleb, walking opposite to how he once walked, the current of his life altered, and running into the channel of piety — this is wholly against nature. When a stone ascends, it is not a natural motion — but a violent. Just so, the motion of the soul heaven-ward is a violent motion, it must be learned; flesh and blood is not skilled in these things; nature can no more cast out nature, than Satan can cast out Satan.

2. Because spiritual things are above nature. There are some things in the world that are hard to find out, which are not learned without study. What then are divine things, which are in sphere above the world, and beyond all human learning? Only God's Spirit can light our candle here. The apostle calls these 'the deep things of God.' The gospel is full of jewels — but they are locked up — away from sense and reason. The angels in heaven are searching into these sacred depths. (1 Pe. 22)

USE. Let us beg the Spirit of God to teach us. We must be 'divinely taught.' God's Spirit must must teach — or we cannot learn. 'All your children shall be taught of the Lord'. (Is. 54:13) A man may read the figure on the dial — but he cannot tell how the day goes, unless the sun shines upon the dial. Just so, we may read the Bible over — but we cannot learn effectually, until the Spirit of God shines into our hearts. (2 Cor. 4:6) O implore this blessed Spirit! 'I am the Lord your God, who teaches you to profit.' (Is. 48:17) Ministers may tell us our lesson, God alone can teach us.

We have lost both our hearing and sight, therefore are very unfit to learn. Ever since Eve listened to the serpent, we have been deaf; and since she looked on the tree of knowledge we have been blind. But when God comes to teach, he removes these impediments. (Is. 35:5)

We are naturally dead. (Ep. 2:1) Who can teach a dead man? Yet, behold, God undertakes to make dead men to understand mysteries! God is the grand teacher. This is the reason the preached Word works so differently upon men. There are two men in one pew — the one is wrought upon effectually by the Spirit; the other lies at the ordinances as a dead child at the breast, and gets no nourishment. What is the reason for this? Because the heavenly gale of the Spirit blows upon the one, and not upon the other. One has the anointing of God, which teaches him all things (1 John 2:27) the other has it not. God's Spirit speaks sweetly — but irresistibly. In that heavenly doxology, none could sing the new song — but those who were sealed in their foreheads, (Re. 14:2) reprobates could not sing it. Those who are skillful in the mysteries of salvation, must have the seal of the Spirit upon them. Let us make this our prayer: 'Lord, breathe your Spirit into your Word!' We have a promise, which may add wings to prayer; 'if you then being evil know how to give good gifts unto your children; how much more shall your heavenly Father give the Holy Spirit to those who ask him?' (Lu. 11:13) And thus much of the first part of the text, the scholar, which I intended only as a short summary.

The Lesson itself, with the Proposition.

I come to the second, which is the main thing—the lesson itself, 'in whatever state I am, therewith to be content.' Here was a rare piece of learning indeed! The text has but few words in it; 'in every state content:' but if that be true—that the most golden sentence is ever measured by brevity and suavity, then, this is a most accomplished speech. The text is like a precious jewel—little in quantity—but great in worth and value!

The main proposition I shall insist upon, is this—that a gracious spirit is a contented spirit. The doctrine of contentment is very superlative, and until we have learned this—we have not learned to be Christians.

1. It is a hard lesson. The angels in heaven had not learned it; they were not contented. Though their estate was very glorious—yet they were still soaring aloft, and aimed at something higher; 'the angels which kept not their first estate.' They kept not their estate, because they were not contented with their estate. Our first parents, clothed with the white robe of innocency in paradise, had not learned to be content; they had aspiring hearts, and would be crowned with the Deity, and 'be as gods.' Though they had the choice of all the trees of the garden—yet none would content them but the tree of knowledge, which they supposed would have been as eye-salve to have made them omniscient. O then, if this lesson was so hard to learn in the original state of innocency, how hard shall we find it, who are clogged with corruption!

2. It is of universal extent, it concerns all people.

(a.) It concerns rich men. One would think it needless to press those to contentment whom God has blessed with great estates—but rather persuade them to be humble and thankful; nay—but I say, be content. Rich men have their discontents as well as others! When they have a great estate—yet they are discontented that they have no more; they would make the hundred into a thousand. The drunkard—the more he drinks, the more he thirsts. Just so with covetousness. An earthly heart is like the grave, which is 'never satisfied;' therefore I say to you, rich men—be content! Rich men are seldom content with their large estates; though they have estate enough, they have not honor enough; if their barns are full enough—yet their turrets are not high enough. They would be somebody in the world, as Theudas, 'who boasted himself to be somebody.' (Ac. 5:36) They never go so cheerfully as when the wind of honor and applause fills their sails; if this wind is low—they are discontented.

One would think Haman had as much as his proud heart could desire; he was set above all the princes, advanced upon the pinnacle of honor, to be the second man in the kingdom; (Es. 3:1) yet in the midst of all his pomp, because Mordecai would not bow to him—he is discontented, and full of wrath, and there was no way to assuage this madness of revenge—but by spilling all the Jews' blood. (The itch of honor is seldom allayed, without blood.) Therefore I say to you rich men—be content!

Rich men, if we may suppose them to be content with their honor and magnificent titles—yet they have not always contentment in their relations. She who lies in the bosom, may sometimes blow the coals; as Job's wife, who would have him curse God himself; 'curse God, and die!' Sometimes children cause discontent. How often is it seen that the mother's milk, nourishes a viper! He who once sucked her breast, goes about to suck her blood! Parents often gather thorns from grapes, and thistles from figs. Children are sweet-briar; like the rose, which is a fragrant flower—but has its prickles. Our family comforts are not all pure wine—but mixed; they have in them more dregs than spirits. They are like that river which in the morning runs sweet—but in the evening runs bitter. We have no charter of exemption granted us in this life; therefore rich men had need be called upon to be content.

(b.) The doctrine of contentment concerns poor men. You who suck so liberally from the breasts of providence—be content; it is an hard lesson, therefore it had need be learned very early. How hard is it when the livelihood is even gone, a great estate boiled away almost to nothing—then to be contented. The means of subsistence is in Scripture called our life, because it is the very sinews of life. The woman in the gospel spent 'all her living upon the physicians;' (Lu. 8:43) in the Greek it is, she spent her whole life upon the physicians, because she spent her means by which she should live. It is hard to be content when poverty has clipped our wings! But, though hard, 'contentment in poverty' is an excellent virtue. ⱽ

The apostle had 'learned in every state to be content.' God had brought Paul into as great variety of conditions as ever we read of any man—and yet he was content; else surely he could never have gone through it with so much cheerfulness. See into what vicissitudes this blessed apostle was cast! 'We are troubled on every side,' (2 Cor 4:8) there was the sadness of his condition; 'but not distressed,' there was his contentment in that condition. 'We are perplexed,' there is his affliction; 'but not in despair,' there is his contentment. And, if we read a little further, 'in afflictions, in necessities, in distresses, in stripes, in imprisonments, in tumults, etc.' (2 Cor 6:4,5) there is his trouble. Behold his contentment, 'as having nothing—yet possessing all ✓ things.' When the apostle was driven out of all—yet in regard of that sweet contentment of mind which was like music in his soul—he possessed all. We read a short map or history of his sufferings; 'in prisons more frequent, in deaths often, etc.' (2 Cor. 11:23, 24, 25) Yet behold the blessed frame and temper of his spirit, 'I have learned, in whatever state I am, therewith to be content.' Whichever way providence blew, Paul had such heavenly skill and dexterity, that he knew how to steer his course. For his outward estate he was indifferent; he could be either on the top—or the bottom; he could sing either the dirge—or the anthem; he could be anything that God would have him to be. 'I know what it is to be in need—and how to abound.' Here is a rare pattern for us to imitate!

Paul, in regard of his faith and courage, was like a cedar, he could not be stirred. But for his outward condition, he was like a reed bending every way with the wind of providence. When a prosperous gale blew upon him, he could bend with that, 'I know how to be full;' and when a boisterous gust of affliction blew, he could bend in humility with that, 'I know how to be hungry.' Paul was like a dice—throw it whichever way you will—it always falls upon a bottom! Let God throw the apostle whichever way he would—he fell upon this bottom of contentment!

A contented spirit is like a watch: though you carry it up and down with you, yet the spring of it is not shaken, nor the wheels out of order—but the watch keeps its perfect motion. So it was with Paul—though God carried him into various conditions—yet he was not overly elated with the one, nor cast down with the other. The spring of his heart was not broken, the wheels of his affections were not disordered—but kept their constant motion towards heaven—still content.

The ship which lies at anchor may sometimes be a little shaken—but never sinks; flesh and blood may have its fears and disquiets—but grace keeps them afloat. A Christian, having cast anchor in heaven, his heart never sinks. A gracious spirit—is a contented spirit. This is a rare art! Paul did not learn it at the feet of Gamaliel. 'I have learned,' (Ph. 4:11) I am initiated into this holy mystery; as if he had said, I have gotten the divine art, I have the knack of it. God must make us right artists. If we should put some men to an art that they are not skilled in, how unfit would they be for it! Put a farmer to drawing pictures—what strange art work would he make? This is out of his sphere. Take a great painter, and put him to plough, or set him to planting, or grafting of trees—this is not his art—he is not skilled in it! Just so, bid a natural man live by faith, and when all things go contrary, to be contented, you bid him do what he has no skill in, you may as well bid an infant to guide the stern of a ship! To live contented upon God in the deficiency of outward comforts, is an art which 'flesh and blood has not learned;' nay, many of God's own children, who excel in some duties of religion, when they come to this art of contentment, how do they bungle! They have scarcely commenced the learning of this art.

The resolving of some questions.

For the illustration of this doctrine, I shall propound these questions.

Question 1. Should a Christian be insensible to his condition?

No — for then he is not a saint — but a stoic. Rachel did well to weep for her children — there was nature. But her fault was, she refused to be comforted — there was discontent. Christ himself was sensible, when he sweat great drops of blood, and said, 'Father, if it is possible, let this cup pass from me;' yet he was contented, and sweetly submitted his will: 'nevertheless, not as I will — but as you will.' The apostle bids us to humble ourselves 'under the mighty hand of God,' (1 Pe. 5:6) which we cannot do unless we are sensible of it.

Question 2. Whether a Christian may lay open his grievances to God.

Yes. 'Unto you have I opened my cause;' (Jer. 20:12) and David poured out his complaint before the Lord. (Psalm 142:2) We may cry to God, and desire him to write down all our injuries. Shall not the child complain to his father? When any burden is upon the heart, prayer gives vent, it eases the heart. Hannah's spirit was burdened; 'I am' says she, 'a woman of a sorrowful spirit.' Now having prayed, and wept, she went away, and was no more sad. Here is the difference between a holy complaint and a discontented complaint; in the one we complain to God; in the other we complain of God.

Question 3. What does contentment exclude?

There are three things which contentment banishes out of its diocese, and which can by no means dwell with it.

1. Contentment excludes a vexatious repining. Murmuring is properly the daughter of discontent. 'I mourn in my complaint.' (Psalm 55:2) He does not say 'I murmur in my complaint'. Murmuring is no better than mutiny in the heart; it is a rising up against God. When the sea is rough and unquiet — it casts forth nothing but foam. Just so, when the heart is discontented — it casts forth the foam of murmuring, anger, and impatience! Murmuring is nothing else, but the scum which boils off from a discontented heart!

2. Contentment excludes an uneven discomposure. When a man says, 'I am in such straits, that I know not how to evolve or get out, I shall be undone!' When his head and heart are so distracted, that he is not fit to pray or meditate, etc. When he is not himself — just as when an army is routed, one man runs this way, and another that, the army is put into disorder; so a man's thoughts run up and down distracted, discontent dislocates and unjoints the soul, it pulls off the wheels.

3. Contentment excludes a childish despondency. This is usually consequent upon the other. A man being in a hurry of mind, not knowing which way to extricate, or wind himself out of the present trouble, begins to faint and sink under it. For worry is to the mind as a burden to the back; it loads the spirits, and with overloading, sinks them. A despondent spirit is a discontented spirit.

Showing the Nature of contentment.

Having answered these questions, I shall in the next place, come to describe this contentment. It is a sweet temper of spirit, whereby a Christian carries himself in an equal poise in every condition. The nature of this will appear more clear in these three aphorisms.

1. Contentment is a divine thing. It becomes ours, not by acquisition—but as a gift from God. It is a slip taken off from the tree of life, and planted by the Spirit of God in the soul. It is a fruit that grows not in the garden of human learning—but is of a heavenly birth. It is therefore very observable that contentment is joined with godliness, 'godliness with contentment is great gain.' (1 Tim. 6:6) Contentment being an outgrowth of godliness, I call it divine, to distinguish it to that contentment, which a moral man may arrive at. Heathens have seemed to have this contentment—but it was only the shadow and picture of it—not the true diamond. Theirs was but civil, this is sacred; theirs was only from principles of human reason, this of religion; theirs was only lighted at nature's torch, this at the lamp of scripture. Reason may a little teach contentment, as thus: whatever my condition be, this is what I am born to; and if I meet with crosses, it is but the universal misery: all have their share, why therefore should I be troubled? Reason may suggest this; and indeed, this may be rather constraint; but to live securely and cheerfully upon God in the abatement of creature supplies, only piety can bring this into the soul's treasury.

2. Contentment is an internal thing. It lies within a man; not in the bark—but the root. Contentment has both its fountain and stream in the soul. The beams of comfort which a contented man has, do not arise from foreign comforts—but from within. As sorrow is seated in the spirit; 'the heart knows its own bitterness;' (Proverbs 14:10) so contentment lies within the soul, and does not depend upon externals. Hence I gather, that outward troubles cannot hinder this blessed contentment. It is a spiritual thing, and arises from spiritual grounds—the apprehension of God's love. When there is a tempest without, there may be music within. A bee may sting through the skin—but it cannot sting to the heart; outward afflictions cannot sting to a Christian's heart, where contentment lies. Thieves may plunder us of our money and goods—but not of this pearl of contentment, unless we are willing to part with it, for it is locked up in the cabinet of the heart. The soul which is possessed of this rich treasure of contentment, is like Noah in the ark—it can sing in the midst of a deluge.

3. Contentment is an habitual thing. It shines with a fixed light in the soul. Contentment does not appear only now and then, as some stars which are seen but seldom; it is a settled temper of the heart. One action does not denominate a person to be a contented person. One is not said to be a liberal man, who gives alms once in his life; a covetous man may do so. But he is said to be liberal, who is 'given to hospitality,' that is, who upon all occasions is willing to relieve the necessities of the poor. Just so, he is said to be a contented man, who is given to contentment. It is not casual but constant. Aristotle distinguishes between colors in the face that arise from passion, and those which arise from complexion. The pale face may look red when it blushes—but this is only a passion. He is said properly to be ruddy who is constantly so—it is his complexion. He is not a contented man, who is so upon some occasions, when things go well with him. A contented man, is so constantly—it is the habit and complexion in his soul.

Reasons Pressing to Holy Contentment.

Having opened the nature of contentment, I come next to lay down some reasons or arguments to contentment, which may preponderate with us.

The first is God's precept. (Contentment is charged upon us as a duty) 'be content with such things as you have.' (Heb. 13:5) The same God, who has bid us believe, has bid us to be content. If we obey not, we run ourselves into sin. God's Word is a sufficient warrant; it has authority in it. God's Word must be the star which guides, and his will the weight that moves our obedience; his will is a law, and has majesty enough in it to captivate us into obedience; our hearts must not be more unquiet than the raging sea, which at his Word is stilled.

The second reason enforcing contentment, is, God's promise. For he has said 'I will never leave you, nor forsake you.' (He. 13:5) Here God has engaged himself, under hand and seal for our necessary provisions. If a king should say to one of his subjects, I will take care of you; as long as I have any crown-revenues, you shall be provided for; if you are in danger – I will secure you; if in need – I will supply you. Would not that subject be content? Behold, God has here made promise to the believer, and as it were, entered into bond for his security, 'I will never leave you;' shall not this charm away the devil of discontent? 'Leave your fatherless children with me, I will preserve them alive.' (Jer. 49:11) Methinks I see the godly man on his death-bed much discontented, and hear him complaining what will become of my wife and children when he is dead and gone. God says, 'trouble not yourself, be content, I will take care of your children; and let your widow trust in me.' God has made a promise to us, that he will not leave us, and has entailed the promise upon our wife and children; and will not this satisfy us? True faith will take God's single bond, without calling for witnesses.

Be content, by virtue of a decree. Whatever our condition is, God the umpire of the world, has from everlasting, decreed that condition for us, and by his providence ordered all details thereunto. Let a Christian often think with himself, 'who has placed me here, whether I am in a high sphere, or in a lower. Not chance or fortune, as the blind heathens imagined. No! it is the wise God who has by his providence fixed me in this orb.'

We must act that scene which God would have us. Say not, 'such an one has occasioned this to me!' Look not too much at the under-wheel. We read in Ezekiel, of a 'wheel within a wheel.' (Ez. 1:16) God's decree is the cause of the turning of the wheels, and his providence is the inner-wheels which move all the rest. God's providence is that helm which turns about the whole ship of the universe. Say then, as holy David, 'I was silent, I opened not my mouth, because you, Lord, did it.' (Psalm 39:9) God's providence, which is nothing else but the carrying on of his decree – should be a counterpoise against discontent. God has set us in our station, and he has done it in wisdom.

We imagine that such a condition of life is good for us; whereas if we were our own carvers, we would often cut the worst piece. Lot, being put to his choice, chose Sodom, which soon after was burned with fire. Rachel was very desirous of children, 'give me children or I die,' and it cost her her life in bringing forth a child. Abraham was earnest for Ishmael, 'O that Ishmael might live before you!' but he had little comfort either from him or his seed; he was born a son of strife, his hand was against every man, and every man's hand against him. The disciples wept for Christ's leaving the world, they chose his physical presence: whereas it was best for them that Christ should be gone, for else 'the comforter would not come.' (John 16:7) David chose the life of his child, 'he wept and fasted for it;' (2 Sam. 12:16) whereas if the child had lived – it would have been a perpetual monument of his shame.

If we would be able to parcel out our own comforts, we would often parcel out that which is harmful to us. Is it not well for the child – that the parent should choose for it? Were it left to itself, it would perhaps choose a knife to cut its own finger. It is well for the patient that he is at the physician's appointment. The consideration of a decree determining, and a providence disposing of all things, should work our hearts to holy contentment. The wise God has ordered our condition; if he sees it better for us to abound – we shall abound; if he sees it better for us to be in need – we shall be in need. Be content to be at God's disposal.

God sees, in his infinite wisdom, the same condition is not best for all; that which is good for one, may be bad for another. One season of weather will not serve all men's occasions, one needs sunshine, another rain. One condition of life will not fit every man, no more than one suit of apparel will fit everybody. Prosperity is not fit for all, nor is adversity fit for all. If one man be brought low, perhaps he can bear it better; he has a greater stock of grace, more faith and patience; he can 'gather grapes from thorns', pick some comfort out of the cross. Everyone cannot do this. Another man is seated in an eminent place of dignity; he is fitter for it; perhaps it is a place which requires more wisdom, which everyone is not capable of; perhaps he can use his estate better, he has a public heart as well as a public place. The wise God sees that condition to be bad for one, which is good for another; hence it is, that he places men in different orbs and spheres; some higher, some lower. One man desires health, God sees sickness is better for him; God will work spiritual health out of physical sickness, by bringing the body of death, into a consumption. Another man desires liberty, God sees bondage to be better for him; he will work his liberty by bondage; when his feet are bound, his heart shall be most enlarged. Did we believe this, it would give a check to the sinful disputes and cavils of our hearts: 'Shall I be discontented at that which is enacted by God's decree, and ordered by His wise providence?' Is this to be God' child — or a rebel?

Use I. Showing how a Christian may make his life comfortable.

It shows how a Christian may come to lead a comfortable life, even an heaven upon earth, be the times what they will — by Christian contentment. The comfort of life does not consist in having much; it is Christ's maxim, 'a man's life consists not in the abundance of the things which he does possess,' (Lu. 12:15) but it is in being contented. Is not the bee as well contented with sucking from a flower — as the ox which grazes on the mountains? Contentment lies within a man, in the heart; and the way to be comfortable, is not by having our barns filled — but our minds quiet. 'The contented man,' says Seneca, 'is the happy man.'

Discontent is a fretting temper, which dries the brains, wastes the spirits, corrodes and eats out the comfort of life. Discontent makes a man not enjoy what he does possess. A drop or two of vinegar will sour a whole glass of wine. Just so, let a man have the affluence and all worldly comforts — a drop or two of discontent will embitter and poison all.

Comfort depends upon contentment. Jacob went halting, when the sinew upon the hollow of his thigh shrank: so, when the sinew of contentment begins to shrink, we go halting in our comforts. Contentment is as necessary to keep the life comfortable, as oil is necessary to keep the lamp burning. The clouds of discontent often drop the showers of tears.

Would we have comfort in our lives? We may have it if we will. A Christian may carve out whatever condition he will to himself. Why do you complain of your troubles? it is not trouble which troubles — but discontentment. It is not outward affliction which can make the life of a Christian sad; a contented mind would sail above these waters — but when discontent gets into the heart, then it is disquieted and sinks.

Use II. A check to the discontented Christian.

Here is a just reproof to such as are discontented with their condition. This disease is almost epidemic. Some not content with the calling which God has set them in, must be a step higher, from the plough to the throne; who like the spider in the Proverbs, will 'be in kings' palaces.' Others desire to go from the shop to the pulpit; (Nu. 12:2) they would be in the temple of honor, before they are in the temple of virtue. They are like apes, which most show their deformity when they are climbing. It is not enough that God has bestowed gifts upon men, in private to edify; that he has enriched them with many mercies — but must they 'seek you the priesthood also?' (Nu. 16:10)

What is this but discontent arising from pride? These secretly tax the wisdom of God, that he has not made their condition a peg higher. Every man is complaining that his estate is no better, though he seldom complains that his heart is no better. One man commends this kind of life, another commends that; one man thinks a country-life best, another a city-life; the soldier thinks it best to be a merchant, and the merchant to be a soldier. Men desire to be anything but what God would have them. How is it that no man is contented? Very few Christians have learned Paul's lesson: neither poor nor rich know how to be content, they can learn anything but this.

If men are poor, they learn to be envious; they malign those who are above them. Another's prosperity is an eye-sore. When God's candle shines upon their neighbor's tabernacle, this light offends them. In the midst of poverty, men can, in this sense, abound — namely, in envy and malice! An envious eye is an evil eye. They learn to be querulous, still complaining, as if God had dealt hardly with them; they are ever telling their needs, they lack this and that comfort, whereas their greatest need is a contented spirit. Those that are well enough content with their sin — yet are not content with their condition.

If men are rich, they learn to be covetous; thirsting insatiably after the world, and by unjust means scraping it together; their 'right hand is full of bribes,' as the Psalmist expresses it. (Psalm 26:10) Put a good cause in one scale, and a piece of gold in the other, and the gold weighs heaviest. There are, says Solomon, four things that say, 'it is not enough:' (Proverbs 30:15) I may add a fifth; the heart of a covetous man.

So we see that neither poor nor rich know how to be content. Never certainly since the creation did this sin of discontent reign, or rather rage, more than in our times; never was God more dishonored; you can hardly speak with any — but the passion of his tongue betrays the discontent of his heart! Everyone lisps out his discontent, and here even the stammering tongue speaks too freely and fluently. If we have not what we desire, God shall not have a good look from us — but presently we are sick with discontent. If God will not forgive the people of Israel for their lusts — they bid him take their lives; they must have quails to their manna! Ahab, though a king, and one would think his crown-lands had been sufficient for him — yet is sullen and discontented for Naboth's vineyard. Jonah though a good man and a prophet — yet ready to die in a peeve; and because God killed his gourd. 'Kill me too!' says he. Rachel complains, 'give me children, or I die;' she had many blessings, if she could have seen them — but lacked this blessing of contentment.

God will supply our needs — but must he satisfy our lusts too! Many are discontented for lack of a trifle — another has a better dress, a richer jewel, a newer fashion. Nero, not content with his empire, was troubled that the musician had more skill in playing than he. How foolish are some, who pine away in discontent for the lack of those things which if they had, would but render them more sad!

Use III. A persuasive to contentment.

It exhorts us to labor for contentment — this is that which does beautify and bespangle a Christian, and as a spiritual embroidery, does set him off in the eyes of the world.

But methinks I hear some bitterly complaining, and saying to me, 'Alas! How is it possible to be contented? The Lord has made my chain heavy! He has cast me into a very sad condition.'

There is no sin — but labors either to hide itself under some mask; or, if it cannot be concealed, then to vindicate itself by some apology. This sin of discontent I find very witty in its apologies, which I shall first unveil it — and then make a reply. We must lay it down as a rule, that discontent is a sin; so that all the pretenses and apologies with which it labors to justify itself — are but the painting and dressing of a strumpet.

The first apology which discontent makes is this: *'I have lost a child!'* Paulina, upon the loss of her children, was so possessed with a spirit of sadness that she had liked to have entombed herself in her own discontent! Our love to relations should never be more than our love to true religion.

1. We must be content, not only when God gives mercies — but when He takes away. If we must 'in everything give thanks,' (1 Th. 5:18) then in nothing should we be discontented.

2. Perhaps God has taken away the cistern — that he may give you the more of the spring. Perhaps he has darkened the starlight — that you may have more sun-light. God intends you shall have more of himself — and is not he better than ten sons? Look not so much upon a temporal loss — as upon a spiritual gain. The comforts of the world run to dregs; those which come out of the granary of the promise, are pure and sweet!

3. Your child was not given — but lent: 'I have, says Hannah, lent my son to the Lord;' (1 Sa. 1:28) she lent him! The Lord has lent him to her. Mercies are not given to us — but lent; what a man lends — he may take back again when he pleases. O be not discontented that a mercy is taken away from you — but rather be thankful that it was lent you so long.

4. Suppose your child to be taken from you, either he was good or bad; if he was rebellious, you have not so much parted with a child, as a burden; you grieve for that which might have been a greater grief to you; if he was pious, then remember, he 'is taken away from the evil to come,' and placed in his center of felicity. This lower region is full of vile and hurtful vapors; how happy are those who are mounted into the celestial orbs! 'The righteous are taken away,' in the original it is, he is gathered. A wicked child is cut off — but the pious child is gathered. Even as we see men gather flowers, and preserve them — so has God gathered your child as a sweet flower that he may preserve it with glory, and preserve it by him forever.

Why then should a Christian be discontented? Why should he weep excessively? 'Daughters of Jerusalem weep not for me — but weep for yourselves!' (Lu. 23:28) Just so, could we hear our children speaking to us out of heaven, they would say, 'Weep not for us who are happy; we lie upon a soft pillow, even in the bosom of Christ! The Prince of Peace is embracing us and kissing us with the kisses of his lips! Don't be troubled at our preferment; weep not for us, but weep for yourselves, who are in a sinful sorrowful world! You are in the valley of tears — but we are on the mountain of spices; we have gotten to our harbor — but you are still tossing upon the waves of trouble'

O Christian! Be not discontented that you have parted with such a child; but rather rejoice that you had such a child to part with. Break forth into thankfulness. What an honor is it to be a parent to beget such a child, that while he lives increases the joy of the glorified angels, (Lu. 20:10) and when he dies increases the number of the glorified saints.

5. If God has taken away one of your children, he has left you more — he might have stripped you of all. He took away Job's comforts, his estate, his children! Indeed his wife was left — but as a cross. Satan made a bow of this rib, and shot a temptation by her at Job, thinking to have him shot to the heart; 'curse God and die!' But Job had upon him the breast-plate of integrity; and though his children were taken away — yet not his graces; still he is content, still he blesses God.

O think how many mercies you still enjoy; yet your base hearts are more discontented at one loss — than thankful for an hundred mercies! God has plucked one bunch of grapes from you — but how many precious clusters are left behind?

You may object — but it was my only child — the staff of my old age — the seed of my comfort — and the only blossom out of which my ancient family did grow.

6. God has promised you, if you belong to him, 'a name better than of sons and daughters.' (Is. 56:5) Is he dead — who would have been the monument to have kept up the name of a family?

God has given you a new name, he has written your name in the book of life! Behold your spiritual heraldry; here is a name which cannot be cut off.

Has God taken away your only child? He has given you his only Son! This is a happy exchange. What needs he complain of losses — who has Christ! He is his Father's brightness, (He. 1:3) his riches, (Col. 2:9) his delight. (Psalm 42:1) Is there enough in Christ to delight the heart of God? and is there not enough in him to ravish us with holy delight? He is wisdom to teach us, righteousness to acquit us, sanctification to adorn us; he is that royal and princely gift, he is the bread of angels, the joy and triumph of saints; he is all in all. (Col. 3:10) Why then are you discontented? Though your child is lost — yet you have him for whom all things are loss.

7. Let us blush to think that nature should outstrip grace. Pulvillus, a heathen, when he was about to consecrate a temple to Jupiter, and news was brought him of the death of his son, would not desist from his enterprise — but with much composure of mind, went through with the burial.

The second apology which discontent makes is, *'I have a great part of my estate suddenly melted away!'* God is pleased sometimes to bring his children very low, and cut them short in their estate; it fares with them as with that widow, who had nothing in her house, but a pot of oil. (2 Ki. 4:2) But be content.

1. God has taken away your estate — but not your eternal portion. This is a sacred paradox, honor and estate are no part of a Christian's portion; they are rather luxuries than essentials, and therefore the loss of those cannot denominate a man miserable. Still the portion remains; 'the Lord is my portion, says my soul.' (Lam. 3:24) Suppose one were worth millions, and he should chance to lose a pin off his sleeve, this is no part of his estate, nor can we say he is undone. Just so, the loss of sublunary comforts is not so much to a Christian's portion, as the loss of a pin is to a million. 'These things shall be added to you,' (Mat. 6:33) they shall be cast in as overplus. When a man buys a piece of cloth he has an inch or two given in to the measure; now, though he lose his inch of cloth — yet he is not undone, for still the whole piece remains. Just so, our outward estate is not so much in regard of the portion, as an inch of cloth is to the whole piece; why then should a Christian be discontented, when the title to his spiritual treasure remains? A thieve may take away all the money that I have — but not my land. Just so, a Christian has a title to the land of promise. Mary has chosen the better part, which shall not be taken from her.

2. Perhaps, if your estate had not been lost — your soul had been lost; outward comforts do often quench inward spiritual heat. God can bestow a jewel upon us — but we fall so in love with it, that we forget Him who gave it. What pity is it, that we should commit idolatry with the creature! God is forced sometimes to drain away an estate: the plate and jewels are often cast over-board to save the passenger. Many a man may curse the time that ever he had such an estate: it has been an enchantment to draw away his heart from God; 'those who will be rich, fall into a snare.' Are you troubled that God has prevented a snare? Riches are thorns; (Mat. 13:7) are you angry because God has pulled away a thorn from you? Riches are compared to 'thick clay;' (Ha. 2:6) perhaps your affections, which are the feet of the soul, might have stuck so fast in this golden clay that they could not have ascended up to heaven. Be content; if God dams up our outward comforts — it is that the stream of our love may run faster to Him!

3. If your estate be small — yet God can bless a little. It is not how much money we have — but how much blessing. He who often curses the bags of gold, can bless the meal in the barrel, and the oil in the cruise. What if you have not the full fleshpots? Yet you have a promise, 'I will abundantly bless your provision,' (Psalm 132:15) and then a little goes a long way. Be content

you have the dew of a blessing distilled; a dinner of green herbs, where love is, is sweet; I may add, where the love of God is. Another may have more estate than you — but more worry; more riches — but less rest; more revenues — but more occasions of expense; he has a greater inheritance — yet perhaps 'God gives a man riches, wealth, and honor so that he lacks nothing of all he desires for himself, but God does not allow him to enjoy them' (Ecc. 6:2) he has the dominion of his estate, not the use; he holds more — but enjoys less. In a word, you has less gold than he, perhaps less guilt.

4. You did never so thrive in your spiritual trade; your heart was never so low — as when your condition was low; you were never so poor in spirit, never so rich in faith. You did never run the ways of God's commandments so fast — as when some of your golden weights were taken off. You never had such trading for heaven all your life; this is most abundant gain. You did never make such adventures upon the promise — as when you left off your sea-adventures. This is the best kind of merchandise. O Christian, you never had such incomes of the Spirit, such spring-tides of joy; and what though weak in estate, if strong in assurance? Be content — what you have lost one way, you have gained another.

5. Be your losses what they will in this kind, remember in every loss there is only a suffering — but in every discontent there is a sin — and one sin is worse than a thousand sufferings. What! Because some of my revenues are gone, shall I part with some of my holiness? Shall my faith and patience go too? Because I do not possess an estate, shall I not therefore possess my own spirit? O learn to be content!

The third apology is, *'It is sad with me in my relations — where I should find most comfort, there I have most grief!'* This apology or objection branches itself into two particulars, whereto I shall give a distinct reply.

[A.] My child goes on in rebellion — I fear I have brought forth a child for the devil. It is indeed, sad to think, that hell should be paved with the skulls of any of our children; and certainly the pangs of grief which the mother has in this kind, are worse than her pangs of travail! But though you ought to be humbled — yet not discontented; for, consider,

1. You may pick something out of your child's undutifulness; the child's sin is sometimes the parent's sermon; the undutifulness of children to us, may be a memento to put us in mind of our undutifulness once to God. Time was, when we were rebellious children; how long did our heart stand out as garrisons against God? How long did he parley with us and beseech us, before we would yield? He walked in the tenderness of his heart towards us — but we walked in the stubbornness of our hearts towards him; and since grace has been planted in our souls, how much of the wild olive is still in us? How many motions of the Spirit do we daily resist? How many unkindnesses and affronts have we put upon Christ? Let this open a spring of repentance; look upon your child's rebellion — and mourn for your own rebellion!

2. Though to see him undutiful is your grief — yet not always your sin. Has a parent given the child, not only the milk of the breast — but 'the sincere milk of the Word?' have you seasoned his tender years with pious education? You can do no more; parents can only work knowledge, God must work grace; they can only lay the wood together, it is God who must make it burn. A parent can only be a guide to show his child the way to heaven — the Spirit of God must be a loadstone to draw his heart into that way. 'Am I in God's stead,' says Jacob, 'who has withheld the fruit of the womb?' (Ge. 30:2) Can I give children? So, is a parent in God's stead to give grace? Who can help it, if a child having the light of conscience, Scripture, education, these three torches in his hand — yet runs willfully into the deep ponds of sin? Weep for your child, pray for him; but do not sin for him by discontent.

3. Say not, you have brought forth a child for the devil; God can reform him; he has promised 'to turn the hearts of the children to their fathers' (Mal. 4:6) and 'to open springs of grace in the desert.' (Is. 35:6) When your child is going full sail to the devil—God can blow with a contrary wind of his Spirit and alter his course. When Paul was breathing out persecution against the saints, and was sailing hellward, God turns him another way; before he was going to Damascus, God sends him to Ananias; before a persecutor, now a preacher. Though our children are for the present fallen into the devil's pond, God can turn them from the power of Satan, and bring them home the twelfth hour. Monica was weeping for her son Augustine: at last God saved him, and he became a famous instrument in the church of God.

[B.] The second branch of the objection is—but my husband takes ill courses; where I looked for honey, behold a sting! It is sad to have the living and the dead tied together; yet, let not your heart fret with discontent; mourn for his sins—but do not murmur. For,

1. God has placed you in your relation, and if you are discontented, you quarrel with God. What! For every cross that befalls us, shall we call the infinite wisdom of God into question? O the blasphemy of our hearts!

2. God can make you a gainer by your husband's sin; perhaps you would have never been so good—if he had not been so bad. The fire burns hottest in the coldest climate. God often by a divine chemistry, turns the sins of others to our good—and makes our maladies into our medicines. The more profane the husband is, often the more holy the wife grows; the more earthly he is, the more heavenly she grows. God makes sometimes the husband's sin a spur to the wife's grace. His exorbitance is often a bellows to blow up the flame of her zeal and devotion the more. Is it not thus? Does not your husband's wickedness send you to prayer? You perhaps would have never prayed so much—if he had not sinned so much. His deadness quickens you the more—the stone of his heart is an hammer to break your heart. The apostle says, 'the unbelieving wife is sanctified by the believing husband;' (1 Cor. 7:14) but in this sense, the believing wife is sanctified by the unbelieving husband; she grows better, his sin is a whetstone to her grace, and a medicine for her soul.

The next apology that discontent makes is — *'But my friends have dealt very unkindly with me, and turned against me.'*

It is sad, when a friend proves like a brook in summer. (Job 6:15) The traveler being parched with heat, comes to the brook, hoping to refresh himself—but the brook is dried up—yet be content.

1. You are not alone, other saints have been betrayed by friends; and when they have leaned upon them, they have been as a foot out of joint. This was true in the type David; 'it was not an enemy that reproached me—but it was you, O man, my equal, my guide, and mine acquaintance; we took sweet counsel together: (Psalm 55:12, 13, 14) and in the antitype Christ; he was betrayed by a friend. So why should we think it strange to have the same measure dealt out to us—as Jesus Christ had? 'The servant is not above his master'.

2. A Christian may often read his sin in his punishment: has not he dealt treacherously with God? How often has he grieved the Comforter, broken his vows, and through unbelief sided with Satan against God! How often has he abused God's love, taken the jewels of God's mercies, and made a golden calf of them—serving his own lusts! How often has he made the free grace of God, which should have been a bolt to keep out sin, rather a key to open the door to it! These wounds has the Lord received in the house of his friends. Look upon the unkindness of your friend—and mourn for your own unkindness against God! Shall a Christian condemn that in another, which he has been too guilty of himself?

3. Has your friend proved treacherous? Perhaps you did repose too much confidence in him. If you lay more weight upon a house than the pillars will bear, it must needs break. God says, 'trust not in a friend:' (Mi. 7:5) perhaps you did put more trust in him, than you did dare to put in God. Friends are as Venice-glasses, we may use them—but if we lean too hard upon them, they will break. Behold matter of humility—but not of sullenness and discontent.

4. You have a friend in heaven who will never fail you; 'there is a friend' says Solomon 'who sticks closer than a brother!' (Proverbs 18:24) such a friend is God; he is very studious and inquisitive on our behalf; he has a debating with himself, a consulting and projecting how he may do us good; he is the best friend, who gives contentment in the midst of all discourtesies of friends. Consider,

(1.) He is a loving friend. 'God is love;' (1 John 4:16) hence he is said sometimes to engrave us on the 'palm of his hand,' (Is. 49:16) that we may never be out of his eye. He carries us in his bosom, (Is. 40:11) near to his heart. There is no interruption or stint in his love; but as the Nile river, it overflows all the banks. His love is as far beyond our thoughts—as it is above our deserts! O the infinite love of God, in giving the Son of his love to be made flesh, which was more than if all the angels had been made worms! God in giving Christ to us gave his very heart to us. Here is love penciled out in all its glory, and engraved as with the 'point of a diamond.' All other love is hatred—in comparison of the love of our Friend.

(2.) He is a caring friend: 'He cares for you!' (1 Pe. 5:7) He minds and transacts our business as his own—he accounts his people's interests and concernments as his interest. He provides for us—grace to enrich us—and glory to ennoble us. It was David's complaint, 'no man cares for my soul!' (Psalm 142:4) a Christian has a friend who cares for him.

(3.) He is a wise friend. (Da. 2:20) A friend may sometimes err through ignorance or mistake, and give his friend poison instead of sugar; but 'God is wise in heart; (Job 9:4) he is skillful as well as faithful; he knows what our disease is, and what remedy is most proper to apply; he knows what will do us good, and what wind will be best to carry us to heaven.

(4.) He is a faithful friend. He is faithful in his promises; 'in hope of eternal life which God, who cannot lie, has promised.' (Titus 1:2) God cannot lie; he will not deceive his people; nay, he cannot: he is called 'the Truth;' he can as well cease to be God—as cease to be true. The Lord may sometimes change his promise, as when he converts a temporal promise into a spiritual promise; but he can never break his promise.

(5.) He is a compassionate friend, hence in Scripture we read of the yearning of his affections. (Jer. 31:20) God's friendship is nothing else but compassion; for there is naturally no affection in us to desire his friendship, nor any goodness in us to deserve it; the loadstone is in himself. When we were full of sin—he was full of love; when we were enemies—he sent an embassage[1] of peace; when our hearts were turned away from God—his heart was turned towards us. O the tenderness and sympathy of our Friend in heaven! We ourselves have some relentings of heart to those which are in misery; but it is God who begets all the mercies and affections that are in us, therefore he is called 'the Father of mercies.' (2 Cor. 1:3)

(6.) He is a constant friend: 'his compassions fail not.' (La. 3:22) Friends do often in adversity, drop off as leaves in autumn; these are rather flatterers than friends. Joab was for a time faithful to King David's house; but within a while proved false to the crown, and went after the treason of Adonijah. (1 Ki. 1:7) God is a friend forever: 'having loved his own which were in the world—he loved them to the end.' (John 13:1) What though I am despised? Yet God loves me.

---

[1] The business or message of an envoy.

What though my friends cast me off? Yet God loves me; he loves to the end, and there is no end of that love. This methinks, in case of discourtesies and unkindnesses, is enough to charm down discontent.

The next apology is, *'I am under great reproaches!'* Let not this discontent you, for,

1. It is a sign there is some good in you. The applause of the wicked, usually denotes some evil in us — and their censure usually imports some good in us. (Psalm 38:20) David wept and fasted, and that was turned to his 'reproach'. (Pe. 4:14) As we must pass to heaven through the spikes of suffering, so through the clouds of reproach.

2. If your reproach be for God, as David's was, 'for your sake I have born reproach;' (Psalm 69:7) then it is rather matter of triumph, than dejection. Christ does not say, when you are reproached be discontented; but rejoice! (Mat. 5:12) Wear your reproach as a diadem of honor, for now a spirit of 'glory and of God rests upon you.' (1 Pe. 4:14) Put your reproaches into the inventory of your riches — as Moses did. (He. 11:26) It should be a Christian's ambition to wear his Savior's livery, though it is sprinkled with blood and sullied with disgrace!

3. God will do us good by reproach: as David of Shimei's cursing; 'it may be, that the Lord will requite[2] me good for his cursing this day.' (2 Sa. 16:12) This puts us upon searching our sin: a child of God labors to read his sin — in every stone of reproach which is cast at him. Besides, now we have an opportunity to exercise patience and humility.

4. Jesus Christ was content to be reproached by us. He 'endured the cross, scorning its shame.' (He. 12:2) It may amaze us to think that he who was God, could endure to be spit upon, and be crowned with thorns; and when he was ready to bow his head upon the cross, to have the Jews in scorn, wag their heads and say, 'he saved others, himself he cannot save.' The shame of the cross was as much as the blood of the cross! His name was crucified before his body. The sharp arrows of reproach which the world shot at Christ, went deeper into his heart, than the spear! His suffering was so ignominious, that the sun blushed to behold it. It withdrew its bright beams and masked itself with a cloud; (and well it might, when the Sun of Righteousness was in an eclipse') All this revilement and reproach, did the God of glory endure for us.

O then let us be content to have our names eclipsed for Christ; let not reproach lie at our heart — but let us bind it as a crown about our head! These who are discontented at a reproach, will avoid any persecution for Christ.

5. Is not many a man contented to suffer reproach for maintaining his lust? And shall not we for maintaining the truth? Some glory in that which is their shame, (Ph. 3:19) and shall we be ashamed of that which is our glory? Be not troubled at these petty things. He whose heart is once divinely touched with the loadstone of God's Spirit, does account it his honor — to be dishonored for Christ, (Ac. 15:4) and does as much despise the world's censure, as he does their praise.

6. We live in an age wherein men dare reproach God himself. The divinity of the Son of God is blasphemously reproached by the Socinian. The blessed Bible is reproached by the Anti-Scripturist, as if it were but a legend of lies, and every man's faith a fable. The justice of God is called to the bar of reason by the Arminians. The wisdom of God in his providential actings, is taxed by the Atheist. The ordinances of God are decried by the Familists, as being too heavy a burden for a free-born conscience, and too low and carnal for a sublime seraphic spirit. The ways of God, which have the majesty of holiness shining in them, are calumniated by the profane. The mouths of men are open against God, as if he were an hard master, and the path of

---

[2] Make appropriate return for (a favor, service, or wrongdoing)

true religion, too strict and severe. If men cannot give God a good word, shall we be discontented or troubled that they speak hardly of us? Such as labor to bury the glory of true religion, shall we wonder that 'their throats are open sepulchers,' (Ro. 3:13) to bury our good name? O let us be contented, while we are in God's scouring-house, to have our names sullied a little; the blacker we seem to be here, the brighter shall we shine when God has set us upon the celestial shelf!

The sixth apology that discontent makes, is disrespect. *'I have not that esteem from men, as is suitable to my worth and grace!'* And does this trouble you? Consider,

1. The world is an unequal judge; as it is full of change—as of partiality. The world gives her respects, as she does her places of preferment; more often by favor, than desert. Have you real worth in you? It is better to deserve respect—and not have it; than have it—and not deserve it!

2. Have you grace? God respects you, and his judgment is most worth prizing. A believer is a person of honor, being born of God: 'Since you were precious in my eyes, you have been honorable, and I have loved you.' (Is. 43:4) Let the world think what they will of you; perhaps in their eyes, you are vile; but in God's eyes, you are his dove, (Ca. 2:14) his spouse, (Ca. 5:1) his jewel. (Mal. 3:17) Others account you the dregs of offscouring of the world, (1 Cor. 4:14) but God will give whole kingdoms for your ransom. (Is. 43:3) Let this content—it does not matter how I am looked upon in the world—if God thinks well of me. It is better that God approves—than man applauds. The world may honor us—and God put us in his black book! What is a man the better that his fellow-prisoners commend him—if his judge condemns him! O labor to keep in with God; prize his love! Let worldlings frown on me—I am contented, being a favorite of the king of heaven!

3. If you are a child of God, you must expect disrespect from the ungodly. A believer is in the world—but not of the world. We are here in a pilgrim condition, out of our own country, therefore must not look for the respect and acclamation of the world. It is sufficient that we shall have honor in our own country. (He. 13:14) It is dangerous to be the world's favorite!

4. Discontent arising from disrespect, savors too much of pride. A humble Christian has a lower opinion of himself—than others can have of him. He who is taken up about the thoughts of his sins, and how he has provoked God, cries out, as Agur, 'I am more brutish than any man!' (Proverbs 30:2) and therefore is contented, though he be set among 'the dogs of my flock.' (Job 30:1) Though he is low in the thoughts of the ungodly—yet he is thankful that he is not laid in 'the lowest hell.' (Psalm 86:13) A proud man sets an high value upon himself; and is angry with others, because they will not come up to his price! Take heed of pride! O had others a window to look into their heart, or did your heart stand where your face does—you would wonder to have so much respect!

The next apology is, *'I meet with very great sufferings for the truth!'* Consider,

1. Your sufferings are not so great as your sins! Put these two in the balance, and see which weighs heaviest; where sin lies heavy, sufferings lie light. A carnal spirit makes more of his sufferings—and less of his sins; he looks upon one at the great end of the telescope—but upon the other at the little end of the telescope. The carnal heart cries out, 'Take away my affliction!' But a gracious heart cries out, 'Take away my iniquity!' (2 Sa. 24:10) The one says, 'Never has anyone suffered as I have done!' But the other says, 'Never has anyone sinned as I have done!' (Mi. 7:7)

2. Are you under sufferings: you have an opportunity to show the valor and constancy of your mind. Some of God's saints would have accounted it a great favor, to have been honored with

martyrdom. One said, 'I am in prison — until I be in prison'. You count that a trouble, which others would have worn as an ensign of their glory.

3. Even those who have gone only upon moral principles, have shown much constancy and contentment in their sufferings. Curtius, being bravely mounted and in armor, threw himself into a great gulf, that the city of Rome might, (according to the oracle,) be delivered from the pestilence. And we, having a divine oracle, 'those who who kill the body, cannot hurt the soul,' shall we not with much constancy and patience devote ourselves to injuries for Christ, and rather suffer for the truth — than the truth suffer for us?

The Decii among the Romans, vowed themselves to death, that their legions and soldiers might be crowned with the honor of the victory. O what should we be content to suffer, to make the truth victorious! Regulus having sworn that he would return to Carthage, though he knew there was a furnace heating for him there — yet not daring to infringe his oath, he did adventure to go. We then who are Christians, having made a vow to Christ in baptism, and so often renewed in the blessed sacrament, should with much contentment rather choose to suffer, than violate our sacred oath! Thus the blessed martyrs, with what courage and cheerfulness did they yield up their souls to God! When the fire was set to their bodies — yet their spirits were not at all fired with passion or discontent. Though others hurt the body, let them not be discontent; show by your heroic courage, that you are above those troubles, which you cannot be without.

The next apology is, *'the prosperity of the wicked.'* 'I envied the arrogant when I saw the prosperity of the wicked!' Psalm 73:3. It is often that the evil enjoy all the good — and the good endure all the evil. David, though a godly man, stumbled at this, and had almost stumbled because of this. Well, be contented; for remember,

1. Worldly goods are not the only things, nor the best things; they are mere temporal blessings. These are but the acorns with which God feeds swine! You who are believers have more choice fruit — the olive, the pomegranate, the fruit which grows on the true vine Jesus Christ! Others have the fat of the earth — you have the dew of heaven! They have muddied puddles — but you have those springs of living water which are purified with Christ's blood, and filled with his love.

2. To see the wicked flourish is rather a matter of pity, than envy! This is all the heaven they will have! 'Woe to you who are rich, for you have your only happiness now!' (Luke 6:24) Hence it was, that David made it his solemn prayer, 'Deliver me from the wicked, from men of the world, who have their portion in this life!' (Psalm 17:15) These words are David's litany — 'good Lord, deliver me!' When the wicked have eaten of their dainty dishes — there comes in a sad reckoning which will spoil all. The world is first musical and then tragical! We should not envy a man who will fry and blaze in hell — let him have enough of the fat of the earth. O remember — for every sand of mercy which runs out of the wicked, God puts a drop of wrath into his vial! 'You are storing up wrath for yourself in the day of wrath, when God's righteous judgment is revealed.' Romans 2:5

Therefore as that soldier said to his fellow, 'do you envy my grapes? They cost me dear, I must die for them!' So I say, do you envy the wicked? Alas their prosperity is like Haman's banquet before execution! If a man were to be hanged, would one envy to see him walk to the gallows through pleasant fields and fine galleries, or to see him go up the ladder in clothes of gold? The wicked may flourish in their bravery for a while; but, when they flourish as the grass, 'it is, that they shall be destroyed forever; (Psalm 92:7) the proud grass shall be mown down. Whatever a sinner enjoys — he has a curse with it, 'I will curse your blessings!' (Malachi 2:2) And shall we envy him? Would we envy a dog--if poisoned food was given to it! The long furrows in the backs of the godly have a seed of blessing in them, when the table of the wicked becomes a snare, and their honor their halter!

The next apology that discontent makes for itself is *'the evils of the times.'* The times are full of heresy and impiety, and this is that which troubles me. This apology consists of two branches, to which I shall answer in specie; and,

[A.] The times are full of heresy! Error is a touch-stone to discover bad men. This is indeed sad; when the devil cannot destroy the church by violence — he endeavors to poison it; when he cannot with Samson's foxtails set the corn on fire, then he sows tares. As he labors to destroy the peace of the church by division, so the truth of it by error. We may cry out, 'We live in times wherein there is a sluice open to all novel opinions, and every man's opinion is his Bible!' Well; this may make us mourn — but let us not murmur or be discontent. Consider,

1. Error makes a discovery of men. Error reveals such as are tainted and corrupt. When the leprosy brake forth in the forehead, then was the leper discovered. Error is a spiritual bastard; the devil is the father, and pride the mother! You never knew an erroneous man, but he was a proud man. Now, it is good that such men should be unveiled, to the intent, first, that God's righteous judgment upon them may be adored; secondly, that others be not infected. If a man has the plague, it is well it breaks forth. For my part, I would avoid a heretic, as I would avoid the devil, for he is sent on the devil's errand. I appeal unto you; if there were a tavern in this city, where under a pretense of selling wine, many bottles of poison were to be sold, were it not well that others should know of it, that they might not buy? It is good that those that have poisoned opinions should be known, that the people of God may not come near either the scent or the taste of that poison!

Error is a touch-stone to discover good men: it tries the gold: 'there must be heresies that those who are approved, may be made manifest.' (1 Cor. 11:19) Thus our love to Christ, and zeal for truth does appear. God shows who are the living fish; such as swim against the stream: who are the sound sheep; such as feed in the green pastures of the ordinances: who are the doves; such as live in the best air, where the spirit breathes. God sets a garland of honor upon these, 'these are those who came out of great tribulation'; (Re. 7:14) so these are they that have opposed the errors of the times, these are they that have preserved the virginity of their conscience, who have kept their judgment sound and their heart soft. God will have a trophy of honor set upon some of his saints, they shall be renowned for their sincerity, being like the cypress, which keeps its greenness and freshness in the winter-season.

2. Be not sinfully discontented, for God can make the errors of the church advantageous to truth. Thus the truths of God have come to be more beaten out and confirmed; as it is in the law, one may lay a false title to a piece of land, the true title has by this means been the more searched into and ratified. Some had never so studied to defend the truth by Scripture, if others had not endeavored to overthrow it by sophistry; all the mists and fogs of error that have risen out of the bottomless pit, have made the glorious Sun of truth to shine so much the brighter. Had not Arius and Sabellius broached their damnable error, the truth of those questions about the blessed Trinity would never have been so discussed and defended by Athanasius, Augustine, and others; had not the devil brought in so much of his princely darkness, the champions for truth had never run so fast to Scripture to light their lamps. So that God with a wheel within a wheel, over-rules these things wisely, and turns them to the best. Truth is a heavenly plant — which settles by shaking.

3. God raises the price of his truth the more; the very shreds and filings of truth are esteemed. When there is much counterfeit metal abroad, we prize the true gold the more; pure wine of truth is never more precious, than when unsound doctrines are broached and vented.

4. Error makes us more thankful to God for the jewel of truth. When you see another infected with the plague – how thankful are you that God has freed you from the infection! When we see others have the leprosy in the head – how thankful are we to God that he has not given us over to believe a lie and so be damned! It is a good use that may be made even of the error of the times – when it makes us more humble and thankful, adoring the free grace of God, who has kept us from drinking of that deadly poison!

[B.] The times are full of impiety! I live and converse among the profane: 'O that I had wings like a dove, for then would I fly away and be at rest.' (Psalm 55:6)

It is indeed sad, to be mixed with the wicked. David beheld 'transgressors and was grieved.' And Lot (who was a bright star in a dark night) was vexed, or, as the word in the original may bear, wearied out, with the filthy lives of the wicked; he made the sins of Sodom, into spears to pierce his own soul. We ought, if there is any spark of divine love in us, to be very sensible of the sins of others – and to have our hearts bleed for them. Yet let us not break forth into mourning and discontent, knowing that God in his providence has permitted it, and surely not without some reasons; for,

1st. The Lord makes the wicked a hedge to defend the godly; the wise God often makes those who are wicked and peaceable, a means to safeguard his people from those who are wicked and cruel. The king of Babylon kept Jeremiah, and gave special order for his looking after, that he did lack nothing. (Jer. 39:11,12) God sometimes makes brazen sinners to be brazen walls to defend his people.

2nd. God does but interline and mingle the wicked with the godly, that the godly may be a means to save the wicked; such is the beauty of holiness that it has a magnetic force in it to allure and draw even the wicked. Sometimes God makes a believing husband a means to convert an unbelieving wife, and vice versa: 'How do you know, wife, whether you will save your husband? Or, how do you know, husband, whether you will save your wife?' (1 Cor. 7:16) The godly living among the wicked, by their prudent advice and pious example, have won them to the embracing of true religion. If there were not some godly among the wicked, how in a practical way, without a miracle, can we imagine that the wicked should be converted? Those who are now shining saints in heaven, once served diverse lusts. (Ti. 3:3) Paul was once a persecutor; Augustine was once a Manichean; Luther was once a monk; but by the kind and holy behavior of the godly, were converted to the faith.

The next apology that discontent makes, is, *smallness of abilities and gifts*. 'I cannot (says the Christian) discourse with that fluency, nor pray with that elegance, as others.'

1. Grace is beyond gifts; you compare your grace with another's gifts, there is a vast difference. Grace without gifts is infinitely better than gifts without grace. In religion, the vitals are best. Gifts are a more extrinsic and common work of the Spirit, which is incident to reprobates. Grace is a more distinguishing work, and is a jewel hung only upon the elect. Have you the seed of God – the holy anointing? Be content!

(1.) You say that you cannot discourse with that fluency as others. Experience in religion, is better than notions; and heart impressions are beyond vocal expressions. Judas (no doubt) could make a learned discourse on Christ – but well-fared the woman in the gospel, who felt virtue coming out of Christ, (Lu. 8:47). A sanctified heart is better than a silver tongue! There is as much difference between gifts and graces, as between a tulip painted on the wall, and one growing in the garden!

(2.) You say that you cannot pray with that elegance as others. Prayer is a matter more of the heart—than the head. In prayer it is not so much fluency which prevails—as fervency, (Ja. 5:16) nor is God so much taken with the elegance of speech, as the efficacy of the Spirit. Humility is better than fluency; here the mourner is the orator; sighs and groans are the best rhetoric!

2. Be contented, for God does usually proportion a man's abilities to the place to which he calls him; some are set in a higher sphere and function, their place requires more gifts and abilities; but the most inferior member is useful in its place, and shall have a power delegated for the discharge of its peculiar office.

The next apology is, the troubles of the church. 'Alas, my disquiet and discontent is not so much for myself, as the church! The church of God suffers.'

I confess it is sad and we ought for this 'to hang our harps upon the willows.' He is a wooden leg in Christ's body that is not sensible of the state of the body. As a Christian must not be proud flesh, so neither dead flesh. When the church of God suffers, he must sympathize; Jeremiah wept for the virgin daughter of Zion. We must feel our brethren's hard cords, through our soft beds. In music, if one string is touched, all the rest sound: when God strikes upon our brethren, our 'affections must sound like a harp'. Be sensible—but give not way to discontent. For consider,

1. God sits at the stern of his church. (Psalm 46:5) Sometimes it is a ship tossed upon the waves, 'afflicted and tossed! (Is. 54:11) but cannot God bring this ship to haven, though it meets with a storm upon the sea? This ship in the gospel was tossed because sin was in it; but it was not overwhelmed, because Christ was in it. Christ is in the ship of this church, fear not sinking; the church's anchor is cast in heaven. God loves his church, and takes much care of it. The names of the twelve tribes were on Aaron's breastplate, signifying how near to God's heart his people are. They are his portion, (De. 27:9) and shall that be lost? They are his glory, (Is. 46:13) and shall that be finally eclipsed? Certainly not! God can deliver his church, not only from opposition—but by opposition; the church's pangs shall help forward her deliverance.

2. God has always propagated true religion by sufferings. The foundation of the church has been laid in blood, and these sanguine showers have ever made it more fruitful. Cain put the knife to Abel's throat, and ever since, the church's veins had bled: but she is like the vine, which by bleeding grows; and like the palm-tree, which the more weight is laid upon it, the higher it rises. The holiness and patience of the saints, under their persecutions, has much added both to the growth of true religion, and the glory of God. Basil and Tertullian observe of the primitive martyrs, that many of the heathen, seeing their zeal and constancy, turned Christians. Religion is that Phoenix which has always revived and flourished in the ashes of holy men. Isaiah sawn asunder, Peter crucified at Rome with his head upside down, Cyprian, bishop of Carthage, and Polycarp of Smyrna, were both martyred for true religion—yet evermore the truth has been sealed by blood, and gloriously dispersed; whereupon Julian did forbear to persecute, not out of pity—but envy, because the church grew so fast, and multiplied, as Nazianzen well observes.

The twelfth apology that discontent makes for itself, is this, 'it is not my afflictions which trouble me—but it is my sins which disquiet and discontent me.'

Be sure it is so; do not prevaricate with God and your own soul; in true mourning for sin when the present suffering is removed—yet the sorrow is not removed. But suppose the apology is real, that sin is the ground of your discontent; yet I answer, a man's disquiet about sin may be beyond its bounds, in these three cases.

1. When it is disheartening, that is, when it sets up sin above mercy. If Israel had only pored over their sting, and not looked up to the brazen serpent — they would never have been healed. That sorrow for sin which drives us away from God, is sinful — for there is more despair in it than remorse; the soul has so many tears in its eyes, that it cannot see Christ! Sorrow, as sorrow, does not save, that were to make a Christ of our tears! But is useful, as it is preparatory in the soul — making sin vile, and Christ precious. O look up to the brazen serpent, the Lord Jesus! A sight of his blood will revive, the plaster of his merits is broader than our sore. It is Satan's policy, either to keep us from seeing our sins; or, if we do see them — that we may be swallowed up with sorrow; (2 Cor. 2:7). Either he would stupify us, or affright us; either keep the looking-glass of the law from our eyes, or else pencil out our sins in such crimson colors, that we may sink in the quicksands of despair!

2. When sorrow is indisposing, it untunes the heart for prayer, meditation, holy conference; it cloisters up the soul. This is not sorrow — but rather sullenness, and renders a man not so much penitential, as cynical.

3. When it is out of season. God made us rejoice — and we hang up our harps upon the willows; he bids us trust — and we cast ourselves down, and are brought even to the margin of despair. If Satan cannot keep us from mourning — he will be sure to put us upon it when it is least in season. When God calls us in a special manner to be thankful for mercy, and put on our white robes — Satan will be putting us into mourning, and instead of a garment of praise, clothe us with a spirit of heaviness; so God loses the acknowledgment of mercy — and we the comfort. If your sorrow has turned and fitted you for Christ, if it has raised in you high prizings of him, strong hungerings after him, sweet delight in him — this is as much as God requires. A Christian does but sin — to vex and torture himself further upon the rack of his own discontent.

And thus I hope I have answered the most material objections and apologies which this sin of discontent does make for itself. I see no reason why a Christian should be discontented, unless for his discontent. Let me, in the next place, propound something which may be both as a loadstone and a whet-stone to contentment.

Divine Motives to Contentment.

I. Consider the excellency of contentment. Contentment is a flower which does not grow in every garden. You would think it were excellent if I could prescribe a remedy or antidote against poverty. Behold, here is that which is more excellent, for a man to be poor — and yet have enough! Contentment teaches a man how to abound — in the midst of poverty. Contentment is a remedy against all our trouble, an alleviation to all our burdens, the cure of to every worry. Contentment, though it be not properly a grace (it is rather a disposition of mind,) yet in it there is a happy mixture of all the graces: it is a most precious compound, which is made up of faith, patience, meekness, humility, etc. which are the ingredients put into it. Now there are these seven rare excellencies in contentment.

First excellency. A contented Christian carries heaven with him. For, what is heaven — but that sweet repose and full contentment that the soul shall have in God. In contentment there are the first-fruits of heaven. There are two things in a contented spirit, which make it like heaven.

(1.) God is there; something of God is to be seen in that heart. A discontented Christian is like a rough tempestuous sea; when the water is rough you can see nothing there; but when it is smooth and serene, then you may behold your face in the water. (Proverbs 27:19) When the heart rages through discontent, it is like a rough sea, you can see nothing there, unless it is passion and murmuring; there is nothing of God, nothing of heaven in that heart! But by virtue of contentment, the heart becomes like the sea when it is smooth and calm, there is a face shining there; you may see something of Christ in that heart, a representation of all the graces.

(2.) Rest and peace are there. O what a peace is kept in a contented heart! What a heaven! A contented Christian, is like Noah in the ark; though the ark was tossed with waves, Noah could sit and sing in the ark. The soul that is gotten into the ark of contentment, sits quiet, and sails above all the waves of trouble; he can sing in this spiritual ark. The wheels of the chariot move — but the axle stirs not; the circumference of the heavens is carried about the earth — but the earth moves not out of its center. When we meet with motion and change in the creatures round about us, a contented spirit is not stirred nor moved out of its center. The sails of a mill move with the wind — but the mill itself stands still, an emblem of contentment; when our outward estate moves with the wind of providence — yet the heart is settled through holy contentment; and when others are shaking and trembling in times of trouble, the contented spirit can say, as David, 'O God my heart is fixed!' (Psalm 57:7) What is this, but a piece of heaven?

Second excellency. Whatever is defective in the creature, is made up in contentment. A Christian may lack the comforts that others have — the land, and possessions; but God has instilled into his heart that contentment which is far better: in this sense that saying of our Savior is true, 'he shall receive a hundred fold.' (Mat. 19:29) Perhaps he who ventured all for Christ, never has his house or land again: yes — but God gives him a contented spirit, and this breeds such joy in the soul, as is infinitely sweeter than all his houses and lands which he left for Christ.

It was sad with David in regard of his outward comforts, he being driven from his kingdom; yet in regard of that sweet contentment he found in God, he had more comfort than men have in the time of harvest and vintage. (Psalm 4:7) One man has house and lands to live upon, another has nothing, only a small trade; yet even that brings in a livelihood. A Christian may have little in the world — but he drives the trade of contentment; and so he knows as well how to lack, as to abound. O the rare art, or rather miracle of contentment!

Wicked men are often disquieted in the enjoyment of all things. But the contented Christian is joyful in the lack of all things! But how does a Christian come to be contented in the deficiency of outward comforts? A Christian finds contentment distilled out of the breasts of the promises. He is poor in purse — but rich in promise. There is one promise that brings much sweet contentment into the soul: 'Those who seek the Lord shall not lack any good thing.' (Psalm 34:10) If the thing we desire is good for us — we shall have it. If it is not good, then the not having is good for us. The resting satisfied with the promise gives contentment.

Third excellency. Contentment makes a man in tune to serve God. It oils the wheels of the soul and makes it more agile and nimble; it composes the heart, and makes it fit for prayer, meditation, etc. How can he who is in a passion of grief, or discontent, 'attend upon the Lord without distraction?' Contentment prepares and tunes the heart. First you prepare the violin, and wind up the strings, before you play a score of music. Just so, when a Christian's heart is wound up to this heavenly frame of contentment, then it is fit for duty. A discontented Christian is like Saul, when the evil spirit came upon him — O what jarrings and discords does he make in prayer! When an army is put into a disorder, then it is not fit for battle; when the thoughts are scattered and distracted about the cares of this life, a man is not fit for devotion. Discontent takes the heart wholly off from God, and fixes it upon the present trouble, so that a man's mind is not upon his prayer — but upon his trouble. Discontent disjoints the soul; and it is impossible now that a Christian should go so steadily and cheerfully in God's service. O how lame is his devotion!

The discontented person gives God but a half-duty, and his religion is nothing but an external exercise, it lacks a soul to animate it. David would not offer that to God that cost him nothing.' (2 Sa. 24:24) Where there is too much worldly care, there is too little spiritual cost in a duty. The discontented person does his duties by halves; he is just like Ephraim, 'a cake not turned;' (Ho. 7:8) he is a cake baked on one side; he gives God the outside but not the spiritual part; his heart is not in duty; he is baked on one side — but the other side dough; and what profit is there of such raw undigested services? He who gives God only the skin of worship, what can he expect more than the shell of comfort? Contentment brings the heart into frame, and only then, do we give God the flower and soul of a duty, when the soul is composed. Now a Christian's heart is intent and serious. There are some duties which we cannot perform as we ought, without contentment, such as:

(1.) To rejoice in God. How can he rejoice — who is discontented? he is fitter for repining, than rejoicing.

(2.) To be thankful for mercy. Can a discontented person be thankful? He can be fretful, not thankful.

(3.) To justify God in his proceedings. How can he do this who is discontented with his condition? He will sooner censure God's wisdom, than clear his justice. O then, how excellent is contentment, which does prepare, and as it were, string the heart for duty? Indeed contentment does not only make our duties light and agile — but acceptable to God. It is this that puts beauty and worth into them; for contentment settles the soul. Now, as it is with milk, when it is always stirring, you can make nothing of it — but let it settle a while, and then it turns to cream: when the heart is overmuch stirred with disquiet and discontent, you can make nothing of those duties. How thin, how fleeting and tedious are they! But when the heart is once settled by holy contentment, now there is some worth in our duties, now they turn to cream.

Fourth excellency. Contentment is the spiritual pillar of the soul. It fits a man to bear burdens. He who has a contented heart — is invincible under sufferings. A contented Christian is like the camomile, the more it is trodden upon — the more it grows. As medicine works disease out of the body — so does contentment work trouble out of the heart. Thus it argues, 'if I am under reproach, God can vindicate me; if I am in need, God can relieve me.' 'You shall not see wind, neither shall you see rain — yet the valley shall be filled with water.' (2 Ki. 3:17) Thus holy contentment keeps the heart from fainting.

In the autumn, when the fruit and leaves are blown off, still there is sap in the root. Just so, when there is an autumn upon our external felicity, the leaves of our estate drop off — still there is the sap of contentment in the heart. A Christian has life inwardly, when his outward comforts do not blossom. The contented heart is never out of heart.

Contentment is the golden shield, which beats back all discouragements. Humility is like the lead to the net — which keeps the soul down when it is rising through passion; and contentment is like the cork in the net — which keeps the heart up when it is sinking through discouragements. Contentment is the great under-prop; it is like the steel beam, which bears whatever weight is laid upon it; nay, it is like a rock which breaks the waves.

It is astonishing to observe the same affliction lying upon two men — how differently they respond to it. The contented Christian is like Samson, who carried away the gates of the city upon his back; he can go away with his cross cheerfully, and makes nothing of it: the other is like Issachar, couching down under his burden. (Ge. 49:14) The reason is, the one is discontent, and that breeds fainting. Discontent swells the grief, and grief breaks the heart. When this sacred sinew of contentment begins to shrink, we go limping under our afflictions. We know not what burdens God may exercise us with; let us therefore preserve contentment; as is our contentment, such will be our courage. David with his five stones and his sling defied Goliath, and overcame him. Get but contentment into the sling of your heart; and with this sacred stone you may both defy the world and conquer it; you may break those afflictions, which otherwise would break you.

Fifth excellency. Contentment prevents many sins and temptations.

First, Contentment prevents many sins. Where contentment is lacking — there is no lack of sin! Discontentedness with our condition is a sin that does not go alone — but is like the first link of the chain, which draws all the other links along with it. In particular, there are two sins which contentment prevents:

(1.) Contentment prevents impatience. Discontent and impatience are twins: 'This evil is of the Lord — why should I wait on the Lord any longer!' (2 Ki. 6:33) As if God were so bound — that he must give us the mercy just when we desire it. Impatience is no small sin; as will appear if you consider whence it arises. It is for lack of faith. Faith gives a right notion of God; it is an intelligent grace; it believes that God's wisdom tempers — and his love sweetens all ingredients. This works patience. 'Shall I not drink the cup which my Father has given me?'

Impatience is the daughter of infidelity. If a patient has a bad opinion of the physician, and thinks that he comes to poison him, he will take none of his remedies. Just so, when we have a prejudice against God, and think that he comes to kill us, and undo us — then we storm and cry out, like a foolish man, who cries out 'away with the remedy!' though it is in order to a cure. Is it not better that the remedy smart a little — than the wound fester and rankle?

Impatience is for lack of love of God. We will bear his reproofs, whom we love not only patiently — but thankfully. 'Love thinks no evil.' (1 Cor. 13:5). Love puts the fairest, and most kind gloss upon the actions of a friend; 'love covers a multitude of evil.' If it were possible for God in the least manner to err, which were blasphemy to think — love would cover that error! Love takes everything in the best sense, it makes us bear any stroke. 'Love endures all things.' (1 Cor. 13:7) Had we love to God — we would have patience.

Impatience is for lack of humility. An impatient man was never humbled under the burden of sin. He who studies his sins, the numberless number of them, how they are twisted together, and sadly accented; is patient and says, 'I will bear the indignation of the Lord, because I have sinned against him.' The greater noise drowns the lesser noise; when the sea roars — the rivers are still. Just so, he who lets his thoughts expatiate about sin, is both silent and amazed — he wonders that it is no worse with him.

How great then is this sin of impatience! And how excellent is contentment, which is a counterpoise against this sin! The contented Christian believing that God does all in love, is patient, and has not one word of complaint. That is the sin that contentment prevents.

(2.) Contentment prevents murmuring, a sin which is a degree higher than the other; murmuring is quarreling with God, and inveighing against him; 'they spoke against God.' (Nu. 21:5) The murmurer essentially says, that God has dealt wrongly with him, and he has deserved better from him. The murmurer charges God with folly and unkindness. This is the language, or rather blasphemy of a murmuring spirit; 'God might have been a wiser and better God to me.' The murmurer is a mutineer. The Israelites are called in the same text murmurers and rebels: (Nu. 17:10) and is not rebellion as the sin of witchcraft? You who are a murmurer, are in the account of God as a witch, a sorcerer, as one that deals with the devil: this is a sin of the first magnitude.

Murmuring often ends in cursing: Micah's mother fell to cursing when the talents of silver were taken away, (Ju. 17:2) so does the murmurer when a part of his estate is taken away. Murmuring is the devil's music. This is that sin which God cannot bear, 'How long shall I bear with this evil congregation, which murmurs against Me?' (Nu. 14:27) Murmuring is a sin which whets the sword against a people: it is a land-destroying sin; 'neither murmur you as some of them also murmured, and were destroyed of the destroyer.' (1 Cor. 10:10) Murmuring is a ripening sin; without mercy it will hasten England's funerals. O then, how excellent is contentment, which prevents this sin! To be contented, and yet murmur is an impossibility. A contented Christian acquiesces in his present condition, and does not murmur — but admire. Herein appears the excellency of contentment; it is a spiritual antidote against sin.

Secondly, Contentment prevents many temptations. Discontent is a devil which is always tempting.

1st. Discontent puts a man upon sinful means. He who is poor and discontented, will attempt anything; he will go to the devil for riches! He who is proud and discontented, will hang himself, as Ahithophel did when his counsel was rejected. Satan takes great advantage of discontent; he loves to fish in these troubled waters. Discontent both eclipses reason, and weakens faith! It is Satan's policy that he usually breaks over the hedge where it is weakest; discontent makes a breach in the soul, and usually at this breach the devil enters by a temptation, and storms the soul.

How easily can the devil by his logic dispute a discontented Christian into sin? He forms such a argument as this, 'he who is in need must study self-preservation: but you are now in need; therefore you ought to study self-preservation.' Hereupon to make good his conclusion, he tempts to the forbidden fruit, not distinguishing between what is needful, and what is lawful. 'What?' says he, 'do you lack a livelihood? Never be such a fool as starve — take the rising side at a venture, be it good or bad; 'eat the bread of deceit, drink the wine of violence.' Thus you see how the discontented man is a prey to that sad temptation to steal.

Contentment is a shield against poverty; for he who is contented, knows as well how to lack, as to abound. He will not sin to get a living; though his food grows short, he is content. He lives as the birds of the air — upon God's providence, and doubts not but he shall have enough to pay for his passage to heaven.

2d. Discontent tempts a man to atheism and apostasy. 'Surely, there is no God to take care of things here below! Would he allow his holy people to be in need?' says discontent. 'Throw off Christ's livery, desist from the religion!' Thus Job's wife being discontented with her condition, says to her husband, 'do you still retain your integrity?' As if she had said, 'do you not see, Job, what has become of all your religion? You fear God and eschew evil — and what are you the better? See how God turns his hand against you; he has smitten you in your body, estate, family — and do you still retain your integrity? What! Still devout? Still weep and pray for him? You fool, cast off religion, turn atheist!' Here was a sore temptation, which the devil handed over to Job by his discontented wife. Only his grace, as a golden shield, did ward off the blow from his heart, 'you speak as one of the foolish women!'

'What profit is it,' says the discontented person, 'to serve the Almighty? Those who never trouble themselves about religion, are the prosperous men, and I in the mean while suffer need. I will just as well give over driving the trade of religion — if this be all my reward!' This logic often prevails. Atheism is the fruit which grows out of the blossom of discontent.

O then, behold the excellency of contentment! 'If God is mine,' says the contented spirit, 'it is enough; though I have no lands or tenements, his smile makes heaven; his loves are better than wine. I have little in hand — but much in hope; my livelihood is short — but this is his promise, even eternal life! I am persecuted by malice — but better is persecuted godliness, than prosperous wickedness.' Thus divine contentment is a spiritual antidote both against sin and temptation.

Sixth excellency. Contentment sweetens every condition. Christ turned the water into wine. Just so, contentment turns the bitter waters of Marah, into spiritual wine.

'Have I but little? Yet it is more than I deserve. This contented spirit is given in mercy; it is the fruit of Christ's blood — it is the legacy of free grace! A small present sent from a king — is highly valued. This little I have is with a good conscience; it is not stolen waters; guilt has not muddied or poisoned it; it runs pure. This little — is a pledge of more: this bit of bread — is a pledge of that bread which I shall eat in the kingdom of God! This little water in the cruise — is a pledge of that heavenly nectar which shall be distilled from the true vine! Do I meet with some crosses? My comfort is, if they are heavy — I have not far to go; I shall but carry my cross to Golgotha and there I shall leave it. My cross is light — in comparison with the weight of glory. Has God taken away my comforts from me? It is well--the Comforter still abides with me.'

Thus contentment, as a honeycomb, drops sweetness into every condition. Discontent is a leaven which sours every comfort; it puts vinegar into every mercy, it doubles every cross. But the contented spirit sucks sweetness from every flower of providence; it can make poison into a choice morsel. Contentment is full of consolation.

Seventh excellency. Contentment is the best commentator upon providence; it makes a fair interpretation of all God's dealings. Let the providences of God be ever so dark or dismal, contentment construes them ever in the best sense. I may say of it, as the apostle of charity, 'it thinks no evil.' (1 Cor. 13:5) 'Sickness (says contentment) is God's furnace to refine his gold, and make it sparkle the more! The prison is an oratory, or house of prayer. What if God melts away the creature from it? he saw perhaps my heart grew so much in love with it; had I been long in that fat pasture, I would have surfeited, and the better my estate had been, the worse my soul would have been. God is wise; he has done this either to prevent some sin — or to exercise some grace.' What a blessed frame of heart is this!

A contented Christian is an advocate for God, against unbelief and impatience: whereas discontent takes everything from God in the worst sense; it censures God — and all that He does. But the contented soul takes all well; and when his condition is ever so bad, he can say, 'truly God is good.' (Psalm 73:1)

II. The second motive to contentment. A Christian has that which may make him content.

1. Has not God given you Christ? In him there are 'unsearchable riches!' (Ep. 3:8) He is such a golden mine of wisdom and grace — that all the saints and angels can never dig to the bottom! As Seneca said to his friend Polybius, 'never complain of your hard fortune — as long as Caesar is your friend.' So I say to a believer, 'never complain of your troubles — as long as Christ is your friend!' He is an enriching pearl, a sparkling diamond; the infinite luster of his merits makes us shine in God's eyes. (Ep. 1:7) In him there is both fullness and sweetness; he is unspeakably good. Pitch up your thoughts to the highest pinnacle, stretch them to the utmost bound, let them expatiate to their full latitude and extent — yet they fall infinitely short of these ineffable and inexhaustible treasures which are locked up in Jesus Christ! Is not this enough to give the soul contentment? A Christian who lacks necessities — yet having Christ, he has the 'one thing needful.'

2. Your soul is exercised and enameled with the graces of the Spirit, and is not here enough to give contentment? Grace is of a divine birth! It is the new plantation!. Grace is the flower of the

heavenly paradise! It is the embroidery of the Spirit! Grace is the seed of God! (1 John 3:9) Grace is the sacred unction! (1 John 2:20) Grace is Christ's portraiture in the soul! Grace is the very foundation on which superstructure of glory is laid! O, of what infinite value is grace! What a jewel is faith! Well may it be called 'precious faith.' (2 Pe. 1:1) What is love—but a divine sparkle in the soul? A soul beautified with grace, is like a room richly hung with tapestry, or the sky bespangled with glittering stars.

These are the 'true riches!' (Lu. 16:11) Is not here enough to give the soul contentment? What are all other things, but like wings of a butterfly, curiously painted—but they defile our fingers! Earthly riches cannot enrich the soul: oftentimes under silken apparel there is a thread-bare soul. Earthly riches are corruptible: 'riches are not forever,' as the wise man says. (Proverbs 27:24) Heaven is a place where gold and silver will not go. A believer is rich towards God! (Lu. 12:21) Why then, are you discontented? Has not God given you that which is better than the world? What if he does not give you the box—if he gives you the jewel! What if he denies you pennies—if he pays you in diamonds! What if he denies you temporal mercies—if he give you spiritual mercies. What if the water in the bottle is spent—you have enough in the fountain! What need he complain of the world's emptiness—who has God's fullness!

'The Lord is my portion,' says David, (Psalm 16:5) then let the lines fall where they will, in a sick-bed or prison, I will say, 'the lines are fallen unto me in pleasant places, yes, I have a goodly heritage!' Are you not heir to all the promises? Have you not a guarantee of heavenly glory? When you let go your hold of natural life—are you not sure of eternal life? Has not God given you the pledge and first fruits of glory? Is not here enough to work your heart to contentment?

III. The third motive is—Be content, for else we confute our own prayers. We pray, 'May your will be done.' It is the will of God that we should are in such a condition; he has decreed it, and he sees it best for us—why then do we murmur, and are discontent at that which we pray for? Either we are not in good earnest in our prayer, which argues hypocrisy; or we contradict ourselves which argues folly.

IV. The fourth motive to contentment is—because now God has his end, and Satan misses of his end.

1. God has his end. God's end in all his providences, is to bring the heart to submit and be content. Indeed, this pleases God much—he loves to see his children satisfied with that portion he carves and allots them; it contents him—to see us contented. Therefore let us acquiesce in God's providence, now God has his end.

2. Satan misses of his end. The end why the devil, though by God's permission, did smite Job in his body and estate—was to perplex his mind; he vexed his body with the purpose that he might disquiet his spirit. He hoped to bring Job into a fit of discontent; and then that he would in anger, break forth against God. But Job being so well-contented with his condition—that he falls to blessing of God, and so he did disappoint Satan of his hope. 'The devil will cast some of you into prison;' (Re. 2:10) why does the devil throw us into prison? It is not so much the hurting our body, as the molesting our mind, that he aims at; he would imprison our contentment, and disturb the regular motion of our souls—this is his design. It is not so much the putting us into a prison—as the putting us into a passion—which he attempts; but by holy contentment, Satan loses his prey, and misses of his end.

The devil has often deceived us; the best way to deceive him, is by contentment in the midst of temptation; our contentment will discontent Satan. O, let us not gratify our enemy! Discontent is the devil's delight! Now it is as he would have it, he loves to warm himself at the fire of our passions. Repentance is the joy of the angels—and discontent is the joy of the devils! As the devil dances at discord, so he sings at discontent. The fire of our passions makes the devil a bonfire! It is a kind of heaven to him—to see us torturing ourselves with our own troubles; but by holy contentment, we frustrate him of his purpose, and do as it were put him out of countenance.

V. The fifth motive is to contentment is—by contentment a Christian gains a victory over himself. For a man to be able to rule his own spirit—this of all others, is the most noble conquest. Passion denotes weakness; to be discontented is suitable to flesh and blood. But to be in every state content, reproached—yet content, imprisoned—yet content; this is above nature; this is some of that holy valor and chivalry which only a divine spirit is able to infuse. In the midst of the affronts of the world, to be patient; and in the changes of the world, to have the spirit calmed—this is a conquest worthy indeed of the garland of honor. Holy Job, divested and turned out of all, leaving his scarlet, and embracing the dunghill, (a sad catastrophe!) yet had learned contentment. It is said, 'he fell down upon the ground and worshiped.' (Job 1:20) One would have thought he should have fallen upon the ground and blasphemed! No, he fell and worshiped! He adored God's justice and holiness! Behold the strength of grace! here was a humble submission—yet a noble conquest; he got the victory over himself! It is no great matter for a man to yield to his own passions, this is facile and cowardly—but to content himself in denying of himself, this is sacred.

VI. The sixth great motive to work the heart to contentment is—the consideration that all God's providences, however cross or difficult, shall do a believer good. 'And we know that all things work together for good, to those who love God.' (Rom. 8:28) Not only all good things—but all evil things work for good; and shall we be discontented at that which works for our good? Suppose our troubles are sadly twisted together: what if sickness, poverty, reproach, law-suits, etc., unite and muster their forces against us? All shall work for good; our maladies shall be our medicines; and shall we repine at which shall undoubtedly do us good? 'Unto the upright, there arises light in darkness.' (Psalm 112:4) Affliction may be baptized Marah; it is bitter—but medicinal. Because this is so full of comfort, and may be a most excellent remedy against discontent, I shall a little expatiate. It will be inquired how the evils of affliction work for good? Several ways.

First, they instruct us—they teach us. The Psalmist having very elegantly described the church's trouble, (Psalm 74) prefixed this title to the psalm, a Maschil, which signifies a psalm giving instruction; and that which seals up instruction, works for good. God puts us sometimes under the black rod of discipline; 'hear the rod, and who has appointed it.' (Mi. 6:9) God makes our adversity our university. Affliction is a preacher; 'blow the trumpet in Tekoa:' (Je. 6:1) the trumpet was to preach to the people; 'be instructed, O Jerusalem.' (Je. 6:8) Sometimes God speaks to the minister to lift up his voice like a trumpet, (Is. 58:1) and here he speaks to the trumpet to lift up its voice like a minister.

Afflictions teach us humility. We are commonly prosperous and proud, but corrections are God's corrosives to eat out the proud flesh. Jesus Christ is the lily of the valleys, (Can. 2:1) he dwells in a humble heart! God brings us into the valley of tears—that He may bring us into the valley of humility; 'remembering my affliction and my misery, the wormwood and the gall; my soul has them still in remembrance, and is humbled in me. (La. 3:19, 20) When men are grown proud, God has no better way with them, than to brew them a cup of wormwood.

Afflictions are compared to thorns, (Ho. 2:6) God's thorns are to prick the bubble of pride. Suppose a man runs at another with a sword to kill him; accidentally, it only lets out his abscess of pride; this does him good: God's sword is to let out the abscess of pride; and shall that which makes us humble, make us discontented?

Afflictions teach us repentance; 'You have disciplined me—and I have been disciplined. After I strayed, I repented.' (Jer. 31:18, 19) Repentance is the precious fruit that grows upon the cross. When the fire is put under the still, the water drops. Just so, fiery afflictions make the waters of repentance drop and distill from the eyes; and is here any cause of discontent?

Afflictions teach us to pray better, 'they poured out a prayer when Your chastening was upon them;' (Is. 26:16) before, they would say a prayer; now they poured out a prayer. Jonah was asleep in the ship—but awake and at prayer in the whale's belly. When God puts under the fire-brands of affliction, now our hearts boil over the more; God loves to have his children possessed with a spirit of prayer. Never did David, the sweet singer of Israel, tune his harp more melodiously, never did he pray better, than when he was in affliction. Thus afflictions instruct us; and shall we be discontent at that which is for our good?

Secondly, Afflictions test us. (Psalm 66:10,11) Gold is not the worse for being tried, or grain for being fanned. Affliction is the touchstone of sincerity, it tries what metal we are made of; affliction is God's fan and his sieve. It is good that men be known; some serve God for a livery; they are like the fisherman, who makes use of the net, only to catch the fish; so they go a-fishing with the net of religion, only to catch preferment: affliction discovers these. Hypocrites will fail in a storm, true grace holds out in the winter-season. That is a precious faith which, like the stars, shines brightest in the darkest night. It is good that our graces should be brought to trial; thus we have the comfort, and the gospel the honor—and why then be discontented?

Thirdly, Afflictions are purgatives. These evils work for our good, because they purge out sin, and shall I be discontented at this? What if I have more trouble, if I have less sin? The brightest day has its clouds; the purest gold its dross; the most refined soul has some measure of corruption. The saints lose nothing in the furnace—but what they can well spare—their dross: is not this for our good? Why then should we murmur? 'I am come to send fire on the earth.' (Lu. 12:49) Tertullian understands it of the fire of affliction. God makes this like the fire of the three children, which burned only their bonds and set them at liberty in the furnace, so the fire of affliction serves to burn the bonds of iniquity. 'By this therefore shall the iniquity of Jacob be purged: and this is all the fruit—to take away his sin.' (Is. 27:9)

When affliction or death comes to a wicked man, it takes away his soul; when it comes to a godly man, it only takes away his sin; is there any cause why we should be discontented? God steeps us in the brinish waters of affliction that he make take out our spots. God's people are his husbandry; (1 Cor. 3:9) the ploughing of the ground kills the weeds, and the harrowing of the earth breaks the hard clods: God's ploughing of us by affliction, is to kill the weeds of sin; his harrowing of us is to break the hard clouds of impenitency, that the heart may be fitter to receive the seeds of grace; and if this is the purpose of affliction, why should we be discontented?

Fourthly, Afflictions both exercise and increase our grace. Afflictions exercise our graces; everything is most in its excellency when it is most in its exercise. Our grace, though it cannot be dead—yet it may be asleep, and has need of awakening. What a dull thing is the fire when it is hid in the embers, or the sun when it is masked behind a cloud! A sick man is living—but not lively; afflictions quicken and excite grace. God does not like to see grace in the eclipse. Now faith puts forth its purest and most noble acts in times of affliction. God makes the fall of the leaf the spring of our graces. What if we are more afflicted—if graces be more active.

Afflictions increase grace; as the wind serves to increase and blow up the flame, so does the windy blasts of affliction augment and blow up our graces; grace is not consumed in the furnace—but it is like the widow's oil in the cruise, which increased by pouring out. The torch, when it is beaten burns brightest, so does grace when it is exercised by sufferings. Sharp frosts nourish the good grain—so do sharp afflictions nourish grace. Some plants grow better in the shade than in the sun; the shade of adversity is better for some than the sun-shine of prosperity. Naturalists observe that the colewort thrives better when it is watered with salt water than with fresh water, so do some thrive better in the salt water of affliction; and shall we be discontented at that which makes us grow and fructify more?

Fifthly, these afflictions do bring more of God's gracious presence into the soul. When we are most assaulted, we shall be most assisted; 'I will be with him in trouble.' (Psalm 91:15) It cannot be ill with that man with whom God is—by his powerful presence in supporting, and his gracious presence in sweetening the present trial. God will be with us in trouble, not only to behold us—but to uphold us, as he was with Daniel in the lion's den, and the three Hebrew children in the fiery furnace. What if we have more trouble than others—if we have more of God with us than others have? We never have sweeter smiles from God's face—than when the world begins to frown upon us. Your statutes have been my song; where? Not when I was upon the throne—but 'in the house of my pilgrimage.' (Psalm 119:54)

We read, the Lord was not in the wind, nor in the earthquake, nor in the fire: (1 Ki. 19:11) but in a metamorphical and spiritual sense, when the wind of affliction blows upon a believer, God is in the wind; when the fire of affliction kindles upon him, God is in the fire—to sanctify, to support, to sweeten. If God is with us, the furnace shall be turned into a festival, the prison into a paradise, the earthquake into a joyful dance. O why should I be discontented, when I have more of God's gracious presence!

Sixthly, these evils of affliction are for good, as they bring with them certificates of God's love, and are evidences of his special favor. Affliction is the saint's livery; it is a badge of honor! That the God of glory should look upon a worm, and take so much notice of him—as to afflict him rather than lose him—is an high act of favor. God's rod is a scepter of dignity, Job calls God's afflicting of us, his magnifying of us. (Job 7:17) Some men's prosperity has been their shame, when others afflictions have been their crown.

Seventhly, these afflictions work for our good, because they work for us a far exceeding weight of glory. (2 Cor. 4:17) That which works for my glory in heaven, works for my good. We do not read in Scripture that any man's honor or riches work for him a weight of glory—but afflictions do; and shall a man be discontented at that which works for his glory? The heavier the weight of affliction, the heavier the weight of glory; not that our sufferings merit glory, (as the papists do wickedly teach,) but though they are not the cause of our crown—yet they are the way to it; and God makes us, as he did our captain, 'perfect through sufferings.' (He. 2:10) And shall not all this make us contented with our condition?

O I beseech you, look not upon the evil of affliction—but the good of affliction! Afflictions in Scripture are called 'visitations.' (Job 7:18) God's afflictions are but friendly visits. Behold here God's rod, like Aaron's rod blossoming; and Jonathan's rod, it has honey at the end of it. Poverty shall starve out our sins; the sickness of the body cures a sin-sick soul; O then, instead of murmuring and being discontented, bless the Lord! Had you not met with such a cross in the way—you might have gone to hell and never stopped!

VII. The seventh motive to contentment is—consider the evil of discontent. Malcontent has a mixture of grief and anger in it, and both of these must needs raise a storm in the soul. Have you not seen the posture of a sick man? Sometimes he will sit up on his bed, by and by he will lie down, and when he is down he is not quiet; first he turns on the one side and then on the other; he is restless; this is just the emblem of a discontented spirit. The man is not sick—yet he is never well; sometimes he likes such a condition of life but is soon weary; and then another condition of life; and when he has it—yet he is not pleased; this is an evil under the sun. Now the evil of discontent appears in three things.

First Evil. The sordidness of it is unworthy of a Christian.

(1.) It is unworthy of his profession. It was the saying of a heathen, 'bear your condition quietly; know you are a man;' so I say, 'bear your condition contentedly; know you are a Christian.' You professes to live by faith: what? And not be content? Faith is a grace which substantiates things not seen; (He. 11:1) faith looks beyond the present—it feeds upon promises; faith lives not by bread alone; when the water is spent in the bottle, faith knows where to have recourse. Now to see a Christian dejected in the lack of visible supplies, where is faith? 'O,' says one, 'my estate in the world is down.' Ay, and which is worse—his faith is down. Unless he has many outward comforts—he will not be content. True faith will trust God's heart—where it cannot trace his hand; and will venture upon God's promise though it has nothing in view.

You who are discontented because you have not all that you would, let me tell you—either your faith is a nonentity—or at best but an embryo. It is a weak faith which must have crutches to support it. Nay, discontent is not only below faith—but below reason: why are you discontented? Is it because you are dispossessed of such comforts? Well, and have you not reason to guide you? Does not reason tell you that you are but tenants at will? And may not God turn you out when he pleases? You hold not your estate by personal right—but upon God's favor and courtesy.

(2.) It is unworthy of the relation we stand in to God. A Christian is invested with the title and privilege of sonship, (Ep. 1:5) he is an heir of the promise. O consider the lot of free-grace which has fallen upon you! You are nearly allied to Christ, and of the blood royal; you are advanced in some sense, above the angels: 'why are you, being the king's son, lean from day to day?' (2 Sa. 13:4) Why are you discontented? O, how unworthy is this! as if the heir to some great monarch should go pining up and down, because he may not pick such a flower.

Second Evil. Consider the sinfulness of discontent; which appears in three things; the causes, the accompaniments, the consequences of it.

(1.) It is sinful in the causes.

The first cause of discontent is pride. He who thinks highly of his

deserts, usually is discontent with his condition. A discontented man is a proud man, he thinks himself better than others, therefore finds fault with the wisdom of God. 'Should the thing that was created say to the One who made it—Why have you made me like this?' (Ro. 9:20) why am I not in better circumstances? Discontent is nothing else but the boiling over of pride!

The second cause of discontent is envy, which Augustine calls the sin of the devil. Satan envied Adam the glory of paradise, and the robe of innocency. He who envies what his neighbor has—is never contented with that portion which God's providence, parcels out to him. As envy stirs up strife, so it creates discontent: the envious man looks so much upon the blessings which another enjoys—that he cannot see his own mercies—and so does continually vex and torture himself. Cain envied that his brother's sacrifice was accepted, and his rejected; hereupon he was discontented, and presently murderous thoughts began to arise in his heart.

The third cause of discontent is covetousness. This is a foul sin. Whence are vexing lawsuits—but from discontent? And whence is discontent—but from covetousness? Covetousness and contentedness cannot dwell in the same heart. Avarice is never satisfied. The covetous man is like Behemoth, 'behold he drinks up a river.' (Job 40:23) 'There are four things (says Solomon) which never have enough.' I may add a fifth—the heart of a covetous man; he is continually craving. Covetousness is like a wolf in the breast, which is ever feeding. Because a man is never satisfied—he is never content.

The fourth cause of discontent is unbelief, which is akin to Atheism. The discontented person is ever distrustful. The provisions grow scanty, and the distrustful person asks, 'I am in these great difficulties, can God help me? Can he prepare a table in the wilderness? Surely he cannot. My estate is exhausted, can God help me? My friends are gone, can God raise me up more? Surely the arm of his power is shrunk. I am like the dry fleece, can any water come upon this fleece? If the Lord would make windows in heaven, might this thing be?' (2 Ki. 7:2) Thus the anchor of hope, and the shield of faith, being cast away, the soul goes pining up and down. Discontent is nothing else but the echo of unbelief. Remember, distrust is worse than distress.

(2.) Discontent is evil in its accompaniments, which are two:

1. Discontent is joined with a sullen melancholy. A Christian of a right temper should be ever cheerful in God: 'serve the Lord with gladness;' (Psalm 100:2) A sign that the oil of grace has been poured into the heart, is when the oil of gladness shines in the countenance. Cheerfulness credits religion; how can the discontented person be cheerful? Discontent is a dogged, sullen humor. Because we have not what we desire, God shall not have a good work or look from us. This is like the bird in the cage, because she is pent up, and cannot fly in the open air, therefore beats herself against the cage, and is ready to kill herself. Thus that peevish prophet; 'I do well to be angry, even unto death!' (Jon. 4:9)

2. Discontent is accompanied with unthankfulness. Because we have not all we desire, we never mind the mercies which we have. We deal with God as the widow of Zarephath did with the prophet: the prophet Elijah had been a means to keep her alive in the famine, for it was for his sake that her meal in the barrel, and her oil in the cruise failed not. But as soon as ever her son dies, she falls into a passion, and begins to quarrel with the prophet: 'O man of God, what have you done to me? Have you come here to punish my sins by killing my son?' (1 Ki. 17:18) So ungratefully do we deal with God: we can be content to receive mercies from God—but if he crosses us in the least thing, then, through discontent, we grow touchy and impatient, and are ready to fly upon God! Thus God loses all his mercies.

We read in Scripture of the thank-offering; the discontented person cuts God short of this; the Lord loses his thank-offering. A discontented Christian repines in the midst of mercies—as Adam who sinned in the midst of paradise. Discontent is a spider which sucks the poison of unthankfulness out of the sweetest flowers of God's mercies! Discontent is a devilish chemistry, which extracts dross out of the most pure gold. The discontented person thinks everything he does for God too much, and everything God does for him too little.

O what a sin is unthankfulness! It is an accumulative sin. I may say of ingratitude: 'there are many sins bound up in this one sin.' It is a voluminous wickedness! How full of sin is discontent! A discontented Christian, because he has not all the world, therefore dishonors God with the mercies which he has. God made Eve out of Adam's rib, to be a helper—but the devil has made an arrow of this rib, and shot Adam to the heart! Just so, discontent takes the rib of God's mercy, and ungratefully shoots at him—every blessing is employed against God. Thus it is oftentimes. Behold then how discontent and ingratitude are interwoven and twisted one within the other: thus discontent is sinful in its accompaniments.

(3.) Discontent is sinful in its consequences, which are these.

1. Discontent makes a man very unlike the Holy Spirit. The Spirit of God is a meek Spirit. The Holy Spirit descended in the likeness of a dove, (Mat. 3:16) a dove is the emblem of meekness; a discontented spirit is not a meek spirit.

2. Discontent makes a man like the devil; the devil being swelled with the poison of envy and malice, is never content. Just so, is the malcontent. The devil is an unquiet spirit, he is still 'walking about,' (1 Pe. 5:8) it is his rest to be walking. And herein is the discontented person like him; for he goes up and down vexing himself, 'seeking rest, and finding none.' The malcontent is the devil's picture!

3. Discontent disjoints the soul, it untunes the heart for duty. 'Is any among you afflicted, let him pray.' (Ja. 5:13) But, is any man discontented? How shall he pray? 'Lift up holy hands without wrath.' (1 Ti. 2:8) Discontent is full of wrath and passion; the malcontent cannot lift up pure hands; he lifts up leprous hands—he poisons his prayers! Will God accept a poisoned sacrifice! Chrysostom compares prayer to a fine garland; those who make a garland, their hands had need to be clean. Prayer is a precious garland, the heart that makes it, had need to be clean. Discontent throws poison into the spring. Discontent puts the heart into a disorder and mutiny, and such as one cannot serve the Lord 'without distraction.'

4. Discontent sometimes unfits for the very use of reason. Jonah, in a passion of discontent, spoke no better than blasphemy and nonsense: 'I do well to be angry—even unto death!' (Jon. 4:9) What? To be angry with God! And to die for anger! Sure he did not know what he said! When discontent rules, then, like Moses, we speak unadvisedly with our lips. This humor even suspends the very acts of reason.

5. Discontent does not only disquiet a man's self—but those who are near him. This evil spirit troubles families, parishes, etc. If there is but one string out of tune, it spoils all the music. Just so, one discontented spirit makes jarrings and discords among others. It is this ill-humor which breeds quarrels and law-suits. Whence are all our contentions—but for lack of contentment? 'What is the source of the wars and the fights among you? Don't they come from the cravings that are at war within you?' (Ja. 4:1) in particular from the craving of discontent. Why did Absalom raise a war against his father, and would have taken off not only his crown—but his head! Was it not his discontent? Absalom would be king. Why did Ahab stone Naboth? Was it not discontent about the vineyard? Oh this devil of discontent! Thus, you have seen the sinfulness of it.

Third Evil. Consider the foolishness of discontent. I may say, as the Psalmist, 'surely they are disquieted in vain:' (Psalm 39:6) which appears thus,

1. Is it not a vain simple thing to be troubled at the loss of that which is in its own nature, perishing and changeable? God has put a vicissitude into the creature; all the world rings changes; and for me to meet with inconstancy here on earth—to lose a friend, estate, to be in constant fluctuation; is no more than to see a flower wither or a leaf drop off in autumn! There is an autumn upon every comfort, a fall of the leaf. Now it is extreme folly to be discontented at the loss of those things which are in their own nature, loseable. What Solomon says of riches, is true of all things under the sun, 'they take wings—and fly away!' Noah's dove brought an olive-branch in its mouth—but presently flew out of the ark, and never more returned. Such and such a comfort, brings to us honey in its mouth—but it has wings; and to what purpose should we be troubled, unless we had wings to fly after and overtake it?

2. Discontent is a heart-breaking. 'By sorrow of the heart, the spirit is broken.' (Proverbs 15:13) It takes away the comfort of life. There is none of us, but may have many mercies if we can see them; now because we have not all we desire, therefore we will lose the comfort of that which we have already. Jonah having his gourd smitten, a withering vanity — was so discontented, that he never thought of his miraculous deliverance out of the whale's belly; he takes no comfort of his life — but wishes that he might die. What folly is this! We must have all or none; herein we are like children that throw away the piece which is cut for them, because they may have no bigger. Discontent eats out the comfort of life!

Besides, it were well if it were seriously weighed, how harmful this is even to our health; for discontent, as it does discruciate the mind — so it does pine the body. It frets as a moth; and by wasting the spirits, weakens the vitals. The cancer of discontent harms both the body and the mind — and is not this folly?

3. Discontent does not ease us of our burden — but it makes it heavier. A contented spirit goes cheerfully under its affliction. Discontent makes our grief as unsupportable as it is unreasonable. If the leg is well, it can endure a fetter and not complain; but if the leg is injured, then the fetters trouble. Discontent of mind, is the sore which makes the fetters of affliction more grievous. Discontent troubles us more than the trouble itself! It steeps the affliction in wormwood. When Christ was upon the Cross, the Jews brought him gall and vinegar to drink, that it might add to his sorrow. Discontent brings to a man in affliction, gall and vinegar to drink! This is worse than the affliction itself. Is it not folly for a man to embitter his own affliction?

4. Discontent spins out our troubles the longer. One is discontented because he is in need, and therefore he is in need because he is discontented; he murmurs because he is afflicted, and therefore he is afflicted, because he murmurs. Discontent delays and adjourns our mercies. God deals herein with us, as we do with our children — when they are quiet and cheerful, they shall have anything; but if we see them cry and fret, then we withhold from them. Just so, we get nothing from God by our discontent, but blows! The more the child struggles, the more it is beaten: when we struggle with God by our sinful passions, he doubles his strokes; God will tame our peevish hearts. What did Israel get by their peevishness? They were within eleven days journey to Canaan; and now they were discontented and began to murmur, so God leads them a march of forty years long in the wilderness. Is it not folly for us to adjourn our own mercies? Thus you have seen the evil of discontent.

VIII. The eighth motive to contentment is this: Why is not a man content with that which he has? Perhaps if he had more he would be less content. Covetousness is cancer which is never satisfied. The world is such that the more we have — the more we crave. The world cannot fill the heart of man. When the fire burns, how do you quench it? Not by putting oil in the flame, or laying on more wood — but by withdrawing the fuel. When the appetite is inflamed after riches, how may a man be satisfied? Not by having just what he desires — but by withdrawing the fuel, and by moderating and lessening his desires. He who is contented has enough! A man in a fever thirsts; how do you satisfy him? Not by giving him liquid things, which will inflame his thirst the more; but by removing the cause, and so curing the distemper. The way for a man to be contented, is not by raising his estate higher — but by bringing his heart lower!

IX. The ninth motive to contentment is — the shortness of life. Life is 'but a vapor,' says James. (Ja. 4:14) Life is a wheel ever-running. The poets painted time with wings to show the volubility and swiftness of it. Job compares it to a swift runner, (Job 9:25). Our life is indeed like a day. Infancy is as it were the day-break, youth is the sun-rising, adulthood is the sun in the meridian, old age is sun-setting, sickness is the evening — then comes the night of death. How quickly is this day of life spent! Oftentimes this sun goes down at noon-day; life ends before the evening of old age comes. Nay, sometimes the sun of life sets presently after sun-rising. Quickly after the dawning of infancy, the night of death approaches. O, how short is the life of man!

The consideration of the brevity of life, may work the heart to contentment. Remember you are to be here but a day; you have but a short way to go—and what is the need of a long provision for a short way? If a traveler has but enough to bring him to his journey's end—he desires no more. We have but a day to live, and perhaps we may be in the twelfth hour of the day. If God gives us but enough to bear our charges, until night, it is sufficient, let us be content. If a man had the lease of a house—but for two or three days, and he should begin building and planting, would he not be judged very foolish? Just so, when we have but a short time here, and death calls us presently off the stage—to thirst immoderately after the world, and pull down our souls to build up an estate—is an extreme folly.

Therefore, as Esau said once, in a profane sense, concerning his birth-right, 'I am at the point of death—so what profit shall this birth-right do to me?' so let a Christian say in a religious sense, 'I am at the point of death, my grave is going to be made—so what good will the world do to me? If I have but enough until sun-setting, I am content.'

X. The tenth motive to contentment is—consider seriously the nature of a prosperous condition. There are in a prosperous estate three things,

1. There is more trouble in a prosperous condition. Many who have abundance of all things to enjoy—yet have not so much contentment and sweetness in their lives, as some who go to their hard labor. Sad, anxious thoughts often attend a prosperous condition. Worry is the evil spirit which haunts the rich man—and will not allow him to be quiet. When his chest is full of gold— his heart is full of worry, either how to manage, or how to increase, or how to secure what he has gotten. O the troubles and perplexities which attend prosperity! The world's high seats are very uneasy. Sunshine is pleasant—but sometimes it scorches with its heat. The bee gives honey—but sometimes it stings! Just so, prosperity has its sweetness—and also its sting! 'But godliness with contentment is great gain.' 1 Timothy 6:6. Never did Jacob sleep better, than when he had the heavens for his canopy, and a hard stone for his pillow. A large estate is but like a long trailing garment, which is more troublesome than useful.

2. In a prosperous condition there is more danger; and that two ways:

First, in respect of a man's self. The rich man's table is often his snare; he is ready to engulf himself too deep in these sweet waters. In this sense it is hard to know how to abound. It must be a strong brain which can bear heady wine. Just so, he has need have of much wisdom and grace, to know how to bear a prosperous condition; either he is ready to kill himself with worry—or to glut himself with luscious delights. O the hazard of honor, the damage of prosperity! Pride, lust, and worldliness, are the three worms which breed in prosperity. (De. 32:15) The pastures of prosperity are dangerous. How soon are we ensnared upon the soft pillow of ease! Prosperity is often a trumpet which sounds a retreat—it calls men off from the pursuit of religion. The sun of prosperity often dulls and puts out the fire of piety! How many souls has the cancer of abundance killed? 'People who want to get rich fall into temptation and a trap and into many foolish and harmful desires that plunge men into ruin and destruction. For the love of money is a root of all kinds of evil. Some people, eager for money, have wandered from the faith and pierced themselves with many griefs.' (1 Timothy 6:9-10)

The world is full of golden sands—but they are quick-sands! Prosperity, like smooth Jacob, will supplant and betray! A great estate, without much vigilance—will be a thief to rob us of heaven! Such as are upon the pinnacle of honor, are in most danger of falling. A more humble condition, is less hazardous. The little boat rides safely along, when the gallant ship with its large mast and top-sail, is cast away. Adam in paradise was overcome, when Job on the dunghill was a conqueror. Samson fell asleep in Delilah's lap. Just so, some have fallen so fast asleep on the lap of ease and plenty, that they have never awaked until they have been in hell!

The world's fawning—is worse than its frowning! It is more to be feared when it smiles—than when it thunders. Prosperity, in Scripture, is compared to a candle; 'his candle shined upon my head:' (Job 29:3) how many have burnt their wings about this candle! The corn being over-ripe, withers; and fruit, when it mellows, begins to rot. Just so, when men mellow with the sun of prosperity, commonly their souls begin to rot in sin! 'How hard it is for the rich to enter the kingdom of God!' (Lu. 18:24) His golden weights keep him from ascending up the hill of God! And shall we not be content, though we are placed in a lower orb? What if we have not as much of the world, as others do? We are not in so much danger! As we lack the riches of the world—so we lack their temptations. O the abundance of danger—which is in abundance!

When men's estates are low, they are more serious about their souls, and more humble. But when they have abundance, then their hearts begin to swell with their estates. Bring a man from the cold, starving climate of poverty—into the hot southern climate of prosperity—and he begins to lose his appetite to godly things, he grows weak—and a thousand to one if all his religion does not die! But bring a Christian from a rich flourishing estate into a low condition—and he has a better appetite after heavenly things, he hungers more after Christ, he thirsts more for grace, he eats more of the Bread of Life; this man is now likely to live and hold out in his piety. Be content then, with moderation; if you have but enough to pay for your passage to heaven, it suffices. 'If we have food and clothing—we will be content with these.' 1 Timothy 6:8

Secondly, a prosperous condition is dangerous in regard of others. A great estate, for the most part, draws envy to it; whereas in little there is quiet. David a shepherd was quiet—but David a king was pursued by his enemies. Envy cannot endure a superior; an envious man knows not how to live—but upon the ruins of his neighbors; he raises himself higher—by bringing others lower. Prosperity is an eye-sore to many. Such sheep as have most wool—are soonest fleeced. The barren tree grows peaceably; but the fruit-laden tree shall have many savage suitors. O then be contented to carry a lesser sail! He who has less revenues, has less envy. Such as make the greatest show in the world, are the bulls-eye for envy and malice to shoot at!

3. A prosperous condition has in it, a greater reckoning; every man must be responsible for his talents. You who have great possessions in the world, do you use them for God's glory? Are you rich in good works? Grace makes a private person—a common good. Do you disburse your money for public uses? It is lawful, in this sense, to put out our money to use. O let us all remember that we are but stewards; and our Lord and Master will before long say, 'give an account of your stewardship!' The greater our estate—the greater our responsibilities; the more our revenues—the more our reckonings. You who have but little in the world—be content. God will expect less from you—where He has sowed more sparingly.

XI. The eleventh motive to contentment is—the example of those who have been eminent for contentment. Examples are usually more forcible than precepts. Abraham being called out to hard service, and such as was against flesh and blood, was content. God bid him offer up his son Isaac. This was great work: Isaac was the son of his old age; the son of his love; the son of the promise; Christ the Messiah was to come from his line, 'in Isaac shall your seed be called.' So that to offer up Isaac seemed not only to oppose Abraham's reason—but his faith too; for, if Isaac dies, the world, for ought he knew—must be without a Mediator. Besides, if Isaac must be sacrificed, was there no other hand to do it, but Abraham's? Must the father needs be the executioner? Must he who was the instrument of giving Isaac his being, be the instrument of taking it away? Yet Abraham does not dispute or hesitate — but believes 'against hope,' and is content with God's prescription: so, when God called him to leave his country, he was content.

Some would have argued thus: 'What! Leave my friends, my native soil, my prosperous situation, and become a wandering pilgrim?' Abraham is content. Besides, Abraham went blindfold, 'He did not know where he was going.' God held him in suspense; he must go wander — he knows not where; and when he does come to the place which God has laid out for him, he knows not what oppositions he shall meet with there. The world seldom casts a favorable aspect upon strangers. Yet he is content, and obeys; 'he sojourned in the land of promise.' (He. 11:9)

Behold a little his pilgrimage. First, he goes to Haran, a city in Mesopotamia. When he had sojourned there a while, his father dies. Then he moved to Canaan; there a famine arises; then he went down to Egypt; after that he returns to Canaan. When he comes there, it is true he had a promise — but he found nothing to answer expectation; he had not there one foot of land — but was an exile. In this time of his sojourning he buried his wife; and as for his dwellings, he had no sumptuous buildings — but lived in tents: all this was enough to have broken any man's heart. Abraham might think thus with himself: 'is this the land I must possess? Here is no probability of any good; all things are against me!' Well, is he discontented? No! God says to him, 'Abraham, go, leave your country,' and this word was enough to lead him all over the world; he is presently upon his march. Here was a man who had learned to be content.

But let us descend a little lower, to heathen Zeno, of who Seneca speaks, who had once been very rich, hearing of a shipwreck, and that all his goods were drowned at sea: 'Fortune,' says he, (he spoke in a heathen dialect) 'has dealt with me, and would have me now study philosophy.' He was content to change his course of life, to leave off being a merchant, and turn a philosopher. And if a heathen said thus, shall not a Christian say, when the world is drained from him, 'God would have me leave off following the world, and study Christ more, and how to get to heaven!' Do I see an heathen contented, and a Christian disquieted? How did heathens vilify those worldly things, which Christians did magnify? Though they knew not God, or what true happiness meant; yet, they would speak very sublimely of a deity, and of the life to come, and for those Elysian delights, which they did but imagine — so they undervalued and despised the things here below! It was the doctrine they taught their scholars, and which some of them practiced, that they should strive to be contented with a little; they were willing to make an exchange, and have less gold — and more learning. And shall not we be content then, to have less of the world — so that we may have more of Christ! May not Christians blush to see the heathens content with little of this world — and to see themselves so elated with the love of earthly things, that if they begin a little to abate, and their provisions grow short, they murmur, and are like Micah, 'You took away the gods I made. What else do I have?' (Judges 18:24) Have heathens gone so far in contentment, and is it not sad for us to be discontent?

These heroes of their time, how did they embrace death itself! Socrates died in prison; Herculus was burnt alive; Cato, who Seneca calls the portrait of virtue, was thrust through with a sword; but how bravely, and with contentment of spirit did they die? 'Shall I (said Seneca) weep for Cato, or Regulus, or the rest of those worthies, who died with so much valor and patience?' These severe afflictions did not make them alter their countenance — and do I see a Christian appalled and amazed? Death did not affright them — and does it distract us? Did the spring-head of nature rise so high? And shall not grace, like the waters of the sanctuary, rise higher? We that pretend to live by faith — may we not go to school to them who had no other pilot but reason to guide them?

Nay, let me come a step lower, to creatures void of reason; we see that every creature is contented with its allowance; the beasts with their provender, the birds with their nests; they live only upon providence. And shall we make ourselves below them? Let a Christian go to school to the ox and the donkey to learn contentedness! We think that we never have enough, and are always storing up. 'Look at the birds of the air; they do not sow or reap or store away in barns, and yet your heavenly Father feeds them. Are you not much more valuable than they?' (Mat. 6:26) It is an motive which Christ brings to make Christians contented with their condition; the birds do not store up—yet they are provided for, and are contented. But if you are discontented, you are much worse than they are. Let these examples quicken us.

XII. The twelfth motive to contentment is—whatever affliction or trouble a child of God meets with—it is all the hell he shall ever have! Whatever eclipse may be upon his name or estate—it is a little cloud which will soon be blown over—and then his hell is past. Death begins a wicked man's hell. Death ends a godly man's hell. Think with yourself, 'What is my affliction? It is but a temporary hell. Indeed if all my hell is here on earth--it is but an easy hell. What is the cup of affliction, compared to the cup of damnation!'

Lazarus could not get a crumb; he was so diseased that the dogs took pity on him, and as if they had been his physicians, licked his sores. But this was an easy hell—the angels quickly fetched him out of it! If all our hell is in this life—and in the midst of this hell we may have the love of God, and then it is no more hell—but paradise! If all our hell is here, we may see to the end of it; it is but skin-deep, it cannot touch the soul. It is a short-lived hell. After a dreary night of affliction, comes the bright morning of glory! Since our lives are short—our trials cannot be long. As our riches take wings and fly away—so do our sufferings. Let us learn to be content, whatever our circumstances.

XIII. The thirteenth motive to contentment is this—to have much of the world, and to lack contentment, is a great judgement. For a man to have a huge stomach, that whatever food you give him—he is still craving and is never satisfied—this is a great judgement upon the man! Likewise, you who are a devourer of money, and yet never have enough—but still cry, 'give, give!' this is a sad judgement! 'They shall eat, and not have enough.' (Ho. 4:10) The throat of a malicious man is an open sepulcher, (Ro. 3:13) so is the heart of a covetous man. Covetousness is not only a sin—but the punishment of a sin! It is a secret curse upon a covetous person; he shall thirst, and thirst, and never be satisfied! 'Whoever loves money never has money enough; whoever loves wealth is never satisfied with his income.' (Ec. 5:10) And is not this a curse!

It was a severe judgement upon the people of Judah, 'You have food to eat, but not enough to fill you up. You have wine to drink, but not enough to satisfy your thirst.' (Haggai 1:6) O let us take heed of this plague! Did not Esau say to his brother, 'I have enough, my brother,' (Gen. 33:9); and shall not a Christian say so much more. It is sad that our hearts should be dead to heavenly things—that they are a sponge to suck in earthly vanities!

All that has been said, should be sufficient to work our minds to heavenly contentment.

Three cautions

In the next place, I come to lay down some necessary cautions. Though I say a man should be content in every estate—yet there are three estates in which he must not be contented.

I. He must not be contented in a natural estate. Here we must learn not to be content.

A sinner in his natural state, is under the wrath of God, (John 3:16) and shall he be content when that dreadful vial is about to be poured out upon him! Is it nothing to lie forever under the scorchings of divine fury? 'Who can dwell with everlasting burnings!'

A sinner, as a sinner, is under the power of Satan, (Ac. 26:18) and shall he be content in this dreadful state! Who would be contented to stay in the enemies' quarters? While we sleep in the lap of sin, the devil does to us as the Philistines did to Samson — he cut out the lock of our strength, and put out our eyes! Be not content, O sinner, in this estate! For a man to be in debt, body and soul; in fear every hour to be arrested and carried prisoner to hell — shall he now be content? Here I preach against contentment. Oh get out of this condition! I would hasten you out of it — as the angel hastened lot out of Sodom (Gen. 19:15). There is the smell of the fire and brimstone upon you!

The longer a man stays in his sin, the more does sin strengthen. It is hard to get out of sin, when the heart as a garrison is supplied and fortified by sin. A young tree is easily removed — but when the tree is once rooted, there is no stirring of it. Just so, you who are rooted in your pride, unbelief, impenitency, it will cost you many a hard pull before you are plucked out of your natural estate! (Jer. 6:16) It is a hard thing to have a brazen face and a broken heart! 'He travails with iniquity;' (Psalm 7:14) be assured, the longer you travail with your sins, the more and the sharper pangs you must expect in the new birth. O be not contented with your natural estate! David says, 'why are you cast down, O my soul?' (Psalm 43:5) But a sinner should say to himself, why are you not disquieted, O my soul? Why is it that you lay afflictions so to heart, and cannot lay sin to heart? It is a mercy when we are disquieted about sin. A man had better be at the trouble of setting a bone, than to be lame, and in pain all his life. Blessed is that trouble that brings the soul to Christ! It is one of the worst sights to see a bad conscience quiet. Of the two, better is a fever than a lethargy. I wonder to see a man in his natural estate content. What! Content to go to hell!

II. Though, in regard of externals, a man should be in every estate content — yet he must not be content is such a condition wherein God is apparently dishonored. If a man's trade be such that he must trespass upon a command of God, and so make a trade of sin — he must not content himself in such a condition; God never called any man to such a calling as is sinful; a man in this case, had better lose some of his gain, so he may lessen some of his guilt. So, for servants who live in a profane family — the suburbs of hell — where the name of God is not called upon, unless when it is taken in vain — they are not to content themselves in such a place, they are to come out of the tents of these sinners; there is a double danger in living among the profane.

1. Lest we come to be infected with the poison of their evil example. Joseph, living in Pharaoh's court, had learned to swear 'by the life of Pharaoh.' (Ge. 42:15) We are prone to suck in example: men take in deeper impressions by the eye — than the ear. Dives was a bad pattern, and he had many brethren that seeing him sin, trod just in his steps, therefore says he, 'I beg you to send him to my father's house — because I have five brothers — to warn them, so they won't also come to this place of torment!' (Lu. 16:27, 28) Dives knew which way they went. It is easy to catch a disease from another — but not to catch health. The bad will sooner corrupt the good — than the good will convert the bad. Take an equal quantity and proportion, so much sweet wine with so much sour vinegar; the vinegar will sooner sour the wine than the wine will sweeten the vinegar.

Sin is compared to the plague, (1 Ki. 8:37) and to leaven, (1 Cor. 5:7) to show of what a spreading nature it is. A bad master makes a bad servant. We do as we see others do before us, especially those who are above us. If the head is sick, the other parts of the body are distempered. If the sun shines not upon the mountains, it must needs set in the valleys. We pray, 'lead us not into temptation!' Lot was the world's miracle, who kept himself fresh, in Sodom's salt water.

2. By living in an evil family, we are liable to incur their punishment. 'Pour out Your wrath on the families that don't call on Your name.' (Jer. 10:25) For lack of pouring out of prayer, the wrath of God was ready to be poured out! It is dangerous living in the tents of Kedar. When God sends his flying scroll, written within and without with curses, it enters into the house of the thief and the perjurer, 'and consumes the timber and the stones thereof.' (Ze. 5:4) Is it not of sad consequence to live in a profane family, when the sin of the master pulls his house about his ears? If the stones and timber be destroyed, how shall the servant escape? And suppose God does not send a temporal scroll of curses in the family, there is a spiritual scroll, and that is worse. 'The Lord's curse is on the household of the wicked!' (Proverbs 3:33) Be not content to live where religion dies.

'Salute the brethren, and Nymphas, and the church which is in his house.' (Col. 4:15) The house of the godly is a little church—but the house of the wicked is a little hell. (Proverbs 7:27) Oh, incorporate yourselves into a pious family; the house of a godly man is perfumed with a blessing. 'The Lord's curse is on the household of the wicked, but He blesses the home of the righteous.' (Proverbs 3:33) When the holy oil of grace is poured on the head, the savor of this ointment sweetly diffuses itself, and the virtue of it runs down upon the skirts of the family. Pious examples are very magnetic and forcible. Seneca said to his sister, 'though I leave you not wealth—yet I leave you a good example.' Let us ingraft ourselves among the saints. By being often among the spices—we come to partake of their fragrance.

III. The third caution is, though in every condition we must be content—yet we are not to content ourselves with a little grace. Grace is the best blessing. Though we should be contented with a competency of estate—yet not with a competency of grace. It was the end of Christ's ascension to heaven, to give gifts; and the end of those gifts, 'that we may grow up into him in all things who is the head, even Christ. (Ep. 4:15) Where the apostle distinguishes between our being in Christ, and our growing in him; our maturing, and our flourishing. Do not be content with a little piety.

It is not enough that there is life—but there must be fruit. Barrenness in the law was accounted a curse: the further we are from the fruit, the nearer we are to cursing. (He. 6:8) It is a sad thing when men are fruitful only in the unfruitful works of darkness. Be not content with a grain or two of grace. 'My Father is glorified by this: that you produce much fruit and prove to be My disciples.' (John 15:8) O covet more grace! Never think you have enough. We are bid to covet the best things. (1 Cor. 12:31) It is a heavenly ambition, when we desire to be high in God's favor. It is a blessed contentment when all the strife is 'who shall be most holy'. Paul, though he was content with a little of the world—yet not with a little grace. 'I do not consider myself to have taken hold of it. But one thing I do: forgetting what is behind and reaching forward to what is ahead, I pursue as my goal the prize promised by God's heavenly call in Christ Jesus.' (Ph. 3:13, 14) A true Christian is a wonder; he is the most contented—and yet the least satisfied. He is contented with a morsel of bread, and a little water in the cruise—yet never satisfied with his grace; he pants and breathes after more. This is his prayer, 'Lord, more conformity to Christ, more communion with Christ!' He would sincerely have Christ's image more lively pictured upon his soul. True grace is always progressive. As the saints are called lamps and stars, in regard of their light—so they are called trees of righteousness, (Is. 61:3) for their growth. They are indeed like the tree of life, bringing forth several sorts of fruit.

A true Christian grows in beauty. Grace is the best complexion of the soul; it is at the first plantation, like Rachel, fair to look upon; but still the more it lives, the more it sends forth its rays of beauty. Abraham's faith was at first beautiful; but at last did shine in its orient colors, and grew so illustrious, that God himself was in love with it, and makes his faith a pattern to all believers.

A true Christian grows in sweetness. A poisonous weed may grow as much as the corn; but the one has a harsh sour taste, the other mellows as it grows. A hypocrite may grow in outward dimensions, as much as a child of God, he may pray as much, profess as much: but he grows only in magnitude, he brings forth only sour grapes, his duties are leavened with pride; the other ripens as he grows; he grows in love, humility, faith, which do mellow and sweeten his duties, and make them come off with a better relish. The believer grows as the flower, he casts a fragrancy and perfume.

A true Christian grows in strength: he grows still more rooted and settled. The more the tree grows, the more it spreads its root in the earth: a Christian who is a plant of the heavenly Jerusalem, the longer he grows, the more he incorporates into Christ, and sucks spiritual juice and sap from him. He is a dwarf in regard of humility — but a giant in regard of strength — he is strong to do duties, to bear burdens, resist temptations.

He grows in the exercise of his grace; he has not only oil in his lamp — but his lamp is also burning and shining. Grace is agile and dexterous. Christ's vines flourish; (Ca. 6:11) hence we read of 'a lively hope, (1 Pe. 1:3) and 'a fervent love;' (1 Pe. 1:22) here is the activity of grace. Indeed sometimes grace is a sleepy habit of the soul, like sap in the vine, not exerting its vigor, which may be occasioned through spiritual sloth, or by reason of falling into some sin; but this is only for a while: the spring of grace will come, 'the flowers will appear, and the fig-tree put forth her green figs.' The fresh gales of the Spirit sweetly revive and nourish grace. The church of Christ, whose heart was a garden, and her graces as precious spices, prays for the heavenly breathings of the Spirit, that her sacred spices might flow out. (Ca. 6:16)

A true Christian grows both in the kind and in the degree of grace. To his spiritual living he gets an augmentation, 'Make every effort to add to your faith goodness; and to goodness, knowledge; and to knowledge, self-control; and to self-control, perseverance; and to perseverance, godliness; and to godliness, brotherly kindness; and to brotherly kindness, love. For if you possess these qualities in increasing measure, they will keep you from being ineffective and unproductive in your knowledge of our Lord Jesus Christ.' (2 Pe. 1:5-8) Here is grace growing in its kind. And he goes on 'from faith to faith;' (Ro. 1:17) there is grace growing in the degree; 'we are bound to thank God always for you, brethren, because your faith grows exceedingly;' (2 Th. 1:3) it increases over and above.

The apostle speaks of those spiritual plants which were laden with gospel-fruit. (Ph. 1:11) A Christian is compared to the vine, (an emblem of fruitfulness) he must bear full clusters: we are bid to perfect that which is lacking in our faith. (1 Th. 3:10) A Christian must never be so old as to be past bearing; he brings forth fruit in his old age. (Psalm 92:14) A heaven-born plant is ever growing; he never thinks he grows enough; he is not content unless he adds every day to his spiritual stature. We must not be content just with so much grace as will keep life and soul together, a grain or two will not suffice — but we must be still increasing, 'with the increase of God.' (Col. 2:19) We had need renew our strength as the eagle. (Is. 40:31) Our sins are renewed, our temptations are renewed, our needs are renewed — and shall not our strength be renewed? O be not content with grace in its infancy! You look for degrees of glory, be Christians of high degrees. Though a believer should be contented with a little estate — yet not with a little piety. A Christian of the right breed, labors still to excel himself, and come nearer to that holiness in God, who is the original, the pattern, and prototype of all holiness.

Showing how a Christian may know whether he has learned this Divine Art of Contentment

Thus having laid down these three cautions, I proceed, in the next place, to an use of trial. How may a Christian know that he has learned this lesson of contentment? I shall lay down some characters by which you shall know it.

1. A contented spirit is SILENT when under afflictions. 'I was silent; I would not open my mouth, for You are the one who has done this!' (Psalm 39:9) Contentment silences all dispute: 'he sits alone and keeps silence.' (La. 3:28)

There is a sinful silence—when God is dishonored, his truth wounded, and men hold their peace, this silence is a loud sin. And there is a holy silence—when the soul sits down quiet and content with its condition. When Samuel tells Eli that dreadful message from God, 'that judgment is coming for his family,' (1 Sa. 3:13, 14) does Eli murmur or dispute? No! He has not one word to say against God: 'It is the Lord's will. Let him do what he thinks best.' A discontented spirit says as Pharaoh, 'who is the Lord?' why should I suffer all this? Why should I be brought into this low condition? 'Who is the Lord?' But a gracious heart says, as Eli, 'It is the Lord's will. Let him do what he thinks best.' When Nadab and Abihu, the sons of Aaron, had offered up strange fire, and fire went from the Lord and devoured them, (Le. 10:1) is Aaron now in a passion of discontent? No! 'Aaron held his peace.' A contented spirit is never angry—unless with himself for having hard thoughts of God. When Jonah said, 'I do well to be angry,' this was not a contented spirit, it was not fitting for a prophet.

2. A contented spirit is a cheerful spirit. Contentment is something more than patience; for patience denotes only submission, contentment denotes cheerfulness. A contented Christian is more than passive; he does not only bear the cross—but take up the cross. (Mat. 6:24) He looks upon God as a wise God; and whatever he does, it is in order to a cure. Hence the contented Christian is cheerful, and with the apostle, 'I delight in weaknesses, in insults, in hardships, in persecutions, in difficulties.' (2 Cor. 12:10) He does not only submit to God's dealings—but rejoices in them! He does not only say, 'just is the Lord in all that has befallen me,' but 'good is the Lord.' This is to be contented. A sullen melancholy is hateful to God. It is said, 'God loves a cheerful giver,' (2 Cor. 9:7) yes and God loves a cheerful liver! We are bid in Scripture, 'not to be anxious,' but we are not bid not to be cheerful. He who is contented with his condition, does not abate of his spiritual joy; and indeed he has that within him which is the ground of cheerfulness; he carries a pardon sealed in his heart! (Mat. 9:2)

3. A contented spirit is a thankful spirit. This is a degree above cheerfulness; 'in everything giving thanks.' (1 Th. 5:18) A gracious heart spies mercy in every condition, therefore has his heart pitched up to thankfulness. Others will bless God for prosperity—but he blesses him for affliction. Thus he reasons with himself; am I in need? God sees it better for me to lack than to abound; God is now dieting me, he sees it better for my spiritual health sometimes to be kept fasting; therefore he does not only submit—but is thankful. The malcontent is ever complaining of his condition; the contented spirit is ever giving thanks. O what height of grace is this! A contented heart is a temple where the praises of God are sung forth—not a sepulcher wherein they are buried.

A contented Christian in the greatest straits, has his heart enlarged and dilated in thankfulness; he often contemplates God's love in election—he sees that he is a monument of mercy, therefore desires to be a pattern of praise. There is always thankful music in a contented soul; the Spirit of grace works in the heart like new wine, which under the heaviest pressures of sorrow, will have a vent open for thankfulness: this is to be content.

4. He who is content, no condition comes amiss to him; so it is in the text, 'in whatever condition I am.' A Christian should be content in any and every situation; either to lack or

abound. The people of Israel knew neither how to abound, nor yet how to lack; when they were in need they murmured; 'can God prepare a table in the wilderness?' and when they ate, and were filled, then they lifted up the heel. Paul knew how to manage every state; he could be either a note higher or lower; he was in this sense an universalist, he learned to be content whatever the circumstances. If he was in prosperity, he knew how to be thankful. If he was in adversity, he knew how to be patient; he was neither lifted up with the one, nor cast down with the other.

Thus a contented Christian knows how to respond to any condition. We have those who can be contented in some conditions — but not in every estate; they can be content in a wealthy estate, when they have the streams of milk and honey; while Gods candle shines upon their head — now they are content — but if the wind turns and is against them — now they are discontented. While they have a silver crutch to lean upon — they are contented; but if God breaks this crutch — now they are discontented. But Paul had learned in every estate to carry himself with an equanimity of mind. Others could be content with their affliction — if God would allow them to pick and choose. They could be content to bear such a cross of their choosing; they could better endure sickness than poverty; or bear loss of estate than loss of children; if they might have a cross of their own choosing — they would be content. A contented Christian does not go to choose his cross — but leaves God to choose for him; he is content both for the kind of the affliction and the duration of the affliction. A contented spirit says, 'let God apply whatever medicine he pleases, and let it lie on as long as it will; I know when it has done its cure, and eaten the venom of sin out of my heart, God will take it away.'

In a word, a contented Christian, being sweetly captivated under the authority of the Word, desires to be wholly at God's disposal, and cheerfully lives in whatever circumstances that God has placed him in.

5. He who is contented with his condition — to rid himself out of trouble, will not turn himself into sin. I deny not but a Christian may lawfully seek to change his condition: so far as God's providence goes before, he may follow. But when men will not follow providence but run before it, as he who said, 'this evil is of the Lord, why should I wait any longer. (2 Ki. 6:33) If God does not open the door of his providence, they will break it open — and wind themselves out of affliction by sin; bringing their souls into trouble! This is far from holy contentment, this is unbelief broken into rebellion. A contented Christian is willing to wait God's leisure, and will not stir until God opens a door. The contented Christian says, with reverence, 'God has cast me into this condition; and though it is sad, and troublesome, yet I will not stir, until God by a clear providence fetches me out.' Thus those brave spirited Christians; 'they accepted not deliverance,' (He. 11:35) that is, upon base dishonorable terms. They would rather stay in prison, than purchase their liberty by carnal compliance.

Estius observes on the place, 'they might not only have had their enlargements — but been raised to honor, and put into offices of trust — yet the honor of Christ was dearer to them, than either liberty or honor.' A contented Christian will not remove, until as the Israelites, he sees a pillar of cloud and fire going before him. 'It is good that a man should both hope, and quietly wait for the salvation of the Lord.' (La. 3:26) It is good to wait God's leisure — and not to extricate ourselves out of trouble — until we see the star of God's providence pointing out a way to us!

A Christian Directory, or Rules about Contentment.

I proceed now to an use of direction, to show Christians how they may attain to this divine art of contentment. Certainly it is feasible, others of God's saints have reached to it. Paul here had it; and what do we think of those we read of, in that little book of martyrs, (Hebrews 11) who had trials of cruel mockings and scourgings, who wandered about in deserts and caves — yet were contented. It is possible to attain to this divine art of contentment. And here I shall lay down some rules for holy contentment.

Rule 1. Advance faith. All our disquiets issue from unbelief. It is this which raises the storm of discontent in the heart. O set faith a-work! It is the property of faith to silence our doubtings, to scatter our fears, to still the heart when the passions are up. Faith works the heart to a sweet serene composure. It is not having fancy food and raiment — but having faith, which will make us content. Faith chides down passion. When reason begins to sink — let faith swim! How does faith work contentment?

1. Faith shows the soul that whatever its trials are — that they are all from the hand of a loving heavenly father. It is indeed a bitter cup — but 'shall I not drink the cup which my father has given me to drink?' Faith shows the soul that whatever its trials are — that they are all sent in love to my soul. God corrects me, with the same love with which he crowns me; God is now training me up for heaven. He is only polishing his 'jewels'. These sufferings bring forth patience, humility, even the peaceful fruits of righteousness. (He. 12:11) And if God can bring such sweet fruit out of our stock, let him graft me wherever and however he pleases. Thus faith brings the heart to holy contentment.

2. Faith sucks the honey of contentment out of the hive of the promise. Christ is the vine, the promises are the clusters of grapes which grow upon this vine, and faith presses the sweet wine of contentment out of these spiritual clusters of the promises. I will show you but one cluster, 'the Lord will give grace and glory;' (Psalm 84:11) here is enough for faith to live upon. The promise is the flower out of which faith distills the spirits and quintessence of divine contentment. In a word, faith carries up the soul, and makes it aspire after more generous and noble delights than the earth affords, and to live in the world — above the world. Would you live contented lives? Live up to the height of your faith.

Rule 2. Labor for assurance. O let us get a saving interest cleared, between God and our souls! O, if there is an interest worth looking after, it is an interest between God and the soul! Labor to say, 'My God.' To be without money, and without friends, and without God too, is sad. But he whose faith flourishes into assurance, who can say, 'I know whom I have believed!' (2 Ti. 1:2) that man has enough to give his heart contentment. When a man's debts are paid, and he can go abroad without fear of being arrested, what contentment is this! O, let your title to heaven be cleared! If God is ours, whatever we lack in the creature, is infinitely made up in him. Do I lack bread? I have Christ, the bread of life. Am I under defilement? His blood is like the trees of the sanctuary; not only for food — but medicine. (Ez. 47:12) If anything in the world be worth laboring for, it is to get sound evidences, that God is ours. If this is once cleared, what can come amiss? No matter what storms I meet with — iit is well with me, so long that I know where to put in for harbor. He who has God to be his God, is so well contented with his condition, that he does not much care whether he has anything else.

To rest in a condition where a person cannot say that God is his God, is matter of fear. If a person can truly say that God is his God — and yet is not contented — this is a matter of shame. 'David encouraged himself in the Lord his God.' (1 Sa. 30:6) It was sad with him — his city burnt, his wives taken captive, his all lost, and likely to have lost his soldiers' hearts too, (for they spoke of stoning him,) yet he had the ground of contentment within him; a saving interest in God, and this was a pillar of support to his spirit. He who knows God is his, and all that is in God is for his good — if this does not satisfy him, I know nothing that will.

Rule 3. Get a HUMBLE spirit. The humble man is the contented man; if his estate is low, his heart is lower than his estate, and therefore he is content. If his esteem in the world is low—he who is little in his own eyes will not be much troubled to be little in the eyes of others. He has a lower opinion of himself, than others can have of him. The humble man studies his own unworthiness; he looks upon himself as 'less than the least of God's mercies:' (Ge. 32:10) and then a little will content him! He cries out with Paul, that he is the chief of sinners, (1 Ti. 1:15) therefore does not murmur—but admire. He does not complain that his comforts are small. He thinks it is mercy that he is out of hell, therefore he is contented. He does not go to carve out a more happy condition to himself; he knows that the worst piece which God cuts for him—is better than he deserves.

A proud man is never contented; he is one that has a high opinion of himself; therefore under small blessings, he is disdainful; and under small crosses, he is impatient. The humble spirit is the contented spirit; if his cross is light—he reckons it the inventory of his mercies; if his cross is heavy—yet he takes it upon his knees, knowing that when his estate is worse, it is to make him the better. Where you lay humility for the foundation, contentment will be the superstructure.

Rule 4. Keep a clear conscience. Contentment is the manna which is laid up in the ark of a good conscience! O take heed of indulging in any sin! It is as natural for guilt to breed disquiet—as for putrid matter to breed vermin. Sin lies as Jonah in the ship, it raises a tempest. If dust or splinters have gotten into the eye, they make the eye water, and cause a soreness in it; if the eye be clear, then it is free from that soreness. Just so, if sin has gotten into the conscience, which is as the eye of the soul, then grief and disquiet breed there. Keep the eye of conscience clear—and all is well. What Solomon says of a good stomach, I may say of a good conscience, 'to the hungry soul every bitter thing is sweet.' (Proverbs 27:7) So to a good conscience, every bitter thing is sweet; it can pick contentment out of the cross! A good conscience turns the bitter waters of Marah into sweet wine.

Would you have a quiet heart? Get a smiling conscience. I do not wonder to hear Paul say that he was content in every situation, when he could make that triumph, 'I have lived in all good conscience to this day!' When once a man's reckonings are clear, it must needs let in abundance of contentment into the heart. Good conscience can suck contentment out of the bitterest slanders; 'our rejoicing is this, the testimony of our conscience.' (2 Cor. 1:12) In case of imprisonment, Paul had his prison songs, and could play the sweet lessons of contentment, when his feet were in the stocks! (Ac. 16:25) Augustine calls contentment, 'the paradise of a good conscience!' And if it is so—then in prison we may be in paradise! When the times are troublesome, a good conscience makes a calm. If conscience be clear, what though the days are cloudy?

Is it not a contentment to have a friend always by to speak a good word for us? Such a friend is conscience. A good conscience, as David's harp, drives away the evil spirit of discontent. When anxious thoughts begin to arise, and the heart is disquieted, conscience says to a man, as the king did to Nehemiah, 'Why is your countenance sad?' So says conscience, 'Have not you the seed of God in you? Are not you an heir of the promise? Have not you a treasure which can never be plundered? Why is your countenance sad?' O keep conscience clear—and you shall never lack contentment! For a man to keep the pipes of his body—the veins and arteries—free from colds and obstructions, is the best way to maintain health. Just so, to keep conscience clear, and to preserve it from the obstructions of guilt—is the best way to maintain contentment. First, conscience is pure—and then peaceable.

Rule 5. Learn to deny yourselves. Look well to your affections, and bridle them in. Do two things: mortify your desires; moderate your delights.

1. Mortify your desires. We must not be of the dragon's temper, which, they say — is so thirsty, that no water will quench its thirst. 'Put to death the sinful, earthly things lurking within you. Have nothing to do with sexual sin, impurity, lust, and shameful desires.' (Col. 3:5) Our desires, when they are inordinate, are evil. Crucify your desires — be as dead men — a dead man has no appetite!

How should a Christian martyr his desires?

(1.) Get a right judgment of the things here below; they are poor beggarly things. 'Do not wear yourself out to get rich; have the wisdom to show restraint. Cast but a glance at riches, and they are gone, for they will surely sprout wings and fly off to the sky like an eagle' (Proverbs 23:4-5). The appetite must be guided by reason. The affections are the feet of the soul; therefore they must follow the judgment, not lead it.

(2.) Often seriously meditate of mortality. Death will soon crop these flowers which we delight in; and pull down the fabric of our bodies which we so garnish and beautify. Think, when you are locking up your money in your chest — that you shall shortly be locked up in your coffin!

2. Moderate your delights. Do not set your heart too much upon any creature comfort. What we over-love, we shall over-grieve. Rachel set her heart too much upon her children, and when she had lost them, she lost herself too! Such a vein of grief was opened, as could not be staunched, 'she refused to be comforted.' Here was discontent. When we let any creature creature lie too near our heart — when God pulls away that comfort — a piece of our heart is torn away with it! Too much fondness ends in frowardness. Those who would be content in the lack of comforts, must be moderate in the enjoyment of comforts. Jonathan dipped the rod in honey — he did not thrust it in. Let us take heed of engulfing ourselves in pleasure! It is better have a spare diet, than, by having too much, to glut ourselves.

Rule 6. Get much of heaven into your heart. 'You satisfy me more than the richest of foods. (Psalm 63:5) Spiritual things truly satisfy! The more that heaven is in us — the less earth that will content us. He who has once tasted the love of God, his thirst is much quenched towards earthly things. The joys of God's Spirit are heart-filling and heart-cheering joys; he who has these, has heaven begun in him! (Ro. 14:27) And shall not we be content to be in heaven? O get a heavenly heart! 'Seek those things which are above.' (Col. 3:1) Fly aloft in your affections, thirst after the graces and comforts of the Spirit! The eagle which flies high in the air, does not fear the stinging of the serpent. The serpent creeps on his belly, and stings only such creatures as creep upon the earth.

Rule 7. Look not so much on the dark side of your condition, as on the bright side. God chequers his providences, white and black — as the pillar of the cloud had its light side and dark side. Look on the light side of the estate; who looks on the back side of a landscape? Suppose you have lost much in a law-suit — there is the dark side; yet you have some land left — there is the light side. You have sickness in your body — there is the dark side; but you also have grace in your soul — there is the light side. You have a child taken away — there is the dark side; your husband lives — there is the light side. God's providences in this life are variously represented by those speckled horses among the myrtle-trees which were red and white. (Ze. 1:1) Mercies and afflictions are interwoven — God speckles his work.

'O,' says one, 'I lack such a comfort!' But weigh all your mercies in the balance — and that will make you content. If a man lacked a finger, would he be so discontented for the loss of that, as not to be thankful for all the other parts and joints of his body? Look on the light side of your condition, and then all your discontents will easily dissolve. Do not pore upon your losses — but ponder upon your mercies. What! Would you have no afflictions at all — and only all good things? Would you have no evil about you—who has so much evil in you? You are not fully sanctified in this life—how then think you to be fully satisfied in this life? Never look for perfection of contentment, until there is perfection of grace.

Rule 8. Consider in what a posture we stand here in the world.

1. We are in a military condition—we are soldiers, (2 Ti. 2:3) A soldier is content with anything. Though he has not his stately house, his rich furniture, his soft bed, his full table—yet he does not complain; he can lie on straw as well as down; he minds not his lodging—but his thoughts run upon dividing the spoil, and the garland of honor which shall be set upon his head. For hope of this, is he content to run any hazard, and endure any hardship. Would it not be absurd to hear him complain, that he lacks such provision and is discontent to lie out in the fields? A Christian is a military person, he fights the Lord's battles, he is Christ's ensign bearer. Now, what though he endures hard fate, and the bullets fly about him? He fights for a crown—and therefore must be content!

2. We are in a nomadic condition—we are pilgrims and travelers. A man who is in a strange country, is contented with anything. Though he has not that respect or attendance which he looks for at home, nor is capable of the privileges and amenities of that place—he is content. He knows, when he comes into his own country, he has lands to inherit, and there he shall have honor and respect. So it is with a child of God, he is in a pilgrim condition; 'I am a stranger with you, and a sojourner, as all my fathers were!' (Psalm 39:12) Therefore let a Christian be content; he is in the world—but not of the world: he is born of God, and is a citizen of the New Jerusalem! (He. 12:22) Therefore, though 'he hungers and thirsts, and has no certain dwelling-place,' (1 Cor. 4:11) yet he must be content: it will be better—when he comes into his own country.

3. We are in a mendicant condition—we are beggars. We beg at heaven's gate, 'give us this day our daily bread.' We live upon God's alms, therefore must be content with anything. A beggar must not pick and choose—he is contented with the scraps. Oh, why do you who are a beggar, murmur? Oh, why do you who are fed out of the alms-basket of God's providence, murmur?

Rule 9. Do not let your hope depend upon external things. Do not lean upon sandy pillars. We often build our comfort upon such a friend or estate—and when that prop is removed—all our joy is gone, and our hearts begin either to fail or fret! A lame man leans on his crutches—and if they break, he is undone! Let not your contentment go upon crutches, which may soon fail. The ground of contentment must be within yourself. The Greek word which is used for contentment, signifies self-sufficiency. A Christian has that within him—which is able to support him—that strength of faith, and good hope through grace, as bears up his heart in the deficiency of outward comforts. The philosophers of old, when their estates were gone—yet could take contentment in the goods of the mind—learning and virtue. And shall not a believer much more in the graces of the Spirit, that rich enamel and embroidery of the soul! Say with yourself, 'if friends leave me, if riches take wings—yet I have that within me, which comforts me—a heavenly treasure! When the blossoms of my estate are blown off, still there is the sap of contentment, in the root of my heart! I have still a saving interest in God, and that interest cannot be broken off!' O never place your felicity in these poor and beggarly things here below!

Rule 10. Let us often compare our condition. Make this fivefold comparison.

1. Let us compare our condition and our desert together. If we have not what we desire—we have more than we deserve. For our mercies—we have deserved less. For our afflictions—we have deserved more.

First. In regard of our mercies—we have deserved less. What can we deserve? Can a man be profitable to the Almighty? We live upon free grace! Alexander gave a great gift to one of his subjects; the man being much taken with it, said, 'this is more than I am worthy of!' 'I do not give you this,' said the king, 'because you are worthy of it—but I give a gift like Alexander!' Whatever we have is not merit—but bounty! The least bit of bread is more than God owes to us! We can bring faggots to our own burning—but not one flower to the garland of our salvation. He who has the least mercy—will die in God's debt!

Secondly. In regard of our afflictions—we have deserved more. 'You have punished us less than our iniquities deserve. (Ex. 9:13) Is our condition sad? We have deserved it should be worse. Has God taken away our estate from us? He might have taken away Christ from us. Has he thrown us into prison? He might have thrown us into hell! He might as well damn us, as whip us! This should make us contented.

2. Let us compare our condition with others—and this will make us content. We look at them who are above us, let us look at them who are below us; we can see one in his silks, another in his sackcloth; one has a full cup of the choicest wine wrung out to him, another is mingling his drink with tears. How many pale faces do we behold, whom poverty has brought into a comsumption! Think of this—and be content.

It is worse with them, who perhaps deserve better than we—and are higher in God's favor. Am I in prison? Was not Daniel in a worse place—the lion's den! Do I live in a poor cottage? Look on those who are banished from their cottages. We read of the primitive saints, 'Some were mocked, and their backs were cut open with whips. Others were chained in dungeons. Some died by stoning, and some were sawed in half; others were killed with the sword. Some went about in skins of sheep and goats, hungry and oppressed and mistreated.' (He. 11:37, 38)

Have you a gentle illness? Look on those who are tormented with the stone, the gout, cancer etc. Others of God's children have had greater afflictions, and have borne them better than we. Daniel fed only upon vegetables and drank only water—yet was fairer than they who ate of the king's portion. (Dan. 1:15) Some Christians who have been in a lower condition, who have had only bread and water, have been more patient and contented, than we who enjoy abundance. Do others rejoice in affliction—and do we repine? Can they take up their cross and walk cheerfully under it—and do we under a lighter cross murmur?

3. Let us compare our condition with Christ's condition, when He was upon earth. What a poor, base condition was He pleased to be in for us! He was contented with anything. 'For you know the grace of our Lord Jesus Christ, that though He was rich—yet for our sakes he became poor!' (2 Cor. 8:9) He could have brought down a house from heaven with him, or taken the high places of the earth—but he was contented to be in the wine-press, that we might be in the wine-cellar; and to live poor that we might be eternally rich! The feeding trough was his cradle, and the cobwebs were his canopy. He who is now preparing mansions for us in heaven—had none for himself on earth, 'he had nowhere to lay his head.' Christ took upon him the form of a servant. (Ph. 2:7) We do not read not that He had any money. When he needed money, he had to work a miracle for it. (Mat. 17:27) Jesus Christ was in a low condition. He was never high—but when he was lifted up upon the cross, and that was his greatest humility! He was content to live poor—and die cursed! O compare your condition with His—and learn to be content!

4. Let us compare our present condition—with what it once WAS—and this will make us content.

First, Let us compare our spiritual estate with what it was once. What were we—when we lay in our blood? We were heirs to hell, having no right to pluck one leaf from the tree of promise! It was a Christless and hopeless condition! (Ep. 2:12) But now God has cut off our destiny of hell and damnation. He has taken you out of the wild olive tree of nature — and engrafted you into Christ, making you living branches of that living vine! He has not only caused the light to shine upon you — but into you, (2 Cor. 6:6) and has made you an heir of all the privileges of divine sonship! Is not this enough to make the soul content.

Secondly, Let us compare our temporal estate with what it was once. Alas! We had nothing when we stepped out of the womb; 'for we brought nothing into this world.' (1 Ti. 6:7) If we have not that which we now desire — we have more than we brought with us! We brought nothing with us — but sin! Other creatures bring something with them into the world; the lamb brings wool, the silk-worm silk, etc. But we brought nothing with us — but sin! What if our condition at present is low? It is better than it was once; therefore, having food and clothing, let us be content. Whatever we have, God's providence fetches it unto us! And if we lose all — yet we have as much as we brought with us! This was what made Job content, 'Naked I came out of my mother's womb!' (Job 1:21) As if he had said, though God has taken away all from me — yet why should I murmur? I am as rich as I was when I came into the world! I have as much left as I brought with me; naked I came I hither! Therefore blessed be the name of the Lord.

5. Let us compare our present condition — with what it shortly shall be. There is a time shortly coming, when, if we had all the riches of the Indies, they would do us no good — we must die, and can carry nothing with us. So says the apostle, 'We didn't bring anything with us when we came into the world — and we certainly cannot carry anything with us when we die!' (1 Ti. 6:7) Therefore it follows, 'So if we have enough food and clothing, let us be content.' Open the rich man's grave — and see what is there — you may find the miser's bones — but not his riches! Were we to live forever here on earth, or could we carry our riches into the eternal world — then indeed we might be discontented, when we look upon our empty money bags. But it is not so; God may presently seal a warrant for death to apprehend us — and when we die, we cannot carry our estate with us! Honor and riches do not descend into the grave — why then are we troubled at our outward condition? Why do we clothe ourselves with discontent? O lay up a stock of grace! Be rich in faith and good works — these riches will follow us! (Re. 14:13) No other coin but grace, will pass current in heaven, silver and gold will not go there. Labor to be rich towards God, (Luke 12:21) and as for other things, be not much concerned — for we shall carry nothing with us into the eternal world!

Rule 11. Do not to bring your condition to your mind — but bring your mind to your condition. The way for a Christian to be contented, is not by raising his estate higher — but by bringing his heart lower! It is not by making his barns wider — but his heart narrower. A whole kingdom will not content one man; another man is satisfied with a poor hut. What is the difference? The one tries to satisfy his lusts — the other his necessity. The one thinks what he may yet obtain — the other what he may spare.

Rule 12. Study the vanity of the creature. It matters not whether we have less or more of these earthly things — for they have vanity written upon their frontispiece. The world is like a shadow which declines. The world is delightful — but deceitful. The world promises more than it has — and it fails us when we have most need of it. All the world rings 'change', and is constant only in its disappointments! What then, if we have less of that which is at best but uncertain and changing? The world is as full of change — as of motion; so what if God cut us short in these passing vanities? The more a man has to do with the world — the more he has to do with vanity! The world may be compared to ice, which is smooth — but slippery! The world may also be compared to the Egyptian temples — very beautiful and sumptuous on the outside — but within nothing to be seen but the image of an ape! Every creature says concerning satisfaction, 'it is not in me!' The world is not a filling comfort—but a flying comfort. The world is like a game at tennis; providence bandies her golden balls, first to one, then to another. Why are we discontented at the loss of these things—but because we expect that from them, that which they cannot give? 'Jonah was exceeding glad of the gourd.' (Jon. 4:6) What a vanity was that! Is it much to see a gourd smitten and withering?

Rule 13. Get the 'imagination' regulated. It is the 'imagination' which raises the price of things, above their real worth. What is the reason one flower is worth five dollars—and another perhaps not worth one penny? 'Imagination' raises the price—the difference is rather imaginary than real. Just so, the reason why it is better to have thousands than hundreds is—because men 'imagine' it so! If we could 'imagine' a lower condition to be better—as having less worry in it, and less accounting to give for it—it would be far more prized. The water from a paper cup, tastes as sweet as if it came out a golden chalice. Things are as we 'imagine' them. Ever since the fall, the 'imagine' is distempered; 'God saw that the imagination of the thoughts of his heart, was only evil all the time.' (Ge. 6:5) 'Imagination' looks at things through a 'magnifying glass'. Pray that God will sanctify your 'imagination'; a lower condition would content you, if the mind and 'imagination' were set right. Diogenes preferred his solitary life before Alexander's royalty. Fabricius was a poor man—yet despised the gold of King Pyrrhus. Could we cure our distempered 'imagination'—we would soon conquer our discontented heart!

Rule 14. Consider how little will suffice nature. The body is but a small thing—and is easily nourished. Christ has taught us to pray for our daily bread. Nature is content with a little. Not to thirst, not to starve—is enough. 'Having food and clothing, let us be content.' The stomach is sooner filled—than the eye! How quickly would a man be content, if he would study rather to satisfy his hunger—than his humor.

Rule 15. Believe that the present condition is best for us. The flesh is not a competent judge. Gluttons are for rich banquets—but a man who regards his health, is rather for solid food. Vain men imagine that a prosperous condition is best for them; whereas a wise Christian has his will melted into God's will, and thinks it best to be at God's will. God is wise—he knows best what we need; and if we could acquiesce in His providencial dealings with us—the quarrel would soon be at an end. O what a strange creature would man be—if he were what he could wish himself to be! Be content to be at God's allowance. God knows which is the fittest pasture to put his sheep in; sometimes a more sparse ground does well—whereas a lush pasture may rot. Do I meet with such a cross? By it, God shows me what the world is; he has no better way to wean me. Does God stint me in my temporals? He is now dieting me. Do I meet with losses? It is, that God may keep me from being lost. Every cross wind shall at last—blow me to the right port! Did we believe that condition best which God parcels out to us, we would cheerfully submit, and say, 'the lines have fallen to me in pleasant places.'

Rule 16. Do not too much indulge the flesh. The flesh is a worse enemy than the devil, it is a bosom-traitor! An enemy within—is worst! If there were no devil to tempt, the flesh would be another Eve—to tempt to the forbidden fruit. O take heed of giving way to it! Whence is all our discontent—but from our flesh? The flesh puts us upon the immoderate pursuit of the world. The flesh hunts for ease and luxury—and if it be not satisfied, then discontent begins to arise! O let it not have the reins! Martyr the flesh! In spiritual things the flesh is a sluggard; but in secular things, it is a horse-leech, crying 'give, give!' The flesh is an enemy to suffering: it will never make a man a martyr. O keep it under control! Put its neck under Christ's yoke, stretch and nail it to his cross! Never let a Christian look for contentment in his spirit—until there is confinement in his flesh.

Rule 17. Meditate much on the glory which shall be revealed. There are great things laid up in heaven. Though things are sad for the present — yet let us be content in that it shortly will be better; it is but a short while — and we shall be with Christ, bathing ourselves in the fountain of love! We shall more never complain of needs and injuries! Our cross may now be heavy — but one sight of Christ will make us forget all our former sorrows! There are two things that should give contentment.

1. That God will make us able to bear our troubles. 'God is faithful; he will not let you be tempted beyond what you can bear. But when you are tempted, he will also provide a way out so that you can stand up under it.' (1 Cor. 10:13)

2. After we have suffered a while — we shall be perfected in glory! The cross shall be our ladder by which we shall climb up to heaven! Be content — the scene will soon alter; God will before long, turn out water into wine — the hope of this is enough to drive away all distempers from the heart. Blessed be God — it will shortly be better! 'We have no continuing city here,' therefore our afflictions cannot continue. A wise man always looks to the end of a matter; 'The end of the just man is peace.' (Psalm 37:37) Methinks the smoothness of the end — should make amends for the ruggedness of the way. O eternity, eternity! Think often of the eternal kingdom prepared. David was advanced from the field — to the throne! First he held his shepherd's staff — and shortly after the royal scepter. God's people may be put to hard services here on earth — but God has chosen them to be kings — to sit upon the throne with the Lord Jesus! This being weighed in the balance of faith, would be an excellent means to bring the heart to contentment.

Rule 18. Be much in prayer. The last rule for contentment is, be much in prayer. Beg of God, that he will work our hearts to this blessed frame. 'Is any man afflicted? Let him pray!' (Ja. 5:14) Just so, is any man discontented? Let him pray. Prayer gives vent: the opening of a vein lets out bad blood. Just so, when the heart is filled with sorrow and disquiet, prayer lets out the bad blood. The key of a prayer, oiled with tears, unlocks the heart of all its discontents! Prayer is a holy charm, to drive away trouble. Prayer is the unbosoming of the soul — the unloading of all our cares into God's breast; and this ushers in sweet contentment. When there is any burden upon our spirits, by opening our mind to a friend we find our hearts greatly eased and quieted. It is not our strong resolutions — but our strong requests to God, which must give the heart ease in trouble. By prayer the strength of Christ comes into the soul — and where that is, a man is able to go through any condition. Paul could be in every state content; but that you may not think he was able to do this himself, he tells you that though he could lack and abound, and 'do all things;' yet it was through Christ strengthening him. (Ph. 4:13)

Consolation to the Contented Christian.

The last use is of comfort — an encouraging word to the contented Christian. If there is an heaven upon earth — you have it! O Christian! You may leap over your troubles, and, with the leviathan, laugh at the shaking of a spear. (Job 41:7) You are a crown to your profession; you hold it out to all the world — that there is virtue enough in piety, to give the soul contentment. You show the highest degree of grace. When grace is reigning in our hearts, it is easy for us to be content. But when grace is declining, and meets with crosses, temptations, agonies; now the heart becomes discontent.

To a contented Christian, I shall say two things for a farewell.

1. God is exceedingly pleased with such a frame of heart. God says of a contented Christian, as David once said of Goliath's sword, 'there is none like that; give it to me!' If you would please God, and be men whom he delights in — be contented. God hates a froward spirit.

2. The contented Christian shall be no loser. What did Job lose, by his patience? God gave him twice as much as he had before. What did Abraham lose, by his contentment? He was content to leave his country at God's call: the Lord makes a covenant with him, that he would be his God. He changes his name; no more Abram — but Abraham, the father of many nations. (Ge. 17) God makes his seed as the stars of heaven; nay, honors, him with this title, 'the father of the faithful.' (Ge. 18:17) The Lord makes known his secrets to him, 'shall I hide from Abraham the things that I will do?' God settles a rich inheritance upon him, that land which was a type of heaven, and afterwards translated him to the blessed paradise of glory!

God will be sure to reward the contented Christian. As our Savior said in another case, to Nathaniel, 'You shall see greater things than these!' (John 1:50) So I say, are you contented, O Christian, with a little? You shall see greater things than these! God will distill the sweet influences of his love into your soul. He will bless the oil in your cruise; and when that is done, He will crown you with an eternal enjoyment of himself! He will give you heaven — where you shall have as much contentment as your soul can possibly thirst after!

The Beatitudes

An exposition of Matthew 5:1-12

Introduction

Christian Reader,

I here present you with a subject full of sweet variety. This Sermon of Christ on the Mount is a piece of spiritual needlework, wrought with divers colors. Here is both usefulness and sweetness. In this portion of Holy Scripture, you have a summary of true religion — the Bible epitomized. Here is a garden of delight, where you may pluck those flowers which will deck the hidden man of your heart. Here is the golden key which will open the gate of Paradise! Here is the conduit of the Gospel, running wine to nourish such as are poor in spirit and pure in heart. Here is the rich cabinet wherein the Pearl of Blessedness is locked up. Here is the golden pot in which is that manna which will feed and revive the soul unto everlasting life. Here is a way chalked out to the Holy of Holies.

Reader, how happy were it if, while others take up their time and thoughts about secular things which perish in the using — you could mind eternity and be guided by this Scripture-clue which leads you to the Beatific Vision. If, after God has set life before you — you indulge your sensual appetite and still court your lusts, how inexcusable will be your neglect, and how inexpressible your misery!

May the Lord grant that while you have an opportunity, and the wind serves you, you may not lie idle at anchor, and when it is too late begin to hoist up sails for Heaven. Oh now, Christian, let your loins be girt, and your lamps burning, that when the Lord Jesus, your blessed Bridegroom, shall knock, you may be ready to go in with Him to the marriage-supper, which shall be the prayer of him who is,

Yours in all true affection and devotion,

Thomas Watson

When Jesus saw the crowds, He went up on the mountain; and after He sat down, His disciples came to Him. He opened His mouth and began to teach them.

Matthew 5:1, 2

The blessed evangelist Matthew, the penman of this sacred history, was at first by profession, a tax collector; and Christ, having called him from the custom-house, made him a gatherer of souls. This holy man in the first chapter records Christ's birth and genealogy. In the second chapter, he records Christ's dignity — a star ushers in the wise men to him, and as a king he is presented with gold and frankincense and myrrh (2:9-11). In the third chapter the evangelist records his baptism. In the fourth, his temptations; in the fifth, his preaching, which chapter is like a rich gold mine. Every verse has some gold in it.

There are four things in this chapter which offer themselves to our view:

1. The Preacher

2. The Pulpit

3. The Occasion

4. The Sermon

1. The Preacher. Jesus Christ. The best of preachers. 'He went up.' He in whom there was a combination of all virtues, a constellation of all beauties. He whose lips were not only sweet as the honey-comb, but did drop as the honey-comb. His words — an oracle; his works — a miracle; his life — a pattern; his death — a sacrifice. 'He went up into a mountain and taught.' Jesus Christ was every way ennobled and qualified for the work of the ministry.

[1] Christ was an intelligent preacher. He had 'the Spirit without measure' (John 3:34) and knew how to speak a word in due season — when to humble, and when to comfort. We cannot know all the faces of our hearers. Christ knew the hearts of his hearers! He understood what doctrine would best suit them, as the farmer can tell what sort of grain is proper for such-and-such a soil.

[2] Christ was a powerful preacher. 'He spoke with authority' (Matthew 7:29). He could set men's sins before them and show them their very hearts! 'Come, see a man who told me all things that I ever did!' (John 4:29). That is the best looking-glass, not which is most richly set with pearl — but which shows the truest face! Christ was a preacher to the conscience. He breathed as much zeal as eloquence. He often touched upon the heart-strings. What is said of Luther is more truly applicable to Christ. He spoke 'as if he had been within a man'. He could drive the wedge of his doctrine in the most knotty piece. He was able with his two-edged sword to pierce a heart of stone! 'Never man spoke like this man!' (John 7:46)

[3] Christ was a successful preacher. He had the art of converting souls. 'Many believed on him.' (John 10:42), yes, people of rank and quality. 'Among the chief rulers many believed' (John 12:42). He who had 'grace poured into his lips' (Psalm 45:2), could pour grace into his hearers' hearts. He had the key of David in his hand, and when he pleased — he opened the hearts of men, and made way both for himself and his doctrine to enter. If he blew the trumpet, his very enemies would come under his banner! Upon his summons, none dare but surrender.

[4] Christ was a lawful preacher. As he had his unction from his Father, so also his mission. 'The Father who sent me, bears witness of me' (John 8:18). Christ, in whom were all perfections concentred — yet he would be solemnly sealed and inaugurated into his ministerial office — as well as his mediatory office.

If Jesus Christ would not enter upon the work of the ministry without a commission, how absurdly impudent are those who without any warrant dare invade this holy function! There must be a lawful admission of men into the ministry. 'No man takes this honor to himself — but he who is called of God, as was Aaron' (Hebrews 5:4). Our Lord Christ gave apostles and prophets — who were extraordinary ministers; so he gives pastors and teachers who were initiated and made in an ordinary way (Ephesians 4:11). He will have a gospel ministry perpetuated; 'Lo I am with you always, even unto the end of the world' (Matthew 28:20). Surely, there is as much need of ordination now, as in Christ's time and in the time of the apostles, there being then extraordinary gifts in the church which have now ceased.

But why should not the gospel ministry be open to all people? 'Has the Lord spoken only by Moses?' (Numbers 12:2). Why should not one preach as well as another? I answer — Because God (who is the God of order) has made the work of the ministry a select, distinct office from any other. As in the body natural the members have a distinct office — the eye is to see, the hand to work. You may as well say, 'why should not the hand see — as well as the eye?' Because God has made the distinction. He has put the seeing faculty into the eye — and not the hand. So here, God has made a distinction between the work of the ministry and other work.

Where is this distinction? We find in Scripture a distinction between pastor and people. 'The elders (or ministers) I exhort ... Feed the flock of God which is among you' (1 Peter 5:2). If anyone may preach, by the same rule all may, and then what will become of the apostle's distinction? What would the flock of God be — if all were pastors?

God has cut out the minister's work — which is proper for him and does not belong to any other. 'Give attendance to reading, to exhortation, to doctrine ... give yourself wholly to them', or, as it is in the Greek, 'Be wholly in them' (1 Timothy 4:13-15). This charge is peculiar to the minister and does not concern any other. It is not spoken to the tradesman that he should give himself wholly to doctrine and exhortation. No! Let him look to his shop. It is not spoken to the ploughman that he should give himself wholly to preaching. No! Let him give himself to his plough. It is the minister's charge. The apostle speaks to Timothy and, in him, to the rest who had the hands of the elders laid on them. And 'Study to show yourself approved ..., a workman who needs not to be ashamed, rightly dividing the word of truth' (2 Timothy 2:15). This is spoken peculiarly to the minister. Everyone who can read the word aright cannot divide the word aright. So that the work of the ministry does not lie open to all people; it is a select, peculiar work. As none might touch the ark but the priests — so none may touch this temple-office but such as are called to it.

But if a man has gifts, is not this sufficient? I answer, No! As grace is not sufficient to make a minister, so neither are gifts. The Scripture puts a difference between gifting and sending. 'How shall they preach unless they are sent?' (Romans 10:15). If gifts were enough to constitute a minister, the apostle would have said, 'How shall they preach unless they be gifted? But he says 'unless they are sent?'

We see this in other callings — gifts do not make a magistrate. The attorney who pleads at the bar may have as good gifts as the judge who sits upon the bench — but he must have a commission before he sit as judge. If it be thus in civil matters, much more in sacred matters, which are, as Bucer says, 'things of the highest importance'. Those therefore, who usurp the ministerial work without any special designation and appointment, reveal more pride than zeal. They act out of their sphere and are guilty of theft. They steal upon a people, and, as they come without a call from God, so they stay without a blessing to the people. 'I sent them not, therefore they shall not profit this people at all' (Jeremiah 23:32). And so much for the first, the preacher.

2. The pulpit where Christ preached. 'He went up on the mountain.'

The law was first given on the mount, and here Christ expounds it on the mount. This mount, as is supposed by the learned — was Mount Tabor. It was a convenient place to speak in, being seated above the people, and in regard of the great confluence of hearers.

3. The occasion of Christ's ascending the mount: 'When Jesus saw the crowds.'

The people thronged to hear Christ, and he would not dismiss the congregation without a sermon — but 'seeing the multitude he went up on the mountain'. Jesus Christ came from heaven — to work for souls. Preaching was his business. The people could not be so desirous to hear — as he was to preach. He who treated faint bodies with compassion (Matthew 15:32), much more pitied dead souls. It was his 'food and drink, to do his Father's will (John 4:34). 'When Jesus saw the crowds', he goes up into the mount and preaches. This he did not only for the consolation of his hearers — but for the imitation of his ministers.

From whence observe — that Christ's ministers according to Christ's pattern must embrace every opportunity of doing good to souls. Praying and preaching and studying must be our work. 'Preach the word; be instant in season, out of season' (2 Timothy 4:2). Peter, seeing the multitude, lets down the net and, at one draught, catches three thousand souls! (Acts 2:41). How zealously industrious have God's champions been in former ages in fulfilling the work of their ministry — as we read of Chrysostom, Augustine, Basil the Great, Calvin, Bucer and others — who for the work of Christ 'were near unto death'. The reasons why the ministers of Christ (according to his pattern) should be ambitiously desirous of all opportunities for soul-service are:

[1] Their commission: God has entrusted them as ambassadors (2 Corinthians 5:20). An ambassador waits for a day of audience, and as soon as a day is granted, he faithfully and impartially delivers the mind of his prince. Thus Christ's ministers, having a commission delegated to them to negotiate for souls, should be glad when there is a day of audience, that they may impart the mind and will of Christ to his people.

[2] Their titles: Ministers are called God's sowers (1 Corinthians 9:11). Therefore they must upon all occasions be scattering the blessed seed of the Word. The sower must go forth and sow; yes, though the seed falls upon stones, as usually it does — yet we must disseminate and scatter the seed of the Word upon stony hearts, because 'even from these stones, God is able to raise up children' to himself.

Ministers are called stars. Therefore they must shine by word and doctrine in the firmament of the church. Thus our Lord Christ has set them a pattern in the text: 'When Jesus saw the crowds, He went up on the mountain.' Here was a light set upon a hill, the bright morning star shining to all who were round about. Christ calls his ministers 'the light of the world' (Matthew 5:14). Therefore they must be always giving forth their luster. Their light must not go out until their last breath — or until violent death as an extinguisher puts it out.

[3] Christ's ministers must take all occasions of doing good to others, in regard of the work which they are about — which is saving of souls. What a precious thing is a soul! Christ takes, as it were, a pair of scales in his hands and he puts the world in one scale and the soul in the other — and the soul outweighs! (Matthew 16:26). The soul is of a noble origin. It is a flower of eternity; here, in the bud; in heaven, fully ripe. The soul is one of the richest pieces of embroidery which God ever made — the understanding bespangled with light, the will invested with liberty, the affections like musical instruments tuned with the finger of the Holy Spirit. Now if the souls of men are of so noble an extract and made capable of glory, oh how zealously industrious should Christ's ministers be to save these souls! If Christ spent his blood for souls, well may we spend our sweat! It was Augustine's prayer that Christ might find him at his coming — either praying or preaching. What a sad sight is it to see precious souls, as so many pearls and diamonds — cast into the dead sea of hell!

[4] The ministers of Christ, 'seeing the multitude', must 'ascend the mount' — because there are so many emissaries of Satan who lie in wait to catch and destroy souls! How the old serpent casts out of his mouth floods of water after the woman to drown her! (Revelation 12:15). What floods of heresy have been poured out in city and country, which have overflowed the banks not only of religion — but morality and civility! Ignatius calls error 'the invention of the devil', and Bernard calls it 'a sweet poison'. Men's ears, like sponges, have sucked in this poison! Never were the devil's commodities more vendible in England, than at present. A fine tongue, can sell bad wares. The Jesuit can color over his lies, and dress error in truth's coat! A weak brain is soon intoxicated. When flattery and subtlety in the speaker, meet with simplicity in the hearer — they easily become an easy prey. The Romish whore entices many to drink down the poison of her idolatry and filthiness, because it is given in 'a golden cup' (Revelation 17:4). If all who have the plague of the head should die, it would much increase the tally of mortality.

Now if there are so many emissaries of Satan abroad, who labor to make proselytes to the church of Rome, how it concerns those whom God has put into the work of the ministry — to bestir themselves and lay hold on all opportunities, that by their spiritual antidotes they may 'convert sinners from the error of their way and save their souls from death!' (James 5:20). Ministers must not only be 'pastors'—but fighters and warriors! In one hand they must hold the bread of life and 'feed the flock of God'; in the other hand, they must hold the sword of the Spirit and fight against those errors which carry damnation in them.

[5] The ministers of Christ should wait for all opportunities of soul-service, because the preaching of the Word meets so many adverse forces which hinder the progress and success of it. Never did a pilot meet with so many crosswinds in a voyage, as the spiritual pilots of God's church do, when they are transporting souls to heaven.

Some hearers have bad memories (James 1:25). Their memories are like leaking vessels. All the precious wine of holy doctrine that is poured in—runs out immediately. Ministers cannot by study find a truth—as fast as others can lose it. If the food does not stay in the stomach, it can never give nourishment. If a truth delivered does not stay in the memory, we can never be, as the apostle says, 'nourished up in the words of faith' (1 Timothy 4:6). How often does the devil, that fowl of the air, pick up the good seed that is sown! If people suffer at the hands of thieves, they tell everyone and make their complaint they have been robbed; but there is a worse thief they are not aware of! How many sermons has the devil stolen from them! How many truths have they been robbed of, which might have been so many cordials! Now if the Word preached slides so fast out of the memory, ministers had need the oftener to go up the preaching mount, that at last some truth may abide and be as 'a nail fastened'.

The ears of many of our hearers are stopped up with earth! I mean the cares of the world, that the Word preached will not enter, according to that in the parable, 'Hearing, they hear not' (Matthew 13:13). We read of Saul, his eyes were open—yet 'he saw no man' (Acts 9:8). A strange paradox! And is it not as strange that men's ears should be open—yet 'in hearing hear not?' They mind not what is said: 'They sit before you as my people—but their heart goes after their covetousness' (Ezekiel 33:31). Many sit and stare the minister in the face—yet scarcely understand a word he says. They are thinking of their wares and are often casting up accounts in the church. If a man is in a grinding-mill, though you speak ever so loud to him—he does not hear you for the noise of the mill. We preach to men about matters of salvation—but the grinding-mill of worldly business makes such a noise that they cannot hear! 'In hearing, they hear not'. It being thus, ministers who are called 'sons of thunder' had need often ascend the mount and 'lift up their voice like a trumpet' (Isaiah 58:1) that the deaf ear may be cleaned and unstopped, and may hear 'what the Spirit says unto the churches' (Revelation 2:7).

As some have earth in their ears—so others have a stone in their hearts! They make 'their hearts as an adamant stone, lest they should hear' (Zechariah 7:12). The ministers of Christ therefore must be frequently brandishing the sword of the Spirit and striking at men's sins, that, if possible, they may at last pierce the heart of stone! When the earth is scorched with the sun, it is so hard and crusted, that one shower of rain will not soften it. There must be shower after shower before it will be either moist or fertile. Such a hardened piece, is the heart of man naturally. It is so stiffened with the scorchings of lust, that there must be 'precept upon precept' (Isaiah 28:10). Our doctrine must 'distill as the dew, as the small rain on the tender herb, and as the showers upon the grass' (Deuteronomy 32:2).

[6] Christ's ministers, according to the example of their Lord and Master, should take all occasions of doing good, not only in regard of God's glory—but their own comfort. What triumph is it, and cause for gladness, when a minister can say on his deathbed, 'Lord, I have done the work which you gave me to do'—I have been laboring for souls! When a minister comes to the mount of glory, the heavenly mount, it will be a great comfort to him that he has

been so often upon the preaching mount. Certainly if the angels in heaven rejoice at the conversion of a sinner (Luke 15:7, 10), how shall that minister rejoice in heaven over every soul that he has been instrumental to convert! As it shall add a member to Christ's body, so a jewel to a minister's crown. 'Those who are wise', or as the original carries it, 'those who are teachers shall shine (not as lamps or candles, but) as stars (Daniel 12:3); not as planets—but as fixed stars in the firmament of glory forever!

And though 'Israel is not gathered'—yet shall God's ministers 'be glorious in the eyes of the Lord' (Isaiah 49:5). God will reward them not according to their success—but their diligence. When they are a 'savor of death' to men—yet they are a 'sweet savor' to God. In an orchard the laborer who plants a tree is rewarded, as well as he who fells a tree. The doctor's bill is paid, even though the patient dies.

First, let me crave liberty to speak a word to the Elishas—my honored brethren in the ministry. You are engaged in a glorious service. God has put great renown upon you. He has entrusted you with two most precious jewels—his truths and the souls of his people. Never was this honor conferred upon any angel—to convert souls! What princely dignity can parallel this? The pulpit is higher than the throne, for a true minister represents no less than God himself. 'As though God did beseech you by us, we beg you in Christ's stead—be reconciled to God' (2 Corinthians 5:20). Give me permission to say as the apostle, 'I magnify my office' (Romans 11:13). Whatever our persons are—the office is sacred. The Christian ministry is the most honorable employment in the world. Jesus Christ has graced this calling by his entering into it. Other men work in their trade; but ministers work with God. 'We are laborers together with God' (1 Corinthians 3:9). O high honor! God and his ministers have one and the same work. They both negotiate about souls. Let the sons of the prophets wear this as their crown and diadem!

But while I tell you of your dignity—do not forget your duty. Imitate this blessed pattern in the text, 'When Jesus saw the crowds—He opened His mouth and began to teach them'. He took all occasions of preaching. Sometimes he taught in the temple (Mark 14:49); sometimes in a ship (Mark 4:1), and here, upon the mount. His lips were a tree of life which fed many. How often did he neglect his food—that he might feast others with his doctrine! Let all the ministers of Christ tread in his steps! Make Christ not only your Savior—but your example. Allow no opportunities to slip away, wherein you may be helpful to the souls of others. Be not content to go to heaven yourselves—but be such shining lamps, that you may light others to heaven with you. I will conclude with that of the apostle: 'Therefore, my beloved brethren, be steadfast, unmoveable, always abounding in the work of the Lord, forasmuch as you know that your labor is not in vain in the Lord' (1 Corinthians 15:58).

Secondly, let me turn myself to the flock of God. If ministers must take all opportunities to preach—you must take all opportunities to hear. If there were twice or thrice a week a certain sum of money to be distributed to all comers, then people would resort there. Now think thus with yourselves— when the Word of God is preached, the bread of life is distributed, which is more precious than 'thousands of gold and silver' (Psalm 119:72). In the Word preached, heaven and salvation is offered to you. In this field, the pearl of great price is hidden. How should you 'flock like doves' to the windows of the sanctuary (Isaiah 60:8)! We read the gate of the temple was called 'beautiful' (Acts 3:2). The gate of God's house is the beautiful gate. Lie at 'these posts of wisdom's doors' (Proverbs 8 34).

Not only hear the Word preached—but encourage those ministers who do preach, by liberal maintaining of them. Though I hope all who have God's Urim and Thummim written upon them, can say, as the apostle, 'I seek not what is yours—but you' (2 Corinthians 12:14)—yet that scripture is still canonical, 'So has the Lord ordained, that those who preach the gospel, should live of the gospel' (1 Corinthians 9:14). Are not laborers in a vineyard, maintained by their labors? The apostle puts the question, 'Who plants a vineyard and does not eat the fruit of it? (1 Corinthians 9:7). Hypocrites love a cheap religion. They like a gospel which will cost them nothing. They are content—so long as they may have golden bags, to have wooden priests. How many by saving their purses—have lost their souls! Is it not pity that the fire on God's altar should go out for lack of pouring in a little golden oil? David would not offer that to God, which cost him nothing (2 Samuel 24:24).

Encourage God's ministers by your fruitfulness under their labors. When ministers are upon the 'mount', let them not sow upon the rocks. What cost has God laid out upon this city! Never, I believe, since the apostles' times, was there a more learned, orthodox, powerful ministry than now. God's ministers are called stars (Revelation 1:20). In this city every morning a star appears, besides the bright constellation on the Lord's Day. Oh you that feed in the green pastures of ordinances—be fat and fertile. You who are planted in the courts of God, flourish in the courts of God (Psalm 92:13). How sad will it be with a people, who shall go laden to hell with Gospel blessings! The best way to encourage your ministers is to let them see the travail of their souls in your new birth. It is a great comfort when a minister not only woos souls—but wins souls! 'He who wins souls is wise' (Proverbs 11:30). This is a minister's glory. 'For what is our joy, or crown of rejoicing? Are not you our crown?' (1 Thessalonians 2:19). A successful preacher wears two crowns, a crown of righteousness in heaven, and a crown of rejoicing here upon earth. 'Are not you our crown?'

Encourage your ministers by praying for them. Their work is great. It is a work which will take up their head and heart. It is a work fitter for angels—than men. 'Who is sufficient for these things?' (2 Corinthians 2:16). Oh pray for them! Christ indeed, when he ascended the mount and was to preach, needed none of the people's prayers for him. He had a sufficient stock—the divine nature to supply him. But all his under-officers in the ministry need prayer. If Paul, who abounded in the graces of the Spirit and supernatural revelations, begged prayer (1 Thessalonians 5:25), then surely those ministers need prayer, who do not have such revelations.

And pray for your ministers that God will direct them what to preach, that he will cut out their work for them. 'Go preach ... the preaching that I bid you' (Jonah 3:2). It is a great matter to preach suitable truths; there are 'acceptable words' (Ecclesiastes 12:10).

Pray that God will go forth with their labors—or else 'they toil and catch nothing'. God's Spirit must fill the sails of our ministry. It is not the hand which scatters the seed, which makes it spring up—but the dews and influences of heaven. So it is not our preaching—but the divine influence of the Spirit, which makes grace grow in men's hearts. We are but pipes and organs. It is God's Spirit blowing through us, which makes the preaching of the Word by a divine enchantment—allure souls to Christ. Ministers are but candles—to light you to Christ. The Spirit is the loadstone—to draw you. All the good done by our ministry is 'due to the Lord's excellent and effectual working' (Bucer).

Oh then pray for us, that God will make his work prosper in our hands. This may be one reason why the Word preached does not profit more—because people do not pray more. Perhaps you complain the tool is dull—the minister is dead and cold. You should have whetted and sharpened him by your prayer! If you would have the door of a blessing opened to you through our ministry, you must unlock it by the key of prayer!

4. The Sermon

Having done with the occasion of the sermon – I come now to the sermon itself. 'Blessed are the poor in spirit'. Christ does not begin his Sermon on the Mount, as the Law was delivered on the mount – with commands and threatenings, the trumpet sounding, the fire flaming, the earth quaking, and the hearts of the Israelites shaking for fear! But our Savior (whose lips 'dropped as the honeycomb') begins with promises and blessings. So sweet and ravishing was the doctrine of this heavenly Orator, that, like music, it was able to charm the most savage natures, yes, to draw hearts of stone to him!

To begin then with this first word, 'Blessed' – or 'Happy'. If there be any blessedness in knowledge, it must needs be in the knowledge of blessedness. For the illustration of this, I shall lay down two principles:

The fullness of blessedness, lies in the future.

That the godly are in some sense already blessed.

A. The fullness of blessedness, lies in the future! The people of God meet with many knotty difficulties and sinking discouragements in the way of religion. Their march is not only tedious, but dangerous, and their hearts are ready to despond. It will not be amiss therefore to set the crown of blessedness before them – to animate their courage and to inflame their zeal. How many scriptures bring this olive-branch in their mouth – the tidings of eternal blessedness to believers! 'Blessed is that servant whom his Lord, when he comes, shall find so doing' (Matthew 24:46). 'Come, you who are blessed by my Father' (Matthew 25:34). Blessedness is the perfection of a rational creature. It is the whetstone of a Christian's industry, the height of his ambition, the flower of his joy. Blessedness is the desire of all men. Aquinas calls it the 'ultimate end'. This is the 'bulls-eye' which every man aims to hit; to this center all the lines are drawn.

In what does blessedness (happiness) consist? Millions of men mistake both the nature of blessedness, and the way there. Some of the learned have set down two hundred and eighty eight different opinions about blessedness, and all have shot wide of the mark. I shall show wherein it does not consist, and then wherein it does consist.

(1) Wherein blessedness does not consist.

It does not lie in the acquisition of worldly things. Happiness cannot by any art or chemistry, be extracted from the world. Christ does not say, 'Blessed are the rich', or 'Blessed are the noble.' Yet too many idolize these things. Man, by the fall, has not only lost his crown – but his wisdom. How ready is he to terminate his happiness in external worldly things! Which makes me call to mind that definition which some of the heathen philosophers give of blessedness, that it was to have a sufficiency of subsistence and to thrive well in the world. And are there not many who pass for Christians, who seem to be of this philosophical opinion? If they have but worldly accommodations, they are ready to sing a requiem to their souls and say with that brutish fool in the gospel, 'Soul, you have much goods laid up for many years, take your ease ...' (Luke 12:19).

'What is more shameful', says Seneca, 'than to equate the rational soul's good with that which is irrational.' Alas, the tree of blessedness does not grow in an earthly paradise. Has not God 'cursed the ground' because of sin? (Genesis 3:17). Yet many are digging for happiness here – as if they would fetch a blessing out of a curse! A man may as well think to extract oil out of a flint, or fire out of water – as blessedness out of earthly things.

King Solomon had more worldly things, than any man. He was the most magnificent prince who ever held the scepter. For his parentage: he sprang from the royal line, not only that line from which many kings came – but of which Christ himself came. Jesus Christ descended from Solomon's line and race, so that for heraldry and nobility none could show a fairer coat of arms.

For the situation of his palace: it was in Jerusalem, the princess and paragon of the earth. Jerusalem, for its renown, was called 'the city of God'. It was the most famous metropolis in the world. For wealth: his crown was hung full of jewels. He had treasures of gold and of pearl and 'made silver to be as common as stones' (1 Kings 10:27). For worldly joy: he had the flower and quintessence of all delights—sumptuous fare, stately edifices, vineyards, farms, all sorts of music to enchant and ravish the senses with joy. If there were any rarity—it was present in King Solomon's court. Thus did he bathe himself in the perfumed waters of pleasure.

For wisdom: he was the oracle of his time. When the queen of Sheba came to pose him with hard questions, he gave a solution to all her queries (1 Kings 10:3). He had a key of knowledge to unlock nature's dark cabinet, so that if wisdom had been lost, it might have been found here, and the whole world might have lighted their understanding at Solomon's lamp! He was an earthly angel, so that a carnal eye surveying his glory would have been ready to imagine that Solomon had entered into that paradise out of which Adam was once driven, or that he had found another as good. Never did the world cast a more smiling aspect upon any man. Yet when he comes to give his impartial verdict, he tells us that the world has 'vanity' written upon its frontispiece, and all those golden delights he enjoyed, were but a painted felicity—a glorious misery! 'Behold! All was vanity!' (Ecclesiastes 2:8). Happiness is too noble and delicate a plant, to grow in this world's soil.

That blessedness does not lie in external worldly things—I shall prove by these five demonstrations:

[1] Those things which are not commensurate to the desires of the soul, can never make a man blessed. Transitory worldly things, are not commensurate to the desires of the soul—therefore they cannot render him blessed. Nothing on earth can satisfy the soul's desires!

'He who loves silver, shall not be satisfied with silver' (Ecclesiastes 5:10). Riches are unsatisfying:

Because they are not real. The world is called a 'fashion' (1 Corinthians 7:31). The word in the Greek signifies an apparition. Riches are but painted over. They are like paint, which glitters a little in our eyes—but at death all this paint will be worn off. Riches are but sugared lies, pleasant deceits, like a gilded cover which has not one leaf of true happiness bound up in it.

Because they are not suitable. The soul is a spiritual thing; riches are of an earthly extract—how can these fill a spiritual substance? A man may as well fill his treasure chest with sunshine, as his heart with gold. If a man were crowned with all the delights of the world, nay, if God should build a house for him among the stars—yet the restless eye of his unsatisfied mind would be looking still higher. He would be prying beyond the heavens for some hidden rarities which he thinks he has not yet attained to! So unquenchable is the thirst of the soul—until it comes to bathes in the river of life and to center upon true blessedness.

[2] That which cannot quiet the heart in a storm—cannot entitle a man to blessedness. A great accumulation of earthly things, cannot rock the troubled heart quiet. Therefore they cannot make one blessed or truly happy. If the heart is wounded—can we pour wine and oil into this wound? If God sets conscience to work, and it flies in a man's face, can worldly comforts take off this angry fury? Is there any harp to drive away the 'evil spirit'? Outward things can no more cure the agony of conscience than a silken stocking can cure a gouty foot. When Saul was 'greatly distressed' (1 Samuel 28:15), could all the jewels of his crown comfort him? If God is angry, whose 'fury is poured out like fire, and the rocks are thrown down by him' (Nahum 1:6), can a wedge of gold be a screen to keep off this fire? 'They shall cast their silver in the streets; their silver and their gold shall not be able to deliver them in the day of the wrath of the Lord'

(Ezekiel 7:19). King Belshazzar was carousing and partying. 'He drank wine in the golden vessels of the temple' (Daniel 5:3) — but when the fingers of a man's hand appeared, 'his countenance was changed' (verse 6), his wine grew sour, his feast was spoiled with that dish, which was served in upon the wall. The things of the world will no more keep out trouble of spirit — than a paper shirt will keep out a bullet!

[3] That which is but 'temporary' cannot make one blessed. All things under the sun are but 'temporary', therefore they cannot enrich with blessedness. Worldly delights are like those foods which are fresh at first — and then presently grow stale or rot. 'The world passes away' (1 John 2:17). Worldly delights are winged. They may be compared to a flock of birds in the garden — which stay a little while — but when you come near to them — they take their flight and are gone! So 'riches make themselves wings; they fly away as an eagle toward heaven' (Proverbs 23:5). They are like a meteor which blazes — but soons burns out. They are like a castle made of snow, lying under the fiery beams of the sun. Augustine says of himself, that when any preferment smiled upon him, he was afraid to accept of it lest it should on a sudden give him the slip. Outward comforts are like tennis balls which are bandied up and down from one to another. Had we the longest lease of worldly comforts, it would soon be run out. Riches and honor are constantly in flight; they pass away like a swift stream, or like a ship that is going full sail. While they are with us — they are going away from us. They are like a bouquet of flowers — which withers while you are smelling it. They are like ice — which melts away while it is in your hand. The world takes its salute and farewell together.

[4] Those things which do more vex than comfort — cannot make a man blessed. Such are all things under the sun, therefore they cannot have blessedness affixed to them. As riches are compared to wind — to show their vanity (Hosea 12:1); so they are compared to thorns — to show their vexation (Matthew 13:17). Thorns are not more apt to tear our garments, than riches to tear our hearts. They are thorns in the gathering — and they prick with anxious care. They pierce the head with care of getting, so they wound the heart with fear of losing. God will have our sweetest wine run into dregs; yes, and taste of a musty cask too — that we may not think that earthly things are the wine of paradise.

[5] Those things which (if we have nothing else) will make us cursed, cannot make us blessed. The sole enjoyment of worldly things will make us cursed, therefore it is far from making us blessed. 'Riches are kept for the hurt of the owner' (Ecclesiastes 5:13). Riches to the wicked are fuel for pride: 'Your heart is lifted up because of your riches' (Ezekiel 28:5). Riches to the wicked are fuel for lust: 'when I had fed them to the full, they then committed adultery' (Jeremiah 5:7). Riches are a snare: 'But those who will be rich fall into temptation and a snare, and into many foolish and hurtful lusts, which drown men in perdition' (1 Timothy 6:9). How many have pulled down their souls — to build up an estate! A ship may be so laden with gold that it sinks. Just so, many a man's gold has sunk him to hell. The rich sinner seals up money in his bag — and God seals up a curse with it! 'Woe to him who ladens himself with thick clay' (Habakkuk 2:6). Augustine says that Judas for money sold his salvation — and with that same money, the Pharisees bought their damnation. So we see that happiness is not to be fetched out of the earth. Those who go to the creature for blessedness go to the wrong box.

If blessedness does not consist in externals — then let us not place our blessedness here. This is to seek the living among the dead. As the angel told Mary concerning Christ, 'He is not here, he is risen' (Matthew 28:6), so I may say of blessedness, 'It is not here, it is risen; it is in a higher region!' How do men thirst after the world, as if the pearl of blessedness hung upon an earthly crown! 'O,' says one, 'if I had but such an estate — then I would be happy! Had I but such a comfort, then I would sit down satisfied!' Well, God gives him that comfort and lets him suck out the very juice of it — but, alas, it falls short of his expectation. It cannot fill the emptiness and longing of his soul which still cries 'Give, give' (Proverbs 30:15).

This is like a sick man, who says, 'If I had but such a food, I could eat it.' But when he has it, his stomach is nauseated, and he can hardly endure to smell it. God has put not only an emptiness — but bitterness into the creature, and it is good for us that there is no perfection here, that we may raise our thoughts higher to more noble and generous delights. Could we distill and draw out the quintessence of the creature, we would say as once the emperor Severus said, who grew from a low estate to be head of the greatest empire in the world: 'I have run through all conditions — yet could never find full contentment.'

To such as are cut short in their allowance, whose cup does not overflow, remember that these outward comforts cannot make you blessed. You might live rich and die cursed. You might treasure up an estate, and God might treasure up wrath. Do not be perplexed about those things the lack of which cannot make you miserable, nor the enjoyment make you blessed.

(2) Having shown wherein blessedness does not consist, I shall next show wherein it DOES consist. Blessedness consists in the fruition of the chief good.

True blessedness consists in fruition; there must not be only possession — but fruition. A man may possess an estate — yet not enjoy it. He may have the dominion of it — but not the comfort, as when he is in a sickness, or under the predominance of melancholy. But in true blessedness there must be a sensible enjoyment of that which the soul possesses.

True blessedness lies in the fruition of the chief good. It is not every good which makes a man blessed — but it must be the supreme good — and that is God. 'Happy is that people whose God is the Lord' (Psalm 144:15). God is the soul's rest (Psalm 116:7). Now, that only in which the soul acquiesces and rests — can make it blessed. The circle, as is observed in mathematics, is of all others the most perfect figure, because the last point of the figure ends in that first point where it began. So, when the soul meets in God, whence it sprang as its first original, then it is completely blessed. That which makes a man blessed must have fixed qualifications or ingredients in it — and these are found nowhere but in God — the chief good.

In true blessedness there must be something better. That which fills with blessedness, must be such a good as is better than a man's self. If you would ennoble a piece of gold, it must be by putting something to it which is better than silver, as by adding a diamond to it. So that which ennobles the soul and enriches it with blessedness, must be by adding something to it which is more excellent than the soul, and that alone is God. The world is below the soul; it is but the soul's footstool; therefore it cannot crown it with happiness.

Another ingredient of true blessedness, is delectability. That which brings blessedness must have a delicious taste in it, such as the soul is instantly ravished with. Delight and quintessence of joy must be in it. And where can the soul suck those pure comforts which amaze it with wonder, and crown it with delight — but in God? 'In God', says Augustine, 'the soul is delighted with such sweetness as enraptures it!' The love of God is a honeycomb which drops such infinite sweetness and satisfaction into the soul as is 'unspeakable and full of glory.' (1 Peter 1:8). A kiss from God's mouth puts the soul into a divine ecstasy, so that now it cries out, 'It is good to be here!'

Another ingredient in blessedness is plenty. That which makes a man blessed — must not be scanty. It is a full draught which quenches the soul's thirst; and where shall we find plenty but in Deity? 'You shall make them drink of the river of your pleasures' (Psalm 36:8); not drops but rivers! The soul bathes itself and is laid, as it were, steeping in the water of life! The river of paradise overflows and empties its silver streams into the souls of the blessed!

In true blessedness there must be variety. Plenty without variety — is apt to nauseate. In God there is 'all fullness'. (Colossians 1:19). What can the soul desire — but it may be had in the chief good? God is 'the good in all good things'. He is a sun, a shield, a portion, a fountain, a rock of strength, a horn of salvation. In God there is a convergence of all excellencies. There are every moment — fresh beauties and delights springing from God.

To make up blessedness there must be perfection; the joy must be perfect, the glory perfect. 'Spirits of just men made perfect' (Hebrews 12:23). Blessedness must run through the whole. If there is the least defect, it destroys the nature of blessedness; as the least symptom of a disease takes away the well-being and right temperature of the body.

True blessedness must have eternity stamped on it. Blessedness is a fixed thing; it admits of no change or alteration. God says of every child of his, 'I have blessed him — and he shall be blessed!' As the sunshine of blessedness is 'without clouds', so it never sets. 'I give unto them eternal life' (John 10:28). 'And so shall we ever be with the Lord' (1 Thessalonians 4:17). Eternity is the highest link of blessedness! Thus we have seen that this diamond of blessedness is only to be found in the Rock of Ages. 'Blessed are the people whose God is the Lord.' 'There remains a rest for the people of God' (Hebrews 4:9).

Revolve this truth often in your mind. There are many truths which swim in the brain, which do not sink into the heart — and those do us no good. Chew the cud! Let a Christian think seriously with himself, 'there is a blessedness feasible and I am capable of enjoying it — if I do not lay bars in the way and block up my own happiness. Though within I see nothing but guilt, and without nothing but curses — yet there is a blessedness to be had, and to be had for me too in the use of means.'

The serious meditation on this, will be a forcible argument to make the sinner break off his sins by repentance, and sweat hard until he finds the golden mine of blessedness. I say — it would be the break-neck of sin! How would a man offer violence to himself by mortification, and to heaven by supplication that at last he may arrive at this state of blessedness! What! Is there a crown of blessedness to be set upon my head! A crown hung with the jewels of honor, delight, magnificence! A crown reached out by God himself! And shall I hazard all this — by sin! Can the pleasure of sin countervail the loss of all this blessedness! What more powerful motive to repentance than this — Sin will rob me of the blessing!

If a man knew certainly that a king would settle all his crown revenues on him after a term of years, would he offend that regal Majesty and cause him to reverse or alter his will? There is a blessedness promised to all who live godly. 'This is the promise he has promised us — even eternal life' (1 John 2:25). We are not excluded — but may come in for a child's part. Now shall we, by living in sin — provoke God and forfeit this blessedness? O what madness is this! Well may the apostle call them 'foolish and hurtful lusts' (1 Timothy 6:9), because every lust does what it can — to cut off the mercy and block up the way to happiness. Every sin may be compared to the 'flaming sword', which shuts the heavenly paradise — so that the sinner cannot enter.

Let us so conduct ourselves — that we may express to others that we do believe a blessedness to come — and that is by seeking an interest in God. For the beams of blessedness shine only from his face. It is our union with God, the chief good — which makes us blessed. Oh, let us never rest until we can say, 'This God is our God forever and ever' (Psalm 48:14). Most men think because God has blessed them with an estate, therefore they are blessed. Alas, God often gives these worldly things in anger. 'God grants a thing when he is angry — which he does not will to give when he is tranquil.' God often loads his enemies with gold and silver — the weight whereof sinks them into hell. Oh, let us pant after heavenly things! Let us get our eyes fixed, and our hearts united to God, the supreme good.

Let us proclaim to the world that we do believe a blessedness to come – by living blessed lives; walk as befits the heirs of blessedness. A blessed crown, and a cursed life – will never agree. Many tell us they are bound for heaven – but they steer their course a quite contrary way. The Devil is their pilot, and they sail hell-ward, as if a man should say he were going a voyage to the east – but sails quite westward. The drunkard will tell you he hopes for blessedness – but he sails another way. You must go weeping to heaven, not reeling. The unclean person talks of blessedness – but he is fallen into that 'deep ditch' (Proverbs 23:27), where he is like sooner to find hell than heaven. A beast may as well be made an angel – as an unclean person in his leprosy, can enter into the paradise of God. The covetous person (of whom it may be said, 'he is a worm and no man', for he is ever creeping in the earth) yet would lay a claim to blessedness; but can earth ascend? Shall a lump of clay be made a bright star in the firmament of glory? Be assured they shall never be blessed – who bless themselves in their sins. 'If,' says God, 'the sinner blesses himself in his heart, saying, I shall have peace, though I walk in the imagination of my heart, to add drunkenness to thirst' – the Lord will not spare him – but then the anger of the Lord and his jealousy shall smoke against that man, and the Lord shall blot out his name under heaven' (Deuteronomy 29:19). A man can no more extract blessedness out of sin – than he can suck health out of poison! O let us lead blessed lives, and so 'declare plainly that we seek a heavenly country' (Hebrews 11:14).

To you who have any good hope through grace, that you have a title to blessedness, let me say as the Levites did to the people, 'Stand up and bless the Lord your God forever and ever' (Nehemiah 9:5). What infinite cause have you to be thankful that the lot of free grace has fallen upon you! Though you had forfeited all – yet God has provided a haven of happiness, and he is carrying you there upon the sea of Christ's blood, with the gale of his Spirit blowing your sails! You are in a better condition through Christ, than when you had the robes of innocence upon you. God has raised you a step higher – by your fall. How many has God passed by – and looked upon you! There are millions who shall lie under the bitter vials of God's curses; whereas he will bring you into his banqueting-house, and pour out the flagons of wine, and feast you eternally with the delicacies of heaven! O adore free grace! Rejoice in this love of God towards you. Spend and be spent for the Lord. Dedicate yourselves to him in a way of resignation, and lay out yourselves for him in a way of thanksgiving. Never think you can do enough – for that God who will shortly set you ashore in the land of heavenly promise!

B. The godly are in some sense already blessed

I proceed now to the second premise – that the godly are in some sense already blessed. The saints are blessed not only when they arrive in heaven – but also while they are travelers to glory. They are blessed before they are crowned. This seems a paradox to flesh and blood. What, reproached and maligned – yet blessed! A man who looks upon the children of God with a carnal eye and sees how they are afflicted, and like the ship in the gospel which was 'covered with waves' (Matthew 8:24), would think they were far from blessedness. Paul brings a catalogue of his sufferings: 'Thrice was I beaten with rods; once I was stoned, thrice I suffered shipwreck ...' (2 Corinthians 11:24-26). And those Christians of the first magnitude, of whom the world was not worthy, 'had trial of cruel mockings and scourgings; they were sawn asunder; they were slain with the sword' (Hebrews 11:36, 37). What! Were all these during the time of their sufferings, blessed? A carnal man would think, 'If this is to be blessed – God deliver me from it!'

But, however sense and reason give their vote, our Savior Christ pronounces the godly man to be blessed. Though he is a mourner, though he is a martyr — yet he is blessed. Job on the dunghill — was blessed Job. The saints are blessed when they are cursed. Shimei cursed David. 'He came forth and cursed him' (2 Samuel 16:5). Yet when he was cursed David, he was blessed David. The saints, though they are bruised — yet they are blessed. Not only shall they be blessed, they are now blessed. 'Blessed are the undefiled' (Psalm 19:1). 'Your blessing is upon your people' (Psalm 3:8).

How are the saints already blessed?

(1) In that they are enriched with heavenly blessings (Ephesians 1:3). They are 'partakers of the divine nature' (2 Peter 1:4), not by an incorporation into the divine essence — but by transformation into the divine likeness. This is blessedness begun. The new-born babe is said to have life in it — as well as he who is fully grown. Just so, the saints, who are partakers of the divine nature, have an incipient blessedness, though they have not arrived yet at perfection. Believers have the seed of God abiding in them (1 John 3:9). And this is a seed of blessedness. The flower of glory grows out of the seed of grace! Grace and glory differ not in kind — but degree. Grace is the root — glory is the fruit. Grace is glory in the dawning; glory is grace in the full meridian. Grace is the first link in the chain of blessedness. Now he who has the first link of the chain in his hand, has the whole chain. The saints have the Spirit of God in them, 'The Holy Spirit, who dwells in us' (2 Timothy 1:14). How can the blessed Spirit be in a man — and he not blessed? A godly man's heart is a paradise, planted with the choicest fruit — and God himself walks in the midst of this paradise — so the man must be blessed!

(2) The saints are already blessed — because their sins are not imputed to them. 'Blessed is the man to whom the Lord does not impute iniquity' (Psalm 32:2). God's not imputing iniquity, signifies God's making of sin not to be. It is as if the man had never sinned. The debt book is crossed out in Christ's blood, and if the debtor owes ever so much — yet if the creditor crosses out the book, it is as if he had never owed anything. God's not imputing sin signifies that God will never call for the debt; or, if it should be called for, it shall be hidden out of sight. 'In those days the iniquity of Israel shall be sought for, and there shall be none; and the sins of Judah, and they shall not be found' (Jeremiah 50:20). Now such a man who has not sin imputed to him, is blessed, and the reason is, because if sin is not imputed to a man, then the curse is taken away; and if the curse be taken away, then he must needs be blessed!

(3) The saints are already blessed — because they are in covenant with God. This is clear by comparing two scriptures: 'I will be their God', (Jeremiah 31:33), and 'Happy is that people whose God is the Lord' (Psalm 144:15). This is the crowning blessing, to have the Lord for our God. Impossible it is to imagine that God should be our God — and we not be blessed.

This sweet word, 'I will be your God', implies propriety — that all that is in God, shall be ours! His love is ours, his Spirit ours, his mercy ours. It implies all relations. It implies the relation of a father, 'I will be a father unto you' (2 Corinthians 6:18). The sons of a prince are happy. How blessed are the saints who are of true royal blood? It implies the relation of a husband, 'Your Maker is your husband' (Isaiah 54:5). The spouse, being contracted to her husband, is happy by having an interest in all that he has. The saints being contracted by faith are blessed, though the marriage supper is kept for heaven. It implies terms of friendship. Those who are in covenant with God are favorites of heaven. 'Abraham my friend' (Isaiah 41:8). It is counted a subject's happiness to be in favor with his prince, though he may live a ways from court. How happy must he needs be — who is God's favorite!

(4) The saints are already blessed because they have a guarantee of heaven; as, on the contrary, the unbeliever has a guarantee of hell, and is said to be already condemned. 'He who believes not, is condemned already' (John 3:18). He is as sure to be condemned, as if he were condemned already. So he who has heaven laid up for him, may be said to be already blessed. A man that has the guarantee of a house, after a short lease is run out — he looks upon that house — as his already. 'This house,' says he, 'is mine.' So a believer has a guarantee of heaven after the lease of life has run out, and he can say at present, 'Christ is mine and glory is mine!' He has a title to heaven, and he is a blessed man who has a title to show; more — faith turns the promise, into a possession!

(5) The saints are already blessed because they have the first-fruits of blessedness here. We read of the pledge of the Spirit, and the seal of the Spirit (2 Corinthians 1:22), and the first-fruits of the Spirit (Romans 8:23). Heaven is already begun in a believer. 'The kingdom of God is peace and joy in the Holy Spirit' (Romans 14:17). This kingdom is in a believer's heart (Luke 17:21). The people of God have a foretaste of blessedness here. As Israel tasted of the grapes before they actually possessed Canaan, so the children of God have those secret incomes of the Spirit, those smiles of Christ's face, those kisses of his lips, those love-tokens — and they think themselves sometimes in heaven. Oftentimes the Comforter is let down to the soul in an ordinance, and now the soul is in the suburbs of Jerusalem above. A Christian sees heaven by faith, end tastes it by joy; end what is this, but blessedness?

(6) The saints may be said in this life to be blessed, because all things tend to make them blessed. 'All things work together for good to them that love God' (Romans 8:28). We say to him that has everything falling out for the best, you are a happy man. The saints are very happy, for all things have a tendency to their good. Prosperity does them good; adversity does them good. Nay, sin turns to their good. Every trip makes them more watchful. Their maladies are their medicines. Are not they happy people that have every wind blowing them to the right port?

(7) A saint may be said to be blessed, because part of him is already blessed. He is blessed in his head; Christ, his head, is in glory; Christ and believers make one mystical body; their head is gotten into heaven.

See the difference between a wicked man and a godly. Let a wicked man have ever so many comforts — still he is cursed. Let a godly man have ever so many crosses — still he is blessed. Let a wicked man have the 'candle of God shining' on him (Job 29:3), let his way be so smooth that he meets with no rubs; let him have success — yet still there is a curse upon him. You may read the sinner's inventory (Deuteronomy 28:16, 17, 18). He is not more full of sin — than he is of a curse. Though perhaps he blesses himself in his wickedness — yet he is heir to God's curse. All the curses of the Bible are his portion, and at the day of death this portion is sure to be paid. But a godly man in the midst of all his miseries is blessed. He may be under the cross — but not under a curse!

It shows the privilege of a believer. He not only shall be blessed — but he is blessed! Blessedness has begun in him. 'You are blessed of the Lord' (Psalm 115:15). Let the condition of the righteous be ever so sad — yet it is blessed. He is blessed in affliction, 'Blessed is he whom you chasten' (Psalm 94:12). He is blessed in poverty, 'poor in the world, rich in faith' (James 2:5). He is blessed in disgrace, 'The spirit of glory and of God rests upon you' (1 Peter 4:14). This may be a cordial to the fainting Christian; he is blessed both in life and death! Satan cannot supplant him of the blessing.

How may this take away murmuring and melancholy from a child of God! Will you repine and be sad—when you are blessed? Esau wept because he lost the blessing. 'Bless me, even me also, O my father, and Esau lifted up his voice and wept' (Genesis 27:38). But shall a child of God be immoderately cast down when he has the blessing? How evil it is to be blessed, and yet murmur!

What an encouragement is this to godliness! We are all ambitious of a blessing, then let us espouse true religion. 'Blessed is the man who fears the Lord' (Psalm 112:1). But you will say, 'This way is everywhere spoken against.' It does not matter, seeing this is the way to get a blessing. Suppose a rich man should adopt another for his heir, and others should reproach him—he does not care as long as he is heir to the grand estate. So, what though others may reproach you for your piety—as long as it entails a blessing on you; the same day you become godly, you become blessed.

Having spoken of the general notion of blessedness, I come next to consider the subjects of this blessedness, and these our Savior has described to be the poor in spirit, the mourners, etc. But before I touch upon these, I shall attempt a little preface upon this sermon of the beatitudes.

1. Observe the divinity in this sermon, which goes beyond all philosophy. The philosophers say that one contrary expels another; but here one contrary begets another. Poverty is accustomed to expel riches—but here poverty begets riches, for how rich are those who have a kingdom! Mourning is accustomed to expel joy—but here mourning begets joy—'they shall be comforted'. Water is accustomed to quench the flame—but the water of tears kindles the flame of joy. Persecution is accustomed to expel happiness—but here it makes happy—'Blessed are those who are persecuted'. These are the sacred paradoxes in our Savior's sermon.

2. Observe how Christ's doctrine and the opinion of carnal men differ. They think, 'Blessed are the rich.' The world would count him blessed who could have Midas' wish—that all that he touched might be turned into gold. But Christ says, 'Blessed are the poor in spirit'. The world thinks, 'Blessed are they on the pinnacle!' But Christ pronounces them blessed, who are in the valley. Christ's reckonings and the world's reckonings—do not agree.

3. Observe the nature of true religion. Poverty leads the van, and persecution brings up the rear. Every true saint is heir to the cross! Some there are, who would be thought religious, displaying Christ's colors by a glorious profession—but to be 'poor in spirit' and 'persecuted'—they cannot take down this bitter pill. They would wear Christ's jewels—but waive his cross! These are strangers to true religion.

4. Observe the certain connection between grace and its reward. Those who are 'poor in spirit' shall have the 'kingdom of God'. They are as sure to go to heaven, as if they were in heaven already. Our Savior would encourage men to piety—by sweetening commands with promises. He ties duty and reward together. As Apelles painted Helena richly drawn in costly and glorious apparel, hung all over with orient pearl, and precious stones; so our Lord Christ, having set down several qualifications of a Christian, 'poor in spirit', 'pure in heart', etc.' draws these heavenly virtues in their fair colors of blessedness, and sets the magnificent crown of reward upon them—that by this brilliance, he might the more set forth their unparalleled beauty, and entice holy love.

5. Observe hence the chain of the graces: poor in spirit, meek, merciful, etc. Where there is one grace—there is all. We may say of the graces of the spirit—they are linked and chained together. He that has poverty of spirit—is a mourner. He who is a mourner—is meek. He who is meek—is merciful, etc. The Spirit of God plants in the heart a habit of all the graces. The graces of the Spirit are like a row of pearls which hang together upon the string of piety, and

serve to adorn Christ's bride. This I note, to show you a difference between a hypocrite and a true child of God. The hypocrite flatters himself with a pretense of grace — but in the meantime he does not have a habit of all the graces. He does not have poverty of spirit, nor purity of heart; whereas a child of God has the habit of all the graces in his heart. These things being premised, I come in particular to those heavenly dispositions of soul to which Christ has affixed blessedness. And the first is Poverty of Spirit: 'Blessed are the poor in spirit'.

Poverty of Spirit

Blessed are the poor in spirit, for theirs is the kingdom of heaven.

Matthew 5:3

Some are of opinion, that this was the first sermon which ever Christ gave, therefore it may challenge our best attention. 'Blessed are the poor in spirit'. Our Lord Christ, beginning to raise a high and stately fabric of blessedness, lays the foundation of it low — in poverty of spirit. But all poverty is not blessed. I shall use a fourfold distinction.

1. I distinguish between 'poor in estate', and 'poor in spirit'. There are the Devil's poor. They are both poor and wicked — whose clothes are not more torn than their conscience. There are some whose poverty is their sin, who through improvidence or excess have brought themselves to poverty. These may be poor in estate — but not poor in spirit.

2. I distinguish between 'spiritually poor' and 'poor in spirit'. He who is without grace is spiritually poor — but he is not poor in spirit; he does not know his own beggary. 'You know not, that you are poor' (Revelation 3:17). He is in the worst sense poor — who has no sense of his poverty.

3. I distinguish between 'poor-spirited' and 'poor in spirit'. They are said to be poor-spirited who have mean, base spirits, who act below themselves. Such are those misers, who having great estates — yet can hardly afford themselves bread; who live sneakingly, and are ready to wish their own throats cut, because they are forced to spend something in satisfying nature's demands. This Solomon calls an evil under the sun. 'There is an evil which I have seen under the sun — a man to whom God has given riches, so that he lacks nothing that he desires — yet God gives him not power to eat thereof' (Ecclesiastes 6:2). True religion makes no man a niggard. Though it teaches prudence — yet not sordidness.

Then there are those who act below themselves as they are Christians, while they sinfully comply and prostitute themselves to the desires of others; a base kind of metal that will take any stamp. They will for a piece of silver — part with the jewel of a good conscience. They will be of the popular religion. They will dance to the devil's pipe, if their superior commands them. These are poor-spirited but not poor in spirit.

4. I distinguish between poor in an evangelical sense — and poor in a popish sense. The papists give a wrong gloss upon the text. By 'poor in spirit', they understand those who, renouncing their estates, vow a voluntary poverty, living retiredly in their monasteries. But Christ never meant these. He does not pronounce them blessed — who make themselves poor, leaving their estates and callings — but such as are evangelically poor.

Well then, what are we to understand by 'poor in spirit'? The Greek word for 'poor' is not only taken in a strict sense for those who live upon charity — but in a more large sense, for those who are destitute as well of inward as outward comfort. Poor in spirit, then, signifies those who are brought to the sense of their sins, and seeing no goodness in themselves, despair in themselves and sue wholly to the mercy of God in Christ. Poverty of spirit is a kind of self-annihilation. 'The poor in spirit' (says Calvin) 'are those who see nothing in themselves — but fly to mercy for sanctuary.' Such an one was the publican: 'God be merciful to me a sinner' (Luke 18:13). Of this temper was Paul: 'That I may be found in Christ, not having my own righteousness' (Philippians 3:9). These are the poor, who are invited as guests to wisdom's banquet (Proverbs 7:3, 4).

Here several questions may be propounded.

[1] Why does Christ here begin with poverty of spirit? Why is this put in the forefront? I answer, Christ does it to show that poverty of spirit is the very basis and foundation of all the other graces which follow. You may as well expect fruit to grow without a root, as the other graces without poverty of spirit. Until a man is poor in spirit, he cannot mourn. Poverty of spirit is like the fire under the still, which makes the water drop from the eyes. When a man sees his own defects and deformities, and looks upon himself as undone — then he mourns after Christ. 'The springs run in the valleys' (Psalm 104:10). When the heart becomes a valley and lies low by poverty of spirit, now the springs of holy mourning run there. Until a man is poor in spirit, he cannot 'hunger and thirst after righteousness'. He must first be sensible of need, before he can hunger. Therefore Christ begins with poverty of spirit — because this ushers in all the rest.

[2] What is the difference between poverty of spirit, and humility? These are so alike that they have been taken one for the other. Chrysostom, by 'poverty of spirit', understands humility. Yet I think there is some difference. They differ as the cause and the effect. I think that poverty of spirit is the cause of humility, for when a man sees his need of Christ, and how he lives on the alms of free grace — this makes him humble. He who is sensible of his own vacuity and indigence, hangs his head in humility with the violet. Humility is the sweet spice which grows from poverty of spirit.

[3] What is the difference between poverty of spirit, and self-denial? I answer, in some things they agree, in some things they differ. In some things they agree; for the one who is poor in spirit is an absolute self-denier. He renounces all good opinion of himself. He acknowledges his dependence upon Christ and free grace.

But in some things they differ. The self-denier parts with the world for Christ; the poor in spirit parts with himself for Christ, that is — his own righteousness. The poor in spirit sees himself nothing without Christ; the self-denier will leave himself nothing for Christ. And thus I have shown what poverty of spirit is.

The words thus opened present us with this truth — that Christians must be poor in spirit. Or thus — poverty of spirit is the jewel which Christians must wear. As the best creature was made out of nothing; so when a man sees himself to be nothing, out of this nothing God makes a most beautiful creature. It is God's usual method to make a man poor in spirit — and then fill him with the graces of the Spirit. As we deal with a watch, we take it first to pieces, and then set all the wheels and pins in order — so the Lord first takes a man all to pieces, shows him his undone condition — and then sets him in frame.

The reasons are:

1. Until we are poor in spirit — we are not capable of receiving grace. He who is swollen with self-excellency and self-sufficiency — is not fit for Christ. He is full already. If the hand is full of pebbles — it cannot receive gold. The glass is first emptied, before you pour in wine. God first empties a man of himself, before he pours in the precious wine of his grace. None but the poor in spirit are within Christ's commission. 'The Spirit of the Lord God is upon me; he has sent me to bind up the broken-hearted' (Isaiah 61:1), that is, such as are broken in the sense of their unworthiness.

2. Until we are poor in spirit—Christ is never precious. Until we see our own wants, we never see Christ's worth. Poverty of spirit is salt and seasoning, which makes Christ relish sweet to the soul. Mercy is most welcome to the poor in spirit. He who sees himself clad in filthy rags (Zechariah 3:4,5), what will he give for change of raiment, the righteousness of Christ! What will he give to have the fair mitre of salvation set upon his head! When a man sees himself almost wounded to death—how precious will the balm of Christ's blood be to him! When he sees himself deep in arrears with God, and is so far from paying the debt that he cannot sum up the debt—how glad would he be for a surety! 'The pearl of great price' is only precious to the one who is poor in spirit. He who needs bread and is ready to starve, will have it whatever it cost. He will lay his garment to pledge; bread he must have—or he is undone! So to him who is poor in spirit, who sees his need of Christ—how precious is a Savior! Christ is Christ and grace is grace to him! He will do anything for the bread of life! Therefore will God have the soul thus qualified—to enhance the value and estimate of the Lord Jesus.

3. Until we are poor in spirit—we cannot go to heaven. 'Theirs is the kingdom of heaven'. Poverty of spirit tunes and prepares us for heaven. By nature a man is puffed up with self-esteem, and the gate of heaven is so narrow that he cannot enter. Now poverty of spirit lessens the soul; it pares off its superfluity, and now he is fit to enter in at the 'narrow gate'. The great rope cannot go through the eye of the needle—but let it be untwisted and made into small threads, and then it may. Poverty of spirit untwists the great rope. It makes a man little in his own eyes, and now an entrance shall be made unto him, 'richly into the everlasting Kingdom' (2 Peter 1:11). Through this temple of poverty, we must go into the temple of glory.

It shows wherein a Christian's riches consist, namely in poverty of spirit. Some think if they can fill their bags with gold—and then they are rich. But those who are poor in spirit, are the rich men. They are rich in poverty. This poverty entitles them to a kingdom! How poor are those who think themselves rich! How rich are those who see themselves poor! I call it the 'jewel of poverty'. There are some paradoxes in piety which the world cannot understand; for a man to become a fool that he may be wise (1 Corinthians 3:18); to save his life by losing it (Matthew 16:25); and by being poor to be rich. Carnal reason laughs at it—but 'Blessed are the poor in spirit, for theirs is the kingdom'. Then this poverty is to be striven for more than all riches. Under these rags is hidden cloth of gold. Out of this carcass comes honey.

If blessed are the poor in spirit, then by the rule of contraries, cursed are the proud in spirit (Proverbs 16:5). There is a generation of men who commit idolatry with themselves; no such idol as self! They admire their own parts, moralities, self-righteousness; and upon this stock graft the hope of their salvation. There are many too good to go to heaven. They have commodities enough of their own growth, and they scorn to live upon the borrow, or to be indebted to Christ. These bladders the Devil has blown up with pride, and they are swelled in their own conceit; but it is like the swelling of a dropsy man whose bigness is his disease. Thus it was with that proud justiciary: 'The Pharisee stood and prayed, God, I thank you that I am not as other men are, extortioners, unjust, adulterers, or even as this publican; I fast twice in the week, I give tithes ...' (Luke 18:11). Here was a man setting up the topsail of pride; but the publican, who was poor in spirit, stood afar off and would not lift up so much as his eyes unto heaven—but smote upon his breast saying, 'God be merciful to me a sinner.' This man carried away the garland. 'I tell you' (says Christ) 'this man went down to his house justified rather than the other'. Paul, before his conversion, thought himself in a very good condition, 'touching the law, blameless' (Philippians 3:6). He thought to have built a tower of his own righteousness, the top whereof should have reached to heaven; but, at last, God showed him there was a crack in the foundation, and then he gets into the 'rock of ages'. 'That I may be found in him'

(Philippians 3:9). There is not a more dangerous precipice than self-righteousness. This was Laodicea's temper: 'Because you say I am rich and I have need of nothing ...' (Revelation 3:17). She thought she wanted nothing when indeed she had nothing. How many does this damn! We see some ships that have escaped the rocks—yet are cast away upon the sands; so some who have escaped the rocks of gross sins—yet are cast away upon the sands of self-righteousness; and how hard is it to convince such men of their danger! They will not believe but that they may be helped out of their dungeon with these rotten rags. They cannot be persuaded their case is so bad as others would make it. Christ tells them they are blind—but they are like Seneca's maid, who was born blind—but she would not believe it. The house, says she, is dark—but I am not blind. Christ tells them they are naked, and offers his white robe to cover them—but they are of a different persuasion; and because they are blind, they cannot see themselves naked. How many have perished by being their own saviors! O that this might drive the proud sinner out of himself! A man never comes to himself until he comes out of himself. And no man can come out, until first Christ comes in.

If poverty of spirit be so necessary – how shall I know that I am poor in spirit? By the blessed effects of this poverty, which are:

1. He who is poor in spirit—is weaned from himself. 'My soul is even as a weaned child' (Psalm 131:2). It is hard for a man to be weaned from himself. The vine catches hold of everything that is near, to prop itself upon. Just so, there is some bough or other a man would be catching hold of to rest upon. How hard is it to be brought quite off himself! The poor in spirit are divorced from themselves; they see they must go to hell without Christ. 'My soul is even as a weaned child'.

2. He who is poor in spirit—is a Christ-admirer. He has high thoughts of Christ. He sees himself naked—and flies to Christ, to be clothed in the garments of His righteousness. He sees himself wounded—and as the wounded deer runs to the water, so he thirsts for Christ's blood, the water of life. 'Lord!' says he, 'give me Christ or I die!' Conscience is turned into a fiery serpent and has stung him; now he will give all the world—for a brazen serpent! He sees himself in a state of death; and how precious is one leaf of the tree of life, which is both for food and medicine! The poor in spirit sees all his riches lie in Christ, 'wisdom, righteousness, sanctification...' In every need, he flies to this storehouse! He adores the all-fullness in Christ.

They say of the oil in Rheims, though they are continually almost using it—yet it is never used up. And such is Christ's blood—it can never be emptied. He who is poor in spirit has recourse still to this fountain. He sets a high value and appreciation upon Christ. He hides himself in Christ's wounds. He bathes himself in his blood. He wraps himself in Christ's robe. He sees a spiritual dearth and famine at home—but he flees to Christ. 'Show me the Lord (says he) and it suffices!'

3. He who is poor in spirit—is ever complaining of his spiritual estate. He is much like a poor man who is ever telling you of his needs. He has nothing to help himself with—he is ready to starve! So it is with him that is poor in spirit. He is ever complaining of his needs, saying, 'I want a broken heart—and a thankful heart.' He makes himself the most indigent creature. Though he dares not deny the work of grace (which would be a bearing false witness again the Spirit)—yet he mourns he has no more grace. This is the difference between a hypocrite and a child of God. The hypocrite is ever telling what good he has. A child of God complains of what good he lacks. The one is glad he is so good; the other grieves he is so bad. The poor in spirit goes from ordinance to ordinance for a supply of his needs; he would gladly have his stock increased. Try by this if you are poor in spirit. While others complain they want children, or they want estates—do you complain you wany grace? This is a good sign. 'There is one who

makes himself poor—yet has great riches' (Proverbs 13:7). Some beggars have died rich. The poor in spirit, who have lain all their lives at the gate of mercy and have lived upon the alms of free grace—have died rich in faith, heirs to an eternal kingdom!

4. He who is poor in spirit—is lowly in heart. Rich men are commonly proud and scornful—but the poor are submissive. The poor in spirit roll themselves in the dust in the sense of their unworthiness. 'I abhor myself in dust' (Job 42:6). He who is poor in spirit looks at another's excellencies—and his own infirmities. He denies not only his sins—but his duties. The more grace he has, the more humble he is—because he now sees himself a greater debtor to God. If he can do any duty, he acknowledges it is Christ's strength more than his own (Philippians 4:13). As the ship gets to the haven more by the benefit of the wind than the sail—so when a Christian makes any swift progress, it is more by the wind of God's Spirit than the sail of his own endeavor. The poor in spirit, when he acts most like a saint, confesses himself 'the chief of sinners'. He blushes more at the defect of his graces—than others do at the excess of their sins. He dares not say he has prayed or wept. He lives—yet not he—but Christ lives in him (Galatians 2:20). He labors—yet not he—but the grace of God (1 Corinthians 15:10).

5. He who is poor in spirit—is much in prayer. He sees how short he is of the standard of holiness, therefore begs for more grace; Lord, more faith, more conformity to Christ. A poor man is ever begging. You may know by this—one who is poor in spirit. He is ever begging for a spiritual alms. He knocks at heaven-gate; he sends up sighs; he pours out tears; he will not leave the gate—until he has his alms. God loves a modest boldness in prayer; such shall not be turned away.

6. He who is poor in spirit—is content to take Christ upon his own terms. The proud sinner will argue and bargain with Christ. He will have Christ—and his pleasures; Christ—and his covetousness. But he who is poor in spirit sees himself lost without Christ, and he is willing to have him upon his own terms, a Prince to rule him—as well as a Saviour to save him: 'Jesus my Lord' (Philippians 3:8). A castle which has long been besieged and is ready to be captured, will surrender on any terms to save their lives. He whose heart has been a garrison for the devil, and has held out long in opposition against Christ, when once God has brought him to poverty of spirit, and he sees himself damned without Christ, let God propound whatever articles he will—he will readily subscribe to them. 'Lord, what will you have me to do?' (Acts 9:6). He who is poor in spirit will do anything—that he may have Christ. He will behead his beloved sin! He will, with Peter, cast himself upon the water to come to Christ.

7. He who is poor in spirit—is an exalter of free grace. None so magnify God's mercy—as the poor in spirit. The poor are very thankful. When Paul had tasted mercy, how thankfully does he adore free grace! 'The grace of our Lord was exceeding abundant' (1 Timothy 1:14). It was super-exuberant grace! He sets the crown of his salvation—upon the head of free grace! As a man who is condemned and has a pardon sent him—how greatly he proclaims the goodness and mercifulness of his prince! So Paul displays free grace in its magnificent colors. He interlines all his epistles with free grace. As a vessel which has been perfumed makes the water taste of it—so Paul, who was a vessel perfumed with mercy, makes all his epistles to taste of this perfume of free grace! Those who are poor in spirit, bless God for the least crumb which falls from the table of free grace! Labor for poverty of spirit. Christ begins with this, and we must begin here if ever we are saved. Poverty of spirit is the foundation stone, on which God lays the superstructure of eternal glory!

There are four things which may persuade Christians to be poor in spirit.

1. This poverty is your riches. You may have the world's riches, and yet be poor. You cannot have this poverty without being made rich. Poverty of spirit entitles you to all Christ's riches.

2. This poverty is your nobility. God looks upon you as people of honor. He who is vile in his own eyes — is precious in God's eyes. The way to rise — is to fall. God esteems the valley highest.

3. Poverty of spirit sweetly quiets the soul. When a man is brought off from himself to rest on Christ, what a blessed calm is in the heart! I am poor — but 'my God shall supply all my needs!' (Philippians 4:19). I am unworthy — but Christ is worthy! I am indigent — but Christ is infinite! 'Lead me to the rock that is higher than I' (Psalm 61:2). A man is safe upon a rock. When the soul goes out of itself and centers upon the rock, Christ — now it is firmly settled upon its basis. This is the way to comfort. You will be wounded in spirit — until you come to be poor in spirit.

4. Poverty of spirit paves the pathway for blessedness. 'Blessed are the poor in spirit.' Are you poor in spirit? You are blessed people! Happy for you that ever you were born! If you ask, 'Wherein does this blessedness appear?' read the next words, 'Theirs is the Kingdom of Heaven'.

5. The poor in spirit are enriched with a heavenly kingdom!

'Theirs is the kingdom of heaven.' Matthew 5:3

Here is high advancement for the saints. They shall be advanced to a heavenly kingdom! There are some who, aspiring after earthly greatness, talk of a temporal reign here — but then God's church on earth would not be militant, but triumphant. But sure it is — that the saints shall reign in a glorious manner: 'Theirs is the Kingdom of Heaven.' A kingdom is the pinnacle and top of all worldly felicity, and 'this honor have all the saints!' So says our Savior, 'Theirs is the kingdom of heaven.' All Christ's subjects are kings! By the kingdom of heaven, is meant that state of glory which the saints shall enjoy when they shall reign with God and the angels forever; sin, hell and death being fully subdued.

A. For the illustration of this, I shall show first — wherein the saints in heaven are like kings. Kings have their insignia or regalia, their ensigns of royalty and majesty.

1. Kings have their CROWNS. So the saints after death have their royal crown. 'Be faithful unto death — and I will give you a crown of life' (Revelation 2:10). Believers are not only pardoned — but crowned! The crown is an ensign of honor. A crown is not for everyone. It will not fit every head. It is only for kings and people of renown to wear (Psalm 21:3). The crown which the poor in spirit shall wear in heaven, is an honorable crown. God himself installs them into their honor and sets the royal crown upon their head. And this crown that the saints shall wear, which is divinely glorious and illustrious, exceeds all other.

[1] It is more pure. Other crowns, though they are made of pure gold — yet they are mixed metal; they have their troubles. A crown of gold, cannot be made without thorns. It has so many vexations belonging to it that it is apt to make the head ache. Which made Cyrus say, did men but know what cares he sustained under the imperial crown, he thought they would not stoop to take it up. But the saints' crown is made without crosses. It is not mingled with care of keeping — or fear of losing. What Solomon speaks in another sense, I may say of the crown of glory, 'It adds no sorrow with it' (Proverbs 10:22). This crown, like David's harp, drives away the evil spirit of sorrow and disquiet. As there can be joy in hell — so there can be no grief in heaven!

[2] This crown of glory does not draw envy to it. David's own son envied him and sought to take his crown from his head. A princely crown is oftentimes the mark for envy and ambition to shoot at! But the crown the saints shall wear is free from envy. One saint shall not envy

another — because all are crowned! And though one crown may be larger than another — yet every one shall have as big a crown as he is able to carry!

[3] This is a never-fading crown. Other crowns quickly wear away and tumble into the dust: 'Does the crown endure to all generations?' (Proverbs 27:24). Henry VI was honored with the crowns of two kingdoms, France and England. The first was lost through the faction of his nobles; the other was twice plucked from his head. The crown has many heirs and successors. The crown is a withering thing. Death is a worm which feeds in it; but the crown of glory is imperishable, 'it fades not away' (1 Peter 5:4). It is not like the rose which loses its color and vernancy. This crown cannot be made to wither — but it keeps always fresh and resplendent. Eternity is a jewel of the saints' crown!

2. Kings have their robes. The robe is a garment with which Kings are arrayed. 'The King of Israel and the King of Judah sat clothed in their robes' (2 Chronicles 18:9). The robe was of scarlet or velvet lined with ermine, sometimes of a purple color; sometimes of an azure brightness. Thus the saints shall have their robes. 'I beheld a great multitude which no man could number of all nations and kindreds, clothed in white robes' (Revelation 7:9). The saints' robes signify their glory and splendor; white robes denote their sanctity. They have no sin to taint or defile their robes. In these robes they shall shine as the angels!

3. Kings have their scepters in token of rule and greatness. King Ahasuerus held out to Esther the golden scepter (Esther 5:2); and the saints in glory have their scepter, and 'palms in their hands' (Revelation 7). It was a custom of great conquerors to have palm branches in their hand, in token of victory. So the saints, those kings have 'palms', an emblem of victory and triumph. They are victors over sin and hell. 'They overcame by the blood of the Lamb' (Revelation 12:11).

4. Kings have their thrones. When Caesar returned from conquering his enemies, there were granted to him four triumphs in token of honor, and there was set for him a chair of ivory in the senate, and a throne in the theater. Just so — the saints in heaven returning from their victories over sin, shall have a throne more rich than ivory or pearl — a throne of glory! (Revelation 3:21).

[1] This shall be a high throne. It is seated high above all the kings and princes of the earth. Nay, it is far above all heavens (Ephesians 4). There is the airy heaven — which is that space from the earth to the sphere of the moon. There is the starry heaven — the place where the stars are. There is the empyrean heaven, which is called the 'third heaven' (2 Corinthians 12:2). In this glorious sublime place, shall the throne of the saints be erected.

[2] It is a safe throne. Other thrones are unsafe; they stand tottering. 'You have set them in slippery places' (Psalm 73:18); but the saints' throne is sure. 'He who overcomes shall sit with me upon my throne' (Revelation 3:21). The saints shall sit with Christ. He keeps them safe, that no hand of violence can pull them from their throne. O people of God, think of this — you shall shortly sit upon the heavenly throne with Jesus!

B. Having shown wherein the saints in glory are like kings — let us see wherein the kingdom of heaven excels other kingdoms.

1. It excels in the founder and maker. Other kingdoms have men for their builders — but this kingdom has God for its builder! (Hebrews 11:10). Heaven is said to be 'made without hands' (2 Corinthians 5:1), to show the excellency of it. Neither man nor angel could ever lay stone in this building. God erects this kingdom. Its 'builder and maker is God'.

2. This kingdom excels in the riches of it. Gold does not so much surpass iron — as this kingdom surpasses all other riches. 'The gates are of pearl' (Revelation 21:21). 'And the foundations of the wall of it are garnished with all precious stones' (verse 19). It is enough for cabinets to have pearl; but were 'gates of pearl' ever heard of before? It is said that 'Kings shall throw down their

crowns and scepters before it (Revelation 4:10), as counting all their glory and riches but dust —
in comparison of it. This kingdom has deity itself to enrich it, and these riches are such as
cannot be weighed in the balance; neither the heart of man can conceive, nor the tongue of
angel express the magnificence of the heavenly kingdom!

3. This kingdom excels in the perfection of it. Other kingdoms are defective. They have not all
provisions within themselves, nor have they all commodities of their own growth — but are
forced to trade abroad to supply their needs at home. King Solomon sent for gold to Ophir (2
Chronicles 8:18). But there is no defect in the kingdom of heaven! Here are all delights and
rarities to be had! 'He who overcomes shall inherit all things!' (Revelation 21:7). Here is beauty,
wisdom, glory and magnificence. Here is the Tree of Life in the midst of this paradise. All
things are to be found here — but sin and sorrow — the absence whereof adds to the blessedness
of this kingdom!

4. This kingdom excels in security. Other kingdoms fear either foreign invasions or internal
divisions. Solomon's kingdom was peaceable a while — but at last he had an alarum given him
by the enemy (1 Kings 11:11,14). But the kingdom of heaven is so impregnable, that it fears no
hostile assaults or inroads. The devils are said to be locked up in chains (Jude 6). The saints in
heaven shall no more need fear them than a man fears a thief who is hanged up in chains. The
gates of this celestial kingdom 'are not shut' (Revelation 21:25). We shut the gates of the city in a
time of danger — but the gates of that kingdom always stand open — to show that there is no fear
of the approach of an enemy. The kingdom has gates for the magnificence of it — but the gates
are not shut because of the security of it.

5. This kingdom excels in its stability. Other kingdoms have vanity written upon them. They
cease and are changed; though they may have a head of gold — yet feet of clay. 'I will cause the
kingdom to cease' (Hosea 1:4). Where is the glory of Athens? the pomp of Troy? What is
become of the Assyrian, Grecian, Persian monarchy? Those kingdoms are demolished and laid
in the dust! But the kingdom of heaven has eternity written upon it! It is an 'everlasting
kingdom' (2 Peter 1:11). Other kingdoms may be lasting — but not everlasting. The apostle calls
it 'a kingdom which cannot be shaken' (Hebrews 12:28). It is fastened upon a strong
foundation — the omnipotence of God. It runs parallel with eternity. 'They shall reign forever
and ever!' (Revelation 22:5).

C. I shall next show the truth of this proposition — that this kingdom is infallibly entailed on the
saints.

In regard of God's free grace. 'It is your Father's good pleasure to give you the kingdom' (Luke
12:32). It is not for any desert in us — but the free grace in God. The papists say we merit the
kingdom — but we disclaim the title of merit. Heaven is a gift of God's grace.

There is a price paid. Jesus Christ has shed his blood for it. All saints come to the kingdom,
through blood. Christ's hanging upon the cross was to bring us to the crown. As the kingdom
of heaven is a gift in regard of the Father — so it is a purchase in regard of the Son.

1. This shows us that true religion is no unreasonable thing. God does not cut us out work — and
give no reward. Godliness enthrones us in a kingdom! When we hear of the doctrine of
repentance, steeping our souls in brinish tears for sin; the doctrine of mortification, pulling out
the right eye, beheading the king-sin; and we are ready to think it is hard to swallow down this
bitter pill. But here is something in the text which may sweeten it. There is a glorious kingdom
reserved for us — and that will make amends for all. This glorious recompense as far exceeds
our thoughts — as it surpasses our defects. No one can say without wrong to God, that he is a
hard master. God gives double pay. He bestows a kingdom upon those who fear him. Satan

may disparage the ways of God, like those spies who raised a bad report of the good land (Numbers 13:32). But will Satan mend your wages if you serve him? He gives damnable pay! Instead of a kingdom—he gives 'chains of darkness' (Jude 6).

2. See here the mercy and bounty of God, who has prepared a kingdom for his people. It is a favor that we poor 'worms and no men' (Psalm 22:6) should be allowed to live. But that worms should be made kings—this is divine bounty! It is mercy to pardon us—but it is rich mercy to crown us! 'Behold, what manner of love' is this! Earthly princes may bestow great gifts on their subjects—but they keep the kingdom to themselves. Though Pharaoh advanced Joseph to honor and gave him a ring from his finger—yet he kept the kingdom to himself. 'Only in the throne will I be greater than you' (Genesis 41:40). But God gives a kingdom to his people, he sets them upon the throne! How David admires the goodness of God in bestowing upon him a temporal kingdom! 'Then went King David in, and sat before the Lord and said, Who am I, O Lord God! and what is my house, that you have brought me hitherto?' (2 Samuel 7:18). He wondered that God should take him from the sheepfold and set him on the throne! That God should turn his shepherd's staff into a king's scepter! O then how may the saints admire the riches of grace, that God should give them a glorious kingdom above all the princes of the earth, nay, far above all heavens! God thinks nothing too good for his children. We many times think much of a tear, a prayer, or to sacrifice a sin for him—but He does not think a kingdom is too much to bestow upon us! How will the saints read over the lectures of free grace in heaven, and trumpet forth the praises of that God, who has crowned them with such astonishing loving-kindness! 'Don't be afraid, little flock, because your Father delights to give you the kingdom.' Luke 12:32

3. This shows us that Christianity is no disgraceful thing. Wise men measure things by the final end. What is the end of godliness? It brings a glorious kingdom! A man's sin brings him to shame (Proverbs 13:5). What fruit had you in those things, whereof you are now ashamed? (Romans 6:21). But religion brings to honor (Proverbs 4:8). It brings a man to a throne, a crown, it ends in eternal glory! It is the sinner's folly to reproach a saint. It is just as if Shimei had reproached David when he was going to be made king. It is a saint's wisdom to despise a reproach. Say as David when he danced before the ark, 'I will yet be more vile' (2 Samuel 6:22). If to pray and hear and serve my God, is be to be vile—'I will yet be more vile'. This is my excellency, my glory. I am doing now, that which will bring me to a kingdom. O think it no disgrace to be a Christian! I speak it chiefly to you who are entering upon the ways of God. Perhaps you may meet with such as will reproach and censure you. Bind their reproaches as a crown about your head. Despise their censure as much as their praise. Remember there is a kingdom entailed upon godliness. Sin draws hell after it; grace draws a crown after it!

4. See here that which may make the people of God long for death. Then they shall enter upon their glorious kingdom! Indeed the wicked may fear death. It will not lead them to a kingdom—but a horrid dungeon. Hell is the jail where they must lie rotting forever with the devil and his demons! To every Christless person—death is the king of terror; but the godly may long for death. It will raise them to a kingdom. When Scipio's father had told him of that glory the soul should be invested with in a state of immortality, 'why then,' says Scipio, 'do I tarry thus long upon the earth? Why do I not hasten to die?' Believers are not perfectly happy until death. When Croesus asked Solon whom he thought happy, he told him one Tellus, a man who was dead. A Christian at death shall be completely installed into his honor. The anointing oil shall be poured on him, and the royal crown set upon his head. The Thracians, in their funerals, used festive music. The heathens (as Theocritus' observes) had their funeral banquet, because of that felicity which they supposed the deceased were entered into. The saints are now 'heirs of the kingdom' (James 2:5). Does not the heir desire to be crowned?

Truly there is enough to wean us and make us willing to be gone from hence. The saints 'eat ashes like bread'. They are here in a suffering condition. 'Our bones are scattered at the grave's mouth, as when one cuts wood' (Psalm 141:7). When a man hews and cuts a tree the chips fly up and down; here and there a chip. So here a saint wounded, there a saint massacred; our bones fly like chips up and down. 'For your sake we are killed all the day long' (Romans 8:36). But there is a kingdom a-coming; when the body is buried the soul is crowned. Who would not be willing to sail in a storm — if he were sure to be crowned as soon as he came at the shore? Why is it that the godly look so ghastly at thoughts of death, as if they were rather going to their execution, than their coronation? Though we should be willing to stay here awhile to do service — yet we should with Paul, 'desire to depart — and be with Christ'. The day of a believer's dissolution — is the day of his inauguration.

But how shall we know that this glorious kingdom shall be settled upon us at death?

1. God has set up his kingdom of grace within each of his children. 'The kingdom of God is within you' (Luke 17:21). By the kingdom of God here — is meant the kingdom of grace in the heart. Grace may be compared to a kingdom. It sways the scepter; it gives out laws. There is the law of love. Grace beats down the devil's garrisons. It brings the heart into a sweet subjection to Christ. Is this kingdom of grace set up in your heart? Do you rule over your sins? Can you bind those kings in chains? (Psalm 149:8). Are you a king over your pride, passion and unbelief? Is the kingdom of God within you? While others aspire after earthly greatness — do you labor for a kingdom within you? Certainly if the kingdom of grace is in your heart, you shall have the kingdom of glory. If God's kingdom of grace enters into you, you shall enter into his kingdom of glory. But let not that man ever think to reign in glory — who now lives a slave to his lusts!

2. If you are a believer — you will go to this blessed kingdom. 'Rich in faith, heirs of the kingdom' (James 2:5). Faith is a heroic act of the soul. It makes a holy adventure on God, by a promise. Faith is the crowning grace. Faith puts us into Christ, and our title to the crown comes in by Christ. By faith we are born of God, and so we become children of the royal blood. By faith our hearts are purified (Acts 15:9, 10), and we are made fit for a kingdom; 'rich in faith, heirs of the kingdom'. Faith paves a highway to heaven. Believers die heirs to the crown.

3. He who has a noble, kingly spirit — shall go to the heavenly kingdom. 'Set your affection on things above, not on things on the earth.' (Colossians 3:2). He who has a heavenly spirit — shall go to the heavenly kingdom. Do you live above the world? The eagle does not catch flies — she soars aloft in the air. Do you pant after glory and immortality? Do you abhor that which is sordid and carnal? Can you trample upon all sublunary things? Is heaven in your eye — and Christ in your heart — and the world under your feet? He who has such a kingly spirit, who looks no lower than a crown — 'he shall dwell on high', and have his throne mounted far above all heavens!

The exhortation has a double aspect.

1. The exhortation looks toward the wicked. Is there a kingdom to be had, a kingdom so enameled and bespangled with glory? Oh then, do not by your folly make yourselves incapable of this glorious blessing! Do not for the satisfying of a base lust, forfeit a kingdom. Do not drink away a kingdom. Do not for the lap of pleasure — lose the crown of life! If men, before they committed a sin, would but sit down and rationally consider whether the present gain and sweetness in sin, would countervail the loss of the heavenly kingdom — it would put them into a cold sweat, and give some check to their unbridled lusts. Jacob took Esau by the heel. Look not upon the smiling face of sin — but 'take it by the heel'. Look at the end of it. It will deprive you of a kingdom, and can anything make amends for that loss? O, is it not madness, for the

unfruitful works of darkness (Ephesians 5:11), to lose a kingdom? How will the devil at the last day reproach and laugh at men, that they should be so stupidly sottish for a rattle—to forgo a crown! They are like those Indians who for glass beads, will part with their gold. Surely it will much contribute to the vexation of the damned—to think how foolishly they missed of a kingdom.

2. The exhortation looks toward the godly, and it exhorts to two things.

[1] Is there a kingdom in reserved for us? Then let this be a motive to duty. Do all the service you can for God while you live. 'Spend and be spent.' The reward is honorable. The thoughts of a kingdom, should add wings to prayer, and fire to zeal. Inquire what you have done for God. What love have you shown to his name? What zeal for his glory? Where is the head of that Goliath lust which you have slain for his sake? Methinks we should sometimes go aside into our closets and weep, to consider how little work we have done for God. What a vast disproportion is there between our service—and our reward! What is all our weeping and fasting—compared to a kingdom! Oh improve all your talents for God. Make seasons of grace, opportunities for service.

And that you may act more vigorously for God, know and be assured—that the more work you do, the more glory you shall have. Every saint shall have a kingdom—but the more service any man does for God, the greater will be his kingdom. There are degrees of glory which I will prove thus:

First, because there are degrees of torment in hell. 'They shall receive greater damnation' (Luke 20:47). Those who make religion a cloak for their sin, shall have a hotter place in hell. Now if there are degrees of torment in hell, then by the rule of contraries, there are degrees of glory in the kingdom of heaven.

Again, seeing God in his free grace rewards men according to their works, therefore, the more service they do the greater shall their reward be. 'Behold I come quickly and my reward is with me, to give every man according as his work shall be' (Revelation 22:12). He who has done more—shall receive more. He who gained ten times what was entrusted to him, was made ruler over ten cities (Luke 19:16, 17). This may very much excite to eminency in religion. The more the lamp of your grace shines, the more you shall shine in the heavenly orb. Would you have your crown brighter, your kingdom larger, your palm-branches more flourishing? Be eminent Christians. Do much work in a little time. While you are laying out, God is laying up. The more glory you bring to God, the more glory you shall have from God.

[2] Walk worthy of this kingdom. 'You should walk worthy of God, who has called you to his kingdom' (1 Thessalonians 2:12). Live as kings! Let the majesty of holiness appear in your faces. Those who looked on Stephen, 'saw his face, as it had been the face of an angel (Acts 6:15). A kind of angelic brightness was seen in his visage. When we shine in zeal, humility, and holiness—this beautifies and honors us in the eyes of others, and makes us look as those who are heirs to a heavenly crown.

Here is comfort to the people of God in case of poverty. God has provided them a kingdom: 'Theirs is the kingdom of heaven'. A child of God is often so low in the world, that he has not a foot of land to inherit. He is poor in purse—as well as in spirit. But here is a fountain of consolation opened. The poorest saint who has lost all his golden fleece, is heir to a kingdom—a kingdom which excels all the kingdoms and principalities of the world, more than diamond excels dirt! This kingdom is peerless and endless. 'The hope of a kingdom,' says Basil, 'should carry a Christian with courage and cheerfulness through all his afflictions!' And it is a saying of Luther, 'The sea of God's mercy, overflowing in spiritual blessings, should drown all the sufferings of this life!' What though you go now in rags? You shall have your white robes! What though you have only bread and water? You shall feast when you come into the kingdom! Here you drink the brinish water of tears—but shortly you shall drink the wine of paradise. Be comforted with the thoughts of your glorious kingdom!

Gospel Mourning

Blessed are those who mourn, for they shall be comforted.

Matthew 5:4

Here are eight steps leading to true blessedness. They may be compared to Jacob's Ladder, the top whereof reached to heaven. We have already gone over one step—and now let us proceed to the second. 'Blessed are those who mourn.' We must go through the valley of tears—to paradise! Mourning would be a sad and unpleasant subject to address—were it not that it has blessedness going before, and comfort coming after. Mourning is put here, for repentance. It implies both sorrow, which is the cloud, and tears which are the rain distilling in this golden shower!

The words fall into two parts, first, an assertion—that mourners are blessed people; second, a reason—because they shall be comforted.

The assertion—mourners are blessed people. 'Blessed are you who weep now' (Luke 6:21). Though the saints' tears are bitter tears—yet they are blessed tears. But will all mourning entitle a man to blessedness? No! There is a twofold mourning which is far from making one blessed. There is a carnal mourning, and a diabolical mourning.

1. There is a carnal mourning when we lament outward losses. 'A cry of anguish is heard in Ramah—weeping and mourning unrestrained. Rachel weeps for her children, refusing to be comforted—for they are dead!' (Matthew 2:18). There are abundance of these carnal tears shed. We have many who can mourn over a dead child—who cannot mourn over a crucified Savior! Worldly sorrow hastens our funerals. 'The sorrow of the world works death' (2 Corinthians 7:10).

2. There is a diabolical mourning and that is twofold:

When a man mourns that he cannot satisfy his impure lust. This is like the devil, whose greatest torture is that he can be no more wicked. Thus Ammon mourned and was sick, until he defiled his sister Tamar (2 Samuel 13:2). Thus Ahab mourned for Naboth's vineyard, 'So Ahab went home angry and sullen. The king went to bed with his face to the wall and refused to eat!' (1 Kings 21:4). This was a devilish mourning.

Again, when men are sorry for the good which they have done. Pharaoh was grieved that 'he had let the children of Israel go' (Exodus 14:5). Many are so devilish that they are troubled they have prayed so much and have heard so many sermons. They repent of their repentance. But if we repent of the good which is past—God will not repent of the evil which is to come.

The objects of spiritual mourning. To illustrate this point of holy mourning, I shall show you what is the adequate object of it. There are two objects of spiritual mourning—sin and misery.

The first object of spiritual mourning is SIN; and that twofold, our own sin; and the sin of others.

1. Our own sin. Sin must have tears. While we carry the fire of sin about with us—we must carry the water of tears to quench it! (Ezekiel 7:16). 'They are not blessed' (says Chrysostom) 'who mourn for the dead—but rather those who mourn for sin.' And indeed it is with good reason we mourn for sin, if we consider the guilt of sin, which binds over to wrath. Will not a

guilty person weep, who is to be bound over to the penalty? Every sinner is to be tried for his life and is sure to be cast away—if sovereign mercy does not become an advocate for him.

The pollution of sin. Sin is a plague spot, and will you not labor to wash away this spot with your tears? Sin makes a man worse than a toad or serpent. The serpent has nothing but what God has put into —but the sinner has that which the devil has put into him. 'Why has Satan filled your heart to lie to the Holy Spirit?' (Acts 5:3). What a strange metamorphosis has sin made! The soul, which was once of an azure brightness, sin has made of a sable color! We have in our hearts the seed of the unpardonable sin. We have the seed of all those sins for which the damned are now tormented! And shall we not mourn? He who does not mourn, has surely lost the use of his reason. But every mourning for sin is not sufficient to entitle a man to blessedness. I shall show what is not the right gospel-mourning for sin, and then what is the right gospel-mourning for sin.

What is NOT the right gospel-mourning for sin? There is a fivefold mourning which is false and spurious.

A despairing kind of mourning. Such was Judas' mourning. He saw his sin, he was sorry, he made confession, he justifies Christ, he makes restitution (Matthew 27). Judas, who is in hell, did more than many nowadays! He confessed his sin. He did not plead necessity or good intentions—but he makes an open acknowledgment of his sin. 'I have sinned!' Judas made restitution. His conscience told him he came wickedly by the money. It was 'the price of blood', and he 'brought back the thirty pieces of silver to the chief priests' (Matthew 27:3). But how many are there who invade the rights and possessions of others—but not a word of restitution! Judas was more honest than they are. Well, wherein was Judas' sorrow blameworthy? It was a mourning joined with despair. He thought his wound broader than the plaster. He drowned himself in tears. His was not repentance unto life (Acts 11:18)—but rather unto death.

An hypocritical mourning. The heart is very deceitful. It can betray as well by a tear—as by a kiss. Saul looks like a mourner, and as he was sometimes 'among the prophets' (1 Samuel 10:12) So he seemed to be among the penitents—'And Saul said unto Samuel, I have sinned, for I have transgressed the commandment of the Lord' (1 Samuel 15:24). Saul played the hypocrite in his mourning, for he did not take shame to himself—but he did rather take honor to himself: 'honor me before the elders of my people' (verse 30). He pared and minced his sin that it might appear lesser, he laid his sin upon the people, 'because I feared the people' (verse 24). They would have me fly upon the spoil, and I dare do no other. A true mourner labors to draw out sin in its bloody colors, and accent it with all its killing aggravations, that he may be deeply humbled before the Lord. 'Our iniquities are increased over our head, and our sin has grown up unto the heavens' (Ezra 9:6). The true penitent labors to make the worst of his sin. Saul labors to make the best of sin; like a patient that makes the best of his disease, lest the physician should prescribe him too sharp remedy. How easy is it for a man to put a cheat upon his own soul— and by hypocrisy to sweep himself into hell!

A forced mourning. When tears are pumped out by God's judgements, these are like the tears of a man who has the stone, or that lies upon the rack. Such was Cain's mourning. 'My punishment is greater than I can bear!' (Genesis 4:13). His punishment troubled him more than his sin! To mourn only for fear of hell is like a thief that weeps for the penalty, rather than the offence. The tears of the wicked are forced by the fire of affliction!

An external mourning; when sorrow lies only on the outside. 'They disfigure their faces' (Matthew 6:16). The eye is tender—but the heart is hard. Such was Ahab's mourning. 'He tore his clothes and put sackcloth on his flesh, and went softly' (1 Kings 21:27). His clothes were torn — but his heart was not torn. He had sackcloth but no sorrow. He hung down his head like a bulrush — but his heart was like granite. There are many who may be compared to weeping marbles, they are both watery and flinty.

A vain fruitless mourning. Some will shed a few tears — but are as bad as ever. They will deceive and be unclean. Such a kind of mourning there is in hell. The damned weep — but they continue to blaspheme God.

What is the right gospel-mourning? That mourning which will entitle a man to blessedness has these qualifications:

It is spontaneous and free. It must come as water out of a spring, not as fire out of a flint. Tears for sin must be like the myrrh which drops from the tree freely without cutting or forcing. Mary Magdalene's repentance was voluntary. 'She stood weeping' (Luke 7). She came to Christ with ointment in her hand, with love in her heart, with tears in her eyes. God is for a freewill offering. He does not love to be put to distrain.

Gospel-mourning is spiritual; that is, when we mourn for sin more than suffering. Pharaoh says, 'Take away the plague!' He never thought of the plague of his heart. A sinner mourns because judgment follows at the heels of sin — but David cries out, 'My sin is ever before me' (Psalm 51:3). God had threatened that the sword should ride in circuit in his family — but David does not say, 'The sword is ever before me' — but 'My sin is ever before me'. The offence against God troubled him. He grieved more for his treason against God — than the bloody axe. Thus the penitent prodigal, 'I have sinned against heaven, and before you' (Luke 15:18, 21). He does not say, 'I am almost starved among the husks' — but 'I have offended my father'. In particular, our mourning for sin, if it is spiritual, must be under this threefold notion:

1. We must mourn for sin, as it is an act of hostility and enmity against God. Sin not only makes us unlike God — but contrary to God: 'They have walked contrary unto me' (Leviticus 26:40). Sin affronts and resists the Holy Spirit (Acts 7:51). Sin is contrary to God's nature; God is holy; sin is an impure thing. Sin is contrary to his will. If God be of one mind — sin is of another. Sin does all it can to spite God. The Hebrew word for 'sin' signifies 'rebellion'. A sinner fights against God (Acts 5:39). Now when we mourn for sin as it is a walking contrary to heaven, this is a gospel-mourning.

2. We must mourn for sin, as it is the highest ingratitude against God. It is a kicking against the breasts of mercy. God sends his Son to redeem us, his Spirit to comfort us. We sin against the blood of Christ, the grace of the Spirit — and shall we not mourn? We complain of the unkindness of others, and shall we not lay to heart our own unkindness against God? Caesar took it unkindly that his son, Brutus, should stab him — 'and you, my son!' May not the Lord say to us, 'These wounds I have received in the house of my friend!' (Zechariah 13:6). Israel took their jewels and earrings and made a golden calf of them. The sinner takes the jewels of God's mercies and makes use of them to sin. Ingratitude is a 'crimson sin' (Isaiah 1:18). Sins against gospel-love are worse in some sense, than the sins of the devils, for they never had an offer of grace offered to them. Now when we mourn for sin as it has its accent of ingratitude upon it, this is an evangelical mourning.

3. We must mourn for sin as it is a privation; it keeps good things from us; it hinders our communion with God. Mary wept for Christ's absence. 'They have taken away my Lord!' (John 20:13). So our sins have taken away our Lord. They have deprived us of his sweet presence. Will not he grieve, who has lost a rich jewel? When we mourn for sin under this notion, as it makes the Sun of Righteousness withdraw from our horizon; when we mourn not so much that peace is gone, and trading is gone — but God is gone, 'My beloved had withdrawn himself' (Canticles

5:6); this is a holy mourning. The mourning for the loss of God's favor — is the best way to regain his favor. If you have lost a friend, all your weeping will not fetch him again — but if you have lost God's presence, your mourning will bring your God again.

Gospel-mourning sends the soul to God. When the prodigal son repented, he went to his father. 'I will arise and go to my father' (Luke 15:18). Jacob wept and prayed (Hosea 12:4). The people of Israel wept and offered sacrifice (Judges 2:4,5). Gospel-mourning puts a man upon duty. The reason is, that in true sorrow there is a mixture of hope, and hope puts the soul upon the use of means. That mourning which like the 'flaming sword' keeps the soul from approaching to God, and beats it off from duty — is a sinful mourning. It is a sorrow hatched in hell. Such was Saul's grief — which drove him to the witch of Endor (1 Samuel 28:7). Evangelical mourning is a spur to prayer. The child who weeps for offending his father goes to his presence and will not leave until his father is reconciled to him. Absalom could not be quiet 'until he had seen the king's face' (2 Samuel 14:32, 33).

Gospel-mourning is for sin in particular. The deceitful man is occupied with generalities. It is with a true penitent as it is with a wounded man. He comes to the surgeon and shows him all his wounds. Here I was cut with the sword; here I was shot with a bullet. So a true penitent bewails all his particular sins. 'We have served Baal' (Judges 10:10). They mourned for their idolatry. And David lays his fingers upon the sore — and points to that very sin which troubled him (Psalm 51:4). 'I have done this evil!' He means his blood-guiltiness. A wicked man will say he is a sinner — but a child of God says, 'I have done this evil!' Peter wept for that particular sin of denying Christ. It is reported that Peter never heard a rooster crow — but he fell a-weeping. There must be a particular repentance, before we have a general pardon.

Gospel tears must drop from the eye of faith. 'The father of the child cried out with tears, 'Lord, I believe' (Mark 9:24). Our disease must make us mourn — but when we look up to our Physician, who has made a remedy of his own blood, we must not mourn without hope. Believing tears are precious. When the clouds of sorrow have overcast the soul, some sunshine of faith must break forth. The soul will be swallowed up of sorrow, it will be drowned in tears — if faith does not keep it up from sinking. Though our tears drop to the earth — yet our faith must reach heaven. After the greatest rain, faith must appear as the rainbow in the cloud. The tears of faith are bottled as precious wine. 'You keep track of all my sorrows. You have collected all my tears in your bottle. You have recorded each one in your book' (Psalm 56:8).

Gospel-mourning is joined with self-loathing. The sinner admires himself. The penitent loathes himself. 'You shall loath yourselves in your own sight for all your evils' (Ezekiel 20:43). A true penitent is troubled not only for the shameful consequence of sin — but for the loathsome nature of sin; not only the sting of sin — but the deformed face of sin. How did the leper loathe himself! (Leviticus 13:45). The true mourner cries out, O these impure eyes! This heart which is a conclave of wickedness! He not only leaves sin — but loathes sin. He who has fallen in the dirt loathes himself (Hosea 14:1).

Gospel-mourning must be purifying. Our tears must make us more holy. We must so weep for sin, as to weep out sin. Our tears must drown our sins. We must not only mourn — but turn. 'Turn to me with weeping' (Joel 2:12). What good is it, to have a watery eye and a whorish heart? It is foolish to say it is day, when the air is full of darkness; so to say you repent, when you draw dark shadows in your life. It is an excellent saying of Augustine, 'He truly bewails the sins he has committed, who never commits the sins he has bewailed'. True mourning is like the 'water of jealousy' (Numbers 5:12-22). It makes the thigh of sin to rot. 'You broke the heads of the monster in the waters.' (Psalm 74:13). The heads of our sins, these monsters, are broken in the waters of true repentance. True tears are cleansing. They are like a flood that carries away all the rubbish of our sins away with it. The waters of holy mourning are like the river Jordan wherein Naaman washed and was cleansed of his leprosy. It is reported that there is a river in Sicily where, if the blackest sheep are bathed, they become white; so, though our sins be as scarlet — yet by washing in this river of repentance, they become white as snow. Naturalists say of the serpent, before it goes to drink it vomits out its poison. In this 'be wise as serpents'. Before you think to drink down the sweet cordials of the promises, cast up the poison that lies at your heart. Do not only mourn for sin — but break from sin.

Gospel-mourning must be joined with hatred of sin. 'What indignation!' (2 Corinthians 7:11). We must not only abstain from sin — but abhor sin. The dove hates the least feather of the hawk. A true mourner hates the least motion to sin. A true mourner is a sin-hater. Amnon hated Tamar more than ever he loved her (2 Samuel 13:15). To be a sin-hater implies two things: first, to look upon sin as the most deadly evil — as the essence of all evil. It looks more ghastly than death or hell. Second, to be implacably incensed against it. A sin-hater will never admit of any terms of peace. The war between him and sin is like the war between Rehoboam and Jeroboam. 'There was war between Rehoboam and Jeroboam all their days' (1 Kings 14:30). Anger may be reconciled — hatred cannot. True mourning begins in the love of God — and ends in the hatred of sin.

Gospel-mourning in some cases is joined with restitution. It is as well a sin to violate the name of another — as the chastity of another. If we have eclipsed the good name of others, we are bound to ask them for forgiveness. If we have wronged them in their estate by unjust, fraudulent dealing, we must make them some compensation. Thus Zacchaeus, 'If I have taken anything from any man by false accusation, I restore him fourfold' (Luke 19:8), according to the law of Exodus 22:1. James bids us not only look to the heart but the hand: 'Cleanse your hands, you sinners, and purify your hearts' (James 4:8). If you have wronged another, cleanse your hands by restitution. Be assured, without restitution — no remission.

Gospel-mourning must be a speedy mourning. We must take heed of adjourning our repentance, and putting it off until death. As David said, 'I will pay my vows now' (Psalm 116:18), so should a Christian say, 'I will mourn for sin now.' 'Blessed are you that weep now' (Luke 6:21). God has encircled us in the compass of a little time, and charges us immediately to bewail our sins. 'Now God calls all men everywhere to repent' (Acts 17:30). We know not whether we may have another day granted us. Oh let us not put off our mourning for sin until the making of our will. Do not think holy mourning is only a deathbed duty. You may seek the blessing with tears, as Esau when it is too late. How long shall I say that I will repent tomorrow? Why not at this instant? 'Delay brings danger'. Caesar's deferring to read his letter before he went to the Senate-house, cost him his life. The true mourner makes haste to meet an angry God, as Jacob did his brother; and the present he sends before, is the sacrifice of tears.

Gospel-mourning for sin is perpetual. There are some who at a sermon will shed a few tears — but they are soon dried up. The hypocrite's sorrow is like a vein opened and presently stopped. The Hebrew word for 'eye' signifies also 'a fountain', to show that the eye must run like a fountain for sin and not cease; but it must not be like the Libyan fountain which the ancients speak of — in the morning the water is hot, at midday cold. The waters of repentance must not overflow with more heat in the morning, at the first hearing of the gospel; and at midday, in the midst of health and prosperity, grow cold and be ready to freeze. No! It must be a daily weeping. As Paul said, 'I die daily' (1 Corinthians 15:31), so a Christian should say, 'I mourn daily'. Therefore keep open an outflow of godly sorrow, and be sure it is not stopped until death. 'Let your tears flow like a river. Give yourselves no rest from weeping day or night' (Lamentations 2:18). It is reported of holy John Bradford that scarcely a day passed him wherein he did not shed some tears for sin. Daily mourning is a good antidote against backsliding. I have read of one that had an epilepsy, and being dipped in seawater, was cured. The washing of our souls daily in the brinish waters of repentance is the best way both to prevent and cure the falling into relapses.

Even God's own children must mourn after pardon; for God, in pardoning, does not pardon at one instant sins past and future; but as repentance is renewed, so pardon is renewed. Should God by one act pardon sins future as well as past, this would make void part of Christ's office. What need were there of his intercession, if sin should be pardoned before it be committed? There are sins in the godly of daily incursion, which must be mourned for. Though sin is pardoned, still it rebels; though it be covered, it is not cured (Romans 7:23). There is that in the best Christian, which is contrary to God. There is that in him, which deserves hell — and shall he not mourn? A ship that is always leaking must have the water continually pumped out. While the soul leaks by sin, we must be still pumping at the leak by repentance. Think not, O Christian, that your sins are washed away only by Christ's blood — but by water and blood. The brazen laver (Exodus 30:18) that the people of Israel were to wash in might be a fit emblem of this spiritual laver, tears and blood; and when holy mourning is thus qualified, this is that 'sorrowing after a godly sort' (2 Corinthians 7:11), which makes a Christian eternally blessed.

2. As we must mourn for our own sins — so we must lay to heart the sins of OTHERS. Thus we should wish with Jeremiah, that our eyes were a fountain of tears, that we might weep day and night for the iniquity of the times. Our blessed Savior mourned for the sins of the Jews: 'Being grieved for the hardness of their hearts' (Mark 3:5). And holy David, looking upon the sins of the wicked, his heart was turned into a spring, and his eyes into rivers. 'Rivers of tears run down my eyes, because they do not keep your law' (Psalm 119:136). Lot's righteous soul 'was vexed with the filthy lives of the wicked' (2 Peter 2:7). Lot took the sins of Sodom and made spears of them to pierce his own soul. Cyprian says that in the primitive times, when a virgin who vowed herself to religion had defiled her chastity, shame and grief filled the whole congregation.

Have not we cause to mourn for the sins of others? The whole axle of the nation is ready to break under the weight of sin. What an inundation of wickedness is there among us? Mourn for the hypocrisy of the times. Jehu says 'Come, see my zeal for the Lord' — but it was zeal for the throne (2 Kings 10:16). This is the hypocrisy of some. They entitle God to whatever they do. They make bold with God to use his name to their wickedness; as if a thief should pretend the king's warrant for his robbery. 'They build up Zion with blood; yet will they lean upon the Lord and say, 'Is not the Lord among us?' (Micah 3:10, 11). Many with a religious kiss smite the gospel under the fifth rib. Could not Ahab be content to kill and take possession — but must he usher it in with religion, and make fasting a preface to his murder? (1 Kings 21:12). The white devil is worst! To hear the name of God in the mouths of scandalous hypocrites, is enough to affright others from the profession of religion.

Mourn for the errors and blasphemies of the nation. There is now a free trade of error. Toleration gives men a patent to sin. Whatever cursed opinion which has been long ago buried in the church — but is now dug out of the grave, and by some worshiped! England is grown as wanton in her religion, as she is antic in her fashions. Did men's faces alter as fast as their religious opinions, we would not know them.

Mourn for covenant violation. This sin is a flying scroll against England. Breach of covenant is spiritual harlotry, and for this God may name us 'Not my people', and give us a bill of divorce (Hosea 1:9).

Mourn for the pride of the nation. Our condition is low — but our hearts are high. Mourn for the profaneness of the land. England is like that man in the gospel who had 'an unclean demonic spirit' (Luke 4:33). Mourn for the removing of landmarks (Deuteronomy 27:17). Mourn for the contempt offered to magistracy, the spitting in the face of authority. Mourn that there are so few mourners. Surely if we mourn not for the sins of others, it is to be feared that we are not sensible of our own sins. God looks upon us as guilty of those sins in others — which we do not lament. Our tears may help to quench God's wrath!

The saints must be sensible of the injuries of God's church. 'We wept when we remembered Zion' (Psalm 137:1). The people of Israel, being debarred from the place of public worship, sat by the rivers weeping. They laid aside all their musical instruments. 'We hung our harps upon the willows' (verse 2). We were as far from joy as those willows were from fruit. 'How shall we sing the Lord's song in a strange land?' (verse 4). We were fitter to weep than to sing. The sound of song is not agreeable to mourning.

When we consider the miseries of many Christians in foreign parts, who have been driven from their habitations because they would not espouse the Popish religion; when instead of a Bible, a crucifix; instead of prayers, mass; instead of going to church, they should go on pilgrimage to some saint or relic. When we consider these things, our eyes should run down. Mourn to see God's church a bleeding vine. Mourn to see Christ's spouse with 'garments rolled in blood'.

Methinks I hear England's death bell ring. Let us shed some tears over dying England. Let us bewail our internal divisions. England's divisions have been fatal. How can we stand, but by a miracle of free grace? Truth has fallen in the streets — and peace has fled. England's fine coat of peace, is torn and, like Joseph's coat, dipped in blood. Peace is the glory of a nation. Some observe, if the top of the beech tree be taken off — that the whole tree withers. Peace is the apex and top of all earthly blessings. This top being cut off, we may truly say the body of the whole nation begins to wither apace.

Mourn for the oppressions of England. The people of this land have laid out their money only to buy mourning.

Though we must always keep open the flow of godly sorrow — yet there are some seasons wherein our tears should overflow, as the water sometimes rises higher. There are three special seasons of extraordinary mourning, when it should be as it were high-water in the soul:

1. When there are tokens of God's wrath breaking forth in the nation. England has been under God's black rod these many years. The Lord has drawn his sword. O that our tears may blunt the edge of this sword! When it is a time of treading down, now is a time of breaking up the fallow ground of our hearts. 'Therefore said I, look away from me, I will weep bitterly for it is a time of treading down' (Isaiah 22:4, 5). 'A day of darkness and of gloominess, a day of clouds ... therefore turn to me with weeping and with mourning' (Joel 2:2, 12). Rain follows thunder. When God thunders in a nation by his judgements, now the showers of tears must distill. When God smites upon our back, we must 'smite upon our thigh' (Jeremiah 31:19). When God seems to stand upon the 'threshold of the temple' (Ezekiel 10:4), as if he were ready to take his wings and fly, then is it a time to lie weeping between 'the porch and the altar'. If the Lord seems to be packing up and carrying away his gospel — it is now high time to mourn, that by our tears possibly his 'repentings may be kindled' (Hosea 11:8).

2. Before the performing solemn duties of God's worship, as fasting or receiving the Lord's Supper. Christian, are you about to seek God in an extraordinary manner? 'Seek him sorrowing' (Luke 2:48). Would you have the smiles of God's face, the kisses of his lips? Set open all the springs of mourning, and then God will draw near to you in an ordinance and say, 'Here I am!'

(Isaiah 58:9). When Jacob wept, then he 'found God in Bethel' (Hosea 12:4). 'He called the name of the place Peniel, for I have seen God face to face' (Genesis 32:30). Give Christ the wine of your tears to drink—and in the sacrament he will give you the wine of his blood to drink.

3. After scandalous relapses. Though I will not say that there is no mercy for sins of relapse— yet I say there is no mercy without bitter mourning. Scandalous sins reflect dishonor upon religion (2 Samuel 12:14). Therefore now our cheeks should be covered with blushing, and our eyes bedewed with tears. Peter, after his denying Christ, wept bitterly. Christian, has God given you over to any enormous sin as a just reward of your pride and carnal security? Go into the 'weeping bath'. Sins of infirmity injure the soul—but scandalous sins wound the gospel. Lesser sins grieve the Spirit—but greater sins vex the Spirit (Isaiah 63:10). And if that blessed Dove weeps, shall not we weep? When the air is dark then the dew falls. When we have by scandalous sin darkened the luster of the gospel, now is the time for the dew of holy tears to fall from our eyes.

Next to the seasons of mourning, let us consider the degree of mourning. The mourning for sin must be a very great mourning. The Greek word imports a great sorrow, such as is seen at the funeral of a dear friend. 'They shall look on me whom they have pierced, and they shall mourn for him, as one that mourns for his only son' (Zechariah 12:10). The sorrow for an only child is very great. Such must be the sorrow for sin. 'In that day there shall be great mourning, as the mourning of Hadadrimmon in the valley of Megiddon' (verse 11). In that valley Josiah, that famous and pious prince, was cut off by an untimely death, at whose funeral there was bitter lamentation. Thus bitterly must we bewail, not the death—but the life of our sins. Now then, to set forth the degree of sorrow.

Our mourning for sin must be so great as to exceed all other grief. Eli's mourning for the ark was such that it swallowed up the loss of his two children. Spiritual grief must preponderate over all other grief. We should mourn more for sin than for the loss of friends or estate.

We should endeavor to have our sorrow rise up to the same height and proportion as our sin does. Manasseh was a great sinner—and a great mourner. 'He humbled himself greatly' (2 Chronicles 33:12). Manasseh made the streets run with blood—and he made the prison in Babylon run with tears. Peter wept bitterly. A true mourner labors that his repentance may be as eminent as his sin.

Having shown the nature of mourning, I shall next show what is the opposite to holy mourning. The opposite to mourning is 'hardness of heart', which in Scripture is called 'a heart of stone' (Ezekiel 36:26). a heart of stone is far from mourning and repenting. This heart of stone is known by two symptoms:

One symptom is insensibility. A stone is not sensible of anything. Lay weight upon it; or grind it to powder—it does not feel. So it is with a hard heart. It is insensible to both its own sin and God's wrath. The stone in the kidneys is felt—but not the stone in the heart. 'Having lost all sensitivity.' (Ephesians 4:19).

A heart of stone is known by its inflexibility. A stone will not bend. That is hard, which does not yield to the touch. So it is with a hard heart. It will not comply with God's command. It will not stoop to Christ's scepter. A heart of stone will sooner break, than bend by repentance. It is so far from yielding to God, that like the anvil—it beats back the hammer. It 'always resists the Holy Spirit' (Acts 7:51).

Oh Christians, if you would be spiritual mourners, take heed of this stone of the heart. 'Harden not your hearts' (Hebrews 3:7, 8). A stony heart is the worst heart. If it were bronze, it might be melted in the furnace; or it might be bent with the hammer. But a stony heart is such, that only the arm of God can break it--and only the blood of Christ can soften it! Oh the misery of a hard heart! A hard heart is void of all grace. While the wax is hard, it will not take the impression of the seal. The heart, while it is hard, will not take the stamp of grace. It must first be made tender and melting. The plough of the Word will not penetrate a hard heart. A hard heart is good for nothing — but to make fuel for hellfire. 'Because of your hardness and unrepentant heart you are storing up wrath for yourself in the day of wrath' (Romans 2:5). Hell is full of hard hearts — there is not one soft heart there. There is weeping there — but no softness. We read of 'vessels of his wrath--prepared for destruction' (Romans 9:22). Hardness of heart, fits these vessels for hell, and makes them like withered wood, which is fit only to burn.

Hardness of heart makes a man's condition worse than all his other sins besides. If one is guilty of great sins — yet if he can mourn, there is hope. Repentance unravels sin, and makes sin not to be. But hardness of heart binds guilt fast upon the soul. It seals a man under wrath. It is not heinousness of sin — but hardness of heart which damns. This makes the sin against the Holy Spirit incapable of mercy, because the sinner who has committed it, is incapable of repentance.

Sundry sharp reproofs

This doctrine draws up a charge against several sorts of people:

1. Those who think themselves good Christians — yet have not learned this art of holy mourning. Luther calls mourning 'a rare herb'. Men have tears to shed for other things — but have none to spare for their sins. There are many murmurers — but few mourners. Most are like the stony ground which 'lacked moisture' (Luke 8:6).

We have many cry out of hard times — but they are not sensible of hard hearts. Hot and dry is the worst temper of the body. To be hot in sin, and to be so dry as to have no tears — is the worst temper of the soul. How many are like Gideon's dry fleece, and like the mountains of Gilboa! There is no dew upon them. Did Christ bleed for sin — and can you not weep! If God's bottle is not filled with tears — his vial will be filled with wrath! We have many sinners in Zion — but few mourners in Zion. It is with most people as with a man on the top of a mast; the winds blow and the waves beat, and the ship is in danger of ship wreck — and he is fast asleep! So when the waves of sin have even covered men and the stormy wind of God's wrath blows, and is ready to blow them into hell — yet they are asleep in carnal security.

2. This doctrine reproves them who instead of weeping for sin, spend their days in mirth and jollity. Instead of mourners we have jesters. 'They sing with tambourine and harp. They make merry to the sound of the flute' (Job 21:12, 13). 'They do not give themselves to mourning — but follow after their pleasures'. They live epicures, and die atheists. James bids us 'turn our laughter to mourning' (James 4:9). But they turn their mourning to laughter. Samson was brought forth to amuse the Philistines (Judges 16:25). The jovial sinner amuses the devil. It is a saying of Theophylact, 'It is one of the worst sights to see a sinner go laughing to hell.' How unseasonable is it to take the harp and violin — when God is taking the sword! 'A sword is being sharpened and polished. It is being prepared for terrible slaughter; it will flash like lightning! Now will you laugh?' (Ezekiel 21:9, 10). This is a sin which enrages God.

'The Lord, the Lord Almighty, called you to weep and mourn. He told you to shave your heads in sorrow for your sins and to wear clothes of sackcloth to show your remorse. But instead, you dance and play; you feast on meat, and drink wine. The Lord Almighty has revealed to me that this sin will never be forgiven you until the day you die. That is the judgment of the Lord, the Lord Almighty' (Isaiah 22:12-14). That is, this your sin shall not be done away by any expiatory sacrifice — but vengeance shall pursue you forever!

3. This doctrine reproves those who, instead of mourning for sin, rejoice in sin (Proverbs 2:14); 'Who take pleasure in iniquity' (2 Thessalonians 2:12). Wicked men in this sense are worse than the damned in hell, for they take little pleasure in their sins. There are some so impudently profane, that they will make themselves and others merry with their sins. Sin is a soul sickness (Luke 5:31). Will a man make merry with his disease? Ah wretch! Did Christ bleed for sin—and do you laugh at sin! Is it a time for a man to be jesting when he is upon the scaffold, and his head is to be stricken off? You who laugh at sin now, 'So I will laugh when you are in trouble! I will mock you when disaster overtakes you—when calamity overcomes you like a storm, when you are engulfed by trouble, and when anguish and distress overwhelm you!' Proverbs 1:24-27

4. This doctrine reproves those that cry down mourning for sin. They are like the Philistines who stopped-up the wells (Genesis 26:15). These would stop-up the wells of godly sorrow. Antinomians say this is a legal doctrine—but Christ here preaches it: 'Blessed are those who mourn.' And the apostles preached it, 'And they went out and preached that men should repent' (Mark 6:12). Holy sincerity will put us upon mourning for sin. He who has the heart of a child cannot but weep for his unkindness against God. Mourning for sin is the very fruit and product of the Spirit of grace (Zechariah 12:10). Such as cry down repentance, cry down the Spirit of grace. Mourning for sin is the only way to keep off wrath from us. Such as with Samson would break this pillar, go about to pull down the vengeance of God upon the land. To all such I say, as Peter to Simon Magus, 'Repent therefore of this your wickedness and pray God if perhaps the thought of your heart may be forgiven you', O sinner (Acts 8:22). Repent that you have cried down repentance.

Motives to holy mourning

Let me exhort Christians to holy mourning. I now persuade to such a mourning as will prepare the soul for blessedness. Oh that our hearts were spiritual stills, distilling the water of holy tears! Christ's doves weep. 'They that escape shall be like doves of the valleys, all of them mourning, everyone for his iniquity' (Ezekiel 7:16).

There are several divine motives to holy mourning:

1. Tears cannot be put to a better use. If you weep for outward losses, you lose your tears. It is like a shower upon a rock, which does no good; but tears for sin are blessed tears. 'Blessed are those who mourn.' These poison our corruptions; salt-water kills the worms. The brinish water of repenting tears will help to kill that worm of sin which would gnaw the conscience.

2. Gospel-mourning is an evidence of grace. 'I will pour upon the house of David and the inhabitants of Jerusalem, the Spirit of grace, and they shall mourn ...' (Zechariah 12:10). The Holy Spirit descended on Christ like a dove (Luke 3:22). The dove is a weeping creature. Where there is a dove-like weeping, it is a good sign the Spirit of God has descended there. Weeping for sin is a sign of the new birth. As soon as the child is born, it weeps: 'And behold the babe wept' (Exodus 2:6). To weep kindly for sin is a good sign we are born of God. Mourning shows a 'heart of flesh' (Ezekiel 36:26). A stone will not melt. When the heart is in a melting frame, it is a sign the heart of stone is taken away.

3. The preciousness of tears. Tears dropping from a mournful, penitent eye, are like water dropping from the roses—very sweet and precious to God. A fountain in the garden makes it pleasant. That heart is most delightful to God—which has a fountain of sorrow running in it. 'Mary stood at Christ's feet weeping' (Luke 7:38). Her tears were more fragrant than her ointment. The incense, when it is broken, smells sweetest. When the heart is broken for sin, then our services give forth their sweetest perfume. 'There is joy in heaven over one sinner that repents' (Luke 15:7). Whereupon Bernard calls tears 'the wine of angels'. And surely, God

delights much in tears, else he would not keep a bottle for them (Psalm 56:8). One calls tears 'a fat sacrifice', which under the law was most acceptable (Leviticus 3:3). Jerome calls mourning a plank after shipwreck. Chrysostom calls tears a sponge to wipe off sin. Tears are powerful orators for mercy. Eusebius says there was an altar at Athens, on which they poured no other sacrifice but tears, as if the heathens thought there was no better way to pacify their angry gods, than by weeping. Jacob wept and 'had power over the angel' (Hosea 12:4). Tears melt the heart of God. When a malefactor comes weeping to the bar, this melts the judge's heart towards him. When a man comes weeping in prayer and smites on his breast, saying, 'God be merciful to me a sinner' (Luke 18:13), this melts God's heart towards him. Prayer (says Jerome) inclines God to show mercy; tears compel him. God seals his pardons upon melting hearts. Tears, though they are silent — yet have a voice, 'The Lord has heard the voice of my weeping!' (Psalm 6:8). Tears wash away sin. Rain melts and washes away a ball of snow. Repenting tears wash away sin. That sin, says Ambrose, which cannot be defended by argument, may be washed away by tears.

4. The sweetness of tears. Mourning is the way to solid joy. 'The sweetest wine is that which comes out of the winepress of the eyes', says Chrysostom. The soul is never more enlarged than when it can weep. Closet tears are better than court music. When the heart is sad, weeping eases it by giving vent. The soul of a Christian is most eased when it can vent itself by holy mourning. Chrysostom observes that David who was the great mourner in Israel — was the sweet singer in Israel. 'My tears were my food' (Psalm 42:3). Ambrose says, 'No food so sweet as tears.' 'The tears of the penitent,' says Bernard, 'are sweeter than all worldly joy.' A Christian thinks himself sometimes in the suburbs of heaven, when he can weep. When Hannah had wept, she went away and was no more sad. Sugar when it melts is sweetest. When a Christian melts in tears, now he has the sweetest joy. When the daughter of Pharaoh descended into the river, she found a babe there among the reeds; so when we descend into the river of repenting tears, we find the babe Jesus there who shall wipe away all tears from our eyes. Well therefore might Chrysostom solemnly bless God for giving us this laver of tears to wash in.

5. A mourner for sin not only does good to himself but to others. He helps to keep off wrath from a land. As when Abraham was going to strike the blow, the angel stayed his hand (Genesis 22:12), so when God is going to destroy a nation, the mourner stays his hand. Tears in the child's eye sometimes move the angry father to spare the child. Penitential tears melt God's heart and bind his hand. Jeremiah, who was a weeping prophet, was a great intercessor. God says to him, 'Pray not for this people' (Jeremiah 7:16), as if the Lord had said, 'Jeremiah, so powerful are your prayers and tears, that if you pray I cannot deny you.' Tears have a mighty influence upon God. Surely God has some mourners in the land, or he would have destroyed us before now.

6. Holy mourning is preventing remedy. Our mourning for sin here — will prevent mourning in hell. Hell is a place of weeping (Matthew 8:12). The damned mingle their drink with weeping. God is said to hold his bottle for our tears (Psalm 56:8). Those who will not shed a bottle-full of tears shall hereafter shed rivers of tears. 'Woe to you that laugh now, for you shall mourn and weep' (Luke 6:25). You have sometimes seen sugar lying in a damp place dissolve to water. All the sugared joys of the wicked dissolve at last to the water of tears. Now, tears will do us good. Now, it is seasonable weeping. It is like a shower in the spring. If we do not weep now, it will be too late in hell. Could we hear the language of the damned, they are now cursing themselves that they did not weep soon enough. Oh is it not better to have our hell here, than hereafter? Is it not better to shed repenting tears, than despairing tears? He who weeps here is a blessed mourner. He who weeps in hell is a cursed mourner. The physician by bleeding the patient prevents death. By the opening a vein of godly sorrow, we prevent the death of our souls.

7. There is no other way the Gospel prescribes to blessedness, but mourning. 'Blessed are those who mourn'. This is the road that leads to the New Jerusalem. There may be several ways leading to a city; some go one way, some another; but there is but one way to heaven, and that is by the house of weeping (Acts 26:20). Perhaps a man may think thus, 'If I cannot mourn for sin, I will get to heaven some other way. I will go to church; I will give alms; I will lead a civil life.' Nay — but I tell you there is but one way to blessedness, and that is, through the valley of tears. If you do not go this way, you will miss of Paradise. 'I tell you, except you repent, you shall all likewise perish' (Luke 13:3). There are many lines leading to the center — but the heavenly center has but one line leading to it, and that is a tear dropping from the eye of faith. A man may have a disease in his body that twenty medicines will heal. Sin is a disease of the soul which makes it sick unto death. Now there is but one medicine will heal, and that is the medicine of repentance.

8. Consider what need every Christian has to be conversant in holy mourning. A man may take physic when he has no need of it. Many go to London when they have no need. It is rather out of curiosity than necessity. But O what need is there for everyone to go into the weeping bath! Think what a sinner you have been. You have filled God's book with your debts, and what need you have to fill his bottle with your tears! You have lived in secret sin. God enjoins you this penance, 'Mourn for sin'. But perhaps some may say, I have no need of mourning, for I have lived a very civil life. Go home and mourn because you are only civil. Many a man's civility, being rested upon — has damned him! It is sad for men to be without repentance — but it is worse to have no need for repentance (Luke 15:7).

9. Tears are but finite. It is but a while that we shall weep. After a few showers that fall from our eyes, we shall have a perpetual sunshine. In heaven the bottle of tears is stopped. 'God shall wipe away all tears ...' (Revelation 7:17). When sin shall cease, tears shall cease. 'Weeping may endure for a night — but joy comes in the morning' (Psalm 30:5). In the morning of the ascension, then shall all tears be wiped away.

10. The benefit of holy mourning. The best of our commodities come by water. Mourning makes the soul fruitful in grace. When a shower falls, the herbs and plants grow. 'I will water you with my tears, O Heshbon!' (Isaiah 16:9). I may allude to it; tears water our graces and make them flourish. 'He sends his springs into the valleys' (Psalm 104:10). That is the reason the valleys flourish with corn, because the springs run there. Where the springs of sorrow run, there the heart bears a fruitful crop. Leah was tender-eyed; she had a watery eye — and was fruitful. The tender-eyed Christian usually brings forth more of the fruits of the Spirit. A weeping eye is the water-pot to water our graces!

Again, mourning fences us against the devil's temptations. Temptations are called 'fiery darts' (Ephesians 6:16), because indeed they set the soul on fire. Temptations enrage anger, inflame lust. Now the waters of holy mourning quench these fiery darts. Wet gunpowder will not easily take fire. When the heart is wetted and moistened with sorrow, it will not so easily take the fire of temptation. Tears are the best engines and waterworks to quench the devil's fire; and if there is so much profit and benefit in gospel-sorrow, then let every Christian wash his face every morning in the laver of tears.

11. And lastly, to have a melting frame of spirit is a great sign of God's presence with us in an ordinance. It is a sign that the Sun of Righteousness has risen upon us, when our frozen hearts thaw and melt for sin. It is a saying of Bernard, 'By this you may know whether you have met with God in a duty — when you find yourselves in a melting and mourning frame'. We are apt to measure everything, by comfort. We think we never have God's presence in an ordinance, unless we have joy. Herein we are like Thomas. 'Unless (says he) I shall see in his hands the

print of the nails, I will not believe' (John 20:25). So are we apt to say that, unless we have incomes of comfort, we will not believe that we have found God in a duty; but if our hearts can melt kindly in tears of love, this is a real sign that God has been with us. As Jacob said, 'Surely the Lord is in this place, and I knew it not' (Genesis 28:16). So, Christian, when your heart breaks for sin and dissolves into holy tears, God is in this duty, though you do not know it.

Methinks all that has been said should make us spiritual mourners. Perhaps we have tried to mourn and cannot. But as a man who has dug so many fathoms deep for water and can find none, at last digs until he finds a spring; so though we have been digging for the water of tears and can find none—yet let us weigh all that has been said and set our hearts again to work, and perhaps at last we may say, as Isaac's servants said, 'We have found water!' (Genesis 26:32). When the herbs are pressed, the watery juice comes out. These eleven serious motives may press out tears from the eye!

But some may say, My constitution is such that I cannot weep. I may as well go to squeeze a rock as think to get a tear.

I answer—but if you cannot weep for sin—can you not grieve? Heart mourning is best. There may be godly sorrow—where there are no tears. The vessel may be full though it lacks vent. It is not so much the weeping eye which God respects—as the broken heart. Yet I would be reluctant to stop their tears of those who can weep. God stood looking on Hezekiah's tears: 'I have seen your tears' (Isaiah 38:5). David's tears made music in God's ears. 'The Lord has heard the voice of my weeping' (Psalm 6:8). It is a sight fit for angels to behold—tears as pearls dropping from a penitent eye!

What shall we do to get our heart into this mourning frame? Do two things. Take heed of those things which will stop these channels of mourning; put yourselves upon the use of all means that will help forward holy mourning. Take heed of those things which will stop the current of tears.

Nine hindrances of mourning.

1. The love of sin. The love of sin is like a stone in the pipe, which stops up the current of water. The love of sin makes sin taste sweet, and this sweetness in sin bewitches the heart. It is worse to love sin than to commit it. A man may be overtaken with sin (Galatians 6:1). He who has stumbled upon sin unawares will weep—but the love of sin hardens the heart and keeps the devil in possession. In true mourning there must be a grieving for sin. But how can a man grieve for that sin which his heart is in love with? Oh, take heed of this sweet poison! The love of sin freezes the soul in impenitence.

2. Despair. Despair affronts God, undervalues Christ's blood and damns the soul! 'But they will say—It's hopeless. We will continue to follow our plans, and each of us will continue to act according to the stubbornness of his evil heart' (Jeremiah 18:12). This is the language of despair. I had as good follow my sins still—and be damned for something. Despair presents God to the soul as a judge clad in the garments of vengeance (Isaiah 59:17). The despair of Judas was in some sense worse than his treason. Despair destroys repentance, for the proper ground of repentance is mercy. 'The goodness of God leads you to repentance' (Romans 2:4)—but despair hides mercy out of sight—as the cloud covered the Ark. Oh, take heed of this. Despair is an irrational sin; there is no ground for it. The Lord shows mercy to thousands. Why may you not be one of a thousand? The wings of God's mercy, like the wings of the Cherubim, are stretched out to every humble penitent. Though you have been a great sinner—yet if you are a weeping sinner—there is a golden scepter of mercy held forth (Psalm 103:11). Despair locks up the soul in impenitence!

3. A conceit that this mourning will make us melancholy. 'We shall drown all our joy in our tears!' But this is a mistake. Lose our joy? Tell me, what joy can there be in a condemned condition? What joy does sin afford? Is not sin compared to a wound and bruise? (Isaiah 1:6). David had his broken bones (Psalm 51:8). Is there any comfort in having the bones out of joint? Does not sin breed a palpitation and trembling of heart? (Deuteronomy 28:65, 66). Is it any joy for a man to be a 'terror to himself'? (Jeremiah 20:4). Surely of the sinner's laughter it may be said, 'It is mad!' (Ecclesiastes 2:2), whereas holy mourning is the breeder of joy. It does not eclipse joy — but refines our joy and makes it better. The prodigal dated his joy from the time of his repentance. 'Then they began to be merry' (Luke 15:24).

4. Checking the motions of the Spirit. The Spirit sets us a-mourning. He causes all our spring-tides. 'All my springs are in you' (Psalm 87:7). Oft we meet with gracious motions to prayer and repentance. Now when we stifle these motions, which is called a quenching the Spirit (1 Thessalonians 5:19), then we do, as it were, hinder the tide from coming in. When the dew falls, then the ground is wet. When the Spirit of God falls as dew in his influences upon the soul, then it is moistened with sorrow. But if the Spirit withdraws, the soul is like Gideon's dry fleece. A ship can as well sail without the wind, a bird can as well fly without wings — as we can mourn without the Spirit! Take heed of grieving the Spirit. Do not drive away this sweet Dove from the ark of your soul. The Spirit is 'gentle and tender'. If he is grieved, he may say, 'I will come no more' — and if he once withdraws, we cannot mourn.

5. Presumption of mercy. Who will take pains with his heart or mourn for sin — who thinks he may be saved at a cheaper rate? How many, spider-like, suck damnation out of the sweet flower of God's mercy? Jesus Christ, who came into the world to save sinners, is the occasion of many a man's perishing. 'Oh,' says one, 'Christ died for me. He has done all. What need I pray or mourn?' Many a bold sinner plucks death from the tree of life, and through presumption, goes to hell by that ladder of Christ's blood, by which others go to heaven. It is sad when the goodness of God, which should 'lead to repentance' (Romans 2:4), leads to presumption. O sinner, do not hope yourself into hell. Take heed of being damned upon a mistake. You say God is merciful, and therefore you go on securely in sin. But whom is mercy for? The presuming sinner or the mourning sinner? 'Let the wicked forsake his way, and return to the Lord, and he will have mercy upon him' (Isaiah 55:7). No mercy without forsaking sin, and no forsaking sin without mourning!

If a king should say to a company of rebels, 'Whoever comes in and submits shall have mercy', such as stood out in rebellion could not claim the benefit of the pardon. God makes a proclamation of mercy to the mourner — but such as are not mourners have nothing to do with mercy. The mercy of God is like the ark, which none but the priests were to meddle with. None may touch this golden ark of mercy but such as are 'priests unto God' (Revelation 1:6), and have offered up the sacrifice of tears.

6. A conceit of the smallness of sin. 'Is it not a little one?' (Genesis 19:20). The devil holds the small end of the telescope to sinners. To imagine that sin less than it is, is very dangerous. An opinion of the littleness of sin keeps us from the use of means. Who will be earnest for a physician, who thinks it is but a trivial disease? And who will seek to God with a penitent heart for mercy, who thinks sin is but a slight thing? But to take off this wrong conceit about sin, and that we may look upon it with watery eyes — consider that sin cannot be little, because it is against the Majesty of heaven. There is no small treason, it being against the king's person. Every sin is sinful, therefore damnable. A penknife or stiletto makes but a little wound — but either of them may kill as well as a large sword. There is death and hell in every sin. 'The wages of sin is death!' (Romans 6:23). What was it for Adam to pluck an apple? But that lost him his

crown! It is not with sin as it is with diseases—some are mortal, some not mortal. The least sin without repentance, will be a lock and bolt to shut men out of heaven.

View sin in the red glass of Christ's sufferings. The least sin cost his blood. Would you take a true view of sin? Go to Golgotha. Jesus Christ was fain to veil his glory and lose his joy, and pour out his soul an offering for the least sin. Read the greatness of your sin in the deepness of Christ's wounds. Let not Satan cast such a mist before your eyes that you cannot see sin in its right colors. Remember, not only do great rivers fall into the sea—but little brooks. Not only do great sins carry men to hell—but lesser sins as well.

7. Procrastination; or an opinion that it is too soon as yet to tune the penitential string. 'When the lamp is almost out, the strength exhausted, and old age comes on—then mourning for sin will be in season—but it is too soon now.' That I may show how pernicious this opinion is, and that I may roll away this stone from the mouth of the well, that so the waters of repentance may be drawn forth—let me propose these four serious and weighty considerations:

First, do you know what it is to be in the state of condemnation? And will you say it is too soon to get out of it? You are under 'the wrath of God' (John 3:36), and is it too soon to get from under the dropping of this vial? You are under 'the power of Satan' (Acts 26:18), and is it too soon to get out of the enemy's quarters?

Second, men do not argue thus in other cases. They do not say, 'It is too soon to be rich.' They will not put off getting the world until old age. No! Here they take the first opportunity. It is not too soon to be rich—and is it too soon to be saved from sin? Is not repentance a matter of the greatest consequence? Is it not more needful for men to lament their sin, than augment their estate?

Third, God's call to mourning is always in the present. 'Today, if you will hear his voice, harden not your hearts' (Hebrews 3:7, 8). A general besieging a garrison summons it to surrender upon such a day—or he will storm it. Such are God's summons to repentance. 'Today if you will hear his voice'. Sinners, when Satan has tempted you to any wickedness, you have not said, 'It is too soon, Satan'—but have immediately embraced his temptation. You have not put the devil off—and will you put God off?

Fourth, it is a foolish thing to adjourn and put off mourning for sin, for the longer you put off holy mourning—the harder you will find the work when you come to it! A bone which is out of joint is easier to set at first—than if you let it go longer. A disease is sooner cured at first—than if it is let alone until advance stages come. You may easily wade over the waters when they are low but if you wait stay until they are risen, then they will be beyond your depth. O sinner, the more treasons against God you commit—the more do you incense him against you, and the harder it will be to get your pardon. The longer you spin out the time of your sinning—the more work you make for repentance!

To adjourn, and put off mourning for sin is folly in respect of the uncertainty of life. How does the procrastinating sinner know that he shall live to be old? 'What is your life? It is but a vapor' (James 4:14). How soon may sickness arrest you, and death strike off your head! May not your sun set at noon? Oh then what impudence is it to put off mourning for sin, and to make a long work, when death is about to make a short work? Caesar, deferring to read the letter which was sent to him, was stabbed in the senate house.

It is folly to put off all until the last—in respect of the improbability of finding mercy. Though God has given you space to repent, he may deny you grace to repent. When God calls for mourning and you are deaf—when you call for mercy God may be dumb 'I called you so often, but you didn't come. I reached out to you, but you paid no attention. You ignored my advice and rejected the correction I offered. So I will laugh when you are in trouble! I will mock you when disaster overtakes you— when calamity overcomes you like a storm, when you are engulfed by trouble, and when anguish and distress overwhelm you. I will not answer when they cry for help. Even though they anxiously search for me, they will not find me!' (Proverbs 1:24-28). Think of it seriously. God may take the latter time to judge you in—because you did not take the former time to repent in.

To put off our solemn turning to God until old age, or sickness, is high imprudence, because 'death bed repentance' is for the most part insincere and spurious. Though true mourning for sin be never too late—yet 'death bed repentance' is seldom true. That repentance is seldom true-hearted, which is grey-headed. It is disputable whether these death-tears are not shed more out of fear of hell—than love to God. The mariner in a storm throws his goods overboard—not that he hates them—but he is afraid they will sink the ship. When men falls to weeping-work late and would cast their sins overboard—it is for the most part, only for fear lest they should sink the ship and drown in hell! It is a great question whether the sickbed penitent begins to mourn—only because he can keep his sins no longer. All which considered may make men take heed of running their souls upon such a desperate hazard, as to put all their work for heaven, upon the last hour.

8. Delay in the execution of justice. 'When the sentence for a crime is not quickly carried out, the hearts of the people are filled with schemes to do wrong.' (Ecclesiastes 8:11). God forbears punishing—therefore men forbear repenting. He does not smite upon their back by correction—therefore they do not smite upon their thigh by humiliation (Jeremiah 31:19). The sinner thinks thus: 'God has spared me all this while; he has eked out patience into longsuffering; surely he will not punish.' 'He says to himself—God has forgotten; he covers his face and never sees' (Psalm 10:11). In infinite patience God sometimes adjourns his judgements a while longer. He is not willing to punish (2 Peter 3:9). God is like the bee, which naturally gives honey—but stings only when it is provoked. The Lord would have men make their peace with him (Isaiah 27:5). God is not like a hasty creditor who requires the payment of the debt, and will give no time for the payment. He is not only gracious—but 'waits to be gracious' (Isaiah 30:18). But God by his patience, would bribe sinners to repentance. But, alas, how is his patience abused! God's longsuffering hardens most. Because God stops the vial of his wrath, sinners stop the conduit of tears! That the patience of God may not (through our corruption) obstruct holy mourning, let sinners remember:

First, God's patience has bounds set to it (Genesis 6:3). Though men will not set bounds to their sin—yet God sets bounds to his patience. There is a time when the sun of God's patience will set, and, being once set—it never returns any degrees backwards. The lease of patience will soon be run out! There is a time when God says, 'My Spirit shall no longer strive.' The angel cried, 'The hour of judgement has come' (Revelation 14:7). Perhaps at the next sin you commit—God may say, 'Your hour has now come!'

Second, to be hardened under God's patience, makes our condition far worse. Incensed justice will revenge abused patience! God was patient towards Sodom—but when they did not repent, he made the fire and brimstone flame about their ears! Sodom, which was once the wonder of God's patience—is now a standing monument of God's severity. All the plants and fruits were destroyed, and, as Tertullian says—that place still smells of fire and brimstone. Long forbearance is no forgiveness. God may keep off the stroke awhile—but justice is not dead—but only sleeps. God has leaden feet but iron hands. The longer God is taking his blow—the sorer it will be when it comes. The longer a stone is falling—the heavier it will be at last. The longer God is whetting his sword—the sharper it cuts. Sins against God's patience are of a deeper dye;

they are worse than the sins of the devils. The fallen angels never sinned against God's patience. How dreadful will their condition be — who sin because God is patient with them. For every crumb of patience, God puts a drop of wrath into his vial. The longer God forbears with a sinner, the more interest he is sure to pay in hell.

9. Mirth and music. 'You sing idle songs to the sound of the harp. You drink wine by the bowlful, and you perfume yourselves with exotic fragrances.' (Amos 6:5, 6). Instead of the dirge, they sing idle songs. Many sing away sorrow, and drown their tears in wine. The sweet waters of pleasure destroy the bitter waters of mourning. How many go dancing to hell — like those fish which swim pleasantly down into the Dead Sea!

Let us take heed of all these hindrances to holy tears. 'Let the harp play sad music, and the flute accompany those who weep.' (Job 30:31).

Some helps to mourning

Having removed the obstructions, let me in propound some helps to holy mourning.

1. Set sin continually before you. 'My sin is ever before me' (Psalm 51:3). David, that he might be a mourner, kept his eye fully upon sin. See what sin is — and then tell me if there be not enough in it to draw forth tears! I know not what name, is bad enough to give to sin. One calls it the devil's excrement. Sin is a combining of all evils. It is the spirit of evil distilled. Sin dishonors God — it denies God's omniscience, it derides his patience, it distrusts his faithfulness. Sin tramples upon God's law, slights his love, grieves his Spirit. Sin wrongs us; sin shames us. 'Sin is a reproach to any people' (Proverbs 14:34). Sin has made us naked. It has plucked off our robe — and taken our crown from us! Sin has spoiled us of our glory. Nay, it has not only made us naked — but impure. 'I saw you polluted in your blood' (Ezekiel 16:6). Sin has not only taken off our golden robe — but it has put upon us 'filthy garments' (Zechariah 3:3).

God made us 'after his likeness' (Genesis 1:26) — but sin has made us 'like the beasts which perish' (Psalm 49:20). We have all become brutish in our affections. Nor has sin made us only like the beasts — but like the devil (John 8:44). Sin has drawn the devil's picture upon man's heart. Sin stabs us. The sinner, like the jailer, draws a sword to kill himself (Acts 16:27). He is bereaved of his judgement and, like the man in the gospel, possessed with the devils, 'he cuts himself with stones' (Mark 5:5), though he has such a stone in his heart that he does not feel it. Every sin is a stroke at the soul. So many sins — so many wounds! Every blow given to the tree, helps forward the felling of the tree. Every sin is a hewing and chopping down the soul for hellfire! If then there is all this evil in sin — if this forbidden fruit has such a bitter core — it should make us mourn. Our hearts should be the spring — and our eyes the rivers!

2. If we would be mourners, let us be orators. Beg a spirit of contrition. Pray to God that he will put us in mourning, that he will give us a melting frame of heart. Let us beg Achsah's blessing, even 'springs of water' (Joshua 15:19). Let us pray that our hearts may be spiritual stills — dropping tears into God's bottle. Let us pray that we who have the poison of the serpent — may have the tears of the dove. The Spirit of God is a spirit of mourning. Let us pray that God would pour out that Spirit of grace upon us, whereby we may 'look on him whom we have pierced and mourn for him' (Zechariah 12:10).

God must breathe in his Spirit — before we can breathe out our sorrows. The Spirit of God is like the fire in a still — which sends up the dews of grace in the heart and causes them to drop from the eyes. It is this blessed Spirit whose gentle breath causes our spices to smell — and our waters to flow! If the spring of mourning is once set open in the heart — there can lack no joy. As tears flow out — comfort flows in! This leads to the second part of the text, 'They shall be comforted'.

The comforts belonging to mourners

Having already presented to your view the dark side of the text, I shall now show you the bright side, 'They shall be comforted.' Where observe:

1. Mourning goes before comfort—as the lancing of a wound precedes the cure. The Antinomian talks of comfort—but cries down mourning for sin. He is like a foolish patient who, having a pill prescribed him, licks the sugar—but throws away the pill. The libertine is all for joy and comfort. He licks the sugar—but throws away the bitter pill of repentance. If ever we have true comfort we must have it in God's way and method. Sorrow for sin ushers in joy: 'I will restore comforts to him, and to his mourners' (Isaiah 57:18). That is the true sunshine of joy—which comes after a shower of tears. We may as well expect a crop without seed—as comfort without gospel-mourning.

2. Observe that God keeps his best wine until last. First he prescribes mourning for sin—and then sets open the wine of consolation. The devil does quite contrary. He shows the best first—and keeps the worst until last. First, he shows the wine sparkling in the glass—then comes the 'biting of the serpent' (Proverbs 23:32). Satan sets his dainty dishes before men. He presents sin to them colored with beauty, sweetened with pleasure, silvered with profit—and then afterwards the sad reckoning is brought in! He showed Judas first the silver bait—and then stuck him with the hook! This is the reason why sin has so many followers, because it shows the best first. First, the golden crowns—then comes the lions' teeth! (Revelation 9:7, 8).

But God shows the worst first. First he prescribes a bitter portion— and then brings a cordial, 'They shall be comforted.'

3. Observe, gospel tears are not lost. They are seeds of comfort. While the penitent pours out tears, God pours in joy. 'If you would be cheerful' (says Chrysostom), 'mourn.' 'Those who sow in tears—shall reap in joy' (Psalm 126:5). It was the end of Christ's anointing and coming into the world—that he might comfort those who mourn (Isaiah 61:3). Christ had the oil of gladness poured on him (as Chrysostom says) that he might pour it upon the mourner. Well then, may the apostle call it 'a repentance not to be repented of' (2 Corinthians 7:10). A man's drunkenness is to be repented of; his uncleanness is to be repented of; but his repentance is never to be repented of, because it is the inlet to joy. 'Blessed are those who mourn, for they shall be comforted.' Here is sweet fruit from a bitter stock. Christ caused the earthen vessels to be filled to the brim with water, and then turned the water into wine (John 2:9). So when the eye, that earthen vessel, has been filled with water to the brim, then Christ will turn the water of tears into the wine of joy. 'Holy mourning,' says Basil, 'is the seed out of which the flower of eternal joy grows.'

The reasons why the mourner shall be comforted.

[1] Because mourning is made on purpose for this end. Mourning is not prescribed for itself but that it may lead on to something else—that it may lay a train for comfort. Therefore we sow in tears—that we may reap in joy. Holy mourning is a spiritual medicine. Now a medicine is not prescribed for itself—but for the sake of health. So gospel-mourning is appointed for this very end—to bring forth joy.

[2] The spiritual mourner is the fittest person for comfort. When the heart is broken for sin— now it is fittest for joy. God pours the golden oil of comfort—into broken vessels. The mourner's heart is emptied of pride—and God fills the empty with his blessing. The mourner's tears have helped to purge out corruption—and then God gives a cordial. The mourner is ready to faint away under the burden of sin—and then the refreshing cordial comes seasonably. The Lord would have the incestuous person (upon his deep humiliation) to be comforted, lest 'he should be swallowed up with overmuch sorrow' (2 Corinthians 2:7).

This is the mourner's privilege: 'He shall be comforted'. The valley of tears brings the soul into a paradise of joy. A sinner's joy brings forth sorrow. The mourner's sorrow brings forth joy. 'Your sorrow shall be turned into joy' (John 16:20). The saints have a sorrowful seedtime — but a joyful harvest. 'They shall be comforted'.

Now to illustrate this, I shall show you what the comforts are, that the mourners shall have. These comforts are of a divine infusion, and they are twofold, either here or hereafter.

They are called 'the consolations of God' (Job 15:11); that is, 'great comforts', such as none but God can give. They exceed all other comforts as far as heaven exceeds earth. The root on which these comforts grow is the blessed Spirit. He is called 'the Comforter' (John 14:26), and comfort is said to be a 'fruit of the Spirit' (Galatians 5:22). Christ purchased peace, and the Spirit speaks peace.

How does the Spirit comfort? Either mediately[3] or immediately.

[1] The Spirit comforts mediately, by helping us to apply the promises to ourselves and draw water out of those 'wells of salvation'. We lie as dead children at the breast — until the Spirit helps us to suck the breast of a promise; and when the Spirit has taught faith this art, now comfort flows in. O how sweet is the breast-milk of a promise!

[2] The Spirit comforts immediately. The Spirit by a more direct act presents God to the soul as reconciled. He 'sheds his love abroad in the heart', from whence flows infinite joy (Romans 5:5). The Spirit secretly whispers pardon for sin — and the sight of a pardon dilates the heart with joy. 'Be of good cheer — your sins are forgiven' (Matthew 9:2).

That I may speak more fully to this point, I shall show you the nature and excellencies of these comforts which God gives his mourners. These comforts are real comforts. The Spirit of God cannot witness to that which is untrue. There are many in this age who pretend to comfort — but their comforts are mere impostures. A man may as well be swelled with false, as true comforts. The comforts of the saints are certain. They have the seal of the Spirit set to them (2 Corinthians 1:22; Ephesians 1:13). A seal is for confirmation. When a deed is sealed, it is firm and unquestionable. When a Christian has the seal of the Spirit stamped upon his heart — now he is confirmed in the love of God.

Wherein do these comforts of the Spirit which are unquestionably sure, differ from those which are false and pretended? Three ways:

First, the comforts of God's Spirit are laid in deep conviction: 'And when he (that is, the Comforter) has come, he shall convict the world of sin' (John 16:7, 8).

Why does conviction go before consolation? Conviction of sin, fits for comfort. By conviction of sin, the Spirit sweetly disposes the heart to seek after Christ and then to receive Christ. Once the soul is convinced of sin and of the hell which follows sin — a Savior is precious. When the Spirit has shot in the arrow of conviction, 'now,' says a poor soul, 'Where may I meet with Christ? How may I come to enjoy Christ?' 'Have you seen him whom my soul loves? All the world for one glimpse of my Savior!'

Again, the Spirit by conviction makes the heart willing to receive Christ upon his own terms. Man, by nature, would bargain with Christ. He would take half Christ. He would take him for a Savior to save him from his sin — but not as a King to rule over him. He would accept of Christ as he has 'a head of gold' (Canticles 5:11) — but not as he has 'the government upon his shoulder' (Isaiah 9:6). But when God lets loose the spirit of bondage and convinces a sinner of

---

[3] Through a mediator

his lost, undone condition – now he is content to have Christ upon any terms. When Paul was struck down to the ground by a spirit of conviction, he cries out, 'Lord, what will you have me to do?' (Acts 9:6). Let God propound whatever articles he will – the soul will subscribe to them. Now, when a man is brought to Christ's terms, to believe and obey, then he is fit for mercy. When the Spirit of God has been a spirit of conviction of sin, then He becomes a spirit of consolation. When the plough of the law has gone upon the heart and broken up the fallow ground – then God sows the seed of comfort. Those who brag of comfort – but were never truly convicted, nor broken, for sin – have cause to suspect their comfort to be a delusion of Satan. It is like a madman's joy, who thinks himself to be a king – but it may be said of 'his laughter, it is mad' (Ecclesiastes 2:2). The seed which lacked 'depth of earth' withered (Matthew 13:5). That comfort which lacks 'depth of earth', deep humiliation and conviction, will soon wither and come to nothing.

The Spirit of God is a sanctifying, before a comforting Spirit. As God's Spirit is called the 'Comforter', so he is called 'a Spirit of grace' (Zechariah 12:10). Grace is the work of the Spirit. Comfort is the seal of the Spirit. The work of the Spirit goes before the seal. The graces of the Spirit are compared to water (Isaiah 44:3) and to oil (Isaiah 61:3). First, God pours in the water of the Spirit and then comes the oil of gladness. The oil (in this sense) runs above the water. Hereby we shall know whether our comforts are true and genuine. Some talk of the comforting Spirit, who never had the sanctifying Spirit. They boast of assurance – but never had grace. These are spurious joys. These comforts will leave men at death. They will end in horror and despair. God's Spirit will never set seal to a blank. First, the heart must be an epistle written with the finger of the Holy Spirit – and then it is 'sealed with the Spirit of promise'.

First, the comforts of the Spirit are humbling. 'Lord,' says the soul, 'what am I that I should have a smile from heaven, and that you should give me a privy seal of your love?' The more water is poured into a bucket – the lower it descends. The fuller the ship is laden with sweet spices – the lower it sails. The more a Christian is filled with the sweet comforts of the Spirit – the lower he sails in humility. The fuller a tree is of fruit – the lower the bough hangs. The more full we are of 'the fruit of the Spirit – love, joy and peace' (Galatians 5:22), the more we bend in humility. Paul, a 'chosen vessel' (Acts 9:15), filled with the wine of the Spirit (2 Corinthians 1:5), did not more abound in joy, than in lowliness of mind. 'Unto me who am less than the least of all saints, is this grace given…' (Ephesians 3:8). He who was the chief of the apostles calls himself the least of the saints.

Those who say they have comfort – but are proud; who have learned to despise others – their comforts are delusions. The devil is able, not only to 'transform himself into an angel of light' (2 Corinthians 11:14) – but he can transform himself into the comforter. It is easy to counterfeit money, to silver over brass and put the king's image upon it. The devil can silver over false comforts and make them look as if they had the stamp of the King of heaven upon them. The comforts of God are humbling. Though they lift the heart up in thankfulness – yet they do not puff it up in pride.

Second, the comforts God gives his mourners are unmixed. They are not tempered with any bitter ingredients. Worldly comforts are like wine that is mixed with dregs. 'In the midst of laughter the heart is sad' (Proverbs 14:13). If the breast of a sinner were anatomized and opened – you would find a worm gnawing at his heart. Guilt is a wolf which feeds in the breast of his comfort. A sinner may have a smiling countenance – but a chiding conscience. His mirth is like the mirth of a man in debt, who is every hour in fear of arrest. The comforts of wicked men are spiced with bitterness. They are worm-wood wine.

'These are the men who tremble, and grow pale at every lightning flash, and when it thunders are half-dead with terror at the very first rumbling of the heavens.'

But spiritual comforts are pure. They are not muddied with guilt, nor mixed with fear. They are the pure wine of the Spirit. What the mourner feels is joy, and nothing but joy.

Third, the comforts God gives his mourners are sweet. 'Truly the light is sweet' (Ecclesiastes 11:7); so is the light of God's countenance. How sweet are those comforts which bring the Comforter along with them! (John 14:10). Therefore the love of God shed into the heart, is said to be 'better than wine' (Canticles 1:2). Wine pleases the palate—but the love of God cheers the conscience. The lips, of Christ 'drop sweet-smelling myrrh' (Canticles 5:13). The comforts which God gives, are a Christian's music. They are the golden pot of manna, the nectar and ambrosia of a Christian. They are the saints' festival, their banqueting delicacies.

So sweet are these divine comforts, that the church had her fainting fits, for lack of them. 'Stay me with flagons' (Canticles 2:5). By these flagons, are meant the comforts of the Spirit. The Hebrew word signifies 'all variety of delights' to show the abundance of delectability and sweetness in these comforts of the Spirit. 'Comfort me with apples.' Apples are sweet in taste, fragrant in smell. Just so, sweet and delicious are those apples which grow upon the tree in paradise. These comforts from above are so sweet that they make all other comforts sweet; health, estate, relations. They are like sauce which makes all our earthly possessions and enjoyments come off with a bitter relish. So sweet are these comforts of the Spirit that they much abate and moderate our joy in worldly things. He who has been drinking choice wine, will not much desire water; and that man who has once 'tasted how sweet the Lord is' (Psalm 34:8), and has drunk the cordials of the Spirit, will not thirst immoderately after carnal delights. Those who play with dogs and birds—it is a sign they have no children. Just so, such as are inordinate in their desire and love of the creature, declare plainly that they never had better comforts.

Fourth, these comforts which God gives his mourners are holy comforts. They are called 'the comfort of the Holy Spirit' (Acts 9:31). Everything propagates in its own kind. The Holy Spirit can no more produce impure joys in the soul, than the sun can produce darkness. He who has the comforts of the Spirit looks upon himself as a person engaged to do God more service. Has the Lord looked upon me with a smiling face? I can never pray enough. I can never love God enough. The comforts of the Spirit raise in the heart a holy antipathy against sin. The dove hates every feather from the hawk. Just so, there is a hatred of every motion and temptation to evil. He who has a principle of life in him, opposes everything that would destroy life—he hates poison. So he who has the comforts of the Spirit living in him, sets himself against those sins which would murder his comforts. Divine comforts give the soul more acquaintance with God. 'Our fellowship is with the Father and with his Son, Jesus.' (1 John 1:3).

Fifth, the comforts reserved for the mourners are filling comforts. 'The God of hope fill you with all joy ...' (Romans 15:13). 'Ask ... that your joy may be full' (John 16:24). When God pours in the joys of heaven, they fill the heart and make it run over. 'I am exceeding joyful ...' (2 Corinthians 7:4). The Greek word is 'I overflow with joy', as a cup that is filled with wine until it runs over. Outward comforts can no more fill the heart—than a triangle can fill a circle. Spiritual joys are satisfying. 'My soul shall be satisfied as with marrow, and I will praise you with joyful lips' (Psalm 63:5). David's heart was full, and the joy broke out at his lips. 'You have put gladness in my heart' (Psalm 4:7). Worldly joys put gladness into the face: 'They rejoice in the face' (2 Corinthians 5:12). But the Spirit of God puts gladness into the heart. Divine joys are heart joys (Zechariah 10:7). 'Your heart shall rejoice' (John 16:22). A believer rejoices in God: 'My Spirit rejoices in God ...' (Luke 1:47).

And to show how filling these comforts are which are of a heavenly extraction, the Psalmist says they create greater joy than when 'their wine and oil increase' (Psalm 4:7). Wine and oil may delight—but they cannot satisfy; they have their emptiness and indigence. We may say as Zechariah 10:2, 'They comfort in vain.' Outward comforts sooner cloy than cheer—and sooner weary than fill. Xerxes offered great rewards to him who could find out a new pleasure—but the comforts of the Spirit are satisfactory. They refresh the heart. 'Your comforts delight my soul' (Psalm 94:19). There is as much difference between heavenly comforts and earthly comforts—as between a banquet which is eaten, and one which is painted on the wall.

Sixth, the comforts God gives his mourners in this life are glorious comforts. 'Joy full of glory' (1 Peter 1:8). They are glorious because they are a foretaste of that joy which we shall have in a glorified estate. These comforts are a pledge of glory. They put us in heaven before our time. 'You were sealed with the Holy Spirit, which is the pledge of the inheritance' (Ephesians 1:13, 14). So the comforts of the Spirit are the pledge, the 'cluster of grapes' at Eshcol (Numbers 13:23), the first-fruits of the heavenly Canaan. The joys of the Spirit are glorious, in opposition to other joys, which compared with these, are inglorious and vile. A carnal man's joy, as it is airy and flashy, so it is sordid. He sucks nothing but dregs. 'You rejoice in a thing of nothing' (Amos 6:13). A carnal spirit rejoices because he can say that this house is his, or that this estate is his. But a gracious spirit rejoices because he can say that this God is his: 'For this God is our God forever and ever' (Psalm 48:14). The ground of a Christian's joy is glorious. He rejoices in that he is an heir of the promise. The joy of a godly man is made up of that which is the angels' joy. He triumphs in the light of God's countenance. His joy is that which is Christ's own joy. He rejoices in the mystical union which is begun here and consummated in heaven. Thus the joy of the saints is a joy 'full of glory'.

Seventh, the comforts which God gives his mourners are infinitely transporting and RAVISHING. So delightful are they and amazing, that they cause a jubilation which is so great, that it cannot be expressed. Of all things joy is the most hard to be deciphered. It is called 'joy unspeakable' (1 Peter 1:8). You cannot tell how sweet honey is, without actually tasting it. The most elevated words can no more set forth the comforts of the Spirit, than the a pencil can draw the life and breath of a man. The angels cannot express the joys they feel. Some men have been so overwhelmed with the sweet raptures of joy, that they have not been able to contain—but as Moses, have died with a kiss from God's mouth. Thus have we seen the glass oft breaking with the strength of the liquor put into it.

Eighth, these comforts of the Spirit are POWERFUL. They are strong cordials, strong consolation, as the apostle phrases it (Hebrews 6:18). Divine comfort strengthens for duty. 'The joy of the Lord is your strength' (Nehemiah 8:10). Joy whets and sharpens industry. A man who is steeled and animated with the comfort of God's Spirit, goes with vigor and alacrity through the exercises of piety. He believes firmly, he loves fervently, he is carried full sail in duty. 'The joy of the Lord is his strength'. Divine comfort supports under affliction: 'Having received the Word in much affliction, with joy' (1 Thessalonians 1:6). The wine of the Spirit can sweeten 'the waters of Marah'. Those who are possessed of these heavenly comforts can 'gather grapes from thorns', and fetch honey out of the 'lion's carcass'. They are 'strong consolations' indeed, which can endure the 'fiery trial', and turn the flame into a bed of roses. How powerful is that comfort which can make a Christian glory in tribulations (Romans 5:3)! A believer is never so sad, but he can rejoice. The bird of paradise can sing in the winter. 'As sorrowing—yet always rejoicing' (2 Corinthians 6:10). Let sickness come, the sense of pardon takes away the sense of pain. 'The inhabitant shall not say, I am sick' (Isaiah 33:24). Let death come, the Christian is above it. 'O death, where is your sting?' (1 Corinthians 15:55). At the end of the rod, a Christian tastes honey. These are 'strong consolations'.

Ninth, the comforts God's mourners have are heart-quieting comforts. They cause a sweet acquiescence and rest in the soul. The heart of a Christian is in a state of discomposure, like the needle in the compass; it shakes and trembles — until the Comforter comes. Some creatures cannot live but in the sun. A Christian is discomposed, unless he has the sunlight of God's countenance. 'Hide not your face from me, lest I be like those who go down into the pit' (Psalm 143:7). Nothing but the breast will quiet the child. It is only the breast of consolation, which quiets the believer.

Tenth, the comforts of the Spirit are abiding comforts. As they abound in us so they abide with us. 'He shall give you another Comforter that he may abide with you forever' (John 14:16). Worldly comforts are always upon the wing, ready to fly. They are like a flash of lightning. 'They will oftentimes pass away and glide from your closest embrace'. All things here are transient — but the comforts with which God feeds his mourners are immortal: 'Who has loved us and given us everlasting consolation' (2 Thessalonians 2:16). Though a Christian does not always have a full beam of comfort — yet he has a dawning of it in his soul. He always has a ground of hope and a root of joy. There is that within him, which bears up his heart, and which he would not on any terms part with.

Behold, then, the mourner's privilege, 'He shall be comforted'. David who was the great mourner of Israel, was the 'sweet singer of Israel'. The weeping dove shall be covered with the golden feathers of comfort. O how rare and superlative are these comforts!

But the question may be asked, *'May not God's mourners lack these comforts?'* Spiritual mourners have a title to these comforts — yet they may sometimes lack them. God is a sovereign agent. He will have the timing of our comforts. He has a self-freedom to do what he will. The Holy One of Israel will not be limited. He reserves his prerogative to give or suspend comfort — as he will; and if we are a while without comfort, we must not quarrel with his dispensations, for as the mariner is not to wrangle with providence because the wind blows out of the east when he desires it to blow out of the west; nor is the farmer to murmur when God stops the bottles of heaven in time of drought; so neither is any man to dispute or quarrel with God, when he stops the sweet influence of comfort — but he ought rather to acquiesce in his sacred will.

But though the Lord might by virtue of his sovereignty withhold comfort from the mourner — yet there may be many pregnant causes assigned why mourners lack comfort in regard of God and also in regard of themselves.

1. Why mourners lack comfort — in regard of God. He sees it fit to withhold comfort that he may raise the value of grace. We are apt to esteem comfort above grace, therefore God locks up our comforts for a time, that he may enhance the price of grace. When farthings go better than gold the king will call in farthings, that the price of gold may be the more raised. God would have his people serve him for himself — and not for comfort alone. It is a harlot love to love the husband's money and gifts, more than his person. Such as serve God only for comfort, do not so much serve God, as serve themselves with God.

2. That God's mourners lack comfort, it is most frequency in regard of themselves.

[1] Through mistake, which is twofold. They do not go to the right spring for comfort. They go to their tears, when they should go to Christ's blood. It is a kind of idolatry to make our tears the ground of our comfort. Mourning is not meritorious. It is the way to joy, not the cause. Jacob got the blessing in the garments of his elder brother. True comfort flows out of Christ's pierced

side. Our tears are stained, until they are washed in the blood of Christ. 'In me you will have peace' (John 16:33).

The second mistake is that mourners are privileged people, and may take more liberty to slacken or sin. They may slacken the strings of duty, and let loose the reins to sin. Christ has indeed purchased a liberty for his people – but a holy liberty, not a liberty for sin – but from sin. 'But you are a chosen people, a royal priesthood, a holy nation, a people belonging to God, that you may declare the praises of him who called you out of darkness into his wonderful light' (1 Peter 2:9). You are not in a state of slavery – but royalty. What follows? Do not make Christian liberty a cloak for sin. 'As free, and not using your liberty for a cover-up for evil' (16). If we quench the sanctifying Spirit, God will quench the comforting Spirit. Sin is compared to a 'cloud' (Isaiah 44:22). This cloud intercepts the light of God's countenance.

[2] God's mourners sometimes lack comfort through discontent and peevishness. David makes his disquiet the cause of his sadness. 'Why are you cast down, O my soul? Why are you disquieted within me?' (Psalm 43:5). A disquieted heart, like a rough sea, is not easily calmed. It is hard to make a troubled spirit receive comfort. This disquiet arises from various causes: sometimes from outward sorrow and melancholy, sometimes from a kind of envy. God's people are troubled to see others have comfort, and they lack it; and now in a peeve, they refuse comfort, and like a froward child, put away the breast. 'My soul refused to be comforted' (Psalm 77:2). Indeed a disquieted spirit is no more fit for comfort, than a madman is fit for counsel. And whence is the mourner's discontent – but pride? As if God had not dealt well with him in stopping the influences of comfort. O Christian, your spirit must be more humbled and broken, before God empty out his golden oil of joy.

[3] The mourner is without comfort for lack of applying the promises. He looks at sin, which may humble him – but not at that Word, which may comfort him. The mourner's eyes are so full of tears that he cannot see the promise. The virtue and comfort of a medicine is in the applying. When the promises are applied by faith, they bring comfort (Hosea 2:19; Isaiah 49:15, 16). Faith milks the breast of a promise. That Satan may hinder us of comfort; it is his policy either to keep the promise from us that we may not know it, or to keep us from the promise that we may not apply it. All the promises in the Bible belong to the mourner – had he but the skill and dexterity of faith to lay hold on it.

[4] The mourner may lack comfort through too much earthly-mindedness. By feeding immoderately on earthly comforts – we miss of heavenly comforts. 'For the iniquity of his covetousness was I angry, and I hid myself' (Isaiah 57:17). The earth puts out the fire. Earthiness extinguishes the flame of divine joy in the soul. An eclipse occurs when the moon, which is a dense body, comes between the sun and the earth. The moon is an emblem of the world (Revelation 12:1). When this comes between, then there is an eclipse in the light of God's face. Such as dig in mines say there is such a damp comes from the earth as puts out the light of a candle. Earthly comforts send forth such a damp as puts out the light of spiritual joy.

[5] Perhaps the mourner has had comfort and lost it. Adam's rib was taken from him, when he was asleep (Genesis 2:21). Our comforts are taken away, when we fall asleep in security. The spouse lost her beloved when she lay upon the bed of sloth (Canticles 5:2, 6).

For these reasons God's mourners may lack comfort – but that the spiritual mourner may not be too much dejected, I shall reach forth 'the cup of consolation' (Jeremiah 16:7), and speak a few words that may comfort the mourner in the lack of comfort.

Jesus Christ was without comfort, therefore no wonder if we are. Our comforts are not better than his. He who was the Son of God's love, was without the sense of God's love. The mourner has a seed of comfort: 'Light is sown for the righteous' (Psalm 97:11). Light is a metaphor put for comfort, and it is sown. Though a child of God does not have comfort always in the flower — yet he has it in the seed. Though he does not feel comfort from God, yet he takes comfort in God. A Christian may be high in grace — and low in comfort. The high mountains are without flowers. The mines of gold have no corn growing on them. A Christian's heart may be a rich mine of grace, though it is barren of comfort. The mourner is heir to comfort, and though for a small moment God may forsake his people (Isaiah 54:7) — yet there is a time shortly coming, when the mourner shall have all tears wiped away, and shall be brim full of comfort. This joy is reserved for heaven, and this brings me to the second particular.

'They shall be comforted'. Though in this life some interviews and love tokens pass between God and the mourner — yet the great comforts are kept in sore for heaven. 'In God's presence is fullness of joy' (Psalm 16:11). There is a time coming (the daystar is ready to appear) when the saints shall bathe themselves in the river of life, when they shall never more see a wrinkle on God's brow — but his face shall shine, his lips drop honey, his arms sweetly embrace them! The saints shall have a spring-tide of joy, and it shall never be low water. The saints shall at that day put off their mourning, and exchange their sables for white robes. Then shall the winter be past, the rain of tears be over and gone (Canticles 2:11, 12). The flowers of joy shall appear, and after the weeping of the dove — 'the time of the singing of birds shall come'. This is the 'great consolation', the Jubilee of the blessed which shall never expire. In this life the people of God taste of joy — but in heaven their vessels shall always overflow. There is a river in the midst of the heavenly paradise which has a fountain to feed it (Psalm 36:8, 9).

The times we are cast into, being for the present sad and cloudy, it will not be amiss for the reviving the hearts of God's people, to speak a little of these comforts which God reserves in heaven for his mourners. 'They shall be comforted'.

The greatness of these celestial comforts is most fitly in Scripture expressed by the joy of a feast. Mourning shall be turned into feasting, and it shall be a marriage-feast, which is usually kept with the greatest solemnity. 'Blessed are those who are called unto the marriage-supper of the Lamb' (Revelation 19:9). Some understand this supper of the Lamb, to be meant of the saints' supping with Christ in heaven. Men after hard labor, go to supper. So when the saints shall 'rest from their labors' (Revelation 14:13), they shall sup with Christ in glory. Now to speak something of the last great supper.

[1] It will be a great supper in regard of the founder of this feast — God. It is the supper of a king, therefore sumptuous and magnificent. 'The Lord is a great God, and a great King above all gods' (Psalm 95:3). Where should there be grandeur and magnificence, but in a king's court?

[2] It will be a great supper in regard of the cheer and provision. This exceeds all hyperboles. What blessed fruit does the tree of life in paradise yield! (Revelation 2:7). Christ will lead his spouse into the 'banqueting house' and feast her with those rare viands, and cause her to drink that spiced wine, that heavenly nectar and ambrosia with which the angelic powers are infinitely refreshed.

First, every dish served in at this heavenly supper shall be sweet to our palate. There is no dish here we do not love. Christ will make such 'savory meat' as he is sure his spouse loves.

Second, there shall be no lack here. There is no lack at a feast. The multifaceted fullness in Christ will prevent a scarcity, and it will be a fullness without surfeit, because a fresh course will continually be served in.

Third, those who eat of this supper shall 'hunger no more'. Hunger is a sharp sauce. The 'Lamb's supper' shall not only satisfy hunger—but prevent it. 'They shall hunger no more!' (Revelation 7:16).

[3] It will be a great supper in regard of the company invited. Company adds to a feast, and is of itself sauce to whet the appetite. Saints, angels, archangels will be at this supper. Nay, Christ himself will be both Founder and Guest. The Scripture calls it 'an innumerable company…' (Hebrews 12:22); and that which makes the society sweeter, is that there shall be perfect love at this feast. The motto shall be 'one heart and one way'. All the guests shall be linked together with the golden chain of love.

[4] It will be a great supper in regard of the holy mirth. 'A feast is made for mirth' (Ecclesiastes 10:19). At this supper there shall be joy, and nothing but joy (Psalm 16:11). There is no weeping at this feast. O what triumph and acclamations will there be! There are two things at this 'supper of the Lamb, which will create joy and mirth. First, when the saints shall think with themselves, that they are kept from a worse supper. The devils have a supper (such an one as it is), a black banquet. There are two dishes served in—weeping and gnashing of teeth. Every bit they eat makes their hearts ache. Who would envy them their feasts here on earth—who must have such a dismal supper in hell? Second, it will be a matter of joy at the 'supper of the Lamb', that the Master of the feast bids all his guests welcome. The saints shall have the smiles of God's face, the kisses of his lips. He will lead them into the wine cellar, and display the banner of love over them. The saints shall be as full of solace as sanctity. What is a feast without mirth? Worldly mirth is flashy and empty. This will be infinitely delightful and ravishing.

[5] It will be a great supper for the music. This will be a marriage supper, and what better music than the Bridegroom's voice, saying, 'My spouse, my undefiled, take your fill of love!' There will be the angels' anthems, the saints' triumphs. The angels, those trumpeters of heaven, shall sound forth the excellencies of Jehovah, and the saints, those noble choristers, shall take 'down their harps from the willows', and join in consort with the angels, praising and blessing God. 'I saw before me what seemed to be a crystal sea mixed with fire. And on it stood all the people who had been victorious over the beast and his statue and the number representing his name. They were all holding harps that God had given them. And they were singing the song of Moses, the servant of God, and the song of the Lamb—Great and marvelous are your actions, Lord God Almighty. Just and true are your ways, O King of the nations!' (Revelation 15:2, 3). O the sweet harmony at this feast! It shall be music without discord.

[6] This supper is great in regard of the place where it shall be celebrated, in the 'paradise of God' (Revelation 2:7). It is a stately palace. It is stately for its situation. It is of a very great height (Revelation 21:10). It is stately for its prospect. All sparkling beauties are centered there, and the delight of the prospect is personal possession! That is the best prospect, where a man cannot see to the furthest end of his own ground. This royal feast shall be kept in a most spacious room, a room infinitely greater than the whole firmament. Though there is such a multitude as no man can number, 'of all nations, kindred, people and tongues' (Revelation 7:9)—yet the table is long enough and the room spacious enough, for all the guests. One of the things which are requisite to a feast, is a fit place. The empyrean heaven bespangled with light, arrayed with rich hangings, embroidered with glory, seated above all the visible orbs, is the place of the marriage-supper. This infinitely transcends the most profound search. I am no more able to express it, than I can span the firmament, or weigh the earth in a scale.

[7] It will be a great supper in regard of its continuance. It has no end. Epicures have a short feast—and a long reckoning. But those who shall sit down at the heavenly banquet—shall never rise from the table. The provisions shall never be taken away—but they shall always be feeding

upon those sweets and delicacies which are set before them. We read that King Ahasuerus made a feast for his princes which lasted 'a hundred and eighty days' (Esther 1:4). But this blessed feast reserved for the saints—is 'forever'. 'At your right hand there are pleasures for evermore' (Psalm 16:11).

For your consolation, consider how this may be as divine cordial to keep the hearts of God's people from fainting! 'They shall be comforted'. They shall sit with Christ 'upon the throne' (Revelation 3:21), and sit down with him 'at the table'. Who would not mourn for sin—that are sure to meet with such rewards! 'They shall be comforted!' The marriage-supper will make amends for 'the valley of tears!' O saint of God, you who are now weeping bitterly for sin, at this last and great feast your 'water shall be turned into wine'. You who now mortify your corruptions, and 'beat down your body' by prayer and fasting—shall shortly sup with Christ and angels! You who refused to touch the forbidden tree—shall feed upon 'the tree of life in the paradise of God!' You impoverished saint, who have scarce a bit of bread to eat, remember for your comfort, 'in your father's house there is bread enough', and he is making ready a feast for you, where all the dainties of heaven are served! O feed with delight upon the thoughts of this marriage-supper! After your funeral, begins your festival! Long for the Lamb's supper! Christ himself, has paid for this supper upon the cross! 'Therefore comfort one another with these words!'

Christian Meekness

Blessed are the meek, for they shall inherit the earth.

Matthew 5:5

We are now got to the third step leading in the way to blessedness, Christian meekness. 'Blessed are the meek'. See how the Spirit of God adorns 'the hidden man of the heart, with a multiplicity of graces! The workmanship of the Holy Spirit is not only astonishing—but various. He makes the heart meek, pure, peaceable etc. The graces therefore are compared to fine needlework, which is intricate and various in its textures and colors (Psalm 45:14). In the words there is the duty of meekness—and that duty like the dove, brings an olive leaf in the mouth of it—'they shall inherit the earth'.

The proposition I shall insist on, is that meek people are blessed people. For the right understanding of this, we must know there is a twofold meekness. Meekness towards God, meekness towards man.

1. Meekness towards god, which implies two things: submission to his will; flexibleness to his Word.

[1] Submission to God's will: when we react calmly, without swelling or murmuring, under the adverse dispensations of providence. 'It is the Lord's will. Let him do what he thinks best' (1 Samuel 3:18). The meek-spirited Christian says thus: 'Let God do what he will with me, let him carve out whatever condition he pleases, I will submit.' God sees what is best for me, whether a fertile soil or a barren. Let him chequer his work as he please, it suffices that God has done it. It was an unmeek spirit in the prophet to struggle with God: 'I do well to be angry to the death!' (Jonah 4:9).

[2] Flexibleness to God's word: when we are willing to let the Word bear sway in our souls and become pliable to all its laws and maxims. He is spiritually meek who conforms himself to the mind of God, and does not quarrel with the instructions of the Word—but with the corruptions of his heart. Cornelius' speech to Peter savored of a meek spirit: 'Now here we are, waiting before God to hear the message the Lord has given you' (Acts 10:33). How happy is it when the Word which comes with majesty, is received with meekness! (James 1:21).

2. Meekness towards man. Basil calls this 'the indelible character of a gracious soul.' 'Blessed are the meek'. To illustrate this, I shall show what this meekness is. Meekness is a grace whereby we are enabled by the Spirit of God to moderate our angry passions. It is a grace. The philosopher calls it a virtue—but the apostle calls it a grace, and therefore reckons it among the 'fruit of the Spirit' (Galatians 5:23). It is of a divine extract and original. By it we are enabled to moderate our passion. By nature the heart is like a troubled sea, casting forth the foam of anger and wrath. Now meekness calms the passions. It sits as moderator in the soul, quieting and giving check to its distempered motions. As the moon serves to temper and allay the heat of the sun, so Christian meekness allays the heat of passion. Meekness of spirit not only fits us for communion with God—but for civil converse with men; and thus among all the graces it holds first place. Meekness has a divine beauty and sweetness in it. It brings credit to true religion; it wins upon all. This meekness consists in three things: the bearing of injuries, the forgiving of injuries, the recompensing good for evil.

1. First, meekness consists in the bearing of injuries. I may say of this grace, 'it is not easily provoked'. A meek spirit, like wet tinder, will not easily take fire. 'Those who seek my hurt spoke mischievous things—but I, as a deaf man, heard not' (Psalm 38:12, 13). Meekness is 'the bridle of anger'. The passions are fiery and headstrong; meekness gives check to them. Meekness 'bridles the mouth', it ties the tongue to its good behavior. Meekness observes that motto, Bear and forbear. There are four things opposite to meekness.

[1] Meekness is opposed to anger. 'Do not be quickly provoked in your spirit, for anger resides in the lap of fools' (Ecclesiastes 7:9). When the heart boils in passion, and anger (as Seneca says) sparkles forth in the eye, this is far from meekness. 'Anger resides in the lap of fools'. Anger may be in a wise man—but it resides in a fool. The angry man is like gunpowder. No sooner do you touch him but he is all on fire. Seneca calls anger 'a short fit of madness'. Sometimes it suspends the use of reason.

How unfitting is rash anger! How it disguises and disfigures! As Plato counseled the great revellers and drinkers of his time, that they should view themselves in a glass when they were in their drunken humor, and they would appear loathsome to themselves, so let a man disguised with passion view himself in the glass, and sure he would ever after be out of love with himself. 'The face swells with anger, the veins become black with blood'. 'Let not the sun go down upon your anger, neither give place to the devil' (Ephesians 4:26, 27). Oh, says one, 'he has wronged me and I will never give place to him!' But better give place to him than to the devil. An angry spirit is not a meek spirit. Not but that we may in some cases be angry. There is a holy anger. Only that anger is without sin—which is against sin. Meekness and zeal may stand together. In matters of religion, a Christian must be clothed with the spirit of Elijah, and be 'full of the fury of the Lord' (Jeremiah 6:11). Christ was meek (Matt. 11:29)—yet zealous (John 2:14, 15). The zeal of God's house ate him up.

[2] Meekness is opposed to malice. Malice is the devil's picture (John 8:44). Malice is mental murder (1 John 3:15). It unfits for duty. How can such a man pray? I have read of two men who lived in malice, who being asked how they could say the Lord's Prayer, one answered, he thanked God there were many good prayers besides. The other answered, when he said the Lord's Prayer he left out those words, 'as we forgive those who trespass against us'. But Augustine brings in God replying, 'Because you do not say my prayer, I will not hear yours'. Were it not a sad judgement if all that a man ate should turn to poison! To a malicious man all the holy ordinances of God turn to poison. 'The table of the Lord, is a snare; 'he eats and drinks his own damnation'. A malicious spirit is not a meek spirit.

[3] Meekness is opposed to revenge. Malice is the scum of anger, and revenge is malice boiling over. Malice is a vermin which lives on blood. Revenge is Satan's nectar and ambrosia. This is the savory meat which the malicious man cooks for the devil. The Scripture forbids revenge: 'Dearly beloved, avenge not yourselves' (Romans 12:19). This is to take God's office out of his hand, who is called 'the God of recompenses' (Jeremiah 51:56) and the 'God of vengeance' (Psalm 94:1). This I urge against those who challenge one another to duels. Indeed, spiritual duels are lawful. It is good to fight with the devil. 'Resist the devil' (James 4:7). It is good to duel with a man's self, the regenerate part against the carnal. Blessed is he who seeks a revenge upon his lusts. 'Yes, what revenge!' (2 Corinthians 7:11). But other duels are unlawful. 'Avenge not yourselves'. The Turks, though a barbarous people, in ancient times burnt such as went to duel, applying hot coals of fire to their sides. Those who were in heat of revenge were punished suitably with fire.

Some may object. *'But if I am thus meek and tame in bearing of injuries and incivilities, I shall lose my credit. It will be a stain to my reputation.'* I answer: To pass by an injury without revenge is no eclipse to a man's credit. Solomon tells us it is the glory of a man to 'pass over a transgression' (Proverbs 19:11). It is more honor to bury an injury than revenge it; and to slight it than to write it down. The weakest creatures (such as the bee) soonest sting with every provocation. The lion, a more majestic creature, is not easily provoked. The bramble tears. The oak and cedar are more peaceable. Passion imports weakness. A noble spirit overlooks an injury.

Again, suppose a man's credit should suffer with those whose censure is not to be valued. Yet think which is worse, shame or sin? Will you sin against God to save your credit? Surely it is little wisdom for a man to venture his blood that he may fetch back his reputation, and to run into hell to be counted valorous!

Not but that a man may stand up in defense of himself when his life is endangered. Some hold it to be unlawful to take up the sword upon any occasion—but without question a man may take up the sword for self-preservation, else he comes under the breach of the sixth commandment. He is guilty of self-murder. In taking up the sword he does not so much seek another's death, as the safeguard of his own life. His intention is not to do hurt—but to prevent it. Self-defense is consistent with Christian meekness. The law of nature and religion justify it. That God who bids us 'put up our sword' (Matthew 26:52) yet will allow us a sword in our own defense, and he who will have us 'innocent as doves' not to offend others, will have us 'wise as serpents' in preserving ourselves.

Though revenge may be contrary to meekness—yet not but that a magistrate may revenge the quarrels of others. Indeed, it is not revenge in him—but doing justice. The magistrate is God's lieutenant on earth. God has put the sword in his hand, and he is not 'to bear the sword in vain'. He must be 'for the punishment of evildoers' (1 Peter 2:14). Though a private person must not render to any man 'evil for evil' (Romans 12:17)—yet a magistrate may; the evil of punishment for the evil of offence. This rendering of evil is good. Private men must 'put their sword into the sheath'—but the magistrate sins if he does not draw it out. As his sword must not surfeit through cruelty, so neither must it rust through partiality. Too much lenity in a magistrate is not meekness—but injustice. For him to indulge offences, and say with a gentle reproof as Eli, 'Why do you such things? Nay, my sons, for it is no good report that I hear' (1 Samuel 2:23, 24), this is but to shave the head that deserves to be cut off. Such a magistrate makes himself guilty.

[4] Meekness is opposed to evil-speaking. 'Let all evil-speaking be put away' (Ephesians 4:31). Our words should be mild, like the waters of Shiloah which run softly. It is too usual for passionate spirits to break out into opprobrious language. The tongues of many are fired, and it

is the devil who lights the match. Therefore they are said in Scripture to be 'set on fire of hell' (James 3:6). Men have learned of the 'old serpent, to spit their venom one at another in disgraceful revilings. 'Whoever shall say, You fool, shall be in danger of hellfire' (Matthew 5:22). Under that word 'fool', all vilifying terms are by our Savior forbidden. Let us take heed of this. It is hateful to God. God is not in this fire — but in the still small voice (1 Kings 19:12).

Some may say — *but did not the apostle Paul call the Galatians 'fools'?* (Galatians 3:1). When Paul uttered those words, it was not by way of reproach — but reproof. It was not to defame the Galatians but to reclaim them; not to vilify them but to humble them. Paul was grieved to see them so soon fall into a relapse. Well might he say 'foolish Galatians' in a holy zeal, because they had suffered so much in the cause of religion, and now made a defection and fell off. 'Have you suffered so many things in vain?' (verse 4). But though Paul, guided by the Spirit of God, did give this epithet to the Galatians, it is no warrant for us when any have wronged us to use disgraceful terms. Meekness does not vent itself in reviling. It does not retaliate by railing.

'Yet Michael the archangel, when contending with the devil he disputed about the body of Moses, dared not bring against him a railing accusation; but said, The Lord rebuke you' (Jude 9). Some understand by Michael, Christ — but more truly it is meant of one of the chief of the angels. The contest or dispute between the archangel and the devil was about the body of Moses. Some divines say that when God disposed of Moses' body, he employed the archangel to inter him so secretly that his burying place might not be known. It is likely if his dead body had been found, the Israelites might have been ready in a preposterous zeal to have worshiped it. The devil opposes the archangel and contends about the dead body — but the archangel 'dared not', or, as some read it, he could not endure to 'bring a railing accusation'. It seems the devil provoked him with evil language, and would fain have extorted passion from him — but the archangel was mild, and said only, 'The Lord rebuke you'. The angel would not so much as rail against the devil. We may learn meekness of the archangel: 'Not rendering railing for railing' (1 Peter 3:9).

Not but that a Christian ought prudentially to clear himself from slanders. When the apostle Paul was charged to be mad, he vindicated himself. 'I am not mad, most noble Festus' (Acts 26:25). Though a Christian's retorts must not be reviling, they may be vindicating. Though he may not scandalize another — yet he may defend himself. There must be Christian prudence, as well as Christian meekness. It is not mildness, but weakness — to part with our integrity (Job 27:6). To be silent when we are slanderously traduced, is to make ourselves appear guilty. We must so affect meekness, as not to lose the honor of innocence. It is lawful to be our own defenders. The fault lies only in this — when we retort injuries with reproachful terms, which is to pay a man back in the devil's coin.

2. The second branch of meekness is in forgiving of injuries. 'And when you stand praying, forgive' (Mark 11:25); as if Christ had said, 'It is to little purpose to pray, unless you forgive.' A meek spirit is a forgiving spirit. This is a herculean work. Nothing more crosses the stream of corrupt nature — than forgiving injuries. Men forget kindnesses — but remember injuries. I once heard of a woman who lived in malice, and being requested by some of her neighbors when she lay on her deathbed, to forgive, she answered, 'I cannot forgive though I go to hell'. Forgiveness is cutting against the grain of human nature. Some can rather sacrifice their lives than their lusts — but forgive we must, and forgive as God forgives. Forgiveness must be:

[1] Really. God does not make a show of forgiveness and keep our sins by him. He 'blots out' our debts (Isaiah 43:25). God passes an act of oblivion (Jeremiah 31:34). He forgives and forgets. So the meek spirit not only makes a show of forgiving his neighbor — but he does it from the heart (Matthew 18:27).

[2] Fully. God forgives all our sins. He does not for 'fourscore write down fifty' — but he gives a full release. 'Who forgives all your iniquities' (Psalm 103:3). Thus a meek-spirited Christian forgives all injuries. False hearts pass by some offences — but retain others. This is but half forgiving. Is this meekness? Would you have God deal so with you? Would you have him forgive your trespasses, as you forgive others?

[3] God forgives often. We are often sinful! We run every day afresh upon the score — but God often forgives. Therefore he is said to 'multiply pardon' (Isaiah 55:7). So a meek spirit reiterates and sends one pardon after another. Peter asks the question, 'Lord, how many times shall I forgive my brother when he sins against me? Up to seven times?' (Matthew 18:21) Christ answers him, 'I tell you, not seven times, but seventy times seven' (verse 22).

Some may object that such an affront has been offered, that flesh and blood cannot put up. I answer: 'Flesh and blood cannot inherit the Kingdom of God' (1 Corinthians 15:50). Christians must walk contrary to their natural dispositions, and with the sword of the Spirit fight against the lusts of the flesh (Galatians 5:24).

Again, you may say: But if I forgive one injury I shall invite more. I answer: It argues a devilish nature to be the worse for kindness; but suppose we should meet with such monsters — yet it is our duty to be ready to forgive (Colossians 3:13). Shall we cease from doing good because others will not cease from being evil? If the more you forgive injuries, the more injuries you meet with, this will make your grace shine the more. Another's vice will be a greater demonstration of your virtue. Frequent forgiving will add the more to the weight of his sin, and the weight of your glory. If any shall say to me, I strive to excel in other graces — but as for this grace of meekness, the bearing and forgiving of injuries, I cannot arrive at it; I desire in this to be excused. What do you talk of other graces? Where there is one grace, there is all. If meekness is lacking, it is but a counterfeit chain of grace. Your faith is a fable: your repentance is a lie; your humility is hypocrisy.

And whereas you say you cannot forgive, think of your own sin. Your neighbor is not so bad in offending you — as you are in not forgiving him. Your neighbor, in offending you — but trespasses against a man — but you, refusing to forgive him, trespass against God. Think also of your danger. You who are implacable, and though you may smother the fire of your rage — yet will not extinguish it, know that if you die this night, you die in an unpardoned condition. If you will not believe me, believe Christ. 'If you do not forgive, neither will your Father who is in heaven forgive your trespasses' (Mark 11:26). He who lives without meekness, dies without mercy!

3. The third branch of meekness is in recompensing good for evil. This is a higher degree than the other. 'Love your enemies, do good to those who hate you, pray for those who despitefully use you' (Matthew 5:44). 'If your enemy is hungry, feed him' (Romans 12:20). 'Not paying back evil for evil or insult for insult but, on the contrary, giving a blessing' (1 Peter 3:9). This threefold cord of Scripture should not easily be broken. To render evil for evil is brutish; to render evil for good is devilish; to render good for evil is Christian. The heathen thought it lawful to wrong none unless first provoked with an injury — but the sunlight of Scripture shines brighter than the lamp of reason. 'Love your enemies.' When grace comes into the heart, it works a strange alteration. When a scion is engrafted into the stock, it partakes of the nature and sap of the tree and brings forth the same fruit. He who was once of a sour disposition, given to revenge, when he once partakes of the sap of the heavenly grace, he bears holy fruits. He is full of love to his enemies. Grace allays the passion — and melts the heart into compassion. As the sun draws up many thick noxious vapors from the earth and sea, and returns them in sweet showers, so a gracious heart returns all the unkindness and discourtesies of his enemies

with the sweet influences and distillations of love. Thus David, 'They repay me with evil for the good I do. Yet when they were ill, I grieved for them. I even fasted and prayed for them.' (Psalm 35:12, 13). Some would have rejoiced;

David wept. Some would have put on scarlet; David put on sackcloth. This is the rarity or rather miracle of meekness. It repays good for evil. Thus we have seen the nature of meekness.

Meekness shows us the badge of a true saint. He is of a forbearing, meek spirit. 'He is not easily provoked'. He takes everything in the best sense and conquers malice with mildness. I would to God all who profess themselves saints were bespangled with this grace. We are known to belong to Christ when we wear his livery. He is a saint whose spirit is made so meek that he can smother injuries, and bury unkindnesses. A flow of tears better befits a Christian than a passion of anger. Every saint is Christ's spouse (Canticles 4:8). It befits Christ's spouse to be meek. If any injury is offered to the spouse, she leaves it to her husband to revenge. It is unseemly for Christ's spouse to fight.

Let me beseech all Christians to labor to be eminent in this superlative grace of meekness. 'Seek meekness' (Zephaniah 2:3). Seeking implies we have lost it. Therefore, we must seek and cry after it to find it. 'Put on therefore as the elect of God, meekness' (Colossians 3:12). Put it on as a garment, never to be left off. Meekness is a necessary ingredient in everything. It is necessary in instruction: 'In meekness instructing ...' (2 Timothy 2:25). Meekness conquers the opposers of truth. Meekness melts the heart. 'Soft words' are softening. Meekness is necessary in hearing or reading the Word. 'Receive with meekness the engrafted Word' (James 1:21). He who come to the Word in anger or malice, gets no good — but hurt. He turns wine into poison, and stabs himself with the sword of the Spirit! Meekness is needful in reproof. 'If a man is overtaken with a fault, restore such a one with the spirit of meekness' (Galatians 6:1). The Greek word is 'put him in joint again'. If a bone is out of joint, the surgeon must not use a rough hand that may chance break another bone. But he must come gently to work, and afterwards bind it up softly. So if a brother is overtaken with a fault, we must not come to him in a fury of passion — but with a spirit of meekness labor to restore him.

I shall lay down several motives or arguments to meeken the spirits of men.

1. Let me propound examples of meekness.

[1] The example of Jesus Christ. 'Your king comes unto you meek' (Matthew 21:5). Christ was the exemplar and pattern of meekness. 'When he was reviled, he reviled not again' (1 Peter 2:23). His enemies' words were more bitter than the gall they gave him — but Christ's words were smoother than oil. He prayed and wept for his enemies. He calls us to learn of him: 'Learn of me, for I am meek' (Matthew 11:29). Christ does not bid us (says Augustine) learn of him to work miracles, to open the eyes of the blind, to raise the dead — but he would have us learn of him to be meek. If we do not imitate his life — we cannot be saved by his death!

[2] Let us set before our eyes the examples of some of the saints who have shined in this grace. Moses was a man of unparalleled meekness. 'Now the man Moses was very meek, above all the men who were upon the face of the earth' (Numbers 12:3). How many injuries did he put up? When the people of Israel murmured against him, instead of falling into a rage, he falls to prayer for them (Exodus 15:24, 25). The text says, they murmured at the waters of Marah. Sure the waters were not so bitter as the spirits of the people — but they could not provoke him to anger — but to petition. Another time when they lacked water, they fell arguing with Moses. 'Why have brought us up out of Egypt — to kill us and our children with thirst?' (Exodus 17:3). As if they had said, If we die we will lay our death to your charge. Would not this exasperate Moses? Surely it would have required the meekness of an angel to bear this — but behold Moses,

meekness. He did not give them a harsh word! Though they were in a storm—he was in a calm. They lambaste him—but he prays. Oh that as the spirit of Elijah rested upon Elisha, so may some of the spirit of Moses, this meek man (or rather earthly angel), rest upon us!

Another eminent pattern of meekness was David. When Shimei cursed David, and Abishai, one of David's lifeguard, would have beheaded Shimei. 'No!' says king David, 'Let him alone, and let him curse' (2 Samuel 16:11). And when Saul had wronged and abused David and it was in David's power to have killed Saul while he was asleep, (1 Samuel 26:7, 12)—yet he would not touch Saul—but called God to be umpire (verse 23). Here was a miracle of meekness.

[3] The examples of meek heathen. Though their meekness could not properly be called grace, because it did not grow upon the right stock of faith—yet it was very beautiful in its kind. When one reviled Pericles and followed him home to his gate at night, railing upon him, he answered not a word—but commanded one of his servants to light a torch, and bring the railer home to his own house. Frederick, Duke of Saxony, when he was angry, would shut himself up in his closet and let none come near him, until he had mastered his passion. Plutarch reports of the Pythagoreans, if they argued in the day, they would embrace and be friends before sunset. Cicero, in one of his Orations, reports of Pompey the Great, that he was a man of a meek disposition. He admitted all to come to him so freely, and heard the complaints of those who were wronged so mildly, that he excelled all the princes before him. He was of that sweet temper that it was hard to say whether his enemies more feared his valor, or his subjects loved his meekness. Julius Caesar not only forgave Brutus and Cassius, his enemies—but advanced them. He thought himself most honored by acts of mercy and meekness. Did the spring-head of nature rise so high, and shall not grace rise higher? Shall we debase faith below reason? Let us write according to these fair copies.

2. Meekness is a great ornament to a Christian. 'The ornament of a meek spirit, which is so precious to God' (1 Peter 3:4). How lovely is a saint in God's eye, when adorned with this jewel! What the psalmist says of praise (Psalm 33:1), the same may I say of meekness. It is 'lovely for the righteous'. No garment is more befitting to a Christian, than meekness. Therefore we are bid to put on this garment. 'Put on therefore as the elect of God, meekness' (Colossians 3:12) A meek spirit brings credit to the gospel, and silences malice. It is the varnish which puts luster upon holiness, and sets off the gospel with a better gloss.

3. This is the way to be like God. God is meek towards those who provoke him. How many black mouths are opened daily against the Majesty of heaven? How do men tear his Name! vex his Spirit! crucify his Son afresh! They walk up and down the earth as so many devils covered with flesh—yet the Lord is meek, 'not willing that any should perish' (2 Peter 3:9). How easily could God crush sinners, and kick them into hell! But he moderates his anger. Though he is full of majesty—yet full of meekness. In him is mixed princely greatness and fatherly mildness. As he has his scepter of royalty, so his throne of grace. Oh how should this make us fall in love with meekness! Hereby we bear a kind of likeness to God. It is not profession which makes us like God—but imitation. Where meekness is lacking, we are like brutes. Where it is present, we are like God.

4. Meekness is a noble and excellent spirit. A meek man is a valorous man. He gets a victory over himself! Anger arises from weakness of character. Therefore we may observe old men and children are more choleric than others. Anger argues weakness of judgement—but the meek man who is able to conquer his fury, is the most strong and victorious. 'He who is slow to anger is better than the mighty; controlling one's temper, is better than capturing a city' (Proverbs 16:32). To yield to one's anger is easy. It is swimming along with the tide of corrupt nature—but to turn against nature, to resist anger, to 'overcome evil with good', this is truly Christian. This

is that spiritual chivalry and fortitude of mind that deserves the trophies of victory and the garland of praise.

5. Meekness is the best way to conquer and melt the heart of an enemy. When Saul lay at David's mercy and David only cut off the skirt of his robe, how was Saul's heart affected with David's meekness? 'Saul called back—Is that really you, my son David? Then he began to cry. And he said to David—You are a better man than I am, for you have repaid me good for evil. Yes, you have been wonderfully kind to me today, for you could have killed me. May the Lord reward you well for the kindness you have shown me today' (1 Samuel 24:16-19). This 'heaping of coals' melts and thaws the heart of others. It is the greatest victory—to overcome an enemy without striking a blow. The fire will go where the wedge cannot. Mildness prevails more than fierceness. Anger makes an enemy of a friend. Meekness makes a friend of an enemy. The meek Christian shall have letters testimonial even from his adversary. It is reported of Philip, king of Macedon, that when it was told him Nicanor openly railed against his Majesty, the king instead of putting him to death (as his council advised), sent Nicanor a rich present, which so overcame the man's heart, that he went up and down to recant what he had said against the king, and highly extolled the king's mercy. Roughness hardens men's hearts; meekness causes them to relent (2 Kings 6:22). When the king of Israel feasted the captives he had taken in war, they were more conquered by his meekness—than by his sword. 'The bands of Syria came no more into the land of Israel' (2 Kings 6:22)

6. Consider the great promise in the text. 'The meek shall inherit the earth'. This argument perhaps will prevail with those who desire to have earthly possessions. Some may object, 'If I forbear and forgive, I shall lose my right at last and be turned out of all.' No! God has here entered into bond, 'The meek shall inherit the earth'. The unmeek man is in a sad condition. There is no place remains for him but hell, for he has no promise made to him either of earth or heaven. It is the 'meek shall inherit the earth'.

How do the meek inherit the earth—when they are strangers in the earth? (Hebrews 11:37).

The meek are said to inherit the earth, not that the earth is their chief inheritance, or that they have always the greatest share there—but:

[1] They are the inheritors of the earth because, though they have not always the greatest part of the earth—yet they have the best right to it. The word 'inherit', says Ambrose, denotes the saints' 'title to the earth'. The saints' title is best, being 'members of Christ', who is Lord of all. Adam not only lost his title to heaven when he fell—but to the earth too; and until we are incorporated into Christ, we do not fully recover our title. I do not deny that the wicked have a civil right to the earth which the laws of the land give them—but not a sacred right. Only the meek Christian has a Scripture-title to his land. The saints hold their right to the earth in their head, Christ, who is 'the prince of the kings of the earth (Revelation 1:5). In this sense, he who has but a foot of land inherits more than he who has a thousand acres, because he has a better and more juridical right to it.

[2] The meek Christian is said to inherit the earth, because he inherits the blessing of the earth. The wicked man has the earth—but not as a fruit of God's favor. He has it as a dog has poisoned bread. It does him more hurt than good. A wicked man lives in the earth as one that lives in an infectious air. He is infected by his mercies. The fat of the earth will but make him fry and blaze the more in hell. So that a wicked man may be said not to have what he has, because he has not the blessing; but the meek saint enjoys the earth as a pledge of God's love. The curse and poison is taken out of the earth: 'The meek shall inherit the earth and shall delight themselves in the abundance of peace' (Psalm 37:11), on which words Augustine gives this

gloss: 'Wicked men' (says he) 'may delight themselves in the abundance of cattle and riches — but the meek man delights himself in the abundance of peace. What he has he possesses with inward serenity and quietness.'

When it is said the meek shall inherit the earth, it does not intimate that they shall not inherit more than the earth. They shall inherit heaven too. If they should only inherit the earth, then (says Chrysostom) how could it be said, 'Blessed are the meek'? The meek have the earth only for their sojourning-house: they have heaven for their mansion-house. 'He will beautify the meek with salvation' (Psalm 149:4). The meek beautify religion, and God will beautify them with salvation. Salvation is the port we all desire to sail to. It is the harvest and vintage of souls. The meek are those who shall reap this harvest. The meek shall wear the embroidered robe of salvation. The meek are lords of the earth and 'heirs of salvation' (Hebrews 1:14).

7. Consider the harm of an unmeek spirit. There is nothing which makes such room for the devil to come into the heart and take possession, as wrath and anger. 'Let not the sun go down upon your wrath, neither give place to the devil' (Ephesians 4:26, 27). When men let forth passion, they let in Satan. The wrathful man has the devil for his bedfellow. Passion hinders peace. The meek Christian has sweet quiet and harmony in his soul — but passion puts the soul into a disorder. It not only clouds reason — but disturbs conscience. He does not possess himself, whom passion possesses. It is no wonder if they have no peace of conscience, who make so little conscience of peace. Wrathfulness grieves the Spirit of God (Ephesians 4:30, 31), and if the Spirit is grieved, he will be gone. We do not care to stay in smoky houses. The Spirit of God does not love to be in that heart which is so full of the vapors and fumes of distempered passion.

8. Another argument to cool the intemperate heat of our cursed hearts, is to consider that all the injuries and unkind usages we meet with from the world, do not fall out by chance — but are disposed of by the all-wise God for our good. Many are like the foolish cur, which snarls at the stone, never looking to the hand that threw it; or like the horse, who being spurred by the rider, bites the snaffle. If we looked higher than instruments our hearts would grow meek and calm. David looked beyond Shimei's rage: 'Let him curse, for the Lord has bidden him' (2 Samuel 16:11). What wisdom is it for Christians to see the hand of God in all the barbarisms and incivilities of men! Job eyed God in his affliction, and that meekened his spirit. 'The Lord has taken away, blessed be the name of the Lord!' (Job 1:21). He does not say, The Chaldeans have taken away — but 'The Lord has taken away'. What made Christ so meek in his sufferings? He did not look at Judas or Pilate — but at his Father. 'The cup which my Father has given me' (John 18:11). When wicked men revile and injure us, they are but God's executioners. Who is angry with the executioner?

And as God has a hand in all the affronts and discourtesies we receive from men (for they but hand them over to us), so God will do us good by all, if we belong to him. 'It may be' (says David) 'that the Lord will look upon my affliction, and requite me good for his cursing' (2 Samuel 16:12). Usually, when the Lord intends us some signal mercy, he fits us for it by some eminent trial. As Moses' hand was first leprous before it wrought salvation (Exodus 4:6), so God may let his people be belepered with the cursings and revilings of men, before he shower down some blessings upon them. 'It may be the Lord will requite me good for his cursing this day.'

9. Lack of meekness evidences lack of grace. True grace inflames love and moderates anger. Grace is like the file which smooths the rough iron. It files off the ruggedness of a man's spirit. Grace says to the heart as Christ did to the angry sea, 'Peace, be still' (Mark 4:39). So where there is grace in the heart, it stills the raging of passion and makes a calm. He who is in a perpetual frenzy, letting loose the reins to wrath and malice — has never yet felt the sweet

efficacy of grace. It is one of the sins of the heathen to be 'implacable' (Romans 1:31). A revengeful cankered heart, is not only heathenish—but devilish. 'If you have bitter envying and strife in your hearts, this wisdom descends not from above—but is devilish' (James 3:14, 15). The old serpent spits forth the poison of malice and revenge.

10. If all that has been said will not serve to master this bedlam-humor of wrath and anger, let me tell you, you are the people whom God steaks of, who hate to be reformed. You are rebels against the Word. Read and tremble: 'Now go, write it before them in a table, and note it in a book, that it may be for the time to come forever and ever; that this is a rebellious people, children that will not hear the law of the Lord' (Isaiah 30:8, 9). If nothing yet said will charm down the wrathful devil, let me tell you, God has charged every man not to meddle or have any league of friendship with you. 'Make no friendship with an angry man, and with a furious man you shall not go' (Proverbs 22:24). What a monster is he among men, that everyone is warned to beware of, and not to come near, as one who is unfit for humane society! Make no league, says God, with that man. If you take him into your society, you take a snake into your bosom. 'With a furious man you shall not go'. Will you walk with the devil? The furious man is possessed with a wrathful devil.

Oh that all this might help to meeken and sweeten Christians, spirits!

But some will say, *'It is my nature to be angry and passionate!'* I answer:

[1] This is sinful arguing. It is secretly to lay our sin upon God. We learned this from Adam. 'The woman whom you gave to be with me, she gave me of the tree, and I did eat' (Genesis 3:12); rather than Adam would confess his sin, he would blame it upon God. 'The woman you gave me'. As if he had said, 'If you had not given this woman to me—I would not have eaten.' So, says one, 'It is my nature; this is the froward, peevish nature God has given me.' Oh no! you charge God falsely. God did not give you such a nature. 'He made man upright' (Ecclesiastes 7:29). God made you straight; you made yourself crooked. All your affections at first, your joy, love, anger were set in order as the stars in their right orb—but you misplaced them and made them move in an evil way. At first the affections like several musical instruments well tuned, made a sweet consort—but sin was the jarring string which brought all out of tune. Vain man, do not plead that it is your nature to be angry; thank yourself for it. Nature's spring was pure—until sin poisoned the spring!

[2] Is it your nature to be fierce and angry? This is so far from being an excuse, that it makes it so much the worse. It is the nature of a toad to poison that makes it the more hateful. If a man were indicted for stealing, and he should say to the judge, 'Spare me; it is my nature to steal', were this any excuse? The judge would say, 'You deserve the rather to die'. Sinner, get a new nature. 'Flesh and blood cannot enter into the kingdom of God'.

What shall I do to be possessed of this excellent grace of meekness?

1. Often look upon the meekness of Christ. The scholar that would write well, has his eye often upon the copy.

2. Pray earnestly that God will meeken your spirit. God is called 'the God of all grace' (1 Peter 5:10). He has all the graces in his gift. Sue to him for this grace of meekness. If one were patron of all the livings in the land, men would sue to him for a living. God is patron of all the graces. Let us sue to him. Mercy comes in at the door of prayer. 'I will yet for this be enquired of by the house of Israel to do it for them' (Ezekiel 36:26, 37). Meekness is the commodity we need. Let us send prayer as our factor over to heaven to procure it for us; and pray in faith. When faith sets prayer on work, prayer sets God on work. All divine blessings come streaming to us through this golden channel of prayer!

Spiritual Hunger

Blessed are those who hunger and thirst after righteousness, for they will be filled.

Matthew 5:6

We are now come to the fourth step of blessedness: 'Blessed are those who hunger'. The words fall into two parts: a duty implied; a promise annexed.

A duty implied: 'Blessed are those who hunger'. Spiritual hunger is a blessed hunger.

What is meant by hunger? Hunger is put for desire (Isaiah 26:9). Spiritual hunger is the rational appetite whereby the soul pants after that which it apprehends most suitable and proportional to itself.

Whence is this hunger? Hunger is from the sense of lack. He who spiritually hungers, has a real sense of his own indigence. He lacks righteousness.

What is meant by righteousness? There is a twofold righteousness: of imputation; of implantation.

A righteousness of imputation, namely, Christ's righteousness. 'He shall be called the Lord our righteousness' (Jeremiah 23:6). This is as truly ours to justify us, as it is Christ's to bestow upon us. By virtue of this righteousness God looks upon us as if we had never sinned (Numbers 23:21). This is a perfect righteousness. 'You are complete in him' (Colossians 2:10). This does not only cover, but adorn. He who has this righteousness is equal to the most illustrious saints. The weakest believer is justified as much as the strongest. This is a Christian's triumph. When he is defiled in himself, he is undefiled in his Head. In this blessed righteousness we shine brighter than the angels. This righteousness is worth hungering after.

A righteousness of implantation: that is, inherent righteousness, namely, the graces of the Spirit, holiness of heart and life, which Cajetan calls 'universal righteousness'. This a pious soul hungers after. This is a blessed hunger. Bodily hunger cannot make a man so miserable, as spiritual hunger makes him blessed. This evidences life. A dead man cannot hunger. Hunger proceeds from life. The first thing the child does when it is born, is to hunger after the breast. Spiritual hunger follows upon the new birth (1 Peter 2:2). Bernard comforts himself with this — that surely he had the truth of grace in him, because he had in his heart a strong desire after God. It is happy when, though we have not what we should, we desire what we have not. The appetite is as well from God, as the food.

1. See here at what a low price God sets heavenly things. It is but hungering and thirsting. 'Ho, everyone who thirsts, come to the waters, buy without money' (Isaiah 55:1). We are not bid to bring any merits as the Papists would do, nor to bring a sum of money to purchase righteousness. All that is required is to bring an appetite. Christ 'has fulfilled all righteousness'. We are only to 'hunger and thirst after righteousness'. This is equal and reasonable. God does not require rivers of oil — but sighs and tears. The invitation of the gospel is free. If a friend invites guests to his table, he does not expect they should bring money to pay for their dinner — only come with an appetite. So, says God, It is not penance, pilgrimage, self-righteousness which I require. Only bring an appetite: 'hunger and thirst after righteousness'. God might have set Christ and salvation at a higher price — but he has much beaten down the price. Now as this shows the sweetness of God's nature — he is not a hard master; so it shows us the inexcusableness of those who perish under the gospel. What apology can any man make at the day of judgement, when God shall ask that question, 'Friend, why did you not embrace Christ? I set Christ and grace at a low rate. If you had but hungered after righteousness, you might have had it — but you slighted Christ. You had such low thoughts of righteousness that you would not hunger after it.' How do you think to escape, who have neglected 'so great

salvation'? The easier the terms of the gospel are — the sorer punishment shall they be thought worthy of who unworthy refuse such an offer!

2. It shows us a true character of a godly man. He hungers and thirsts after spiritual things (Isaiah 26:9; Psalm 73:25). A true saint is carried upon the wing of desire. It is the very temper and constitution of a gracious soul to thirst after God (Psalm 42:2). In the word preached, how he is big with desire! These are some of the pantings of his soul: 'Lord, you have led me into your courts. O that I may have your sweet presence, that your glory may fill the temple! Will you draw some sacred lineaments of grace upon my soul that I may be more assimilated and changed into the likeness of my dear Savior?' In prayer, how is the soul filled with passionate longings after Christ! Prayer is expressed by 'unutterable groans' (Romans 8:26). The heart sends up whole volleys of sighs to heaven, 'Lord, one beam of your love! Lord, one drop of your blood!'

It reproves such as have none of this spiritual hunger. They have no winged desires. The edge of their affections is blunted. Honey is not sweet to those who are sick with a fever and have their tongues embittered with cholera.' So those who are soul-sick and 'in the gall of bitterness', find no sweetness in God or religion. Sin tastes sweeter to them; they have no spiritual hunger. That men do not have this 'hunger after righteousness' appears by these seven demonstrations:

1. Men do not hunger after righteousness, because they never felt any emptiness. They are full of their own righteousness (Romans 10:3). Now 'the full stomach loathes the honeycomb'. This was Laodicea's disease. She was full and had no appetite either to Christ's gold or eye-salve (Revelation 3:17). When men are filled with pride, this swelling distemper hinders holy longings. As when the stomach is bloated with air, it spoils the appetite. None so empty of grace as he who thinks he is full. He has most need of righteousness, who least feels the need of it.

2. Men do not hunger after righteousness, because they think that they can do well enough to be without it. If they have oil in the cruse, and the world coming in — they are well content. Grace is a commodity that is least missed. You shall hear men complain they lack health, they lack trading — but never complain they lack righteousness. If men lose a meal or two they think themselves half undone — but they can stay away from ordinances which are the conduits of grace. Do they hunger after righteousness, who are satisfied without it? Nay, who desire to be excused from feeding upon the gospel banquet (Luke 14:18). Sure he has no appetite, who entreats to be excused from eating.

3. It is a sign they have none of this spiritual hunger, who desire rather sleep than food. They are more drowsy than hungry. Some there are, who come to the Word that they may get a nap, to whom I may say as Christ did to Peter, 'Could you not watch one hour?' (Mark 14:37). It is strange to see a man asleep at his dining table. Others there are who have a 'deep sleep' fallen upon them. They are asleep in security and they hate a soul-awakening ministry. While they sleep, 'their damnation slumbers not' (2 Peter 2:3).

4. It appears that men have no spiritual hunger because they refuse their food. Christ and grace are offered, nay, pressed upon them — but they put away salvation from them as the froward child puts away the breast (Psalm 81:11; Acts 13:46). Such are your fanatics and enthusiasts who put away the blessed ordinances and pretend to revelations. That is a strange revelation that tells a man he may live without food. These prefer husks before manna. They live upon airy notions, being fed by the 'prince of the air'.

5. It is a sign they have none of this spiritual hunger who delight more in the garnishing of the dish, than in food. These are those who look more after elegance and notion in preaching, than

solid matter. It argues either a wanton palate or a surfeited stomach — to feed on sweets, and neglecting wholesome food. 'If any man consent not to wholesome words, he is proud, knowing nothing ...' (1 Timothy 6:3, 4). The plainest truth has its beauty. They have no spiritual hunger, who desire only to feast their fancy. Of such the prophet speaks: 'You are to them as a very lovely song of one who has a pleasant voice, and can play well on an instrument' (Ezekiel 33:32). If a man were invited to a feast, and there being music at the feast, he should so listen to the music that he did not mind his food, you would say, 'Surely he is not hungry.' So when men are for jingling words and gallantry of speech, rather than spirituality of matter — it is a sign they have surfeited stomachs and 'itching ears'.

6. They evidence little hunger after righteousness who prefer other things before it, namely, their profits and recreations. If a boy when he should be at dinner is playing in the street, it is a sign that he has no appetite for his food. Were he hungry — he would not prefer his play before his food. So when men prefer 'vain things which cannot profit' before the blood of Christ and the grace of the Spirit, it is a sign they have no palate or stomach to heavenly things.

7. It is a sign that men have no spiritual hunger when they are more for religious disputes — than the practice of piety. Some men feed only on difficult questions and controversies (1 Timothy 6:3, 4). These pick bones — and do not feed on the meat. They have hot brains but cold hearts. Did men hunger and thirst after righteousness, they would propound to themselves such questions as these, 'How shall we do to be saved? How shall we make our calling and election sure? How shall we mortify our corruptions?' But such as ravel out their time in frothy and useless theological disputes, I call heaven to witness, they are strangers to this text. They do not 'hunger and thirst after righteousness'.

The Word reproves those who, instead of hungering and thirsting after righteousness, thirst after riches. This is the thirst of covetous men. They desire mammon not manna. 'They pant after the dust of the earth' (Amos 2:7). This is the disease most are afflicted with — an immoderate appetite after the world. But these things will no more satisfy, than drink will quench the thirst of a man with the dropsy. Covetousness is idolatry (Colossians 3:5). Too many professors set up the idol of gold, in the temple of their hearts. This sin of covetousness is the most hard to root out. Commonly, when other sins leave men, this sin abides. Wantonness is the sin of youth; worldliness the sin of mature age.

The Word reproves those who hunger and thirst after unrighteousness. Here I shall indict three sorts of people:

1. It reproves such as thirst after other men's lands and possessions. This the Scripture calls a 'mighty sin' (Amos 5:12). Thus Ahab thirsted after Naboth's vineyard. This is a hungry age wherein we live. Men have fleeced others to feather themselves. What a brave challenge did Samuel make; 'Behold, here I am, witness against me before the Lord, and before his anointed: Whose ox have I taken? Or whose donkey have I taken? Or whom have I defrauded? Of whose hand have I received any bribe?' (1 Samuel 12:3). Few who have been in power that can say thus, 'Whose ox have we taken? Whose house have we plundered? Whose estate have we sequestered? Nay, whose ox have they not taken?' 'Goods unjustly gotten, seldom go to the third heir'. Read the plunderer's curse: 'Woe to you who plunder — when you shall cease to plunder, you shall be plundered' (Isaiah 33:1). Ahab paid dearly for the vineyard when the devil carried away his soul — and the 'dogs licked his blood' (1 Kings 21:19). He who lives on rapine, dies a fool. 'He who gets riches unjustly, at his end shall be a fool' (Jeremiah 17:11).

2. It reproves such as hunger and thirst after revenge. This is a devilish thirst. Though it were more Christian and safe to smother an injury — yet our nature is prone to this disease of

revenge. We have the sting of the bee, not the honey. Malice having broken the bars of reason, grows savage and carries its remedy in the scabbard. Heathens who have stopped the vein of revengeful passion when it has begun to vent, will rise up against Christians. I have read of Phocion who, being wrongfully condemned to die, desired that his son might not remember the injuries which the Athenians had done to him, nor revenge his blood.

3. It reproves such as hunger and thirst to satisfy their impure lusts. Sinners are said to sin 'with greediness' (Ephesians 4:19). So Amnon was sick until he had defiled Tamar's chastity (2 Samuel 13). Never does a hungry man come with more eagerness to his food — than a wicked man does to his sin! And when Satan sees men have such an appetite — he will provide a dish they love. He will set the 'forbidden tree' before them. Those who thirst to commit sin — shall thirst as Dives did in hell, and not have a drop of water to cool their tongue!

Let us put ourselves upon a trial — whether we hunger and thirst after righteousness. I shall give you five signs by which you may judge of this hunger.

1. Hunger is a painful thing. Esau, when he was returning from hunting, was famished with hunger (Genesis 25:32). 'Hungry and thirsty, their soul fainted in them' (Psalm 107:5). So a man who hungers after righteousness, is in anguish of soul and ready to faint away for it. He finds a lack of Christ and grace. He is distressed and in pain until he has his spiritual hunger stilled and allayed.

2. Hunger is satisfied with nothing but food. Bring a hungry man flowers or music; tell him pleasant stories — nothing will content him but food. 'Shall I die for thirst!' says Samson (Judges 15:18). So a man who hungers and thirsts after righteousness says, 'Give me Christ or I die! Lord, what will you give me seeing I go Christless? What though I have abilities, wealth, honor and esteem in the world? All is nothing without Christ. Give me Jesus — and it will suffice me. Let me have Christ to clothe me, Christ to feed me, Christ to intercede for me!' While the soul is Christless, it is restless. Nothing but the water-springs of Christ's blood, can quench its thirst.

3. Hunger wrestles with difficulties and hunts for food. We say hunger breaks through stone walls (Genesis 42:1, 2). The soul that spiritually hungers is resolved — Christ it must have; grace it must have. And to use Basil's expression, the hungry soul is almost distracted until it enjoys the thing it hungers after.

4. A hungry man goes to his food with a strong appetite. You need not make an oration to a hungry man and persuade him to eat. So he who hungers after righteousness feeds eagerly on an ordinance. 'Your words were found, and I did eat them' (Jeremiah 15:16). In the sacrament he feeds with appetite upon the body and blood of the Lord. God loves to see us feed hungrily on the bread of life.

5. A hungry man tastes sweetness in his food. So he who hungers after righteousness relishes a sweetness in heavenly things. Christ is to him all marrow, yes the quintessence of delights. 'You have tasted that the Lord is gracious' (1 Peter 2:3). He who spiritually hungers, tastes the promises sweet — nay tastes a reproof sweet. 'To the hungry soul, every bitter thing is sweet' (Proverbs 27:7). A bitter reproof is sweet. He can feed upon the myrrh of the gospel as well as the honey. By these evidences, we may judge of ourselves whether we hunger and thirst after righteousness.

The words may serve to comfort the hearts of those who hunger and thirst after righteousness; I doubt not but it is the grief of many a gracious heart — that he cannot be more holy, that he cannot serve God better. 'Blessed are those who hunger'. Though you do not have as much righteousness as you would — yet you are blessed because you hunger after it. Desire is the best evidence of a Christian. Actions may be counterfeit. A man may do a good action for a bad end.

So did Jehu. Actions may be compulsory. A man may be forced to do that which is good – but not to will that which is good. Therefore we are to nourish good desires and to bless God for them. Oftentimes a child of God has nothing to show for himself, but desires. 'Your servants, who desire to fear your name' (Nehemiah 1:11). These hungerings after righteousness proceed from love. A man does not desire that which he does not love. If you did not love Christ, you could not hunger after him.

But some may say, *'If my hunger were right then I could take comfort in it – but I fear it is counterfeit. Hypocrites have their desires.'*

In reply, that I may the better settle a doubting Christian I shall show the difference between true and false desires, spiritual hunger and carnal hunger.

1. The hypocrite does not desire grace for itself. He desires grace only as a bridge to lead him over to heaven. He does not so much search after grace – as glory. He does not so much desire the way of righteousness – as the crown of righteousness. His desire is not to be made like Christ – but to reign with Christ. This was Balaam's desire. 'Let me die the death of the righteous' (Numbers 23:10). Such desires as these are found among the damned. This is the hypocrite's hunger. But a child of God desires grace for itself, and Christ for himself. To a believer not only is heaven precious, but Christ is precious, 'Yes, He is very precious to you who believe!' (1 Peter 2:7).

2. The hypocrite's desire is conditional. He would have heaven and his sins too, heaven and his pride, heaven and his covetousness. The young man in the gospel would have had heaven, provided he might keep his earthly possessions. Many a man would have Christ – but there is some sin he must gratify. This is the hypocrites' hunger; but true desire is absolute. Give me, says the soul, Christ on any terms. Let God propound whatever articles he will, I will subscribe to them. Would he have me deny myself? Would he have me mortify sin? I am content to do anything – just so I may have Christ. Hypocrites would have Christ – but they will not part with their beloved lust for Him!

3. Hypocrites' desires are but desires. They are lazy and sluggish. 'The desire of the slothful kills him, for his hands refuse to labor' (Proverbs 21:25). Men would be saved but they will take no pains. Does he desire water. Who will not let down the bucket into the well? But true desire is quickened into endeavor. 'All night long I search for you; earnestly I seek for God.' (Isaiah 26:9). The 'violent take heaven by force (Matthew 11:12). The lovesick spouse, though she was wounded, and her veil taken away – yet she seeks after Christ (Canticles 5:7). Desire is the weight of the soul, which sets it a going; as the eagle which desires her prey makes haste to it. 'Where the slain are, there is she' (Job 39:30). The eagle has sharpness of sight to discover her prey, and swiftness of wing to fly to it. So the soul who hungers after righteousness, is carried swiftly to it in the use of all holy ordinances.

4. The hypocrite's desires are cheap. He would have spiritual things – but will be spend nothing for them. He cares not how much money he parts with for his lusts; he has money to spend upon a drunken companion; but he has no money to part with for the maintaining of God's ordinances. Hypocrites cry up religion – but cry down supporting the church. But true desires are costly. David would not offer burnt-offerings without cost (1 Chronicles 21:24). A hungry man will give anything for food; as it fell out in the siege of Samaria (2 Kings 6:25). That man never hungered after Christ, who thinks much of parting with a little silver for 'the Pearl of great price'.

5. Hypocrites' desires are flashy and transient. They are quickly gone, like the wind which does not stay long in one corner. Or like a hot fit which is soon over. While the hypocrite is under

terror of conscience, or in affliction, he has some good desires—but the hot fit is soon over. His goodness, like a fiery comet, soon spends and evaporates. But true desire is constant. It is observable that the word in the text is: 'Blessed are those who are hungering.' Though they have righteousness—yet they are still hungering after more. Hypocrites desire it like the motion of a watch—which is quickly run down. The desire of a godly man is like the beating of the pulse—which lasts as long as life. 'My soul breaks for the longing that it has to your judgments' (Psalm 119:20). And that we might not think this pang of desire would soon be over he adds, 'at all times'. David's desire after God was not a high color in a fit—but the constant complexion of his soul. In the temple the fire was not to go out by night. 'The fire shall ever be burning upon the altar' (Leviticus 6:13). There was, says Cyril, a mystery in it, to show that we must be ever burning in holy affections and desires.

6. Hypocrites' desires are unseasonable. They are not well-timed. They put off their hungering after righteousness until it is too late. They are like the foolish virgins, who came knocking when the door was shut (Matthew 25:11). In time of health and prosperity the stream of their affections ran another way. It was sin the hypocrite desired, not righteousness. When he is about to die and can keep his sins no longer, now he would have grace as a passport to carry him to heaven (Luke 13:25). This is the hypocrite's fault. His desires are too late. He sends forth his desires when his last breath is going forth; as if a man should desire a pardon after the sentence is passed. These bedridden desires are bogus! But true desires are timely and seasonable. A gracious heart 'seeks first the Kingdom of God' (Matthew 6:33). David's thirst after God was early (Psalm 63:1). The wise virgins got their oil early before the bridegroom came. Thus we see the difference between a true and false hunger. Those who can find this true hunger are blessed, and may take comfort in it.

But some may object: *'My hunger after righteousness is so weak, that I fear it is not true.'*

I answer: Though the pulse beats but weak—it shows there is life. And that weak desires should not be discouraged, there is a promise made to them. 'A bruised reed he will not break' (Matthew 12:20). A reed is a weak thing—but especially when it is bruised—yet this 'bruised reed' shall not be broken—but like Aaron's dry rod, 'bud and blossom'. In case of weakness— look to Christ your High Priest. He is merciful, therefore will bear with your infirmities; he is mighty, therefore will help them.

Further, if your desires after righteousness seem to be weak and languid—yet a Christian may sometimes take a measure of his spiritual estate as well by the judgment as by the affections. What is that you esteem most in your judgment? Is it Christ and grace? This is good evidence for heaven. It was a sign that Paul bore entire love to Christ because he esteemed this Pearl above all. He counted other things 'but dung, that he might win Christ' (Philippians 3:8).

'But,' says a child of God, 'that which much eclipses my comfort is, I have not that hunger which I once had. Time was when I hungered after a Sabbath because then the manna fell. 'I called the Sabbath a delight'. I remember the time when I hungered after the body and blood of the Lord. I came to a sacrament as a hungry man to a feast—but now it is otherwise with me. I do not have those hungerings as formerly.'

I answer: It is indeed an ill sign for a man to lose his appetite—but, though it is a sign of the decay of grace to lose the spiritual appetite—yet it is a sign of the truth of grace to bewail the loss. It is sad to lose our first love—but it is happy when we mourn for the loss of our first love.

If you do not have that appetite after heavenly things as formerly—yet do not be discouraged, for in the use of means you may recover your appetite. The ordinances are for the recovering of the appetite when it is lost. In other cases, feeding takes away the appetite—but here, feeding on an ordinance begets an appetite.

The text exhorts us all to labor after this spiritual hunger. Hunger less after the world—and more after righteousness. Say concerning spiritual things, 'Lord, evermore give us this bread! Feed me with this angels' food!' That manna is most to be hungered after, which will not only preserve life, but prevent death (John 6:50). That is most desirable which is most durable. Riches are not forever (Proverbs 27:24) but righteousness is forever (Proverbs 8:18). 'The beauty of holiness' never fades (Psalm 110:3). 'The robe of righteousness' (Isaiah 61:10) never waxes old! Oh hunger after that righteousness which 'delivers from death' (Proverbs 10:12). This is the righteousness which God himself is in love with. 'He loves him who follows after righteousness' (Proverbs 15:9). All men are ambitious of the king's favor. Alas, what is a prince's smile but a transient glance? This sunshine of his royal countenance soon masks itself with a cloud of displeasure—but those who are endued with righteousness are God's favorites, and how sweet is his smile! 'Your loving-kindness is better than life' (Psalm 63:3).

To persuade men to hunger after this righteousness, consider two things.

1. Unless we hunger after righteousness we cannot obtain it. God will never throw away his blessings upon those who do not desire them. A king may say to a rebel, 'Do but desire a pardon and you shall have it.' But if through pride and stubbornness he disdains to sue out his pardon, he deserves justly to die. God has set spiritual blessings at a low rate. Do but hunger and you shall have righteousness; but if we refuse to come up to these terms there is no righteousness to be had for us. God will stop the current of his mercy and set open the sluice of his indignation!

2. If we do not thirst here we shall thirst when it is too late. If we do not thirst as David did 'My soul thirsts for God' (Psalm 42:2) we shall thirst as Dives did for a drop of water (Luke 16:24). Those who do not thirst for righteousness shall be in perpetual hunger and thirst. They shall thirst for mercy—but no mercy will be received. Heat increases thirst. When men shall burn in hell and be scorched with the flames of God's wrath, this heat will increase their thirst for mercy—but there will be nothing to allay their thirst. Oh is it not better to thirst for righteousness while it is to be had, than to thirst for mercy when there is none to be had? Sinners, the time is shortly coming when the drawbridge of mercy will be quite pulled up!

I shall next briefly describe some helps to spiritual hunger.

1. Avoid those things which will hinder your appetite. As 'windy things'. When the stomach is full of wind a man has little appetite to his food. So when one is filled with a windy opinion of his own righteousness, he will not hunger after Christ's righteousness. He who, being puffed up with pride, thinks he has grace enough already, will not hunger after more. These windy vapors spoil the appetite.

'Sweet things' spoil the appetite. So by feeding immoderately upon the sweet luscious delights of the world, we lose our appetite to Christ and grace. You never knew a man who glutted himself upon the world, and at the same time was greatly in love with Christ. While Israel fed with delight upon garlic and onions, they never hungered after manna. The soul cannot be carried to two extremes at once. As the eye cannot look intent on heaven and earth at once, so a man cannot at the same instant hunger excessively after the world, and after righteousness! The earth puts out the fire. The love of earthly things will quench the desire of spiritual things. 'Love not the world' (1 John 2:15). The sin is not in the having the world—but in the loving the world.

2. Do all that may nourish spiritual appetite. There are two things which nourish appetite.

Exercise: a man by walking and excercising gets an appetite for his food. So by the exercise of holy duties the spiritual appetite is increased. 'Exercise yourself unto godliness' (1 Timothy 4:7). Many have left off closet prayer. They hear the Word but seldom, and for lack of exercise they have lost their appetite to religion.

Sauce: sauce whets and sharpens the appetite. There is a twofold sauce which provokes holy appetite: first, the 'bitter herbs' of repentance. He who tastes gall and vinegar in sin, hungers after the body and blood of the Lord. Second, affliction. God often gives us this sauce to sharpen our hunger after grace. 'Reuben found mandrakes in the field' (Genesis 30:14). The mandrakes are a herb of a very strong savor, and among other virtues they have, they are chiefly medicinal for those who have weak and bad appetites. Afflictions may be compared to these mandrakes, which sharpen men's desires after that spiritual food which in time of prosperity they began to loathe and nauseate. Poverty is the sauce which cures the gluttony of plenty. In sickness people hunger more after righteousness, than in health. 'The full soul loathes the honeycomb' (Proverbs 27:7).

Christians, when glutted on the world, despise the rich cordials of the gospel. I wish we did not slight those truths now, which would taste sweet in a prison. How precious was a leaf of the Bible in Queen Mary's days! The wise God sees it good sometimes to give us the sharp sauce of affliction, to make us feed more hungrily upon the bread of life. And so much for the first part of the text, 'Blessed are those who hunger.

Spiritual hunger shall be satisfied

'Blessed are those who hunger and thirst for righteousness, for they will be filled.' Matthew 5:6

I proceed now to the second part of the text. A promise annexed. 'They shall be filled'. A Christian fighting with sin is not like one who 'beats the air' (1 Corinthians 9:26), and his hungering after righteousness is not like one who sucks in only air, 'Blessed are those who hunger, for they shall be filled.'

Those who hunger after righteousness shall be filled. God never bids us to seek him 'in vain' (Isaiah 45:19). Here is a honeycomb dropping into the mouths of the hungry —'they shall be filled'. 'He has filled the hungry with good things' (Luke 1:53). 'He satisfies the longing soul' (Psalm 107:9). God will not let us lose our longing. Here is the excellency of righteousness above all other things. A man may hunger after the world and not be filled. The world is fading, not filling. Cast three worlds into the heart—yet the heart is not full. But righteousness is a filling thing; nay, it so fills that it satisfies. A man may be filled and not satisfied. A sinner may take his fill of sin—but that is a sad filling. It is far from satisfaction. 'The backslider in heart shall be filled with his own ways' (Proverbs 14:14). He shall have his belly full of sin; he shall have enough of it—but this is not a filling to satisfaction. This is such a filling that the damned in hell have! They shall be full of the fury of the Lord!

But he who hungers after righteousness shall be satisfyingly filled. 'My people shall be satisfied with my goodness' (Jeremiah 31:14). 'My soul shall be satisfied as with marrow' (Psalm 63:5). Joseph first opened the mouth of the sacks, and then filled them with grain and put money in them (Genesis 42:25). So God first opens the mouth of the soul with desire and then fills it with good things (Psalm 81:10). For the illustration of this, consider these three things: that God can fill the hungry soul; why he fills the hungry soul; how he fills the hungry soul.

1. God can fill the hungry soul. He is called a fountain. 'With you is the fountain of life' (Psalm 36:9). The cistern may be empty and cannot fill us. Creatures are often 'broken cisterns' (Jeremiah 2:13). But the fountain is filling. God is a fountain. If we bring the vessels of our desires to this fountain, he is able to fill them. The fullness in God is an infinite fullness. Though

he fills us, and the angels which have larger capacities to receive — yet he has never the less himself. As the sun, though it shines, has never the less light. 'I perceive that virtue is gone out of me' (Luke 8:46). Though God lets virtue go out of him — yet he has never the less. The fullness of the creature is limited. It arises just to such a degree and proportion; but God's fullness is infinite; as it has its resplendence, so its abundance.' It has neither bounds nor bottom!

It is a constant fullness. The fullness of the creature is a mutable fullness; it ebbs and changes. 'I would like to have helped you — but now my estate is low', says one. The blossoms of the fig-tree are soon blown off. But God is a constant fullness. 'You are the same' (Psalm 102:27). God and his bounty, can never be exhausted. His fullness is overflowing and ever-flowing. Then surely 'it is good to draw near to God' (Psalm 73:28). It is good bringing our vessels to this spring-head. It is a never-failing goodness.

2. Why God fills the hungry soul. The reasons are:

[1] God will fill the hungry soul out of his tender compassion. He knows that otherwise, 'the spirit would fail before him and the soul which he has made' (Isaiah 57:16). If the hungry man is not satisfied with food, he dies. God has more affections than to allow a hungry soul to be famished. When the multitude had nothing to eat, Christ was moved with compassion and he wrought a miracle for their supply (Matthew 15:32). Much more will he compassionate such as hunger and thirst after righteousness. When a poor sinner sees himself almost starved in his sins (as the prodigal among his husks) and begins to hunger after Christ, saying, 'there is bread enough and to spare in my Father's house', God will then out of his infinite compassion, bring forth the fatted calf and refresh his soul with the delicacies and provisions of the gospel. Oh the melting of God's affections to a hungry sinner! 'My heart is torn within me, and my compassion overflows' (Hosea 11:8) We cannot see a poor creature at the door ready to perish with hunger — but our affections begin to be stirred, and we afford him some relief. And will the Father of mercies let a poor soul that hungers after the blessings of the gospel go away without an alms of free grace? No! he will not; he cannot! Let the hungry sinner think thus, 'Though I am full of needs — yet my God is full of affection!'

[2] God will fill the hungry that he may fulfill his Word. 'Blessed are you who hunger now: for you shall be filled' (Psalm 107:9; Jeremiah 31:14; Luke 6:21). 'I will pour water upon him who is thirsty, I will pour my Spirit upon your seed ...' (Isaiah 44:3). Has the Lord spoken and shall it not come to pass? Promises are obligatory. If God has passed a promise — he cannot go back on his word. You who hunger after righteousness have God engaged for you. He has (to speak with reverence) pawned his truth for you. As 'his compassions fail not' (Lamentations 3:22), so 'he will not allow his faithfulness to fail' (Psalm 89:33). If the hungry soul should not be filled — the promise would not be fulfilled.

[3] God will fill the hungry soul because he himself has excited and stirred up this hunger. He plants holy desires in us, and will not he satisfy those desires which he himself has wrought in us? As in the case of prayer, when God prepares the heart to pray, he prepares his ear to hear (Psalm 10:17); so in the case of spiritual hunger, when God prepares the heart to hunger, he will prepare his hand to fill. It is not rational to imagine that God should deny to satisfy that hunger which he himself has caused. God does nothing in vain. Should the Lord inflame the desire after righteousness and not fill it, he might seem to do something in vain.

[4] God will fill the hungry because of those sweet relations he stands unto them — they are his children. We cannot deny our children when they are hungry. We will rather spare it from our own selves (Luke 11:13). When he who is born of God shall come and say, 'Father, I hunger,

give me Christ! Father, I thirst, refresh me with the living streams of your Spirit!' can God deny him? Does God hear the raven when it cries, and will he not hear the righteous when they cry? When the earth opens its mouth and thirsts, God satisfies it (Psalm 65:9, 10). Does the Lord satisfy the thirsty earth with showers and will he not satisfy the thirsty soul with grace?

[5] God will satisfy the hungry because the hungry soul is most thankful for mercy. When the restless desire has been drawn out after God, and God fills it, how thankful is a Christian! The Lord loves to bestow his mercy where he may have most praise. We delight to give to those who are thankful. Musicians love to play where there is the best praise. God loves to bestow his mercies where he may hear of them again. The hungry soul sets the crown of praise upon the head of free grace! 'Whoever offers praise glorifies me' (Psalm 50:23).

3. how God fills the hungry soul. There is threefold filling: with grace; with peace; with bliss.

[1] God fills the hungry soul with grace. Grace is filling, because it is suitable to the soul. Stephen was 'full of the Holy Spirit' (Acts 7:55). This fullness of grace is in respect of parts, not of degrees. There is something of every grace given, though not perfection in any grace.

[2] God fills the hungry soul with peace. 'The God of hope fill you with all joy and peace' (Romans 15:13). This flows from Christ. Israel had honey out of the rock. This honey of peace comes out of the rock, Christ. 'That in me you might have peace' (John 16:33). So filling is this peace that it sets the soul a-longing after heaven. This cluster of grapes quickens the appetite and pursuit after the full crop.

[3] God fills the hungry soul with bliss. Glory is a filling thing. 'When I awake I shall be satisfied with your image' (Psalm 17:15). When a Christian awakes out of the sleep of death — then he shall be satisfied, having the glorious beams of God's image shining upon him. Then shall the soul be filled to the brim! The glory of heaven is so sweet, that the soul shall still thirst — yet so infinite that it shall be filled. 'Those who drink of you, O Christ, being refreshed with sweet torrents, shall continue to thirst — yet they shall continue to be filled'.

What an encouragement is this to hunger after righteousness! Such shall be filled. God charges us to fill the hungry (Isaiah 58:10). He blames those who do not fill the hungry (Isaiah 32:6). And do we think he will be slack in that which he blames us for not doing? Oh come with hungerings after Christ and be assured of satisfaction! God keeps open house for hungry sinners. He invites his guests and bids them come without money (Isaiah 55:1, 2). God's nature inclines him, and his promise obliges him — to fill the hungry. Consider, why did Christ receive 'the Spirit without measure'? (John 3:34). It was not for himself. He was infinitely full before. But he was filled with the holy unction for this end — that he might distill his grace upon the hungry soul. Are you ignorant? Christ was filled with wisdom that he might teach you. Are you polluted? Christ was filled with grace that he might cleanse you. Shall not the soul then come to Christ who was filled on purpose to fill the hungry? We love to knock at a rich man's door. In our Father's house there is bread enough. Come with desire — and you shall go away with comfort! You shall have the virtues of Christ's blood, the influences of his Spirit, the communications of his love!

There are two objections made against this.

The carnal man's objection: *'I have hungered after righteousness — yet am not filled.'*

You say you hunger and are not satisfied? Perhaps God is not satisfied with your hunger. You have 'opened your mouth wide' (Psalm 81:10) — but have not 'opened your ear' (Psalm 49:4). When God has called you to family prayer and mortification of sin, you have, like the 'deaf adder', stopped your ear against God (Zechariah 7:11). No wonder then that you have not that comfortable filling as you desire. Though you have opened your mouth—you have stopped your ear. The child that will not hear his parent, is made to do penance by fasting.

Perhaps you thirst as much after a temptation, as after righteousness. At a sacrament you seem to be inflamed with desire after Christ—but the next temptation that comes either to drunkenness or lust—you imbibe the temptation. Satan but beckons to you—and you come. You open faster to the tempter—than to Christ! And do you wonder you are not filled with the fat things of God's house?

Perhaps you hunger more after the world than after righteousness. The young man in the gospel would have Christ—but the world lay nearer to his heart, than Christ. Hypocrites pant more after the dust of the earth (Amos 2:7) than the 'water of life'. Israel had no manna while their dough lasted. Such as feed immoderately upon the dough of earthly things, must not think to be filled with manna from heaven. If your money is your God—never think to receive another God in the sacrament.

The godly man's objection: '*I have had sincere desires after God—but am not filled*'

You may have a filling of grace—though not of comfort. If God does not fill you with gladness—yet with goodness (Psalm 107:9). Look into your heart and see the distillations of the Spirit. The dew may fall—though the honeycomb does not drop.

Wait a while, and you shall be filled. The gospel is a spiritual banquet. It feasts the soul with grace and comfort. None eat of this banquet, but such as wait at the table. 'In this mountain shall the Lord Almighty make unto all people a feast of fat things, a feast of wines on the lees well refined. And it shall be said in that day, Lo, this is our God, we have waited for him; we will be glad and rejoice in his salvation' (Isaiah 25:6,9). Spiritual mercies are not only worth desiring—but worth waiting for.

If God should not fill his people to satisfaction here on earth—yet they shall be filled in heaven. The vessels of their desires shall be filled as those water pots--'up to the brim!' (John 2:7)

A Discourse of Mercifulness

Blessed are the merciful, for they shall obtain mercy.

Matthew 5:7

These verses, like the stairs of Solomon's temple, cause our ascent to the holy of holies. We are now mounting up a step higher. 'Blessed are the merciful.' There was never more need to preach of mercifulness, than in these unmerciful times wherein we live. It is reported in the life of Chrysostom that he preached much on this subject of mercifulness, and for his much pressing Christians to mercy, he was called of many, 'the alms-preacher,' or 'the preacher for mercy'. Our times need many Chrysostoms.

'Blessed are the merciful'. Mercy stands both in the van and back end of the text. In the beginning of the text, it stands as a duty. In the end of the text it stands as a reward. The Hebrew word for 'godly' signifies 'merciful'. The more godly—the more merciful. The doctrine I shall gather out of the words, which will comprehend and bring in the whole, is this: That the merciful man is a blessed man.

Just so, there is a curse which hangs over the head of the unmerciful man. 'When his case is called for judgment, let him be pronounced guilty. Count his prayers as sins. Let his years be few; let his position be given to someone else. May his children become fatherless, and may his wife become a widow. May his children wander as beggars; may they be evicted from their ruined homes. May creditors seize his entire estate, and strangers take all he has earned. Let no one be kind to him; let no one pity his fatherless children. 'May all his offspring die.' (Psalm

109:6-9). Why, what is this crime? 'Because he refused all kindness to others' (verse 16). See what a large vial full of the plagues of God, is poured out upon the unmerciful man! So by the rule of contraries, the blessings of the Almighty crown and encompass the merciful man. 'The merciful man is a blessed man' (2 Samuel 22:26; Psalm 37:26; Psalm 41:1). For the illustrating this I shall show, first, what is meant by mercifulness; second, the several kinds of mercy.

1. *What is meant by mercifulness?* I answer, it is a melting disposition whereby we lay to heart the miseries of others and are ready on all occasions to be instrumental for their good.

How do mercy and love differ? In some things they agree, in some things they differ, like waters that may have two different spring-heads — but meet in the stream. Love and mercy differ thus: love is more extensive. The diocese that love walks and visits in, is larger. Mercy properly respects those who are miserable. Love is of a larger consideration. Love is like a friend who visits those who are well. Mercy is like a physician who visits only those who are sick. Again, love acts more out of affection. Mercy acts out of a principle of conscience. Mercy lends its hand to another. Love gives its heart to another. Thus they differ — but love and mercy agree in this, they are both ready to do good offices. Both of them have healing under their wings.

Whence does mercy spring? Its spring-head rises higher than nature. Mercy taken in its full latitude, proceeds from a work of grace in the heart. Naturally we are far from being merciful. The sinner is a bramble, not a fig tree yielding sweet fruit. It is the character and sign of a natural man to be 'unmerciful' (Romans 1:31). 'They made their hearts as hard as stone' (Zechariah 7:12). Their heart does not melt in mercy. Before conversion the sinner is compared to a wolf for his savageness (Matthew 7:15), to a lion for his fierceness (Isaiah 11:6), to a bee for his sting (Psalm 118:12), to an adder for his poison (Psalm 140:3). By nature we do not send forth oil — but poison; not the oil of mercifulness — but the poison of maliciousness.

Besides that inbred unmercifulness which is in us, there is something infused too by Satan. 'The prince of the air works in men' (Ephesians 2:2). He is a fierce spirit, therefore called 'the Red Dragon' (Revelation 12:3). And if he possesses men, then it is no wonder if they are implacable and without mercy. What mercy can be expected from hell? So that, if the heart is tuned into mercifulness, it is from the change that grace has made (Colossians 3:12). When the sun shines the ice melts. When the Sun of righteousness once shines with beams of grace upon the soul, then it melts in mercy and tenderness. You must first be a new man, before you can be a merciful man. You cannot help a member of Christ, until you yourself are a member of Christ.

2. The several kinds of mercy, or how many ways a man may be said to be merciful. Mercy is a fountain which runs in five streams. We must be merciful to the souls, names, estates, offences, needs of others.

We must be merciful to the souls of others. This is a spiritual alms. Indeed soul-mercy is the chief of mercies. The soul is the most precious thing; it is a vessel of honor; it is a bud of eternity; it is a sparkle lighted by the breath of God; it is a rich diamond set in a ring of clay. The soul has the blood of God to redeem it, the image of God to beautify it. It being therefore of so high a descent, sprung from the Ancient of days, that mercy which is shown to the soul must needs be the greatest. This soul-mercy to others, consists in four things.

1. In pitying them. 'If I weep,' says Augustine, 'for that body from which the soul is departed — how should I weep for that soul from which God is departed!' Had we seen that man in the gospel cutting himself with stones — it would have moved our pity (Mark 5:5). To see a sinner stabbing himself and having his hands imbrued in his own blood, should cause pity in our affections. Our eye should affect our heart. God was angry with Edom because he 'cast off all pity (Amos 1:11).

2. Soul-mercy is in advising and exhorting sinners. Tell them in what a sad condition they are, even 'in the gall of bitterness'. Show them their danger. They tread upon the banks of the bottomless pit. If death gives them a jog—they tumble in. And we must dip our words in honey; use all the mildness we can: 'Gently teach those who oppose the truth.' (2 Timothy 2:25). Fire melts; ointment mollifies. Words of love may melt hard hearts into repentance. This is soul-mercy. God made a law that, 'If you see the donkey of someone who hates you struggling beneath a heavy load, do not walk by. Instead, stop and offer to help.' (Exodus 23:5). Says Chrysostom, 'We should help a donkey which is struggling beneath a heavy load; and shall we not extend relief to those who are fallen under a worse burden of sin?'

3. Soul-mercy is in reproving refractory sinners. That is a cruel mercy—when we see men go on in sin and we let them alone. And there is a merciful cruelty—when we are sharp against men's sins and will not let them go to hell quietly. 'Do not hate your brother in your heart. Rebuke your neighbor frankly so you will not share in his guilt.' (Leviticus 19:17). Fond sentimentality is no better than cruelty. 'Rebuke them sharply', cuttingly (Titus 1:13). The surgeon cuts and lances the flesh—but it is in order to a cure. They are healing wounds. So by cutting reproof when we lance men's consciences and let out the blood of sin, we exercise spiritual surgery. This is showing mercy. 'Rescue others by snatching them from the fire' (Jude 23). If a man had fallen into the fire, though you did hurt him a little in pulling him out, he would be thankful and take it as a kindness. Some men, when we tell them of sin say, 'O, you are unloving!' No! it is showing mercy. If a man's house were on fire, and another should see it and not tell him of it for fear of waking him—would not this be cruelty? When we see others sleeping in their sin, and the fire of God's wrath ready to burn about to burn them up--and we are silent, is not this to be accessory to their damnation?

4. Soul-mercy is in praying for others. Prayer is the remedy used in a desperate case, and often it recovers the sick patient. 'The effectual fervent prayer of a righteous man avails much' (James 5:16). As the remedy cures the sick body, so prayer cures the sin-sick soul. There is a story of one who gave his soul to the devil, who was saved through the prayers of Luther. When 'Eutychus was overcome by sleep he fell down from the third story, and was picked up dead, Paul fell on him', that is, he effectually prayed over him and he prayed him alive (Acts 20:9-12). By sin the soul is fallen from a high loft, namely, a state of innocence. Now fervent prayer oftentimes fetches life into such a dead soul.

See what a blessed work the work of the ministry is! The preaching of the Word is nothing but showing mercy to souls. This is a mighty and glorious engine in the hand of the Lord Almighty for the beating down of the devil's strongholds. The ministry of the Word not only brings light with it—but eye-salve, anointing the eyes to see that light. It is a sin-killing and soul-quickening ordinance. It is the 'power of God to salvation'. What enemies are they to their own souls, who question the ministry! It is said that the people that live at the equator, curse the sun and are glad when the sun sets, because of its burning heat. Foolish sinners curse the sun-rising of the ministry and are offended at the light of it—because it comes near their sins and scorches their consciences, though in the end it saves their souls!

It reproves those who have no mercy to souls: evil magistrates; evil ministers.

Evil magistrates who either 'take away the key of knowledge' (Luke 11:52), or give a toleration to wickedness, allowing men to sin by a licence. The meaning of toleration is this, that if men will themselves to hell—none shall stop them. Is not nature enough poisoned? Do not men sin fast enough—but must have such political engines as serve them up higher in wickedness? Must they have such favorable gales from the breath of magistrates, as serve to carry them full sail to the devil? This is far from soul-mercy. What a heavy reckoning will these magistrates have in the day of the Lord!

Evil ministers are such as have no affections to the souls of their people. They do not pity them or pray for them. They seek not their souls — but only their money. They preach not for love — but filthy lucre. Their care is more for tithes, than souls. How can they be called spiritual fathers, who are without affections? These are mercenaries, not ministers.

Such men feed not the souls of their people with solid truths. When Christ sent out his apostles, he gave them their text, and told them what they must preach, 'Preach, saying the kingdom of heaven is at hand' (Matthew 10:7). 'Upon which place,' says Luther, 'the ministers of Christ must preach things which pertain to the kingdom of God — pardon of sin, sanctification, living by faith.' They are unmerciful ministers who, instead of breaking the bread of life, fill their people's heads with airy speculations and notions; who tickle the fancy — rather than touch the conscience; and give precious souls music — rather than food.

Some there are who darken knowledge with words, and preach as if they were speaking in 'an unknown tongue'. Some ministers love to soar aloft like the eagle and fly above their people's capacities, endeavoring rather to be admired than understood. It is unmercifulness to souls to preach so as not to be understood. Ministers should be stars to give light, not clouds to obscure the truth. Paul was learned — yet plain. Clearness and perspicuity is the grace of speech. It is cruelty to souls when we go about to make easy things hard. This many are guilty of in our age, who go into the pulpit only to tie knots, and think it their glory to amuse the people. This savors more of pride, than mercifulness.

Such there are, too, as see others going on in sin but do not tell them of it. When men declare their sin as Sodom, it is the minister's duty to 'lift up his voice like a trumpet and show the house of Jacob their sin' (Isaiah 58:1). Zeal in the ministry is as proper as fire on the altar. He who lets another sin and holds his peace, is a man-slayer. That sentinel deserves death, who sees the enemy approaching, and gives not warning (Ezekiel 3:20).

Some ministers poison souls with error. How dangerous is the leprosy of the head! A frenzy is worse than a fever. What shall we say to such ministers as give poison to their people in a golden cup? Are not these unmerciful? Others there are (unworthy the name of ministers), itineraries, the devil's ambassadors, who ride up and down, and with Satan compass the earth to deceive and devour souls! It would pity one's heart to see poor unstable creatures misled by crude and illiterate men, who diet the people with blasphemy and nonsense, and make them fitter for bedlam than the New Jerusalem. All these are unmerciful to souls.

Let me beseech all who fear God to show soul-mercy. Strengthen the weak; reduce the wandering; raise up those who are fallen. 'He which converts the sinner from the error of his way shall save a soul from death' (James 5:20).

We must be merciful to the names of others. A good name is one of the greatest blessings upon earth. No chain of pearl so adorns, as this. This being so, we ought to be very merciful to the reputations of others. They are to be accounted in a high degree unmerciful, who make no conscience of taking away the good names of their brethren. Their throats are open sepulchers, to bury the fame and renown of men (Romans 3:13). It is a great cruelty to murder a man in his name. 'The keepers of the walls took away my veil from me' (Canticles 5:7). Some expositors interpret it of her honor and fame which covered her, as a beautiful veil. The ground of this unmercifulness to names is:

1. Pride. Pride is such a thing as cannot endure to be out-shined. Pride cannot endure to see itself exceeded in abilities and eminency; therefore it will behead another in his good name —

that he may appear something lower. The proud man will be pulling down of others in their reputation, and so by their eclipse—he thinks he shall shine the brighter. The breath of a proud man causes a blast or mildew, upon the reputations of others.

2. Envy (1 Peter 2:1). An envious man maligns the dignity of another, therefore seeks to harm him in his name. Piety teaches us to rejoice in the esteem and fame of others. 'I thank my God for you all, that your faith is spoken of throughout the whole world' (Romans 1:8). Envy, consulting with the devil, fetches fire from hell to blow up the good name of another.

In how many ways may we be unmerciful to the names of others? Diverse ways.

First, by slander, a sin forbidden. 'You shall not raise a false report' (Exodus 23:1). Eminency is commonly blasted by slander. 'They sharpen their tongues like swords and aim their words like deadly arrows' (Psalm 64:3). The tongue of a slanderer shoots out words to wound the fame of another and make it bleed to death. The saints of God in all ages have met with unmerciful men who have fathered things upon them, which they have not been guilty of. Surius, the Jesuit, reported of Luther that he learned his divinity of the Devil and that he died drunk; but Melanchthon, who wrote his life, affirms that he died in a most pious holy manner and made a most excellent prayer before his death. It was David's complaint, 'They laid to my charge things which I knew not' (Psalm 35:11).

The Greek word for 'devil' signifies slanderer (1 Timothy 3:11). 'Not slanderers'—in the Greek it is 'not devils'. Some think that it is no great maker to defame and traduce another—but know, this is to act the part of a devil. O how many unmerciful men are there, who indeed pass for Christians—but play the devil in venting their lies and calumnies! Wicked men in Scripture are called 'dogs' (Psalm 22:16). Slanderers are not like those dogs which licked Lazarus' sores to heal them—but like the dogs which ate Jezebel. They rend and tear the precious names of men. Valentinian the Emperor decreed that he who was openly convicted of this crime of slander should die for it.

Second, we are unmerciful to the names of others when we receive a slander, and then report what we hear. 'You shall not go up and down as a talebearer among your people' (Leviticus 19:16). A good man is one who 'has no slander on his tongue, who does his neighbor no wrong and casts no slur on his fellowman' (Psalm 15:3). We must not only not raise a false report—but not take it up. To divulge a report before we speak with the party and know the truth of it, is unmercifulness and sin. The same word in the Hebrew, 'to raise a slander', signifies to receive it (Exodus 23:1). The receiver is even as bad as the thief. It is well if none of us have (in this sense) received stolen goods. When others have stolen away the good names of their brethren, have not we received these stolen goods? There would not be so many to broach false rumors—but that they see this liquor pleases other men's taste.

Third, we deal unmercifully with the names of others when we diminish from their just worth and dignity; when we make more of their infirmities and less of their virtues. 'Speak not evil one of another' (James 4:11). I have read a story of one, Idor, that he was never heard to speak evil of any man. Augustine could not endure that any should eclipse and lessen the fame of others, therefore he wrote those two verses upon his table:

> *'Whoever loves another's name to blast,*
>
> *This table's not for him; so let him fast.'*

Wicked men are still paring off the credit of their neighbors, and they make thick parings. They pare off all that is good. Nothing is left but the core, something which may tend to their disparagement. Unmerciful men know how to boil a quart to a pint. They have a devilish art so to extenuate and lessen the merit of others, that it is even boiled away to nothing. Some, though they have not the power of creation—yet they have the power of annihilation. They can sooner annihilate the good which is in others, than imitate it.

Fourth, we are unmerciful to the names of others when we know them to be calumniated yet do not vindicate them. A man may sometimes as well wrong another by silence, as slander. He who is merciful to his brother is an advocate to plead in his behalf when he is injuriously traduced. When the apostles, who were filled with the wine of the Spirit, were charged with drunkenness, Peter vindicated them openly (Acts 2:15). A merciful man will take the dead fly out of the box of ointment.

Fifth, they are in a high degree unmerciful to the names of others who bear false witness against them (Psalm 27:12). 'Put not your hand with the wicked to be a false witness' (Exodus 23:1). 'Putting the hand' is taking an oath falsely, as when a man puts his hand upon the book and swears to a lie. This 'false-witness' is a two-edged sword. The party forsworn wounds another's name and his own soul. A false witness is compared to a maul or hammer (Proverbs 25:18). It is true in this sense, because he is hardened in impudence he blushes at nothing and in unmercifulness. There is no softness in a maul or hammer, nor is there any mercy to be found in a false witness. In all these ways men are unmerciful to the names of others.

Let me persuade all Christians, as they make conscience of religion, so to show mercy to the names of others. Be very watchful and tender of men's good name.

Consider what a sin it is to defame any man. 'Laying aside all envy and evil speakings' (Titus 3:2; 1. Peter 2:1). Envy and evil speaking are put together: 'laying aside', 'putting away', as a man would put away a thing from him with indignation; as Paul shook off the viper (Acts 28:5).

Consider also the injuriousness of it. You, who take away the good name of another, wound him in that which is most dear to him. Better take away a man's life—than his good name. By eclipsing his name, you bury him alive. It is an irreparable injury; something will remain. A wound in the name is like a flaw in a diamond, which will never die out. No physician can heal the wounds of the tongue!

God will require it at men's hands. If idle words must be accountable for, shall not reproachful slanders? God will make inquisition one day as well for names, as for blood. Let all this persuade to caution and circumspection. You would be opposed to steal the goods of others. A man's name is of more worth, and he who takes away the good name of another sins more than if he had taken the the wares out of his shop!

Especially take heed of wounding the names of the godly. God has set a crown of honor on their head, and will you take it off? 'Why then were you not afraid to speak against my servant Moses?' (Numbers 12:8). To defame the saints is no less than the defaming God himself, they having his picture drawn upon them and being members of Christ. Oh think how ill Christ will take this at your hand in the day of reckoning! It was under the old law a sin to violate a virgin, and what is it to calumniate Christ's spouse? Are the names of the saints written in heaven, and will you blot them out upon earth? Be merciful to the names of others.

Be merciful to the estates of others. If a man is your debtor and providence has frowned upon him, so that he has not the means to pay, do not crush him when he is sinking—but remit something of the rigor of the law. 'Blessed are the merciful'. The wicked are compared to beasts of prey, which live upon rapine and robbery. They do not care what harm they do. 'Their mouths are full of cursing, lies, and threats. Trouble and evil are on the tips of their tongues. They lurk in dark alleys, murdering the innocent who pass by. They are always searching for some helpless victim. Like lions they crouch silently, waiting to pounce on the helpless. Like hunters they capture their victims and drag them away in nets.' (Psalm 10:7-9).

It is not justice but cruelty, when others lie at our mercy, to be like that hardhearted creditor in the gospel who took his debtor by the throat saying, 'Pay me what you owe!' (Matthew 18:28). God made a law, 'No man shall take the nether or the upper millstone, for the owner uses it to make a living' (Deuteronomy 24:6). If a man had lent another money, he must not take both his millstones for a pawn. He must show mercy and leave the man something to get a livelihood with. We should in this imitate God who in the midst of anger remembers mercy. God does not take the extremity of the law upon us — but when we have nothing to pay, if we confess the debt, he freely forgives (Proverbs 28:13; Matthew 18:27).

Not but that we may justly seek what is our own — but if others are brought low and plead for mercy, we ought in conscience to remit something of the debt. 'Blessed are the merciful.'

We must be merciful to the offences of others. Be ready to show mercy to those who have injured you. Thus Stephen the proto-martyr, 'He kneeled down and cried with a loud voice, Lord, lay not this sin to their charge' (Acts 7:60). When he prayed for himself he stood — but when he came to pray for his enemies, he kneeled down, to show, says Bernard, his earnestness in prayer and how greatly he desired that God would forgive them. This is a rare kind of mercy. 'It is a man's glory to pass over a transgression' (Proverbs 19:11). Mercy in forgiving injuries, as it is the touchstone, so the crown of Christianity. Cranmer was of a merciful disposition. If any who had wronged him came to ask a favor from him, he would do all that lay in his power for him, insomuch that it grew to a proverb: 'Do Cranmer an injury and he will be your friend as long as he lives.' To 'overcome evil with good', and answer malice with mercy is truly heroic, and renders piety glorious in the eyes of all. But I leave this and proceed.

We must be merciful to the needs of others. This the text chiefly intends. A good man does not, like the snake, twist within himself. His motion is direct, not circular. He is ever merciful and lends (Psalm 37:26). This merciful charity to the needs of others stands in three things.

1. A judicious consideration. 'Blessed is he who considers the poor' (Psalm 41:1); and you must consider these things.

It might have been your own case. You yourselves might have stood in need of another's charity — and then how welcome and refreshing would those streams have been to you!

Consider how sad a condition poverty is. Though Chrysostom calls poverty the highway to heaven — yet he who walks this road will go weeping there. Consider the poor; behold their tears, their sighs, their dying groans. Look upon the deep furrows made in their faces, and consider if there is not reason why you should scatter your seed of mercy in these furrows. 'For a cloak he has a tattered vesture, for a couch a stone.' 'You have fed us with sorrow and made us drink tears by the bucketful' (Psalm 80:5). Like Jacob, in a windy night he has the clouds for his canopy and a stone for his pillow.

Nay further, consider that oftentimes poverty becomes not only a cross — but a snare. It exposes to much evil, which made Agur pray, 'Give me not poverty' (Proverbs 30:8). Need puts men upon sinful courses. The poor will venture their souls for money, which is like throwing diamonds into the sea. If the rich would wisely consider this, their alms might prevent much sin.

Consider why the wise God has allowed an inequality in the world. It is for this very reason — because he would have mercy exercised. If all were rich, there were no need of alms, nor could the merciful man have been so well known. If he who traveled to Jericho had not been wounded and left half dead, the Good Samaritan who poured oil and wine into his wounds had not been known.

Consider how quickly the balance of providence may turn. We ourselves may be brought to poverty and then it will be no small comfort to us, that we relieved others while we were in a capacity to do it. 'Give a portion to seven or even to eight, for you don't know what disaster may happen on earth' (Ecclesiastes 11:2). We cannot promise ourselves always halcyon days. God alone knows how soon many of us may change our pasture. The cup which now runs over with wine—may soon be filled with the waters of Marah. 'I went out full—and the Lord has brought me home again empty' (Ruth 1:21). How many have we seen invested with great possessions, who have suddenly brought their manor to a morsel?

So that it is wisdom to consider the needs of others. Remember how soon the scene may alter. We may be put in the poor's dress and, if adversity comes, it will be no trouble of mind to us, to think that while we had an estate we laid it out upon Christ's indigent members. This is the first thing in mercifulness, a judicious consideration

2. A tender commiseration. 'If you draw out your soul to the hungry' (Isaiah 58:10). Bounty begins in pity. Christ first 'had compassion on the multitude'. Then he wrought a miracle to feed them (Matthew 15:32). Charity which lacks compassion, is brutish. The brute creatures can relieve us in many ways—but cannot pity us. It is a kind of cruelty (says Quintilian) to feed one in need—and not to sympathize with him. True religion begets tenderness. As it melts the heart in tears of contrition towards God, so in affections of compassion towards others. 'My heart shall sound as a harp' (Isaiah 16:11). Likewise, when our hearts of pity sound, then our alms make sweet music in the ears of God.

3. Mercifulness consists in a liberal contribution. 'If there is a poor man within your gates, you shall open your hand wide unto him' (Deuteronomy 15:7, 8). The Hebrew word to 'disperse' (Psalm 112:9) signifies 'a largeness of bounty'. It must be like water, which overflows the banks. 'Not a meager dispersing of a mere trifle'. If God has enriched men with estates and made 'his candle (as Job says) to shine upon their tabernacle', they must not encircle and engross all to themselves, but be as the moon which, having received its light from the sun, lets it shine to the world. The ancients made oil to be the emblem of charity. The golden oil of mercy must, like Aaron's oil, run down upon the poor which are the lower skirts of the garment. This liberal disbursement to the needs and necessities of others—God commands, and grace compels.

God Commands. There is an express statute law, 'If one of your countrymen becomes poor and is unable to support himself among you, help him' (Leviticus 25:35). The Hebrew word is 'strengthen him'; put under him a silver crutch when he is falling. It is worth our observation what great care God took of the poor, besides what was given them privately. God made many laws for the public and visible relief of the poor. 'The seventh year you shall let the land rest and lie still, that the poor of the people may eat' (Exodus 23:11). God's intention in his law was that the poor should be liberally provided for. They might freely eat of anything which grew of itself this seventh year, whether of herbs, vines or olive trees. If it be asked how the poor could live only on these fruits, there being (as it is probable) no grain growing then, for answer Cajetan is of opinion that they lived by selling these fruits and, so converting them into money, lived upon the price of the fruits.

There is another law made: 'And when you reap the harvest of your land, you shall not wholly reap the corners of your field, neither shall you gather the gleanings of your harvest' (Leviticus 19:9). See how God indulged the poor. Some corners of the field were for the poor's sake to be left uncut, and when the owners reaped they must not go too near the earth with their sickle. The Vulgate Latin reads, 'You shall not shear to the very ground'. Something like an after-crop must be left. 'The shorter ears of corn and such as lay bending to the ground, were to be reserved for the poor,' says Tostatus.

And God made another law in favor of the poor. 'At the end of every third year bring the tithe of all your crops and store it in the nearest town. Give it to the Levites, who have no inheritance among you, as well as to the foreigners living among you, the orphans, and the widows in your towns, so they can eat and be satisfied. Then the Lord your God will bless you in all your work.' (Deuteronomy 14:28, 29). The Hebrews write that every third year, besides the first tithe given to Levi which was called the perpetual tithe (Numbers 18:21), the Jews set apart another tithe of their increase for the use of the widows and orphans, and that was called 'the tithe of the poor'. Besides, at the Jews' solemn festivals, the poor were to have a share (Deuteronomy 16:11).

And as relieving the needy was commanded under the law, so it stands in force under the gospel. 'Command those who are rich in this present world, to do good, to be rich in good deeds, and to be generous and willing to share.' (1 Timothy 6:17, 18). It is not only a counsel but a command, and non-attendance to it runs men into a gospel offense. Thus we have seen the mind of God in this particular of charity. Let all good Christians comment upon it in their practice. What benefit is there of gold — while it is locked up in the mine? And what is it the better to have a great estate — if it is so hoarded up as never to see the light?

As God commands, so grace compels to works of mercy and beneficence. 'The love of Christ constrains' (2 Corinthians 5:14). Grace comes with majesty upon the heart. Grace does not lie as a sleepy habit in the soul — but will put forth itself in vigorous and glorious actings. Grace can no more be concealed, than fire. Like new wine it will have vent. Grace does not lie in the heart as a stone in the earth — but as seed in the earth. It will spring up into good works.

The Church of Rome lays upon us this aspersion — that we are against good works. Indeed we plead not for the merit of them — but we are for the use of them. 'Our people must also learn to devote themselves to good works' (Titus 3:14). We preach that they are needful both as they are enforced by the precept, and as they are needful for the general good of men. We read that the angels had wings, and hands under their wings (Ezekiel 1:8). It may be emblematic of this truth. Christians must not only have the wings of faith to fly — but hands under their wings to work the works of mercy.

'This saying is trustworthy. I want you to insist on these things, so that those who have believed God might be careful to devote themselves to good works.' (Titus 3:8). The lamp of faith must be filled with the oil of charity. Faith alone justifies — but justifying faith is not alone. You may as well separate weight from lead, or heat from fire, as works from faith. Good works, though they are not the causes of salvation — yet they are evidences of salvation. Though they are not the foundation — yet they are the superstructure. Faith must not be built upon works — but works must be built upon faith. 'You are married to Christ — that we should bring forth fruit unto God' (Romans 7:4). Faith is the grace which marries Christ, and good works are the children which faith bears. For the vindication of the doctrine of our Church, and in honor of good works, I shall lay down four aphorisms.

1. Works are distinct from faith. It is vain to imagine that works are included in faith, as the diamond is enclosed in the ring. No! they are distinct, as the sap in the vine is different from the clusters of fruit which grow upon it.

2. Works are the touchstone of faith. 'Show me your faith by your works' (James 2:18). Works are faith's letters of credence to show. 'If,' says Bernard, 'you see a man full of good works, then by the rule of charity you are not to doubt his faith.' We judge the health of the body by the pulse where the blood stirs and operates. O Christian, judge of the health of your faith by the pulse of mercy and charitableness. It is with faith as with a deed in law. To make a deed valid, there are three things requisite — the writing, the seal, the witnesses. So for the trial and

confirmation of faith there must be these three things the writing, the Word of God; the seal, the Spirit of God; the witnesses, good works. Bring your faith to this Scripture touchstone. Faith justifies works; works testify faith.

3. Works honor faith. These fruits adorn the 'trees of righteousness'. 'Let the liberality of your hand' (says Clemens Alexandrinus) 'be the ornament of your faith, and wear it as a holy bracelet about your wrists.' 'I served as eyes for the blind and feet for the lame. I was a father to the poor' (Job 29:14-15). While Job was the poor's benefactor and advocate, this was the ensign of his honor; it clothed him as a robe and crowned him as a diadem. This is that which takes off the odium and obloquy — and makes others speak well of piety — when they see good works as handmaids waiting upon this queen — faith.

4. Good works are in some sense more excellent than faith; in two respects:

Because they are of a more noble diffusive nature. Though faith is more needful for ourselves — yet good works are more beneficial to others. Faith is a receptive grace. It is all for self-interest. It moves within its own sphere. Works are for the good of others, and it is a more blessed thing to give, than to receive.

Good works are more visible and conspicuous than faith. Faith is a more hidden grace. It may lie hidden in the heart and not be seen — but when works are joined with it, now it shines forth in its native beauty. Though a garden is ever so decked with flowers — yet they are not seen until the light comes. So the heart of a Christian may be enriched with faith — but it is like a flower in the night. It is not seen until works come. When this light shines before men, then faith appears in its orient colors.

If this be the effigy of a good man, that he is of a merciful disposition, then it sharply reproves those who are far from this temper. Their hearts are like the scales of the Leviathan, 'shut up together as with a close seal' (Job 41:15). They move only within their own circle — but do not help the necessities of others. They have a flourishing estate — but they have a withered hand and cannot stretch it out to good uses. They have all as for themselves, not for Christ. These are akin to the churl Nabal. 'Shall I take my bread and my water and give it unto men, whom I know not whence they come?' (1 Samuel 25:11). It was said of the emperor Pertinax, that he had a large empire — but a narrow scanty heart.

There was a temple at Athens which was called the Temple of Mercy. It was dedicated to charitable uses; and it was the greatest reproach to upbraid one with this — that he had never been in the Temple of Mercy. It is the greatest disgrace to a Christian to be unmerciful. Covetous men, while they enrich themselves, debase themselves, setting up a monopoly and committing idolatry with Mammon. In the time of pestilence, it is sad to have your houses shut up — but it is worse to have your hearts shut up. How miserable it is — to have a sea of sin and not a drop of mercy! Covetous hearts, like the Leviathan, are 'firm as a stone' (Job 41:24). One may as well extract oil out of a flint, as the golden oil of charity out of their flinty hearts. They say that coldness of the heart, is a presage of death. When men's affections to works of mercy are frozen, this coldness of heart is ominous and sadly portends that they are dead in sin! We read in the law that the shellfish was accounted unclean. This might probably be one reason, because its meat was enclosed in the shell and it was hard to get to. They are to be reckoned among the unclean who enclose all their estate within the shell of their own cabinet and will not let others be the better for it. How many have lost their souls — by being so selfish!

There are some who perhaps will give the poor good words — and that is all. 'Suppose a brother or sister is without clothes and daily food. If one of you says to him, 'Go, I wish you well; keep warm and well fed,' but does nothing about his physical needs, what good is it?' (James 2:15).

Good words are but a cold kind of charity. The poor cannot live upon this air. Let your words be as smooth as oil, they will not heal the wounded. Let them drop as the honeycomb, they will not feed the hungry. 'Though I speak with the tongues of angels and have not charity, I would only be making meaningless noise like a loud gong or a clanging cymbal' (1 Corinthians 13:1). It is better to be charitable as a saint — than eloquent as an angel. Such as are cruel to the poor, let me tell you — you unchristian yourselves! Unmercifulness is the sin of the heathen (Romans 1:31). When you put off the affections of mercy — you put off the badge of Christianity. Ambrose says that when we do not relieve one whom we see ready to perish with hunger, we are guilty of his death. If this rule holds true, there are more guilty of the breach of the sixth commandment than we are aware of.

James speaks a sad word: 'For he shall have judgment without mercy — who has showed no mercy' (James 2:13). How do they think to find mercy from Christ, who never showed mercy to Christ in his members? Dives denied Lazarus a crumb of bread — and Dives was denied a drop of water. At the last day behold the sinner's indictment, 'I was hungry, and you didn't feed me. I was thirsty, and you didn't give me anything to drink. I was a stranger, and you didn't invite me into your home. I was naked, and you gave me no clothing. I was sick and in prison, and you didn't visit me.' (Matthew 25:42). Christ does not say, 'You took away my food' — but 'You didn't feed me; you did not feed my members'. Then follows the sentence, 'Depart from Me, you who are cursed, into the eternal fire prepared for the Devil and his angels!' When Christ's poor come to your doors and you bid them depart from you, the time may come when you shall knock at heaven's gate, and Christ will say, 'Depart from Me, you who are cursed, into the eternal fire prepared for the Devil and his angels!'

In short, covetousness is a foolish sin. God gave the rich man in the gospel that appellation, 'You fool!' (Luke 12:20). The covetous man does not enjoy what he possesses. He embitters his own life. He troubles himself with care either how to get, or how to increase, or how to secure an estate. And what is the result? Often as a just reward of sordid penuriousness, God blasts and withers him in his outward estate. That saying of Gregory Nazianzen is to be seriously weighed: 'God many times lets the thief take away, and the moth consume — that which is unmercifully withheld from the poor.'

Before I leave this matter, I am sorry that any who profess Christianity should be impeached as guilty of this sin of covetousness and unmercifulness. Sure I am that God's elect put on 'heartfelt compassion' (Colossians 3:12). I tell you, that devout misers are the reproach of Christianity. They are blemishes and spots in the face of true religion. They report that in India there is a creature having four feet and wings, and a bill like an eagle. It is hard whether to rank him among the beasts or the birds. So I may say of penurious professors — they have the wings of profession by which they seem to fly to heaven — but the feet of beasts, walking on earth and even licking the dust! It is hard where to rank these, whether among the godly or the wicked. Oh take heed that, seeing your religion will not destroy your covetousness, at last your covetousness does not destroy your religion! One tells a story of the hedgehog which came to the cony-burrows in stormy weather and desired harbor, promising that he would be a quiet guest — but when once he had gotten entertainment, he set up his prickles and never left until he had thrust the poor conies out of their burrows. So covetousness, though it has many fair pleas to insinuate and wind itself into the heart — yet as soon as you have let it in, this thorn will never leave pricking until it has choked all good beginnings and thrust all piety out of your hearts.

I proceed next to the exhortation to beseech all Christians to put on 'heartfelt compassion'. Be ready to relieve the miseries and necessities of others. Ambrose calls charity, the sum of

Christianity, and the apostle makes it the very definition of true religion. 'Pure and undefiled religion before our God and Father is this: to look after orphans and widows in their distress' (James 1:27).

The Hebrew word for 'poor' signifies 'one who is empty' or 'drawn dry'. So the poor are exhausted of their strength, beauty, substance; like ponds they are dried up. Therefore let them be filled again with the silver streams of charity. The poor are as it were in the grave. The comfort of their life is buried. Oh Christians, help with your merciful hands to raise them out of the sepulcher! God 'sends his springs into the valleys' (Psalm 104:10). Let the springs of your liberality run among the valleys of poverty. Your sweetest and most gracious influence should fall upon the the needy. What is all your seeming devotion, without bounty and mercifulness? 'I have known many,' says Basil, 'pray and fast—but will not relieve those who are in distress. They are for a zeal which will put them to no expense. What are they the better for all their seeming virtue?'

We read that the incense was to be laid upon the fire (Leviticus 16:13). The flame of devotion must be perfumed with the incense of charity. Aaron was to have a bell and a pomegranate. The pomegranate, as some of the learned observe, was a symbol of good works. 'They lack the pomegranate' (says Gregory Nazianzen) 'who have no good works.' The wise men not only bowed the knee to Christ—but presented him with gold, myrrh and frankincense (Matthew 2:11). Pretenses of zeal are insufficient. We must not only worship Christ—but bestow something upon his members. This is to present Christ with gold and frankincense. Isaac would not bless Jacob by the voice—but he feels his hands, and supposing them to be Esau's hands, he blessed him. God will not bless men by their voice, their loud prayers, their devout discourses—but if he feels Esau's hands, if their hands have wrought good works, then he blesses them.

Let me exhort you therefore to deeds of mercy. Let your fingers drop with the myrrh of liberality. Sow your golden seed. Remember that excellent saying of Augustine, 'Give those things to the poor which you cannot keep—that you may receive those things which you cannot lose.' There are many occasions of exercising your mercifulness. Hear the orphans' cry; pity the widows' tears. Some need employment. It would do well to set their wheel a-going. Others are to old or sick to work—be as eyes to the blind and feet to the lame. In some cases whole families are sinking—if some merciful hand does not help to shore them up! Before I press arguments to liberality and munificence, there are three objections which lie in the way, which I shall endeavor to remove:

1. We may give and so in time come ourselves to need. Let Basil answer this. 'Wells, which have their water drawn, spring ever more freely.' 'The liberal soul shall be made fat' (Proverbs 11:25). There is nothing lost by relieving the needy. An estate may be imparted—yet not impaired. The flowers yield honey to the bee—yet do not hurt their own fruit. When the candle of prosperity shines upon us, we may light our neighbor who is in the dark, and have never the less light ourselves. Whatever is disbursed to pious uses, God brings it back to us some other way. As the loaves in breaking multiplied—or as the widow's oil increased by pouring out (1 Kings 17:10).

2. I cannot do so much as others—erect churches, build hospitals, augment libraries, maintain scholars at the university.

If you cannot do so much—yet do something. Let there be much goodwill, though there is not much wealth to go with it. The widow's two mites cast into the treasury were accepted (Luke 21:14). God (as Chrysostom observes) looked not at the smallest of her gift—but at the largeness of her heart. In the law, he who could not bring a lamb for an offering, if he brought but two turtledoves, it sufficed. We read that the people brought 'gold and silver, and goats' hair, to the building of the tabernacle' (Exodus 35:22-24); on which place (says Origen), 'I desire, Lord, to bring something to the building of your temple, if not gold to make the mercy-seat, if not silk to make the curtains—yet a little goats' hair, that I may not be found in the number of those who have brought nothing to your temple'.

3. But I do not have anything to bestow upon the necessities of others. Have you anything to bestow upon your lusts? Have you money to feed your pride, your Epicurianism? And can you find nothing to relieve the poor members of Christ?

Admit this excuse to be real, that you do not have such an estate; yet you may do something wherein you may express your mercy to the poor. You may sympathize with them, pray for them, speak a word of comfort to them. 'Speak you comfortably to Jerusalem' (Isaiah 40:2). If you can give them no gold, you may speak a word in season which may be as 'apples of gold in pictures of silver'. Nay more, you may be helpful to the poor in stirring up others who have estates to relieve them. As it is with the wind, if a man be hungry the wind will not fill him— but it can blow the sails of the mill and make it grind grain for the use of man. So though you do not have an estate yourself to help him who is in need—yet you may stir up others to help him. You may blow the sails of their compassion, causing them to show mercy, and so you may help your brother by a proxy.

Having answered these objections let me now pursue the exhortation to mercifulness. I shall lay down several arguments which I desire may be weighed in the balance of reason and conscience.

1. To be diffusively good is the great end of our creation. 'Created in Christ Jesus unto good works' (Ephesians 2:10). Every creature answers the end of its creation. The star shines, the bird sings, the plant bears fruit; the end of life is service. He who does not answer his end in respect of usefulness, cannot enjoy his end in respect of happiness. Many have been long in the world— but have not lived. They have done no good: 'a useless weight of earth'. A useless person serves for nothing but to 'cumber the ground'. And because he is barren in figs—he shall be fruitful in curses (Hebrews 6:8).

2. By mercifulness we resemble God who is a God of mercy. He is said to 'delight in mercy' (Micah 7:18). 'His tender mercies are over all his works, (Psalm 145:9). He gives good for evil, like the clouds which receive ill vapors from us—but return them to us again in sweet showers. There is not a creature which lives, but tastes of the mercies of God. Every bird sings hymns of praise to God for his bounty—but men and angels in a more particular manner taste the cream and quintessence of God's mercies.

What temporal mercies have you received! Every time you draw your breath you suck in mercy. Every bit of bread you eat, the hand of mercy carves it to you. You never drink but in a golden cup of mercy.

What spiritual mercies has God enriched some of you with! Pardoning, adopting, saving mercy! The picture of God's mercy can never be drawn to the full. You cannot take the breadth of his mercy, for it is infinite, nor the height of it, for it 'reaches above the clouds', nor the length of it, for it is 'from everlasting to everlasting' (Psalm 103:17). The works of mercy are the glory of the Godhead. Moses prays, 'Lord, show me your glory' (Exodus 33:18). Says God, 'I will make all my goodness to pass before you' (verse 19). God accounts himself most glorious in the shining robes of his mercy. Now by works of mercy we resemble the God of mercy. We are bid to draw our lines according to this copy. 'Be you merciful—as your Father also is merciful' (Luke 6:36).

3. Alms are a sacrifice to God. 'Do good and to share with others, for with such sacrifices God is pleased' (Hebrews 13:16). When you are distributing to the poor — it is as if you were praying, as if you were worshiping God. There are two sorts of sacrifices; expiatory — the sacrifice of Christ's blood; and thanksgiving — the sacrifice of alms. This (says holy Greenham) is more acceptable to God than any other sacrifice. The angel said to Cornelius, Your acts of charity have come up as a memorial offering before God' (Acts 10:4). The backs of the poor, are the altar on which this sacrifice is to be offered.

4. We ourselves live upon alms. Other creatures liberally contribute to our necessities. The sun does not have its light for itself but for us; it enriches us with its golden beams. The earth brings us a fruitful crop, and to show how joyful a mother she is in bringing forth, the psalmist says 'The meadows are clothed with flocks of sheep, and the valleys are carpeted with grain. They all shout and sing for joy!' (Psalm 65:13). One creature gives us wool, another oil, another silk. We are glad to go a-begging to the creation. Shall every creature be for the good of man — and man only be for himself? How absurd and irrational is this!

5. We are to extend our liberality by virtue of a membership. 'I want you to share your food with the hungry and to welcome poor wanderers into your homes. Give clothes to those who need them, and do not hide from relatives who need your help.' (Isaiah 50:7). The poor are 'of the same clay'. The members by a law of equity and sympathy contribute one to another. The eye conveys light to the body, the heart blood, the head spirits. That is a dead member in the body which does not communicate to the rest. Thus it is in the body politic. Let no man think it is too far below him to mind the needs and necessities of others. That hand should be cut off, which disdains to pluck a thorn out of the foot. It is spoken in the honor of that renowned princess, the Empress of Theodosius the Great, that she herself visited the sick and prepared relief for them with her own imperial hands.

6. We are not lords of an estate — but stewards, and how soon may we hear the word, 'Give an account of your stewardship, for you may be no longer steward!' (Luke 16:2). An estate is a talent to trade with. It is as dangerous to hide our talent — as to waste it (Matthew 25:25, 30). If the covetous man keeps his gold too long, it will begin to rust, and the rust will witness against him (James 5:3).

7. The examples of others who have been renowned for acts of mercy and munificence.

Our Lord Christ is a great example of charity, he was not more full of merit, than bounty. Trajan the Emperor rent off a piece of his own robe to wrap his soldiers' wounds. Christ did more. He rent his flesh; He made a medicine of his body and blood to heal us. 'By his stripes we are healed' (Isaiah 53:5). Here was a pattern of charity without a parallel.

The Jews are noted in this kind. It is a rabbinic observation that those who live devoutly among the Jews distribute a tenth part of their estate among the poor, and they give so freely (says Philo the Jew) as if by giving they hope to receive some great gratuity. Now if the Jews are so devoted to works of mercy, who live without Messiah, shall not we much more profess our faith in the blessed Messiah!

Let me tell you of some heathen. I have read of Titus Vespasian, he was so inured to works of mercy that remembering he had given nothing that day, cried out, 'I have lost a day'. It is reported of some of the Turks that they have servants whom they employ on purpose to enquire what poor they have and they send relief to them. And the Turks have a saying in their Koran, that if men knew what a blessed thing it were to distribute alms, rather than spare, they would give some of their own flesh to relieve the poor. And shall not a Christian's creed be better than a Turk's Koran?

Let all this persuade to works of mercy. Believe me, it is a royal deed to support the fallen.

When poor indigent creatures like Moses are laid in the ark of bulrushes weeping and ready to sink in the waters of affliction, be as temporal saviors to them and draw them out of the waters with a golden cord. Let the breasts of your mercy nurse the poor. Be like the trees of the sanctuary both for food and medicine (Ezekiel 47:12). When distressed and even starved souls are fainting, let your spiritual cordials revive them. Let others see the coats and garments which you have made for the poor (Acts 9:39).

8. The sin of unmercifulness. The unmerciful man is an unthankful man, and what worse can be said? You to whom the Lord has given an estate, your cup runs over — but you have a miserly heart and will not part with anything for good uses; it is death to you to relieve those who are dying. Know that you are in the highest degree ungrateful; you are not fit for human society. The Scripture has put these two together 'unthankful, without natural affection' (2 Timothy 3:2, 3). God may repent that ever he gave such men estates, and may say as Hosea 2:9: 'I will take back the wine and ripened grain I generously provided each harvest season. I will take away the linen and wool clothing I gave her.'

The unmerciful man lacks love to Christ. They would be very angry with those who should question their love; but do they love Christ who let the members of Christ starve? No! these love their money more than Christ, and come under that fearful 'Anathema' 'If anyone does not love the Lord, that person is cursed' (1 Corinthians 16:22).

9. Lastly, I shall use but one argument more to persuade to works of mercy, and that is the reward which follows alms-deeds. Giving of alms is a glorious work, and let me assure you it is not unfruitful work. Whatever is disbursed to the poor brethren, is given to Christ! 'Inasmuch as you have done it to one of the least of these my brethren, you have done it unto me' (Matthew 25:40). The poor man's hand is Christ's treasury, and there is nothing lost that is put there. 'Whatever you give by stretching forth your hand on earth is as it were given in heaven'. The text says, 'the merciful shall obtain mercy'. In the Greek it is, 'they shall be bemercied'. What is it, that we need most? Is it not mercy? Pardoning and saving mercy? What is it we desire on our deathbed? Is it not mercy? You who show mercy, shall find mercy. You who pour in the oil of compassion to others, God will pour in the golden oil of salvation unto you (Matthew 7:2).

The Shunammite woman showed mercy to the prophet and she received kindness from him another way (2 Kings 4:8-37). She welcomed him to her house — and he restored her dead child to life. Those who sow mercy, shall reap in kind; 'they shall obtain mercy'. Such is the sweetness and mercifulness of God's nature, that he will not allow any man to be a loser. No kindness shown to him shall be unregarded or unrewarded. God will be in no man's debt. For a cup of cold water — he shall have a draught of Christ's warm blood to refresh his soul. 'For God is not unrighteous to forget your work and labor of love, which you have shown toward his name, in that you have ministered to the saints ...' (Hebrews 6:10). God's mercy is a tender mercy, a pure mercy, a rich mercy. Mercy shall follow and overtake the merciful man. He shall be rewarded in this life — and in the life to come.

The merciful man shall be rewarded in this life. He shall be blessed —

In his person: 'Blessed is he who considers the poor' (Psalm 41:1). Let him go where he will, a blessing goes along with him. He is in favor with God. God casts a smiling aspect upon him.

Blessed in his name: 'He shall be had in everlasting remembrance' (Psalm 112:6). When the niggard's name shall rot, the name of a merciful man shall be embalmed with honor, and give forth its scent as the wine of Lebanon.

Blessed in his estate: 'He shall abound in all things'. 'The liberal soul shall be made fat' (Proverbs 2:25). He shall have the fat of the earth and the dew of heaven. He shall not only have the venison—but the blessing.

Blessed in his posterity: 'He is ever merciful and lends; and his seed is blessed' (Psalm 37:26). He shall not only leave an estate behind—but a blessing behind to his children, and God will see that the entail of that blessing shall not be cut off.

Blessed in his negotiations: 'For this thing the Lord your God shall bless you in all your works, and in all that you put your hand unto' (Deuteronomy 15:10). The merciful man shall be blessed in his building, planting, journeying. Whatever he is about, a blessing shall empty itself upon him. 'Wherever he treads there shall be a rose'. He shall be a prosperous man. The honeycomb of a blessing shall be still dropping upon him.

Blessed with long life: 'The Lord will preserve him and keep him alive' (Psalm 41:2). He has helped to keep others alive, and God will keep him alive. Is there anything then, lost by mercifulness? It spins out the silver thread of life. Many are taken away the sooner for their unmercifulness. Because their hearts are straitened, their lives are shortened.

Again, the merciful man shall be rewarded in the life to come. Aristotle joins these two together, liberality and utility. God will reward the merciful man hereafter, though not for his works—yet according to his works. 'I saw the dead, small and great, stand before God, and the books were opened, and the dead were judged out of those things which were written in the books, according to their works' (Revelation 20:12). As God has a bottle to put our tears in, so he has a book to write our alms in. As God will put a veil over his people's sins, so he will in free grace set a crown upon their works! The way to lay up—is to lay out. Other parts of our estate are left behind (Ecclesiastes 2:18)—but that which is given to Christ's poor is hoarded up in heaven. That is a blessed kind of giving, which though it makes the purse lighter, it makes the crown heavier.

You who are mercifully inclined, remember whatever alms you distribute:

You shall have good security. 'He who gives to the poor lends to the Lord; and that which he has given will he pay him again' (Ecclesiastes 11:1; Luke 6:38; Proverbs 19:17). There is God's pledge. Yet here is our unbelief—we will not take God's bond.

You shall be abundantly repaid. For a wedge of gold which you have parted with—you shall have a weight of glory. For a cup of cold water—you shall have rivers of pleasure, which run at God's right hand for evermore. The interest comes to infinitely more than the principal. Pliny writes of a country in Africa where the people for every bushel of seed they sow receive a hundred and fifty-fold increase. For every penny you drop into Christ's treasury, you shall receive above a thousand-fold increase. Your after-crop of glory will be so great that, though you are still reaping, you will never be able to gather the whole harvest. Let all this persuade rich men to honor the Lord with their substance.

Before I conclude this subject, let me lay down some brief rules concerning works of mercy.

1. Charity must be free. 'You shall give, and your heart must not be grieved' (Deuteronomy 15:10). That is, you must not be troubled at parting with your money. He who gives grievingly, gives grudgingly. It is not a gift—but a tax. Charity must flow like spring-water. The heart must be the spring, the hand the pipe, the poor the cistern. God loves a cheerful giver. Do not be like the fruit which has all the juice squeezed and pressed out. You must not give to the poor as if you were delivering your purse to the robber. Charity without cheerfulness, is rather a fine than an offering. It is rather doing of penance than giving of alms. Charity must be like the myrrh which drops from the tree without cutting or forcing.

2. We must give that which is our own (Isaiah 58:7). To give bread to the hungry, it must be 'your bread'. The Scripture puts them together, 'To do justice, to love mercy.' (Micah 6:8). 'For I the Lord love justice; I hate robbery and injustice' (Isaiah 61:8). He who shall build an almshouse or hospital with ill-gotten goods, displays the ensign of his pride and sets up the monument of his shame!

3. Do all in Christ and for Christ.

Do all in Christ. Labor that you may be in Christ. We are 'accepted in him' (Ephesians 1:6). Origen, Chrysostom, and Peter Martyr affirm that the best works not springing from faith, are lost. The Pelagians thought to have posed Augustine with that question, Whether it was sin in the heathen to clothe the naked? Augustine answered rightly: 'The doing of good is not in itself evil—but proceeding from infidelity it becomes evil'. 'To those who are unbelieving is nothing pure' (Titus 1:15). That fruit is most sweet and genuine which is brought forth in the vine (John 15:4). Outside of Christ, all our alms-deeds are but the fruit of the wild olive tree. They are not good works—but dead works.

Do all for Christ, namely, for his sake, that you may testify your love to him. Love to Christ mellows and ripens our alms-deeds. It makes them a precious perfume to God. As Mary did out of love bring her ointments and sweet spices to anoint Christ's dead body, so out of love to Christ bring your ointments and anoint his living body, namely, saints and members.

4. Works of mercy are to be done in humility. Away with ostentation! The worm breeds in the fairest fruit; and the moth in the finest cloth. Pride will be creeping into our best things. Beware of this dead fly in the box of ointment. When Moses' face shone, he put a veil over it. So while your light shines before men and they see your good works, cover yourselves with the veil of humility. As the silkworm, while she weaves her curious works, hides herself within the silk and is not seen, so we should hide ourselves from pride and vainglory.

It was the sin of the Pharisees while they were distributing alms that they blew the trumpet (Matthew 6:2). They did not give their alms—but sold them for applause. A proud man 'casts his bread upon the waters', as a fisherman casts his angle upon the waters. He angles for vainglory. I have read of one Cosmus Medices, a rich citizen of Florence, that he confessed to a near friend of his, he built so many magnificent structures, and spent so much on scholars and libraries, not for any love to learning but to raise up to himself trophies of fame and renown.

A humble soul denies himself, yes, even annihilates himself. He thinks how little it is he can do for God, and if he could do more, it were but a due debt. Therefore he looks upon all his works as if he had done nothing. The saints are brought in at the last day as disowning their works of charity. 'Lord, when did we ever see you hungry and feed you? Or thirsty and give you something to drink? Or a stranger and show you hospitality? Or naked and give you clothing? When did we ever see you sick or in prison, and visit you?' (Matthew 25:37-39). A holy Christian not only empties his hand of alms—but empties his heart of pride. While he raises the poor out of the dust, he lays himself in the dust. Works of mercy must be like the cassia, which is a sweet spice—but grows low.

5. Dispose your alms prudentially. It is said of the merciful man, 'He orders his affairs with discretion' (Psalm 112:5). There is a great deal of wisdom in distinguishing between those who have sinned themselves into poverty, and those who by the hand of God are brought into poverty. Discretion in the distribution of alms consists of two things: in finding out a fit object; in taking a fit season.

The finding out a fit object comes under a double notion. Give to those who are in most need. Raise the hedge where it is lowest. Feed the lamp which is going out. Give to those who may probably be more serviceable. Though we bestow cost and dressing upon a weak plant — yet not upon a dead plant. Breed up such as may help to build the house of Israel (Ruth 4:11), that may be pillars in church and state, not caterpillars making your charity to blush. 'Whenever we have the opportunity, we should do good to everyone, especially to our Christian brothers and sisters.' (Galatians 6:10)

Discretion in giving alms is in taking the fit season. Give to charitable uses in time of health and prosperity. Distribute your silver and gold to the poor before 'the silver cord is loosed or the golden bowl is broken' (Ecclesiastes 12:6). 'He who gives early, gives double'. Do not be as some, who reserve all they give until the term of life is ready to expire. Truly what is then bestowed is not given away — but taken away by death! It is not charity — but necessity. Oh do not so marry yourselves to money that you are resolved nothing shall part you from it — but death! A covetous man may be compared to a Christmas-box. He receives money — but parts with none until death breaks this box in pieces. Then the silver and the gold come tumbling out. Give in time of health. These are the alms which God takes notice of, and (as Calvin says) puts in his book of accounts.

6. Give thankfully. They should be more thankful who give an alms — than those who receive it. We should give a thank-offering to God that we are in the number of givers and not receivers. Bless God for a willing mind. To have not only an large estate — but a large heart, is matter of thankfulness!

Heart Purity

Blessed are the pure in heart, for they shall see God.

Matthew 5:8

The holy God, who is 'of purer eyes than to behold iniquity' calls here for heart-purity, and to such as are adorned with this jewel, he promises a glorious and beatific vision of himself: 'they shall see God'. Two things are to be explained the nature of purity; the subject of purity.

1. The nature of purity. Purity is a sacred refined thing. It stands diametrically opposed to whatever defiles. We must distinguish the various kinds of purity.

First, there is a primitive purity which is in God originally and essentially, as light is in the sun. Holiness is the glory of the Godhead: 'Glorious in holiness' (Exodus 15:11). God is the origin, pattern and prototype of all holiness.

Second, there is a created purity. Thus holiness is in the angels, and was once in Adam. Adam's heart did not have the least spot or tincture of impurity. We call that wine pure which has no mixture; and that gold pure which has no dross mingled with it. Such was Adam's holiness. It was like the wine which comes from the grape, having no mixture. But this is not to be found on earth. We must go to heaven for it.

Third, there is an evangelical purity; whence grace is mingled with some sin — like gold in the ore; like wine which has a dreg in it; like fine cloth with a blemish; like Nebuchadnezzar's image, part of silver, and part of clay (Daniel 2:35). This mixture God calls purity in a gospel-sense; as a face may be said to be fair, which has some freckles in it. Where there is a study of purity and a loathing ourselves for our impurity — this is to be 'pure in heart'.

Some by pure in heart, understand chastity, others sincerity (Psalm 32:2). But I suppose purity here is to be taken in a larger sense for the several kinds and degrees of holiness. They are said to be pure, who are consecrated people, having the oil of grace poured upon them. This purity is much mistaken.

Civility and morality are not purity. A man may be clothed with great moral virtues, such as justice, charity, prudence, temperance—and yet go to hell.

Profession is not purity. A man may have a name to live and yet be dead (Revelation 3:1). He may be swept by civility and garnished by profession—yet the devil may dwell in the house. The blazing comet is no star. The hypocrite's tongue may be silver—yet his heart stone.

Purity consists in two things; rectitude of mind, a prizing holiness in the judgment (Psalm 119:30); conformity of will, an embracing of holiness in the affections (Psalm 119:97). A pure soul is cast into the mold of holiness. Holiness is a blood that runs in his veins.

2. The subject of purity. The heart—'pure in heart'. Purity of heart does not exclude purity of life, no more than the pureness of the fountain excludes the pureness of the stream. But it is called purity of heart, because the heart is the main thing in true religion, and there can be no purity of life without it. A Christian's great care should be to keep the heart pure, as one would especially preserve the spring from being poisoned. In a duel, a man will chiefly guard and fence his heart, so a wise Christian should above all things keep his heart pure. Take heed that the love of sin does not get in there—lest it prove fatal.

Christians should above all things breathe after heart purity: 'Holding the mystery of the faith in a pure conscience' (1 Timothy 3:9). Justification causes our happiness, sanctification evidences it.

1. The reasons for purity.

[1] Purity is a thing called for in Scripture. 'Be holy for I am holy' (1 Peter 1:16). It is not only the minister bids you be holy—but God himself calls for it. What would the Holy God do with unholy servants?

[2] Because of that filthy and cursed condition we are in, before purity is wrought in us. We are a lump of clay and sin mingled together! Sin not only blinds us—but defiles us. It is called filthiness (James 1:21). And to show how befilthying a thing it is, it is compared to a plague of the heart (1 Kings 8:38), to corruption (Deuteronomy 32:5), to vomit (2 Peter 2:22), to infants 'helplessly kicking about in their own blood' (Ezekiel 16:6), and to a 'menstrual cloth' (Isaiah 30:22), which (as Jerome says) was the most defiling thing under the law. All the legal warnings which God appointed, were but to put men in mind of their loathsomeness before they were washed in the blood of Christ. If all the evils in the world were put together and their quintessence strained out, they could not make a thing so black and polluted as sin does! A sinner is a devil in a man's shape! When Moses' rod was turned into a serpent, he fled from it. Would God open men's eyes and show them their deformities and damnable spots—they would fly from themselves, as from serpents! This shows what need we have of purity. When grace comes—it washes off this hellish filth. It makes Ethiopians into true Israelites! It turns ravens into swans! It makes those who are as black as hell—to become as white as snow!

[3] Because none but the pure in heart are savingly interested in the covenant of grace. Covenanted people have 'the sprinkling with clean water' (Ezekiel 36:25). Now, until we are thus sprinkled, we have nothing to do with either the new covenant, or with the new Jerusalem. If a will is made only to such people as are so qualified, none can come in for a share—but such as have those qualifications. Just so, God has made a will and covenant that he will be our God, and will settle eternal glory upon us—but with this clause or proviso in the will—that we be purified people, having the 'clean water sprinkled, upon us. Now until then, we have nothing to do with God or mercy.

[4] Purity is the end of our election. 'He has chosen us—that we should be holy' (Ephesians 1:4). Not for holiness—but to holiness. 'Whom he did foreknow, he also did predestinate to be

conformed to the image of his Son' (Romans 8:29). God predestinates us to Christ's image, which image consists 'in righteousness and true holiness' (Ephesians 4:24). So that until you are holy, you cannot show any sign of election upon you — but rather the devil's brand-mark!

[5] Purity is the end of our redemption. If we could have gone to heaven in our sins, Christ needed not have died. Why did he shed his blood, but to redeem us from an 'empty way of life'? (1 Peter 1:18, 19). 'Christ gave himself for us to redeem us from all wickedness and to purify for himself a people that are his very own' (Titus 2:14). Christ shed his blood — to wash off our filth! The cross was both an altar and a laver. Jesus died not only to save us from wrath (1 Thessalonians 1:10) — but to save us from sin (Matthew 1:21). Out of his side came water which signifies our cleansing, as well as blood which signifies our justifying (1 John 5:6). The truth is, it would make Christ monstrous, if the head should be pure and not the members.

2. Why purity must be chiefly in the heart.

[1] Because if the heart is not pure, we differ nothing from a Pharisaic purity. The Pharisees' holiness consisted chiefly in externals. Theirs was an outside purity. They never minded the inside of the heart. 'Woe unto you, scribes and Pharisees, hypocrites! You are so careful to clean the outside of the cup and the dish, but inside you are filthy — full of greed and self-indulgence! Hypocrites! You are like whitewashed tombs — beautiful on the outside but filled on the inside with dead people's bones and all sorts of impurity!' (Matthew 23:25, 27). The Pharisees were good only on the surface. They were whited-over, not white. They were like a rotten post overlaid with fine paint. They were like a gold chimney — but within nothing but soot. Of such hypocrites Salvian complains, who had Christ in their mouths — but not in their lives.

We must go further. Be 'pure in heart', like the king's daughter 'all glorious within' (Psalm 45:13); else ours is but a Pharisaic purity; and Christ says, 'For I tell you that unless your righteousness surpasses that of the Pharisees and the teachers of the law, you will certainly not enter the kingdom of heaven.' (Matthew 5:20).

[2] The heart must especially be kept pure, because the heart is the chief seat or place of God's residence. God dwells in the heart. He takes up the heart for his own lodging (Isaiah 57:15; Ephesians 3:17), therefore it must be pure and holy. A king's palace must be kept from defilement, and especially his throne. How holy ought that to be! If the body is the temple of the Holy Spirit (1 Corinthians 6:19), the heart is the holy of holies! Oh take heed of defiling the room where God chiefly dwells! Let that room be washed with holy tears.

[3] The heart must especially be pure, because it is the heart which sanctifies all that we do. If the heart is holy, all is holy — our affections holy, our duties holy. 'The altar sanctifies the gift' (Matthew 23:19). The heart is the altar that sanctifies the offering. The Romans kept their springs from being poisoned. The heart is the spring of all our actions; let us keep this spring from poison. Be 'pure in heart'.

See here what that beauty is, which beautifies a soul in God's eye, namely, purity of heart. You are but a spiritual leper — until you are pure in heart. God is in love with the pure heart, for he sees his own picture drawn there.

Holiness is the angels' glory. They are pure virgin-spirits. Take away purity from an angel — and he is but a devil! You who are pure in heart — have the angels' glory shining in you. You have the embroidery and workmanship of the Holy Spirit upon you.

The pure heart is God's paradise where he delights to walk. It is his lesser heaven. The dove delights in the purest air. The Holy Spirit who descended in the likeness of a dove, delights in the purest soul. God says of the pure in heart, as of Zion, 'This is my rest forever, here will I dwell' (Psalm 132:14). God loves the loveliest complexion. The pure in heart is Christ's bride, decked and bespangled with the jewels of holiness. 'You have ravished my heart with one of your eyes' (Canticles 4:9). Your eyes, that is, your graces; these as a chain of diamonds, have drawn my heart to you. Of all hearts God loves the pure heart best. You who dress yourself by the looking-glass of the Word and adorn 'the hidden person of your heart' (1 Peter 3:4), are most precious in God's eyes, though you may be as bleary-eyed as Leah, or as lame as Barzillai. Yet being 'pure in heart, you are the mirror of beauty and may say 'Yet shall I be glorious in the eyes of the Lord' (Isaiah 49:5). How may this raise the esteem of purity! This is a beauty which never fades and which makes God himself fall in love with us.

If we must be pure in heart—then we must not rest in outward purity. Morality is not sufficient. A swine may be washed—yet a swine still. Morality does but wash a man, grace changes him. Morality may shine in the eyes of the world—but it differs as much from purity, as a pebble differs from the diamond. Morality is but strewing flowers on a dead corpse. A man who is but highly moral—is but a tame devil. How many have made 'morality' their Savior! Morality will damn, as well as heinous vice. A boat may be sunk with gold, as well as with dung.

Observe two things:

1. The moral person, though he will not commit gross sins—yet he is not sensible of heart sins. He does not discern the 'law in his members' (Romans 7:23). He is not troubled for unbelief, hardness of heart, vanity of thoughts. He abhors gaol-sins, not gospel-sins.

2. The moral person rises against holiness. The snake has a fine appearance—but has a deadly sting. The moral man is fair to look to—but has a secret antipathy against the holy ways of God. He hates grace, as much as vice. Zeal is as odious to him as uncleanness. Morality is not to be rested in. The heart must be pure. God would have Aaron wash the inner parts of the sacrifice (Leviticus 9:14). Morality does but wash the outside; the inside must be washed. 'Blessed are the pure in heart'.

Let us put ourselves on trial whether we are pure-hearted or not. Here I shall show the signs of an impure heart; and then, signs of a pure heart.

I. Signs of an impure heart

1. An ignorant heart is an impure heart. To be ignorant of sin or Christ, argues impurity of heart. Nahash the Ammonite would enter into covenant with the men of Jabesh-Gilead, so he might thrust out their right eyes (1 Samuel 11:2). Satan leaves men their left eye. In worldly knowledge they are quick-sighted enough—but the right eye of spiritual knowledge is quite put out! (2 Corinthians 4:4). Ignorance is Satan's stronghold (Acts 26:18). The devils are bound in chains of darkness (Jude 6). So are all ignorant people. Impossible it is that an ignorant heart should be holy. It is knowledge which makes the heart good. 'That the soul is without knowledge is not good' (Proverbs 19:2). For any to say that, though their mind is ignorant—yet their heart is good; they may as well say that, though they are blind—yet their eyes are good.

In the law, when the plague of leprosy was in a man's head—the priest was to pronounce him unclean. This is the case of an ignorant man. The leprosy is in his head, 'he is unclean'. That heart cannot be very pure, which is a dungeon. Grace cannot reign, where ignorance reigns. An ignorant man can have no love to God. 'He cannot love that which he does not know'. He can have no faith. Knowledge must usher in faith (Psalm 9:10). He cannot worship God aright (John 4:22). Though he may worship the true God—yet in a wrong manner. Ignorance is the root of sin. Blindness leads to lasciviousness (Ephesians 4:18, 19; Proverbs 7:23). Ignorance is the mother of pride (Revelation 3:17). It is the cause of error (2 Timothy 3:7), and, which is worse, a willful ignorance. 'It is one thing to be ignorant; it is another thing to be unwilling to know'.

Many are in love with ignorance. They hug their disease (Job 21:14; 2. Peter 3:5). Ignorant minds are impure. There is no going to heaven in the dark!

2. A self-righteous heart is an impure heart. It sees no need of purity. 'I am rich and have need of nothing' (Revelation 3:17). Not to be sensible of a disease — is worse than the disease! You do not hear a sick man say, 'I am well'. There are some who 'need no repentance' (Luke 15:7). Some sinners are too well to be cured. Heart purity is as great a wonder to the natural man — as the new birth was to Nicodemus (John 3:4). It is sad to think how many go on confidently and are ready to bless themselves, never suspecting their dreadful condition — until it is too late!

3. He has an impure heart who regards iniquity in his heart. 'If I regard iniquity in my heart, the Lord will not hear me' (Psalm 66:18). In the original it is 'If I look upon sin', that is, with a lustful look. Sin-regarding is inconsistent with heart-purity.

What is it to 'regard iniquity'?

[1] We regard iniquity, when we indulge in sin. When sin not only lives in us — but when we live in sin. Some will leave all their sins but one. Jacob would let all his sons go but Benjamin. Satan can hold a man by one sin. The fowler holds the bird fast enough by one claw. Others HIDE their sins like one who shuts up his shop windows, but follows his trade within doors. Many deal with their sins as Moses' mother dealt with her son. She hid him in the ark of bulrushes, as if she had left him — but her eye was still upon him and in the end, she became his nurse (Exodus 2:9). Just so, many seem to leave their sins — but they only hide them from the eye of others. Their heart still goes after them, and at last they nurse and give breast to their sins.

[2] To regard iniquity, is to delight in iniquity. Though a child of God sins — yet he does not take a delight in sin. 'I do the very thing I hate' (Romans 7:15). But impure souls make a recreation of sin. They 'delight in wickedness' (2 Thessalonians 2:12). Never did one feed with more delight on a meal he loves — than a wicked man does upon the forbidden fruit. This delight in sin — shows that the will is in the sin. And 'the will is the rule and measure of the deed'.

[3] To regard iniquity is to make provision for sin. 'Make no provision for the flesh, to fulfill the lusts thereof' (Romans 13:14). The wicked are caterers for their lusts. It is a metaphor taken from such as make provision for a family — to feed them. The Greek word here signifies a projecting and planning in the mind, how to bring a thing about. This is to make provision for the flesh — when one studies to satisfy the flesh and provide fuel for lust. Thus Amnon made provision for the flesh (2 Samuel 13:5). He pretends himself to be sick, and his sister, Tamar, must be his nurse. She must cook and serve his food to him. By which means he defiled her virginity. It is sad when men's concern is not to be holy — but to satisfy lust.

[4] To regard iniquity, is to give it respect and entertainment, as Lot showed respect to the angels. 'He bowed himself with his face toward the ground and said, Behold now, my lords, turn in, I beg you ...' (Genesis 19:2). When the Spirit of God comes He is repulsed and grieved — but when temptation comes, the sinner bows to it, sets open the gates, and says 'Turn in here, my lord'. This is to regard iniquity.

[5] He is said to regard sin, who does not regard the threatenings of God against sin. We read of 'seven thunders uttering their voices' (Revelation 10:3). How many thunders in Scripture utter their voice against sin! 'Surely God will crush the heads of his enemies, the hairy crowns of those who go on in their sins.' (Psalm 68:21). Here is a thundering scripture — but sinners fear not this thunder. Let a minister come as a Boanerges, clothed with the spirit of Elijah, and denounce all the curses of God against men's sins — they have no regard for it. They can laugh at the shaking of a spear (Job 41:29). This is to regard iniquity, and argues an impure heart.

4. An unbelieving heart is an impure heart. The Scripture calls it expressly 'an evil heart of unbelief' (Hebrews 3:12). An unbelieving heart is evil in the highest degree. It is full of the poison of hell. Unbelief is the foul medley of all sins—the root and receptacle of sin.

[1] Unbelief is a God-affronting sin. It puts the lie upon God. It calls in question his power (Psalm 78:19), mercy and truth. 'The one who does not believe God, is actually calling God a liar' (1 John 5:10). Can a greater affront be cast upon the God of glory! It makes us trust to second causes, which is setting the creature in the place of God. 'Asa in his disease sought not to the Lord—but to the physicians' (2 Chronicles 16:12). He relied more on the physician than upon God. Saul seeks to the witch of Endor. O high affront, to lean upon the reed and neglect the Rock of Ages!

[2] Unbelief hardens the heart. These two sins are linked together. 'He upbraided them with their unbelief and hardness of heart' (Mark 16:14). Unbelief breeds the stone of the heart. He who does not believe God's threatenings—will never fear him. He who does not believe God's promises—will never love him. What is said of the Leviathan, is true of the unbeliever. 'Its heart is as hard as rock, as hard as a millstone' (Job 41:24). Unbelief first pollutes the heart—and then hardens it!

[3] Unbelief breeds hypocrisy. Professors do not believe that God is a jealous God, and will call them to account. Therefore it is they put on a mask of religion and are saints in jest, that they may play the devil in earnest (2 Timothy 3:4, 5). They pretend to worship God—but Self is the idol they worship. Like rowers—they look one way and row another. The unbeliever is the greatest hypocrite.

[4] Unbelief causes the fear of men. 'Fear is proof of a baseborn soul'. Fear is a debasing thing. It unmans a man. It makes him afraid to be godly. The fearful man studies rather compliance, than conscience. 'The fear of man brings a snare' (Proverbs 29:25). What made Abraham equivocate, David pretend to be mad, and Peter deny Christ? Was it not their fear? And whence does fear spring—but from unbelief? Therefore the Scripture joins them together. 'The fearful and unbelieving' (Revelation 21:8).

[5] Unbelief is the root of apostasy. 'an evil heart of unbelief in departing from the living God' (Hebrews 3:12). What is the reason those who seemed once zealous—now despise God, and leave off prayer in their families? Is it not their unbelief? They believed not that God is, and that he is a rewarder of those who diligently seek him (Hebrews 11:6). Infidelity is the cause of apostasy. In the Greek, 'apistia' (unbelief) leads to 'apostasia' (apostasy). And if unbelief is the breeder and fomenter of so much sin, then the unbelieving heart must needs be an impure heart.

5. A covetous heart is an impure heart. The earth is the most impure element. The purity of the heart lies in the spirituality of it, and what is more opposite to spiritualness than earthiness? Covetousness is 'the root of all evil' (1 Timothy 6:10). 'To what cost do you drive mortal hearts—you accursed lust for gold!'

[1] Covetousness is the root of discontent. Why do any repine at their condition—but because they think they do not have enough? The Greek word for covetousness signifies an immoderate desire of getting. Because the covetous man is never satisfied, his heart frets in discontent and impatience.

[2] Covetousness is the root of theft. Achan's covetous heart made him steal that wedge of gold—which served to cleave asunder his soul from God (Joshua 7:21).

[3] Covetousness is the root of treason. It made Judas betray Christ. 'How much will you pay me to betray Jesus to you?' (Matthew 26:15). Absalom's covetousness made him attempt to

pluck the crown from his father's head. He who is a Demas, will soon prove a Judas. 'Men shall be covetous' (2 Timothy 3:2), and it follows in the next verse, 'traitors'. Where covetousness is in the preface, treason will be in the conclusion.

[4] Covetousness is the root of murder. Why did Ahab stone Naboth to death but to possess his vineyard? (1 Kings 21:13). Covetousness has made many swim to the crown in blood. And can the heart be pure, when the 'hands are full of blood'? (Isaiah 1:15).

[5] Covetousness is the root of perjury. 'Men shall be covetous, and it follows, 'trucebreakers' (2 Timothy 3:2, 3). For love of money will take a false oath and break a just oath. He who lives a Midas, will die a perjurer.

[6] Covetousness is the root of necromancy. Why do people indent with the devil—but for money? They study the black art—for yellow gold. Alexander the Sixth pawned his soul to the devil for a popedom.

[7] Covetousness is the root of fraud and theft. Such as would be over-rich, will overreach. It is the covetous hand which holds false weights (Amos 8:5).

[8] Covetousness is the root of bribery and injustice. It makes the courts of law, 'great places of robbery', as Augustine speaks. At Athens, court cases were bought and sold for money.

[9] Covetousness is the cause of uncleanness. The Scripture mentions 'the hire of a whore' (Deuteronomy 23:18). For money both conscience and chastity are sold.

[10] Covetousness is the root of idolatry: 'Covetousness which is idolatry' (Colossians 3:5). The covetous person bows down to the image of gold. His money is his god, for he puts his trust in it. Money is his creator. When he has abundance of wealth, then he thinks he is made. Money is his redeemer. If he is in any strait or trouble, he flies to his money and that must redeem him. Money is his comforter. When he is sad he counts over his money and with this golden harp he drives away the evil spirit. When you see a covetous man, you may say, 'There goes an idolater!'

[11] Covetousness is the cause of unprofitableness under the means of grace. In the parable, the thorns choked the seed (Matthew 13:7). This is the reason the Word preached does no more good. The seed often falls among thorns. Thousands of sermons lie buried in earthly hearts!

[12] Covetousness is the root of selfishness and stinginess. It hinders hospitality. A covetous man has a withered hand. He cannot reach it out to clothe or feed those who are in need. The covetous person is so sordid, that if his estate may flourish he is content to let his name lie dead and buried. What a cursed sin is avarice! And can he be pure in heart—who has such a 'root of bitterness' growing in him? We may as well say that the body is pure which is full of plague-sores.

6. Those hearts are impure which are 'haters of purity' (Micah 3:2). They 'hate knowledge' (Proverbs 1:29). Some things in nature have an antipathy; the serpent will not come near the boughs of the wild ash. There is an antipathy in a carnal heart against holiness; and when hatred is boiled up to malice—it is dangerous. Thus Julian maliciously opposed holiness. Receiving a mortal wound when in battle, he threw up a handful of his blood into the air in indignation saying, 'O Galilean, you have overcome me!'

7. He who scoffs at purity, has an impure heart. 'There shall come in the last days scoffers' (Luke 16:14; 2. Peter 3:3). There are some who make a jeer of religion. It is a sign of an Ishmael spirit to scoff at holiness. Are we not commanded to be perfect as God is perfect? (Matthew 5:48). One would wonder that those who dare open their mouths in derision against holiness — the earth does not open her mouth to swallow them up as it did Korah and Dathan. These are

devils covered over with flesh! They have damnation written on their foreheads! Lucian who in the time of the Emperor Trajan had professed religion, afterwards became so profane as to make a mock at the Christians and by his jeers and taunts went about to destroy religion. At last he himself was rent asunder and devoured by dogs. When the scab of the leper appeared, he was to be shut out of the camp (Leviticus 13:8, 46). Those who flout at religion, if God does not give them repentance, are sure to be shut out of the camp of heaven.

II. I shall next show you the signs of a pure heart.

1. A sincere heart is a pure heart. 'In whose spirit there is no deceit' (Psalm 32:2). There are four characters of a sincere-hearted Christian.

[1] A sincere heart serves God with the whole heart.

First, he serves God with the heart. The hypocrite does but make a show of obedience. 'You are always on their lips — but far from their hearts' (Jeremiah 12:2). There may be a fair complexion when the lungs and vitals are diseased. The hypocrite is fair to look on. He has a devout eye — but a hollow heart. But he who is sincere, his inside is his best side! In the law God would have 'the inner parts' offered up (Leviticus 4:11). A good Christian gives God 'the inner parts'. When he prays — his heart prays. 'Hannah prayed in her heart' (1 Samuel 1:13). In his thanksgiving the heart is the chief instrument of praise (Psalm 111:1). Then is the sweetest music when we 'make melody in our hearts to the Lord' (Ephesians 5:19).

Secondly, the sincere Christian serves God with the 'whole heart' (Psalm 119:2). Hypocrites have a double heart (Psalm 12:2) — a heart for God, and a heart for sin. 'Their heart is divided' (Hosea 10:2). God loves a broken heart — but not a divided heart. An upright heart is a whole heart. The full stream and torrent of the affections runs out after God. A sincere heart 'follows God fully' (Numbers 14:24).

[2] A sincere heart is willing to come under a trial. 'Search me, O God, and try me' (Psalm 139:23). That metal is to be suspected which men are afraid to bring to the touchstone. A sound heart likes the touchstone of the Word. It is for a searching ministry. Hypocrites fly from the light of truth; they fly from that light which would reveal their sin. They hate that physic of the Word which, meeting with their ill humours, begins to make them sick, and trouble their conscience. A gracious soul loves that preaching best, which makes a heart-anatomy.

[3] A man of sincere heart, dares not act in the least against his conscience. He is the most magnanimous — yet the most cautious. He is bold in suffering (Proverbs 28:1) but fearful of sin (Genesis 39:9). He dares not get an estate by sinful shifts, or rise upon the ruins of another. Jacob got his father's blessing by fraud — but that is not the way to get God's blessing.

[4] A sincere heart is a suspicious heart. The hypocrite suspects others of sin — but has charitable thoughts of himself! The sincere Christian has charitable thoughts of others — and suspects himself of sin. He calls himself often to account: 'O my soul, have you any evidences for heaven? Is there no flaw in your evidences? You may mistake common grace — for saving grace. Weeds in the cornfields look like flowers. The foolish virgins' lamps looked as if they had oil in them. O my soul, is it not so with you?' The man of sincere soul, being ever jealous, plays the critic upon himself and so traverses things in the court of conscience as if he were presently to be cited to God's bar. This is to be pure in heart.

2. A pure heart breathes after purity. If God should stretch out the golden scepter and say to him, 'Ask, and it shall be given you — up to half the kingdom', he would say, 'Lord, give me a pure heart! Let my heart have this inscription — Holiness to the Lord. Let my heart be your temple for you to dwell in. Lord, what would I do in heaven with this unholy heart? What

converse could I have with You?' A gracious soul is so in love with purity — that he prizes a pure heart above all blessings.

[1] He prizes a pure heart above riches. He knows that he may be clothed in purple and fine linen — and yet go to hell. He is content to be poor — so long as he may be pure. He knows heart-purity is a special certificate of God's love. 'The pure in heart' shall see God.

[2] He prizes a pure heart above gifts. Gifts do not at all commend us in God's eye. A pure heart is the jewel! 'O woman, great is your faith!' (Matthew 15:28). It was not her rhetorical language Christ was taken with — but her faith. Hypocrites have had rare gifts. Saul had the spirit of prophecy. Judas no doubt could make an elegant oration. Hypocrites have come into God's church loaded with the Egyptian gold of human learning. There may be illumination without sanctification. A small diamond is better than a great deal of brass. A little grace excels the most flourishing abilities. Now if the out-goings of your soul are after holiness — you desire a pure heart, rather than an eloquent tongue. You have the oil of the Spirit poured on you and you shall be crowned with a glorious sight of God.

3. A pure heart abhors all sin. A man may forbear and forsake sin — yet not have a pure heart.

[1] A man may forbear sin — for lack of occasion to sin. He may forbear sin as one may hold his breath while he dives under water, and then take breath again. The gunpowder makes no noise until the fire is put to it. The clock stands still until the weights are put on. Let a temptation come, which is like the hanging on of the weights, and the heart goes as fast in sin as ever!

[2] He may forbear sin — for fear of the penalty. A man forbears a dish he loves — for fear it should bring his disease upon him of the stone or gout. There is conflict in a sinner between the passions of desire — and fear. Desire spurs him on to sin — but fear as a curb and bit checks him. Nor is it the crookedness of the serpent he fears — but the sting of the serpent!

[3] He may forbear sin — out of a design. He has a plot in hand and his sin might spoil his plot. Some rich heir would fly out in excess — but he behaves properly, to prevent being cut off from the inheritance. How good was Joash while Jehoiada the priest lived! Prudence as well as conscience may restrain from sin.

Again, a man may forsake sin — yet not have a pure heart. It is a great matter, I confess, to forsake sin. So dear is sin to men, that they will part with the fruit of their body for the sin of their souls. Sin is the Delilah that bewitches, and it is much to see men divorced from it. There may be a forsaking of sin — yet no heart purity. Sin may be forsaken upon wrong principles.

[1] A man may forsake sin, from morality. Moral arguments may suppress sin. I have read of a debauched heathen who, hearing Socrates read an ethical lecture on virtue and vice — he went away changed and no more followed his former vices. Cato, Seneca, Aristides, seeing beauty in virtue, led unblamable lives.

[2] A man may forsake sin, from policy. A man may forsake sin, not out of respect to God's glory — but his own credit. Vice will waste his estate, eclipse the honor of his family, therefore out of policy he will divorce his sin.

[3] A man may forsake sin, from necessity. Perhaps he cannot follow the trade of sin any longer. The adulterer is grown old, the drunkard has become too poor. His heart is toward sin — but either his purse fails him or his strength; as a man who loves hunting — but his prison-fetters will not allow him to follow the sport. This man, who is necessitated to put a stop to sin — does not so much forsake sin, as sin forsakes him.

But he is pure in God's eye, who abhors sin. 'I hate every false way' (Psalm 119:104). This is excellent indeed, because now the love of sin is crucified. A hypocrite may leave sin — yet love it; as the serpent sheds her coat—yet keeps her sting. But when a man can say he abhors sin—now is sin killed in the root. A pure heart abstains from sin—as a man does from a dish that he has an antipathy against. This is a sign of a new nature—when a man hates what he once loved! And because he hates sin, therefore he fights against it with the 'sword of the Spirit'—as a man who hates a serpent seeks the destruction of it.

4. A pure heart avoids the appearance of evil. 'Abstain from all appearance of evil' (1 Thessalonians 5:22). A pure heart avoids that which may be interpreted as evil. He who is loyal to his prince, not only forbears to have his hand in treason—but he takes heed of that which has an appearance of treason. A gracious heart is shy of that which looks like sin. When Joseph's mistress took hold of him and said, 'Lie with me!'—he left his garment in her hand and fled from her (Genesis 39:12). He avoided the appearance of evil. He would not be seen in her company. Thus a pure heart avoids whatever may have the suspicion of sin:

[1] A pure heart avoids the suspicion of sin—in regard of himself, and that two ways.

First, because the appearance of evil is oftentimes an occasion of evil. Dalliance is an appearance of evil, and many times occasions evil. Had Joseph been familiar with his mistress in a wanton sporting manner, he might in time have been drawn to commit immorality with her. Some out of novelty and curiosity have gone to hear mass, and afterwards have lent the idol not only their ear—but their knee! There are many who have gone with itching ears to hear false teachers, and have come home with the plague in their head! When Dinah would be gadding about, she lost her chastity (Genesis 34:2). A pure heart foreseeing the danger avoids the appearance of evil. It is dangerous to go near a hornet's nest. The men who went near the furnace were burned (Daniel 3:22).

Second, because the appearance of evil may eclipse his good name. A good name is a precious ointment. It is better than 'fine gold' (Proverbs 22:1). It commends us to God and angels, which riches cannot do. Now a godly man avoids the appearance of evil—lest he wounds his good name. What comfort can there be of life, when the name lies buried?

[2] A pure heart avoids the suspicion of sin—out of reverence and respect to the holiness of god. God hates the very appearance of evil. God abhors hypocrites because they have no more than the appearance of good—and he is angry with his children if they have so much as the appearance of evil. A gracious heart knows God is a jealous God and cannot endure that his people should border upon sin. Therefore he keeps aloof from sin, and will not come near the smell of infection.

[3] A pure heart avoids the very appearance of sin—in regard of the godly. The appearance of evil may scandalize a weak brother. A gracious heart is not only fearful lest he should defile his own conscience—but lest he should offend his brother's conscience. Were it only an indifferent thing—yet if it is an appearance of evil and may grieve another—we are to forbear (1 Corinthians 10:25-28). For 'when we sin against the brethren and wound their weak conscience, we sin against Christ' (1 Corinthians 8:12). The weak Christian is a member of Christ. Therefore the sinning against a member—is a sinning against Christ.

[4] A pure heart avoids the very appearance of evil—in regard of the wicked. The apostle would have us walk wisely towards unbelievers. (1 Thessalonians 4:12). The wicked watch for our halting. How glad would they be of anything to reproach religion! Professors are placed as stars in the highest orb of the church, and if there is but the appearance of any eccentric, or irregular motion, the wicked would presently open their mouths with a fresh cry against piety. Now to a godly heart the fame and honor of the gospel is so dear that he had rather die than incriminate or eclipse it.

By this then let us try ourselves whether we are pure in heart—do we avoid the least appearance of sin? Alas, how many run themselves into the occasions of sin! They tempt the devil to tempt them! Some go to plays and comedies—the very fuel and temptation to lust! Others frequent heretical meetings, and truly God often in just judgment leaves them to the acts of sin, who do not avoid the appearance of sin. 'They were mingled among the heathen and learned their works' (Psalm 106:35). Pure hearts flee the occasion of sin! John would not endure the company of the heretic Cerinthus. Polycarp would have no conference with Marcion the heretic—but called him 'the devil's firstborn'. Basil says that the Christians in his time avoided the meetings of heretics as the 'very schools of error'. Oh, avoid the appearance of evil. The apostle bids us to follow those things which are 'of good report' (Philippians 4:8).

5. A pure heart performs holy duties in a holy manner. This holy manner, or due order, consists in three things:

[1] Preparing the heart before a duty. An unholy heart does not care how it rushes upon an ordinance. It comes without preparation and goes away without profit. The pure heart is a prepared heart. It dresses itself, before it comes to a duty—by examination and prayer. When the earth is prepared—then it is fit to receive the seed. When the instrument is prepared and tuned—then it is fit for music.

[2] Watching the heart in a duty. A holy heart labors to be affected and wrought upon by the Spirit. His heart burns within him. There was no sacrifice without fire. A pure saint labors to have his heart broken in a duty (Psalm 51:17). The incense, when it was broken, cast the sweetest savor. Impure souls care not in what a dead or perfunctory manner they serve God (Ezekiel 33:31). They pray more out of fashion, than out of faith. They are no more affected with an ordinance, than the dead in the church graveyard. God complains of offering up the blind (Malachi 1:8). And is it not as bad to offer up the dead? O Christian, say to yourself, How can this deadness of heart stand with pureness of heart? Do not dead things putrefy?

[3] Outward reverence. Purity of heart will express itself by the reverend posture of the body — the lifting up of the eye and hand, the bending the knee. When God gave the law, 'the mount was on fire and trembled' (Exodus 19:18). The reason was that the people might prostrate themselves more reverently before the Lord. The ark wherein the law was put, was carried upon poles, so that the Levites might not touch it—to show what reverence God would have about holy things (Exodus 25:11, 14). We must not only offer up our souls—but our bodies (Romans 12:1). The Lord takes notice what posture and gesture we use in his worship. If a man were to deliver a petition to the king, would he deliver it with a foolish jest? The careless irreverence of some would make us think they did not much regard whether God heard them or not. We are run from one extreme to another, from superstition to irreverence. Let Christians think of the dreadful majesty of God who is present. 'How dreadful is this place! This is none other but the house of God and this is the gate of heaven!' (Genesis 28:17). The blessed angels 'cover their faces crying, Holy, holy holy' (Isaiah 6:3). A holy heart will have a holy posture.

6. A pure heart will have a pure life. 'Let us cleanse ourselves from all filthiness of the flesh and spirit, perfecting holiness in the fear of God'. (2 Corinthians 7:1). Where there is a holy heart, there will be a holy life. Some bless God they have good hearts—but their lives are evil. 'There is a generation that are pure in their own eyes, and yet is not washed from their filthiness' (Proverbs 30:12). If the stream is corrupt—we may suspect the spring-head to be impure. Aaron was called the saint of the Lord (Psalm 106:16). He had not only a holy heart—but there was a golden plate on his forehead on which was written 'Holiness to the Lord'. Purity must not only be woven into the heart—but engraved upon the life! Grace is most beautiful when it shines

abroad with its golden beams. The clock has not only its motion within – but the hand moves outside upon the dial. Just so, pureness of heart, shows itself upon the dial of the life.

[1] A pure soul talks of God (Psalm 37:30). His heart is seen in his tongue. He who is pure in heart – his mouth is full of heaven.

[2] A pure soul walks with God (Genesis 6:9). He is still doing angel's work, praising God, serving God. He lives as Christ did upon earth. Holy duties are the Jacob's ladder by which he is still ascending to heaven. Purity of heart and life, are in Scripture made twins. 'I will put my Spirit within you' – there is purity of heart. 'And cause you to walk in my statutes' – there is purity of life (Ezekiel 36:27). Shall we account them pure, whose life is not in heaven (Philippians 3:20) – but rather in hell? 'Shall I count them pure – who have wicked balances and a bag of deceitful weights?' (Micah 6:11). How justly may others reproach religion when they see it kicked down with our unholy feet! A pure heart has a golden frontispiece. Grace, like new wine, will have vent; it can be no more concealed than lost. The saints are called 'jewels' (Malachi 3:17), because of that shining luster which they cast in the eyes of others!

7. A pure heart is so in love with purity that nothing can draw him off from it.

[1] Let others reproach purity, he loves it. As David, when he danced before the ark, and Michal scoffed. David replied, 'if this is to be vile – I will yet be more vile!' (2 Samuel 6:22). So says a pure heart: 'If to follow after holiness is to be vile – I will yet be more vile!' The more others deride holiness, the more a gracious soul burns in love and zeal to it. If a man had an inheritance befallen him, would he be laughed out of it? What is a Christian the worse for another's reproach? A blind man's disparaging a diamond does not make it sparkle the less!

[2] Let others persecute holiness, a pure heart will pursue it. Holiness is the queen every gracious soul is espoused to – and he will rather die than be divorced. Paul would be holy, 'though bonds and persecutions awaited him' (Acts 20:23). The way of religion is often thorny and bloody – but a gracious heart prefers inward purity before outward peace. I have heard of one who, having a jewel he much prized, the king sent for his jewel. 'Tell the king' (says he) 'I honor his Majesty – but I will rather lose my life than part with my jewel.' He who is enriched with the jewel of holiness, will rather die than part with this jewel. When his honor and riches will do him no good – his holiness will end in bliss, 'You have your fruit unto holiness, and the end everlasting life'.

Let me persuade Christians to heart purity. The harlot 'wipes her mouth' (Proverbs 30:20). But that is not enough. 'Wash your heart, O Jerusalem' (Jeremiah 4:14). And here I shall lay down some arguments or motives to persuade to heart purity.

1. The necessity of heart-purity.

[1] Heart-purity is necessary, in respect of ourselves. Until the heart is pure, all our holy things (that is, our religious duties) are polluted. They are but splendid sins! 'Everything is pure to those whose hearts are pure. But nothing is pure to those who are corrupt and unbelieving, because their minds and consciences are defiled' (Titus 1:15). Their offering is unclean. Under the law, if a man who was unclean by a dead body, and carried a piece of holy meat, the holy meat could not cleanse him – but the dead body polluted that. (Haggai 2:12,13). He who had the leprosy, whatever he touched was unclean. If he had touched the altar or sacrifice, the altar would not cleanse him – but he would defiled the altar. A filthy hand defiles the purest water. An impure heart defiles all religious duties – he drops poison upon them all. A pure stream running through muddy ground, is polluted. Just so, the holiest duties, running through an impure heart, are polluted. A sinner's works are called 'dead works' (Hebrews 6:1). And those works which are dead cannot please God. A dead wife cannot please her husband.

[2] Heart purity is necessary, in respect of god. God is holy. Purity is the chief robe with which God adorns himself. 'You are of purer eyes than to behold evil' (Habakkuk 1:13). And will this holy God endure to have an impure heart come near him? Will a man lay a viper in his bosom! The holy God and the unrepentant sinner, cannot dwell together. None can dwell together but friends—but there is no friendship between God and the sinner, both of them being of a contrary judgment and disposition. An impure heart is more odious to God than a serpent! God gave the serpent its venom—but Satan fills the heart with sin. 'Satan has filled your heart!' (Acts 5:3). The Lord abhors a sinner. He will not come near him, having his plague-sores running. 'My soul loathed them!' (Zechariah 11:8).

[3] Heart purity is necessary, in regard of angels. They are pure creatures. The Cherubim, which typified the angels, were made of fine gold to denote the purity of their essence. No unholy thought enters into the angels, therefore there must be purity of heart that there may be some resemblance between us and them. What would unholy hearts do, among those pure angelic spirits?

[4] Heart purity is necessary, in regard of the glorified saints. They are pure, being refined from all the dregs of sin. They are 'spirits of just men made perfect' (Hebrews 12:23). Now what would profane spirits do among 'spirits made perfect'? I tell you, if you who wallow in your sins, could come near God and angels and spirits of men made perfect, and have a sight of their luster—you would soon wish yourselves out of their company. As a man who is dirty and in his rags, if he should stand before the king and his nobles and see them glistening in their cloth of gold and sparkling with their jewels—he would be ashamed of himself, and wish himself out of their presence.

[5] Heart purity is necessary, in regard of heaven. Heaven is a pure place. It is an 'undefiled inheritance' (1 Peter 1:4). No unclean beasts come into the heavenly ark! 'Nothing evil will be allowed to enter!' (Revelation 21:27). The Lord will not put the new wine of glory, into a musty impure heart! All these things considered, shows the necessity of heart purity.

2. It is the will of God that we should be pure in heart. 'This is the will of God—your sanctification' (1 Thessalonians 4:3). Are you low in the world? Perhaps it is not the will of God that you should be rich. But it is the will of God that you should be holy. 'This is the will of God—your sanctification.' Let God have his will by being holy—and you shall have your will by being happy. God's will must either be fulfilled by us or upon us!

3. Purity of heart is the characteristic note of God's people. 'God is good to Israel—to those whose hearts are pure' (Psalm 73:1). Heart-purity denominates us, the 'Israel of God'. It is not profession which makes us the Israel of God. 'Not all who are descended from Israel, are Israel' (Romans 9:6). Purity of heart is the jewel which is hung only upon the elect! Chastity distinguishes a virtuous woman from a harlot. Just so, the true Christian is distinguished from the hypocrite—by his heart-purity. This is like the nobleman's star, which is a peculiar ensign of honor, differing him from the vulgar. When the bright star of purity shines in a Christian's heart, it distinguishes him from a formal professor.

4. Purity of heart makes us like God. It was Adam's unhappiness once, that he aspired to be like God in omniscience; but we must endeavor to be like God in sanctity. God's image consists in holiness. To those who do not have this image and superscription upon them, he will say 'I never knew you!' God delights in no heart but where he may see his own face and likeness. You cannot see your face in a looking-glass when it is dusty. God's face cannot be seen in a dusty impure soul. A pure heart (like a clean looking-glass) gives forth some idea and representation of God. There is little comfort in being like God in other things besides purity. Are we like God

in that we have a being? So have stones. Are we like him in that we have motion? So have stars. Are we like him in that we have life? So have trees and birds. Are we like him in that we have knowledge? So have devils. There is no likeness to God, which will prove comfortable and blissful — but our being like him in purity. God loves the pure in heart. Love is founded upon likeness.

5. The excellency of the heart, lies in the purity of it. Purity was the glory of the soul in innocence. The purer a thing is — the better. The purer the air is, and the more free from noxious vapors — the better it is. Pure water is most sweet. The purer the gold is, the more valuable. The purer the wine is when it is taken off from the lees and dregs — the more excellent it is. The more the soul is purified by grace and taken off from the lees and dregs of sin — the more precious in God's eyes. The purer the heart is — the more spiritual it is; and the more spiritual it is — the more fit to entertain him who is pure Spirit.

6. God is good to the pure in heart. 'God is good to Israel — to those whose hearts are pure' (Psalm 73:1). We all desire that God should be good to us. It is the sick man's prayer, 'May the Lord be good to me'. God is good to those whose hearts are pure. But how is God good to them? Two ways —

[1] To those who are pure, all things are sanctified. 'To the pure — all things are pure' (Titus 1:15). Estate is sanctified, relations are sanctified — just as the temple sanctified the gold and the altar sanctified the offering. To the unclean — nothing is clean. Their table is a snare; and their devotions are sin. There is a curse entailed upon a wicked man (Deuteronomy 28:15-20) — but holiness removes the curse and cuts off the punishment. 'To the pure all things are pure'.

[2] The pure-hearted have all things work for their good (Romans 8:28). Mercies and afflictions shall turn to their good. The most poisonous drug shall be medicinal. The most cross providence shall carry on the design of their salvation. Who then would not be pure in heart? 'God is good to those who are pure in heart'.

7. Heart purity makes way for heaven. The pure in heart 'shall see God'. Happiness is nothing but the quintessence of holiness. Purity of heart is heaven begun in a man. Holiness is called in Scripture 'the anointing of God' (1 John 2:27). Solomon was first anointed with the holy oil, and then he was made king (1 Kings 1:39). Just so, the people of God are first anointed with the oil of the Spirit and made pure in heart, and then the crown of glory is set upon their head. And is not purity to be highly valued? It lays a path for glory. 'Purity of heart' and 'seeing of God' are linked together.

8. Note the examples of those who have been eminent for heart-purity. The Lord Jesus was a pattern of purity. 'Who of you convicts me of sin?' (John 8:46). In this we are to imitate Christ. We are not to imitate him in raising the dead or in working miracles — but in being holy (1 Peter 1:16).

Besides this golden pattern of Christ, we are to write after the fair copy of those saints who have been of a dove-like purity. David was so pure in heart, that he was a man 'after God's heart'. Abraham was so purified by faith that he was one of God's cabinet-counsel (Genesis 18:17). Moses was so holy that God spoke with him face to face. What were the rest of the patriarchs but so many plants of renown, flourishing in holiness? The fathers in the primitive church were exemplary for purity. Gregory Nazianzen, Basil, Augustine, they were so inlaid and adorned with purity, that envy itself could not tax them. We wish we had such saints as were in the primitive times, so just were they in their dealings, so decent in their attire, so true in their promises, so devout in their religion, so unblamable in their lives, that they were living sermons, walking Bibles, genuine pictures of Christ, and helped to keep up the credit of godliness in the world.

9. Heart-purity is the only jewel you can carry out of the world. Have you a child you delight in, or an estate? You can 'carry nothing out of the world' (1 Timothy 6:7). Purity of heart is the only commodity that can be with comfort transported. This is that which will stay longest with you. Usually we love those things which last longest. We prize a diamond or piece of gold above the most beautiful flower, because the flower is fading. Heart-purity has perpetuity! It will go with us beyond the grave!

But how shall we attain to heart-purity?

1. Often look into the Word of God. 'Now you are clean, through the word' (John 15:3). 'Your word is very pure' (Psalm 119:140). God's Word is pure, not only for the matter of it—but the effect of it, because it makes us pure. 'Sanctify them through your truth; your word is truth' (John 17:17). By looking into this pure crystal—we are changed into the image of it. The Word is both a looking-glass to show us the spots of our souls—and a laver to wash them away! The Word breathes nothing but purity; it enlightens the mind; it consecrates the heart.

2. Go to the bath. There are two baths Christians should wash in.

[1] The bath of tears. Go into this bath. Peter had sullied and defiled himself with sin and he washed himself with penitential tears. Mary Magdalene, who was an impure sinner, 'stood at Jesus' feet weeping' (Luke 7:38). Mary's tears washed her heart—as well as Christ's feet! Oh sinners, let your eyes be a fountain of tears! Weep for those sins which are so many as have passed all arithmetic. This water of contrition is healing and purifying.

[2] The bath of Christ's blood. This is that 'fountain opened for sin and uncleanness' (Zechariah 13:1). A soul steeped in the brinish tears of repentance and bathed in the blood of Christ is made pure. This is that 'spiritual washing'. All the legal washings and purifications were but types and emblems representing Christ's blood. This blood whitens the black soul.

3. Get faith. It is a soul-cleansing grace. 'Having purified their hearts by faith' (Acts 15:9). The woman in the gospel who but touched the hem of Christ's garment was healed. A touch of faith heals. If I believe Christ and all his merits are mine, how can I sin against him? We do not willingly injure those friends who, we believe, love us. Nothing can have a greater force and efficacy upon the heart to make it pure, than faith. Faith will remove mountains, the mountains of pride, lust, envy. Faith and the love of sin are incompatible.

4. Breathe after the Spirit. He is called the Holy Spirit (Ephesians 1:13). He purifies the heart as lightning purifies the air. That we may see what a purifying virtue the Spirit has, he is compared to various things:

[1] The Spirit is compared to fire (Acts 2:3). Fire is of a purifying nature. It refines and cleans metals. It separates the dross from the gold. The Spirit of God in the heart refines and sanctifies it. He burns up the dross of sin.

[2] The Spirit is compared to wind. 'There came a sound from heaven as of a mighty rushing wind, and they were all filled with the Holy Spirit' (Acts 2:24). The wind purifies the air. When the air by reason of foggy vapors is unwholesome, the wind is a fan to winnow and purify it. Thus when the vapors of sin arise in the heart—vapors of pride and covetousness, earthly vapors—the Spirit of God arises and blows upon the soul and purges away these impure vapors. The spouse in the Canticles prays for a gale of the Spirit, that she might be made pure (4:16).

[3] The Spirit is compared to water. 'He who believes on me, out of his belly shall flow rivers of living water; but this spoke he of the Spirit' (John 7:38, 39). The Spirit is like water, not only to make the soul fruitful, for it causes the desert to blossom as the rose (Isaiah 32:15; 35:1) — but the Spirit is like water to purify. Whereas, before, the heart of a sinner was unclean and whatever he touched had a tincture of impurity (Numbers 19:22), when once the Spirit comes into the heart, with his continual showers, he washes off the filthiness of it, making it pure and fit for God to dwell in.

5. Take heed of close converse and fellowship with the wicked. One vain mind makes another vain. One hard heart makes another. The stone in the body is not infectious — but the stone in the heart is. One profane person poisons another. Beware of the society of the wicked.

Some may object: But what hurt is in this? Did not Jesus converse with sinners? (Luke 5:29).

[1] There was a necessity for that. If Jesus had not come among sinners, how could any have been saved? He went among sinners — but not to join with them in their sins. He was not a companion of sinners — but a physician of sinners.

[2] Though Christ did converse with sinners, he could not be polluted with their sin. His divine nature was a sufficient antidote to preserve him from infection. Christ could be no more defiled with their sin — than the sun is defiled by shining on a dunghill. Sin could no more stick on Christ — than a burr on a crystal. The soil of his heart was so pure — that no viper of sin could breed there. But the case is altered with us. We have a storehouse of corruption within, and the least thing will increase this storehouse. Therefore it is dangerous mingling ourselves among the wicked. If we would be pure in heart — let us shun their society. He who would preserve his garment clean, avoids the dirt. The wicked are as the mire (Isaiah 57:20). The fresh waters running among the salt waters, taste brackish.

6. If you would be pure, walk with those who are pure. As the communion of the saints is in our Creed, so it should be in our company. 'He who walks with the wise, shall be wise' (Proverbs 13:20), and he who walks with the pure, shall be pure. The saints are like a bed of spices. By intermixing ourselves with them we shall partake of their savouriness. Association begets assimilation. Sometimes God blesses godly society, to the conversion of others.

7. Wait at the posts of wisdom's doors. Reverence the Word preached. The Word of God sucked in by faith (Hebrews 4:2) transforms the heart into the likeness of it (Romans 6:17). The Word is a holy seed (James 1:18), which being cast into the heart makes it partake of the divine nature (2 Peter 1:4).

8. Pray for heart purity. Job propounds the question, 'Who can bring a clean thing out of an unclean?' (Job 14:4; 15:14). God can do it. Out of an impure heart — he can produce grace. Pray that prayer of David, 'Create in me a clean heart, O God' (Psalm 51:10). Most men pray more for full purses, than pure hearts. We should pray for heart-purity fervently. It is a matter we are most nearly concerned in. 'Without holiness no man shall see the Lord' (Hebrews 12:14). Our prayer must be with sighs and groans (Romans 8:23-26). There must not only be elocution but affection. Jacob wrestled in prayer (Genesis 32:24). Hannah poured out her soul (1 Samuel 1:15). We often pray so coldly (our petitions even freezing between our lips), as if we would teach God to deny our prayers. We pray as if we did not care whether God heard us or not!

Oh Christian, be earnest with God for a pure heart! Lay your heart before the Lord and say, 'Lord, You who have given me a heart, give me a pure heart. My heart is good for nothing as it is. It defiles everything it touches. Lord, I am not fit to live with this heart — for I cannot honor you; nor fit to die with it — for I cannot see you. Oh purge me with hyssop. Let Christ's blood be sprinkled upon me. Let the Holy Spirit descend upon me. 'Create in me a clean heart, O God'. You who bid me to give you my heart—Lord, make my heart pure and you shall have it!'

The blessed PRIVILEGE of seeing God explained

'They shall see God!' Matthew 5:8

These words are linked to the former and they are a great incentive to heart-purity. The pure heart shall see the pure God. There is a double sight which the saints have of God.

1. In this life; that is, spiritually by the eye of faith. Faith sees God's glorious attributes in the looking-glass of his Word. Faith beholds him showing forth himself through the lattice of his ordinances. Thus Moses saw him who was invisible (Hebrews 11:27). Believers see God's glory as it were—veiled over. They behold his 'back parts' (Exodus 33:23).

2. In the life to come; and this glorious sight is meant in the text, 'They shall see God.' A glorious prospect! This divines call 'the beatific vision'. At that day the veil will be pulled off, and God will show himself in all his glory to the soul, just as a king on a day of coronation, shows himself in all his royalty and magnificence. This sight of God, will be the heaven of heaven. We shall indeed have a sight of angels, and that will be sweet—but the quintessence of happiness and the diamond in the ring will be this—'We shall see God!' It would be night in heaven, if the Sun of Righteousness did not shine there. It is the king's presence, which makes the court. Absalom counted himself half-alive, unless he might see the king's face (2 Samuel 14:32).

'Blessed are the pure in heart—for they shall see God!' This sight of God in glory is, first, partly mental and intellectual. We shall see him with the eyes of our mind.

But second, it is partly physical; not that we can with bodily eyes behold the bright essence of God. Indeed, some erroneously held that God had a visible shape and figure. As man was made in God's image, so they thought that God was made in man's image; but God is a Spirit (John 4:24), and being a Spirit, he is invisible (1 Timothy 1:17). He cannot be beheld by bodily eyes. 'Whom no man has seen, nor can see' (1 Timothy 6:16). A sight of his glory would overwhelm us. This wine is too strong for our weak heads.

But when I say our seeing of God in heaven is physical, my meaning is that we shall with bodily eyes behold Jesus Christ, through whom the glory of God, his wisdom, holiness, and mercy, shall shine forth to the soul. Put a back of steel to the glass—and you may see a face in it. So the human nature of Christ is as it were a back of steel through which we may see the glory of God (2 Corinthians 4:6). In this sense that scripture is to be understood, 'With these eyes shall I see God' (Job 19:26, 27).

Now concerning this blessed sight of God, it is so sublime and sweet, that I can only draw a dark shadow of it. We shall better understand it—when we come to heaven. At present I shall lay down these nine maxims concerning this beatific vision.

1. Our sight of God in heaven shall be a clear sight. Here we see him 'through a glass darkly' (1 Corinthians 13:12). But through Christ we shall behold God in a very illustrious manner. God will unveil himself and show forth his glory—so far as the soul is capable to receive. If Adam had not sinned, it is probable that he would never have had such a clear sight of God—as the saints in glory shall have. 'We shall see him as he is' (1 John 3:2). Now we see him as he is not. There we shall see him 'as he is' in a very clear manner. 'Then shall I know—even as also I am known' (1 Corinthians 13:12), that is, 'clearly'. Does not God know us clearly and fully? Then shall the saints know him (according to their capacity) as they are known. As their love to God, so their sight of God—shall be perfect.

2. This sight of God will be a transcendent sight. It will surpass in glory. Such glittering beams shall sparkle forth from the Lord Jesus, as shall infinitely amaze and delight the eyes of the beholders! Imagine what a blessed sight it will be, to see Christ wearing the robe of our human nature and to see that nature sitting in glory above the angels. If God is so beautiful here in his ordinances, Word, prayer, sacraments; if there is such excellency in him when we see him by the eye of faith through the telescope of a promise, O what will it be when we shall see him 'face to face'!

When Christ was transfigured on the mount, he was full of glory (Matthew 17:2). If his transfiguration was so glorious, what will his exaltation be! What a glorious time will it be when (as it was said of Mordecai) we shall see him in the presence of his Father, 'arrayed in royal apparel, and with a great crown of gold upon his head' (Esther 8:15). This will be glory beyond hyperbole! If the sun were ten thousand times brighter than it is—it could not so much as shadow out this glory. In the heavenly horizon we behold beauty in its first magnitude and highest elevation. There we shall 'see the king in his glory' (Isaiah 33:17). All lights are but eclipses, compared with that glorious vision. Apelles' pencil could but blot it; angels' tongues could but dishonor it.

3. This sight of God will be a transforming sight. 'We shall be like him' (1 John 3:2). The saints shall be changed into glory. As when the light springs into a dark room, the room may be said to be changed from what it was; the saints shall so see God—as to be changed into his image! (Psalm 17:15). Here on earth, God's people are blackened and sullied with infirmities—but in heaven they shall be as the dove covered with silver wings. They shall have some rays and beams of God's glory shining in them. The crystal, by having the sun shine on it, sparkles and looks like the sun. Just so, the saints by beholding the brightness of God's glory shall have a tincture of that glory upon them. Not that they shall partake of God's very essence, for as the iron in the fire becomes fire—yet remains iron still, so the saints by beholding the luster of God's majesty shall be glorious creatures—but yet creatures still.

4. This sight of God will be a joyful sight. 'You shall make me glad with the light of your countenance' (Acts 2:28). After a sharp winter, how pleasant will it be to see the Sun of Righteousness displaying himself in all his glory! Does faith breed joy? 'Even though you do not see him now, you believe in him and are filled with an inexpressible and glorious joy' (1 Peter 1:8). If the joy of faith is such, what will the joy of vision be! The sight of Christ will amaze the eye with wonder, and ravish the heart with joy. If the face of a friend whom we entirely love so affects us and drives away sorrow—O how cheering will the sight of God be to the saints in heaven! Then indeed it may be said, 'Your heart shall rejoice!' (John 16:22). There are two things which will make the saints' vision of God in heaven joyful.

[1] Through Jesus Christ, the dread and terror of the divine essence shall be taken away. Majesty shall appear in God to preserve reverence—but however, it will be a majesty clothed with beauty and tempered with sweetness, to excite joy in the saints. We shall see God as a friend, not as guilty Adam did, who was afraid, and hid himself (Genesis 3:10)—but as Queen Esther looked upon King Ahasuerus holding forth the golden scepter (Esther 5:2). Surely this sight of God will not be dreadful, but delightful!

[2] The saints shall not only have vision, but fruition. They shall so see God, as to enjoy him. True blessedness lies partly in the understanding—by seeing the glory of God richly displayed; and partly in the will—by a sweet delicious taste of it and acquiescence of the soul in it. We shall so see God—as to love him—and so love him as to be filled with him. The seeing of God implies fruition. 'Enter into the joy of your Lord' (Matthew 25:21) not only behold it—but enter into it. 'In your light we shall see light' (Psalm 36:9); there is vision. 'At your right hand there

are pleasures for evermore' (Psalm 16:11); there is fruition. So great is the joy which flows from the sight of God—as will make the saints break forth into triumphant praises and hallelujahs.

5. This sight of God will be a satisfying sight. Cast three worlds into the heart, and they will not fill it—but the sight of God satisfies! 'I shall be satisfied when I awake with your likeness' (Psalm 17:15). Solomon says 'The eye is never satisfied with seeing' (Ecclesiastes 1:8). But there the eye will be satisfied with seeing. God, and nothing but God, can satisfy. The saints shall have their heads so full of knowledge, and their hearts so full of joy—that they shall have no lack.

6. This sight of God will be an unwearying sight. Let a man see the rarest sight that is—he will soon be cloyed. When he comes into a garden and sees delightful walks, lovely arbours, pleasant flowers, within a little while he grows weary; but it is not so in heaven. There is no cloying there. We shall never be weary of seeing God, for the divine essence being infinite, there shall be every moment new and fresh delights springing forth from God into the glorified soul! The soul shall be full and satisfied—yet still desire more of God. So sweet will God be—that the more the saints behold God—the more they will be ravished with desire and delight!

7. This sight of God will be a beneficial sight. It will tend to the bettering and advantaging of the soul. Some colors, while they delight the eyes, hurt them. But this knowledge and vision of God, shall better the soul and tend to its infinite happiness. Eve's looking upon the tree of knowledge, was harmful to her. But the saints can receive no detriment from the eternal beholding of God's glory. This sight will be beneficial. The soul will never be in its perfection, until it comes to see God. This will be the crowning blessing.

8. This sight of God shall be perpetual. Here we see objects awhile, and then our eyes grow dim and we need eye-glasses. But the saints shall always behold God. As there shall be no cloud upon God's face, so the saints shall have no mote in their eye. Their sight shall never grow dim—but they shall be to all eternity looking on God, that beautiful and delightful object! O what a soul-ravishing sight will this be! God must make us able to bear it. We can no more endure a sight of glory—than a sight of wrath. But the saints in heaven, shall have their capacities enlarged, and they shall be made fit to receive the delightful beams of divine glory!

9. This sight of God will be an immediate sight. There are some who deny that the soul is immediately after death admitted to the sight of God—but I assert that the saints shall have an immediate transition and passage from death to glory. As soon as death has closed their eyes—they shall see God. If the soul is not immediately after death translated to the beatific vision—then what becomes of the soul in that period of time, until the resurrection?

Does the soul go into torment? That cannot be, for the soul of a believer is a member of Christ's mystical body, and if this soul should go to hell—a member of Christ might be for a time damned. But that is impossible.

Does the soul sleep in the body as some drowsily imagine? How then shall we make good sense of that scripture 'We are willing rather to be absent from the body—and to be present with the Lord'? (2 Corinthians 5:8) If the soul at death is absent from the body, then it cannot sleep in the body.

Does the soul die? It appears that the soul of a believer after death, goes immediately to God. 'This day shall you be with me in paradise' (Luke 23:43). That word 'with me' shows clearly that the thief on the cross was translated to heaven. For there Christ was (Ephesians 4:10). And the word 'this day' shows that the thief on the cross had an immediate passage from the cross to paradise. Therefore, the souls of believers have an immediate vision of God after death. It is but winking—and they shall see God!

See the misery of an impure sinner.

He shall never be admitted to the blessed sight of God. Only the pure in heart shall see God. Such as live in sin, whose souls are dyed black with the filth of hell — they shall never come where God is. They shall have an affrighting vision of God — but not a beatific vision. They shall see the flaming sword and the burning lake — but not the mercy-seat! God in Scripture is sometimes called a 'consuming fire', sometimes the 'Father of lights'. The wicked shall feel the fire — but not see the light. Impure souls shall be covered with shame and darkness as with a mantle, and shall never see the king's face. Those who would not see God in his Word and ordinances — shall not see him in his glory.

Is there such a blessed privilege after this life? Then let me persuade all who hear me this day:

1. To get into Christ. We can come to God — only by Christ. Moses when he was in the rock saw God (Exodus 33:32). Only in this blessed rock, Christ — shall we see God.

2. To be purified people. It is only the pure in heart, who shall see God. It is only a clear eye, which can behold a bright transparent object. Only those who have their hearts cleansed from sin, can have this blessed sight of God. Sin is such a cloud as, if it is not removed, will forever hinder us from seeing the Sun of Righteousness. Christian, have you upon your heart 'holiness to the Lord'? Then you shall see God. 'There are many,' says Augustine, 'who want to go to heaven — but they will not take the holy way which alone leads there!'

There are several sorts of eyes which shall never see God — the ignorant eye, the unchaste eye, the scornful eye, the malicious eye, the covetous eye. If you would see God when you die, you must be purified people while you live! 'We know that when He appears, we will be like Him, because we will see Him as He is. And everyone who has this hope in Him purifies himself just as He is pure.' (1 John 3:2, 3).

Let me turn myself to the pure in heart.

1. Stand amazed at this privilege — that you who are worms crept out of the dust — should be admitted to the blessed sight of God, for all eternity! It was Moses' prayer, 'I beseech you, show me your glory' (Exodus 33:18). The saints shall behold God's glory! The pure in heart shall have the same blessedness that God himself has. For what is the blessedness of God — but the contemplating his own infinite glory and beauty!

2. Begin your sight of God here on earth. Let the eye of your faith be ever upon God. Moses by faith 'saw him who is invisible' (Hebrews 11:27). Often look upon him with believing eyes — whom you hope to see with glorified eyes. 'My eyes are ever towards the Lord' (Psalm 25:15). While others are looking towards the earth as if they would fetch all their comforts thence — let us look up to heaven! There is the best sight. The sight of God by faith would let in much joy to the soul. 'You love Him, though you have not seen Him. And though not seeing Him now, you believe in Him and rejoice with inexpressible and glorious joy!' (1 Peter 1:8).

3. Let this be a cordial, to revive the pure in heart. Be comforted with this — you shall shortly see God! The godly have many sights here on earth, which they do not desire to see. They see a body of death; they see evil and sin; they see unholy people wearing the mask of religion; they see the white devil. These sights occasion sorrow. But there is a blessed sight a-coming! 'They shall see God!' And in him, are all sparkling beauties and ravishing joys to be found!

4. Do not be discouraged at sufferings. All the hurt that affliction and death can do — is to give you a sight of God. As one said to his fellow-martyr, 'One half-hour in glory, will make us forget all our pain!' When the sun rises — all the dark shadows of the night flee away. When the pleasant beams of God's countenance begin to shine upon the soul in heaven — then sorrows

and sufferings shall be no more! The dark shadows of the night, shall fly away. The thoughts of this coming beatific vision, should carry a Christian full sail with joy through the waters of affliction! This made Job so willing to embrace death: 'But as for me, I know that my Redeemer lives! And after my body has decayed, yet in my body I will see God! I will see him for myself. Yes, I will see him with my own eyes! I am overwhelmed at the thought!' (Job 19:25-27).

Concerning Peaceableness

Blessed are the peacemakers.

Matthew 5:9

This is the seventh step of the golden ladder which leads to blessedness. The name of peace is sweet, and the work of peace is a blessed work. 'Blessed are the peacemakers'.

Observe the connection. The Scripture links these two together, pureness of heart and peaceableness of spirit. 'The wisdom from above is first pure, then peaceable' (James 3:17). 'Follow peace and holiness' (Hebrews 12:14). And here Christ joins them together 'pure in heart, and 'peacemakers', as if there could be no purity where there is not a study of peace. That religion is suspicious which is full of faction and discord.

In the words there are three parts:

1. A duty implied, namely — Peaceable-mindedness.

2. A duty expressed — to be peacemakers.

3. A title of honor bestowed — 'They shall be called the children of God'.

1. The duty implied, 'peaceable-mindedness'. For before men can make peace among others, they must be of peaceable spirits themselves. Before they can be promoters of peace, they must be lovers of peace.

Christians must be peaceable-minded. This peaceableness of spirit is the beauty of a saint. It is a jewel of great price: 'The ornament of a quiet spirit which is in the sight of God of great price' (1 Peter 3:4). The saints are Christ's sheep (John 10:27). The sheep is a peaceable creature. They are Christ's doves (Canticles 2:14), therefore they must be without gall. It becomes not Christians to be Ishmaels but Solomons. Though they must be lions for courage — yet lambs for peaceableness. God was not in the earthquake, nor in the fire — but in the 'still small voice' (1 Kings 19:12). God is not in the rough fiery spirit, but in the peaceable spirit.

There is a fourfold peace that we must study and cherish.

[1] There is a home peace — peace in families. It is called 'the bond of peace' (Ephesians 4:3). Without this all drops in pieces. Peace is a belt which ties together members in a family. It is a golden clasp which knits them together, so that they do not fall in pieces. We should endeavor that our houses should be 'houses of peace'. It is not the beauty of the rooms which makes a house pleasant — but peaceableness of dispositions. There can be no comfortableness in our dwellings, until peace is the atmosphere of our houses.

[2] There is a town peace — when there is a sweet harmony, a tuning and chiming together of affections in a town; when all draw one way and, as the apostle says, are 'perfectly joined together in the same mind' (1 Corinthians 1:10). One jarring string brings all the music out of tune. One bad member in a town endangers the whole. 'Be at peace among yourselves' (1 Thessalonians 5:13). It is little comfort to have our houses joined together if our hearts be asunder.

[3] There is a political peace — peace in a nation. This is the fairest flower of a prince's crown. Peace is the best blessing of a nation. It is well with bees when there is a noise; but it is best with

Christians when (as in the building of the Temple) there is no noise of hammer heard. Peace brings plenty along with it. How many miles would some go on pilgrimage to purchase this peace! Political plants thrive best in the sunshine of peace. 'He makes peace in your borders, and fills you with the finest of the wheat' (Psalm 147:14). 'Peace makes all things flourish'.

The ancients made the harp the emblem of peace. How sweet would the sounding of this harp be, after the roaring of the cannon! All should study to promote this political peace. The godly man when he dies 'enters into peace' (Isaiah 57:2). But while he lives peace must enter into him.

[4] There is an ecclesiastical peace — a church-peace, when there is unity and verity in the church of God. Never does religion flourish more, than when her children spread themselves as olive-plants round about her table. Unity in faith and conduct is a mercy we cannot prize enough. This is that which God has promised (Jeremiah 32:39) and which we should pursue (Zechariah 8:18-23). Ambrose says of Theodosius the Emperor, that when he lay sick he took more care for the Church's peace than for his own recovery.

The reasons why we should be peaceable-minded are two:

First, we are called to peace (1 Corinthians 7:15). God never called any man to division. That is a reason why we should not be given to strife, because we have no call for it. But God has called us to peace.

Second, it is the nature of grace to change the heart and make it peaceable. By nature we are of a fierce cruel disposition. When God cursed the ground for man's sake, the curse was that it should bring forth 'thorns and thistles' (Genesis 3:18). The heart of man naturally lies under this curse. It brings forth nothing but the thistles of strife and contention. But when grace comes into the heart, it makes it peaceable. It infuses a sweet, loving disposition. It smoothes and polishes the most knotty piece. It files off the ruggedness in men's spirits. Grace turns the vulture into a dove, the briar into a myrtle tree (Isaiah 55:13), the lion-like fierceness into a lamb-like gentleness. 'In that day the wolf and the lamb will live together' (Isaiah 11:6-9). It is spoken of the power which the gospel shall have upon men's hearts; it shall make such a metamorphosis that those who before were full of rage and hatred, shall now be made peaceable and gentle. 'Nothing will hurt or destroy in all my holy mountain.'

It shows us the character of a true saint. He is given to peace. He is the keeper of the peace. He is 'a son of peace'.

Caution: Not but that a man may be of a peaceable spirit — yet seek to recover that which is his due. If peace has been otherwise sought and cannot be attained, a man may go to law and yet be a peaceable man. It is with going to law as it is with going to war, when the rights of a nation are invaded (as 2. Chronicles 20:2, 3), and peace can be purchased by no other means than war; here it is lawful to beat the ploughshare into a sword. So when there is no other way of recovering one's right but by going to law, a man may commence a suit in law yet be of a peaceable spirit. Going to law (in this case) is not so much striving with another — as contending for a man's own. It is not to do another wrong — but to do himself right. It is a desire rather of equity than victory. I say as the apostle, 'the law is good if a man uses it lawfully' (1 Timothy 1:8).

Is all peace to be sought? How far is peace lawful? I answer, Peace with men must have this double limitation:

1. The peace a godly man seeks is not to have a league of amity with sinners. Though we are to be at peace with their persons — yet we are to have war with their sins. We are to have peace with their persons as they are made in God's image — but to have war with their sins as they have made themselves in the devil's image. David was for peace (Psalm 120:7) — but he would

not sit on the ale-bench with sinners (Psalm 26:4, 5). Grace teaches kindness. We are to be civil to the worst — but not twist into a cord of friendship. That were to be 'brethren in iniquity'. 'Have no fellowship with the unfruitful works of darkness' (Ephesians 5:11). Jehoshaphat (though a good man) was blamed for this: 'Should you help the ungodly and love those who hate the Lord?' (2 Chronicles 19:2). The fault was not that he entertained civil peace with Ahab — but that he had a league of friendship and was assistant to Ahab when he went contrary to God. 'Therefore was wrath upon Jehoshaphat from before the Lord' (verse 2). We must not so far have peace with others, as to endanger ourselves. If a man has the plague, we will be helpful to him and send him our best remedies — but we are careful not to have too much of his company or suck in his infectious breath. So we may be peaceable towards all, and helpful to all. Pray for them, counsel them, relieve them — but let us take heed of too much familiarity, lest we suck in their infection. In short we must so make peace with men that we do not break our peace with conscience. 'Follow peace and holiness' (Hebrews 12:14). We must not purchase peace with the loss of holiness.

2. We must not so seek peace with others as to wrong truth. 'Buy the truth — and sell it not' (Proverbs 23:23). Peace must not be bought with the sale of truth. Truth is the ground of faith, and the rule of life. Truth is the most orient gem of the churches' crown. Truth is a deposit, or charge that God has entrusted us with. We trust God with our souls. He trusts us with his truths. We must not let any of God's truths fall to the ground. Luther says, 'It is better that the heavens fall — than one crumb of truth perish.' The least filings of this gold are precious. We must not so seek the flower of peace — as to lose the diamond of truth.

We ought not to unite with error. 'What communion has light with darkness?' (2 Corinthians 6:14). There are many who would have peace, by the destroying of truth; peace with Arminian, Socinian, and other heretics. This is a peace of the devil's making. Cursed be that peace which makes war with the Prince of peace. Though we must be peaceable — yet we are bid to 'contend for the faith' (Jude 3). We must not be so in love with the golden crown of peace, as to pluck off the jewels of truth. Rather let peace go — than truth. The martyrs would rather lose their lives — than let go the truth.

If Christians must be peaceable-minded, what shall we say to those who are given to strife and contention? To those who, like flax or gunpowder, if they be but touched, are all on fire? How far is this from the spirit of the gospel! It is made the note of the wicked. 'They are like the troubled sea' (Isaiah 57:20). There is no rest or quietness in their spirits — but they are continually casting forth the foam of passion and fury. We may with Strigelius wish even to die to be freed from the bitter strifes which are among us. There are too many who live in the fire of broils and contentions. 'If you have bitter envying and strife, this wisdom descends not from above — but is devilish' (James 3:14, 15). The lustful man is brutish; the wrathful man is devilish. Everyone is afraid to dwell in a house which is haunted with evil spirits — yet how little afraid are men of their own hearts, which are haunted with the evil spirit of wrath and anger.

And then, which is much to be laid to heart, there are the divisions of God's people. God's own tribes go to war with each other. In Tertullian's time it was said, 'See how the Christians love one another.' But now it may be said, 'See how the Christians snarl one at another, They are like ferocious bears!' Wicked men agree together, when those who pretend to be led by higher principles are full of animosities and heart-burnings. Was it not sad to see Herod and Pilate uniting, and to see Paul and Barnabas arguing? (Acts 15:39). When the disciples called for fire from heaven, 'You know not (says Christ) what manner of spirit you are of' (Luke 9:55). As if the Lord had said, This fire you call for is not zeal — but is the wildfire of your own passions. This spirit of yours does not suit with the Master you serve, the Prince of peace, nor with the work I am sending you about, which is a mission of peace. It is Satan who kindles the fire of contention in men's hearts—and then stands and warms himself at the fire! When men's spirits begin to bluster and storm, the devil has conjured up these winds. Discords and animosities among Christians bring their godliness much into question, for 'the wisdom which is from above is peaceable, gentle, and easy to be entreated' (James 3:17).

Be of a peaceable disposition. 'If it be possible, as much as lies in you, live peaceably with all men' (Romans 12:18). The curtains of the tabernacle were to be looped together (Exodus 26:3, 4). So should the hearts of Christians be looped together in peace and unity. That I may persuade to peaceable-mindedness, let me speak both to reason and conscience.

1. A peaceable spirit seems to be agreeable to the natural frame and constitution. Man by nature seems to be a peaceable creature, fitter to handle the plough than the sword. Other creatures are naturally armed with some kind of weapon with which they are able to revenge themselves. The lion has his paw, the boar his tusk, the bee his sting. Only man has none of these weapons. He comes naked and unarmed into the world as if God would have him a peaceable creature. 'White-robed peace is befitting to men, fierce anger is fitting for wild beasts.' Man has his reason given him—that he should live amiably and peaceably.

2. A peaceable spirit is honorable. 'It is a honor for a man to cease from strife' (Proverbs 20:3). We think it a brave thing to give way to strife and let loose the reins to our passions. Oh no, 'it is an honor to cease from strife'. Noble spirits are lovers of peace. It is the bramble which rends and tears whatever is near it. The cedar and fig-tree, those more noble plants, grow pleasantly and peaceably. Peaceableness is the ensign and ornament of a noble mind.

3. To be of a peaceable spirit is wise. 'The wisdom from above is peaceable' (James 3:17). A wise man will not meddle with strife. It is like putting one's finger into a hornets nest; or to use Solomon's similitude, 'The beginning of strife is as when one lets out water' (Proverbs 17:14). To set out the folly of strife, it is as letting out of water in two respects:

[1] When water begins to be let out, there is no end of it. So there is no end of strife when once begun.

[2] The letting out of water is dangerous. If a man should break down a bank and let in the sea, the water might overflow his fields and drown him in the flood. So is he who intermeddles with strife. He may harm himself and open such a sluice as may engulf and swallow him up. True wisdom espouses peace. A prudent man will keep off from the briars as much as he can.

4. To be of a peaceable spirit brings peace along with it. A contentious person vexes himself and eclipses his own comfort. He is like the bird which beats itself against the cage. 'A kind man benefits himself, but a cruel man brings trouble on himself' (Proverbs 11:17). He is just like one who pares off the sweet of the apple and eats nothing but the core. So a quarrelsome man pares off all the comfort of his life and feeds only upon the bitter core of trouble. He is a self-tormentor. The wicked are compared to a 'troubled sea' (Isaiah 57:20). And it follows 'there is no peace to the wicked' (verse 21). The Septuagint renders it 'There is no joy to the wicked'. Angry people do not enjoy what they possess—but peaceableness of spirit brings the sweet music of peace along with it. It makes a calm and harmony in the soul. Therefore the psalmist says, it is not only good—but pleasant, to live together in unity (Psalm 133:1).

5. A peaceable disposition is a Godlike disposition.

God the Father is called 'the God of peace' (Hebrews 13:20). Mercy and peace surround his throne. He signs the articles of peace and sends the ambassadors of peace to publish them (2 Corinthians 5:20).

God the Son is called 'the Prince of peace' (Isaiah 9:6). His name is Emmanuel, God with us, a name of peace. His office is to be a mediator of peace (1 Timothy 2:5). He came into the world with a song of peace; the angels sang it: 'Peace on earth' (Luke 2:14). He went out of the world with a legacy of peace: 'Peace I leave with you, my peace I give unto you' (John 14:27).

God the Holy Spirit is a Spirit of peace. He is the Comforter. He seals up peace (2 Corinthians 1:22). This blessed dove brings the olive-branch of peace in his mouth. A peaceable disposition evidences something of God in a man. Therefore God loves to dwell there. 'In Salem is God's tabernacle' (Psalm 76:2). Salem signifies 'peace'. God dwells in a peaceable spirit.

6. Christ's earnest prayer was for peace. He prayed that his people might be one (John 17:11, 21, 23), that they might be of one mind and heart. And observe the argument Christ uses in prayer [it is good to use arguments in prayer. They are as the feathers to the arrow, which make it fly swifter, and pierce deeper. Affections in prayer are as the powder in the gun; arguments in prayer are as the bullet]. The argument Christ urges to his Father is 'that they may be one, even as we are one' (verse 22). There was never any discord between the Father and Christ. Though God parted with Christ out of his bosom — yet not out of his heart. There was ever dearness and oneness between them. Now Christ prays that, as he and his Father were one, so his people might be all one in peace and concord. Did Christ pray so earnestly for peace, and shall not we endeavor what in us lies to fulfill Christ's prayer? How do we think Christ will hear our prayer, if we cross his prayer?

7. Christ not only prayed for peace — but bled for it. 'Having made peace through the blood of his cross' (Colossians 1:20). Peace of all kinds! He died not only to make peace between God and man — but between man and man. Christ suffered on the cross that he might cement Christians together with his blood. As he prayed for peace — so he paid for peace. Christ was himself bound — to bring us into the 'bond of peace'.

8. Strife and contention hinder the growth of grace. Can good seed grow in a ground where there is nothing but thorns and briars to be seen? 'The thorns choked the seed' (Matthew 13:7). When the heart is, as it were, stuck with thorns and is ever tearing and rending, can the seed of grace ever grow there? Historians report of the Isle of Patmos that its natural soil is such that nothing will grow upon that ground. A froward heart is like the Isle of Patmos. Nothing of grace will grow there — until God changes the soil and makes it peaceable. How can faith grow in an unpeaceable heart? For 'faith works by love'. It is impossible that he should bring forth the sweet fruits of the Spirit, who is 'in the gall of bitterness'. If a man has received poison into his body, the most excellent food will not nourish until he takes some antidote to expel that poison. Many come to the ordinances, but being poisoned with wrath and animosity they receive no spiritual nourishment. Christ's body mystical 'builds itself up in love' (Ephesians 4:16). There may be praying and hearing — but no spiritual growth, no edifying of the body of Christ — without love and peace.

9. Peaceableness among Christians is a powerful loadstone to draw the world to receive Christ. Not only gifts and miracles and preaching may persuade men to embrace the truth of the gospel — but peace and unity among its professors. When as there is one God and one faith, so there is one heart among Christians — this is as bird-seed, which makes the doves flock to the windows. The temple was adorned with 'goodly stones' (Luke 21:5). This makes Christ's spiritual temple look beautiful, and the stones of it appear goodly, when they are cemented together in peace and unity.

10. Unpeaceableness of spirit is to make professors turn heathens. It is the sin of the heathens to be 'implacable' (Romans 1:31). They cannot be pacified. Their hearts are like adamant. No oil

can supple them; no fire can melt them. It is a heathenish thing to be so fierce and violent, as if with Romulus men had sucked the milk of wolves!

11. To add yet more weight to the exhortation, it is the mind of Christ that we should live in peace. 'Have peace one with another' (Mark 9:50). Shall we not be at peace for Christ's sake? If we ought to lay down our life for Christ's sake, shall we not lay down our strife for his sake?

To conclude: If we will neither be under counsels nor commands — but still feed the vile disposition, nourishing in ourselves a spirit of dissension and unpeaceableness — then Jesus Christ will never come near us. The people of God are said to be his house: 'Whose house are we ...' (Hebrews 3:6). When the hearts of Christians are a spiritual house, adorned with the furniture of peace, then they are fit for the Prince of peace to inhabit. But when this pleasant furniture is lacking and instead of it nothing but strife and debate, Christ will not own it for his house, nor will he grace it with his presence. Who will dwell in a house which is all on fire?

How shall we attain to peaceableness?

1. Take heed of those things which will hinder peace. There are several impediments of peace which we must beware of, and they are either outward or inward.

Take heed of outward destroyers to peace. Such as whisperers (Romans 1:29). There are some who will be buzzing things in our ears purposely to exasperate and provoke us. Among these we may rank talebearers (Leviticus 19:16). The talebearer carries reports up and down. The devil sends his letters by this post! The talebearer is an incendiary. He blows the coals of contention. 'Did you hear' (says he) 'what such a one says of you? Will you put up with such a wrong? Will you allow yourself to be so abused?' Thus does he, by throwing in his fireballs, foment differences and set men against each other. We are commanded indeed to provoke one another to love (Hebrews 10:24) — but nowhere to provoke to anger. We should stop our ears to such people, as are known to come on the devil's errand.

Take heed of INWARD destroyers to peace. For example:

[1] Self-love. 'Men shall be lovers of themselves' (2 Timothy 3:2). And it follows they shall be 'fierce' (verse 3). The setting up of this idol of self has caused so many lawsuits, plunders, massacres in the world. 'All seek their own interests' (Philippians 2:21). Nay, it were well if they would seek but their own interests. Self-love angles away the estates of others, either by force or fraud. Self-love is a bird of prey which lives upon rapine. Self-love cuts asunder the bond of peace. We Christians must lay aside self! Even some heathen could say 'We are not born for ourselves alone'.

[2] Pride. 'He who is of a proud heart, stirs up strife' (Proverbs 28:25). Pride and contention are twins — born at the same time. A proud man thinks himself better than others, and will contend for superiority. 'Diotrephes, who loves to have the pre-eminence' (3. John 9). A proud man would have all strike sail to him. Because Mordecai would not bow to Haman — he gets a bloody warrant signed for the death of all the Jews (Esther 3:9). What made all the strife between Pompey and Caesar, but pride? They were too proud to yield one to another. When this wind of pride gets into a man's heart, it causes sad earthquakes of division. The poets feign that when Pandora's box was broken open, it filled the world with diseases. When Adam's pride had broken the box of original righteousness it has ever since filled the world with debates and dissensions! Let us shake off this viper of pride! Humility solders Christians together in peace.

[3] Envy. Envy stirs up strife. The apostle has linked them together. 'Envy, strife' (1 Timothy 6:4). Envy cannot endure a superior. An envious man seeing another to have a fuller crop, a better trade, is ready to pick a quarrel with him. 'Who can stand before envy?' (Proverbs 27:4).

Envy is a vermin which lives on blood. Take heed of it. Peace will not dwell with this vile inmate.

[4] Credulity. 'The simple believes every word' (Proverbs 14:15). A credulous man is akin to a fool. He believes all that is told him and this often creates differences. As it is a sin to be a talebearer, so it is a folly to be a tale-believer. A wise man will not take a report at the first hearing—but will sift and examine it before he gives credit to it.

2. Let us labor for those things which will maintain and nourish peace.

[1] Faith. Faith and peace keep house together. Faith believes the Word of God. The Word says, 'Live in peace' (2 Corinthians 13:11). And as soon as faith sees the King of heaven's warrant, it obeys. Faith persuades the soul that God is at peace, and it is impossible to believe this and live in disagreement. Nourish faith. Faith knits us to God in love, and to our brethren in peace.

[2] Christian communion. There should be much familiarity among Christians. The primitive saints had their 'agape meals' that is, love-feasts. The apostle exhorting to peace brings this as an expedient: 'Be kind one to another' (Ephesians 4:32).

[3] Do not look upon the failings of others—but upon their graces. There is no perfection here on earth. We read of the 'spots of God's children' (Deuteronomy 32:5). The most golden Christians are some grains too light. Oh, let us not so quarrel with the infirmities of others—as to pass by their virtues. If in some things they fail, in other things they excel. It is the manner of the world to look more upon the sun in an eclipse—than when it shines in its full luster.

[4] Pray to God that he will send down the Spirit of peace into our hearts. We should not as vultures, prey upon one another—but pray for one another. Pray that God will quench the fire of contention, and kindle the fire of compassion in our hearts one to another. So much for the first thing in the text implied, that Christians should be peaceable-minded.

I proceed to the second thing expressed, that Christians should be peace-makers.

All Christians ought to be peacemakers; they should not only be peaceable themselves—but make others to be at peace. As in the body when a joint is out—we set it again, so it should be in the body of Christ. When a garment is torn—we sew it together again. When others are rent asunder in their affections—we should with a spirit of meekness sew them together again. Had we this excellent skill we might glue and unite dissenting hearts. I confess it is often a thankless office to go about to reconcile differences (Acts 7:27). Handle a briar ever so gently—and it may scratch! He who goes to interpose between two brawlers, many times receives the blow. But this duty, though it may lack success as from men—yet it shall not lack a blessing from God. 'Blessed are the peacemakers.' O how happy were England, if it had more peacemakers! Abraham was a peacemaker (Genesis 13:8). Moses was a peacemaker (Exodus 2:13). Constantine, when he called the bishops together at that first Council of Nicaea to end church controversies, they having prepared bitter invectives and accusations one against another, Constantine took their papers and rent them, gravely exhorting them to peace and unanimity.

It sharply reproves those who are so far from being peacemakers that they are peace-breakers. If 'blessed are the peacemakers', then cursed are the peace-breakers. If peacemakers are the children of God, then peace-breakers are the children of the devil. Heretics destroy the truth of the church by error, and schismatics destroy the peace of it by division. The apostle sets a brand upon such. 'Mark those who cause divisions—and avoid them' (Romans 16:17). Have no more to do with them than with witches or murderers. The devil was the first peace-breaker. He divided man from God. There are too many in England whose sweetest music is in discord, who never unite but to divide. How many in our days may be compared to Samson's foxtails, which were tied together only to set the Philistines' grain on fire! (Judges 15:4, 5). Sectaries unite to set the church's peace on fire. These are the people God's soul hates — 'Sowers of discord among brethren' (Proverbs 6:19). These are the children of a curse: 'Cursed be he who smites his neighbor secretly' (Deuteronomy 27:24), that is, who backbites and so sets one friend against another. If there be a devil in man's shape, it is the incendiary schismatic.

The text exhorts to two things:

1. Let us take up a bitter lamentation for the divisions of England. The wild beast has broken down the hedge of our peace. We are like a house falling to ruin, if the Lord does not mercifully under-prop and shore us up. Will not a sincere child grieve to see his mother rent and torn in pieces? It is reported of Cato that from the time the civil wars began in Rome, that he was never seen to laugh. That our hearts may be sadly affected with these our church and state divisions let us consider the great harm of divisions.

[1] They are a prognostic of much evil to a nation. Here that rule in philosophy holds true, 'All division tends to destruction'. When the veil of the temple was rent in pieces, it was a sad omen and forerunner of the destruction of the temple. The rending the veil of the church's peace betokens the ruin of it. Josephus observes that the city of Jerusalem when it was besieged by Titus Vespasian had three great factions in it, which destroyed more than the enemy and was the occasion of the taking it. How fatal internal divisions have been to this land! How is the bond of peace broken! We have so many schisms and are run into so many different churches, that God may justly un-church us, as he did Asia.

[2] It may afflict us to see the garment of the church's peace rent, because divisions bring infamy and scandal upon religion. These make the ways of God to be evil spoken of — as if religion itself, were the fomenter of strife and sedition. Julian, in his invective against the Christians, said that they lived together as tigers rending and devouring one an other. And shall we make good Julian's words? It is unfitting to see Christ's doves fighting; to see his lily become a bramble. Alexander Severus, seeing two Christians contending, commanded them that they should not take the name of Christians any longer upon them, for (says he) you dishonor your Master Christ. Let men either lay down their contentions, or lay off the coat of their profession.

[3] Divisions obstruct the progress of piety. The gospel seldom thrives where the weed of strife grows. The building of God's spiritual temple is hindered by the confusion of tongues. Division eats as a worm and destroys the 'peaceable fruits of righteousness' (Hebrews 12:11). In the Church of Corinth, when they began to divide into parties, one was for Paul, another for Apollos; there were but few for Christ. Confident I am, that England's divisions have made many turn atheists.

2. Let us labor to heal differences, and be repairers of breaches. 'Blessed are the peacemakers.' Jesus Christ was a great peacemaker. He took a long journey from heaven to earth to make peace. Peace and unity are a great means for the corroborating and strengthening the church of God. The saints are compared to living stones, built up for a spiritual house (1 Peter 2:5). You know the stones help to preserve and bear up one another. If the stones become loosened and drop out, all the house falls in pieces. When the Christians in the primitive church were of one heart (Acts 4:32) what a supporting was this! How did they counsel, comfort, build up one another in their holy faith! We see while the members of the body are united, so long they do administer help and nourishment one to another; but if they are divided and broken off, they are in no way useful — but the body languishes. Therefore let us endeavor to be peacemakers.

The church's unity tends much to her stability. Peace makes the church of God on earth, in some measure like the church in heaven. The cherubim (representing the angels) are set out with their faces 'looking one upon another' to show their peace and unity. There are no jarrings or discords among the heavenly spirits. One angel is not of an opinion differing from another. Though they have different orders, they are not of different spirits. They are seraphim, therefore burn, not in heat of contention — but in love. The angels serve God not only with pure hearts — but united hearts. By a harmonious peace, we would resemble the church triumphant.

He who sows peace shall reap peace. 'To the counselors of peace is joy' (Proverbs 12:20). The peacemaker shall have peace with God, peace in his own bosom, and that is the sweetest music which is made in a man's own breast. He shall have peace with others. The hearts of all shall be united to him. All shall honor him. He shall be called 'the repairer of the breach' (Isaiah 58:12). To conclude, the peacemaker shall die in peace. He shall carry a good conscience with him and leave a good name behind him. So I have done with the first part of the text 'Blessed are the peacemakers'. I proceed to the next part.

'They shall be called the children of God.' Matthew 5:9

In these words, the glorious privilege of the saints is set down. Those who have made their peace with God and labor to make peace among brethren, this is the great honor conferred upon them, 'They shall be called the children of God'.

'They shall be called', that is, they shall be so reputed and esteemed by God. God never miscalls anything. He does not call them children — who are not children. 'You shall be called the prophet of the Highest' (Luke 1:76), that is, you shall be so. They shall be 'called the children of God', that is, they shall be accounted and admitted for children.

The proposition resulting is this: that peacemakers are the children of the Most High. God is said in Scripture to have many children:

By eternal generation. Christ alone, is the natural Son of his Father. 'You are my Son — this day have I begotten you' (Psalm 2:7).

By creation. So the angels are the sons of God. 'When the morning stars sang together and all the sons of God shouted for joy' (Job 38:7).

By participation of dignity. So king and rulers are said to be children of the high God. 'All of you are children of the Most High' (Psalm 82:6).

By visible profession. So God has many children. Hypocrites forge a title of sonship. 'The sons of God saw the daughters of men that they were fair' (Genesis 6:2).

By real sanctification. So all the faithful are peculiarly and eminently the children of God.

That I may illustrate and amplify this, and that believers may suck much sweetness out of this gospel-flower, I shall discuss and demonstrate these seven particulars:

1. That naturally we are not the children of God.

2. What it is to be the children of God.

3. How we come to be made children.

4. The signs of God's children.

5. The love of God in making us children.

6. The honor of God's children.

7. The privileges of God's children.

1. Naturally we are not the children of God. As Jerome says, we are not born God's children but made so. By nature we are strangers to God, swine not sons (2 Peter 2:22). Will a man settle his estate upon his swine? He will give them his acorns, not his jewels. By nature we have the devil

for our father: 'You are of your father the devil (John 8:44). A wicked man may search the records of hell for his pedigree.

2. What it is to be the children of God. This child-ship consists in two things. Adoption; infusion of grace.

Child-ship consists in adoption: 'That we might receive the adoption of sons' (Galatians 4:5).

Wherein does the true nature of adoption consist? In three things:

[1] A transition or translation from one family to another. He who is adopted is taken out of the old family of the devil and hell (Ephesians 2:2, 3), and is made of the family of heaven, of a noble family (Ephesians 2:19). God is his Father, Christ is his elder-brother, the saints co-heir, the angels fellow-servants in that family.

[2] Adoption consists in an immunity and removal of obligation from all the laws of the former family. 'Forget also your father's house' (Psalm 45:10). He who is spiritually adopted has now no more to do with sin. 'Ephraim shall say, what have I to do any more with idols?' (Hosea 14:8). A child of God has indeed to do with sin as with an enemy to which he gives battle — but not as with a master to which he yields obedience. He is freed from sin (Romans 6:7). I do not say he is freed from duty. Was it ever heard that a child should be freed from duty to his parents? This is such a freedom as rebels take.

[3] Adoption consists in a legal investiture into the rights and royalties of the family into which the person is to be adopted. These are chiefly two:

The first royalty is a new name. He who is divinely adopted assumes a new name; before — a slave; now — a son; before — a sinner; now — a saint. This is a name of honor better than any title of prince or monarch. 'To him that overcomes I will give a white stone, and in the stone a new name written' (Revelation 2:17). The white stone signifies remission. The new name signifies adoption, and the new name is put in the white stone to show that our adoption is grounded upon our justification; and this new name is written to show that God has all the names of his children enrolled in the book of life.

The second royalty is a giving the party adopted an interest in the inheritance. The making one a heir, implies a relation to an inheritance. A man does not adopt another to a title but to an estate. So God in adopting us for his children gives us a glorious inheritance: 'The inheritance of the saints in light' (Colossians 1:12).

It is pleasant; it is an inheritance in light.

It is safe; God keeps the inheritance for his children (1 Peter 1:4), and keeps them for the inheritance (1 Peter 1:5), so that they cannot be hindered from taking possession.

There is no disinheriting, for the saints are co-heirs with Christ (Romans 8:17). Nay, they are members of Christ (Colossians 1:18). Until Christ is disinherited, his members cannot be disinherited.

The heirs never die. Eternity is a jewel of their crown. 'They shall reign forever and ever' (Revelation 22:5).

Before I pass to the next, here a question may arise: *How do God's adopting, and man's adopting differ?*

1. Man adopts to supply a defect, because he has no children of his own — but God does not adopt upon this account. He had a Son of his own, the Lord Jesus. He was his natural Son and the Son of his love, testified by a voice from heaven, 'This is my beloved Son' (Matthew 3:17). Never was there any Son so like the Father. He was his exact image, 'the express image of his person' (Hebrews 1:3). He was such a Son as was worth more than all the angels in heaven:

'Being made so much better than the angels' (Hebrews 1:4); so that God adopts not out of necessity — but pity.

2. When a man adopts, he adopts but one heir — but God adopts many: 'In bringing many sons to glory' (Hebrews 2:10). Oh may a poor trembling Christian say, Why should I ever look for this privilege to be a child of God! It is true, if God did act as a man, if he adopted only one son, then you might despair. But he adopts millions. He brings 'many sons to glory'. Indeed this may be the reason why a man adopts but one, because he does not have enough estate for more. If he should adopt many, his land would not hold out. But God has enough land to give to all his children. 'In my Father's house are many mansions' (John 14:2).

3. Man when he adopts, does it with ease. It is but sealing a deed and the thing is done. But when God adopts, it puts him to a far greater expense. It sets his wisdom on work to find out a way to adopt us. It was no easy thing to reconcile hell and heaven, to make the children of wrath, into the children of the promise; and when God in his infinite wisdom had found out a way, it was no easy way. It cost God the death of his natural Son, to make us his adopted sons. When God was about to constitute us sons and heirs, he could not seal the deed but by the blood of his own Son. It did not cost God as much to make us creatures, as to make us sons. To make us creatures cost but the speaking of a word. To make us sons cost the effusion of blood!

4. Man, when he adopts, settles earthly privileges upon his heir — but God settles heavenly privileges, such as justification and glorification. Men but entail their land upon the people they adopt. God does more. He not only entails his land upon his children — but he entails himself upon them. 'I will be their God' (Hebrews 8:10). Not only heaven is their portion — but God himself is their portion!

God's making of children, is by infusion of grace. When God makes any his children, he stamps his image upon them. This is more than any man living can do. He may adopt another — but he cannot alter the child's disposition. But God in making of children, fits them for sonship. He prepares and sanctifies them for this privilege. He changes their disposition. He files off the ruggedness of their nature. He makes them not only sons — but saints. They are of another spirit (Numbers 14:24). They become meek and humble. They are 'partakers of the divine nature' (2 Peter 1:4).

3. How we come to be the children of God. There is a double cause of our filiation or child-ship.

The impulsive cause is God's free grace. We were rebels and traitors, and what could move God to make sinners into his sons — but free grace? 'Having predestinated us unto the adoption of children according to the good pleasure of his will' (Ephesians 1:5). Free grace gave the casting voice. Adoption is a mercy spun out of the affections of free grace. It were much for God to take a clod of earth and make it a star — but it is more for God to take a piece of clay and sin and instate it into the glorious privilege of sonship. How will the saints read over the lectures of free grace in heaven!

The instrumental cause of our sonship is faith. Baptism does not make us children of God. The thing which makes God take cognizance of us for children, is faith. 'You are all the children of God by faith in Christ Jesus' (Galatians 3:26). Before faith is wrought in us, we have nothing to do with God. We are (as the apostle speaks in another sense) bastards and not sons (Hebrews 12:8). An unbeliever may call God his Judge — but not his Father. Wicked men may hope that God will be their Father — but while they are unbelievers they are bastards, and God will not father them but will lay them at the devil's door! 'You are the children of God by faith'. Faith legitimates us. It confers upon us the title of sonship and gives us right to inherit the kingdom of heaven.

How then should we labor for faith! Without faith we are creatures, not children. Without faith we are spiritually illegitimate. This word 'illegitimate' is a term of infamy. Such as are illegitimate are looked upon with disgrace. We call them baseborn. You who ruffle it in your silks and velvets — but are in the state of nature, you are illegitimate. God looks upon you with an eye of scorn and contempt. You are a vile person, a son of the earth, 'of the seed of the serpent'. The devil can show as good a coat of arms as you!

This word 'illegitimate' also imports infelicity and misery. Illegitimate people cannot inherit legally. The land goes only to such as are lawful heirs. Until we are the children of God, we have no right to heaven, and there is no way to be children but by faith. 'You are the children of God by faith'.

Here two things are to be discussed:

1. What faith is.

2. Why faith makes us children.

1. What faith is. If faith instates us into sonship, it concerns us to know what faith is. There is a twofold faith.

[1] A mere notional faith. When we believe the truth of all that is revealed in the Holy Scriptures. This is not the faith which privileges us to sonship. The devils believe all the articles in the creed. It is not the bare knowledge of a medicine, or believing the sovereign virtue of it — which will cure one who is ill. This notional faith (so much cried up by some) will not save. This a man may have, and not love God. He may believe that God will come to judge the living and the dead, and still hate God — as the prisoner believes the judge's coming to the court, and abhors the thought of him. Take heed of resting in a mere notional faith. You may have this and be no better than devils!

[2] There is a special faith, when we not only believe the report we hear of Christ — but rest upon him, embrace him, 'taking hold of the horns of this altar', resolving there to abide. In the body there are sucking veins, which draw the food into the stomach and concoct it there. So faith is the sucking vein which draws Christ into the heart and applies him there. By this faith, we are made the children of God. Wherever this faith is, it is not like medicine in a dead man's mouth — but is exceedingly operative. It obliges to duty. It works by love (Galatians 5:6).

2. *But why does faith makes us children?* Why should not other graces, repentance, love etc., do so? I answer: Because faith is instituted by God and honored to this work of making us children. God's institution gives faith its value and validity. It is the king's stamp makes the coin pass current. If he would put his stamp upon brass or leather, it would go as current as silver. The great God has authorized and put the stamp of his institution upon faith, and that makes it pass for current and gives it a privilege above all the graces, to make us children.

Again, faith makes us children as it is the vital principle. 'The just shall live by faith' (Habakkuk 2:4). All God's children are living. None of them are stillborn. Now 'by faith we live'. As the heart is the fountain of life in the body — so faith is the fountain of life in the soul.

Faith also makes us children, as it is the uniting grace. It knits us to Christ. The other graces cannot do this. By faith we are one with Christ, and so we are akin to God. Being united to the natural Son, we become adopted sons. The kindred relationship comes in by faith. God is the Father of Christ. Faith makes us Christ's brethren (Hebrews 2:11), and so God comes to be our Father.

4. The fourth particular to be discussed is to show the signs of God's children. It concerns us to know whose children we are. Augustine says that all mankind are divided into two ranks; either they are the children of God—or the children of the devil.

1. The first sign of our heavenly sonship, is tenderness of heart. 'Because your heart was tender' (2 Chronicles 34:27). A childlike heart is a tender heart. He who before had a flinty heart—has now a fleshy heart. A tender heart is like melting wax to God. He may set whatever seal he will upon it. This tenderness of heart shows itself three ways.

[1] A tender heart grieves for sin. A child weeps for offending his father. Peter showed a tender heart when Christ looked upon him and he remembered his sin, and wept as a child. It is reported that Peter never heard a rooster crow, but he wept. And some tell us that by much weeping there seemed to be as it were, channels made in his blessed face. The least hair makes the eye weep. The least sin makes the heart smite. David's heart smote him when he cut off the lap of King Saul's garment! What would it have done if he had cut off his head!

[2] A tender heart melts under mercy. Though when God thunders by affliction, the rain of tears falls from a gracious eye—yet the heart is never so kindly dissolved as under the sunbeams of God's mercy. See how David's heart was melted with God's kindness: 'Who am I, O Sovereign Lord, and what is my family, that you have brought me this far?' (2 Samuel 7:18). There was a gracious thaw upon his heart. So says a child of God, 'Lord, who am I--a piece of dust and sin kneaded together--that the orient beams of free grace should shine upon me? Who am I, that You should pity me when I lay in my blood--and spread the golden wings of mercy over me!' The soul is overcome with God's goodness--the tears drop, and the love flames. God's mercy has a melting influence upon the soul.

[3] A tender heart trembles under God's threatenings. 'My flesh trembles in fear of you' (Psalm 119:120). 'Because your heart was tender, and you humbled yourself before God when you heard what he spoke against this place and its people, and because you humbled yourself before me and tore your robes and wept in my presence' (2 Chronicles 34:27). If the father is angry—the child trembles. When ministers denounce the threats of God against sin—tender souls sit in a trembling posture. This trembling frame of heart, God delights in. 'To this man will I look, even to him who trembles at your word' (Isaiah 66:2). A wicked man, like the Leviathan, 'is made without fear' (Job 41:33). He neither believes God's promises—nor dreads God's threatenings. Let judgment be denounced against sin, he laughs. He thinks that God is either ignorant and does not see—or impotent and cannot punish. 'The mountains quake before him and the hills melt away. The earth trembles at his presence' (Nahum 1:5). But the hearts of the ungodly are more obdurate than the rocks! A hardened sinner like Nebuchadnezzar has 'the heart of a beast given to him' (Daniel 4:16). A childlike heart is a tender heart. The heart of stone is taken away.

2. The second sign of sonship, is assimilation. 'You have taken off your old self with its practices and have put on the new self, which is being renewed in knowledge in the image of its Creator' (Colossians 3:9-10). The child resembles the father. God's children are like their heavenly Father. They bear his very image and impress. Wicked men say they are the children of God— but there is too great a dissimilitude and unlikeness. The Jews bragged they were Abraham's children—but Christ disproves them by this argument, because they were not like him. 'You are determined to kill me, a man who has told you the truth that I heard from God. Abraham did not do such things' (John 8:40). 'You—Abraham's children, and go about to kill me! Abraham would not have murdered an innocent. You are more like Satan than Abraham!' 'You are of your father the devil' (verse 44). Such as are proud, earthly, malicious may truly say, 'Our father which art in hell'. It is blasphemy to call God our Father, and make the devil our pattern.

God's children resemble him in meekness and holiness. They are his walking pictures. As the seal stamps its print and likeness upon the wax, so does God stamp the print and image of his own beauty upon his children.

3. The third sign of God's children is, they have the spirit of God. He is called the Spirit of adoption; 'you have received the Spirit of adoption.' (Romans 8:15).

How shall we know that we have received the Spirit of adoption, and so are in the state of adoption? The Spirit of God has a threefold work in those who are made children:

A regenerating work.

A supplicating work.

A witnessing work.

[1] A regenerating work. Whoever the Spirit adopts, he regenerates. God's children are said to be 'born of the Spirit'. 'Unless a man is born of water and of the Spirit—he cannot enter into the kingdom of God' (John 3:5). We must first be born of the Spirit, before we are baptized with this new name of sons and daughters of God. We are not God's children by creation—but by recreation; not by our first birth—but by our new birth. This new birth produced by the Word as the instrumental cause (James 1:18), and by the Spirit as the efficient cause, is nothing else but a change of nature (Romans 12:2), which though it is not a perfect change—yet is a thorough change (1 Thessalonians 5:23). This change of heart is as necessary as salvation.

How shall we know that we have this regenerating work of the Spirit? Two ways: by the pangs; by the products.

The new birth is known by the pangs. There are spiritual pangs before the new birth—some bruisings of soul, some groanings and cryings out, some strugglings in the heart between flesh and Spirit. 'They were pricked at their heart' (Acts 2:37). The child has sharp throws before the birth; so it is in the new birth. The new birth is marked by pangs—'more and less'. All do not have the same pangs of humiliation—yet all have pangs; all feel the hammer of the law upon their heart, though some are more bruised with this hammer than others. God's Spirit is a Spirit of bondage, before he is a Spirit of adoption (Romans 8:15). What then shall we say to those who are as ignorant about the new birth as Nicodemus: 'What do you mean? How can an old man go back into his mother's womb and be born again?' (John 3:4). Some thank God they never had any trouble of spirit—they were always quiet. These bless God for the greatest curse! It is a sign they are not God's children. The child of grace is always born with pangs.

The new birth is known by the products, which are:

Sensibility. The new-born infant is sensible of the least touch. If the Spirit has regenerated you, you are sensible of the ebullitions and first risings of sin, which before you did not perceive. Paul cries out of the 'law of sin at work within my members' (Romans 7:23). The new-born saint sees sin in the root.

Circumspection. He who is born of the Spirit is careful to preserve grace. He plies the breast of the ordinances (1 Peter 2:1). He is fearful of that which may endanger his spiritual life (1 John 5:18). He lives by faith—yet passes the time of his sojourning in fear (1 Peter 1:17). This is the first work of the Spirit in those who are made children—a regenerating work.

[2] The Spirit of God has a supplicating work in the heart. The Spirit of adoption is a Spirit of supplication. 'You have received the Spirit of adoption whereby we cry Abba, Father' (Romans 8:15). While the child is in the womb it cannot cry. While men lie in the womb of their natural estate, they cannot pray effectually—but when they are born of the Spirit, then they cry 'Abba, Father'. Prayer is nothing else but the soul's breathing itself into the bosom of its Father. It is a

sweet and familiar fellowship with God. As soon as ever the Spirit of God comes into the heart, He sets it a-praying. No sooner was Paul converted but the next act is, 'Behold, he prays!' (Acts 9:11). It is reported of Luther that, when he prayed, it was with so much reverence – as if he were praying to God, and with so much boldness – as if he had been speaking to his friend. God's Spirit tunes the strings of the affections, and then we make melody in prayer. For any to say, in derision, 'you pray by the Spirit', is a blasphemy against the Spirit. It is a main work of the Spirit of God in the hearts of his children to help them to pray: 'Because you are sons, God has sent forth the Spirit of his Son into your hearts, crying, Abba, Father' (Galatians 4:6).

But many of the children of God do not have such abilities to express themselves in prayer. How then does the Spirit help their infirmities?

Though they do not have always the gifts of the Spirit in prayer – yet they have the groans of the Spirit (Romans 8:26). Gifts are the ornaments of prayer – but not the life of prayer. A carcass may be hung with jewels. Though the Spirit may deny fluency of speech – yet He gives fervency of desire, and such prayers are most prevalent. The prayers which the Spirit indites[4] in the hearts of God's children, have these threefold qualifications.

The prayers of God's children are believing prayers. Prayer is the key. Faith is the hand which turns this key of prayer. Faith feathers the arrow of prayer, and makes it pierce the throne of grace. 'Whatever you shall ask in prayer believing, you shall receive' (Matthew 21:22). Whereupon, says Jerome, I would not presume to pray unless I bring faith along with me. To pray and not believe is (as one says) a kind of jeer offered to God, as if we thought either he did not hear – or he would not grant.

That faith may be animated in prayer, we must bring Christ in our arms when we appear before God. 'Samuel took a young lamb and offered it to the Lord as a whole burnt offering. He pleaded with the Lord to help Israel, and the Lord answered' (1 Samuel 7:9). This young lamb typified Christ. When we come to God in prayer we must bring the Lamb – Christ, along with us. Themistocles carried the king's son in his arms and so pacified the king when he was angry. The children of God present Christ in the arms of their faith.

The prayers of God's children indited by the Spirit, are ardent prayers. 'You have received the Spirit, whereby we cry Abba, Father' (Romans 8:15). 'Father' – that implies faith. We 'cry' – that implies fervency. The incense was to be laid upon burning coals (Leviticus 16:12). The incense was a type of prayer; the burning coals, of ardency in prayer. 'Elijah prayed earnestly, James 5:17). That is, he did it with vehemence. In prayer, the heart must boil over with heat of affection. Prayer is compared to unutterable groans (Romans 8:26). It alludes to a woman who is in the pangs of childbirth. We should be in pangs when we are travailing for mercy. Such prayer 'commands God himself' (Isaiah 45:11).

The prayers of God's children are heart-cleansing prayers. They purge out sin. Many pray against sin – and then sin against prayer. God's children not only pray against sin – but pray down sin.

[3] The Spirit of God has a witnessing work in the heart. God's children have not only the influence of the Spirit – but the witness. 'The Spirit itself bears witness with our spirit that we are the children of God' (Romans 8:16). There is a threefold witness a child of God has – the witness of the Word, the witness of conscience, the witness of the Spirit. The Word makes the major proposition – he who is in such a manner qualified, is a child of God. Conscience makes the minor proposition – that you are so divinely qualified. The Spirit makes the conclusion –

---

[4] writes

therefore you are a child of God. The Spirit joins with the witness of conscience. 'The Spirit witnesses with our spirits' (Romans 8:16). The Spirit teaches conscience to search the records of Scripture and find its evidences for heaven. It helps conscience to spell out its name in a promise. The Spirit bears witness with our spirit.

But how shall I know the witness of the Spirit — from a delusion?

The Spirit of God always witnesses according to the Word, as the echo answers the voice. Religious enthusiasts speak much of the Spirit — but they leave the Word. That inspiration which is either without the Word or against it — is an imposture. The Spirit of God indited the Word (2 Peter 1:21). Now if the Spirit should witness otherwise than according to the Word, the Spirit would be divided against Himself. He would be a spirit of contradiction, witnessing one thing for a truth in the Word — and another thing different from it in a man's conscience.

4. The fourth sign of God's children is zeal for God. They are zealous for his truth, and his glory. Those who are born of God are zealous for his honor. Moses was cool in his own cause — but hot in God's. When the people of Israel had wrought folly in worshiping the golden calf, he breaks the tables. When Paul saw the people of Athens given to idolatry 'his spirit was stirred within him' (Acts 17:16). In the Greek it is his spirit was 'embittered', or, as the word may signify, he was in a burning fit of zeal. He could not contain himself — but with this fire of zeal, speaks against their sin. As we shall answer for idle words, so for sinful silence. It is dangerous in this sense to be possessed with a 'dumb devil'. David says, 'zeal for Your house has consumed me, and the insults of those who insult You have fallen on me' (Psalm 69:9). Many Christians whose zeal once had almost consumed them, now they have consumed their zeal. They are grown tepid and indifferent. The breath of the world blowing upon them has cooled their heat. I can never believe that he has the heart of a child in him — who can be silent when God's glory suffers. Can a loving child endure to hear his father reproached? Though we should be silent under God's displeasure — yet not under his dishonor. When there is a holy fire kindled in the heart, it will break forth at the lips! Zeal tempered with holiness, gives the soul its best complexion.

Of all others, let ministers be zealous when God's glory is impeached and eclipsed. A minister without zeal is like 'salt which has lost its savor'. Zeal will make men take injuries done to God — as done to themselves. It is reported of Chrysostom, that he reproved any sin against God as if he himself had received a personal wrong. Let not ministers be either shaken with fear — or seduced with flattery. God never made ministers to be as false looking-glasses, to make bad faces look good. For lack of this fire of zeal, they are in danger of another fire, even the 'burning lake' (Revelation 21:8), into which the fearful shall be cast!

5. Those who are God's children and are born of God, are of a more noble and celestial spirit than men of the world. They 'set their minds on things above, not on earthly things' (Colossians 3:2). 'Whoever is born of God, overcomes the world' (1 John 5:4). The children of God live in a higher region. They are compared to eagles (Isaiah 40:31), in regard of their sublimeness and heavenly-mindedness. Their souls are fled aloft. Christ is in their heart (Colossians 1:27) and the world is under their feet (Revelation 12:1). Men of the world are ever tumbling in thick clay. They are 'sons of earth'; not eagles — but earthworms. The saints are of another spirit. They are born of God and walk with God as the child walks with the father. 'Noah walked with God' (Genesis 6:9). God's children show their high pedigree in their heavenly life (Philippians 3:20).

6. Another sign of adoption is love to those who are children. God's children are knit together with the bond of love, as all the members of the body are knit together by several nerves and ligaments. If we are born of God, then we 'love the brotherhood' (1 Peter 2:17); He who loves

the person, loves the picture. The children of God are his walking pictures, and if we are of God, we love those who have his effigy and portraiture drawn upon their souls. If we are born of God, we love the saints notwithstanding their infirmities. Children love one another, though they have some imperfections of nature — a squint-eye, or a crooked back. We love gold in the ore, though it has some drossiness in it. The best saints have their blemishes. We read of the 'spot of God's children' (Deuteronomy 32:5). A saint in this life is like a fair face with a scar in it. If we are born of God we love his children though they are poor. We love to see the image and picture of our Father, though hung in ever so poor a frame. We love to see a rich Christ in a poor man.

And if we are children of the Highest, we show our love to God's children:

[1] We show our love to the children of God — by prizing them above others. He who is born of God 'honors those who fear the Lord' (Psalm 15:4). The saints are the 'dearly beloved of God's soul' (Jeremiah 12:7). They are his 'jewels' (Malachi 3:17). They are of the true blood-royal, and he who is divinely adopted sets a higher estimate upon these, than upon others.

[2] We show our love to the children of God — by prizing their company above others. Children love to associate and be together. The communion of saints is precious. Christ's doves will flock together in company. 'Like associates with like'. 'I am a companion of all those who fear you' (Psalm 119:63). A child of God has a love of civility to all — but a love of delight only to such as are fellow-heirs with him of the same inheritance.

By this, people may test their adoption. It appears plainly that they are not the children of God — who hate those who are born of God. They soil and blacken the silver wings of Christ's doves by their aspersive reproaches. They cannot endure the society of the saints. As vultures hate sweet smells, and are killed with them — so the wicked hate to come near the godly. They cannot tolerate the precious perfume of their graces. They hate these sweet smells. It is a sign they are of the serpent's brood — who hate the seed of the woman.

7. The seventh sign of God's children is to delight to be much in God's presence. Children love to be in the presence of their father. Where the king is — there is the court. Where the presence of God is — there is heaven. God is in a special manner present in his ordinances. They are the ark of his presence. Now if we are his children, we love to be much in holy duties. In the use of ordinances we draw near to God. We come into our Father's presence. In prayer we have secret conference with God. In the Word we hear God speaking from heaven to us, and how does every child of God delight to hear his Father's voice! In the sacraments God kisses his children with the 'kisses of his lips'. He gives them a smile of his face and a secret seal of his love. Oh it is 'good to draw near to God' (Psalm 73:28). It is sweet being in his presence. Every true child of God says, 'Better is one day in your courts, than a thousand elsewhere' (Psalm 84:10). Slighters of ordinances are not God's children, because they care not to be in his presence. They love the tavern better than the temple! 'Cain went out from the presence of the Lord' (Genesis 4:16); not that he could go out of God's sight (Psalm 139:7) — but the meaning is, Cain went from the church of God where the Lord gave the visible signs of his presence to his people.

8. The eighth sign sign of God's children is compliance with the will of our heavenly Father. A childlike heart answers to God's call — as the echo answers to the voice. It is like the flower which opens and shuts with the sun. So it opens to God — and shuts to temptation. This is the motto of a new-born saint, 'Speak, Lord, for your servant is listening' (1 Samuel 3:9). When God bids his children pray in their closets, mortify sin, suffer for his name — they are ambitious to obey. They will lay down their lives at their Father's call. Hypocrites court God and speak him fair — but refuse to go on his errands. They are not children — but rebels.

9. The last sign of God's children is—he who is a child of God will labor to make others the children of God. The holy seed of grace propagates (Galatians 4:19; Philemon 10). He who is of the seed royal will be ambitiously desirous to bring others into the kindred. Are you divinely adopted? You will studiously endeavor to make your child a child of the Most High.

How Christians should bring up their children

There are two reasons why a godly parent will endeavor to bring his child into the heavenly family:

[1] Out of conscience. A godly parent sees the injury he has done to his child. He has conveyed the plague of sin to him, and in conscience he will endeavor to make some recompense. In the old law, he who had smitten and wounded another was bound to see him healed and pay for his cure. Parents have given their children a wound in their souls, and therefore must do what in them lies by admonition, prayers, and tears—to see the wound healed.

[2] Out of flaming zeal to the honor of God. He who has tasted God's love in adoption, looks upon himself as engaged to bring God all the glory he can. If he has a child or acquaintance who are strangers to God, he would gladly promote the work of grace in their hearts. It is a glory to Christ when multitudes are born to him.

How far are they from being God's children who have no care to bring others into the family of God! To blame are those masters, who mind more their servants' work than their souls. To blame are those parents who disregard the spiritual welfare of their children. They do not drop in principles of knowledge into them—but allow them to have their own way. They will let them lie and swear—but not pray for them. They will let them read play-books—but not Scripture.

'These words which I command you this day, you shall teach them diligently to your children' (Deuteronomy 6:6, 7). 'Train up a child in the way he should go, and when he is old he will not depart from it' (Proverbs 22:6). 'Fathers, do not exasperate your children; instead, bring them up in the training and instruction of the Lord' (Ephesians 6:4). This threefold cord of Scripture is not easily broken.

The saints of old were continually grafting principles of holy knowledge in their children. 'I know that Abraham will command his children, and they shall keep the way of the Lord' (Genesis 18:19). 'And you Solomon, my son, know the God of your father and serve him with a perfect heart' (1 Chronicles 28:9). What need is there of instilling holy instructions to overtop the poisonful weeds of sin which grow in our children's hearts! As farmers, when they have planted young trees, they set stays to them to keep them from bending. Children are young plants. The heavenly precepts of their parents are like stays set about them, to keep them from bending to error and profaneness. When can there be a fitter season to disseminate and infuse knowledge into children, than when they are young? Now is a time to give them the breast and let them suck in the 'sincere milk of the word' (1 Peter 2:2).

But some may object that it is to no purpose to teach our children the knowledge of God. They have no sense of spiritual things, nor are they the better for our instructions.

I answer:

We read in Scripture of children who by virtue of instruction have had their tender years sanctified. Timothy's mother and grandmother taught him the Scriptures from his cradle: 'And that from a child you have known the holy Scriptures' (2 Timothy 3:15). Timothy sucked in Scripture, as it were with his milk. We read of young children who cried 'Hosanna' to Christ and trumpeted forth his praises (Matthew 21:15).

And again, suppose our counsel and instruction does not at present prevail with our children, it may afterwards take effect. The seed a man sows in his ground does not immediately spring up—but in its season it brings forth a crop. He who plants a tree does not see the full growth until many years after. If we must not instruct our children because at present they do not reap the benefit, by the same reason ministers should not preach the Word, because at present many of their hearers have no benefit.

Again, if our counsels and admonitions do not prevail with our children—yet 'we have delivered our own souls'. There is comfort in the discharge of conscience. We cannot control the outcome of our instructions. Duty is our work; success is God's work.

All which considered, should make parents persevere in giving holy instructions to their children. Those who are of the family of God and whom he has adopted for children, will endeavor that their children may be more God's children than theirs. They will 'travail in birth until Christ is formed in them'. A true saint is a loadstone that will be drawing others to God. Let this suffice to have spoken of the signs of adoption. I proceed.

5. The fifth particular to be discussed is the love of God in making us children. 'Behold! How great is the love the Father has lavished on us, that we should be called children of God!' (1 John 3:1). God showed power in making us his creatures—but his love in making us his sons. Plato gave God thanks that he had made him a man and not a beast—but what cause have they to adore God's love, who has made them his children! The apostle adds a 'Behold!' to it. That we may the better behold God's love in making us children, consider three things.

1. We were deformed—so did not deserve to be made God's children. 'When I passed by you and saw you polluted in your own blood, it was the time of love' (Ezekiel 16:6, 8). Mordecai adopted Esther because she was lovely—but we were in our blood, and then God adopted us. He did not adopt us when we were clothed with the robe of innocence in paradise, when we were hung with the jewels of holiness; but when we were in our blood and had our leprous spots upon us! The time of our loathing—was the time of God's loving!

2. As we did not deserve to be made God's children, so neither did we desire it. No rich man will force another to become his heir against his will. If a king should go to adopt a beggar and make him heir of the crown, if the beggar should refuse the king's favor and say, 'I had rather be a beggar still—I do not want your riches'; the king would take it in high contempt of his favor, and would not adopt him against his will. Thus it was with us. We had no willingness to be made God's children. We desired to be beggars still—but God out of his infinite mercy and indulgence, not only offers to make us children—but makes us willing to embrace the offer (Psalm 110:3). What stupendous love was this!

3. It is the wonder of love that God should adopt us for his children, when we were enemies. If a man would make another heir of his land, he would adopt one who is near akin to him. No man would adopt an enemy. But that God should make us his children—when we were his enemies; that he should make us heirs to the crown—when we were traitors to the crown—oh amazing, astonishing love! What stupendous love was this! We were not akin to God. We had by sin lost and forfeited our pedigree. We had done God all the injury and spite we could, defaced his image, violated his law, trampled upon his mercies—but when we had angered him, he adopted us. What stupendous love was this! Such love was never shown to the angels! When they fell (though they were of a more noble nature, and in probability might have done God more service than we can)—yet God never gave this privilege of adoption to them. He did not make them children—but prisoners. They were heirs only to 'the treasures of wrath'! (Romans 2:5).

Let all who are thus nearly related to God, stand admiring his love. When they were like Saul, breathing forth enmity against God; when their hearts stood out as garrisons against him, the Lord conquered their stubbornness with kindness, and not only pardoned — but adopted them. It is hard to say which is greater — the mystery, or the mercy. This is such amazing love as we shall be searching into and adoring to all eternity! The bottom of it cannot be fathomed by any angel in heaven. God's love in making us children is a rich love. It is love in God to feed us — but it is rich love to adopt us! It is love to give us a crumb — but it is rich love to make us heirs to a crown!

It is a distinguishing love, that when God has passed by so many millions, he should cast a favorable aspect upon you! Most are made vessels of wrath, and fuel for hell. And that God should say to you, 'You are my son', here is the depth of mercy, and the height of love! Who, O who, can tread upon these hot coals, and his heart not burn in love to God!

6. The sixth particular, is the honor and renown of God's children. For the illustration of this, observe two things:

1. God makes a precious account of them.

2. He looks upon them as people of honor.

1. God makes a precious account of them. 'Since you were precious in my sight' (Isaiah 43:4). A father prizes his child above his estate. How dearly did Jacob prize Benjamin! His 'life was bound up in the life of the lad' (Genesis 44:30). God makes a precious valuation of his children. The wicked are of no account with God. They are vile people. 'I will prepare your grave, for you are vile' (Nahum 1:14). Therefore the wicked are compared to chaff (Psalm 1:4), to dross (Psalm 119:119). There is little use of a wicked man while he lives — and no loss of him when he dies! There is only a little chaff blown away, which may well be spared. But God's children are precious in his sight. They are his jewels (Malachi 3:17). The wicked are but lumber which serves only to 'cumber the ground'. But God's children are his jewels locked up in the cabinet of his decree from all eternity. God's children are 'the apple of his eye' (Zechariah 2:8), very dear and very tender to him, and the eyelid of his special providence covers them. The Lord accounts everything about his children, to be precious.

Their name is precious. The wicked leave their name for a curse (Isaiah 65:15). The names of God's children are embalmed (Isaiah 60:15). So precious are their names that God enters them in the book of life, and Christ carries them on his breast. How precious must their name needs be, who have God's own name written upon them! 'Him who overcomes, I will write upon him the name of my God' (Revelation 3:12).

Their prayers are precious. 'O my dove, in the clefts of the rock, let me hear your voice, for your voice is sweet' (Canticles 2:14). Every child of God is this dove. Prayer is the voice of the dove, and 'this voice is sweet'. The prayer of God's children is as sweet to him as music. A wicked man's prayer is as the 'howling' of a dog (Hosea 7:14). The prayer of the saints is as the singing of the bird. The finger of God's Spirit touching the lute-strings of their hearts — they make pleasant melody to the Lord. 'Their sacrifices shall be accepted upon my altar' (Isaiah 56:7).

Their tears are precious. Their tears drop as pearls from their eyes. 'I have seen your tears' (Isaiah 38:5). The tears of God's children drop as precious wine into God's bottle. 'You keep track of all my sorrows. You have collected all my tears in your bottle. You have recorded each one in your book' (Psalm 56:8). A tear from a broken heart, is a present for the King of heaven!

Their blood is precious. 'Precious in the sight of the Lord is the death of his saints' (Psalm 116:15). This is the blood which God will chiefly make inquisition for. Athaliah shed the blood of the king's children (2 Kings 11:1). The saints are the children of the Most High God, and such as shed their blood shall pay dear for it. 'You have given their murderers blood to drink. It is their just reward' (Revelation 16:6).

2. God looks upon his children as people of honor. 'Because you are precious in My sight and honored, and I love you.' (Isaiah 43:4).

God esteems them honorable. He calls them a crown and a royal diadem (Isaiah 62:3). He calls them his glory: 'Israel my glory' (Isaiah 46:13)

God makes them honorable. As a king creates dukes, marquises, earls, barons etc., so God installs his children into honor. He creates them noble people, people of renown. David thought it no small honor to be the king's son-in-law. 'Who am I that I should be son-in-law to the king?' (1 Samuel 18:18). What an infinite honor is it to be the children of the High God, to be of the blood-royal of heaven! The saints are of an ancient family. They are sprung from 'the Ancient of days' (Daniel 7:9). That is the best pedigree, which is fetched from heaven! Here the youngest believer is an heir, a co-heir with Christ who is heir of all (Hebrews 1:2; Romans 8:17). Consider the honor of God's children positively and comparatively.

Consider the honor of God's children positively. They have titles of honor. They are called 'kings' (Revelation 1:6); 'the excellent of the earth' (Psalm 16:3); 'vessels of honor' (2 Timothy 2:21).

They have their escutcheon. You may see the saints' escutcheon or coat of arms. The Scripture has set forth their heraldry. Sometimes they give the lion in regard of their courage (Proverbs 28:1). Sometimes they give the eagle in regard of their sublimeness. They are ever flying up to heaven upon the two wings of faith and love. 'They shall mount up with wings as eagles' (Isaiah 40:31). Sometimes they give the dove in regard of their meekness and innocence (Canticles 2:14). This shows the children of God, to be people of renown.

Consider the honor of God's children comparatively. This comparison is double. Compare the children of God with Adam; with the angels.

Compare the children of God with Adam in a state of innocence. Adam was a person of honor. He was the sole monarch of the world. All the creatures bowed to him as their sovereign. He was placed in the garden of Eden, which was a paradise of pleasure. He was crowned with all the contentments of the earth. Nay more, Adam was God's living picture. He was made in the likeness of God himself. Yet the state of the lowest of God's children by adoption — is far more excellent and honorable than the state of Adam was, when he wore the robe of innocence, for Adam's condition, though it was glorious yet it was mutable — and was soon lost! Adam was a bright star — yet a falling star.

But God's children by adoption are in an unalterable state. Adam had a possibility of standing — but believers have an impossibility of falling; once adopted, they are forever adopted. As Isaac said, when he had given the blessing to Jacob, 'I have blessed him — and he shall be blessed!' (Genesis 27:33). So may we say of all God's children, they are adopted, and they shall be adopted! So that God's children are in a better and more glorious condition now than Adam was, in all his regal honor and majesty.

Let us ascend as high as heaven and compare God's children with the glorious and blessed angels. God's children are equal to the angels, in some sense above them, so that they must be people of honor.

God's children are equal to the angels. This is acknowledged by some of the angels themselves. 'I am your fellow-servant' (Revelation 19:10). Here is a parallel made between John and the angel. The angel says to John, 'I am your fellow-servant.'

The children of God by adoption are in some sense above the angels, and that two ways.

The angels are servants to God's children (Hebrews 1:14). Though they are 'glorious spirits' — yet they are 'ministering spirits'. The angels are the saints' servants. We have examples in Scripture of angels attending the people of God's children. We read of angels waiting upon Abraham, Moses, Daniel, Mary etc. Nor do the angels only render service to God's children while they live — but at their death also. Lazarus had a convoy of angels to carry him into the paradise of God. Thus we see the children of God have a pre-eminence and dignity above the angels. The angels are their servants both living and dying; and this is more to be observed, because it is never said in Scripture that the children of God are servants to the angels.

God's children are above the angels, because Christ by taking their nature has ennobled and honored it above the angelic nature. 'He in no wise took the nature of angels' (Hebrews 2:16). God by uniting us to Christ has made us nearer to himself than the angels. The children of God are members of Christ (Ephesians 5:30). This was never said of the angels. How can they be members of Christ, who are of a different nature from him? Indeed metaphorically Christ may be called the head of the angels, as they are subject to him (1 Peter 3:22). But that Christ is head of the angels in that near and sweet conjunction, as he is head of the believers, we nowhere find in Scripture. In this respect therefore I may clearly assert that the children of God have a superiority and honor even above the angels! Though by creation they are 'a little lower than the angels' — yet by adoption and mystical union, they are above the angels!

How may this comfort a child of God in the midst either of calumny or poverty! He is a person of honor. He is above the angels. A gentleman who is fallen to decay will sometimes boast of his parentage and noble blood. Just so, a Christian who is poor in the world — yet by virtue of his adoption — he is of the family of God. He has the true blood-royal running in his veins. He has a fairer coat of arms to show than the angels themselves.

7. The seventh particular to be explained is to show the glorious privileges of God's children. And what I shall say now belongs not to the wicked. It is 'children's bread'. The fruit of paradise was to be kept with a flaming sword. So these sweet and heart-ravishing privileges are to be kept with a flaming sword — that impure worldly people may not touch them. There are twelve rare privileges which belong to the children of God.

1. If we are his children, then God will be full of tender love and affection towards us. A father compassionates his child. 'Like as a father pities his children, so the Lord pities those who fear him' (Psalm 103:13). Oh the yearning of God's affections to his children! 'Is Ephraim my dear son? Is he a pleasant child? My affections are troubled for him, I will surely have mercy upon him, says the Lord' (Jeremiah 31:20). Towards the wicked God's wrath is kindled (Psalm 2:12). Towards those who are children, God's repentings are kindled (Hosea 11:8). Mercy and pity as naturally flow from our heavenly Father — as light from the sun.

Some may object: But God is angry and writes bitter things. How is this consistent with his love?

God's love and his anger towards his children are not in opposition. They may stand together. He is angry in love. 'As many as I love — I rebuke and chasten' (Revelation 3:19). We have as much need of afflictions as ordinances. A bitter pill may be as needful for preserving health, as a cordial. God afflicts with the same love as he adopts. God is most angry when he is not angry! His hand is heaviest when it is lightest (Hosea 14:4). Affliction is a proof of sonship. 'If you endure chastening, God deals with you as with sons' (Hebrews 12:7).

Why, it is a sign of child-ship to be sometimes under the rod. God had one son without sin — but no son without stripes! God puts his children to the school of the cross — and there they learn best. God speaks to us in the Word, 'Children, do not be proud, do not love the world; walk in wisdom.' But, we are 'dull of hearing'; nay we 'stop our ear'. 'I spoke to you in your prosperity — but you said, I will not hear' (Jeremiah 22:21). 'Now,' says God, 'I shall lose my child if I do not correct him.' Then God in love smites — that he may save.

Aristotle speaks of a bird which lives among thorns — yet sings sweetly. God's children make the best melody in their heart, when God 'hedges their way with thorns' (Hosea 2:6). Afflictions are refining. 'The refining pot is for silver, and the furnace for gold' (Proverbs 17:3). Fiery trials make golden Christians. Afflictions are purifying. 'Many shall be tried and made white' (Daniel 12:10). We think God is going to destroy us — but he only lays us a-whitening. Some birds will not hatch but in time of thunder. Christians are commonly best in affliction. God will make his children at last bless him for sufferings. The eyes that sin shuts — affliction opens! When Manasseh was in chains, 'then he knew the Lord was God' (2 Chronicles 33:13). Afflictions fit for heaven.

First the stones of Solomon's temple were hewn and polished — and then set up into a building. First the saints (who are called 'living stones') must be hewn and carved by sufferings, as the corner stone was, and so made fit for the celestial building (Colossians 1:12). And is there not love in all God's Fatherly chastisements?

But there may be another objection, that sometimes God's children are under the black clouds of desertion. Is not this far from love?

Concerning desertion, I must needs say that this is the saddest condition that can betide God's children. When the sun is gone — the dew falls. When the sunlight of God's countenance is removed — then the dew of tears falls from the eyes of the saints. In desertion God rains hell out of heaven (to use Calvin's expression). 'The arrows of the Almighty are within me, the poison whereof drinks up my spirit, Job 6:4). This is the poisoned arrow that wounds to the heart. Desertion is a taste of the torments of the damned. God says, 'In a little wrath I hid my face from you' (Isaiah 54:8). I may here gloss with Bernard, 'Lord, do you call that a little wrath when you hide your face? Is it but a little? What can be more bitter to me than the eclipsing of your face?'

God is in the Scripture called a light and a fire. The deserted soul feels the fire but does not see the light. But yet you who are adopted may see love in all this. They say of Hercules' club, that it was made of wood of the olive tree. The olive is an emblem of peace. So God's club, whereby he beats down the soul in desertion, has something of the olive tree. There is peace and mercy in it. I shall hold forth a spiritual rainbow wherein the children of God may see the love of their Father, in the midst of the clouds of desertion.

Therefore I answer:

[1] In time of desertion God leaves in his children a seed of comfort. 'His seed remains in him' (1 John 3:9). This seed of God is a seed of comfort. Though God's children in desertion lack the seal of the Spirit — yet they have the unction of the Spirit (1 John 2:27). Though they lack the sun — yet they have a daystar in their hearts. As the tree in winter, though it has lost its leaves and fruit — yet there is sap in the root; so in the winter of desertion there is the sap of grace in the root of the heart. As it is with the sun masking itself with a cloud when it denies light to the earth — yet it gives forth its influence; so though God's dear adopted ones may lose sight of his countenance — yet they have the influence of his grace.

What grace appears in the time of desertion?

I answer:

A high prizing of God's love. If God should say to the deserted soul, 'Ask what will you, and it shall be granted' he would reply, 'Lord that I might see you; that I may have one golden beam of your love!' The deserted soul slights all other things in comparison. It is not gardens or orchards, or the most delightful objects which can give him contentment. They are like music to a sad heart. He desires, as Absalom, 'to see the king's face'.

A lamenting after the Lord. It is the saddest day for him when the sun of righteousness is eclipsed. A child of God can better bear the world's stroke — than God's absence. He is even melted into tears; the clouds of desertion produce spiritual rain, and whence is this weeping — but from love?

Willingness to suffer anything so he may have sight of God. A child of God could be content with Simon of Cyrene to carry the cross — if he were sure Christ were upon it. He could willingly die — if with Simeon he might die with Christ in his arms. Behold here, 'the seed of God' in a believer, the work of sanctification, when he lacks the wine of consolation.

[2] I answer, God has a design of mercy in hiding his face from his adopted ones.

First, it is for the trial of grace, and there are two graces brought to trial in time of desertion, faith and love.

Faith: When we can believe against sense and feeling; when we are without experience — yet can trust to a promise; when we do not have the 'kisses of God's mouth' — yet can cleave to 'the word of his mouth'; this is faith indeed. Here is the sparkling of the diamond.

Love: When God smiles upon us — it is not difficult to love him. But when he seems to put us away in anger (Psalm 27:9), now to love him — this is love indeed. That love sure is as 'strong as death' (Canticles 8:6) which the waters of desertion cannot quench.

Secondly, it is for the exercise of grace. We are all for comfort. If it be put to our choice, we would be ever upon Mount Pisgah, looking into Canaan. We are loath to be in trials, agonies, desertions — as if God could not love us except he had us in his arms. It is hard to lie long in the lap of spiritual joy — and not fall asleep. Too much sunshine causes a drought in our graces. Oftentimes when God lets down comfort into the heart, we begin to let down our efforts. As it is with musicians, before they have money they will play you many a sweet lesson — but as soon as you throw them down money they are gone. You hear no more of them. Before joy and assurance, O the sweet music of prayer and repentance! But when God bestows the comforts of his Spirit, we either leave off duty or at least slacken the strings of our violin, and grow remiss in it. You are taken with the money — but God is taken with the music. Grace is better than comfort. Rachel is more beautiful — but Leah is more fruitful. Comfort is fair to look upon — but grace has the fruitful womb. Now the only way to exercise grace and make it more vigorous and lively, is sometimes to 'walk in darkness and have no light' (Isaiah 50:16). Faith is a star which shines brightest in the night of desertion. 'I said, I am cast out of your sight; yet will I look again toward your holy temple' (Jonah 2:4). Grace usually puts forth its most heroic acts at such a time.

[3] I answer: God may forsake his children in regard of vision — but not in regard of union. Thus it was with Jesus Christ when he cried out, 'my God, my God! Why have you forsaken me?' There was not a separation of the union between him and his Father, only a suspension of the vision. God's love, through the interposition of our sins, may be darkened and eclipsed — but still he is our Father. The sun may be hidden in a cloud — but it is not out of the sky. The promises in time of desertion may be, as it were, sequestered. We do not have the comfort from them as formerly — but still the believer's union holds good.

[4] I answer: when God hides his face from his child — his heart may be towards him. As Joseph, when he spoke roughly to his brethren and made them believe he would take them for spies, still his heart was towards them and he was as full of love as ever. He had to go aside and

weep. So God is full of love to his children even when he seems to appear withdrawn. And as Moses' mother when she put her child into the basket in the river, and went away a little from it—yet still her eye was toward it. 'The babe wept'; yes, and the mother wept too. So God, when he goes aside as if he had forsaken his children—yet he is full of sympathy and love towards them. God may change his countenance—but not break his covenant. It is one thing for God to desert, another thing to disinherit.

'Oh, how can I give you up, Israel? How can I let you go? My heart is torn within me, and my compassion overflows.' (Hosea 11:8). It is a metaphor taken from a father going to disinherit his son, and while he is setting his hand to the deed, his affections begin to melt and to yearn over him and he thinks thus within himself, 'Though he is a prodigal child—yet he is my child; I will not disinherit him.' So says God, 'How shall I give you up? Though Ephraim has been a rebellious son—yet he is my son, I will not disinherit him.' God's thoughts may be full of love when there is a veil upon his face. The Lord may change his dispensation towards his children—but not his disposition. He may have the look of an enemy—but still, the heart of a Father. So that the believer may say, 'I am adopted; let God do what he will with me; let him take the rod or the staff; it is all the same; He loves me.'

2. The second privilege of adoption is this—if we are his children, then God will bear with many infirmities. A father bears much with a child he loves. 'I will spare them as a father spares an obedient and dutiful child' (Malachi 3:17). We often grieve the Spirit, and abuse his kindness. God will pass by much disobedience in his children. 'He has not seen iniquity in Jacob' (Numbers 23:21). His love does not make him blind. He sees sin in his people—but not with an eye of revenge. He see their sins with an eye of pity. He sees sin in his children as a physician does a disease in his patient. He has not seen iniquity in Jacob, so as to destroy him. God may use the rod (2 Samuel 7:14), not the scorpion. O how much is God willing to pass by in his children, because they are his children!

God takes notice of the good that is in his children, and passes by the infirmity. God does quite contrary to us. We often take notice of the evil that is in others and overlook the good. Our eye is upon the flaw in the diamond—but we do not observe its sparkling. But God takes notice of the good that is in his children. God sees their faith—and winks at their failings (1 Peter 3:6). 'Sarah obeyed Abraham, calling him Lord'; the Holy Spirit does not mention her unbelief and laughing at the promise—but takes notice of the good in her, namely, her obedience to her husband. 'She obeyed Abraham, calling him Lord'. God puts his finger upon the scars and infirmities of his children! How much did God wink at—in Israel his firstborn! Israel often provoked him with their murmurings (Deuteronomy 1:27)—but God answered their murmurings with mercies. He spared them as a father spares his son.

3. The third privilege of adoption is this—if we are his children then God will accept of our imperfect services. A parent takes anything in good part from his child. God accepts of the will for the deed (2 Corinthians 8:12). Often times we come with broken prayers—but if we are children, God spells out our meaning and will take our prayers as a grateful present. A father loves to hear his child speak, though he but lisps and stammers. Like a 'crane, so did I chatter' (Isaiah 38:14). Good Hezekiah looked upon his praying as chattering—yet that prayer was heard (verse 5). A sigh and groan from a humble heart, goes up as the smoke of incense to God. 'My groaning is not hidden from you' (Psalm 38:9).

When all the glistening shows of hypocrites evaporate and come to nothing—a little that a child of God does in sincerity is crowned with acceptance. A father is glad for a letter from his young son, though there are blots in the letter, though there are wrong spellings and broken English. O what blottings are there in our holy things! What broken English sometimes! Yet coming from broken hearts it is accepted. Though there be weakness in duty—yet if there be willingness, the Lord is much taken with it. Says God, 'It is my child, and he would do better if he could!' 'He has accepted us in the beloved!' (Ephesians 1:6).

4. If we are his children—then God will provide for us. A father will take care for his children. He gives them allowance and lays up a portion (2 Corinthians 12:14). So does our heavenly Father.

He gives us our allowance: 'The God who fed me all my life long unto this day' (Genesis 48:15). Whence is our daily bread—but from his daily care? God will not let his children starve, though our unbelief is ready sometimes to question his goodness and say, 'Can God prepare a table in this wilderness?' See what arguments Christ brings to prove God's paternal care for his children. 'Look at the birds of the air; they do not sow or reap or store away in barns, and yet your heavenly Father feeds them. Are you not much more valuable than they?' (Matthew 6:26). Does a man feed his bird—and will he not feed his child? 'See how the lilies of the field grow. They do not labor or spin. Yet I tell you that not even Solomon in all his splendor was dressed like one of these. If that is how God clothes the grass of the field, which is here today and tomorrow is thrown into the fire, will he not much more clothe you?' (Luke 12:27). Does God clothe the lilies—and will he not clothe his lambs? 'Cast all your cares on him—because he cares for you' (1 Peter 5:7). As long as his heart is full of love—so long his head will be full of care for his children. This should be as medicine—to kill the worm of unbelief.

As God gives his children a portion along the way—so he lays up a portion for them in eternity. 'It is your Father's good pleasure to give you the kingdom' (Luke 12:32). Our Father keeps the purse and will give us enough to bear our charges here—and when at death we shall be set upon the shore of eternity, then will our heavenly Father bestow upon us an eternal and glorious kingdom upon us! Lo, here is a portion which can never be summed up!

5. If we are his children—then God will shield off dangers from us. A father will protect his child from injuries. God ever lies sentinel to keep off evil from his children—both temporal evil and spiritual evil.

[1] God screens off temporal evil. There are many casualties and contingencies which are incident to life. God mercifully prevents them. He keeps watch and ward for his children. 'My defense is of God' (Psalm 7:10). 'He who keeps Israel shall neither slumber nor sleep' (Psalm 121:4). The eye of providence is ever awake! God gives his angels charge over his children (Psalm 91:11). A believer has a guard of angels for his lifeguard. We read of the wings of God in Scripture. As the breast of his mercy feeds his children—so the wings of his power cover and protect them. How miraculously did God preserve Israel his firstborn! He with his wings sometimes covered, sometimes carried them. 'He bore you as upon eagles wings' (Exodus 19:4), an emblem of God's providential care. The eagle fears no bird from above to hurt her young, only the arrow from beneath. Therefore she carries them upon her wings that the arrow must first hit her before it can come at her young ones. Thus God carries his children upon the wings of providence, and they are such that there is no clipping these wings, nor can any arrow hurt them.

[2] God shields off spiritual evils from his children. 'There shall no evil befall you' (Psalm 91:10). God does not say that no affliction shall befall us—but no evil.

But some may say, that sometimes evil in this sense befalls the godly. They spot themselves with sin. I answer:

But that evil shall not be fatal. As sin is in itself deadly — but being tempered with repentance and mixed with the sacred ointment of Christ's blood, the venomous damning nature of it is taken away!

6. If we are his children — then God will reveal to us the great and wonderful things of his Word. 'I praise you, Father, Lord of heaven and earth, because you have hidden these things from the wise and learned, and revealed them to little children' (Matthew 11:25). A father will teach his children. The child goes to his father, saying, 'Father, teach me my lesson'. So David goes to God: 'Teach me to do your will, for you are my God' (Psalm 143:10). The Lord glories in this title, 'I am the Lord your God — who teaches you to profit' (Isaiah 48:17). God's children have that anointing which teaches them all things necessary to salvation. They see those mysteries which are veiled over to carnal eyes, as Elisha saw those horses and chariots of fire which his servant did not see (2 Kings 6:17). The adopted see their own sins, Satan's snares, and Christ's beauty — but those whom the god of the world has blinded, cannot discern these truths.

Whence was it that David understood more than the ancients? (Psalm 119:100) He had a Father to teach him. God was his instructor. 'O God, you have taught me from my youth' (Psalm 71:17). Many a child of God complains of ignorance and dullness. Remember this — your Father will be your tutor. He has promised to give 'his Spirit to lead you into all truth' (John 16:13). And God not only informs the understanding — but inclines the will. He not only teaches us what we should do — but enables us to do it. 'I will cause you to walk in my statutes' (Ezekiel 36:27). What a glorious privilege is this, to have the star of the Word pointing us to Christ, and the loadstone of the Spirit drawing us to Christ!

7. If we are his children — this gives us boldness in prayer. The child goes with confidence to his father, and he cannot find in his heart to deny him: 'How much more shall your heavenly Father give his Holy Spirit to those who ask him!' (Luke 11:13). All the father has, is for his child. If you come to God for pardon, for brokenness of heart — God cannot deny his child. Whom does he keep his mercies in store for — but his children?

And that which may give God's children holy boldness in prayer is this; when they consider God not only in the relation of a father — but as having the disposition of a father. Some parents are of a morose, rugged nature — but God is 'the Father of mercies and the God of all comfort' (2 Corinthians 1:3). He begets all the affections which are in the world. In prayer we should look upon God under this notion, 'a Father of mercy', sitting upon a 'throne of grace'. We should run to this heavenly Father in all conditions!

We should run to our heavenly Father with our sins — as that sick child who, as soon as he found himself ill, he ran to his father to support him — 'My head! My head!' (2 Kings 4:19). So in case of sin, run to God and say: 'My heart, my heart! O this dead heart, Father, quicken it! This hard heart, Father, soften it! Father, my heart, my heart!'

In our temptations: A child, when another strikes him, runs to his father and complains. So when the devil strikes us by his temptations, let us run to our Father: 'Father, Satan assaults and hurls in his fiery darts at me! He would not only wound my peace — but your glory. Father, take off the tempter! It is your child who is assaulted by this 'red dragon'. Father, will you not 'bruise Satan' under my feet?' What a sweet privilege is this! When any burden lies upon our hearts, we may go to our Father and unload all our cares and griefs into his loving bosom!

8. If we are God's children — then we are in a state of freedom. Claudius Lysias valued his Roman freedom at a high rate (Acts 22:20). A state of sonship is a state of freedom. This is not to be understood in an Antinomian sense — that the children of God are freed from the rule of the moral law. This is such a freedom as rebels take. Was it ever heard that a child should be freed

from duty to his parents? But the freedom which God's children have, is a holy freedom. They are freed from 'the law of sin' (Romans 8:2).

It is the sad misery of an unregenerate person, that he is in a state of vassalage. He is under the tyranny of sin. Justin Martyr used to say, 'It is the greatest slavery in the world for a man to be a slave to his own passions!' A wicked man is as much a slave as he who works in the galley! Look into his heart and there are legions of lusts ruling him. He must do what sin will have him to do. A slave is at the service of a usurping tyrant. If he bids him dig in the mine, or hew in the quarries, or tug at the oar—he must do it. Thus every wicked man must do what corrupt nature inspired by the devil, bids him to do. If sin bids him be drunk, be unchaste—he is at the command of sin, as the donkey is at the command of the driver. Sin first enslaves—and then damns!

But the children of God, though they are not free from the indwelling of sin—yet they are freed from the dominion of sin. All sin's commands are like laws repealed, which are not in force. Though sin lives in a child of God—it does not reign. 'Sin shall not have dominion over you' (Romans 6:14). Sin does not have a coercive power over a child of God. There is a principle of grace in his heart which gives check to corruption. This is a believer's comfort—though sin is not removed—yet it is subdued; and though he cannot keep sin out—yet he keeps sin under.

The saints of God are said to 'crucify the flesh' (Galatians 5:24). Crucifying was a lingering death. First one member died, then another. Every child of God crucifies sin. Some limb of the old man is ever and anon dropping off. Though sin does not die totally—it dies daily. This is the blessed freedom of God's children, they are freed from the dominion of sin. They are led by the Spirit of God (Romans 8:14). This Spirit makes them free and cheerful in obedience. 'Where the Spirit of the Lord is, there is liberty' (2 Corinthians 3:17).

9. If we are God's children then we are heirs to all the promises. The promises are called precious (2 Peter 2:4). The promises are a cabinet of jewels. They are breasts full of the milk of the gospel. The promises are enriched with variety—and are suited to a Christian's every condition. Does he need pardoning grace? There is a promise which carries forgiveness in it (Jeremiah 31:34). Does he need sanctifying grace? There is a promise of healing (Hosea 14:4). Does he need assisting grace? There is a promise of strength (Isaiah 41:10). And these promises are the children's bread. The saints are called 'heirs of the promise' (Hebrews 6:17). There is Christ and heaven in a promise; and there is never a promise in the Bible but an adopted person may lay a legal claim to it and say, 'This is mine!'

The natural man who remains still in the old family has nothing to do with these promises. He may read over the promises (as one may read over another man's will or inventory) but has no right to them. The promises are like a garden of flowers, guarded in and enclosed, which no stranger may gather, only the children of the family. Ishmael was the son of the bond-woman. He had no right to the family. 'Cast out the bond-woman and her son,' as Sarah once said to Abraham (Genesis 21:10). So the unbeliever is not adopted, he is not of the household, and God will say at the Day of Judgment, 'Cast out this son of the bond-woman into utter darkness, where there is weeping and gnashing of teeth.'

10. If we are children, then we shall have our Father's blessing. 'They are the seed which the Lord has blessed' (Isaiah 61:9). We read that Isaac blessed his son Jacob: 'May God give you of heaven's dew and of earth's richness-- an abundance of grain and new wine' (Genesis 27:28), which was not only a prayer for Jacob—but (as Luther says) a prophecy of that happiness and blessing which should come upon him and all his posterity. Thus every adopted child has his heavenly Father's benediction. There is a special blessing distilled into all that he possesses.

'The Lord will bless his people with peace' (Exodus 23:25; Psalm 29:11). He will not only give them peace — but they shall have it with a blessing. The wicked have the things they enjoy with God's permission — but the adopted have them with God's love. The wicked have them by providence; the saints by promise. Isaac had but one blessing to bestow. 'Have you but one blessing, my father?' (Genesis 27:38). But God has many blessings for his children. He blesses them in their souls, bodies, names, estate, posterity. He blesses them with the upper springs and the nether springs. He multiplies to bless them and his blessing cannot be reversed. As Isaac said concerning Jacob, 'I have blessed him, yes and he shall be blessed' (Genesis 27:33), so God blesses his children and they shall be blessed.

11. If we are God's children, then all things which happen to them, shall turn to our good. 'All things work together for good to those who love God' (Romans 8:28). Both good things and evil things work to their eternal good.

[1] Good things work for good to God's children.

Mercies shall do them good. The mercies of God shall soften them. David's heart was overcome with God's mercy. 'Who am I, O Sovereign Lord, and what is my family, that you have brought me this far?' (2 Samuel 7:18). I who was of a poor family, I who held the shepherd's staff — that now I should hold the royal scepter! Nay, you have spoken of your servant's house for a great while to come. You have made a promise that my children shall sit upon the throne; yes, that the blessed Messiah shall come of my line and race. And is this the manner of man, O Lord God! As if he had said, 'Do men show such undeserved kindness?' See how this good man's heart was dissolved and softened by mercy! The flint is soonest broken upon a soft pillow.

Mercies make the children of God more fruitful. The ground bears the better crop for the labor which is spent upon it. God gives his children health — and they spend and are spent for Christ. He gives them estates — and they honor the Lord with their substance. The backs and bellies of the poor are the field where they sow the precious seed of their charity. A child of God makes his estate a golden clasp to bind his heart faster to God, a footstool to raise him up higher towards heaven.

Ordinances shall work for good to God's children. The Word preached shall do them good. It is a savor of life; it is a lamp to the feet and a laver to their hearts. The word preached is a means of spiritual health, a chariot of salvation. It is an engrafting and a transforming word; it is a word with unction, anointing their eyes to see that light. The preaching of the Word is that lattice where Christ looks forth and shows himself to his saints. This golden pipe of the sanctuary conveys the water of life. To the wicked the Word preached works for evil; even the Word of life becomes a savor of death. The same cause may have divers, nay, contrary effects. The sun dissolves the ice — but hardens the clay. To the unregenerate and profane, the Word is not humbling — but hardening. Jesus Christ, the best of preachers, was to some a rock of offence. The Jews sucked death from his sweet lips. It is sad that the breast should kill any. The wicked suck poison from that breast of ordinances, where the children of God suck milk and are nourished unto salvation.

The sacrament works for good to the children of God. In the Word preached the saints hear Christ's voice; in the sacrament they have his kiss. The Lord's Supper is to the saints 'a feast of fat things'. It is a healing and a sealing ordinance. In this chalice, a bleeding Savior is brought in to revive drooping spirits. The sacrament has glorious effects in the hearts of God's children. It quickens their affections, strengthens their faith, mortifies their sin, revives their hopes, increases their joy. It gives a foretaste of heaven.

[2] Evil things work for good to God's children. 'Unto the upright arises light in the darkness' (Psalm 112:4).

Poverty works for good to God's children. It starves their lusts. It increases their graces. 'Poor in the world – rich in faith' (James 2:5). Poverty tends to prayer. When God has clipped his children's wings by poverty – they fly swiftest to the throne of grace.

Sickness works for their good. It shall bring the body of death into a consumption. 'Though our outward man perishes – yet the inward man is renewed day by day' (2 Corinthians 4:16). Like those two laurels at Rome – when the one withered the other flourished.' When the body withers – the soul of a Christian flourishes. How often have we seen a lively faith – in a languishing body! Hezekiah was better on his sick bed – than upon his throne. When he was upon his sickbed he humbles himself and weeps. When he was on his throne he grew proud (Isaiah 39:2). God's children recover spiritual health, by physical sickness. In this sense, 'out of weakness they are made strong' (Hebrews 11:34).

Reproach works for good to God's children; it increases their grace and their glory.

Disgrace increases their grace. The farmer by fertilizing his ground makes the soil more rich and fertile. God lets the wicked fertilize his people with reproaches and calumnies, that their hearts may be a richer soil for grace to grow in.

Reproach increases their glory. He who unjustly takes from a saint's credit, shall add to his crown. The sun shines brighter after an eclipse. The more a child of God is eclipsed by reproaches, the brighter he shall shine in the kingdom of heaven.

Persecution to God's children works for good. The godly may be compared to that plant which grows by cutting. The zeal and love of the saints is blown up by sufferings. Their joy flourishes. Tertullian says the primitive Christians rejoiced more in their persecutions than in their deliverances.

Death works for good to the children of God. It is like the whirlwind to the prophet Elijah, which blew off his mantle – but carried him up to heaven. So death to a child of God is like a boisterous whirlwind which blows off the mantle of his flesh (for the body is but the mantle the soul is wrapped in) – but it carries up the soul to God. This is the glorious privilege of the sons of God. Everything which happens, shall do them good. The children of God, when they come to heaven, shall bless God for all cross providences.

12. And lastly, if we are children of God, we shall never finally perish (John 5:24; 10:28). Those who are adopted – are out of the power of damnation. 'There is no condemnation to those who are in Christ' (Romans 8:1). Will a father condemn his own son? God will never disinherit any of his children. Earthly fathers may disinherit for some fault. Reuben for incest lost his birthright (Genesis 49:4). What is the reason parents disinherit their children? Surely this, because they can make them no better. They cannot make them fit for the inheritance. But when we are bad – our heavenly Father knows how to make us better. He can make us fit to inherit. 'Giving thanks to the Father who has made us fit for the inheritance' (Colossians 1:12). Therefore it being in his power to make us better, and to work in us fitness for the inheritance, certainly he will never finally disinherit.

Because this is so sweet a privilege, and the life of a Christian's comfort lies in it, therefore I shall clear it by arguments that the children of God cannot finally perish. The curse of hell and damnation is cut off. Not but that the best of God's children have that guilt which deserves hell – but Christ is the friend at court, who has purchased their pardon. Therefore the damning power of sin is taken away, which I prove thus:

The children of God cannot finally perish, because God's justice is satisfied for their sins. The blood of Christ is the price paid not only meritoriously — but efficaciously for all those who believe. This being the 'blood of God' (Acts 20:28), justice is fully satisfied and cannot condemn those for whom this blood was shed, and to whom it is applied. Jesus Christ was a substitute. He stood bound for every child of God as a surety. He said to justice, 'Have patience with them and I will pay you all', so that the believer cannot be liable to wrath. God will not require the debt twice, both of the surety and the debtor (Romans 3:24, 26). God is not only merciful in pardoning his children — but righteous, 'He is just to forgive' (1 John 1:9). It is an act of God's equity and justice — to spare the sinner when he has been satisfied in the surety.

A damnatory sentence cannot pass upon the children of God, because they are so God's children, as also they are Christ's spouse (Canticles 4:11). There is a marriage union between Christ and the saints. Every child of God is a part of Christ. Now, shall a member of Christ perish? A child of God cannot perish — unless Christ perishes. Jesus Christ who is the Husband, is the Judge, and will he condemn his own spouse?

Every child of God is transformed into the likeness of Christ. He has the same Spirit, the same judgment, the same will. He is a living picture of Christ. As Christ bears the saints' names upon his breast, so they bear his image upon their hearts (Galatians 4:19). Will Christ allow his own image to be destroyed? Theodosius counted them traitors, who defaced his image. Christ will not let his image in believers be defaced and rent. He will not endure to see his own picture take fire. The sea has not only stinking carrion — but jewels thrown into it — but none of God's jewels shall ever be thrown into the dread sea of hell.

If God's children could be capable of final perishing, then pardon of sin is no privilege. The Scripture says, 'Blessed is he whose transgression is forgiven' (Psalm 32:1). But what blessedness is there in having sin forgiven, if afterwards a final and damnatory sentence should pass upon the heirs of promise? What is a man the better for the king's pardon — if he were condemned after he were pardoned?

If the children of God should be finally disinherited, then the Scripture could not be fulfilled which tells us of glorious rewards. 'Truly there is a reward for the righteous' (Psalm 58:11). God sweetens his commands with promises. He ties duty and reward together. One part of the Word carries duty in it, and another part of the Word carries reward. Now if the adopted of God should eternally miscarry, what reward is there for the righteous? And Moses was deceived, in looking to the 'recompense of the reward' (Hebrews 11:26). And so by consequence there would be a door opened to despair.

By all which it appears that the children of God cannot be disinherited or reprobated. If they should lose eternal happiness — then Christ would lose his purchase and would die in vain.

Thus we have seen the glorious privileges of the children of God. What an encouragement is here to true religion! How may this tempt men to turn godly! Can the world vie with a child of God? Can the world give such privileges as these? Can the world do that for you, which God does for his children? Can it give you pardon of sin and eternal life? Is not godliness gain? What is there in sin that men should love it? The work of sin is drudgery — and the wages death! Those who see more in sin, than in the privileges of adoption — let them go on and have their ears bored to the devil's service!

Exhortations

1. There is a bill of indictment against those who declare to the world they are not the children of God — all profane people. These have damnation written upon their forehead.

Scoffers at religion. It were blasphemy to call these the children of God. Will a true child jeer at his Father's picture?

Drunkards, who drown reason and stupefy conscience. These declare their sin as Sodom! They are children indeed — but 'cursed children!' (2 Peter 2:14).

2. Exhortation to believers, which consists of two branches.

[1] Let us prove ourselves to be the children of God.

[2] Let us carry ourselves as the children of God.

[1] Let us prove ourselves to be the children of God. There are many false and unscriptural evidences.

Says one, 'The minister thinks me to be godly, and can he be mistaken?'

Others can but see the outward carriage and deportment. If that is fair, the minister may by the rule of charity, judge well of you. But what does God say? He is your judge. Are you a saint in God's calendar? It is a poor thing to have an applauding world — and an accusing God.

'Oh but,' says another, 'I hope I am a child of God; I love my heavenly Father.'

Why do you love God? Perhaps because God gives you food and wine. This is a mercenary love, a love to yourself more than to God. You may lead a sheep all the field over with a bunch of hay in your hand — but throw away the hay, now the sheep will follow you no longer. So the squint-eyed hypocrite loves God only for the provender. When this fails, his affection fails too.

But leaving these vain and false evidences of adoption, let us enquire for a sound evidence. The main evidence of adoption is sanctification. Search, O Christian, whether the work of sanctification has passed upon your soul! Is your understanding sanctified to discern the things which are excellent? Is your will sanctified to embrace heavenly objects? Do you love where God loves — and hate where God hates? Are you a holy person? This argues the heart of a child of God. God will never reject those who have his image and superscription upon them!

[2] Let us walk as befits the children of God, and let us deport ourselves as the children of the holy God.

Let us walk as the children of God, in obedience. 'As obedient children' (1 Peter 1:14). If a stranger bids a child to do a thing, he regards him not. But if his father commands — he presently obeys. Obey God out of love, obey him readily, obey every command. If he bids you to part with your bosom-sin, leave and loathe it. 'I set cups and jugs of wine before them and invited them to have a drink, but they refused. 'No,' they said. 'We don't drink wine, because Jehonadab son of Recab, our ancestor, gave us this command — You and your descendants must never drink wine.' (Jeremiah 35:5, 6). Thus when Satan and your own heart would be tempting you to a sin and set cups of wine before you, refuse to drink. Say, 'My heavenly Father has commanded me not to drink!' Hypocrites will obey God in some things which are consistent either with their credit or profit — but in other things they desire to be excused. Like Esau who obeyed his father in bringing him venison, because probably he liked the sport of hunting — but refused to obey him in a business of greater importance, namely, in the choice of his wife.

Let us walk as the children of God, in humility. 'Be clothed with humility' (1 Peter 5:5). Humility is a lovely garment. Let a child of God look at his face every morning in the looking-glass of God's Word and see his sinful spots. This will make him walk humbly all the day after. God cannot endure to see his children grow proud. He allows them to fall into sin, as he did Peter, that their plumes of pride may fall off, and that they may walk humbly.

Let us walk as the children of God, in sobriety. 'But let us who are of the day be sober' (1 Thessalonians 5:8). God's children must not do as others. They must be sober.

Our speech must be sober—not rash, not unfitting. 'Let your speech be seasoned with salt' (Colossians 4:6). Grace must be the salt which seasons our words and makes them savory. Our words must be solid and weighty, not feathery. God's children must speak the language of Canaan. Many pretend to be God's children—but their speech betrays them. Their lips do not drop as a honeycomb—but are like the sink, where all the filth of the house is carried out.

The children of God must be sober in their opinions; hold nothing but what a sober man would hold. 'Error,' as Basil says, 'is a spiritual intoxication, a kind of frenzy.' If Christ were upon the earth again, he would have patients enough. There are an abundance of spiritual lunatics among us which need healing.

The children of God must be sober in their attire. 'Don't be concerned about the outward beauty that depends on fancy hairstyles, expensive jewelry, or beautiful clothes. You should be known for the beauty that comes from within, the unfading beauty of a gentle and quiet spirit, which is so precious to God' (1 Peter 3:3-4). God's children must not be conformed to the world (Romans 12:2). It is not for God's children to do as others, taking up every fashion. What is a naked breast but a looking-glass in which you may see a vain heart? Walk soberly.

Let us walk as the children of God, in our labors. We must be diligent in our calling. Religion does not seal warrants to idleness. It was Jerome's advice to his friend, to be always well employed. 'Six days shall you labor'. God sets all his children to work. They must not be like the 'lilies which neither toil nor spin'. Heaven indeed is a place of rest. 'They rest from their labors' (Revelation 14:13). There the saints shall lay aside all their working tools, and take the harp and violin—but while we are here, we must labor in a calling. God will bless our diligence, not our laziness.

Let us walk as the children of God, in magnanimity and courage. The saints are highborn. They are of the true blood-royal, born of God. They must do nothing sneakingly or sordidly. They must not fear the faces of men. As said that brave-spirited Nehemiah, 'Shall such a man as I flee?' (Nehemiah 6:11) so should a child of God say, Shall I be afraid to do my duty? Shall I unworthily comply and prostitute myself to the lusts and desires of men? The children of the Most High should do nothing to stain or dishonor their noble birth. A king's son scorns to do anything that is below him.

Let us walk as the children of God, in sanctity (1 Peter 1:16). Holiness is the diadem of beauty. In this let us imitate our heavenly Father. A debauched child is a disgrace to his father. There is nothing which more casts a reflection on our heavenly Father, than the unholy lives of such as profess themselves his children. What will others say? 'Are these the children of the holy God? Can God be their Father?' 'The world blasphemes the name of God because of you' (Romans 2:24). Oh let us do nothing unworthy of our heavenly Father.

Let us walk as the children of God, in cheerfulness. 'Why should the son of a king look so dejected morning after morning?' (2 Samuel 13:4). Why do the children of God walk so pensively? Are they not 'heirs of heaven'? Perhaps they may meet with hard usage in the world—but let them remember they are the seed-royal, and are of the family of God. Suppose a man were in a strange land, and should meet there with unkind usage—yet he rejoices that he has a great estate in his own country. Just so, should the children of God comfort themselves with this, though they are now in a strange country—yet they have a title to the Jerusalem above; and though sin at present hangs about them (for they still have some relics of their disease) yet shortly they shall get rid of it. At death they shall shake off this viper!

Let us walk as the children of God, in holy longings and expectations. Children are always longing to be at home. 'Meanwhile we groan, longing to be clothed with our heavenly dwelling.' (2 Corinthians 5:2). There is bread enough in our Father's house. How should we long for home! Death carries a child of God to his Father's house! Paul desired 'to depart and be with Christ, which is better by far!' It is comfortable dying, when by faith we can resign up our souls into our Father's hands. 'Father, into your hands I commend my spirit' (Luke 23:46).

Concerning Persecution

Blessed are those who are persecuted for righteousness sake; for theirs is the kingdom of heaven.

Matthew 5:10

We are now come to the last beatitude: 'Blessed are those who are persecuted . . '. Our Lord Christ would have us reckon the cost. 'Which of you intending to build a tower sits not down first and counts the cost, whether he have enough to finish it?' (Luke 14:28). Religion will cost us the tears of repentance and the blood of persecution. But we see here a great encouragement that may keep us from fainting in the day of adversity. For the present, blessed; for the future, crowned.

The words fall into two general parts.

1. The condition of the godly in this life: 'They are persecuted'.

2. Their reward after this life: 'Theirs is the kingdom of heaven'.

I shall speak chiefly of the first, and wind in the other in the application. The observation is that true godliness is usually attended with persecution. 'We must through much tribulation enter into the kingdom of God' (Acts 14:22). 'The Jews stirred up the chief men of the city and raised persecution against Paul ...' (Acts 13:50). Luther makes persecution the very definition of a Christian. Though Christ died to take away the curse from us – yet not to take away the cross from us. Those stones which are cut out for a building are first under the saw and hammer – to be hewed and squared. The godly are called 'living stones' (1 Peter 2:5). And they must be hewn and polished by the persecutor's hand, that they may be fit for the heavenly building.

The saints have no charter of exemption from trials. Though they live ever so meek, merciful, and pure in heart – their piety will not shield them from sufferings. They must hang their harp on the willows and take the cross. The way to heaven is by way of thorns and blood. Though it be full of roses in regard of the comforts of the Holy Spirit – yet it is full of thorns in regard of persecutions. Before Israel got to Canaan, a land flowing with milk and honey, they must go through a wilderness of serpents and a Red Sea. So the children of God in their passage to the holy land must meet with fiery serpents and a red sea of persecution. It is a saying of Ambrose, 'There is no Abel, but has his Cain.' Paul fought with beasts at Ephesus (1 Corinthians 15:32). Set it down as a maxim – if you will follow Christ, you must see the swords and staves. 'Yes, and everyone who wants to live a godly life in Christ Jesus will suffer persecution.' (2 Timothy 3:12). Put the cross in your creed. For the amplification of this, there are several things we are to take cognizance of.

1. What is meant by persecution.

2. The several kinds of persecution.

3. Why there must be persecution.

4. The chief persecutions are raised against the ministers of Christ.

5. What that persecution is, which makes a man blessed.

1. *What is meant by persecution?* The Greek word 'to persecute', signifies 'to vex and molest', sometimes 'to prosecute another', to 'arraign him at the bar', and 'to pursue him to the death'. A persecutor is a 'pricking briar' (Ezekiel 28:24); therefore the church is described to be a 'lily among thorns' (Canticles 2:2).

2. *What are the several kinds of persecution?* There is a twofold persecution; a persecution of the hand; a persecution of the tongue.

1. A persecution of the hand. 'Which of the prophets have not your fathers persecuted?' (Acts 7:52). 'For your sake we are killed all the day long' (Romans 8:36; Galatians 4:29). This I call a bloody persecution, when the people of God are persecuted with fire and sword. So we read of the ten persecutions in the time of Nero, Domitian, Trajan etc.; and of the Marian persecution. England for five years drank a cup of blood, and lately Christians in Bohemia have been scourged to death with the rod of the persecutor. God's Church has always, like Abraham's ram, been tied in a bush of thorns.

2. The persecution of the tongue, which is twofold.

[1] Reviling. This few think of or lay to heart — but it is called in the text, persecution. 'When men shall revile you and persecute you'. This is tongue persecution. 'His words were drawn swords' (Psalm 55:21). You may kill a man as well in his name, as in his person. A good name is as 'precious ointment' (Ecclesiastes 7:1). A good conscience and a good name is like a gold ring set with a rich diamond. Now to smite another by his name, is by our Savior called persecution. Thus the primitive Christians endured the persecution of the tongue. 'They had trial of cruel mockings' (Hebrews 2:36). David was 'the song of the drunkards' (Psalm 69:12). They would sit on their ale-bench and jeer at him. How frequently do the wicked cast out the squibs of reproach at God's children: 'These are the holy ones!' Little do they think what they do. They are now doing Cain's work! They are persecuting.

[2] Slandering. So it is in the text: 'When they shall persecute you and say all manner of evil against you falsely'. Slandering is tongue persecution. Thus Paul was slandered in his doctrine. Report had it that he preached, 'Men might do evil that good might come of it' (Romans 3:8). Thus Christ who cast out devils — was charged to have a devil (John 8:48). The primitive Christians were falsely accused for killing their children, and for incest. 'They laid to my charge things that I knew not' (Psalm 35:11)

Let us take heed of becoming persecutors. Some think there is no persecution but fire and sword. Yes, there is persecution of the tongue. There are many of these persecutors nowadays, who by a devilish chemistry can turn gold into dung — the precious names of God's saints into reproach and disgrace! There have been many punished for clipping of coin. Of how much sorer punishment shall they be thought worthy, who clip the names of God's people to make them weigh lighter!

3. Why there must be persecution. I answer for two reasons.

1. In regard of God: his decree and his design.

God's decree: 'We are appointed 'hereunto' (1 Thessalonians 3:3). Whoever brings the suffering — God sends it! God bade Shimei curse. Shimei's tongue was the arrow — but it was God who shot it!

God's design. God has a twofold design in the persecutions of his children.

[1] Trials. 'Many shall be tried' (Daniel 12:10). Persecution is the touchstone of sincerity. It discovers true saints from hypocrites. Unsound hearts look good in prosperity — but in time of persecution fall away (Matthew 13:20, 21). Hypocrites cannot sail in stormy weather. They will

follow Christ to Mount Olivet—but not to Mount Calvary. Like green timber they shrink in the scorching sun of persecution. If trouble arises, hypocrites will rather make Demas their choice than, Moses their choice. They will prefer thirty pieces of silver before Christ. God will have persecutions in the world to make a discovery of men. Suffering times are sifting times. 'When I am tried I shall come forth as gold' (Job 23:10). Job had a furnace-faith. A Christian of right breed (who is born of God), whatever he loses, will 'hold fast his integrity' (Job 2:3). Christ's true disciples will follow him upon the water.

[2] Purity. God lets his children be in the furnace that they may be 'partakers of his holiness' (Hebrews 12:10). The cross is cleansing. It purges out pride, impatience, love of the world. God washes his people in bloody waters to get out their spots and make them look white (Daniel 12:10). 'I am black—but lovely' (Canticles 1:5). The torrid zone of persecution made the spouse's skin black—but her soul lovely. See how differently afflictions work upon the wicked and godly. They make the wicked worse; they make the godly better. Take a cloth that is rotten. If you scour and rub it, it frets and tears; but if you scour a piece of plate, it looks brighter. When afflictions are upon the wicked, they fret against God and tear themselves in impatience—but when the godly are scoured by these, they look brighter.

2. There will be persecutions in regard of the enemies of the church. These vultures prey upon God's doves. The church has two sorts of enemies.

Open enemies. The wicked hate the godly. There is 'enmity between the seed of the woman and the seed of the serpent' (Genesis 3:15). As in nature there is an antipathy between the elephant and the dragon; and as vultures have an antipathy against sweet smells; so in the wicked there is an antipathy against the people of God. They hate the sweet perfumes of their graces. It is true the saints have their infirmities—but the wicked do not hate them for these—but for their holiness, and from this hatred arises open violence. The thief hates the light, therefore would blow it out.

Secret enemies, who pretend friendship but secretly raise persecutions against the godly. Such are hypocrites and heretics. Paul calls them 'false brethren' (2 Corinthians 11:26). The church complains that her own sons had vexed her (Canticles 1:6). That is, those who had been bred up in her bosom and pretended religion and sympathy, these false friends vexed her. The church's enemies are those 'of her own house'. Such as are open pretenders, but secret opposers of the faith, are ever worst. They are the vilest and basest of men, who hang forth Christ's colors—yet fight against him.

4. The fourth particular, is that the chief persecutions are raised against the ministers. Our Lord Christ turns himself directly to the apostles whom he was ready to commission and send abroad to preach: 'Blessed are you when men shall persecute you' (verse 11). 'So persecuted they the prophets before you' (verse 12). 'Take, my brethren, the prophets for an example of suffering affliction' (James 5:10). No sooner is any man a minister—but he is part martyr. The ministers of Christ are his chosen vessels. Now as the best vessel of gold and silver passes through the fire, so God's chosen vessels pass often through the fire of persecution. Ministers must expect an alarm.

Peter knew how 'to cast the net on the right side of the ship', and at one sermon he converted three thousand souls. Yet neither the divinity of his doctrine nor the sanctity of his life could exempt him from persecution. 'When you shall be old, another shall gird you, and carry you where you would not'. It alludes to his suffering death for Christ. He was (says Eusebius) bound with chains and afterwards crucified at Jerusalem with his head downwards.

Paul, a holy man, who is steeled with courage, and fired with zeal, as soon as he entered into the ministry 'bonds and persecutions awaited him' (Acts 9:16; 20:23). He was made up of sufferings. 'I am ready to be offered up' (2 Timothy 4:6). He alludes to the drink offerings wherein the wine or blood used in sacrifice was poured out, thereby intimating by what manner of death he would glorify God; not by being sacrificed in the fire—but by pouring out his blood, which was when he was beheaded. And that it might seem no strange thing for God's ministers to be under the heat and rage of persecution, Stephen puts the question, 'Which of the prophets have not your fathers persecuted?' (Acts 7:52). Ignatius was torn with wild beasts. Cyprian and Polycarp were martyred. Maximus, the emperor gave charge to his officers to put none to death but the governors and pastors of the Church.

The reasons why the storm of persecution has chiefly fallen upon the ministers are:

1. They have their corruptions as well as others, and lest they should be lifted up 'through the abundance of revelation', God lets loose some 'messenger of Satan' to vex and persecute them. God sees they have need of the flail to thresh off their husks. The fire which God puts them into, is not to consume, but to refine them.

2. The ministers are Christ's ensign-bearers. They are the captains of the Lord's army, therefore they are the most shot at. 'I am set for the defense of the gospel' (Philippians 1:17). The Greek word here used alludes to a soldier that is set in the forefront of the battle and has all the bullets flying about his ears. The minister's work is to preach against men's sins, which are as dear to them as their right eye—and they cannot endure this. Every man's sin is his king to which he yields love and subjection. Now as Pilate said, 'Shall I crucify your king?' Men will not endure to have their king-sin crucified. This then being the work of the ministry—to divide between men and their lusts, to part these two old friends—it is no wonder that it meets with so much opposition. When Paul preached against Diana, all the city was in an uproar. We preach against men's Dianas, those sins which bring them in pleasure and profit—this causes an uproar.

3. From the malice of Satan. The ministers of Christ come to destroy his kingdom, therefore the old serpent will spit all his venom at them. If we tread upon the devil's head, he will bite us by the heel. The devil sets up several forts and garrisons in men's hearts—pride, ignorance, unbelief. Now the weapons of the ministry beat down these strongholds (2 Corinthians 10:4). Therefore Satan raises his militia, all the force and power of hell against the ministry. The kingdom of Satan is a 'kingdom of darkness' (Acts 26:18; Revelation 16:10), and God's ministers are called the 'light of the world' (Matthew 5:14). They come to enlighten those who sit in darkness. This enrages Satan. Therefore he labors to eclipse the lights, to pull down the stars—that his kingdom of darkness may prevail. The devil is called a lion (1 Peter 5:8). The souls of people are the lion's prey. The ministers' work is to take away this prey from this lion. Therefore how will he roar upon them, and seek to destroy them!

[1] It shows us what a work the ministry is; though full of dignity—yet full of danger. The persecution of the tongue is the most gentle persecution can be expected. 'It is not possible' (says Luther) 'to be a faithful preacher and not to meet with trials and oppositions.'

[2] It shows the corruption of men's nature since the fall. They are their own enemies. They persecute those who come to do them most good. What is the work of the ministry, but to save men's souls from hell? to pull them as 'brands out of the fire'. Yet worldly men are angry at this. We do not hate the physician who brings such a remedy as makes us nauseated, because it is to make us well; nor the surgeon who lances the flesh, because it is in order to a cure. Why then should we quarrel with the minister? What is our work but to bring men to heaven? 'We

are ambassadors for Christ ...' (2 Corinthians 5:20). We would have a peace made up between you and God; yet this is the folly of depraved nature, to requite evil for good.

Aristoxenus used to moisten his flowers with wine, honey, and perfumes that they might not only smell more fragrantly but put forth more fruit. So should we do with our ministers. Give them wine and honey. Encourage them in their work that they might act more vigorously. But instead of this we give them gall and vinegar to drink. We hate and persecute them. Most deal with their ministers as Israel did with Moses. He prayed for them and wrought miracles for them — yet they were continually quarreling with him and sometimes ready to take away his life.

[3] If the fury of the world is against the ministers, then you who fear God had need pray much for them. 'Pray for us, that the Word of the Lord may have free course, and that we may be delivered from unreasonable and wicked men.' (2 Thessalonians 3:1, 2). People should pray for their ministers that God would give them wisdom of the serpent — that they may not betray themselves to danger by indiscretion; and the boldness of the lion — that they may not betray the truth by fear.

5. What that suffering persecution is, which makes a man blessed.

1. I shall show what that suffering is, which will not make us blessed.

[1] That is not Christian suffering, when we pull a cross upon ourselves. There is little comfort in such suffering. Augustine speaks of some in his time who were called Circumcellions, who out of a zeal for martyrdom, would run themselves into sufferings. These were accessory to their own death, like King Saul who fell upon his own sword. We are bound by all lawful means to preserve our own lives. Jesus Christ did not suffer until he was called to it. Suspect that to be a temptation, which bids us cast ourselves down into sufferings. When men through rashness run themselves into trouble, it is a cross of their own making and not of God's laying upon them.

[2] That is not Christian suffering, when we suffer for our offences. 'Let none of you suffer as an evildoer' (1 Peter 4:15). 'We indeed suffer justly' (Luke 23:41). I am not of Cyprian's mind that the thief on the cross suffered as a martyr. No! he suffered as an evildoer! Christ indeed took pity on him and saved him. He died a saint — but not a martyr. When men suffer by the hand of the magistrate for their uncleanness, blasphemies etc., these do not suffer persecution — but execution. They die not as martyrs — but as malefactors. They suffer evil — for being evil.

[3] That is not Christian suffering, when they suffer, out of sinister respects, to be cried up as head of a party, or to keep up a faction. The apostle implies that a man may give his body to be burned — yet go to hell (1 Corinthians 13:3). Ambitious men may sacrifice their lives to purchase fame. These are the devil's martyrs.

2. What that suffering persecution is, which will make us blessed, and shall wear the crown of martyrdom.

[1] We suffer as a Christian, when we suffer in a good cause. So it is in the text. 'Blessed are those who suffer for righteousness sake'. It is the cause which makes a martyr. When we suffer for the truth and espouse the quarrel of true religion, this is to suffer for righteousness' sake. 'For the hope of Israel, I am bound with this chain' (Acts 28:20).

[2] We suffer as a Christian, when we suffer with a good conscience. A man may have a good cause — and a bad conscience. He may suffer for 'righteousness sake' — yet he himself be unrighteous. Paul, as he had a just cause, so he had a pure conscience. 'I have lived in all good conscience to this day' (Acts 23:1). Paul kept a good conscience to his dying day. It has made the

saints go as cheerfully to the stake—as if they had been going to a crown. See to it that there is no flaw in conscience. A ship that is to sail upon the waters must be preserved from leaking. When Christians are to sail on the waters of persecution, let them take heed there be no leak of guilt in their conscience. He who suffers (though it is in God's own cause) with a bad conscience, suffers two hells; a hell of persecution, and a hell of damnation.

[3] We suffer as a Christian, when we have a good call. 'You shall be brought before kings ...' (Matthew 10:18). There is no question but a man may so far consult for his safety that if God by his providence opens a door, he may flee in time of persecution (Matthew 10:23). But when he is brought before kings, and the case is such that either he must suffer, or the truth must suffer— here is a clear call to suffering, and this is reckoned for martyrdom.

[4] We suffer as a Christian, when we have good ends in our suffering, namely, that we may glorify God, set a seal to the truth, and show our love to Christ. 'You shall be brought before kings for my sake' (Matthew 10:18). The primitive Christians burned more in love, than in fire. When we look at God in our sufferings and are willing to make his crown flourish, though it be in our ashes—this is that suffering which carries away the garland of glory.

[5] When we suffer with Christian virtues. 'If any man suffers as a Christian, let him not be ashamed' (1 Peter 4:16). To suffer as a Christian is to suffer with such a spirit as becomes a Christian, which is:

When we suffer with patience. 'Take, my brethren, the prophets for an example of suffering affliction and of patience' (James 5:10). A Christian must not repine but say, 'Shall I not drink the cup' of martyrdom which my Father has given me? There should be such a spirit of meekness in a Christian's suffering, that it should be hard to say which is greater—his persecution or his patience. When Job had lost all, he kept the breastplate of innocence and the shield of patience. An impatient martyr is a contradiction.

To suffer as Christians is when we suffer with courage. Courage is a Christian's armor. It steels and animates him. The three Hebrew children, or rather the three champions, were of brave heroic spirits. They do not say to the king, 'We ought not to serve your gods'—but 'We will not!' (Daniel 3:18). Neither Nebuchadnezzar's music nor his furnace could alter their resolution. Tertullian was called an adamant, for his invincible courage. Holy courage makes us (as one of the fathers says) 'have such faces of brass that we are not ashamed of the cross'. This is to suffer as Christians, when we are meek yet resolute. The more the fire is blown—the more it flames. So it is with a brave-spirited Christian. The more opposition he meets with—the more zeal and courage flames forth.

To suffer as Christians is to suffer with cheerfulness. Patience is a bearing the cross; cheerfulness is a taking up the cross. Christ suffered for us cheerfully. His death was a freewill offering (Luke 12:50). He thirsted to drink of that cup of blood! Such must our sufferings be for Christ. Cheerfulness perfumes suffering and makes it the sacrifice of a sweet-smelling savor to God. Thus Moses suffered cheerfully. 'Moses, when he was come to years, chose to suffer affliction with the people of God, rather than to enjoy the pleasures of sin for a season' (Hebrews 11:24, 25). Observe: 'When he was come to years': It was no childish act. It was when he was of years of discretion. 'He chose to suffer affliction.' Suffering was not so much his task—as his choice. The cross was not so much imposed—as embraced. This is to suffer as Christians, when we are volunteers; we take up the cross cheerfully, nay, joyfully. 'They departed from the presence of the council, rejoicing that they were counted worthy to suffer shame for his name' (Acts 5:41). Or as it is more emphatic in the original, 'They rejoiced that they were so far graced as to be disgraced for the name of Christ'. Tertullian says of the primitive Christians, that they took more comfort in their sufferings than in their deliverance. And indeed well may a Christian be joyful in suffering, because it is a great favor when God honors a man to be a witness to the truth. Christ's marks in Paul's body were prints of glory. The saints have worn their sufferings as ornaments. Ignatius' chains were his jewels. Never have any princes been so famous for their victories, as the martyrs for their sufferings.

We suffer as Christians when we suffer and pray for our persecutors. 'Love your enemies, do good to those who hate you, bless those who curse you, pray for those who mistreat you' (Luke 6:27-28).

There are two reasons why we should pray for our persecutors.

Because our prayers may be a means to convert them. Stephen prayed for his persecutors: 'Lord, lay not this sin to their charge' (Acts 7:60). And this prayer was effectual to some of their conversions. Augustine says that the church of God was indebted to Stephen's prayer for all that benefit which was reaped by Paul's ministry.

We should pray for our persecutors because they do us good, though against their will. They shall increase our reward. Every reproach shall add to our glory. Every injury shall serve to make our crown heavier. As Gregory Nazianzen speaks in one of his orations, Every stone which was thrown at Stephen was a precious stone which enriched him and made him shine brighter in the kingdom of heaven.

Thus have I shown what that suffering is, which makes us blessed, and shall wear the crown of martyrdom.

1. It shows us what the nature of Christianity is, namely, sanctity joined with suffering. A true saint carries Christ in his heart—and the cross on his shoulders. 'All who will live godly in Christ Jesus shall suffer persecution' (2 Timothy 3:12). Christ and his cross are never parted. It is too much for a Christian to have two heavens, one here and another hereafter. Christ's kingdom on earth is the kingdom of the cross. What is the meaning of the shield of faith, the helmet of hope, the breastplate of patience—but to imply that we must encounter sufferings? It is one of the titles given to the church, 'afflicted' (Isaiah 54:11). Persecution is the legacy bequeathed by Christ to his people. 'In the world you shall have tribulation' (John 16:33). Christ's spouse is a lily among thorns. Christ's sheep must expect to lose their golden fleece. This the flesh does not like to hear of. Therefore Christ calls persecution 'the cross' (Matthew 16:24). It is cross to flesh and blood. We are all for reigning. 'When will you restore the kingdom again to Israel?' (Acts 1:6). But the apostle tells of suffering before reigning. 'If we suffer—we shall also reign with him' (2 Timothy 2:12). How loath is corrupt flesh to put its neck under Christ's yoke, or stretch itself upon the cross!

True religion gives no charter of exemption from suffering. To have two heavens is more than Christ had. Was Christ crowned with thorns—and do we think to be crowned with roses! 'Don't be surprised at the fiery trials you are going through, as if something strange were happening to you' (1 Peter 4:12). If we are God's gold, it is not strange to be cast into the fire. Some there are, who picture Erasmus as half in heaven and half out. Methinks it represents a Christian in this life. In regard of his inward consolation—he is half in heaven. In regard of his outward persecution—he is half in hell.

2. See hence that persecutions are not signs of God's anger or fruits of the curse, for 'blessed are those who are persecuted'. If they are blessed who die in the Lord, are they not blessed who die for the Lord? We are very apt to judge them hated and forsaken of God, who are in a suffering condition. 'If you are the Son of God, come down from the cross' (Matthew 27:40). The Jews made a question of it. They could hardly believe Christ was the Son of God when he hung upon

the cross. Would God let him be reproached and forsaken—if he were the Son of God? When the barbarians saw the viper on Paul's hand, they thought he was a great sinner. 'No doubt this man is a murderer' (Acts 28:4). So when we see the people of God afflicted and the viper of persecution fastens upon them, we are apt to say, 'These are greater sinners than others, and God does not love them.' This is for lack of judgment. 'Blessed are those who are persecuted'. Persecutions are pledges of God's love, badges of honor (Hebrews 12:7). In the sharpest trial, there is the sweetest comfort. God's fanning his wheat, is but to make it purer.

1. It reproves such as would be thought good Christians, but will not suffer persecution for Christ's sake. Their care is not to take up the cross—but to avoid the cross. 'When trouble or persecution comes because of the word, he quickly falls away' (Matthew 13:21). There are many professors who will suffer nothing for him. These may be compared to the crystal which looks like diamond until it comes to the hammering, then it breaks. Many, when they see the palm-branches and garments spread, cry 'Hosanna!' to Christ—but if the swords and staves appear, then they slink away. It is to be feared there are some among us, who, if persecutions should come, would rather make Demas' choice—than Moses' choice, and would study rather to keep their skin whole—than their conscience pure. Erasmus highly extolled Luther's doctrine—but when the Emperor threatened all who should favor Luther's cause, he unworthily deserted it. Hypocrites will sooner renounce Christ, than take up the cross. If ever we should show ourselves Christians to purpose, we must with Peter throw ourselves upon the water to come to Christ. He who refuses to suffer, let him read over that sad scripture, 'Whoever shall deny me before men, him will I also deny before my Father which is in heaven' (Matthew 10:33).

2. It reproves them who are the opposers and persecutors of the saints. How great is their sin! They resist the Holy Spirit. 'You always resist the Holy Spirit! Which of the prophets have your not fathers persecuted?' (Acts 7:51, 52). Persecutors offer affront to Christ in heaven. They tread his jewels in the dust, touch the apple of his eye, and pierce his sides. 'Saul, Saul, why persecute you me?' (Acts 9:4). When the foot was trodden on, the head cried out. As the sin is great, so the punishment shall be proportionable. 'Because they poured out the blood of the saints and the prophets, You also gave them blood to drink; they deserve it!' (Revelation 16:6). Will not Christ avenge those who die in this quarrel?

1. Let it exhort Christians to think beforehand and make account of sufferings. This reckoning beforehand can do us no hurt; it may do us much good.

[1] The fore-thoughts of suffering will make a Christian very serious. The heart is apt to be feathery and frothy. The thoughts of suffering persecution would solidify it. Why am I thus light? Is this a posture fit for persecution? Christians grow serious in the casting up their spiritual accounts. They reckon what religion must cost them, and may cost them. It must cost them the blood of their sins. It may cost them the blood of their lives.

[2] The fore-thoughts of persecution will be as sauce to season our delights, that we do not surfeit upon them. How soon may there be an alarum sounded? How soon may the clouds drop blood? The thoughts of this would take off the heart from the immoderate love of the creature. Our Savior at a great feast breaks out into mention of his death. 'She has prepared this against my burial' (Mark 14:8). So the fore-thoughts of persecution would be an excellent antidote against a surfeit.

[3] The fore-thoughts of sufferings would make them lighter when they come. The suddenness of an evil adds to the sadness. This was ill news to the fool in the gospel, 'This night shall your soul be required of you' (Luke 12:20). This will be an aggravation of Babylon's miseries: 'Her plagues shall come in one day' (Revelation 18:8). Not that antichrist shall be destroyed in a

day—but ('in a day') that is, suddenly. The blow shall come unawares, when he does not think of it. The reckoning beforehand of suffering, alleviates and shakes off the edge of it when it comes. Therefore Christ, to lighten the cross, still forewarns his disciples of sufferings that they might not come unlooked for (John 16:33; Acts 1:7).

[4] Fore-thoughts of persecution would put us in mind of getting our armor ready. It is dangerous as well as imprudent, to have all to seek when the trial comes—as if a soldier should have no weapons when the enemy is in the field. He who reckons upon persecution will be in a ready posture for it. He will have the shield of faith and the sword of the Spirit ready, that he may not be surprised unawares.

Let us prepare for persecution. A wise pilot in a calm, will prepare for a storm. God knows how soon persecution may come. There seems to be a cloud of blood hanging over the nation.

How shall we prepare for sufferings? Do three things.

1. Be people rightly qualified for suffering.

2. Avoid those things which will hinder suffering.

3. Promote all helps to suffering.

1. Labor to be people rightly qualified for suffering. Be righteous people. That man who would suffer 'for righteousness sake' must himself be righteous. I mean evangelically righteous. In particular I call him righteous:

[1] A righteous person breathes after holiness (Psalm 119:5). Though sin cleaves to his heart—yet his heart does not cleave to sin. Though sin has an alliance—yet no allowance. 'I do the very thing I hate!' (Romans 7:15). A godly man hates the sin to which Satan most tempts and his heart most inclines (Psalm 119:128).

[2] A righteous person is one who makes God's grace his center. The glory of God is more worth than the salvation of all men's souls. He who is divinely qualified, is so zealously ambitious for God's glory, that he does not care what he loses, so long God may be a gainer. He prefers the glory of God before credit, estate, relations. It was the speech of Kiliaz, that blessed martyr, 'Had I all the gold in the world to dispose of, I would give it to live with my family (though in prison)—yet Jesus Christ is dearer to me than all.'

[3] A righteous person is one who values the jewel of a good conscience at a high rate. Good conscience is a saint's festival, his music, his paradise, and he will rather hazard anything than violate his conscience. They say of the Irish, if they have a good scimitar, a warlike weapon—that they had rather take a blow on their arm than their scimitar should be hurt. To this I may compare a good conscience. A good man had rather sustain hurt in his body or estate than his conscience should be hurt. He had rather die than violate the virginity of his conscience. Such a man as this is evangelically righteous, and if God calls him to it—he is fit to suffer.

2. Avoid those things which will hinder suffering.

[1] The love of the world. God allows us the use of the world (1 Timothy 6:7, 8). But take heed of the love of it. He who is in love with the world will be out of love with the cross. 'Demas has forsaken me, having loved this present world' (2 Timothy 4:10). He not only forsook Paul's company but his doctrine. The love of the world chokes our zeal. A man wedded to the world will for thirty pieces of silver betray Christ and his cause. Let the world be as a loose garment that you may throw off at pleasure. Before a man can die for Christ—he must be dead to the world. Paul was crucified to the world (Galatians 6:14). It will be an easy thing to die, when we are already dead in our affections.

[2] Carnal fear. There is a twofold fear:

A filial fear, when a man fears to displease God. When he fears he should not hold out, this is a good fear. 'Blessed is he who fears always'. If Peter had feared his own heart better, and said, 'Lord Jesus, I fear I shall forsake you; Lord strengthen me'; doubtless Christ would have kept him from falling.

There is a cowardly fear, when a man fears danger more than sin, when he is afraid to be godly; this fear is an enemy to suffering. God proclaimed that those who were fearful should not go to the wars (Deuteronomy 20:8). The fearful are unfit to fight in Christ's wars. A man possessed with fear does not consult what is best — but what is safest. If he may save his estate, he will snare his conscience. 'In the fear of man, there is a snare' (Proverbs 29:25). Fear made Peter deny Christ, Abraham equivocate, David pretend to be mad. Fear will put men upon sinful courses. Fear makes sin appear little, and suffering great. The fearful man sees double. He looks upon the cross through his microscope, and it appears twice as big as it is. Fear argues sordidness of spirit. It will put one upon things most ignoble and unworthy. A fearful man will vote against his conscience. Fear enfeebles. It is like the cutting off Samson's locks. Fear melts away the courage. 'Their hearts melt because of you' (Joshua 2:9). And when a man's strength is gone he is very unfit to carry Christ's cross. Fear is the root of apostasy. Spira's fear made him abjure and recant his religion.

Fear hurts one more than the adversary. It is not so much an enemy outside the castle, as a traitor within, which endangers it. It is not so much sufferings without, as traitorous fear within, which undoes a man. A fearful man is versed in no posture so much as in retreating. Oh take heed of this! Be afraid of this fear. 'Fear not those who can kill the body' (Luke 12:4). Persecutors can but kill the body, which must shortly die anyway. The fearful are set in the forefront of those who shall go to hell (Revelation 21:8). Let us get the fear of God into our hearts. As one wedge drives out another, so the fear of God will drive out all other base fear.

[3] Take heed of a vacillating spirit. A vacillating man will be turned any way with a word. He will be wrought as wax. He is so tame that you may lead him where you will. 'With fair speeches they deceive the hearts of the simple' (Romans 16:18). A vacillating man is malleable to anything. He is like wool that will take any dye. He is a weak reed that will be blown any way with the breath of men. One day you may persuade him to engage in a good cause, the next day to desert it. He is not made of oak — but of willow. He will bend every way. Oh take heed of a vacillating spirit! It is folly to allow one's self to be abused. A good Christian is like Mount Zion that cannot be moved (Psalm 125:1). He is like Fabricius of whom it was said, a man might as well alter the course of the sun as turn him aside from doing justice. A good Christian must be firm to his resolution. If he be not a fixed star, he will be a falling star.

[4] Take heed of listening to the voice of the flesh. Paul 'conferred not with flesh and blood' (Galatians 1:16). The flesh will give bad counsel. First King Saul consulted with the flesh — and afterwards he consulted with the devil. He sends to the witch of Endor. 'Oh,' says the flesh, 'the cross of Christ is heavy! There are nails in that cross which will lacerate, and fetch blood!' Be as a deaf adder stopping your ears to the charmings of the flesh!

3. Promote those things which will help to suffer.

[1] Inure yourselves to suffering. 'As a good soldier of Christ endure hardship' (2 Timothy 2:3). Jacob made the stone his pillow (Genesis 28:18). 'It is good for a man that he bear the yoke in his youth' (Lamentations 3:27). The bearing of a lighter cross, will fit for the bearing of a heavier cross. Learn to bear a reproach with patience, and then you will be fitter to bear an iron chain. Paul died daily. He began with lesser sufferings and so by degrees learned to be a martyr. As it is in sin — a wicked man learns to be expert in sin by degrees. First he commits a lesser sin, then

a greater, then he arrives at a habit in sin, then he grows impudent in sin, then he glories in sin (Philippians 3:19); so it is in suffering. First a Christian takes up the chips of the cross — mockings and scornings — and then he carries the cross itself.

Alas how far are they from suffering, who indulge the flesh: 'They lie upon beds of ivory and stretch themselves upon their couches' (Amos 6:4); a very unfit posture for suffering. That soldier is likely to make but poor work of it, who is stretching himself upon his bed when he should be in the field exercising and drilling. 'What shall I say,' says Jerome, 'to those professors who make it all their care to perfume their clothes, to crisp their hair, to sparkle their diamonds — but if sufferings come, and the way to heaven has any difficulty in it, they will not endure to set their feet upon it!' Most people are too delicate. They pamper themselves too tenderly. Those 'silken Christians' (as Tertullian calls them) who pamper the flesh, are unfit for the school of the cross. The naked breast and bare shoulder, is too soft and tender to carry Christ's cross. Inure yourselves to hardship. Do not make your pillow too easy.

[2] Be well skilled in the knowledge of Christ. A man can never die for one he does not know. 'For which cause I suffer those things; for I know whom I have believed' (2 Timothy 1:12). Blind men are always fearful. A blind Christian will be fearful of the cross. Enrich yourselves with knowledge. Know Christ in his virtues, offices, privileges. See the preciousness in Christ. 'To you who believe, he is precious' (1 Peter 2:7). His name is precious; it is as ointment poured forth. His blood is precious; it is as balm poured forth. His love is precious; it is as wine poured forth. Jesus Christ is made up of all sweets and delights. He himself is all that is desirable. He is light to the eye, honey to the taste, joy to the heart. Get but the knowledge of Christ and you will part with all for him. You will embrace him though it be in the fire. An ignorant man can never be a martyr. He may set up an altar — but he will never die for an unknown God.

[3] Prize every truth of God. The filings of gold are precious. The least ray of truth is glorious. 'Buy the truth — and sell it not' (Proverbs 23:23). Truth is the object of faith (2 Thessalonians 2:13), the seed of regeneration (James 1:18), the spring of joy (1 Corinthians 13:6). Truth crowns us with salvation (1 Timothy 2:4). If ever you would suffer for the truth — prize it above all things. He who does not prize truth above life will never lay down his life for the truth. The blessed martyrs sealed the truth with their blood. There are two things God counts most dear to him, his glory and his truth.

[4] Keep a good conscience. If there is any sin allowed in the soul, it will unfit for suffering. A man who has a boil upon his shoulders cannot carry a heavy burden. Guilt of conscience is like a boil. He who has this can never carry the cross of Christ. If a ship is sound and well-rigged, it will sail upon the water — but if it is full of holes and leaks, it will sink in the water. If conscience be full of guilt (which is like a leak in the ship), it will not sail in the bloody waters of persecution. If the foundation is rotten, the house will not stand in a storm. If a man's heart is rotten, he will never stand in a storm of tribulation. How can a guilty person suffer when for ought he knows, he is likely to go from the fire at the stake — to hell-fire! Let conscience be pure. 'Holding the mystery of the faith in a pure conscience' (1 Timothy 3:9). A good conscience will abide the fiery trial. This made the martyrs' flames, to be beds of roses. A good conscience is a wall of brass. With the Leviathan, 'it laughs at the shaking of a spear' (Job 41:29). Let one be in prison — a good conscience is a bird that can sing in this cage. Augustine calls it 'the paradise of a good conscience'.

[5] Make the Scripture familiar to you (Psalm 119:50). The Scripture well digested by meditation, will fit for suffering. The Scripture is a Christian's armory. It may be compared to the 'tower of David on which there hang a thousand shields' (Canticles 4:4). From these breasts of Scripture, divine strength flows into the soul. 'Let the word of Christ dwell in you richly'

(Colossians 3:16). Jerome speaks of one who by frequent studying the Scripture made his breast 'the library of Christ'. The blessed Scripture as it is a honeycomb for comfort, so an armory for strength. First, the martyrs 'hearts did burn within them' (Luke 24:32) by reading the Scripture, and then their bodies were fit to burn. The Scripture arms a Christian both against temptation and persecution.

The Scripture arms a Christian both against temptation. Christ himself, when he was tempted by the devil ran to Scripture for armor: 'It is written'. Three times he wounds the old serpent with his sword. Jerome says of Paul, he could never have gone through so many temptations, but for his Scripture-armor. Christians, are you tempted? Go to Scripture; gather a stone hence to fling in the face of a Goliath-temptation. Are you tempted to pride? Read that scripture, 'God resists the proud' (1 Peter 5:5). Are you tempted to lust? Read James 1:15, 'When lust has conceived, it brings forth sin; and sin when it is finished, brings forth death'.

The Scripture arms a Christian both against persecution. When the flesh draws back the Scripture will recruit us. It will put armor upon us — and courage into us. 'Do not be afraid of what you are about to suffer. I tell you, the devil will put some of you in prison to test you, and you will suffer persecution for ten days. Be faithful, even to the point of death, and I will give you the crown of life' (Revelation 2:10). O, says the Christian, I am not afraid to suffer. 'Do not be afraid of what you are about to suffer.' But why should I suffer? I love God and is not this sufficient? Nay — but God will test your love. God's gold is best tried in the furnace. But this persecution is so long! No! it is but for 'ten days'. It may be lasting — but not everlasting. What are ten days put in balance with eternity? But what am I the better if I suffer? What comes of it? 'Be faithful, even to the point of death, and I will give you the crown of life.' Though your body is martyred, your soul shall be crowned. 'But I shall faint when trials come.' 'My grace shall be sufficient' (2 Corinthians 12:9). The Christian though weak, has omnipotence to underprop him.

[6] Get a suffering frame of heart.

'What is that?', you say. I answer: A self-denying frame. 'If anyone would come after me, he must deny himself and take up his cross daily and follow me.' (Luke 9:23). Self-denial is the foundation of godliness, and if this foundation is not well-laid, the whole building will fall. If there is any lust in our souls which we cannot deny — it will turn at length either to scandal or apostasy. Self-denial is the thread which must run along through the whole work of piety. The self-denying Christian will be the suffering Christian. 'Let him deny himself and take up his cross'.

For the further explication of this, I shall do two things.

1. Show what is meant by this word deny.

2. What is meant by self.

1. What is meant by deny? The word 'to deny' signifies to lay aside, to put off, to annihilate oneself. Beza renders it 'let him renounce himself'.

2. What is meant by self? Self is taken four ways:

Worldly self,

Relative self,

Natural self,

Carnal self.

A man must deny worldly self, that is, his estate. 'Behold we have forsaken all and followed you' (Matthew 19:27). The gold of Ophir must be denied — for the pearl of great price. Let their money perish with them (said that noble Marquess of Vico) who esteem all the gold and silver in the world worth one hour's communion with Christ.

A man must deny relative self, that is, his dearest relations – if God calls. If our nearest relative, father or mother, stand in our way and would hinder us from doing our duty, we must either leap over them or tread upon them! 'If you want to be my follower you must love me more than your own father and mother, wife and children, brothers and sisters – yes, more than your own life. Otherwise, you cannot be my disciple' (Luke 14:26). Relations must not weigh heavier than Christ.

A man must deny natural self. He must be willing to become a sacrifice and make Christ's crown flourish, though it be in his ashes. 'They loved not their lives unto the death' (Luke 14:26; Revelation 12:11). Jesus Christ was dearer to them, than their own heart's blood.

A man must deny carnal self. This I take to be the chief sense of the text. He must deny carnal ease. The flesh cries out for ease. It is loath to put its neck under Christ's yoke or stretch itself upon the cross. The flesh cries out, 'There is a lion in the way' (Proverbs 22:13). We must deny our self-ease. Those who lean on the soft pillow of sloth, will hardly take up the cross. 'You as a good soldier of Christ endure hardness' (2 Timothy 2:3). We must force a way to heaven through sweat and blood. Caesar's soldiers fought with hunger and cold.

A man must deny self-esteem. Every man by nature has a high opinion of himself. He is drunk with spiritual pride, and a proud man is unfit for suffering. He thinks himself too good to suffer. What (says he) I who am of such a noble descent, such high abilities, such repute and credit in the world – shall I suffer? A proud man disdains the cross. Oh deny self-esteem! How did Christ come to suffer? 'He humbled himself and became obedient unto death' (Philippians 2:8). Let the plumes of pride fall off!

A man must deny self-confidence. Peter's self-confidence undid him. 'Even if everyone else deserts you, I never will! Not even if I have to die with you! I will never deny you!' (Matthew 26:33, 35). How did this man presume upon his own strength, as if he had more grace than all the apostles besides! His denying Christ was for lack of denying himself. Oh deny your own strength! Samson's strength was in his locks. A Christian's strength lies in Christ. He who trusts to himself – shall be left to himself. He who goes out in his own strength comes off to his own shame.

A man must deny self-wisdom. We read of the 'wisdom of the flesh' (2 Corinthians 1:12). Self-wisdom is carnal policy. It is wisdom (says the flesh) to keep out of suffering. It is wisdom not to declare against sin. It is wisdom to find out subtle ways to avoid the cross. The wisdom of the flesh – is to save the flesh. Indeed there is a Christian prudence to be used. The serpent's eye must be in the dove's head. Wisdom and innocence do well – but it is dangerous to separate them. Cursed be that policy which teaches to avoid duty. This wisdom is not from above, but is devilish (James 3:15). It is learned from the old serpent. This wisdom will turn to folly at last. It is like a man who to save his gold – throws himself overboard into the water. Many, to save their skin – will damn their souls.

A man must deny self-will. Gregory calls the will the commander-in-chief of all the faculties of the soul. Indeed, in innocence, Adam had rectitude of mind and conformity of will. The will was like an instrument in tune. It was full of harmony and tuned sweetly to God's will – but now the will is corrupt and like a strong tide carries us violently to evil. The will has not only an indisposition to good – but an opposition to good. 'You have always resisted the Holy Spirit' (Acts 7:51). There is not a greater enemy than the will. It is up in arms against God (2 Peter 2:10). The will loves sin – and hates the cross. Now if ever we suffer for God we must cross our own will. The will must be martyred. A Christian must say, 'Not my will — but may your will be done.'

A man must deny self-reasonings. The fleshy part will be reasoning and disputing against sufferings. 'Why are you reasoning about these things in your hearts?' (Mark 2:8). Such reasonings as these will begin to arise in our hearts:

1. Persecution is bitter.

Oh but it is blessed! 'Blessed is he who endures temptation ...' (James 1:12). The cross is heavy — but the sharper the cross, the brighter the crown.

2. But it is sad to part with estate and relations.

But Christ is better than all. He is manna to strengthen; he is wine to comfort; he is salvation to crown.

3. But liberty is sweet.

This restraint makes way for enlargement. 'You have enlarged me in distress' (Psalm 4:1). When the feet are bound with irons, the heart may be sweetly dilated and enlarged.

Thus should we put to silence those self-reasonings which are apt to arise in the heart against sufferings.

This self-denying frame of heart is very hard. This is 'to pluck out the right eye'. It is easier to overcome men and devils, than to overcome self. 'Stronger is he who conquers himself, than he who conquers the strongest walled city'. Self is the idol, and how hard it is to sacrifice this idol and to turn self-seeking into self-denial! But though it is difficult, it is essential to suffering. A Christian must first lay down self, before he can take up the cross.

Alas! How far are they then from suffering that cannot deny themselves in the least things; who in their diet or apparel, instead of martyring the flesh, pamper the flesh! Instead of taking up the cross take up their cups! Is this self-denial, to let loose the reins to the flesh? It is sure that those who cannot deny themselves, if sufferings come, will deny Christ. Oh Christians, as ever you would be able to carry Christ's cross, begin to deny yourselves. Consider:

Whatever you deny for Christ, you shall find again in Christ. 'Everyone who has given up houses or brothers or sisters or father or mother or children or property, for my sake, will receive a hundred times as much in return and will have eternal life.' (Matthew 19:29). Here is a very choice bargain!

It is but equity that you should deny yourselves for Christ. Did not Jesus Christ deny himself for you? He denied his joy; he left his Father's house; he denied his honor; he endured the shame (Hebrews 12:2); he denied his life; he poured out his blood as a sacrifice upon the altar of the cross (Colossians 1:20). Did Christ deny himself for you, and will not you deny yourselves for him?

Self-denial is the highest sign of a sincere Christian. Hypocrites may have great knowledge and make large profession — but it is only the true-hearted saint who can deny himself for Christ. I have read of a holy man who was once tempted by Satan, to whom Satan said, 'Why do you take all these pains? You watch and fast and abstain from sin. O man, what do you do, more than I? Are you no drunkard, no adulterer? Neither am I. Do you watch? Let me tell you, I never sleep. Do you fast? I never eat. What do you do, more than I?' 'Why,' says the godly man, 'I will tell you, Satan; I pray; I serve the Lord; nay, more than all, I deny myself.' 'Nay, then,' says Satan, 'you go beyond me for I exalt myself!' And so he vanished. Self-denial is the best touchstone of sincerity. By this you go beyond hypocrites.

To deny yourselves is but what others have done before you. Moses was a self-denier. He denied the honors and profits of the court (Hebrews 11:24-26). Abraham denied his own country at God's call (Hebrews 11:8). Marcus Arethusus endured great torments for Christ. If he would but have given a half-penny towards the rebuilding of the idol's temple, he might have been released – but he would not do it, though the giving of a half-penny might have saved his life. Here was a self-denying saint.

There is a time shortly coming, that if you do not deny the world for Christ, the world will deny you. The world now denies satisfaction, and before long it will deny place. It will not allow you so much as to breathe in it. It will turn you out of possession; and, which is worse, not only the world will deny you – but Christ will deny you. 'Whoever shall deny me before men, him will I also deny before my Father which is heaven' (Matthew 10:33).

[7] Get suffering graces; these three in particular:

Faith; Love; Patience.

The first suffering grace is faith. 'In every situation take the shield of faith, and with it you will be able to extinguish the flaming arrows of the evil one' (Ephesians 6:16). The pretense of faith is one thing, the use of faith another. The hypocrite makes faith a cloak, the martyr makes it a shield. A shield is useful in time of danger; it defends the head; it guards the vitals. Such a shield is faith.

Faith is a furnace grace. 'Though it is tried with fire, it is found unto praise and honor' (1 Peter 1:7). Faith, like Hercules' club, beats down all oppositions. By faith we resist the devil (1 Peter 5:9). By faith we resist unto blood (Hebrews 11:34).

Faith is a victorious grace. The believer will make Christ's crown flourish, though it is in his own ashes. An unbeliever is like Reuben: 'Unstable as water he shall not excel' (Genesis 49:4). A believer is like Joseph, who, though the archers shot at him, 'his bow abode in strength.' Cast a believer upon the waters of affliction – he can follow Christ upon the water, and not sink. Cast him into the fire, his zeal burns hotter than the flame. Cast him into prison, he is enlarged in spirit. Paul and Silas had their prison songs. 'You shall tread upon the lion and adder' (Psalm 91:13). A Christian, armed with faith as a coat of armor, can tread upon those persecutions which are fierce as the lion, and sting as the adder! Get faith.

But how does faith come to be such strong armor? I answer – in six ways.

(1) Faith unites the soul to Christ, and that blessed Head sends forth grace into the members. 'I can do all things through Christ, who give me strength.' (Philippians 4:13). Faith is a grace which lives upon borrowed strength. As when we need water, we go to the well and fetch it; when we need gold, we go to the mine; so faith goes to Christ and fetches his strength into the soul, whereby it is enabled both to do and suffer. Hence it is that faith is such a wonderworking grace.

(2) Faith works in the heart, a contempt of the world. Faith gives a true map of the world, 'When I surveyed all that my hands had done and what I had toiled to achieve, everything was meaningless, a chasing after the wind; nothing was gained under the sun!' (Ecclesiastes 2:11). Faith shows the world in its night-dress, having all its jewels pulled off. Faith makes the world appear in its true state. Faith shows the soul better things than the world. It gives a sight of Christ and eternal glory. It gives a prospect of heaven. As the mariner in a dark night climbs up to the top of the mast and cries out, 'I see a star', so faith climbs up above sense and reason into heaven and sees Christ, that bright and morning star; and the soul, having once viewed his superlative excellencies, becomes crucified to the world. Oh, says the Christian, shall not I suffer the loss of all these things that I may enjoy Jesus Christ! 'Yes, everything else is worthless

when compared with the priceless gain of knowing Christ Jesus my Lord. I have discarded everything else, counting it all as garbage, so that I may have Christ!' Philippians 3:8

(3) Faith gets strength from God's promises. Faith lives upon the promises. Take the fish out of the water—and it dies. Take faith out of a promise—and it cannot live. The promises are breasts of consolation. The child by sucking the breast gets strength. Faith gets strength by sucking the breast of a promise. When a garrison is besieged and is ready almost to yield to the enemy, auxiliary forces are sent in to relieve it. So when faith begins to be weak and is ready to faint in the day of battle, then the promises muster their forces together, and all come in for faith's relief and now it is able to hold out in the fiery trial.

(4) Faith gives the soul a right notion of suffering. Faith draws the true picture of sufferings. What is suffering? Faith says, it is but the suffering of the body—which must shortly by the course of nature drop into the dust. Persecution can but take away my life. An ague or fever may do as much. Now faith giving the soul a right notion of sufferings and taking (as it were) a just measure of them, enables a Christian to prostrate his life at the feet of Christ.

(5) Faith reconciles God's providences with His promises. As it was on Paul's voyage, providence seemed to be against him. There was a 'northeaster' which arose (Acts 27:14)—but God had given him a promise that he would save his life, and the lives of all who sailed with him in the ship (verse 24). Therefore when the wind blew ever so contrary, Paul believed it would at last blow him to the haven. So when sense says, 'Here is a cross providence. Great sufferings are coming—and I shall be undone!' Then faith says 'we know that God causes everything to work together for the good of those who love God and are called according to his purpose' (Romans 8:28). This providence, though bloody, shall fulfill the promise. Affliction shall work for my good. It shall heal my corruption, and save my soul. Thus faith, making the wind and tide go together, the wind of a providence with the tide of the promise, enables a Christian to suffer persecution.

(6) Faith picks sweetness out of suffering. Faith shows God reconciled and sin pardoned; and then how sweet is every suffering! The bee gathers the sweetest honey from the bitterest herb. 'A bitter medicine often gives strength to the weary'. So faith gathers the sweetest comforts—from the sharpest trials. Faith looks upon suffering as God's love-token. 'Afflictions are sharp arrows—but they are shot from the hand of a loving Father!' Faith can taste honey at the end of the afflicting rod. Faith fetches joy out of suffering, 'your sorrow will turn to joy!' (John 16:20). Faith gets honey from the belly of the lion. Faith finds a jewel under the cross!

Thus you see how faith comes to be such a wonder-working grace. 'Above all, taking the shield of faith'. A believer having cast his anchor in heaven cannot sink in the waters of persecution.

The next suffering grace is love. Get hearts fired with love to the Lord Jesus. Love is a grace both active and passive.

(1) Love is active. It lays a law of constraint upon the soul. 'The love of Christ constrains us' (2 Corinthians 5:14). Love is the wing of the soul, which sets it flying. Love is also the weight of the soul, which sets it going. Love never thinks it can do enough for Christ—as he who loves the world never thinks he can take enough pains for it. Love is never weary. It is not tired unless with its own slowness.

(2) Love is passive. It enables to suffer. A man who loves his friend will suffer anything for him, rather than he shall be wronged. Love made our dear Lord suffer for us. The pelican out of her love to her young ones, when they are bitten with serpents, feeds them with her own blood to recover them again. Just so, when we had been bitten by the old serpent, that Christ might recover us—he fed us with his own blood. Jacob's love to Rachel made him almost hazard his

life for her. 'Many waters cannot quench love' (Canticles 8:7). No! not the waters of persecution. 'Love is as strong as death' (Canticles 8:6). Death makes its way through the greatest oppositions. So love will make its way to Christ — through the prison and the furnace.

But all pretend love to Christ. How shall we know that we have such a love to him, as will make us suffer for him?

I answer:

True love is a love of friendship, which is genuine and sincere — when we love Christ for himself. There is a mercenary and spurious love, when we love divine objects for something else. A man may love the queen of truth for the jewel at her ear — because she brings preferment. A man may love Christ for his 'head of gold' (Canticles 5:11), because he enriches with glory. But true love is when we love Christ for his loveliness, namely, that infinite and superlative beauty which shines in him, as Augustine says, 'We love Jesus on account of Jesus'; that is, as a man loves sweet wine for itself.

True love is a love of desire — when we desire to be united to Christ as the fountain of happiness. Love desires union. The one who sincerely loves Christ, desires death because death ushers into full union and communion with Christ. 'I desire to depart and be with Christ, which is better by far!' (Philippians 1:23). Death slips one knot and ties another.

True love is a love of benevolence — when so far as we are able, we endeavor to lift up Christ's name in the world. As the wise men brought him 'gold and frankincense' (Matthew 2:11), so we bring him our tribute of service and are willing that he should rise — though it is by our fall. In short, that love which is kindled from heaven makes us give Christ the pre-eminence of our affection. 'I would give you spiced wine to drink — my sweet pomegranate wine' (Canticles 8:2). If the spouse has a cup which is more juicy and spiced — Christ shall drink of that! Indeed we can never love Christ too much. We may love gold in excess — but not Christ. The angels do not love Christ comparable to his worth. Now when love is boiled up to this height, it will enable us to suffer. 'Love is as strong as death'. The martyrs first burned in love — and then in fire!

The third suffering grace is patience. Patience is a grace made and cut out for suffering. Patience is the sweet submission to the will of God, whereby we are content to bear anything which he is pleased to lay upon us. Patience makes a Christian invincible. It is like the anvil which bears all strokes. We cannot be men without patience. Impatience unmans a man. It puts him beside the use of reason. We cannot be martyrs without patience. Patience makes us endure (James 5:10).

We read of a beast 'like unto a leopard and his feet were as the feet of a bear and the dragon gave him his power ...' (Revelation 13:2). This beast is to be understood of the anti-christian power. Antichrist may be compared to a leopard for subtlety and fierceness, and on his head was the name of blasphemy (verse 1), which agrees with that description of the man of sin, 'He sits in the temple of God showing himself that he is God' (2 Thessalonians 2:4); and the 'dragon gave him power' (verse 2), that is the devil, and 'it was given to him to make war with the saints' (Revelation 13:7). Well, how do the saints bear the heat of this fiery trial? (verse 10): 'Here is the patience of the saints.' Patience overcomes by suffering.

A Christian without patience is like a soldier without arms. Faith keeps the heart up from sinking. Patience keeps the heart from murmuring. Patience is not provoked by injuries. It is sensible — but not peevish. Patience looks to the end of sufferings. This is the motto: 'God will guarantee the end also.' As the watchman waits for the dawning of the morning, so the patient Christian suffers and waits until the day of glory begins to dawn upon him. Faith says, 'God will come,' and patience says, 'I will wait for his perfect time.' These are those suffering graces which are a Christian's armor of proof.

[8] Treasure up suffering promises. The promises are faith's bladders to keep it from sinking. They are the breast-milk a Christian lives on, in time of sufferings. They are honey at the end of the rod. Hoard up the promises!

God has made promises of direction—that he will give us a spirit of wisdom in that hour, teaching us what to say. 'Make up your mind not to worry beforehand how you will defend yourselves. For I will give you words and wisdom that none of your adversaries will be able to resist or contradict' (Luke 21:14-15). You shall not need to study. God will put an answer into your mouth. This many of God's sufferers can set their seal to. The Lord has suddenly darted such words into their mouths—as their enemies could easier censure than contradict.

God has made promises of protection. 'No man shall set on you to hurt you' (Acts 18:10). How safe was Paul when he had omnipotence itself to screen off danger! 'Not a hair of your head shall perish' (Luke 21:18). Persecutors are lions—but chained lions. *Words can't hurt me.*

God has made promises of his special presence with his saints in suffering. 'I will be with him in trouble' (Psalm 91:15). If we have such a friend to visit us in prison, we shall do well enough. Though we change our place—we shall not change our keeper. 'I will be with him.' God will uphold our head and heart, when we are fainting! What if we have more afflictions than others—if we have more of God's company! God's honor is dear to him. It would not be for his honor to bring his children into sufferings, and leave them there. He will be with them to invigorate and support them. Yes, when new troubles arise; 'He shall deliver you in six troubles' (Job 5:19).

The Lord has made promises of deliverance. 'I will deliver him and honor him' (Psalm 91:15). God will open a back door for his people to escape out of sufferings. 'He will with the temptation, make a way to escape' (1 Corinthians 10:13). Thus he did to Peter (Acts 12:7-10). Peter's prayers had opened heaven—and God's angel opens the prison! God can either prevent a snare or break it. 'Our God is a God who saves! The Sovereign Lord rescues us from death' (Psalm 68:20). He who can strengthen our faith—can break our fetters. The Lord sometimes makes enemies the instruments of breaking those snares which themselves have laid (Esther 8:8).

In the case of martyrdom God has made promises of consolation. 'Your sorrow shall be turned into joy' (John 16:20). There is the water—turned into wine. 'Be of good cheer, Paul' (Acts 23:11). In time of persecution, God broaches the wine of consolation. Cordials are kept for fainting. Stephen 'saw the heavens opened' (Acts 7:56). Glover, that blessed martyr, cried out at the stake in a holy rapture, 'He is come! He is come!' meaning the Comforter. 'Do not be afraid, for I have ransomed you. I have called you by name; you are mine. When you go through deep waters and great trouble, I will be with you. When you go through rivers of difficulty, you will not drown! When you walk through the fire of oppression, you will not be burned up; the flames will not consume you. For I am the Lord, your God, the Holy One of Israel, your Savior.' (Isaiah 43:1-3)

The Lord has made promises of compensation. God will abundantly recompense all our sufferings, 'Everyone who has given up houses or brothers or sisters or father or mother or children or property, for my sake, will receive a hundred times as much in return and will have eternal life' (Matthew 19:29). Augustine calls this the best and greatest interest. Our losses for Christ are gainful. 'He who loses his life for my sake, shall find it' (Matthew 10:39).

[9] Set before your eyes suffering examples. Look upon others as patterns to imitate. 'Take my brethren the prophets for an example of suffering affliction' (James 5:10). Examples have more influence upon us than precepts. Precepts instruct us—but examples animate us. As they show

elephants the blood of grapes and mulberries to make them fight the better, so the Holy Spirit shows us the blood of saints and martyrs to infuse a spirit of zeal and courage into us. Micaiah was in the prison; Jeremiah in the dungeon; Isaiah was sawn asunder. The primitive Christians, though they were boiled, roasted, and dismembered—yet like the adamant they remained invincible. Such was their zeal and patience in suffering, that their persecutors stood amazed and were more weary in tormenting—than they were in enduring!

When John Huss was brought to be burned, they put upon his head a triple crown of paper printed with red devils, which when he saw, he said, 'My Lord Jesus Christ wore a crown of thorns for me, why then shall I not wear this paper crown, however ignominious?' Polycarp, when he came before the court, was bidden to deny Christ and swear by the Emperor; he replied: 'I have served Christ these eighty-six years and he has not once hurt me—and shall I deny him now?' Saunders that blessed martyr, said, 'Welcome the cross of Christ; my Savior drank the bitter cup for me—shall not I suffer for him? I feel no more pain in the fire than if I were in a bed of down!'

Another of the martyrs said, 'The ringing of my chain has been sweet music in my ears. O what a comforter is a good conscience!' Another martyr, kissing the stake, said, 'I shall not lose my life—but change it for a better one! Instead of coals—I shall have pearls!' Another, when the chain was fastening to him, said, 'Blessed be God for this wedding belt!' These suffering examples we should lay up. God is still the same God. He has as much love in his heart to pity us—and as much strength in his arm to help us!

Let us think what courage the very heathens have shown in their sufferings. Julius Caesar was a man of a heroic spirit. When he was foretold of a conspiracy against him in the senate-house, he answered he had rather die than fear. Mutius Scaevola held his hand over the fire until the flesh fried and his sinews began to shrink—yet he bore it with an undaunted spirit. Lysimachus, a brave captain, being adjudged to be cast to a lion, when the lion came roaring upon him, Lysimachus thrust his hand into the lion's mouth and taking hold of his tongue, killed the lion. Did nature infuse such a spirit of courage and gallantry into heathens! How should grace much more into Christians! Let us be of Paul's mind: 'I consider my life worth nothing to me, if only I may finish the race and complete the task the Lord Jesus has given me--the task of testifying to the gospel of God's grace' (Acts 20:24).

[10] Let us lay in considerations. A wise Christian will consider several things.

Consider whom we suffer for. It is for Christ, and we cannot suffer for a better friend. There is many a man will suffer shame and death for his lusts. He will suffer disgrace for a drunken lust. He will suffer death for a revengeful lust. Shall others die for their lusts—and shall not we die for Christ? Will a man suffer for that lust which damns him—and shall not we suffer for that Christ who saves us? Oh remember, we espouse God's own quarrel and he will not allow us to be losers. Surely no man shall sacrifice himself for God for nothing.

Consider that it is a great honor to suffer persecution. Ambrose, in the eulogy of his sister said, 'I will say this of her—she was a martyr'. It is a great honor to be singled out to bear witness to the truth. 'They departed from the council rejoicing that they were counted worthy to suffer shame for his name' (Acts 5:41). It is a title that has been given to kings, 'Defender of the faith'. A martyr is in a special manner, a 'defender of the faith'. Kings are defenders of the faith by their swords, martyrs by their blood. It is a credit to appear for God. Martyrs are not only Christ's followers—but his ensign-bearers. The Romans had their brave warriors which graced the field. God calls out none but his champions to fight his battles. We read that Abraham called forth his trained soldiers (Genesis 14:14), such as were more expert and valiant. What a honor is it to be one of Christ's trained band!

The disciples dreamed of a temporal reign (Acts 1:6). Christ tells them (verse 8), 'You shall be witnesses unto me in Jerusalem...' To bear witness by their sufferings to the truth of Christ's divinity and passion was a greater honor to the disciples than to have had a temporal reign upon earth. A bloody cross is more honorable than a purple robe. Persecution is called the 'fiery trial' (1 Peter 4:12).

'I have refined you in the furnace of affliction.' (Isaiah 48:10). 'Away with you, you cursed ones, into the eternal fire prepared for the Devil and his demons! And they will go away into eternal punishment!' (Matthew 25:41, 46). God has two fires—one where He puts His gold, and another where He puts His dross. The fire where He puts His gold, is the fire of suffering and affliction--to purify them. The fire where He puts His dross, is the fire of damnation--to punish them.

God honors his gold when he puts it into the fire. 'A spirit of glory rests upon you' (1 Peter 1:7; 1. Peter 4:14). Persecution, as it is a badge of our honor, so an ensign of our glory. What greater honor can be put upon a mortal man, than to stand up in the cause of God? And not only to die in the Lord but to die for the Lord? Ignatius called his fetters his spiritual pearls. Paul gloried more in his iron chain than if it had been a gold chain! (Acts 28:20).

Consider what Jesus Christ suffered for us. Calvin says that Christ's whole life, was a series of sufferings. Christian, what is your suffering? Are you poor? So was Christ. 'Foxes have holes and the birds of the air have nests—but the Son of Man has nowhere to lay his head' (Matthew 8:20). Are you surrounded with enemies? So was Christ. 'Against your holy child Jesus whom you have anointed, both Herod and Pontius Pilate with the Gentiles ... were gathered together' (Acts 4:27). Do our enemies lay claim to religion? So did his. 'The chief priests took the silver pieces and said—It is not lawful to put them into the treasury because it is the price of blood' (Matthew 27:6). Godly persecutors! Are you reproached? So was Christ. 'They bowed the knee before him, and mocked him, saying, 'Hail, King of the Jews!' (Matthew 27:29). Are you slandered? So was Christ. 'He casts out devils by the prince of devils' (Matthew 9:34). Are you ignominiously treated? So was Christ. 'Some began to spit upon him' (Mark 14:65). Are you betrayed by friends? So was Christ. 'Judas, are you betraying the Son of Man with a kiss?' (Luke 22:48). Is your estate taken from you? And do the wicked cast lots for it? So Christ was dealt with. 'They parted his garments, casting lots' (Matthew 27:35). Do we suffer unjustly? So did Christ. His very judge acquitted him. 'Then Pilate said to the chief priests and to the people, I find no fault in this man' (Luke 23:4). Are you barbarously dragged and hauled away to suffering? So was Christ. 'When they had bound him, they led him away' (Matthew 27:2). Do you suffer death? So did Christ. 'When they were come to Calvary, there they crucified him' (Luke 23:33). They gave him gall and vinegar to drink; the gall picturing the bitterness of his death, the vinegar picturing the sharpness of his death. Christ underwent not only the blood of the cross but the curse of the cross (Galatians 3:13). He had agony in his soul. 'My soul is exceeding sorrowful unto death' (Matthew 26:38). The soul of Christ was overcast with a cloud of God's displeasure. The Greek Church speaking of the sufferings of Christ, calls them 'unknown sufferings'. Did the Lord Jesus endure all this for us—and shall not we suffer persecution for his name? Say, as holy Ignatius, 'I am willing to die for Christ, for Christ my love was crucified!' Our cup of suffering is nothing, compared to the cup which Christ drank. His cup was mixed with the wrath of God, and if he bore God's wrath for us—well may we bear man's wrath of him.

Consider the honor we bring to Christ and the gospel by suffering. It was a honor to Caesar that he had such soldiers as were able to fight with hunger and cold and endure hardship in their marches. It is a honor to Christ that he has such people listed under him, as will leave all for him. It proclaims him to be a good Master—when his servants will wear his livery though it be sullied with disgrace and lined with blood. Paul's iron chain made the gospel wear a golden chain. Tertullian says of the saints in his time that they took their sufferings more kindly, than if they had had deliverance. Oh, what a glory was this to the truth, when they dared embrace it in the flame!

And as the saints' sufferings adorn the gospel, so they propagate it. Basil says that the zeal and constancy of the martyrs in the primitive times made some of the heathens to be Christianised. 'The Church is founded in blood and by blood it increases'. The showers of blood have ever made the church fruitful. Paul's being bound made the truth more enlarged (Philippians 1:13). The gospel has always flourished in the ashes of martyrs.

Consider who it is, that we have engaged ourselves to in baptism. We solemnly vowed that we would be true to Christ's interest and fight under his banner, to the death. And how often have we in the blessed supper, taken the oath of allegiance to Jesus Christ that we would be his servants and that death should not part us! Now if when being called to it, we refuse to suffer persecution for his name—Christ will bring our baptism as an indictment against us. Christ is called 'the Captain of our salvation' (Hebrews 2:10). We have listed ourselves by name under this Captain. Now if, for fear, we shall fly from our colors, it is perjury in the highest degree, and how shall we be able to look Christ in the face at the Day of Judgment? That oath which is not kept inviolably—shall be punished infallibly. Where does the 'flying scroll' of curses land— but in the house of him that 'swears falsely' (Zechariah 5:4)?

Consider that our sufferings are light. This 'light affliction ...' (2 Corinthians 4:17) 1. It is heavy to flesh and blood—but it is light to faith. Affliction is light in a threefold respect:

1. It is light—in comparison to sin. He who feels sin heavy, feels suffering light. Sin made Paul cry out, 'O wretched man that I am!' (Romans 7:24). He does not cry out of his iron chain—but of his sin. The greater noise drowns the lesser. When the sea roars, the rivers are silent. He who is taken up with his sins, and sees how he has provoked God—thinks the yoke of affliction to be light (Micah 7:9).

2. Affliction is light—in comparison of hell. What is persecution, compared to damnation? What is the fire of martyrdom, compared to the fire of the damned? It is no more than the pricking of a pin, compared to a death's wound. 'Who knows the power of your anger!' (Psalm 90:11) Christ himself could not have borne that anger, had he not been more than a man.

3. Affliction is light—in comparison of glory. The weight of glory makes persecution light. 'If,' says Chrysostom, 'the torments of all the men in the world could be laid upon one man, it were not worth one hour's being in heaven!' And if persecution is light, we should not be overly downcast by it. Let us neither faint through unbelief, nor fret through impatience.

Consider that our sufferings are short. 'After you have suffered a little while' (1 Peter 5:10). Our sufferings may be lasting, not everlasting. Affliction is compared to a 'cup' (Lamentations 4:21). The wicked drink of a 'sea' of wrath which has no bottom. It will never be emptied. But it is only a 'cup' of martyrdom, and God will say, 'Let this cup pass away'. 'The rod of the wicked shall not rest upon the lot of the righteous' (Psalm 125:3). The rod may be there, it shall not rest. Christ calls his sufferings 'an hour' (Luke 22:53). Can we not suffer one hour? Persecution is sharp—but short. Though it has a sting to torment—yet it has a wing to fly! 'Sorrow shall fly away' (Isaiah 35:10). It is but a little while when the saints shall have a writ of ease granted them. They shall weep no more—and suffer no more. They shall be taken off the torturing rack—and laid in Christ's bosom. The people of God shall not always be in the iron furnace; a year of Jubilee will come. The water of persecution like a land-flood, will soon be dried up.

Consider that while we suffer for Christ—we suffer with Christ. 'If we suffer with him ...' (Romans 8:17). Jesus Christ bears part of the suffering with us. 'Oh,' says the Christian, 'I shall never be able to hold out!' But remember—you suffer with Christ. He helps you to suffer. As our blessed Savior said: 'I am not alone; the Father is with me' (John 16:32); so a believer may say, 'I am not alone, my Christ is with me'. He bears the heaviest end of the cross. 'My grace is sufficient for you' (2 Corinthians 12:9). 'Underneath are the everlasting arms' (Deuteronomy 33:27). If Christ puts the yoke of persecution over us—he will put his arms under us. The Lord Jesus will not only crown us when we conquer—but he will enable us to conquer. When the dragon fights against the godly, Christ is that Michael who stands up for them and helps them to overcome (Daniel 12:1).

Consider that he who refuses to suffer persecution shall never be free from suffering:

He will have internal sufferings. He who will not suffer for conscience, shall suffer in conscience. Thus Francis Spira, after he had abjured that doctrine which once he professed for fear of persecution, was in great terror of mind. He professed he felt the very pains of the damned in his soul. He who was afraid of the stake, was set upon the wrack of a tormenting conscience!

He will have external sufferings. Pendleton refused to suffer for Christ; not long after, his house was on fire and he was burned in it. He who would not burn for Christ—was afterwards made to burn for his sins.

He will have eternal sufferings. 'Suffering the vengeance of eternal fire' (Jude 7).

These present sufferings cannot hinder a man from being blessed. 'Blessed are those who are persecuted ...' We think, 'Blessed are those who are rich'; nay—but 'Blessed are those who are persecuted'. 'Blessed is the man who endures temptation ...' (James 11, 12). 'If you suffer for righteousness, sake, happy are you' (1 Peter 3:14).

Persecution cannot hinder us from being blessed. I shall prove this by these demonstrations:

1. They are blessed who have God for their God. 'Happy is that people whose God is the Lord' (Psalm 144:15). But persecution cannot hinder us from having God for our God. 'Our God is able to deliver us' (Daniel 3:17). Though persecuted—yet they could say, 'our God'. Therefore persecution cannot hinder us from being blessed.

They are blessed whom God loves—but persecution cannot hinder the love of God. 'Who shall separate us from the love of Christ? Shall persecution?' (Romans 8:35). The goldsmith loves his gold as well when it is in the fire—as when it is in his bag. God loves his children as well in adversity, as in prosperity. 'As many as I love—I rebuke' (Revelation 3:19). God visits his children in prison. 'Be of good cheer, Paul' (Acts 23:11). God sweetens their sufferings. 'As the sufferings of Christ abound in us, so our consolation also abounds' (2 Corinthians 1:5). As the mother, having given her child a bitter pill, gives it afterwards a lump of sugar; persecution is a bitter pill—but God gives the comforts of his Spirit to sweeten it. If persecution cannot hinder God's love, then it cannot hinder us from being blessed.

2. They are blessed, for whom Christ prays. Such as are persecuted, have Christ praying for them. 'Keep through your own name, those whom you have given me' (John 17:11); which prayer, though made for all believers—yet especially for his apostles which he foretold should be martyrs (John 16:2). Now if persecution cannot hinder Christ's prayer for us, then it cannot impede or obstruct our blessedness.

3. They are blessed, who have sin purged out. Persecution purges out sin (Isaiah 27:9; Hebrews 12:11). Persecution is a corrosive to eat out the proud flesh. It is a fan to winnow us, a fire to refine us. Persecution is the remedy which God applies to his children, to carry away their ill humours. That surely which purges out sin cannot hinder blessedness.

[11] The great suffering-consideration is the glorious reward which follows sufferings: 'Theirs is the kingdom of heaven.' 'The hope of reward,' says Basil, 'is very powerful and moving.' Moses had an eye to the 'recompense of reward' (Hebrews 11:26). Yes, so did Christ himself (Hebrews 12:2). Many have done great things for hope of a temporal reward. Camillus, when his country was oppressed by the Gauls, ventured his life for his country, to purchase fame and honor. If men will hazard their lives for a little temporal honor, what should we do for the reward of eternal glory! 'A merchant,' says Chrysostom, 'does not mind a few storms at sea—but he thinks of the gain when the ship comes fraught home.' So a Christian should not be overly concerned about his present sufferings—but think of the rich reward he shall receive, when he shall arrive at the heavenly port. 'Great is your reward in heaven' (verse 12). The cross is a golden ladder by which we climb up to heaven! A Christian may lose his life—but not his reward. He may lose his head—but not his crown. If he who gives 'a cup of cold water' shall not lose his reward, then much less he who gives a draught of warm blood. The rewards of glory may sweeten all the bitter waters of Marah. It should be a spur to martyrdom.

Not that we can merit this reward by our sufferings. 'I will give you a crown of life' (Revelation 2:10). The reward is the legacy which free grace bequeaths. Alas, what proportion is there between a drop of blood—and an eternal weight of glory? Christ himself, as he was man only (setting aside his Godhead), did not merit by his sufferings, for Christ, as he was man only, was a creature. Now a creature cannot merit from the Creator. Christ's sufferings, as he was man only, were finite, therefore could not merit infinite glory. Indeed, as he was God, his sufferings were meritorious; but considering him purely as man, they were not. This I urge against the Papists. If Christ's sufferings, as he was man only (though as man he was above the angels), could not merit, then what man upon earth, what prophet or martyr is able to merit anything by his sufferings?

But though we have no reward *ex merito*, by merit—we shall have it *ex gratia*, by grace. So it is in the text, 'Great is your reward in heaven'. The thoughts of this reward should animate Christians. Look upon the eternal crown of glory—and faint if you can. The reward is as far above your thoughts—as it is beyond your deserts. A man who is to wade through a deep water, fixes his eyes upon the firm land before him. While Christians are wading through the deep waters of persecution—they should fix the eyes of their faith on the land of promise. 'Great is your reward in heaven!' Those who bear the cross patiently—shall wear the crown triumphantly!

Christ's suffering saints shall have greater degrees in glory (Matthew 19:28). God has his highest seats, yes, his thrones—for his martyrs. It is true, he who has the least degree of glory—a doorkeeper in heaven, will have enough; but as Joseph gave to Benjamin a double portion above the rest of his brethren, so God will give to his sufferers a double portion of glory. Some orbs in heaven are higher, some stars brighter. God's martyrs shall shine brighter in the heavenly horizon.

Oh, often look upon 'the recompense of the reward'. Not all the silks of Persia, nor all the spices of Arabia, nor all the gold of Ophir—can be compared to this glorious reward. How should the thoughts of this sharpen and steel us with courage in our sufferings! When they threatened Basil with banishment, he comforted himself with this—that he should be either under heaven, or in heaven. It was the hope of this reward which so animated those primitive martyrs, who, when there was incense put into their hands and there was no more required of them for the saving of their lives, but to sprinkle a little of that incense upon the altar in honor of the idol — they would rather die than do it!

This glorious reward in heaven, is called a reigning with Christ. 'If we suffer, we shall also reign with him!' First martyrs for Christ — then kings for Christ. Julian honored all those who were slain in his battles. So does the Lord Jesus. After the saints' crucifixion, follows their coronation. 'They shall reign!' The wicked first reign — and then suffer. The godly first suffer — and then reign. The saints shall have a happy reign. It shall be both peaceable and durable. Who would not swim through blood — to this crown! Who would not suffer joyfully? Christ says, 'Be exceeding glad' (verse 12). The Greek word signifies 'to leap for joy'. Christians should have their spirits elevated and exhilarated when they contemplate the eternal weight of glory!

If you would be able to suffer, pray much. Beg of God to clothe you with a spirit of zeal and magnanimity. 'To you it is given in the behalf of Christ, not only to believe on him — but also to suffer for his sake' (Philippians 1:29). It is a gift of God to be able to suffer. Pray for this gift. Do not think you can be able of yourselves, to lay down life and liberty for Christ. Peter was overconfident of himself. 'I will lay down my life for your sake!' (John 13:37). But Peter's strength undid him. Peter had habitual grace — but he lacked auxiliary grace. Christians need fresh gales from heaven. Pray for the Spirit to animate you in your sufferings. As the fire hardens the potter's vessel, which is at first weak and limber — so the fire of the Spirit hardens men against sufferings. Pray that God will make you like the anvil — that you may bear the strokes of persecutors with invincible patience!

Appendix

His commandments are not grievous.

1 John 5:3

You have seen that Christ calls for poverty of spirit, pureness of heart, meekness, mercifulness, cheerfulness in suffering persecution, etc. Now that none may hesitate or be troubled at these commands of Christ, I thought it good (as a closure to the former discourse) to take off the surmises and prejudices in men's spirits by this sweet, mollifying Scripture, 'His commandments are not grievous.'

The censuring world objects against piety — that it is difficult and irksome. 'Behold what a weariness is it!' (Malachi 1:13). Therefore the Lord, that he may invite and encourage us to obedience, draws religion in its fair colors and represents it to us as beautiful and pleasant, in these words: 'His commandments are not grievous.' this may well be called a sweetening ingredient put into religion and may serve to take off that asperity and harshness which the carnal world would put upon the ways of God.

For the clearing of the terms, let us consider:

1. What is meant here by 'commandments'?

By this word, commandments, I understand gospel-precepts; faith, repentance, self-denial etc.

2. What is meant by 'not grievous'?

The Greek word signifies they are not tedious or heavy to be borne. There is a train of thought in the words. 'His commands are not grievous', that is, they are easy, sweet, excellent.

Hence observe that none of God's commandments are grievous, when he calls us to be meek, merciful, pure in heart. These commandments are not grievous. 'My burden is light' (Matthew 11:30). The Greek word there for 'burden', signifies properly 'the ballast of a ship' which glides through the waves as swiftly and easily as if the ship had no weight or pressure in it. Christ's commandments are like the ballast of a ship—useful, but not troublesome. All his precepts are sweet and easy, therefore called 'pleasantness' (Proverbs 3:17). To illustrate and amplify this, consider two things:

1. Why Christ lays commands upon his people.

2. That these commands are not grievous.

1. Why Christ lays commands upon his people. There are two reasons.

[1] In regard of christ—it is suitable to his dignity and state. He is Lord paramount. This name is written on his thigh and vesture, 'King of kings' (Revelation 19:16). And shall not a king appoint laws to his subjects? It is one of the regal rights, the flowers of the crown, to enact laws and statutes. What is a king without his laws? And shall not Christ (by whom 'kings reign', Proverbs 8:15) put forth his royal edicts by which the world shall be governed?

[2] In regard of the saints—it is well for the people of God that they have laws to bind and check the exorbitancies of their unruly hearts. How far would the vine spread its luxuriant branches— were it not pruned and tied? The heart would be ready to run wild in sin—if it did not have affliction to prune it, and the laws of Christ to bind it. The precepts of Christ are called 'a yoke' (Matthew 11:30). The yoke is useful. It keeps the oxen from straggling and running out. So the precepts of Christ as a yoke—keep the godly from straggling into sin. Where would we not run, into what damnable opinions and practices— did not Christ's laws lay a check and restraint upon us! Blessed be God for precepts! That is a blessed yoke, which yokes our corruptions. We would run to hell were it not for this yoke! The laws of Christ are a spiritual hedge, which keeps the people of God within the pastures of ordinances. Some that have broken this hedge and have straggled off, are now in the devil's pound! Thus we see what need the saints have of the royal law.

2.The second thing I am to demonstrate, is that Christ's commands are not grievous. I confess they are grievous to the unregenerate man. To mourn for sin, to be pure in heart, to suffer persecution for righteousness' sake—is a hard work, and grievous to flesh and blood. Therefore Christ's commands are compared to bands and cords—because carnal men look upon them so. God's commands restrain men from their excess, and bind them to their good behavior. Therefore, they hate these bonds and instead of breaking off sin, say, 'Let us break their bands asunder and cast away their cords from us!' (Psalm 2:3). A carnal man is like an untamed heifer which will not endure the yoke—but kicks and flings, or like a 'wild bull in a net' (Isaiah 51:20). Thus to an unsaved person, Christ's commands are grievous.

Nay, to a child of God, so far as corruption prevails (for he is but in part regenerate), Christ's laws seem irksome. The flesh cries out that it cannot pray or suffer. 'The law in the members' rebels against Christ's law. Only as the spiritual part prevails, does it make the flesh stoop to Christ's injunctions. A regenerate person, so far as he is regenerate, does not count God's commandments grievous. They are not a burden—but a delight.

Divine commands are not grievous, if we consider them first positively, in these eight particulars:

(1) A Christian consents to God's commands, therefore they are not grievous. 'I consent to the law, that it is good' (Romans 7:16). What is done with consent is easy. If the virgin gives her consent, the match goes on cheerfully. A godly man in his judgment approves of Christ's laws, and in his will consents to them. Therefore they are not grievous. A wicked man is under a force; terror of conscience forces him to duty. He is like a slave that is chained to the galley. He must work whether he will or not. He is forced to pull the rope, tug at the oar. But a godly man is like a free subject, who consents to his prince's laws and obeys out of choice as seeing the

equity and rationality of them. Thus a gracious heart sees a beauty and equity in the commands of heaven, which draws forth consent, and this consent makes them pleasant.

(2) They are Christ's commands, therefore not grievous. 'Take my yoke' (Matthew 11:29). Gospel commands are not the laws of a tyrant — but of a Savior. The husband's commands are not grievous to the wife. It is her desire to obey. This is enough to animate and excite obedience — it is Christ's who commands. As Peter said in another sense, 'Lord if it is you, bid me come unto you upon the water' (Matthew 14:28), so says a gracious soul; 'Lord, if it is you who would have me mourn for sin and breathe after heart purity; if it is you (dear Savior) who bids me to do these things — I will cheerfully obey. Your commandments are not grievous'. A soldier at the word of his general, makes a brave fight.

(3) Christians obey out of a principle of love, and then God's commandments are not grievous. Therefore in Scripture serving and loving of God, are put together. 'They join themselves to the Lord, to serve him and to love the name of the Lord' (Isaiah 56:6). Nothing is grievous to him who loves. Love lightens a burden; it adds wings to obedience. A heart who loves God, counts nothing tedious but its own dullness and slowness of motion. Love makes sin heavy — and Christ's burden light.

(4) A Christian is carried on by the help of the Spirit, and the Spirit makes every duty easy. 'The Spirit helps our infirmities' (Romans 8:26). The Spirit works in us 'both to will and to do' (Philippians 2:13). When God enables us to do what he commands, then 'his commandments are not grievous'. If two carry a burden, it is easy. The Spirit of God helps us to do duties, and to bear burdens. He draws as it were in the yoke with us. If the teacher guides the child's hand and helps it to frame its letter — it is not hard for the child to write. If the loadstone draw the iron — it is not hard for the iron to move. If the Spirit of God as a divine loadstone draws and moves the heart — it is not hard to obey. When the bird has wings given it, it can fly. Though the soul of itself be unable to do that which is good — yet having two wings given it — the wing of faith and the wing of the Spirit, now it flies swiftly in obedience! 'The Spirit lifted me up' (Ezekiel 11:1). The heart is heavenly in prayer, when the Spirit lifts it up. The sails of a mill cannot move by themselves — but when the wind blows then they turn round. When a gale of the Spirit blows upon the soul, now the sails of the affections move swiftly in duty.

(5) All Christ's commands are beneficial, not grievous. 'And now, O Israel, what does the Lord your God require of you — but to fear the Lord your God, to love him, to keep his statutes which I command you this day — for your good' (Deuteronomy 10:12, 13). Christ's commands carry food in the mouth of them, and then surely they are not grievous. Salvation runs along in every precept. To obey Christ's laws is not so much our duty — as our privilege. All Christ's commands center in blessedness. Medicine is in itself very unpleasant — yet because it tends to health, no man refuses it. Divine precepts are irksome to the fleshy part — yet, having such excellent operation as to make us both holy and happy — they are not to be accounted grievous. The apprentice is content to go through hard service, because it makes way for his freedom. The scholar willingly wrestles with the knotty difficulties of arts and sciences, because they serve both to ennoble and advance him. How cheerfully does a believer obey those laws which reveal Christ's love! That suffering is not grievous — which leads to a crown. This made Paul say, 'I take pleasure in infirmities, in persecutions' (2 Corinthians 12:10).

(6) It is honorable to be under Christ's commands. Therefore they are not grievous. The precepts of Christ do not burden us — but adorn us. It is a honor to be employed in Christ's service. How cheerfully did the rowers row the barge which carried Caesar! The honor makes the precept easy. A crown of gold is in itself heavy — but the honor of the crown makes it light and easy to be worn. I may say of every command of Christ, as Solomon speaks of wisdom,

'She shall give to your head an ornament of grace: a crown of glory shall she deliver to you' (Proverbs 4:9). It is honorable working at the King's court. The honor of Christ's yoke, makes it easy and pleasant.

(7) Christ's commands are sweetened with joy—so then they are not grievous. Cicero questions whether that can properly be called a burden—which is carried with joy and pleasure. When the wheels of a chariot are oiled they run swiftly. Just so, when God pours in the oil of gladness, how fast does the soul run in the ways of his commandments! Joy strengthens for duty. 'The joy of the Lord is your strength' (Nehemiah 7:10); and the more strength—the less weariness. God sometimes drops down comfort—and then a Christian can run in the yoke!

(8) Gospel commands are finite, therefore not grievous. Christ will not always be laying his commands upon us. Christ will shortly take off the yoke from our neck—and set a crown upon our head! There is a time coming when we shall not only be free from our sins—but our duties too. Prayer and fasting are irksome to the flesh. In heaven there will be no need of prayer or repentance. Duties shall cease there. Indeed in heaven the saints shall love God—but love is no burden. God will shine forth in his beauty—and to fall in love with beauty is not grievous. In heaven the saints shall praise God—but their praising of him shall be so sweetened with delight, that it will not be a duty any more—but part of their reward. It is the angels' heaven to praise God. This then makes Christ's commands not grievous—they are temporary; it is but a while and duties shall be no more. The saints shall not so much be under commands as embraces! Wait but a while, and you shall put off your armor—and end your weary marches!

Thus we have seen that Christ's commands considered in themselves, are not grievous.

Let us consider Christ's commands comparatively—and we shall see they are not grievous. Let us make a fourfold comparison. Compare Gospel commands:

1. With the severity of the moral law.

2. With the commands of sin.

3. With the torments of the damned.

4. With the glory of heaven.

1. Christ's commands in the gospel are not grievous, when compared with the severity of the MORAL LAW. The moral law was such a burden as neither we nor our fathers could bear. 'Cursed is everyone who continues not in all things which are written in the book of the law to do them' (Galatians 3:10). Impossible it is that any Christian should come up to the strictness of this. The golden mandates of the gospel comparatively are easy. For:

(1) In the gospel, if there is a desire to keep God's commandments, it is accepted. 'If there be first a willing mind, it is accepted' (Nehemiah 1:11; 2 Corinthians 8:12). Though a man had had ever so good an intention to have fulfilled the moral law, it would not have been accepted. He must 'de facto' (in actual deed) have obeyed (Galatians 3:12). But in the gospel God crowns the desire. If a Christian says in humility, 'Lord, I desire to obey you, I would be more holy' (Isaiah 26:8), this desire, springing from love—is accepted by God.

(2) In the gospel a surety is admitted in the court. The law would not admit of a surety. It required personal obedience. But now, God so far indulges us that, what we cannot of ourselves do, we may do by a proxy. Christ is called 'a surety of a better testament' (Hebrews 7:22). We cannot walk so exactly. We tread awry, and fall short in everything—but God looks upon us in our surety, and Christ 'having fulfilled all righteousness' (Matthew 3:15), it is as if we had fulfilled the law in our own person.

(3) The law commanded and threatened—but gave no strength to perform. It Egyptianized, requiring the full tally of bricks—but gave no straw. But now, God gives power with his commands. Gospel-precepts are sweetened with promises. God commands, 'Make a new heart' (Ezekiel 18:31). 'Lord,' may the soul say, 'I cannot make a new heart! I could as well make a new world!' But see Ezekiel 36:26, 'A new heart also will I give you'. God commands us to cleanse ourselves: 'Wash, make yourself clean' (Isaiah 1:16). 'Lord, I have no power to cleanse myself! Who can bring a clean thing out of an unclean?' (Job 14:4). See the precept turned into a promise: 'From all your filthiness and from your idols—I will cleanse you' (Ezekiel 36:25). If, when the child cannot go, the father takes it by the hand and leads it, now it is not hard for the child to go. When we cannot go, God takes us by the hand, 'I taught Ephraim to go, taking them by their arms' (Hosea 11:3).

(4) In the gospel God winks at infirmities, where the heart is right. The law called for perfect obedience. It was death to have shot but a hairbreadth short of the mark. It would be sad if the same rigor should continue upon us. 'Woe to the holiest man who lives' (says Augustine) 'if God comes to weigh him in the balance of his justice!' It is with our best duties as with gold. Put the gold in the fire and you will see dross come out. What drossiness is in our holy things! But in the gospel, God will pass by our failings. Thus Christ's commands in the gospel are not grievous, compared with the severity of the moral law.

2. Christ's commands are not grievous, when compared with the commands of sin. Sin lays a heavy yoke upon men. Sin is compared to heavy lead (Zechariah 5:7) to show the weightiness of it. The commands of sin are burdensome. Let a man be under the power and rage of any lust (whether it be covetousness or ambition), how he tires and excruciates himself! What hazards does he run, even to the endangering of his health and soul, that he may satisfy his lust! 'They wear themselves out with all their sinning' (Jeremiah 9:5). And are not Christ's precepts easy and sweet in comparison of sin's austere and inexorable commands? Therefore Chrysostom says well that 'virtue is easier than vice'. Temperance is less burdensome than drunkenness. Doing justice is less burdensome than crime. There is more difficulty and perplexity in the contrivement (Micah 2:1) and pursuit of wicked ends—than in obeying the sweet and gentle precepts of Christ. Hence it is that a wicked man is said to 'pregnant with evil and conceives trouble' (Psalm 7:14), to show what anxious pain and trouble he has in bringing about his wickedness! Many have gone with more pain to hell--than others have to heaven!

3. Christ's commands are not grievous, when compared with the grievous torments of the damned. The rich man cries out 'I am tormented in this flame!' (Luke 16:24). Hell fire is so inconceivably torturing—that the wicked do not know either how to bear or how to avoid it. The torment of the damned may be compared to a yoke—but it differs from other yokes. Usually the yoke is laid but upon the neck of the beast—but the hell-yoke is laid upon every part of the sinner. His eyes shall behold nothing but bloody tragedies. His ears shall hear the groans and shrieks of blaspheming spirits. He shall suffer in every member of his body and faculty of his soul, and this agony though violent, is yet perpetual. The yoke of the damned shall never be taken off. 'The footprints to hell show no return.' Sinners might break the golden chain of God's commands—but they cannot break the iron chain of his punishments! It is as impossible for them to file this chain, as to scale heaven.

And are not gospel-commands easy in comparison of hell-torments? What does Christ command? He bids you repent. Is it not better to weep for sin—than bleed for it! Christ bids you pray in your families and closets. Is it not better praying—than roaring in hell! He bids you sanctify the Sabbath. Is it not better to keep a holy rest to the Lord than to be forever without rest? Hell is a restless place. There is no intermission of torment for one moment in all eternity! I appeal to the consciences of men. Are not Christ's commands sweet and pleasant—in comparison of the insupportable pains of reprobates? Is not obeying better than damning! Are not the cords of love—better than the chains of darkness!

4. Gospel commands are not grievous, when compared with the glory of heaven. What an infinite disproportion is there between our service and our reward! What are all the saints' labors and travails in religion—compared with the eternal crown of glory? The weight of glory makes duty light.

Behold here an encouraging argument to true religion. How may this make us in love with the ways of God! 'His commandments are not grievous'. Believers are not now under the thundering curses of the law—no, nor under the ceremonies of it, which were both numerous and burdensome. The ways of God are reasonable, his statutes pleasant! He bids us mourn— that we may be comforted. He bids us be poor in spirit—that he may settle a kingdom upon us. God is no hard Master. 'His commandments are not grievous.' O Christian, serve God out of choice (Psalm 119:3). Think of the joy, the honor, and the reward of godliness. Never more grudge God your service. Whatever he prescribes—let your hearts cheerfully subscribe.

It reproves those who refuse to obey these sweet and gentle commands of Christ. 'Israel would not submit to me' (Psalm 81:11). The generality of men choose rather to put their neck in the devil's yoke than to submit to the sweet and easy yoke of Christ. What should be the reason that, when God's 'commandments are not grievous', his ways pleasantness, his service perfect freedom—yet men should not bow to Christ's scepter, nor stoop to his laws?

Surely the cause is that inbred hatred which is naturally in men's hearts against Christ. Sinners are called 'God-haters' (Romans 1:30). Sin begets not only a dislike of the ways of God—but hatred to God! And from disaffection, flows disloyalty. 'His citizens hated him and sent a message after him, saying—We will not have this man to reign over us!' (Luke 19:14)

Besides this inbred hatred against Christ, the devil labors to blow the coals and increase this odium and antipathy. He raises an evil report upon religion as those spies did on Canaan. 'They brought up an evil report of the land' (Numbers 13:32). Satan is implacably malicious, and as he sometimes accuses us to God—so he accuses God to us, and says, 'He is a hard Master and his commandments are grievous.' It is the devil's design to do as the sons of Eli, 'who made the offering of God to be abhorred' (1 Samuel 2:17). If there is any hatred and prejudice in the heart against true religion, 'an enemy has done this!' (Matthew 13:28, 38). The devil raises in the hearts of men a twofold prejudice against Christ and his ways:

(1) The small number of those who embrace religion. The way of Christ is but a pathway (Psalm 119:35), whereas the way of pleasure and vanity is the roadway. Many ignorantly conclude that must be the best way—which most people travel on.

I answer: There are but few that are saved, and will not you be saved because so few are saved? A man does not argue thus in other things: 'there are but few rich, therefore I will not labor to be rich.' Nay, therefore, he the rather strives to be rich. Why should not we argue thus wisely about our souls? There are but few that go to heaven, therefore we will labor the more to be of the number of that few.

What a weak argument is this: there are but few who embrace true religion, therefore you will not! Those things which are more excellent are more rare. There are but few diamonds. There are but few kings. The fewness of those who embrace true religion, argues the way of religion to be excellent. We are warned not to sail with the multitude (Exodus 23:2). Most fish go to the Devil's net! 'Enter through the narrow gate. For wide is the gate and broad is the road that leads to destruction, and many enter through it. But small is the gate and narrow the road that leads to life, and only a few find it.' (Matthew 7:13-14)

(2) The ways of religion are rendered deformed and unlovely by the scandals of professors.

I answer: I acknowledge the luster of religion has been much eclipsed and sullied by the scandals of men. This is an age of scandals. Many have made the pretense of religion, to be a key to open the door to all ungodliness. Never was God's name more taken in vain. This is that our Savior has foretold. 'It must needs be that offences come' (Matthew 18:7). But to take off this prejudice, consider: scandals are not from true religion — but for lack of true religion. True religion is not the worse, though some abuse it. To dislike piety because some of the professors of it are scandalous, is as if one should say, 'Because the servant is dishonest, therefore he will not have a good opinion of his master.' Is Christ the less glorious because some who wear his livery are scandalous? Is true religion the worse — because some of her followers are bad? Is wine the worse — because some are drunkards? Shall a woman dislike chastity because some of her neighbors are unchaste? Let us argue soberly. 'Judge righteous judgment' (John 7:24).

God sometimes permits scandals to fall out in the church out of a design:

(1) As a just judgment upon hypocrites. These squint-eyed devotionists who serve God for their own ends, the Lord in justice allows them to fall into horrid debauched practices, that he may lay open their baseness to the world, and that all may see they were but pretend Christians, but painted devils! Judas was first a sly hypocrite, afterwards a visible traitor!

(2) Scandals are for hardening of the profane. Some desperate sinners who would not be won by piety — they shall be wounded by it. God lets scandals occur, to be a break neck to men and to engulf them more in sin. Jesus Christ ('God blessed forever') is to some a 'rock of offence' (Romans 9:33). His blood, which is to some balm, is to others poison. If the beauty of piety does not allure — the scandals of some of its followers shall spur men to hell.

(3) Scandals in the church are for the caution of the godly. The Lord would have his people walk tremblingly. 'Be not high-minded — but fear' (Romans 11:20). When cedars fall, let the 'bruised reed' tremble. The scandals of professors are not to discourage us — but to warn us. Let us tread more warily. The scandals of others are sea-marks for the saints to avoid.

Let all this serve to take off these prejudices from true religion. Though Satan may endeavor by false disguises to render the gospel odious — yet there is a beauty and a glory in it. God's 'commandments are not grievous'.

Let me persuade all men cordially to embrace the ways of God. 'His commandments are not grievous'. God never burdens us — but that he may unburden us of our sins. His commands are our privileges. There is joy in the way of duty (Psalm 19:11) — and heaven at the end!

The Christian's Charter

Showing the Privileges of a Believer

All things are yours: whether Paul or Apollos or Cephas or the world or life or death or things present or things to come — all are yours, and you belong to Christ, and Christ to God.

1 Corinthians 3:21-23

Chapter 1. The Porch or Entrance into the Words, together with the Proposition.

Happiness is the mark and center which every man aims at. The next thing that is sought after being, is being happy. Surely, the nearer the soul comes to God, who is the fountain of life and peace, the nearer it approaches to happiness. Who is so near to God as the believer, who is mystically one with him? he must needs be the happy man. If you would survey his blessed estate, cast your eyes upon this text, which points to it, as the finger to the dial: 'All things are yours.' The text may not unfitly be compared to the tree of life, which bore twelve kinds of fruits, and yielded her fruit every month; there are many precious clusters growing out of this text, and being skillfully improved, will yield much excellent fruit.

In the words we have the inventory of a Christian, 'All things are yours!' A strange paradox! when a believer can call nothing his, yet he can say, all things are his. I have often thought a poor Christian who lives in a prison, or some old cottage, is like the banker, who, though he goes poor, and can hardly find himself bread, yet has thousands at his fingertips. So it is with a child of God, 'as having nothing — yet possessing all things.' What once the philosopher said, 'Only the wise man is the rich man.' But I say, 'only the believer is the rich man!' Here is his estate summed up, 'all things are his.'

Objection: Before I come to the words, there is an objection must be removed. If all things are ours, there seems to be a community; what is one man's is another's.

Answer: The apostle does not speak here of civil possessions. Paul was no leveler, he did not go about to destroy any man's property; for though he says, 'all things are yours'; yet he does not say, what any man has is yours.

Objection: But is it not said, They had all things common? Acts 2:44.

Answer: It is true; but this was purely voluntary; there was no precept for it, or obligation to do it.

If it be objected, that this was set down as an example to imitate;

1. I answer — Examples in scripture are not always precepts. The prophet Elijah called for fire from heaven, to consume the captains and their fifties; but it does not therefore follow, that when one Christian is angry with another, he may call for fire from heaven. Thus the primitive saints, out of prudence and charity, had all things common; it will not therefore follow, that in every age and century of the church, there should be a common stock, and everyone have a share.

2. I answer — Though the disciples had all things common — yet still they held their ownership, as is clear by Peter's speech to Ananias, 'While it remained, was it not your own? and after it was sold, was it not in your own power?' It is true in one sense, what the primitive church had, was not their own; so much as could be spared, was for the relief of the saints; thus all things were common. But still they kept a part of their estate in their own hand. There is a double right to an estate, a right of Ownership, and a right of Charity. The right of charity belongs to the poor — but the right of ownership belongs to the owner. For instance, God made a law, that a man must not put his sickle into his neighbor's grain. We read that the disciples being hungry

when they went through the fields on the Sabbath, did pluck the ears of corn — there was Charity; but they must not put the sickle into the corn — here was ownership. This I the rather speak, because there are some, that when God has made a gift to one, would make all common. The Lord has set the eighth commandment as a fence about a man's estate; and he who breaks this hedge, a serpent shall bite him. Thus having taken that objection out of the way, I come now to the next.

The text falls into three parts.

1. The inventory, 'all things,'

2. The proprietors, 'all things are yours.'

3. The tenure, 'You are Christ's.'

Which three branches will make up this one proposition.

Doctrine: That all things in heaven and earth are the portion and privilege of a believer. 'He who overcomes shall inherit all things.' A large inventory! 'All things!' We cannot have more than all; and the apostle doubles it, to take away all hesitancy and doubting from faith.

Chapter 2. The Arguments proving the Proposition.

There are two reasons which will serve to illustrate and confirm the proposition, 'All things are a believer's.'

Reason 1. All things are a believer's, because the covenant of grace is his. The covenant is our Great Charter, by virtue of which God settles all things in heaven and earth upon us. By sin we had forfeited all; therefore if all things are ours, the title comes in by a covenant: until then we had nothing of our own. This covenant is the plan and outcome of God's love; it is the legacy of free-grace. This covenant is enriched with mercy, it is embroidered with promises: you may read the Charter, 'I will be their God.' And there is a parallel to it, 'I am God, even your God.' This is a sufficient dowry. If God is ours, then all things are ours.

1. God is eminently good. One diamond does virtually contain many lesser pearls: the excellencies in the creature are single, and lack their adjuncts. Learning has not always noble parentage; honor has not always virtue. No individual can be the receptacle of all perfections. Those excellencies which lie scattered in the creature, are all united and concentrated in God — as the beams in the sun, or the drops in the ocean.

2. God is superlatively good. Whatever is in the creature, is to be found in God after a most transcendent manner. A man may be said to be wise — but God is infinitely so. A man may be said to be powerful — but God is eternally so. A man may be said to be faithful — but God is unchangeably so. Now in the covenant of grace, God passes himself over to us to be our God, 'I am God, your God!' Psalm 50:7

This expression, 'I am your God,' imports three things:

1. Pacification. You shall find grace in my sight, I will cast a favorable aspect upon you. I will take off my armor, I will take down my standard, I no more will be enemy.

2. Donation. God makes himself over to us by a deed of gift, and gives away himself to us. He says to the believer, as the king of Israel said to the king of Syria, 'I am yours — and all that I have!' This is a hive of divine comfort! All that is in God is ours! His wisdom is ours to teach us; his love is ours to pity us; his Spirit is ours to comfort us; his mercy is ours to save us. When God says to the soul, 'I am yours,' — He cannot say no more!

3. Duration. I will be your God — as long as I am a God. 'For this God is our God for ever and ever; he will be our guide even to the end.' Psalm 48:14.

Reason 2. All things are a believer's, because christ is his. Jesus Christ is the pillar and hinge upon which the covenant of grace turns. Without Christ, we have nothing to do with a covenant. The covenant is founded upon Christ, and is sealed in his blood. We read of the mercy-seat, Exod. 25:17, which was a divine emblem, typifying Jesus Christ. 'There will I meet you, and I will commune with you from above the mercy-seat,' verse 22, to show that in Christ, God is propitious. From above this mercy-seat he communes with us, and enters into covenant. Therefore it is observable, when the Apostle had said, 'All things are yours,' he presently adds, 'You are Christ's.' Belong to Christ, gives us the title to all things. This golden chain, 'Things present, and things to come,' are linked to us, by virtue of our being linked to Christ. By faith we have a saving interest in Christ; having an interest in Christ, we have an interest in God; having an interest in God, we have a title to all things.

Chapter 3. Things Present are a Believer's.

Question. And now I come to that great question, What are the things contained in the Charter?

Answer. There are two words in the text that express it, 'Things present, and things to come.' I begin with the first.

1. Things present, are a believer's. Among these things present, there are three specified in the text; Paul and Apollos, the world, life, etc. Here is, methinks, a chain of pearls! I will take every one of these pearls asunder, and show you their worth; then see how rich a believer is, who wears such a chain of pearl about him.

Section 1. Paul and Apollos are yours.

1. Under these words, 'Paul and Apollos,' by a figure are comprehended all the ministers of Christ, the weakest as well as the most eminent. 'Paul and Apollos are yours,' namely, their labors are for edifying the church. They are the helpers of your faith; the abilities of a minister are not given for himself, they are the church's. If the people have a taint of error, the ministers of Christ must season them with wholesome words; therefore they are called 'the salt of the earth.' If any soul is fainting under the burden of sin, it is the work of a minister to drop in comfort, therefore he is said to hold forth the breast as a nursing mother.

In this way, Paul and Apollos are yours—all the gifts of a minister, all his graces, are not only for himself, they are the Church's. A minister must not monopolize his gifts to himself, this is 'to hide his talents in a napkin.' 'Paul and Apollos are yours.' The ministers of Christ should be as musk among linen, which casts a fragrancy; or like that box of spikenard, which being broken open, filled the house with its fragrance. So should they do by the fragrance of their ointments.

A minister by sending out a sweet perfume in his doctrine and life, makes the church of God as a garden of spices. 'Paul and Apollos are yours,' that is, they are as a lamp or torch to light souls to heaven. Chrysostom's hearers thought they had better be without the sun in the sky, than Chrysostom in the pulpit. Paul and Apollos are springs which hold the water of life; as these springs must not be poisoned, so neither must they be shut up or sealed. A minister of Christ is both a granary to hold the corn, and a steward to give it out. It is little better than theft—to withhold the bread of life! The lips of Apollos must be as a honeycomb, dropping in season and out of season. The graces of the Spirit are sacred flowers, which though they cannot die—yet being apt to wither, Apollos must come with his water-pot. It is not enough that there is grace in the believer's heart—but it must be poured into his lips. As Paul is a believer, so all things are his; but as Paul is a minister, so he is not his own, he is the church's. There are three corollaries I shall draw from this.

Use 1. If 'Paul and Apollos are yours,' every minister of Christ is given for the edifying of the church; take heed that you despise not the least of these, for all are for your profit. The least star gives light, the least drop moistens, the least minister is no less than an angel. There is some use to be made even of the lowest abilities of men: there are 'gifts differing,' but all are yours. The weakest minister may help to strengthen your faith. In the law, all the Levites did not sacrifice, only the priests, as Aaron, and his sons; but all were serviceable in the worship of God. Those who did not sacrifice — yet they helped to carry the ark.

As in a building, some bring stones, some timber, some perhaps bring only nails; yet all these are useful, these all serve to fasten the work in the building. The church of God is a spiritual building, some ministers bring stones, are more eminent and useful; others timber; others less, they have but a nail in the work — yet all serve for the good of this building. The least nail in the ministry serves for the fastening of souls to Christ, therefore let no true minster be despised. Though all are not apostles, all are not evangelists, all have not the same dexterous abilities in their work; yet remember, 'All are yours,' all edify. Oftentimes God crowns his labors, and sends most fish into his net, who, though he may be less skillful — is more faithful; and though he has less brain — yet he has more heart. An ambassador may deliver his message with a trembling lip, and a stammering tongue — but he is honorable for his work's sake — he represents the king's person.

Use 2. If 'Paul and Apollos are yours,' all Christ's ministers have a subserviency to your good, they come to make up the match between Christ and you — then love Paul and Apollos. All the labors of a minister, his prayers, his tears, the usefulness of his abilities, the torrent of his affections — all are yours; then, by the law of equity — there must be some reflections of love from your hearts towards Paul and Apollos, such as are 'set over you in the Lord.'

1. Show your love, by honoring them. Manoah would know the angel's name, that he might honor him. And the apostle calls for this, 'We beseech you, brethren, know those who labor among you, and are over you in the Lord, and esteem them very highly.' They are co-workers with God. God and his ministers (to speak with reverence) drive one and the same trade; and 'they labor among you,' therefore esteem them very highly. Next to sending out Christ and the Spirit, God never honored the world more than in sending out his Pauls and Apolloses. Kings may be your fathers to nurse you up in peace — but ministers are your fathers to beget you to Christ. The earthly father is an instrument of conveying nature, the spiritual father of conveying grace. Therefore Chrysostom thinks that the ministers should not only more reverenced than kings and judges — but more than our natural parents as well. What shall we say then to those who make no more reckoning of their ministers, than the Egyptians did of their shepherds! 'Every shepherd was an abomination to the Egyptians.'

'Know those who labor among you'; many can be content 'to know them' in the baseness of their parentage; 'Is not this the carpenter's son?' Or to know them in their infirmities — but not to know them in the apostle's sense, so as to give them double honor. Surely, were it not for the ministry, you would not be a vineyard — but a wilderness! Were it not for the ministry, you would be destitute of the two seals of the covenant, baptism and the Lord's supper; you would be infidels, for 'faith comes by hearing.' 'How shall they hear without someone preaching to them?' O therefore honor Paul and Apollos; though they may be lowly — yet their office is honorable.

2. Show your love to the ministers, by pleading their cause, when they are unjustly traduced and calumniated. It is counted by some, a piece of their religion — to defame a minister. Others who would be thought more modest, though they do not raise a report — yet they can receive it as a welcome present. This is contrary to that apostolical rule, 'against an elder' (or minister)

'receive not an accusation — but before two or three witnesses.' Constantine was a great honorer of the ministry; it is reported of him, that he would not read the envious accusations brought in against them — but burned them. O, if you love Paul and Apollos, stand up in their defense, become their advocates! It was a law the Egyptians made, that if a man found another in the hands of thieves, and did not deliver him when it was in his power, he was condemned to die. Just so, when your ministers fall among thieves who would rob them of their good name — you must seek to deliver them. We have too many who labor to clip the credit of God's ministers, to make them weigh lighter. O, you must put some grains into the scales! Do they open their mouths to God for you, and will not you open your mouths in their behalf? Certainly if they labor to save your souls, you ought to save their reputation.

3. Show your love to your ministers, by encouraging them, and by being a screen to keep off injuries from them. If they seek your establishment, you must seek their encouragement. If they endeavor your salvation, you must endeavor their safety. The very name of an ambassador, has been a protection from wrongs. What an unnatural thing is it, that any should strive to bring them to death, whose very calling is to bring men to life! The minister is a spiritual father; it was a brand of infamy on them, 'For this people are as those who strive with their priest.' Was there none to strive with, but the priest, even he who offered up their sacrifices for them! Is is right for men to quarrel with their spiritual fathers! even those whom they once had a venerable opinion of, and acknowledged to be the means of their conversion! Either love your spiritual fathers, or there is ground of suspicion that yours was but a false birth.

Use 3. If 'Paul and Apollos are yours,' they are for the building you up in your faith; then endeavor to get good by the labors of Paul and Apollos, I mean such as labor in the word and doctrine. Let them not plough upon the rock; answer God's end in sending them among you. 'Labor to profit;' you may get some knowledge by the word, such as is discursive and polemical, and yet not profit.

Question. What is it to profit?

Answer. The apostle tells us, 'When we mingle the word with faith,' that is, when we so hear that we believe, and so believe that we are transformed into the image of the word. 'You have obeyed from the heart that form of doctrine into which you were delivered.' It is one thing for the truth to be delivered to us, and another thing for us to be delivered into the truth. These words are a metaphor taken from lead or silver cast into a mold. This is to profit when our hearts are cast into the mold of the word preached: as the seed is spiritual, so the heart is spiritual. We should do as the bee, when she has sucked sweetness from the flower, she works it in her own hive, and so turns it to honey. So when we have sucked any precious truth, we should by holy meditation work it in the hive of our hearts, and then it would turn to honey. Then we would profit by it.

O, let the labors of Paul and Apollos have an influence upon us. A good hearer should labor to go out from the ministry of the word, as Naaman out of Jordan — his leprous flesh was healed! So though we came to the word proud — we should go home humble. Though we came to the word earthly — we should go home heavenly. Our leprosy should be healed. Ambrose observes of the woman of Samaria, who came to Jacob's well — she came a sinner — she went away a prophetess. Such a metamorphosis should the word of God make. Let not the ministers of Christ say upon their deathbeds, that they have spent their lungs and exhausted their strength; but know not whether they have done anything, unless they preached men to hell.

It is Augustine's note upon those words of the apostle, 'That they may give up their accounts with joy.' 'When' (says he) 'does a minister give up his account with joy — but when he has been working in the vineyard and sees fruit appear?' Brethren, this will be his joy, and your joy also in the day of the Lord. O, labor to grow; some grow not at all, others grow worse for hearing. 'Evil men shall wax worse and worse,' as Pliny speaks of some fish which swim backward: they grow dead-hearted under preaching; they grow covetous, they grow apostates. It were far easier to write a book of apostates in this age, than a book of martyrs! Men grow riper for hell every day!

O, labor to thrive under the spiritual dew that falls upon you. Let not the ministers of Christ be as those 'which beat the air.' Is it not sad when the spiritual clouds shall drop their rain upon a barren desert! — when the minister's tongue 'is as the pen of a ready writer,' and the peoples' heart is like oiled paper that will take no impression. O, improve in grace. If you have a barren piece of ground, you do all you can to improve it, and will you not improve a barren heart!

It is a great compliment and honor to the ministry, when people thrive under it: 'Need we as some others, epistles of commendation?' Paul esteemed the Corinthians his glory and his crown; hence says he, though other ministers have need of letters of commendation — yet he needed none; for when men should hear of the faith of these Corinthians, which was wrought in them by Paul's preaching; this was sufficient certificate for him, that God had blessed his labors, there should need no other epistle; they themselves were walking certificates, they were his testimonial letters. This was a high commendation; what an honor is it to a minister, when it shall be said of him, as once of Octavius when he came to Rome — he found the walls of brick — but he left them walls of marble! So when the minister came among the people, he found hearts of stone — but he left hearts of flesh.

On the other side, it is a dishonor to a minister when his people are like Laban's sickly lambs, or Pharaoh's lean cows. There are some diseases which they call the reproach of physicians — as they cannot be healed. And there are some people who may be called the reproach of ministers — as they will not be mended. What greater dishonor to a minister, than when it shall be said of him, he has lived so many years in a parish, he found them an ignorant people — and they are so still! That he found them a dull slothful people, (as if they went to the church as some use to go to the apothecary's shop — to take a medicine to make them sleep) and they are so still! That he found them a profane people — and so they are still. Such a people are not a minister's crown — but his heart-breaking. Beloved, when God's stars shine in the sky of the church, will you still walk in the dark! when for the work of Christ they are 'near unto death,' will you be as near unto hell as ever? when these golden bells of Aaron sound, shall you not chime in with Christ? I beseech you, 'let your profiting appear to all.' God sends Paul and Apollos as blessings among a people, they are to be helpers of your faith; if they 'toil all night and catch nothing,' it is to be feared that Satan caught the fish, before the ministers threw their net.

Section 2. Showing, that the world is a Believer's.

1. The lawful use of the world is a believer's.

2. The special use of the world is a believer's.

1. The lawful use of the world is yours. The gospel does somewhat enlarge our charter. We are not in all things so tied up as the Jews were; there were several kinds of meat which were prohibited to them; they might eat of those beasts only, which chewed the cud, and parted the hoof. They might not eat of the swine, because though it divided the hoof — yet it did not chew the cud; it was unclean. But to Christians who live under the gospel, there is not this prohibition. 'The world is yours,' that is — the lawful use of it is yours. Every creature 'being sanctified by the word and prayer,' is good, and we may eat, asking no question for conscience

sake. The world is a garden; God has given us permission to pick off any flower. The world is a paradise; we may eat of any tree that grows in it—but the forbidden tree—that is, sin. Yet even in things lawful, beware of excess. We are apt to offend in lawful things. The world is yours to use; only let those who buy, 'be as if they bought not.' Take heed that you do not drive such a trade in the world, that you are likely to break in your trading for heaven.

2. The special use of the world is yours.

1. The world was made for your sake.

2. All things which happen in the world, are for your good.

1. The world 'was made for your sake.' God has raised this great fabric of the world, chiefly for a believer. The saints are 'God's jewels.' The world is the cabinet where God locks up these jewels for a time. The world is yours—it was made for you. The creation is but a theater to act the great work of redemption upon. The world is the Field, the saints are the Corn, the ordinances are the Showers, the mercies of God are the Sunshine which ripens this corn, death is the Sickle which cuts it down, the angels are the Harvesters who carry it into the barn. The world is yours; God would never have made this field, were it not for the corn growing in it. What use then is there of the wicked? They are as a hedge to keep the corn from foreign invasions, though ofttimes they are a thorn hedge.

Question. But alas, a child of God has often the least share in the world; how then is the world his?

Answer. If you are a believer, that little you have, though it be but a handful of the world, it is blessed to you. If there is any consecrated ground in the world, that is a believer's. The world is yours! Esau had the venison—but Jacob got the blessing. A little blessed is sweet. A little of the world with a great deal of peace, is better than the 'revenues of the wicked.' Every mercy a child of God has, swims to him in Christ's blood, and this sauce makes it relish the sweeter. Whatever he tastes is seasoned with God's love; he has not only corn, but money in the mouth of the sack; not only the gift but the blessing. Thus, the world is a believer's. An unbeliever may be wealthy—yet the world is not his—as he does not taste the quintessence of it. 'Thorns and thistles does the ground bring forth to him.' He feeds upon the fruit of the curse, 'I will curse your blessings'; he eats 'with bitter herbs'. Thus, properly the world is a believer's. He only has a scripture-tenure, and that little he has, turns to cream! Every mercy is a present sent him from heaven.

2. All things which happen in the world, are for your good.

1. The lack of the world is for your good.

2. The hatred of the world is for your good.

1. The lack of the world is for your good. By lacking the honors and revenues of the world—you lack the temptations which others have. Physicians observe that men die sooner by eating an abundance of food, than by scarcity. It is hard to say which kills most—the sword or surfeit. A glutton digs his own grave with his teeth! The world's beauty tempts—but it is like a fair plant to the eye—but poison to the taste. The lack of the world is a mercy.

2. The hatred of the world is for your good. Wicked men are instruments in God's hand for good—albeit they do not intend this. They are flails to thresh off our husks, files to brighten our graces, leeches to suck out the noxious blood. Out of the most poisonous drug—God distills his glory, and our salvation. A child of God is indebted even to his enemies; 'The ploughers ploughed upon my back'; if they did not plough and harrow us, we should bear but a very thin crop. After a man has planted a tree, he prunes and dresses it. Persecutors are God's pruning-

scissors, to cut off the protrusions of sin! The bleeding vine is most fruitful. The envy and malice of the wicked shall do us good. God stirred up the people of Egypt to hate the Israelites, and that was a means to usher in their deliverance. The frowns of the wicked, make us the more ambitious for God's smile! Their incensed rage, shall only carry on God's decree (for while they sit backward to his command, they shall row forward to his decree) so it shall have a subserviency to our good. Every cross wind of Providence shall blow a believer nearer to the port of glory! What a blessed condition is a child of God in! Kill him — or save him alive — it is all working to his good. The opposition of the world is for his good. The world is yours.

Section 3. Showing, that Life is a Believers.

'Life is yours.' Hierom understands it of the life of Christ. It is true, Christ's life is ours; the life which he lived on earth, and the life which he now lives in heaven; his satisfaction and his intercession both are ours, and they are of unspeakable comfort to us. But I conceive by life in the text, is meant natural life, that which is contra-distinguished to death. But how is life a believer's? Two ways.

1. The privilege of life is his.

2. The comfort of life is his.

1. The privilege of life is a believer's. That is, life to a child of God is an advantage for heaven; this life is given him to make provision for a better life. Life is the porch of eternity; here on earth, the believer dresses himself, that he may be fit to enter in with the Bridegroom. We cannot say of a wicked man, that life is his. Though he lives — yet life is not his, he is 'dead while he lives.' He does not improve the life of nature — to get the life of grace. He is like a man who takes the lease of a farm, and makes no benefit of it. He has been so long in the world — but he has not lived. He was born in the reign of such a king, his father left him such an estate, he was of such an age, and then he died. There is the end of him — his life was not worth a prayer — nor his death worth a tear. But life is yours; it is a privilege to a believer; while he has natural life, he 'lays hold upon eternal life.' How does he work out his salvation! What ado is there to get his evidences sealed! What weeping! What wrestling! How does he even take heaven by storm! Just so, that life is yours. It is to a child of God a season of grace, the seed-time of eternity; the longer he lives — the riper he grows for heaven. The life of a believer is as a figure engraved in marble; the life of an unbeliever, as letters written in dust.

2. The comfort of life is a believer's. 'As sorrowful — yet always rejoicing.' Take a child of God at the greatest disadvantage, let his life be overcast with clouds — yet if there be any comfort in life, the believer has it. Our life is often sickly and weak — but the spiritual life administers comfort to the natural life. 'Man' (says Augustine) 'is compounded of the mortal part, and the rational part; the rational serves to comfort the mortal part.' So, I may say, a Christian consists of a natural life, and a spiritual life; the spiritual revives the natural. Observe how the spiritual life distills sweetness into the natural, in three cases.

1. In case of Poverty. This often eclipses the comfort of life. But what though poverty has clipped your wings? 'Poor in the world — yet rich in faith,' James 2:5. Poverty humbles, faith revives.

2. In case of Reproach. This is a heart-breaking, Psalm 69:20. 'Reproach has broken my heart.' Yet a Christian has his cordial by him, 2 Cor. 1:12. 'For this is our rejoicing, the testimony of our conscience.' Who would desire a better jury to acquit him — than God and his own conscience!

3. In case of Losses. It is in itself sad, to have an interposition between us and our dear relations. A limb as it were pulled from our body, and sometimes our estates strangely melted away. Yet a believer has some gleanings of comfort left, and such gleanings as are better than the world's

vintage. 'You took joyfully the confiscation of your goods, knowing in yourselves that you have in heaven a better and an enduring substance,' Heb. 10:34. They had lost their estate — but not their God. Here is you see, the dry rod, blossoming. The spiritual life distills comfort into the natural life. Take the sourest part of a Christian's life, and there is comfort in it. When you hear him sighing bitterly, it is for sin; and such a sigh, though it may break the heart — yet it revives it. The tears of the godly are sweeter than the triumph of the wicked. The comfort that a wicked man has is only imaginary, it is but a pleasant delusion. He is as rejoicing — yet always sorrowing. He has that within, which spoils his music.

But life is yours! When a believer's life is at the lowest ebb — yet he has a spring-tide of comfort.

Chapter 4. The Augmentation of the Charter.

Among these 'things present,' there are yet two other eminent privileges which are in the believer's charter.

1. Remission of sin.

2. Regeneration.

Section 1. Remission of Sin is a Jewel of the Believer's Crown.

To pardon sin, is a privilege belonging to God alone. Pope's pardons are like blanks in a lottery — good for nothing but to be torn up and thrown away. Who can forgive sins but God alone? Mark 2:7. Now this remission or pardon is,

1. A costly mercy.

2. A choice mercy.

1. Pardon of sin is a costly mercy. That which enhances the price of it is that it is the great fruit of Christ's sacrificial death. 'Without shedding of blood is no remission.' Christ bled out our pardon: he was not only 'a lamb without spot,' but a lamb slain. Every pardon a sinner has, is written in Christ's blood.

2. Pardon of sin is a choice mercy. This jewel God hangs upon none but his elect. It is put into the charter; 'I will forgive their iniquity, and I will remember their sin no more.' This is an enriching mercy, it entitles us to blessedness; 'Blessed is he whose transgressions are forgiven, whose sins are covered. Blessed is the man whose sin the Lord does not count against him.' Psalm 32:1-2. Of all the debts we owe, our sins are the worst! To have the book cancelled and God appeased; to hear God whisper by his Spirit, 'son, be of good cheer, your sins are forgiven; I will not blot your Name out of my book — but I will blot your Sins out of my book,' — this is a mercy of the first magnitude. 'Blessed is that man'; in the original it is in the plural, 'blessednesses.' 'Have you but one blessing, my father,' says Esau. But here is a plurality, a whole chain of blessings. Pardon of sin draws the silver link of grace, and the golden link of glory after it. It is a voluminous mercy, there are many mercies bound up with it. You may name it Gad, for behold, 'a troop comes.'

When God pardons a sinner, now he puts on (if I may so speak) his brightest robe. Therefore when he would proclaim himself in his glory to Moses, it was after this manner, 'The Lord, the Lord merciful.' Exod. 34:6. His mercy is his glory: and if you read a little further, you shall see it was no other than pardoning mercy: 'Forgiving iniquity, and transgression and sin,' etc. This is a high act of indulgence. God seals the sinner's pardon with a kiss. This made David put on his best clothes and anoint himself. It was strange, his child newly dead, and God had told him that the sword should not depart from his house; yet now he falls anointing himself. The reason was, David had heard good news, God sent him his pardon by Nathan the prophet; 'The Lord has put away your sin!' This oil of gladness which God had poured into his heart, made way for the anointing oil.

Question. How shall I know that this privilege is mine?

Answer. He whose sins are pardoned, has something to show for it. There are three scripture-evidences:

1. The pardoned sinner is a weeping sinner. Never did any man read his pardon with dry eyes. Look upon that weeping penitent, 'she stood behind Christ weeping.' Tears were distilled out of her penitent heart! O, how precious were Mary's tears! surely more costly in Christ's esteem than her ointment. They dropped from her eyes—as so many pearls. Her amorous eyes, whose sparkles had so often set on fire all her lovers, she now seeks to be revenged on them, and washes Christ's feet with her tears! Her embroidered hair, which had so often as a net, ensnared others—she now makes it a towel to wipe Christ's feet! Here was a pardoned penitent. A pardon will turn the stony heart into a spring of tears! O sinner, ask yourself the question—Is your heart dissolved into tears? does it melt for sin? God seals his pardons only upon melting hearts.

Question. But to what purpose is all this cost? What is the need of weeping after pardon?

Answer. Because now sin and mercy are drawn out in more lively colors than ever. The Spirit comes thus to a sinner; 'You have sinned against God, who never intended you evil; you have abused his mercy; all this you have done—yet behold, here is your pardon! I will set up my mercy above your sin, nay, in spite of it!' The sinner being sensible of this, falls a weeping, and wishes himself even dissolved into tears. He looks upon a bleeding Christ with a bleeding heart. Nothing can so melt the heart of a sinner as the love of God, and the blood of Christ.

2. He whose sins are pardoned, his heart burns in a flame of LOVE. Thus we read of Mary Magdalene—as her eyes were broached with tears—so her heart was red with love to Christ, 'for she loved much.' God's love in pardoning a sinner has an attracting power. The law has a driving power—but love has a drawing power.

3. He whose sins are pardoned, is willing to pardon others. He does forbear and forgive those who have offended him, Eph. 4:32. Some will pray, go to church, give alms—anything but forgive! It is the brand set upon the heathens, 'unmerciful,' Romans 1:31. Those who live without forgiveness, cannot pray the Lord's Prayer, or if they do, they must pray against themselves; they pray that God will forgive them 'as they forgive others,' which is in effect to pray that God will not forgive them. Surely he who has tasted of pardon will think it but rational and Christian, that he should forgive his offending brother.

Section 2. Showing that Regeneration goes along with Remission, and is a Branch of the Charter.

Privilege 2. Regeneration—which is nothing else but the transforming the heart, and casting it into a new mold. You have a pregnant verse for this, Romans 12:2, 'Be transformed by the renewing of your mind.' In the Incarnation, Christ did assume our human nature; and in Regeneration, we partake of his divine nature.

This blessed work of regeneration, is in scripture called sometimes the 'new birth,' because it is begotten of a new seed, the Word, James 1:18, and sometimes the 'new creature'; new, not in substance but in quality. This is the great promise, Ezek. 36:26, 'A new heart also will I give you.' Observe, remission of sin and regeneration are two twins; when God pardons he takes away the rebel's heart. Where this work of regeneration is wrought, the heart has a new bias, and the life a new bent. How great a privilege this is, will appear two ways.

1. Until this blessed work of regeneration, we are in a spiritual sense, DEAD. 'Dead in trespasses and sins,' Eph. 2:1.

A. He is dead in respect of working. A dead man cannot work. The works of a sinner in scripture are called 'dead works'; bid a natural man do anything, you had as good set a dead man about your work; bring him to a sermon, you do but bring a dead corpse to church; bring him to the sacrament, he poisons the sacramental cup; it is as if you should put bread and wine into a dead man's mouth. 'Reprove him sharply for sin'; to what purpose do you strike a dead man?

B. He is dead in respect of honor. He is dead to all privileges; he is not fit to inherit mercy. Who sets the crown upon a dead man? The apostle calls it the crown of life, Rev. 2:10. It is only the living Christian, who shall wear the crown of life.

2. Until this blessed work of regeneration, we are in a spiritual sense, illegitimate. The Devil is his father. 'You are of your father the Devil.' Thus it is, until Christ be formed in the heart of a sinner; then his reproach is rolled away from him. Regeneration ennobles a person; therefore such a one is said to be 'born of God,' 1 John 3:9. O how beautiful is that soul! I may say with Bernard, 'O divine soul, invested with the image of God, espoused to him by faith, dignified with the Spirit! A person regenerate is embroidered with all the graces; he has the silver spangles of holiness, the angels' glory shining in him; he has upon him the image of Christ's beauty. The new creature is a new paradise set full of the heavenly plants. A heart ennobled with grace (to speak with reverence) is God's lesser heaven.

Chapter V. Showing that things to come are a Believer's.

And so I slide into the second part of the text, 'Things to come,' are yours! Here is portion enough! It is a great comfort that when things present are taken away — yet things to come are ours. Methinks the very naming this word, 'things to come,' should make the spirits of a Christian revive. It is a sweet word; our happiness is 'to come' — the best is ahead! Truly if we had nothing but what we have here on earth, we would be miserable; here on earth, are disgraces and martyrdoms; we must taste some of that gall and vinegar which Jesus Christ drank upon the cross. But, O Christian, be of good cheer, there is something to come! The best part of our portion is yet to be given — 'all things to come are yours!' God deals with us as a merchant who shows the worst piece of cloth first. We meet sometimes with coarse usage in the world; that piece which is of the finest spinning, is kept until we come at heaven. It is true, God does chequer his work in this life — white and black. He gives us something to sweeten our pilgrimage here — some tastes of his love — these are the pledge and first-fruits. But what is this to that which is to come? 'Now we are the sons of God,' 1 John 3:2, 'But it does not yet appear what we shall be.' Expect that God should keep his best wine until last; 'things to come are yours!'

What are those things which are to come? There are twelve things yet to come, the which I call Twelve Royal Privileges, with which the believer shall be invested. The first is set down in the text, which I will begin with.

Chapter VI. The first Royal Privilege of a Christian, is death.

'Death is yours!' Death in scripture is called an enemy, 1 Cor. 15:26. Yet here it is put in a Christian's inventory of royal privileges, 'death is yours.' Death is an enemy to the mortal part — but a friend to the spiritual. Death is one of our best friends, next to Christ. When Moses saw his rod turned into a serpent, it did at the first affright him, and he fled from it; but when God bade him take hold of it, he found by the miraculous effects which it wrought, it did him and the people of Israel much good. Just so, death at the first sight is like the rod turned into a serpent—it affrights. But when by faith we take hold of it, then we find much benefit and comfort in it. As Moses' rod divided the waters, and made a passage for Israel into Canaan; so death divides the waters of tribulation, and makes a passage for us into the 'land of promise.' Death is called the king of terrors—but it can do a child of God no hurt; this snake may hiss and wind about the body—but the sting is pulled out. The bee by stinging, loses its sting. While death did sting Christ upon the cross, it has quite lost its sting to a believer; it can hurt the soul no more than David did king Saul, when he cut off the lap of his garment. Death to a believer is but like the arresting of a man for debt—after the debt is paid! Death, as God's sergeants at arms, may arrest us, and carry us before God's justice; but Christ will show our discharge—the debt-book is crossed in his blood!

Question. How is death ours?

Answer. Two ways

1. Death is the outlet to sin.

2. Death is the inlet to happiness.

1. Death to a believer, is an outlet to sin. We are in this life under a sinful necessity; even the best saint: 'There is not a just man upon earth, that does good and sins not.' Evil thoughts are continually arising out of our hearts, as sparks out of a furnace. Sin keeps house with us whether we will or not; the best saint alive is troubled with these evil inhabitants; though he forsakes his sins—yet his sins will not forsake him.

Sin does indispose to good. 'How to perform that which is good I find not,' Romans 7:18. When we would pray, the heart is a violin out of tune; when we would weep, we are as clouds without rain.

Sin tempts to evil. 'The flesh lusts against the spirit.' There needs be no external wind of temptation, we have tide strong enough in our hearts, to carry us to hell. Consider sin under this threefold notion.

1. Sin is a 'body of death,' and that not impertinently.

First, it is a body for its weight. The body is a heavy and weighty substance: so is sin a body, it weighs us down. When we would pray, the weights of sin are tied to our feet that we cannot ascend. Anselm, seeing a little boy playing with a bird, he let her fly up, and presently pulls the bird down again by a string: so, says he, it is with me as with this bird; when I would fly up to heaven upon the wings of meditation, I find a string tied to my leg; I am overpowered with corruption; but death pulls off these weights of sin, and lets the soul free.

Secondly, sin is a body of death, for its annoyance. It was a cruel torment that one used, he tied a dead man to a living man, that the dead man might annoy and infest the living. Thus it is with a child of God, he has two men within him—flesh and spirit—grace and corruption. There is the dead man tied to the living man. A proud sinful heart is worse to a child of God, than the smell of a dead corpse. Indeed to a natural man sin is not offensive; for, being 'dead in sin,' he is not sensible: but where there is a vital principle of spiritual life, there is no greater annoyance than the body of death: insomuch that the pious soul often cries out, as David, 'Woe is me, that I dwell in Meshech, and sojourn in the tents of Kedar.' So says he, 'Woe is me, that I am constrained to abide with sin! How long shall I be troubled with evil inhabitants! How long shall I offend that God whom I love! When shall I leave these tents of Kedar!'

2. Sin is a tyrant, it carries in it the nature of a law; the apostle calls it the 'law in his members.' Romans 7:14. There is the law of pride, the law of unbelief; it has a kind of jurisdiction, as Caesar over the senate. 'What I hate, that I do'; verse 15. The apostle was for the present like a

man carried down the stream, and was not able to bear up against it. Whence are our carnal fears? whence our sinful passions? whence is it that a child of God does that which he does not want to do? yes, sometimes against knowledge? The reason is, he is captivated under sin. But be of good cheer, where grace makes a combat — death shall make a conquest!

3. Sin is a leprous spot. It makes everything we touch unclean. Thus in every man naturally, there is a fretting leprosy of sin, pride, unbelief, impenitency, etc. These are leprous spots. In conversion, God makes a change in the heart of a sinner — but still the leprosy of sin spreads; then at last death comes and pulls down the stones and timber of the house, and the soul is quite freed from the leprosy. Sin is a defiling thing, it makes us red with guilt — and black with filth Sin is compared to a 'menstruous cloth'; we need carry it no higher. Hierom says, there was nothing in the law more unclean than the menstruous cloth: this is sin. Sin draws the Devil's picture in a man; malice is the Devil's eye; oppression is his hand; hypocrisy is his cloven foot!

But behold, death will give us our discharge; death is the last and best physician, which cures all diseases and sins — the aching head and the unbelieving heart. Sin was the midwife which brought death into the world, and death shall be the grave to bury sin! O the privilege of a believer! he is not taken away in his sins — but he is taken away from his sins. The Persians had a certain day in the year, wherein they used to kill all serpents and venomous creatures: such a day as that will the day of death be to a man in Christ. This day the old serpent dies in a believer, which has so often stung him with his temptations! This day the sins of the godly, these venomous creatures, shall all be destroyed. They shall never more be proud; they shall never more grieve the Spirit of God; the death of the body shall quite destroy the body of death.

2. To a believer, death is the inlet to eternal happiness. Samson found a honeycomb in the lion's carcass; so may a child of God suck much sweetness from death. Death is the gate of life! Death pulls off our rags, and gives us glorious raiment. All the hurt death does to us — is to put us into a blissful condition. Death is called in scripture a sleep, 1 Thess. 4:14. 'Those who sleep in Jesus'; as after sleep the spirits are exhilarated and refreshed, so after death, 'the times of refreshing come from the presence of the Lord.' Death is yours. Death is a believer's ferryman, to ferry him over to the land of rest! Death opens the portal into heaven! The day of a Christian's death — is the birthday of his heavenly life! Death is his ascension-day to glory! Death is his marriage-day with Jesus Christ! After his funeral, he begins his marriage!

Well then might Solomon say, 'The day of one's death is better than the day of one's birth.' Death is the spiritual man's advancement, why then should he fear it? Death, I confess, has a grim visage to an impenitent sinner; so it is ghastly to look upon; it is a messenger to carry him to hell. But to such as are in Christ, 'death is yours!' Death is like the 'pillar of cloud,' it has a dark side to a sinner: but it has a light side to a believer. Death's pale face looks ruddy, when the 'blood of sprinkling' is upon it; in short, faith gives us a property in heaven, death gives us a possession: fear not your privilege, the thoughts of death should be delightful. Jacob, when he saw the wagons, his spirits revived. Death is the chariot which carries us to our Father's house! What were the martyrs' flames but a fiery chariot to carry them up to heaven! This world we live in, is but a desert; shall we not be willing to leave it for paradise! We say, it is good to be here; we try to have an earthly paradise. But grace must curb nature.

Think of the privileges of death. Though naturally we desire to live here on earth, as we are made up of flesh — yet grace should be as the master wheel, which sways our will, making us long for death. 'I desire to depart and be with Christ, which is better by far!' 2 Cor. 5:2, 'We groan, longing to be clothed with our heavenly dwelling.' We would put off the earthly clothes of our body, and put on the bright robe of immortality. 'We groan,' it is a metaphor taken from a mother, who being pregnant, groans and cries out for delivery. Augustine longed to die, that he might see that head which was once crowned with thorns. We pray, 'May Your kingdom come'; and when God is leading us into his kingdom, shall we be afraid to go! The times we live in should, methinks, make us long for death. We live in dying times, we may hear, as it were, God's death bell ringing over these nations. They are well—who are out of the storm—and have gotten already to the haven!

Question. But who shall have this privilege?

Answer. Death is certain; but there are only two sorts of people to whom we may say 'Death is yours!' It is your preferment.

1. Such as die daily. We are not born angels; die we must, therefore we had need carry always a death's head with us. The basilisk, if it sees a man first—it kills him; but if he sees it first—it does him no hurt. The basilisk death, if it sees us first, before we see it—it is dangerous; but if we see it first by meditating upon it, it does us no hurt. Study death, often walk among the tombs. It is the thoughts of death beforehand, that must do us good. In a dark night, one torch carried before a man is worth many torches carried after him: one serious thought of death beforehand, one tear shed for sin before death—is worth a thousand shed after, when it is too late. It is good to make death our familiar friend, and in this sense to be in deaths often: that if God should presently send us a letter of summons this night, we might have nothing to do but to die.

Alas, how do many put off the thoughts of death! It is almost death to them—to think of death. There are some who are in the very threshold of the grave, who have one foot in the grave, and the other foot in hell; yet 'put far from them the evil day.' I have read of one Lysicrates, who in his old age dyed his gray hairs black, that he might seem young again. When we should be building our tombs, we are building our houses! Die daily, lest you die eternally! The holy patriarchs in purchasing for themselves a burying place, showed us what thoughts they still had of death. Joseph of Arimathea erected his sepulcher in his garden: we have many that set up the trophies of their victories; others that set up their trophies, that they may blaze their honor. But how few that set up their sepulchers; who erect in their hearts the serious thoughts of death! O remember when you are in your gardens, in places most delicious and fragrant, to keep a place for your tombstone; die daily! There is no better way to bring sin into a consumption, than by often looking on the pale horse, and the one that sits thereon. By thinking on death, we begin to repent of an evil life; and so we disarm death before it comes, and cut the lock where its strength lies.

2. Such as are in heaven before they die. Death is yours! If we must be high-minded, let it be in setting our mind upon heavenly things. Heaven must come down into us before we go up there. A child of God breathes his faith in heaven; his thoughts are there: 'When I awake I am still with you,' Psalm 139:17. David awaked in heaven; his conversation is there; Philip. 3:20, 'For our conversation is in heaven.' The believer often ascends mount Tabor, and takes a prospect of glory. O that we had this celestial frame of heart! When Zaccheus was in the crowd, he was too low to see Christ; therefore he climbed up into the Sycamore tree. When we are in a crowd of worldly business, we cannot see Christ. Climb up into the tree by divine contemplation! If you would get Christ into your heart, let heaven be in your eye! 'Set your affections upon things above,' Col. 3:2. There needs be no exhortation for us to set our hearts on things below. How is the curse of the serpent upon most men! 'Upon your belly shall you go, and dust shall you eat all the days of your life.' Those who feed only upon dust, golden dust, will be unwilling to return to dust. To them, death will be terrible!

The tribes of Reuben and Gad desired that they might stay on this side Jordan — and have their portion there; it being a place convenient for their cattle. It seems they minded their cattle more than their passage into the holy land! Just so, many professors, if they may have but a little grazing here in the world, in their shops, and in their farms, they are content to live on this side the river, and mind not their passage into the land of promise! But you who are in heaven before you die — death is yours!

An earthly saint is a contradiction. The Greek word for saint signifies a man refined and separated from the earth. If an astronomer, instead of observing the planets, and the motions of the heavens, should take a reed in his hand, and fall a measuring of the earth, would not this be counted a contradiction! And is not it as great a contradiction in religion, when men pretend to have Christ and heaven in their eye — yet mind earthly things! Phil. 3:19. Our souls, methinks should be like to a ship, which is made little and narrow downwards — but more wide and broad upwards. So our affections should be very narrow downwards to the earth — but wide and large upwards towards heavenly things.

Thus we see death is a privilege to believers; death is yours! The heir while he is under age, is heir of the land he is born to — but he has not the use or the benefit of it, until he comes of age. Be as old as you will, you are never of age for heaven — until you die. Death brings us to age, and then the possession comes into our hands!

Chapter 7. The second Royal Privilege of a Christian, is that he shall be carried up by the angels.

Now I proceed to the second privilege, which is yet to come: what holy David says of Zion, 'Glorious things are spoken of you, O you city of God,' Psalm 87:3.

In this life, a believer is carried by the saints; they lift him upon the wings of their prayers; and when they can carry him no longer, after death, the angels take him, and carry him up. Wicked men, when they die, they shall have a black guard of angels to carry them. You who are an old sinner (who has a hoary head — but your heart is as young in sin as ever) I may say to you as Christ said in another sense to Peter: 'When you are old, you shall stretch forth your hands, and another shall gird you, and carry you where you would not.' So I say, You old sinner, the time is shortly coming, when you shall stretch forth your hands on your death-bed, and another shall bind you, and carry you where you would not; you shall be carried by a black guard!

But a believer shall be carried by the angels into heaven: 'The beggar died, and was carried by the angels into Abraham's bosom.' Abraham's bosom is a figurative speech, representing the seat of the blessed. There poor Lazarus was carried by the angels. When he was upon earth, he had no friends but the dogs which licked his sores. But when he died, he had a convoy of angels. After our fall, the angels (as well as God) fell out with us, and became our enemies; hence we read that the angels (the cherubim) stood with a flaming sword, to keep our first parents out of Paradise, Gen. 3:24. But being now at peace with God, we are at peace with the angels. Therefore the angel comes with an olive-branch of peace in his mouth, and proclaims with triumph the news of Christ's incarnation. Luke 2:11, 'For unto you is born, in the city of David, a Savior which is Christ the Lord!' The angels bless God for man's redemption, verse 13. 'And suddenly there was with the angel a multitude of the heavenly multitude praising God, and saying, glory be to God in the highest.'

The angels love mankind (especially where there is the new man) and are ready to do all friendly offices for us. As in our lifetime, they are our supporters, Psalm 91:11. 'He shall give his angels charge to keep you;' so after death they are our porters. Lazarus was carried by the angels. The angels are called ministering spirits; they are willing to minister for the good of the saints. Hence some observe, it is said, Lazarus was carried by the angels, in the plural, not by one angel—as if the angels had been ambitious to carry Lazarus, and each one strived which should have a part. O in what pomp and triumph did Lazarus's soul now ride! Never was Dives so honored in his life—as Lazarus was at his death. For a king to help to carry the coffin of one of his subjects, were a high honor; but a believer shall have a guard of angels to conduct him. Amasis king of Egypt, that he might set forth his magnificence, would have his chariot drawn by four princes, which he had conquered in the war. But what was all this, compared to the chariot in which Lazarus, and the soul of every believer, shall be drawn at their death! They shall be carried by the angels of God!

Chapter 8. The Third Royal Privilege of a Believer is—that he shall 'be with Christ in glory.'

Phil. 1:23, 'I desire to be depart,' or loosen anchor—and to be with Christ! This is a privilege of the first magnitude! Surely we can be no losers, by being with Christ. A graft or scion, though it is taken out of the tree, it does not perish—but is set into a better stock. Thus it is with a Christian, while he is here, (even after conversion) there is much of the wild olive still in him; now when this scion, by death is cut off, he does not perish—but is set into a more noble stock—he is with Christ, which is far better. Well might the apostle say, 'I desire to depart and be with Christ, which is better by far!' Is not a state of perfection better than a state of imperfection?

Our graces are our best jewels—but they are imperfect, and do not give out their full luster; grace is but in its infancy here on earth, it will not be of full growth until we are with Christ. The best Christian in this life—is but a child in grace. Here on earth, we have but some imperfect buddings of grace; when we are with Christ, our graces shall be fully ripe and matured. In this life we are said to receive but 'the first fruits of the Spirit.' We must not expect a full crop until we are with Christ! Grace while we are here in this world, is mingled with corruption. It is like gold in the ore; or as the pillar of cloud, it has its dark side as well as its light side. Our faith is mingled with unbelief; our humility is stained with pride! The flame of grace is not so pure, but it has some smoky vapors. Our life of grace is said to be hidden. It is hidden indeed, under much corruption, as the sun is hidden under a cloud; or as the corn is hidden under chaff; or as a pearl may be hidden in the mire. Though grace cannot be lost—yet it may be hidden. David so clouded his graces by sin, that others could hardly see the cloth of gold under the filthy garments. Is it not far better to be with Christ? our graces then shall shine forth in their perfection! This is a glorious privilege, we shall be with Christ.

It is a blessed thing to be with Christ while we are here on earth. 'I am ever with you.' What is it, which the pious soul desires in this life? Is it not to have the sweet presence of Christ! He cares for nothing, but what has something of Christ in it. He loves duties only as they carry him to Christ. Why is prayer so sweet—but because the soul has private conference with Christ! Why is the Word precious—but because it is a means to convey Christ to him! He comes down to us upon the wings of the Spirit; and we go up to him upon the wings of faith! An ordinance without Christ—is but feeding upon the dish—instead of the meat. Why does the wife love the letter—but because it brings news of her husband! Here on earth, we enjoy Christ by letters, and that is sweet; but what will it be to enjoy his presence in glory! Here is that which may amaze us—we shall be with Christ! Christ is all that is desirable! Nay, he is more than we can desire! A man that is thirsty, he desires only a little water to quench his thirst; but bring him to the lake—and here he has more than he can desire. In Christ there is not only a fullness of sufficiency—but a fullness of abundance; it overflows all the banks! A Christian that is most energized by faith, has neither a head to devise, nor a heart to desire—all that which is in Christ! Only when we come to heaven, will God enlarge the vessel of our desire, and will fill us as Christ did the waterpots with wine—'up to the brim.' Now this privilege of being with Christ, has six privileges growing out of it.

1. The First Privilege of being with Christ—vision.

Job 19:26. 'In my flesh shall I see God'; the sight of Jesus Christ will be the most sublime and ravishing object to a glorified saint. When Christ was upon earth, his beauty was hidden. 'He has no form or loveliness;' the light of the divine nature was hidden in the dark lantern of the human; it was hidden under reproaches, sufferings; yet even at that time there was enough of beauty in Christ to delight the heart of God. 'My Elect in whom my soul delights.' His veil was then upon his face; but what will it be when the veil shall be taken off, and he shall appear in all his embroidery! It is heaven enough—to see Christ. 'Whom have I in heaven but you!' Angels and archangels do not make heaven. Christ is the most sparkling diamond in the ring of glory!

2. The Second Privilege of being with Christ—UNION. We shall enter into a marriage union with Christ. We shall so behold him, as to be made one with him. What nearer than union? what sweeter? Union is the spring of joy, the ground of privilege; by virtue of this blessed union with Christ, all those rare beauties with which the human nature of the Lord Jesus is bespangled, shall be ours. Let us compare two scriptures: John 17:24, 'Father, I will that they also whom you have given me, be with me where I am, that they may behold my glory.' That is, the glory of the human nature. But this is not all, verse 22, 'The glory that you have given me, I have given them.' Christ has not his glory only for himself—but for us; we shall shine by his beams. Here on earth, Christ puts his graces upon his spouse, and in heaven he will put his glory upon her.

No wonder then the king's daughter is 'all glorious within,' and 'her clothing of wrought gold.' How glorious will the spouse be, when she has Christ's jewels upon her! Judge not of the saints by what they are—but by what they shall be. 'It does not yet appear what we shall be,' 1 John 3:1. Why, what shall we be? 'We shall be like him.' The spouse of Christ shall not only be made one with Christ—but she shall be made like Christ; in other marriages, the spouse changes her condition—but here she changes her complexion! Not that the saints in glory shall receive of Christ's essence, they shall have as much glory as the human nature is capable of; though Christ conveys his image—yet not his essence. The sun shining upon a glass leaves a print of its beauty there; and it is hard to distinguish between the glass and the sunbeam: but the glass is not the beam, the sun conveys only its likeness, not its essence.

3. The Third Privilege of being with Christ—nobility. This consists in two things.

1. The saints shall sit with Jesus Christ when he judges the world. 'Know you not, that the saints shall judge the world?' The saints shall sit with Christ in judicature, as the justices of peace with the judge. The saints are Christ's assessors; they shall be with him upon the bench, applauding his righteous sentence. O what a glorious tribunal will that be! Here on earth, the world judges the saints—but there the saints shall judge the world.

2. They shall sit nearer the throne than the angels. The angels are noble and sublime spirits—but by virtue of our marriage union, we shall be ennobled with greater honor than the angels! The angels are Christ's friends—but not his spouse! This honor have all his saints. As the saints' robes in glory shall be brighter than the angels: theirs being only the righteousness of creatures—but these having upon them the righteousness of God, so their dignity shall be greater. Here on earth, we are prisoners at bar—but there favorites at court! The saints shall sit down in glory above the angels.

4. The Fourth Privilege of being with Christ — joy. This joy of the saints proceeds from union; when our union with Christ is perfect, then our joy shall be full. Rev. 21:4, 'And God shall wipe away all tears, and there shall be no more sorrow.'

1. There shall be no weeping. Jesus Christ has provided a handkerchief to wipe off the tears of the saints. Here on earth, the spouse is in sable, it being a time of absence from her husband. But in heaven, Christ will take away the spouse's mourning; he will take off all her black and bloody apparel, and will clothe her in white robes, Rev. 7:13. White, as it is an emblem of the saints' purity, so it is a type of their joy. Heaven would not be heaven — if there were weeping there. Hell indeed is called a place of weeping; those who would not shed a tear for their sins while they lived, shall have weeping enough; but we never read of weeping in heaven. Christ will take down our harps from the willows; there he will call for his heralds and trumpeters. The angels, those blessed choristers, shall sing the divine anthems of praise, and the saints shall join in that heavenly concert. If it were possible that any tears could be shed when we are with Christ, they should be the tears of joy, as sometimes we have seen a man weep for excessive joy! Christ will turn all our water there, into wine.

2. There shall be no sorrow. One smile from Christ's face will make us forget all the afflictions of our earthly life. Sorrow is a cloud gathered in the heart, upon the apprehension of some evil: and weeping is the cloud of grief dropping into rain. But in heaven the sun of righteousness shall shine so bright, that there shall not be the least interposition of any cloud. There shall be no sorrow there, nor anything to breed it. There shall be no sin to humble. Heaven is such a pure soil, that the viper of sin will not breed there. There shall be no enemy to molest. When Israel had conquered Canaan — yet they could not get rid of all the Canaanites, they would live among them; 'But the Canaanites would dwell in that land!' But when we are with Christ, we shall never more be troubled with Canaanites. 'In that day, there shall be no more the Canaanite in the house of the Lord.' God will keep the heavenly paradise with a flaming sword, that none shall come near to hurt: 'Upon all that glory shall be a defense.' There shall be nothing to breed sorrow in heaven. There are two things that usually raise the clouds of sorrow, and both shall be removed when we are with Christ.

1. The frowns of great men. How ambitious are men of the King's smile? but alas, that quickly sets in a cloud, and then their comforts are in the wane, they are sad! But when we are with Christ, we shall have a perpetual smile from God! The saints shall never be out of favor, Jesus Christ is the great favorite at court; and as long as God smiles upon Christ, so long he will smile upon the saints, they having on Christ's beauty; and being part of Christ.

2. The loss of dear friends. Friends imparts secrets; friendship is the marriage of affections, it makes two become one spirit. David and Jonathan took sweet counsel together, their heart was knit in one. Now here is the grief — when this precious knot must be untied. But be of good cheer, if your friend is one of the elect, after you have parted with your sins — you shall meet with him and never part. If your friend is wicked, though he were your friend on earth, you will cease to be his friend in heaven. The pious wife will not complain she has lost her wicked husband; nor the pious parent, that he has lost his wicked child. All relations are infinitely made up in Christ, as the whole constellation in the sun, that great lamp of heaven. When a man comes to the lake, he does not complain that he lacks his cistern of water. Though you sucked comfort from your relations; yet when you come to the ocean, and are with Christ, you shall never complain that you have left your cistern behind!

There will be nothing to breed sorrow in heaven; there shall be joy — and nothing but joy. Heaven is set out by that phrase, 'Enter into the joy of your Lord.' Here on earth, joy enters into us; there we enter into joy. The joys we have here on earth, are from heaven; those joys are in heaven! The joys that we shall have with Christ, are without measure and without mixture. 'In your presence is fullness of joy,' Psalm 16:11.

1. The heart shall be filled with joy. Nothing but Christ can replenish the heart with joy: the understanding, will, and affections, are such a triangle, that none can fill but the Trinity. As Christ's beauty shall amaze the eye, so his love shall ravish the heart of a glorified saint! Must it not needs be joy to be with Christ? What joy, when a Christian shall pass the great gulf between heaven and hell! What joy when Christ shall take a believer into the wine cellar, and kiss him with the kisses of his lips! What joy when the match shall be at once made up, and solemnized between Christ and the soul! These are the more noble and entire delights.

2. All the senses shall be filled with joy—and at once! The eye shall be filled. What joy shall it be, to see that orient brightness in the face of Christ! There you may see the lily and the rose mixed, white and ruddy, Cant. 5:10. The ear shall be filled. What joy to the spouse—to hear Christ's voice! The voice of God was dreadful to Adam, after he had listened to the serpent's voice. 'I heard your voice in the garden—and was afraid,' Gen. 3:10. But how sweet will the bridegroom's voice be! What joy to hear him say, 'My love, my dove, my undefiled one!' What joy to hear the music of angels, even the heavenly multitude praising God? If the eloquence of Origin, and the golden mouth of Chrysostom, did so affect and charm the ears of their auditors, O then what will it be to hear the glorious tongues of saints and angels, as so many divine trumpets sounding forth the excellencies of God, and singing hallelujahs to the lamb!

The smell shall be filled. What joy to smell that fragrance and perfume which comes from Christ! All his garments smell of myrrh, aloes, and cassia. The sweet breath of his Spirit blowing upon the soul, shall give forth its scent as the wine of Lebanon. The taste shall be filled. Christ will bring his spouse into the banqueting-house, and she shall be inebriated with his love! O what joy to be drinking in this heavenly nectar! This is the water of life! This is the wine on the lees well refined. The touch shall be filled—the saints shall be ever in the embraces of Christ; 'Behold my hands and my feet; handle me, and see me,' Luke 24:39. That will be our work in heaven; we shall be forever handling the Lord of life! Thus all the senses shall be filled with joy. Well might the apostle say, to be with Christ is better by far! If Christ's sufferings are full of joy, what then are his embraces! If the dew of Hermon hill is so sweet—the first-fruits of Christ's love; what will the full crop be!

In short, there will be nothing in heaven but what shall add infinitely to the joy of the saints. The very torments of the damned shall create matter of joy and triumph. I may allude to that of the Psalmist, 'The righteous shall rejoice when he sees the vengeance.' 'And again they shouted: Hallelujah! The smoke from her goes up for ever and ever!' Revelation 19:3. The Elect shall rejoice upon a double account— to see God's justice magnificently exalted, and to see themselves miraculously delivered. There shall be no unpleasant object represented; nothing but joy. Such will that joy be, when we are with Christ, that it is not possible to now even imagine! 'He was caught up to paradise. He heard inexpressible things, things that man is not permitted to tell.' 2 Cor. 12:4. We read that Joseph gave his brethren money and provisions for the way; but the full sacks were kept until they came to their father's house. Just so, God gives us something by the way; some of the hidden manna; some taste of his heavenly joy in this life—but the full sacks of blessing are kept for heaven! O what joy to be with Christ! Surely if there were such joy and triumph at Solomon's coronation, that all the earth rang with the sound of it, what joy will be on the saints' coronation-day, when they shall be eternally united to Jesus Christ!

5. The Fifth Privilege of being with Christ—rest. A Christian in this life is like quicksilver, which has a principle of motion in itself—but not of rest. We are never quiet—but are like the ship

upon the waves. As long as we have sin—we will not have rest. A child of God is full of motion and disquiet; 'I have no rest in my bones by reason of my sin,' Psalm 38:3. While there are wicked men in the world, never look for rest. If a man is poor, he is thrust away by the rich. If he be rich, he is envied by the poor. Sometimes losses disquiet, sometimes law-suits vex. The saints in this life are in a pilgrim condition; the apostles had no certain dwelling place, 1 Cor. 4:11. We are here on earth, in a perpetual hurry, in a constant fluctuation. Our life is like the tide, sometimes ebbing, sometimes flowing.

Here on earth, is no rest—and the reason is, because we are out of center; everything is in motion until it comes at the center; Christ is the center of the soul. The needle of the compass trembles—until it turns to the North pole. Noah's dove found no rest for the sole of her foot—until she came at the ark. This ark was a type of Christ. When we come to heaven, the kingdom which cannot be shaken, we shall have rest, Heb. 4:9. 'There remains therefore a rest for the people of God.' Heaven in scripture is compared to a granary, Matt. 3:12, an emblem of rest. Wheat, while it stands on the ground, is shaken to and fro with the wind—but when it is laid up in the granary it is at rest. The elect are spiritual wheat, who while they are in the field of this world, are never quiet—the wind of persecution shakes this wheat, and everyone who passes by, will be plucking these sacred ears of corn. But when the wheat is in the heavenly garner, it is at rest. There remains a rest for the people of God. Not but that there shall be motion in heaven, (for spirits cannot be idle) but it shall be without lethargy and weariness. It shall be a labor full of ease; a motion full of rest. When a believer is in heaven, he has his rest. The lower earthly region is windy and tempestuous. When we are once gotten into the upper region of glory, there are no winds or noxious vapors—but a serene calmness; this is to be with Christ.

6. The Sixth Privilege of being with Christ—security. It is possible that a man may have a few minutes of rest; but he is not secure, he knows not how soon eclipses and changes may come. He is still in fear, and fear makes a man a slave, though he knows it not. There is torment in fear, 1 John 4:18. He who has great possessions thinks thus: 'How soon may I fall from this pinnacle of honor? how soon may the plunderer come?' Nay, a believer who has durable riches—may still be wavering and doubting concerning his condition.

1. He sometimes questions whether he is in the state of grace or not; and thus he thinks with himself; 'Perhaps I believe; I have something that glitters, perhaps it is but a counterfeit pearl. Perhaps my faith is presumption, my love to Christ is but self-love.' And after the Spirit of God has wrought the heart to some sound persuasion, he is soon shaken again; as a ship that lies at anchor, though it is safe—yet it is shaken and tossed upon the water; and these fears leave impressions of sadness upon the heart.

2. But secondly, he fears that though he is in the state of grace—yet he may fall into some scandalous sin, and so grieve the Spirit of God, sadden the hearts of the righteous, wound his own conscience, harden sinners, discourage new beginners, put a song into the mouth of the profane, and at last God hide his face in a cloud. A child of God after a sad declension, having by his sin put black spots in the face of religion, though I deny not but he has a title to the promise; yet be may be in such a condition, that he cannot for the present apply any promise—he may go weeping to his grave.

These sad fears, like black vapors, are still arising out of a gracious heart. But when once a believer is with Christ, there is full security of heart; he is not only out of danger—but out of fear. Take it thus; a man that is upon the top of a mast, he may sit safe for the present—but not secure. Perhaps the pirates may shoot at the ship, and take it; perhaps the winds may arise suddenly, and the ship may sink in the storm. But a man who is upon a rock, he stands impregnable; his heart is secure. A Christian in this life is like a man upon the top of a mast; sometimes the pirates come aboard, namely, cruel persecutors, and they shoot at his ship, and often, though the passenger (the precious soul) escapes — yet they sink the ship; sometimes the winds of temptation blow; those northern winds; and now the Christian questions whether God loves him, or whether his name is enrolled in the book of life. And though being in Christ, there is no danger — yet his heart hesitates and trembles. But when he is with Christ, off from the top of the mast, and is planted upon the rock — his heart is fully secure; and you shall hear him say thus, now I am sure I have passed the gulf, I am now passing from death unto life, and none shall pluck me out of my Savior's arms!

Chapter 9. The Fourth Royal Privilege — the blessed inheritance.

Let worldlings place their happiness in this life; a believer's happiness is in the future — the golden world is yet to come. I pass to the next privilege, which is the blessed inheritance. Col. 1:12, 'Giving thanks unto the Father, who has made us fit to be partakers of the inheritance of the saints in light.' This world is but a tenement, which we may be soon turned out of; heaven is an inheritance, and a glorious one. Heaven cannot be hyperbolized. If the skirts and suburbs of the palace, namely, the stars and planets are so glorious, that our eyes cannot behold the dazzling luster of them; what glory then is there in the celestial palace itself!

Of this blessed place we have a figurative description in Rev. 21. John was carried away in the Spirit, and had a vision of heaven, verse 2. 'And I saw no temple therein;' while we dwell upon earth, there is need for a temple, we shall not be above ordinances until we are above sin; but in heaven, God will be our meeting place — instead of a temple, 'he shall be all in all.'

Verse 25, 'there shall be no night there.' No city is to be found, not the most glorious metropolis under heaven, where it is always day: for though some regions which lie immediately under the pole, have light for several months together; yet when the sun withdraws from the horizon, they have as long a night as before they had a day. But says the text, 'There shall be no night there.' In hell it is all night — but in heaven the day will be ever lengthening. Now this blessed inheritance which the saints shall possess, has eight properties, or rather privileges worth our serious thoughts.

1. Sublimeness. It is set out by a great and high mountain, Rev. 21:10. It is placed above the airy and starry heaven, says Musculus. It is the empyrean heaven which Paul calls the third heaven. For the situation of it; it is far above all heavens, where Christ himself is. This is the royal palace where saints shall dwell. The men of this world are high in power and in pride — and if they could build their nests among the stars, the elect shall shortly be above them; they shall take their flight as high as Christ: here is a preferment worth looking after.

2. Magnificence. It is set out by gems and precious stones, the richest jewels. If the streets are of gold — what is the furniture and decorations! What is the cabinet of jewels! No wonder that 'the violent take it by force!' Mat. 11:12. I rather wonder, why others are not more earnest for this inheritance. What are all the rarities of the world, compared to this! The coasts of pearl, the islands of spices, the rocks of diamonds! What a rich place must that needs be, where God will lay out his cost — where infinite wisdom contrives, and infinite bounty disburses!

Fulgentius, beholding the pomp and splendor of the Roman senate-house, cried out, 'If the earthly senate-house is so glorious — O how beautiful is the celestial Jerusalem!' In this blessed inheritance there is nothing but glory. There is the king of glory; there are the vessels of glory; there are the thrones of glory; there is the weight of glory; there are the crowns of glory; there is the kingdom of glory; there is the brightness of glory! This is a purchase worth getting! What will not men adventure for a kingdom!

3. Purity. Heaven is set forth under the metaphor of 'pure gold, and transparent glass,' Rev. 21:11. The apostle calls it 'an undefiled inheritance.' Heaven is a pure place; it is compared to the sapphire, 21:19. The sapphire is a precious stone of a bright sky color, and it has a virtue in it, says Pliny, to preserve chasteness and purity. Thus heaven is represented by the sapphire; it is a place where only the refined pure spirits enter. Heaven is compared to the emerald, verse 19, which (as writers say) has a precious virtue to expel poison. Heaven is such a pure soil, that as no fever of lust, so no venom of malice shall be there. There shall not enter into it anything 'which defiles,' Rev. 21:27. It is a kingdom wherein 'dwells righteousness,' 2 Pet. 3:13.

In this lower earthly region, there is little righteousness; 'They set up wickedness by a law,' Psalm 94:20. The wicked devours his neighbor, 'who is more righteous than he,' Hab. 1:13. The just man is oppressed because he is just. One says, there is more justice to be found in hell — than upon earth. For in hell no innocent person is oppressed; but here on earth, righteousness is the thing that is persecuted. A man can hardly tread two steps — but either into sin or into suffering. In this world, the sinner need not fear any punitive vindictive act of justice; rather he who reproves sin may fear. Holiness is the mark which the Devil shoots at! But heaven is a kingdom wherein dwells righteousness; there is the judge of the world, 'who puts on righteousness as a breastplate; who loves righteousness.'

4. Peaceableness. The word Peace, comprehends all blessings. Peace is the glory of a kingdom: this white lily is the best flower of a prince's crown. How happy was the reign of Pompilius — when it was so peaceful, that the bees made their hives in the soldiers helmets! But where shall we find an uninterrupted peace upon earth? Either there are divisions at home, or wars abroad, the beating of the drums, the roaring of the cannons, the sounding of the trumpets. Solomon's kingdom was peaceable a while — but how soon had he an alarm given him! 1 Kings 11:14, 'The Lord stirred up an adversary against him.' How soon do the clouds of blood drop after a little sunshine of peace!

But the heavenly inheritance to come is peaceable. There is the 'Prince of Peace'; there the saints enter into peace. The harp, in ancient times, was made the emblem of peace; in heaven there shall be the 'voice of harpers harping.' The saints in this life wear 'garments rolled in blood'; but in a state of glory, they are said to wear 'white robes,' which shall not be stained with the blood of war anymore! In heaven righteousness and peace shall kiss each other.

5. Amplitude. The inheritance is sufficiently spacious for all the saints. The garner is wide enough to receive all those infinite grains of wheat which shall be laid in it. Though there are innumerable companies of saints and angels in heaven — yet there is infinitely room enough to receive them: 'In my Father's house are many mansions.' Some are of opinion that every believer shall have a particular mansion in glory. 'Every saint shall have his kingdom,' says Jansenius. We know our Savior told his apostles that they would sit upon twelve thrones. Certainly the saints shall not be straitened for room. The world of glory is wide enough for the most sublime spirits to expatiate in!

6. Safety. It is an inheritance which the saints cannot be defrauded of; it is in safe hands. God keeps the inheritance for them, 1 Pet. 1:4, and keeps them for the inheritance, 1 Pet. 1:5, so that there can be no defalcation, nothing can hinder the saints from taking possession.

7. Light. It is called an inheritance 'in light.' If every star were a sun, it could never shadow out the bright luster of this celestial paradise. Light is a glorious creature; without light, what would all the world be — but a dark prison? What beauty is there in the sun when it is masked with a cloud? Light does actuate the colors, and makes every flower appear in its fresh beauty. Heaven is a bright body, all over embroidered with light. It is not like the starry heaven — here and there

bespangled with stars – but other parts of it like chequer-work interwoven with darkness. Here Christ as a continual sun, shall give light to the whole heaven. 'The Lamb shall be the light thereof!' Indeed all other light, in comparison of this, is but like the twilight, or rather the midnight. Here alone are the shining rays of beauty, which every glorified eye shall be enabled both to behold and to possess! This light shall have no night to eclipse or extinguish it; when once the Sun of Righteousness has risen upon the soul, it shall never set any more. This is a high privilege of the glory of heaven – that it is an inheritance in light. When the scripture would set forth the blessedness of God himself; it makes it consist in this, 'He dwells in light.'

8. Permanency. It is an incorruptible inheritance. It runs parallel with eternity. Eternity is a circle which has neither beginning nor end. Eternity is a sea which has neither bottom nor banks! This is the glory of the celestial paradise – it abides forever! If we could by our arithmetic reckon up more millions of ages than there have been minutes since the creation, after all this time (which were a short eternity) the inheritance of the saints shall be as far from ending as it was at the beginning. 'This world is fading away, along with everything it craves. But if you do the will of God, you will live forever.' 1 John 2:17. Everything is fading away! It is good to look upon the world as the heathens did upon pleasure; they looked upon the back parts of pleasure, and saw it going away from them and leaving a sting. The world is fading away – but heaven never fades, therefore heaven's eminency is its permanency.

With evil things, (such as pain and misery,) length of time makes them worse; but good things, (as joy and pleasure,) length of time makes them better! Heaven's eminency is its permanency. Things are prized and valued by the time we have in them. Lands or houses which are owned – are esteemed far better than leases, which soon expire. The saints do not lease heaven; it is not their landlord's house – but their Father's house!

This house never falls to decay; it is a mansion-house, John 14:2. There is nothing excellent (says Nazianzene) that is not perpetual. The comforts of the world are wavering and uncertain, like a fading garland; therefore they are shadowed out by the tabernacle, which was transient. But heaven is set out by the temple, which was fixed and permanent. It was made of strong materials, built with stone, covered with cedar, over-laid with gold. Eternity is the highest link of the saint's happiness! The believer shall be forever bathing in the pure and pleasant fountain of bliss! The lamp of glory shall be ever burning, never wasting. As there is no intermission in the joys of heaven, so no expiration. When once God has set his plants in the celestial paradise, he will never more pluck them up! He will never transplant them; never will Christ lose any member of this body; you may sooner separate light from the sun, than a glorified saint from Jesus Christ. O eternity, eternity! what a spring of delight will that be – which shall have no autumn! What a day will that be – which shall have no night! Methinks I see the morning-star appear, it is break of day already!

Concerning the glory of this blessed inheritance, let me super-add these four things.

1. The glory of heaven is ponderous and weighty. It is called 'a weight of glory,' 2 Cor. 4:17. God must make us able to bear it. This weight of glory should make sufferings light: this weight should make us throw away the weights of sin – though they be golden weights! Who would for the indulging of a lust, forfeit so glorious an inheritance! Lay the whole world in scales with it – it is lighter than vanity!

2. The glory of heaven is infinitely satisfying. There is neither lack, nor excess. This can be said properly of nothing but heaven. You who court the world for honor and preferment, remember what the creature says concerning satisfaction, 'It is not in me!' Heaven alone, is commensurate to the vast desires of the soul. Here the Christian cries out in a divine ecstasy, 'I have enough,

my Savior, I have enough!' 'You will fill me with joy in your presence, with eternal pleasures at your right hand!' Psalm 16:11. 'You feed them from the abundance of your own house, letting them drink from your rivers of delight!' Psalm 36:8. Not drops—but rivers! These only can quench the thirst. Every day in heaven, shall be a feast! There is no lack at this feast! There shall excellency shine in its perfection.

This present world is but a jail, the body is the fetter with which the soul is bound. If there is anything in a jail to delight—what is the eternal palace and the throne! If we meet with any comfort in Mount Horeb, what is in Mount Zion! All the world is like a picture of a landscape; you may see orchards and gardens curiously drawn in the landscape—but you cannot enter into them. But you may enter into this heavenly paradise, 2 Pet. 1:11, 'For so an entrance shall be ministered unto you abundantly into the everlasting kingdom,' etc. Here is soul-satisfaction.

3. Though an innumerable company of saints and angels have a part in this inheritance, there is never the less for you. Another man's beholding the sun, does not make me to have the lesser light: thus will it be in glory. Usually here on earth, all the inheritance is divided among the several heirs—some are put off with smaller portions. In heaven all the saints are heirs; the youngest believer is an heir, and God has land enough to give to all his heirs. All the angels and archangels have their portion paid out; yet a believer shall never have the less. Is not Christ the heir of all things? Heb. 1:2, and the saints co-heirs? Romans 8:17. They share with Christ in the same glory. It is true, one vessel may hold more than another—but every vessel shall be full.

4. The souls of the elect shall enter upon possession immediately after death! 2 Cor. 5:8, 'We are willing rather to be absent from the body—and to be present with the Lord.' There is an immediate transition and passage from death—to glory, 'the soul returns to God who gave it.' Christ's resurrection was before his ascension; but the saints' ascension is before their resurrection. The body may be compared to the bubble in the water, the soul to the wind that fills it; you see the bubble rises higher and higher, at last it breaks into the open air; so the body is but like a bubble, which rises from infancy to youth, from youth to age, higher and higher; at last this bubble breaks, and dissolves into dust, and the spirit ascends into the open air—it returns unto God who gave it.

Be of good comfort, we shall not wait long for our inheritance. It is but winking—and we shall see God. O the glory of this paradise! When we are turned out of all, let us think of this inheritance which is to come; faith itself is not able to reach it! It is more than we can hope for— or even imagine! I may say of this celestial paradise, as once the children of Dan said of Laish, Judges 18:9, 10. 'We have seen the land, and behold it is very good; a place where there is no lack of anything.' Faith being sent out as a spy to search the land of promise, returns this answer, 'There is no lack of anything.' There can be no lack where Christ is, who is 'all in all,' Col. 3:11.

In heaven there is health without sickness, plenty without famine, riches without poverty, life without death. There is unspotted purity, unstained honor, unparalleled beauty. There is the tree of life in the midst of paradise; there is the river which waters the garden; there is the vine flourishing, and the pomegranates budding, Cant. 6:11. There is the banqueting house, where are all those delicacies and rarities, with which God himself is delighted. While we are sitting at that table, Christ's 'spikenard will send forth its fragrance,' Cant. 1:12. There is the bed of love, there are the curtains of Solomon, there are the mountains of spices, and the streams from Lebanon! There are the cherubim, not to keep us out—but to welcome us into paradise! There shall the saints be adorned, as a bride with gems of glory! There will God give us abundantly, 'infinitely more than we would ever dare to ask or hope for!' Eph. 3:20. Is not this enough? What more could we ask for!

Haman's aspiring heart could have asked not only the king's royal robe, and the ring from his hand — but the crown from his head too. A man can ask for million of worlds — but in heaven God will give us more than we can ask; nay, more than we can ever imagine! We could imagine — what if all the dust of the earth were turned to silver; what if every stone were a wedge of gold; what if every flower were a ruby; what if every blade of grass were a pearl; what if every sand in the sea were a diamond! Yet all this is nothing — compared to the glory of heaven! It is as impossible for any man in his deepest thoughts, to comprehend glory, as it would be for him to measure the heavens with a ruler; or drain the great ocean with a thimble. O incomparable place!

Methinks our souls should be big with longing for this blessed inheritance! All this that I have told you of heaven, may make you say as Monica, Augustine's mother, 'What am I doing here? Why is my soul held with the earthen fetter of this flesh?' Cleombrotus having read Plato's piece of the immortality of the soul, being ravished with desire of those golden delights in the other world, killed himself. Though we must not break prison — until God opens it — yet how should we long for delivery from this earthly jail! How should we be inflamed with desire to taste of those rare and sweet delicacies, which are above at God's right hand! O what madness is it for men to spin out their time, and tire out their strength--in pursuing the vanities of this world! This is to imitate Dionysius, who busied himself in catching flies!

Surely, were we 'carried away in the Spirit,' I mean, elevated by the power of faith — to the contemplation of this royal and stately palace of glory — I know not whether we should more wonder at the luster of heaven, or at the dullness of such as mind earthly things. The world adored — though is but a painted pageant or shadow! It is reported of Caesar, that traveling through a certain city, as he passed along, he saw the women, for the most part, playing with monkeys and parrots; at which sight he said, 'What! have they no children to play with!' So I say, when I see men toying with these earthly and beggarly vanities, 'What! are there not more glorious and sublime things to mind!'

That which our Savior said to the woman of Samaria, 'If you knew the gift of God, and who it is that says to you, Give me to drink, you would have asked of him, and he would have given you living water!' The same may I say, did men know these eternal mansions, and what it were to be digging in these rich mines of glory. Would God give them a vision of heaven a while, as he did Peter, who saw 'heaven opened,' Acts 10:11, how would they fall into a trance, (being amazed and filled with joy!) and being a little recovered out of it, how importunately would they beg of God, that they might be adopted into this stately inheritance!

But why do I expatiate? These things are unspeakable and full of glory. Had I as many tongues as hairs on my head, I could never sufficiently set forth the beauty and resplendency of this blissful inheritance! Such was the curious art of Apelles in drawing of pictures, that if another had taken up the pencil to touch up the painting, he would have spoiled all Apelles' work. Such is the excellency of this celestial paradise, that if the angels should take up their pencil to delineate it in its colors, they would but stain and eclipse the glory of it. I have given you only the dark shadow the picture, and that but crudely and imperfectly! Such is the beauty and bliss of this inheritance, that as Chrysostom says, 'if it were possible that all the sufferings of the saints could be laid upon one man — it would not compare with his being in heaven for one hour!'

Some of the learned are of opinion, that we shall know our friends in heaven. This seem very probable to me — for surely our knowledge there shall not be eclipsed or diminished, but increased. And that which Anselm asserts — that we shall have a knowledge of the patriarchs, and prophets, and apostles, all that were before us, and shall be after us, our predecessors and successors, to me seems very rational. For society without acquaintance is not comfortable, and methinks the scripture does hint this much. If Peter and James, having but a glimpse of glory, (when our Lord was transfigured on the mount), were able to know Moses and Elijah, whom they had never seen before; how much more shall we, being infinitely irradiated and enlightened with the Sun of Righteousness, know all the saints, though we were never acquainted with them before! This will be very comfortable. Certainly there will be nothing lacking—which may complete the saints' happiness!

Now that this glorious inheritance is the saints' privilege, I shall evince by two arguments.

1. It is so—in respect of the many obligations which lie upon God for performing this. As,

1. In regard of his promise, Titus 1:2, 'In hope of eternal life, which God, who cannot lie, has promised.' God's promise is better than any man's bond.

2. In regard of his oath. 'He who is truth has sworn.' Heb. 6:17.

3. In regard to the price that is paid for it—Christ's blood. Heaven is not only a promised possession—but a purchased possession, Eph. 1:14.

4. In regard of Christ's prayer for it: 'Father, I will that they also whom you have given me, be with me where I am.' Now God can deny Christ nothing, being his only favorite. 'I know you always hear me,' John 11:42.

5. In regard of Christ's ascension. He is gone before us to take possession of heaven for us. He is now making preparations for our coming; John 14:2, 'I go before to prepare a place for you.' We read that our Lord sent two of his disciples to prepare 'a large upper room for the Passover,' Mark 14:15. Just so has Jesus Christ gone before—to prepare a large upper room in heaven for the saints.

6. In regard of the dwelling of the Spirit in the hearts of the godly, giving them an assurance of heaven; and stirring up in them passionate desires after this glorious inheritance. Hence it is, we read of the pledge of the Spirit, 2 Cor. 1:22, and the first-fruits of the Spirit, Romans 8:23, and the seal of the Spirit, Eph. 1:13. God does not still his children with rattles. Heaven is already begun in a believer, so that the inheritance is certain. You see how many obligations lie upon God, and to speak with reverence, it stands not only upon God's mercy—but upon his faithfulness to make all this good to us!

2. The second argument is in respect of the union which the saints have with Jesus Christ. They are members of Christ, therefore they must have a part in this blessed inheritance. The member must be where the head is. Indeed the Arminians tell us that a justified person may fall finally from grace, and so his union with Christ may be dissolved, and the inheritance lost. But how absurd is this doctrine! Is Christ divided? can he lose a member of his body? then his body is not perfect; for how can that body be perfect which lacks a limb? If Christ might lose one member from his body—he might lose all! And so he would be a head without a body. But be assured, the union with Christ cannot be broken, John 17:12, and the inheritance cannot be lost. What was said of Christ's natural body, is as true of the mystical body: 'a bone of it shall not be broken.' See how every bone and limb of Christ's natural body was raised up out of the grave, and carried into heaven. Just so, shall every member of his mystical body, joined to him by the eternal Spirit, be carried up into glory. Fear not, O you saints, neither sin nor Satan can dissolve your union with Christ, nor hinder you from going to that blessed place where your Head is.

Question. Here it will be asked, 'Who shall ascend into the hill of the Lord?' Psalm 24:3. Who shall be a citizen of this new Jerusalem which is above?

Answer. The new creature: this you read of, 2 Cor. 5:17. This new creature does prepare us for the new Jerusalem. This is the divine and curious artifice of the Holy Spirit in our hearts, forming Christ in us. The same Holy Spirit who overshadowed the Virgin Mary, and formed the human nature of Christ in her womb—does work and produce this new creature. O blessed man and woman—in whom this new creature is formed! I may say to you, as the angel to Mary, 'That which is conceived in you, is of the Holy Spirit!' Of all God's creatures, the new creature is the best.

Let me ask—are you a new creature? are you a branch cut off from the wild olive tree of nature, and ingrafted into a new stock, the tree of life? Has God defaced and dismantled the old man in you? Does some limb drop off every day? Have you a new heart? Until then you are not fit for the new heaven! Are you new all over? Do you have a new eye to discern the things that differ? Do you have a new appetite? Does the pulse of your soul beat after Christ? It is only the new creature, who shall be the heir of the New Jerusalem.

When you were sailing to hell, (for we have both wind and tide to carry us there), have the north and south winds awaked? Has the gale of the Spirit blown upon you, and turned your course? Are you now sailing to a new port? Has the seal of the Scripture stamped a new and heavenly print upon you? Then I am speaking all this while to you; this blessed inheritance is entailed upon you!

But if you are an old unrepenting sinner, expect that heaven should be kept, as paradise, with a flaming sword—that you may not enter! Be assured, God will never put the new wine of glory, into an old musty bottle. Heaven is not like Noah's ark, which received both clean and unclean animals into it! Nor is heaven like Pharoah's court, where the vermin came! This inheritance does not receive all comers. It is only the wheat, which goes into Christ's garner; what has the chaff to do there! This inheritance is only for 'those who are sanctified,' Acts 20:32. Is your heart consecrated ground? We read that in the time of Ezra, after the return of the people from the captivity, some who were ambitious for the priesthood, sought the writings of the genealogies—but they were not found among the numbers of the priests, 'therefore they were put aside as polluted, from the priesthood.' So whoever they are, who think to have a part in this blessed place, if their names be not found; that is, if they are not enrolled among the new creatures, they shall be put away from this inheritance, as polluted!

Chapter 10. The Fifth Royal Privilege—our knowledge shall be clear.

Knowledge is a beautiful thing; such was Adam's ambition to know more, that by tasting the tree of knowledge, he lost the tree of life. In heaven our knowledge shall be full and clear. Many things we have now but in the notion, which then we shall see perfectly; now, 'we know but in part.' The best Christian has a veil on his eye, as the Jews have upon their heart; hereafter the veil shall be taken off. Here on earth, we see through a glass darkly—in a riddle, mystery; then, we shall see face to face; that is, clearly.

There are five mysteries which God will clear up to us when we are in heaven.

1. The great mystery of the trinity. This we know but in part. Unity in Trinity, and Trinity in Unity, where one makes three, and three make but one: this is bad arithmetic—but good divinity. We have but dark conceptions of it: it is a mystery so deep, that we may soon wade beyond our depth.

Augustine being to write his books of the Trinity, was taught modesty by a child, who was attempting to empty the sea into a little spoon; to whom Augustine said, that he labored in vain; for his little spoon would not contain the sea. To whom the child answered, 'my little spoon will sooner hold this vast ocean, than your shallow brain can contain the depth of the

Trinity!' How little a portion is known of God! If Job asked the question, 'who can understand the thunder?' We may much more ask, 'who can understand the Trinity?' But in heaven we shall see God as he is, that is, perfectly.

Question. But shall every saint enjoy God so perfectly, that he shall have the same knowledge that God has?

Answer. We shall have a full knowledge of God — but not know him fully — yet we shall take in so much of God as our human nature is capable of; it will be a bright and glorious knowledge. Here on earth, we know him but by his power, wisdom, mercy — we see but his back-parts; there we shall see him face to face.

2. The mystery of the incarnation. Christ assuming our human nature, and marrying it to the divine. Therefore called God-man, God with us. A mystery which the angels in heaven adore. God said, 'The man has become as one of us,' Gen. 3:22 — but now we may say, God himself is become as one of us! There was nothing within the sphere of natural causes to produce it. The incarnation of Christ is a golden chain made up of several links of miracles. For instance, that the Creator of heaven should become a creature; that eternity should be born; that he whom the heaven of heavens cannot contain, should be enclosed in the womb; that he who thunders in the clouds, should cry in the cradle; that he who rules the stars, should suck the breasts; that he who upholds all things by the word of his power, should himself be upheld; that a virgin should conceive; that Christ should be made of a woman, and of that woman which himself made; that the creature should give a being to the Creator; that the star should give light to the sun; that the branch should bear the vine; that the mother should be younger than the child she bore; and the child in the womb bigger than the mother; that he who is a Spirit, should be made flesh; that Christ should be without father, and without mother — yet have both; without mother in the God-head, without father in the manhood; that Christ being incarnate, should have two natures, (the divine and human), and yet but one person; that the divine nature should not be infused into the human, nor the human mixed with the divine — yet assumed into the person of the Son of God; the human nature not God — yet one with God. Here is, I say, a chain of miracles.

I acknowledge the mercy of the incarnation was great, we having now both affinity and consanguinity with Jesus Christ: Christ's incarnation is the saint's inauguration.

The love of Christ in the incarnation was great; for herein he did set a pattern without a parallel. In clothing himself with our flesh, which is but walking ashes, he has sewed, as it were, sackcloth to cloth of gold — the humanity to the Deity. But though the incarnation is so rich a blessing — yet it is hard to say which is the greater, the mercy or the mystery. It is a sacred depth — how does it transcend reason, and even puzzle faith! We know but in part, we see this only in a glass darkly — but in heaven our knowledge shall be cleared up, we shall fully understand this divine riddle!

3. The mystery of Scripture. The hard knots of scripture shall be untied, and dark prophecies fulfilled. There is a sacred depth in scripture which we must adore: some places of scripture are hard in the sense, others dark in the phrase, and cannot well be translated in regard of ambiguity; one Hebrew word having such various, and sometimes contrary significations, that it is very difficult to know which is the genuine sense. As it is with a traveler who is not skilled in his way, when he comes to a turning where the way parts, he is at a standstill, and knows not which of the ways to take; such difficulties and labyrinths are there in scripture. It is true, all things purely necessary to salvation, are clear in the word of God; but there are some sacred

depths that we cannot fathom, and this may make us long after heaven, when our light shall be clear.

Just so for prophecies, some are very abstruse and profound; divines may shoot their arrows — but it is hard to say how near they may come to the mark: it is dubious whether in such a particular age and century of the church, such a prophecy was fulfilled. The Jews have a saying when they meet with a hard scripture they don't understand, 'Elijah will come and interpret these things to us.' We do not expect Elijah; but when we are in heaven, we shall understand prophecies; our knowledge shall be clear.

4. The great mystery of providence shall be cleared up. Providence is the queen of the world; it is the hand which turns all the wheels in the universe! Chrysostom calls it 'the pilot which steers the ship of the creation.' Providences are often dark; God sometimes writes in short-hand. The characters of providence are so various and strange, and our eyes are so dim, that we know not what to make of providence. Hence we are ready to censure that which we do not understand. We think that things are very eccentric and disorderly; God's providence is sometimes secret — but always wise. The dispensations of providence are often sad, 'Judgment beginning at the house of God,' and the 'just man perishing in his righteousness,' Eccles. 7:15; that is, while he is pursuing a righteous cause. Though his way be pious, it is not always prosperous. On the other side, 'those who do evil get rich, and those who dare God to punish them go free of harm,' Mal. 3:15.

Though now our candle is in a dark lantern, and the people of God cannot tell what God is a doing — yet when they are in heaven they shall see the reason of these transactions: they shall see that every providence served for the fulfilling of God's promise, namely, 'That all things shall work together for good,' Romans 8:28. In a watch the wheels seem to move contrary one to another — but all carry on the motion of the watch, all serve to make the watch work properly. Just so, the wheels of providence seem to move contrary — but all shall carry on the good of the elect; all the lines shall meet at last in the center of the promise. In heaven, as we shall see mercy and justice, so we shall see promises and providences kissing each other. Our light shall be clear.

When a man is at the bottom of a hill, he cannot see very far; but when he is on the top, he may see many miles distant. Here on earth, the saints of God are in the valley of tears, they are at the bottom of the hill, and cannot tell what God is a doing. But when they come to heaven, and shall be on the top of the mount, they shall see all the glorious transactions of God's providence; never a providence but they shall see either a wonder or a mercy enrapt up in it. A painter first makes a crude draught in the picture — here an eye, there a hand; but when he has painted it out in all its parts and lineaments, and laid them in their colors — it is beautiful to behold. We who live in this age of the church, see but a crude draught, as it were some dark pieces of God's providence represented; and it is impossible that we should be able to correctly judge of God's work, by pieces. But when we come to heaven, and see the full body and portraiture of God's providence drawn out in its lively colors, it will be a most glorious sight to behold! Providence shall be unriddled!

5. The mystery of hearts. We shall see a heart-anatomy. 'For God will bring every act to judgment, including every hidden thing, whether good or evil.' Ecclesiastes 12:14. We shall see the designs and cabinet-counsels of men's hearts revealed; then the hypocrite's mask shall fall off. Oh the black conclave that is in the heart of man! The heart is deep: it may be compared to a river which has fair streams running on the top — but when this river comes to be drained, there lies abundance of vermin at the bottom. Thus it is with man's heart, there are fair streams running on the top — a civil life, a religious profession; but at the Day of Judgment, when God

shall drain this river, and unveil hearts; then all the vermin of ambition, lust, and covetousness shall appear—all shall come out! Then we shall see whether Jehu's design was zeal for God, or the kingdom. We shall see clearly whether Jezebel had more mind to keep a fast, or to get Naboth's vineyard. Then we shall see whether Herod had more mind to worship Christ, or to worry him. All the secrets of men's hearts shall be laid open! Methinks it would be worth dying to see this sight. We shall then see who is the Achan, who is the Judas. The women's paint falls off from their faces when they come near the fire. Just so, before the scorching heat of God's justice, the hypocrite's paint will drop off, and the hidden motives of his heart will be visible! These mysteries will God reveal to us—our knowledge shall be clear.

Chapter 11. The Sixth Royal Privilege—our love shall be perfect.

Love is the jewel with which Christ's bride is adorned. In one sense, love is more excellent than faith; for love never ceases, 1 Cor. 13:8. The spouse shall put off her jewel of faith, when she goes to heaven—but she shall never put off her jewel of love. Her love shall be perfect.

1. Our love to God shall be perfect. The saint's love shall be joined with reverence; for a filial disposition shall remain—but there shall be no servile fear in heaven. Horror and trembling is proper to the damned in hell; though in heaven there shall be a reverencing fear—yet a rejoicing fear: we shall see that in God which will work such a delight that we cannot but love him! This love to God shall be,

1. A fervent love. Our love to God in this life, is rather a faint desire—but in heaven the smoke of desire shall be blown up into a flame of love. We shall love God with an intenseness of love, and thus the saints shall be like the seraphim who are so called, from their burning. Here on earth, our love is lukewarm, and sometimes frozen: a child of God weeps that he can love God no more. But there is a time shortly coming, when our love to God shall be fervent, it shall burn as hot as it can! The damned shall be in a flame of fire, the elect in a flame of love!

2. A fixed love. Alas, how soon is our love taken off from God! Other objects presenting themselves, steal away our love. 'Your goodness is like a morning cloud, and as the early dew it goes away': in the morning you shall see the grass covered with drops of dew, as so many pearls—but before noon all is vanished; so it is with our love to God. Perhaps at a sermon, when our affections are stirred, the heart melts in love; and at a sacrament, when we see Christ's blood, as it were, trickling down upon the cross, some love-drops fall from our heart; but within a few days all is vanished, and we have lost our first love: this is matter of humiliation while we live. But O you saints, comfort yourselves, in heaven your love shall be fixed, as well as fervent; it shall never more be taken off from God! Such beauty and excellency shall shine in God, that as a divine magnet, it will be always drawing your eyes and heart after him.

2. Our love to the saints shall be perfect. Love is a sweet harmony, a tuning and chiming together of affections.

1. It is our duty to love the saints—though they are of bad dispositions; sometimes their nature is so abrasive and unpolished, that grace does not cast forth such a luster. It is like a gold ring on a leprous hand, or a diamond set in iron. Yet if there is anything of Christ—it is our duty to love it.

2. It is our duty to love the saints—though they in some things differ from us. Yet if we see Christ's image or portraiture drawn upon their hearts, we are to separate the precious from the vile. But alas, how defective is this grace! how little love is there among God's people! Herod and Pilate can agree: wicked men unite when saints divide. Contentions were never more hot,

love never more cold. Many there are whose music consists all in discord; they pretend to love truth—but hate peace. Divisions are Satan's powder-plot to blow up religion.

It would not be strange to hear the harlot say, 'Let the child be divided;' but to hear the mother say so, this is sad! If pope, cardinal, Jesuit, all conspire against the church of God, it would not be strange; but for one saint to persecute another—this is strange! For a wolf to worry a lamb is usual—but for a lamb to worry a lamb is unnatural. For Christ's lily to be among the thorns, is ordinary; but for this lily to become a thorn, to tear and fetch blood—this is strange! How will Christ take this at our hands! Would he not have his coat rent, and will he have his body rent! O that I could speak here weeping!

Well, this will be a bright foil to set off heaven the more—there is a time shortly coming when our love shall be perfect, there shall be no difference of judgment in heaven; there the saints shall be all of one mind. Though we fall out along the way—we shall all agree in the journey's end. The cherubim, representing the angels, are set out 'with their faces looking one upon another'; in this life Christians turn their backs one upon another—but in heaven they shall be like the cherubim with their faces looking one upon another.

It is observed that the olive tree and the myrtle tree have a wonderful sympathy, and if they grow near together, will mutually embrace, and twist about each others' roots and branches. Christians in this life are like tearing brambles—but in heaven they shall be like the olive and myrtle—and sweetly embrace one another! When once the blessed harp of Christ's voice has sounded in the ears of the saints, the evil spirit shall be quite driven away! When our strings shall be wound up to the highest pitch of glory, you shall never more hear discord in the saints' music! In heaven there shall be a perfect harmony!

Chapter 12. The Seventh Royal Privilege—the resurrection of our bodies.

Trajan's ashes after death were brought to Rome and honored, being set upon the top of a famous pillar. So the ashes of the saints at the resurrection shall be honored, and shine as silver dust! This is an article of our faith. Now for the illustration of this, there are three things considerable: 1. That there is such a thing as the resurrection. 2. That this is not yet past. 3. That the same body that dies, shall rise again.

1. I shall prove the proposition that there is a resurrection of the body. There are some of the Sadducees of opinion that there is no resurrection; then 'let us eat and drink, for tomorrow we die,' 1 Cor. 15:32. To what purpose are all our prayers and tears? and indeed it were well for them who are in their lifetime as brute beasts, if it might be with them as beasts after death. But there is a resurrection of the body, as well as an ascension of the soul; which I shall prove by two arguments.

1. Because Christ is risen, therefore we must rise. The head being raised, the rest of the body shall not always lie in the grave, for then it would be a head without a body. His rising is a pledge of our resurrection, 1 Thess. 4:14.

2. In regard of justice and equity. The bodies of the wicked have been weapons of unrighteousness, and have joined with the soul in sin! Their eyes have been a casement to let in vanity! Their hands have been full of bribes! Their feet have been swift to shed blood! Therefore justice and equity require that they should rise again, and their bodies be punished with their souls!

Again, the bodies of the saints have been members of holiness! Their eyes have dropped down tears for sin! Their hands have relieved the poor! Their tongues have been trumpets of God's praise. Therefore justice and equity require that they should rise again, that their bodies as well as their souls may be crowned!

There must be a resurrection, else how should there be a remuneration? We are more sure to rise out of our graves — than out of our beds! The bodies of the wicked are locked up in the grave as in a prison, that they may not infest the church of God; and at the Day of Judgment they shall be brought out of the prison to trial. And the bodies of the saints are laid in the grave as in a bed of perfume, where they mellow and ripen until the resurrection. Noah's olive tree springing after the flood, the blossoming of Aaron's dry rod, the flesh and sinews coming to Ezekiel's dry bones — what were these, but lively emblems of the resurrection!

2. That this resurrection is not yet past. Some hold that it is past, and make the resurrection to be nothing else but regeneration, which is called a rising from sin, and a 'being risen with Christ'; and do affirm, that there is no other resurrection but this, and that only the soul is with God in happiness, not the body. Of this opinion were Hymeneus and Philetus, 2 Tim. 2:18. But the rising from sin is called the first resurrection, Rev. 1:6, which implies that there is a second resurrection; and that second I shall prove out of Dan. 12:2. 'And many of those who sleep in the dust of the earth, shall awake.' He does not say they are already awake — but they shall awake. And John 5:28, 'The hour is coming, in which all that are in the graves shall hear his voice, and shall come forth; those who have done good, unto the resurrection of life; and those who have done evil, unto the resurrection of damnation.' Observe, Christ does not say, they have come forth of the grave already — but they shall come forth.

Here a question may be moved, 'Whether the bodies of some of the saints are not in heaven already?' Then it will seem that their resurrection is not yet to come; as we read that Elijah was taken up to heaven in a fiery chariot; and Enoch, Heb. 11:5, 'was translated, that he might not see death.'

Answer. I know the question is controverted among divines. Should it be granted that they are bodily in heaven, by an extraordinary writ, or dispensation from God — this does not at all disprove a general resurrection to come. But there are some reasons do incline me to think that Enoch and Elijah are not yet bodily in heaven, nor shall be until the resurrection of all flesh, when the rest of the elect, like a precious crop, being fully ripe, shall be translated into glory. The first is Heb. 11:13, where it is said, 'these all died in faith,' where Enoch was included: now why we should restrain this word, these, only to Abel, Noah, Abraham, and not also to Enoch, I see no rational ground.

Question. But is it not said, he was translated, 'that he might not see death'; how can these two stand together, that Enoch died — yet he did not see death?

Answer. These words, that he might not see death, I conceive (with some other divines) the meaning is, that he might not see it in that painful and horrid manner as others: his soul had an easy and joyful passage out of his body; he died not after the common manner of men. Seeing and feeling are often in scripture — the one is put for the other.

2. My second argument is, 1 John 3:2: 'We know when he shall appear, we shall be like him.' We read in scripture but of two appearings of Christ, his appearing in the flesh, and his appearing at the Day of Judgment. Now his appearing in this text, must needs be meant of his last appearing: and what then? 'We shall be like him,' that is, in our bodies, Phil. 3:21. The spirits of just men being already made perfect, Heb. 12:23, whence I infer, Enoch is not yet ascended bodily into heaven, because none of the bodies of the saints shall be fully made like Christ until his second appearing.

3. Besides this, may be added the judgment of many of the Fathers, who were pious and learned. It is not probable that Enoch and Elijah should be taken up in their bodies into heaven, says Peter Martyr; and he urges that saying of our Lord, 'No man has ascended into heaven'; (that is, physically) 'but the Son of man that descended from heaven.' Of this opinion also is the

learned Doctor Fulk, who in his marginal notes upon the 11th to the Hebrews, has this descant: 'It appears not,' says he, 'that Enoch now lives in the body, no more than Moses; but that he was translated by God out of the world, and died not after the common manner of men.' And concerning Elijah, the same author has this passage: 'It is evident that he was taken up alive; but not that he continues alive.' And again, 'Because we read expressly, that he was taken up into heaven, 2 Kings 2:1, it is certain' (says he) 'that his body was not carried into heaven.' Christ being the first that in perfect humanity ascended there, 1 Cor. 15:20, 'Christ has become the first fruits of those who sleep.' He is called the first fruits, not only because he was the most excellent, and sanctified the rest—but because he was the first cluster which was gathered; the first that went up in a physical manner into the place of the blessed: hence we see that the resurrection is yet to come.

3. At the resurrection every soul shall have its own body. The same body that dies, shall arise. Some hold that the soul shall be clothed with a new body—but then it were improper to call it a resurrection of the body, it should be rather a creation. It was a custom in the African churches to say, I believe the resurrection of this body. I confess, the doctrine of the resurrection is such, that it is too deep for reason to wade: you must let faith swim. For instance, suppose a man dying is cast into the sea, several fish come and devour him, the substance of his body goes into these fishes, afterwards, these fish are taken and eaten, and the substance of these fishes go into several men. Now how this body, thus devoured, and as it were, crumbled into a thousand fractions, should be raised the same individual body, is infinitely above reason to imagine; we have scarcely faith enough to believe it.

Question. How can this be?

Answer. To such I say as our blessed Savior, Matt. 22:19, 'You are in error—not knowing the scriptures, nor the power of God.'

1. You are in error—not knowing the scriptures. The scripture tells us expressly that the same body that dies shall rise again; Job 29:26, 'In my flesh shall I see God,' not in another flesh. And verse 27, 'My eyes shall behold him,' not other eyes. So 1 Cor. 15:53, 'This mortal shall put on immortality,' not another mortal—but this mortal, and, 2 Cor. 5:10, 'For we must all appear before the judgment seat of Christ, that each one may receive what is due him for the things done while in the body, whether good or bad.' Not in another body. Death in scripture is called a sleep. It is far easier with God to raise the body, than it is for us to awaken a man when he is asleep!

2. You are in error—not knowing the power of God. That God, who created all things out of nothing—can he not reduce many things to one thing? When the body is gone into a thousand substances, cannot he make a compilation, and bring that body together again? The chemist can, out of several metals mingled together—as gold, silver, and tin—extract the one from the other, the silver from the gold, the tin from the silver, and can reduce every metal to its own kind? And shall we not much more believe that when our bodies are mingled and confounded with other substances, the wise God is able to make a divine extraction, and reinvest every soul with its own body!

Use 1. This is comfort to a child of God. As Christ said to Martha, John 11:23, 'Your brother shall rise again,' so I say to you, your body shall rise again. The body is sensible of joy as well as the soul; and indeed, we shall not be perfect in glory until our bodies are reunited to our souls. Therefore in scripture, the doctrine of the resurrection is made matter of joy and triumph! Isaiah 26:19, 'Yet we have this assurance: Those who belong to God will live; their bodies will rise again! Those who sleep in the earth will rise up and sing for joy!' Death is as it were the fall of the leaf—but our bodies shall flourish as a herb, in the spring of the resurrection. That body which is mouldered to dust shall revive.

Sometimes the saints sow the land with their bodies, Psalm 142:7, and water it with their blood, Psalm 79:3. But these bodies, whether imprisoned, beheaded, sawn asunder—shall arise and sit down with Christ upon the throne! O consider what joy there will be at the reuniting of the body and soul at the resurrection! As there will be a sad meeting of the body and soul of the wicked, they shall be joined together as briars, to scratch and tear one another; so, what unspeakable joy will there be at the meeting together of the soul and body of the saints—how will they greet one another (they two being the nearest acquaintance that ever were). What a welcome will the soul give to the body! 'O blessed body, you allowed yourself to be martyred, and crucified, you were kept under control by watchings, fastings, etc. When I prayed, you attended my prayers with hands lifted up, and knees bowed down. You were willing to suffer with me, and now you shall reign with me! Cheer up, my dear friend; you were sown as seed in the dust of the earth with ignominy—but now are raised a spiritual body. O my dear body, I will enter into you again as a heavenly sparkle, and you shall clothe me again as a glorious vestment!'

Use 2. It shows the great love and respect God bears to the weakest believer; God will not glorify the bodies of his dearest and most eminent saints, not the patriarchs or prophets, not the body of Moses or Elijah, until you rise out of your grave. God is like a master of a feast that stays until all his guests are come. Abraham, the father of the faithful, must not sit down in heaven until all his children are born, and the body of every saint perfectly mellow and ripe for the resurrection.

3. If the bodies of the saints must arise—then consecrate your bodies to the service of God! These bodies must be made one with Christ's body. The Apostle makes this use of the doctrine of the resurrection, 1 Cor. 6:14, 'And God will raise our bodies from the dead by his marvelous power, just as he raised our Lord from the dead.' There is the doctrine. 'Don't you realize that your bodies are actually parts of Christ? Should a man take his body, which belongs to Christ, and join it to a prostitute? Never!' Verse 15; There is the use. It is enough for wicked men to adulterate and defile their bodies. The drunkard makes his body a tunnel for the wine and liquor to run through. The epicure makes his body a living tomb to bury the good creatures of God. The adulterer makes his body a slave to his lust. The body is called a vessel in scripture; these vessels will be found musty at the resurrection, fit only to hold that wine which you read of, Psalm 75:8, 'In the hand of the Lord there is a cup, and the wine is red'; this is the wine of God's wrath. It is enough for those bodies to be defiled, which shall be joined to the devil! But you who are believers, that expect your bodies shall be joined with Christ's body, oh cleanse these vessels! Take heed of putting your bodies to any impure services. Present your bodies a living sacrifice, Romans 12:1. Have a care to guard all the passages which sin might come in at. Sometimes the devil comes in at the eye; therefore Job made a covenant with his eyes. Sometimes sin goes out at the tongue; therefore David set a watch before his lips. Surely those who have their hearts sprinkled from an evil conscience, that is, the guilt of known sin, will have a care to have their bodies washed with clean water.

Chapter 13. The eighth Royal Privilege—The bodies of the saints shall be enameled with glory!

'So will it be with the resurrection of the dead. The body that is sown is perishable, it is raised imperishable; it is sown in dishonor, it is raised in glory; it is sown in weakness, it is raised in power; it is sown a natural body, it is raised a spiritual body. If there is a natural body, there is also a spiritual body! For our perishable earthly bodies must be transformed into heavenly bodies that will never die!' 1 Corinthians 15:42-44, 53. In this life the body is infirm, physicians have much work to repair it and keep it going! It is like a house out of repair—every storm of sickness it rains through. How does a holy soul often lodge in a sickly or deformed body! The body is like a piece of rotten wood, diseases like worms, breed there. Fevers, aches, etc. But this body shall be made glorious at the resurrection; it shall neither have diseases nor defects! Leah shall no more complain of her bleary eyes, nor Barzillai of his lameness. There are five properties of our glorified bodies.

1. They shall be agile and nimble. The bodies of the saints on earth are heavy and weary in their motion—but in heaven there shall be no gravity hindering; but our bodies being refined, shall be swift and facile in their motion, and made fit to ascend, as the body of Elijah. This is the apostle's meaning when he calls it a spiritual body; that is not only a body made fit to serve God without weariness—but a body that can move swiftly from one place to another. In this life the body is a great hindrance to the soul in its operation: 'The spirit is willing—but the flesh is weak.' When the soul would fly up to Christ, the body as a leaden lump keeps it down. Here on earth, the body is a clog; in heaven it shall be a wing. The bodies of the saints shall be agile and lively, they shall be made fully subject to the soul, and will in no way, impede or hinder the soul in its progress.

2. The bodies of the saints shall be transparent, full of clarity and brightness. They shall be as Christ's body when it was transfigured, Matt. 17:2. Our bodies shall have a divine luster put upon them! Here on earth, they are as iron when it is rusty; there they shall be as iron when it is filed and made bright, as the sun in its splendor; nay, 'seven times brighter!' says Chrysostom. Here on earth, our bodies are as the gold in the ore—drossy and impure. In heaven they shall be as gold when it spangles and glitters! So clear shall they be, that the soul may venture out at every part, and sparkle through the body as the wine through the glass.

3. They shall be beautiful. Beauty consists in two things.

1. Symmetry and proportion, when all the parts are drawn out in their perfect lineaments.

2. Complexion, when there is a mixture and variety in the colors. Thus the bodies of the saints shall have a transcendency of beauty upon them. Here on earth, the body is called a vile body. It is vile in its origin—it is made of the dust of the earth. The earth is the most ignoble element. The body is also vile in the use that it is put to; the soul often uses the body as a weapon to fight against God. But this vile body shall be ennobled and beautified with glory; it shall be made like Christ's body!

How beautiful was Christ's body upon earth! In it there was the rose and the lily; it was a mirror of beauty! For all deformities of body issue immediately from sin—but Christ being conceived by the Holy Spirit, and so without sin, he must needs have a beautiful body, and in this sense he was fairer than the children of men, Psalm 45:2. There was graceful majesty in his looks. Christ's body, as some writers aver, was so fair by reason of the beauty and grace which shined in it, that no artist could ever draw it exactly. And if it was so glorious a body on earth, how great is the luster of it now in heaven! That light which shone upon Paul, 'surpassing the glory of the sun,' was no other than the beauty of Christ's body in heaven. O then what beauty and resplendency will be put upon the bodies of the saints! they shall be made 'like Christ's glorious body.'

4. The bodies of the saints shall be impeccable. Not but that the body when it is glorified, shall have such a passion as is delightful, (for the body is capable of joy) but it will have no passion which is hurtful; it shall not be capable of any noxious impression; in particular,

1. The bodies of the saints shall be free from the necessities of nature, such as hunger and thirst. Here on earth, we are pinched with hunger: 'David waxed faint,' 2 Sam. 21:15. Here on earth, we need continual supplies for nature. Christ 'took compassion on the multitude,' and wrought a miracle, lest they should 'faint by the way,' Matt. 15:32. Nature must have its supplies; these are as necessary to maintain life, as the oil is to maintain the lamp. But in heaven we shall hunger no more, Rev. 7:16. Hunger implies a need and lack, which cannot be in heaven; there we need not pray, 'Give us our daily bread.'

Question. But does not Christ say, 'I will not drink this day of the fruit of the vine, until that day when I drink it new with you in my Father's kingdom'; which implies there will be eating and drinking in heaven, and by consequence hunger?

Answer. We must not understand the words literally; our Savior only alludes to the metaphor of the vine. It is as if Christ had said, as drinking the fruit of the vine now with you, is an action of familiarity and pleasantness; so when you shall be with me in the kingdom of heaven, you shall be filled with such joy and delight, as if all the time were a time of feasting and banqueting.

2. Glorified bodies shall be free from the infirmities of nature, such as cold and heat. Heaven is a temperate zone: there is no nipping frost or scorching heat, nothing will be there in extremity — but joy.

3. The bodies of the saints shall be free from the burdens of nature, such as labor and sweating. There will be no more ploughing or sowing — what is the need of that — when the saints shall receive the full crop of joy! When the farmer works in the field, he needs his rake, his spade, etc. But let this same farmer be advanced to the throne, and now he has no more use for the spade — he is freed from all those labors! So though now we must 'eat our bread with the sweat of our brows,' yet when we are in heaven, and shall be advanced to the throne — there will be no more need of our working tools! Labor shall cease! Our sweat as well as our tears shall be dried up!

4. The bodies of the saints shall be free from the injuries of nature, such as sufferings. We run the race of our life on the track of misery! We go from one suffering to another. We never finish our troubles — but merely change them! 'Man is born to trouble,' he is the natural heir to it. Where the body is, there will afflictions like vultures be gathered together. Job was smitten with boils, and Paul did bear in his body the marks of the Lord Jesus. Afflictions, like hard frosts, nip the tender buds of our comfort; but before long the saints shall be impeccable, they shall have a protection from injuries granted them.

5. The bodies of the saints shall be immortal. Here on earth, our bodies are always dying. It is improper to ask, 'When shall we die?' We should rather ask, 'When shall we be finished dying?' First, the infancy dies, then the childhood, then the youth, then the old age — and then we are finished dying! It is not only the running out of the last sand in the glass which spends it — but all the sands which run out before. Death is a worm that is ever feeding at the root of our gourds! But in heaven 'our mortal shall put on immortality.' As it was with Adam in innocency, if he had not sinned, such was the excellent temperature and harmony in all the qualities of his body, that it is probable he would have never died — but had been translated from paradise to heaven! Indeed, Belarmine says that Adam would have died, though he had not sinned. But I know no ground for that assertion, for sin is made the formal cause of death!

However there is no such thing disputable in heaven, as the bodies there are immortal. Luke 20:36, 'Neither can they die any more': heaven is a healthful place, there is no sickness or dying; we shall never more hear a death-bell ring! As our souls shall be eternal, so our bodies immortal. If God made manna (which is in itself corruptible) to last many years in the golden pot, much more is he able by a divine power, so to fashion the bodies of the saints, that they shall be preserved to eternity. God 'will wipe every tear from their eyes. There will be no more death or mourning or crying or pain.' Revelation 21:4.

Chapter 14. The Ninth Royal Privilege is—that we shall be as the angels in heaven!

Matthew 22:30, 'The will be like the angels in heaven.' Christ does not say, we shall be angels— but like the angels.

Question. How is that?

Answer. Two ways.

1. In regard of our manner of worship. The angels fulfill the will of God, 1. Readily. 2. Perfectly.

1. The angels fulfill the will of God readily. When God sends the angels upon a commission, they do not hesitate or dispute the case with God—but immediately obey. The cherubim are pictured with wings displayed—to show how ready they are in their obedience, it is as if they had wings, Dan. 9:21. As soon as God speaks the word, the angels are eager to obey. When we get to heaven—we shall be as the angels!

This is a singular comfort to a weak Christian! Alas, we are not as the angels in this life! When God commands us to service, or to mourn for sin, or to take up the cross—O what a dispute is there! how long is it sometimes before we can get permission from our stubborn hearts to go to prayer! Jesus Christ went more willingly to suffer, than we do often to pray! How badly do we perform our duties! God had as good almost be without it! O but (if this is our grief) be of good comfort—in heaven we shall serve God swiftly—we shall be winged in our obedience, even as the angels!

2. The angels fulfill the will of God perfectly. They fulfill God's whole will; they leave nothing undone! When God commands them upon duty, they can shoot to a hair's breadth. Alas, our services—how lame and bedridden are they! We do things by halves. We pray as if we prayed not; we weep for sin as if we wept not; how many blemishes are there in our holy things! as the moon when it shines brightest, has a dark spot in it. How many grains would we lack, if Christ did not put his merits into the scales! Our duties, like good wine, do smell of a bad cask. The angel pouring sweet fragrances into the prayers of the saints, Rev. 8:3, shows that in themselves they yield no sweet savor, unless perfumed with Christ's incense. But in heaven we shall be even as the angels—we shall serve God perfectly! How should we long for that time!

2. We shall be as the angels in regard of dignity. There is no question—but in regard of our marriage-union with Christ, we shall be above the angels. But behold our human nature, simply and entirely considered, shall be parallel with the angelic nature. Luke 20:36, 'they shall be equal to the angels.' I shall show the dignity of the angelic nature, and the analogies between the saints glorified, and the angels. The dignity of the angels appears,

1. The dignity of the angels appears in their sagacity[5]. The angels (who are God's courtiers) are wise, intelligent creatures. Tyre in regard of wisdom is styled a cherubim, or angel, Ezek. 28:3, 4, 16. The angels have a most critical exquisite judgment, they are discerning spirits. Thus the saints shall be as the angels—for wisdom and sagacity. Christ the wisdom of God is their oracle.

2. The dignity of angels appears in their majesty. An angel is a beautiful glorious creature. They saw Stephen's face 'as it had been the face of an angel,' Acts 6:15. The angels are compared to lightning, in regard of their sparkling luster, Matt. 28:3. Such beams of majesty fall from the angels, that we are not able to bear a sight of them. John the apostle was so amazed at the sight

---

[5] Sagacious: having or showing keen mental discernment and good judgment; shrewd:

of an angel, that he fell at his feet to worship him, Rev. 19:10. Thus shall we be as the angels—for splendor and majesty. 'Then shall the righteous shine forth as the sun in the kingdom of their Father,' Matt. 13:43, not that the saints shall not surpass the sun in brightness, says Chrysostom; but the sun being the most noble and excellent creature, therefore our Savior takes a resemblance thence, to express the saints' glory. They shall not only be of a sun-like brightness—but angel-like brightness! The beams of Christ's glory will be transparent in them.

3. The dignity of angels is seen in their power. Angels 'excel in strength,' Psalm 103:20. We read of one angel which destroyed an army of a hundred and eighty-five thousand at one blow! An angel would be able to merely look us dead! Thus shall we be as the angels. Here on earth, we have our fainting fits, we wrestle continually with infirmities; but in heaven the weak reed shall be turned into a cedar! We shall put on strength, and be as the angels of God.

4. The dignity and nobility of angels consists in their purity. Take away holiness from an angel, and he is no more an angel—but a devil. Those blessed spirits are sinless, spotless creatures; no unholy thought enters into their mind. They are virgin spirits; therefore they are said to be 'clothed in pure white linen,' Rev. 15:6. And they are represented by the cherubim overshadowing the mercy-seat, which were made 'all of fine gold,' to denote the purity of their essence. In this sense we shall be as the angels—of a refined, pure, sublime nature. Therefore the saints are said to have 'washed their robes, and made them white in the blood of the Lamb,' Rev. 7:14. Christ's blood washes white! We read of 'the spirits of just men made perfect.'

5. The dignity of angels appears in their immunity. The angels are privileged by their immunities—and thus shall we be as the angels. There is a two-fold immunity.

1. We shall be immune from the difficulties of piety. Duties are irksome to the flesh. But in heaven, we shall be as the angels; no more praying or fasting, no more repenting or mortification. When we are above sin—then we shall be above ordinances! I do not say we shall be free from serving God—but we shall be freed from all that is tedious and unpleasant! The angels serve God—but it is with cheerfulness. It is their heaven to serve God—when they are singing hallelujahs they are ravished with holy delight! Though being spirits, they need no food—yet it is their food and drink to be doing the will of God: 'the joy of the Lord is their strength.' Thus the saints shall be as the angels, 'they shall rest from their labors,' Rev. 14:13. They shall not rest from serving God—but from their labor in serving him. Their service shall be sweetened with so much pleasure and delight, that it shall not be a task—but a recreation! What joy will it be to sing in the heavenly choir! The angels begin the music—and the saints join in the concert!

2. We shall be immune from temptation. The angels, those blessed spirits, have no temptations to sin—thus shall we be as the angels. It is sad to have atheistical, blasphemous thoughts forced upon us. It is sad always to lie under the Devil's spout, to have temptations dropping upon us! And though we do not yield to the enemy—yet to have the garrison continually assaulted, is a great grief to a child of God! But this is a believer's privilege—he shall be shortly as the angels—not subject to temptation. The Devil is cast out of paradise! The old serpent shall never sneak into the New Jerusalem. Heaven is pictured out by an exceeding high mountain, Rev. 21:10. This heavenly mount is so high, that Satan's fiery darts cannot shoot up to it—it is above the reach of his arrow!

6. The dignity of angels consist in their impeccability. The blessed angels are not only without sin—but they are in an impossibility of sinning. The angels have a clear sight of God! They are, by the sweet influence of that vision, so enamored with the beauty and love of God, that they

have not the least motion or will to sin. 'They are confirmed by the power of God,' says Augustine, 'that they cannot sin!' The angels are immoveable in holiness.

Indeed Origen affirms that there is a possibility of sinning even in the angels; but this opinion is, 1. Contrary to the current of the fathers — that the angels are of that invincible sanctity, that they cannot be drawn by any violence to sin. 2. That it should be possible for the angels to be stained with the least tincture of sin — is repugnant to scripture; for if the angels may sin, then they may fall — but they cannot fall. The minor proposition is clear: elected angels cannot fall — but the angels are elected; the apostle proves the election of angels. 1 Tim. 5:21, 'I charge you before God and the elect angels.'

The angels are called stars, Job. 38:7. These angelical stars are so fixed in their orb of sanctity, that they cannot have the least erring, or retrograde motion to sin. Does not all this set forth the privilege and comfort of believers? They shall be in this sense as the angels — in an impossibility of sinning! Here on earth, it is impossible that we should not sin; in heaven it is impossible that we should sin! There we shall not only be exempted from the act of sinning — but from the capacity of sinning — for we shall be as the angels of God! What a blessed privilege is this! We who are now accounted as the off-scouring of men — shall be as the angels!

Oh how may this excite the most profane people to the study of piety! Fly from sin! Sin will not make you angels — but devils! 'Follow after holiness!' The huntsmen pursue the deer with earnestness. Pursue holiness as the huntsman pursues his game! Here is reason enough — you shall not only be with the angels — but you shall be like the angels! If while you live, you live as saints — when you die, you shall be as angels!

Chapter 15. The Tenth Royal Privilege is — the vindication of our reputations.

Fulgentius calls a good name the godly man's heir, because it lives when he is dead. A good reputation is the best temporal blessing — yet all do not wear this garland. Those who have a good conscience, have not always a good name. The old serpent spits his venom at the godly — through the mouths of wicked men! If Satan cannot strike his fiery dart into our conscience — he will put a dead fly into our reputation.

The people of God are represented to the world, in a very bad light. How strangely does a saint look — when he is put in the Devil's dress! Some primitive Christians that were clothed with bear's skins, and painted with red devils. Job was represented to the world as a hypocrite — and by his friends too — which was very painful to him. Paul was called a seditious man. He suffered (in the opinion of some) as an evildoer, 2 Tim. 2:9. 'Wherein I suffer trouble as an evildoer, even unto bonds.' He did not only bear Christ's mark in his body — but in his name. Our blessed Savior was called a glutton and a drunkard, and a deceiver of the people. It has always been the manner of the wicked world — to paint God's children in very strange colors.

It is a great sin to defame a saint, it is murder; better take away his life than his name! It is a sin which we can never make him reparation for; a flaw in a man's credit being like a blot in white paper, which will never come out. The defaming of a saint is no less than the defaming of God himself! The saints have God's picture drawn in their hearts: a man cannot abuse the picture of Caesar, without some reflection upon Caesar's person. Well, either God will clear his peoples' innocency here, which he has promised, Psalm 37:6, 'And he shall bring forth your righteousness as the light.' Your good name may be in a cloud — but it shall not set in a cloud; or else God will clear his peoples' innocency at the Day of Judgment.

In this life the godly are called the troublers of Israel, seditious, rebellious and what not! but a day is shortly coming, when God himself will proclaim their innocency. Believe it, as God will make inquisition for blood, so also for names! The name of a saint is precious in God's esteem —

it is like a statue of gold which the polluted breath of men cannot stain. And though the wicked may throw dust upon it—yet as God will wipe away all tears from the eyes of his people—so he will wipe off the dust from their name! The time is shortly coming when God will say to us, as once to Joshua, 'I have rolled away the reproach of Egypt from off you.' Even as it was with Christ, the Jews rolled a great stone upon him, and as they thought, it was impossible he should rise again; but an angel came and rolled away the stone, and he arose in a glorious triumphant manner. So it shall be with the godly, their good names or titles are buried, a stone of calumny and reproach is rolled upon them; but at the Day of Judgment, not an angel—but God himself will roll away the stone, and they shall come forth from among the pots, where they have been blackened and sullied, 'as the wings of a dove covered with silver, and her feathers with yellow gold.' O what a blessed day will that be, when God himself shall be the saints' vindicator.

Chapter 16. The Eleventh Royal Privilege is—the sentence of absolution.

Here take notice of two things.

1. The process in law. 'And I saw the dead, great and small, standing before the throne, and books were opened. Another book was opened, which is the book of life. The dead were judged according to what they had done as recorded in the books.' Revelation 20:12. This is a metaphor taken from the manner of our courts of judicature, where there is the whole process, every circumstance considered, and the witnesses examined. So here—the books are opened, the book of God's accounting, and the book of conscience! Now observe, 'another book was opened, which is the book of life'; that is, the book of God's decree, the book of free grace, the book which has the saints' names written in it, and their pardon! The elect shall be judged out of this book! Surely the sentence cannot be dismal, when our husband is judge—and will judge us by the book of life!

2. The sentence itself. Matt. 25:34, 'Come you who are blessed by my Father!'

1. This implies the saints' acquittance. The curse is taken off; they have their discharge in the court of justice, and shall have the broad seal of heaven, Father, Son, and Holy Spirit—all setting their hands to the pardon, and this Christ shall proclaim.

2. This implies the saints' installment. 'Come you who are blessed.' As if Christ should say, 'You are the heirs to the crown of heaven! Come in—enter upon possession!' And this sentence can never be reversed to eternity; but as Isaac said, 'I have blessed him, and he shall be blessed!' At the hearing of this wondrous sentence, O with what ineffable joy will the saints be filled! it will be like music in the ear, and a jubilee in the heart! Even as Elizabeth once said to the virgin Mary, as soon as the voice of your salutation sounded in my ears, the babe leaped in my womb for joy! Just so, the heart of a believer will leap inside him—at the hearing of this blessed sentence, and be ready to leap out of him for joy. O what trembling now among the devils! What triumph among the angels!

Chapter 17. The Last Royal Privilege is—that God will make a public and honorable mention of all the good which the saints have done.

This I ground upon three scriptures. Matt. 15:21, 'Well done—good and faithful servant!' The world maligns and censures us. When we discharge our conscience, they say 'Badly done!' But God will say, 'Well done—good and faithful servant!' He will set a trophy of honor upon his people, 'He will place the sheep at his right hand and the goats at his left. Then the King will say to those on the right—Come, you who are blessed by my Father, inherit the Kingdom prepared for you from the foundation of the world. For I was hungry, and you fed me. I was thirsty, and you gave me a drink. I was a stranger, and you invited me into your home. I was naked, and you gave me clothing. I was sick, and you cared for me. I was in prison, and you visited me!' Matthew 25:33-36.

King Ahasuerus had his book of records; and when he read in his book, he took notice of Mordecai's good service, and caused him to have public honor. Be assured—God has his book of record, and will openly take notice of all the good service you have done, and he himself will be the herald to proclaim your praises! 2 Cor. 4:5, 'Then shall every man have praise from God.'

I speak this the rather, to encourage you in God's service. Perhaps you have laid out yourself for the cause of God, but it came to nothing, and you begin to think that it was a foolish venture—and all is lost. No! your faith and zeal are recorded; your service iw written in heaven, and God will give you a public testimony of honor, 'Well done—good and faithful servant!' What a whetstone is this to duty? How should it add oil to the flame of our devotion? You perhaps have prayed a great while, and watered this seed with your tears. Be of good comfort— your tears are not lost! God bottles them as precious wine, and it will not be long before he will open his bottle, and this wine which came from the wine-press of your eyes—shall sparkle forth in the sight of men and angels!

More—God will not only take notice of what we have done for him—but what we would have done, if we could have. David had an intention to build God a house, and the Lord interpreted it as if he had done it, 1 Kings 8:18. 'Whereas it was in your heart to build a house unto my name, you did well that it was in your heart.' Intentional goodness is recorded, and shall add to our crown!

What a good and generous God we serve! Who would ever change such a master! It were, one would think, enough that God should give us wages for our work (especially seeing that he was the one who gave us the ability to work). But what a marvel it this—that God should applaud us with a 'Well done!' Think how sweet it will be to hear such a word from God—how amazing and ravishing, when he shall say openly, 'These are the servants of the most high God! These are those who feared to sin! These are those who have wept in secret for that which it was not in their power to perform! These are those who have kept their garments pure—who have valued my favor above life—who rather choose to honor me than humor men! These are those who were willing to wash off the stains from the face of religion with their blood, and to make my crown flourish, though it were in their ashes! Well done, good and faithful servant, enter into the joy of your Lord!' Thus shall it be done to those whom God delights to honor!

These are those glorious things which are to come! I have led you to the top of the mount, and given you a prospect of heaven! I have shown you just a glimpse. I shall say of this glory of heaven, as once the queen of Sheba said of Solomon's pomp and magnificence, 'The half of it has not been told!'

Chapter 18. The First Inference drawn from the Proposition.

It shows us what a high valuation and esteem we should set upon the godly. They are, we see, men 'greatly in favor with God,' as the angel once proclaimed to Daniel, and they are invested with glorious privileges. They are of a heavenly descent, born of the Spirit; they are very rich, for they are heirs of the kingdom! God has not only laid out some parcels of land, or divided heaven to them, as Canaan was divided to Israel by lot: the tribe of Judah to inhabit in one country, the tribe of Reuben in another, etc. God, I say, does not parcel out heaven thus to the saints. No! heaven is theirs, with all its privileges, blessings, and royalties. There are no enclosures or fences in heaven; there can be no confinement where everything is infinite. Oh what a high value and estimate then should be put upon the saints! they are heirs of God! How does the world respect great heirs! What honor then should we give to the godly! They are adopted into all the stately privileges of heaven. How rich is he when possessed of the inheritance! How rich shall the saints be, when God shall pour out of his love, and shall empty all the treasures of glory into them! The saints are jewels—but their worth and riches are not known; therefore they are trampled upon by the world. 'It does not yet appear what they shall be!' All things are theirs!

Chapter 19. The Second Inference drawn from the Proposition.

It shows us a main difference between the godly and the wicked. he godly man has all his best things to come. The wicked man has all his worst things to come. As their way is different, so their end. 'You in your lifetime received your good things.' The wicked have all their good things here on earth; their worst things are to come. Why—what is to come? The apostle answers, 1 Thes. 1:10, 'Wrath to come!' And here I shall briefly show you the wicked man's charter—which consists in five things.

Section 1. The first thing to come, is the awakening of conscience. Conscience is God's deputy in the soul, his viceroy. A wicked man does what he can to unthrone conscience, and put it out of office. Conscience is God's echo, and sometimes it is so shrill and clamorous, that the sinner cannot endure the noise—but silences conscience. By frequent sinning, conscience begins to be sleepy and seared; 'having their conscience seared with a hot iron,' 1 Tim. 4:2. This conscience is quiet—but not good; for the silence of conscience proceeds from the numbness of it. It is with him as with a sick patient, who having a confluence of diseases upon him—yet being asleep, is insensible of his diseases.

Time was when conscience was tender—but by often sinning, he is like the ostrich which can digest iron; or as it is said of Mithridates, that by often accustoming his body to poison, it never hurt him—but he could live upon it as his food. That sin which was before as the wounding of the sensitive eye; now is no more painful than the cutting of the finger nail.

Well, there is a time coming when this sleepy conscience shall be awakened! Belshazzar was drinking wine in bowls, when 'the fingers of a human hand writing on the plaster wall of the king's palace. The king himself saw the hand as it wrote, and his face turned pale with fear! Such terror gripped him that his knees knocked together and his legs gave way beneath him!' There conscience began to be awakened.

Conscience is like a looking-glass; if it is foul and dusty, you can see nothing in it; but wipe away the dust, and you may see your face in it clearly. There is a time coming, when God will wipe off the dust from the looking-glass of a man's conscience, and he shall see his sins clearly represented! Conscience is like a sleeping lion; when he awakes—he roars and tears his prey. When conscience awakes, then it roars upon a sinner, and tears him!—as the devil did the man into which he entered; he 'rent him, and threw him into the fire.' When Moses' rod was turned into a serpent, he was afraid and fled from it. Oh what is it when conscience is turned into a serpent!

Conscience is like the bee, if a man does well—then conscience gives honey, it speaks comfort; if he does evil—it puts forth a sting. Conscience is called a worm, Mark 9:44, 'where the worm never dies.' It is like Prometheus' vulture, it is ever gnawing. Conscience is God's bloodhound, which pursues a man. When the jailor saw the prison doors open, and, as he thought, the prisoners were missing, he drew his sword and would have killed himself. Just so, when the eye of conscience is opened, and the sinner begins to look about him for his evidences, faith, repentance, etc. and sees they are missing, he will be ready to kill himself! A troubled conscience is the first-fruits of hell; indeed it is a lesser hell. That it is so, appears two ways:

1. By the testimony of scripture. Proverbs 18:14, 'A wounded spirit who can bear?' a wound in the name, in the estate, in the body, is sad; but a wound in the conscience, who can bear? especially when the wound can never be healed — I speak of such as awake in the night of death.

2. By the experience both of good and bad.

A. By the experience of good men; when the storm has risen in their conscience (though afterwards it has been allayed) yet for the present, they have been in the suburbs of hell. David complains of his broken bones, he was like a man that had all his bones out of joint. What is the matter? You may see where his pain lay, Psalm 51:3, 'My sin is ever before me!' He was in a spiritual agony: it was not the sword which threatened; it was not the death of the child — but it was the roarings of his conscience! Some of God's arrows fast stuck there! Though God will not damn his children — yet he may send them to hell in this life!

B. By the experience of bad men, who have been in the perpetual convulsions of conscience. 'I have sinned!' says Judas. Before, he was nibbling at the silver bait — the thirty pieces. But now the hook troubles him, conscience wounds him. Such was Judas' horror, being now like a man upon the rack, that he hangs himself to quiet his conscience. This shows what the hell of conscience is; that men account death easy — to get rid of conscience; but in vain. It is with them as with a sick man, he moves out of one room into another, and changes the air — but still he carries his disease with him. O sinner, what will you do when conscience will begin to fly upon you, and shall probe you with scourgings? It is a mercy when conscience is awakened in time; but the misery is when the wound is too late, there being then, no balm in Gilead.

Section 2. The second thing to come is, his appearing before the judge. 'For we must all appear before the judgment-seat of Christ.' Hierome thought he ever heard that sounding in his ears, 'Arise you dead, and come to judgment!' What solemnity is there at court, when the judge comes to the bench, and the trumpets are sounded! Thus Christ the Judge shall be accompanied with angels and archangels, and the trumpets shall be blown; 1 Thess. 4:16, 'For the Lord himself shall descend from heaven with a shout, with the voice of the archangel, and with the trumpet of God!' This is the great and general judgement. Then shall Christ sit down upon the throne of judgement, holding his sword in his hand, and a flame coming out of his mouth. Now the sinner being summoned before him as a prisoner at bar, he has his guilt written in his forehead; he is condemned before he comes, I mean in his conscience, which is the petty judgement; and appearing before Christ, he begins to tremble and be amazed with horror! And not being covered with Christ's righteousness, for lack of a better covering, he cries to the mountains to cover him! 'And the kings and the great men said to the mountains and rocks — fall on us, and hide us from the face of him who sits on the throne, and from the wrath of the Lamb!' Nothing so dreadful as the sight of mercy abused. Now the Lamb will be turned into a Lion; and he who was once a Savior will be a Judge!

Section 3. The third thing to come is, his charge read. 'I will reprove you, and set your sins in order before you,' Psalm 50:21. As God has a bottle for the tears of his people; so he has a book to register men's sins, Rev. 20:12, 'the books were opened.' Oh what a black charge will be read against a sinner! not only the sins which have damnation written in their forehead — such as drunkenness, swearing, blasphemy, shall be brought into the charge — but those sins which he slighted, as,

1. Secret sins, such as the world never took notice of. Many a man does not forsake his sins — but grows more cunning in concealing them. His heart gives as much vent to sin as ever. His care is rather that sin should be concealed, than cured. He is like him who shuts up his shop

windows—but follows his trade within doors; he sits brooding upon sin. He does with his sins, as Rachel did with her father's idols, she put them under her that he might not find them; so does he put his sins in a secret place. But all these sins shall be set in order before him! Luke 12:2, 'For there is nothing covered that shall not be revealed!' God has a key for the heart!

2. Little sins, as the world calls them. The majesty of God — against which it is committed, does accent and enhance the sin. Besides, little sins (suppose them so) yet multiplied, become great! What is less than a grain of sand? Yet when multiplied, what is heavier than the sands of the sea? A little sum multiplied, is great. A little sin, unrepented of, will damn! Just as one leak in the ship, if it be not looked to, will sink it. You would think it is no great matter to merely forget God — yet it has a heavy doom, 'Consider this, you who forget God, or I will tear you to pieces, with none to rescue!' Psalm 50:22. 'The wicked shall be turned into hell, and all the nations that forget God.' Psalms 9:17. The non-improvement of talents, the world looks upon as a small thing; yet we read of him who 'hid his talent in the earth,' Matt. 25:25. He had not wasted it. Only not trading it, is sentenced. 'You wicked and lazy servant!' 'Now throw this useless servant into outer darkness, where there will be weeping and gnashing of teeth!'

3. Sins that in the eye of the world were looked upon as virtues; sins that were colored and masked over with zeal of God, and good intentions, etc. Men put fine glosses upon their sins, that they may obtain credit, and be the more commendable. It is said of Alcibiades, that he embroidered a curtain with lions and eagles, that he might hide the picture underneath, full of witches and satyrs. So does Satan embroider the curtain with the image of virtue, that he may hide the foul picture of sin underneath. The devil is like the spider — first she weaves her web, and then hangs the fly in it. Just so, the devil helps men to weave the web of sin with religious pretenses, and then he hangs them in the snare! All these sins shall be read in the sinner's charge, and set in order before him!

Section 4. The next thing is, the passing of the sentence. Matt. 25:41, 'Depart from me, you who are cursed, into the eternal fire prepared for the devil and his angels!' At the hearing of this sentence, the heart of a sinner will be rent through with horror; that heart which before would not break with sorrow for sin, shall now break with despair. At the pronouncing of this dreadful sentence, 'depart from me,' the sinner would be glad if he could depart from himself, and be annihilated. O it will be a sad departing! We use to say, when a man is dead, he is departed. But this will be a departing without a deceasing. As soon as Christ has pronounced the curse, the sinner will begin to curse himself. 'Oh what have I been doing! I have lain in wait for my own blood! I have twisted the noose of my own damnation!' While he lived, he blessed himself; 'oh how happy am I, how does providence smile upon me!' Psalm 49:18, 'Though while he lived he blessed his soul,' yet when this sentence is passed, he is the first who will curse himself.

Section 5. The pouring out of the vial. Psalm 75:8, 'For the Lord holds a cup in his hand; it is full of foaming wine mixed with spices. He pours the wine out in judgment, and all the wicked must drink it, draining it to the dregs!' This is the sad execution. Hell is pictured out by Tophet, Isaiah 30:33, which was a place situated near Jerusalem, where they offered their children in the fire to Moloch. This is a fit metaphor to picture out the infinite torments of hell — the sinner shall lie in the furnace of God's wrath, and the breath of the Lord, as a pair of bellows, shall blow the fire!

Hell is said to be prepared, as if God had been sitting down to study and devise some exquisite torment. Hell is pictured out as fire, and in another place by darkness — to show that hell is a fire without light. The hypocrite, while he lived, was all light, no fire; and in hell he shall be all fire, no light! In hell there is nothing to give comfort! There is no music but the shrieks of the damned! There is no wine but what is burnt with the flame of God's wrath: 'There shall be weeping, and wailing, and gnashing of teeth!' The weeping hypocrite shall go to the place of weeping: while he lived, he lifted up his eyes in a false devotion, and now being in hell he shall lift up his eyes in torment. He who gnashed his teeth at the godly, shall now have gnashing enough! Before he gnashed in envy — now in despair — and this forever!

'He will burn up the chaff with unquenchable fire!' The word unquenchable scorches hotter than the fire! The fire of hell is like that stone in Arcadia, I have read of, which being once kindled, could not be extinguished. Eternity is the hell of hell! The loss of the soul is irreparable! If all the angels in heaven should put together a purse, they could not make up this loss. When a sinner is in hell, shall another Christ be found to die for him? or will the same Christ be crucified again? Oh no! They are everlasting burnings!

Thus the sinner has all worst things to come; but a believer has all his best things to come — the things which eye has not seen, nor ear heard, namely, the beatific vision, the crystal streams of joy that run at God's right hand! His heaven is to come!

Chapter 20. A Serious Scrutiny about the Believer's Charter.

I hear, methinks, a Christian say, 'Great are the privileges of a believer; but I fear I have no title to this glorious charter.' Were there a dispute about our estate, whether such an inheritance did belong to us, we would desire that there should be a trial in law to decide it. Here is a large inheritance, 'things present and things to come;' but the question is — whether we are the true heirs to whom it belongs? Now for the deciding this, we must seriously examine what right we have to Christ; for all this estate is made over to us through Christ. 'All things are yours, and you are Christ's' — there comes in the title. Jesus Christ is the great treasury and storehouse of a Christian, he has purchased heaven with his blood. If we can say we are Christ's, then we may say, 'all things are ours!'

Question. But how shall we know that we are Christ's?

Answer. Those that are Christ's — Christ is in them, 2 Cor. 13:5. 'Know you not that Christ is in you?'

Question. But how shall we know that?

Answer. If we are in the faith. It is observable, before the apostle had said, 'Know you not that Christ is in you'; first he puts this query, 'Examine whether you are in the faith.' Christ is in you, if you are in the faith. Here lies the question, Have you faith? Now for the deciding this, I shall show,

The antecedents, the concomitants, the genuine act, and the fruits of faith.

Section 1. Showing the antecedents of Faith.

1. Antecedent to faith, is knowledge. Faith is an intelligent grace; though there can be knowledge without faith — yet there can be no faith without knowledge. 'Those who know your name will put their trust in you,' Psalm 9:10. One calls it, quick-sighted faith. Knowledge must carry the torch before faith, 2 Tim. 1:12, 'For I know whom I have believed.' As in Paul's conversion, a light from heaven 'shined round about him,' Acts 9:3; so before faith be wrought, God shines in with a light upon the understanding. A blind faith is as bad as a dead faith. That eye may as well be said to be a good eye, which is without sight; as that faith is good, which is without knowledge. Devout ignorance damns! This condemns the church of Rome, which teaches that ignorance is the mother of devotion! But surely, where the sun is set in the understanding, it must needs be night in the affections. So necessary is knowledge to the being of faith, that the scriptures do sometimes baptize faith with the name of knowledge, Isaiah

53:11, 'By his knowledge shall my righteous servant justify many;' knowledge is put there for faith. This knowledge which is antecedent to faith and does usher it in, consists in the apprehension of four things: the soul through this optic glass of knowledge sees,

1. The soul, by faith, sees a preciousness in Christ, 'he is the chief of ten thousand.' There is nothing in Christ but what is precious: he is precious in his name, in his nature, in his influences, in his privileges. He is called a precious stone, Isaiah 28:16. He must needs be a precious stone—who has made us living stones, 1 Pet. 2:5.

2. The soul, by faith, sees a fullness in Christ, the fullness of the Godhead. Col. 2:9, 'all fullness,' Col. 1:19. Christ has a fullness of merit—his blood is able to satisfy God's justice. Christ has a fullness of spirit—his grace able to supply our needs.

3. The soul, by faith, sees a suitableness in Christ; nothing can be satisfactory but what is suitable. If a man is hungry, bring him fine flowers, this is not suitable; he desires food. If he be sick, bring him music, this is not suitable, he desires medicine. In this sense there is a suitableness in Christ to the soul: there is a fitness as well as a fullness. He is (as Origen speaks) everything which is desirable. If we hunger, he is the food of the soul, therefore he is called the bread of life. If we are sick unto death, his blood is the balm of Gilead. He may be compared to the trees of the sanctuary, which were both for food and medicine, Ezek. 47:12.

4. The soul, by faith, sees a propensity and readiness in Christ to GIVE out his fullness. There is bounty in Christ as well as beauty. Isaiah 55:1, 'Come, all you who are thirsty, come to the waters; and you who have no money, come, buy and eat! Come, buy wine and milk without money and without cost!' Behold, at what a low price does God set his heavenly blessings! it is but thirsting: bring but desires. Behold the readiness in Christ to dispense and give out his fullness: 'Come, buy wine and milk without money and without cost!' A strange kind of buying! As he is all fullness, so he is all sweetness—he is of a noble and generous disposition. This is the enticer of the affections; this draws the eyes and heart of a sinner after him. What are the promises—but Christ's golden scepter held forth? What are the motions of the Spirit—but Jesus Christ coming a wooing?

Such a knowledge of Christ does necessarily precede and go before faith; now the soul begins to move towards him.

2. The second antecedent to faith is credence; a setting our seal to the truth of the word; a giving credit to that which the Word asserts concerning Christ: namely, that he is the true Messiah, that there is no other name under heaven whereby we can be saved; that whoever believes in him shall not perish; that he delights in mercy. It is delightful to the mother to have her breasts drawn. Just so, it is pleasing to Christ, that sinners should draw the breasts of the promises. An assent, and giving credence to all that the scripture holds forth concerning Christ, is necessary to precede faith. Dogmatic faith goes before justifying faith.

3. The third preparatory or antecedent to faith, is deep conviction and humiliation. The seed that lacked depth of earth withered; so will that faith which is not laid in deep humiliation. Christ is never sweet, until sin is bitter! He never gives ease, but to those who feel their burden, Matt. 11:28. Indeed, until a man feels his burden, he cannot cast it upon Christ. A man must see himself as lost. Many are lost for lack of knowing their lostness. Acts 2:37, 'they were pricked at their hearts,' etc. as if a balloon were pricked and the wind let out. Just so, the swelling of pride, was let out by humiliation, Romans 7:9, 'when the commandment came, sin revived and I died.' As if Paul had said, 'when the law of God came, and showed me the spots of my soul, sin revived; that is—sin began to appear in its bloody colors, striking horror and amazement into my soul, and I died! The good opinion which before I had of myself—died!' As it was with the

people of Israel, they saw the Red Sea before them, and Pharaoh pursuing behind. So the sinner after some legal bruisings, being affrighted, sees the sea of his sins before ready to swallow him up, and the justice of God pursuing and ready to overtake him, and no way to extricate or help himself; only there is a brazen serpent lifted up, and if he can look upon that, he may be saved!

4. The fourth antecedent to faith is self-renunciation, or a disclaiming and renouncing anything in a man's self that can save. This is certain — before a man can come to Christ, he must come out of himself. Before he can trust in Christ, he must despair in himself; Phil. 3:7, 'Not having my own righteousness.' Men would like to have something of their own, to trust to. They would bow down to their own righteousness, their duties and moralities, Romans 10:3. Oh but if you will lean on Christ — throw away these rotten crutches! You must use duty, as the dove did her wings — to fly. But trust to Christ the ark — for safety. A man must be first transplanted; he must be taken out of the old soil, and have nothing of his own to grow upon, before he can be engrafted into Christ the true olive tree. As the angel said to Mary when she looked for Christ in the sepulcher, 'he is not here,' Matt. 28:6, so I may say to that man who seeks to make a Christ of his duties, and moral excellencies, 'Christ is not here, you must look higher! Salvation is not to be found within you — but in something without you, in something above you.'

5. The fifth antecedent, or that which goes before faith, is a secret persuasion in the soul of man, that Christ is willing to show mercy to him in particular. Mark 10:49, 'Arise, he calls you.' Just so, the Spirit secretly whispers to the soul, 'Arise out of your sins, Jesus Christ calls you! He bids you believe in him.' Then the soul begins to think thus, 'Did Jesus Christ come to save sinners, such as are humble and penitent? Does he not only invite them — but command them to believe in him, 1 John. 3:23. Then why do I not believe? What is it which keeps me off from Christ? Is it my unworthiness? Behold there is merit enough in Christ to make me worthy! Is it my impurity? 'The blood of Jesus cleanses from all sin,' 1 John 1:7. His blood is a balsam to heal me, a laver to wash me! Though I have nothing whereby to ingratiate myself into his favor — yet my comfort is, that Jesus Christ does not require that I should carry anything to him — but, fetch everything from him. I need carry no water to this well of salvation — only an empty vessel — only a humble broken heart. If God justifies the ungodly — why should I hold off from Christ any longer? Romans 4:5. Why then should not I think that there is mercy for me? Surely there is! Methinks I see Christ beckoning to me to come to him, methinks I hear the soundings of his affections. These are the preparations to faith.

SECTION 2. Showing the attendants of faith.

1. Consent is the first attendant of faith. The soul now consents to have Christ, and to have him upon his own terms.

1. As a Head. The head has a double office — it is the fountain of spirits, and the seat of government. The head is, as it were, the pilot of the body, it rules and steers it in its motion. The believer consents to have Christ, not only as a head to send forth spirits, that is comfort — but as a head to rule. A hypocrite would take Christ's promises — but not his laws. He would be under Christ's benediction — but not his jurisdiction. A believer consents to have whole Christ; he does not pick and choose. As he expects to one day to sit down with Christ upon the throne, so he now makes his heart Christ's throne.

2. The believer consents to have Christ for better for worse — a naked Christ, a persecuted Christ; for he sees a beauty and glory — in the reproaches of Christ, 1 Pet. 4:14, and will have Christ not only in his royal purple — but when with John Baptist he is clothed in camel's hair. He can embrace the fire — if Christ is in it. He looks upon the cross as Jacob's ladder by which he

ascends up to heaven. He says, 'Blessed be that affliction, welcome that cross — which carries Christ upon it.'

3. He consents to have Christ purely for love. If the wife should give her consent only for her husband's riches, she would marry his estate rather than his person; it were not properly to make a marriage with him — but rather to make a merchandise of him. The believer consents for love. He loves Christ for Christ. Heaven without Christ is not a sufficient dowry for a believer; there is no ulterior motive in his consent — it is not sinister; there is nothing forced — it is not for fear; that would rather be a constraint than consent; a forced consent will not hold in law. The believer's consent is voluntary; the beauty of Christ's person and the sweetness of his disposition draws the will, which as the master-wheel, carries the whole soul with it.

4. The believer consents to have Christ, never more to part. He would have an uninterrupted communion with him. He will part with life — but not with Christ. Death, when it slips the knot between the soul and the body — it ties it faster between the soul and Christ!

5. The believer does so consent to have Christ, as he makes a deed of gift — resigning up all the interest in himself, to Christ. He is willing to lose his own name, and surname himself by the name of Christ. He is willing to lose his own will and be wholly at Christ's disposal, 1 Cor. 6:19. He resigns up his love to Christ. In this sense the spouse is said to be a spring shut up, Cant. 4:12; she has love for relations — but the best of her love is kept for Christ. The world has the milk of her love — but Christ has the cream of it. The choicest and purest of her love is a spring shut up; it is broached only for Christ to drink!

2. The second attendant of faith is desire. Psalm 42:1, 'As the deer pants after the water-brooks, so pants my soul after you, O God!' 'Oh!' (says the soul) 'that I had Christ, that I might but touch the hem of his garment!' 'Oh that one would give me drink of the water of the well of Bethlehem!' 2 Sam. 23:15. So says the thirsty sinner, 'Who will give me to drink of those streams of living water, which run in Christ's blood? O that I had this morning star — to enlighten me! O that I had this pearl of great price — to enrich me! O that I this tree of life — to quicken me. Oh that I had a sight of Christ's beauty, a taste of his sweetness! There is such a thirst raised in the soul, that nothing can quench it but the blood of Christ! Nothing but the breast will quiet the child; nothing will quiet the longing soul — but God's opening the breasts of free-grace, and giving his Son out of his bosom!

3. The third attendant of faith is a spirit of contrition. The soul is even melted into tears, Zech. 12:10, 'They shall look upon me whom they have pierced — and shall mourn!' The Spirit of grace drops as dew upon the heart, and makes it soft and tender. The poor sinner weeps for his sins of unkindness against Christ! 'Oh,' says he, 'that I should sin against so sweet a Savior!' He looks upon a broken Christ with a broken heart! He washes Christ's wounds with his tears! Before, he wept for fear; now, he weeps for love! Mary stood at Jesus feet — weeping!

Section 3. Showing the genuine act of Faith.

Then follows the genuine and proper act of faith, namely recumbency. The soul rests upon Christ, and Christ alone for salvation. This is the very door by which we enter into heaven. Faith casts itself upon Christ, as a man that casts himself upon the stream to swim. The believer stays himself upon Christ, therefore faith is called a 'leaning upon Christ,' Cant. 5:8. Believers are called living stones, 1 Pet. 2:5, and they rest upon Christ the corner-stone, Isaiah 28:16. The believer caches hold of Christ, as Adonijah caught hold of the horns of the altar, 1 Kings 1:51, or as a man that is sinking caches hold of a bough. Faith makes a holy venture upon Christ, as Queen Esther did upon king Ahasuerus, 'If I perish, I perish!' Esther 4:16; and this venturing upon Christ, is by virtue of a promise: else it is not faith — but presumption. Faith has its warrant in its hand, John 6:37, 'he who comes to me, I will never cast out.'

This is the proper act of faith — the soul's resting with a humble affiance upon Jesus Christ. Bernard, being a little before his death (as he thought) brought before God's tribunal, and Satan standing at his right hand to accuse him for his sins, he runs to Christ, and he says, 'Satan I am sinful and unworthy as you say — but though you do magnify my disease, I will magnify my physician. I know the Lord Jesus has a double right to the kingdom of glory, not only by heritage — but conquest; and he has conquered for me. So that I am not confounded while I look on Christ as my Savior, and heaven as my inheritance!' It was a saying of Augustine, 'I can rest securely, while I lay my head on Christ's bleeding side.'

Now concerning this faith, I shall lay down two rules.

1. That faith justifies not as a formal cause — but purely as an instrument, namely, as it lays hold on Christ the blessed object, and fetches in his fullness. In this sense it is called a precious faith. But the worth lies not in the faith — but in Christ, on which it does center and terminate. Faith in itself considered, is not more excellent than other graces. Take a piece of wax, and a piece of gold of the same magnitude, the wax is not valuable with the gold; but as the wax seals the label of some will, by virtue of which a great estate is confirmed and conveyed, so it may be of more worth than the gold. So faith considered purely in itself, does challenge nothing more than other graces, nay in some sense, it is inferior, it being an empty hand. But as this hand receives the precious alms of Christ's merits, and is an instrument or channel through which the blessed streams of life flow to us from him; so it does challenge a superiority above other graces.

Indeed, some affirm that the very act of believing, without reference to the merits of Christ, justifies. To which I shall say but this,

1. Faith cannot justify, as it is an act; for it must have an object. We cannot (if we make good sense) separate between the act and the object. What is faith, if it does not fix upon Christ — but fancy! It was not the people of Israel's looking up that cured them — but the fixing their eye upon the brazen serpent!

2. Faith does not justify, as it is a grace. This would be to substitute faith in Christ's place, it were to make a savior of faith. Faith is a good grace — but a bad savior!

3. Faith does not justify, as it is a work. Which must needs be, if the stress and virtue of faith lies only in the act, but then we should be justified by works, which is contrary to Eph. 2:9, where the apostle says expressly, 'not of works.' So that it is clear, faith's excellency lies in the apprehending and applying the object Christ! Therefore in scripture we are said to be justified through faith — as an instrument which lays hold on Christ the blessed object, and fetches in his fullness.

2. The second rule is, that faith does not justify, as it exercises grace. It cannot be denied but faith has an influence upon the graces; it is like a silver thread which runs through a chain of pearls. Faith puts strength and vivacity into all the virtues; but it does not justify under this notion. Faith begets obedience. By faith Abraham obeyed — but Abraham was not justified because he obeyed — but as he believed. Faith works by love — but it does not justify as it works by love. For as the sun shines by its brightness, not by its heat (though both are inseparably joined); so faith and love are tied together by an indissoluble knot. Yet faith does not justify as it works by love — but as it lays hold on Christ. Though faith is accompanied with all the graces — yet in point of justification, it is alone, and has nothing to do with any of the graces. Hence that speech of Luther, 'In the justification of a sinner, Christ and faith are alone; as the bridegroom

and bride in the bed-chamber.' Faith is never separated from the graces — yet sometimes it is alone. And thus I have shown you the essentials of faith.

Section 4. Showing what are the fruits and Products of Faith.

I proceed to the products of faith. There are many rare and supernatural fruits of faith.

1. Faith is a heart-quickening grace. It is the vital artery of the soul: 'The just shall live by his faith,' Hab. 2:4. When we begin to believe, we begin to live. Faith grafts the soul into Christ, as the scion into the stock, and fetches all its sap and juice from the blessed vine. Faith is the great quickener; it quickens our graces and our duties.

Faith quickens our graces. The Spirit of God infuses all the seeds and habits — but faith is the fountain of all the acts of grace; it is as the spring in the watch, which moves the wheels. Not a grace stirs, until faith sets it to work. How does love work? By faith! When I apprehend by faith, Christ's love to me — this attracts and draws up my love to Him in return. How does humility work? By faith! Faith humbles the soul; it has a double aspect; it looks upon sin, and a sight of sin humbles: it looks upon free-grace, and a sight of mercy humbles. How does patience work? By faith! If I believe God is a wise God, who knows what is best for me, and can deliver not only from affliction — but by affliction. This spins out patience. Thus faith is not only alive — but gives life. It puts forth a divine energy and operation into all the graces.

2. Faith animates and quickens our duties. What was the blood of bulls and goats, to take away sin? It was their faith in the Messiah which made their dead sacrifices become living sacrifices. What are ordinances, but a dumb show, without the breathings of faith in them? therefore in scripture it is called the prayer of faith, the hearing of faith, and the obedience of faith. Dead things have no beauty in them; it is faith which quickens and beautifies our duties.

3. Faith is a heart-purifying grace. 'Having purified their hearts by faith,' Acts 15:9. Faith is a virgin grace, of a pure and heavenly nature. Faith is in the soul, as the storm, which purifies the air. Faith is in the soul, as fire to the metals, which refines them. Faith is in the soul, as medicine in the body, which works out the disease. Faith works out pride, self-love, hypocrisy. Faith consecrates the heart. That which was before the devil's thoroughfare, is now made into God's enclosure; 1 Tim. 3:9, 'Holding the mystery of faith in a pure conscience.' Faith is a heavenly plant, which will not grow in an impure soil. Faith does not only justify — but sanctify. As it has one work in heaven, so it has another work in the heart. He who before was under the power of some debasing corruption, as soon as faith is wrought, there is a sacred virtue coming from Christ, for the enervating and weakening of that sin: 'the waters are abated.' The woman that did but touch the hem of Christ's garment, felt virtue coming out of him. The touch of faith has a healing power! Faith casts the devil out of the castle of the heart, though still he keeps the outworks. Satan has a party in a believer — but there is a duel fought every day: and faith will never give up, until, as a prince, it prevails. 'This is the faith of God's elect.'

You that say you Believe, has your faith removed the mountain of sin, and cast it into the sea? What, a believer — and a drunkard! A believer — and a swearer! A believer — and a worldling! Shame! Either leave your sins, or leave your profession! Faith and the love of sin can no more exist together, than light and darkness.

4. Faith is a heart-pacifying grace. Peace is the daughter of faith, Romans 5:1. 'Being justified by faith — we have peace with God.' Faith is the dove that brings an olive branch of peace in its mouth. Faith presents a reconciled God — and that gives peace. What is it which makes heaven — but the smile of God? Faith puts the soul into Christ — and there is peace. 'That in me — you may have peace.' When the conscience is in a fever, and burns as hell, faith opens the orifice in Christ's side, and sucks in his blood — which has a cooling and pacifying virtue in it!

Faith gives us peace in trouble; nay, out of trouble as well!

1. Faith gives peace in trouble. Faith is a heart-pacifying, because a heart-securing grace. When Noah was in the ark, he did not fear the deluge; he could sing in the ark. Faith shuts a believer into the ark, Christ! 'Lead me to the rock which is higher than I,' was David's prayer. Faith plants the soul upon this rock. The West Indians built their palaces upon the tops of hills: in the flood the waters covered the hills. But a believer is built higher: 'These are the ones who will dwell on high. The rocks of the mountains will be their fortress of safety.' Isaiah 33:16. His place of defense shall be the munition of rocks. But a man may starve upon a rock; therefore it follows, 'Food will be supplied to them, and they will have water in abundance.' Faith builds a Christian upon the power, wisdom, and faithfulness of God — this is the munition of rocks. And faith feeds him with the hidden manna of God's love — here is bread given him. The way to be safe in evil times, is to get faith; this ushers in peace, and it is such a peace as does garrison the heart, Phil. 4:7. 'The peace of God shall guard your heart'; it shall guard it as in a tower or garrison.

2. Faith gathers peace out of trouble. It gathers joy out of sorrow; glory out of reproach. This is the key to Samson's riddle, 'out of the eater came meat'; this explains that paradox, 'Can a man gather grapes of thorns, or figs of thistles?' Yes, of trials and persecutions, faith gathers joy and peace: here are figs of thistles. How were the martyrs ravished in the flames! the Apostles were whipped in prison — but it was with sweet-briar. O how sweet is that peace which faith breeds! it is a plant of the heavenly paradise; it is a Christian's festival! it is his music: it is as Chrysostom speaks, the anticipation of heaven.

5. Faith is a heart-strengthening grace. A believer has a heart of oak — he is strong to resist temptation, to bear afflictions, to foil corruptions; he gives check to them, though not full mate. An unbeliever is like Rueben, unstable as water, he shall not excel. A state of unbelief is a state of impotency. A believer is as Joseph, who though the archers shot at him, his bow abode in strength. If a Christian is to do anything, he consults with faith; this is the sinew, which if it be cut, all his strength goes from him. When he is called out to suffering, he harnesses himself with faith — he puts on this coat of armor. Faith gives suffering strength, furnishes the soul with suffering promises, musters together suffering graces, and propounds suffering rewards.

Question. But how is it, that faith is so strong?

Answer 1. Because it is a piece of God's armor. It is a shield which God puts into our hand. Eph. 6:16, 'Above all, taking the shield of faith.' A shield will serve for a breast-plate; a sword, if need be; and a helmet; it defends the head, it guards the vitals; such a shield is faith.

Answer 2. Faith brings the strength of Christ into the soul. Phil. 4:13, 'I can do all things through Christ, who strengthens me.' The strength of faith lies outside of itself, it grafts upon another stock — Christ. When it would have wisdom, it consults with Christ, whose name is Wonderful, Counselor. When it would have strength, it goes to Christ, who is called the Lion of the tribe of Judah. Christ is a Christian's armory, faith is the key that unlocks it! Faith hangs upon the lock of Christ, all its strength lies here; cut it off from this lock, and it is weaker than any other grace. Christ may be compared to that tower of David, on which there hung a thousand bucklers, all shields of mighty men: the faith of all the elect, these shields hang upon Christ. Faith is a heroical grace; the crown of martyrdom is set upon the head of faith. 'By faith they quenched the violence of the fire'; the fire overcame their bodies — but their faith overcame the flame.

5. Faith is a life-fructifying grace. It is fruitful. Julian, upbraiding the Christians, said, that their motto was, 'only believe.' Indeed, when faith is alone, and views all the rare beauties in Christ,

then faith sets a low value and esteem upon works. But when faith goes abroad in the world, good works are the handmaids which wait on this queen! Though we place faith in the highest orb, in matter of justification — yet good works are in conjunction with it — in matter of sanctification. It is no wrong to good works — to give faith the upper hand, which goes hand in hand with Christ. Good works are not separated from faith — only faith claims the higher rank. Faith believes as if it did not work, and it works as if it did not believe. Faith has Rachel's clear eye, and Leah's fruitful womb! Romans 7:4, 'That you should be married to another, even to him who is raised from the dead — that you should bring forth fruit unto God.' Faith is that spouse-like grace which marries Christ; and good works are the children which faith bears.

Thus having briefly shown you the nature of faith, I now come to the application: Have you true faith or not?

And here let me turn myself, first to unbelievers, such as cannot find that they have this uniting, this espousing grace. What shall I say to you? Go home and mourn; think with yourselves, 'What if you should die this night? what if God should send you a letter of summons to judgement? 'What would become of you? You lack that faith, which entitles you to Christ and heaven! Oh, I say, mourn! Yet mourn not as those who are without hope, for in the use of means, you may recover a title to Christ. I know it is otherwise in our law-courts; if a title to an estate is once lost, it can never be recovered. But it is otherwise here; though you have no title to Christ today — yet you may recover a title: you have not sinned away the hope of a title, unless you have sinned away the sense of sinning. To such as are resolved to go on in sin, I have not a word to say — except that they shall shortly go to hell. But to you that have been prodigal sons — but are now taking up serious resolutions to give a bill of divorce to your sins, let me encourage you to come to Christ, and to throw yourselves upon his blood; for yet a title to heaven is recoverable.

Objection 1. 'But,' says the sinner, 'Is there hope of mercy for me? surely this is too good news to be true! I would believe, and repent — but I am a great sinner.'

Answer. And whom else does Christ come to save! whom does God justify — but the ungodly! Did Christ take our flesh on him, and not our sins?

Objection 2. 'But my sins are of no ordinary dye.'

Answer. And is not Christ's blood of a deeper purple than your sins? Is there not more virtue in his blood, than there can be venom in the your sin? What if the devil magnifies your sins? Can you not magnify your physician? Cannot God drown one sea in another — your sea of sins, in the ocean of his mercy?

Objection 3. 'But my sins are of a long standing.'

Answer. Can Christ's blood only heal new and fresh wounds? We read that Christ raised not only the daughter of Jairus, who was newly dead, and the widow's son who was carried forth to burying; but he also Lazarus, who had lain four days in the grave, and had begun to putrefy! Has Christ less virtue now in heaven, than he had upon earth? if yours is an old wound — yet the medicine of Christ's blood, applied by faith, is able to heal it! Therefore, do not sink in these quicksands of despair! Judas' despair was worse in some sense than his treason. I would not encourage any to go on in sin, God forbid! It is sad to have old age and old sins. It is hard to pull up an old tree that is deeply rooted; it is easier to cut it down for the fire! But let not such despair: God can give an old sinner a new heart! He can 'make springs in the desert!' Have not others been set forth as patterns of mercy, who have come in at the twelfth hour? Therefore break off your league with sin, throw yourself into Christ's arms! Say, 'Lord Jesus, you have said — Those who come to you, you will never cast out!'

2. Let me turn myself to the people of God, such as upon a serious scrutiny with their own hearts, have solid grounds to think that they have faith, and being in the faith, are engrafted into Christ. Read over your charter, 'All things are yours!' Things present and to come! You are the heir on which God has settled all these glorious privileges. 'Give wine,' says Solomon, 'to those who are of heavy hearts.' But while I am going to pour in this wine of consolation, methinks I hear the Christian sadly disputing against himself, that he has no right to this charter.

Chapter 21. The Believer's Objections answered.

There are three great objections which he makes.

Objection. 1. 'Alas!' says he, 'I cannot tell whether I have faith or not.'

Answer. Have you no faith? How did you come to see that? A blind man cannot see. You cannot see the lack of grace—but by the light of grace.

Question. 'But surely, if I had faith I would be able to discern it?'

Answer 1. You may have faith, and not know it. A man may sometimes seek for that, which he has in his hand. Mary was with Christ, she saw him, she spoke with him—yet her eyes were blurred, that she did not know it was Christ. The child lives in the womb—yet does not know that it lives.

Answer 2. Faith often lies hidden in the heart, and we see it not, for lack of search. The fire lies hidden in the embers—but blow aside the ashes, and it is discernable. Faith may be hidden under fears, or temptations; but blow away the ashes! You prize faith. If had you a thousand jewels lying by, you would part with all of them—for this jewel of faith! No man can prize grace—but he who has it. You desire faith; the true desire of faith, is faith. You mourn for lack of faith; dispute not—but believe! What are these tears—but the seeds of faith.

Objection. 2. 'But my faith is weak. The hand of faith so trembles, that I fear it will hardly lay hold upon Christ.'

Answer. There are seven things which I shall say in reply to this.

1. A little faith is faith; as a sparkle of fire is fire. Though the pearl of faith be little—yet if it be a true pearl, it shines in God's eyes. This little grace is the seed of God, and it shall never die—but live as a sparkle in the main sea.

2. A weak faith will entitle us to Christ, just as well as a stronger faith. 'To those who have obtained like precious faith,' 2 Pet. 1:1. Not but that there are degrees of faith—as faith sanctifies, so all faith is not alike, one is more than another. But as faith justifies, so faith is alike precious. The weakest faith justifies, just as well as the faith of the most eminent saint! A weak hand is able to receive great alms. For a man to doubt of his grace because it is weak, is to rely upon his grace, rather than upon Christ.

3. The promise is not made to strong faith—but to true faith. The promise does not say, Whoever has a faith which can move mountains, or which can stop the mouths of lions—shall be saved; but whoever believes—be his faith ever so small. The promise is made to true faith, and for the most part to weak faith. What is a grain of mustard seed, what is a bruised reed—but the emblems of a weak faith? Yet the promise is made to these: 'A bruised reed he will not break.' The words are a figure of speech, where the lesser is put for the greater. He will not break, that is, he will bind it up! Though Christ chides a weak faith—yet that it may not be discouraged, he makes a promise to it. Hierome observes upon the beatitudes, there are many of the promises made to weak grace; Matt. 5:3, 'Blessed are the poor in spirit'; 'blessed are those who mourn,' verse 4, 'blessed are those who hunger,' verse 5.

4. A weak faith may be fruitful. Weakest things may multiply most. The vine is a weak plant, it must be borne up and under-propped—but it is fruitful; it is made in scripture the emblem of fruitfulness. The thief on the cross, when he was newly converted, had but a weak faith; but how many precious clusters grew upon that vine! Luke 23:40. He chides his fellow-thief, 'Do you not fear God?' He falls to self-judging, 'we indeed suffer justly.' He makes a heavenly prayer, and believes in Christ when he says, 'Lord, remember me when you come into your kingdom!' Here was a young plant—but very fruitful. Weak Christians often are most fruitful in affections. How strong is the first love to Christ, which is after the first planting of faith!

5. A Christian may mistake, and think he is weak in faith, because he is weak in assurance. But faith may be strongest—when assurance is weakest. Assurance is rather the fruit of faith. The woman of Canaan was weak in assurance—but was strong in faith. Christ gives her three repulses—but her faith stands the shock. She pursues Christ with a holy obstinacy of faith, insomuch that Christ sets a trophy of honor upon her faith, 'O woman, great is your faith!' It may be a strong faith, though it does not see the print of the nails! It is a heroic faith which can swim against wind and tide, and believe against hope. Christ sets the crown upon the head of faith—not of assurance! John 20:29, 'Blessed are those who have not seen, and yet have believed.'

6. God has most care of weak believers. The mother tends the weak child the most. 'God will gather the lambs with his arms, and carry them in his bosom.' The Lord has a great care of his weak tribes: when Israel marched towards Canaan, the tribes were divided into several companies or brigades: now it is observable, all the weak tribes were not put together, lest they should discourage one another, and so have fainted in their march. But God puts a strong tribe with two weak tribes; as Issachar, Zebulun, two weak tribes, and Judah a victorious tribe. Therefore he gives the lion in his standard. Surely this was not without a mystery, to show what care God has of his weak children! Christ the lion of the tribe of Judah shall be joined to them.

7. Weak faith is a growing faith. It is resembled by the grain of mustard-seed, which, of all seeds, is the least. But when it is full-grown, it is the 'greatest among herbs, and becomes a tree, so that the birds of the air come and lodge in its branches.' Faith must have a growing time. The seed springs up by degrees, first the blade, and then the ear; and then the full corn in the ear. The strongest faith had once been weak. The faith that has been renowned in the world, was once in its infancy. Grace is like the waters of the sanctuary, which rose higher and higher. Wait on the ordinances, these are the breasts to nourish faith. Do not be discouraged at your weak faith; though it be now in the blossom and bud, it will come to the full flower.

Objection 3. 'But,' says a child of God, 'I fear I am not elected!'

Answer. What! a believer—and not elected? Who told you that you were not elected? Have you seen your name in the black book of reprobation? Even the angels cannot unclasp this book—and will you meddle with it? Which is our duty to study, God's secret will, or his revealed will? It is a sin for any man to say he is a reprobate—as that which keeps him in sin, must needs be a sin. This opinion keeps him in sin, it cuts the sinews of endeavor. Who will take pains for heaven—who gives himself up for lost? O believer, be of good comfort, you need not look into the book of God's decree—but look into the book of your heart, see what is written there! He who finds the Bible copied out into his heart—his nature transformed, the bias of his will changed, the signature and engravings of the Holy Spirit upon him—this man does not look like a reprobate!

When you see the fruits of the earth spring up, you conclude the sun has been there! It is hard to climb up into election. But if we find the fruits of holiness springing up in our hearts—we may conclude the Sun of Righteousness has risen there, 2 Thes. 2:13. 'God has from the beginning chosen you to salvation through sanctification of the Spirit.' By our sanctification we must calculate our election. Indeed, God in saving us, begins at the highest link of the chain, election; but we must begin at the lowest link of the chain, sanctification, and so ascend higher.

Therefore laying aside all disputes, let me pour in of the wine of consolation. You who are a believer, (and though you will not affirm it—yet you cannot deny it without sin) let me do two things, show you your happiness, then your duty.

1. Behold your happiness! All the things which you have heard of, present and to come—are your portion and privilege! What shall I say to you? All my expressions fall short! When I speak of things to come, I know not how to express myself but by a deep silence and astonishment. O the magnitude and magnificence of the saints' glory! The ascent to it is so high, that it is too high for any man's thoughts to climb! The most sublime spirit, would here be too low and insipid. How happy are you, O believer! If God himself can make you blessed, you shall be so! If being invested with Christ's robes, enameled with his beauty, replenished with his love—if all the dimensions of glory will make you blessed, you shall be so! O the infinite superlative happiness of a believer! All things to come are his!

What! To have a partnership with the angels, those blessed spirits! Nay, to speak with reverence, to have a partnership with God himself! To be enriched with the same glory which sparkled forth in the human nature of Christ! How amazing is this! The thoughts of it are enough to swallow us up! O what an inheritance is he born to, who is new-born! Suppose he is poor in the world, and despised, I say to him as our Savior, 'Blessed are you who are poor, for yours is the kingdom of God!' All things to come are yours! Who would not be a believer! O that I might tempt such to Christ—who as yet hold out against him!

Chapter 22. Showing the duties of a believer—in response to God's astonishing mercy.

There are several duties which I would press upon believers; and they branch themselves into ten particulars.

1. If you have such a glorious inheritance to come—admire, and thankfully adore the love of God in settling this rich charter upon you! You who are mirrors of mercy should be monuments of praise. How was David affected with God's goodness? 2 Sam. 7:19, 'You have spoken of your servant's house for a great while to come.' So should we say, 'Lord, you have not only given us things present—but you have spoken of your servants for a great while to come, nay, forever!' It will be a great part of our work in heaven, to admire God; let us begin to do that work now—which we shall be forever doing.

Adore free grace! Free grace is the hinge on which all this astonishing mercy turns! Every link in this golden chain is richly enameled with free grace! Free grace has provided us a plank after shipwreck. When things past were forfeited—God has given us things to come! When we had lost paradise—he has provided heaven! Thus are we raised a step higher—by our fall. Set the crown upon the head of free grace! O to what a seraphic frame of spirit, should our hearts be raised! How should we join with angels and archangels in blessing God for this! It is well there is an eternity coming; and truly that will be little enough time, to praise God.

Say as that sweet singer of Israel, Psalm 103:1, 'Bless the Lord, O my soul'; or as the original will bear, 'Bow the knee, O my soul, before the Lord!' Thus should a Christian say, 'All things in heaven and earth are mine, God has settled this great portion upon me! Bow the knee, O my soul!' Praise God with the best instrument, the heart, and let the instrument be pitched up to the highest pitch—do it with the whole heart. When God is tuning upon the string of mercy—a Christian should be tuning upon the string of praise! I have given you a taste of this new wine — yet so full of spirits is it, that a little of it would inflame the heart in thankfulness. Let me call upon you, who are the heirs apparent to this rich inheritance, 'Things present and to come;' that you would get your hearts elevated, and wound up to a thankful frame!

It is not a handsome posture, to see a Christian ever complaining when things go contrary. O do not so look upon your troubles — as to forget your mercies. Bless God for what is to come! To heighten your praises, consider God gives you not only these things — but he gives you himself! It was Augustine's prayer: 'Lord,' says he, 'Whatever you have given me, take all away, only give me yourself!' Christian! You have not only the gift but the Giver! O take the harp and violin! If you do not bless God — who shall? Where will God get his praise? He has but a little in the world. Praise is in itself a high angelic work, and requires the highest spirited Christians to perform it. Wicked men cannot praise God. Indeed, who can praise God for these glorious privileges to come — but he who has the seal of the Spirit to assure him that all is his? O that I might persuade the people of God to be thankful, 'make God's praise glorious.' Let me tell you, God is much pleased with this thankful frame. Repentance is the joy of heaven; but thankfulness is the music of heaven! Let not God lack his music! Let it not be said, that God has more murmurers than musicians. 'Whoever offers praise, glorifies me.'

2. If we have such a glorious inheritance to come — live suitable to these glorious hopes! You who look for things to come, let me tell you, God looks for something present from you; namely, that you live suitably to your hopes. 'What kind of people ought you to be?' 2 Pet. 3:21. You have heard what kind of privileges you shall have; yes — but what kind of people ought you to be! Those who look to differ from others in their condition, must differ from them also in their conversation and lifestyle. Therefore beloved, 'seeing you look for such things, be diligent that you may be found of him in peace, without spot.' We would all be glad to be found of God in peace — then labor to be found without spot. Spot not your faces, spot not your consciences; live as those who are the citizens and nobles of this New Jerusalem above. Walk as Christ did, when he was upon earth. There are three steps, in which we should follow Christ.

1. Live HOLY. His life was a holy life. 'Who of you convinces me of sin?' Though he was made sin — yet he knew no sin. The very devils acknowledged his holiness: 'We know you who you are — the Holy One of God.' O be like Christ; tread in his steps. In the sacrament, 'we show forth the Lord's death,' and in a holy walk, we show forth his life. The holy oil, with which the vessels of the sanctuary were to be consecrated, was compounded of the purest ingredients. This was a type and emblem of that sanctity which should rest upon the godly: their hearts and lives should be consecrated with the holy oil of the Spirit. Holiness of life is the ornament of the gospel, it credits religion. Sozomen observes, that the devout life of a poor captive Christian woman moved a king and his whole family to embrace the Christian faith. Whereas how does it eclipse, and as it were, entomb the honor of religion, when men profess they are going to heaven — yet there is nothing of heaven in them? If there is light in the lantern — it will shine out. Just so, if grace is in the heart — it will shine forth in the life.

The looseness of professors' lives — is a great sin to be bewailed. Even those whom we hope (by the rule of charity) have the sap of grace in their heart — yet do not give forth such a sweet fragrance in their lives! How many under the notion of Christian liberty, degenerate into libertinism! The lives of some professors are so bad — that it would make profane men afraid to embrace the Christian religion!

If a stranger should come from beyond the ocean, and see the loose lives of many professors — their covetousness, and their licentiousness; and had he no other Bible to read in, but the lives of some professors, he would turn back again and resolve never to be made a Christian. What a shame is this! Did Christ walk thus — when he was upon earth? His life was a pattern of sanctity! You who are professors, your sins are sins of unkindness; they go nearest to Christ's heart. Do you live as those who have hope of eternal felicity? Is Christ preparing heaven for you—and are you preparing war against him? Is this your kindness to your friend! O consider how you wound religion! Your sins are worse than others! A stain in a black cloth is not easily seen or taken notice of; but a spot in a piece of white linen, everyone's eye is upon it.

The sins of wicked men are not much wondered at, they can do nothing else but sin—theirs is a spot on black. But a sin in a professor, this is like a spot on white linen, everyone's eye is upon it! How does this dishonor the gospel? Is it not sad, that others should make a rod of your sin—to lash the gospel? The deviation of the godly, is as odious as the devotion of the profane. O that there were such a luster and majesty of holiness in the lives of professors, that others might say, 'These look as if they had been with Jesus! They live as if they were in heaven already!' Aaron must not only have bells for sound—but pomegranates, which were for savor. It is not enough to discourse of godliness, or to make a noise by a profession. What are these bells without the pomegranates; namely, a life which casts no fragrance in the church of God!

2. Walk as Christ did, in humility. His life was a pattern of humility. He was the heir of heaven, the Godhead was in him, 'yet he took on him the form of a servant,' Phil. 2:7. O infinite humility—for a Savior to become a servant; for the Lord of glory to lay aside his robe, and put on rags; as if a king should leave his throne, and serve at table! Nay, that is not all—but Christ washes his disciples' feet. 'He poured water into a basin, and began to wash his disciples' feet, and to wipe them with the towel,' John 13:5. No wonder it is said that he came in the form of a servant; he stands here with his basin of water and a towel! Yes, to express the depth of his humility, he was made in the likeness of men. O how did Christ abase himself in taking flesh! it was more humility in Christ to humble himself to the womb—than to the cross. It was not so much for flesh to suffer—but for God to be made flesh—this was the wonder of humility! We read that Christ's flesh is called a veil, Heb. 10:20. 'Through the veil, his flesh'; indeed the taking of flesh was the wearing of a veil. By putting this dark veil upon himself, he eclipsed the glory of the Deity. This was Christ's 'emptying of himself,' Phil. 2. The metaphor may allude to a vessel full of wine that is drawn out; Christ, in whom all fullness dwells, by humility seemed to be so drawn out, as if there had been nothing left in him. Behold here a rare pattern of humility!

You who look for the eternal inheritance—tread in this step of Christ— be humble! Grace shines brightest through the mask of humility! Humility is such a precious herb as grows not in the garden of philosophy, that is rather humanity than humility. Humility beautifies us. The humble saint looks like a citizen of heaven. Humility is the veil of a Christian: Christ's bride never looks more beautiful in his eyes, than when she has on this veil of humility. 'Be clothed with humility.' Or as the Greek word is, be knotted. Humility is the spangled knot in the garment of our graces.

Humility sweetens our duties. Incense smells sweetest when it is beaten small. When the incense of our duties is beaten small with humility, then it sends forth its most fragrant perfume. The violet is a sweet flower; it hangs down the head so low, that it can hardly be seen, and only discovers itself by its scent. This is the emblem of humility.

The humble Christian studies his own unworthiness. He looks with one eye upon grace—to keep his heart cheerful; and with the other eye upon sin—to keep it humble. Better is that sin which humbles me, than that duty which makes me proud! As humility hides another's error—so it hides its own graces. Humility looks upon another's virtues—and its own infirmities. The humble man admires that in another which he slights in himself. He is one who does not deny only his evil things—but his good things. He is one who does not deny only his sins but his duties. He desires to have atonement made even for the pious duties.

The humble Christian is no murmurer — yet he is ever complaining. The more knowledge he has, the more he complains of ignorance. The more faith he has, the more he complains of unbelief. In short, the humble Christian translates all the glory — from himself — to Christ. Constantine use to write the name of Christ upon his doors. Just so, does the humble soul write Christ and free-grace upon his duties! 'I labored more abundantly than they all; yet not I — but the grace of God which was with me!' When he prays, he says — 'it is the Spirit who helps my infirmities.' When he mourns for sin, he says, 'the Almighty makes my heart soft.' When his heart is in a good frame, he says, 'By the grace of God I am what I am.' When he conquers a corruption, he says, 'It is through Christ, who strengthens me.'

As Joab, when he had gotten a victory, sends for king David that he might carry away the crown; just so does the humble Christian, when he has gotten the victory over a corruption, he sets the crown upon the head of Christ! O blessed humility! You who look for things above, let me tell you — the way to ascend is to descend! The lower the tree roots — the higher it shoots up! Would you shoot up in glory, would you be tall cedars in the kingdom of God? Be deeply rooted in humility. Humility is compared by some — to a valley. We must walk to heaven, through this valley of humility. Humility distinguishes Christ's spouse, from harlots. Hypocrites grow in knowledge — but not in humility. 'Knowledge puffs up,' 1 Cor. 8:1. It is a metaphor taken from a pair of bellows that are blown up and filled with wind. He who is proud of his knowledge, the devil cares not how much he knows. It is observable in the old law, that God hated the very semblance of the sin of pride. He would have no honey mingled in their offering; 'You shall burn no leaven, nor any honey in any offering of the Lord made by fire,' Lev. 2:1. Indeed, leaven is sour — but what is there in honey that should offend? Why no honey? because honey, when it is mingled with meal, makes it to rise and swell: therefore the people of Israel must mingle no honey in their offering. This was to let us see how God hated the semblance of this sin of pride. Be humble.

3. Be like Christ in love. Christ's life was a life of love. He breathed nothing but love; he was full of this sweet perfume! As his person was lovely, so was his disposition! He was composed all of love: his lips dropped honey, his side dropped blood, his heart dropped love. You who expect these glorious things to come — live as Christ did — live in love! O that this spice might send out its fragrant smell among Christians! 'We know that we have passed from death to life, because we love the brethren.' Do you love the person of Christ, and hate the picture? 'Everyone who loves the Father loves his children, too.' There are two devils which are not fully cast out of God's own people; the devil of vain-glory, and the devil of uncharitableness! Are we not fellow-citizens? Do we not all expect the same heaven? Nay, are we not brethren? This should be a sufficient bond to knit us together in amity. We have all the same Father, God; we are born of the same mother, the Church; we are begotten of the same seed, the Word; we suck the same breasts, the promises; we feed at the same table, the Table of the Lord; we all wear the same clothing, the Robe of Christ's Righteousness; we are partners in the same glory, the inheritance of the saints in light. Shall we not love one another!

You who look for things to come — live suitably to your hopes! Walk as Christ did, that some of his beams may shine in you, and his life may be copied out in yours!

3. If we have such a glorious inheritance to come — be content, though you have the less of present things. A believer is to be valued, according to that which is in eternity. Things to come are his. If you were to take an estimate of a man's estate — would you value it by that which he has in his house, or by his land? Perhaps he has little in his house, little money or decorations. But he has a rich inheritance coming — there lies his estate. While we are in this house of clay, we have but little. Many a Christian can hardly keep life and soul together; but he has a rich

inheritance coming! So be content with less of present things. It is sufficient if we have but enough for our necessities, until we come to heaven!

An heir who has a great estate beyond the sea, will be content, though he has but little money for his voyage there! Should not Hagar have been content, though the water were spent in her bottle, when there was a well so near? God has given Christ to a believer, and in him all things, 'things present and to come,' grace and glory! Is not this enough to make him content? 'But,' says the Christian, 'I want present comforts.' Consider, the angels in heaven are rich — yet they have no money. You have things to come — angels' riches, so be content then, with the less of present things. If you complain of anything — let it be of your complaining.

4. If we have such a glorious inheritance to come — labor for such a high degree of faith, as to make these future blessings, to become present realities. Faith and hope are two sisters, and are very alike. But they differ thus; hope looks at the excellency of the promise, faith looks at the certainty of it. Now faith looking at the infallible truth of him who promises, thus it makes things to come, present. Faith does antedate glory; it does substantiate things not seen. Faith alters the tenses — it puts the future into the present tense, Psalm 60:7, 'Gilead is mine, Manasseh is mine, Ephraim is the strength of my head,' etc. Those places were not yet subdued — but God had spoken in his holiness, he had made David a promise, and he believed it, therefore he looked upon it as already subdued: Gilead is mine, etc. 'Just so,' says faith, 'God has spoken in his holiness; he has made me a promise of things to come; therefore heaven is mine already!'

When one will shortly have the inheritance of a house, he says, 'this house is mine!' O that we had this art of faith, thus to anticipate heaven, and make things to come present. You who are a believer — heaven is yours now! Your head is already glorified; nay, heaven is begun in you — you have some of those joys which are the first fruits of it. A Christian, by the eye of faith, through the telescope of the promise — may see into heaven. Faith sees the promise fulfilled before it is fulfilled. Faith sets it down as already recieved — before it is paid. Had we a vigorous faith, we might be in heaven before our time! That which a weak believer hopes for — a strong believer does in some measure, possess. Oh that we could often take a prospect of the heavenly paradise: 'Go, inspect the city of Jerusalem. Walk around and count the many towers. Take note of the fortified walls, and tour all the citadels,' Psalm 48:12, 13. So, go and inspect your heavenly inheritance, see what a glorious situation it is, go count her towers, see what an inheritance you have! O that every day — we could thus look by faith into our heavenly inheritance!

Do not say, 'all this shall be mine;' but say, 'all this is mine already! My head is there, my faith is there, my heart is there!' Could we thus, living up to the height of our faith, realize and enter into things to come — how would all present things vanish! If a man could live in the sun — the earth would not appear! When Paul had been enraptured up into the third heaven, the earth did hardy appear ever after! See how he scorns it, 'I am crucified to the world!' It was a dead thing to him, he had begun heaven already. Thus it is with a man who is heavenized. You saints who are earthly — the eye of your faith is bloodshot! It is the character of a sinner, 'he cannot see afar off'; like a man who has bad eyes, who can see only things which are just before him. Faith carries the heart up to heaven — and brings heaven down into the heart!

5. If we have such a glorious inheritance to come — then walk CHEERFULLY with God. Put on your white robes! Has a believer a title to heaven? What — and sad! 'We rejoice in hope of the glory of God!' Romans 5:2. It is but a little while — it is but putting off the earthly clothes of our body — and we shall be clothed with the bright robes of glory! And can a believer be sad! See how Christ does secretly check his disciples for this, Luke 24:17. What, sad — and Christ risen!

So I say to believers — things to come are yours! How can you be sad? Let them be sad — who have no hope. O rejoice in God!

When the lead of the flesh begins to sink, let the cork of faith swim above! How does the heir rejoice in hope of the inheritance! How does the slave rejoice to think of ending his time of service! Here on earth, we are harassed by sin, and a child of God is forced sometimes to do the devil's work — but shortly death will make us free! There is an eternal jubilee coming, therefore 'rejoice in hope of the glory of God!' Can wicked men rejoice that have their portion in this life? And cannot he rejoice, who has an inheritance in heaven? Can the waters of Abanah and Pharphar compare to the waters of Jordan?

O you saints, think into what a blessed condition you are now brought! Is it not a sweet thing to have God appeased? Is it not a matter of joy to be an heir of the promise? Adam in paradise had choice of all the trees, one only excepted. The promises are the trees of life — you may walk in the garden of the Bible, and pluck from all these trees. Who should rejoice — if not a Christian? He has never so much cause to be sad — as he has to be cheerful.

Objection: 1. But my sins trouble me.

Answer. This is true. That sin will not forsake you — is matter of sadness; but that you have forsaken sin — is matter of joy! Sin is a heavy weight upon you. That you cannot run so fast as you desire, in the ways of God, is matter of sadness. But that you go without halting (in regard of righteousness) this is matter of joy! And for your comfort remember, shortly you shall sin no more — all things shall be yours — but sin!

Objection 2. But we are bid to mourn.

Answer. I would not speak against holy mourning; while we carry fire about us, we must carry water. That is, as long as the fire of sin burns in our breasts, we must carry tears to quench it. But consider,

1. Spiritual joy and mourning are not inconsistent. Sometimes it rains and shines at once: when there is a shower in the eyes, there may be a sunshine in our heart. Mourning and music may stand together; the great mourner in Israel, was the sweet singer of Israel.

2. The end why God makes us sad, is to make us rejoice; he does not require sorrow for sorrow — but it is ordained to be as sauce to make our joy relish the better. We sow in tears — that we may reap in joy.

3. The sweetest joy is from the sourest tears. Christ made the best wine — from water. The purest and most excellent joy, is made of the waters of true repentance. The bee gathers the best honey from the bitterest herbs. Tears are the breeders of spiritual joy. After Hannah had wept, she went away, and was no longer sad. Those clouds are very uncomfortable, which never have any sunshine. Just so, that mourning which dyes the soul all in sable, which has no place for rejoicing, I would rather think it despair, than true remorse. The same God who has bid us mourn, has also bid us rejoice, Phil. 4:4. It is an excellent temper to be serious — yet cheerful. Jesus Christ loves the joyful Christian. Joy puts liveliness and activity into a Christian, it oils the wheels of the affections. A heavy mind makes a dull action. The joy of the Lord is your strength.

The pensive, melancholy Christian, disparages the glory of heaven. What will others say? Here is one who speaks of future glory — but surely he does not believe it — see how sad he is! What ado is here on earth, to make a child of God cheerful! Must we have to force an heir, to rejoice in the estate which has befallen him? Let me tell you, you who refuse consolation, are not fit people to praise God — it is a contradiction to praise God with a sad heart: 'I will sing praises,' Psalm 108:1. It is more proper to sing praises, than to weep them. Rejoice, O Christian, lift up your crest, triumph in the hope of these things to come. It is not enough that there is joy within the Christian's heart—but it must shine forth in his countenance.

6. If we have such a glorious inheritance to come—let him not envy those who have only present things. God often wrings out the waters of a full cup to wicked men; but there are dregs at the bottom! Indeed, the prosperity of sinners is a great temptation. David stumbled at it, and had almost fallen. Psalm 73, 'My feet had well near slipped!' It is not matter of envy but pity—to see men thrive in a way of sin! Do you envy a fool is in mirthful clothes? Do you envy a condemned man, who is going up the ladder to be hung—simply because he has a rich coat? 'Those who will be rich, fall into temptations and a snare,' 1 Tim. 6:9. Do you envy a man who is fallen into a snare? Wicked men have that guilt which embitters their comforts. They are like a man who has great possessions—yet having a fit of the stone or gout, while he is in that torment, he may be said not to have them, because the comfort of them is taken away. A believer has better things than these—an blissful inheritance! Wicked men have a crown of unrighteousness, but you have a crown of righteousness! They have rich robes, but you have the bright robe of glory. 'Envy not the oppressor, and choose none of his ways.' Better is sanctified adversity than successful impiety.

7. If we have such a glorious inheritance to come—be supported in lack of spiritual comfort. Spiritual joy is a sweet thing; this is the hidden manna, the cluster of grapes which grow upon the true vine; this is the saints' banqueting stuff; how sweet is it to have Word, and Spirit, and Conscience speaking peace! in the mouth of these three witnesses, faith is confirmed. 'But,' says the poor soul that goes mourning, 'It is not so with me, I have not the secret seal of heaven, I lack assurance.' Well, do not give up waiting. We read that the disciples were in the ship, and there arose a great storm, 'And when they had rowed about three or four miles, they saw Jesus.' This, O Christian, may be your case: there is a tempest of sorrow risen in your heart; and you have rowed from one ordinance to another, and have no comfort! Well, be not discouraged, do not give up rowing; you have but rowed three or four miles; perhaps when you has rowed a little more—you may see Jesus, and have a comfortable evidence of his love!

But suppose you should row all your life long, and not have assurance—yet this may be a pillar of support—things to come are yours! It is but waiting a while—and you shall be brimful of comfort! A believer is now an heir of this joy; let him wait until he is of age, and he shall be fully possessed of the joys of heaven. For the present, God leaves a seed of comfort in the heart; there is a time shortly coming, when we shall have the full flower; we shall drink of the fruit of the vine in the kingdom of heaven! As Paul said of Onesimus, Philem. verse 15, 'For perhaps he therefore departed for a season, that you might receive him forever.' So I say of the comforts of God's Spirit—that they may be withdrawn for a season, that we may have them forever! There is a time coming when we shall bathe ourselves in the rivers of divine pleasure.

8. If we have such a glorious inheritance to come—let us zealously contend for it against all oppositions. We have a city above—but there are enemies in the way which we must give battle to. God would give Israel Canaan, a land flowing with milk and honey; but first they must encounter with the sons of Anak. So he will bestow upon us a crown—but we must fight for it. Heaven is not taken without storm. Hence it is the scripture bids us to 'fight the good fight of faith,' 1 Tim. 6:12, that we may not through a slothful negligence lose the recompense of a reward. Christians must be military people; it befits the children of light to put on the armor of light. The apostle reckons up our several pieces of armor; the shield of faith, the helmet of hope, the breastplate of righteousness; and our weapons—the sword of the Spirit, the cannon-bullet of prayer. Indeed in heaven our armor shall be hung up in token of victory and triumph; but now

it is a day of battle, and no cessation of arms, until death. And there is a threefold regiment we must fight against, which would hinder us of our eternal crown.

1. The enemy within, namely, a treacherous heart. This is a sly enemy; 'A man's enemies are those of his own house,' Mic. 7:6, nay, of his own heart! Man by his fall lost his head-piece, namely, spiritual wisdom, and ever since he is an enemy to himself. He lays a snare for his own blood, Proverbs 1:18, therefore Augustine prays, 'Lord deliver me from that evil man—myself!' The heart is a conclave of wickedness. It is an armory and magazine, where all the weapons of unrighteousness lie. The heart holds conference with Satan—and it sides with him—at every turn is ready to deliver up the keys to him. This is good reason why we should gird on our armor, and give battle to this bosom traitor, which stands in our way to the heavenly crown.

It is reported of Basil, that to shun the allurements and flatteries of the world, he retired and fled into the wilderness; but when he was there, he cries out against his heart, 'I have forsaken all—but my evil heart is still tempting me!' Luther used to say, that he feared his heart more than pope or cardinals. Your heart, O Christian, would supplant you of the eternal inheritance. O therefore make a brave fight, run the sword of the Spirit up to the hilt, in the blood of your sins! Stab your heart-lusts to the heart with the knife of mortification! If the flesh does war against us, good reason we should war against the flesh.

2. The second regiment that stands in the way to salvation, and which we must arm against, is the devil. He may be called a regiment, for his name being Legion. This is the red regiment! How furiously does he make his onset upon us, sometimes with temptations, sometimes with persecutions, that if possible we might let fall our armor, and so let go our crown! The devil, that roaring lion, while we are marching to heaven, raises all the bands of hell against us; 'whom resist, steadfast in the faith,' 1 Pet. 5:9. Our enemy is beaten in part already, he knows no march but running away.

3. The third regiment which stands in our way to heaven is the world. This enemy courts us. It smiles that it may deceive. It kills by embracing! It has a golden apple in one hand—and a dagger in the other! Marcia gave to the emperor Commodus poison, in sweet wine. Such an aromatic cup does the world present us with—that we may drink and die. The ivy, while it clasps about the oak, sucks away the heart of it for its own leaves and berries; such are the world's embraces. 'The one I kiss,' says Judas, 'is the man; arrest him and lead him away.' So, whom the world kisses—it often betrays. The world is a silken halter. The world is a golden fetter. Some have been drowned in the sweet waters of pleasure! Others have been choked in silver mines! Oh arm, arm against this flattering enemy! 'You adulterous people, don't you know that friendship with the world is hatred toward God? Anyone who chooses to be a friend of the world becomes an enemy of God.' James 4:4

If the world's music enchants us, and we fall asleep upon our guard, then the devil falls on, and wounds us. Fight it out against all these regiments.

Consider the excellency of the prize! Things to come! What striving is there for earthly crowns and scepters! with what zeal and alacrity did Hannibal continue his march over the Alps, and Caesar's soldiers fight with hunger and cold? Men will break through laws and oaths, run a thousand hazards for those things which, when they have them, will prove damnable gains. But 'things to come are yours.' You expect salvation, which is the crown of your desires, the flower of your ambition; oh therefore muster and rally together all your forces against this three-headed adversary which stands in your way to hinder you from taking possession. Fight it out to the death, you have a good captain; Christ is 'the Captain of your salvation,' Heb. 2:10. If a flock of sheep have a lion for their captain, what need they fear? So, fear not little flock, you fight under the Lion of the tribe of Judah.

9. If we have such a glorious inheritance to come — if all Christ's things are ours — then all our things must be Christ's.

Justice and equity require it. There is a joint interest between Christ and a believer Christ says, 'All that is mine — is yours!' Then the heart of a believer must echo back to Christ, 'Lord, all that is mine — is yours!' It was the saying of a holy man, 'Lord, you are my all; and my all is yours.' Oh be willing to spend, and be spent; do, and suffer for Christ.

1. Let us, with all our might, advance the honor and interest of Jesus Christ! Alas, what is all that we can do? If a king should bestow upon a person, a million dollars per year, with this proviso — that this person shall pay a peppercorn every year to the king; what proportion is there between this man's payment — and his revenue? Alas, we are but unprofitable servants; all that we can do for Christ is not so much as this peppercorn! Yet up, and be doing! Christ hates compliments: we must not only bow the knee to him — but, with the wise men, present him with gifts of gold, frankincense, and myrrh. Do not be like the sons of Belial, who brought their king no presents. 'But,' says the Christian, 'I am poor, and can do little for Christ.' Can you not bestow your love upon Christ? In the law, he who could not afford a lamb for an offering, if he brought but two turtle-doves, it was sufficient. The woman in the gospel threw in only her two mites — yet she was accepted. God is not angry with any man because he has but one talent — but because he does not use it.

2. Suffer for Christ, be willing to sell all, nay, to lose all for Christ. We may be losers for him, we shall never be losers by him. If he calls for our blood, let us not deny it him; we have no such blood to shed for Christ — as he has shed for us. It was Luther's saying, 'That in the cause of God he was content to endure the odium and fury of the whole world.' Basil affirms of the primitive saints, they had so much courage in their sufferings, that many of the heathens, seeing their heroic zeal, turned Christians. They snatched up torments as so many crowns! O think nothing too dear for Christ! We who look for things to come, should be willing to part with things present for Christ.

10. Lastly, If we have such a glorious inheritance to come — be content to wait for these great privileges. It is not incongruous to long for Christ's appearing, and yet to wait for it. You see the glory which a believer shall be invested with; but though the Lord gives a large portion, he may set a long day for the payment. David had the promise of a crown — but was long before he came to wear it. God will not deny his promise — yet he may delay his promise, to teach us to wait. It is but a shortsighted faith, which cannot wait. The farmer waits for the seed. There is a seed of glory sown in a believer's heart; wait until it springs up into a harvest.

Truly, it is a hard thing to wait for these things to come. There are so many discouragements from without, so many distempers from within, that the Christian desires to be at home with Christ. Therefore we need patience, Heb. 10:36, 'For you have need of patience.' But how shall we get it? Nourish faith. verse 35, 'So do not throw away your confidence; it will be richly rewarded.' Patience is nothing else but faith spun out; if you would lengthen patience, be sure to strengthen faith.

There are great reasons why a believer should be content to wait for heaven.

1. God is faithful who promises. God's word is security enough to venture upon. All the world hangs upon the word of his power; and cannot our faith hang upon the word of his promise? We have His hand and seal, nay, his oath!

2. While we are waiting, God is tuning and fitting us for glory. 'Giving thanks to the Father, who has made us fit for the inheritance,' Col. 1:12. We must be made fit. Perhaps our hearts are not humble enough, or not patient enough. Perhaps our faith is but in its infancy. We should be content to wait a while, until we have gotten such a vigorous faith as will carry us full sail to heaven! As there is a ripening and a fitting of vessels for hell, Romans 9:22, so there is a ripening and a preparing of the vessels of mercy, verse 23. A Christian should be willing to wait for glory, until he is fit to take his inheritance.

3. While we are waiting, our glory is increasing. While we are laying out for God – he is laying up for us, 2 Tim. 4:8. If we suffer for God, the heavier our cross – the heavier shall be our crown. Would a Christian be in the meridian of glory? Would he have his robes shine bright? Let him stay here and do service; God will reward us, though not for our works – yet according to our works, Mark 16:27. The longer we keep the principal, the greater will the interest be.

The longer a Christian lives, the more glory he may bring to God. Faith is an ingenuous grace; as it has one eye at the reward, so it has another eye at duty. The time of life is the only time we have to work for God. Heaven is a place of receiving; this world is a place of doing. Hence the apostle being inflamed with divine love, though he desired with all his heart be with Christ – yet he was content to live a while longer, that he might build up souls, and make the crown flourish upon the head of Christ.

It is self-love which says, 'Who will show us any good?' Divine love says, 'How may I do good?' The prodigal son could say, 'Father, give me my portion!' He thought more of his portion than his duty. A gracious spirit is content to stay out of heaven a while – that he may be a means to bring others there. He whose heart has been divinely touched with the love of God, his care is not so much for receiving the talents of gold, as for improving the talents of grace. O wait a while! Learn from the saints of old, they waited patiently. If we cannot wait now, what would we have done in the times of the long-lived patriarchs? Look upon worldly men, they wait for pleasures. Shall they wait for earth – and cannot we wait for heaven! If a man has the promise of a grand estate, when such a lease is out, will he not wait for it? We have the promise of heaven when the lease of life is run out; and shall we not wait?

Look upon wicked men, they wait for an opportunity to sin; the adulterer waits for the twilight; sinners 'lie in wait for their own blood,' Proverbs 1:18. Shall men wait for their damnation, and shall not we be content to wait for our salvation? Wait without murmuring, wait without fainting! The things we expect are infinitely more than we can hope for.

And let me add one caution; 'wait on the Lord and keep to his ways,' Psalm 37:34. While we are waiting, let us take heed of wavering. Go not a step out of God's way, though a lion be in the way. Do not avoid duty – to meet with safety. Keep to God's highway, 'the good old way,' Jer. 6:16, the way which is paved with holiness, Isaiah 25:8. 'And a highway shall be there, and it shall be called the way of holiness.' Avoid crooked paths, take heed of turning to the left hand, lest you be set on the left hand! Sin crosses our hopes; it barricades up our way. A man may as well expect to find heaven in hell, as in a sinful way.

My last use is to such as have only present things – that they would labor for things to come. You have seen the blessed condition of a man in Christ; never rest until this be yours. Alas, how poor and contemptible are these present earthly enjoyments, when laid in balance with things to come!

1. What is honor – which is the highest elevation of men's ambition? One calls honor – the gallant madness. It was foretold to Agrippina, Nero's mother, that her son would be emperor, and that he would afterward kill his own mother; to which Agrippina replied, 'let my son be

emperor, and then let him kill me and spare not' — so thirsty was she of honor. Alas, what are swelling titles but rattles to applaud men's ambition? Honor is like a gale of wind which carries the ship; sometimes this wind is down, a man has lost his honor, and lives to see himself entombed: sometimes this wind is too high: how many have been blown to hell, while they have been sailing with the wind of popular applause! Honor is but a glorious nothing! Acts 25:23. It does not make a man really the better — but often the worse. A man swelled with honor, lacking grace — his bigness is his disease and doom.

2. What are riches — that men so thirst after them? Amos 2:7, 'Who pant after the dust of the earth.' Golden dust will sooner choke than satisfy! How many have pulled down their souls to build up their houses! What a transiency and deficiency is there in all things under the sun? Christ, who had all riches, scorned these earthly riches. He was born poor — the feeding-trough was his cradle, the cobwebs his curtains. He lived poor — he had nowhere to lay his head. He died poor; he made no will; he had no crown-lands, only his coat was left, and that the soldiers parted among them. His funeral was fitting; for as he was born in another man's stable, so he was buried in another man's tomb; to show how he did despise earthly dignities and possessions. His kingdom was not of this world.

Suppose an hour of adversity comes, can these present earthly things quiet the mind in trouble? Riches are called thick clay, which will sooner break the back, than lighten the heart. When pangs of conscience and pangs of death come, and there is no hope of things to come, what peace can the world give at such a time? Surely it can yield no more comfort, than a silken stocking to a man whose leg is out of joint. A fresh color delights the eye; but if the eye be sore, this color will not heal it. 'Riches avail not in the day of wrath.' You can not hold your wedge of gold as a screen to keep off the fire of God's justice.

Let this sound a retreat to call us off from the immoderate pursuit of present things, to labor for things to come. What are these lower springs — compared to the upper springs? As Abraham said, 'Lord, what will you give me, seeing I go childless?' So say, 'Lord, what will you give me, seeing I go Christless?' Luther did solemnly protest, God should not put him off with these worldly things. Oh labor for those blessings in heavenly places. Earthly things may be pleasing — but they are not permanent.

Do not be content with a few earthly gifts: Abraham gave gifts unto the sons of the concubines, and sent them away; 'but unto Isaac, he gave all that he had.' Reprobates may have a few jewels and earrings which God scatters with an indifferent hand: these, like the sons of the concubines, are put off with a few earthly gifts. But labor for the eternal inheritance! Get into Christ, and then all is yours! So says the Apostle, 'All things are yours, and you belong to Christ!'

A Divine Cordial

And we know that all things work together for good to those who love God, to those who are the called according to His purpose.

Romans 8:28

Introduction

Christian Reader,

There are two things, which I have always looked upon as difficult. The one is — to make the wicked sad; the other is — to make the godly joyful. Dejection in the godly arises from a double spring: either because their inward comforts are darkened, or their outward comforts are disturbed. To cure both these troubles, I have put forth this ensuing treatise, hoping, by the blessing of God, that it will buoy up their desponding hearts, and make them look with a more pleasant aspect. I would prescribe them to take, now and then, a little of this Cordial: 'all things work together for good to those who love God.' To know that nothing hurts the godly, is a matter of comfort; but to be assured that all things which fall out shall cooperate for their good, that their crosses shall be turned into blessings, that showers of affliction water the withering root of their grace and make it flourish more — this may fill their hearts with joy until they run over!

If the whole Scripture be the feast for the soul (as Ambrose says) — then Romans 8 may be a dish at that feast, and with its sweet variety may very much refresh and animate the hearts of Gods people. In the preceding verses the apostle had been wading through the great doctrines of justification and adoption, mysteries so arduous and profound, that without the help and conduct of the Spirit, he might soon have waded beyond his depth. In this verse the apostle touches upon that pleasant string of consolation, 'we know that all things work together for good, to those who love God.' Not a word but is weighty; therefore I shall gather up every filing of this gold, that nothing will be lost.

In the text there are three general branches.

First, a glorious privilege. *All things work for good.*

Second, the people interested in this privilege. They are doubly specified. They are lovers of God; they are called.

Third, the origin and spring of this effectual calling, set down in these words, 'according to His purpose.'

I. First, the glorious privilege.

Here are two things to be considered:

1. The certainty of the privilege — 'We know.'

2. The excellency of the privilege — 'All things work together for good.'

1. The certainty of the privilege: 'We know.' It is not a matter wavering or doubt. The apostle does not say, 'We hope, or conjecture.' 'We know that all things work for good.' Hence observe that the truths of the gospel are evident and infallible.

A Christian may come not merely to a vague opinion, but to a certainty of what he holds. As axioms and aphorisms are evident to reason, so the truths of true religion are evident to faith. 'We know,' says the apostle. Though a Christian has not a perfect knowledge of the mysteries of the gospel — yet he has a certain knowledge. 'We see through a glass darkly' (1 Cor. x3:12), therefore we have not perfection of knowledge; but 'we behold with open face' (2 Cor. 3:18), therefore we have certainty. The Spirit of God imprints heavenly truths upon the heart, as with the point of a diamond. A Christian may know infallibly that there is an evil in sin, and a beauty in holiness. He may know that he is in the state of grace. 'We know that we have passed from death to life' (1 John 3:14).

He may know that he shall go to heaven. 'We know that if our earthly tabernacle were dissolved, we have a building of God, a house not made with hands, eternal in the heavens' (2 Cor. 5:1). The Lord does not leave His people at uncertainties in matters of salvation. The apostle says, 'We know. We have arrived at a holy confidence. We have both the Spirit of God, and our own experience, setting seal to it.'

Let us then not rest in skepticism or doubts—but labor to come to a certainty in the things of religion. As that martyr woman said, 'I cannot dispute for Christ—but I can burn for Christ.' God knows whether we may be called forth to be witnesses to His truth; therefore it concerns us to be well-grounded and confirmed in it. If we are doubting Christians, we shall be wavering Christians. Whence is apostasy, but from incredulity? Men first question the truth, and then fall from the truth. Oh, beg the Spirit of God, not only to anoint you, but to seal you (2 Cor. 1:22).

2. The excellency of the privilege. 'All things work together for good.'

This is as Jacob's staff in the hand of faith, with which we may walk cheerfully to the mount of God! What will satisfy or make us content, if this will not? All things work together for good. This expression 'work together' refers to medicine. Several poisonous ingredients put together, being tempered by the skill of the apothecary, make a sovereign medicine, and work together for the good of the patient. So all God's providences being divinely tempered and sanctified, do work together for the best to the saints. He who loves God and is called according to His purpose, may rest assured that everything in the world shall be for his good. This is a Christian's cordial, which may warm him—and make him like Jonathan who, when he had tasted the honey at the end of the rod, 'his eyes were enlightened' (1 Sam. xiv. 27). Why should a Christian destroy himself? Why should he kill himself with care, when all things shall sweetly concur, yes, conspire for his good? The result of the text is this—all the various dealings of God with His children, do by a special providence turn to their good. 'All the paths of the Lord are mercy and truth unto such as keep his covenant' (Psalm 25:10). If every path has mercy in it, then it works for good.

We shall consider, first, what things work for good to the godly; and here we shall show that both the best things and the worst things work for their good. We begin with the best things.

The best things work for good to the godly

1. God's attributes work for good to the godly.

(1). God's power works for good. It is a glorious power (Col. 1:11), and it is engaged for the good of the elect.

God's power works for good, in supporting us in trouble. 'Underneath are the everlasting arms' (Deut. 33:27). What upheld Daniel in the lion's den? What upheld Jonah in the whale's belly? What upheld the three Hebrews in the furnace? Only the power of God! Is it not strange to see a bruised reed grow and flourish? How is a weak Christian able, not only to endure affliction— but to rejoice in it? He is upheld by the arms of the Almighty. 'My strength is made perfect in weakness' (2 Cor. 12:9).

The power of God works for us by supplying our needs. God creates comforts, when means fail. He who brought food to the prophet Elijah by ravens, will bring sustenance to His people. God can preserve the 'oil in the cruse' (1 Kings x7:14). The Lord made the sun on Ahaz's dial go ten degrees backward: so when our outward comforts are declining, and the sun is almost setting, God often causes a revival, and brings the sun many degrees backward.

The power of God subdues our corruptions. 'He will subdue our iniquities' (Micah 7:19). Is your sin strong? God is powerful, He will break the head of this leviathan. Is your heart hard? God will dissolve that stone in Christ's blood. 'The Almighty makes my heart soft' (Job 23:16). When we say as Jehoshaphat, 'We have no might against this great army'; the Lord goes up with us, and helps us to fight our battles. He strikes off the heads of those goliath lusts which are too strong for us!

The power of God conquers our enemies. He stains the pride, and breaks the confidence of adversaries. 'You shall break them with a rod of iron' (Psalm 2:9). There is rage in the enemy, and malice in the devil—but omnipotence in God. How easily can He rout all the forces of the wicked! 'It is nothing for you, Lord, to help' (2 Chr. xiv. 11). God's power is on the side of His church. 'Happy are you, O Israel, O people saved by the Lord, who is the shield of your help, and the sword of your excellency' (Deut. 33:29).

(2). The wisdom of God works for good. God's wisdom is our oracle to instruct us. As He is the mighty God, so also the Counselor (Isaiah 9:6). We are oftentimes in the dark, and, in intricate and doubtful matters, know not which way to take; here God comes in with light. 'I will guide you with my eye' (Psalm. 32:8). 'Eye,' there, is put for God's wisdom. Why is it, that the saints can see further than the most quick-sighted politicians? They foresee the evil, and hide themselves; they see Satan's sophisms. God's wisdom is the pillar of fire to go before, and guide them.

(3). The goodness of God works for good to the godly. God's goodness is a means to make us good. 'The goodness of God leads to repentance' (Romans 2:4). The goodness of God is a spiritual sunbeam to melt the heart into tears. 'Oh,' says the soul, 'has God been so good to me? Has He reprieved me so long from hell, and shall I grieve His Spirit any more? Shall I sin against God's goodness?'

The goodness of God works for good, as it ushers in all blessings. The favors we receive, are the silver streams which flow from the fountain of God's goodness. This divine attribute of goodness brings in two sorts of blessings. Common blessings: all partake of these, the bad as well as the good; this sweet dew falls upon the thistle as well as the rose. Crowning blessings: these only the godly partake of. 'Who crowns us with loving-kindness' (Psalm 103. 4). Thus the blessed attributes of God work for good to the saints.

2. The promises of God work for good to the godly.

The promises are God's bank notes. The promises are the milk of the gospel; and is not the milk for the good of the infant? They are called 'precious promises' (2 Pet. 1:4). They are as cordials to a soul that is ready to faint. The promises are full of virtue.

Are we under the guilt of sin? There is a promise, 'The Lord is merciful and gracious' (Exod. 34:6), where God as it were puts on His glorious embroidery, and holds out the golden scepter, to encourage poor trembling sinners to come to Him. 'The Lord is merciful and gracious.' God is more willing to pardon—than to punish. Mercy does more multiply in Him, than sin in us. Mercy is His nature. The bee naturally gives honey; it stings only when it is provoked. 'But,' says the guilty sinner, 'I cannot deserve mercy.' Yet He is gracious: He shows mercy, not because we deserve mercy—but because He delights in mercy. But what is that to me? Perhaps my name is not in the pardon. 'He keeps mercy for thousands!' The treasury of mercy is not exhausted. God has treasures lying by, and why should not you come in for a child's part?

Are we under the defilement of sin? There is a promise working for good. 'I will heal their backslidings' (Hos. 14:4). God will not only bestow mercy — but grace. And He has made a promise of sending His Spirit (Isaiah 44:3), which for His sanctifying nature, is in Scripture compared sometimes to water — which cleanses the vessel; sometimes to the fan — which winnows corn, and purifies the air; sometimes to fire — which refines metals. Thus the Spirit of God shall cleanse and consecrate the soul, making it partake of the divine nature.

Are we in great trouble? There is a promise which works for our good, 'I will be with him in trouble' (Psalm 91. 15). God does not bring His people into troubles, and leave them there. He will stand by them; He will hold their heads and hearts when they are fainting. And there is another promise, 'He is their strength in the time of trouble' (Psalm 37:39). 'Oh,' says the soul, 'I shall faint in the day of trial.' But God will be the strength of our hearts; He will join His forces with us. Either He will make His hand lighter — or our faith stronger!

Do we fear outward needs? There is a promise. 'Those who seek the Lord shall not lack any good thing' (Psalm 34:10). If it is good for us, we shall have it; if it is not good for us, then the withholding of it is good. 'I will bless your bread and your water' (Exod. 33:25). This blessing falls as the honey dew upon the leaf; it sweetens that little we possess. Let me lack the venison, so I may have the blessing. But I fear I shall not get a livelihood? Peruse that Scripture, 'I have been young, and now am old — yet have I not seen the righteous forsaken, nor his seed begging bread' (Psalm 37:25). How must we understand this? David speaks it as his own observation; he never beheld such an eclipse, he never saw a godly man brought so low that he had not a bit of bread to put in his mouth. David never saw the righteous and their seed lacking. Though the Lord might try godly parents a while by need — yet not their seed too; the seed of the godly shall be provided for. David never saw the righteous begging bread, and forsaken. Though he might be reduced to great straits — yet not forsaken; still he is an heir of heaven, and God loves him.

Question. How do the promises work for good?

Answer. They are food for faith; and that which strengthens faith works for good. The promises are the milk of faith; faith sucks nourishment from them, as the child from the breast. 'Jacob feared exceedingly' (Gen. 32:7). His spirits were ready to faint; now he goes to the promise, 'Lord, you have said you will do me good' (Gen. 32:12). This promise was his food. He got so much strength from this promise, that he was able to wrestle with the Lord all night in prayer, and would not let Him go until He had blessed him.

The promises also are springs of joy. There is more in the promises to comfort — than in the world to perplex. Ursin was comforted by that promise: 'No man shall pluck them out of my Father's hands' (John 10:29). The promises are cordials in a fainting fit. 'Unless your word had been my delight, I had perished in my affliction' (Psalm 119:92). The promises are as cork to the net, to bear up the heart from sinking in the deep waters of distress!

3. The mercies of God world for good to the godly.

The mercies of God humble. 'Then King David went in and sat before the Lord and prayed, 'Who am I, O Sovereign Lord, and what is my family, that you have brought me this far?' (2 Sam. 7:18). Lord, why is such honor conferred upon me, that I should be king? That I who followed the sheep, should be king over Your people? So says a gracious heart, 'Lord, who am I, that it should be better with me than others? That I should drink of the fruit of the vine, when others drink, not only a cup of wormwood — but a cup of blood (or suffering to death). Who am I, that I should have those mercies which others lack, who are better than I? Lord, why is it, that with all my unworthiness, a fresh tide of mercy comes in every day?' The mercies of God make a sinner proud—but a saint humble.

The mercies of God have a melting influence upon the soul; they dissolve it in love to God. God's judgments make us fear Him—but His mercies make us love Him. How was Saul wrought upon by kindness! David had him at the advantage, and might have cut off, not only the skirt of his robe—but his head; yet he spares his life. This kindness melted Saul's heart. 'Is this your voice, my son David? and Saul lifted up his voice, and wept' (1 Sam. 24:16). Such a melting influence has God's mercy; it makes the eyes drop with tears of love.

The mercies of God make the heart fruitful. When you lay out more cost upon a field, it bears a better crop. A gracious soul honors the Lord with his substance. He does not do with his mercies, as Israel with their jewels and ear rings, make a golden calf; but, as Solomon did with the money thrown into the treasury, build a temple for the Lord. The golden showers of Gods' mercy, cause fertility.

The mercies of God make the heart thankful. 'What shall I render unto the Lord for all his benefits towards me? I will take the cup of salvation' (Psalm 116:12, 13). David alludes to the people of Israel, who at their peace offerings used to take a cup in their hands, and give thanks to God for deliverances. Every mercy is an gift of free grace; and this enlarges the soul in gratitude. A godly Christian is not a grave to bury God's mercies—but a temple to sing His praises. 'If every bird in its kind,' as Ambrose says, 'chirps forth thankfulness to its Maker, much more will a sincere Christian, whose life is enriched and perfumed with mercy.'

The mercies of God quicken. As they are loadstones to love, so they are whetstones to obedience. 'I will walk before the Lord in the land of the living' (Psalm 116. 9). He who takes a review of his blessings, looks upon himself as a person engaged for God. He argues from the sweetness of mercy—to the swiftness of duty. He spends and is spent for Christ; he dedicates himself to God. Among the Romans, when one had redeemed another, he was afterwards to serve him. A soul encompassed with mercy, is zealously active in God's service.

The mercies of God work compassion to others. A Christian is a temporal Savior. He feeds the hungry, clothes the naked, and visits the widow and orphan in their distress; among them he sows the golden seeds of his charity. 'A godly man shows favor, and lends' (Psalm 112. 5). Charity drops from him freely, as myrrh from the tree. Thus to the godly, the mercies of God work for good; they are wings to lift them up to heaven.

Spiritual mercies also work for good.

The word preached works for good. It is a savor of life, it is a soul transforming word, it assimilates the heart into Christ's likeness; it produces assurance. 'Our gospel came to you not in word only—but in power, and in the Holy Spirit, and in much assurance' (1 Thess. 1:5). It is the chariot of salvation.

Prayer works for good. Prayer is the bellows of the affections; it blows up holy desires and ardours of soul. Prayer has power with God. 'Command me' (Isaiah 14:11). Prayer is a key which unlocks the treasury of God's mercy. Prayer keeps the heart open to God—and shut to sin. Prayer assuages the swellings of lust. It was Luther's counsel to a friend, when he perceived a temptation begin to arise, to betake himself to prayer. Prayer is the Christian's gun, which he discharges against his enemies. Prayer is the sovereign medicine of the soul. Prayer sanctifies every mercy (1 Tim. 4:5). Prayer is the dispeller of sorrow—by venting the grief it, eases the heart. When Hannah had prayed, 'she went away, and was no more sad' (1 Sam. 1:18). And if it has these rare effects, then it works for good.

The Lord's Supper works for good. It is an emblem of the marriage supper of the Lamb (Rev. 19:9), and a pledge of that communion we shall have with Christ in glory. It is a feast of fat things; it gives us bread from Heaven, such as preserves life, and prevents death. It has glorious effects in the hearts of the godly. It quickens their affections, strengthens their graces, mortifies their corruptions, revives their hopes, and increases their joy. Luther says, 'It is as great a work to comfort a dejected soul, as to raise the dead to life'; yet this may and sometimes is done to the souls of the godly in the blessed supper.

4. The graces of the Spirit work for good.

Grace is to the soul, as light to the eye, as health to the body. Grace does to the soul, as a virtuous wife to her husband, 'She will do him good all the days of her life' (Proverbs 31:12). How incomparably useful are the graces! Faith and fear go hand in hand. Faith keeps the heart cheerful, fear keeps the heart serious. Faith keeps the heart from sinking in despair, fear keeps it from floating in presumption. All the graces display themselves in their beauty: hope is 'the helmet' (1 Thess. 5:8), meekness 'the ornament' (1 Pet. 3:4), love 'the bond of perfectness' (Col. 3:14). The saints' graces are weapons to defend them, wings to elevate them, jewels to enrich them, spices to perfume them, stars to adorn them, cordials to refresh them. And does not all this work for good? The graces are our evidences for heaven. Is it not good to have our evidences at the hour of death?

5. The angels work for the good of the Saints.

The good angels are ready to do all offices of love to the people of God. 'Are not all angels ministering spirits, sent to serve those who will inherit salvation?' (Heb. 1:14). Some of the fathers were of opinion that every believer has his guardian angel. This subject needs no hot debate. It may suffice us to know the whole hierarchy of angels is employed for the good of the saints.

The good angels do service to the saints in life. The angel comforted the virgin Mary (Luke 1:28). The angels stopped the mouths of the lions — that they could not hurt Daniel (Dan. 6:22). A Christian has an invisible guard of angels about him. 'He shall give his angels charge over you, to keep you in all your ways' (Psalm 91. 11). The angels are of the saints' life guard, yes, the chief of the angels: 'Are they not all ministering spirits?' The highest angels take care of the lowest saints.

The holy angels do service at death. The angels are about the saints' sick beds to comfort them. As God comforts by His Spirit, so by His angels. Christ in His agony was refreshed by an angel (Luke xx2:43); so are believers in the agony of death: and when the saints' breath expires, their souls are carried up to heaven by a convoy of angels (Luke 16:22).

The holy angels also do service at the Day of Judgment. The angels shall open the saints' graves, and shall conduct them into the presence of Christ, when they shall be made like His glorious body. 'He shall send his angels, and they shall gather together his elect from the four winds, from the one end of heaven to the other' (Matt. 26:31). The angels at the Day of Judgment shall rid the godly of all their enemies. Here the saints are plagued with enemies. 'They are my adversaries, because I follow that which is good' (Psalm 38:20). Well, the angels will shortly give God's people a writ of ease, and set them free from all their enemies: 'The tares are the children of the wicked one, the harvest is the end of the world, the reapers are the angels; as therefore the tares are gathered and burnt in the fire, so shall it be in the end of the world: the Son of man shall send forth his angels, and they shall gather out of his kingdom all things which offend, and them which do iniquity, and cast them into a furnace of fire' (Matt. 13:38 42). At the Day of Judgment the angels of God will take the wicked, which are the tares, and will bundle them up, and throw them into hell furnace, and then the godly will not be troubled with enemies any more: thus the good angels work for good.

See here the honor and dignity of a believer. He has God's name written upon him (Rev. 3:12), the Holy Spirit dwelling in him (2 Tim. 1:14), and a guard of angels attending him!

6. The Communion of Saints works for good.

'We are helpers of your joy' (2 Cor. 1:24). One Christian conversing with another is a means to confirm him. As the stones in an arch help to strengthen one another, one Christian by imparting his experience, heats and quickens another. 'Let us provoke one another to love, and to good works' (Heb. 10:24). How does grace flourish by holy conference! A Christian by good discourse drops that oil upon another, which makes the lamp of his faith burn the brighter.

7. Christ's intercession works for good.

Christ is in heaven, as Aaron with his golden plate upon his forehead, and his precious incense; and He prays for all believers as well as He did for the apostles. 'My prayer is not for them alone. I pray also for those who will believe in me' (John 17:20). When a Christian is weak, and can hardly pray for himself, Jesus Christ is praying for him; and He prays for three things.

First, that the saints may be kept from sin (John 17:15). 'I pray that you should keep them from the evil.' We live in the world as in a pest-house; Christ prays that His saints may not be infected with the contagious evil of the times.

Second, for His people's progress in holiness. 'Sanctify them' (John 17:17). Let them have constant supplies of the Spirit, and be anointed with fresh oil.

Third, for their glorification 'Father, I will that those which you have given me, be with me where I am' (John 17:24). Christ is not content until the saints are in His arms. This prayer, which He made on earth, is the copy and pattern of His prayer in heaven. What a comfort is this — when Satan is tempting, Christ is praying! This works for good.

Christ's prayer takes away the sins of our prayers. As a child who present his father with a posy, goes into the garden, and there gathers some flowers and some weeds together — but coming to his mother, she picks out the weeds and binds the flowers, and so it is presented to the father. Just so — when we have put up our prayers, Christ comes, and picks away the weeds, the sin of our prayer, and presents nothing but flowers to His Father, which are a sweet smelling savor.

8. The prayers of Saints work for good to the godly.

The saints pray for all the members of the mystical body, their prayers prevail much. They prevail for recovery from sickness 'Your prayer of faith shall save the sick, and the Lord shall raise him up' (James 5:15). They prevail for victory over enemies. 'Lift up your prayer for the remnant that is left' (Isaiah 37:4). That night the angel of the Lord went out to the Assyrian camp and killed 185,000 Assyrian troops' (Isaiah 37:36). They prevail for deliverance out of prison. 'But while Peter was in prison, the church prayed very earnestly for him. The night before Peter was to be placed on trial, he was asleep, chained between two soldiers, with others standing guard at the prison gate. Suddenly, there was a bright light in the cell, and an angel of the Lord stood before Peter. The angel tapped him on the side to awaken him and said, 'Quick! Get up!' And the chains fell off his wrists.' (Acts 12:5-7). The angel fetched Peter out of prison — but it was prayer which fetched the angel. They prevail for forgiveness of sin. 'My servant Job shall pray for you, for him will I accept' (Job 13:8).

Thus the prayers of the saints work for good to the mystical body. And this is no small privilege to a child of God that he has a constant trade of prayer driven for him. When he comes into any place, he may say, 'I have some prayer here, nay, all the world over I have a stock of prayer going for me. When I am indisposed, and out of tune, others are praying for me, who are quick and lively.' Thus the best things work for good to the people of God.

The worst things work for good to the godly.

Do not mistake me, I do not say that of their own nature, the worst things are good, for they are a fruit of the curse. But though they are naturally evil — yet the wise overruling hand of God disposing and sanctifying them — they are morally good. As the elements, though of contrary qualities — yet God has so tempered them, that they all work in a harmonious manner for the good of the universe. Or as in a watch, the wheels seem to move contrary one to another — but all carry on the motions of the watch: so things that seem to move cross to the godly — yet by the wonderful providence of God, work for their good. Among these worst things, there are four sad evils which work for good to those who love God.

1. The evil of affliction works for good, to the godly.

It is one heart-quieting consideration in all the afflictions which befall us — that God has a special hand in them: 'The Almighty has afflicted me' (Ruth 1:21). Instruments can no more stir until God gives them a commission, than the axe can cut, by itself, without a hand. Job eyed God in his affliction: therefore, as Augustine observes, he does not say, 'The Lord gave — and the devil took away,' but, 'The Lord has taken away.' Whoever brings an affliction to us, it is God who sends it.

Another heart quieting consideration is — that afflictions work for good. 'I have sent them into captivity for their own good.' (Jer. 24:6). Judah's captivity in Babylon was for their good. 'It is good for me that I have been afflicted' (Psalm 119:71). This text, like Moses' tree cast into the bitter waters of affliction, may make them sweet and wholesome to drink. Afflictions to the godly are medicinal. Out of the most poisonous drugs God extracts our salvation. Afflictions are as needful as ordinances (1 Peter 1:6). No vessel can be made of gold without fire; so it is impossible that we should be made vessels of honor, unless we are melted and refined in the furnace of affliction. 'All the paths of the Lord are mercy and truth' (Psalm 35:10). As the painter intermixes bright colors with dark shadows; so the wise God mixes mercy with judgment. Those afflictive providences which seem to be harmful, are beneficial. Let us take some instances in Scripture.

Joseph's brethren throw him into a pit; afterwards they sell him; then he is cast into prison; yet all this did work for his good. His abasement made way for his advancement, he was made the second man in the kingdom. 'You thought evil against me — but God meant it for good' (Gen. 50:20).

Jacob wrestled with the angel, and the hollow of Jacob's thigh was put out of joint. This was sad; but God turned it to good, for there he saw God's face, and there the Lord blessed him. 'Jacob called the name of the place Peniel, for I have seen God face to face' (Gen. 32:30). Who would not be willing to have a bone out of joint, so that he might have a sight of God?

King Manasseh was bound in chains. This was sad to see — a crown of gold changed into fetters. But it wrought for his good, for, 'So the Lord sent the Assyrian armies, and they took Manasseh prisoner. They put a ring through his nose, bound him in bronze chains, and led him away to Babylon. But while in deep distress, Manasseh sought the Lord his God and cried out humbly to the God of his ancestors. And when he prayed, the Lord listened to him and was moved by his request for help.' (2 Chron. 33:11-13). He was more indebted to his iron chain — than to his golden crown. The one made him proud — the other made him humble.

Job was a spectacle of misery; he lost all that he ever had; he abounded only in boils and ulcers. This was sad; but it wrought for his good, his grace was proved and improved. God gave a testimony from heaven of his integrity, and did compensate his loss by giving him twice as much as ever he had before (Job 13:10).

Paul was smitten with blindness. This was uncomfortable — but it turned to his good. God did by that blindness, make way for the light of grace to shine into his soul; it was the beginning of a happy conversion (Acts 9:6).

As the hard frosts in winter bring on the flowers in the spring; as the night ushers in the morning star: so the evils of affliction produce much good to those who love God. But we are ready to question the truth of this, and say, as Mary did to the angel, 'How can this be?' Therefore I shall show you several ways how affliction works for good.

(1). Affliction works for good, as it is our preacher and teacher — 'Hear the rod' (Micah 6:9). Luther said that he could never rightly understand some of the Psalms — until he was in affliction.

Affliction teaches what sin is. In the word preached, we hear what a dreadful thing sin is, that it is both defiling and damning — but we fear it no more than a painted lion; therefore God lets loose affliction — and then we feel sin bitter in the fruit of it. A sick bed often teaches more than a sermon. We can best see the ugly visage of sin in the looking-glass of affliction!

Affliction teaches us to know ourselves. In prosperity we are for the most part strangers to ourselves. God afflicts us — that we may better know ourselves. We see that corruption in our hearts, in the time of affliction, which we would not believe was there. Water in the glass looks clear — but set it on the fire, and the scum boils up. In prosperity, a man seems to be humble and thankful, the water looks clear; but set this man a little on the fire of affliction, and the scum boils up — much impatience and unbelief appear. 'Oh,' says a Christian, 'I never thought I had such a bad heart, as now I see I have! I never thought my corruptions had been so strong, and my graces so weak.'

(2). Afflictions work for good, as they are the means of making the heart more upright. In prosperity the heart is apt to be divided (Hos. 10:2). The heart cleaves partly to God — and partly to the world. It is like a needle between two loadstones: God draws, and the world draws. Now God takes away the world — that the heart may cleave more to Him in sincerity. Correction is a setting the heart right and straight. As we sometimes hold a crooked rod over the fire to straighten it; so God holds us over the fire of affliction to make us more straight and upright. Oh, how good it is, when sin has bent the soul awry from God, that affliction should straighten it again!

(3). Afflictions work for good, as they conform us to Christ. God's rod is a pencil to draw Christ's image more lively upon us. It is good that there should be symmetry and proportion between the Head and the members. Would we be parts of Christ's mystical body, and not like Him? His life, as Calvin says, was a series of sufferings, 'a man of sorrows, and acquainted with grief' (Isaiah 53:3). He wept, and bled. Was His head crowned with thorns, and do we think to be crowned with roses? It is good to be like Christ, though it be by sufferings. Jesus Christ drank a bitter cup, it made Him sweat drops of blood to think of it; and, though He drank the poison in the cup (the wrath of God) yet there is some wormwood in the cup left, which the saints must drink: only here is the difference between Christ's sufferings and ours; His were atoning, ours are only chastening.

(4). Afflictions work for good to the godly, as they are destructive to sin. Sin is the mother, affliction is the daughter; the daughter helps to destroy the mother. Sin is like the tree which breeds the worm, and affliction is like the worm that eats the tree. There is much corruption in the best heart: affliction does by degrees work it out, as the fire works out the dross from the gold, 'The Lord did this to purge away his sin' (Isaiah 37:9). What if we have more of the rough file — if we have less rust! Afflictions carry away nothing but the dross of sin. If a physician should say to a patient, 'Your body is distempered, and full of bad humours, which must be cleared out, or you will die. But I will prescribe physic which, though it may make you sick — yet it will carry away the dregs of your disease, and save your life.' Would not this be for the good of the patient? Afflictions are the medicine which God uses to carry off our spiritual diseases; they cure the swelling of pride, the fever of lust, the cancer of covetousness. Do they not then work for good?

(5). Afflictions work for good, as they are the means of loosening our hearts from the world. When you dig away the earth from the root of a tree, it is to loosen the tree from the earth. Just so, God digs away our earthly comforts to loosen our hearts from the earth. A thorn grows up with every flower. God would have the world hang as a loose tooth which, being twitched away does not much trouble us. Is it not good to be weaned? The oldest saints need it. Why does the Lord break the conduit pipe — but that we may go to Him, in whom are 'all our fresh springs' (Psalm 87:7).

(6). Afflictions work for good, as they make way for comfort. 'In the valley of Achor, is a door of hope' (Hos. 2:15) Achor signifies trouble. God sweetens outward pain with inward peace. 'Your sorrow shall he turned into joy' (John 16:20). Here is the water turned into wine. After a bitter pill, God gives sugar. Paul had his prison songs. God's rod has honey at the end of it. The saints in affliction have had such sweet raptures of joy, that they thought themselves in the borders of the heavenly Canaan.

(7). Afflictions work for good, as they are a magnifying of us. 'What is man, that you should magnify him, and that you should visit him every morning?' (Job 7:17). God does by affliction magnify us three ways.

(1st.) In that He will condescend so low as to take notice of us. It is an honor that God will mind dust and ashes. It is a magnifying of us that God thinks us worthy to be smitten. God's not striking is a slighting: 'Why should you be stricken anymore?' (Isaiah 1:5). If you will go on in sin, take your course — sin yourselves into hell.

(2nd.) Afflictions also magnify us, as they are ensigns of glory, signs of sonship. 'If you endure chastening, God deals with you as with sons' (Heb. 12:7). Every print of the rod is a badge of honor.

(3rd.) Afflictions tend to the magnifying of the saints, as they make them renowned in the world. Soldiers have never been so admired for their victories, as the saints have been for their sufferings. The zeal and constancy of the martyrs in their trials have rendered them famous to posterity. How eminent was Job for his patience! God leaves his name upon record: 'You have heard of the patience of Job' (James 5:11). Job the sufferer, was more renowned than Alexander the conqueror.

(8.) Afflictions work for good, as they are the means of making us happy. 'Happy is the man whom God corrects' (Job 5:17). What politician or moralist ever placed happiness in afflictions? Job does. 'Happy is the man whom God corrects.'

It may be said, 'How do afflictions make us happy?' We reply that, being sanctified, they bring us nearer to God. The moon in the full is furthest off from the sun: so are many further off from God in the full moon of prosperity; afflictions bring them nearer to God. The magnet of mercy does not draw us so near to God as the cords of affliction. When Absalom set Joab's corn on fire, then he came running to Absalom (2 Sam. 16:30). When God sets our worldly comforts on fire, then we run to Him, and make our peace with Him. When the prodigal was pinched with need, then he returned home to his father (Luke 15:13). When the dove could not find any rest for the sole of her foot, then she flew to the ark. When God brings a deluge of affliction upon us, then we fly to the ark, Christ. Thus affliction makes us happy, in bringing us nearer to God. Faith can make use of the waters of affliction, to swim faster to Christ.

(9). Afflictions work for good, as they put to silence the wicked. How ready are they to asperse and calumniate the godly, that they serve God only for self-interest. Therefore God will have His people endure sufferings for religion, that He may put a padlock on the lying lips of wicked men. When the atheists of the world see that God has a people, who serve Him not for a livery—but for love, this stops their mouths. The devil accused Job of hypocrisy, that he was a mercenary man, all his religion was made up of ends of gold and silver. 'Does Job serve God for naught? Have not you made a hedge about him?' Etc. 'Well,' says God, 'put forth your hand, touch his estate' (Job 1:9). The devil had no sooner received a commission—but he falls a breaking down Job's hedge; but still Job worships God (Job 1:20), and professes his faith in Him. 'Though he slays me—yet will I trust in him' (Job 13:15). This silenced the devil himself. How it strikes a damp into wicked men, when they see that the godly will keep close to God in a suffering condition, and that, when they lose all, they yet will hold fast their integrity.

(10). Afflictions work for good, as they make way for glory (2 Cor. 4:17). Not that they merit glory—but they prepare for it. As ploughing prepares the earth for a crop, so afflictions prepare and make us meet for glory. The painter lays his gold upon dark colors—so God first lays the dark colors of affliction, and then He lays the golden color of glory. The vessel is first seasoned before wine is poured into it: the vessels of mercy are first seasoned with affliction, and then the wine of glory is poured in. Thus we see afflictions are not harmful—but beneficial, to the saints. We should not so much look at the evil of affliction, as the good; not so much at the dark side of the cloud, as the light. The worst that God does to His children, is to whip them to heaven!

2. The evil of temptation is overruled for good to the godly.

The evil of temptation works for good. Satan is called the tempter (Mark 4:15). He is ever lying in ambush, he is continually at work with one saint or another. The devil has his circuit that he walks every day: he is not yet fully cast into prison—but, like a prisoner that goes under bail, he walks about to tempt the saints. This is a great molestation to a child of God. Now concerning Satan's temptations; there are three things to be considered:

(1). His method in tempting.

(2). The extent of his power.

(3). These temptations are overruled for good.

(1). Satan's method in tempting. Here take notice of two things. His violence in tempting; and so he is the red dragon. He labors to storm the castle of the heart, he throws in thoughts of blasphemy, he tempts to deny God. These are the fiery darts which he shoots, by which he would inflame the passions. Also, notice his subtlety in tempting; and so he is the old serpent. There are five chief subtleties the devil uses.

(a.) He observes the temperament and constitution—he lays suitable baits of temptation. Like the farmer, he knows what grain is best for the soil. Satan will not tempt contrary to the natural disposition and temperament. This is his policy—he makes the wind and tide go together; that way the natural tide of the heart runs, that way the wind of temptation blows. Though the devil cannot know men's thoughts—yet he knows their temperament, and accordingly he lays his baits. He tempts the ambitious man with a crown, the lustful man with beauty.

(b.) Satan observes the fittest time to tempt—as a cunning angler casts in his angle when the fish will bite best. Satan's time of tempting is usually after an ordinance—and the reason is, he thinks he shall find us most secure. When we have been at solemn duties, we are apt to think all is done, and we grow remiss, and leave off that zeal and strictness as before; just as a soldier, who after a battle leaves off his armor, not once dreaming of an enemy. Satan watches his time, and, when we least suspect, then he throws in a temptation.

(c.) He makes use of near relations; the devil tempts by a proxy. Thus he handed over a temptation to Job by his wife. Are you still trying to maintain your integrity? Curse God and die!' (Job 2:9). A wife in the bosom may be the devil's instrument to tempt to sin.

(d.) Satan tempts to evil by those who are good; thus he gives poison in a golden cup. He tempted Christ by Peter. Peter dissuades him from suffering. 'Master, pity Yourself!' Who would have thought to have found the tempter in the mouth of an apostle?

(e.) Satan tempts to sin under a pretense of religion. He is most to be feared when he transforms himself into an angel of light. He came to Christ with Scripture in his mouth: 'It is written.' The devil baits his hook with religion. He tempts many a man to covetousness and extortion under a pretense of providing for his family; he tempts some to do away with themselves, that they may live no longer to sin against God; and so he draws them into sin, under a pretense of avoiding sin. These are his subtle stratagems in tempting.

(2). The extent of his power; how far Satan's power in tempting reaches.

(a.) He can propose the object; as he set a wedge of gold before Achan.

(b.) He can poison the imagination, and instill evil thoughts into the mind. As the Holy Spirit casts in good suggestions, so the devil casts in bad ones. He put it into Judas' heart to betray Christ (John 13:2).

(c.) Satan can excite and irritate the corruption within, and work some kind of inclinableness in the heart to embrace a temptation. Though it is true Satan cannot force the will to yield consent—yet he being a cunning suitor, by his continual solicitation, may provoke to evil. Thus he provoked David to number the people (1 Chron. 21:1). The devil may, by his subtle arguments, dispute us into sin.

(3). These temptations are overruled for good to the children of God. A tree that is shaken by the wind is more settled and rooted. Just so, the blowing of a temptation does but settle a Christian the more in grace. Temptations are overruled for good in eight ways:

(a.) Temptation sends the soul to prayer. The more furiously Satan tempts, the more fervently the saint prays. The deer being shot with the dart, runs faster to the water. When Satan shoots his fiery darts at the soul, it then runs faster to the throne of grace. When Paul had the messenger of Satan to buffet him, he says, 'For this I besought the Lord thrice, that it might depart from me' (2 Cor. 12:8). Temptation is a medicine for carnal security. That which makes us pray more, works for good.

(b.) Temptation to sin, is a means to keep from the perpetration of sin. The more a child of God is tempted, the more he fights against the temptation. The more Satan tempts to blasphemy, the more a saint trembles at such thoughts, and says, 'Get you hence, Satan.' When Joseph's mistress tempted him to folly, the stronger her temptation was, the stronger was his opposition. That temptation which the devil uses as a spur to sin, God makes a bridle to keep back a Christian from it.

(c.) Temptation works for good, as it abates the swelling of pride. 'Lest I should be exalted above measure, there was given me a thorn in the flesh, a messenger of Satan to buffet me' (2

Cor. 12:7). The thorn in the flesh was to puncture the puffing up of pride. Better is that temptation which humbles me—than that duty which makes me proud. Rather than a Christian shall be haughty minded, God will let him fall into the devil's hands awhile, to be cured of his swelling pride.

(d.) Temptation works for good, as it is a touchstone to try what is in the heart. The devil tempts, that he may deceive; but God allows us to be tempted, to try us. Temptation is a trial of our sincerity. It argues that our heart is chaste and loyal to Christ, when we can look a temptation in the face, and turn our back upon it. Also it is a trial of our courage. 'Ephraim is a silly dove, without heart' (Hosea 8:11). So it may be said of many, they are without a heart; they have no heart to resist temptation. No sooner does Satan come with his bait—but they yield; like a coward who, as soon as the thief approaches, gives him his purse. But he is the valorous Christian, who brandishes the sword of the Spirit against Satan, and will rather die than yield. The courage of the Romans was never more seen than when they were assaulted by the Carthaginians: the valor and courage of a saint is never more seen than on a battlefield, when he is fighting the red dragon, and by the power of faith puts the devil to flight. That grace is tried gold, which can stand in the fiery trial, and withstand Satan's fiery darts!

(e.) Temptations work for good, as God makes those who are tempted, fit to comfort others in the same distress. A Christian must himself be under the buffetings of Satan, before he can speak a word in due season to him that is weary. Paul was versed in temptations. 'We are not ignorant of his devices' (2 Cor. 2:11). Thus he was able to acquaint others with Satan's cursed wiles (1 Cor. 10:13). A man that has ridden over a place where there are bogs and quicksands, is the fittest to guide others through that dangerous way. He who has felt the claws of the roaring lion, and has lain bleeding under those wounds, is the fittest man to deal with one who is tempted. None can better discover Satan's subtle devices, than those who have been long in the fencing school of temptation.

(f.) Temptations work for good, as they stir up fatherly compassion in God, to those who are tempted. The child who is sick and bruised is most looked after. When a saint lies under the bruising of temptations, Christ prays, and God the Father pities. When Satan puts the soul into a fever, God comes with a cordial; which made Luther say, that temptations are Christ's embraces, because He then most sweetly manifests Himself to the soul.

(g.) Temptations work for good, as they make the saints long more for heaven. There they shall be out of gunshot; heaven is a place of rest, no bullets of temptation fly there. The eagle which soars aloft in the air, and sits upon high trees—is not troubled with the stinging of the serpent. Just so, when believers are ascended to heaven, they shall not be molested by the old serpent, the devil. In this life, when one temptation is over, another comes. This makes God's people wish for death—to call them off the battlefield where the bullets fly so quick—and to receive a victorious crown, where neither the drum nor cannon—but the harp and violin, shall be eternally sounding.

(h.) Temptations work for good, as they engage the strength of Christ. Christ is our Friend, and when we are tempted, He sets all His power working for us. 'Since he himself has gone through suffering and temptation, he is able to help us when we are being tempted' (Heb. 2:18). If a poor soul was to fight alone with the Goliath of hell, he would be sure to be vanquished—but Jesus Christ brings in His auxiliary forces, He gives fresh supplies of grace. 'We are more than conquerors through him who loved us!' (Romans 8:37). Thus the evil of temptation is overruled for good.

Question. But sometimes Satan foils a child of God. How does this work for good?

Answer. I grant that, through the suspension of divine grace, and the fury of a temptation, a saint may be overcome; yet this foiling by a temptation shall be overruled for good. By this foil God makes way for the augmentation of grace. Peter was tempted to self-confidence, he presumed upon his own strength; and Christ let him fall. But this wrought for his good, it cost him many a tear. 'He went out, and wept bitterly' (Matt. 26:75). And now he grows less self-reliant. He dared not say he loved Christ more than the other apostles. 'Do you love me more than these?' (John 21:15). He dared not say so — his fall into sin broke the neck of his pride!

The foiling by a temptation causes more circumspection and watchfulness in a child of God. Though Satan did before decoy him into sin — yet for the future he will be the more cautious. He will have a care of coming within the lion's chain any more. He is more vigilant and fearful of the occasions of sin. He never goes out without his spiritual armor, and he girds on his armor by prayer. He knows he walks on slippery ground, therefore he looks wisely to his steps. He keeps close sentinel in his soul, and when he spies the devil coming, he grasps his spiritual weapons, and displays the shield of faith (Eph. 6:16). This is all the hurt the devil does when he foils a saint by temptation — he cures him of his careless neglect; he makes him watch and pray more. When wild beasts get over the hedge and damage the grain, a man will make his fence the stronger. Just so, when the devil gets over the hedge by a temptation, a Christian will be sure to mend his fence; he will become more fearful of sin, and careful of duty. Thus the being worsted by temptation works for good.

Objection. But if being foiled works for good, this may make Christians careless whether they are overcome by temptations or not.

Answer. There is a great deal of difference between falling into a temptation, and running into a temptation. The falling into a temptation shall work for good, not the running into it. He who falls into a river is fit for help and pity — but he who desperately runs into it, is guilty of his own death. It is madness running into a lion's den. He who runs himself into a temptation is like King Saul — who fell upon his own sword.

From all that has been said, see how God disappoints the old serpent, making his temptations turn to the good of His people. Surely if the devil knew how much benefit accrues to the saints by temptation, he would forbear to tempt. Luther once said, 'There are three things which make a godly man — prayer, meditation, and temptation.' Paul, in his voyage to Rome, met with a contrary wind (Acts 27:4). So the wind of temptation is a contrary wind to that of the Spirit; but God makes use of this cross wind, to blow the saints to heaven!

3. The evil of desertion works for good to the godly.

The evil of desertion works for good. The spouse complains of desertion. 'My beloved had withdrawn himself, and was gone!' (Cant. 5:6). There is a twofold withdrawing; either in regard of grace, when God suspends the influence of His Spirit, and withholds the lively actings of grace. If the Spirit is gone, grace freezes into a chillness and indolence. Or, a withdrawing in regard of comfort. When God withholds the sweet manifestations of His favor, He does not look with such a pleasant aspect — but veils His face, and seems to be quite gone from the soul.

God is just in all His withdrawings. We desert Him before He deserts us. We desert God — when we leave off close communion with Him; when we desert His truths and dare not appear for Him; when we leave the guidance and conduct of His word, and follow the deceitful light of our own corrupt affections and passions. We desert God first; therefore we have none to blame but ourselves.

Desertion is very sad, for as when the light is withdrawn, darkness follows in the air — so when God withdraws, there is darkness and sorrow in the soul. Desertion is an agony of conscience.

God holds the soul over hell. 'The arrows of the Almighty are within me, the poison whereof drinks up my spirits' (Job 6:4). It was a custom among the Persians in their wars, to dip their arrows in the poison of serpents to make them more deadly. Thus did God shoot the poisoned arrow of desertion into Job, under the wounds of which his spirit lay bleeding. In times of desertion the people of God are apt to be dejected. They dispute against themselves, and think that God has quite cast them off. Therefore I shall prescribe some comfort to the deserted soul.

The mariner, when he has no star to guide him — yet he has light in his lantern, which is some help to him to see his compass; so, I shall lay down four consolations, which are as the mariner's lantern, to give some light when the poor soul is sailing in the darkness of desertion, and needs the bright morning star.

(1). None but the godly are capable of desertion. Wicked men do not know what God's love means — nor what it is to lack it. They know what it is to lack health, friends, trade — but not what it is to lack God's favor. You fear that you are not God's child because you are deserted. The Lord cannot be said to withdraw His love from the wicked, because they never had it. The being deserted, evidences you to be a child of God. How could you complain that God has estranged Himself, if you had not sometimes received smiles and tokens of love from Him?

(2). There may be the seed of grace, where there is not the flower of joy. The earth may lack a crop of grain — yet may have a mine of gold within! A Christian may have grace within, though the sweet fruit of joy does not grow. Vessels at sea, which are richly fraught with jewels and spices, may be in the dark and tossed in the storm. A soul enriched with the treasures of grace, may yet be in the dark of desertion, and so tossed as to think it shall be cast away in the storm! David, in a state of dejection, prays, 'Take not your Holy Spirit from me' (Psalm 51:11). He does not pray, says Augustine, 'Lord, give me your Spirit' — but 'Take not away your Spirit', so that still he had the Spirit of God remaining in him.

(3). These desertions are but for a time. Christ may withdraw, and leave the soul awhile — but He will come again. 'In a little wrath I hid my face from you for a moment — but with everlasting kindness will I have mercy on you' (Isaiah 64:8). When it is low water — the tide will come in again. 'I will not always show my anger.' (Isaiah 57:16). The tender mother sets down her child in anger — but she will take it up again into her arms, and kiss it. God may put away the soul in anger — but He will take it up again into His dear embraces, and display His banner of love over it.

(4). These desertions work for good to the godly.

Desertion cures the soul of sloth. We find the spouse fallen upon the bed of sloth: 'I sleep' (Cant. 5:2). And presently Christ was gone. 'My beloved had withdrawn himself' (Cant. 5:6). Who will speak to one that is drowsy?

Desertion cures inordinate affection to the world. 'Love not the world' (1 John 2:15). We may hold the world as a posy in our hand — but it must not lie too near our heart! We may use it as an inn where we take a meal — but it must not be our home. Perhaps these secular things steal away the heart too much. Godly men are sometimes weighed down with an overabundance of temporal things, and drunk with the luscious delights of prosperity. And having spotted their silver wings of grace, and much defaced God's image by rubbing it against the earth — the Lord, to recover them of this, hides His face in a cloud. This eclipse has good effects — it darkens all the glory of the world, and causes it to disappear.

Desertion works for good, as it makes the saints prize God's countenance more than ever. 'Your loving-kindness is better than life' (Psalm 63:3). Yet the commonness of this mercy lessens it in our esteem. When pearls grew common at Rome, they began to be slighted. God has no better way to make us value His love, than by withdrawing it awhile. If the sun shone but once a year, how would it be prized! When the soul has been long benighted with desertion, oh how welcome now is the return of the Sun of righteousness!

Desertion works for good, as it is the means of embittering sin to us. Can there be a greater misery than to have God's displeasure? What makes hell — but the hiding of God's face? And what makes God hide His face — but sin? 'They have taken away my Lord, and I know not where they have laid him' (John 20:13). So, our sins have taken away the Lord, and we know not where He is laid. The favor of God is the best jewel; it can sweeten a prison, and unsting death. Oh, how odious then is that sin, which robs us of our best jewel! Sin made God desert His temple (Ezek. 8:6). Sin causes Him to appear as an enemy, and dress Himself in armor. This makes the soul pursue sin with a holy malice, and seek to be avenged on it! The deserted soul gives sin gall and vinegar to drink, and, with the spear of mortification, lets out the heart-blood of it!

Desertion works for good, as it sets the soul to weeping for the loss of God. When the sun is gone, the dew falls; and when God is gone, tears drop from the eyes. How Micah was troubled when he had lost his gods! 'You've taken away all my gods — and I have nothing left!' (Judges 18:24). So when God is gone, what more do we have left? It is not the harp and violin, which can comfort — when God is gone. Though it is sad to lack God's presence — yet it is good to lament His absence.

Desertion sets the soul to seeking after God. When Christ was departed, the spouse pursues after Him, she 'searched for him in all its streets and squares' (Cant. 3:2). And not having found Him, she makes a cry after Him, 'Have you seen him anywhere, this one I love so much?' (Cant. 3:3). The deserted soul sends up whole volleys of sighs and groans. It knocks at heaven's gate by prayer — it can have no rest until the golden beams of God's face shine!

Desertion puts the Christian upon inquiry. He inquires the cause of God's departure. What is the accursed thing which has made God angry? Perhaps pride, perhaps sloth, perhaps worldliness. 'I was angry and punished these greedy people. I withdrew myself from them' (Isaiah 57:17). Perhaps there is some secret sin allowed. A stone in the pipe hinders the current of water; so, sin lived in, hinders the sweet current of God's love. Thus conscience, as a bloodhound, having found out sin and overtaken it — this Achan is stoned to death!

Desertion works for good, as it gives us a sight of what Jesus Christ suffered for us. If the sipping of the cup is so bitter, how bitter was that full cup which Christ drank to the dregs upon the cross? He drank a cup of deadly poison, which made Him cry out, 'My God, my God, why have you forsaken me?' (Matt. 22:46). None can so appreciate Christ's sufferings, none can be so fired with love to Christ — as those who have been humbled by desertion, and have been held over the flames of hell for a time.

Desertion works for good, as it prepares the saints for future comfort. The nipping frosts prepare for spring flowers. It is God's way, first to cast down, then to comfort (2 Cor. 7:6). When our Savior had been fasting — then the angels came and ministered to Him. When the Lord has kept His people long fasting — then He sends the Comforter, and feeds them with the hidden manna. 'Light is sown for the righteous' (Psalm 97:11.) The saints' comforts may be hidden like seed underground — but the seed is ripening, and will increase, and flourish into a crop!

These desertions work for good, as they will make heaven the sweeter to us. Here on earth, our comforts are like the moon, sometimes they are in the full, sometimes in the wane. God shows Himself to us awhile, and then retires from us. How will this set off heaven the more, and make it more delightful and ravishing, when we shall have a constant aspect of love from God! (1 Thess. 4:17).

Thus we see desertions work for good. The Lord brings us into the deep of desertion — that He may not bring us into the deep of damnation! He puts us into a seeming hell — that He may keep us from a real hell. God is fitting us for that time when we shall enjoy His smiles forever, when there shall be neither clouds in His face or sun setting, when Christ shall come and stay with His spouse, and the spouse shall never say again, 'My beloved has withdrawn himself!'

4. The evil of sin works for good to the godly.

Sin in its own nature, is damnable — but God in His infinite wisdom overrules it, and causes good to arise from that which seems most to oppose it. Indeed, it is a matter of wonder that any honey should come out of this lion! We may understand it in a double sense.

(1). The sins of others are overruled for good to the godly. It is no small trouble to a gracious heart to live among the wicked. 'Woe is me — that I dwell in Mesech' (Psalm 120:5). Yet even this the Lord turns to good. For,

(a.) The sins of others work for good to the godly — as they produce holy sorrow. God's people weep for what they cannot reform. 'Rivers of tears run down my eyes, because they keep not your law' (Psalm 119. 136). David was a mourner for the sins of the times; his heart was turned into a spring — and his eyes into rivers! Wicked men make merry with sin. 'When you do evil, then you rejoice' (Jer. 11:15). But the godly are weeping doves; they grieve for the oaths and blasphemies of the age. The sins of others, like spears, pierce their souls!

This grieving for the sins of others is good. It shows a childlike heart, to resent with sorrow the injuries done to our heavenly Father. It also shows a Christ-like heart. 'He was grieved for the hardness of their hearts' (Mark 3:5). The Lord takes special notice of these tears. He likes it well — that we should weep when His glory suffers. It argues more grace to grieve for the sins of others, than for our own. We may grieve for our own sins — out of fear of hell; but to grieve for the sins of others — is from a principle of love to God. These tears drop as water from roses — they are sweet and fragrant, and God puts them in His bottle! 'You keep track of all my sorrows. You have collected all my tears in your bottle. You have recorded each one in your book!' (Psalm 56:8)

(b.) The sins of others work for good to the godly — as they set them the more a praying against sin. If there were not such a spirit of wickedness abroad, perhaps there would not be such a spirit of prayer. Crying sins cause crying prayers! The people of God pray against the iniquity of the times — that God will give a check to sin, that He will put sin to the blush. If they cannot pray down sin, they pray against it; and this God takes kindly. These prayers shall both be recorded and rewarded. Though we do not prevail in prayer, we shall not lose our prayers. 'My prayer returned into my own bosom' (Psalm 35:13).

(c.) The sins of others work for good — as they make us the more in love with grace. The sins of others are a foil to set off the luster of grace the more. One contrary sets off another: deformity sets off beauty. The sins of the wicked do much disfigure them. Pride is a disfiguring sin; now the beholding another's pride makes us the more in love with humility! Malice is a disfiguring sin, it is the devil's picture; the more of this we see in others the more we love meekness and charity. Drunkenness is a disfiguring sin, it turns men into beasts, it deprives of the use of reason; the more intemperate we see others, the more we must love sobriety. The black face of sin, sets off the beauty of holiness so much the more.

(d.) The sins of others work for good — as they work in us the stronger opposition against sin. 'The wicked have broken your law; therefore I love your commandments' (Psalm 119:126, 127).

David would never have loved God's law so much, if the wicked had not set themselves so much against it. The more violent others are against the truth, the more valiant the saints are for it. Living fish swim against the stream. Just so, the more the tide of sin comes in, the more the godly swim against it! The impieties of the times provoke holy passions in the saints! That anger is without sin — which is against sin. The sins of others are as a whetstone to set the sharper edge upon us; they whet our zeal and indignation against sin the more!

(e.) The sins of others work for good — as they make us more earnest in working out our salvation. When we see wicked men take such pains for hell — this makes us more industrious for heaven. The wicked have nothing to encourage them — yet they sin. They venture shame and disgrace, they break through all opposition. Scripture is against them, and conscience is against them, there is a flaming sword in the way — yet they sin. Godly hearts, seeing the wicked thus mad for the forbidden fruit, and wearing out themselves in the devil's service — are the more emboldened and quickened in the ways of God. They will take heaven as it were, by storm. The wicked are like camels — running after sin (Jer. 2:23). And do we creep like snails in piety? Shall impure sinners do the devil more service — than we do Christ? Shall they make more haste to go to the prison of hell — than we do to the kingdom of heaven? Are they never weary of sinning — and are we weary of praying? Have we not a better Master than they? Are not the paths of virtue pleasant? Is not there joy in the way of duty, and heaven at the end? The activity of the sons of Belial in sin — this is a spur to the godly to make them mend their pace, and run the faster to heaven!

(f.) The sins of others work for good — as they are looking-glasses in which we may see our own hearts. Do we see a heinous, impious wretch? Behold a picture of our own hearts! Such would we be — if God left us! What is in wicked men's practice — is in our nature. Sin in the wicked is like fire which flames and blazes forth; sin in the godly is like fire in the embers. Christian, though you do not break forth into a flame of scandalous sin — yet you have no cause to boast, for there is as much sin in the embers of your nature. You have the root of all sin in you, and would bear as hellish fruit as any ungodly wretch — if God did not either curb you by His power, or change you by His grace!

(g.) The sins of others work for good — as they are the means of making the people of God more thankful. When you see another infected with the plague, how thankful are you that God has preserved you from it! It is a good use that may be made of the sins of others — to make us more thankful. Why might not God have left us to the same excess of wickedness? Think with yourself, O Christian — why should God be more merciful to you than to another? Why should He snatch you, as brand plucked out of the fire — and not him? How may this make you to adore free grace! What the Pharisee said boastingly, we may say thankfully, 'God, I thank you that I am not like other men — robbers, evildoers, adulterers, etc.' (Luke 18:11).

If we are not as wicked as others — we should adore the riches of free-grace! Every time we see men hastening on in sin — we are to thank God that we are not such. If we see a crazy person — we thank God that it is not so with us. Much more when we see others under the power of Satan — how thankful we should be, that this is no longer our condition! 'For we too were once foolish, disobedient, deceived, captives of various passions and pleasures, living in malice and envy, hateful, detesting one another.' Titus 3:3

(h.) The sins of others work for good — as they are means of making God's people better. Christian, God can make you a gainer by another's sin. The more unholy others are — the more holy you should be. The more a wicked man gives himself to sin — the more a godly man gives himself to prayer. 'But I give myself to prayer' (Psalm 109:4).

(i.) The sins of others work for good — as they give an occasion to us of doing good. Were there no sinners, we could not be in such a capacity for service. The godly are often the means of converting the wicked; their prudent advice and pious example is a lure and a bait to draw sinners to the embracing of the gospel. The disease of the patient, works for the good of the physician; by healing the patient, the physician enriches himself. Just so, by converting sinners from the error of their way, our crown comes to be enlarged. 'Those who turn many to righteousness, shall shine as the stars forever and ever' (Dan. 12:31). Not as lamps or candles — but as the stars forever! Thus we see the sins of others are overruled for our good.

(2). The sense of their own sinfulness, will be overruled for the good of the godly. Thus our own sins shall work for good. This must be understood carefully, when I say the sins of the godly work for good — not that there is the least good in sin. Sin is like poison, which corrupts the blood, and infects the heart; and, without a sovereign antidote, sin always brings death. Such is the venomous nature of sin — it is deadly and damning. Sin is worse than hell. But yet God, by His mighty over ruling power, makes sin in the outcome turn to the good of His people. Hence that golden saying of Augustine, 'God would never permit evil — if He could not bring good out of evil.' The feeling of sinfulness in the saints, works for good several ways.

(a.) Sin makes them weary of this life. That sin is in the godly — is sad; but that it is their burden — is good. Paul's afflictions (pardon the expression) were but child's play to him — in comparison of his sin. He rejoiced in tribulation (2 Cor. 7:4). But how did this bird of paradise weep and bemoan himself under his sins! 'Who shall deliver me from the body of this death?' (Romans 8:24). A believer carries his sins as a prisoner his shackles; oh, how does he long for the day of release! This sense of sin is good.

(b.) This indwelling of corruption, makes the saints prize Christ more. He who feels his sin, as a sick man feels his sickness — how welcome is Christ the physician to him! He who feels himself stung with sin — how precious is the brazen serpent to him! When Paul had bemoaned his body of death — how thankful was he for Christ! 'I thank God through Jesus Christ our Lord!' (Romans 8:25). Christ's blood saves from sin, and is the sacred ointment which kills this deadly disease of sin.

(c.) This sense of sin works for good, as it is an occasion of putting the soul upon six special duties:

(i) Sin puts the soul upon self-searching. A child of God being conscious of sin, takes the candle and lantern of the Word, and searches into his heart. He desires to know the worst of himself; as a man who is diseased in body, desires to know the worst of his disease. Though our joy lies in the knowledge of our graces — yet there is some benefit in the knowledge of our corruptions. Therefore Job prays, 'Reveal to me my transgression and sin' (Job 13:23). It is good to know our sins — that we may not flatter ourselves, or take our condition to be better than it is. It is good to find out our sins — lest they find us out!

(ii) Sin puts a child of God upon self-abasing. Sin is left in a godly man — as a cancer in the breast, or a hunch upon the back — to keep him from being proud. Gravel and dirt are good to ballast a ship, and keep it from overturning; the sense of sin helps to ballast the soul, that it be not overturned with pride. We read of the 'spots of God's children' (Deut. 32:5). When a godly man beholds his face in the looking-glass of Scripture, and sees the spots of pride, lust and hypocrisy. They are humbling spots — and make the plumes of pride fall off! It is a good use that may be made even of our sins, when they occasion low thoughts of ourselves. Better is that sin which humbles me — than that duty which makes me proud! Holy Bradford uttered these words of himself, 'I am but a painted hypocrite'; and Hooper said, 'Lord, I am hell—and You are heaven.'

(iii) Sin puts a child of God on self-judging. He passes a sentence upon himself. "I am more brutish than any man' (Proverbs 30:2). It is dangerous to judge others—but it is good to judge ourselves. But if we judged ourselves, we would not come under judgment' (1 Cor. 11:31). When a man has judged himself, Satan is put out of office. When Satan lays anything to a saint's charge, he is able to retort and say, 'It is true, Satan, I am guilty of these sins; but I have judged myself already for them; and having condemned myself in the lower court of conscience, God will acquit me in the upper court of heaven.'

(iv) Sin puts a child of God upon self-conflicting. Spiritual self-conflicts with carnal self. 'The spirit lusts against the flesh' (Gal. 5:17). Our life is a wayfaring life—and a war-faring life. There is a duel fought every day between the two seeds. A believer will not let sin have peaceable possession. If he cannot keep sin out, he will keep sin down; though he cannot quite overcome—yet he is overcoming. 'To him who is overcoming' (Rev. 2:7).

(v) Sin puts a child of God upon self-observing. He knows sin is a bosom traitor, therefore he carefully observes himself. A subtle and deceitful heart, needs a watchful eye. The heart is like a castle which is continually in danger to be assaulted; this makes a child of God to be always a sentinel, and keep a guard over his heart. A believer has a strict eye over himself, lest he fall in to any scandalous sin—and so open a sluice to let all his comfort run out.

(vi) Sin puts the soul upon self-reforming. A child of God does not only find out sin—but drives out sin! One foot he sets upon the neck of his sins—and the other foot he 'turns to God's testimonies' (Psalm 119. 59). Thus the sins of the godly work for good. God makes the saints' maladies—their medicines.

But let none abuse this doctrine. I do not say that sin works for good to an impenitent person. No, it works for his damnation! Sin only works for good to those who love God; and for you who are godly, I know you will not draw a wrong conclusion from this—either to make light of sin, or to make bold with sin. If you should do so, God will make it cost you dearly! Remember David. He ventured presumptuously on sin, and what did he get? He lost his peace, he felt the terrors of the Almighty in his soul, though he had all helps to cheerfulness. He was a king; he had skill in music; yet nothing could administer comfort to him; he complains of his 'broken bones' (Psalm 51:8). And though he did at last come out of that dark cloud—yet perhaps he never recovered his full joy to his dying day. If any of God's people should be tampering with sin, because God can turn it to good; though the Lord does not damn them—He may send them to hell in this life. He may put them into such bitter agonies and soul convulsions, as may fill them full of horror, and make them draw near to despair. Let this be a flaming sword to keep them from coming near the forbidden tree!

And thus have I shown, that both the best things and the worst things, by the overruling hand of the great God—do work together for the good of the saints.

Again, I say—think not lightly of sin!

Why all things work for good

1. The grand reason why all things work for good, is the near and dear interest which God has in His people. The Lord has made a covenant with them. 'They shall be my people, and I will be their God' (Jer. 32:38). By virtue of this compact, all things do, and must work, for good to them. 'I am God, even your God' (Psalm 50:7). This word, 'Your God,' is the sweetest word in the Bible, it implies the best relations; and it is impossible there should be these relations between

God and His people, and everything not work for their good. This expression, 'I am your God,' implies,

(1). The relation of a physician. 'I am your Physician.' God is a skillful Physician. He knows what is best. God observes the different temperaments of men, and knows what will work most effectually. Some are of a more sweet disposition, and are drawn by mercy. Others are more rugged and knotty pieces; these God deals with in a more forcible way. Some things are kept in sugar, others are kept in brine. God does not deal alike with all; He has trials for the strong and cordials for the weak. God is a faithful Physician, and therefore will turn all to the best. If God does not give you that which you like — He will give you that which you need. A physician does not so much study to please the taste of the patient — as to cure his disease. We complain that very sore trials lie upon us; let us remember God is our Physician, therefore He labors rather to heal us — than humor us. God's dealings with His children, though they are sharp — yet they are safe, and in order to cure; 'that he might do you good in the latter end' (Deut. 8:16).

(2). This word, 'your God', implies the relation of a father. A father loves his child; therefore whether it be a smile or a stroke, it is for the good of the child. I am your God, your Father, therefore all I do is for your good. 'As a man chastens his son, so the Lord your God chastens you' (Deut. 8:5). God's chastening is not to destroy — but to reform. God cannot hurt His children, for He is a tender hearted Father, 'Like as a father pities his children, so the Lord pities those who fear him' (Psalm 103. 13). Will a father seek the ruin of his child, the child that came from himself, that bears his image? All his care and skill is for his child. Whom does he settle the inheritance upon — but his child? God is the tender hearted 'Father of mercies' (2 Cor. 1:3). He begets all the mercies and kindnesses in the creatures.

God is an everlasting Father (Isaiah 9:6). He was our Father from eternity; before we were children, God was our Father, and He will be our Father to all eternity. A father provides for his child while he lives; but the father dies, and then the child may be exposed to injury. But God never ceases to be a Father! You who are a believer, have a Father who never dies; and if God is your father, you can never be undone. All things must needs work for your good.

(3). This word, 'your God,' implies the relation of a husband. This is a near and sweet relation. The husband seeks the good of his spouse — not to destroy his wife. 'No man ever yet hated his own flesh,' (Ephes. 5:29). There is a marriage relation between God and His people. 'Your Maker is your Husband' (Isaiah 54:5). God entirely loves His people. He engraves them upon the palms of His hands (Isaiah 49:16). He sets them as a seal upon His breast (Cant. 8:6). He will give kingdoms for their ransom (Isaiah 43:3). This shows how near they lie to His heart. If He is a Husband whose heart is full of love, then He will seek the good of His spouse. Either He will shield off an injury — or will turn it to the best.

(4). This word, 'your God,' implies the relation of a friend. 'This is my friend' (Cant. 5:16). 'A friend is,' as Augustine says, 'half one's self.' He is studious and desirous how he may do his friend good; he promotes his welfare as his own. Jonathan ventured the king's displeasure for his friend David (1 Sam. 19:4). God is our Friend, therefore He will turn all things to our good. There are false friends; Christ was betrayed by a friend. But God is the best Friend.

He is a faithful Friend. 'Know therefore that the Lord your God, he is God — the faithful God' (Deut. 7:9). He is faithful in His love. He gave His very heart to us, when He gave the Son out of His bosom. Here was a pattern of love without a parallel. He is faithful in His promises. 'God, who cannot lie, has promised' (Titus 1:2). He may change His promise — but cannot break it. He is faithful in His dealings; when He is afflicting He is faithful. 'In faithfulness you have afflicted me' (Psalm 119:75). He is sifting and refining us as silver (Psalm 66:10).

God is an immutable Friend. 'I will never leave you, nor forsake you' (Heb. 13:5). Friends often fail at a pinch. Many deal with their friends as women do with flowers; while they are fresh — they put them in their bosoms; but when they begin to wither — they throw them away. Or as the traveler does with the sun-dial; if the sun shines upon the dial, the traveler will step out of the road, and look upon the dial. But if the sun does not shine upon it, he will ride by, and never take any notice of it. So, if prosperity shines on men, then friends will look upon them; but if there is a cloud of adversity on them, they will not come near them. But God is a Friend forever; He has said, 'I will never leave you.' Though David walked in the shadow of death, he knew he had a Friend by him. 'I will fear no evil, for you are with me' (Psalm 23:4). God never takes off His love wholly from His people. 'He loved them unto the end' (John 13:1). God being such a Friend, will make all things work for our good. There is no friend but will seek the good of his friend.

(5). This word, 'your God,' implies yet a nearer relation, the relation between the Head and the members. There is a mystical union between Christ and the saints. He is called, 'the Head of the church' (Eph. 5:23). Does not the head consult for the good of the body? The head guides the body, it sympathizes with it. The head is the fountain of spirits, it sends forth influence and comfort into the body. All the parts of the head are placed for the good of the body. The eye is set as it were in the watchtower, it stands sentinel to spy any danger that may come to the body, and prevent it. The tongue is both a taster and an orator. If the body be a microcosm, or little world, the head is the sun in this world, from which proceeds the light of reason. The head is placed for the good of the body. Christ and the saints make one body mystical. Our Head is in heaven, and surely He will not allow His body to be hurt — but will work for the safety of it, and make all things work for the good of the body mystical.

2. Inferences from the proposition that all things work for the good of the saints.

(1). If all things work for good, hence learn that there is a providence. Things do not work by themselves — but God sets them working for good. God is the great Disposer of all events and issues, He sets everything working. 'His kingdom rules over all' (Psalm 103:19). It is meant of His providential kingdom. Things in the world are not governed by second causes, by the counsels of men, by the stars and planets — but by divine providence. Providence is the queen and governess of the world. There are three things in providence: God's foreknowing, God's determining, and God's directing all things to their proper outcomes. Whatever things do work in the world, God sets them a working. We read in the first chapter of Ezekiel, of wheels, and eyes in the wheels, and the moving of the wheels. The wheels are the whole universe, the eyes in the wheels are God's providence, the moving of the wheels is the hand of Providence, turning all things here below. That which is by some called chance is nothing else but the result of God's providence.

Learn to adore providence. Providence has an influence upon all things here below. God's providence mingles the ingredients, and makes up the whole compound.

(2). Observe the happy condition of every child of God. All things work for his good — the best and worst things. 'Unto the upright arises light in darkness' (Psalm 112:4). The most dark cloudy providences of God, have some sunshine in them. What a blessed condition is a true believer in! When he dies, he goes to God; and while he lives, everything shall do him good. Affliction is for his good. What hurt does the fire to the gold? It only purifies it. What hurt does the winnowing fan do to the grain? It only separates the chaff from it. God never uses His staff — but to beat out the dust. Affliction does that which the Word many times will not, it 'opens the ear to discipline' (Job 36:10). When God lays men upon their backs — then they look up to heaven! God's smiting His people is like the musician's striking upon the violin, which makes it put forth a melodious sound. How much good comes to the saints by affliction! Like bruised flowers—when they are pounded and broken—they send forth their sweetest smell.

Affliction is a bitter root—but it bears sweet fruit. 'It yields the peaceable fruits of righteousness' (Heb. 12:11). Affliction is the highway to heaven; though it be flinty and thorny—yet it is the best way. Poverty shall starve our sins; sickness shall make grace more helpful (2 Cor. 4:16). Reproach shall cause 'the Spirit of God and of glory to rest upon us' (1 Pet. 4:14). Death shall stop the bottle of tears—and open the gate of Paradise! A believer's dying day is his ascension day to glory. Hence it is, the saints have put their afflictions, in the inventory of their riches (Heb. 11:26). A child of God say, 'If I had not been afflicted, I would have been destroyed; if my health and estate had not been lost—my soul had been lost.'

(3). See then what an encouragement there is to become godly. All things shall work for good. Oh, that this may induce men to fall in love with piety! Can there be a greater loadstone to piety? Can anything more prevail with us to be good, than this—that all things shall work for our good? Piety is the true magic stone which turns everything into gold. Take the sourest part of religion, the suffering part, and there is comfort in it. God sweetens suffering with joy; He candies our wormwood with sugar. Oh, how may this bribe us to godliness! 'Acquaint now yourself with God, and be at peace; thereby good shall come unto you' (Job 22:21). No man did ever come off a loser by his acquaintance with God. By this, good shall come unto you, abundance of good, the sweet distillations of grace, the hidden manna, yes, everything shall work for good. Oh, then get acquaintance with God, espouse His interest.

(4). Notice the miserable condition of wicked men. To those who are godly—evil things work for good; to those who are evil—good things work for hurt.

(a.) Temporal good things work for hurt to the wicked. Riches and prosperity are not benefits, but snares to them. Worldly things are given to the wicked, as Michal was given to David, for a snare (1 Sam. 18:21). The vulture is said to draw sickness from a perfume; so do the wicked get hurt from the sweet perfume of prosperity. Their mercies are like poisoned bread; their tables are sumptuously spread—but there is a hook under the bait! 'Let their table become a snare' (Psalm 69:22). All their enjoyments are like Israel's quail—which were sauced with the wrath of God (Numb. 11:33). Pride and luxury are the twin offspring of prosperity. 'You are waxen fat' (Deut. 32:15). Then he forsook God. Riches are not only like the spider's web, unprofitable—but like the cockatrice's egg, pernicious. 'Riches kept for the hurt of the owner' (Eccles. 5:13). The common mercies wicked men have, are not loadstones to draw them nearer to God—but millstones to sink them deeper in hell (1 Tim. 6:9). Their delicious dainties are like Haman's banquet; after all their lordly feasting, death will bring in the bill, and they must pay it in hell.

(b.) Spiritual good things work for hurt to the wicked. From the flower of heavenly blessings—they suck poison!

The ministers of God work for their hurt. The same wind that blows one ship to the haven, blows another ship upon a rock. The same breath in the ministry that blows a godly man to heaven, blows a profane sinner to hell. They who come with the word of life in their mouths—yet to many are a savor of death. 'Make the heart of this people fat, and their ears heavy' (Isaiah 6:10). The prophet was sent upon a sad message, to preach their funeral sermon. Wicked men are worse for preaching. 'They hate him who rebukes' (Amos 5:10). Sinners grow more resolved in sin; let God say what He will, they will do what they desire. 'As for the word which you have spoken to us in the name of the Lord—we will not hearken unto you!' (Jer. 44:16). The word preached is not healing—but hardening. And how dreadful is this for men to be sunk to hell with sermons!

Prayer works for their hurt. 'The sacrifice of the wicked is an abomination to the Lord' (Proverbs 15:8). A wicked man is in a great strait: if he prays not — he sins; if he prays — he sins. 'Let his prayer become sin' (Psalm 109:7). It were a sad judgment if all the food a man ate, should breed diseases in the body. And so it is with a wicked man. That prayer which should do him good, works for his hurt; he prays against sin, and sins against his prayer; his duties are tainted with atheism, and flyblown with hypocrisy. God abhors them! 'The plowing of the wicked, is sin.' (Proverbs 21:4)

The Lord's Supper works for their hurt. 'You cannot eat of the Lord's table — and the table of devils. Do we provoke the Lord to jealousy?' (1 Cor. 10:21, 22). Some professors kept their idol-feasts — yet would come to the Lord's table. The apostle says, 'Do you provoke the Lord to wrath?' Profane people feast with their sins; yet will come to feast at the Lord's table. This is to provoke God to wrath. To a sinner there is death in the cup, he 'eats and drinks his own damnation' (1 Cor. 11:29). Thus the Lord's Supper works for hurt to impenitent sinners. After the sop — the devil enters!

Christ Himself works for hurt to desperate sinners. He is 'a stone of stumbling, and rock of offence' (1 Pet. 2:8). He is so, through the depravity of men's hearts; for instead of believing in Him, they are offended at Him. The sun, though in its own nature pure and pleasant — yet it is hurtful to sore eyes. Jesus Christ is set for the fall, as the rising, of many (Luke 2:34). Sinners stumble at a Savior, and pluck death from the tree of life! As strong medicines recover some patients — but destroy others, so the blood of Christ, though to some it is medicine, to others it is condemnation. Here is the unparalleled misery of such as live and die in sin. The best things work for their hurt; cordials themselves, kill.

(5). See here the wisdom of God, who can make the worst things imaginable, turn to the good of the saints. He can by a divine chemistry extract gold out of dross. 'Oh the depth of the wisdom of God!' (Romans 11:33). It is God's great design to set forth the wonder of His wisdom. The Lord made Joseph's prison a step to advancement. There was no way for Jonah to be saved — but by being swallowed alive by the fish. God allowed the Egyptians to hate Israel (Psalm 106:41), and this was the means of their deliverance. Paul was bound with a chain, and that chain which did bind him was the means of enlarging the gospel (Phil. 1:12). God enriches by impoverishing; He causes the augmentation of grace by the diminution of an estate. When the creature goes further from us, it is that Christ may come nearer to us. God works strangely. He brings order out of confusion, and harmony out of discord. He frequently makes use of unjust men to do that which is just.

'He is wise in heart' (Job. 9:4). He can reap His glory out of men's fury (Psalm 86:10). Either the wicked shall not do the hurt that they intend — or they shall do the good which they do not intend. God often helps when there is least hope, and saves His people in that way which they think will destroy. He made use of the high priest's malice and Judas' treason — to redeem the world. Through indiscreet passion, we are apt to find fault with things that happen: which is as if an illiterate man should censure learning, or a blind man find fault with the work in a landscape. 'Vain man would be wise' (Job 11:12). Silly men will be taxing Providence, and calling the wisdom of God to the bar of human reason. God's ways are 'past finding out' (Romans 9:33). They are rather to be admired than fathomed. There is never a providence of God — but has either a mercy, or a wonder in it. How stupendous and infinite is that wisdom, that makes the most adverse dispensations work for the good of His children!

(6). Learn how little cause we have then to be discontented at outward trials and troubles! What! Discontented at that which shall do us good! All things shall work for good. There are no sins God's people are more subject to, than unbelief and impatience. They are ready either to faint through unbelief, or to fret through impatience. When men fly out against God by discontent and impatience, it is a sign they do not believe this text. Discontent is an ungrateful sin, because we have more mercies than afflictions; and it is an irrational sin, because afflictions work for good. Discontent is a sin which puts us upon sin. 'Fret not yourself to do evil' (Psalm 37:8). He who frets will be ready to do evil: fretting Jonah was sinning Jonah (Jonah 4:9). The devil blows the coals of passion and discontent, and then warms himself at the fire. Oh, let us not nourish this angry viper in our bosom! Let this text produce patience, 'All things work for good to those who love God' (Romans 8:28). Shall we be discontented at that which works for our good? If one friend should throw a bag of money at another, and in throwing it, should graze his head — he would not be troubled much, seeing by this means he had got a bag of money. Just so, the Lord may bruise us by afflictions — but it is to enrich us. These light afflictions work for us an eternal weight of glory — and shall we be discontented!

(7). See here that Scripture fulfilled, 'God is good to Israel' (Psalm 73:1). When we look upon adverse providences, and see the Lord covering His people with ashes, and 'making them drunk with wormwood' (Lam. 3:15), we may be ready to call in question the love of God, and to say that He deals harshly with His people. Yet God is good to His people, because He makes all things work for good. Is not He a good God — who turns all to good? He works out sin, and works in grace; is not this good? 'We are chastened of the Lord, that we should not be condemned with the world' (1 Cor. 11:32). The depth of affliction — is to save us from the depth of damnation! Let us always justify God; when our outward condition is ever so bad, let us say, 'Yet God is good.'

(8). See what cause the saints have to be frequent in the work of thanksgiving. In this, Christians are defective, though they are much in supplication — yet little in thanksgiving. The apostle says, 'In everything giving thanks' (Thess. 5:18). Why so? Because God makes everything work for our good. We thank the physician, though he gives us a bitter medicine which makes us sick, because it is to make us well. We thank any man who does us a good turn; and shall we not be thankful to God, who makes everything work for good to us? God loves a thankful Christian. Job thanked God when He took all away: 'The Lord has taken away — blessed be the name of the Lord!' (Job 1:21). Many will thank God when He gives; Job thanks Him when He takes away, because he knew God would work good out of it. We read of saints with harps in their hands (Rev. 14:2), an emblem of praise. We meet many Christians who have tears in their eyes, and complaints in their mouths. But there are few with their harps in their hands, who praise God in affliction. To be thankful in affliction is a work peculiar to a saint. Every bird can sing in spring — but some birds will sing in the dead of winter. Everyone, almost, can be thankful in prosperity — but a true saint can be thankful in adversity. A godly Christian will bless God, not only at sun-rise — but at sun-set. Well may we, in the worst which befalls us, have a psalm of thankfulness, because all things work for good. Oh, be much in blessing of God. We will thank Him who befriends us — and makes all things work out to our good.

(9). Think — if the worst things work for good to a believer, what shall the best things — Christ, and heaven! How much more shall these work for good! If the cross has so much good in it — what has the crown! If such precious clusters grow in Golgotha — how delicious is that fruit which grows in Canaan! If there is any sweetness in the bitter waters of Marah — what is there in the sweet wine of Paradise! If God's rod has honey at the end of it — what has His golden scepter! If the bread of affliction tastes so savory — then how savory is His manna! What is the heavenly ambrosia? If God's blow and stroke work for good — what shall the smiles of His face do! If temptations and sufferings have matter of joy in them — what shall glory have! If there is so much good out of evil — how great is that good where there shall be no evil? If God's chastening mercies are so great—what will His crowning mercies be? 'Therefore comfort one another with these words.'

(10). Consider, that if God makes all things to turn to our good—how right is it that we should make all things tend to His glory! 'Do all to the glory of God' (1 Cor. 10:31). The angels glorify God, they sing divine anthems of praise. How then ought redeemed man to glorify Him, for whom God has done more than for angels! He has dignified us above them in uniting our nature with the Godhead. Christ has died for us—and not the angels. The Lord has given us, not only out of the common stock of His bounty—but He has enriched us with covenant blessings. He has bestowed upon us His Spirit. He studies our welfare, He makes everything work for our good. Free grace has laid a plan for our salvation! If God seeks our good—shall we not seek His glory?

Question. How can we be said properly to glorify God. He is infinite in His perfections, and can receive no augmentation from us?

Answer. It is true that in a strict sense we cannot bring glory to God—but in an evangelical sense we may. When we do what in us lies to lift up God's name in the world, and to cause others to have high reverential thoughts of God—this the Lord interprets a glorifying of Him. Likewise, a man is said to dishonor God—when he causes the name of God to be evil spoken of.

We are said to advance God's glory in three ways:

(1.) We glorify God—when we aim at His glory—when we make Him the first in our thoughts, and the end of our life. As all the rivers run into the sea, and all the lines meet in the center—so all our actions should terminate and center in God!

(2.) We advance God's glory—by being fruitful in grace. 'Herein is my Father glorified—that you bring forth much fruit' (John 15:8). Barrenness reflects dishonor upon God. We glorify God when we grow in beauty as the lily, in tallness as the cedar, in fruitfulness as the vine.

(3.) We glorify God—when we give the praise and glory of all we do unto God. It was an excellent and humble speech of a king of Sweden; he feared lest the people's ascribing that glory to him which was due to God, should cause him to be removed before the work was done. When the silk worm weaves her curious work, she hides herself under the silk—and is not seen. When we have done our best, we must vanish away in our own thoughts—and transfer the glory of all to God. The apostle Paul said, 'I labored more abundantly than them all' (1 Cor. 15:10). One would think this speech savored of pride; but the apostle pulls off the crown from his own head, and sets it upon the head of free grace, 'Yet not I—but the grace of God which was with me!' Constantine used to write the name of Christ over the door, so should we over our duties. 'Therefore, whether you eat or drink, or whatever you do, do everything for God's glory.' 1 Corinthians 10:31

Thus let us endeavor to make the name of God glorious and renowned. If God seeks our good—let us seek His glory. If He makes all things tend to our edification—let us make all things tend to His exaltation. So much for the privilege mentioned in the text.

I proceed to the second general branch of the text—the people interested in this privilege.

II. The people interested in this privilege.

They are lovers of God. 'All things work together for good, to those who love God.'

Despisers and haters of God have no lot or part in this privilege. It is children's bread—it belongs only to those who love God. Because love to God is the very heart and spirit of true religion, I shall the more fully treat upon this; and for the further discussion of it, let us notice these five things concerning love to God.

1. The nature of love to God. Love is an expansion of soul, or the inflaming of the affections, by which a Christian breathes after God as the supreme and sovereign good. Love is to the soul as the weights to the clock, it sets the soul a-going towards God, as the wings by which we fly to heaven. By love we cleave to God, as the needle to the loadstone.

2. The ground of love to God; that is, knowledge. We cannot love that which we do not know. That our love may be drawn forth to God, we must know these three things in Him:

(1.) A fullness (Col. 1:19). He has a fullness of grace to cleanse us, and of a fullness glory to crown us; a fullness not only of sufficiency — but of redundancy. God is a sea of goodness without bottom and banks!

(2.) A freeness. God has an innate propensity to dispense mercy and grace; He drops as the honeycomb. 'Whoever will, let him take of the water of life freely' (Rev. 22:17). God does not require that we should bring money with us, only appetite.

(3.) A propriety, or property. We must know that this fullness in God is ours. 'This God is our God' (Psalm 48:14). Here is the ground of love — His Deity, and the saving interest we have in Him.

3. The kinds of love — which I shall branch into these three:

(1.) There is a love of appreciation. When we set a high value upon God as being the most sublime and infinite good. We so esteem God, as that if we have Him, we do not care though we lack all other things. The stars vanish, when the sun appears. All creatures vanish in our thoughts, when the Sun of righteousness shines in His full splendor.

(2.) A love of delight. As a man takes delight in a friend whom he loves. The soul that loves God, rejoices in Him as in his treasure — and rests in Him as his center. The heart is so set upon God — that it desires no more. 'Show us the Father, and it suffices' (John 14:8).

(3.) A love of benevolence. Which is a wishing well to the cause of God. He who is endeared in affection to his friend, wishes all happiness to him. This is to love God — when we are well-wishers. We desire that His interest may prevail. Our desire and prayer is that His name may be had in honor; that His gospel, which is the rod of His strength, may, like Aaron's rod — blossom and bring forth fruit!

4. The properties of love.

(1.) Our love to God must be entire, and that, in regard of the subject, it must be with the whole heart. 'You shall love the Lord your God with all your heart' (Mark 12:30). In the old law, a high priest was not to marry with a widow, nor with a harlot — not with a widow, because he had not her first love; nor with a harlot, because he had not all her love. God will have the whole heart. 'Their heart is divided' (Hos. 10:2). The true mother would not have the child divided; and God will not have the heart divided. God will not have only one room in the heart, and all the other rooms let out to sin. It must be an entire love.

(2.) Love to God must be sincere. 'Grace be with all those who love our Lord Jesus in sincerity' (Eph. 6:24). Sincere; it alludes to honey that is quite pure. Our love to God is sincere, when it is pure and without self-interest: this the school-men call a love of friendship. We must love Christ, as Augustine says, for Himself — as we love sweet wine for its taste. God's beauty and love must be the two loadstones to draw our love to Him. Alexander had two friends, Hephestion and Craterus, of whom he said, 'Hephestion loves me because I am Alexander; Craterus loves me became I am King Alexander.' The one loved his person, the other loved his gifts. Many love God because He gives them food and wine, and not for His intrinsic excellencies. We must love God more for what He is — than for what He bestows. True love is not mercenary. You need not hire a mother to love her child: a soul deeply in love with God needs not be hired by rewards. It cannot but love Him, for that luster of beauty which sparkles forth in Him.

(3.) Love to God must be fervent. The Hebrew word for love signifies ardency of affection. Saints must be seraphim, burning in holy love. To love one coldly, is the same as not to love him. The sun shines as hot as it can. Our love to God must be intense and vehement; like coals of juniper, which are most acute and fervent (Psalm 120:4). Our love to transitory things must be indifferent; we must love as if we loved not (1 Cor. 7:30). But our love to God must flame forth. The spouse was love-sick for Christ (Cant. 2:5). We can never love God as much as He deserves. As God's punishing us is less than we deserve (Ezra 9:13), so our loving Him is less than He deserves.

(4.) Love to God must be active. It is like fire, which is the most active element; it is called the labor of love (1 Thess. 1:3). Love is no idle grace; it sets the head a-studying for God, and the feet a-running in the ways of His commandments. 'The love of Christ constrains' (2 Cor. 5:14). Pretenses of love are insufficient. True love is not only seen at the tongue's end — but at the finger's end; it is the labor of love. The living creatures, mentioned in Ezekiel 1:8, had wings — an emblem of a godly Christian. He has not only the wings of faith to fly — but hands under his wings: he works by love, he spends and is spent for Christ.

(5.) Love to God must be liberal. It has love tokens to bestow (1 Cor. 13:4). Love is kind. Love has not only a smooth tongue — but a kind heart. David's heart was fired with love to God, and he would not offer that to God which cost him nothing (2 Sam. 24:24). Love is not only full of benevolence — but beneficence. Love which enlarges the heart, never straitens the hand. He who loves Christ, will be liberal to His members. He will be eyes to the blind, and feet to the lame. The backs and bellies of the poor shall be the furrows where he sows the golden seeds of liberality. Some say they love God — but their love is lame of one hand, they give nothing to good uses. Indeed faith deals with invisibles — but God hates that love which is invisible. Love is like new wine, which will have vent; it vents itself in good works. The apostle speaks it in honor of the Macedonians, that they gave to the poor saints, not only up to — but beyond their power (2 Cor. 8:3). Love is bred at court, it is a noble munificent grace.

(6.) Love to God must be special. He who is a lover of God gives Him such a love as he bestows upon none else. As God gives His children such a love as He does not bestow upon the wicked — electing, adopting love; so a gracious heart gives to God such a special distinguishing love as none else can share in. 'I have espoused you to one husband, that I may present you as a chaste virgin to Christ' (2 Cor. 11:2). A wife espoused to one husband gives him such a love as she has for none else; she does not part with her marital love, to any but her husband. So a saint espoused to Christ gives Him a special love — a love incommunicable to any other, namely, a love joined with adoration. Not only is the love is given to God — but the soul. 'A garden enclosed is my sister, my spouse' (Cant. 4:12). The heart of a believer is Christ's garden. The flower growing in it is love mixed with divine worship, and this flower is for the use of Christ alone. The spouse keeps the key of the garden, that none may come there, but Christ.

(7.) Love to God must be permanent. It is like the fire the vestal virgins kept at Rome — it does not go out. True love boils over — but does not give over. Love to God, as it is sincere without hypocrisy, so it is constant without apostasy. Love is like the pulse of the body, always beating. Wicked men are constant in love to their sins — neither shame, nor sickness, nor fear of hell, will make them give over their sins. Just so, nothing can hinder a Christian's love to God. Nothing can conquer love, not any difficulties, or oppositions. 'Love is as strong as the grave' (Cant. 8:6). The grave swallows up the strongest bodies — so love swallows up the strongest difficulties.

'Many waters cannot quench love' (Cant. 8:7). Neither the sweet waters of pleasure, nor the bitter waters of persecution. Love to God abides firm to death. 'Being rooted and grounded in love' (Ephes. 3:17). Light things, as chaff and feathers, are quickly blown away — but a tree that is rooted, abides the storm; he who is rooted in love, endures. True love never ends — but with the life.

5. The degree of love.

We must love God above all other objects. 'There is nothing on earth that I desire beside you' (Psalm 73:25). God is the quintessence of all good things, He is superlatively good. The soul seeing a super eminency in God, and admiring in Him that constellation of all excellencies, is carried out in love to Him in the highest degree. 'The measure of our love to God,' says Bernard, 'must be to love Him without measure.' God, who is the chief of our happiness, must have the chief of our affections. The creature may have the milk of our love — but God must have the cream. Love to God must be above all other things, as the oil swims above the water.

We must love God more than relations. As in the case of Abraham's offering up Isaac; Isaac being the son of his old age, no question he loved him entirely, and doted on him; but when God said, 'Abraham, offer up your son' (Gen. 22:2), though it were a thing which might seem, not only to oppose his reason — but his faith, for the Messiah was to come of Isaac, and if he be cut off, where shall the world have a Mediator! Yet such was the strength of Abraham's faith and ardency of his love to God — that he will take the sacrificing knife, and let out Isaac's blood. Our blessed Savior speaks of hating father and mother (Luke 14:26). Christ would not have us be unnatural; but if our dearest relations stand in our way, and would keep us from Christ — either we must step over them, or know them not (Deut. 33:9). Though some drops of love may run beside to our kindred and friends — yet the full torrent must run out after Christ. Relations may lie on the bosom — but Christ must lie in the heart!

We must love God more than our estate. 'You took joyfully the confiscation of your goods' (Heb. 10:34). They were glad they had anything to lose for Christ. If the world be laid in one scale, and Christ in the other — He must weigh heaviest. And is it thus? Has God the highest room in our affections? Plutarch says, When the love of God bears sway in the heart — all other love is as nothing in comparison of this love.

Use. A sharp reproof to those who do not love God. This may serve for a sharp reproof to such as have not a grain of love to God in their hearts — and are there such reprobates alive? He who does not love God — is a beast with a man's head! Oh wretch! Do you live upon God's bounty every day — yet not love Him? If one had a friend that supplied him continually with money, and gave him all his allowance, were not he worse than a barbarian, if he did not respect and honor that friend? Such a friend is God — He gives you your breath, He bestows a livelihood upon you — and will you not love Him? You will love your prince if he saves your life, and will you not love God who gives you your life? What loadstone so powerful to draw love, as the blessed Deity? He is blind whom beauty does not tempt, he is sottish who is not drawn with the cords of love. When the body is cold and has no heat in it, it is a sign of death — that man is dead who has no heat of love in his soul to God. How can he expect love from God, who shows no love to Him? Will God ever lay such a viper in His bosom, as casts forth the poison of malice and enmity against Him?

This reproof falls heavy upon the infidels of this age, who are so far from loving God, that they do all they can to show their hatred of Him. 'They declare their sin as Sodom' (Isaiah 3:9). 'They set their mouth against the heavens' (Psalm 73:9), in pride and blasphemy, and bid open defiance to God. These are monsters in nature, devils in the shape of men! Let them read their doom: 'If anyone does not love the Lord, that person is cursed!' (1 Cor. 16:22), that is, let him be accursed from God, until Christ's coming to judgment. Let him be heir to a curse while he lives, and at the dreadful day of the Lord, let him hear that heart rending sentence pronounced against him, 'Depart, you who are cursed!'

The tests of love to God

Let us test ourselves impartially whether we are in the number of those that love God. For the deciding of this, as our love will be best seen by the fruits of it, I shall lay down fourteen signs, or fruits, of love to God, and it concerns us to search carefully whether any of these fruits grow in our garden.

1. The first fruit of genuine love to God — is the musing of the mind upon God. He who is in love — his thoughts are ever upon the object of his love. He who loves God is ravished and transported with the contemplation of God. 'When I awake, I am still with You!' (Psalm 139:18). The thoughts are as travelers in the mind. David's thoughts kept on the heaven-road, 'I am still with You!' God is the treasure, and where the treasure is, there is the heart. By this we may test our love to God. What are our thoughts most upon? Can we say we are ravished with delight, when we think on God? Have our thoughts got wings? Are they fled aloft? Do we contemplate Christ and glory? Oh, how far are they from being lovers of God — who scarcely ever think of God! 'God is not in all his thoughts' (Psalm 10:4). A sinner crowds God out of his thoughts. He never thinks of God, unless with horror, as the prisoner thinks of the judge!

2. The next fruit of genuine love to God — is desire of communion with Him. Love desires familiarity and fellowship. 'My heart and flesh cry out for the living God' (Psalm 84:2). King David being debarred the house of God where the tabernacle was, the visible token of His presence, he breathes after God, and in a holy pathos of desire, cries out for the living God. Lovers desire to be conversing together. If we love God we prize His ordinances, because there we meet with God. He speaks to us in His Word — and we speak to Him in prayer. By this let us examine our love to God. Do we desire intimacy of communion with God? Lovers cannot be long away from each other. Such as love God have a holy affection for Him — and desire to be with Him. They can bear the lack of anything — but God's presence. They can do without health and friends, they can be happy without a full table — but they cannot be happy without God. 'Hide not your face from me, lest I be like those who go down into the grave' (Psalm 143:7). Lovers have their fainting fits. David was ready to faint away and die, when he had not a sight of God. They who love God cannot be contented with having ordinances, unless they may enjoy God in them; that would be to lick the glass, and not the honey.

What shall we say to those who can be all their lives long without God? They think that God may be ignored: they complain they lack health and trading — but not that they lack God! Wicked men are not acquainted with God. How can they love Him — who are not acquainted with him! Nay, which is worse, they do not desire to be acquainted with Him. 'They say to God, Depart from us, we desire not the knowledge of your ways' (Job 21:14). Sinners shun acquaintance with God, they count His presence a burden; and are these lovers of God? Does that woman love her husband, who cannot endure to be in his presence?

3. Another fruit of genuine love to God — is grief for sin. Where there is love to God — there is a grieving for our sins of unkindness against Him. A child who loves his father, cannot but weep for offending him. The heart which burns in love — melts in tears. Oh! That I should abuse the love of so dear a Savior! Did not my Lord suffer enough upon the cross — but must I make Him suffer more? Shall I give Him more gall and vinegar to drink? How disloyal and hypocritical have I been! How have I grieved His Spirit, trampled upon His royal commands, slighted His

blood! This opens a vein of godly sorrow, and makes the heart bleed afresh. 'Peter went out, and wept bitterly' (Matt. 26:75). When Peter thought how dearly Christ loved him; how he was taken up into the mount of transfiguration, where Christ showed him the glory of heaven in a vision; that he should deny Christ after he had received such amazing love from Him, this broke his heart with grief—he went out, and wept bitterly.

By this let us test our love to God. Do we shed the tears of godly sorrow? Do we grieve for our unkindness against God, our abuse of His mercy, our non-improvement the talents which He has given us? How far are they from loving God—who sin daily, and their hearts never smite them! They have a sea of sin—and not a drop of sorrow! They are so far from being troubled, that they make merry with their sins. 'When you engage in your wickedness, then you rejoice!' (Jer. 11:15). Oh wretch! Did Christ bleed for sin—and do you laugh at it? These are far from loving God. Does he love his friend—who loves to do him an injury?

4. Another fruit of genuine love to God—is courage. Love is valorous—it turns cowardice into courage. Love will make one venture upon the greatest difficulties and hazards. The fearful hen will fly upon a dog or serpent—to defend her young ones. Just so, love infuses a spirit of gallantry and fortitude into a Christian. He who loves God will stand up in His cause, and be an advocate for Him. 'We cannot but speak the things which we have seen and heard' (Acts 4:20). He who is afraid to own Christ, has but little love to Him. Nicodemus came sneaking to Christ by night (John 3:2). He was fearful of being seen with Him in the day time. Love casts out fear. As the sun expels fogs and vapors, so divine love in a great measure expels carnal fear. Does he love God—who can hear His blessed truths spoken against and be silent? He who loves his friend will stand up for him, and vindicate him when he is reproached. Does Christ appear for us in heaven—and are we afraid to appear for Him on earth? Love animates a Christian, it fires his heart with zeal, and steels him with courage.

5. The fifth fruit of genuine love to God—is sensitiveness. If we love God, our hearts ache for the dishonor done to God by wicked men. To see piety and morality broken down—and a flood of wickedness coming in; to see God's name dishonored—if there is any love to God in us, we shall lay these things to heart. Lot's righteous soul was 'vexed with the filthy lives of the wicked' (2 Pet. 2:7). The sins of Sodom were as so many spears to pierce his soul. How far are they from loving God, who are not at all affected with His dishonor? If they have but peace and trading, they lay nothing to heart. A man who is dead drunk, never minds nor is affected by it—though another is bleeding to death by him. Just so, many, being drunk with the wine of prosperity, when the honor of God is wounded and His truths lie a-bleeding, are not affected by it. Did men love God, they would grieve to see His glory suffer, and piety itself become a martyr.

6. The sixth fruit of genuine love to God—is hatred against sin. Fire purges the dross from the metal. The fire of love purges out sin. 'Ephraim shall say, What have I to do any more with idols!' (Hos. 14:8). He who loves God, will have nothing to do with sin, unless to give battle to it. Sin strikes not only at God's honor—but His being. Does he love his prince—who harbors a traitor to the prince? Is he a friend to God—who loves that which God hates? The love of God and the love of sin, cannot dwell together. The affections cannot be carried to two contrarieties at the same time. A man cannot love health and love poison too. Just so, one cannot love God and sin too. He who has any secret sin in his heart allowed, is as far from loving God as heaven and earth are distant one from the other.

7. Another fruit of genuine love to God—is crucifixion to the world. He who is a lover of God—is dead to the world. 'The world has been crucified to me, and I to the world.' (Gal. 6:14). That is, 'I am dead to the honors and pleasures of the world.' He who is in love with God is not much

in love with anything else. The love of God, and ardent love of the world—are incompatible. 'If any man loves the world, the love of the Father is not in him' (1 John 2:15). Love to God swallows up all other love—as Moses' rod swallowed up the Egyptian rods. If a man could live as high as the sun—what a small point would all the earth be. Just so, when a man's heart is raised above the world in the admiring and loving of God, how poor and diminutive are these things below! They seem as nothing in his eye. It was a sign the early Christians loved God, because their property did not lie near their hearts; but they 'laid down their money at the apostles' feet' (Acts 4:35).

Test your love to God by this. What shall we think of those who have never enough of the world? They have the cancer of covetousness, thirsting insatiably after riches: 'That pant after the dust of the earth' (Amos 2:7). 'Never talk of your love to Christ,' says Ignatius,' when you prefer the world before the Pearl of price!' Are there not many such, who prize their gold above God? If they have a good farm—they care not for the water of life. They will sell Christ and a good conscience for money. Will God ever bestow heaven upon those who so basely undervalue Him, preferring glittering dust before the glorious Deity? What is there in the earth, that we should so set our hearts upon it? The devil makes us look upon it through a magnifying glass! The world has no real intrinsic worth, it is but paint and deception.

8. The next fruit of genuine love to God—is reverential fear of God. In the godly, love and fear kiss each other. There is a double fear arises from love.

(1.) A fear of displeasing. The spouse loves her husband, therefore will rather deny herself than displease him. The more we love God, the more fearful we are of grieving His Spirit. 'How then can I do this great wickedness, and sin against God?' (Gen. 39:9). When Eudoxia, the empress, threatened to banish Chrysostom; 'Tell her' (said he) 'I fear nothing but sin!' That is a blessed love which puts a Christian into a hot fit of zeal, and a cold fit of fear, making him shake and tremble, and not dare willingly to offend God.

(2.) A fear mixed with jealousy. 'Eli's heart trembled for the ark' (1 Sam. 4:13). It is not said, his heart trembled for Hophni and Phinehas, his two sons—but his heart trembled for the ark, because if the ark were taken, then the glory was departed. He who loves God is full of fear lest it should go ill with the church. He fears lest worldliness (which is the plague of leprosy) should increase; lest popery should get a footing; lest God should go from His people. The presence of God in His ordinances is the beauty and strength of a nation. So long as God's presence is with a people, so long they are safe; but the soul inflamed with love to God fears lest the visible tokens of God's presence should be removed.

By this touchstone let us test our love to God. Many fear lest peace and trading might leave them—but not lest God and His gospel might leave them. Are these lovers of God? He who loves God is more afraid of the loss of spiritual blessings than temporal blessings. If the Sun of righteousness removes out of our horizon, what can follow but darkness? What comfort can an anthem give, if the gospel is gone? Is it not like the sound of a trumpet at a funeral?

9. If we are lovers of God—we love what God loves.

(1.) We love God's word. David esteemed the Word, for the sweetness of it—above honey (Psalm 119. 103), and for the value of it—above gold (Psalm 119. 72). The lines of Scripture are richer than the mines of gold. Well may we love the Word; it is the pole-star which directs us to heaven, it is the field in which the Pearl of great price is hidden. That man who does not love the Word—but thinks it too strict and could wish any part of the Bible torn out (as an adulterer did the seventh commandment), he has not the least spark of love in his heart.

(2.) We love God's day. We do not only keep a sabbath—but love a sabbath. 'If you call the Sabbath a delight' (Isaiah 58:13). The Sabbath is that which keeps up the face of religion among us; this day must be consecrated as glorious to the Lord. The house of God is the palace of the great King, on the Sabbath God shows Himself there through the lattice. If we love God we prize His day above all other days. All the week would be dark if it were not for this day; on this day manna falls double. Now, if ever, heaven gate stands open, and God comes down in a golden shower. This blessed day the Sun of righteousness rises upon the soul. How does a gracious heart prize that day which was made on purpose to enjoy God in.

(3.) We love God's laws. A gracious soul is glad of the law because it checks his sinful excesses. The heart would be ready to run wild in sin, if it had not some blessed restraints put upon it by the law of God. He who loves God, loves His law—the law of repentance, the law of self-denial. Many say they love God but they hate His laws. 'Let us break their bands asunder, and cast away their cords from us' (Psalm 2:3). God's precepts are compared to cords, they bind men to their good behavior; but the wicked think these cords too tight, therefore they say, 'Let us break them!' They pretend to love Christ as a Savior—but hate Him as a King. Christ tells us of His yoke (Matt. 11:29). Sinners would have Christ put a crown upon their head—but not a yoke upon their neck! He would be a strange king—who would rule without laws.

(4.) We love God's picture, we love His image shining in the saints. 'Everyone who loves the Father loves his children, too' (1 John 5:1). It is possible to love a saint—yet not to love him as a saint; we may love him for something else, for his ingenuity, or because he is affable and bountiful. A beast loves a man—but not as he is a man—but because he feeds him, and gives him provender. But to love a saint as he is a saint, this is a sign of love to God. If we love a saint for his saintship, as having something of God in him, then we love him in these four cases.

(a) We love a saint, though he be poor. A man who loves gold—loves a piece of gold, though it is wrapped in a rag. Just so, though a saint is in rags, we love him, because there is something of Christ in him.

(b) We love a saint, though he has many personal failings. There is no perfection here on earth. In some, rash anger prevails; in some, fickleness; in some, too much love of the world. A saint in this life is like gold in the ore, much dross of infirmity cleaves to him—yet we love him for the grace that is in him. A saint is like a fair face with a scar—we love the beautiful face of holiness, though there is a scar in it. The best emerald has its blemishes, the brightest stars have their twinklings, and the best of the saints have their failings. You who cannot love another because of his infirmities, how would you have God love you?

(c) We love the saints though in some lesser things they differ from us. Perhaps another Christian has not so much light as you, and that may make him err in some things; will you presently unsaint him because he cannot come up to your light? Where there is union in fundamentals, there ought to be union in affections.

(d) We love the saints, though they are persecuted. We love precious metal, though it is in the furnace. Paul bore in his body the marks of the Lord Jesus (Gal. 6:17). Those marks were, like the soldier's scars, honorable. We must love a saint as well in chains, as in scarlet. If we love Christ, we love His persecuted members.

If this is love to God, when we love His image sparkling in the saints, oh then, how few lovers of God are to be found! Do they love God, who hate those who are like God? Do they love Christ's person, who are filled with a spirit of revenge against His people? How can that wife be said to love her husband, who tears his picture? What greater crime than holiness—if the devil is the judge! Wicked men seem to bear great reverence to the departed saints; they canonize dead saints – but persecute living saints. In vain do men stand up at the creed, and tell the world they believe in God, when they abominate one of the articles of the creed, namely, the communion of saints. Surely, there is not a greater sign of a man ripe for hell, than this – not only to lack grace – but to hate it.

10. Another blessed sign of genuine love to God – is to entertain good thoughts of God. He who loves his friend interprets what his friend does, in the best sense. 'Love thinks no evil' (1 Cor. 13:5). Malice interprets all in the worst sense; love interprets all in the best sense. Love is an excellent commentator upon God's providence; it thinks no evil. He who loves God, has a good opinion of God; though He afflicts sharply – the soul takes all well. This is the language of a gracious spirit: 'My God sees what a hard heart I have, therefore He drives in one wedge of affliction after another, to break my heart. He knows how full I am of the cancer of covetousness, or the swelling of pride, or the fever of lust – therefore He gives me bitter remedies, to save my life. This severe dispensation is either to mortify some corruption, or to exercise some grace. How good is God, who will not let me alone in my sins – but smites my body to save my soul! Thus he who loves God, receives all of God's dealings in the best sense. Love puts a good gloss upon all God's actions. You who are apt to murmur at God, as if He had dealt ill with you – be humbled for this; say thus with yourself, 'If I loved God more, I would have better thoughts of God.' It is Satan who makes us have high thoughts of ourselves, and hard thoughts of God. 'But take away everything he has, and he will surely curse You to Your face!' (Job 1:11) Love takes all in the fairest sense; it thinks no evil. 'Then Job fell to the ground in worship and said, 'Naked I came from my mother's womb, and naked I will depart. The Lord gave and the Lord has taken away; may the name of the Lord be praised.' In all this, Job did not sin by charging God with wrongdoing.' (Job 1:20-22) 'It is the Lord's will. Let him do what he thinks best.' (1 Samuel 3:18)

11. Another fruit of genuine love to God – is obedience. 'He who has my commandments, and keeps them, he it is that loves me' (John 14:21). It is a vain thing to say we love Christ – if we slight His commands. Does that child love his father, who refuses to obey him? If we love God, we shall obey Him in those things which cross flesh and blood. (1.) In things difficult, and (2.) In things dangerous.

(1.) In things difficult. As, in mortifying sin. There are some sins which are not only as near to us as our garment – but dear to us as our eye. If we love God, we shall set ourselves against these, both in purpose and practice.

Also, in forgiving our enemies. God commands us upon pain of death to forgive. 'Forgive one another' (Ephes. 4:32). This is hard; it is crossing the stream. We are apt to forget kindnesses, and remember injuries; but if we love God, we shall pass by offences. When we seriously consider how many talents God has forgiven us, how many affronts and provocations He has put up with at our hands; this makes us write after His copy, and endeavor rather to bury an injury, than to retaliate it.

(2.) In things dangerous. When God calls us to suffer for Him, we shall obey. Love made Jesus suffer for us. 'Because of His great love for us.' (Ephesians 2:4) 'Because of the Lord's great love we are not consumed, for His compassions never fail.' (Lamentations 3:22) Love was the chain which fastened Jesus to the cross; so, if we love God, we shall be willing to suffer for Him. Love has a strange quality, it is the least suffering grace, and yet it is the most suffering grace. It is the least suffering grace in one sense; it will not suffer known sin to lie in the soul unrepented of, it will not suffer abuses and dishonors done to God; thus it is the least suffering grace. Yet it is the most suffering grace; it will suffer reproaches, bonds, and imprisonments, for Christ's sake. 'I am ready not only to be bound – but to die, for the name of the Lord Jesus' (Acts 21:13). It is true that every Christian is not a martyr — but he has the spirit of martyrdom in him. He says as Paul, 'I am ready to be bound.' He has a disposition of mind to suffer, if God calls him to suffer.

Love will carry men out above their own strength. Tertullian observes how much the heathen suffered, for love to their country. If the spring head of nature rises so high, surely grace will rise higher. If love to their country will make men suffer, much more should love to Christ. 'Love endures all things' (1 Cor. 13:7). Basil speaks of a virgin condemned to the fire, who having her life and estate offered her if she would fall down to worship the idol, answered, 'Let life and money go, welcome Christ!' It was a noble and zealous speech of Ignatius, 'Let me be ground with the teeth of wild beasts — if I may be God's pure wheat.' How did divine affection carry the early saints above the love of life, and the fear of death! Stephen was stoned; Luke was hanged on an olive tree; Peter was crucified at Jerusalem with his head downwards. These divine heroes were willing to suffer, rather than by their cowardice to make the name of God suffer. How did Paul prize his chain that he wore for Christ! He gloried in it, as a woman who is proud of her jewels! And holy Ignatius wore his fetters as a bracelet of diamonds. 'Not accepting deliverance' (Heb. 11:35). They refused to come out of prison on sinful terms, they preferred their innocence before their liberty.

By this let us test our love to God. Have we the spirit of martyrdom? Many say they love God — but how does it appear? They will not forego the least comfort, or undergo the least cross for His sake. If Jesus Christ should have said to us, 'I love you much, you are dear to me — but I cannot suffer for you, I cannot lay down my life for you,' we would have questioned the genuineness of His love. And may not Christ suspect us, when we pretend to love Him, and yet will endure nothing for Him!

12. He who sincerely loves God — will endeavor to make Him appear glorious in the eyes of others. Such as are in love will be commending and setting forth the amiableness of those people whom they love. If we love God, we shall spread abroad His excellencies, that so we may raise His fame and esteem, and may induce others to fall in love with Him. Love cannot be silent. We shall be as so many trumpets, sounding forth the freeness of God's grace — the transcendence of His love — and the glory of His kingdom. Love is like fire — where it burns in the heart, it will break forth at the lips. It will be elegant in setting forth God's praise. Love must have vent.

13. Another fruit of genuine love to God — is to long for Christ's appearing. 'Henceforth there is a crown of righteousness laid up for me, and not for me only — but for those who love Christ's appearing' (2 Tim. 4:8). Love desires union; Aristotle gives the reason — because joy flows upon union. When our union with Christ is perfect in glory, then our joy will be full. He who loves Christ loves His appearing. Christ's appearing will be a happy appearing to the saints. His appearing now is very comforting, when He appears for us as an Advocate (Heb. 9:24). But the other appearing will be infinitely more so, when He shall appear for us as our Husband. He will at that day bestow two jewels upon us! His love; a love so great and astonishing, that it is better felt than expressed. And He will also bestow His likeness upon us! 'When he shall appear, we shall be like him' (1 John 3:2). And from both these, love and likeness, infinite joy will flow into the soul! No wonder then that he who loves Christ longs for His appearance. 'The Spirit and the bride say come; even so come, Lord Jesus!' (Rev. 22:17, 20). By this let us test our love to Christ. A wicked man is afraid of Christ's appearing, and wishes He would never appear; but such as love Christ, are joyful to think of His coming in the clouds. They shall then be delivered from all their sins and fears, they shall be acquitted before men and angels, and shall be forever translated into the paradise of God!

14. Genuine love to God—will make us stoop to the lowest offices. Love is a humble grace, it does not walk abroad in state, it will creep upon its hands, it will stoop and submit to anything whereby it may be serviceable to Christ. As we see in Joseph of Arimathea, and Nicodemus, both of them honorable people—yet one takes down Christ's body with his own hands, and the other embalms it with sweet odors. It might seem much for people of their rank to be employed in that service—but love made them do it. If we love God, we shall not think any work too low for us, by which we may be helpful to Christ's members. Love is not squeamish; it will visit the sick, relieve the poor, wash the saints' wounds. The mother who loves her child is not squeamish; she will do those things for her child which others would scorn to do. He who loves God will humble himself to the lowest office of love to Christ and His members.

These are the fruits of love to God. Happy are they who can find these fruits so foreign to their natures, growing in their souls.

1. An exhortation to love God

Let me earnestly persuade all who bear the name of Christians to become lovers of God. 'O love the Lord, all you his saints' (Psalm 31:23). There are but few that love God: many give Him hypocritical kisses—but few love Him. It is not so easy to love God as most imagine. The affection of love is natural—but the grace of love is not. Men are by nature haters of God (Romans 1:30). The wicked would flee from God; they would neither be under His rules, nor within His reach! They fear God—but do not love Him. All the strength in men or angels cannot make the heart love God. Ordinances will not do it of themselves, nor will judgments. Only the almighty and invincible power of the Spirit of God can infuse love into the soul. This being so hard a work, it calls upon us for the more earnest prayer and endeavor after this angelic grace of love to god. To excite and inflame our desires after it, I shall prescribe twenty motives for loving God.

(1). Without love to God, all our religion is vain. It is not duty—but love to duty, which God looks at. It is not how much we do—but how much we love. If a servant does not do his work willingly, and out of love, it is not acceptable. Duties not mingled with love, are as burdensome to God as they are to us. David therefore counsels his son Solomon to serve God with a willing mind (1 Chron. 28:9). To do duty without love, is not sacrifice—but penance.

(2). Love to God is the most noble and excellent grace. It is a pure flame kindled from heaven; by it we resemble God, who is love. Believing and obeying do not make us like God—but by love we grow like Him (1 John 4:16). Love is a grace which most delights in God, and is most delightful to Him. That disciple who was most full of love, lay in Christ's bosom. Love puts a verdure and luster upon all the graces: the graces seem to be eclipsed, unless love shines and sparkles in them. Faith is not true, unless it works by love. The waters of repentance are not pure, unless they flow from the spring of love. Love is the incense which makes all our services fragrant and acceptable to God.

(3). Is that unreasonable, which God requires? It is but our love. If He should ask our estate, or the fruit of our bodies, could we deny Him? But He asks only our love! He would only pick this flower! Is this a hard request? Was there ever any debt so easily paid as this? We do not at all impoverish ourselves by paying it. Love is no burden. Is it any labor for the bride to love her husband? Love is delightful.

(4). God is the most adequate and complete object of our love. All the excellencies which lie scattered in the creatures, are united in Him! He is wisdom, beauty, love, yes, the very essence of goodness. There is nothing in God which can cause a loathing. The creature sooner surfeits than satisfies — but there are fresh beauties continually sparkling forth in God. The more we love Him — the more we enjoy Him and are ravished with delight!

There is nothing in God to deaden our affections or quench our love. There is neither infirmity nor deformity — such as usually weaken and cool love. There is that excellence in God, which may not only invite — but command our love. If there were more angels in heaven than there are, and all those glorious seraphim had an immense flame of love burning in their breasts to eternity — yet could they not love God equivalently to that infinite perfection and transcendence of goodness which is in Him. Surely then here is enough to induce us to love God — we cannot spend our love upon a better object!

(5). Love to God facilitates religion. It oils the wheels of the affections, and makes them more lively and cheerful in God's service. Love takes off the tediousness of duty. Jacob thought seven years but little, for the love he bore to Rachel. Love makes duty a pleasure. Why are the angels so swift and winged in God's service? It is because they love Him. Love is never weary. He who loves God, is never weary of telling it. He who loves God, is never weary of serving Him.

(6). God desires our love. We have lost our beauty, and stained our blood — yet the King of heaven is a suitor to us! What is there in our love, that God should seek it? What is God the better for our love? He does not need it, He is infinitely blessed in Himself. If we deny Him our love, He has more sublime creatures who pay the cheerful tribute of love to Him. God does not need our love — yet He seeks it.

(7). God has deserved our love; how has He loved us! Our affections should be kindled at the fire of God's love. What a miracle of love is it, that God should love us, when there was nothing lovely in us. 'When you were in your blood, I said unto you, Live' (Ezek. 16:6). The time of our loathing, was the time of God's loving. We had something in us to provoke God's fury — but nothing to excite His love. What love, passing understanding, was it, to give Christ to us! That Christ should die for sinners! God has set all the angels in heaven wondering at this love. Augustine says, 'The cross is a pulpit, and the lesson Christ preached on it is love.' Oh the living love of a dying Savior! I think I see Christ upon the cross bleeding all over! I think I hear Him say to us, 'Put your hand into the wound in My side. Feel My bleeding heart. See if I do not love you! And will you not bestow your love upon Me? Will you love the world more than me? Did the world appease the wrath of God for you? Have I not done all this? And will you not love Me?' It is natural to love where we are loved. Christ having set us a copy of love, and written it with His blood, let us labor to write after so fair a copy, and to imitate Him in love. 'We love Him because He first loved us.' 1 John 4:19

(8). Love to God is the best self-love. It is self-love to get the soul saved; by loving God, we forward our own salvation. 'He who dwells in love, dwells in God, and God in him' (1 John 4:16). And he is sure to dwell with God in heaven — who has God dwelling in his heart. So that to love God is the truest self-love; he who does not love God, does not love himself.

(9). Love to God evidences sincerity. 'The upright love you' (Cant. 1:4). Many a child of God fears he is a hypocrite. Do you love God? When Peter was dejected with the sense of his sin, he thought himself unworthy that ever Christ should take notice of him, or employ him more in the work of his apostleship; see how Christ goes about to comfort him. 'Peter, do you love me?' (John 21:15). As if Christ had said, 'Though you have denied me through fear — yet if you can say from your heart you love me, you are sincere and upright.' To love God is a better sign of sincerity, than to fear Him. The Israelites feared God's justice. 'When he slew them, they sought him, and inquired early after God' (Psalm 78:34). But what did all this come to? 'Nevertheless, they did but flatter him with their mouth, and lied to him with their tongue; for their heart was not right with him' (verses 36, 37). That repentance is no better than flattery, which arises only from fear of God's judgments, and has no love mixed with it. Loving God evidences that God has the heart; and if the heart is His, that will command all the rest!

(10). By our love to God, we may conclude God's love to us. 'We love Him, because He first loved us' (1 John 4:19). Oh, says the soul, if I knew God loved me, I could rejoice! Do you love God? Then you may be sure of God's love to you. If our hearts burn in love to God, it is because God's love has first shined upon us, else we could not burn in love. Our love is nothing but the reflection of God's love.

(11). If you do not love God, you will love something else, either the world or sin; and are those worthy of your love? Is it not better to love God than these? It is better to love God than the world, as appears in the following particulars.

If you set your love on worldly things, they will not satisfy. You may as well satisfy your body with air, as your soul with earth! 'In the fullness of his sufficiency, he shall be in straits' (Job 22:22). Plenty has its poverty. If the globe of the world were yours, it would not fill your soul. Will you set your love on that which will never give you contentment? Is it not better to love God? He will give you that which shall satisfy your soul to all eternity! 'When I awake, I shall be satisfied with your likeness' (Psalm 17:15). When I awake out of the sleep of death, and shall have some of the rays and beams of God's glory put upon me, I shall then be satisfied with His likeness.

If you love worldly things, they cannot remove trouble of mind. If there is a thorn in the conscience, all the world cannot pluck it out. King Saul, being perplexed in mind, all his crown jewels could not comfort him (1 Sam. 28:15). But if you love God, He can give you peace when nothing else can; He can turn the 'shadow of death into the morning' (Amos 5:8). He can apply Christ's blood to refresh your soul; He can whisper His love by the Spirit, and with one smile scatter all your fears and disquiets.

If you love the world, you love that which may keep you out of heaven. Worldly contentments may be compared to the wagons in an army; while the soldiers have been entertaining themselves at the wagons, they have lost the battle. 'How hard it is for those who have wealth to enter the kingdom of God!' (Mark 10:23). Prosperity to many is like a large sail to a small boat, which quickly overturns it; so that by loving the world, you love that which will endanger you. But if you love God, there is no fear of losing heaven. He will be a Rock to hide you — but not to hurt you. By loving Him, we come to enjoy Him forever.

You may love worldly things — but they cannot love you in return. You love gold and silver — but your gold cannot love you in return. You love a picture — but the picture cannot love you in return. You give away your love to the creature — and receive no love back. But if you love God, He will love you in return. 'If any man loves me, my Father will love him, and we will come unto him, and make our abode with him' (John 14:23). God will not be behindhand in love to us. For our drop of love to Him, we shall receive an ocean of His love!

When you love the world, you love that which is worse than yourselves. The soul, as Damascen says, is a sparkle of celestial brightness; it carries in it an idea and resemblance of God. While you love the world, you love that which is infinitely below the worth of your souls. Will any one lay out cost upon sackcloth? When you lay out your love upon the world, you hang a pearl upon a swine — you love that which is inferior to yourself. As Christ speaks in another sense of the fowls of the air, 'Are you nor much better than they?' (Matt. 6:26), so I say of worldly things, Are you not much better than they? You love a fair house, or a beautiful garment — are you not much better than they? But if you love God, you place your love on the most noble and sublime object—you love that which is better than yourselves. God is better than the soul, better than angels, better than heaven!

You may love the world, and receive hatred for your love. 'Because you are not of the world, therefore the world hates you' (John 15:19). Would it not vex one to lay out money upon a piece of ground which, instead of bringing forth grain or fruit, should yield nothing but nettles? Thus it is with all earthly things—we love them, and they prove nettles to sting us! We meet with nothing but disappointment. 'Let fire come out of the bramble, and devour the cedars of Lebanon' (Judg. 9:15). While we love the creature, fire comes out of this bramble to devour us; but if we love God, He will not return hatred for love. 'I love those who love me' (Proverbs 7:17). God may chastise His children—but He cannot hate them. Every believer is part of Christ, and God can as well hate Christ as hate a believer.

You may over-love the creature. You may love wine too much, and silver too much; but you cannot love God too much. If it were possible to exceed, excess here were a virtue; but it is our sin that we cannot love God enough. 'How weak is your heart!' (Ezek. 16:30). So it may be said, How weak is our love to God! It is like water of the last drawing from the still—which has less spirit in it. If we could love God far more than we do--yet it can never be proportionate to His worth; so that there is no danger of excess in our love to God.

You may love worldly things, and they die and leave you. Riches take wings! Relations drop away! There is nothing here abiding. The creature has a little honey in its mouth--but it has wings! It will soon fly away. But if you love God, He is 'a portion forever' (Psalm 73:26). As He is called a Sun for comfort, so a Rock for eternity; He abides forever. Thus we see it is better to love God than the world.

If it is better to love God than the world—surely also it is better to love God than SIN. 'They are haters of God, insolent, proud, and boastful. They are forever inventing new ways of sinning.' (Romans 1:30). What is there in sin, that any should love it? Sin is a debt. 'Forgive us our debts' (Matt. 6:12). It is a debt which binds over to the wrath of God; why should we love sin? Does any man love to be in debt? Sin is a disease. 'The whole head is sick' (Isaiah 1:5). And will you love sin? Will any man hug a disease? Will he love his plague sores? Sin is a pollution. The apostle calls it 'filthiness' (James 1:21). It is compared to leprosy and to poison of asps. God's heart rises against sinners. 'My soul loathed them' (Zech. 11:8). Sin is a hideous monster. Lust makes a man brutish; malice makes him devilish. What is in sin to be loved? Shall we love deformity? Sin is an enemy. It is compared to a 'serpent' (Proverbs 23:32). Sin has five sharp stings—shame, guilt, horror, death, damnation. Will a man love that which seeks his death? Surely then it is better to love God than sin. God will save you, sin will damn you! Is he not a fool—who loves damnation? Many love sin, more than God.

(12). The relation we stand in to God calls for love. There is near affinity. 'Your Maker is your husband' (Isaiah liv. 5). And shall a wife not love her husband? He is full of tenderness. His spouse is to him as the apple of his eye. He rejoices over her, as the bridegroom over his bride (Isaiah 62:5). He loves the believer—as He loves Christ (John 17:26). The same love for quality, though not equally. Either we must love God, or we give ground of suspicion that we are not yet united to Him.

(13). Love to God is the most abiding grace. This will stay with us when other graces take their farewell. In heaven we shall need no repentance—because we shall have no sin. In heaven we shall not need patience—because there will be no affliction. In heaven we shall need no faith—because faith looks at unseen things (Heb. 11:1). Then we shall see God face to face; and where there is vision, there is no need of faith.

But when the other graces are out of date, love continues; and in this sense the apostle says that love is greater than faith or hope—because it abides the longest. 'Love will last forever' (1 Cor. 13:8). Faith is the staff which we walk with in this life. 'We walk by faith' (2 Cor. 5:7). But we shall leave this staff at heaven's door—and only love shall enter. Thus love carries away the crown from all the other graces. Love is the most long-lived grace—it is a blossom of eternity. How should we strive to excel in this grace, which alone shall live with us in heaven, and shall accompany us to the marriage supper of the Lamb!

(14). Love to God will never let sin thrive in the heart. Some plants will not thrive when they are near together: the love of God withers sin. Though the old man lives—yet as a sick man, it is weak. The flower of love kills the weed of sin. Though sin does not die totally—yet it dies daily. How should we labor for that grace, which is the only corrosive to destroy sin!

(15). Love to God is an excellent means for growth of grace. 'But grow in grace' (2 Peter 3:18). Growth in grace is very pleasing to God. Christ accepts the reality of grace—but commends the maturity of grace; and what can more promote and augment grace than love to God? Love is like watering of the root, which makes the tree grow. Therefore the apostle uses this expression in his prayer, 'May the Lord direct your hearts into the love of God' (2 Thess. 3:5). He knew this grace of love would nourish all the graces.

(16). The great benefit which will accrue to us, if we love God. 'No eye has seen, no ear has heard, and no mind has imagined what God has prepared for those who love him!' (1 Cor. 2:9). The eye has seen rare sights, the ear has heard sweet music; but eye has not seen, nor ear heard, nor can the heart of man imagine what God has prepared for those who love Him! Such glorious rewards are laid up that, as Augustine says, 'faith itself is not able to comprehend them!' God has promised a crown of life to those who love Him (James 1:12). This crown encircles within it, all blessedness—riches, and glory, and delight: and it is a crown which is unfading! (1 Pet. 5:4). Thus God would draw us to Him by rewards.

(17). Love to God is armor against error. For lack of hearts full of love—men have heads full of error; unholy opinions are for lack of holy affections. Why are men given up to strong delusions? Because 'they receive not the love of truth' (2 Thess. 2:10, 11). The more we love God, the more we hate those heterodox opinions that would draw us off from God into libertinism.

(18). If we love God, we have all winds blowing for us, everything in the world shall conspire for our good. We know not what fiery trials we may meet with—but to those who love God all things shall work for good. Those things which work against them, shall work for them; their cross shall make way for a crown; every crosswind shall blow them to the heavenly port!

(19). Lack of love to God is the ground of apostasy. The seed in the parable, which had no root, fell away. He who has not the love of God rooted in his heart, will fall away in time of temptation. He who loves God will cleave to Him, as Ruth to Naomi. 'Where you go I will go, and where you die I will die' (Ruth 1:16, 17). But he who lacks love to God will do as Orpah to her mother in law; she kissed her, and took her farewell of her. That soldier who has no love to his commander, when he sees an opportunity, will leave him, and run over to the enemy's side. He who has no love in his heart to God, you may set him down for an apostate.

(20). Love is the only thing which we can give back to God. If God is angry with us, we must not be angry back. If He chides us, we must not chide Him back. But if God loves us, we must love Him back. There is nothing in which we give back to God—but love. We must give Him our love for His love.

Thus we have seen twenty motives to excite and inflame our love to God.

Question. What shall we do to love God?

Answer. Study God. Did we study Him more, we would love Him more. Take a view of His superlative excellencies, His holiness, His incomprehensible goodness. The angels know God better than we, and clearly behold the splendor of His majesty; therefore they are so deeply enamored with Him.

Labor for an interest in God. 'O God, you are my God' (Psalm lx3:1). That pronoun 'my', is a sweet loadstone to love; a man loves that which is his own. The more we believe, the more we love. Faith is the root, and love is the flower which grows upon it. 'Faith which works by love' (Gal. 5:6).

Make it your earnest request to God, that He will give you a heart to love Him. This is an acceptable request, surely God will not deny it. When king Solomon asked for wisdom from God, (1 Kings 3:9), 'the request pleased the Lord' (verse 10). So when you cry to God, 'Lord, give me a heart to love You. It is my grief, I can love You no more. Oh, kindle this fire from heaven upon the altar of my heart!' Surely this prayer pleases the Lord, and He will pour of His Spirit upon you — whose golden oil shall make the lamp of your love burn bright!

2. An exhortation to preserve your love to God.

You who have love to God, labor to preserve it; let not this love die, or be quenched.

As you would have God's love to be continued to you, let your love be continued to Him. Love, as fire, will tend to die out. 'You have left your first love' (Rev. 2:4). Satan labors to blow out this flame, and through neglect of duty we lose it. When a frail body leaves off clothes, it is apt to get cold: so when we leave off duty, by degrees we cool in our love to God. Of all graces, love is most apt to decay; therefore we had need to be the more careful to preserve it. If a man has a precious jewel, he will keep it safe. What care then should we have to keep this precious jewel of love to God! It is sad to see professors declining in their love to God; many are in a spiritual declension, their love is decaying.

There are four signs by which Christians may know that their love is decaying.

(1). When they have lost their taste. He who is in a severe illness, has no taste; he does not find that savory relish in his food as formerly. So when Christians have lost their taste, and they find no sweetness in a promise, it is a sign of a spiritual decay. 'If so be you have tasted that the Lord is gracious' (1 Pet. 2:3). Time was, when they found comfort in drawing near to God. His Word was as the dropping honey, very delicious to the palate of their soul — but now it is otherwise. They can taste no more sweetness in spiritual things than in the 'white of an egg' (Job 6:6). This is a sign they are in a decay; to lose the taste, argues the loss of the first love.

(2). When they have lost their appetite. A man in a deep decay has not that relish for his food as formerly. Time was, when Christians did 'hunger and thirst after righteousness' (Matt. 5:6). They minded things of a heavenly aspect, the grace of the Spirit, the blood of the cross, the light of God's countenance. They had a longing for ordinances, and came to them as a hungry man to a feast. But now the case is altered. They have no appetite, they do not so prize Christ, they have not such strong affections to the Word, their hearts do not burn within them; a sad presage, they are in a decay, their love is decaying. It was a sign David's natural strength was abated, when they covered him with clothes, and yet he get no heat (1 Kings 1:1). So when men are plied with hot clothes (1 mean ordinances) — yet they have no heat of affection — but are cold and stiff, as if they were ready to be laid forth; this is a sign their first love is declined, they are in a deep decay.

(3). When they grow more in love with the world, it argues the decrease of spiritual love. They were once of a sublime, heavenly temper, they did speak the language of Canaan: but now they are like the fish in the gospel, which had money in its mouth (Matt. x7:27). They cannot lisp out three words—but one is about mammon. Their thoughts and affections, like Satan, are still compassing the earth, a sign they are going down the hill apace, their love to God is in a decay. We may observe, when nature decays and grows weaker, people go more stooping: and truly, when the heart goes more stooping to the earth, and is so bowed together that it can scarcely lift up itself to a heavenly thought, it is now sadly declining in its first love. When rust cleaves to metal, it not only takes away the brightness of the metal—but it cankers and consumes it: so when the earth cleaves to men's souls, it not only hinders the shining luster of their graces—but by degrees it cankers them.

(4). When they make little reckoning of God's worship. Duties of religion are performed in a dead, formal manner; if they are not left undone—yet they are ill done. This is a sad symptom of a spiritual decay; remissness in duty shows a decay in our first love. The strings of a violin being slack, the violin can never make good music; when men grow slack in duty, they pray as if they prayed not; this can never make any harmonious sound in God's ears. When the spiritual motion is slow and heavy, and the pulse of the soul beats low, it is a sign that Christians have left their first love.

Let us take heed of this spiritual decay; it is dangerous to abatement in our love. Love is such a grace as we know not how to be without. A soldier may as well be without his weapons, an artist without his pencil, a musician without his instrument, as a Christian can be without love. The body cannot lack its natural heat. Love is to the soul as the natural heat is to the body—there is no living without it. Love influences the graces, it excites the affections, it makes us grieve for sin, it makes us cheerful in God; it is like oil to the wheels; it quickens us in God's service. How careful then should we be to keep alive our love for God!

Question. How may we keep our love from going out?

Answer. Watch your hearts every day. Take notice of the first declinings in grace. Observe yourselves when you begin to grow dull and listless, and use all means for quickening. Be much in prayer, meditation, and holy conference. When the fire is going out you throw on fuel: so when the flame of your love is going out, make use of ordinances and gospel promises, as fuel to keep the fire of your love burning.

3. An exhortation to increase your love to God.

Let me exhort Christians to increase your love to God. Let your love be raised up higher. 'And this I pray, that your love may abound more and more' (Phil. 1:9). Our love to God should be as the light of the morning: first there is the day break, then it shines brighter, to the full meridian. They who have a few sparks of love should blow up those divine sparks into a flame. A Christian should not be content with so small a grain of grace, as may make him wonder whether he has any grace or not—but should be still increasing the stock. He who has a little gold, would have more; you who love God a little, labor to love Him more. A godly man is contented with a very little of the world; yet he is never satisfied—but would have more of the Spirit's influence, and labors to add one degree of love to another. To persuade Christians to put more oil to the lamp, and increase the flame of their love, let me propose these four divine incentives.

(1). The growth of love evinces its reality. If I see the almond tree bud and flourish, I know there is life in the root. Paint will not grow; a hypocrite, who is but a picture, will not grow. But where we see love to God increasing and growing larger, as Elijah's cloud, we may conclude it is true and genuine.

(2). By the growth of love we imitate the saints in the Bible. Their love to God, like the waters of the sanctuary, did rise higher. The disciples love to Christ at first was weak, they fled from

Christ; but after Christ's death it grew more vigorous, and they made an open profession of Him. Peter's love at first was more infirm and languid, he denied Christ; but afterwards how boldly did he preach Him! When Christ put him to a trial of his love, 'Simon, love you Me?' (John 21:16), Peter could make his humble yet confident appeal to Christ, 'Lord, you know that I love You.' Thus that tender plant which before was blown down with the wind of a temptation, now is grown into a cedar, which all the powers of hell cannot shake!

(3). The growth of love will amplify the reward. The more we burn in love — the more we shall shine in glory! The higher our love — the brighter our crown!

(4). The more we love God, the more love we shall have from Him. Would we have God unbosom the sweet secrets of His love to us? Would we have the smiles of His face? Oh, then let us strive for higher degrees of love. Paul counted gold and pearl but dung for Christ, 'Yes, everything else is worthless when compared with the priceless gain of knowing Christ Jesus my Lord. I have discarded everything else, counting it all as garbage, so that I may have Christ.' (Phil. 3:8). Yes, he was so inflamed with love to God, that he could have wished himself accursed from Christ for his brethren the Jews (Romans 9:3). Not that he could be accursed from Christ; but such was his fervent love and pious zeal for the glory of God, that he would have been content to have suffered, even beyond what is fit to speak, if God might have had more honor.

Here was love screwed up to the highest pitch that it was possible for a mortal to arrive at: and behold how near he lay to God's heart! The Lord takes him up to heaven a while, and lays him in His bosom, where he had such a glorious sight of God, and heard those 'unspeakable words, which it is not lawful for a man to utter' (2 Cor. 12:4). Never was any man a loser by his love to God.

If our love to God does not increase — it will soon decrease. If the fire is not blown up — it will quickly go out. Therefore Christians should above all things endeavor to cherish and excite their love to God. This exhortation will be out of date when we come to heaven, for then our light shall be clear, and our love perfect; but now it is in season to exhort, that our love to God may abound yet more and more.

Effectual Calling

The second qualification of the people to whom this privilege in the text belongs, is — they are the called by God. 'All things work for good to those who are called.' Though this word called is placed in order after loving of God — yet in reality, it goes before it. Love is first named — but not first wrought; we must be called of God, before we can love God.

Calling is made (Romans 8:30) the middle link of the golden chain of salvation. It is placed between predestination and glorification; and if we have this middle link fast, we are sure of the two other ends of the chain. For the clearer illustration of this, there are six things observable.

1. A distinction about calling. There is a two-fold call.

(1.) There is an outward call, which is nothing else but God's blessed offer of grace in the gospel, His parleying with sinners, when He invites them to come in and accept of mercy. Of this our Savior speaks: 'Many are called — but few chosen' (Matt. 20:16). This external call is insufficient to salvation — yet sufficient to leave men without excuse.

(2.) There is an inward call, when God wonderfully overpowers the heart, and draws the will to embrace Christ. This is an effectual call. God, by the outward call, blows a trumpet in the ear; by the inward call, He opens the heart, as He did the heart of Lydia (Acts 16:14). The outward call may bring men to a profession of Christ—the inward call brings them to a possession of Christ. The outward call curbs a sinner—the inward call changes him.

2. Our deplorable condition before we are called.

(1.) We are in a state of bondage. Before God calls a man, he is the devil's slave. If he says, 'Go!'—the man goes. The deluded sinner is like the slave who digs in the mine, hews in the quarry, or tugs at the oar. He is at the command of Satan, as the donkey is at the command of the driver.

(2.) We are in a state of darkness. 'You were once darkness' (Ephes. 5:8). Darkness is very disconsolate. A man in the dark is full of fear, he trembles every step he takes. Darkness is dangerous. He who is in the dark may quickly go out of the right way, and fall into rivers or whirlpools. Just so, in the darkness of ignorance, we may quickly fall into the whirlpool of hell.

(3.) We are in a state of impotency. 'When we were without strength' (Romans 5:6). We had no strength to resist a temptation, or grapple with a corruption. Sin cut the lock where our strength lay (Judg. 16:20). Nay, there is not only impotency—but obstinacy, 'You do always resist the Holy Spirit' (Acts 8:51). Besides indisposition to holiness, there is opposition to holiness.

(4.) We are in a state of pollution. 'I saw you polluted in your blood' (Ezek. 16:6). The mind coins only earthly thoughts; the heart is the devil's forge, where the sparks of lust fly.

(5.) We are in a state of damnation. We are born under a curse. The wrath of God abides on us (John 3:36). This is our condition before God is pleased by a merciful call to bring us near to Himself, and free us from that misery in which we were before engulfed.

3. The means of our effectual call. The ordinary means which the Lord uses in calling us, is not by raptures and revelations—but is,

(1.) By His word, which is 'the rod of his strength' (Psalm 105:2). The voice of the Word is God's call to us; therefore He is said to speak to us from heaven (Heb. 12:25). That is, in the ministry of the Word. When the Word calls from sin, it is as if we heard a voice from heaven.

(2.) By His spirit. This is the loud call. The Word is the instrumental cause of our conversion, the Spirit is the efficient cause of our conversion. The ministers of God are only the pipes and organs; it is the Spirit blowing in them, which effectually changes the heart. 'While Peter spoke, the Holy Spirit fell on all those who heard the word' (Acts 10:44). It is not the farmer's industry in ploughing and sowing, which will make the ground fruitful, without the early and latter rain. Just so, it is not the seed of the Word that will effectually convert, unless the Spirit puts forth His sweet influence, and drops as rain upon the heart. Therefore the aid of God's Spirit is to be implored, that He would put forth His powerful voice, and awaken us out of the grave of unbelief. If a man knocks at a gate of brass, it will not open; but if he comes with a key in his hand, it will open. Just so, when God, who has the key of David in His hand (Rev. 3:7) comes, He opens the heart, though it be ever so fast locked against Him.

4. The method God uses in calling of sinners.

The Lord does not tie Himself to a particular way, or use the same order with all. He comes sometimes in a still small voice. Such as have had godly parents, and have sat under the warm sunshine of religious education, often do not know how or when they were called. The Lord did secretly and gradually instill grace into their hearts, as the dew falls unnoticed. They know by the heavenly effects that they are called—but the time or manner they know not. The hand moves on the clock—but they do not perceive when it moves.

Thus God deals with some. Others are more stubborn and knotty sinners, and God comes to them in a rough wind. He uses more wedges of the law to break their hearts; He deeply humbles them, and shows them they are damned without Christ. Then having ploughed up the fallow ground of their hearts by humiliation, He sows the seed of consolation. He presents Christ and mercy to them, and draws their wills, not only to accept Christ – but passionately to desire, and faithfully to rest upon Him. Thus He wrought upon Paul, and called him from a persecutor – to a preacher. This call, though it is more visible than the other – yet is not more real. God's method in calling sinners may vary – but the effect is still the same.

5. The properties of this effectual calling.

(1.) This call is a sweet call. God so calls – as He allures. He does not force – but draw. The freedom of the will is not taken away – but the stubbornness of it is conquered. 'Your people shall be willing in the day of your power' (Psalm 110:3). After this call there are no more disputes, the soul readily obeys God's call – as when Christ called Zacchaeus, he joyfully welcomed Him into his heart and house.

(2.) This call is a holy call. 'Who has called us with a holy calling' (2 Tim. 1:9). This call of God calls men out of their sins – by it they are consecrated, and set apart for God. The vessels of the tabernacle were taken from common use, and set apart to a holy use. Just so, those who are effectually called are separated from sin, and consecrated to God's service. The God whom we worship is holy, the work we are employed in is holy, the place we hope to arrive at is holy; all this calls for holiness. A Christian's heart is to be the presence chamber of the blessed Trinity; and shall not holiness to the Lord be written upon it? Believers are children of God the Father, members of God the Son, and temples of God the Holy Spirit; and shall they not be holy? Holiness is the badge and livery of God's people. 'The people of your holiness' (Isaiah 63:18). As chastity distinguishes a virtuous woman from a harlot, so holiness distinguishes the godly from the wicked. It is a holy calling, 'God has called us to be holy, not to live impure lives' (1 Thess. 4:7).

Let not any man say he is called by God – who lives in sin. Has God called you to be a swearer, to be a drunkard? Nay, let not the merely moral person say he is effectually called. What is civility without sanctity? It is but a dead carcass strewed with flowers. The king's picture stamped upon brass, will not go current for gold. The merely moral man looks as if he had the King of heaven's image stamped upon him – but he is no better than counterfeit metal, which will not pass for current with God.

(3.) This call is an irresistible call. When God calls a man by His grace, he cannot but come. You may resist the minister's call – but you cannot the Spirit's call. The finger of the blessed Spirit can write upon a heart of stone, as once He wrote His laws upon tables of stone. God's words are creating words; when He said 'Let there be light, there was light'; and when He says, 'Let there be faith', it shall be so. When God called Paul, he answered to the call. 'I was not disobedient to the heavenly vision' (Acts 26:19). God rides forth conquering in the chariot of His gospel; He makes the blind eyes see, and the stony heart bleed. If God will call a man, nothing shall lie in the way to hinder; difficulties shall be untied, the powers of hell shall disband. 'Who has resisted his will?' (Romans 9:19). God bends the iron sinew, and cuts asunder the gates of brass (Psalm 107:16). When the Lord touches a man's heart by His Spirit, all proud imaginations are brought down, and the fort-royal of the will yields to God. The man that before was as a raging sea of sin, foaming forth wickedness; now he suddenly flies back and trembles, he falls down as the jailer, 'What shall I do to he saved?' (Acts 16:30). What has happened this man? The Lord has effectually called him. God has been working powerfully by grace, and now his stubborn heart is conquered by a sweet violence.

(4.) This call is a high calling. 'I press toward the mark, for the prize of the high calling of God' (Phil. 3:14). It is a high calling, because we are called to high exercises of piety — to die to sin, to be crucified to the world, to live by faith, to have fellowship with the Father (1 John 1:3). This is a high calling: here is a work too high for men in a state of nature to perform. It is a high calling, because we are called to high privileges — to justification and adoption, to be made co-heirs with Christ. He who is effectually called, is higher than any of the kings of the earth.

(5.) This call is a gracious call. It is the fruit and product of free grace. That God should call some, and not others; that some should be taken, and others left; that one should be called who is of a more wicked disposition, while another of a sweeter temper, is rejected; here is free grace! That the poor should be rich in faith, heirs of a kingdom (James 2:5), and the nobles and great ones of the world for the most part rejected, 'Not many noble are called' (1 Cor. 1:26); this is free and rich grace! 'Even so, Father, for so it seemed good in your sight' (Matt. 11:26). That under the same sermon one should be effectually wrought upon — while another is no more moved than a dead man with the sound of music; that one should hear the Spirit's voice in the Word — while another does not hear it; that one should be softened and moistened with the influence of heaven — while another, like Gideon's dry fleece, has no dew upon him; behold here distinguishing, sovereign grace! The same affliction which converts one — hardens another. Affliction to one is as the bruising of spices, which cast forth a fragrant smell; to the other it is as the crushing of weeds in a mortar, which are more unsavory. What is the cause of this — but the free grace of God! It is a gracious calling; it is all enameled and interwoven with free grace! 'Brothers, think of what you were when you were called. Not many of you were wise by human standards; not many were influential; not many were of noble birth. But God chose the foolish things of the world to shame the wise; God chose the weak things of the world to shame the strong. He chose the lowly things of this world and the despised things--and the things that are not--to nullify the things that are, so that no one may boast before Him.' 1 Corinthians 1:26-29

(6.) This call is a glorious call. 'In his kindness God called you to his eternal glory.' (1 Peter 5:10). We are called to the enjoyment of the ever blessed God. It is as if a man were called out of a prison to sit upon a throne. Curtius writes of one, who while digging in his garden was called to be king. Thus God calls us to glory and virtue (2 Pet. 1:3). First to virtue, then to glory. At Athens there were two temples, the temple of Virtue, and the temple of Honor; and no man could go to the temple of honor — but through the temple of virtue. Just so, God calls us first to virtue, and then to glory.

What is the glory among men, which most so hunt after — but a feather blown in the air? What is it, compared to the weight of eternal glory? Is there not great reason we should follow God's call? He calls to eternal glory; can there be any loss or harm in this? God would have us part with nothing for Him — but that which will damn us if we keep it. He has no design upon us — but to make us happy. He calls us to salvation, He calls us to a heavenly kingdom! Oh, how should we then, with Bartimeus, throw off our ragged coat of sin, and follow Christ when He calls!

(7.) This call is a rare call. But few are savingly called. 'Few are chosen' (Matt. 22:14). Few, not collectively — but comparatively. The word 'to call' signifies to choose out some from among others. Many have the light brought to them — but few have their eyes anointed to see that light. 'You have a few names in Sardis who have not defiled their garments' (Rev. 3:4). How many millions sit in the region of darkness! And in those climates where the Sun of righteousness does shine, there are many who receive the light of the truth, without the love of it. There are many formalists — but few believers. There is something that looks like faith, which is not. The Cyprian diamond sparkles like the true diamond — but it is not of the right kind, it will break with the hammer. Just so, the hypocrite's faith will break with the hammer of persecution. But few are truly called. The number of precious stones is few, compared to the number of pebble stones. Most men shape their religion according to the fashion of the times; they are for the music and the idol (Dan. 3:7). The serious thought of this, should make us work out our salvation with fear, and labor to be in the number of those few whom God has translated into a state of grace.

(8.) This call is an unchangeable call. 'God's gracious gifts and calling are irrevocable' (Romans 11:29). That is, as a learned writer says, those gifts which flow from election. When God calls a man, He does not repent of it. God does not, as many friends do, love one day, and hate another; or as princes, who make their subjects favorites, and afterwards throw them into prison. This is the blessedness of a saint—his condition admits of no alteration. God's call is founded upon His decree—and His decree is immutable. Acts of grace cannot be reversed. God blots out His people's sins—but not their names. Let the world ring changes every hour, a believer's condition is unchangeable and unalterable.

6. The end of our effectual calling is the honor of God. 'That we should be to the praise of his glory' (Ephes. 1:12). He who is in the state of nature, is no more fit to honor God, than a brute beast can put forth acts of reason. A man before conversion continually reflects dishonor upon God. As black vapors which arise out of moorish grounds, cloud and darken the sun, so out of the natural man's heart arise black vapors of sin, which cast a cloud upon God's glory. The sinner is versed in treason—but understands nothing of loyalty to the King of heaven. But there are some whom the lot of free grace falls upon, and these shall be taken as jewels from among the rubbish and be effectually called, that they may lift up God's name in the world. The Lord will have some in all ages who shall oppose the corruptions of the times, bear witness to His truths, and convert sinners from the error of their ways. He will have His worthies, as king David had. Those who have been monuments of God's mercies, will be trumpets of His praise.

These considerations show us the necessity of effectual calling. Without it there is no going to heaven. We must be 'made fit for the inheritance' (Col. 1:12). As God makes heaven fit for us, so He makes us fit for heaven; and what gives this fitness—but effectual calling? A man remaining in the filth and rubbish of nature, is no more fit for heaven, than a dead man is fit to inherit an estate. The high calling is not a thing arbitrary or indifferent—but as needful as salvation; yet alas, how is this one thing needful neglected! Most men, like the people of Israel, wander up and down to gather straw—but do not mind the evidences of their effectual calling.

Take notice what a mighty power God puts forth in calling of sinners! God does so call, as to draw (John 6:44). Conversion is styled a resurrection. 'Blessed is he who has part in the first resurrection' (Rev. 20:6). That is, a rising from sin to grace. A man can no more convert himself than a dead man can raise himself. It is called a creation (Col. 3:10). To create is above the power of nature.

Objection. 'But,' say some, 'the will is not dead, but asleep; and God, by a moral persuasion, does only awaken us—and then the will can obey God's call, and move of itself to its own conversion.'

Answer. To this I answer, Every man is by sin bound in fetters. 'I perceive that you are in the bond of iniquity' (Acts 7:23). A man that is in fetters, if you use arguments, and persuade him to go, is that sufficient? There must be a breaking of his fetters, and setting him free, before he can walk. So it is with every natural man; he is fettered with corruption; now the Lord by converting grace must file off his fetters, nay, give him legs to run too—or he can never obtain salvation!

Use. An exhortation to make your calling sure.

'Give diligence to make your calling sure' (2 Peter 1:10). This is the great business of our lives — to get sound evidences of our effectual calling. Do not acquiesce in outward privileges, do not cry as the Jews, 'The temple of the Lord!' (Jer. 7:4). Do not rest in baptism; what is it to have the water — and lack the Spirit? Do not be content that Christ has been preached to you. Do not satisfy yourselves with an empty profession; all this may be, and yet you are no better than empty professors. But labor to evidence to your souls that you are called of God. Give diligence to make your calling sure — it is both feasible and probable. God is not lacking to those that seek Him. Let not this great business hang in hand any longer. If there were a controversy about your land, you would use all means to clear your title; and is salvation nothing? Will you not clear your title here? Consider how sad your case is, if you are not effectually called.

If you are not effectually called, you are strangers to God. The prodigal went into a far country (Luke 14:13), which implies that every sinner, before conversion, is a far off from God. 'At that time you were without Christ, strangers to the covenants of promise' (Ephes. 2:12). Men dying in their sins have no more right to promises, than strangers have to the privilege of free-born citizens. If you are strangers, what language can you expect from God — but this, 'I know you not!'

If you are not effectually called, you are enemies to God. 'Alienated and enemies' (Col. 1:21). There is nothing in the Bible you can lay claim to — but the threatenings! You are heirs to all the plagues written in the book of God! Though you may resist the commands of the law, you cannot flee from the curses of the law. Such as are enemies to God, let them read their doom. 'Bring here these enemies of mine, who did not want me to rule over them, and slaughter them in my presence!' (Luke 19:27). Oh, how it should concern you therefore to make your calling sure! How miserable and damnable will your condition be, if death calls you before the Spirit calls you!

Question. But is there any hope of my being effectually called? I have been a great sinner.

Answer. Great sinners have been called. Paul was a violent persecutor — yet he was called. Some of the Jews who had a hand in crucifying Christ, were called. God loves to display His free grace to sinners. Therefore be not discouraged. You see a golden cord let down from heaven for poor trembling souls to lay hold upon!

Question. But how shall I know I am effectually called?

1. He who is savingly called is called out of himself, not only out of sinful self — but out of righteous self. 'Not having my own righteousness' (Phil. 3:9). He whose heart God has touched by His Spirit, lays down the idol of self-righteousness at Christ's feet, for Him to tread upon. The true Christian denies not only sinful self — but righteous self. He becomes moral and pious-- but he does not trust to his morality or piety. Noah's dove made use of her wings to fly — but trusted to the ark for safety. This is to be effectually called — when a man is called out of himself. Self-renunciation is the first step to saving faith.

2. He who is effectually called — has a great change wrought. Not a change of the faculties — but of the qualities. He is altered from what he was before. His body is the same — but not his mind; he has another spirit. Paul was so changed after his conversion that people did not know him (Acts 9:21). Oh what a metamorphosis does grace make! 'Do you not know that the wicked will not inherit the kingdom of God? Do not be deceived: Neither the sexually immoral nor idolaters nor adulterers nor male prostitutes nor homosexual offenders nor thieves nor the greedy nor drunkards nor slanderers nor swindlers will inherit the kingdom of God. And that is what some of you were! But you were washed, you were sanctified, you were justified in the name of

the Lord Jesus Christ and by the Spirit of our God. (1 Corinthians 6:9-11). Grace changes the heart!

In effectual calling there is a three-fold change wrought:

(1). There is a change wrought in the understanding. Before, there was ignorance—but now there is light, 'Now you are light in the Lord' (Ephes. 5:8). The first work of God in the creation of the world was light: so it is in the new creation. He who is savingly called says with that man in the gospel: 'I once was blind—but now I see!' (John 9:25). He sees such evil in sin, and excellency in the ways of God, as he never saw before. Indeed, this light which the blessed Spirit brings, may well be called a marvelous light. 'That you should show forth the praises of Him who has called you into his marvelous light' (1 Pet. 2:9). It is a marvelous light in six respects.

(1.) Because it is supernaturally conveyed. It does not come from the celestial orbs where the planets are—but from the Sun of righteousness.

(2.) It is marvelous in the effect. This light does that which no other light can. It makes a man perceive himself to be blind.

(3.) It is a marvelous light, because it is more penetrating. Other light may shine upon the face—but this light shines into the heart, and enlightens the conscience (2 Cor. 4:6).

(4.) It is a marvelous light, because it sets those who have it a marveling. They marvel at themselves, how they could be contented to be so long without it. They marvel that their eyes should be opened, and not others. They marvel that notwithstanding their previous hatred and opposition this light—yet it should shine in their souls. This is what the saints will stand wondering at to all eternity.

(5.) It is a marvelous light, because it is more vital than any others. It not only enlightens—but quickens! It makes alive those who 'were dead in trespasses and sins' (Ephes. 2:1). Therefore it is called the 'light of life' (John7:12).

(6.) It is a marvelous light, because it is the beginning of everlasting light. The light of grace is the morning star which ushers in the sunlight of glory.

Now then, reader, can you say that this marvelous light of the Spirit has dawned upon you? When you were enveloped in ignorance, and neither knew God nor yourself—did suddenly a light from heaven shined in your mind? This is one part of that blessed change which is wrought in the effectual calling.

(2). There is a change wrought in the will. 'To will is present with me' (Romans 8:18). The will, which before opposed Christ, now embraces Him. The will, which was an iron sinew against Christ, is now like melting wax—it readily receives the stamp and impression of the Holy Spirit. The will moves heavenward, and carries all the orbs of the affections along with it. The regenerate will answers to every call of God, as the echo answers to the voice, 'Lord, what will you have me to do?' (Acts 9:6). The will now becomes a volunteer, it enlists itself under the Captain of salvation (Heb. 2:10). Oh what a happy change is wrought here! Before, the will kept Christ out; now, it keeps sin out!

(3). There is a change in the conduct. He who is called of God, walks directly contrary to what he did before. He walked before in envy and malice—now he walks in love! Before he walked in pride—now he walks in humility. The current is carried quite another way. As in the heart there is a new birth, so in the life a new conduct. Thus we see what a mighty change is wrought, in all who are called by God.

How far are they from this effectual call, who never had any change! They are the same as they were forty or fifty years ago — as proud and carnal as ever! They have seen many changes in their times — but they have had no change in their heart. Let not men think to leap out of the harlot's lap (the world) into Abraham's bosom! They must either have a gracious change while they live — or a cursed change when they die! 'Therefore, if anyone is in Christ, he is a new creation; the old has gone, the new has come!' 2 Corinthians 5:17

3. He who is called of God — esteems this call as the highest blessing. A king whom God has called by His grace, esteems it more that he is called to be a saint, than that he is called to be a king. He values his high calling more than his high birth. Theodosius thought it a greater honor to be a Christian, than to be an emperor. A carnal person can no more value spiritual blessings than an infant can value a diamond necklace. He prefers his worldly grandeur, his ease, plenty, and titles of honor, before conversion. He had rather be called duke than saint — this is a sign he is a stranger to effectual calling. He who is enlightened by the Spirit, counts holiness his best heraldry, and looks upon his effectual calling as his choicest blessing. When he has taken this degree, he is a candidate for heaven.

4. He who is effectually called — is called out of the world. It is a 'heavenly calling' (Heb. 3:1). He who is called of God, minds the things of a heavenly aspect. He is in the world — but not of the world. Naturalists say of precious stones, though they have their matter from the earth — yet their sparkling luster is from the influence of the heavens. So it is with a godly man — though his body is from the earth — yet the sparkling of his affections is from heaven; his heart is drawn into the upper region, as high as Christ. He not only casts off every wicked work — but every earthly weight. He is not a worm — but an eagle!

5. Another sign of our effectual calling — is diligence in our ordinary calling. Some boast of their high calling — but they lie idly at anchor. True religion does not give warrant to idleness. Christians must not be slothful. Idleness is the devil's bath; a slothful person becomes a prey to every temptation. Grace, while it cures the heart, does not make the hand lame. He who is called of God, as he works for heaven, so he works in his trade.

Exhortations to those who are called

If, after searching you find that you are effectually called, I have three exhortations to you.

1. Admire and adore God's free grace in calling you — that God should pass over so many, that He should pass by the wise and noble, and that the lot of free grace should fall upon you! That He should take you out of a state of vassalage, from grinding the devil's mill, and should set you above the princes of the earth, and call you to inherit the throne of glory! Fall upon your knees, break forth into a thankful triumph of praise! Let your hearts be ten stringed instruments, to sound forth the memorial of God's saving mercy. There are none so deep in debt to free grace — as you are; and none should be so high mounted upon the pinnacle of thanksgiving. Say as the sweet singer; 'I will extol you, O God my King, every day will I bless you, and I will praise your name forever!' (Psalm 145:1, 2). Those who are monuments of mercy — should be trumpets of praise! O long to be in heaven, where your thanksgivings shall be purer and shall be raised a note higher!

2. Pity those who are not yet called. Sinners in scarlet are not objects of envy — but pity; they are under 'the power of Satan' (Acts 26:18). They tread every day on the brink of the bottomless pit! What if death should cast them in! O pity unconverted sinners. If you pity an ox or an donkey going astray, will you not pity a soul going astray from God, who has lost his way and his wits, and is upon the precipice of damnation!

Nay, not only pity sinners — but pray for them. Though they curse you — you must pray for them. You will pray for people who are demented; sinners are demented. 'When he came to his senses' (Luke 15:17). It seems the prodigal before conversion, was in his senses. Wicked men are going to execution; sin is the halter which strangles them; death removes them off the ladder; and hell is their burning place! Will you not pray for them, when you see them in such danger?

3. You who are effectually called, honor your high calling. 'I beg you to lead a life worthy of your calling' (Ephes. 4:1). Christians must keep a decorum, they must observe what is lovely. This is a seasonable advice, when many who profess to be called of God — yet by their loose and irregular walking — cast a blemish on religion, whereby the ways of God are evil spoken of. It is Salvian's speech, 'What do pagans say when they see Christians live scandalously? Surely Christ taught them no better.' Will you reproach Christ, and make Him suffer again, by abusing your heavenly calling?

It is one of the saddest sights — to see a man lift up his hands in prayer, and with those hands oppress; to hear the same tongue praise God at one time, and at another lie and slander; to hear a man in words profess God, and in works deny Him. Oh how unworthy is this! Yours is a holy calling, and will you be unholy? Do not think you may take liberty as others do. The Nazarite had a vow on him, separated himself to God, and promised abstinence; though others did drink wine, it was not fit for the Nazarite to do it. So, though others are loose and vain, it is not fit for those who are set apart for God by effectual calling. Are not flowers sweeter than weeds? You must be now 'a peculiar people' (1 Pet. 2:9); not only peculiar in regard of dignity — but deportment. Abhor all motions of sin, because it would disparage your high calling.

Question. What is it to walk worthy of our heavenly calling?

1. It is to walk regularly, to tread with an even foot, and walk according to the rules and axioms of the Word. A true saint is for canonical obedience, he follows the canon of Scripture. 'As many as walk according to this canon' (Gal. 6:16). When we leave men's inventions, and cleave to God's institutions; when we walk after the Word, as Israel after the pillar of fire; this is walking worthy of our heavenly calling.

2. To walk worthy of our calling is to walk singularly. 'Among all the people of the earth, I consider you alone to be righteous.' (Genesis 7:1). When others walked with the devil, Noah walked with God. We are forbidden to run with the multitude (Exod. 23:2). Though in civil things singularity is not commendable — yet in religion it is good to be singular. Melanchthon was the glory of the age he lived in. Athanasius was singularly holy; he appeared for God when the stream of the times ran another way. It is better to be a pattern of holiness, than a partner in wickedness. It is better to go to heaven with a few, than to hell in the crowd! We must walk in an opposite course to the people of the world.

3. To walk worthy of our calling is to walk cheerfully. 'Rejoice in the Lord always' (Phil. 4:4). Too much drooping of spirit disparages our high calling, and makes others suspect a godly life to be melancholy. Christ loves to see us rejoicing in Him. Causinus speaks of a dove, whose wings being perfumed with sweet ointments, drew the other doves after her. Cheerfulness is a perfume to draw others to godliness. True religion does not banish joy. As there is a seriousness without sourness, so there is a cheerful liveliness without lightness. When the prodigal was converted 'they began to be merry' (Luke 15:24). Who should be cheerful — if not the people of God? They are no sooner born of the Spirit — but they are heirs to a crown! God Himself is their portion, and heaven is their mansion — and shall they not rejoice?

4. To walk worthy of our calling is to walk wisely. Walking wisely implies three things.

(a) To walk watchfully. 'The wise man's eyes are in his head' (Eccles. 2:14). Others watch for our halting, therefore we had need look to our standing. We must beware, not only of scandals — but of all that is unfitting, lest thereby we open the mouth of others with a fresh cry against religion. If our piety will not convert men — our prudence may silence them.

(b) To walk courteously. The spirit of the gospel is full of meekness and politeness. 'Be courteous' (1 Pet. 3:8). Take heed of a morose, or haughty behavior. Religion does not take away civility — but refines it. 'Abraham stood up, and bowed himself to the children of Heth' (Gen. 23:7). Though they were of a heathenish race — yet Abraham gave them a civil respect. Paul was of an affable temper. 'I am made all things to men, that I might by all means save some' (1 Cor. 9:22). In lesser matters the apostle yielded to others — that by his winning manner, he might win upon them.

(c) To walk magnanimously. Though we must be humble — yet not base. It is unworthy to prostitute ourselves to the lusts of men. What is sinfully imposed, ought to be zealously opposed. Conscience is God's diocese, where none has right to visit — but He who is the Bishop of our souls (1 Pet. 2:25). We must not be like hot iron, which may be beaten into any form. A brave spirited Christian will rather suffer, than let his conscience be violated. Here is the serpent and the dove united — sagacity and innocence. This prudential walking corresponds with our high calling, and much adorns the gospel of Christ.

5. To walk worthy of our calling is to walk influentially — to do good to others, and to be rich in acts of mercy (Heb. 13:16). Good works honor religion. As Mary poured the ointment on Christ, so by good works we pour ointments on the head of the gospel, and make it give forth a fragrant smell. Good works, though they are not causes of salvation — yet they are evidences. When with our Savior we go about doing good, and send abroad the refreshing influence of our liberality, we walk worthy of our high calling.

Here is matter of consolation to you who are effectually called. God has magnified rich grace toward you. You are called to great honor to be co-heirs with Christ; this should revive you in the worst of times. Let men reproach and miscall you; set God's calling of you against man's miscalling. Let men persecute you to death: they do but give you a pass, and send you to heaven the sooner! How may this cure the trembling of the heart! What, though the sea roars, though the earth is unsettled, though the stars are shaken out of their places, you need not fear. You are effectually called — and therefore are sure to be crowned!

Concerning God's purpose

1. God's purpose is the cause of salvation.

The last thing in the text, which I shall but briefly glance at, is the ground and origin of our effectual calling, in these words, 'according to His purpose' (Eph. 1:11). Anselm renders it, 'According to his good will.' Peter Martyr reads it, 'According to His decree.' This purpose, or decree of God, is the fountainhead of our spiritual blessings. It is the moving cause of our effectual calling, justification, and glorification. It is the highest link in the golden chain of salvation. What is the reason that one man is effectually called, and not another? It is from the eternal purpose of God! God's decree gives the casting vote in man's salvation.

Let us then ascribe the whole work of grace to the pleasure of God's will. God did not choose us because we were worthy — but by choosing us He makes us worthy. Proud men are apt to assume and arrogate too much to themselves, in being sharers with God. While many cry out against church sacrilege, they are in the meantime guilty of a far greater sacrilege, in robbing God of His glory, while they go to set the crown of salvation upon their own head. But we must resolve all into God's purpose. The evidences of salvation are in the saints — but the cause of salvation is in God.

If it is God's purpose which saves — then it is not free will. Pelagians are strenuous asserters of free will. They tell us that a man has an innate power to affect his own conversion; but this text confutes it. Our calling is 'according to God's purpose.' The Scripture plucks up the root of free will. 'It is not of him who wills' (Romans 9:16). All depends upon the purpose of God. When the prisoner is cast at the bar, there is no saving him, unless the king has a purpose to save him. God's purpose is His prerogative royal.

If it is God's purpose which saves — then it is not merit. Bellarmine holds that good works do expiate sin and merit glory; but the text says that we are called according to God's purpose, and there is a parallel Scripture, 'Who has saved us, and called us, not according to our works — but according to his own purpose and grace' (2 Tim. 1:9). There is no such thing as merit. Our best works have in them both defection and infection, and so are but glittering sins; therefore if we are called and justified, it is God's purpose brings it to pass.

Objection. But the Papists allege that Scripture for merit: 'Henceforth is laid up for me a crown of righteousness, which the Lord, the righteous fudge, shall give me at that day' (2 Tim. 4:8). This is the force of their argument. If God in justice rewards our works, then they merit salvation.

Answer. To this I answer, God gives a reward as a just Judge, not to the worthiness of our works — but to the worthiness of Christ. God as a just Judge rewards us, not because we have deserved it — but because He has promised it. God has two courts, a court of mercy, and a court of justice: the Lord condemns those works in the court of justice, which He crowns in the court of mercy. Therefore that which carries the main stroke in our salvation, is the purpose of God.

Again, if the purpose of God is the spring-head of happiness, then we are not saved for foreseen faith. It is absurd to think anything in us could have the least influence upon our election. Some say that God foresaw that such people would believe — and therefore choose them. Just so, they would make the business of salvation to depend upon something within us. Whereas God does not choose us for faith — but to faith. 'He has chosen us — that we should be holy' (Eph. 1:4), not because we were holy — but that we might be holy. We are elected to holiness, not for any inherent holiness. What could God foresee in us — but pollution and rebellion! If any man be saved, it is according to God's purpose.

Question. How shall we know that God has a purpose to save us?

Answer. By being effectually called. 'Give diligence to make your calling and election sure' (2 Pet. 1:10). We make our election sure, by making our calling sure. 'God has chosen you to salvation through sanctification' (2 Thess. 2:13). By the stream, we come at last to the fountain. If we find the stream of sanctification running in our souls, we may by this come to the spring-head of election. Though I cannot look up into the secret of God's purpose — yet I may know I am elected, by the shining of sanctifying grace in my soul. Whoever finds the word of God transcribed and copied out into his heart, may undeniably conclude his election.

2. God's purpose is the ground of assurance.

Here is a sovereign elixir of unspeakable comfort, to those who are the called of God. Their salvation rests upon God's purpose. 'The foundation of God stands sure, having this seal. The Lord knows those who are his. Let everyone who names the name of Christ depart from iniquity' (2 Tim. 2:19). Our graces are imperfect, our comforts ebb and flow — but God's foundation stands sure. They who are built upon this rock of God's eternal purpose, need not fear falling away; neither the power of man, nor the violence of temptation, shall ever be able to overturn them!

The Doctrine of Repentance

The Epistle to the Reader

Reader,

The two great graces essential to a saint in this life, are faith and repentance. These are the two wings by which he flies to heaven. Faith and repentance preserve the spiritual life — as heat and water preserve the physical life. The grace which I am going to discuss is repentance. Chrysostom thought that repentance was the fittest subject for him to preach upon before the Emperor. Augustine kept the penitential psalms with him as he lay upon his bed, and he often perused them with tears. Repentance is never out of season; it is of as frequent use as the artificer's tool or the soldier's weapon. If I am not mistaken, practical points are more needful in this age than controversial and disputable matters.

Repentance is purgative — do not fear the working of this pill. 'Smite your soul,' said Chrysostom, 'smite it; it will escape death by that stroke!' How happy it would be, if we were more deeply affected with sin, and our eyes did swim in tears of repentance. We may clearly see the Spirit of God moving in the waters of repentance, which though troubled, are yet pure. Moist tears of repentance dry up sin — and quench the wrath of God. Repentance is the nourisher of piety, the procurer of mercy. The more regret and trouble of spirit we have first at our conversion, the less we shall feel afterwards.

Christians, do you have a sad regret of other things — and not of sin? Worldly tears fall to the earth — but godly tears of repentance are kept in a bottle. 'You keep track of all my sorrows. You have collected all my tears in your bottle. You have recorded each one in your book.' (Psalm 56:8). Do not judge holy weeping to be wasted. Tertullian thought he was born for no other end — but to repent. Either sin must drown in the tears of repentance — or the soul must burn in hell.

Let it not be said that repentance is difficult. Things that are excellent deserve labor. Will not a man dig for gold — though it makes him sweat? It is better to go with difficulty to heaven — than with ease to hell! What would the damned give, that they might have a herald sent to them from God, to proclaim forgiveness upon their repentance? What volleys of sighs and groans of repentance, would they send up to heaven? What floods of tears would their eyes pour forth? But it is now too late! They may keep their tears to lament their folly — sooner than to procure God's pity. O that we would therefore, while we are on this side of the grave, make our peace with God! Tomorrow may be our dying day; let this be our repenting day. How we should imitate the saints of old, who embittered their souls and sacrificed their lusts, and put on sackcloth in the hope of white robes. Peter baptized himself with tears; and that devout lady Paula, like a bird of paradise, bemoaned herself and humbled herself to the dust for sin.

Besides our own personal sins, the deplorable condition of the land calls for a contribution of tears. Have we not lost much of our pristine fame and renown? The time was when we sat as princes among the provinces (Lam. 1:1), and God made the sheaves of other nations do obeisance to our sheaf (Gen. 37:7) But has not our glory fled away as a bird (Hos. 9:11)? And what severe dispensations are yet ahead, we cannot tell. Our black and hideous vapors having ascended, we may fear loud thunder-claps should follow. And will not all this bring us to our senses and excite in us a spirit of humiliation? Shall we sleep on the top of the mast when the winds are blowing from all the quarters of heaven? 'Cry aloud before the Lord! Let your tears flow like a river. Give yourselves no rest from weeping day or night!' (Lam. 2:18)

I will not launch forth any further in a prefatory discourse — but that God would add a blessing to this work and so direct this arrow, that though shot at random — it may hit the mark, and that some sin may be shot to death — shall be the ardent prayer of him who is the well-wisher of your soul's happiness,

Thomas Watson, May 25, 1668

A Preliminary Discourse

Paul, having been falsely accused of sedition by Tertullus — 'we have him to be a troublemaker, a man who is constantly inciting the Jews throughout the world to riots and rebellions against the Roman government' (Acts 24:5) — makes an apology for himself before Festus and King Agrippa in Chapter 26 of the Book of Acts. Paul treats of three things with such conviction, as almost to have converted King Agrippa:

(1.) He speaks of the manner of his life before his conversion. 'I have been a member of the Pharisees, the strictest sect of our religion.' During the time of his unregeneracy he was zealous for religious traditions, and his false fire of zeal was so hot, that it scorched all who stood in his way; 'I did everything I could to oppose the followers of Jesus of Nazareth. I caused many of the believers in Jerusalem to be sent to prison!'

(2.) He speaks of the manner of his conversion. 'About noon, Your Majesty, a light from heaven brighter than the sun shone down on me.' This light was no other than what shone from Christ's glorified body. 'And I heard a voice speaking unto me, Saul, Saul, why are you persecuting me?' The body being hurt, the head in heaven cried out. At this light and voice — Paul was amazed and fell to the earth: 'Then I asked, 'Who are you, Lord?' 'I am Jesus, whom you are persecuting,' the Lord replied.' All opinion of self-righteousness now vanished, and Paul grafted his hope of heaven upon the stock of Christ's righteousness.

(3) He speaks of the manner of his life after his conversion. He who had been a persecutor before — now became a preacher: 'Now get up and stand on your feet. I have appeared to you to appoint you as a servant and as a witness of what you have seen of me and what I will show you.' When Paul, this 'elect vessel', was savingly wrought upon, he labored to do as much good — as previously he had done hurt. He had persecuted saints to death before, now he preached sinners to life. God first sent him to the Jews at Damascus and afterwards enlarged his commission to preach to the Gentiles. And the message he preached was this, 'I preached that they should repent and turn to God and prove their repentance by their deeds.' (verse 20). A weighty and excellent subject!

I shall not dispute whether faith or repentance comes first into the soul. Doubtless repentance shows itself first in a Christian's life. Yet I am apt to think that the seeds of faith are first wrought in the heart. As when a burning candle is brought into a room — the light shows itself first — but the candle was before the light. Just so, we see the fruits of repentance first — but the beginnings of faith were there before. That which inclines me to think that faith is in the heart before repentance — is because repentance, being a grace, must be exercised by one who is living. Now, how does the soul live — but by faith? 'The just shall live by his faith' (Heb. 10:38). Therefore there must be first, some seeds of faith in the heart of a penitent, otherwise it is a dead repentance and so of no value. Whether faith or repentance goes first — I am sure that repentance is of such importance, that there is no being saved without it.

After Paul's shipwreck he swam to shore on planks and broken pieces of the ship (Acts 27:44). In Adam we all suffered shipwreck, and repentance is the only plank left us after shipwreck — to swim to heaven. It is a great duty incumbent upon Christians solemnly to repent and turn unto God: 'Repent! for the kingdom of heaven is at hand!' (Matt. 3:2) 'Repent therefore, and be converted that your sins may be blotted out!' (Acts 3:19) 'Repent of this your wickedness' (Acts 8:22). In the mouths of three witnesses this truth is confirmed.

Repentance is a foundation grace: 'Not laying again the foundation of repentance' (Heb. 6:1). That religion which is not built upon this foundation must needs fall to the ground. Repentance is a grace required under the gospel. Some think it legal; but the first sermon that Christ preached, indeed, the first word of his sermon, was 'Repent!' (Matt. 4:17) And his farewell that he left when he was going to ascend was that 'repentance should be preached in his name' (Luke 24:47).

The apostles plucked upon this same string: 'They went out and preached that men should repent' (Mark 6:12). Repentance is a pure gospel grace. The covenant of works admitted no repentance; there it was, sin and die! Repentance came in by the gospel. Christ has purchased in his death — that repenting sinners shall be saved. The Law required personal, perfect, and perpetual obedience. It cursed all who could not come up to this: 'Cursed is everyone who does not continue to do everything written in the Book of the Law' (Gal. 3:10). It does not say, 'he who obeys not all things, let him repent' — but, 'let him be cursed.' Thus repentance is a doctrine that has been brought to light, only by the gospel.

How is repentance wrought? The manner in which repentance is wrought is:

Partly by the Word. 'When they heard this, they were pierced to the heart!' (Acts 23:7). The Word preached, is the engine God uses to effect repentance. It is compared to a hammer and to a fire (Jer. 23:29), the one to break, the other to melt the heart. 'Does not my word burn like fire? Is it not like a mighty hammer that smashes rock to pieces?' How great a blessing it is to have the Word, which is of such virtue, when dispensed by the Holy Spirit! Those who will not be melted into repentance by the fire of the Word, will never escape hell!

By the Spirit. Ministers are but the pipes and organs. It is the Holy Spirit breathing in them — which makes their words effectual: 'While Peter yet spoke these words, the Holy Spirit fell on all those who heard the Word' (Acts 10:44). The Spirit in the Word illuminates and converts. When the Spirit touches a heart — it dissolves with tears: 'I will pour upon the inhabitants of Jerusalem the spirit of grace — and they shall look upon me whom they have pierced, and they shall mourn' (Zech. 12:10).

It is astonishing to consider what different effects the Word has upon men. Some at a sermon are like Jonah: their heart is tender and they let tears fall. Others are no more affected with it than a deaf man with music. Some grow better by the Word — others grow worse. The same earth which causes sweetness in the grape — causes bitterness in the wormwood. What is the reason the Word works so differently? It is because the Spirit of God carries the Word to the conscience of one — and not another. One has received the divine annointing — and not the other (1 John 2:20). I pray that the dew may fall with the manna — that the Spirit may go along with the Word. The chariot of ordinances will not carry us to heaven unless the Spirit of God joins himself to this chariot (Acts 8:29).

COUNTERFEITS of Repentance

To discover what true repentance is, I shall first show what it is not. There are several counterfeits of repentance, which might occasion that saying of Augustine that 'repentance damns many'. He meant a false repentance; a person may delude himself with counterfeit repentance:

1. The first counterfeit of repentance, is legal terror.

A man has gone on long in sin. At last God arrests him, shows him what desperate hazard he has run—and he is filled with anguish. But after a while, the tempest of conscience is blown over, and he is quiet. Then he concludes that he is a true penitent because he has felt some bitterness in sin. Do not be deceived! This is not true repentance! Both Ahab and Judas had great trouble of mind. It is one thing to be a terrified sinner—and another to be a repenting sinner. Sense of guilt is enough to breed terror in the conscience. Only infusion of divine grace, breeds true repentance. If pain and trouble were sufficient to repentance, then the damned in hell should be most penitent, for they are most in anguish. 'Men gnawed their tongues in agony and cursed the God of heaven because of their pains and their sores, but they refused to repent of what they had done!' Revelation 16:10-11. Repentance depends upon a change of heart. There may be terror—yet with no change of heart. 'I preached that they should repent and turn to God and prove their repentance by their deeds.' Acts 26:20

2. Another counterfeit about repentance, is resolution against sin.

A person may purpose and make vows—yet be no penitent. 'You said, I will not transgress' (Jer. 2:20). Here was a good resolution. But see what follows: 'but still you would not obey me. On every hill and under every green tree, you have prostituted yourselves by bowing down to idols!' Notwithstanding her solemn engagements, they played fast and loose with God—and ran after their idols!

We see by experience what protestations against sin, a person will make when he is on his sick-bed, if God should recover him again. Yet if that person does recover—he is as bad as ever. He shows his old heart in a new temptation. Resolutions against sin may arise:

(1) From present extremity; not because sin is sinful—but because it is painful. This kind of resolution will vanish.

(2) From fear of future evil, an apprehension of death and hell. 'I looked, and there before me was a pale horse! Its rider was named Death, and Hell was following close behind him!' (Rev. 6:8). What will a sinner not do—what vows will he not make—when he knows he must die and stand before the God in judgment? Self-love raises a sickbed repentance. But if he recovers—the love of sin will prevail against it. Trust not to a such passionate resolution; it is raised in a storm—and will die in a calm!

3. The third counterfeit about repentance, is the leaving of many sinful ways.

It is a great matter, I confess, to leave sin. So dear is sin to a man—that he will rather part with a child than with a lust! 'Shall I give the fruit of my body—for the sin of my soul?' (Micah 6:7). Sin may be parted with—yet without repentance.

(1) A man may part with some sins and keep others. Herod reformed many things which were amiss—but could not leave his beloved Herodias.

(2) An old sin may be left in order to entertain a new sin—as you get rid an old servant to take another. This is to exchange a sin. Sin may be exchanged—and the heart remained unchanged. He who was a profligate in his youth, turns to be a miser in his old age. A slave is sold to a Jew; the Jew sells him to a Turk. Here the master is changed—but he is a slave still. So a man moves from one vice to another—but remains an unrepentant sinner still.

(3) A sin may be left not so much from strength of grace—as from reasons of prudence. A man sees that though such a sin is for his pleasure—yet it is not for his best interest. It will eclipse his credit, harm his health, or impair his estate. Therefore, for prudential reasons, he dismisses it. But true leaving of sin, is when the acts of sin cease from a principle of grace infused into the soul—as the air ceases to be dark from the infusion of light.

The Nature of True Repentance

I shall next show what gospel repentance is. Repentance is a grace of God's Spirit, whereby a sinner is inwardly humbled and outwardly reformed. For a further amplification, know that repentance is a spiritual medicine made up of six special ingredients:

1. Sight of sin

2. Sorrow for sin

3. Confession of sin

4. Shame for sin

5. Hatred for sin

6. Turning from sin

If any one ingredient is left out, it loses its virtue.

Ingredient 1. Sight of Sin

The first ingredient of Christ's gospel-medicine is eye-salve. 'I am sending you to them to open their eyes and turn them from darkness to light' (Acts 26:17-18). It is the great thing noted in the prodigal's repentance: 'he came to himself' (Luke 15:17). He saw himself a sinner — and nothing but a sinner. Before a man can come to Christ — he must first come to himself. A man must first recognize and consider what his sin is, and know the plague of his heart — before he can be duly humbled for it.

The first thing God made was light. So the first thing in a penitent, is illumination: 'For you were once darkness, but now you are light in the Lord' (Eph. 5:8). The eye is made both for seeing and weeping. Sin must first be seen — before it can be wept for. Hence I infer that where there is no sight of sin — there can be no repentance.

Many who can spy faults in others — see none in themselves. They cry that they have good hearts. Is it not strange that two should live together, and eat and drink together — yet not know each other? Such is the case of a sinner. His body and soul live together, work together — yet he is unacquainted with himself. He knows not his own heart, nor what a hell he carries about him. Under a veil — a deformed face is hidden. People are veiled over with ignorance and self-love; therefore they see not what deformed souls they have! The devil does with them as the trainer with the hawk. He covers their eyes, and carries them hooded to hell! 'The sword will pierce his right eye!' (Zechariah 11:17) Men have insight enough into worldly matters — but the right eye of their mind is blind. They do not see any evil in sin; the sword has pierced their right eye!

Ingredient 2. Sorrow for Sin

'I will be sorry for my sin.' (Psalm 38:18) Ambrose calls sorrow the embittering of the soul. The Hebrew word 'to be sorrowful' signifies 'to have the soul, as it were, crucified'. This must be in true repentance: 'They shall look upon me whom they have pierced — and they shall mourn' (Zech. 12:10), as if they did feel the nails of the cross sticking in their sides. A woman may as well expect to have a child without pangs — as one can have repentance without sorrow! He who can repent without sorrowing, suspect his repentance. Martyrs shed blood for Christ, and penitents shed tears for sin: 'she stood at Jesus' feet weeping' (Luke 7:38). See how this tear dropped from her heart. The sorrow of her heart — ran out at her eye!

The brazen laver for the priests to wash in (Exod. 30:18) typified a double laver: the laver of Christ's blood we must wash in by faith — and the laver of tears we must wash in by repentance. A true penitent labors to work his heart into a sorrowing frame. He blesses God when he can weep. He is glad of a rainy day, for he knows that it is a repentance he will have no cause to repent of. Though the bread of sorrow is bitter to the taste – yet it strengthens the heart (Psalm 104:15; 2 Cor. 7:10).

This sorrow for sin is not superficial: it is a holy agony. It is called in scripture a breaking of the heart: 'The sacrifices of God are a broken and a contrite heart' (Psalm 51:17); and a rending of the heart: 'Rend your heart' (Joel 2:13). The expressions of smiting on the thigh (Jer. 31:19), beating on the breast (Luke 18:13), putting on of sackcloth (Isaiah 22:12), plucking off the hair (Ezra 9:3), all these are but outward signs of inward sorrow. This sorrow is:

(1) To make Christ precious. O how desirable is a Savior to a troubled soul! Now Christ is Christ indeed – and mercy is mercy indeed. Until the heart is full of sorrow for sin – it is not fit for Christ. How welcome is a surgeon – to a man who is bleeding from his wounds!

(2) To drive out sin. Sin breeds sorrow – and sorrow kills sin! Holy sorrow purges out the evil humours of the soul. It is said that the tears of vine-branches are good to cure the leprosy. However that may be, it is certain that the tears which drop from the penitential eye, will cure the leprosy of sin. The saltwater of tears – kills the worm of conscience.

(3) To make way for solid comfort. 'Those who sow in tears shall reap in joy' (Psalm 126:5). The penitent has a wet sowing-time – but a delicious harvest. Repentance breaks the abscess of sin – and then the soul is at ease! Hannah, after weeping, went away and was no longer sad (1 Sam. 1:18). God's troubling of the soul for sin, is like the angel's troubling of the pool (John 5:4), which made way for healing.

But not all sorrow evidences true repentance. There is as much difference between true and false sorrow – as between water in the spring, which is sweet – and water in the sea, which is briny. The apostle speaks of 'godly sorrow' (2 Cor. 7:9). What is this godly sorrowing? There are six qualifications of it:

1. True godly sorrow is internal. It is inward in two ways:

(1) It is a sorrow of the heart. The sorrow of hypocrites lies in their faces: 'they disfigure their faces' (Matt. 6:16). They make a sour face – but their sorrow goes no further. It is like the dew which wets the leaf, but does not soak to the root. Ahab's repentance was in outward show. His garments were rent – but not his heart (1 Kings 21:27). Godly sorrow goes deep, like a vein which bleeds inwardly. The heart bleeds for sin: 'they were pricked in their heart' (Acts 2:37). As the heart bears a chief part in sinning – so it must in sorrowing.

(2) It is a sorrow for heart-sins, the first outbreaks and risings of sin. Paul grieved for the law of sin in his members (Romans 7:23). The true mourner weeps for the stirrings of pride and lust. He grieves for the 'root of bitterness' even though it never blossoms into overt act. A wicked man may be troubled for scandalous sins; a real convert laments heart sins.

2. Godly sorrow is sincere. It is sorrow for the offence – rather than for the punishment. God's law has been infringed – and his love abused. This melts the soul in tears. A man may be sorry – yet not repent. A thief is sorry when he is caught, not because he stole – but because he has to pay the penalty! Hypocrites grieve only for the bitter consequence of sin. Their eyes never pour out tears – except when God's judgments are approaching. Pharaoh was more troubled for the frogs – than for his sin.

Godly sorrow, however, is chiefly for the trespass against God – so that even if there were no conscience to smite, no devil to accuse, no hell to punish – yet the soul would still be grieved because of the offense done to God. 'My sin is ever before me' (Psalm 51:3); David does not say, The sword is ever before me – but 'my sin'. 'O that I should offend so good a God, that I should grieve my Comforter! This breaks my heart!' Godly sorrow shows itself to be sincere, because when a Christian knows that he is out of the gun-shot of hell and shall never be damned — yet he still grieves for sinning against that free grace which has pardoned him!

3. Godly sorrow is always intermixed with faith. Sorrow for sin, is chequered with faith, as we have seen a bright rainbow appear in a watery cloud. Spiritual sorrow will sink the heart — if the pulley of faith does not raise it. As our sin is ever before us, so God's promise must be ever before us. As we much feel our sting, so we must look up to Christ our brazen serpent. Some have faces so swollen with worldly grief, that they can hardly look out of their eyes. That weeping is not good — which blinds the eye of faith. If there are not some dawnings of faith in the soul — it is not the sorrow of humiliation, but of despair.

4. Godly sorrow is a great sorrow. 'In that day shall there be a great mourning' (Zech. 12:11). Two suns did set that day when Josiah died, and there was a great funeral mourning. To such a height must sorrow for sin be boiled up.

Question 1. Do all have the same degree of sorrow?

Answer: No, there may be greater or lesser sorrow. In the new birth all have pangs — but some have sharper pangs than others.

(1) Some are naturally of a more rugged disposition, of higher spirits — and are not easily brought to stoop. These must have greater humiliation, as a knotty piece of timber must have sharper wedges driven into it.

(2) Some have been more heinous offenders — and their sorrow must be suitable to their sin. Some patients have their abscess let out with a needle, others with a lance. Heinous sinners must be more bruised with the hammer of the law.

(3) Some are designed and cut out for higher service, to be eminently instrumental for God — and these must have a mightier work of humiliation pass upon them. Those whom God intends to be pillars in his church — must be more hewn. Paul, the prince of the apostles, who was to be God's ensign-bearer to carry his name before the Gentiles and kings, was to have his heart more deeply lanced by repentance.

Question 2. But how great must sorrow for sin be in all?

Answer: It must be as great as for any worldly loss. 'They shall look upon me whom they have pierced — and they shall mourn as for an only son' (Zech. 12:10). Sorrow for sin must surpass worldly sorrow. We must grieve more for offending God — than for the loss of dear relations. 'The Lord, the Lord Almighty, called you on that day to weep and to wail, to tear out your hair and put on sackcloth' (Isaiah 22:12). This repentance was for sin. But in the case of the burial of the dead, we find God prohibiting tears (Jer. 22:10; 16:6), to intimate that sorrow for sin must exceed sorrow at the grave. And with good reason, for in the burial of the dead it is only a friend who departs — but in sin God departs!

Sorrow for sin should be so great as to swallow up all other sorrow, as when the pain of the kidney-stone and gout meet — the pain of the kidney-stone swallows up the pain of the gout. We are to find as much bitterness in weeping for sin — as ever we found sweetness in committing it. Surely David found more bitterness in repentance — than ever he found comfort in Bathsheba.

Our sorrow for sin must be such as makes us willing to let go of those sins which brought in the greatest income of profit or delight. The medicine shows itself strong enough — when it has purged out our disease. Just so, the Christian has arrived at a sufficient measure of sorrow — when the love of sin is purged out.

5. Godly sorrow in some cases is joined with restitution. Whoever has wronged others by unjust fraudulent dealing, ought to make them recompense. There is an express law for this: 'He must make full restitution for his wrong, add one fifth to it and give it all to the person he has wronged.' (Num. 5:7). Thus Zaccheus made restitution: 'if I have cheated anybody out of anything, I will pay back four times the amount' (Luke 19:8). When Selymus the great Turk, lay upon his death-bed, being urged to put to charitable use that wealth he had wronged the Persian merchants of — he commanded that it should be sent back to the right owners. Shall not a Christian's creed be better than a Turk's Koran? It is a bad sign when a man on his death-bed bequeaths his soul to God, and his ill-gotten goods to his friends. I can hardly think God will receive his soul. Augustine said, 'Without restitution, no remission'.

Question 1. Suppose a person has wronged another — and the wronged man is dead. What should he do?

Answer: Let him restore his ill-gotten goods to that man's heirs and family. If none of them are living, let him restore to God — that is, let him put his unjust gain into God's treasury by relieving the poor.

Question 2. What if the party who did the wrong is dead?

Answer: Then those who are his heirs ought to make restitution. Mark what I say — if there are any who has an estate left to them, and he knows that the one who left his estate had defrauded others and died with that guilt upon him — then the heir who now possesses the estate, is bound to make restitution, otherwise he entails the curse of God upon his family.

Question 3. If a man has wronged another and is not able to restore, what should he do?

Answer: Let him deeply humble himself before God, promising to the wronged party full satisfaction, if the Lord makes him able, and God will accept the will for the deed.

6. Godly sorrow is abiding. It is not a few tears shed in a passion, which will serve the turn. Some will fall a-weeping at a sermon — but it is like an April shower, it is soon over — or like a vein opened and presently stopped again. True sorrow must be habitual. O Christian, the disease of your soul is chronic and frequently returns upon you; therefore you must be continually medicating yourself by repentance. This is 'godly sorrow.'

Application: How far are they from repentance, who never had any of this godly sorrow! Such are:

(1) Deluded Papists, who leave out the very soul of repentance, making all penitential work consist in external fasting, penance, pilgrimages, in which there is nothing of spiritual sorrow. They torture their bodies — but their hearts are not torn. What is this, but the carcass of repentance?

(2) Carnal Protestants, who are strangers to godly sorrow. They cannot endure a serious thought, nor do they trouble their heads about sin. One physician spoke of a frenzy some have — which will make them die dancing. Likewise, sinners spend their days in mirth — they fling away sorrow — and go dancing to damnation! Some have lived many years — yet never put a drop of repentant tears in God's bottle, nor do they know what a broken heart means. They weep and wring their hands as if they were undone, when their estates are gone — but have no agony of soul for sin!

There is a two-fold sorrow: Firstly, there is a rational sorrow, which is an act of the soul whereby it has an animosity against sin, and chooses any torture rather than to admit sin. Secondly, there is a sensitive sorrow, which is expressed by many tears. The first of these is to be found in every child of God — but the second, which is a sorrow running out at the eye, all have not.

Yet it is very commendable to see a weeping penitent. Christ counts as great beauties — those who are tender-eyed; and well may sin make us weep. We usually weep for the loss of some great good; by sin we have lost the favor of God. If Micah did so weep for the loss of his idols, saying, 'You've taken away all my gods, and I have nothing left!' (Judges 18:24). Then well may we weep for our sins, which have taken away the true God from us!

Some may ask the question — whether our repentance and sorrow must always be at the same level. Although repentance must be always kept alive in the soul — yet there are two special times when we must renew our repentance in an extraordinary manner:

(1) Before the receiving of the Lord's Supper. This spiritual Passover is to be eaten with bitter herbs. Now our eyes should be fresh broached with tears, and the stream of sorrow overflow. A repenting frame is a sacramental frame. A broken heart and a broken Christ do well agree. The more bitterness we taste in sin — the more sweetness we shall taste in Christ! When Jacob wept — he found God: 'Jacob named the place Peniel — face of God — for I have seen God face to face!' (Gen. 32:30). The way to find Christ comfortably in the sacrament, is to go weeping there. Christ will say to a humble penitent, as to Thomas: 'Put your hand into the wound in my side' (John 20:27), and let those bleeding wounds of mine heal you.

(2) Another time of extraordinary repentance is at the hour of death. This should be a weeping season. Now is our last work to be done for heaven, and our best wine of tears should be kept until such a time. We should repent now — that we have sinned so much — and wept so little; that God's bag of our sins has been so full — and his bottle of our repenting tears has been so empty (Job 14:17). We should repent now — that we repented no sooner; that the garrisons of our hearts held out so long against God before they were leveled by repentance. We should repent now — that we have loved Christ no more — that we have fetched no more virtue from him and brought no more glory to him. It should be our grief on our death-bed that our lives have had so many blanks and blots in them — that our duties have been so tainted with sin, that our obedience has been so imperfect — and we have gone so lame in the ways of God. When the soul is going out of the body — it should swim to heaven in a sea of tears!

Ingredient 3. Confession of Sin

Sorrow is such a vehement passion — that it will have vent. It vents itself at the eyes by weeping, and at the tongue by confession. 'The children of Israel stood and confessed their sins (Neh. 9:2). 'I will go and return to my place, until they acknowledge their offence' (Hos. 5:15). This is a metaphor alluding to a mother who, when she is angry, goes away from the child and hides her face until the child acknowledges its fault and begs pardon. Gregory Nazianzen calls confession 'a salve for a wounded soul.' Confession is self-accusing: 'I have sinned!' (2 Sam. 24:17). When we come before God, we must accuse ourselves. The truth is — that by this self-accusing we prevent Satan's accusing. In our confessions we accuse ourselves of pride, infidelity, passion, so that when Satan, who is called 'the accuser of the brethren', shall lay these things to our charge, God will say, 'They have accused themselves already; therefore, Satan, you have no suit; your accusations come too late.'

The humble sinner does more than accuse himself; he, as it were, sits in judgment and passes sentence upon himself. He confesses that he has deserved to be bound over to the wrath of God. Hear what the apostle Paul says: 'if we judged ourselves, we would not come under judgment' (1 Cor. 11:31). But have not wicked men, like Judas and Saul, confessed sin? Yes! but theirs was not a true confession. That confession of sin may be right and genuine, these eight qualifications are requisite:

1. Confession must be voluntary.

It must come as water out of a spring—freely. The confession of the wicked is extorted, like the confession of a man upon a rack. When a spark of God's wrath flies into their conscience, or they are in fear of death—then they will fall to their confessions! Balaam, when he saw the angel's naked sword, could say, 'I have sinned!' (Num. 22:34). But true confession drops from the lips—as myrrh from the tree, or honey from the comb—freely. 'I have sinned against heaven, and before you' (Luke 15:18). The prodigal charged himself with sin, before his father charged him with it.

2. Confession must be with remorse.

The heart must deeply resent it. A natural man's confessions run through him as water through a pipe. They do not affect him at all. But true confession leaves heart-wounding impressions on a man. David's soul was burdened in the confession of his sins: 'as a heavy burden, they are too heavy for me' (Psalm 38:4). It is one thing to confess sin—and another thing to feel sin's wounds.

3. Confession must be sincere.

Our hearts must go along with our confessions. The hypocrite confesses sin—but loves it; like a thief who confesses to stolen goods—yet loves stealing. How many confess pride and covetousness with their lips—but roll them as honey under their tongue. Augustine said that before his conversion he confessed sin and begged power against it—but his heart whispered within him, 'not yet, Lord'. He really did not want to leave his sin. A good Christian is more honest. His heart keeps pace with his tongue. He is convinced of the sins he confesses, and abhors the sins he is convinced of.

4. In true confession a man particularizes sin.

A wicked man acknowledges he is a sinner in general. He confesses sin by wholesale. A wicked man says, 'Lord, I have sinned'—but does not know what the sin is; whereas a true convert acknowledges his particular sins. As it is with a wounded man, who comes to the surgeon and shows him all his wounds—here I was cut in the head, there I was shot in the arm; so a mournful sinner confesses the various sins of his soul. Israel drew up a particular charge against themselves: 'we have served Baal' (Judg. 10:10). The prophet recites the very sin which brought a curse with it: 'Neither have we hearkened unto your servants the prophets, which spoke in your name' (Dan. 9:6). By a diligent inspection into our hearts, we may find some particular sin indulged—point to that sin with a repentant tear!

5. A true penitent confesses sin in the fountain.

He acknowledges the pollution of his nature. The sin of our nature is not only a privation of good—but an infusion of evil. It is like rust to iron or stain to scarlet. David acknowledges his birth-sin: 'I was shaped in iniquity; and in sin did my mother conceive me' (Psalm 51:5). We are ready to charge many of our sins to Satan's temptations—but this sin of our nature is wholly from ourselves; we cannot shift it off to Satan. We have a root within, which bears gall and wormwood (Deut. 29:18). Our nature is an abyss and seed of all sin, from whence come those evils which infest the world. It is this depravity of nature which poisons our holy things; it is this which brings on God's judgments. Oh confess sin in the fountain!

6. Sin is to be confessed with all its circumstances and aggravations.

Those sins which are committed under the gospel horizon, are aggravated sins. Confess sins against knowledge, against grace, against vows, against experiences, against judgments. 'The wrath of God came upon them and slew the fattest of them. For all this they sinned still' (Psalm 78:31-2). Those are killing aggravations, which enhance our sins.

7. In confession, we must so charge ourselves as to clear God.

Should the Lord be severe in his providences and unsheathe his bloody sword — yet we must acquit him and acknowledge he has done us no wrong. Nehemiah in his confessing of sin vindicates God's righteousness: 'Every time you punished us you were being just. We have sinned greatly, and you gave us only what we deserved' (Neh. 9:33). Mauritius the emperor, when he saw his wife slain before his eyes by Phocas, cried out, 'Righteous are you, O Lord, in all your ways'.

8. We must confess our sins with a resolution not to commit them over again. Some run from the confessing of sin — to the committing of sin, like the Persians who have one day in the year when they kill serpents; and after that day allow them to swarm again. Likewise, many seem to kill their sins in their confessions, and afterwards let them grow as fast as ever. 'Cease to do evil' (Isaiah 1:16). It is vain to confess, 'We have done those things we ought not to have done', and continue still in doing so. Pharaoh confessed he had sinned (Exod. 9:27) — but when the thunder ceased he fell to his sin again: 'he sinned yet more, and hardened his heart' (Exod. 9:34). Origen calls confession 'the vomit of the soul whereby the conscience is eased of that burden which did lie upon it.' Now, when we have vomited up sin by confession — we must not return to this vomit! What king will pardon that man who, after he has confessed his treason, practices new treason? Thus we see how confession must be qualified.

Use 1. Is confession a necessary ingredient in repentance? Here is a bill of indictment against four kinds of people:

(1) It reproves those who hide their sins, as Rachel hid her father's idols under her saddle (Gen. 31:34). Many had rather have their sins covered — than cured. They do with their sins as with their pictures: they draw a curtain over them. But though men will have no tongue to confess — God has an eye to see! He will unmask their treason: 'But I will rebuke you and accuse you to your face!' (Psalm 50:21). Those iniquities which men hide in their hearts — shall be written one day on their foreheads as with the point of a diamond! They who will not confess their sin as David did — that they may be pardoned; shall confess their sin as Achan did — that they may be punished. It is dangerous to keep the devil's counsel — to hide our sins. 'He who covers his sins shall not prosper' (Proverbs 28:13).

(2) It reproves those who do indeed confess sin, but only by halves. They do not confess all; they confess the pence — but not the pounds. They confess vain thoughts or badness of memory — but not the sins they are most guilty of, such as rash anger, extortion, and immorality. They are like one who complains that his head aches — when his lungs are full of cancer! But if we do not confess all, how should we expect that God will pardon all? It is true that we cannot know the exact catalogue of our sins — but the sins which come within our view and cognizance, and which our hearts accuse us of, must be confessed as ever we hope for mercy.

(3) It reproves those who in their confessions, mince and mitigate their sins. A gracious soul labors to make the worst of his sins — but hypocrites make the best of them. They do not deny they are sinners — but they do what they can to lessen their sins. They indeed offend sometimes — but it is their nature. These are excuses rather than confessions. 'I have sinned: for I have transgressed the commandment of the Lord: because I feared the people' (1 Sam. 15:24).

Saul lays his sin upon the people: they would have him spare the sheep and oxen. It was an excuse, not a self-indictment. This runs in the blood. Adam acknowledged that he had tasted the forbidden fruit — but instead of aggravating his sin he transferred it from himself to God: 'The woman you gave me, she gave me the fruit — and I ate' (Gen. 3:12), that is, if I had not had this woman to be a tempter, I would not have transgressed. How apt we are to pare and curtail sin, and look upon it through the small end of the telescope, that it appears but as 'a little cloud, like a man's hand' (1 Kings 18:44).

(4) It reproves those who are so far from confessing sin, that they boldly plead for it. Instead of having tears to lament it, they use arguments to defend it. If their sin is anger, they will justify it: 'I do well to be angry!' (Jon. 4:9). If it be covetousness, they will vindicate it. When men commit sin, they are the devil's servants; when they plead for it they are the devil's attorneys, and he will give them a fee.

Use 2. Let us show ourselves penitents by sincere confession of sin. The thief on the cross made a confession of his sin: 'we indeed are condemned justly' (Luke 23:41). And Christ said to him, 'Today shall you be with me in paradise!' (Luke 23:43), which might have occasioned that speech of Augustine's, that 'confession of sin shuts the mouth of hell and opens the gate of paradise.' That we may make a free and sincere confession of sin, let us consider:

(1) Holy confession gives glory to God. 'Give glory to the Lord, the God of Israel — and make a confession to Him' (Josh. 7:19). A humble confession exalts God. When we confess sin, God's patience is magnified in sparing, and his free grace in saving such sinners.

(2) Confession is a means to humble the soul. He who subscribes himself a hell-deserving sinner, will have little heart to be proud. Like the violet, he will hang down his head in humility. A true penitent confesses that he mingles sin with all he does — and therefore has nothing to boast of. Uzziah, though a king — yet had a leprosy in his forehead; he had enough to abase him (2 Chron. 26:19). So a child of God, even when he does good — yet acknowledges much evil to be in that good. This lays all his plumes of pride in the dust.

(3) Confession gives vent to a troubled heart. When guilt lies boiling in the conscience, confession gives ease. It is like the lancing of an abscess, which gives ease to the patient.

(4) Confession purges out sin. Augustine called it 'the expeller of vice'. Sin is bad blood; confession is like the opening of a vein to let it out. Confession is like the dung-gate, through which all the filth of the city was carried forth (Neh. 3:13). Confession is like pumping at the leak; it lets out that sin which would otherwise drown. Confession is the sponge which wipes the spots from off the soul.

(5) Confession of sin endears Christ to the soul. If I say I am a sinner — how precious will Christ's blood be to me! After Paul has confessed a body of sin, he breaks forth into a thankful triumph for Christ: 'I thank God through Jesus Christ' (Romans 7:25). If a debtor confesses a judgment but the creditor will not exact the debt, instead appointing his own son to pay it, will not the debtor be very thankful? So when we confess the debt, and that even though we should forever lie in hell we cannot pay it — but that God should appoint his own Son to lay down his blood for the payment of our debt — how is free grace magnified and Jesus Christ eternally loved and admired!

(6) Confession of sin makes way for pardon. No sooner did the prodigal come with a confession in his mouth, 'I have sinned against heaven', then his father's heart did melt towards him, 'Filled with love and compassion, he ran to his son, embraced him, and kissed him' (Luke 15:20). When David said, 'I have sinned', the prophet brought him a box with a pardon, 'The Lord has put away your sin' (2 Sam. 12:13). He who sincerely confesses sin, has God's bond for

a pardon: 'If we confess our sins, he is faithful and just to forgive us our sins' (1 John 1:9). Why does not the apostle say that if we confess, God is merciful to forgive our sins? He says that God is just, because he has bound himself by promise to forgive such. God's truth and justice are engaged for the pardoning of that man who confesses sin and comes with a penitent heart by faith in Christ.

(7) How reasonable and easy is this command that we should confess sin!

(a) It is a reasonable command, for if one has wronged another, what is more rational than to confess he has wronged him? We, having wronged God by sin, how equal and consonant to reason is it that we should confess the offence.

(b) It is an easy command. What a vast difference is there between the first covenant and the second! In the first covenant it was, if you commit sin you die! In the second covenant it is, if you confess sin you shall have mercy! In the first covenant no surety was allowed; under the covenant of grace, if we do but confess the debt, Christ will be our surety. What way could be thought of as more ready and facile for the salvation of man, than a humble confession? 'Only acknowledge your iniquity' (Jer. 3:13). God says to us, I do not ask for sacrifices of rams to expiate your guilt; I do not bid you part with the fruit of your body for the sin of your soul, 'only acknowledge your iniquity.' Do but draw up an indictment against yourself and plead guilty—and you shall be sure of mercy. All this should render this duty amiable. Throw out the poison of sin by confession, and 'this day is salvation come to your house'.

There remains one case of conscience: are we bound to confess our sins to men? The papists insist much upon auricular confession; that is—one must confess his sins in the ear of the priest or he cannot be absolved. They urge, 'Confess your sins one to another' (James 5:16)—but this scripture is little to their purpose. It may as well mean that the priest should confess to the people as well as the people to the priest. Auricular confession is one of the Pope's golden doctrines. Like the fish in the Gospel, it has money in its mouth: 'when you have opened its mouth, you shall find a piece of money' (Matt. 17:27). But though I am not for confession to men in a popish sense—yet I think in three cases there ought to be confession to men:

(1) Firstly, where a person has fallen into scandalous sin and by it has been an occasion of offence to some and of falling to others, he ought to make a solemn and open acknowledgment of his sin, that his repentance may be as visible as his scandal (2 Cor. 2:6-7).

(2) Secondly, where a man has confessed his sin to God—yet still his conscience is burdened, and he can have no ease in his mind—it is very requisite that he should confess his sins to some prudent, pious friend, who may advise him and speak a word in due season (James 5:16). It is a sinful modesty in Christians, that they are not more free with their ministers and other spiritual friends in unburdening themselves and opening the sores and troubles of their souls to them. If there is a thorn sticking in the conscience, it is good to make use of those who may help to pluck it out.

(3) Thirdly, where any man has slandered another and by clipping his good name has made it weigh lighter, he is bound to make confession. The scorpion carries its poison in its tail—the slanderer in carries its poison in his tongue! His words pierce deep like swords. That person who has murdered another in his good name or, by bearing false witness, or has damaged him in his estate, ought to confess his sin and ask forgiveness: 'if you are standing before the altar in the Temple, offering a sacrifice to God, and you suddenly remember that someone has something against you, leave your sacrifice there beside the altar. Go and be reconciled to that person. Then come and offer your sacrifice to God' (Matt. 5:23-24). How can this reconciliation be effected but by confessing the injury? Until this is done, God will accept none of your

services. Do not think the holiness of the altar will privilege you; your praying and hearing are in vain, until you have appeased your brother's anger by confessing your fault to him.

Ingredient 4. Shame for Sin

The fourth ingredient in repentance is shame: 'that they may be ashamed of their iniquities' (Ezek. 43:10). Blushing is the color of virtue. When the heart has been made black with sin, grace makes the face red with blushing: 'I am ashamed and blush to lift up my face' (Ezra 9:6). The repenting prodigal was so ashamed of his sinfulness, that he thought himself not worthy to be called a son any more (Luke 15:21). Repentance causes a holy bashfulness. If Christ's blood were not at the sinner's heart, there would not so much blood come in the face. There are nine considerations about sin which may cause shame:

(1) Every sin makes us guilty, and guilt usually breeds shame. Adam never blushed in the time of innocency. While he kept the whiteness of the lily, he had not the blushing of the rose. But when he had deflowered his soul by sin—then he was ashamed. Sin has tainted our blood. We are guilty of high treason against the Crown of heaven. This may cause a holy modesty and blushing.

(2) In every sin there is much unthankfulness, and that is a matter of shame. He who is upbraided with ingratitude will blush. We have sinned against God when he has given us no cause: 'What iniquity have your fathers found in me?' (Jer. 2:5). Wherein has God wearied us, unless his mercies have wearied us? Oh the silver drops which have fallen on us! We have had the finest of the wheat; we have been fed with angels' food. The golden oil of divine blessing has run down on us from the head of our heavenly Aaron. And to abuse the kindness of so good a God—how may this make us ashamed!

Julius Caesar took it unkindly at the hands of Brutus, on whom he had bestowed so many favors, when he came to stab him: 'What, you, my son Brutus?' O ungrateful—to be the worse for mercy! One reports of the vulture, that it draws sickness from perfumes. To contract the disease of pride and luxury, from the perfume of God's mercy—how unworthy is that! It is to requite evil for good, to kick against our feeder, 'He nourished him with honey from the rock, and with oil from the flinty crag, with curds and milk from herd and flock and with fattened lambs and goats, with choice rams of Bashan and the finest kernels of wheat. You drank the foaming blood of the grape. Jeshurun grew fat, and kicked. He abandoned the God who made him and scorned the Rock of his salvation' (Deut. 32:13-15). This is to make an arrow of God's mercies—and shoot at him! This is to wound him with his own blessing! O horrid ingratitude! Will not this dye our faces a deep scarlet? Unthankfulness is a sin so great, that God himself stands amazed at it: 'Hear, O heavens, and give ear, O earth: I have nourished and brought up children—and they have rebelled against me!' (Isaiah 1:2).

(3) Sin has made us naked, and that may breed shame. Sin has stripped us of our white linen of holiness. It has made us naked and deformed in God's eye—which may cause blushing. When Hanun had abused David's servants and cut off their garments so that their nakedness appeared, the text says, 'the men were greatly ashamed' (2 Sam. 10:5).

(4) Our sins have put Christ to shame, and should not we be ashamed? The Jews arrayed him in purple; they put a reed in his hand, spit in his face, and in his greatest agonies reviled him. Here was 'the shame of the cross'. And that which aggravated the shame, was to consider the eminency of his person—as he was the Lamb of God. Did our sins put Christ to shame—and shall they not put us to shame? Did he wear the purple—and shall not our cheeks wear crimson? Who can behold the sun as it were blushing at Christ's passion, and hiding itself in an eclipse—and his face not blush?

(5) Many sins which we commit are by the special instigation of the devil — and should not this cause shame? The devil put it into the heart of Judas to betray Christ (John 13:2). He filled Ananias' heart to lie (Acts 5:3). He often stirs up our passions (James 3:6). Now, as it is a shame to bring forth a child illegitimately, so too is it to bring forth such sins as may call the devil father. It is said that the virgin Mary conceived by the power of the Holy Spirit (Luke 1:35) — but we often conceive by the power of Satan. When the heart conceives pride, lust, and malice — it is very often by the power of the devil. May not this make us ashamed to think that many of our sins are committed in copulation with the old serpent?

(6) Sin turns men into beasts (2 Peter 2:12), and is not that matter for shame? Sinners are compared to foxes (Luke 13:32), to wolves (Matt. 7:15), to donkeys (Job 28 11:12), to swine (2 Pet. 2:22). A sinner is a swine with a man's head. He who was once little less than the angels in dignity — has now become like the beasts. Grace in this life does not wholly obliterate this brutish temper. Agur, that good man, cried out, 'surely I am more brutish than any!' (Proverbs 30:2). But common sinners are in a manner wholly brutified; they do not act rationally, but are carried away by the violence of their lusts and passions. How may this make us ashamed, who are thus degenerated below our own species? Our sins have taken away that noble, holy spirit which once we had. The crown has fallen from our head. God's image is defaced, reason is eclipsed, conscience stupefied! We have more in us of the brute, than of the angel.

(7) In every sin there is folly (Jer. 4:22). A man will be ashamed of his folly. Is not he a fool who labors more for the bread which perishes — than for the bread of life! Is not he a fool who for a lust or a trifle — will lose heaven! They are like Tiberius, who for a drink of water forfeited his kingdom? Is not he a fool who, to safeguard his body, will injure his soul? As if one should let his head be cut, to save his shirt! Is not he a fool who will believe a temptation of Satan — before a promise of God? Is not he a fool who minds his recreation more than his salvation? How may this make men ashamed — to think that they inherit not land — but folly (Proverbs 14:18).

(8) That which may make us blush, is that the sins we commit are far worse than the sins of the heathen. We act against more light. To us have been committed the oracles of God. The sin committed by a Christian is worse than the same sin committed by an heathen, because the Christian sins against clearer conviction, which is like weight put into the scale, which makes it weigh heavier.

(9) Our sins are worse than the sins of the devils. The fallen angels never sinned against Christ's blood. Christ did not die for them. The medicine of his merit was never intended to heal them. But we have affronted his blood by unbelief. The devils never sinned against God's patience. As soon as they apostatized, they were damned. God never waited for the angels — but we have spent upon the stock of God's patience. He has pitied our weakness, borne with our rebelliousness. His Spirit has been repulsed — yet has still importuned us and will take no denial. Our conduct has been so provoking as to have tired not only the patience of a Job, but of all the angels. The devils never sinned against example. They were the first that sinned and were made the first example. We have seen the angels, those morning stars, fall from their glorious orb; we have seen the old world drowned, Sodom burned — yet have ventured upon sin. How desperate is that thief who robs in the very place where his fellow hangs in chains. And surely, if we have out-sinned the devils, it may well put us to the blush.

Use 1. Is shame an ingredient of repentance? If so, how far are they from being penitents who have no shame? Many have sinned away shame: 'the wicked know no shame' (Zeph. 3:5). It is a great shame not to be ashamed. The Lord sets it as a brand upon the Jews: 'Are they ashamed of their loathsome conduct? No, they have no shame at all; they do not even know how to blush!' (Jer. 6:15). The devil has stolen shame from men. When one of the persecutors in Queen Mary's time was upbraided for murdering the martyrs, he replied, 'I see nothing to be ashamed of!' When men have hearts of stone and foreheads of brass—it is a sign that the devil has taken full possession of them.

There is no creature capable of shame but man. The brute beasts are capable of fear and pain—but not of shame. You cannot make a beast blush. Those who cannot blush for sin, do too much resemble the beasts. There are some so far from this holy blushing that they are proud of their sins. They are so far from being ashamed of sin, that they glory in their sins: 'whose glory is in their shame' (Phil. 3:19). Some are ashamed of that which is their glory: they are ashamed to be seen with a good book in their hand. Others glory in that which is their shame: they look on sin as a piece of gallantry. The swearer thinks his speech most graceful when it is interlarded with oaths. The drunkard counts it a glory that he is mighty to drink (Isaiah 5:22). But when men shall be cast into the fiery furnace, heated seven times hotter by the breath of the Almighty—then let them boast of sin!

Use 2. Let us show our penitence by a modest blushing: 'O my God, I blush to lift up my face' (Ezra 9:6). 'My God'—there was faith; 'I blush'—there was repentance. Hypocrites will confidently avouch God to be their God—but they know not how to blush. O let us take holy shame to ourselves for sin. Be assured, the more we are ashamed of sin now—the less we shall be ashamed at Christ's coming. If the sins of the godly are mentioned at the Day of Judgment, it will not be to shame them—but to magnify the riches of God's grace in pardoning them. Indeed, the wicked shall be ashamed at the last day. They shall sneak and hang down their heads—but the saints shall then be as without spot (Eph. 5:27), so without shame; therefore they are bid to lift up their heads (Luke 21:28).

Ingredient 5. Hatred of Sin

The fifth ingredient in repentance is hatred of sin. The Schoolmen distinguished a two-fold hatred: hatred of abominations, and hatred of enmity.

Firstly, there is a hatred or loathing of abominations: 'Then you will remember your evil ways and wicked deeds, and you will loathe yourselves for your sins and detestable practices!' (Ezek. 36:31). A true penitent is a sin-loather. If a man loathes that which makes his stomach sick, much more will he loathe that which makes his soul sick! It is greater to loathe sin—than to leave it. One may leave sin for fear, as in a storm the jewels are cast overboard—but the nauseating and loathing of sin argues a detestation of it. Christ is never loved—until sin is loathed. Heaven is never longed for—until sin is loathed. When the soul sees its filthiness, he cries out, 'Lord, when shall I be freed from this body of death! When shall I put off these filthy garments of sin—and be arrayed in the robe of Your perfect righteousness! Let all my self-love be turned into self-loathing!' (Zech. 3:4-5). We are never more precious in God's eyes—than when we are lepers in our own eyes!

Secondly, there is a hatred of enmity. There is no better way to discover life—than by motion. The eye moves, the pulse beats. So to discover repentance there is no better sign than by a holy antipathy against sin. Sound repentance begins in love to God—and ends in the hatred of sin. How may true hatred of sin be known?

1. When a man's heart is set against sin.

Not only does the tongue protest against sin—but the heart abhors it. However lovely sin is painted—we find it odious—just as we abhor the picture of one whom we mortally hate, even though it may be well drawn. Suppose a dish be finely cooked and the sauce good—yet if a man has an antipathy against the meat—he will not eat it. So let the devil cook and dress sin with pleasure and profit — yet a true penitent has a secret abhorrence of it, is disgusted by it, and will not meddle with it.

2. True hatred of sin is universal.

True hatred of sin is universal in two ways: in respect of the faculties, and of the object.

(1) Hatred is universal in respect of the faculties. That is, there is a dislike of sin not only in the judgment — but in the will and affections. Many a one is convinced that sin is a vile thing, and in his judgment, has an aversion to it — yet he tastes sweetness in it — and has a secret delight in it. Here is a disliking of sin in the judgment and an embracing of it in the affections! Whereas in true repentance, the hatred of sin is in all the faculties, not only in the intellectual part — but chiefly in the will: 'I do the very thing I hate!' (Romans 7:15). Paul was not free from sin — yet his will was against it.

(2) Hatred is universal in respect of the object. He who truly hates one sin — hates all sins. He who hates a serpent — hates all serpents. 'I hate every false way!' (Psalm 119:104). Hypocrites will hate some sins which mar their credit. But a true convert hates all sins — gainful sins, complexion sins, the very stirrings of corruption. Paul hated the motions of sin within him (Romans 7:23).

3. True hatred against sin is against sin in all forms.

A holy heart detests sin for its intrinsic pollution. Sin leaves a stain upon the soul. A regenerate person abhors sin not only for the curse — but for the contagion. He hates this serpent not only for its sting but for its poison. He hates sin not only for hell — but as hell.

4. True hatred is implacable.

It will never be reconciled to sin any more. Anger may be reconciled — but hatred cannot. Sin is that Amalek which is never to be taken into favor again. The war between a child of God and sin is like the war between those two princes: 'there was war between Rehoboam and Jeroboam all their days' (1 Kings 14:30).

5. Where there is a real hatred, we not only oppose sin in ourselves but in OTHERS too. The church at Ephesus could not bear with those who were evil (Rev. 2:2). Paul sharply censured Peter for his deception, although he was an apostle. Christ in a holy anger, whipped the money-changers out of the temple (John 2:15). He would not allow the temple to be made an exchange. Nehemiah rebuked the nobles for their usury (Neh. 5:7) and their Sabbath profanation (Neb. 13:17).

A sin-hater will not endure wickedness in his family: 'He who works deceit shall not dwell within my house' (Psalm 101:7). What a shame it is when magistrates can show height of spirit in their passions — but no heroic spirit in suppressing vice.

Those who have no antipathy against sin, are strangers to repentance. Sin is in them — as poison in a serpent, which, being natural to it, affords delight. How far are they from repentance who, instead of hating sin, love sin! To the godly — sin is as a thorn in the eye; to the wicked sin is as a crown on the head! 'They actually rejoice in doing evil!' (Jer. 11:15).

Loving of sin is worse than committing it. A good man may run into a sinful action unawares — but to love sin is desperate. What is it, which makes a swine love to tumble in the mire? Its love of filth. To love sin shows that the will is in sin, and the more of the will there is in a sin, the greater the sin. Willfulness makes it a sin not to be purged by sacrifice (Heb. 10:26). O how many there are — who love the forbidden fruit! They love their oaths and adulteries; they love the sin and hate the reproof. Solomon speaks of a generation of men: 'madness is in their heart while they live' (Eccles. 9:3). So for men to love sin, to hug that which will be their death, to sport with damnation, 'madness is in their heart'. It persuades us to show our repentance, by a bitter hatred of sin. There is a deadly antipathy between the scorpion and the crocodile; such should there be between the heart and sin.

Question: What is there in sin, which may make a penitent hate it?

Answer: Sin is the accursed thing, the most deformed monster. The apostle Paul uses a very emphatic word to express it: 'that sin might become exceedingly sinful' (Romans 7:13), or as it is in the Greek, 'exaggeratedly sinful'. That sin is an exaggerated mischief, and deserves hatred will appear if we look upon sin as a fourfold conceit:

(1) Look upon the origin of sin, from whence it comes. It fetches its pedigree from hell: 'He who commits sin is of the devil!' (1 John 3:8). Sin is the devil's special work. God has a hand in ordering sin, it is true—but Satan has a hand in acting it out. How hateful is it to be doing that which is the special work of the devil, indeed, that which makes men into devils!

(2) Look upon sin in its nature, and it will appear very hateful. See how scripture has penciled sin out: it is a dishonoring of God (Romans 2:23); a despising of God (1 Sam. 2:30); a fretting of God (Ezek. 16:43); a wearying of God (Isaiah 7:13); a grieving the heart of God, as a loving husband is with the unchaste conduct of his wife: 'I have been grieved by their adulterous hearts, which have turned away from me, and by their eyes, which have lusted after their idols' (Ezek. 6:9). Sin, when acted to the height, is a crucifying Christ afresh and putting him to open shame (Heb. 6:6), that is, impudent sinners pierce Christ in his saints, and were he now upon earth they would crucify him again in his person. Behold the odious nature of sin.

(3) Look upon sin in its comparison, and it appears ghastly. Compare sin with affliction and hell, and it is worse than both. It is worse than affliction, sickness, poverty, or death. There is more malignity in a drop of sin than in a sea of affliction—for sin is the cause of affliction, and the cause is more than the effect. The sword of God's justice lies quiet in the scabbard—until sin draws it out! Affliction is good for us: 'It is good for me that I have been afflicted' (Psalm 119:71). Affliction causes repentance (2 Chron. 33:12). The viper, being stricken, casts up its poison. Just so, when God's rod strikes us with affliction, we spit away the poison of sin! Affliction betters our grace. Gold is purest, and juniper sweetest—when in the fire. Affliction prevents damnation. 'We are being disciplined—so that we will not be condemned with the world.' (1 Cor. 11:32). Therefore, Maurice the emperor prayed to God to punish him in this life—that he might not be punished hereafter.

Thus, affliction is in many ways for our good—but there is no good in sin. Manasseh's affliction brought him to humiliation and repentance—but Judas' sin brought him to desperation and damnation. Affliction only reaches the body—but sin goes further: it poisons the mind, disorders the affections. Affliction is but corrective; sin is destructive. Affliction can but take away the life; sin takes away the soul (Luke 12:20).

A man who is afflicted may have his conscience quiet. When the ark was tossed on the flood waves, Noah could sing in the ark. When the body is afflicted and tossed, a Christian can 'make melody in his heart to the Lord' (Eph. 5:19). But when a man commits sin, conscience is terrified. Witness Spira, who upon his abjuring the faith, said that he thought the damned spirits did not feel those torments which he inwardly endured. In affliction, one may have the love of God (Rev. 3:19). If a man should throw a bag of money at another, and in throwing it should hurt him a little—he will not take it unkindly—but will look upon it as a fruit of love. Just so, when God bruises us with affliction—it is to enrich us with the golden graces and comforts of his Spirit. All is in love. But when we commit sin, God withdraws his love. When David sinned, he felt nothing but displeasure from God: 'Clouds and thick darkness surround him' (Psalm 97:2). David found it so. He could see no rainbow, no sunbeam, nothing but clouds and darkness about God's face.

That sin is worse than affliction is evident, because the greatest judgment God lays upon a man in this life is to let him sin without control. When the Lord's displeasure is most severely kindled against a person, he does not say, I will bring the sword and the plague on this man – but, I will let him sin on: 'I gave them up unto their own hearts lust, living according to their own desires' (Psalm 81:12). Now, if the giving up of a man to his sins (in the account of God himself) is the most dreadful evil, then sin is far worse than affliction. And if it is so, then how should it be hated by us!

Compare sin with hell, and you shall see that sin is worse. Torment has its epitome in hell – yet nothing in hell is as bad as sin. Hell is of God's making – but sin is not of God's making. Sin is the devil's creature. The torments of hell are a burden only to the sinner – but sin is a burden to God. In the torments of hell, there is something that is good, namely, the execution of divine justice. There is justice to be found in hell – but sin is a piece of the highest injustice. It would rob God of his glory, Christ of his purchase, the soul of its happiness. Judge then if sin is not a most hateful thing – which is worse than affliction, or the torments of hell.

(4) Look upon sin in the consequence, and it will appear hateful. Sin reaches the BODY. It has exposed it to a variety of miseries. We come into the world with a cry – and go out with a groan! It made the Thracians weep on their children's birthday – to consider the calamities they were to undergo in the world. Sin is the Trojan horse out of which comes a whole army of troubles. I need not name them because almost everyone feels them. While we suck the honey – we are pricked with the briar. Sin puts a dreg in the wine of all our comforts. Sin digs our grave (Romans 5:12).

Sin reaches the soul. By sin we have lost the image of God, wherein did consist both our sanctity and our majesty. Adam in his pristine glory, was like a herald who has his king's coat of arms upon him. All reverence him because he carries the king's coat of arms – but pull this coat off, and no man regards him. Sin has done this disgrace to us. It has plucked off our coat of innocency. But that is not all. This virulent arrow of sin would strike yet deeper. It would forever separate us from the beautiful vision of God, in whose presence is fullness of joy. If sin be so foully sinful, it should stir up our implacable indignation against it. As Ammon's hatred of Tamar was greater than the love with which he had loved her (2 Sam. 13:15), so we should hate sin infinitely more, than ever we loved it.

Ingredient 6. Turning from Sin

The sixth ingredient in repentance, is a turning from sin. Reformation is left last, to bring up the rear of repentance. What though one could, with Niobe, weep himself into a stone – if he did not weep out sin? True repentance, like acid, eats asunder the iron chain of sin! Therefore weeping fro sin, and turning from sin – are put together, 'return to me with all your heart, with fasting and weeping and mourning!' (Joel 2:12). After the cloud of sorrow has dropped in tears, the sky of the soul is clearer: 'Repent, and turn from your idols; and turn away your faces from all your abominations' (Ezek. 14:6).

This turning from sin is called a forsaking of sin (Isaiah 55:7), as a man forsakes the company of a thief or sorcerer. It is called 'a putting of sin far away' (Job 11:14), as Paul put away the viper and shook it into the fire (Acts 28:5). Dying to sin – is the life of repentance. The very day a Christian turns from sin – he must enjoin himself a perpetual fast. The eye must fast from impure glances. The ear must fast from hearing slanders. The tongue must fast from unwholesome speech. The hands must fast from bribes. The feet must fast from the path of the harlot. And the soul must fast from the love of wickedness.

This turning from sin implies a great change. There is a change wrought in the heart. The flinty heart has become fleshly. Satan would have Christ prove his deity — by turning stones into bread. Christ has wrought a far greater miracle — in making stones become flesh. In repentance Christ turns a heart of stone — into a heart of flesh.

There is a change wrought in the life. Turning from sin is so visible, that others may discern it. Therefore it is called a change from darkness to light (Eph. 5:8). Paul, after he had seen the heavenly vision, was so different — that all men wondered at the change (Acts 9:21). Repentance changed the jailer into a nurse and a servant (Acts 16:33). He took the apostles and washed their wounds and set food before them. A ship is going eastward; there comes a wind which turns it westward. Likewise, a man was turning hell-ward before the contrary wind of the Spirit blew, turned his course, and caused him to sail heaven-ward.

Chrysostom, speaking of the Ninevites' repentance, said that if a stranger who had seen Nineveh's excess had gone into the city after they repented, he would scarcely have believed it was the same city — because it was so transformed and reformed. Such a visible change does repentance make in a person — it is as if another soul lodged in the same body!

That the turning from sin be rightly qualified, these few things are requisite:

1. It must be a turning from sin with the heart.

The heart is the first thing which lives — and it must be the first thing which turns. The heart is that which the devil strives hardest for. Never did he so strive for the body of Moses — as he does for the heart of man. In true religion — the heart is all. If the heart is not turned from sin — it is no better than a pretense: 'her unfaithful sister Judah did not return to me with all her heart, but only in pretense' (Jer. 3:10). Judah did make a show of reformation; she was not so grossly idolatrous as the ten tribes. Yet Judah was worse than Israel: she is called 'unfaithful' Judah — that is, 'treacherous'. She pretended to a reformation — but it was not in truth. Her heart was not for God — she did not turn with the whole heart. It is odious to make a show of turning from sin — while the heart is yet in league with sin! I have read of one of our Saxon kings who was baptized, who in the same church had one altar for the Christian religion and another for an idol. God will have the whole heart turned from sin. True repentance must have no reserves or idols.

2. It must be a turning from all sin.

'Let the wicked forsake his way' (Isaiah 55:7). A real penitent turns out of the road of sin. Every sin is abandoned. As Jehu would have all the priests of Baal slain (2 Kings 10:24) — not one must escape — so a true convert seeks the destruction of every lust — not one must escape. He knows how dangerous it is to entertain any one sin. He who hides one rebel in his house, is a traitor to the King. Just so, he who indulges one sin, is a traitorous hypocrite!

3. It must be a turning from sin upon a spiritual ground.

A man may restrain the open acts of sin — yet not turn from sin in a right manner. Acts of sin may be restrained out of fear or design — but a true penitent turns from sin out of a pious principle, namely, out of love to God. Even if sin did not bear such bitter fruit — if death did not grow on this tree — a gracious soul would forsake sin, out of love to God.

This is the most easy turning from sin. When things are frozen and congealed, the best way to separate them is by fire. When men and their sins are congealed together, the best way to separate them is by the fire of love. Three men, asking one another what made them leave sin:

one said, 'I think of the joys of heaven!' Said the second, 'I think of the torments of hell!' But the third said, 'I think of the love of God, and that makes me forsake sin!' How shall I offend the God of love?

4. It must be such a turning from sin — and turning unto God.

This is in the text, 'that they should repent and turn to God' (Acts 26:20). Turning from sin is like pulling the arrow out of the wound; turning to God is like pouring in the balm. We read in scripture of a repentance from dead works (Heb. 6:1), and a repentance toward God (Acts 20:21). Unsound hearts pretend to leave old sins — but they do not turn to God or embrace his service. It is not enough to forsake the devil's quarters — but we must get under Christ's banner and wear his colors. The repenting prodigal did not only leave his harlots — but he arose and went to his father! It was God's complaint, 'They do not turn to the Most High God' (Hos. 7:16). In true repentance the heart points directly to God — as the compass needle to the North Pole.

5. True turning from sin is such a turn — as has no return.

'What have I to do any more with idols?' (Hos. 14:8). Forsaking sin must be like forsaking one's native soil — never more to return to it. Some have seemed to be converts and to have turned from sin — but they have returned to their sins again. This is a returning to folly (Psalm 85:8). It is a fearful sin, for it is against clear light. It is to be supposed that he who did once leave his sin, felt it bitterly in the pangs of conscience. Yet he returned to it again; he therefore sins against the illuminations of the Spirit. Such a return to sin reproaches God: 'What evil did your fathers find in me, that they strayed so far from me? They followed worthless idols and became worthless themselves!' (Jer. 2:5). He who returns to sin, by implication charges God with some evil. If a man divorces his wife, it implies he knows some fault by her. To leave God and return to sin — is tacitly to asperse the Deity. God, who 'hates divorce' (Mal. 2:16), hates that he himself should be divorced.

To return to sin gives the devil more power over a man than ever. When a man turns from sin, the devil seems to be cast out of him — but when he returns to sin, the devil enters into his house again and takes possession, and 'the last state of that man is worse than the first!' (Matt. 12:45). When a prisoner has broken prison, and the jailer gets him again, he will lay stronger irons upon him. He who leaves off a course of sinning, as it were, breaks the devil's prison — if Satan takes him returning to sin, he will hold him faster and take fuller possession of him than ever! Oh take heed of this! A true turning from sin is a divorcing it, so as never to come near it any more. Whoever is thus turned from sin is a blessed person: 'When God raised up his servant, he sent him to bless you — by turning each of you back from your sinful ways' (Acts 3:26).

Use 1. Is turning from sin a necessary ingredient in repentance? If so, then there is little true repentance to be found. People are not turned from their sins; they are still the same as they ever were! They were proud — and so they are still. They are like the beasts in Noah's ark, they went into the ark unclean — and came out unclean. Men come to gospel ordinances impure — and go away impure. Though men have seen so many changes on the outside — yet there is no change wrought within: 'after all this punishment, the people will still not repent and turn to the Lord Almighty' (Isaiah 9:13).

How can they say they repent — who do not turn? Are they washed in Jordan — who still have their leprosy upon their forehead? May not God say to the unreformed, as once to Ephraim, 'Ephraim is joined to idols — let him alone!' (Hos. 4:17)? Likewise, here is a man joined to his drunkenness and uncleanness — let him alone! Let him go on in sin! If there is either justice in heaven, or vengeance in hell — he shall not go unpunished!

Use 2. It reproves those who are but half-turned. And who are these? Such as turn in their judgment, but not in their practice. They cannot but acknowledge that sin is a dreadful evil, and will weep for sin—yet they are so bewitched with it that they have no power to leave it! Their corruptions are stronger than their convictions. These are half-turned, 'almost Christians' (Acts 26:28). They are like Ephraim, 'as worthless as a half-baked cake!' (Hos. 7:8).

They are but half-turned, who turn only from gross sin—but have no intrinsic work of grace. They do not prize Christ—or love holiness. It is with mere moral people as with Jonah; he got a gourd to shield the heat of the sun, and thought that he was safe—but a worm presently arose and devoured the gourd. So men, when they are turned from gross sin, think that their morality will be a gourd to defend them from the wrath of God—but at death there arises the worm of conscience, which smites this gourd, and then their hearts fail, and they are in a dreadful condtion!

They are but half-turned, who turn from many sins—but are unturned from some special sin. There is a harlot in the bosom which they will not let go! This is as if a man should be cured of several diseases—but has a cancer in his breast, which kills him. It reproves those whose turning is as good as no turning, who expel one devil and welcome another. They turn from swearing—to slandering, from extravagance—to covetousness. Such turning will turn men to hell!

Use 3. Let us show ourselves penitents, in turning from sin to God. There are some people I have little hope to prevail with. Let the trumpet of the Word sound ever so shrill, let threatenings be thundered out against them, let some flashes of hell-fire be thrown in their faces—yet they will keep their beloved sin. These people seem to be like the swine in the Gospel, carried down by the devil violently into the sea. They will rather be damned—than turn from their sin! 'These people keep going along their self-destructive path, refusing to turn back, even though I have warned them!' (Jer. 8:5).

But if there is any sincerity in us, if conscience is not cast into a deep sleep, let us listen to the voice of the charmer, and turn to God as our supreme good. How often does God call upon us to turn to him? He swears, 'As surely as I live, says the Sovereign Lord, I take no pleasure in the death of wicked people. I only want them to turn from their wicked ways so they can live. Turn! Turn from your wickedness! Why should you die?' (Ezek. 33:11). God would rather have our repenting tears—than our blood.

Turning to God is for our benefit. Our repentance is of no benefit to God—but to ourselves. If a man drinks of a fountain—he benefits himself, not the fountain. If he beholds the light of the sun—he himself is refreshed by it, not the sun. If we turn from our sins to God, God is not advantaged by it. It is only we ourselves who reap the benefit. In this case self-love should prevail with us: 'If you become wise, you will be the one to benefit. If you scorn wisdom, you will be the one to suffer.' (Proverbs 9:12).

If we turn to God—he will turn to us. He will turn his anger from us—and his face to us. It was David's prayer, 'O turn unto me, and have mercy upon me' (Psalm 86:16). Our turning will make God turn: 'Turn unto me, says the Lord—and I will turn unto you' (Zech. 1:3). He who was our enemy—will turn to be our friend. If God turns to us—the angels are turned to us. We shall have their tutelage and guardianship (Psalm 91:11). If God turns to us—all things shall turn to our good, both mercies and afflictions. We shall taste honey at the end of the afflicting rod.

Thus we have seen the several ingredients of repentance:

1. Sight of sin

2. Sorrow for sin

3. Confession of sin

4. Shame for sin

5. Hatred for sin

6. Turning from sin

Reasons Which Enforce Repentance

1. God's sovereign command. 'He commands all men everywhere to repent' (Acts 17:30). Repentance is not optional. It is not left to our choice, whether or not we will repent – but it is an indispensable command. God has enacted a law in the High Court of heaven – that no sinner shall be saved, except the repenting sinner – and he will not break his own law. Though all the angels should stand before God and beg for the salvation of an unrepenting person – God would not grant it. 'The Lord God, the compassionate and gracious God, slow to anger, abounding in love and faithfulness, maintaining love to thousands, and forgiving wickedness, rebellion and sin. Yet he does not leave the guilty unpunished' (Ex 34:6-37). Though God is more full of mercy than the sun is of light – yet he will not forgive a sinner while he goes on in his guilt! 'He will not leave the guilty unpunished!'

2. The pure nature of God denies communion with an impenitent creature

Until the sinner repents, God and he cannot be friends: 'Wash yourselves and be clean! Let me no longer see your evil deeds. Give up your wicked ways.' (Isa 1:16). 'Go, steep yourselves in the brinish waters of repentance! Then,' says God, 'I will parley with you!' 'Come now, and let us reason together' (Isa 1:18). But otherwise, do not come near me! 'What communion has light with darkness?' (2 Cor 6:14). How can the righteous God befriend him who goes on still in his trespasses? 'I will not justify the wicked' (Ex 23:7). If God should be at peace with a sinner before he repents – God would seem to accept and approve all that evil he has done. He would go against his own holiness. It is inconsistent with the sanctity of God's nature, to pardon a sinner while he is in the act of rebellion.

3. Sinners continuing in impenitence are out of Christ's commission

See his commission: 'The Spirit of the Lord God is upon me; he has sent me to bind up the brokenhearted' (Isa 61:1). Christ is a Prince and Savior – but not to save men in an capricious way, whether or not they repent. If ever Christ brings men to heaven, it shall be through the gate of repentance. 'Him has God exalted to be a Prince and a Savior – to give repentance' (Acts 5:31). A king pardons rebels if they repent and yield themselves to the mercy of their prince – but not if they persist in open defiance.

4. We have by sin wronged God

There is a great deal of equity in it that we should repent. We have by sin wronged God. We have eclipsed his honor. We have infringed his law, and we should, reasonably, make him some reparation. By repentance we humble and judge ourselves for sin. We set to our seal that God is righteous if he should destroy us, and thus we give glory to God and do what lies in us to repair his honor.

5. If God should save men without repentance, making no discrimination, then by this rule he must save all, not only all men – but all devils. And so consequently the decrees of election and reprobation must fall to the ground. How diametrically opposed this is to sacred writ – let all judge. There are two kinds of people who will find it harder to repent than others:

(1) Those who have sat a great while under the ministry of God's ordinances – but grow no better. The ground soaks up the rain that falls on it – yet 'bears thistles and thorns, it is useless.

The farmer will condemn that field and burn it.' (Heb 6:8). There is little hope of the metal which has lain long in the fire—but is not melted and refined. When God has sent his ministers one after another, exhorting and persuading men to leave their sins—but they settle upon the lees of external formality and can sit and sleep under a sermon—it will be hard for these ever to be brought to repentance. They may fear lest Christ should say to them as once he said to the fig-tree, 'May you never bear fruit again!' (Matt 21:19).

(2) Those who have sinned frequently against the convictions of the Word, the checks of conscience, and the motions of the Spirit. Conscience has stood as the angel, with a flaming sword in its hand. It has said, 'Do not this great evil!' But sinners regard not the voice of conscience—but march on resolvedly under the devil's colors. These will not find it easy to repent: 'They are those who rebel against the light' (Job 24:13). It is one thing to sin for lack of light—and another thing to sin against light. Men begin by sinning against the light of conscience, and proceed gradually to despising the Spirit of grace.

This serves sharply to reprove all unrepenting sinners whose hearts seem to be hewn out of a rock, and are like the stony ground which lacked moisture. This disease, I fear, is epidemic: 'Is anyone sorry for sin? Does anyone say, 'What a terrible thing I have done?' No! All are running down the path of sin as swiftly as a horse rushing into battle!' (Jer 8:6). Men's hearts are marbled into hardness: 'They made their hearts as hard as stone, so they could not hear the law or the messages that the Lord Almighty had sent them by his Spirit through the earlier prophets. That is why the Lord Almighty was so angry with them.' (Zech 7:12). They are not at all dissolved into a penitential frame.

It is fabled that witches never weep. I am sure of this—that those who have no grief for sin are spiritually bewitched by Satan! We read that Christ 'denounced the cities where he had done most of his miracles, because they hadn't turned from their sins and turned to God' (Matt 11:20). And may he not denounce many now for their impenitence? Though God's heart is broken with their sins—yet their hearts are not broken. They say, as Israel did, 'I love foreign gods, and I must go after them!' (Jer 2:25).

The justice of God, like the angel, stands with a drawn sword in its hand, ready to strike—but sinners have not eyes as good as those of Balaam's donkey to see the sword! God smites on men's backs—but they do not, as Ephraim did, smite upon their thigh (Jer 31:19). It was a sad complaint the prophet took up: 'you have stricken them—but they have not grieved' (Jer 5:3). That is surely reprobate silver which becomes harder in the furnace. 'When trouble came to King Ahaz, he became even more unfaithful to the Lord' (2 Chron 28:22).

A hard heart is a dwelling for Satan. As God has two places he dwells in—heaven and a humble heart; so the devil has two places he dwells in—hell and a hard heart. It is not falling into water which drowns—but lying in it. It is not falling into sin which damns—but lying in it without repentance: 'having their conscience seared with a hot iron' (1 Tim 4:2). Hardness of heart results at last in the conscience being seared. Men have silenced their consciences, and God has seared them. And now he lets them sin and does not punish them, 'Why should you be beaten any more?' (Isa 1:5) —as a father stops correcting a child whom he intends to disinherit.

A Serious Exhortation to Repentance

Let me in the next place persuade you to this great duty of repentance. Sorrow is not good for anything—except for sin. If you shed tears for outward losses, it will not advantage you. Water for the garden, if poured in the sink—does no good. Medicine for the eye, if applied to the arm, is of no benefit. Sorrow is medicinal for the sinful soul—but if you apply it to worldly things it does no good. Oh that our tears may run in the right channel—and our hearts burst with sorrow for sin! That I may the more successfully press this exhortation, I shall show you that repentance is necessary, and that it is necessary for all people and for all sins.

1. Repentance is necessary

Repentance is necessary: 'except you repent — you shall all likewise perish!' (Luke 13:5). There is no rowing to paradise — except upon the stream of repenting tears. Repentance is required as a qualification. It is not so much to endear us to Christ — as to endear Christ to us. Until sin be bitter — Christ will not be sweet.

2. Repentance is necessary for all people

Thus God commands all men: 'now God commands all men everywhere to repent' (Acts 17:30).

(1) Repentance is necessary for great people: 'Say unto the king and to the queen, Humble yourselves' (Jer. 13:18). The king of Nineveh and his nobles changed their robes for sackcloth (Jon. 3:6). Great men's sins do more hurt than the sins of others. The sins of leaders are leading sins, therefore they of all others have need to repent. If such as hold the scepter repent not, God has appointed a day to judge them — and a fire to burn them! (Isaiah 30:33).

(2) Repentance is necessary for the flagitious[6] sinners in the nation. England needs to put itself in mourning and be humbled by solemn repentance. What horrible impieties are chargeable upon the nation! We see people daily listing themselves under Satan. Not only the banks of religion — but those of civility, are broken down. Men seem to contend, as the Jews of old, who should be most wicked. 'It is the filth and corruption of your lewdness and idolatry. And now, because I tried to cleanse you but you refused, you will remain filthy until my fury against you has been satisfied' (Ezek. 24:13). If oaths and drunkenness, if perjury and luxury will make a people guilty, then it is to be feared that England is in God's black book. Men have cancelled their vow in baptism and made a private contract with the devil! Instead of crying to mercy to save them, they cry, 'God damn us!' Never was there such riding posthaste to hell — as if men despaired of getting there in time. They have boasted how many they have debauched and made drunk. Thus 'they declare their sin as Sodom' (Isaiah 3:9). Indeed, men's sins are grown daring, as if they would hang out their flag of defiance against God — like the Thracians who, when it thunders, gather together in a body and shoot their arrows against heaven. 'For they have clenched their fists against God, defying the Almighty. Holding their strong shields, they defiantly charge against him.' (Job 15:25-26). They are desperate in sin — and run furiously against God.

Oh to what a height is sin boiled up! Men count it a shame not to be impudent. May it not be said of us, as Josephus speaks of the Jews. Such was the excessive wickedness of those times, that if the Romans had not come and sacked their city, Jerusalem would have been swallowed up with some earthquake, or drowned with a flood, or consumed with fire from heaven. And is it not high time then for England to enter into a course of remedy, and take this pill of repentance, which has so many vile sins spreading in her? England is an island encompassed by two oceans, an ocean of water — and an ocean of wickedness. O that it might be encompassed with a third ocean — that of repenting tears!

If the book of the law chances to fall upon the ground, the Jews have a custom presently to proclaim a fast. England has let both law and gospel fall to the ground, therefore needs to fast and mourn before the Lord. The ephah of wickedness seems to be full. There is good reason for tears to fall apace, when sin fills so fast! Why then, are the wells of repentance stopped up? Do not the sinners of the land know that they should repent? Have they no warning? Have not

---

[6] criminal; villainous.

God's faithful messengers lifted up their voice as a trumpet—and cried to them to repent? But many of these tools in the ministry have been spent and worn out upon rocky hearts. Has not God blessed us with many preachers to call men to repentance—but still they are settled on their lees (Zeph. 1:12)? Do we think that God will always put up with our affronts? Will he endure thus to have his name and glory trampled upon? The Lord has usually been more swift in the process of his justice, against the sins of a professing people. I say therefore with Bradford, 'Repent, O England!' You have belepered[7] yourself with sin, and must needs go and wash in the spiritual Jordan. You have kindled God's anger against you. Throw away your weapons, and bring your holy tears of repentance, that God may be appeased in the blood of Christ. Let your tears run—or God's scroll of curses will fly (Zech. 5:2). Either men must turn—or God will overturn. Either the fallow ground of their hearts must be broken up—or the land broken down. If no words will prevail with sinners, it is because God has a purpose to slay them (1 Sam. 2:25). Those who, by their prodigious sins have so far incensed the God of heaven that he denies them the tears of repentance, may look upon themselves as condemned people.

(3) Repentance is necessary for the cheating crew. 'They are wise to do evil' (Jer. 4:22), making use of their invention only for circumvention. Instead of living by their faith, they live by their shifts. These are those who make themselves poor so that by this artifice they may grow rich. I would not be misunderstood. I do not mean such as the providence of God has brought low, whose estates have failed, but not their honesty—but rather such as feign a break, that they may cheat their creditors. There are some who get more by breaking than others can by trading. These are like beggars that discolor and blister their arms—that they may move others to charity. As they live by their sores, so these live by their breaking. When the frost breaks, the streets are more full of water. Likewise, many tradesmen, when they break, are fuller of money. These make as if they had nothing—but out of this nothing great estates are created. Remember, the kingdom of heaven is taken by force, not by fraud.

Let men know that after this golden sop, the devil enters. They squeeze a curse into their estates. They must repent quickly. Though the bread of falsehood is sweet (Proverbs 20:17)—yet many vomit up their sweet morsels in hell!

(4) Repentance is necessary for moral people. These have no visible spots on them. They are free from gross sin, and one would think they had nothing to do with the business of repentance. They are so good, that they scorn God's offer of mercy. Indeed these are often in the worst condition: these are they who think they need no repentance (Luke 15:7). Their morality undoes them. They make a 'savior' of it, and so on this rock they suffer shipwreck. Morality shoots short of heaven. It is only nature refined. A moral man is but old Adam dressed in fine clothes. The king's image counterfeited and stamped upon brass will not go current. The moral person seems to have the image of God—but he is only brass metal, which will never pass for current. Morality is insufficient for salvation. Though the life is moralized, the lust may be unmortified. The heart may be full of pride and atheism. Under the fair leaves of a tree, there may be a worm.

I am not saying, repent that you are moral—but that you are no more than moral. Satan entered into the house that had just been swept and garnished (Luke 11:26). This is the emblem of a moral man, who is swept by civility and garnished with common gifts—but is not washed by true repentance. The unclean spirit enters into such a one. If morality were sufficient to

---

[7] To infect oneself with leprosy

salvation, Christ need not have died. The moral man has a fair lamp — but it lacks the oil of grace.

(5) Repentance is needful for hypocrites. I mean such as allow themselves in the sin. Hypocrisy is the counterfeiting of sanctity. The hypocrite or stage-player has gone a step beyond the moralist, and dressed himself in the garb of religion. He pretends to a form of godliness, but denies the power (2 Tim. 3:5). The hypocrite is a saint in disguise. He makes a magnificent show, like an ape clothed in fine purple. The hypocrite is like a house with a beautiful facade — but every room within is dark. He is a rotten post, which is beautifully pointed over. Under his mask of profession, he hides his plague-sores.

The hypocrite is against painting of faces — but he has but painted holiness. He is seemingly good — so that he may be really bad. In Samuel's mantle, he plays the devil. Therefore the same word in the original signifies to use hypocrisy — and to be profane. The hypocrite appears to have his eyes lifted to heaven — but his heart is full of impure lustings. He lives in secret sin against his conscience. He can be as his company is, and act both the dove and the vulture. He hears the word — but is all ear. He is for temple-devotion, where others may look upon him and admire him — but he neglects family and closet prayer. Indeed, if prayer does not make a man leave sin — sin will make him leave prayer. The hypocrite feigns humility — but it is that he may rise in the world. He is a pretender to faith — but he makes use of it rather for a cloak than a shield. He carries his Bible under his arm — but not in his heart! His whole religion is a sly lie (Hos 11:12).

But is there such a generation of men to be found? The Lord forgive them their painted holiness! Hypocrites are 'in the gall of bitterness' (Acts 8:23). O how they need to humble themselves in the dust! They are far gone with their disease, and if anything can cure them, it must be feeding upon the salt marshes of repentance. Let me speak my mind freely. None will find it more difficult to repent — than hypocrites. They have so juggled in religion, that their treacherous hearts know not how to repent. Hypocrisy is harder to cure than insanity. The hypocrite's abscess in his heart, seldom breaks.

Such as are guilty of prevailing hypocrisy, let them fear and tremble. Their condition is sinful and sad. It is sinful because they do not embrace religion out of choice but design; they do not love it, only pretend it. It is sad upon a double account.

Firstly, because this art of deceit cannot hold long; he who hangs out a sign of holiness — but has not the commodity of grace in his heart — must needs break at last!

Secondly, because God's anger will fall heavier upon hypocrites. They dishonor God more and take away the gospel's good name. Therefore the Lord reserves the most deadly arrows in his quiver to shoot at them. If heathen are damned, hypocrites shall be double-damned. Hell is called the place of hypocrites (Matt. 24:51), as if it were chiefly prepared for them.

(6) Repentance is necessary for God's own people, who have a real work of grace. They must offer up a daily sacrifice of tears. The Antinomians hold that when any come to be believers, they have a writ of ease, and there remains nothing for them now to do but to rejoice. Yes, they have something else to do, and that is to repent. Repentance is a continuous act. The outlet of godly sorrow, must not be quite stopped until death. Jerome, writing in a letter to Laeta, tells her that her life must be a life of repentance. Repentance is called crucifying the flesh (Gal. 5:24), which is not done on all at once — but continuously, all our life. And are there not many reasons why God's own people should go into the weeping bath? 'Are there not with you, even with you — sins against the Lord?' (2 Chron. 28:10). Have not you sins of daily living? Though you are diamonds, you still have flaws. Do we not read of the 'spot of God's children' (Deut. 32:5).

Search with the candle of the Word into your hearts—and see if you can find no matter for repentance there!

(a) Repent of your rash censuring. Instead of praying for others, you are ready to pass a verdict upon them. It is true that the saints shall judge the world (1 Cor. 6:2)—but wait your time; remember the apostle's caution in 1 Corinthians 4:5: 'judge nothing before the time, wait until the Lord comes'.

(b) Repent of your vain thoughts. These swarm in your minds as the flies did in Pharaoh's court (Exod. 8:24). What bewilderings there are in the imagination! If Satan does not possess your bodies, he does your imaginations. 'How long shall your vain thoughts lodge within you?' (Jer. 4:14). A man may think himself into hell. O you saints, be humbled for this lightness in your head.

(c) Repent of your vain fashions. It is strange that the garments which God has given to cover shame—should reveal pride! The godly are bid not to be conformed to this world (Romans 12:2). People of the world are garish and mirthful in their dresses. It is in fashion nowadays—to go to hell. But whatever others do—yet let not Judah offend (Hos. 4:15). The apostle Paul has set down what outer garment Christians must wear: 'modest apparel' (1 Tim. 2:9); and what undergarment: 'be clothed with humility' (1 Pet. 5:5).

(d) Repent of your decays in grace. 'You have left your first love' (Rev. 2:4). Christians, how often is it low water in your souls! How often does coldness of heart come upon you! Where are those flames of affection, those sweet meltings of spirit—which you once had? I fear they are melted away. Oh repent for leaving your first love!

(e) Repent of your non-improvement of talents. Health is a talent; estate is a talent; wit and abilities are talents; and these God has entrusted you with, to improve for his glory. He has sent you into the world as a merchant sends his steward beyond the seas to trade for his advantage—but you have not done the good you might. Can you say, 'Master, your talent has earned five more talents' (Luke 19:18)? O mourn at the burial of your talents! Let it grieve you that so much of your life has not been time lived but time lost; that you have filled up your golden hours more with froth than with devotion.

(f) Repent of your forgetfulness of sacred vows. A vow is a binding one's soul to God (Num. 30:2). Christians, have you not served for common uses after you have been the Lord's by solemn dedication? Thus, by breach of vows, you have made a breach in your peace. Surely this calls for a fresh laver of tears.

(g) Repent of your unanswerableness to blessings received. You have lived all your life upon free grace. You have been bemiracled with mercy. But where are your returns of love to God? The Athenians would have ungrateful people sued at law. Christians, may not God sue you at law—for your unthankfulness? 'I will recover my wool and my flax' (Hos. 2:9); I will recover them by law.

(h) Repent of your worldliness. By your profession you seem to resemble the birds of paradise—which soar aloft and live upon the dew of heaven. Yet as serpents you lick the dust! Baruch, a good man, was taxed with this: 'do you seek great things for yourself?' (Jer. 45:5).

(i) Repent of your divisions. These are a blot in your coat of armor, and make others stand aloof from true religion. Indeed, to separate from the wicked, resembles Christ, who was 'separate from sinners' (Heb. 63 7:26). But for the godly to divide among themselves, and look askew one upon another—had we as many eyes as there are stars, they were few enough to weep for this! Divisions eclipse the church's beauty and weaken her strength. God's Spirit brought in cloven tongues among the saints (Acts 2:3) — but the devil has brought in cloven hearts. Surely this deserves a shower of tears!

(j) Repent for the iniquity of your holy things. How often have the services of God's worship been frozen with formality and soured with pride? There have been more of the peacock's plumes — than the moans of the dove. It is sad that pious duties should be made a stage for vainglory to act upon. O Christians, there is such a thick crust upon your duties, that it is to be feared there is but little substance left in them for God to feed upon. Behold here repenting work, cut out for the best. And that which may make the tide of grief swell higher, is to think that the sins of God's people do more provoke God, than do the sins of others (Deut. 32:19). The sins of the wicked pierce Christ's side. The sins of the godly go to his heart! Peter's sin, being against so much love, was most unkind, which made his cheeks to be furrowed with tears: 'When he thought about it, he began to weep' (Mark 14:72).

3. Repentance is necessary for all sins.

Let us be deeply humbled and mourn before the Lord for original sin. We have lost that pure frame of soul that once we had. Our nature is vitiated with corruption. Original sin has diffused itself as a poison into the whole man, like the Jerusalem artichoke which, wherever it is planted, soon overruns the ground. There are not worse natures in hell, than we have! The hearts of the best are like Peter's sheet, in which there were a number of unclean creeping things (Acts 10:12). This primitive corruption is bitterly to be bewailed because we are never free from it. It is like a spring underground, which though it is not seen — yet it still runs. We may as well stop the beating of the pulse — as stop the motions to sin! This inbred depravity retards and hinders us in that which is spiritual: 'I do not do the good that I want to do' (Romans 7:19).

Original sin may be compared to that fish Pliny speaks of, which cleaves to the keel of the ship and hinders it when it is under sail. Sin hangs weights upon us — so that we move but slowly to heaven. O this adherence of sin! Paul shook the viper which was on his hand into the fire (Acts 28:5) — but we cannot shake off original corruption in this life. Sin does not come as a lodger for a night — but as an indweller: 'sin which dwells in me' (Romans 7:17). It is with us as with one who has a cancer in him; though he changes the air — yet still he carries his disease with him. Original sin is inexhaustible. This ocean cannot be emptied. Though we sin much — yet the stock of sin is not at all diminished. The more we sin — the fuller we are of sin. Original corruption is like the widow's oil — which increased by pouring out.

Another wedge to break our hearts, is that original sin mixes with the very habits of grace. Hence it is that our actings towards heaven are so dull and languid. Why does faith act no stronger — but because it is clogged by sin? Why does love to God burn no purer — but because it is hindered with lust? Original sin mixes with our graces. As bad lungs cause shortness of breath — so original sin having infected our heart, our graces breathe now very faintly. Thus we see much in original sin, which may draw forth our tears.

In particular, let us lament the corruption of our will and our affections. Let us mourn for the corruption of our will. The will, not following the dictates of right reason, is biased to evil. The will has a distaste for God, not as he is good — but as he is holy. It contumaciously affronts him: 'We will do whatever we want. We will burn incense to the Queen of Heaven and sacrifice to her just as much as we like!' (Jer. 44:17). The greatest wound has fallen upon our will.

Let us grieve for the corruption of our affections. They are taken off from their proper object. The affections, like faulty arrows, shoot beside the mark. At the beginning, our affections were wings to fly to God; now they are weights to pull us away from him. Let us grieve for the sinful inclination of our affections. Our love is set on sin — our joy on the creature. Our affections, like the lapwing, feed on dung. How justly may the corruption of our affections bear a part in the scene of our grief? We of ourselves are falling into hell, and our affections would thrust us there.

Let us lay to heart actual sins. Of these I may say, 'Who can understand his errors?' (Psalm 19:12). They are like sparks of a furnace. We have sinned in our eyes; they have been conduits to let in vanity. We have sinned in our tongues; they have been fired with passion. What action proceeds from us—wherein we do not betray some sin? To compute all these, would outnumber the drops in the ocean. Let actual sins be solemnly repented of, before the Lord.

Powerful Motives to Repentance

That the exhortation to repentance may be more quickened, I shall lay down some powerful motives to excite repentance.

1. Sorrow and melting of heart fits us for every holy duty.

A piece of lead, while it is in the lump, can be put to no use—but melt it, and you may then cast it into any mold, and it is made useful. So a heart that is hardened into a lump of sin is good for nothing—but when it is dissolved by repentance, it is useful. A melting heart is fit to pray. When Paul's heart was humbled and melted, then 'behold, he prays' (Acts 9:11). It is fit to hear the Word. Now the Word works kindly. When Josiah's heart was tender, he humbled himself and rent his clothes at the hearing of the words of the law (2 Chron. 34:19). His heart, like melting wax, was ready to take any seal of the Word. A melting heart is fit to obey. When the heart is like metal in the furnace, it is facile and malleable to anything: 'Lord, what will you have me to do?' (Acts 9:6). A repenting soul subscribes to God's will and answers to his call—as the echo answers to the voice.

2. Repentance is highly acceptable to God.

When a spiritual river runs to water this garden, then our hearts are a garden of Eden, delightful to God. I have read that doves delight to be about the waters. And surely God's Spirit, who descended in the likeness of a dove, takes great delight in the waters of repentance. The Lord esteems no heart sound, but the broken heart: 'The sacrifices of God are a broken spirit' (Psalm 51:17). Mary stood at Jesus' feet weeping (Luke 7:38). She brought two things to Christ, ointment and tears. Her tears were better than her ointment. Tears are powerful orators for mercy. They are silent—yet they have a voice: 'the Lord has heard the voice of my weeping' (Psalm 6:8).

3. Repentance commends all our services to God.

That which is seasoned with the bitter herbs of godly sorrow, is God's savory meat. Hearing of the Word is then good, when we are pricked at the heart (Acts 2:37). Prayer is delightful to God when it ascends from the altar of a broken heart. The publican smote upon his breast saying, 'God be merciful to me a sinner'. This prayer pierced heaven: 'he went away justified rather than the other' (Luke 18:14). No prayer touches God's ear—but what comes from a heart touched with the sense of sin.

4. Without repentance nothing will avail us.

Some bless themselves that they have a stock of knowledge—but what is knowledge good for, without repentance? It is better to mortify one sin, than to understand all mysteries. Impure notionalists[8] do but resemble Satan transformed into an angel of light. Learning and a bad

---

[8] Those who put their faith in their fleeting notions.

heart—is like a fair face with a cancer in the breast. Knowledge without repentance, will be but a torch to light men to hell.

5. Repenting tears are delicious.

They may be compared to myrrh, which though it is bitter in taste, has a sweet smell and refreshes the spirits. So repentance, though it is bitter in itself—yet it is sweet in the effects. It brings inward peace. The soul is never more enlarged and inwardly delighted—than when it can kindly melt. How oft do the saints fall aweeping for joy! The Hebrew word for 'repent' signifies 'to take comfort'. None so joyful as the penitent!

They say that tears have four qualities: they are hot, moist, salty, and bitter. It is true of repenting tears. They are hot, to warm a frozen conscience; moist, to soften a hard heart; salty, to season a soul putrefying in sin; bitter, to wean us from the love of the world. And I will add a fifth. They are sweet, in that they make the heart inwardly rejoice 'Your sorrow shall be turned into joy!' (John 16:20). 'Sorrowful, yet always rejoicing.' (2 Corinthians 6:10)

'Let a man,' said Augustine, 'grieve for his sin and rejoice for his grief.' Tears are the best sweetmeats. David, who was the great weeper in Israel, was the sweet singer of Israel. The sorrows of the penitent are like the sorrows of a woman giving birth: 'A woman giving birth to a child has pain because her time has come; but when her baby is born she forgets the anguish because of her joy that a child is born into the world' (John 16:21). So the sorrows of humbled sinners bring forth grace, and what joy there is when this child is born!

6. Great sins repented of, shall find mercy.

Mary Magdalene, a great sinner, obtained pardon when she washed Christ's feet with her tears. For some of the Jews who had a hand in crucifying Christ, upon their repentance, the very blood they shed was a sovereign balm to heal them! 'Though your sins be as scarlet, they shall be as white as snow' (Isaiah 1:18). Scarlet in the Greek is called *dibasson*, because it is 'twice dipped', and the arts of man cannot wash out the dye again. But though our sins are of a scarlet color, God's mercy can wash them away. This may comfort those whom the heinousness of their sin discourages, as if there were no hope for them. Yes, upon their serious turning to God, their sins shall be expunged and done away with!

'Oh—but my sins are sinful beyond measure!' Do not make them greater, by not repenting. Repentance unravels sin and makes it as if it had never been. 'Oh—but I have relapsed into sin after pardon, and surely there is no mercy for me!' The children of God have relapsed into the same sin: Abraham did twice equivocate; Lot committed incest twice; Asa, a good king—yet sinned twice by creature-confidence, and Peter twice by carnal fear (Matt. 26:70; Gal. 2:12). But for the comfort of such as have relapsed into sin more than once, if they solemnly repent, a white flag of mercy shall be held forth to them.

Christ commands us to forgive our trespassing brother seventy times seven in one day, if he repents (Matt. 18:22). If the Lord bids us do it, will not he be much more ready to forgive upon our repentance? What is our forgiving mercy, compared to his? This I speak not to encourage any impenitent sinner—but to comfort a despondent sinner that thinks it is in vain for him to repent and that he is excluded from mercy.

7. Repentance is the inlet to spiritual blessings.

It helps to enrich us with grace. It causes the desert to blossom as the rose. It makes the soul as the Egyptian fields after the overflowing of the Nile, flourishing and fruitful. Never do the flowers of grace grow more, than after a shower of repentant tears! Repentance causes knowledge: 'When their heart shall turn to the Lord, the veil shall be taken away' (2 Cor. 3:16).

The veil of ignorance which was drawn over the Jews' eyes shall by repentance be taken away. Repentance inflames love. Weeping Mary Magdalene loved much (Luke 7:47). God preserves these springs of sorrow in the soul — to water the fruit of the Spirit (Gal. 5:22).

8. Repentance ushers in temporal blessings.

The prophet Joel, persuading the people to repentance, brings in the promise of secular good things: 'rend your heart, and not your garments, and turn unto the Lord ... the Lord will answer and say to his people, Behold, I will send you corn, and wine, and oil' (Joel 2:13,19). When we put water into the pump, it fetches up only water — but when we put the water of tears into God's bottle, this fetches up wine: 'I will send you wine, and oil'. Sin blasts the fruits of the earth: 'You have sown much, and bring in little' (Hag. 1:6). But repentance makes the pomegranate bud and the vine flourish with full clusters. Fill God's bottle — and he will fill your basket! 'If you return to the Almighty, you shall lay up gold as dust' (Job 22:2324). Repenting is a returning to God, and this brings a golden harvest.

9. Repentance staves off judgments from a land.

When God is going to destroy a nation, the penitent sinner stays his hand, as the angel did Abraham's (Gen. 22:12). The Ninevites repentance caused God to repent: 'God saw that they turned from their evil way; and God repented of the evil, that he had said that he would do unto them; and he did it not' (Jonah 3:10). An outward repentance has adjourned and kept off wrath. Ahab sold himself to work wickedness; yet upon his fasting and rending his garments, God said to Elijah, 'I will not bring the evil in his days' (1 Kings 21:29). If the rending of the clothes kept off judgment from the nation, what will the rending of the heart do!

10. Repentance makes joy in heaven.

The angels do, as it were, keep festive day: 'There is joy in the presence of the angels of God over one sinner that repents' (Luke 15:10). As praise is the music of heaven, so repentance is the joy of heaven. When men neglect the offer of salvation and freeze in sin, this delights the devils — but when a soul is brought home to Christ by repentance, this makes joy among the angels.

11. Consider how dearly our sins cost Christ.

To consider how dearly our sins cost Christ, may cause tears to distill from our eyes. Christ is called the Rock (1 Cor. 10:4). When his hands were pierced with nails, and the spear thrust in his side, then was this Rock smitten, and there came out water and blood. And all this Christ endured for us: 'the Messiah shall be cut off — but not for himself' (Dan. 9:26). We tasted the apple — and he drank the vinegar and gall. We sinned in every faculty — and he bled in every vein! Can we look upon a suffering Savior with dry eyes? Shall we not be sorry for those sins — which made Christ a man of sorrow? Shall not our enormities, which drew blood from Christ — draw tears from us? Shall we sport any more with sin and so rake in Christ's wounds? Oh that by repentance we could crucify our sins afresh! The Jews said to Pilate, 'If you let this man go, you are not Caesar's friend' (John 19:12). Likewise, if we let our sins go and do not crucify them — we are not Christ's friends.

12. This is the end of all afflictions which God sends, whether it is sickness in our bodies or losses in our estates — that he may awaken us out of our sins and make the waters of repentance flow. Why did God lead Israel in that march in the wilderness among fiery serpents, but that he might humble them (Deut:8:2)? Why did he bring Manasseh so low, changing his crown of gold into fetters of iron — but that he might learn repentance? 'He humbled himself greatly before the God of his fathers. Then Manasseh knew that the Lord he was God' (2 Chron. 33:12,13). One of the best ways to cure a man of his lethargy — is to cast him into a fever. Likewise when a person

is stupefied and his conscience grown lethargic — God, to cure him of this distemper, puts him to extremity and brings one burning calamity or another, that he may startle him out of his security and make him return to him by repentance.

13. The days of our mourning will soon be ended.

After a few showers that fall from our eyes — we shall have perpetual sunshine! Christ will provide a handkerchief to wipe off his people's tears: 'God shall wipe away all tears' (Rev. 7:17). Christians, you will shortly put on your garments of praise. You will exchange your sackcloth for white robes. Instead of sighs — you will have triumphs; instead of groans — anthems; instead of the water of tears — the water of life! The mourning of the dove will be past — and the time of the singing of birds will come. This brings me to the next point.

14. The happy and glorious reward which follows upon repentance.

'But now that you have been set free from sin and have become slaves to God, the benefit you reap leads to holiness, and the result is eternal life!' (Romans 6:22). The leaves and root of the fig-tree are bitter — but the fruit is sweet. Repentance to the fleshy part seems bitter — but behold sweet fruit — everlasting life. The Turks imagine that after this life is a paradise of pleasure, where dainty dishes will be served in, and they will have gold in abundance, silken and purple apparel, and angels will bring them red wine in silver cups, and golden plates. Here is an epicure's heaven. But in the true paradise of God there are astonishing delights and rare viands served in. 'No eye has seen, no ear has heard, and no mind has imagined what God has prepared for those who love him.' (1 Cor. 2:9). God will lead his penitents from the house of mourning — to the banqueting house. There will be no sight there — but of glory; no sound there — but of music; no sickness — unless of love. There shall be unspotted holiness — and unspeakable joy. Then the saints shall forget their solitary hours and be sweetly solacing themselves in God — and bathing in the rivers of divine pleasure!

O Christian, what are your duties — compared to the recompense of reward? What an infinite disproportion is there between repentance enjoined — and glory prepared? There was a feast-day at Rome, when they used to crown their fountains. God will crown those heads which have been fountains of tears. Who would not be willing to be a while in the house of mourning — who shall be possessed of such glory as put Peter and John into an ecstasy to see it even darkly shadowed and portrayed in the transfiguration! (Matt. 17) This reward which free grace gives, is so transcendently great that could we have but a glimpse of glory revealed to us here, we would need patience to be content to live any longer. O blessed repentance, that has such a great light side — with the small dark side; and has so much sugar — at the bottom of the bitter cup!

15. The next motive to repentance is to consider the evil of impenitence.

A hard heart is the worst heart. It is called a heart of stone (Ezek. 36:26). If it were iron — it might be mollified in the furnace — but a stone put in the fire will not melt; it will sooner fly in your face. Impenitence is a sin which grieves Christ: 'being grieved for the hardness of their hearts' (Mark 3:5). It is not so much the disease which offends the physician — as the contempt of his remedy. It is not so much the sins we have committed which so provoke and grieve Christ — as that we refuse the remedy of repentance which he prescribes. This aggravated Jezebel's sin: 'I gave her space to repent, and she repented not' (Rev. 2:21).

A hard heart receives no impression. Oh the plague of an obdurate heart! Pharaoh's heart turned into stone — was worse than his waters turned into blood. David had his choice of three judgments plague, sword, and famine — but he would have chosen them all rather than a hard heart. An impenitent sinner is neither allured by entreaties nor affrighted by menaces. Such as will not weep with Peter — shall weep like Judas! A hard heart is the anvil — on which the hammer of God's justice will be striking to all eternity!

16. The last motive to repentance, is that the Day of Judgment is coming

This is the apostle's own argument: 'God commands all men everywhere to repent; because he has appointed a day, in which he will judge the world' (Acts 17:3031). There is that in the Day of Judgment, which may make a stony heart bleed. Will a man go on thieving — when the the Judge is looking upon him! Will the sinner go on sinning — when the Day of Judgment is so near? You can no more conceal your sin — than you can defend it. And what will you do when all your sins shall be written in God's book — and engraved on your forehead! O direful day, when Jesus Christ clothed in his judge's robe shall say to the sinner, 'Stand forth; answer to the indictment brought against you. What can you say for all your oaths, adulteries, and your desperate impenitence?' O how amazed and stricken with terror will the sinner be! And after his conviction he must hear the sad sentence, 'Depart from Me, you who are cursed, into the eternal fire prepared for the Devil and his angels!' Then, he who would not repent of his sins — shall repent of his folly! If there is such a time coming, wherein God will judge men for their impieties — what a spur should this be to repentance! The penitent soul shall at the last day lift up his head with comfort and have a discharge to show — written by the Judge's own hand!

Exhortations to Speedy Repentance

The second branch of the exhortation is to press people to speedy repentance: 'God now commands all men everywhere to repent' (Acts 17:30). The Lord would not have any of the late autumn fruits offered to him. God loves early penitents, who consecrate the spring and flower of their age to him. Early tears, like pearls bred of the morning dew, are more orient and beautiful. O do not reserve the dregs of your old age for God, lest he reserve the dregs of his cup of wrath for you! Be as speedy in your repentance as you would have God speedy in his mercies: 'the King's business required haste' (1 Sam. 21:8). Therefore repentance requires haste.

It is natural to us to procrastinate and put off repentance. We say, as Haggai did, 'The time is not yet come' (Hag. 1:2). No man is so bad, but he purposes and intends to repent — but he procrastinates so long, until at last all his purposes and intentions prove abortive. Many are now in hell — who purposed and intended to repent!

Satan does what he can to keep men from repentance. When he sees that they begin to take up serious thoughts of repentance, he bids them 'wait a little longer.' 'If this traitor, sin, must die' (says Satan), 'let it not die yet.' So the devil gets a reprieve for sin; it shall not die at present. At last men put off repentance so long — that death seizes on them, and their work is not done! Let me therefore lay down some effective arguments to persuade to speedy repentance:

1. Now is the season of repentance — and everything is best done in its season. 'Now is the accepted time' (2 Cor. 6:2); now God has a mind to show mercy to the penitent. He is on the giving hand. Kings set apart days for healing. Now is the healing day for our souls. Now God hangs forth the white flag and is willing to parley with sinners. A prince at his coronation, as an act of royalty — gives money, proclaims pardons, fills the conduits with wine. Now God promises pardons to penitent sinners. Now the conduit of the gospel runs wine. Now is the accepted time. Therefore come in now and make your peace with God. Break off your iniquities now by repentance. It is wisdom to take the season. The farmer takes the season for sowing his seed. Now is the seedtime for our souls.

2. The sooner you repent — the fewer sins you will have to answer for. At the deathbed of an old sinner, where conscience begins to be awakened, you will hear him crying out: 'Here are all my old sins come about me, haunting my deathbed as so many evil spirits — and I have no

forgiveness! Here is Satan, who was once my tempter, now become an accuser — and I have no advocate; I am now going to be dragged before God's judgment seat where I must receive my final doom!' O how dismal is the case of this man. He is in hell — before his time! But you who repent early of your sinful courses, this is your privilege — you will have the less to answer for. Indeed, let me tell you, you will have nothing to answer for. Christ will answer for you. Your judge will be your advocate (1 John 2:1). 'Father,' Christ will say, 'here is one that has been a great sinner — yet a broken-hearted sinner; if he owes anything to your justice, charge it to my account!'

3. The sooner we repent, the more glory we may bring to God. It is the purpose of our living — to be useful in our generation. Better lose our lives — than the purpose of our living. Late converts who have for many years taken pay on the devil's side, are not in a capacity of doing so much work in the vineyard. The thief on the cross could not do that service for God — as Paul did. But when we turn early from sin, then we give God the first fruits of our lives. We spend and are spent for Christ. The more work we do for God — the more willing we shall be to die — and the sweeter death will be. He who has wrought hard at his labor is willing to go to rest at night. Such as have been honoring God all their lives, how sweetly will they sleep in the grave! The more work we do for God — the greater will our reward be. He whose pound had gained ten pounds, Christ did not only commend him — but advance him: 'you will be governor of ten cities as your reward' (Luke 19:17). By late repentance, though we do not lose our crown — yet we make it lighter.

4. It is of dangerous consequence to put off repentance longer. It is dangerous, if we consider what sin is. Sin is a poison — it is dangerous to let poison lie long in the body. Sin is a bruise. If a bruise is not soon cured, it gangrenes and kills. Just so, if sin is not soon cured by repentance, it festers the conscience and damns! Why should any love to dwell in the tents of wickedness? They are under the power of Satan (Acts 26:18), and it is dangerous to stay long in the enemy's quarters.

It is dangerous to procrastinate repentance because the longer any go on in sin the harder they will find the work of repentance. Delay strengthens sin — and hardens the heart — and gives the devil fuller possession. A tree at first may be easily plucked up — but when it has spread its roots deep in the earth, a whole team cannot remove it. It is hard to remove sin when once it comes to be rooted. The longer the ice freezes — the harder it is to be broken. The longer a man freezes in sin — the harder it will be to have his heart broken. The longer any travail with iniquity — the sharper pangs they must expect in the new birth. When sin has long been fastened in the heart — it is not easily shaken off. Sin comes to a sinner as the elder brother came to his father: 'I have been slaving many years for you, and I have never disobeyed your orders' (Luke 15:29), and will you cast me off now? What, in my old age, after you have had so much pleasure by me? See how sin pleads custom, and that is a leopard's spot (Jer. 13:23). It is dangerous to procrastinate and delay repentance because there are three days which may soon expire:

(1) The day of the GOSPEL may expire. This is a sunshiny day. It is sweet, but swift. Jerusalem had a day but lost it: 'but now they are hidden from your eyes' (Luke 19:42). The Asian churches had a gospel day — but at last the golden candlestick was removed. It would be a sad time in England to see the glory departed. With what hearts could we follow the gospel to the grave? To lose the gospel were far worse than to have our freedom taken from us. 'Gray hairs are here and there' (Hos. 7:9). I will not say the sun of the gospel has set in England — but I am sure it is under a cloud. That was a sad speech, 'The kingdom of God shall be taken from you'

(Matt. 21:43). Therefore it is dangerous to delay repentance, lest the market of the gospel should depart, and the vision cease.

(2) A man's personal day of grace may expire. What if that time should come, when God should say the means of grace shall do no good: that ordinances shall have 'a miscarrying womb and dry breasts' (Hos. 9:14)? Were it not sad to adjourn repentance until such a decree came forth? It is true, no man can justly tell that his day of grace is past — but there are two helpful signs by which he may fear it:

(a) When conscience has done preaching. Conscience is a bosom-preacher. Sometimes it convinces, sometimes it reproves. It says, as Nathan to David, 'You are the man!' (2 Sam. 12:7). But men imprison this preacher, and God says to conscience, 'Preach no more! He who is filthy, let him be filthy still!' (Rev. 22:11). This is a fatal sign that a man's day of grace is past.

(b) When a person is in such a spiritual lethargy that nothing will work upon him or make him sensible. There is 'the spirit of deep sleep poured out upon you' (Isaiah 29:10). This is a sad presage that his day of grace is past. How dangerous then is it to delay repentance when the day of grace may so soon expire!

(3) The day of life may expire. What security have we — that we shall live another day? We are marching rapidly out of the world. We are going off the stage. Our life is a candle, which is soon blown out. Man's life is compared to the flower of the field, which withers sooner than the grass (Psalm 103:15). 'Show me, O Lord, my life's end and the number of my days; let me know how fleeting is my life. You have made my days a mere handbreadth; the span of my years is as nothing before you. Each man's life is but a breath. Man is a mere phantom as he goes to and fro.' (Psalm 39:4-6). Life is but a flying shadow. The body is like a vessel filled with a little breath. Sickness broaches this vessel; death draws it out. O how soon may the scene alter! Many a virgin has been dressed the same day in her bride-apparel, and her winding-sheet! How dangerous then is it to adjourn repenting when death may so suddenly make a thrust at us.

Say not that you will repent tomorrow. Remember that speech of Aquinas: 'God who pardons him who repents — has not promised to give him tomorrow to repent in.' I have read of Archias, who was feasting among his cups, when one delivered him a letter and desired him to read the letter immediately, for it was of serious business. He replied, 'I will mind serious things tomorrow'; and that day he was slain. Thus while men think to spin out their silver thread, death cuts it. Olaus Magnus observes of the birds of Norway, that they fly faster than the birds of any other country. Not that their wings are swifter than others — but by an instinct of nature they, knowing the days in that climate to be very short, not above three hours long, do therefore make the more haste to their nests. So we, knowing the shortness of our lives and how quickly we may be called away by death — should fly so much the faster on the wing of repentance to heaven!

But some will say that they do not fear a sudden death; they will repent upon their deathbed. I do not much like a deathbed repentance. He who will venture his salvation within the circle of a few short minutes, runs a desperate hazard. You who put off repentance until your deathbed, answer me to these four queries:

(a) How do you know that you shall have a time of sickness? Death does not always give its warning, by a lingering illness. Some it arrests suddenly. What if God should presently send you a summons to surrender your life?

(b) Suppose you should have a time of sickness, how do you know that you shall have the use of your senses? Most are demented, on their deathbed.

(c) Suppose you should have your senses—yet how do you know your mind will be in a frame for such a work as repentance? Sickness does so discompose body and mind, that one is in no condition, at such a time, to take care for his soul. In sickness a man is scarcely fit to make his will, much less to make his peace with God! The apostle said, 'Is any sick among you? let him call for the elders of the church' (James 5:14). He does not say, let him pray—but let him call for the elders, that they may pray over him. A sick man is very unfit to pray or repent; he is likely to make but sick work of it. When the body is out of tune, the soul must needs jar in its devotion. Upon a sick bed a person is more fit to exercise impatience than repentance. We read that at the pouring out of the fourth vial, when God did smite the inhabitants and scorched them with fire, that 'they blasphemed the name of God, and repented not' (Rev. 16:9). So when the Lord pours out his vial and scorches the body with a fever—the sinner is fitter to blaspheme than to repent!

(d) How do you who put off all to a deathbed, know that God will give you in that very juncture of time, grace to repent? The Lord usually punishes neglect of repentance in time of health—with hardness of heart in time of sickness. You have in your lifetime repulsed the Spirit of God, and are you sure that he will come at your call? You have not taken the first season, and perhaps you shall never see another springtide of the Spirit again. All this considered may hasten our repentance. Do not lay too much weight upon a deathbed. 'Do your best to come before winter' (2 Tim. 4:21). There is a winter of sickness and death a-coming. Therefore make haste to repent. Let your work be ready before winter. 'Today, if you hear his voice--do not harden your hearts' (Heb. 3:7-8).

The Trial of Our Repentance, and Comfort for the Penitent

A. A trial.

If any shall say they have repented, let me desire them to try themselves seriously by those seven fruits or effects of repentance which the apostle lays down in 2 Corinthians 7:11, 'See what this godly sorrow has produced in you: what earnestness, what eagerness to clear yourselves, what indignation, what alarm, what longing, what concern, what readiness to see justice done.'

1. Earnestness. The Greek word signifies a solicitous diligence or careful shunning all temptations to sin. The true penitent flies from sin, as Moses did from the serpent.

2. Eagerness to clear yourselves. The Greek word is 'apology'. The sense is this: though we have much care—yet through strength of temptation we may slip into sin. Now in this case, the repenting soul will not let sin lie festering in his conscience but judges himself for his sin. He pours out tears before the Lord. He begs mercy in the name of Christ and never leaves until he has gotten his pardon. Here he is cleared of guilt in his conscience, and is able to make an apology for himself against Satan.

3. Indignation. He who repents of sin, his spirit rises against it, as one's blood rises at the sight of him whom he mortally hates. Indignation is a being fretted at the heart with sin. The penitent is vexed with himself. David calls himself a fool and a beast (Psalm 73:22). God is never better pleased with us, than when we fall out with ourselves, for sin.

4. Alarm. A tender heart is ever a trembling heart. The penitent has felt sin's bitterness. This hornet has stung him and now, having hopes that God is reconciled, he is afraid to come near sin any more. The repenting soul is full of fear. He is afraid to lose God's favor which is better than life. He is afraid he should, for lack of diligence, come short of salvation. He is afraid lest, after his heart has been soft, the waters of repentance should freeze and he should harden in sin again. 'Blessed is the man who always fears the Lord' (Proverbs 28:14). A sinner is like the

leviathan who is made without fear (Job 41:33). A repenting person fears and sins not; a graceless person sins and fears not.

5. Longing. As sauce sharpens the appetite, so the bitter herbs of repentance sharpen desire. But what does the penitent desire? He desires more power against sin and to be released from it. It is true, he has got loose from Satan — but he goes as a prisoner that has broken out of prison — with a fetter on his leg. He cannot walk with that freedom and swiftness in the ways of God. He desires therefore to have the fetters of sin taken off. He would be freed from corruption. He cries out with Paul: 'who shall deliver me from the body of this death?' (Romans 7:24). In short, he desires to be with Christ — as everything desires to be in its center.

6. Zeal. Desire and zeal are fitly put together to show that true desire puts forth itself in zealous endeavor. How does the penitent bestir himself in the business of salvation! How does he take the kingdom of heaven by force! (Matt. 11:12) Zeal quickens the pursuit after glory. Zeal, encountering difficulty — is emboldened by opposition and tramples upon danger. Zeal makes a repenting soul persist in godly sorrow against all discouragements and oppositions whatever. Zeal carries a man above himself for God's glory. Paul before conversion, violently opposed the saints (Acts 26:11), and after conversion, he was judged mad for Christ's sake: 'Paul, you are beside yourself' (Acts 26:24). But it was zeal, not frenzy. Zeal animates spirit and duty. It causes fervency in religion, which is as fire to the sacrifice (Romans 12:11). As fear is a bridle to sin — so zeal is a spur to duty.

7. Readiness to see justice done. A true penitent pursues his sins with a holy malice. He seeks the death of them as Samson was avenged on the Philistines for his two eyes. He uses his sins as the Jews used Christ — he gives them gall and vinegar to drink. He crucifies his lusts (Gal. 5:24). A true child of God seeks to be revenged most of those sins which have dishonored God most. Cranmer, who had with his right hand subscribed the popish articles, was revenged on himself; he put his right hand first into the fire. David defiled his bed by sin; afterwards by repentance he watered his bed with tears. Israel had sinned by idolatry, and afterwards they defiled their idols: 'You will defile your silver-plated idols and your gold-plated images. You will throw them away like menstrual cloths, and call them filth!' (Isaiah 30:22).

Mary Magdalene had sinned in her eye by adulterous glances, and now she will be revenged on her eyes. She washes Christ's feet with her tears. She had sinned in her hair. It had entangled her lovers. Now she will be revenged on her hair; she wipes the Lord's feet with it. The Israelite women who had been dressing themselves by the hour and had abused their looking-glasses unto pride, afterwards by way of revenge as well as zeal, offered their looking-glasses to the use and service of God's tabernacle (Exod. 38:8). So those conjurers who used magic arts, when once they repented, brought their books and, by way of revenge, burned them (Acts 19:19).

These are the blessed fruits and effects of repentance, and if we can find these in our souls we have arrived at that repentance which is never to be repented of (2 Cor. 7:10).

A Necessary Caution

Such as have solemnly repented of their sins, let me speak to them by way of caution. Though repentance is so necessary and excellent, as you have heard — yet take heed that you do not ascribe too much to repentance. The papists are guilty of a double error:

(1) They make repentance a sacrament. Christ never made it so. And who may institute sacraments, but he who can give virtue to them?

(2) The papists make repentance meritorious. They say it merits pardon. This is a gross error. Indeed repentance fits us for mercy. As the plough, when it breaks up the ground, fits it for the seed, so when the heart is broken up by repentance, it is fitted for forgiveness of sin — but it

does not merit it. God will not save us without repentance, nor yet for it. I grant, that repenting tears are precious. They are, as Gregory said, 'the fat of the sacrifice;' as Basil said, 'the medicine of the soul;' and as Bernard said, 'the wine of angels.' But yet, tears do not merit pardon for sin. Christ's blood alone can merit pardon. We please God by repentance — but we do not merit pardon by it. To trust to our repentance is to make it a savior. Though repentance helps to purge out the filth of sin — yet it is Christ's blood which washes away the guilt of sin. Therefore do not idolize repentance. Do not rest upon this — that your heart has been wounded for sin — but rather that your Savior has been wounded for sin. When you have wept, say, 'Lord Jesus, wash my tears in your blood.'

B. Comfort for the Repenting Sinner.

Let me in the next place speak by way of comfort. Christian, has God given you a repenting heart? Know these three things for your everlasting comfort:

1. Your sins are pardoned.

Pardon of sin brings blessedness within it. (Psalm 32:1). Whom God pardons — he crowns. 'Who forgives all your iniquities, who crowns you with loving-kindness' (Psalm 103:34). A repenting condition is a pardoned condition. Christ said to that weeping woman, 'Your sins, which are many — are forgiven' (Luke 7:47). Pardons are sealed upon soft hearts. O you whose head has been a fountain to weep for sin — Christ's side will be a fountain to wash away sin! (Zech. 13:1). Have you repented? God looks upon you as if you had not offended. He becomes a friend, a father. He will now bring forth the best robe and put it on you. God is pacified towards you and will, with the father of the prodigal, fall upon your neck and kiss you. Sin in scripture is compared to a cloud (Is. 44:22). No sooner is this cloud scattered by repentance, than pardoning love shines forth. Paul, after his repentance, obtained mercy, (1 Tim. 1:16). When a spring of repentance is open in the heart — a spring of mercy is open in heaven!

2. God will pass an act of oblivion.

He so forgives sin as he forgets. 'I will remember their sin no more' (Jer. 31:34). Have you been penitentially humbled? The Lord will never upbraid you with your former sins. After Peter wept we never read that Christ upbraided him, with his denial of him. God has cast your sins into the depths of the sea (Mic. 7:19). How? Not as cork — but as lead. The Lord will never in a judicial way account for them. When he pardons, God is as a creditor that blots the debt out of his book (Isaiah 43:25). Some ask the question, whether the sins of the godly shall be mentioned at the last day. The Lord said he will not remember them, and he is blotting them out, so if their sins are mentioned, it shall not be to their harm, for the debt-book is crossed out.

3. Conscience will now speak peace.

O the music of a clean conscience! Conscience is turned into a paradise, and there a Christian sweetly solaces himself and plucks the flowers of joy (2 Cor. 1:12). The repenting sinner can go to God with boldness in prayer, and look upon him not as a judge — but as a father. He is 'born of God' and is heir to a kingdom (Luke 6:20). He is encircled with promises. He no sooner shakes the tree of the promise, but some fruit falls.

To conclude, the true penitent may look on death with comfort. His life has been a life of tears — and now at death all tears shall be wiped away! Death shall not be a destruction — but a deliverance from jail. Thus you see what great comfort remains for repenting sinners. Luther said that before his conversion he could not endure that bitter word 'repentance' — but afterwards he found much sweetness in it.

The Removing of 10 Impediments to Repentance

Before I lay down the expedients and means conducive to repentance, I shall first remove the impediments. In this great city, when you lack water, you search the cause, whether the pipes are broken or stopped, that the current of water is hindered. Likewise when no water of repentance comes (though we have the conduit pipes of ordinances), see what the cause is. What is the obstruction which hinders these penitential waters from running? There are ten impediments to repentance:

1. Men do not understand that they need repentance.

They thank God that all is well with them, and they know nothing they should repent of: 'you say, I am rich, and have need of nothing' (Rev. 3.17). He who does not think that there is any illness in his body, will not take the physic prescribed. This is the mischief sin has done; it has not only made us sick — but senseless. When the Lord bade the people return to him, they answered stubbornly, 'Why shall we return?' (Mal. 3:7). So when God bids men repent, they say, 'Why should we repent?' They know nothing they have done amiss. There is surely no disease worse, than that which is not felt.

2. People think that it is an easy thing to repent.

They think that it is but saying a few prayers: a sigh, or a 'Lord have mercy', and the work is done. This mistake of the easiness of repentance is a great hindrance to it. That which makes a person bold and adventurous in sin, must needs obstruct repentance. This opinion makes a person bold in sin. The angler can let out his line as far as he will — and then pull it in again. Likewise when a man thinks he can lash out in sin as far as he will — and then pull in by repentance when he pleases — this must needs embolden him in wickedness. But to take away this false conceit of the easiness of repentance, consider:

(1) A wicked man has a mountain of guilt upon him, and is it easy to rise up under such a weight? Is salvation obtained with a leap? Can a man jump out of sin — into heaven? Can he leap out of the devil's arms — into Abraham's bosom?

(2) If all the power in a sinner is employed against repentance, then repentance is not easy. All the faculties of a natural man join forces with sin: 'I have loved strangers, and after them will I go' (Jer. 2:25). A sinner will rather lose Christ and heaven — than his lusts! Death, which parts man and wife, will not part a wicked man and his sins; and is it so easy to repent? The angel rolled away the stone from the sepulcher — but no angel, only God himself, can roll away the stone from the heart!

3. Another impediment of repentance, is presuming thoughts of God's mercy.

Many suck poison from this sweet flower. Christ who came into the world to save sinners (1 Tim. 1:15) is coincidentally the occasion of many a man's perishing. Though to the elect he is the 'bread of life' — yet to the wicked he is 'a stone of stumbling' (1 Pet. 2:8). To some his blood is sweet wine — to others the water of Marah. Some are softened by this Sun of righteousness (Mal. 4:2), others are hardened. 'Oh,' says one, 'Christ has died; he has done all for me; therefore I may sit still and do nothing.' Thus they suck death from the tree of life; and perish by the Savior.

So I may say of God's mercy. It is coincidentally the cause of many a one's ruin. Because of God's mercy, men presume and think they may go on in sin. Should a king's clemency, make his subjects rebel? The psalmist says, 'there is mercy with God, that he may be feared' (Psalm 130:4) — but not that we may live in sin. Can men expect God's mercy — by provoking his justice? God will hardly show those mercy who sin, because mercy abounds. 'Shall we go on sinning so that grace may increase? By no means!' (Romans 6:1-2)

4. The next impediment of repentance, is a slothful sluggish disposition.

Repentance is looked upon as a toilsome thing, and such as requires much industry; and men are settled upon their lees and care not to stir. They had rather go sleeping to hell — than weeping to heaven! 'A slothful man hides his hand in his bosom' (Proverbs 19:24); he will not be at the labor of smiting on his breast. Many will rather lose heaven, than ply the oar and row there upon the waters of repentance. We cannot have the world without labor and diligence — and would we have that which is more excellent? Sloth is the cancer of the soul: 'slothfulness casts into a deep sleep' (Proverbs 19:15).

It was a witty fiction of the poets, that when Mercury had cast Argus into a sleep and with an enchanted wand closed his eyes, he then killed him. When Satan has by his witcheries lulled men asleep in sloth, then he destroys them. Some report that while the crocodile sleeps with its mouth open, the Indian rat gets into its belly and eats up its entrails. So while men sleep in security they are devoured.

5. The next impediment of repentance, is the bewitching pleasure of sin.

'Who had pleasure in unrighteousness' (2 Thess. 2:12) Sin is a sugared draught, mixed with poison. The sinner thinks there is danger in sin — but there is also delight, and the danger does not terrify him as much as the delight bewitches him. Plato calls love of sin, a great devil. Delighting in sin hardens the heart. In true repentance there must be a grieving for sin — but how can one grieve for that which he loves? He who delights in sin, can hardly pray against it. His heart is so bewitched with sin that he is afraid of leaving it too soon. Samson doted on Delilah's beauty — and her lap proved his grave. When a man rolls iniquity as a sugared lump under his tongue, it infatuates him and is his death at last. Delight in sin is a silken halter. Will it not be bitterness in the latter end (2 Sam:2:26)?

6. An opinion that repentance will take away our joy.

But that is a mistake. It does not kill our joy — but refines our joy, and removes the foul lees of sin. What is all earthly joy? It is but a pleasant insanity. Worldly mirth is but like a pretended laugh. It has sorrow following at the heels. Like the magician's rod, it is instantly turned into a serpent; but divine repentance, like Samson's lion, has a honeycomb in it.

God's kingdom consists as well in joy — as in righteousness (Romans 14:17). None are so truly cheerful as penitent ones. The oil of joy is poured chiefly into a broken heart! 'He will give beauty for ashes, joy instead of mourning' (Isaiah 61:3). In the fields near Palermo grow a great many reeds in which there is a sweet juice from which sugar is made. Likewise in a penitent heart, which is the bruised reed, grow the sugared joys of God's Spirit. God turns the water of tears into the juice of the grape — which exhilarates and makes glad the heart. Who should rejoice if not the repenting soul? He is heir to all the promises — and is not that matter for joy? God dwells in a contrite heart — and must there not needs be joy there? 'I live with those whose spirits are contrite and humble' (Isaiah 57:15). Repentance does not take away a Christian's music — but raises it a note higher and makes it sweeter.

7. Another obstacle to repentance, is despondency of mind.

'It is a vain thing for me,' says the sinner, 'to set upon repentance; my sins are of that magnitude that there is no hope for me.' 'Return now everyone from his evil way ... And they said, There is no hope' (Jer. 18:11,12). Our sins are mountains — and how shall these ever be cast into the sea? Where unbelief represents sin in its bloody colors, and God in his judge's robes — the soul would sooner fly from him than to him. This is dangerous. Our sins need mercy — but despair rejects mercy. It throws the cordial of Christ's blood on the ground. Judas was not damned only for his treason and murder — but it was his distrust of God's mercy that destroyed him. Why should we entertain such hard thoughts of God? He has affections of love to repenting sinners (Joel 2:13). Mercy rejoices over justice. God's anger is not so hot — but mercy can cool it; nor so sharp — but mercy can sweeten it. God counts his mercy — his glory (Exod. 33:18,19).

We have some drops of mercy ourselves — but God is 'the Father of mercies' (2 Cor. 1:3), who begets all the mercies that are in us. He is the God of tenderness and compassion. No sooner do we mourn — than God's heart melts. No sooner do our tears fall — than God's relentings kindle (Hos. 11:8). Do not say then, that there is no hope. Disband the army of your sins, and God will sound a retreat to his judgments. Remember, great sins have been swallowed up in the sea of God's infinite compassions. Manasseh made the streets run with blood — yet when his head was a fountain of tears, God grew merciful.

8. The next impediment of repentance, is hope of sinning with impunity.

Men flatter themselves in sin, and think that God, having spared them all this while, never intends to punish them. Because the judgment is put off, they think therefore, 'surely there will be no judgment'. 'The wicked say to themselves, God has forgotten; He hides His face and will never see.' (Psalm 10:11). The Lord indeed is longsuffering towards sinners and would by his patience allure them to repentance — but here is their wretchedness; because he forbears to punish — they forbear to repent. Know, that the lease of patience will soon run out. There is a time when God will say, 'My Spirit shall not always strive with man' (Gen. 6:3). A creditor may forbear his debtor — but forbearance does not excuse the payment. God takes notice how long the hour-glass of his patience has been running: I gave her time to repent, but she would not turn away from her immorality' (Rev. 2:21). Jezebel added impenitence to her immorality, and what followed? 'So I will cast her on a bed of suffering' (Rev. 2:22), not a bed of pleasure — but a bed of languishing where she will consume away in her iniquity. The longer God's arrow is drawing, the deeper it will wound! Sins against God's patience will make a man's hell so much the hotter.

9. The next impediment of repentance, is fear of reproach.

'If I repent — I will expose myself to men's scorns.' The heathen could say, 'when you apply yourself to the study of wisdom, prepare for sarcasms and reproaches.' But consider well — who they are, who reproach you. They are such as are ignorant of God and spiritually insane. And are you troubled to have them reproach you, who are insane? Who minds a madman laughing at him? What do the wicked reproach you for? Is it because you repent? You are doing your duty. Bind their reproaches as a crown about your head. It is better that men should reproach you for repenting — than that God should damn you for not repenting! If you cannot bear a reproach for true religion, never call yourself a Christian. Luther said, 'a Christian is a crucified one.' Suffering is a saint's badge. And alas, what are reproaches? They are but chips off the cross, which are rather to be despised than laid to heart!

10. The last impediment of repentance, is immoderate love of the world.

No wonder Ezekiel's hearers were hardened into rebellion — when their hearts went after covetousness (Ezek. 33:31). The world so engrosses men's time and bewitches their affections that they cannot repent. They had rather put gold in their bag — than tears in God's bottle! Many scarcely ever give heed to repentance; they are more for the plough and breaking of clods — than breaking up the fallow ground of their hearts. The thorns choke the Word. We read of those who were invited to Christ's supper who put him off with worldly excuses. 'But they all began making excuses. One said he had just bought a field and wanted to inspect it, so he asked to be excused. Another said he had just bought five pair of oxen and wanted to try them out. Another had just been married, so he said he couldn't come.' (Luke 14:18-20).

The farm and the shop so take up people's time, that they have no leisure for their souls. Their golden weights hinder their silver tears. There is an herb in the country of Sardinia, like balm, which if they eat much of, will make them die laughing. Such an herb (or rather, weed) is the world, if men eat too immoderately of it—instead of dying repenting, they will die laughing.

These are the obstructions to repentance which must be removed so that the current may be clearer. In the last place I shall prescribe some rules or means conducive to repentance.

Means for Repentance

I. The first means to repentance is serious consideration.

The first means conducive to repentance, is serious consideration: 'I thought on my ways—and turned my feet unto your testimonies' (Psalm 119:59). The prodigal, when he came to himself, seriously considered his riotous luxuries, and then he repented. Peter, when he thought of Christ's words, wept. There are certain things which, if they were well considered, would be a means to make us break off a course of sinning.

A. Firstly, consider seriously what sin is, and sure enough there is enough evil in it to make us repent. There are in sin these twenty evils:

(1) Sin is a parting from God. (Jer. 2:5). God is the supreme good, and our blessedness lies in union with him. But sin, like a strong bias, draws away the heart from God. The sinner parts from God. He bids farewell to Christ and mercy. Every step forward in sin, is a step backward from God: 'they have forsaken the Lord, they have gone away backward' (Isaiah 1:4). The further one goes from the sun, the nearer he approaches to darkness. The further the soul goes from God, the nearer it approaches to misery.

(2) Sin is a walking contrary to God. (Lev. 26:27). The same word in the Hebrew signifies both to commit sin and to rebel. Sin is God's opposite. If God is of one mind, sin will be of another. Sin strikes at God's very being. If sin could help it, God would no longer be God, 'Rid us of the Holy One of Israel!' (Isaiah 30:11). What a horrible thing is this, for a piece of proud dust to rise up in defiance against its Maker!

(3) Sin is an injury to God. It violates his laws. Here is grievous high treason! What greater injury can be offered to a prince—than to trample upon his royal edicts? A sinner offers contempt to the statute laws of heaven: 'they cast your law behind their backs' (Neh. 9:26), as if they scorned to look upon it. Sin robs God of his due. You injure a man when you do not give him his due. The soul belongs to God. He lays a double claim to it: it is his by creation and by purchase. Now sin steals the soul from God and gives the devil that which rightly belongs to God.

(4) Sin is profound ignorance. Some say that all sin is founded in ignorance. If men knew God in his purity and justice—they would not dare go on in a course of sinning: 'they proceed from evil to evil, and they know not me, says the Lord' (Jer. 9:3). Therefore ignorance and lust are joined together 'As obedient children, do not conform to the evil desires you had when you lived in ignorance' (1 Pet. 1:14). Ignorance is the womb of lust. Vapors arise most in the night. The black vapors of sin arise most in a dark ignorant soul. Satan casts a mist before a sinner—so that he does not see the flaming sword of God's wrath. The eagle first rolls himself in the sand and then flies at the stag, and by fluttering its wings, so bedusts the stag's eyes that it cannot see—and then it strikes it with its talons! So Satan, that eagle or prince of the air, first blinds men with ignorance and then wounds them with his darts of temptation. Is sin ignorance? There is great cause to repent of ignorance.

(5) Sin is hazardous. In every transgression a man runs an apparent hazard of his soul. He treads upon the brink of the bottomless pit! Foolish sinner, you never commit a sin, but you do that which may undo your soul forever. He who drinks poison, it is a wonder if it does not cost him his life. One taste of the forbidden tree lost Adam paradise. One sin of the angels lost them heaven. One sin of Saul lost him his kingdom. The next sin you commit—God may clap you up prisoner among the damned! You who gallop on in sin—it is a question whether God will spare your life a day longer or give you a heart to repent.

(6) Sin besmears with filth. In James 1:21 it is called 'filthiness'. The Greek word signifies the putrid exudate of ulcers. Sin is called an abomination (Deut. 7:25), indeed, in the plural, abominations (Dent. 20:18). This filthiness in sin is inward. A spot on the face may easily be wiped off—but to have the liver and lungs cancered, is far worse. Such a pollution is sin, it has gotten into mind and conscience (Titus 1:15). It is compared to a menstruous cloth (Isaiah 30:22), the most unclean thing under the law. A sinner's heart is like a field spread with dung. Some think sin is an ornament; it is rather an excrement. Sin so besmears a person with filth—that God cannot abide the sight of him: 'My soul loathed them!' (Zech. 11:8).

(7) In sin there is odious ingratitude. God has fed you, O sinner, with angels' food. He has crowned you with a variety of mercies—yet do you go on in sin? As David said of Nabal: 'in vain have I kept this man's sheep' (1 Sam. 25:21). Likewise in vain has God done so much for the sinner. All God's mercies may upbraid, yes, accuse, the ungrateful person. God may say, I gave you wit, health, riches, and you have employed all these against me: 'I was the one who gave her the grain, the new wine and oil, and lavished on her the silver and gold—which they used for Baal' (Hos. 2:8). I sent in provisions and they served their idols with them. The snake in the fable which was frozen, stung him who brought it to the fire and gave it warmth. Likewise, a sinner goes about to sting God with his own mercies. 'Is this your kindness to your friend?' (2 Sam. 16:17). Did God give you life—to sin? Did he give you wages—to serve the devil?

(8) Sin is a debasing thing. It degrades a person of his honor: 'I will make your grave; for you are vile' (Nah. 1:14). This was spoken of a king. He was not vile by birth—but by sin. Sin blots our name, and taints our blood. Nothing so changes a man's glory into shame—as sin. It is said of Naaman, 'He was a great man and honorable—but he was a leper' (2 Kings 5:1). Let a man be ever so great with worldly pomp—yet if he is wicked, he is a leper in God's eye. To boast of sin is to boast of that which is our infamy; as if a prisoner should boast of his fetters—or be proud of his halter.

(9) Sin is infinite loss. Never did any thrive by grazing in sin's pasture. What does one lose? He loses God; he loses his peace; he loses his soul. The soul is a divine spark lighted from heaven; it is the glory of creation. And what can countervail this loss (Matt. 16:26)? If the soul is gone, the treasure is gone; therefore in sin there is infinite loss. Sin is such a trade, that whoever follows it—is sure to be ruined.

(10) Sin is a burden. 'My iniquities have gone over my head—as an heavy burden they are too heavy for me' (Psalm 38:4). The sinner goes with his weights and fetters on him. The burden of sin is always worst—when it is least felt. Sin is a burden wherever it comes. Sin burdens God: 'I am pressed under you, as a cart is pressed that is full of sheaves' (Amos 2:13). Sin burdens the soul. What a weight did the apostate Spira feel! How was the conscience of Judas burdened, so much so that he hanged himself to quiet his conscience! Those who know what sin is, will repent that they carry such a burden.

(11) Sin is a debt. It is compared to a debt of millions (Matt. 18:24). Of all the debts we owe, our sins are the worst. With other debts a sinner may flee to foreign countries—but with sin he

cannot. 'Where shall I flee from your presence?' (Psalm 139:7). God knows where to find out all his debtors. Death frees a man from other debts – but it will not free him from his debt of sin. It is not the death of the debtor, but of the creditor – which discharges this debt.

(12) There is deceitfulness in sin. 'The deceitfulness of sin' (Heb. 3:13). 'The wicked works a deceitful work' (Proverbs 11:18). Sin is a mere cheat. While it pretends to please us, it beguiles us! Sin does as Jael did. First she brought the milk and butter to Sisera, then she pounded the tent peg through his head, so that he died (Judg. 5:26). Sin first courts, and then kills. It is first a fox, and then a lion. Whoever sin betrays – it kills. Those locusts in Revelation are perfect emblems of sin: 'They had gold crowns on their heads ... They had tails that stung like scorpions, with power to torture people' (Rev. 9:7-10). Sin is like the usurer who feeds a man with money and then makes him mortgage his land. Sin feeds the sinner with delightful objects and then makes him mortgage his soul. Judas pleased himself with the thirty pieces of silver – but they proved deceitful riches. Ask him now, how he likes his bargain.

(13) Sin is a spiritual sickness. One man is sick with pride, another with lust, another with malice. It is with a sinner as it is with a sick patient: his palate is distempered, and the sweetest things taste bitter to him. So the Word of God, which is sweeter than the honeycomb, tastes bitter to a sinner: 'They put sweet for bitter' (Isaiah 5:20). And if sin be a disease it is not to be nourished – but rather cured by repentance.

(14) Sin is a bondage. It binds a man to the devil as his slave. Of all conditions, servitude is the worst. Every man is held with the cords of his own sin. 'I was held before conversion,' said Augustine, 'not with an iron chain – but with the obstinacy of my will.' Sin is imperious and tyrannical. It is called a law (Romans 8:2) because it has such a binding power over a man. The sinner must do as sin will have him. He does not so much enjoy his lusts – as serve them, and he will have work enough to do to gratify them all. 'I have seen princes going on foot' (Eccles. 10:7); the soul, that princely thing, which once was crowned with knowledge and holiness – is now made a lackey to sin and runs the devil's errand!

(15) Sin has a spreading malignity in it. It does hurt not only to a man's self – but to others. One man's sin may occasion many to sin. One man may help to defile many. A person who has the plague, going into company, does not know how many will be infected with the plague by him. You who are guilty of open sins, know not how many have been infected by you. There may be many, for anything you know, now in hell, crying out that they would never have come there – if it had not been for your bad example!

(16) Sin is a vexatious thing. It brings trouble with it. The curse which God laid upon the woman is most truly laid upon every sinner: 'in sorrow you shall bring forth' (Gen. 3:16). A man vexes his thoughts with plotting sin, and when sin has conceived, in sorrow he brings forth. Like one who takes a great deal of pain to open a floodgate, when he has opened it, the flood comes in upon him and drowns him! So a man beats his brains to contrive sin, and then it vexes his conscience, brings trouble to his estate, rots the wall and timber of his house (Zech. 5:4).

(17) Sin is a foolish thing. What greater foolishness is there, than to gratify an enemy! Sin gratifies Satan. When lust or anger burn in the soul – Satan warms himself at the fire! Men's sins feast the devil. Samson was called out to amuse the Philistines (Judg. 16:25). Likewise the sinner amuses the devil! Nothing more satisfies him – than to see men sin. How he laughs to see them hazarding their souls for the world, as if one would trade diamonds for straws; or would fish for gudgeons with golden hooks! Every wicked man shall be indicted as a fool, at the Day of

Judgment. 'But God said to him—You fool! This very night your soul will be demanded from you. Then who will get what you have prepared for yourself?' Luke 12:20

(18) There is cruelty in every sin. With every sin you commit—you give a stab to your soul. While you are kind to sin—you are cruel to yourself, like the lunatic man in the Gospel who would cry out and cut himself with stones (Mark 5:5). The sinner is like the jailer—who drew a sword to kill himself (Acts 16:27). The soul may cry out, 'I am being murdered!' Naturalists say the hawk chooses to drink blood, rather than water. So sin drinks the blood of souls.

(19) Sin is a spiritual death. 'Dead in trespasses and sins' (Eph. 2:1). The life of sin—is the death of the soul. A dead man has no sense. So an unregenerate person has no sense of God. 'Having lost all sensitivity, they have given themselves over to sensuality so as to indulge in every kind of impurity, with a continual lust for more.' (Eph. 4:19). Try to persuade him to mind his salvation. To what purpose do you make orations to a dead man? Go to reprove him for vice? To what purpose do you strike a dead man?

He who is dead has no taste. Set a banquet before him, and he does not relish it. Likewise a sinner tastes no sweetness in Christ, or in precious Scripture promises. They are but as cordials in a dead man's mouth!

The dead putrefy; and if Martha said of Lazarus, 'by now the smell will be terrible because he has been dead for four days' (John 11:39). How much more may we say of a wicked man, who has been dead in sin for thirty or forty years, 'by now the smell will be terrible!'

(20) Sin without repentance, will bring to final damnation. As the rose perishes by the canker which breed in itself—so do men perish by the corruptions which breed in their souls. What was once said to the Grecians of the Trojan horse, 'This engine is made to be the destruction of your city!' the same may be said to every impenitent person, 'This engine of sin will be the destruction of your soul!' Sin's last scene is always tragic. Diagoras Florentinus would drink poison in a frolic—but it cost him his life. Men drink the poison of sin in a merriment—but it costs them their souls! 'The wages of sin is death' (Romans 6:23). What Solomon said of wine may also be said of sin: at first 'it sparkles in the cup, when it goes down smoothly. In the end it bites like a poisonous serpent; it stings like a viper!' (Proverbs 23:31-32). Christ tell us of the worm and the fire (Mark 9:48).

Sin is like oil, and God's wrath is like fire. As long as the damned continue sinning, so the fire will continue scorching! 'Who of us can dwell with everlasting burnings?' (Isaiah 33:14). 'They cursed the God of heaven for their pains and sores. But they refused to repent of all their evil deeds!' (Revelation 16:11)

But men question the truth of this and are like impious Devonax who, being threatened with hell for his villainies, mocked at it and said, 'I will believe there is a hell when I come there, and not before!' We cannot make hell enter into men—until they enter into hell.

Thus we have seen the deadly evil in sin which, seriously considered, may make us repent and turn to God. If, for all this, men will persist in sin and are resolved upon a voyage to hell—who can hinder their damnation? They have been told what a soul-damning rock sin is—but if they will voluntarily run upon it and damn themselves—their blood is upon their own head!

B. The second serious consideration to work repentance, is to consider the mercies of God. A stone is soonest broken upon a soft pillow, and a heart of stone is soonest broken upon the soft pillow of God's mercies. 'The goodness of God leads you to repentance' (Romans 2:4). The clemency of a prince sooner causes relenting in a malefactor. While God has been storming others by his judgments—he has been wooing you by his mercies.

(1) What preventative mercies have we had? What troubles have been prevented, what fears blown over? When our foot has been slipping, God's mercy has held us up! (Psalm 94:18). His mercy has always been a screen between us and danger. When enemies like lions have risen up against us to devour us — free grace has snatched us out of the mouth of these lions! In the deepest waves the arm of mercy has upheld us — and has kept our head above water. And will not all of God's preventative mercies lead us to repentance?

(2) What positive mercies have we had!

Firstly, in supplying mercy. God has been a bountiful benefactor, 'the God who fed me all my life long unto this day' (Gen. 48:15). What man will spread a table for his enemy? We have been enemies — yet God has fed us! He has given us the horn of oil. He has made the honeycomb of mercy drop on us. God has been as kind to us — as if we had been his best servants. And will not this supplying mercy lead us to repentance?

Secondly, in delivering mercy. When we have been at the gates of the grave, God has miraculously preserved our lives. He has turned the shadow of death into morning, and has put a song of deliverance into our mouth. And will not delivering mercy lead us to repentance?

The Lord has labored to break our hearts with his mercies. In Judges, chapter 2, we read that when the angel had preached a sermon of mercy, 'the people wept loudly.' If anything will move tears, it should be the mercy of God. He is an obstinate sinner indeed — whom these great cable-ropes of God's mercy will not draw to repentance!

C. The third serious consideration to work repentance, is to consider God's afflictive providences. God has sent us in recent years to the school of affliction. He has twisted his judgments together. He has made good upon us, those two threatenings, 'I will be to Ephraim as a moth' (Hos. 5:12). Has not God been so to England in the decay of trading? And 'I will be unto Ephraim as a lion' (Hos. 5:14) has he not been so to England in the devouring plague? All this while God waited for our repentance. But we went on in sin: 'I hearkened and heard — but no man repented of his wickedness, saying, What have I done?' (Jer. 8:6).

And of late, God has been whipping us with a fiery rod in those tremendous flames of the great fire of London — which is emblematic of the great conflagration at the last day when 'the elements shall melt with fervent heat' (2 Pet. 3:10). When Joab's grain was on fire — then he went running to Absalom (2 Sam. 14:31). God has set our houses on fire — that we may run to him in repentance. 'The Lord's voice cries unto the city: 'Hear the rod — and him who has appointed it!' (Mic. 6:9). This is the language of the rod — that we should humble ourselves under God's mighty hand and 'break off our sins by righteousness' (Dan. 4:27). Manasseh's affliction ushered in repentance (2 Chron. 33:12).

God uses affliction, as the proper medicine for carnal security. 'Their mother has played the harlot' (Hos. 2:5), by idolatry. What course now will God take with her? 'Therefore I will hedge up your way with thorns' (Hos. 2:6). This is God's method, to set a thorn-hedge of affliction in the way. Thus to a proud man — contempt is a thorn. To a lustful man — sickness is a thorn, both to stop him in his sin and to goad him forward in repentance. The Lord teaches his people as Gideon did the men of Succoth: 'Gideon taught them a lesson, punishing them with thorns and briers from the wilderness' (Judg. 8:16). Here was a sharp lesson. Likewise God has of late been teaching us humiliation, by thorny providences. He has torn our golden fleece from us; he has brought our houses low — that he might bring our hearts low. When shall we dissolve into tears — if not now?

God's judgments are so proper a means to work repentance that the Lord wonders at it, and makes it his complaint that his severity did not break men off from their sins: 'I kept the rain from falling when you needed it the most, ruining all your crops.' (Amos 4:7). 'I struck your farms and vineyards with blight and mildew. Locusts devoured all your fig and olive trees.' (Amos 4:9). 'I sent plagues against you like the plagues I sent against Egypt long ago. I killed your young men in war and slaughtered all your horses. The stench of death filled the air!' (Amos 4:10). But still this is the theme of God's complaint, 'Yet you have not returned to me!'

The Lord proceeds gradually in his judgments. First he sends a lesser trial—and if that will not do, then a greater one. He sends upon one a gentle illness to begin with—and afterwards a burning fever. He sends upon another a loss at sea—then the loss of a child—then a loss of a husband. Thus by degrees he tries to bring men to repentance.

Sometimes God makes his judgments go in circuit—from family to family. The cup of affliction has gone round the nation; all have tasted it. And if we repent not now, we stand in contempt of God, and by implication we bid God do his worst! Such an epitome of wickedness, will hardly be pardoned. 'The Lord, the Lord Almighty, called you to weep and mourn. He told you to shave your heads in sorrow for your sins and to wear clothes of sackcloth to show your remorse. But instead, you dance and play; you feast on meat, and drink wine. 'Let's eat, drink, and be merry,' you say. The Lord Almighty has revealed to me that this sin will never be forgiven you until the day you die! That is the judgment of the Lord, the Lord Almighty!' (Isaiah 22:12-14). That is, this sin shall not be expiated by sacrifice.

If the Romans severely punished a young man who in a time of public calamity was seen sporting—of how much sorer punishment shall they be thought worthy, who strengthen themselves in wickedness and laugh in the very face of God's judgments! The heathen mariners in a storm repented (Jon 1:14). Not to repent now and throw our sins overboard is to be worse than heathens.

D. The fourth serious consideration to work repentance, is to consider how much we shall have to answer for at last—if we do not repent. How many prayers, counsels, and admonitions will be put upon the account book. Every sermon will come in as an indictment. As for such as have truly repented, Christ will answer for them. His blood will wash away their sins. The mantle of free grace will cover them. 'In those days, search will be made for Israel's guilt—but there will be none; and for the sins of Judah—but none will be found, for I will forgive the remnant I spare' (Jer. 50:20). Those who have judged themselves in the lower court of conscience shall be acquitted in the High Court of heaven. But if we do not repent—our sins must be all accounted for at the last day, and we must answer for them in our own persons, with no counsel allowed to plead for us.

O impenitent sinner, think with yourself now, how you will be able to look your infallible Judge in the face! You have a damned cause to plead and will be sure to be damned on the Day of Judgment! 'What could I do when God stands up to judge? How should I answer Him when He calls me to account?' (Job 31:14). Therefore, either repent now, or else provide your answers and see what defense you can make for yourselves when you come before God's dread tribunal. When he calls you to account—how will you answer him!

II. The second means to repentance, is a prudent comparison.

Compare penitent and impenitent conditions together—and see the difference. Spread them before your eyes and by the light of the Word—see the impenitent condition as most deplorable—and the penitent as most comfortable. How sad was it with the prodigal before he returned to his father! He had spent all; he had sinned himself into beggary, and had nothing left but a few husks! He was fellow inhabitant with the swine! But when he came home to his father, nothing was thought too good for him. The robe was brought forth to cover him, the ring to adorn him, and the fatted calf to feast him. If the sinner continues in his impenitency, then farewell Christ and mercy and heaven! But if he repents, then presently he has a heaven within him. Then Christ is his, then all is peace. He may sing a song to his soul and say, 'soul, you have enough stored away for years to come. Eat, drink, and be merry!' (Luke 12:19).

Upon our turning to God, we have more restored to us in Christ — than ever was lost in Adam. God says to the repenting soul, 'I will clothe you with the robe of righteousness; I will enrich you with the jewels and graces of my Spirit. I will bestow my love upon you! I will give you a kingdom! Son, all I have is yours!'

O my friends, do but compare your estate before repentance and after repentance together. Before your repenting, there were nothing but clouds and storms to be seen — clouds in God's face and storms in conscience. But after repenting how is the weather altered! What sunshine above! What serene calmness within! A Christian's soul is like the hill Olympus — all light and clear, and no winds blowing!

III. A third means conducive to repentance, is a settled determination to leave sin. Not a faint wish — but a resolved vow. 'I have sworn that I will keep your righteous judgments' (Psalm 119:106). 'All the delights and artifices of sin, shall not make me break my vow!' There must be no hesitation, no consulting with flesh and blood, 'Had I best leave my sin — or not?' But as Ephraim, 'What have I to do any more with idols!' (Hos:14:8). I will be deceived no more by my sins! I will no longer be fooled by Satan! This day I will put a bill of divorce into the hands of my lusts! Until we come to this settled resolution, sin will gain ground of us — and we shall never be able to shake off this viper! It is no wonder that he who is not resolved to be an enemy of sin — is conquered by it.

This resolution must be built upon the strength of Christ more than our own. It must be a humble resolution. As David, when he went against Goliath put off his presumptuous self-confidence, as well as his armor, 'I come to you in the name of the Lord' (1 Sam. 17:45) so we must go out against our Goliath lusts — in the strength of Christ! Being conscious of our own inability to leave sin, let us get Christ to be bound with us, and engage his strength for the mortifying of corruption!

IV. The fourth means conducive to repentance, is earnest prayer. The heathens laid one of their hands on the plough — and the other they lifted up to Ceres, the goddess of corn. So when we have used the means, let us look up to God for a blessing. Pray to him for a repenting heart: 'You, Lord, who bid me repent — give me grace to repent'. Pray that our hearts may be holy stills, dropping tears. Beg of Christ to give to us such a look of love as he did to Peter, which made him go out and weep bitterly. Implore the help of God's Spirit. It is the Spirit's smiting on the rock of our hearts — which makes the waters gush out! 'He causes his wind to blow — and the waters to flow' (Psalm 147:18). When the wind of God's Spirit blows — then the water of tears will flow.

There is good reason we should go to God for repentance:

(1) Because repentance is God's gift: 'God has granted even the Gentiles, repentance unto life.' (Acts 11:18). The Arminians hold that it is in our power to repent. True — we can harden our hearts — but we cannot soften them. This crown of freewill has fallen from our head! Nay, there is in us not only impotency — but obstinacy! (Acts 7:51). Therefore beg of God a repentant spirit. He alone can make the stony to heart bleed! His is a word of creative power.

(2) We must have recourse to God for blessing because he has promised to bestow it. 'I will sprinkle clean water on you, and you will be clean; I will cleanse you from all your impurities and from all your idols. I will give you a new heart and put a new spirit in you; I will remove

from you your heart of stone and give you a heart of flesh.' (Ezekiel 36:25-26). I will soften your adamant hearts—in my Son's blood! Show God his hand and seal.

Here is another gracious promise: 'They shall return unto me with their whole heart' (Jer. 24:7). Turn this promise into a prayer: 'Lord, give me grace to return unto you with my whole heart!'

V. The fifth means conducive to repentance, is endeavor after clearer discoveries of God. 'I had heard about you before, but now I have seen you with my own eyes! Therefore I abhor myself, and repent in dust and ashes!' (Job 42:5 6). Job, having surveyed God's glory and purity—as a humble penitent, he abhorred himself. By looking into the clear looking-glass of God's holiness—we see our own blemishes and so learn to bewail them.

VI. Lastly, we should labor for faith. But what is faith to repentance? Faith breeds union with Christ, and there can be no separation from sin, until there is union with Christ. The eye of faith looks on God's mercy—and that thaws the frozen heart! Faith carries us to Christ's blood, and that blood mollifies the hard heart! Faith persuades of the love of God, and that love sets us a-weeping!

Thus I have laid down the means or helps to repentance. What remains now—but that we set upon the work. And let us be in earnest—not as actors, but as warriors. I will conclude all, with the words of the psalmist: 'He who goes out weeping—will return with songs of joy!' (Psalm 126:6).

The Godly Man's Picture

Drawn with a Scripture Pencil, or, Some Characteristic Marks of a Man who is going to Heaven

The Epistle to the Reader

Christian Reader,

The soul being so precious, and salvation so glorious — it is the highest point of prudence to make preparations for the eternal world. It is beyond all dispute, that there is an inheritance in light; and it is most strenuously asserted in Holy Scripture that there must be a fitness and suitability for it (Col. 1:12). If anyone asks, 'Who shall ascend into the hill of the Lord?' the answer is, 'He who has clean hands, and a pure heart' (Psalm 24:4). To describe such a person is the work of this ensuing treatise. Here you have the godly man's portrait, and see him portrayed in his full lineaments.

What a rare thing godliness is! It is not airy and puffed up — but solid, and such as will take up the heart and spirits. Godliness consists in an exact harmony between holy principles and practices. Oh, that all into whose hands this book shall providentially come, may be so enamored with piety as to embrace it heartily. So sublime is godliness that it cannot be delineated in its perfect radiance and luster, though an angel should take the pencil. Godliness is our wisdom. 'The fear of the Lord, that is wisdom' (Job 28:28). Morality without piety is profound madness. Godliness is a spiritual queen, and whoever marries her, is sure of a large dowry with her. Godliness has the promise of the present life and of that which is to come (1 Tim. 4:8). Godliness gives assurance, yes, holy triumph in God; and how sweet is that! (Isaiah 32:17).

It was old Latimer who said, 'When sometimes I sit alone, and have a settled assurance of the state of my soul, and know that God is my God — I can laugh at all troubles, and nothing can daunt me.' Godliness puts a man in heaven before his time. Christian, aspire after piety; it is a lawful ambition. Look at the saints' characteristics here, and never leave off until you have got them stamped upon your own soul. This is the grand business which should swallow up your time and thoughts. Other speculations and quaint notions are nothing, compared to the priceless soul. They are like wafers which have fine words printed upon them, and are curious to the eye — but are thin, and yield little nourishment. But I will not keep you longer in the porch. Should I have enlarged upon any one characteristic of the godly man, it would have required a volume — but designing to go over many, I have contracted my sails, and given you only a brief summary of things. If this piece conduces to the good of souls, I shall have my desire. That the God of grace will effectually accomplish this shall be the prayer of him who is

Yours in all Christian affection,

Thomas Watson

Introduction

For this cause shall everyone who is godly pray unto you.

Psalm 32:6

Holy David at the beginning of this psalm, shows us wherein true happiness consists; not in beauty, honor, riches (the world's trinity) — but in the forgiveness of sin. 'Blessed is he whose transgression is forgiven' (v. 1). The Hebrew word 'to forgive' signifies 'to carry out of sight', which agrees well with the words of Jeremiah: 'In those days, says the Lord, the sins of Judah shall be sought for, and they shall not be found' (Jer. 50:20). This is an incomprehensible blessing, and such as lays a foundation for all other mercies. I shall just glance at it, and lay down these five assertions about it:

1. Forgiveness of sin is an act of God's free grace.

The Greek word for 'forgive' (*charizomai*) makes clear the source of pardon. Pardon does not arise from anything inherent in us — but is the pure result of free grace (*charis*). 'I, even I, am he who blots out your transgressions for my own sake' (Isaiah 43:25). When a creditor forgives a debtor, he does it freely. Pardon of sin is a royal thread, spun out of the heart of free grace. Paul cries out, 'I obtained mercy' (1 Tim. 1:13) — 'I was be-mercied'. He who is pardoned, is all bestrewn with mercy. When the Lord pardons a sinner, he does not only pay a debt — but gives an inheritance!

2. God, in forgiving sin, remits the guilt and penalty.

Guilt cries for justice. No sooner had Adam eaten the apple, than he saw the 'flaming sword' and heard the curse. But in forgiveness of sin, God indulges the sinner. He seems to say to him, 'Though you have fallen into the hands of my justice and deserve to die — yet I will absolve you, and whatever is charged against you shall be discharged.'

3. Forgiveness of sin is through the blood of Christ.

Free grace is the impulsive cause; Christ's blood is the meritorious cause. 'Without shedding of blood is no remission of sin' (Heb. 9:22). Justice would be revenged either on the sinner, or on the surety. Every pardon is the price of Christ's blood.

4. Before sin is forgiven, it must be repented of.

Therefore repentance and remission are linked together: 'that repentance and forgiveness of sins should be preached in his name' (Luke 24:47). Not that repentance in a popish sense merits forgiveness. Christ's blood must wash our tears away — but repentance is a qualification, though not a cause of forgiveness. He who is humbled for sin, will value pardoning mercy the more. When there is nothing in the soul but clouds of sorrow, and now God brings a pardon — which is a setting up of a rainbow in the cloud, to tell the sinner that the flood of wrath shall not overflow him — oh, what joy there is at the sight of this rainbow! The soul that before was steeped in tears, now melts in love to God (Luke 7:38, 47).

5. God having forgiven sin, he will no longer call it to remembrance. (Jer. 31:34)

The Lord will not upbraid us with former unkindness. 'He will cast all our sins into the depths of the sea' (Mic. 7:19). Sin shall not be cast in like cork which rises up again — but like lead which sinks to the bottom. How we should all labor for this covenant blessing!

(i) How sad it is to lack pardon! It must of necessity go badly with the malefactor, who lacks his pardon. All the curses of God stand in full force against the unpardoned sinner; his very blessings are cursed (Mal. 2:2). Caesar wondered at one of his soldiers, who was so merry when he was in debt. Can that sinner be merry who is heir to all God's curses — and does not know how soon he may take up his lodgings among the damned!

(ii) How sweet it is to have pardon!

(a) The pardoned soul is out of the gunshot of hell (Romans 8:33). Satan may accuse — but Christ will show a discharge!

(b) The pardoned soul may go to God with boldness in prayer. Guilt clips the wings of prayer, so that it cannot fly to the throne of grace — but forgiveness breeds confidence. He who has his pardon, may look his prince in the face with comfort.

This great mercy of pardon David had obtained, as appears in verse 5: 'You forgave me'. And because he had found God 'a God of pardons' (Neh. 9:17), he therefore encouraged others to seek God in the words of the text: 'For this cause shall everyone who is godly pray unto you.'

The Nature of Godliness

It will first be enquired, 'What is godliness?' I answer in general, 'Godliness is the sacred impression and workmanship of God in a man, whereby from being carnal he is made spiritual.' When godliness is wrought in a person, he does not receive a new soul – but he has 'another spirit' (Numb. 14:24). The faculties are not new – but the qualities are; the strings are the same – but the tune is corrected. Concerning godliness, I shall lay down these seven maxims or propositions:

1. Godliness is a real thing

It is not a fantasy, but a fact. Godliness is not the feverish fantasy of a sick brain; a Christian is no enthusiast, one whose religion is all made up of theory. Godliness has truth for its foundation; it is called 'the way of truth' (Psalm 119:30). Godliness is a ray and beam that shines from God. If God is true, then godliness is true.

2. Godliness is an intrinsic thing

It lies chiefly in the heart: 'circumcision is that of the heart' (Romans 2:29). The dew lies on the leaf, the sap is hidden in the root. The moralist's religion is all in the leaf; it consists only in externals – but godliness is a holy sap which is rooted in the soul: 'Surely you desire truth in the inner parts; you teach me wisdom in the inmost place' (Psalm 51:6).

3. Godliness is a supernatural thing

By nature, we inherit nothing but evil. 'When we were in the flesh, the motions of sins did work in our members' (Romans 7:5). We sucked in sin as naturally as our mother's milk; but godliness is the 'wisdom from above' (Jas. 3:17). It is breathed in from heaven. God must light up the lamp of grace in the heart. Weeds grow by themselves; flowers are planted. Godliness is a celestial plant which comes from the New Jerusalem. Therefore it is called a 'fruit of the Spirit' (Gal. 5:22). A man has no more power to make himself godly, than to create himself.

4. Godliness is an extensive thing

It is a sacred leaven which spreads itself into the whole soul: 'May the God of peace sanctify you wholly' (1 Thess. 5:23). There is light in the understanding, order in the affections, pliableness in the will, exemplariness in the life. We do not call a black man white, because he has white teeth. He who is good only in some part is not godly. Grace is called 'the new man' (Col. 3:10), not a new eye, or tongue – but a new man. He who is godly is good all over; though he is regenerate only in part – yet it is in every part.

5. Godliness is an intense thing

It does not lie in a dead formality and indifference – but is vigorous and flaming: 'fervent in spirit' (Romans 12:11). We call water hot when it is so in the third or fourth degree. He whose devotion is inflamed is godly, and his heart boils over in holy affections.

6. Godliness is a glorious thing

As the jewel to the ring, so is piety to the soul, bespangling it in God's eyes. Reason makes us men; godliness makes us earthly angels; by it we 'partake of the divine nature' (2 Pet. 1:4). Godliness is near akin to glory: 'glory and virtue' (2 Pet. 1:3). Godliness is glory in the seed, and glory is godliness in the flower.

7. Godliness is a permanent thing

Aristotle says, 'Names are given from the habit'. We do not call the one who blushes ruddy – but the one who is of a ruddy complexion (1 Sam. 17:42). A blush of godliness is not enough to distinguish a Christian – but godliness must be the temper and complexion of the soul.

Godliness is a fixed thing. There is a great deal of difference between a stake in the hedge — and a tree in the garden. A stake rots and molders — but a tree, having life in it, abides and flourishes. When godliness has taken root in the soul, it abides to eternity: 'his seed remains in him' (1 John 3:9). Godliness being engraved in the heart by the Holy Spirit, as with the point of a diamond, can never be erased.

A reproof to such as are only Pretenders to Godliness

'Woe to you, teachers of the law and Pharisees, you hypocrites! You are like whitewashed tombs, which look beautiful on the outside but on the inside are full of dead men's bones and everything unclean. In the same way, on the outside you appear to people as righteous but on the inside you are full of hypocrisy and wickedness.' Matthew 23:27-28

Here is a sharp rebuke to such as are 'glittering dross' Christians, who only make a show of godliness, like Michal, who put 'an image in the bed', and so deceived Saul's messengers (1 Sam. 19:16). These our Savior calls 'whited sepulchers' (Matt. 23:27) — their beauty is all paint! In ancient times a third part of the inhabitants of England were called Picts, which signifies 'painted'. It is to be feared that they still retain their old name. How many are painted over with a religious profession, whose seeming luster dazzles the eyes of beholders — but within there is nothing but putrefaction! Hypocrites are like the swan, which has white feathers — but a black skin; or like that flower, which has a lovely appearance — but a bad scent. 'You have a name that you live, and are dead' (Rev. 3:1). These the apostle Jude compares to 'clouds without water' (Jude 12). They claim to be full of the Spirit — but they are empty clouds; their goodness is but a religious cheat.

Question: But why do people content themselves with a show of godliness?

Answer: This helps to keep up their fame. Men are ambitious of credit, and wish to gain repute in the world, therefore they will dress themselves in the garb and mode of religion, so that others may write them down for saints. But alas, what is one the better for having others commend him — and his conscience condemn him? What good will it do a man when he is in hell — that others think he has gone to heaven? Oh, beware of this! Counterfeit piety is double iniquity.

1. To have only a show of godliness is a God-enraging sin

The man who is a pretender to saintship — but whose heart tells him he has nothing but the name, carries Christ in his Bible but not in his heart. Some political design spurs him on in the ways of God; he makes religion a lackey to his carnal interest. What is this but to abuse God to his face, and to serve the devil in Christ's livery? Hypocrisy makes the fury rise up in God's face; therefore he calls such people 'the generation of his wrath' (Isaiah 10:6). God will send them to hell, to do penance for their hypocrisy!

2. To make only a show of godliness is self-delusion

It is a horrible mistake to take a show of grace, for grace. This is to cheat yourself: 'deceiving your own souls' (Jas. 1:22). He who has counterfeit gold instead of true gold, wrongs himself most. The hypocrite deceives others while he lives — but deceives himself when he dies.

3. To have only a name, and make a show of godliness, is odious to God and man

The hypocrite is abhorred by all. Wicked men hate him because he makes a show, and God hates him because he only makes a show. The wicked hate him because he has so much as a mask of godliness, and God hates him because he has no more. 'You have almost persuaded me to be a Christian' (Acts 26:28). The wicked hate the hypocrite because he is almost a Christian, and God hates him because he is only almost one.

4. To make a show of piety is a vain thing

Hypocrites lose all they have done. Their sham tears drop beside God's bottle; their prayers and fasts prove abortive. 'When you fasted and mourned, did you at all fast unto me, even to me?' (Zech. 7:5). As God will not recompense a slothful servant, neither will he recompense a treacherous one. The hypocrites' full reward is in this life: 'They have their reward' (Matt. 6:5). A poor reward — the empty breath of men. The hypocrite may make his receipt and write, 'Received in full payment'. Hypocrites may have the praise of men — but though these triumphs are granted them, they shall never have the privilege of sitting in heaven. What acceptance can he look for from God, whose heart tells him he is no better than a charlatan in divinity?

5. To have only a pretense of godliness will yield no comfort at death

Will painted gold enrich a man? Will painted wine refresh him who is thirsty? Will the paint of godliness stand you in any stead? How were the foolish virgins better for their 'blazing lamps', when they had no oil? What is the lamp of profession without the oil of grace? He who has only a painted holiness shall have only a painted happiness.

6. You who have nothing but a specious pretext and mask of piety expose yourself to Satan's scorn

You shall be brought forth at the last day, as was Samson, to make the devil sport (Judges 16:25). He will say, 'What has become of your vows, tears, confessions? Has all your religion come to this? Did you so often defy the devil, and have you now come to dwell with me? Could you meet with no weapon to kill you — but what was made of gospel metal? Could you not suck poison anywhere but out of ordinances? Could you find no way to hell — but by counterfeit godliness?' What a vexation this will be, to have the devil thus reproach a man! What will it be to have the devil triumph over a man at the last day!

Let us therefore take heed of this pious pageantry or devout stage-play. That which may make us fear our hearts the more is when we see tall cedars in the church worm-eaten with hypocrisy. Balaam a prophet, Jehu a king, Judas an apostle — all of them stand to this day on record as hypocrites.

It is true that there are the seeds of this sin in the best Christian; but as it was with leprosy under the law, all who had swellings or spots in the skin of the flesh were not reputed unclean and put out of the camp (Lev. 13:6); so all who have the swellings of hypocrisy in them are not to be judged hypocrites, for these may be the spots of God's children (Deut. 32:5). But that which distinguishes a hypocrite is when hypocrisy is predominant and is like a spreading cancer in the body.

Question: When is a man under the dominion and power of hypocrisy?

Answer: There are two signs of its predominance:

(i) When one serves God for sinister ends.

(ii) When there is some sin dear to a man, which he cannot part with. These two are as clear signs of a hypocrite as any I know.

Oh, let us take David's candle and lantern, and search for this leaven, and burn it before the Lord!

Christian, if you mourn for hypocrisy — yet find this sin so potent that you cannot get the mastery of it, go to Christ. Beg of him that he would exercise his kingly office in your soul, that he would subdue this sin, and put it under the yoke. Beg of Christ to exercise his spiritual surgery upon you. Desire him to lance your heart and cut out the rotten flesh, and that he would apply the medicine of his blood to heal you of your hypocrisy. Say that prayer of David often: 'Let my heart be sound in your statutes' (Psalm 119:80). 'Lord, let me be anything rather than a hypocrite.' A double-heart will exclude from one heaven.

The Characteristics of a godly man

It will be enquired in the next place, 'Who is the godly man?' For the full answer to this I shall lay down several specific signs and characteristics of a godly man.

1. A godly man is a man of knowledge.

'The prudent are crowned with knowledge' (Proverbs 14:18). The saints are called 'wise virgins' (Matt. 25:4). A natural man may have some head knowledge of God — but he 'knows nothing yet as he ought to know' (1 Cor. 8:2). He does not know God savingly. He may have the eye of natural reason open — but he does not discern the things of God in a spiritual manner. Waters cannot go beyond their spring-head. Vapors cannot rise higher than the sun draws them. A natural man cannot act above his sphere; he is no more able to judge sacred things aright than a blind man is to judge colors.

(i) He does not see the evil of his heart. If a face is ever so black and deformed — yet it is not seen under a veil; the heart of a sinner is so black that nothing but hell can pattern it — yet the veil of ignorance hides it.

(ii) He does not see the beauties of a Savior. Christ is a pearl of great price — but a hidden pearl.

But a godly man is taught by God: 'this anointing teaches you of all things' (1 John 2:27), that is, all things essential to salvation. A godly man has 'the good knowledge of the Lord' (2 Chron. 30:22). He has 'Sound wisdom' (Proverbs 3:21). He knows God in Christ. To know God out of Christ is to know him as an enemy — but to know him in Christ is sweet and delicious. A gracious soul has 'the savor of his knowledge' (2 Cor. 2:14). There is a great difference between one who has read of a country, or viewed it on the map — and another who has lived in the country, and tasted its fruits and spices. The knowledge with which a godly man is adorned has these eight rare ingredients in it:

1. It is a grounded knowledge

'If you continue in the faith grounded' (Col. 1:23). It is not simply believing 'as my church believes.' Saving knowledge rests upon a double basis: the Word and Spirit. The one is a guide, the other a witness. Saving knowledge is not changeable or doubtful — but has a certainty in it. 'We believe and are sure that you are that Christ' (John 6:69); 'being always confident' (2 Cor. 5:6). A godly man holds no more than he will die for. The martyrs were so confirmed in the knowledge of the truth, that they would seal it with their blood.

2. It is an appreciative knowledge

The jeweler who has the skill to value a jewel is said to know it. He who esteems God above the comforts of the earth knows him (Psalm 73:25). To compare other things with God is to debase deity; as if you should compare a glow-worm with the sun.

3. It is an enlivening knowledge

'I will never forget your precepts, for with them you have quickened me' (Psalm 119:93). Bible knowledge in a natural man's head is like a torch in a dead man's hand. True knowledge animates. A godly man is like John the Baptist, 'a burning and a shining lamp'. He not only shines by illumination — but he burns by affection. The spouse's knowledge made her 'love-sick' (Cant 2:5). 'I am wounded with love.' I am like a deer that is struck with an arrow; my soul lies bleeding, and nothing can cure me — but a sight of him whom my soul loves!

4. It is an applied knowledge

'I know that my redeemer lives' (Job 19:25). A medicine is best when it is applied. This applicative knowledge is joyful. Christ is called a 'surety' (Heb. 7:22). Oh what joy, when I am drowned in debt, to know that Christ is my surety! Christ is called an 'advocate' (1 John 2:1). The Greek word for advocate, *parakletos*, signifies a comforter. Oh, what comfort it is when I have a bad cause, to know Christ is my advocate, who never lost any cause he pleaded!

Question: But how shall I know that I am making a right application of Christ? A hypocrite may think he applies when he does not. Balaam, though a sorcerer, still said, 'my God' (Numb. 22:18).

Answer:

(i) He who rightly applies Christ puts these two together, Jesus and Lord. 'Christ Jesus my Lord' (Phil. 3:8). Many take Christ as Jesus — to save them; but refuse him as Lord — to rule them. Do you join 'Prince and Savior' (Acts 5:31)? Would you as well be ruled by Christ's laws as saved by his blood? Christ is 'a priest upon his throne' (Zech. 6:13). He will never be a priest to intercede — unless your heart is the throne where he sways his scepter. A true applying of Christ is when we so take him as a husband, that we give up ourselves to him as Lord.

(ii) He who rightly applies Christ derives virtue from him. The woman in the Gospel, having touched Christ, felt virtue coming from him and her fountain of blood was dried up (Mark 5:29). This is to apply Christ — when we feel a sin-mortifying virtue flow from him. That knowledge which is applicatory, has an antipathy against sin, and will not allow the heart to be dominated by sin.

5. It is a transforming knowledge

'We all, with open face beholding as in a glass the glory of the Lord, are changed into the same image' (2 Cor. 3:18). As a painter looking at a face draws a face like it in the picture; so looking at Christ in the mirror of the gospel, we are changed into his likeness. We may look at other objects that are beautiful — yet not be made beautiful by them. A deformed face may look at beauty, and yet not be made beautiful. A wounded man may look at a surgeon, and yet not be healed. But this is the excellence of divine knowledge, that it gives us such a sight of Christ as makes us partake of his nature! Like Moses when he had seen God's back parts, his face shone; some of the rays and beams of God's glory fell on him.

6. It is a self-emptying knowledge

Carnal knowledge makes the head giddy with pride (1 Cor. 8:1,2). True knowledge brings a man out of love with himself. The more he knows — the more he blushes at his own ignorance. David, a bright star in God's church, still thought himself rather a cloud than a star (Psalm 73:22).

7. It is a growing knowledge

'Increasing in the knowledge of God' (Col. 1:10). True knowledge is like the light of the morning, which increases on the horizon until it comes to the full meridian. So sweet is spiritual knowledge that the more a saint knows — the more thirsty he is for knowledge. It is called 'the riches of knowledge' (1 Cor. 1:5). The more riches a man has, the more still he desires. Though Paul knew Christ — yet he wanted to know him more: 'That I may know him, and the power of his resurrection' (Phil. 3:10).

8. It is a practical knowledge

'His sheep follow him because they know his voice.' (John 10:4). God requires a knowledge accompanied by obedience. True knowledge not only improves a Christian's sight — but improves his pace. It is a reproach to a Christian to live in a contradiction to his knowledge, to know he should be strict and holy — yet to live loosely. Not to obey — is the same as not to know: 'the sons of Eli knew not the Lord' (1 Sam. 2:12). They could not but know, for they taught others the knowledge of the Lord; yet they are said not to know — because they did not obey. When knowledge and practice appear together, then they herald much happiness.

Use 1: Let us test ourselves by this characteristic:

1. Are they godly, who are still in the region of darkness? 'It is not good to have zeal without knowledge, nor to be hasty and miss the way.' (Proverbs 19:2). Ignorant people cannot give God 'a reasonable service' (Romans 12:1). It is sad that after the Sun of righteousness has shone so long in our hemisphere, people should still be under the power of ignorance. Perhaps in the things of the world they know enough, none shall outreach them — but in the things of God — they have no knowledge. Nahash wanted to make a covenant with Israel, that he might 'put out their right eyes' (1 Sam. 11:2). Though men have knowledge in secular matters; the devil has put out their right eye — they do not understand the mystery of godliness. It may be said of them as of the Jews, 'to this day the veil is upon their heart' (2 Cor. 3:15). Many Christians are no better than baptized heathen! What a shame it is to be without knowledge! 'Some have not the knowledge of God; I speak this to your shame' (1 Cor. 15:34). Men think it a shame to be ignorant of their trade — but no shame to be ignorant of God. There is no going to heaven blindfold. 'For this is a people without understanding; so their Maker has no compassion on them, and their Creator shows them no favor.' (Isaiah 27:11).

Surely ignorance in these days is great. It is one thing not to know, another thing not to be willing to know: 'men loved darkness rather than light' (John 3:19). It is the owl which loves the dark. Sinners are like the Athlantes, a people in Ethiopia, who curse the sun. Wicked men shut their eyes willfully (Matt. 13:15), and God shuts them judicially (Isaiah 6:10).

2. Are they godly, who, though they have knowledge — yet do not know 'as they ought to know'? They do not know God experimentally. How many knowledgeable people are ignorant? They have illumination — but not sanctification. Their knowledge has no powerful influence upon them to make them better. If you set up a hundred torches in a garden they will not make the flowers grow — but the sun is influential. Many are so far from being better for their knowledge, that they are worse: 'your knowledge has perverted you' (Isaiah 47:10). The knowledge of most people makes them more cunning in sin; these have little cause to glory in their knowledge. Absalom might boast of the hair of his head — but that hanged him; so these may boast of the knowledge of their head — but it will destroy them!

3. Are they godly, who, though they have some glimmering of knowledge — yet have no trustful application of Christ? Many in the old world knew there was an ark — but were drowned, because they did not get into it! Knowledge which is not personally applied, will only light a man to hell! It would be better to live a savage — than to die an infidel under the gospel. Christ not believed in is dreadful. Moses' rod, when it was in his hand, did a great deal of good. It wrought miracles; but when it was out of his hand, it became a serpent. So Christ, when laid hold on by the hand of faith, is full of comfort — but not laid hold on, will prove a serpent to bite!

Use 2: As we would prove ourselves to be godly, let us labor for this good knowledge of the Lord. What pains men will take for the achievement of natural knowledge! Many spend years, searching out the knowledge of an earthly trifle. What pains, then, should we take in finding out the knowledge of God in Christ! There must be digging and searching for it, as one would search for a vein of silver: 'If you look for it as for silver and search for it as for hidden treasure, then you will understand the fear of the Lord and find the knowledge of God' (Proverbs 2:4-5).

This is the best knowledge. It as far surpasses all other knowledge, as the diamond surpasses a stone. No jewel we wear so adorns us as this: 'she is more precious than rubies' (Proverbs 3:15). 'But where can wisdom be found? Where does understanding dwell? Man does not comprehend its worth. It cannot be bought with the finest gold, nor can its price be weighed in silver. It cannot be bought with the gold of Ophir, with precious onyx or sapphires. Neither gold nor crystal can compare with it, nor can it be had for jewels of gold. The price of wisdom is beyond rubies.' (Job 28:12-18). The dark chaos was a fit emblem of an ignorant soul (Gen. 1:2) — but when God lights up the lamp of knowledge in the mind, what a new creation is there! Here the soul sparkles like the sun in its glory.

This knowledge is encouraging. We may say of worldly knowledge, as did Solomon, 'He who increases knowledge increases sorrow' (Eccles. 1:18). To know arts and science is to gather straw — but to know God in Christ is to gather pearl. This knowledge ushers in salvation (1 Tim. 2:4).

Question: But how shall we get this saving knowledge?

Answer: Not by the power of nature. Some speak of how far reason will go if put to good use; but, alas! the plumb line of reason is too short to fathom the deep things of God! A man can no more reach the saving knowledge of God by the power of reason, than a pigmy can reach the top of the pyramids. The light of nature will no more help us to see Christ, than the light of a candle will help us to understand. 'The natural man receives not the things of the Spirit of God: neither can he know them' (1 Cor. 2:14).

What shall we do, then, to know God in a soul-saving manner? I answer, let us implore the help of God's Spirit. Paul never saw himself blind — until a light shone from heaven (Acts 9:3). God must anoint our eyes before we can see! What need did Christ have to bid Laodicea to come to him for eye salve, if she could see before (Rev. 3:18)? Oh, let us beg the Spirit, who is 'the Spirit of revelation' (Eph. 1:17). Saving knowledge is not by speculation — but by inspiration, 'the inspiration of the Almighty gives them understanding' (Job 32:8).

We may have excellent notions in divinity — but the Holy Spirit must enable us to know them in a spiritual manner. A man may see the figures on a sun-dial — but he cannot tell how the time, unless the sun shines. We may read many truths in the Bible — but we cannot know them savingly until God's Spirit shines upon us: 'the Spirit searches all things, yes, the deep things of God' (1 Cor. 2:10). The Scripture reveals Christ to us — but the Spirit reveals Christ in us (Gal. 1:16). The Spirit makes known that which all the world cannot do, namely, the sense of God's love.

Use 3: You who have this saving, sanctifying knowledge flourishing in you, bless God for it! This is the heavenly anointing. The most excellent objects cannot be seen in the dark — but when the light appears, then every flower shines in its native beauty. So while men are in the midnight of a natural state, the beauty of holiness is hidden from them; but when the light of the Spirit comes in a saving manner, then those truths which they slighted before, appear in that glorious luster, and transport them with wonder and love.

Bless God, you saints, that he has removed your spiritual cataract, and has enabled you to discern those things which by nature's spectacles you could never see. How thankful Christ was to his Father for this! 'I thank you, O Father, Lord of heaven and earth, because you have hidden these things from the wise and prudent, and have revealed them unto babes' (Matt. 11:25). How you should admire free grace, that God has not only brought the light to you — but given you eyes to see it; that he has enabled you to know the truth 'as it is in Jesus' (Eph. 4:21); that he has opened, not only the eye of your understanding — but the eye of your conscience! It is a mercy you can never be thankful enough for — that God has so enlightened you that you should not 'Sleep the sleep of death'.

2. A godly man is a man moved by faith.

As gold is the most precious among the metals, so is faith among the graces. Faith cuts us off from the wild olive tree of nature, and grafts us into Christ. Faith is the vital artery of the soul: 'The just shall live by his faith' (Hab. 2:4). Such as are destitute of faith may breathe — but they lack spiritual life.

Faith enlivens all the graces; not a grace stirs until faith sets it working. Faith is to the soul what the animal spirits are to the body, exciting lively activity in it. Faith excites repentance. When I believe God's love to me, this makes me weep that I should sin against so good a God. Faith is the mother of hope; first we believe the promise, then we hope for it. Faith is the oil which feeds the lamp of hope. Faith and hope are two turtledove graces; take away one, and the other languishes. If the sinews are cut, the body is lame; if this sinew of faith is cut, hope is lame. Faith is the ground of patience; he who believes that God is his God, and that all providences work for his good, patiently yields himself to the will of God. Thus faith is a living principle.

The life of a saint is nothing but a life of faith. His prayer is the breathing of faith (Jas. 5:15). His obedience is the result of faith (Romans 16:26). A godly man lives by faith in Christ, as the beam lives in the sun: 'I live; yet not I — but Christ lives in me' (Gal. 2:20). A Christian, by the power of faith, sees above human reason, trades above the moon (2 Cor. 4:18). By faith his heart is calmed and quieted; he trusts himself and all his affairs to God (Psalm 112:7). As in a time of war, men get into a garrison and trust themselves and their treasures there, so 'the name of the Lord is a strong tower' (Proverbs 18:10), and a believer trusts all that he is worth in this garrison. 'I know whom I have believed, and am persuaded that he is able to keep that which I have committed unto him against that day' (2 Tim. 1:12). God trusted Paul with his gospel, and Paul trusted God with his soul.

Faith is a panacea — a remedy against all troubles. It is a godly man's anchor which he casts out into the sea of God's mercy, and is kept from sinking in despair. 'If only faith is firm, no ruin harms.'

Use: Let us test ourselves by this characteristic. Alas, how far from being godly are those who are destitute of faith! Such are altogether drowned in sense. Most men are spiritually blind; they can only see just before them (2 Pet. 1:9). I have read of a people in India who are born with one eye. Such are they who are born with the eye of reason — but lack the eye of faith, who because they do not see God with bodily eyes, do not believe in a God. They may as well not believe they have souls, because they cannot be seen.

Oh, where is he who lives in the heights, who has gone into the upper region and sees 'things not seen' (Heb. 11:27)? 'If men lived by faith, would they use sinful means for a livelihood?' (Chrysostom). If there were faith, would there be so much fraud? If theirs were living faith, would men, like dead fish, swim downstream? In this age there is scarcely so much faith to be found among men, as there is among the devils, 'for they believe and tremble' (Jas. 2:19).

3. A godly man is fired with love to God.

'I love the Lord, for he heard my voice; he heard my cry for mercy.' Psalm 116:1

Faith and love are the two hinges on which all religion turns. A true saint is carried in that chariot, 'the midst whereof is paved with love' (Cant 3:10). As faith enlivens, so love sweetens every duty. The sun mellows the fruit, so love mellows the services of religion, and gives them a better relish. A godly man is sick with love: 'Lord, you know that I love you' (John 21:16).

'Though, dear Savior, I denied you — yet it was for lack of strength, not for lack of love.' God is the fountain and quintessence of goodness. His beauty and sweetness lay constraints of love upon a gracious heart. God is the saint's portion (Psalm 119:57). And what more loved than a portion? 'I would hate my own soul,' says Augustine, 'if I found it not loving God.' A godly man loves God and therefore delights to be in his presence; he loves God and therefore takes comfort in nothing without him. 'Have you seen him whom my soul loves?' (Cant 3:3).

The pious soul loves God and therefore thirsts for him. The more he has of God, the more still he desires. A sip of the wine of the Spirit whets the appetite for more. The soul loves God and therefore rejoices to think 'of his appearing' (2 Tim. 4:8). He loves him and therefore longs to be with him. Christ was in Paul's heart, and Paul would be in Christ's bosom (Phil. 1:23). When the soul is once like God, it would gladly be with God. A gracious heart cries out, 'O that I had wings, that I might fly away, and be with my love, Christ!' The bird desires to be out of the cage, though it is hung with pearl.

Such is the love a gracious soul has to God, that many waters cannot quench it. He loves a frowning God.

A godly man loves God, though he is reduced to straits. A mother and her nine-year-old child were about to die of hunger. The child looked at its mother and said, 'Mother, do you think God will starve us?' 'No, child,' said the mother, 'he will not.' The child replied, 'But if he does, we must love him, and serve him.'

Use: Let us test our godliness by this touchstone: Do we love God? Is he our treasure and center? Can we, with David, call God our 'joy', yes, our 'exceeding joy' (Psalm 43:4)? Do we delight in drawing near to him, and 'come before his presence with singing'? (Psalm 100:2) Do we love him for his beauty more than his jewels? Do we love him, when he seems not to love us?

If this be the sign of a godly man, how few will be found in the number! Where is the man whose heart is dilated in love to God? Many court him — but few love him. People are for the most part eaten up with self-love; they love their ease, their worldly profit, their lusts — but they do not have a drop of love to God. If they loved God, would they be so willing to be rid of him? 'They say unto God, Depart from us' (Job 21:14). If they loved God, would they tear his name by their oaths? Does he who shoots his father in the heart, love him? Though they worship God, they do not love him; they are like the soldiers who bowed the knee to Christ, and mocked him (Matt. 27:29). He whose heart is a grave in which the love of God is buried, deserves to have that curse written upon his tombstone, 'Let him be Anathema Maranatha' (1 Cor. 16:22). A soul devoid of divine love is a temper which best suits damned spirits. But I shall waive this, and pass to the next.

4. A godly man is like God.

He has the same judgment as God; he thinks of things as God does; he has a Godlike disposition; he 'partakes of the divine nature' (2 Pet. 1:4). A godly man bears both God's name and image; godliness is Godlikeness. It is one thing to profess God, another thing to resemble him.

A godly man is like God in holiness. Holiness is the most brilliant pearl in the King of Heaven's crown: 'glorious in holiness' (Exod. 15:11). God's power makes him mighty; his mercy makes him lovely; but his holiness makes him glorious. The holiness of God is the intrinsic purity of his nature and his abhorrence of sin. A godly man bears some kind of analogy with God in this. He has the holy oil of consecration upon him: 'Aaron the saint of the Lord' (Psalm 106:16). Holiness is the badge and mark of Christ's people: 'The people of your holiness' (Isaiah 63:18).

The godly are a holy as well as a royal priesthood (1 Pet. 2:9). Nor have they only a frontispiece of holiness, like the Egyptian temples which were fair outside – but they are like Solomon's temple, which had gold inside. They have written upon their heart, 'Holiness to the Lord'. The holiness of the saints consists in their conformity to God's will, which is the rule and pattern of all holiness.

Holiness is a man's glory. Aaron put on garments 'for glory and for beauty' (Exod. 28:2). So when a person is invested with the embroidered garment of holiness, it is for glory and beauty.

The goodness of a Christian lies in his holiness, as the goodness of the air lies in its clarity, the worth of gold in its purity.

Question: In what do the godly reveal their holiness?

Answer:

1. In hating 'the garment spotted by the flesh' (Jude 23). The godly set themselves against evil, both in purpose and in practice. They are fearful of that which looks like sin (1 Thess. 5:22). The appearance of evil may harm a weak Christian. If it does not defile a man's own conscience, it may offend his brother's conscience; and to sin against him is to sin against Christ (1 Cor. 8:12). A godly man will not go as far as he may, lest he go further than he should; he will not swallow all that others may plead for. It is easy to put a golden color on rotten material.

2. In being advocates for holiness. 'I will speak of your testimonies also before kings, and will not be ashamed' (Psalm 119:46). When piety is calumniated in the world, the saints will stand up in its defense; they will wipe off the dust of a reproach, from the face of religion. Holiness defends the godly, and they will defend holiness; it defends them from danger, and they will defend it from disgrace.

Use 1: How can those who are unlike God be reputed to be godly? They have nothing of God in them, not one shred of holiness. They call themselves Christians – but blot out the word holiness; you may as well call it day at midnight.

So impudent are some, that they boast they are none of the holy ones. Is it not the Spirit of holiness which marks off the sheep of Christ, from the goats? 'You were sealed (or marked) with the Holy Spirit' (Eph. 1:13). And is it a matter for men to boast of, that they have none of the Spirit's earmark upon them? Does not the apostle say that 'without holiness no man shall see the Lord' (Heb. 12:14)? Such as bless themselves in their unholiness had best go and ring the bells for joy, that they shall never see God.

There are others who hate holiness. Sin and holiness never meet but they fight. Holiness discharges its fire of zeal against sin, and sin spits its venom of malice at holiness. Many pretend to love Christ as a Savior – but hate him as he is the Holy One (Acts 3:14).

Use 2: Let us strive to be like God in holiness.

1. This is God's great design which he drives on in the world. It is the object of the Word preached. The silver drops of the sanctuary are to water the seed of grace, and make a crop of holiness spring up. What use is there in the promises, if not to bribe us to holiness? What are all God's providential dispensations for – but to promote holiness? As the Lord makes use of all the seasons of the year, frost and heat, to produce the harvest, so all prosperous and adverse providences are for the promoting of the work of holiness in the soul. What is the object of the mission of the Spirit – but to make the heart holy? When the air is unwholesome by reason of fog and mist, the wind is a fan to winnow and purify the air. So the blowing of God's Spirit upon the heart is to purify it, and make it holy.

2. Holiness is that alone, which God is delighted with. When Tamerlane was presented with a pot of gold, he asked whether the gold had his father's stamp upon it. But when he saw it had the Roman stamp, he rejected it. Holiness is God's stamp and impress; if he does not see this stamp upon us, he will not own us.

3. Holiness fits us for communion with God. Communion with God is a paradox to the men of the world. Not everyone who hangs about the court speaks with the king. We may approach God in duties, and as it were hang about the court of heaven — yet not have communion with God. That which keeps up fellowship with God, is holiness. The holy heart enjoys much of God's presence; he feels heartwarming and heart-comforting virtue in an ordinance. Where God sees his likeness, there he gives his love.

5. A godly man is very exact and careful about the worship of God.

The Greek word for 'godly' signifies a true worshiper of God. A godly man reverences divine institutions — and is more for the purity of worship than the pomp. Mixture in sacred things is like a dash in the wine, which though it gives it a color — yet only adulterates it. The Lord wanted Moses to make the tabernacle 'according to the pattern showed to you in the mount' (Exod. 25:40). If Moses had left out anything in the pattern, or added anything to it, it would have been very offensive to God. The Lord has always given testimonies of his displeasure against such as have corrupted his worship. Nadab and Abihu offered 'Strange fire' (different than what God had sanctified on the altar), 'and fire went out from the Lord, and devoured them' (Lev. 10:1,2). Whatever is not of God's own appointment in his worship, he looks upon as 'Strange fire'. And no wonder he is so highly incensed at it, for it is as if God were not wise enough to appoint the manner in which he will be served. Men will try to direct him, and as if the rules for his worship were defective, they will attempt to correct the copy, and superadd their inventions.

A godly man dares not vary from the pattern which God has shown him in the Scripture. This is probably not the least reason why David was called 'a man after God's own heart', because he kept the springs of God's worship pure, and in matters sacred did not add anything of his own devising.

Use: By this characteristic we may test ourselves, whether we are godly. Are we careful about the things of God? Do we observe that mode of worship which has the stamp of divine authority upon it? It has dangerous consequences to make a medley in religion.

1. Those who will add to one part of God's worship will be as ready to take away from another. 'Laying aside the commandment of God, you hold the tradition of men' (Mark 7:8). They who will bring in a tradition, will in time lay aside a command. This the Papists are very guilty of; they bring in altars and crucifixes, and lay aside the second commandment. They bring in oil in baptism, and leave out the cup in the Lord's Supper. They bring in praying for the dead, and lay aside reading the Scriptures intelligibly to the living. Those who will introduce into God's worship that which he has not commanded, will be as ready to blot out that which he has commanded.

2. Those who are for outward mixtures in God's worship usually disregard of the vitals of religion — such as living by faith, leading a strict mortified life; these things are of less concern to them. Wasps have their combs — but no honey in them.

3. Superstition and profanity kiss each other. Has it not been known that those who have kneeled at a pillar, have reeled in drunkenness against a post?

4. Such as are devoted to superstition are seldom or never converted: 'publicans and harlots go into the kingdom of God before you' (Matt. 21:31). This was spoken to the chief priests, who

were great formalists, and the reason why such people are seldom wrought upon savingly is because they have a secret antipathy to the power of godliness. The serpent has a fine color — but it has a sting. So outwardly men may look zealous and devout — but retain a sting of hatred in their hearts against holiness. Hence it is that they who have been most hot on superstition have been most hot on persecution. The Church of Rome wears white linen (an emblem of innocence) — but the Spirit of God paints her out in scarlet (Rev. 17:4). Why is this? Not only because she puts on a scarlet robe — but because she is of a scarlet dye, having imbrued her hands in the blood of the saints (Rev. 17:6).

Let us, then, as we would show ourselves to be godly, keep close to the rule of worship, and in the things of Jehovah go no further than we can say, 'It is written'.

6. A godly man is a servant of God, not a servant of men.

This characteristic has two distinct branches. I shall speak of both in order.

1. A godly man is a servant of God

'We are the servants of the God of heaven' (Ezra 5:11); 'Epaphras, a servant of Christ' (Col. 4:12).

Question: In what sense is a godly man a servant of God?

Answer: In seven respects:

1. A servant leaves all others, and confines himself to one master. So a godly man leaves the service of sin, and betakes himself to the service of God (Romans 6:22). Sin is a tyrannizing thing; a sinner is a slave when he sins with most freedom. The wages which sin gives, may deter us from its service: 'the wages of sin is death' (Romans 6:23). Here is damnable pay! A godly man enlists himself in God's family, and is one of his menial servants: 'O Lord, truly I am your servant; I am your servant' (Psalm 116:16). David repeats himself, as if he had said, 'Lord, I have given my pledge; no one else can lay claim to me; my ear is bored to your service'.

2. A servant is not independent, at his own disposal — but at the disposal of his master. A servant must not do what he pleases — but be at the will of his master. Thus a godly man is God's servant. He is wholly at God's disposal. He has no will of his own. 'May your will be done on earth'. Some will say to the godly, 'Why cannot you behave like others? Why will you not drink and swear as others do?' The godly are God's servants; they must not do what they want — but be under the rules of the family; they must do nothing but what they can show their master's authority for.

3. A servant is bound. There are agreements and indentures sealed between him and his master. Thus there are indentures drawn in baptism, and in conversion the indentures are renewed and sealed. There we bind ourselves to God to be his sworn servants: 'I have sworn, and I will perform it, that I will keep your righteous judgments' (Psalm 119:106). A godly man has tied himself to the Lord by vow, and he makes conscience of his vow. He would rather die by persecution than live by perjury (Psalm 56:12).

4. A servant not only wears his master's uniform — but does his work. Thus a godly man works for God. Paul 'spent and was spent for Christ' (2 Cor. 12:15). He worked harder than all the other apostles (1 Cor. 15:10). A godly man is active for God to his last breath, 'even unto the end' (Psalm 119:112). Only 'the dead rest from their labors' (Rev. 14:13).

5. A servant follows his master; thus a godly man is a servant of God. While others follow after the beast, he follows after the Lamb (Rev. 13:3; 14:4). He wants to tread in the steps of Christ. If a master leaps over hedge and ditch, the servant will follow him. A godly man will follow Christ through afflictions: 'If any man will come after me, let him take up his cross daily, and

follow me' (Luke 9:23). Peter wanted to follow Christ on the water. A godly man will follow Christ though it is death at every step. He will keep his goodness when others are bad. As all the water in the salt sea cannot make the fish salty — but they still retain their freshness; so all the wickedness in the world cannot make a godly man wicked — but he still retains his piety. He will follow Christ in the worst times.

6. A servant is satisfied with his master's allowance. He does not say, 'I will have such provisions made ready'. If he has meager fare, he does not find fault. He knows he is a servant, and accepts his master's carving. In this sense, a godly man is God's servant; he is willing to live on God's allowance; if he has only some leftovers, he does not grumble. Paul knew he was a servant, therefore whether more or less fell to his share, he was indifferent (Phil. 4:11). When Christians complain at their condition, they forget that they are servants, and must live on the allowance of their heavenly Master. You who have the least grace from God, are debtors to his mercy.

7. A servant will stand up for the honor of his master. He cannot hear his master reproached — but will vindicate his credit. Thus, every godly man will stand up for the honor of his Master, Christ. 'My zeal has consumed me' (Psalm 119:139). A servant of God stands up for his truths. Some can hear God's name reproached, and his ways spoken against — yet remain silent. God will be ashamed of such servants, and reject them before men and angels.

Use: Let us declare ourselves godly by being servants of the most high God. Consider:

1. God is the best Master. He is punctilious in all his promises: 'There is no God like you, in heaven above, or on earth beneath, who keeps covenant and mercy with your servants ... not one word of all his good promise has failed' (1 Kings 8:23,56). God is of a most sweet, gracious disposition. He has this quality that he is 'Slow to anger' and 'ready to forgive' (Psalm 103:8; 86:5). In our needs, he relieves us; in our weakness, he pities us. He reveals his secrets to his servants (Psalm 25:14; Proverbs 3:32). He waits on his servants. Was there ever such a Master? 'It will be good for those servants whose master finds them watching when he comes. I tell you the truth, he will dress himself to serve, will have them recline at the table and will come and wait on them' (Luke 12:37). When we are sick, he makes our bed: 'you will make all his bed in his sickness' (Psalm 41:3). He holds our head when we are fainting. Other masters may forget their servants, and cast them off when they are old — but God will not: 'you are my servant: O Israel, you shall not be forgotten of me' (Isaiah 44:21). It is a slander to say that God is a hard Master.

2. God's service is the best service. There are six privileges in God's service:

(i) Freedom. Though the saints are bound to God's service — yet they serve him freely. God's Spirit, who is called a 'free Spirit' (Psalm 51:12), makes them free and cheerful in obedience. The Spirit carries them on the wings of delight; he makes duty a privilege; he does not force — but draw. He enlarges the heart in love and fills it with joy. God's service is perfect freedom.

(ii) Honor. David the king professed himself one of God's pensioners: 'I am your servant' (Psalm 143:12). Paul, when he wants to blaze his coat of arms, and set forth his best heraldry, does not call himself 'Paul, a Hebrew of the Hebrews', or 'Paul, of the tribe of Benjamin' — but 'Paul, a servant of Jesus Christ' (Romans 1:1). Theodosius thought it a greater dignity to be God's servant, than to be an emperor. Christ himself, who is equal with his Father, is nevertheless not ashamed of the title 'servant' (Isaiah 53:11). Every servant of God is a son; every subject is a prince! It is more honor to serve God than to have kings serve us. The angels in heaven are servants of the saints on earth.

(iii) Safety. God takes care of his servants. He gives them protection: 'You are my servant; fear not; for I am with you' (Isaiah 41:9,10). God hides his servants: 'in the secret of his tabernacle shall he hide me' (Psalm 27:5). That is, he shall keep me safe, as in the most holy place of the sanctuary, where none but the priests might enter. Christ's wings are both for healing and for hiding, for curing and securing us (Mal. 4:2). The devil and his instruments would soon devour the servants of God, if he did not set an invisible guard about them, and cover them with the golden feathers of his protection (Psalm 91:4). 'I am with you, and no man shall set on you to hurt you' (Acts 18:10). God's watchful eye is always on his people, and the enemies shall not do the mischief they intend to do; they shall not be destroyers — but physicians.

(iv) Gain. Atheists say, 'It is vain to serve God: and what profit is it that we have kept his ordinances?' (Mal. 3:14). Besides the advantages which God gives in this life (sweet peace of conscience), he reserves his best wine until last; he gives a glorious kingdom to his servants (Heb. 12:28). The servants of God may for a while be enslaved and abused — but they shall have promotion at last: 'where I am, there shall also my servant be' (John 12:26).

(v) Assistance. Other masters cut out work for their servants — but do not help them in their work. But our Master in heaven gives us not only work — but strength: 'you strengthened me with strength in my soul' (Psalm 138:3). God bids us serve him, and he will enable us to serve him: 'I will cause you to walk in my statutes' (Ezek. 36:27). The Lord not only fits work for us — but fits us for our work; with his command he gives enablement.

(vi) Supplies. A master will not let his servants be in need. God's servants shall be provided for: 'truly you shall be fed' (Psalm 37:3). Does God give us a Christ, and will he deny us a crust? 'The God who fed me all my life long' (Gen. 48:15). If God does not give us what we crave, he will give us what we need. The wicked, who are dogs, are fed (Phil. 3:2). If a man feeds his dog, surely he will feed his child! Oh, then, who would not be in love with God's service?

3. We are engaged to serve God. We are 'bought with a price' (1 Cor. 6:20). This is a metaphor taken from such as ransom captives from prison by paying a sum of money for them. They are to be at the service of those who ransomed them. So when the devil had taken us prisoners, Christ ransomed us with a price, not of money — but of blood. Therefore we are to be only at his service. If any can lay a better claim to us than Christ, we may serve them; but Christ having the best right to us, we are to cleave to him and enroll ourselves forever in his service.

2. A godly man is not the servant of men

'Be not you the servants of men' (1 Cor. 7:23).

Question: But is there no service we owe to men?

Answer: There is a threefold serving of men:

1. There is a civil service we owe to men, as the inferior to the superior. The servant is a living tool, as Aristotle says. 'servants, obey your masters' (Eph. 6:5).

2. There is a religious service we owe to men, when we are serviceable to their souls: 'your servants for Jesus' sake' (2 Cor. 4:5).

3. There is a sinful serving of men. This consists of three things:

(i) When we prefer men's injunctions before God's institutions. God commands one thing; man commands another. God says, 'Sanctify the Sabbath'; man says, 'Profane it.' When men's edicts have more force with us than God's precepts, this is to be the servants of men.

(ii) When we voluntarily prostitute ourselves to the impure lusts of men, we let them lord it over our consciences. When we are pliable and conformable to any beliefs, either Arminian or atheist, for either the gospel or the Koran. When we will be what others will have us be, then we are just like Issachar, who is 'a strong donkey crouching down between two burdens' (Gen. 49:14). This is not humility — but sordidness, and it is men-serving.

(iii) When we are advocates in a bad cause, pleading for any impious, unjustifiable act; when we baptize sin with the name of religion, and with our oratory wash the devil's face — this is to be the servants of men. In these cases, a godly person will not so unman himself, as to serve men. He says, like Paul, 'If I yet pleased men, I would not be the servant of Christ' (Gal. 1:10); and like Peter, 'We ought to obey God rather than men' (Acts 5:29).

Use: How many leagues distant from godliness, are those who serve men, who either for fear of punishment, or from hope of promotion, comply with the sinful commands of men, who will put their conscience under any yoke, and sail with any wind which blows profit. These are the 'Servants of men'; they have abjured their baptismal vow, and renounced the Lord who bought them.

To the one who is so bendable as to change into any form, and bow as low as hell to please men, I would say two things:

1. You who have learned all your postures, who can cringe and tack about — how will you look Christ in the face another day? When you say on your death bed, 'Lord, look on your servant', Christ shall disclaim you, and say, 'My servant? No! you renounced my service, you were 'a servant of men'; depart from me; I do not know you.' What a cold shoulder this will be at that day!

2. What does a man get, by sinfully enslaving himself? He gets a blot on his name, a curse on his estate, a hell in his conscience; no, even those who he basely stoops to, will scorn and despise him. How the high priests kicked off Judas! 'What do we care? That's your problem' (Matt. 27:4).

That we may not be the servants of men, let us abandon fear and advance faith (Esther 8:17). Faith is a world-conquering grace (1 John 5:4). It overcomes the world's music and threats; it steels a Christian with divine courage, and makes him stand immovable, like a rock in the midst of the sea.

7. A godly man prizes christ.

To illustrate this, I shall show:

A. That Jesus Christ is in himself precious.

B. That a godly man esteems him precious.

A. Jesus Christ is precious in himself.

'Behold, I lay a stone in Zion, a chosen and precious cornerstone' (1 Pet. 2:6).

1. Christ is compared to 'a bundle of myrrh' (Cant 1:13). Myrrh is very precious; it was one of the chief spices of which the holy anointing oil was made (Exod. 30:25).

(i) Myrrh is of a perfuming nature. So Christ perfumes our persons and services, so that they are a sweet odor to God. Why is the church, that heavenly bride, so perfumed with grace? Because Christ, that myrrh tree, has dropped his perfume upon her (Cant 3:6).

(ii) Myrrh is of an exhilarating nature. Its fragrance comforts and refreshes the spirits. So Christ comforts the souls of his people, when they are fainting under their sins and suffering.

2. Christ is compared to a pearl: 'when he had found one pearl of great price' (Matt. 13:46). Christ, this pearl, was little with regard to his humility — but of infinite value. Jesus Christ is a pearl that God wears in his bosom (John 1:18); a pearl whose luster drowns the world's glory (Gal. 6:14); a pearl that enriches the soul, the angelic part of man (1 Cor. 1:5); a pearl that

enlightens heaven (Rev. 21:23); a pearl so precious that it makes us precious to God (Eph. 1:6); a pearl that is consoling and restorative (Luke 2:25). This pearl of more value than heaven (Col. 1:16,17).

3. The preciousness of Christ is seen in three ways:

(i) He is precious in his person; he is the picture of his Father's glory (Heb. 1:3).

(ii) Christ is precious in his offices, which are several rays of the Sun of righteousness:

(a) Christ's prophetic office is precious (Deut. 18:15). He is the great oracle of heaven; he has a preciousness above all the prophets who went before him; he teaches not only the ear — but the heart! He who has 'the key of David' in his hand opened the heart of Lydia (Acts 16:14).

(b) Christ's priestly office is precious. This is the solid basis of our comfort. 'Now once has he appeared to put away sin by the sacrifice of himself' (Heb. 9:26). By virtue of this sacrifice, the soul may go to God with boldness: 'Lord, give me heaven; Christ has purchased it for me; he hung upon the cross — that I might sit upon the throne!' Christ's blood (death) and incense (intercession), are the two hinges on which our salvation turns.

(c) Christ's regal office is precious: 'On his robe and on his thigh he has this name written: KING OF KINGS AND LORD OF LORDS!' (Rev. 19:16). Christ has a pre-eminence above all other kings for majesty; he has the highest throne, the richest crown, the largest dominions, and the longest possession: 'Your throne, O God, is forever and ever' (Heb. 1:8). Though Christ has many assessors — those who sit with him (Eph. 2:6) — he has no successors. Christ sets up his scepter where no other king does; he rules the will and affections; his power binds the conscience. The angels take the oath of allegiance to him (Heb. 1:6). Christ's kingship is seen in two royal acts:

(1) In ruling his people. He rules with mercy and mildness; his regal rod has honey at the end of it. Christ displays the ensign of mercy, which makes so many volunteers run to his rule (Psalm 110:3). Holiness without mercy, and justice without mercy, would be dreadful — but mercy encourages poor sinners to trust in him.

(2) In overruling his enemies. He pulls down their pride, befools their policy, restrains their malice. That stone 'cut out of the mountain without hands, which smote the image' (Dan. 2:34) was an emblem, says Augustine, of Christ's monarchical power, conquering and triumphing over his enemies.

(iii) Christ is precious in his benefits. By Christ all dangers are removed; through Christ all mercies are conveyed. In his blood flows justification (Acts 13:39); sanctification (Heb. 9:14); fructification (John 1:16); pacification (Romans 5:1); adoption (Gal. 4:5); perseverance (Heb.12:2); glorification (Heb. 9:12). This will be a matter of sublimest joy to eternity. We read that those who had passed over the sea of glass stood with their harps and sang the song of Moses and the Lamb (Rev. 15:2,3). So when the saints of God have passed over the glassy sea of this world, they shall sing hallelujahs to the Lamb who has redeemed them from sin and hell, and has translated them into that glorious paradise, where they shall see God forever and ever.

B. A godly man esteems Christ as precious

'Yes, he is very precious to you who believe!' (1 Pet. 2:7). In the Greek it is 'an honor'. Believers have an honorable esteem of Christ. The psalmist speaks like one captivated with Christ's amazing beauty: 'there is none upon earth that I desire beside you' (Psalm 73:25). He did not say he had nothing; he had many comforts on earth — but he desired none but God; as if a wife should say that there is no one's company she prizes like her husband's. How did David prize Christ? 'You are fairer than the children of men' (Psalm 45:2). The spouse in the Song of

Solomon looked upon Christ as the the most incomparable one, 'the chief among ten thousand' (Cant 5:10). Christ outvies all others: 'Like an apple tree among the trees of the forest is my lover among the young men. I delight to sit in his shade, and his fruit is sweet to my taste.' (Cant 2:3). Christ infinitely more excels all the beauties and glories of this visible world than the apple tree surpasses the trees of the wild forest.

Paul so prized Christ that he made him his chief study: 'I determined not to know anything among you, save Jesus Christ' (1 Cor. 2:2). He judged nothing else of value. He knew Christ best: 'have I not seen Jesus Christ our Lord?' (1 Cor. 9:1). He saw him with his bodily eyes in a vision, when he was caught up into the third heaven (2 Cor. 12:2), and he saw him with the eye of his faith in the blessed supper. Therefore he knew him best. Consider how he slighted and despised other things in comparison with Christ: 'I count all things but loss for the excellency of the knowledge of Christ Jesus my Lord' (Phil. 3:8). Gain he esteemed loss, and gold he esteemed dung, in comparison with Christ. Indeed, a godly person cannot choose but set a high valuation upon Christ; he sees a fullness of value in him:

1. A fullness in regard to variety. 'In whom are hidden all the treasures' (Col. 2:3). No country has all commodities of its own growth — but Christ has all kinds of fulness — fullness of merit, of spirit, of love. He has a treasury adequate for all our needs.

2. A fullness in regard to degree. Christ has not only a few drops, or rays — but is more full of goodness than the sun is of light; he has the fullness of the Godhead (Col. 2:9).

3. A fullness in regard to duration. The fullness in the creature, like the brooks of Arabia, is soon dried up — but Christ's fullness is inexhaustible; it is a fullness overflowing and ever-flowing.

And this fullness is for believers: Christ is a common treasury or storehouse for the saints: 'of his fullness have all we received' (John 1:16). Put a glass under a still and it receives water out of the still, drop by drop. So those who are united to Christ have the dews and drops of his grace distilling on them. Well, then, may Christ be admired by all those who believe.

Use 1: Is a godly man a high prizer of Christ? Then what is to be thought of those who do not put a value upon Christ? Are they godly or not? There are four kinds of people who do not prize Christ:

1. The Jews. They do not believe in Christ: 'unto this day, the veil is upon their heart' (2 Cor. 3:15). They expect their future age and a Messiah still to come, as their own Talmud reports. They blaspheme Christ; they slight imputed righteousness; they despise the virgin Mary, calling her in derision Marah, which signifies bitterness; they vilify the gospel; they hold Christians in abomination; they regard it as not lawful for a Jew to take medicine from a Christian. Schecardus relates the story of one, Bendema, a Jew who was bitten by a snake. A Christian came to heal him — but he refused his help and chose rather to die than to be healed by a Christian. So do the Jews hate Christ and all that wear his uniform.

2. The Socinians, who acknowledge deny Christ's divinity. This is to set him below the angels, for human nature, simply considered, is inferior to the angelic (Psalm 8:5).

3. Proud nominal Christians, who do not lay the whole stress of their salvation upon Christ — but would mingle their dross with his gold, their duties with his merits. This is to steal a jewel from Christ's crown and implicitly to deny him to be a perfect Savior.

4. Airy theorists, who prefer the study of the arts and sciences before Christ. Not that the knowledge of these is not commendable: 'Moses was learned in all the wisdom of the Egyptians' (Acts 7:22). Human learning is of good use to prepare for the study of better things, as a coarser dye prepares the cloth for a richer and a deeper dye. But the fault is when the study

of Christ is neglected. The knowledge of Christ ought to have the preeminence. It was surely not without a mystery, that God allowed all Solomon's writings about birds and plants to be lost—but what he wrote about spiritual wisdom to be miraculously preserved, as if God would teach us that to know Christ (the true Wisdom) is the crowning knowledge (Proverbs 8:12). One leaf of this tree of life will give us more comfort on a deathbed than the whole realm of human science. What is it to know all the motions of the orbs and influences of the stars, and in the meantime to be ignorant of Christ, the bright Morning Star (Rev. 22:16)? What is it to understand the nature of minerals or precious stones, and not to know Christ the true Cornerstone (Isaiah 28:16)? It is undervaluing, yes, despising Christ, when with the loadstone we draw iron and straw to us—but neglect him who has tried gold to bestow on us (Rev. 3:18).

Use 2: Is it the sign of a godly person to be a Christ prizer? Then let us test our godliness by this: Do we set a high estimation on Christ?

Question: How shall we know if we truly prize Christ?

Answer 1: If we are prizers of Christ, then we prefer him in our judgments before other things. We value Christ above honor and riches; the Pearl of Great Price lies nearest our heart. He who prizes Christ esteems the gleanings of Christ, better than the world's vintage. He counts the worst things of Christ, better than the best things of the world. Moses 'regarded disgrace for the sake of Christ as of greater value than the treasures of Egypt' (Heb. 11:26). And is it thus with us? Has the price of worldly things fallen? Gregory Nazianzen solemnly blessed God that he had something to lose for Christ's sake. But alas, how few Nazianzens are to be found! You will hear some say they have honorable thoughts of Christ—but they prize their land and estate above him. The young man in the Gospel preferred his bags of gold before Christ. Judas valued thirty pieces of silver above him. May it not be feared, if an hour of trial comes, that there are many who would rather renounce their baptism, and throw off Christ's uniform—than hazard the loss of their earthly possessions for him?

Answer 2: If we are the prizers of Christ, we cannot live without him; things which we value, we know not how to be without. A man may live without music—but not without food. A child of God can lack health and friends—but he cannot lack Christ. In the absence of Christ, he says, like Job, 'I went mourning without the sun' (Job 30:28). I have the starlight of creature comforts—but I need the Sun of righteousness. 'Give me children,' said Rachel, 'or else I die' (Gen. 30:1). So the soul says, 'Lord, give me Christ, or I die. Give me one drop of the water of life to quench my thirst.' Let us test by this—do they prize Christ—who can manage well enough to be without him? Give a child a rattle--and it will not want gold. Give a worldling his lusts--and he will be content enough without Christ. Christ is a spiritual Rock (1 Cor. 10:4). Just let men have 'oil in the cruse' and they do not care about honey from this rock. If their trade has gone, they complain—but if God takes away the gospel, which is the ark wherein Christ the manna is hidden, they are quiet and tame enough. Do those prize Christ who can sit down content without him?

Answer 3: If we are prizers of Christ, then we shall not complain at any pains to get him. He who prizes gold, will dig for it in the mine. 'My soul follows hard after God' (Psalm 63:8). Plutarch reports of the Gauls, an ancient people in France, that after they had tasted the sweet wine of the Italian grape, they enquired after the country, and never rested until they had arrived at it. He in whose eye Christ is precious, never rests until he has gained him: 'I sought him whom my soul loves; I held him, and would not let him go' (Cant 3:1,4).

Test by this! Many say they have Christ in high veneration—but they are not industrious in the use of means to obtain him. If Christ would drop as a ripe fig into their mouth, they could be content to have him—but they will not put themselves to too much trouble to get him. Does he who will not exercise, or take the healing medicine, prize his health?

Answer 4: If we are prizers of Christ, then we take great pleasure in Christ. What joy a man takes in, that which he counts his treasure! He who prizes Christ makes him his greatest joy. He can delight in Christ when other delights have gone: 'Even though the fig trees have no blossoms, and there are no grapes on the vine; even though the olive crop fails, and the fields lie empty and barren; even though the flocks die in the fields, and the cattle barns are empty, yet I will rejoice in the Lord! I will be joyful in the God of my salvation!' (Habakkuk 3:17-18). Though a flower in a man's garden dies, he can still delight in his money and jewels. He who esteems Christ can solace himself in Christ, when there is a dearth of all other comforts..

Answer 5: If we are prizers of Christ, then we will part with our dearest pleasures for him. Paul said of the Galatians that they so esteemed him that they were ready to pull out their own eyes and give them to him (Gal. 4:15). He who esteems Christ, will pull out that lust which is as precious as his right eye! A wise man will throw away a poison for a medicine. He who sets a high value on Christ will part with his pride, unjust gain and sinful ways (Isaiah 30:32). He will set his feet on the neck of his sins.

Test by this! How can they be said to prize Christ--who will not leave a vanity for Him; or who prefer a damning pleasure before a saving Christ!

Answer 6: If we are prizers of Christ, we shall think we cannot have him at too dear a rate. We may buy gold too dearly but we cannot purchase Christ too dearly. Though we part with our blood for him, it is no lost bargain. The apostles rejoiced that they were graced so much as to be disgraced for Christ (Acts 5:41). They esteemed their fetters more precious than bracelets of gold. Do not let him who refuses to bear his cross, say that he prizes Christ. 'But since he has no root, he lasts only a short time. When trouble or persecution comes because of the word, he quickly falls away.' (Matt. 13:21).

Answer 7: If we are prizers of Christ, we will be willing to help others to get a part in him. That which we esteem excellent, we are desirous our friend should have a share in it. If a man has found a spring of water, he will call others that they may drink and satisfy their thirst. Do we commend Christ to others? Do we take them by the hand and lead them to Christ? This shows how few prize Christ, because they do not make more effort that their relations should have a part in him. They get land and riches for their posterity—but have no care to leave them the Pearl of Great Price as their portion.

Answer 8: If we are prizers of Christ, then we prize him in health as well as in sickness; when we are in wealth, as well as when we are in poverty. A friend is prized at all times; the Rose of Sharon is always sweet. He who values his Savior aright has as precious thoughts of him in a day of prosperity—as in a day of adversity. The wicked make use of Christ only when they are in straits—as the elders of Gilead went to Jephthah, when they were in distress (Judges 11:7). Themistocles complained of the Athenians, that they only ran to him as they did to a tree, to shelter them in a storm. The wicked desire Christ only for shelter. The Hebrews never chose their judges except when they were in some imminent danger. Godless people never look for Christ except at death, when they are in danger of hell.

Use 3: As we would prove to the world that we have the impress of godliness on us, let us be prizers of Jesus Christ; he is elect, precious. Christ is the wonder of beauty. Pliny said of the mulberry tree that there is nothing in it but what is therapeutic and useful: the fruit, leaves and bark. So there is nothing in Christ but what is precious. His name is precious, his virtues precious, his blood precious—more precious than the world.

Oh, then, let us have endearing thoughts of Christ, let him be accounted our chief treasure and delight. This is the reason why millions perish — because they do not prize Christ. Christ is the door by which men are to enter heaven (John 10:9). If they do not know this door, or are so proud that they will not stoop to go in at it, how can they be saved? That we may have Christ-admiring thoughts, let us consider:

1. We cannot prize Christ at too high a rate. We may prize other things above their value. That is our sin. We commonly overrate the creature; we think there is more in it than there is; therefore God withers our gourd, because we over-prize it. But we cannot raise our esteem of Christ high enough. He is beyond all value! There is no ruby or diamond but the jeweler can set a fair price on it. He can say it is worth so much and no more. But Christ's worth can never be fully known. No seraphim can set a due value on him. His are unsearchable riches (Eph. 3:8). Christ is more precious than the soul, than the angels, than heaven.

2. Jesus Christ has highly prized us. He took our flesh upon him (Heb. 2:16). He made his soul an offering for us (Isaiah 53:10). How precious our salvation was to Christ! Shall not we prize and adore him who has put such a value upon us?

3. Not to prize Christ is great imprudence. Christ is our guide to glory. It is folly for a man to slight his guide. He is our physician (Mal. 4:2). It is folly to despise our physician.

The ungodly choose things of no value, before Christ! 'You blind fools!' (Matthew 23:17). If a person chooses an apple before a priceless diamond, he is judged to be a fool. How many such idiots are there, who choose the gaudy, empty things of this life--before the Prince of Glory! Will not Satan beggar them at last for fools?

4. Some slight Christ now and say, 'There is no beauty that we should desire him' (Isaiah 53:2). There is a day coming shortly when Christ will as much slight them. He will set as light by them as they do by him. He will say, 'I know you not' (Luke 13:27). What a slighting word that will be, when men cry, 'Lord Jesus, save us!' and he says, 'I was offered to you but you would would not have me; you scorned me, and now I will scorn you. Depart from me, I do not know you!' This is all that sinners get by rejecting the Lord of life. At the Day of Judgment, Christ will slight those who have slighted him in the day of grace.

8. A godly man weeps.

David sometimes sang with his harp; and sometimes the organ of his eye wept: 'I water my couch with my tears' (Psalm 6:6). Christ calls his spouse his 'dove' (Cant 2:14). The dove is a weeping creature. Grace dissolves and liquefies the soul, causing a spiritual thaw. The sorrow of the heart runs out at the eye (Psalm 31:9).

The Rabbis report that the same night on which Israel departed from Egypt towards Canaan, all the idols of Egypt were broken down by lightning and earthquake. So at that very time at which men go forth from their natural condition towards heaven, all the idols of sin in the heart must be broken down by repentance! A melting heart is the chief branch of the covenant of grace (Ezek. 36:26), and the product of the Spirit: 'I will pour upon the house of David the spirit of grace, and they shall look upon me whom they have pierced, and they shall mourn for him' (Zech. 12:10).

Question: But why is a godly man a weeper? Is not sin pardoned, which is the ground of joy? Has he not had a transforming work upon his heart? Why, then, does he weep?

Answer: A godly man finds enough reasons for weeping:

1. He weeps for indwelling sin, the law in his members (Romans 7:23), the outbursts and first risings of sin. His nature is a poisoned fountain. A regenerate person grieves that he carries

with him, that which is enmity to God! His heart is like a wide sea in which there are innumerable creeping things (Psalm 104:25) — vain, sinful thoughts. A child of God laments hidden wickedness; he has more evil in him than he knows of. There are those windings in his heart which he cannot trace — an unknown world of sin. 'Who can understand his errors?' (Psalm 19:12).

2. A godly man weeps for clinging corruption. If he could get rid of sin, there would be some comfort — but he cannot shake off this viper! Sin cleaves to him like leprosy! Though a child of God forsakes his sin — yet sin will not forsake him. 'Concerning the rest of the beasts, they had their dominion taken away: yet their lives were prolonged for a season' (Dan. 7:12). So though the dominion of sin is taken away — yet its life is prolonged for a season; and while sin lives, it molests! The Persians were daily enemies to the Romans and would always be invading their frontiers. So sin 'wars against the soul' (1 Pet. 2:11). And there is no cessation of war — until death. Will not this cause tears?

3. A child of God weeps that he is sometimes overcome by the prevalence of corruption. 'For I do not do the good that I want to do, but I practice the evil that I do not want to do.' (Romans 7:19). Paul was like a man carried downstream. How often a saint is overpowered by pride and passion! When David had sinned, he steeped his soul in the brinish tears of repentance. It cannot but grieve a regenerate person to think he should be so foolish as, after he has felt the smart of sin — still to put this fire in his bosom again!

4. A godly heart grieves that he can be no more holy. It troubles him that he shoots so short of the rule and standard which God has set. 'I would', says he, 'love the Lord with all my heart. But how defective my love is! How far short I come of what I should be; no, of what I might have been! What can I see in my life — but either blanks or blots?'

5. A godly man sometimes weeps out of the sense of God's love. Gold is the finest and most solid of all the metals — yet it is soonest melted in the fire. Gracious hearts, which are golden hearts, are the soonest melted into tears by the fire of God's love. I once knew a holy man, who was walking in his garden and shedding plenty of tears, when a friend came on him accidentally and asked him why he wept. He broke forth into this pathetic expression: 'Oh, the love of Christ! Oh, the love of Christ!' Thus have we seen the cloud melted into water, by the sunbeams.

6. A godly person weeps because the sins he commits are in some sense worse than the sins of other men. The sin of a justified person is very odious:

(i) The sin of a justified person is odious — because he acts contrary to his own principles. He sins not only against the rule — but against his principles, against his knowledge, vows, prayers, hopes, experiences. He knows how dearly sin will cost him — yet he adventures upon the forbidden fruit!

(ii) The sin of a justified person is odious, because it is a sin of unkindness (1 Kings 11:9). Peter's denying of Christ was a sin against love. Christ had enrolled him among the apostles. He had taken him up into the Mount of Transfiguration and shown him the glory of heaven in a vision. Yet after all this dazzling mercy — it was base ingratitude, that he should deny Christ! This made him go out and 'weep bitterly' (Matt. 26:75). He baptized himself, as it were, in his own tears! The sins of the godly go nearest to God's heart. The sins of others anger God; the sins of the godly grieve him! The sins of the wicked pierce Christ's side! The sins of the godly wound his heart! The unkindness of a spouse, goes nearest to the heart of her husband.

(iii) The sin of a justified person is odious, because it reflects more dishonor upon God. 'By this deed you have given great occasion to the enemies of the Lord to blaspheme' (2 Sam. 12:14).

The sins of God's people put black spots on the face of piety. Thus we see what cause there is why a child of God should weep even after conversion. 'Can whoever sows such things refrain from tears?'

Now this sorrow of a godly man for sin, is not a despairing sorrow. He does not mourn without hope. 'Iniquities prevail against me' (Psalm 65:3) — there is the holy soul weeping. 'As for our transgressions, you shall purge them away' — there is faith triumphing.

Godly sorrow is excellent. There is as much difference between the sorrow of a godly man, and the sorrow of a wicked man — as between the water of a spring which is clear and sweet, and the water of the sea which is salt and brackish. A godly man's sorrow has these three qualifications:

(a) Godly sorrow is inward. It is a sorrow of soul. Hypocrites 'disfigure their faces' (Matt. 6:16). Godly sorrow goes deep. It is a 'pricking at the heart' (Acts 2:37). True sorrow is a spiritual martyrdom, therefore called 'soul affliction' (Lev. 23:29).

(b) Godly sorrow is sincere. It is more for the evil that is in sin — than the evil which follows after sin. It is more for the spot — than the sting. Hypocrites weep for sin only as it brings affliction. Hypocrites never send forth the streams of their tears, except when God's judgments are approaching.

(c) Godly sorrow is influential. It makes the heart better: 'by the sadness of the countenance, the heart is made better' (Eccles. 7:3). Divine tears not only wet — but wash; they purge out the love of sin!

Use 1: How far from being godly are those who scarcely ever shed a tear for sin! If they lose a near relation — they weep. But though they are in danger of losing God and their souls — they do not weep. How few know what it is to be in an agony for sin, or what a broken heart means! Their eyes are not like the 'fishpools in Heshbon', full of water (Cant 7:4) — but rather like the mountains of Gilboa, which had 'no dew' upon them (2 Sam. 1:21). It was a greater plague for Pharaoh to have his heart turned into stone — than to have his rivers turned into blood.

The wicked, if they sometimes shed a tear — are never the better. They go on in wickedness, and do not drown their sins in their tears!

Use 2: Let us strive for this divine characteristic. Be weepers! This is 'a repentance not to be repented of' (2 Cor. 7:10). It is reported of Bradford, the martyr, that he was of a melting spirit; he seldom sat down to his meal but some tears trickled down his cheeks. There are two lavers to wash away sin: blood and tears. The blood of Christ washes away the guilt of sin; our tears wash away the filth of sin.

Repenting tears are precious. God puts them in his bottle (Psalm 56:8). Repenting tears are beautifying. To God — a tear in the eye, adorns more than a ring on the finger. Oil makes the face shine (Psalm 104:15). Tears make the heart shine. Repenting tears are comforting. A sinner's mirth turns to melancholy. A saint's mourning turns to music! Repentance may be compared to myrrh, which though it is bitter to the taste — is comforting to the spirits. Repentance may be bitter to the flesh, but it is most refreshing to the soul. Wax which melts is fit for the seal. A melting soul is fit to take the stamp of all heavenly blessing. Let us give Christ the water of our tears — and he will give us the wine of his blood!

9. A godly man is a lover of the Word

'O how love I your law!' Psalm 119:97

1. A godly man loves the written Word

Chrysostom compares the Scripture to a garden set with nuts and flowers. A godly man delights to walk in this garden and sweetly solace himself. He loves every branch and part of the Word:

1. He loves the counseling part of the Word, as it is a directory and rule of life. The Word is the sole rule of Christian duty. It contains in it things to be believed and practiced. A godly man loves the teachings of the Word.

2. He loves the threatening part of the Word. The Scripture is like the Garden of Eden: as it has a tree of life in it, so it has a flaming sword at its gates. This is the threatening of the Word. It flashes fire in the face of every person who goes on obstinately in wickedness. 'Surely God will crush the heads of his enemies, the hairy crowns of those who go on in their sins.' (Psalm 68:21). The Word gives no indulgence to evil. It will not let a man halt between God and sin. The true mother would not let the child be divided (1 Kings 3:26), and God will not have the heart divided. The Word thunders out threatenings against the very appearance of evil. It is like that flying roll full of curses (Zech. 5:1).

A godly man loves the imprecations of the Word. He knows there is love in every threat. God would not have us perish; he therefore mercifully threatens us, so that he may scare us from sin. God's threats are like the life-buoy, which shows the rocks in the sea and threatens death to such as come near. The threat is a curbing bit to check us, so that we may not run in full stride to hell. There is mercy in every threat.

3. He loves the consolatory part of the Word—the promises. He goes feeding on these as Samson went on his way eating the honeycomb (Judges 14:8,9). The promises are all marrow and sweetness. They are our refreshing draught when we are fainting; they are the conduits of the water of life. 'In the multitude of my thoughts within me your comforts delight my soul' (Psalm 94:19). The promises were David's harp to drive away sad thoughts; they were the breast which gave him the milk of divine consolation.

A godly man shows his love to the Written Word:

(1) By diligently reading it. The noble Bereans 'searched the Scriptures daily' (Acts 17:11). Apollos was mighty in the Scriptures (Acts 18:24). The Word is our Magna Charta for heaven; we should be daily reading over this charter. The Word shows what is truth, and what is error. It is the field where the pearl of great price is hidden. How we should dig for this pearl! A godly man's heart is the library to hold the Word of God; it dwells richly in him (Col. 3:16). It is reported of Melanchthon that when he was young, he always carried the Bible with him and read it greedily. The Word has a double work: to teach us and to judge us. Those who will not be taught by the Word, shall be judged by the Word. Oh, let us make ourselves familiar with the Scripture! What if it should be as in the times of Diocletian, who commanded by proclamation that the Bible be burned? Or as in Queen Mary's days, when it spelled death to have a Bible in English? By diligent conversing with Scripture, we may carry a Bible in our heads!

(2) By frequently meditating on it. 'It is my meditation all the day' (Psalm 119:97). A pious soul meditates on the truth and holiness of the Word. He not only has a few transient thoughts—but leaves his mind steeping in the Scripture. By meditation, he sucks honey from this sweet flower, and ruminates on holy truths in his mind.

(3) By delighting in it. It is his recreation. 'When your words came, I ate them; they were my joy and my heart's delight' (Jer. 15:16). Never did a man take such delight in a dish that he loved, as the prophet did in the Word. And indeed, how can a saint choose but take great pleasure in the

Word? All of his eternal hopes are contained in it. Does not a son take pleasure in reading his father's will and testament, in which he bequeaths his estate to him?

(4) By hiding it. 'Your word have I hid in my heart' (Psalm 119:11) — as one hides a treasure so that it should not be stolen. The Word is the jewel; the heart is the cabinet where it must be locked up. Many hide the Word in their memory — but not in their heart. And why would David enclose the Word in his heart? 'That I might be kept from sinning against you.' As a man would carry an antidote about him when he comes near an infected place, so a godly man carries the Word in his heart as a spiritual antidote to preserve him from the infection of sin. Why have so many been poisoned with error, others with moral vice — but because they have not hidden the Word as a holy antidote in their heart?

(5) By defending it. A wise man will not let his land be taken from him; but will defend his title. David looked upon the Word as his land of inheritance: 'Your testimonies have I taken as a heritage forever' (Psalm 119:111). And do you think he would let his inheritance be wrested out of his hands? A godly man will not only dispute for the Word but die for it: 'I saw under the altar the souls of those who were slain for the word of God' (Rev. 6:9).

(6) By preferring it above most precious things.

(a) Above food. 'I have esteemed the words of his mouth more than my necessary food' (Job 23:12).

(b) Above riches. 'The law of your mouth is better unto me than thousands of gold and silver' (Psalm 119:72).

(c) Above worldly honor. Memorable is the story of King Edward the Sixth. On the day of his coronation, when they presented three swords before him, signifying to him that he was monarch of three kingdoms, the king said, 'There is still one sword missing.' On being asked what that was, he answered, 'The Holy Bible, which is the 'Sword of the Spirit' and is to be preferred before these ensigns of royalty.'

(7) By talking about it. 'My tongue shall speak of your word' (Psalm 119:172). As a covetous man talks of his rich purchase, so a godly man speaks of the Word. What a treasure it is, how full of beauty and sweetness! Those whose mouths the devil has gagged, who never speak of God's Word, indicate that they never reaped any good from it.

(8) By conforming to it. The Word is his sundial, by which he sets his life, the balance in which he weighs his actions. He copies out the Word in his daily walk: 'I have kept the faith' (2 Tim. 4:7). Paul kept the doctrine of faith, and lived the life of faith.

Question: Why is a godly man a lover of the Word?

Answer: Because of the excellence of the Word.

1. The Word is our pillar of fire to guide us. It shows us what rocks we are to avoid; it is the map by which we sail to the new Jerusalem.

2. The Word is a spiritual mirror through which we may see our own hearts. The mirror of nature, which the heathen had, revealed spots in their lives — but this mirror reveals spots in the imagination; that mirror revealed the spots of their unrighteousness, this reveals the spots of our righteousness. 'When the commandment came, sin revived, and I died' (Romans 7:9). When the Word came like a mirror, all my opinion of self-righteousness died.

3. The Word of God is a sovereign comfort in distress. While we follow this cloud, the rock follows us — 'This is my comfort in my affliction: for your word has quickened me' (Psalm 119:50). Christ is the fountain of living water, the Word is the golden pipe through which it runs! What can revive at the hour of death but the word of life (Phil. 2:16)?

A godly man loves the Word, because of the efficacy it has had upon him. This day-star has risen in his heart, and ushered in the Sun of righteousness.

2. A godly man loves the preached Word, which is a commentary upon the Written Word. The Scriptures are the sovereign oils and balsams; the preaching of the Word is the pouring of them out. The Scriptures are the precious spices; the preaching of the Word is the beating of these spices, which causes a wonderful fragrance and delight. The Preached Word is 'the rod of God's strength' (Psalm 110:2) and 'the breath of his lips' (Isaiah 11:4). What was once said of the city of Thebes, that it was built by the sound of Amphius' harp, is much more true of soul conversion—it is built by the sound of the gospel harp. Therefore the preaching of the Word is called 'the power of God to salvation' (1 Cor. 1:24). By this, Christ is said now to speak to us from heaven (Heb. 12:25). This ministry of the Word is to be preferred before the ministry of angels.

A godly man loves the preached Word, partly from the good he has found by it—he has felt the dew fall with this manna—and partly because of God's institution. The Lord has appointed this ordinance to save him. The king's image makes the coin current. The stamp of divine authority on the Preached Word makes it an instrument conducive to men's salvation.

Use: Let us test by this characteristic whether we are godly: Are we lovers of the Word?

1. Do we love the written Word? What sums of money the martyrs gave for a few leaves of the Bible! Do we make the Word our bosom friend? As Moses often had 'the rod of God' in his hand, so we should have 'the Book of God' in our hand. When we need direction, do we consult this sacred oracle? When we find corruptions strong, do we make use of this 'sword of the Spirit' to hew them down? When we are disconsolate, do we go to this bottle of the water of life for comfort? Then we are lovers of the Word!

But alas, how can they who are seldom conversant with the Scriptures say they love them? Their eyes begin to be sore when they look at a Bible. The two testaments are hung up like rusty armor, which is seldom or never made use of. The Lord wrote the law with his own finger—but though God took pains to write, men will not take pains to read. They would rather look at a pack of cards, than at a Bible!

2. Do we love the preached Word? Do we prize it in our judgments? Do we receive it into our hearts? Do we fear the loss of the preached Word more than the loss of peace and trade? Is it the removal of the ark, which troubles us?

Again, do we attend to the Word with reverential devotion? When the judge is giving his charge on the bench, all attend. When the Word is preached, the great God is giving us his charge. Do we listen to it as to a matter of life and death? This is a good sign that we love the Word.

Again, do we love the holiness of the Word (Psalm 119:140)? The Word is preached to beat down sin and advance holiness. Do we love it for its spirituality and purity? Many love the Preached Word only for its eloquence and notion. They come to a sermon as to a music lecture (Ezek. 33:31,32) or as to a garden to pick flowers—but not to have their lusts subdued or their hearts bettered. These are like a foolish woman who paints her face—but neglects her health!

Again, do we love the convictions of the Word? Do we love the Word when it comes home to our conscience and shoots its arrows of reproof at our sins? It is the minister's duty sometimes to reprove. He who can speak smooth words in the pulpit—but does not know how to reprove, is like a sword with a fine handle, but without an edge! 'Rebuke them sharply' (Titus 2:15). Dip the nail in oil—reprove in love—but strike the nail home! Now Christian, when the Word touches on your sin and says, 'You are the man!' do you love the reproof? Can you bless God that 'the sword of the Spirit' has divided between you and your lusts? This is indeed a sign of grace and shows that you are a lover of the Word.

A corrupt heart loves the comforts of the Word—but not the reproofs: 'You hate the one who reproves in court and despise him who tells the truth!' (Amos 5:10). 'Their eyes flash with fire!' Like venomous creatures that at the least touch spit poison, 'When they heard these things, they were enraged in their hearts and gnashed their teeth at him!' (Acts 7:54). When Stephen touched their sins, they were furious and could not endure it.

Question: How shall we know that we love the reproofs of the Word?

Answer 1: When we desire to sit under a heart-searching ministry. Who cares for medicines that will not work? A godly man does not choose to sit under a ministry that will not work upon his conscience.

Answer 2: When we pray that the Word may meet with our sins. If there is any traitorous lust in our heart, we would have it found out and executed. We do not want sin covered—but cured! We can open our breast to the sword of the Word and say, 'Lord, smite this sin!'

Answer 3: When we are thankful for a reproof: 'Let a righteous man strike me--it is a kindness; let him rebuke me--it is oil on my head. My head will not refuse it.' (Psalm 141:5). David was glad for a reproof. Suppose a man were in the mouth of a lion, and another should shoot the lion and save the man, would he not be thankful? So, when we are in the mouth of sin, as of a lion, and the minister by a reproof shoots this sin to death, shall we not be thankful?

A gracious soul rejoices when the sharp lance of the Word has pierced his abscess. He wears a reproof like a jewel on his ear: 'Like an earring of gold or an ornament of fine gold is a wise man's rebuke to a listening ear.' (Proverbs 25:12). To conclude, it is convincing preaching which must do the soul good. A nipping reproof prepares for comfort, as a nipping frost prepares for the sweet flowers of spring.

10. A godly man has the Spirit of God residing in him

'The Holy Spirit which dwells in us' (2 Tim. 1:14; Gal. 4:6). The Holy Spirit is in the godly, in whom he flows in measure. They have his presence and receive his sacred influences. When the sun comes into a room, it is not the body of the sun which is there, but the beams which sparkle from it. Indeed, some divines have thought that the godly have more than the indwelling of the Spirit; though to say how it is more is ineffable—is fitter for a more seraphic pen than mine to describe. The Spirit of God reveals himself in a gracious soul in two ways:

1. By his motions

These are some of that sweet perfume, which the Spirit breathes upon the heart, by which it is raised into a kind of angelic frame.

Question 1: But how may we distinguish the motions of the Spirit from a delusion?

Answer: The motions of the Spirit are always consonant with the Word. The Word is the chariot in which the Spirit of God rides; whichever way the tide of the Word runs—that way the wind of the Spirit blows.

Question 2: How may the motions of the Spirit in the godly be distinguished from the impulses of a natural conscience?

Answer 1: A natural conscience may sometimes provoke to the same thing as the Spirit does— but not from the same principle. Natural conscience is a spur to duty—but it drives a man to do his duties for fear of hell—as the galley slave tugs at the oar for fear of being beaten. Whereas the Spirit moves a child of God from a more noble principle — it makes him serve God out of choice, and esteem duty his privilege.

Answer 2: The impulses of a natural conscience drive men only to easier duties of religion, in which the heart is less exercised, like perfunctory reading or praying. But the motions of the Spirit in the godly go further, causing them to do the most irksome duties, like self-reflection, self-humbling; yes, perilous duties, like confessing Christ's name in times of danger. Divine motions in the heart are like new wine which seeks vent. When God's Spirit possesses a man, he carries him full sail through all difficulties!

2. By his virtues. These are various:

(1) God's Spirit has a teaching virtue. The Spirit teaches convincingly (John 16:8). He so teaches as to persuade.

(2) God's Spirit has a sanctifying virtue. The heart is naturally polluted — but when the Spirit comes into it, he works sin out and grace in. The Spirit of God was represented by the dove, an emblem of purity. The Spirit makes the heart a temple of purity and a paradise for pleasantness. The holy oil of consecration was nothing but a prefiguring of the Spirit (Exod. 30:25). The Spirit sanctifies a man's mind, causing it to mint holy meditations. He sanctifies his will, biasing it to good, so that now it shall be as delightful to serve God as before it was to sin against him. Sweet powders perfume the linen. So God's Spirit in a man, perfumes him with holiness and makes his heart a picture of holiness.

(3) God's Spirit has a vivifying virtue. 'The Spirit gives life' (2 Cor. 3:6). As the blowing in an flute makes it sound, so the breathing of the Spirit causes life and motion. When the prophet Elijah stretched himself upon the dead child, it revived (1 Kings 17:22); so God's Spirit stretching himself upon the soul, infuses life into it.

As our life is from the Spirit's operations, so is our liveliness: 'the Spirit lifted me up' (Ezek. 3:14). When the heart is bowed down and is listless to duty, the Spirit of God lifts it up. He puts a sharp edge upon the affections; he makes love ardent, and hope lively. The Spirit removes the weights of the soul and gives it wings: 'Before I was aware, my soul became like the chariots of Amminadib' (Cant 6:12). The wheels of the soul were pulled off before, and it drove on heavily — but when the Spirit of the Almighty possesses a man, now he runs swiftly in the ways of God, and his soul is like the chariots of Amminadib.

(4) God's Spirit has a regulating virtue. He rules and governs. God's Spirit sits paramount in the soul; he gives check to the violence of corruption; he will not allow a man to be vain and loose like others. The Spirit of God will not be put out of office; he exercises his authority over the heart, 'bringing into captivity every thought to the obedience of Christ' (2 Cor. 10:5).

(5) The Spirit has a mollifying virtue. Therefore he is compared to fire which softens the wax. The Spirit turns flint into flesh: 'I will give you a heart of flesh' (Ezek. 36:26). How shall this be effected? 'I will put my Spirit within you' (v.27). While the heart is hard, it lies like a log, and is not wrought upon either by judgments or by mercies — but when God's Spirit comes in, he makes a man's heart as tender as his eye — and now it is made yielding to divine impressions.

(6) The Spirit of God has a fortifying virtue. He infuses strength and assistance for work; he is a Spirit of power (2 Tim. 1:7). God's Spirit carries a man above himself: 'strengthened with might by his Spirit in the inner man' (Eph. 3:16). The Spirit confirms faith and animates courage. He lifts one end of the cross, and makes it lighter to bear. The Spirit gives not only a sufficiency of strength — but an abundance.

Question: How shall we know whether we are acting in the strength of God's Spirit, or in the strength of our own abilities?

Answer 1: When we humbly cast ourselves upon God for assistance, as David going out against Goliath cast himself upon God for help: 'I come to you in the name of the Lord' (1 Sam. 17:45).

Answer 2: When our duties are divinely qualified, and we do them with pure aims.

Answer 3: When we have found God going along with us, we give him the glory for everything (1 Cor. 15:10). This clearly evinces that the duty was carried on by the strength of God's Spirit more than by innate abilities of our own.

(7) God's Spirit has a comforting virtue. The sky, though it is a bright and transparent body, still has interposed clouds. Just so, sadness may arise in a gracious heart (Psalm 43:5). This sadness is caused usually through the malice of Satan, who, if he cannot destroy us, will disturb us. But God's Spirit within us, sweetly cheers and revives. He is called the parakletos, 'the Comforter' (John 14:16). These comforts are real and palpable. Hence it is called 'the seal of the Spirit' (Eph. 1:13). When a deed is sealed, it is firm and unquestionable. So when a Christian has the seal of the Spirit, his comforts are confirmed. Every godly man has these revivings of the Spirit in some degree; he has the seeds and beginnings of joy, though the flower is not fully ripe and blown.

Question: How does the Spirit give comfort?

Answer 1: By showing us that we are in a state of grace. A Christian cannot always see his riches. The work of grace may be written in the heart, like shorthand which a Christian cannot read. The Spirit gives him a key to open these dark characters, and spell out his adoption, whereupon he has joy and peace. 'We have received the Spirit which is of God; that we might know the things that are freely given to us of God' (1 Cor. 2:12).

Answer 2: The Spirit comforts by giving us some ravishing apprehensions of God's love. 'The love of God is shed abroad in our hearts by the Holy Spirit' (Romans 5:5). God's love is a box of precious ointment, and it is only the Spirit who can break this box open, and fill us with its sweet perfume.

Answer 3: The Spirit comforts by taking us to the blood of Christ. As when a man is weary and ready to faint, we take him to the water, and he is refreshed; so when we are fainting under the burden of sin, the Spirit takes us to the fountain of Christ's blood: 'In that day there shall be a fountain opened ... ' (Zech. 13:1). The Spirit enables us to drink the waters of justification which run out of Christ's side. The Spirit applies whatever Christ has purchased; he shows us that our sins are done away in Christ, and though we are spotted and defiled in ourselves—we are undefiled in our Head, Christ.

Answer 4: The Spirit comforts by enabling conscience to comfort. The child must be taught, before it can speak. The Spirit opens the mouth of conscience, and helps it to speak and witness to a man that his state is good, whereupon he begins to receive comfort: 'conscience also bearing me witness in the Holy Spirit' (Romans 9:1). Conscience draws up a certificate for a man, then the Holy Spirit comes and signs the certificate.

Answer 5: The Spirit conveys the oil of joy through two golden pipes:

1. The Ordinances. As Christ in prayer had his countenance changed (Luke 9:29) and there was a glorious luster upon his face; so often in the use of holy ordinances the godly have such raptures of joy and soul transfigurations, that they have been carried above the world, and despised all things below.

2. The Promises. The promises are comforting:

(1) For their sureness (Romans 4:16). God in the promises has put his truth in pawn.

(2) For their suitableness, being calculated for the Christian's every condition. The promises are like an herb garden. There is no disease but some herb may be found there to cure it. The promises of themselves cannot comfort--but only as the Spirit enables us to suck consolation from these honeycombs. The promises are like a still full of herbs — but this still will not drop unless the fire is put under it. So when the Spirit of God (who is compared to fire) is put to the still of the promises, then they distill consolation into the soul. Thus we see how the Spirit is in the godly by his virtues.

Objection: But is being filled with the Spirit the sign of a godly man? Are not the wicked said to partake of the Holy Spirit (Heb. 6:4)?

Answer: Wicked men may partake of the Spirit's working — but not of his indwelling. They may have God's Spirit move upon them; but the godly have him enter into them (Ezek. 3:24).

Objection: But the unregenerate taste the heavenly gift (Heb. 6:4).

Answer: It is with them as it is with cooks who may have a smack and taste of the meat they are dressing — but they are not nourished by it. Tasting there is opposed to eating. The godly have not only a drop or taste of the Spirit — but he is in them like a river of living water (John 7:38).

Use 1: It brands those as ungodly who do not have God's Spirit. 'If anyone does not have the Spirit of Christ, he does not belong to Christ' (Romans 8:9). And if he does not belong to Christ — then whose is he? To what regiment does he belong? It is the misery of a sinner — that he does not have God's Spirit. I think it is very offensive to hear men who never had God's Spirit say, 'Take not your holy spirit from us' (Psalm 51:11). Will those who are drunkards and swearers say they have God's Spirit in them? Do those who are malicious and unclean have God's Spirit? It would be blasphemy to say these have the Spirit. Will the blessed Spirit leave his celestial palace to come and live in a foul prison? A sinner's heart is a jail, both for darkness and obnoxiousness, and will God's free Spirit be confined to a prison (Psalm 51:12)? A sinner's heart is the emblem of hell. What would God's Spirit do there? Wicked hearts are not a temple — but a pigsty, where the unclean spirit makes his abode — 'the prince of the power of the air, the spirit who now works in the children of disobedience' (Eph. 2:2).

We would be loath to live in a house haunted by evil spirits; a sinner's heart is haunted. 'After the sop Satan entered' (John 13:27). Satan abuses the godly — but enters into the wicked. When the devils went into the herd of swine, 'the whole herd rushed down the steep bank into the sea and perished in the water' (Matt. 8:32). Why is it that men rush so greedily to the commission of sin — but because the devil has entered into these swine!

Secondly, this cuts off from godliness those who not only lack the Spirit — but deride him — like those Jews who said, 'These men are full of new wine' (Acts 2:13). And indeed, so the apostles were — they were full of the wine of the Spirit. How God's Spirit is scoffed at by the sons of Belial! O wretches, to make those tongues which should be organs of God's praise, into instruments to blaspheme! Have you none to throw your jests at but the Spirit? Deriding the Spirit comes very near to despising him. How can men be sanctified but by the Spirit? Therefore to reproach him is to make merry with their own damnation.

Use 2: As you would be listed in the number of the godly, strive for the blessed indwelling of the Spirit. Pray with Melanchthon, 'Lord, inflame my soul with your Holy Spirit'; and with the spouse, 'Awake, O north wind; and come, O south wind; and blow upon my garden' (Cant 4:16). As a mariner would desire a wind to drive him to sea, so beg for the prosperous gales of the Spirit and the promise may add wings to prayer. 'If you then, being evil, know how to give good gifts unto your children: how much more shall your heavenly Father give the Holy Spirit to those who ask him?' (Luke 11:13). God's Spirit is a rich jewel. Go to God for him: 'Lord, give me your Spirit. Where is the jewel you promised me? When shall my soul be like Gideon's fleece, wet with the dew of heaven?'

Consider how necessary the Spirit is. Without him we can do nothing acceptable to God:

1. We cannot pray without him. He is a Spirit of supplication (Zech. 12:10). He helps both the inventiveness and the affection: 'The Spirit helps us with sighs and groans' (Romans 8:26).

2. We cannot resist temptation without him. 'You will receive power when the Holy Spirit has come upon you' (Acts 1:8). He who has the tide of corrupt nature, and the wind of temptation, must of necessity be carried down the stream of sin — if the contrary wind of the Spirit does not blow.

3. We cannot be fruitful without the Spirit. 'The golden rain from heaven waters the thirsty hearts.' Why is the Spirit compared to dew and rain — but to show us how unable we are to bring forth a crop of grace unless the dew of God falls upon us?

4. Without the Spirit, no ordinance is effectual to us. Ordinances are the conduit pipes of grace — but the Spirit is the spring. Some are content that they have a 'Levite for their priest' (Judges 17:13) — but never look any further. As if a merchant should be content that his ship has good tackling and is well manned, though it never has a gale of wind. The ship of ordinances will not carry us to heaven, though an angel is the pilot, unless the wind of God's Spirit blows. The Spirit is the soul of the Word, without which it is but a dead letter. Ministers may prescribe medicine — but it is God's Spirit who must make it work! Our hearts are like David's body when it grew old: 'they covered him with clothes — but he got no heat' (1 Kings 1:1). So though the ministers of God ply us with prayers and counsel as with hot clothes — yet we are cold and chilly until God's Spirit comes; and then we say, like the disciples, 'Did not our heart burn within us!' (Luke 24:32). Oh, therefore, what need we have of the Spirit!

Thirdly, you who have the blessed Spirit manifested by his energy and vital operations:

1. Acknowledge God's distinguishing love. The Spirit is an earmark of election (1 John 3:24). Christ gave the bag to Judas but not his Spirit. The Spirit is a love token. Where God gives his Spirit as a pawn, he gives himself as a portion. The Spirit is a comprehensive blessing; he is put for all good things (Matt. 7:11). What would you be without the Spirit but like so many carcasses? Without this, Christ would not profit you. The blood of God is not enough without the breath of God. Oh then, be thankful for the Spirit. This lodestone will never stop drawing you until it has drawn you up to heaven.

2. If you have this Spirit, do not grieve him (Eph. 4:30). Shall we grieve our Comforter?

Question: How do we grieve the Spirit?

Answer 1: When we unkindly repel his motions. The Spirit sometimes whispers in our ears and calls to us as God did to Jacob, 'Arise, go up to Bethel' (Gen. 35:1). So the Spirit says, 'Arise, go to prayer, retire to meet your God.' Now when we stifle these motions and entertain temptations to vanity, this is grieving the Spirit. If we check the motions of the Spirit, we shall lose the comforts of the Spirit.

Answer 2: We grieve the Spirit when we deny the work of the Spirit in our hearts. If someone gives another person a gift, and he should deny it and say he never received it, this would be to abuse the love of his friend. So, Christian, when God has given you his Spirit, witnessed by those meltings of heart and passionate desires for heaven — yet you deny that you ever had any renewing work of the Spirit in you, this is base ingratitude and grieves the good Spirit. Renounce the sinful works of the flesh — but do not deny the gracious work of the Spirit.

11. A godly man is a humble man

Augustine calls humility 'the mother of the grace.' But before I show you who the humble man is, I shall lay down three distinctions:

1. I distinguish between being humbled and humble

A man may be humbled and not humble. A sinner may be humbled by affliction. His condition is low, but not his disposition. A godly man is not only humbled, but humble. His heart is as low as his condition.

2. I distinguish between outward and inward humility

There is a great deal of difference between humble behavior and a humble spirit.

(1) A person may behave humbly towards others — yet be proud. Who more humble than Absalom in his outward behavior? 'When people tried to bow before him, Absalom wouldn't let them. Instead, he took them by the hand and embraced them.' (2 Sam. 15:5). But though he acted humbly, he aspired to the crown (v. 10). Here was pride dressed in humility's mantle!

(2) A person may behave humbly towards God — yet be proud. 'Ahab put on sackcloth and fasted and went softly' (1 Kings 21:27) — but his heart was not humble. A man may bow his head like a bulrush — yet lift up the ensigns of pride in his heart.

3. I distinguish between humility and policy

Many make a show of humility to achieve their own ends. The Papists seem to be the most humble, mortified saints — but it is rather subtlety than humility. For by this means, they get the revenues of the earth into their possession. All this they may do, and yet have no godliness.

Question: How may a Christian know that he is humble — and consequently godly?

Answer 1: A humble soul is emptied of all swelling thoughts of himself. Bernard calls humility a self-annihilation. 'You will save the humble' (Job 22:29). In the Hebrew it is 'him that is of low eyes'. A humble man has lower thoughts of himself than others can have of him. David, though a king, still looked upon himself as a worm: 'I am a worm, and no man' (Psalm 22:6). Bradford, a martyr, still subscribes himself a sinner. 'If I be righteous — yet will I not lift up my head' (Job 10:15) — like the violet which is a sweet flower — but hangs down the head.

Answer 2: A humble soul thinks better of others than of himself. 'Let each esteem others better than themselves' (Phil. 2:3). A humble man values others at a higher rate than himself, and the reason is because he can see his own heart better than he can another's. He sees his own corruption and thinks surely it is not so with others; their graces are not so weak as his; their corruptions are not so strong. 'Surely', he thinks, 'they have better hearts than I.' A humble Christian studies his own infirmities, and another's excellences and that makes him put a higher value upon others than himself. 'Surely I am more brutish than any man' (Proverbs 30:2). And Paul, though he was the chief of the apostles, still calls himself 'less than the least of all saints' (Eph. 3:8).

Answer 3: A humble soul has a low esteem of his duties. Pride is apt to breed in our holy things, as the worm breeds in the sweetest fruit, and froth comes from the most tasty wine. A humble person bemoans not only his sins — but also his duties. When he has prayed and wept, 'Alas,' he says, 'how little I have done! God might damn me for all this!' He says, like good Nehemiah, 'Remember me, O my God, concerning this also, and spare me' (Neh. 13:22). 'Remember, Lord, how I have poured out my soul — but spare me and pardon me.' He sees that his best duties weigh too light; therefore he desires that Christ's merits may be put into the scales. The humble saint blushes when he looks at his copy. He sees he cannot write evenly, nor without blotting. This humbles him to think that his best duties run to seed. He drops poison upon his sacrifice. 'Oh,' he says, 'I dare not say I have prayed or wept; those which I write down as duties, God might write down as sins!'

Answer 4: A humble man is always giving bills of indictment against himself. He complains, not of his poor circumstances — but of his poor heart! 'Oh, this evil heart of unbelief!' 'Lord,' says Hooper, 'I am hell — but you are heaven.' A hypocrite is forever telling how good he is. A humble soul is forever saying how bad he is. Paul, that high-flown saint, was caught up into the third heaven — but how this bird of paradise bemoans his corruptions! 'O wretched man that I am!' (Romans 7:24). Holy Bradford subscribes himself, 'the hard-hearted sinner'. The more knowledge a humble Christian has, the more he complains of ignorance; the more faith a humble Christian has, the more he bewails his unbelief.

Answer 5: A humble man will justify God in an afflicted condition. 'You are just in all that is brought upon us' (Neh. 9:33). If men oppress and calumniate, the humble soul acknowledges God's righteousness in the midst of severity: 'Lo, I have sinned' (2 Sam. 24:17). 'Lord, my pride, my barrenness, my worldliness have been the procuring cause of all these judgments.' When clouds are around about God — yet 'righteousness is the habitation of his throne' (Psalm 97:2).

Answer 6: A humble soul is a Christ-magnifier (Phil. 1:20). He gives the glory of all his actions to Christ and free grace. King Canute took the crown off his own head and set it upon a crucifix. So a humble saint takes the crown of honor from his own head and sets it upon Christ's. And the reason is the love that he bears to Christ. Love can part with anything to the object loved. Isaac loved Rebekah and he gave away his jewels to her (Gen. 24:53). The humble saint loves Christ entirely, therefore can part with anything to him. He gives away to Christ the honor and praise of all he does. 'Let Christ wear those jewels!'

Answer 7: A humble soul is willing to take a reproof for sin. A wicked man is too high to stoop to a reproof. The prophet Micaiah told King Ahab of his sin, and the King said, 'I hate him!' (1 Kings 22:8). Reproof to a proud man is like pouring water on lime, which grows the hotter. A gracious soul loves the one who reproves: 'rebuke a wise man, and he will love you' (Proverbs 9:8). The humble-spirited Christian can bear the reproach of an enemy, and the reproof of a friend.

Answer 8: A humble man is willing to have his name and gifts eclipsed, so that God's glory may be increased. He is content to be outshone by others in gifts and esteem, so that the crown of Christ may shine the brighter. This is the humble man's motto: 'Let me decrease; let Christ increase.' It is his desire that Christ should be exalted, and if this is effected, whoever is the instrument, he rejoices. 'some preach Christ of envy' (Phil. 1:15). They preached to take away some of Paul's hearers. 'Well,' says he, 'Christ is preached; and I therein do rejoice' (v.18). A humble Christian is content to be laid aside, if God has any other tools to work with which may bring him more glory.

Answer 9: A humble saint is content with that condition which God sees is best for him. A proud man complains that he has no more; a humble man wonders that he has so much: 'I am not worthy of the least of all your mercies!' (Gen. 32:10). When the heart lies low, it can stoop to a low condition. A Christian looking at his sins wonders that things are no worse with him. He says that his mercies are greater than he deserves. He knows that the worst piece which God carves for him, is better than he deserves; therefore he takes it thankfully upon his knees.

Answer 10: A humble Christian will stoop to the lowest person and the lowest office; he will visit the poorest member of Christ. Lazarus' sores are more precious to him than Dives' royal robes. He does not say, 'Stand aside, come not near to me, for I am holier than you' (Isaiah 65:5) — but 'condescends to men of low estate' (Romans 12:16).

Use 1: If humility is the inseparable character of a godly man, let us test our hearts by this touchstone. Are we humble? Alas, where does their godliness appear—who are swollen with pride and ready to burst? But though men are proud, they will not confess it. This bastard of pride is born—but none are willing to father it. Therefore let me ask a few questions and let conscience answer:

1. Are not those proud, who are given to boasting? 'Your boasting is not good.' (1 Corinthians 5:6).

(1) Many are proud of their riches. Their hearts swell with their estates. Bernard calls pride the rich man's cousin. 'Your heart has become proud because of your wealth.' (Ezek. 28:5).

(2) Many are proud of their apparel. They dress themselves in such fashions as to make the devil fall in love with them. Painted faces, gaudy attire, naked breasts, what are these, but the banners which sinful pride displays?

(3) Many are proud of their beauty. The body is but dust and blood kneaded together. Solomon says, 'Beauty is vain' (Proverbs 31:30). Yet some are so vain as to be proud of vanity!

(4) Many are proud of their gifts and abilities. These trappings and ornaments do not approve them in God's eyes. An angel is a creature of great abilities; but take away humility from an angel—and he is a devil!

2. Are not those who have a high opinion of their own excellences proud? Those who look at themselves in the magnifying mirror of self-love, appear in their own eyes better than they are. Simon Magus boasted that he was some great one (Acts 8:9). Alexander felt the need to be the son of Jupiter and of the race of the gods. Sapor, King of Persia, styles himself 'Brother of the Sun and Moon'. I have read of a pope who trod upon the neck of Frederick the Emperor and as a cloak for his pride cited that text, 'You shall tread upon the lion, and the dragon shall you trample under feet' (Psalm. 91:13). There is no idol like self; the proud man bows down to this idol.

3. Are not those who despise others proud? 'The Pharisees trusted in themselves, that they were righteous, and despised others' (Luke 18:9). The Chinese people say that Europe has one eye and they have two, and all the rest of the world is blind. A proud man looks upon others with such an eye of scorn, as Goliath did upon David: 'when the Philistine looked about, and saw David, he disdained him' (1 Sam. 17:42). Those who stand upon the pinnacle of pride, look upon other men as no bigger than crows.

4. Are not those who trumpet their own praise proud? 'Theudas rose up, claiming to be somebody' (Acts 5:36). A proud man is the herald of his own good deeds; he blazes his own fame, and therein lies his vice, to paint his own virtue.

5. Are not those proud, who take the glory due to God, to themselves? 'Is not this great Babylon, which I have built?' (Dan. 4:30). So says the proud man, 'Are not these the prayers I have made? Are not these the works of charity I have done?' When Herod had made an oration and the people cried him up for a god (Acts 12:22), he was well content to have that honor done to him. Pride is the greatest sacrilege; it robs God of his glory!

6. Are not those who are never pleased with their condition proud? They speak harshly of God, charging his care and wisdom, as if he had dealt badly with them. God himself cannot please a proud man. He is forever finding fault, and flying in the face of heaven.

Oh, let us search if there is any of this leaven of pride in us. Man is naturally a proud piece of flesh. This sin of pride runs in the blood. Our first parents fell by their pride. They aspired to deity. There are the seeds of this sin of pride in the best—but the godly do not allow themselves in it. They strive to kill this weed, by mortification. But certainly where this sin reigns and prevails, it cannot stand with grace. You may as well call him who lacks wisdom, a prudent man; as him who lacks humility, a godly man.

Use 2: Strive for this characteristic: be humble. It is an apostolic exhortation, 'Clothe yourselves with humility toward one another, because, 'God opposes the proud but gives grace to the humble.' (1 Pet. 5:5). Put humility on as an embroidered robe. It is better to lack anything, rather than humility. It is better to lack gifts rather than humility. No, it is better to lack 'the comforts of the Spirit' rather than lack humility. 'What does the Lord require of you — but to walk humbly with your God?' (Mic. 6:8).

1. The more value any man has, the more humble he is. Feathers fly up — but gold descends! The golden saint descends in humility. Some of the ancients have compared humility to the Celidonian stone, which is little for substance — but of rare virtue.

2. God loves a humble soul. It is not our high birth — but our humble hearts, which God delights in. A humble spirit is in God's view: 'to this man will I look, even to him that is poor and of a contrite spirit' (Isaiah 66:2). A humble heart is God's palace! 'For this is what the high and lofty One says — he who lives forever, whose name is holy — I live in a high and holy place, but also with him who is contrite and lowly in spirit, to revive the spirit of the lowly and to revive the heart of the contrite.' (Isaiah 57:15). Great personages, besides their houses of state, have lesser houses which upon occasion they retreat to. Besides God's house of state in heaven, he has the humble soul for his retiring house, where he takes up his rest, and solaces himself. Let Italy boast that it is, for pleasure, the garden of the world. A humble heart glories in this, that it is the presence chamber of the great and glorious King!

3. The times we live in are humbling. The Lord seems to say to us now, as he did to Israel, 'Remove your jewelry and ornaments until I decide what to do with you.' (Exod. 33:5). 'My displeasure is breaking forth — I have eclipsed the light of the sanctuary, I have stained the waters with blood, I have shot the arrow of pestilence — therefore lay down your pride — 'Remove your jewelry and ornaments!' Woe to those who lift themselves up, when God is casting them down. When should people be humble — if not when under the rod? 'Humble yourselves under the mighty hand of God' (1 Pet. 5:6). When God afflicts his people, and cuts them short in their privileges, it is time then to 'sit in sackcloth — and sit in the dust' (Job 16:15).

4. What a horrid sin pride is! Chrysostom calls it 'the mother of hell'. Pride is a complicated evil, as Aristotle said. Justice encompasses all virtue in itself; so pride encompasses all vice. Pride is a spiritual drunkenness; it flies up like wine into the brain and intoxicates it. Pride is idolatry; a proud man is a self-worshiper. Pride is revenge; Haman plotted Mordecai's death because he would not bow the knee. How odious is this sin to God! 'Everyone who is proud in heart, is an abomination to the Lord!' (Proverbs 16:5). 'I hate pride and arrogance!' (Proverbs 8:13)

5. The mischief of pride. It is the breakneck of souls! 'As surely as I live,' says the Lord Almighty, the God of Israel, 'Moab and Ammon will be destroyed as completely as Sodom and Gomorrah. Their land will become a place of stinging nettles, salt pits, and eternal desolation. They will receive the wages of their pride!' (Zeph. 2:9,10). 'Doves', says Pliny, 'take a pride in their feathers, and in their flying high; at last they fly so high that they are a prey to the hawk.' Men fly so high in pride that at last they are a prey to the devil, the prince of the air.

6. Humility raises one's esteem in the eyes of others. All give respect to the humble: 'Before honor is humility' (Proverbs 15:33).

Question: What means may we use to be humble?

Answer 1: Let us set before us the golden pattern of Christ. His degree is 'doctorate in humility'. 'But made himself of no reputation, and was made in the likeness of men' (Phil. 2:7). O what abasement it was for the Son of God to take our flesh! No, that Christ should take our nature when it was in disgrace, being stained with sin — this was the wonder of humility. Look at a humble Savior — and let the plumes of pride fall off!

Answer 2: Study God's immensity and purity; a sight of glory humbles. Elijah wrapped his face in a mantle when God's glory passed before him (1 Kings 19:13). The stars vanish when the sun appears.

Answer 3: Let us study ourselves.

First, our dark side. By looking at our faces in the mirror of the Word, we see our spots. What a world of sin swarms in us! We may say with Bernard, 'Lord, I am nothing but sin or sterility, either sinfulness or barrenness.'

Secondly, our light side. Is there any good in us?

1. How disproportionate is our good — compared to the means of grace we have enjoyed! There is still something lacking in our faith (1 Thess. 3:10). O Christian, do not be proud of what you have — but be humble for what you lack.

2. The grace we have is not of our own growth. We are indebted to Christ and free grace for it. As he said of that axe which fell in the water, 'Alas, master, for it was borrowed' (2 Kings 6:5), so I may say of all the good and excellence in us, 'It is borrowed'. Would it not be folly to be proud of a ring that is loaned to us? 'For who makes you to differ from another? And what have you that you did not receive?' (1 Cor. 4:7). The moon has no cause to be proud of her light — as she borrows it from the sun.

3. How far short we come of others! Perhaps other Christians are giants in grace; they are in Christ not only before us — but above us. We are but like the foot in Christ's body; they are like the eye.

4. Our beauty is spotted. The church is said to be 'fair as the moon' (Cant 6:10), which when it shines brightest, has a dark spot in it. Faith is mixed with unbelief. A Christian has that in his very grace, which may humble him.

5. If we would be humble, let us contemplate our mortality. Shall dust exalt itself? The thoughts of the grave should bury our pride. They say that when there is a swelling in the body, the hand of a dead man stroking that part cures the swelling. The serious meditation of death is enough to cure the swelling of pride.

12. A godly man is a praying man.

'Let everyone who is godly pray to You.' Psalm 32:6

As soon as grace is poured in — prayer is poured out! 'But I give myself unto prayer' (Psalm 109:4). In the Hebrew it is, 'but I prayer'. Prayer and I are all one. Prayer is the soul's communion with heaven. God comes down to us by his Spirit — and we go up to him by prayer. Caligula placed his idols — as whispering in Jupiter's ear. Prayer is a whispering in God's ear! A godly man cannot live without prayer. A man cannot live unless he takes his breath, nor can the soul, unless it breathes forth its desires to God. As soon as the babe of grace is born, it cries. No sooner was Paul converted than 'behold, he prays!' (Acts 9:11). No doubt he prayed before, being a Pharisee — but it was either superficially or superstitiously. But when the work of grace had been done in his soul, behold, now he prays!

A godly man is on the mount of prayer every day. He begins the day with prayer. Before he opens his shop — he opens his heart to God! We burn sweet incense in our houses; a godly man's house is 'a house of incense'; he airs it with the incense of prayer. He engages in no business without seeking God. A godly man consults God in everything; he asks God's permission and his blessing. The Greeks asked counsel at their oracles; just so, a godly man enquires at the divine oracle (Gen. 24:12; 1 Sam. 23:3,4). A true saint continually shoots up his heart to heaven, by sacred prayers.

Question: Is prayer a sign of a godly man? May not a hypocrite pray eloquently and with seeming devotion?

Answer: He may: 'they seek me daily' (Isaiah 58:2). But a hypocrite does not pray 'in the Spirit' (Eph. 6:18). A man may have the gift of prayer, and not have the spirit of prayer.

Question: How shall we know that we have the spirit of prayer?

Answer: When the prayer which we make is spiritual.

Question: What is it to make a spiritual prayer?

Answer 1: When we pray with knowledge. Under the law, Aaron was to 'light the lamps' when he burned the incense on the altar (Exod. 30:7). Incense typified prayer, and the lighting of the lamps typified knowledge. When the incense of prayer burns, the lamp of knowledge must be lit: 'I will pray with the understanding' (1 Cor. 14:15). We must know the majesty and holiness of God, so that we may be deeply affected with reverence when we come before him. We must put up such petitions as are exactly adequate and agreeable to God's will. 'Be not rash with your mouth, to utter anything before God' (Eccles. 5:2). The Lord would not have the blind offered to him (Mal. 1:8). How can we pray with affection when we do not pray with judgment? The Papists pray in an unknown tongue. Christ may reply to them as he did to the mother of Zebedee's children, 'You know not what you ask' (Matt. 20:22). He who prays he knows not how, shall be heard he knows not when.

Answer 2: A spiritual prayer is when the heart and spirit pray. There are not only words but desires. It is excellent when a man can say, 'Lord, my heart prays.' Hannah 'prayed in her heart' (1 Sam. 1:13). The sound of a trumpet comes from within — and the excellent music of prayer comes from within the heart. If the heart does not accompany duty — it is speaking, not praying.

Answer 3: A spiritual prayer is a fervent prayer. 'The effectual fervent prayer ... avails much' (Jas. 5:16). The heart, like the mainspring, should carry the affections in a most zealous and rapid manner. Fervency is the wing of prayer by which it ascends to heaven. Prayer is expressed by sighs and groans (Romans 8:26). It is not so much the gifts of the Spirit — as the groans of the Spirit, which God likes. Prayer is called a 'wrestling' (Gen. 32:24) and a 'pouring out of the soul' (1 Sam. 1:15). Prayer is compared to incense (Psalm 141:2). Incense without fire makes no sweet smell. Prayer without fervency is like incense without fire. Christ prayed with 'Strong crying and tears' (Heb. 5:7); crying prayer prevails. When the heart is inflamed in prayer, a Christian is carried as it were in a fiery chariot up to heaven.

Answer 4: A spiritual prayer is such as comes from a broken heart. 'The sacrifices of God are a broken spirit' (Psalm 51:17). The incense was to be beaten, to typify the breaking of the heart in prayer. It is not the eloquent tongue — but the melting heart — which God accepts.

Moses said to the Lord, 'I am not eloquent.' 'Oh,' says a Christian, 'I cannot pray like others.' But can you weep and sigh? Does your soul melt out at your eyes? God accepts broken expressions, when they come from broken hearts. I have read of a plant which bears no fruit — but it weeps forth a kind of gum which is very costly. So, though you do not flourish with those gifts and expressions like others — yet if you can weep forth tears from a contrite heart, these are exceedingly precious to God, and he will put them in his bottle. Jacob wept in prayer and had 'power over the angel' (Hos. 12:4).

Answer 5: A spiritual prayer is a believing prayer. 'Whatever you shall ask in prayer, believing, you shall receive' (Matt. 21:22). The reason why so many prayers suffer shipwreck, is because they split against the rock of unbelief. Praying without faith, is like shooting without bullets. When faith takes prayer by the hand, then we draw near to God. We should come to God in prayer like the leper: 'Lord, if you will, you can make me clean' (Matt. 8:2). It is a disparagement to deity to have such a whisper in the heart, that 'God's ear is heavy and cannot hear' (Isaiah 59:1). What is said of the people of Israel may be applied to prayer — 'They could not enter in, because of unbelief' (Heb. 3:19).

Answer 6: A spiritual prayer is a holy prayer. 'Lift up holy hands in prayer' (1 Tim. 2:8). Prayer must be offered on the altar of a pure heart. Sin lived in — makes the heart hard, and God's ear deaf. Sin stops the mouth of prayer. Sin does what the thief does to the traveler — puts a gag in his mouth so that he cannot speak. Sin poisons and infests prayer. A wicked man's prayer carries the plague, and will God come near him? The loadstone loses its virtue when it is spread with garlic; so does prayer when it is polluted with sin. 'If I regard iniquity in my heart, the Lord will not hear me' (Psalm 66:18). It is foolish to pray against sin and then to sin against prayer. A spiritual prayer, like the spirits of wine, must be refined and taken off the lees and dregs of sin: 'that they may offer unto the Lord an offering in righteousness' (Mal. 3:3). If the heart is holy — this altar will sanctify the gift.

Answer 7: A spiritual prayer is a humble prayer. 'Lord, you have heard the desire of the humble' (Psalm 10:17). Prayer is the asking of an alms, which requires humility. 'The publican, standing afar off, would not lift up so much as his eyes unto heaven — but smote upon his breast, saying, God be merciful to me a sinner' (Luke 18:13). God's incomprehensible glory may even amaze us and strike a holy consternation into us, when we approach near to him: 'O my God, I blush to lift up my face to you' (Ezra 9:6). It is lovely to see a poor nothing lie prostrate at the feet of its Maker. 'Behold now, I have taken upon me to speak unto the Lord — who am but dust and ashes' (Gen. 18:27). The lower the heart descends — the higher the prayer ascends.

Answer 8: A spiritual prayer is when we pray in the name of Christ. To pray in the name of Christ is not only to name Christ in prayer — but to pray in the hope and confidence of Christ's mediation. As a child claims his estate in the right of his father who purchased it, so we come for mercy in the name of Christ, who has purchased it for us in his blood. Unless we pray thus, we do not pray at all; no, we rather provoke God. As it was with Uzziah, when he wanted to offer incense without a priest, God was angry and struck him with leprosy (2 Chron. 26:16-19). So when we do not come in Christ's name in prayer, we offer up incense without a priest, and what can we expect but to meet with wrath?

Answer 9: A spiritual prayer is when we pray out of love to prayer. A wicked man may pray — but he does not love prayer. 'Will he delight himself in the Almighty?' (Job 27:10). A godly man is carried on the wings of delight. He is never so well, as when he is praying. He is not forced with fear — but fired with love. 'I will make them joyful in my house of prayer' (Isaiah 56:7).

Answer 10: A spiritual prayer is when we have spiritual goals in prayer. There is a vast difference between a spiritual prayer and a carnal desire. The goals of a hypocrite are selfish and carnal. He looks asquint in prayer. It is not the sense of his spiritual needs which moves him — but rather his lusts. 'You ask amiss, that you may consume it upon your lusts' (Jas. 4:3). The sinner prays more for food, than for grace. This, God does not interpret as praying — but as howling: 'They do not cry out to me from their hearts but howl upon their beds. They gather together for grain and new wine but turn away from me. ' (Hos. 7:14).

Prayers which lack a good aim—lack a good answer. A godly man has spiritual goals in prayer. He sends out his prayer as a merchant sends out his ship, so that he may have large returns of spiritual blessings. His design in prayer is that his heart may be more holy and that he may have more communion with God. A godly man engages in the trade of prayer—so that he may increase the stock of grace.

Answer 11: A spiritual prayer is accompanied with the use of means. There must be works—as well as prayer. When Hezekiah was sick he did not only pray for recovery—but he 'prepared a poultice of figs and applies it to the boil' (Isaiah 38:21). Thus it is in the case of the soul when we pray against sin and avoid temptations. When we pray for grace and use opportunities to the full, this is laying a fig on the boil which will make us recover. To pray for holiness and neglect the means—is like winding up the clock and taking off the weights.

Answer 12: A spiritual prayer is that which leaves a spiritual mood behind upon the heart. A Christian is better after prayer. He has gained more strength over sin, as a man by exercise gets strength. The heart after prayer keeps a tincture of holiness, as the vessel favors and relishes of the wine which is put into it. Having been with God on the mount—Moses' face shone. So, having been on the mount of prayer—our graces shine and our lives shine. This is the sign of a godly man—he prays in the Spirit. This is the right kind of praying. The gift of prayer is ordinary—like culinary fire. But spiritual prayer is more rare and excellent—like elemental fire which comes from heaven.

Use 1: Is a godly man of a praying spirit? Then this excludes from being godly:

1. Those who do not pray at all. Their houses are unhallowed houses. It is made the note of a reprobate that 'he does not call upon God' (Psalm 14:4). Does that poor creature who never asks for alms, think that he will receive any? Do those who never seek mercy from God, think that they will receive it? Truly, then God should befriend them more than he did his own Son. 'He offered up prayers and supplications with strong cries' (Heb. 5:7). None of God's children are tongue-tied. 'Because you are sons, God has sent forth the Spirit of his Son into your hearts, crying, Abba, Father' (Gal. 4:6). Creatures by the instinct of nature cry to God: 'the young ravens which cry' (Psalm 147:9). 'The lions seek their meat from God' (Psalm 104:21). Not to cry to God, is worse than brutish.

2. Others pray—but it is seldom. Like that profane atheist of whom Heylin speaks, who told God that 'he was no common beggar; he had never troubled him before and if he would hear him now, he would never trouble him again.'

3. Others pray—but not 'in the Holy Spirit' (Jude 20). They are more like parrots, than weeping doves. Their hearts do not melt in prayer: they exercise their tongues more than their hearts and affections.

Use 2: As you would prove the new birth, cry 'Abba, Father'; be men of prayer. Pray at least twice a day. In the temple there was the morning and evening sacrifice. Daniel prayed three times a day. No, he so loved prayer that he would not neglect prayer to save his life (Dan. 6:10). Luther spent three hours every day in prayer.

Objection: But what need is there of prayer, when God has made so many promises of blessings?

Answer: Prayer is the condition annexed to the promise. Promises turn upon the hinge of prayer: 'I will yet for this be inquired of by the house of Israel' (Ezek. 36:37). A king promises a pardon — but it must be sued for. David had a promise that God would build him a house — but he sues for the promise by prayer (2 Sam. 7:25). Christ himself had all the promises made sure to him — yet he prayed and spent whole nights in prayer.

Therefore if you would be counted godly, be given to prayer. Prayer sanctifies your mercies (1 Tim. 4:5). Prayer weeds out sin. Prayer waters grace.

That I may encourage Christians and hold up their heads in prayer, as Aaron and Hur held up Moses' hands (Exod. 17:12), let me propound these few considerations:

1. Prayer is a seed sown in God's ear. Other seed sown in the ground may be picked up by the birds — but this seed (especially if watered with tears) is too precious to lose.

2. Consider the power of prayer. The apostle, having set out the whole armor of a Christian, brings in prayer as the chief part (Eph. 6:18). Without this (says Zanchius), all the rest are of little value. By prayer, Moses divided the Red Sea. . By prayer, Joshua stopped the course of the sun and made it stand still (Josh. 10: 13). More, prayer made the Sun of righteousness stand still: 'and Jesus stood still' (Luke 18:40). Prayer is the entrance to all blessings, spiritual and temporal. Prayer has a power in it to destroy the insolent enemies of the church. We read that 'the two witnesses' have a flame on their lips — fire proceeds out of their mouths which devours their enemies (Rev. 11:3,5). This fire is certainly to be interpreted of their prayers. David prayed, 'Lord, turn the counsel of Ahithophel into foolishness' (2 Sam. 15:31). This prayer made Ahithophel hang himself. Moses' prayer against Amalek, did more than Joshua's sword. Prayer has a kind of omnipotency in it; it has raised the dead, overcome angels, cast out devils. It has influence upon God himself (Exod. 32:10). Jacob's prayer held God: 'I will not let you go, except you bless me' (Gen. 32:26). Prayer finds God free — but leaves him bound.

3. Jesus Christ prays our prayers over again. He takes the dross out, and presents nothing but pure gold to his Father. Christ mingles his sweet fragrances, with the prayers of the saints (Rev. 5:8). Think of the dignity of his person — he is God; and the sweetness of his relationship — he is a Son. Oh then, what encouragement there is here for us to pray! Our prayers are put in the hands of a Mediator. Though, as they come from us, they are weak and imperfect — yet as they come from Christ, they are mighty and powerful.

4. The sweet promises which God has made to prayer. 'He will be very gracious unto you at the voice of your cry' (Isaiah 30:19). 'Then shall you go and pray unto me, and I will hearken unto you. And you shall seek me, and find me, when you shall search for me with all your heart' (Jer. 29:12,13); and 'before they call, I will answer; and while they are yet speaking, I will hear' (Isaiah 65:24). These promises keep the head of prayer above water. God is bound with his own promises, as Samson was bound with his own hair.

Let us, then, close ranks and with our Savior pray yet more earnestly (Luke 22:44). Let us be importunate suitors, and resolve with Bernard that we will not come away from God without God. Prayer is a bomb which bursts heaven's gates open.

Question: How shall we go about praying aright?

Answer: Implore the Spirit of God: 'praying in the Holy Spirit' (Jude 20). The Holy Spirit both originates prayer and inflames it. God understands no other language, but that of his Spirit. Pray for the Holy Spirit that you may pray in the Holy Spirit.

13. A godly man is a sincere man

'Behold an Israelite indeed, in whose spirit there is no deceit' (John 1:47). The word for sincere, haplous, signifies 'without pleats and folds'. A godly man is plain-hearted, having no subtle subterfuges. Religion is the uniform a godly man wears, and this uniform is lined with sincerity.

Question: In what does the godly man's sincerity appear?

Answer 1: The godly man is what he seems to be. He is a Jew inwardly (Romans 2:29). Grace runs through his heart, as silver through the veins of the earth. The hypocrite is not what he seems. A picture is like a man — but it lacks breath. The hypocrite is a picture; he does not breathe forth sanctity. A godly man answers to his profession as the transcript to the original.

Answer 2: The godly man strives to approve himself to God in everything. 'We labor, that, whether present or absent, we may be accepted of him' (2 Cor. 5:9). It is better to have God approve, than the world applaud. Those who ran in the Olympic race strove to have the approval of the judge and umpire of the race. There is a time coming shortly, when a smile from God's face will be infinitely better than all the applause of men. How sweet that word will be, 'Well done, good and faithful servant!' (Matt. 25:21). A godly man is ambitious of God's testimonial letters. The hypocrite desires the praise of men. Saul was for the approval of the people (1 Sam. 15:30) A godly man approves his heart to God, who is both the spectator and the judge.

Answer 3: The godly man is sincere in laying open his sins. 'I acknowledged my sin unto you, and my iniquity have I not hid' (Psalm 32:5). The hypocrite veils and cloaks his sin. He does not cut off his sin but conceals it. Like a patient who has some loathsome disease in his body, he will rather die than reveal his disease. But a godly man's sincerity is seen in this — he will confess and shame himself for sin: 'Lo, I have sinned, and I have done wickedly' (2 Sam. 24:17). No, a child of God will confess sin in particular. An unsound Christian will confess sin wholesale, he will acknowledge he is a sinner in general. Whereas David does, as it were, point with his finger to the sore: 'I have done this evil' (Psalm 51:4). He does not say, 'I have done evil' — but 'this evil'. He points at his blood-guiltiness.

Answer 4: The godly man has blessed designs in all he does. He propounds this objective in every ordinance — that he may have more acquaintance with God, and bring more glory to God. As the herb heliotropium turns about according to the motion of the sun, so a godly man's actions all move towards the glory of God. A godly man's praying and worshiping, is so that he may honor God. Though he shoots short — yet he takes correct aim. The hypocrite thinks of nothing but self-interest; the sails of his mill move only when the wind of self promotion blows. He never dives into the waters of the sanctuary — except to fetch up a piece of gold from the bottom.

Answer 5: The godly man abhors deception. His heart goes along with his tongue; he cannot both flatter and hate; both commend and censure (Psalm 28:3). Love must be sincere' (Romans 12:9). Insincere love is worse than hatred; counterfeiting of friendship is no better than a lie (Psalm 78:36), for there is a pretense of that which is not. Many are like Joab: 'He took Amasa by the beard to kiss him — and smote him with his sword in the fifth rib, and he died' (2 Sam. 20:9,10). 'Horrible poisons lie hidden under sweet honey.'

There is a river in Spain where the fish seem to be of a golden color — but take them out of the water and they are like other fish. All is not gold that glitters; there are some who pretend much kindness — but they are like great veins which have little blood. If you lean upon them, they are like a leg out of joint. For my part I seriously question a man's sincerity with God — if he flatters and lies to his friend. 'He who conceals his hatred has lying lips' (Proverbs 10:18). By all that has been said, we may test whether we have this mark of a godly man — being sincere.

Sincerity (as I conceive it) is not strictly a grace, but rather the ingredient in every grace. Sincerity is that which qualifies grace and without which grace is not true: 'Grace be with all those who love our Lord Jesus Christ in sincerity' (Eph. 6:24). Sincerity qualifies our love; sincerity is to grace what the blood and spirits are to the body. There can be no life without the blood, so there can be no grace without sincerity.

Use: As we would be reputed godly, let us strive for this characteristic of sincerity.

1. Sincerity renders us lovely in God's eyes. God says of the sincere soul, as of Zion, 'This is my rest forever: here will I dwell; for I have desired it' (Psalm 132:14). A sincere heart is God's paradise of delight. 'Noah found grace in God's eyes.' Why, what did God see in Noah? He was girt with the girdle of sincerity (Gen. 6:9). Noah was perfect in his generation. Truth resembles God, and when God sees a sincere heart, he sees his own image, and he cannot choose but fall in love with it: 'He who is upright in his way, is God's delight' (Proverbs 11:20).

2. Sincerity makes our services find acceptance with God. The church of Philadelphia had only 'a little strength'; her grace was weak, her services slender; yet of all the churches Christ wrote to, he found the least fault with her. What was the reason? Because she was most sincere: 'You have kept fast my word, and have not denied my name' (Rev. 3:8). Though we cannot pay God all we owe — yet a little in current coin, is accepted. God takes sincerity for full payment. A little gold, though rusty, is better than tin, be it ever so bright. A little sincerity, though rusted over with many infirmities, is of more value with God than all the glorious flourishes of hypocrites.

3. Sincerity is our safety. False hearts that will step out of God's way and use carnal policy, when they think they are most safe, are least secure. 'He who walks uprightly walks surely' (Proverbs 10:9). A sincere Christian will do nothing but what the Word warrants, and that is safe, as to the conscience. More, often the Lord takes care of the outward safety of those who are upright in their way: 'I laid me down and slept' (Psalm 3:5). David was now beleaguered by enemies — yet God so encamped about him by his providence, that he could sleep as securely as in a garrison. 'The Lord sustained me.' The only way to be safe is to be sincere.

4. Sincerity is gospel perfection. 'Have you considered my servant Job, that there is none like him in the earth, a perfect and an upright man?' (Job 1:8). Though a Christian is full of infirmities and, like a young child, weak and feeble — God still looks on him as if he were completely righteous. Every true saint has the Thummim of perfection on his breastplate.

5. Sincerity is what the devil attacks most. Satan's spite was not so much at Job's estate, as his integrity; he would have wrested the shield of sincerity from him — but Job held that fast (Job 27:6). A thief does not fight for an empty purse — but for money. The devil would have robbed Job of the jewel of a good conscience, and then he would have been poor Job indeed. Satan does not oppose mere profession — but sincerity. Let men go to church and make glorious pretenses of holiness. Satan does not oppose this; this does him no hurt — and them no good! But if men desire to be sincerely pious, then Satan musters up all his forces against them. Now what the devil most assaults — that we must strive most to maintain. Sincerity is our fort royal, where our chief treasure lies. This fort is most shot at, therefore let us be more careful to preserve it. While a man keeps his castle, his castle will keep him. While we keep sincerity, sincerity will keep us.

6. Sincerity is the beauty of a Christian. Wherein does the beauty of a diamond lie — but in this, that it is a true diamond? If it is counterfeit, it is worth nothing. So wherein does the beauty of a Christian lie — but in this, that he has truth in the inward parts (Psalm 51:6)? Sincerity is a Christian's ensign of glory; it is both his breastplate to defend him and his crown to adorn him.

7. See the vileness of hypocrisy. The Lord would have no leaven offered up in sacrifice; leaven typified hypocrisy (Luke 12:1). The hypocrite does the devil double service; under the mask of

piety, he can sin more and be less suspected: 'Woe unto you, scribes and Pharisees, hypocrites! for you devour widows' houses, and for a pretense make long prayers' (Matt. 23:14). Who would think that those who pray for so many hours on end, would be guilty of extortion? Who would suspect of false weights, the man who has the Bible so often in his hand? Who would think that the one who seems to fear an oath, would slander? Hypocrites are the worst sort of sinners; they reflect infinite dishonor upon religion. Hypocrisy for the most part ends in scandal, and that brings an evil report on the ways of God. One scandalous hypocrite makes the world suspect that all professing Christians are like him. The hypocrite was born to spite religion, and bring it into disrepute.

The hypocrite is a liar. He worships God with his knee — but the passions with his heart, like those who 'feared the Lord, and served their own gods' (2 Kings 17:33).

The hypocrite is an impudent sinner. He knows his heart is false — yet he goes on. Judas knew himself to be a hypocrite; he asks, 'Master, is it I?' Christ replies, 'You have said it' (Matt. 26:25). Yet so shameless was he as to persist in his falseness and betray Christ. All the plagues and curses written in the Book of God are the hypocrite's portion! Hell is his place of rendezvous (Matt. 24:51). Hypocrites are the chief guests whom the devil expects, and he will make them as welcome as fire and brimstone can make them!

8. If the heart is sincere, God will wink at many failings. 'He has not beheld iniquity in Jacob' (Numb. 23:21). God's love does not make him blind; he can see infirmities. But how does God look at a believer's sins? Not with an eye of revenge — but of pity, as a physician sees a disease in his patient — so as to heal him. God does not see iniquity in Jacob — so as to destroy him — but to heal him! 'He kept on in his willful ways. I have seen his ways, but I will heal him' (Isaiah 57:17,18). How much pride, vanity, passion, does the Lord pass by in his sincere ones! He sees the integrity — and pardons the infirmity. How much God overlooked in Asa! The 'high places were not removed' — yet it is said, 'The heart of Asa was perfect all his days' (2 Chron. 15:17). We esteem a picture, though it is not drawn full length. Just so, the graces of God's people are not drawn to their full length! They have many scars and spots — yet having something of God in sincerity, they shall find mercy. God loves the sincere, and it is the nature of love to cover infirmity.

9. Nothing but sincerity will give us comfort in an hour of trouble. King Hezekiah thought he was dying — yet this revived him, that his conscience drew up a certificate for him: 'Remember, O Lord, how I have walked before you in truth ... ' (Isaiah 38:3). Sincerity was the best flower in his crown. What a golden shield this will be against Satan! When he roars at us by his temptations, and sets our sins before us on our death-bed, then we shall answer, 'It is true, Satan; these have been our misdeeds — but we have bewailed them; if we have sinned, it was against the bent and purpose of our heart.' This will stop the devil's mouth and make him retreat; therefore strive for this jewel of sincerity. 'If our heart condemn us not, then have we confidence toward God' (1 John 3:21). If we are cleared at the petty sessions in our conscience, then we may be confident we shall be acquitted at the great assizes on the Day of Judgment.

'Our conscience testifies that we have conducted ourselves in the world, and especially in our relations with you — in the holiness and sincerity that are from God.' 2 Corinthians 1:12. 'Let us draw near to God with a sincere heart.' Hebrews 10:22.

14. A godly man is a heavenly man

Heaven is in him — before he is in heaven! The Greek word for saint, hagios, signifies a man taken away from the earth. A person may live in one place — yet belong to another. He may live in Spain yet be a citizen of England. So a godly man is a while in the world — but he belongs to the Jerusalem above. That is the place to which he aspires. Every day is Ascension Day with a believer. The saints are called 'stars' for their sublimity; they have gone above into the upper region: 'The way of life is above, to the wise' (Proverbs 15:24). A godly man is heavenly in six ways:

1. In his election.

2. In his disposition.

3. In his communication.

4. In his actions.

5. In his expectation.

6. In his conduct.

1. A godly man is heavenly in his choices

He chooses heavenly objects. David chose to be a resident in God's house (Psalm 84:10). A godly person chooses Christ and grace, before the most illustrious things of this world. What a man chooses — that is what he is. This choosing of God is best seen in a critical hour. When Christ and the world come into competition, and we part with the world to keep Christ and a good conscience, that is a sign we have chosen 'the better part' (Luke 10:42). Moses 'chose to be mistreated along with the people of God, rather than to enjoy the pleasures of sin for a short time.' Hebrews 11:25

2. A godly man is heavenly in his disposition

He sets his affections on things above (Col. 3:2). He sends his heart to heaven before he gets there. He looks upon the world as but a beautiful prison and he cannot be much in love with his fetters, though they are made of gold. A holy person contemplates glory and eternity; his desires have gotten wings and have fled to heaven. Grace is in the heart like fire, which makes it sparkle upwards in divine desires and prayers.

3. A godly man is heavenly in his speech

His words are sprinkled with salt to season others (Col. 4:6). As soon as Christ had risen from the grave, he was 'speaking of the things pertaining to the kingdom of God' (Acts 1:3). No sooner has a man risen from the grave of unregeneracy than he is speaking of heaven. 'The words of a wise man's mouth are gracious' (Eccles. 4:12). He speaks in such a heavenly manner, as if he were already in heaven. The love he has for God, will not allow him to be silent. The spouse being sick with love, her tongue was like the pen of a ready writer: 'My beloved is white and ruddy, his head is as the most fine gold ... ' (Cant 5:10,11). Where there is a principle of godliness in the heart — it will vent itself at the lips!

(1) How can they be termed godly — who are possessed with a dumb devil? They never have any good discourse. They are fluent and discursive enough in secular things: they can speak of their wares and shops, they can tell what a good crop they have — but in matters of religion they are as if their tongue cleaved to the roof of their mouth! There are many people in whose company you cannot tell what to make of them — whether they are Turks or atheists, for they never speak a word of Christ!

(2) How can they be termed godly — whose tongues are set on fire by hell? Their lips do not drop honey — but poison, to the defiling of others! Plutarch says that speech ought to be like gold, which is of most value when it has least dross in it. Oh, the unclean, malicious words that some people utter! What an unsavory stench comes from these dunghills! Those lips that gallop so fast in sin, need David's muzzle. 'I will watch my ways and keep my tongue from sin; I will

put a muzzle on my mouth,' (Psalm 39:1). Can the body be healthy — when the tongue is black? Can the heart be holy — when the devil is in the lips? A godly man speaks 'the language of Canaan.' 'Those who feared the Lord spoke often one to another' (Mal. 3:16).

4. A godly man is heavenly in his actions

The motions of the planets are celestial. A godly man is sublime and sacred in his motions; he works out salvation; he puts forth all his strength, as they did in the Greek Olympics, so that he may obtain the garland made of the flowers of paradise. He prays, fasts, watches, and takes heaven by storm. He is divinely actuated, he carries on God's interest in the world, he does angels' work, he is seraphic in his actions.

5. A godly man is heavenly in his hopes

His hopes are above the world (Psalm 39:7). 'In hope of eternal life' (Titus 1:2). A godly man casts anchor within the veil. He hopes to have his fetters of sin filed off; he hopes for such things as eye has not seen; he hopes for a kingdom when he dies — a kingdom promised by the Father, purchased by the Son, assured by the Holy Spirit. As an heir lives in hope of the time when such a great estate shall fall to him, so a child of God, who is a co-heir with Christ, hopes for glory. This hope comforts him in all varieties of condition: 'we rejoice in hope of the glory of God' (Romans 5:2).

(1) This hope comforts a godly man in affliction. Hope lightens and sweetens the most severe dispensations. A child of God can rejoice when tears are in his eyes; the time is shortly coming when the cross shall be taken off his shoulders and a crown set on his head! A saint at present is miserable, with a thousand troubles; in an instant, he will be clothed with robes of immortality, and advanced above seraphim!

(2) This hope comforts a godly man in death. 'The righteous has hope in his death' (Proverbs 14:32). If one should ask a dying saint, when all his earthly comforts have gone, what he had left, he would say, 'the helmet of hope.' I have read of a woman martyr who, when the persecutors commanded that her breasts should be cut off, said, 'Tyrant, do your worst; I have two breasts which you cannot touch, the one of faith and the other of hope.' A soul that has this blessed hope is above the desire of life or the fear of death. Would anyone be troubled at exchanging the lease of a poor hut — for an inheritance that will be for him and his heirs? Who would worry about parting with life, which is a lease that will soon run out, to be possessed of a glorious inheritance in light?

6. A godly man is heavenly in his conduct

He casts such a luster of holiness as adorns his profession. He lives as if he had seen the Lord with his bodily eyes. What zeal, sanctity, humility, shines forth in his life! A godly person emulates not only the angels — but imitates Christ himself (1 John 2:6). The Macedonians celebrate the birthday of Alexander, on which day they wear his picture round their necks, set with pearl and rich jewels. So a godly man carries the lively picture of Christ about him, in the heavenliness of his deportment: 'our conversation is in heaven' (Phil. 3:20).

Use 1: Those who are eaten up with the world will be rejected, as ungodly, at the bar of judgment. To be godly and earthly is a contradiction: 'For, as I have often told you before and now say again even with tears — many live as enemies of the cross of Christ. Their destiny is destruction, their god is their stomach, and their glory is in their shame. Their mind is on earthly things.' (Philippians 3:18-19). We read that the earth swallowed up Korah alive (Numb. 16:32). This judgment is on many — the earth swallows up their time, thoughts and discourse. They are buried twice; their hearts are buried in the earth before their bodies. How sad it is that the soul, that princely thing, which is made for communion with God and angels, should be put to the mill to grind, and made a slave to the earth! How like the prodigal the soul has become, choosing rather to converse with swine and feed upon husks—than to aspire after communion with the blessed Deity! Thus does Satan befool men, and keep them from heaven by making them seek a heaven here on earth.

Use 2: As we would prove ourselves to be 'born of God', let us be of a sublime, heavenly temper. We shall never go to heaven when we die—unless we are in heaven while we live. That we may be more noble and raised in our affections, let us seriously weigh these four considerations:

1. God himself sounds a retreat to us to call us off the world. 'Love not the world' (1 John 2:15). We may use it as a bouquet of flowers to smell—but it must not lie like a bundle of myrrh between our breasts. 'Be not conformed to this world' (Romans 12:2). Do not hunt after its honors and profits. God's providences, like his precepts, are to beat us off the world. Why does he send war and epidemics? What does the heat of this great anger mean? Surely dying times are to make men die to the world.

2. Consider how much below a Christian it is to be earthly-minded. We sometimes laugh at children when we see them busying themselves with toys, kissing and hugging their dolls, etc., when we do the same! At death, what will all the world be, which we so hug and kiss—but like a rag doll? It will yield us no more comfort then. How far it is below a heaven-born soul to be taken up with these things! No, when such as profess to be ennobled with a principle of piety and to have their hopes above, have their hearts below, how they disparage their heavenly calling and spot their silver wings of grace, by besmirching them with earth!

3. Consider what a poor, contemptible thing the world is. It is not worth setting the affections on; it cannot fill the heart. If Satan should take a Christian up the mount of temptation and show him all the kingdoms and glory of the world, what could he show him but a deceitful dream? Nothing here can be proportionate to the immense soul of man. 'In the fullness of his sufficiency he shall be in straits' (Job 20:22). Here is lack in plenty. The creature will no more fill the soul than a drop will fill the bucket. That little sweet which we suck from the creature, is intermixed with bitterness, like that cup which the Jews gave Christ. 'They gave him to drink wine mingled with myrrh' (Mark 15:23). And this imperfect sweet will not last long: 'the world passes away' (1 John 2:17). The creature merely greets us, and is soon on the wing. The world constantly changes. It is never constant except in its disappointments. How quickly we may remove our lodgings and make our pillow in the dust! The world is but a great inn where we are to stay a night or two, and then be gone. What madness it is so to set our heart upon our inn—as to forget our eternal home!

4. Consider what a glorious place heaven is. We read of an angel coming down from heaven who 'set his right foot upon the sea, and his left foot on the earth' (Rev. 10:2). Had we only once been in heaven, and viewed its superlative glory, how we might in holy scorn trample with one foot on the earth and with the other foot on the sea! Heaven is called a better country: 'But now they desire a better country, that is, a heavenly one' (Heb. 11:16). Heaven is said to be a better country, in opposition to the country where we are now staying. What should we seek, but that better country?

Question: In what sense is heaven a better country?

Answer 1: In that country above there are better delights. There is the tree of life, and the rivers of pleasure. There is amazing beauty, and unsearchable riches. There are the delights of angels. There is the flower of joy fully blown. There is more than we can ask or think (Eph. 3:20). There is glory in its full dimensions—and beyond all hyperbole.

Answer 2: In that country there is a better home.

(1) It is a house 'not made with hands' (2 Cor. 5:1). To denote its excellence, there was never any house, but was made with hands. But the house above surpasses the art of man or angel; none besides God could lay a stone in that building.

(2) It is 'eternal in the heavens.' It is not a guest house but a mansion house. It is a house that will never be out of repair. 'Wisdom has built her house, she has hewn out her seven pillars' (Proverbs 9:1), which can never moulder[9].

Answer 3: In that country there are better provisions. In our Father's house, there is bread enough. Heaven was typified by Canaan, which flowed with milk and honey. There is the royal feast, the spiced wine; there is angels' food. There they serve up those rare foods and dainties, such as exceed not only our expressions—but our imaginations.

Answer 4: In that country there is better society. There is God blessed forever. How infinitely sweet and ravishing will a smile of his face be! The king's presence makes the court. There are the glorious cherubim. In this terrestrial country where we now live, we are among wolves and serpents; in that country above, we shall be among angels! There are 'the spirits of just men made perfect' (Heb. 12:23). Here on earth, the people of God are clouded with infirmities; we see them with spots on their faces; they are full of pride, passion, censoriousness. In that Jerusalem above, we shall see them in their royal attire, decked with unparalleled beauty, not having the least tincture or shadow of sin on them!

Answer 5: In that country there is a better air to breathe in. We go into the country for air; the best air is only to be had in that better country:

(1) It is a more temperate air; the climate is calm and moderate; we shall neither freeze with the cold, nor faint with the heat.

(2) It is a brighter air; there is a better light shining there. The Sun of righteousness enlightens that horizon with his glorious beams: 'the Lamb is the light thereof' (Rev. 21:23).

(3) It is a purer air. The marshes, which are full of foul vapors, we count a bad air and unwholesome to live in. This world is a place of bogs and marshes, where the noxious vapors of sin arise, which make it pestilential and unwholesome to live in. But in that country above, there are none of these vapors—but a sweet perfume of holiness. There is the smell of the orange-tree and the pomegranate. There is the myrrh and cassia coming from Christ, which send forth a most fragrant scent.

Answer 6: In that country there is a better soil. The land or soil is better:

(1) For its altitude. The earth, lying low, is of a baser pedigree; the element which is nearest heaven is purer and more excellent, like the fire. That country above is the high country; it is seated far above all the visible orbs (Psalm 24:3).

(2) For its fertility; it bears a richer crop. The country above yields noble commodities. There are celestial pearls; there is the spiritual vine; there is the honeycomb of God's love dropping; there is the water of life, the hidden manna. There is which that does not rot, flowers which never fade. There is a crop which cannot be fully reaped; it will always be reaping time in heaven, and all this the land yields, without the labor of ploughing and sowing.

(3) For its inoffensiveness. There are no briars there. The world is a wilderness where there are wicked men, and the 'best of them is a brier' (Micah 7:4). They tear the people of God in their

---

[9] slowly decay or disintegrate, especially because of neglect

spiritual liberties—but in the country above there is not one briar to be seen; all the briars are burned.

(4) For the rarity of the prospect; all that a man sees there is his own. I account that the best prospect, where a man can see furthest on his own ground.

Answer 7: In that country there is better unity. All the inhabitants are knit together in love. The poisonous weed of malice does not grow there. There is harmony without division, and charity without envy. In that country above, as in Solomon's temple, no noise of hammer is heard.

Answer 8: In that country there is better employment. While we are here, we are complaining of our needs, weeping over our sins—but there we shall be praising God. How the birds of paradise will chirp when they are in that celestial country! There the morning stars will sing together, and all the saints of God will shout for joy.

Oh, what should we aspire after but this country above? Such as have their eyes opened, will see that it infinitely excels! An ignorant man looks at a star and it appears to him like a little silver spot—but the astronomer, who has his instrument to judge the dimension of a star, knows it to be infinitely larger than the earth. So a natural man hears of the heavenly country that it is very glorious—but it is at a great distance. And because he has not a spirit of discernment, the world looks bigger in his eye. But such as are spiritual artists, who have the instrument of faith to judge heaven, will say it is by far the better country and they will hasten there with the sails of desire.

15. A godly man is a zealous man

Grace turns a saint into a seraph—it makes him burn in holy zeal. Zeal is a mixed affection, a compound of love and anger. It carries forth our love to God, and anger against sin—in the most intense manner. Zeal is the flame of the affections; a godly man has a double baptism—of water and fire. He is baptized with a spirit of zeal; he is zealous for God's honor, truth, worship: 'My zeal has consumed me' (Psalm 119:139). It was a crown set on Phineas' head that he was zealous for his God (Numb. 25:13). Moses is touched with a coal from God's altar and in his zeal he breaks the tablets (Exod. 32:19). Our blessed Savior in his zeal whips the buyers and sellers out of the temple: 'Zeal for your house will consume me' (John 2:17).

But there is a false heat—something looking like zeal, which it is not. A comet looks like a star. I shall therefore show some differences between a true and a false zeal:

1. A false zeal is a blind zeal

'They have a zeal of God—but not according to knowledge' (Romans 10:2). This is not the fire of the spirit—but wildfire. The Athenians were very devout and zealous—but they did not know for all that. 'I found an altar with this inscription, To the unknown God' (Acts 17:23). Thus the Papists are zealous in their way—but they have taken away the key of knowledge.

2. A false zeal is a self-seeking zeal

Jehu cries, 'Come, see my zeal for the Lord!' (2 Kings 16). But it was not zeal—but ambition; he was fishing for a crown. Demetrius pleads for the goddess Diana—but it was not her temple—but her silver shrines, that he was zealous for (Acts 19:25-27). Such zealots Ignatius complains of in his time, that they made a trade of Christ and religion, by which to enrich themselves. It is probable that many in King Henry VIII's time were eager to pull down the abbeys, not out of any zeal against popery—but that they might build their own houses upon the ruins of those abbeys, like vultures which fly aloft but their eyes are down upon their prey. If blind zeal is punished sevenfold, hypocritical zeal shall be punished seventy-sevenfold.

3. A false zeal is a misguided zeal

It occurs most in things which are not commanded. It is the sign of a hypocrite to be zealous for traditions and useless of institutions. The Pharisees were more zealous about washing their cups, than their hearts.

4. A false zeal is fired with anger

James and John, when they wished to call down for fire from heaven, were rebuked by our Savior: 'You know not what manner of spirit you are of' (Luke 9:55). It was not zeal—but anger. Many have espoused the cause of religion, rather out of faction and fancy, than out of zeal for the truth.

But the zeal of a godly man is a true and holy zeal which evidences itself in its effects:

1. True zeal cannot bear an injury done to God

Zeal makes the blood rise when God's honor is impeached. 'I know your works, and your labor, and your patience, and how you cannot tolerate those who are evil' (Rev. 2:2). He who zealously loves his friend, cannot hear him spoken against and be silent.

2. True zeal will encounter the greatest difficulties

When the world holds out of danger to discourage us, zeal casts out fear. Zeal is quickened by opposition. Zeal does not say, 'There is a lion in the way!' Zeal will charge through an army of dangers, it will march in the face of death. Let news be brought to Paul that he was waylaid; 'in every city bonds and afflictions' awaited him. This set a keener edge upon his zeal: 'I am ready not to be bound only—but also to die for the name of the Lord Jesus!' (Acts 21:13). As sharp frosts by force of contrast make the fire burn hotter, so sharp oppositions only inflame zeal the more.

3. As true zeal has knowledge to go before it, so it has sanctity to follow after it

Wisdom leads the van of zeal, and holiness brings up the rear. A hypocrite seems to be zealous—but he is wicked. The godly man is white and ruddy; white in purity, as well as ruddy in zeal. Christ's zeal was hotter than the fire, and his holiness purer than the sun.

4. Zeal that is genuine loves truth when it is despised and opposed

'They have made void your law. Therefore I love your commandments above gold' (Psalm 119:126,127). The more others deride holiness, the more we love it. What is religion the worse, for others disgracing it? Does a diamond sparkle the less because a blind man disparages it? The more outrageous the wicked are against the truth, the more courageous the godly are for it. When Michal scoffed at David's pious dancing before the ark, he said, 'If this is to be vile, I will yet be more vile' (2 Sam. 6:22).

5. True zeal causes fervency in duty

'Fervent in spirit' (Romans 12:1). Zeal makes us—hear with reverence, pray with affection, love with ardency. God kindled Moses' sacrifice from heaven: 'Fire came out from the presence of the Lord and consumed the burnt offering' (Lev. 9:24). When we are zealous in devotion, and our heart waxes hot within us—here is a fire from heaven kindling our sacrifice. How odious it is for a man to be all fire when he is sinning, and all ice when he is praying! A pious heart, like water seething hot, boils over in holy affections!

6. True zeal is persevering

Though it is violent, it is perpetual. No waters can quench the flame of zeal, it is torrid in the frigid zone. The heat of zeal is like the natural heat coming from the heart, which lasts as long as life. That zeal which is not constant, was never true.

Use 1: How opposite to godliness are those who cry down zeal, and count it a religious frenzy! They are for the light of knowledge — but not for the heat of zeal. When Basil was earnest in preaching against the Arian heresy, it was interpreted as folly. Religion is a matter requiring zeal; the kingdom of heaven will not be taken, except by violence (Matt. 11:12).

Objection: But why so much fervor in religion? What becomes of prudence then?

Answer: Though prudence is to direct zeal — yet it is not to destroy it. Because sight is requisite, must the body therefore have no heat? If prudence is the eye in religion, zeal is the heart.

Question: But where is moderation?

Answer: Though moderation in things of indifference is commendable, and doubtless it would greatly tend to settling the peace of the church — yet in the main articles of faith, wherein God's glory and our salvation lie at stake, here moderation is nothing but sinful neutrality.

Objection: But the apostle urges moderation: 'Let your moderation be known to all' (Phil. 4:5).

Answer:

1. The apostle is speaking there of moderating our passion. The Greek word for 'moderation' signifies candor and meekness — the opposite of rash anger. And so the word is rendered in another place 'patient' (1 Tim. 3:3). By moderation, then, is meant meekness of spirit. That is made clear by the subsequent words, 'The Lord is at hand' — as if the apostle had said, 'Avenge not yourselves, for the Lord is at hand.' He is ready to avenge your personal wrongs — but this in no way hinders a Christian from being zealous in matters of religion.

2. What strangers they are to godliness, who have no zeal for the glory of God! They can see his ordinances despised, his worship adulterated — yet their spirits are not at all stirred in them. How many are of a dull, lukewarm temper, zealous for their own secular interest — but with no zeal for the things of heaven! Hot in their own cause — but cool in God's cause. The Lord most abominates lukewarm nominal Christians. I almost said that he is sick of them. 'I wish you were either one or the other!' (anything but lukewarm); 'because you are neither cold nor hot, I will spew you out of my mouth' (Rev. 3:15,16). A lukewarm Christian is only half-baked, just like Ephraim: 'Ephraim is a cake not turned' (Hos. 7:8).

I would ask these tepid, neutral professing Christians this question, 'If religion is not a good cause, why did they undertake it at first? If it is, why do they go about it so faintly? Why have they no more holy ardor of soul?' These people would gladly go to heaven on a soft bed — but are loath to be carried there in a fiery chariot of zeal. Remember, God will be zealous against those who are not zealous; he provides the fire of hell for those who lack the fire of zeal!

Use 2: As you would be found in the catalogue of the godly, strive for zeal. It is better to be of no religion — than not to be zealous in religion. Beware of carnal policy. This is one of those three things which Luther feared would be the death of religion. Some men have been too wise to be saved. Their discretion has quenched their zeal. Beware of sloth, which is an enemy to zeal: 'be zealous therefore, and repent' (Rev. 3:19). Christians, what do you reserve your zeal for? Is it for your gold which perishes; or for your sinful passions which will make you perish? Can you bestow your zeal better than upon God?

How zealous men have been in a false religion! 'They lavish gold out of the bag, and weigh silver in the balance' (Isaiah 46:6). The Jews did not spare any cost in their idolatrous worship. No, they 'cause their sons and daughters to pass through the fire to Molech' (Jer. 32:35). They were so zealous in their idol worship that they would sacrifice their sons and daughters to their false gods. How far the blind heathen went in their false zeal! When the tribunes of Rome complained that they needed gold in their treasuries to offer to Apollo, the Roman matrons plucked off their chains of gold, and rings, and bracelets — and gave them to the priests to offer up sacrifice. Were these so zealous in their sinful worship, and will you not be zealous in the worship of the true God?

Do you lose anything by your zeal? Shall it not be superabundantly recompensed? What is heaven worth? What is a sight of God worth? Was not Jesus Christ zealous for you? He sweat drops of blood, he conflicted with his Father's wrath. How zealous he was for your redemption, and have you no zeal for him? Is there anything you yourselves hate more than dullness and slothfulness in your servants? You are weary of such servants. Do you dislike a dull spirit in others, and not in yourselves? What are all your duties without zeal but mere fancies and nonentities?

Do you know what a glorious thing zeal is? It is the luster that sparkles from grace; it is the flame of love; it resembles the Holy Spirit: 'There appeared cloven tongues like fire, which sat upon each of them, and they were all filled with the Holy Spirit' (Acts 2:3,4). Tongues of fire were an emblem to represent that fire of zeal which the Spirit poured upon them.

Zeal makes all our pious performances prevail with God. When the iron is red hot it enters best; and when our services are red hot with zeal, they pierce heaven soonest!

16. A godly man is a patient man

'You have heard of the patience of Job' (Jas. 5:11). Patience is a star which shines in a dark night. There is a twofold patience:

1. Patience in waiting

If a godly man does not obtain his desire immediately, he will wait until the mercy is ripe: 'My soul waits for the Lord' (Psalm 130:6). There is good reason why God should have the timing of our mercies: 'I, the Lord, will bring it all to pass at the right time' (Isaiah 60:22). Deliverance may delay beyond our time — but it will not delay beyond God's time.

Why should we not wait patiently for God? We are servants; it becomes servants to be in a waiting posture. We wait for everything else; we wait for the seed until it grows (Jas. 5:7). Why can we not wait for God? God has waited for us (Isaiah 30:18). Did he not wait for our repentance? How often did he come, year after year, before he found fruit? Did God wait for us, and can we not wait for him? A godly man is content to await God's leisure; though the vision is delayed, he will wait for it (Hab. 2:3).

2. Patience in bearing trials

This patience is twofold:

(a) Patience in regard to man — when we bear injuries without revenging.

(b) Patience in regard to God — when we bear his hand without repining. A good man will not only do God's will — but bear his will: 'I will bear the indignation of the Lord' (Mic. 7:9). This patient bearing of God's will is not:

(1) A stoical apathy; patience is not insensitivity under God's hand; we ought to be sensitive.

(2) Enforced patience, to bear a thing because we cannot help it, which (as Erasmus said) is rather necessity than patience. But patience is a cheerful submission of our will to God. 'May the will of the Lord be done' (Acts 21:14). A godly man acquiesces in what God does, as being not only good, but best for himself. The great quarrel between God and us is, 'Whose will shall stand?' Now the regenerate will falls in with the will of God. There are four things which are opposite to this patient frame of soul:

(a) Disquiet of spirit, when the soul is discomposed and pulled off the hinges, insomuch that it is unfit for holy duties. When the strings of a lute are snarled up, the lute is not fit to make music. So when a Christian's spirit is perplexed and disturbed, he cannot make melody in his heart to the Lord.

(b) Discontent, which is a sullen, dogged mood. When a man is not angry at his sins — but at his condition, this is different from patience. Discontent is the daughter of pride.

(c) Defection, which is a dislike of God and his ways, and a falling off from religion. Sinners have hard thoughts of God, and if he just touches them on a sore spot, they will at once go away from him and throw off his livery.

(d) Self-vindication, when instead of being humbled under God's hand, a man justifies himself, as if he had not deserved what he suffers. A proud sinner stands upon his own defense, and is ready to accuse God of unrighteousness, which is as if we should accuse the sun with darkness. This is far from patience. A godly man subscribes to God's wisdom, and submits to his will. He says not only, 'Good is the word of the Lord' (Isaiah 39:8) — but 'Good is the rod of the Lord!'

Use: As we would demonstrate ourselves to be godly, let us be eminent in this grace of patience: 'the patient in spirit is better than the proud in spirit' (Eccles. 7:8). There are some graces which we shall have no need of in heaven. We shall have no need of faith when we have full vision, nor patience when we have perfect joy — but in a dark sorrowful night there is need of these stars to shine (Heb. 10: 36). Let us show our patience in bearing God's will. Patience in bearing God's will is twofold:

1. When God removes any comfort from us.

2. When God imposes any trouble on us.

1. We must be patient when God removes any comfort from us. If God takes away any of our relations — 'I take away the desire of your eyes with a stroke' (Ezek. 24:16) — it is still our duty patiently to acquiesce in the will of God. The loss of a dear relation is like pulling away a limb from the body. 'A man dies every time he loses his own kith and kin.' But grace will make our hearts calm and quiet, and produce holy patience in us under such a severe dispensation. I shall lay down eight considerations which may act like spiritual medicine to kill the worm of impatience under the loss of relations:

(1) The Lord never takes away any comfort from his people, without giving them something better. The disciples parted with Christ's physical presence, and he sent them the Holy Spirit. God eclipses one joy, and augments another. He simply makes an exchange; he takes away a flower, and gives a diamond.

(2) When godly friends die, they are in a better condition. They are taken away 'from the evil to come' (Isaiah 57:1). They are out of the storm, and have gone to the haven! 'Blessed are the dead who die in the Lord' (Rev. 14:13). The godly have a portion promised them upon their marriage to Christ — but the portion is not paid until the day of their death. The saints are promoted at death to communion with God; they have what they so long hoped for, and prayed for. Why, then, should we be impatient at our friends' promotion?

(3) You who are a saint, have a friend in heaven whom you cannot lose. The Jews have a saying at their funerals, 'Let your consolation be in heaven.' Are you mourning somebody close to you? Look up to heaven and draw comfort from there; your best kindred are above. 'When my father and my mother forsake me, then the Lord will take me up' (Psalm 27:10). God will be with you in the hour of death: 'though I walk through the valley of the shadow of death, you

are with me' (Psalm 23:4). Other friends, you cannot keep. God is a friend you cannot lose. He will be your guide in life; your hope in death; your reward after death!

(4) Perhaps God is correcting you for a fault, and if so, it befits you to be patient. It may be your friend had more of your love than God did, and therefore God took away such a relation, so that the stream of your love might run back to him again. A gracious woman had been deprived, first of her children, then of her husband. She said, 'Lord, you intend to have all my love.' God does not like to have any creature set upon the throne of our affections; he will take away that comfort, and then he shall lie nearest our heart. If a husband bestows a jewel on his wife, and she so falls in love with that jewel as to forget her husband, he will take away the jewel so that her love may return to him again. A dear relation is this jewel. If we begin to idolize it, God will take away the jewel, so that our love may return to him again.

(5) A godly relation is parted with—but not lost. That is lost, which we have no hope ever of seeing again. Pious friends have only gone a little ahead of us. A time will shortly come when there shall be a meeting without parting (1 Thess. 5:10). How glad one is to see a long-absent friend! Oh, what glorious joy there will be, when old relations meet together in heaven, and are in each other's embraces! When a great prince lands at the shore, the guns go off in token of joy; when godly friends have all landed at the heavenly shore and congratulate one another on their happiness, what stupendous joy there will be! What music in the choir of angels! How heaven will ring with their praises! And that which is the crown of all, those who were joined in the flesh here on earth, shall be joined nearer than ever in the mystic body, and shall lie together in Christ's bosom, that bed of perfume (1 Thess. 4:17).

(6) We have deserved worse at God's hand. Has he taken away a child, a wife, a parent? He might have taken away his Spirit. Has he deprived us of a relation? He might have deprived us of salvation. Does he put wormwood in the cup? We have deserved poison. 'You have punished us less than our iniquities deserve' (Ezra 9:13). We have a sea of sin—but only a drop of suffering.

(7) The patient soul enjoys itself most sweetly. An impatient man is like a troubled sea which cannot rest (Isaiah 57:20). He tortures himself upon the rack of his own griefs and passions. Whereas patience calms the heart, as Christ did the sea, when it was rough. Now there is a sabbath in the heart, yes, a heaven. 'In your patience possess your souls' (Luke 21:19). By faith a man possesses God, and by patience he possesses himself.

(8) How patient many of the saints have been, when the Lord has broken the very staff of their comfort in bereaving them of relations. The Lord took away Job's children and he was so far from murmuring that he fell to blessing: 'Naked I came from my mother's womb, and naked I will depart. The Lord gave and the Lord has taken away; may the name of the Lord be praised.' (Job 1:21). God foretold the death of Eli's sons: 'in one day both of them shall die,' (1 Sam. 2:34). But how patiently he took this sad news: 'It is the Lord's will. Let him do what he thinks best.' (1 Sam. 3:18). See the difference between Eli and Pharaoh! Pharaoh said, 'Who is the Lord?' (Exod. 5:2). Eli said, 'It is the Lord.' When God struck two of Aaron's sons dead, 'Aaron held his peace' (Lev. 10:2,3). Patience opens the ear—but shuts the mouth! It opens the ear to hear the rod—but shuts the mouth so that it has not a word to say against God. See here the patterns of patience; and shall we not copy them? These are heart-quietening considerations when God sets a death's-head upon our comforts and removes dear relations from us.

2. We must be patient when God inflicts any trouble on us. 'Patient in tribulation' (Romans 12:12).

(1) God sometimes lays heavy affliction on his people: 'Your arrows have struck deep, and your blows are crushing me.' (Psalm 38:2). The Hebrew word for 'afflicted' signifies 'to be melted.' God seems to melt his people in a furnace.

(2) God sometimes lays various afflictions on the saints: 'he multiplies my wounds' (Job 9:17). As we have various ways of sinning, so the Lord has various ways of afflicting. Some he deprives of their estates; others he chains to a sick bed; others he confines to a prison. God has various arrows in his quiver, which he shoots.

(3) Sometimes God lets the affliction lie for a long time: 'None of us knows how long this will last' (Psalm 74:9). As it is with diseases — some are chronic and linger and hang about the body several years — so it is with afflictions. The Lord is pleased to exercise many of his precious ones with chronic afflictions, which they suffer for a long time. Now in all these cases, it befits the saints to rest patiently in the will of God. The Greek word for 'patient' is a metaphor and alludes to one who stands invincibly under a heavy burden. This is the right notion of patience, when we bear affliction invincibly without fainting or fretting.

The test of a pilot is seen in a storm; so the test of a Christian is seen in affliction. That man has the right art of navigation who, when the boisterous winds blow from heaven, steers the ship of his soul wisely, and does not dash upon the rock of impatience. A Christian should always maintain decorum, not behaving himself in an unseemly manner or acting with intemperate passion when the hand of God lies upon him. Patience adorns suffering. Affliction in Scripture is compared to a net: 'You brought us into the net' (Psalm 66:11). Some have escaped the devil's net — yet the Lord allows them to be taken in the net of affliction. But they must not be 'as a wild bull in a net' (Isaiah 51:20), kicking and flinging against their Maker — but lie patiently until God breaks the net and makes a way for their escape. I shall propound four potent arguments to encourage patience under those troubles which God inflicts on us:

(a) Afflictions are for our profit, for our benefit: 'God disciplines us for our good, that we may share in his holiness.' (Heb. 12:10). We pray that God would take such a course with us as may do our souls good. When God is afflicting us, he is hearing our prayers; he does it 'for our good.' Not that afflictions in themselves profit us — but as God's Spirit works with them. For as the waters of Bethesda could not give health of themselves, unless the angel descended and stirred them (John 5:4), so the waters of affliction are not in themselves healing until God's Spirit co-operates and sanctifies them to us. Afflictions are profitable in many ways:

(1) They make men sober and wise. Physicians have mental patients bound in chains and put on a frugal diet to bring them to the use of reason. Many run stark mad in prosperity; they know neither God nor themselves. The Lord therefore binds them with cords of affliction, so that he may bring them to their right minds. 'If they are held in cords of affliction, then he shows them their transgressions. He opens also their ear to discipline' (Job 36:8-10).

(2) Afflictions are a friend to grace:

(A) They beget grace. Beza acknowledged that God laid the foundation of his conversion, during a violent sickness in Paris.

(B) They augment grace. The people of God are indebted to their troubles; they would never have had so much grace, if they had not met with such severe trials. Now the waters run, and the spices flow forth. The saints thrive by affliction as the Lacedemonians grew rich by war. God makes grace flourish most in the fall of the leaf.

(3) Afflictions quicken our pace on the way to heaven. It is with us as with children sent on an errand. If they meet with apples or flowers by the way, they linger and are in no great hurry to get home — but if anything frightens them, then they run with all the speed they can, to their

father's house. So in prosperity, we gather the apples and flowers and do not give much thought to heaven—but if troubles begin to arise and the times grow frightful, then we make more haste to heaven and with David 'run the way of God's commandments' (Psalm 119:32).

(b) God intermixes mercy with affliction. He steeps his sword of justice in the oil of mercy. There was no night so dark but Israel had a pillar of fire in it. There is no condition so dismal but we may see a pillar of fire to give us light. If the body is in pain, and conscience is at peace—there is mercy. Affliction is for the prevention of sin; there is mercy. In the ark there was 'a rod and a pot of manna', the emblem of a Christian's condition: 'mercy interlined with judgment' (Psalm 101:1). Here is the rod and manna.

(c) Patience proves that there is much of God in the heart. Patience is one of God's titles: 'the God of patience' (Romans 15:5). If you have your heart cast in this blessed mold, it is a sign that God has imparted much of his own nature to you; you shine with some of his beams.

Impatience proves that there is much unsoundness of heart. If the body is of such a type that every little scratch of a pin makes the flesh fester, you say, 'Surely this man's flesh is very unsound.' So impatience with every petty annoyance, and quarreling with providence—is the sign of a disturbed Christian. If there is any grace in such a heart, they who can see it must have good eyes. But he who is of a patient spirit is a graduate in religion, and participates in much of the divine nature.

(d) The end of affliction is glorious. The Jews were captive in Babylon, but what was the end? They departed from Babylon with vessels of silver, gold and precious things (Ezra 1:6). So, what is the end of affliction? It ends in endless glory (Acts 14:22; 2 Cor. 4:17). How this may rock our impatient hearts quiet! Who would not willingly travel along a little dirty path—at the end of which is a priceless inheritance!

Question: How shall I get my heart tuned to a patient mood?

Answer: Get faith; all our impatience proceeds from unbelief. Faith is the breeder of patience. When a storm of passion begins to arise, faith says to the heart, as Christ did to the sea, 'Peace, be still', and there is at once a calm.

Question: How does faith work patience?

Answer: Faith argues the soul into patience. Faith is like that town clerk in Ephesus who allayed the contention of the multitude and argued them soberly into peace (Acts 19:35,36). So when impatience begins to clamor and make a hubbub in the soul, faith appeases the tumult and argues the soul into holy patience. Faith says, 'Why are you disquieted, O my soul?' (Psalm 42:5). Are you afflicted? Is it not your Father who has done it? He is carving and polishing you, and making you fit for glory. He smites that he may save. What is your trial? Is it sickness? God shakes the tree of your body so that some fruit may fall, even 'the peaceable fruit of righteousness' (Heb. 12:11). Are you driven from your home? God has prepared a city for you (Heb. 11:16). Do you suffer reproach for Christ's sake? 'The spirit of glory and of God rests upon you' (1 Pet. 4:14). Thus faith argues and disputes the soul into patience.

Pray to God for patience. Patience is a flower of God's planting. Pray that it may grow in your heart, and send forth its sweet perfume. Prayer is a holy charm, to charm down the evil spirit of impatience. Prayer composes the heart and puts it in tune, when impatience has broken the strings and put everything into confusion. Oh, go to God. Prayer delights God's ear; it melts his heart; it opens his hand. God cannot deny a praying soul. Seek him with importunity and either he will remove the affliction—or, which is better, he will remove your impatience!

17. A godly man is a thankful man

Praise and thanksgiving is the work of heaven; and he begins that work here which he will always be doing in heaven. The Hebrew word for 'praise' comes from a root that signifies 'to shoot up.' The godly man sends up his praises like a volley of shots towards heaven. David was modeled after God's heart and how melodiously he warbled out God's praises! Therefore he was called 'the sweet psalmist of Israel' (2 Sam. 23:1). Take a Christian at his worst — yet he is thankful. The prophet Jonah was a man of waspish spirit. The sea was not so stirred with the tempest, as Jonah's heart was stirred with passion (Jonah 1:13). Yet through this cloud you might see grace appear. He had a thankful heart: 'I will sacrifice unto you with the voice of thanksgiving; I will pay that that I have vowed' (Jonah 2:9). To illustrate this more clearly, I shall lay down these four particulars:

1. Praise and thanksgiving is a saint-like work

We find in Scripture that the godly are still called upon to praise God: 'Praise the Lord; you who fear him, praise the Lord' (Psalm 135:20). 'Let the saints be joyful in glory: let the high praises of God be in their mouth' (Psalm 149:5,6). Praise is a work proper to a saint:

(1) None but the godly can praise God aright. As all do not have the skill to play the lute, so not everyone can sound forth the harmonious praises of God. Wicked men are bound to praise God — but they are not fit to praise him. None but a living Christian can tune God's praise. Wicked men are dead in sin; how can they who are dead, lift up God's praises? 'The grave cannot praise you' (Isaiah 38:18). A wicked man stains and eclipses God's praise. If a filthy hand works in satin, it will slur its beauty. God will say to the sinner, 'What have you to do, to take my covenant in your mouth?' (Psalm 50:16).

(2) Praise is not lovely, for any but the godly: 'praise is lovely for the upright' (Psalm 33:1). A profane man with God's praises is like a dunghill with flowers. Praise in the mouth of a sinner, is like a proverb in the mouth of a fool. How unfitting it is for anyone to praise God — if his whole life dishonors God! It is as indecent for a wicked man to praise God, as it is for a thief to talk of living by faith, or for the devil to quote Scripture. The godly alone are fit to be choristers in God's praises. It is called 'the garment of praise' (Isaiah 61:3). This garment fits handsomely only on a saint's back.

2. Thanksgiving is a more noble part of God's worship

Our needs may send us to prayer, but it takes a truly honest heart to praise God. The raven cries; the lark sings. In petition we act like men; in thanksgiving we act like angels.

3. Thanksgiving is a God-exalting work

'Whoever offers praise glorifies me' (Psalm 50:23). Though nothing can add the least mite to God's essential glory — yet praise exalts him in the eyes of others. Praise is a setting forth of God's honor, a lifting up of his name, a displaying of the trophy of his goodness, a proclaiming of his excellence, a spreading of his renown, a breaking open of the box of ointment, whereby the sweet fragrance of God's name is sent abroad into the world.

4. Praise is a more distinguishing work

By this a Christian excels all the infernal spirits. Do you talk of God? So can the devil; he brought Scripture to Christ. Do you profess religion? So can the devil; he transforms himself into an angel of light. Do you fast? He never eats. Do you believe? The devils have a faith of assent; they believe, and tremble (Jas. 2:19). But as Moses worked such a miracle as none of the magicians could reproduce, so here is a work Christians may be doing, which none of the devils can do — and that is the work of thanksgiving. The devils blaspheme — but do not bless. Satan has his fiery darts but not his harp and violin.

Use 1: See here the true genius and characteristic of a godly man. He is much in doxologies and praises. It is a saying of Lactantius that he who is unthankful to his God cannot be a godly man. A godly man is a God-exalter. The saints are temples of the Holy Spirit (1 Cor. 3:16). Where should God's praises be sounded — but in his temples? A good heart is never weary of praising God: 'his praise shall continually be in my mouth' (Psalm 34:1). Some will be thankful while the memory of the mercy is fresh — but afterwards leave off. The Carthaginians at first to send the tenth of their yearly revenue to Hercules — but by degrees they grew weary and stopped sending. David, as long as he drew his breath, would chirp forth God's praise: 'I will sing praises unto my God while I have any being' (Psalm146:2). David would not now and then give God a snatch of music, and then hang up the instrument — but he would continually be celebrating God's praise.

A godly man will express his thankfulness in every duty. He mingles thanksgiving with prayer: 'in everything by prayer with thanksgiving let your requests be made known unto God' (Phil. 4:6). Thanksgiving is the more divine part of prayer. In our petitions we express our own necessities; in our thanksgivings we declare God's excellences. Prayer goes up as incense, when it is perfumed with thanksgiving.

And as a godly man expresses thankfulness in every duty, he does so in every condition. He will be thankful in adversity as well as prosperity: 'In everything give thanks' (1 Thess. 5:18). A gracious soul is thankful and rejoices that he is drawn nearer to God, though it be by the cords of affliction. When it goes well with him, he praises God's mercy; when it goes badly with him, he magnifies God's justice. When God has a rod in his hand, a godly man will have a psalm in his mouth. The devil's smiting of Job was like striking a musical instrument; he sounded forth praise: 'Naked I came from my mother's womb, and naked I will depart. The Lord gave and the Lord has taken away; may the name of the Lord be praised' (Job 1:21). When God's spiritual plants are cut and bleed, they drop thankfulness; the saints' tears cannot drown their praises.

If this is the sign of a godly man, then the number of the godly appears to be very small. Few are in the work of praise. Sinners cut God short of his thank offering: 'Where are the nine?' (Luke 17:17). Of ten lepers healed there was but one who returned to give praise. Most of the world are sepulchers to bury God's praise. You will hear some swearing and cursing — but few who bless God. Praise is the rent which men owe to God — but most are behindhand with their rent. God gave King Hezekiah a marvelous deliverance, 'but Hezekiah rendered not again according to the benefit done unto him' (2 Chron. 32:25). That 'but' was a blot on his escutcheon.

Some, instead of being thankful to God, 'render evil for good.' They are the worse for mercy: 'Do you thus requite the Lord, O foolish and unwise people?' (Deut. 32:6). This is like the toad which turns the most wholesome herb to poison. Where shall we find a grateful Christian? We read of the saints 'having harps in their hands' (Rev 5:8) — the emblem of praise. Many have tears in their eyes and complaints in their mouths — but few have harps in their hand and are blessing and praising the name of God.

Use 2: Let us scrutinize ourselves and examine by this characteristic whether we are godly: Are we thankful for mercy? It is a hard thing to be thankful.

Question: How may we know whether we are rightly thankful?

Answer 1: We are rightly thankful — when we are careful to register God's mercies: 'David appointed certain of the Levites to record, and to thank and praise the Lord God of Israel' (1

Chron. 16:4). Physicians say that the memory is the first thing which decays. It is true in spiritual matters: 'They soon forgot his works' (Psalm 106:13). A godly man enters his mercies, as a physician does his remedies, in a book, so that they may not be lost. Mercies are jewels that should be locked up. A child of God keeps two books always by him: one to write his sins in — so that he may be humble; the other to write his mercies in — so that he may be thankful.

Answer 2: We are rightly thankful — when our hearts are the chief instrument in the music of praise: 'I will praise the Lord with my whole heart' (Psalm 111:1). David would tune not only his violin — but also his heart. If the heart does not join with the tongue, there can be no true praise. Where the heart is not engaged, the parrot is as good a chorister as the Christian.

Answer 3: We are rightly thankful — when the favors which we receive, endear our love to God the more. David's miraculous preservation from death drew forth his love to God: 'I love the Lord' (Psalm 116:1). It is one thing to love our mercies; it is another thing to love the Lord. Many love their deliverance, but not their deliverer. God is to be loved more than his mercies.

Answer 4: We are rightly thankful when, in giving our praise to God, we see no worthiness from ourselves: 'I am not worthy of the least of all the mercies you have showed unto your servant' (Gen. 32:10). As if Jacob had said, 'Lord, the worst bit you carve for me, is better than I deserve.' Mephibosheth bowed himself and said, 'What is your servant, that you should look upon such a dead dog as I am?' (2 Sam. 9:8). So when a thankful Christian makes a survey of his blessings and sees how much he enjoys, that others better than he lack, he says, 'Lord, what am I, a dead dog, that free grace should look upon me, and that you should crown me with such loving kindness!'

Answer 5: We are rightly thankful — when we put God's mercy to good use. We repay God's blessings — with service. The Lord gives us health — and we spend and are spent for Christ (2 Cor. 12:15). He gives us an estate — and we honor the Lord with our substance (Proverbs 3:9). He gives us children — and we dedicate them to God and educate them for God. We do not bury our talents — but use them for God's glory. This is to put our mercies to good use. A gracious heart is like a piece of good ground that, having received the seed of mercy, produces a crop of obedience.

Answer 6: We are rightly thankful — when we can have our hearts more enlarged for spiritual mercies — than for temporal mercies: 'Blessed be God, who has blessed us with all spiritual blessings' (Eph. 1:3). A godly man blesses God more for a fruitful heart — than a full crop. He is more thankful for Christ — than for a kingdom. Socrates was accustomed to say that he loved the king's smile — more than his gold. A pious heart is more thankful for a smile of God's face — than he would be for all the gold of the Indies.

Answer 7: We are rightly thankful — when mercy is a spur to duty. It causes a spirit of activity for God. Mercy is not like the sun to the fire, to dull it — but like oil to the wheel, to make it run faster. David wisely argues from mercy to duty: 'You have delivered my soul from death. I will walk before the Lord in the land of the living' (Psalm 116:8,9). It was a saying of Bernard, 'Lord, I have two mites, a soul and a body, and I give them both to you.'

Answer 8: We are rightly thankful — when we motivate others to this angelic work of praise. David does not only wish to bless God himself — but calls upon others to do so: 'Praise the Lord, all you nations; extol him, all you peoples.' (Psalm 117:1). The sweetest music is that which is in unison. When many saints join together in unison, then they make heaven ring with their praises. As one drunkard will be calling upon another — so in a holy sense, one Christian must be stirring up another to the work of thankfulness.

Answer 9: We are rightly thankful—when we not only speak God's praise—but live his praise. It is called an expression of gratitude. We give thanks when we live thanks. Such as are mirrors of mercy should be patterns of piety. 'Upon Mount Zion shall be deliverance, and there shall be holiness' (Obad. 17). To give God oral praise and dishonor him in our lives, is to commit a barbarism in religion, and is to be like those Jews who bowed the knee to Christ and then spit on him (Mark 15:19).

Answer 10: We are rightly thankful—when we propagate God's praises to posterity. We tell our children what God has done for us: in such a need he supplied us; from such a sickness he raised us up; in such a temptation he helped us. 'O God, our fathers have told us, what work you did in their days, in the times of old' (Psalm 44:1). By transmitting our experiences to our children, God's name is eternalized, and his mercies will bring forth a plentiful crop of praise when we are gone. Heman puts the question, 'shall the dead praise you?' (Psalm 88:10). Yes, in the sense that when we are dead, we praise God because, having left the chronicle of God's mercies with our children, we start them on thankfulness and so make God's praises live when we are dead.

Use 3: Let us prove our godliness by gratefulness: 'Give unto the Lord the glory due unto his name' (Psalm 29:2).

1. It is a good thing to be thankful. 'It is good to sing praises unto our God' (Psalm 147:1). It is bad when the tongue (that organ of praise) is out of tune and jars by murmuring and discontent. But it is a good thing to be thankful. It is good, because this is all the creature can do to lift up God's name; and it is good because it tends to make us good. The more thankful we are, the more holy. While we pay this tribute of praise, our stock of grace increases. In other debts, the more we pay, the less we have; but the more we pay this debt of thankfulness, the more grace we have.

2. Thankfulness is the rent we owe to God. 'Kings of the earth, and all people; let them praise the name of the Lord' (Psalm 148:11,13), Praise is the tribute or custom to be paid into the King of heaven's treasury. Surely while God renews our lease, we must renew our rent.

3. The great cause we have to be thankful. It is a principle grafted in nature—to be thankful for mercies received. Even the heathen praised Jupiter for their victories.

What full clusters of mercies hang on us when we go to enumerate God's mercies! We must, with David, confess ourselves to be bewildered: 'Many, O Lord my God, are your wonderful works which you have done, they cannot be reckoned up in order' (Psalm 40:5). And as God's mercies are past numbering, so they are past measuring. David takes the longest measuring line he could get. He measures from earth to the clouds, no, above the clouds—yet this measure would not reach the heights of God's mercies: 'Your mercy is great above the heavens' (Psalm 108:4). Oh, how God has enriched us with his silver showers! A whole constellation of mercies has shone in our hemisphere.

(1) What temporal favors we have received! Every day we see a new tide of mercy coming in. The wings of mercy have covered us; the breast of mercy has fed us: 'the God who fed me all my life long unto this day' (Gen. 48:15). What snares laid for us have been broken! What fears have blown over! The Lord has made our bed, while he has made others' graves. He has taken such care of us, as if he had no one else to take care of. Never was the cloud of providence so black—but we might see a rainbow of love in the cloud. We have been made to swim in a sea of mercy! Does not all this call for thankfulness?

(2) That which may put another string into the instrument of our praise and make it sound louder—is to consider what spiritual blessings God has conferred on us. He has given us water

from the upper springs; he has opened the wardrobe of heaven and fetched us out a better garment than any of the angels wear! He has given us the best robe, and put on us the ring of faith, by which we are married to him. These are mercies of the first magnitude, which deserve to have an asterisk put on them. More—God keeps the best wine until last! Here on earth, he gives us mercies only in small quantities; the greatest things are laid up in heaven! Here on earth, there are some honey drops and foretastes of God's love; the rivers of pleasure are reserved for paradise! Well may we take the harp and violin and triumph in God's praise. Who can tread on these hot coals of God's love—and his heart not burn in thankfulness!

4. Thankfulness is the best policy. There is nothing lost by it. To be thankful for one mercy is the way to have more. It is like pouring water into a pump which fetches out more. Musicians love to sound their trumpets where there is the best echo, and God loves to bestow his mercies where there is the best echo of thankfulness.

5. Thankfulness is a frame of heart that God delights in. If repentance is the joy of heaven, praise is the music. Bernard calls thankfulness, 'the sweet balm that drops from a Christian.'

Four sacrifices God is very pleased with: the sacrifice of Christ's blood; the sacrifice of a broken heart; the sacrifice of alms; and the sacrifice of thanksgiving. Praise and thanksgiving (says Greenham) is the most excellent part of God's worship, for this shall continue in the heavenly choir when all other exercises of religion have ceased.

6. What a horrid thing ingratitude is! It gives a dye and tincture to every other sin and makes it crimson. Ingratitude is the spirit of baseness: 'Your trusted friends will set traps for you' (Obad. 7). Ingratitude is worse than brutish (Isaiah 1:3). It is reported of Julius Caesar that he would never forgive an ungrateful person. Though God is a sin-pardoning God, he scarcely knows how to pardon for this. 'How shall I pardon you for this? your children have forsaken me, when I had fed them to the full, they then committed adultery' (Jer. 5:7). Draco (whose laws were written in blood) published an edict that if any man had received a benefit from another, and it could be proved against him that he had not been grateful for it, he should be put to death. An unthankful person is a monster in nature—and a paradox in Christianity. He is the scorn of heaven and the plague of earth. An ungrateful man never does well, except in one thing—that is, when he dies. Then he becomes a monument of God's justice.

7. Not being thankful is the cause of all the judgments which have lain on us. Our unthankfulness for health has been the cause of so much mortality. Our gospel unthankfulness and sermon-surfeiting has been the reason why God has put so many lights under a bushel. Who will spend money on a piece of ground that produces nothing but briars? Unthankfulness stops up the golden vial of God's bounty, so that it will not drop.

Question: What shall we do to be thankful?

Answer 1: If you wish to be thankful, get a heart deeply humbled with the sense of your own vileness. A broken heart is the best pipe to sound forth God's praise. He who studies his sins wonders that he has anything and that God should shine on such a dunghill: 'I was once a blasphemer and a persecutor and a violent man, but I was shown mercy' (1 Tim. 1:13). How thankful Paul was! How he trumpeted forth free grace! A proud man will never be thankful. He looks on all his mercies as either of his own procuring or deserving. If he has an estate, this he has got by his wits and industry, not considering that scripture, 'Always remember that it is the Lord your God who gives you power to become rich' (Deut. 8:18). Pride stops the current of gratitude. O Christian, think of your unworthiness; see yourself as the least of saints, and the chief of sinners—and then you will be thankful.

Answer 2: Strive for sound evidences of God's love to you. Read God's love in the impress of holiness upon your hearts. God's love poured in will make the vessels of mercy run over with thankfulness: 'Unto him that loved us, be glory and dominion forever!' (Rev. 1:5,6). The deepest springs yield the sweetest water. Hearts deeply aware of God's love yield the sweetest praises

18. A godly man is a lover of the saints

The best way to discern grace in oneself — is to love grace in others: 'We know that we have passed from death unto life, because we love the brethren' (1 John 3:14). What is religion — but a knitting together of hearts? Faith knits us to God — and love knits us one to another. There is a twofold love to others:

1. A civil love. A godly man has a love of civility to all: 'Abraham stood up, and bowed to the children of Heth' (Gen. 23:7). Though they were extraneous and not within the pale of the covenant — yet Abraham was affable to them. Grace sweetens and refines nature. 'Be sympathetic, love as brothers, be compassionate and humble' (1 Pet. 3:8). We are to have a love of civility to all:

(1) Because they are of the same clay, of the same lump and mold with ourselves and are a piece of God's intricate needlework.

(2) Because our sweet deportment towards them may be a means to win them over and put them in love with the ways of God. Morose, crude behavior, often alienates the hearts of others and hardens them most against holiness, whereas loving behavior is very obliging and may be like a loadstone to draw them to true religion.

2. A pious and a holy love. This, a godly man has chiefly for those who are 'of the household of faith' (Gal. 6:10). The first was a love of courtesy, this of delight. Our love to the saints (says Augustine) should be more than to our natural relations, because the bond of the Spirit is closer than that of blood. This love to the saints which shows a man to be godly must have seven ingredients in it:

(1) Love to the saints must be sincere. 'Let us not love in word, neither in tongue — but in deed and in truth' (1 John 3:18). The honey that drops from the comb is pure; so love must be pure, without deceit. Many are like Naphtali: 'He gives goodly words' (Gen. 49:21). Pretended love is like a painted fire, which has no heat in it. Some hide malice under a false veil of love. I have read of Antoninus the Emperor that where he made a show of friendship, he intended the most mischief.

(2) Love to the saints must be spiritual. We must love them because they are saints, not out of self-respect because they are affable or have been kind to us.

But we must love them from spiritual considerations, because of the good that is in them. We are to reverence their holiness, else it is a carnal love.

(3) Love to the saints must be extensive. We must love all who bear God's image:

(a) We must love the saints, though they have many infirmities. A Christian in this life is like a good face full of freckles. You who cannot love another because of his imperfections, have never yet seen your own face in the mirror. Your brother's infirmities may make you pity him; his graces must make you love him.

(b) We must love the saints, though in some things they do not agree with us. Another Christian may differ from me in lesser matters, either because he has more light than I, or because he has less light. If he differs from me because he has more light, then I have no reason to censure him. If he differs from me because he has less light, then I ought to bear with him as the weaker vessel. In things of an indifferent nature, there ought to be Christian forbearance.

(c) We must love the saints, though their graces outvie and surpass ours. We ought to bless God for the eminence of another's grace, because hereby religion is honored. Pride is not quite slain in a believer. Saints themselves are apt to grudge and repine at each other's excellences. Is it not strange that the same person should hate one man for his sin and envy another for his virtue? Christians need to look to their hearts. Love is right and genuine, when we can rejoice in the graces of others though they seem to eclipse ours.

(4) Love to the saints must be appreciating. We must esteem them above others: 'He honors those who fear the Lord' (Psalm 15:4). We are to look upon the wicked as chaff — but upon the saints as jewels. These must be had in high veneration.

(5) Love to the saints must be social. We should delight in their company: 'I am a companion of all those who fear you' (Psalm 119:63). It is a kind of hell to be in the company of the wicked, where we cannot choose but hear God's name dishonored. It was a capital crime to carry the image of Tiberius, engraved on a ring or coin, into any sordid place. Those who have the image of God engraved on them should not go into any sinful, sordid company. I have only ever read of two living people who desired to keep company with the dead, and they were possessed by the devil (Matt. 8:28). What comfort can a living Christian have from conversing with the dead (Jude 12)? But the society of saints is desirable. This is not to walk 'among the tombs' — but 'among beds of spices.' Believers are Christ's garden; their graces are the flowers; their savory discourse is the fragrant scent of these flowers.

(6) Love to the saints must be demonstrative. We should be ready to do all offices of love to them, vindicate their names, contribute to their necessities and, like the good Samaritan, pour oil and wine into their wounds (Luke 10:34,35). Love cannot be concealed — but is active in its sphere and will lay itself out for the good of others.

(7) Love to the saints must be constant. 'He who dwells in love' (1 John 4:16). Our love must not only lodge for a night — but we must dwell in love: 'Let brotherly love continue' (Heb. 13:1). As love must be sincere, without hypocrisy; so it must be constant, without deficiency. Love must be like the pulse, always beating, not like those Galatians who at one time were ready to pluck out their eyes for Paul (Gal. 4:15) and afterwards were ready to pluck out his eyes. Love should expire only with our life. And surely if our love to the saints is thus divinely qualified, we may hopefully conclude that we are enrolled among the godly. 'By this shall all men know that you are my disciples — if you have love one to another' (John 13:35).

What induces a godly man to love the saints is the fact that he is closely related to them. There ought to be love among relations; there is a spiritual kinship among believers. They all have one head, therefore should all have one heart. They are stones of the same building (1 Pet. 2:5), and shall not these stones be cemented together with love?

Use 1: If it is the distinguishing mark of a godly man to be a lover of the saints, then how sad it is to see this grace of love in eclipse! This characteristic of godliness is almost blotted out among Christians. England was once a fair garden where the flower of love grew — but surely now this flower is either plucked, or withered. Where is that amity and unity which there should be among Christians? I appeal to you — would there be that censuring and despising, that reproaching and undermining one another — if there were love? Instead of bitter tears, there are bitter spirits. It is a sign that iniquity abounds when the love of many grows cold. There is that distance among some professing Christians as if they had not received the same Spirit, or as if they did not hope for the same heaven. In primitive times there was so much love among the godly — that it set the heathen wondering; and now there is so little love — that it may set Christians blushing.

Use 2: As we would be written down for saints in God's calendar, let us love the brotherhood (1 Pet. 2:17). Those who shall one day live together, should love together. What is it that makes a disciple, but love (John 13:35)? The devil has knowledge — but that which makes him a devil is that he lacks love. To persuade Christians to love, consider:

(1) The saints have that in them which may make us love them. They are the intricate embroidery and workmanship of the Holy Spirit (Eph. 2:10). They have those rare lineaments of grace that none but a pencil from heaven could draw. Their eyes sparkle forth beauty, 'their breasts are like clusters of grapes' (Cant 7:7). This makes Christ himself delight in his spouse: 'The king is held in the galleries' (Cant 7:5). The church is the daughter of a prince (Cant 7:1). She is waited on by angels (Heb 1:14). She has a palace of glory reserved for her (John 14:2), and may not all this draw forth our love?

(2) Consider how evil it is for saints not to love:

(a) It is unnatural. The saints are Christ's lambs (John 21:15). For a dog to worry a lamb is usual — but for one lamb to worry another is unnatural. The saints are brethren (1 Peter 3:8). How barbarous it is for brethren not to love!

(b) Not to love is a foolish thing. Have not God's people enemies enough, that they should fly in the faces of one another? The wicked confederate against the godly: 'They have taken crafty counsel against your people' (Psalm 83:3). Though there may be a private grudge between such as are wicked — yet they will all agree and unite against the saints. If two greyhounds are snarling at a bone and you put a hare between them, they will leave the bone and chase the hare. So if wicked men have private differences among themselves, and the godly are near them, they will leave snarling at one another and chase the godly. Now, when God's people have so many enemies abroad, who watch for their halting and are glad when they can do them a mischief, shall the saints fall out and divide into parties among themselves?

(3) Not to love is very unseasonable. God's people are in a common calamity. They all suffer in the cause of the gospel, and for them to disagree is altogether unseasonable. Why does the Lord bring his people together in affliction, except to bring them together in affection? Metals will unite in a furnace. If ever Christians unite, it should be in the furnace of affliction. Chrysostom compares affliction to a shepherd's dog, which makes all the sheep run together. God's rod has this loud voice in it: 'Love one another.' How unworthy it is when Christians are suffering together, to be then striving together.

(4) Not to love is very sinful.

(a) For saints not to love, is to live in contradiction to Scripture. The apostle is continually plucking this string of love, as if it made the sweetest music in religion: 'This commandment have we from him, That he who loves God love his brother also' (1 John 4:21). (See also Romans 13:8; Col. 3:14; 1 Peter 1:22; 1 John 3:11). Not to love is to walk contrary to the Word. Can he who goes against the rules of medicine, be a good physician? Can he who goes against the rules of piety, be a good Christian?

(b) Lack of love among Christians greatly silences the spirit of prayer. Hot passions make cold prayers. Where animosities and contentions prevail, instead of praying for one another, Christians will be ready to pray against one another, like the disciples who prayed for fire from heaven on the Samaritans (Luke 9:54). And will God, do you think, hear such prayers as come from a wrathful heart? Will he eat our leavened bread? Will he accept those duties which are soured with bitterness of spirit? Shall that prayer which is offered with the strange fire of our sinful passions, ever go up as incense?

(c) These heart-burnings hinder the progress of piety in our own souls. The flower of grace will not grow in a wrathful heart. The body may as soon thrive, while it has the plague—as a soul can thrive, which is infected with malice. While Christians are debating, grace is abating. As the spleen grows, health decays. As hatred increases, holiness declines.

(5) Not to love is very fatal. The differences among God's people portend ruin. All mischiefs come in at this gap of division (Matt. 12:25). Animosities among saints may make God leave his temple: 'the glory of the Lord went up from the cherub, and stood upon the threshold' (Ezek. 10:4). Does not God seem to stand upon the threshold of his house, as if he were taking wings to fly? And woe to us if God departs from us (Hos. 9:12)! If the master leaves the ship, it is nearly sinking indeed. If God leaves a land, it must of necessity sink in ruin.

Question: How shall we attain this excellent grace of love?

Answer 1: Beware of the devil's couriers—I mean such as run on his errand, and make it their work to blow the coals of contention among Christians, and render one party odious to another.

Answer 2: Keep up friendly meetings. Christians should not be shy of one another, as if they had the plague.

Answer 3: Let us plead that promise: 'I will give them one heart, and one way' (Jer. 32:39). Let us pray that there may be no contests among Christians, except as to who shall love most. Let us pray that God will divide Babylon—and unite Zion.

Use 3: Is it a mark of a godly man to love the saints? Then those who hate the saints must stand indicted as ungodly. The wicked have an implacable malice against God's people, and how can antipathies be reconciled? To hate the holy children of God, is a brand of the reprobate. Those who malign the godly, are the curse of creation. If all the scalding drops from God's vial will make them miserable—they shall be so! Never did any who were the haters and persecutors of saints thrive at that trade. What became of Julian, Diocletian, Maximinus, Valerian, Cardinal Crescentius and others? They are standing monuments of God's vengeance! 'Calamity will surely overtake the wicked, and those who hate the righteous will be punished. ' (Psalm 34:21).

19. A godly man does not indulge in any sin

Though sin lives in him—yet he does not live in sin. A godly man may step into sin through infirmity—but he does not keep on that road. He prays, 'Search me, O God, and know my heart; test me and know my thoughts. Point out anything in me that offends you, and lead me along the path of everlasting life.' (Psalm 139:23-24).

Question: What is it to indulge sin?

Answer 1: To give the breast to it and feed it. As a fond parent humors his child and lets him have what he wants, so to indulge sin is to humor sin.

Answer 2: To indulge sin is to commit it with delight. The ungodly 'delight in wickedness' (2 Thess. 2:12).

In this sense, a godly man does not indulge sin. Though sin is in him, he is troubled at it and would gladly get rid of it. There is as much difference between sin in the wicked and sin in the godly—as between poison being in a serpent and poison being in a man. Poison in a serpent is in its natural place and is delightful—but poison in a man's body is harmful and he uses antidotes to expel it. So sin in a wicked man is delightful, being in its natural place—but sin in a child of God is burdensome and he uses all means to expel it. The sin is trimmed off. The will is against it. A godly man enters his protest against sin: 'Oh, what a miserable person I am! Who will free me from this life that is dominated by sin?' (Romans 7:24). A child of God, while he commits sin, hates the sin he commits (Romans 7).

In particular there are four kinds of sin, which a godly man will not allow himself:

1. Secret sins. Some are more modest than to commit open gross sin. That would be a stain on their reputation. But they will sit brooding upon sin in a corner: 'Saul secretly practiced mischief' (1 Sam. 23:9). All will not sin on a balcony — but perhaps they will sin behind the curtain. Rachel did not carry her father's images like a saddle cloth to be exposed to public view — but she put them under her and sat on them (Gen. 31:34). Many carry their sins secretly.

But a godly man dare not sin secretly:

(1) He knows that God sees in secret, 'for he knows the secrets of every heart.' (Psalm 44:21). As God cannot be deceived by our subtlety, so he cannot be excluded by our secrecy.

(2) A godly man knows that secret sins are in some sense worse than others. They reveal more guile and atheism. The curtain-sinner makes himself believe that God does not see: 'Son of man, have you seen what the leaders of Israel are doing with their idols in dark rooms? They are saying — The Lord doesn't see us!' (Ezek. 8:12). Those who have bad eyes think that the sun is dim. How it provokes God, that men's atheism should give the lie to his omniscience! 'He who formed the eye, shall he not see?' (Psalm 94:9).

(3) A godly man knows that secret sins shall not escape God's justice. A judge on the bench can punish no offence but what is proved by witnesses. He cannot punish the treason of the heart — but the sins of the heart are as visible to God as if they were written upon the forehead. As God will reward secret duties, so he will revenge secret sins.

2. Gainful sins. Gain is the golden bait, with which Satan fishes for souls! 'The sweet smell of money.' This was the last temptation he used with Christ: 'All these things will I give you' (Matt. 4:9). But Christ saw the hook under the bait. Many who have escaped gross sins, are still caught in a golden net. To gain the world, they will use indirect routes.

A godly man dare not travel for riches along the devil's highway. Those are sad gains, which make a man lose peace of conscience and heaven at last. He who gets an estate by injustice stuffs his pillow with thorns, and his head will lie very uneasy when he comes to die. 'What good will it be for a man if he gains the whole world, yet forfeits his soul?' Matthew 16:26.

3. A beloved besetting sin. 'Let us throw off everything that hinders and the sin that so easily entangles, and let us run with perseverance the race marked out for us.' Hebrews 12:1. There is usually one sin that is the favorite — the sin which the heart is most fond of. A beloved sin lies in a man's bosom as the disciple whom Jesus loved, leaned on his bosom (John 13:23). A godly man will not indulge a darling sin: 'I kept myself from my iniquity' (Psalm 18:23). 'I will not indulge the sin of my constitution, to which the bias of my heart more naturally inclines.' 'Fight neither with small nor great — but only with the king' (1 Kings 22:31). A godly man fights this king sin. The oracle of Apollo answered the people of Cyrrha that if they would live in peace among themselves, they must make continual war with those strangers who were on their borders. If we would have peace in our souls, we must maintain a war against our favorite sin and never leave off until it is subdued.

Question: How shall we know what our beloved sin is?

Answer 1: The sin which a man does not love to have reproved is the darling sin. Herod could not endure having his incest spoken against. If the prophet meddles with that sin — it shall cost him his head! 'Do not touch my Herodias!' Men can be content to have other sins reproved — but if the minister puts his finger on the sore, and touches this sin — their hearts begin to burn in malice against him!

Answer 2: The sin on which the thoughts run most, is the darling sin. Whichever way the thoughts go, the heart goes. He who is in love with a person cannot keep his thoughts off that person. Examine what sin runs most in your mind, what sin is first in your thoughts and greets you in the morning—that is your predominant sin.

Answer 3: The sin which has most power over us, and most easily leads us captive, is the one beloved by the soul. There are some sins which a man can better resist. If they come for entertainment, he can more easily put them off. But the bosom sin comes as a suitor, and he cannot deny it—but is overcome by it. The young man in the Gospel had repulsed many sins—but there was one sin which soiled him, and that was covetousness. Christians, mark what sin you are most readily led captive by—that is the harlot in your bosom! It is a sad thing that a man should be so bewitched by lust, that if it asks him to part with not only half the kingdom (Esther 7:2) but the whole kingdom of heaven, he must part with it, to gratify that lust!

Answer 4: The sin which men use arguments to defend, is the beloved sin. He who has a jewel in his bosom, will defend it to his death. So when there is any sin in the bosom, men will defend it. The sin we advocate and dispute for, is the besetting sin. If the sin is anger, we plead for it: 'I do well to be angry' (Jonah 4:9). If the sin is covetousness and we vindicate it and perhaps wrest Scripture to justify it—that is the sin which lies nearest the heart.

Answer 5: The sin which most troubles us, and flies most in the face in an hour of sickness and distress, that is the Delilah sin! When Joseph's brethren were distressed, their sin in selling their brother came to remembrance: 'We are truly guilty concerning our brother ... therefore is this distress come upon us' (Gen. 42:21). So, when a man is on a sickbed and conscience says, 'You have been guilty of such a sin; you went on in it, and rolled it like honey under your tongue!' Conscience is reading him a sad lecture. That was the beloved sin for sure.

Answer 6: The sin which a man finds most difficulty in giving up, is the endeared sin. Of all his sons, Jacob found most difficulty in parting with Benjamin. So the sinner says, 'This and that sin I have parted with—but must Benjamin go, must I part with this delightful sin? That pierces my heart!' As with a castle that has several forts about it, the first and second fort are taken—but when it comes to the castle, the governor will rather fight and die than yield that. So a man may allow some of his sins to be demolished—but when it comes to one sin, that is the taking of the castle; he will never agree to part with that! That is the master sin for sure.

The besetting sin is a God-provoking sin. The wise men of Troy counseled Priam to send Helena back to the Greeks, not permitting himself to be abused any longer by the charms of her beauty, because keeping her within the city would lay the foundation of a fatal war. So we should put away our Delilah sin, lest it incense the God of heaven, and make him commence a war against us.

The besetting sin is, of all others, most dangerous. As Samson's strength lay in his hair, so the strength of sin, lies in this beloved sin. This is like a poison striking the heart, which brings death. A godly man will lay the axe of repentance to this sin and hew it down! He sets this sin, like Uriah, in the forefront of the battle, so that it may be slain. He will sacrifice this Isaac, he will pluck out this right eye, so that he may see better to go to heaven.

4. Those sins which the world counts lesser. There is no such thing as little sin—yet some may be deemed less comparatively. But a godly man will not indulge himself in these. Such as:

(1) Sins of omission. Some think it no great matter to omit family, or private prayer. They can go for several months and God never hears from them. A godly man will as soon live without food, as without prayer. He knows that every creature of God is sanctified by prayer (1 Tim.

4:5). The bird may shame many Christians; it never takes a drop — but the eye is lifted up towards heaven.

(2) A godly man dares not allow himself vain, frothy discourse, much less that which looks like an oath. If God will judge for idle words, will he not much more for idle oaths?

(3) A godly man dare not allow himself rash censuring. Some think this a small matter. They will not swear — but they will slander. This is very evil. This is wounding a man in that which is dearest to him. He who is godly turns all his censures upon himself! He judges himself for his own sins — but is very watchful and concerned, about the good name of another.

Use: As you would be numbered among the genealogies of the saints, do not indulge yourselves in any sin. Consider the mischief which one sin lived in, will do:

1. One sin lived in, gives Satan as much advantage against you as more sins. The fowler can hold a bird by one wing. Satan held Judas fast by one sin.

2. One sin lived in, proves that the heart is not sound. He who hides one rebel in his house is a traitor to the crown. The person who indulges one sin is a traitorous hypocrite.

3. One sin lived in, will make way for more, as a little thief can open the door to more. Sins are linked and chained together. One sin will draw on more. David's adultery made way for murder. One sin never goes alone! If there is only one nest egg — the devil can brood on it.

4. One sin lived in, is as much a breach of God's law as more sins. 'Whoever keeps the entire law, yet fails in one point, is guilty of breaking it all' (Jas. 2:10). The king may make a law against felony, treason and murder. If a man is guilty of only one of these, he is a transgressor.

5. One sin lived in, prevents Christ from entering. One stone in the pipe keeps out the water. One sin indulged in, obstructs the soul and keeps the streams of Christ's blood from running into it.

6. One sin lived in, will spoil all your good duties. A drop of poison will spoil a glass of wine. Abimelech, a bastard-son, destroyed seventy of his brethren (Judges 9:5). One bastard-sin will destroy seventy prayers. One dead fly will spoil the whole box of precious ointment.

7. One sin lived in will be a cankerworm to eat out the peace of conscience. It takes away the manna from the ark, and leaves only a rod. 'Alas! What a scorpion lies within!' (Seneca). One sin is a pirate — to rob a Christian of his comfort. One jarring string puts all the music out of tune. One sin lived in — will spoil the music of conscience.

8. One sin lived in, will damn as well as more sins. One disease is enough to kill. If a fence is made ever so strong, and only one gap is left open; the wild beast may enter and tread down the corn. If only one sin is allowed in the soul, you leave open a gap for the devil to enter! A soldier may have only one gap in his armor--and the bullet may enter there. He may as well be shot there--as if he had no armor on at all. So if you favor only one sin, you leave a part of your soul unprotected--and the bullet of God's wrath may enter there — and shoot you! One sin lived in, may shut you out of heaven! What difference is there, between being shut out of heaven for one sin--or for many sins? One millstone will sink a man into the sea--as well as a hundred!

9. One sin harbored in the soul will unfit us for suffering. How soon an hour of trial may come. A man who has hurt his shoulder cannot carry a heavy burden, and a man who has any guilt in his conscience cannot carry the cross of Christ. Will he who cannot deny his lust for Christ — deny his life for Christ? One unmortified sin in the soul — will bring forth the bitter fruit of apostasy.

If, then, you would show yourselves godly, give a certificate of divorce to every sin. Kill the Goliath sin! 'Let not sin reign' (Romans 6:12). In the original it is 'Let not sin king it over you.'

Grace and sin may be together—but grace and the love of sin cannot. Therefore parley with sin no longer—but with the spear of mortification, spill the heart-blood of every sin! 'For if you live after the flesh, you shall die: but if you through the Spirit do mortify the deeds of the body, you shall live.' Romans 8:13. 'So put to death the sinful, earthly things lurking within you.' Colossians 3:5.

20. A godly man is good in his relationships

To be good in general is not enough—but we must show piety in our relationships.

1. He who is good as a magistrate is godly. The magistrate is God's representative. A godly magistrate holds the balance of justice, and gives everyone his right: 'You must never twist justice or show partiality. Never accept a bribe, for bribes blind the eyes of the wise and corrupt the decisions of the godly' (Deut. 16:19). A magistrate must judge the cause, not the person. He who allows himself to be corrupted by bribes, is not a judge but a party. A magistrate must do that which is 'according to law' (Acts 23:3). And in order that he may do justice, he must examine the cause. The archer who wishes to shoot right, must first see the target.

2. He who is good as a minister is godly. Ministers must be:

(1) Painstaking. 'Preach the Word; be prepared in season and out of season; correct, rebuke and encourage--with great patience and careful instruction' (2 Tim. 4:2). The minister must not be idle. Sloth is as inexcusable in a minister, as sleeping in a sentry. John the Baptist was a 'voice crying' (Matt. 3:3). A dumb minister is of no more use, than a dead physician. A man of God must work in the Lord's vineyard. It was Augustine's wish that Christ might find him at his coming either praying or preaching.

(2) Knowledgeable. 'For the lips of a priest ought to preserve knowledge, and from his mouth men should seek instruction--because he is the messenger of the Lord Almighty' (Mal. 2:7). It was said in honor of Gregory Nazianzene that he was an ocean of divinity. The prophets of old were called 'seers' (1 Sam. 9:9). It is absurd to have blind seers. Christ said to Peter, 'Feed my sheep' (John 21:16). But how sad it is when the shepherd needs to be fed! Ignorance in a minister is like blindness in an optometrist. Under the law, he who had the plague in his head, was unclean (Lev. 13:44).

(3) A plain preacher, suiting his matter and style to the capacity of his audience (1 Cor. 14:19). Some ministers, like eagles, love to soar aloft in abstruse metaphysical notions, thinking they are most admired when they are least understood. They who preach in the clouds, instead of hitting their people's conscience, shoot over their heads.

(4) Zealous in reproving sin. 'Rebuke them sharply' (Titus 1:13). Epiphanius said of Elijah, that he sucked fire out of his mother's breasts. A man of God must suck the fire of zeal out of the breasts of Scripture! Zeal in a minister is as proper as fire on the altar. Some are afraid to reprove, like the swordfish which has a sword in his head, but is without a heart. So they carry the sword of the Spirit with them—but have no heart to draw it out in reproof against sin. How many have sown pillows under their people (Ezek. 13:18), making them sleep so securely, that they never awoke until they were in hell!

(5) Holy in heart and life:

(a) In heart. How sad it is for a minister to preach that to others, which he never felt in his own soul; to exhort others to holiness and himself be a stranger to it. Oh, that this were not too often so! How many blow the Lord's trumpet with foul breath!

(b) In life. Under the law, before the priests served at the altar, they washed in the laver. Such as serve in the Lord's house must first be washed from gross sin in the laver of repentance. The life of a minister should be a walking Bible. Basil said of Gregory Nazianzene that he thundered in his doctrine, and lightened in his conduct. A minister must imitate John the Baptist, who was not only 'a voice crying' — but 'a light shining' (John 5:35). Those who live in contradiction to what they preach, disgrace this excellent calling. And though they are angels by office — yet they are devils in their lives (Jer. 23:15).

3. He who is good as a husband is godly. He fills up that relationship with love: 'Husbands, love your wives' (Eph. 5:25). The vine twisting its branches about the elm and embracing it may be an emblem of that entire love which should be in the marital relationship. A married condition would be sad--if it had cares to embitter it and not love to sweeten it. Love is the best diamond in the marriage ring! 'Isaac loved Rebekah' (Gen. 24:67). Unkindnesses in this close relationship are very unhappy. We read in heathen authors that Clytemnestra, the wife of Agamemnon, in order to revenge an injury received from her husband, first rent the veil of her chastity and afterwards consented to his death. The husband should show his love to his wife by covering infirmities; by avoiding occasions of strife; by sweet, endearing expressions; by pious counsel; by love tokens; by encouraging what he sees amiable and virtuous in her; by mutual prayer; by being with her, unless detained by urgency of business. The pilot who leaves his ship and abandons it entirely to the merciless waves, declares that he does not value it or reckon there is any treasure in it.

The apostle gives a good reason why there should be mutual love between husband and wife: 'that your prayers be not hindered' (1 Pet. 3:7). Where anger and bitterness prevail, there prayer is either intermitted or interrupted.

4. He who is good as a father is godly

(1) A father must drop holy instructions into his children: 'bring them up in the nurture and admonition of the Lord' (Eph. 6:4). This is what Abraham did: 'I know Abraham, that he will command his children and his household, and they shall keep the way of the Lord' (Gen. 18:19). Children are young plants which must be watered with good education, so that they may, with Obadiah, fear the Lord 'from their youth up' (1 Kings 18:12). Plato said, 'In vain does he expect a harvest, who has been negligent in sowing.' Nor can a parent expect to reap any good from a child, where he has not sown the seed of wholesome instruction. And though, notwithstanding all counsel and admonition, the child should die in sin — yet it is a comfort to a godly parent to think that before his child died, he gave it spiritual medicine.

(2) A parent must pray for his children. Monica, the mother of Augustine, prayed for his conversion, and someone said 'it was impossible that a son of so many prayers and tears should perish.' The soul of your child is in a trap--and will you not pray that it may 'escape from the Devil's trap?' (2 Tim. 2:26) Many parents are careful to lay up portions for their children — but they do not lay up prayers for them.

(3) A parent must give his children discipline: 'Do not withhold discipline from a child; if you punish him with the rod, he will not die. Punish him with the rod and save his soul from death' (Proverbs 23:13-14). The rod beats out the dust and moth of sin. A child indulged and humored in wickedness, will prove a burden instead of a blessing. David pampered Adonijah: 'his father had never disciplined him at any time' (1 Kings 1:6). And afterwards he was a grief of heart to his father, and wanted to put him off his throne. Discipline is a hedge of thorns--to stop children in their mad race to hell.

5. He who is good as a master is godly

A godly man promotes true religion in his family; he sets up piety in his house, as well as in his heart: 'I will walk within my house with a perfect heart' (Psalm 101:2). 'I and my household will serve the Lord' (Josh. 24:15). I find it written in honor of Cramer, that his family was a nursery of piety. A godly man's house is a little church: 'the church which is in his house' (Col. 4:15).

(1) A good man makes known the oracles of God to those who are under his roof. He reads the Word and perfumes his house with prayer. It is recorded of the Jews, that they had sacrifices in their family as well as in the tabernacle (Exod. 12:3).

(2) A godly man provides necessities. He relieves his servants in health and sickness. He is not like that Amalekite who shook off his servant when he was sick, (1 Sam. 30:13) — but rather like the good centurion, who sought Christ for the healing of his sick servant (Matt. 8:5).

(3) A godly man sets his servants a good example. He is sober and heavenly in his deportment; his virtuous life is a good mirror for the servants in the family to dress themselves by.

6. He who is good in the relationship of a child is godly

He honors his parents. Philo the Jew, placed the fifth commandment in the first table — as if children had not performed their whole devotion to God until they had given honor to their parents. This honoring of parents consists in two things:

(1) In respecting them--which respect is shown both by humility of speech and by attitude. The opposite of this is when a child behaves himself in an unseemly and proud manner. Among the Lacedemonians, if a child had behaved rebelliously towards his parent, it was lawful for the father to appoint someone else to be his heir, and to disinherit that child.

(2) Obeying their commands: 'Children, obey your parents in the Lord' (Eph. 6:1). Duty is the interest which children pay their parents, on the capital they have had from them. Christ has set all children a pattern of obedience to their parents: 'He was subject unto them' (Luke 2:51). The Rechabites were eminent for this: 'I set cups and jugs of wine before them and invited them to have a drink, but they refused. 'No,' they said. 'We don't drink wine, because Jehonadab our ancestor, gave us this command: You and your descendants must never drink wine' (Jer. 35:5,6). Solon was asked why, among the many laws he made, none was against disobedient children. He answered that it was because he thought none would be so wicked.

God has punished children who have refused to pay the tribute of obedience. Absalom, a disobedient son, was hanged in an oak between heaven and earth, as being worthy of neither. Manlius, an old man, being reduced to much poverty, and having a rich son, entreated him only for charity — but could not obtain it. The son disowned him as his father, using reproachful language. The poor old man let tears fall (as witnesses of his grief) and went away. God, to revenge this disobedience of his son, soon afterwards struck him with madness. He in whose heart godliness lives, makes as much conscience of the fifth commandment as of the first.

7. He who is good as a servant is godly

'Obey your earthly masters in everything; and do it, not only when their eye is on you and to win their favor, but with sincerity of heart and reverence for the Lord.' (Col. 3:22; Eph. 6:5). The goodness of servants lies in:

(1) Diligence. Abraham's servant quickly dispatched the business his master entrusted him with (Gen. 24:33).

(2) Cheerfulness. Servants must be cheerful workers, like the centurion's servants: 'If I say to one, 'Go,' he goes' (Luke 7:8).

(3) Faithfulness, which consists in two things:

(a) In not defrauding. 'Not stealing' (Titus 2:10).

(b) In keeping counsel. It proves the badness of a stomach, when it cannot retain what is put into it, and the badness of a servant when he cannot retain those secrets which his master has committed to him.

(4) Submissiveness. 'Be submissive to their masters in everything, and to be well-pleasing, not talking back' (Titus 2:9). It is better to correct a fault than to minimize it. And what may stimulate a servant in his work is that encouraging scripture, 'Work hard and cheerfully at whatever you do, as though you were working for the Lord rather than for people. Remember that the Lord will give you an inheritance as your reward, and the Master you are serving is Christ.' (Col. 3:24). If Christ should bid you do a piece of work for him, would you not do it? While you serve your master, you serve the Lord Christ. If you ask what salary you shall have, 'the Lord will give you an inheritance as your reward.'

Use 1: Is it the grand sign of a godly man to be holy in his relationships? Then the Lord be merciful to us. How few godly ones are to be found! Many put on the coat of profession. They will pray and discourse on points of religion — but 'What means this bleating of the sheep?' (1 Sam. 15:14). They are not good in their relationships. How bad it is when Christians are defective in family piety!

Can we call a bad magistrate, godly? He perverts equity: 'Justice — do you rulers know the meaning of the word? Do you judge the people fairly? No, all your dealings are crooked; you hand out violence instead of justice' (Psalm 58:1,2). Can we call a bad parent, godly? He never teaches his child the way to heaven. He is like the ostrich which is cruel to her young (Job 39:16). Can we call a bad employer, godly? Many employers leave their religion at church (as the clerk does his book). They have nothing of God at home; their houses are not Bethels — but Bethavens — not little temples but little hells. How many employers at the last day must plead guilty at the bar. Though they have fed their servants' bellies, they have starved their souls. Can we call a bad child, godly? He stops his ear to his parents' counsel. You may as well call him who is disloyal--a good subject. Can we call a bad servant, godly? He is slothful and wilful; he is more ready to spy a fault in another than to correct it in himself. To call one who is bad in his relationships godly, is a contradiction; it is to call evil good (Isaiah 5:20).

Use 2: As we desire to have God approve of us, let us show godliness in our relationships. Not to be good in our relationships spoils all our other good things. Naaman was an honorable man — but he was a leper (2 Kings 5:1). That 'but' spoiled everything. So such a person is a great hearer — but he neglects relative duties. This stains the beauty of all his other actions. As in printing, though the letter is ever so well shaped — yet if it is not set in the right place, it spoils the sense. So let a man have many things commendable in him — yet if he is not good in his right place, making conscience of how he walks in his relationships, he does harm to religion. There are many to whom Christ will say at last, as to the young man, 'There is still one thing you lack' (Luke 18:22). You have misbehaved in your relative capacity. As therefore we cherish our salvation and the honor of true religion, let us shine in that orb of relationships where God has placed us.

21. A godly man does spiritual things in a spiritual manner

'We are the true circumcision, who worship God in the spirit' (Phil. 3:3). Spiritual worship is pure worship: 'You are built up a spiritual house, a holy priesthood, to offer up spiritual sacrifices' (1 Peter 2:5) — spiritual not only in the matter — but also in the quality. A wicked man either lives in the total neglect of duty--or else discharges it in a dull, careless manner. Instead of 'using the world as if he used it not' (1 Cor. 7.31), he serves God as if he did not serve him. A godly man spiritualizes duty; he is not only for the doing of holy things--but for the holy doing of things.

Question: What is it to perform spiritual duties spiritually?

Answer: It consists in three things:

1. To do duties from a spiritual principle, namely, a renewed principle of grace. A man may have gifts which attract admiration; he may have the most melting, ravishing expressions; he may speak like an angel come down from heaven; yet his duties may not be spiritual because he lacks the grace of the Spirit. Whatever a moral, unregenerate person does--is only nature refined. Though he may do duties better than a godly man — yet not so well — better as to the matter and elegance — yet not so well, as lacking a renewed principle. A crab-tree may bear as well as an apple tree; the fruit may be big and lovelier to the eye — yet it is not such good fruit as the other, because it does not come from so good a stock. So an unregenerate person may perform as many duties as a child of God, and these may seem to be more glorious to the outward view — but they are harsh and sour, because they do not come from the sweet and pleasant root of grace. A true saint gives God that wine, which comes from the pure grape of the Spirit.

2. To perform duties spiritually is to do them with the utmost intention. A Christian is very serious and strives to keep his thoughts close to the work in hand: 'that you may attend upon the Lord without distraction' (1 Cor. 7:35).

Question: But may not a godly man have roving thoughts in duty?

Answer: Yes, sad experience proves it. The thoughts will be dancing up and down in prayer. The saints are called stars, and many times in duty they are wandering stars. The heart is like quicksilver which will not settle. It is hard to tie two good thoughts together. We cannot lock our hearts so close but that distracting thoughts, like wind, will get in. Jerome complains about himself. 'Sometimes,' he says, 'when I am doing God's service, I am walking in the galleries or casting up accounts.'

But these wandering thoughts in the godly are not allowed: 'I hate vain thoughts' (Psalm 119:113). They come like unwelcome guests who are no sooner spied, than they are turned out.

Question: From where do these wandering thoughts arise in the godly?

Answer 1: From the depravity of nature. They are the mud which the heart casts up.

Answer 2: From Satan. The devil, if he cannot hinder us from duty, will hinder us in duty. When we come before the Lord, he is at our right hand to resist us (Zech. 3:1). Like when a man is going to write, and another stands at his elbow and jogs him, so that he cannot write evenly. Satan will set vain objects before the imagination, to cause a diversion. The devil does not oppose formality, but fervency. If he sees that we are setting ourselves in good earnest to seek God, he will be whispering things in our ears, so that we can scarcely attend to what we are doing.

Answer 3: These wandering thoughts arise from the world. These vermin are bred out of the earth. Worldly business often crowds into our duties, and while our mouths are speaking to God, our hearts are thinking of the world: 'They sit before me as my people — but their heart goes after their covetousness' (Ezek. 33:31). While we are hearing the Word or meditating, some worldly business or other commonly knocks at the door and we are called away from the duty while we are doing it. It is the same with us as it was with Abraham when he was going to worship — the birds came down on the sacrifice (Gen. 15:11).

Question: How may we get rid of these wandering thoughts, so that we may be more spiritual in duty?

Answer 1: Fix your eyes on God's purity. He whom we serve is a holy God, and when we are worshiping him, he cannot tolerate our conversing with vanity. While a king's subject is speaking to him, will the king like him to be playing with a feather? Will God endure light, feathery hearts? How devout and reverent the angels are! They cover their faces and cry, 'Holy, holy.'

Answer 2: Think of the grand importance of the duties we are engaged in. As David said, concerning his building a house for God, 'the work is great' (1 Chron. 29:1). When we are hearing the Word, 'the work is great.' This is the Word by which we shall be judged. When we are at prayer, 'the work is great.' We are pleading for the life of our souls, and is this a time to trifle?

Answer 3: Come with delight to duty. The nature of love is to fix the mind upon the object. The thoughts of a man who is in love, are on the person he loves, and nothing can distract them. The thoughts of a man who loves the world are always intent on it. If our hearts were more fired with love, they would be more fixed in duty, and oh, what cause we have to love duty! Is not this the direct road to heaven? Do we not meet with God here? Can the spouse be better than in her husband's company? Where can the soul be better than in drawing near to God?

Answer 4: Consider the mischief that these vain distracting thoughts do. They blow away our duties; they hinder fervency; they show great irreverence; they tempt God to turn his ear away from us. Why do we think God should heed our prayers--when we ourselves scarcely heed them?

3. To do duties spiritually is to do them in faith. 'By faith Abel offered unto God, a better sacrifice than Cain' (Heb. 11:4). The holy oil for the tabernacle had several spices put into it (Exod. 30:34). Faith is the sweet spice which must be put into duty. It is a wrong done to God--to doubt either his mercy or his truth. A Christian may venture his soul upon the promises of God in Scripture.

Use 1: How far from godliness, are those who are unspiritual in their worship, who do not do duties from a renewed principle and with the utmost intention of soul—but merely to stop the mouth of conscience! Many people look no further than the bare doing of duties—but never heed how they are done. God does not judge our duties by their length—but by love. When men put God off with the dreggish part of duty, may he not say, like Isaiah, 'Is it such a fast that I have chosen?' (Isaiah 58:5). 'Are these the duties I required? I called for the heart and spirit--and you bring nothing but the carcass of duty. Should I receive this?' 'The Lord says--These people come near to me with their mouth and honor me with their lips, but their hearts are far from me.' Isaiah 29:13

Use 2: Let us show ourselves godly by being more spiritual in duty. It is not the quantity, but the quality--which God is concerned with. It is not how much we do--but how well. A musician is commended, not for playing long--but for playing well. We must not only do what God appoints--but as God appoints. Oh, how many are unspiritual in spiritual things! They bring their services but not their hearts. They give God the skin, not the fat of the offering. 'God is a Spirit' (John 4:24)—and it is the spirituality of duty he is best pleased with: 'Spiritual sacrifices, acceptable to God' (1 Pet. 2:5). The spirits of the wine are best. So is the spiritual part of duty: 'making melody in your heart to the Lord' (Eph. 5:19). It is the heart which makes the music; the spiritualizing of duty gives life to it. Without this--it is only dead praying, dead hearing—and dead things are not pleasing. A dead flower has no beauty, a dead breast has no sweetness.

Question: What may we do, to perform duties in a spiritual manner?

Answer 1: Let the soul be kept pure. Lust besots and dispirits a man. Beware of any tincture of uncleanness (Jas. 1:21). Wood that is full of sap will not easily burn. Just so, a heart steeped in sin is not fit to burn in holy devotion. Can he who feeds carnal lust be spiritual in worship? 'Whoredom and wine and new wine take away the heart' (Hos. 4:11). Any sin lived in, takes away the heart. Such a person has no heart to pray or meditate. The more alive the heart is in sin, the more it dies to duty.

Answer 2: If we wish to be spiritual in duty, let us revolve these two things in our mind:

(1) The profit which comes from a duty performed in a spiritual manner. It enfeebles corruption; it increases grace; it defeats Satan; it strengthens our communion with God; it breeds peace of conscience; it procures answers of mercy; and it leaves the heart always in better tune.

(2) The danger of doing duties in an unspiritual manner. They are as if they had not been done. For what the heart does not do--is not done. Duties carelessly performed, turn ordinances into judgments. Therefore many, though they are often doing duty--go away worse from duty! If medicine is not well made and the ingredients rightly mixed, it is as bad as poison for the body. Just so, if duties are not well performed, they leave the heart harder and more sinful than before.

Unspiritual duties often create temporal judgments: 'the Lord our God made a breach upon us, for that we sought him not after the due order' (1 Chron. 15:13). Therefore God makes breaches in families and relationships, because people do not worship him in that manner and due order which he requires.

Answer 3: If we want to have our duties spiritual, we must get our hearts spiritual. An earthly heart cannot be spiritual in duty. Let us beg from God, a spiritual palate to relish a sweetness in holy things. For lack of spiritual hearts, we come to duty without delight--and go away without profit! If a man wants to have the wheels of his watch move regularly, he must mend the spring. Christian, if you want to move more spiritually in duty, get the spring of your heart mended.

22. A godly man is thoroughly trained in piety

He obeys every command of God: 'I have found David a man after my own heart, for he will carry out all My will' (Acts 13:22). In the Greek it is 'all my wills.' A godly man strives to walk according to the full breadth and latitude of God's law. Every command has the same stamp of divine authority on it, and he who is godly will obey one command as well as another: 'Then shall I not be ashamed, when I have respect to all your commandments' (Psalm 119:6). A godly man goes through all the body of piety--as the sun through all the signs of the Zodiac. Whoever is to play a ten-stringed instrument must strike every string or he will spoil all the music. The ten commandments may be compared to a ten-stringed instrument. We must obey every commandment, strike every string, or we cannot make any sweet music in piety.

True obedience is filial. It is fitting that the child should obey the parent in all just and sober commands. God's laws are like the curtains of the tabernacle which were looped together. They are like a chain of gold where all the links are coupled. A godly man will not willingly break one link of this chain. If one command is violated, the whole chain is broken: 'whoever shall keep the whole law — yet offend in one point, he is guilty of all' (Jas. 2:10). A voluntary breach of one of God's laws involves a man in the guilt, and exposes him to the curse of the whole law. True obedience is entire and uniform. A good heart, like the needle, points the way in which the loadstone draws.

This is one great difference between a child of God and a hypocrite. The hypocrite picks and chooses in religion. He will perform some duties which are easier, and gratify his pride or interest—but other duties he takes no notice of: 'Woe to you, teachers of the law and Pharisees, you hypocrites! You give a tenth of your spices--mint, dill and cummin. But you have neglected the more important matters of the law--justice, mercy and faithfulness' (Matt. 23:23). To sweat in some duties of religion, and freeze in others--is the symptom of a disordered Christian. Jehu was zealous in destroying the idolatry of Baal—but let the golden calves of Jeroboam stand (2 Kings 10:29). This shows that men are not good in truth--when they are good by halves. If your servant should do some of your work you command him, and leave the rest undone, how would you like that? The Lord says, 'Walk before me, and be perfect' (Gen. 17:1). How are our hearts perfect with God--when we prevaricate with him? Some things we will do and other things we leave undone. He is godly who is godly universally. 'Here I am, Father; command what you will' (Plautus).

There are ten duties that God calls for, which a godly man will conscientiously perform, and indeed these duties may serve as so many other characteristics and touchstones to test our godliness by:

1. A godly man will often be calling his heart to account

He takes the candle of the Word and searches his innermost being: 'I commune with my own heart: and my spirit made diligent search' (Psalm 77:6). A gracious soul searches whether there is any duty omitted--or any sin cherished. He examines his evidences for heaven. As he will not take his gold on trust, so neither will he take his grace. He is a spiritual merchant; he casts up the estate of his soul to see what he is worth. He 'sets his house in order.' Frequent reckonings keep God and conscience friends. A carnal person cannot abide this heart-work; he is ignorant how the affairs go in his soul. He is like a man who is well acquainted with foreign countries, but a stranger in his own country.

2. A godly man is much in private prayer

He keeps his hours for private devotion. Jacob, when he was left alone, wrestled with God (Gen. 32:24). So when a gracious heart is alone, it wrestles in prayer and will not leave God until it has a blessing. A devout Christian exercises 'eyes of faith' and 'knees of prayer'.

Hypocrites who have nothing of religion besides the frontispiece, love to be seen. Christ has characterized them: 'they love to pray in the corners of the streets--that they may be seen' (Matt. 6:5). The hypocrite is devout in the temple. There everyone will gaze at him—but he is a stranger to secret communion with God. He is a saint in the church—but an atheist in private. A good Christian holds secret communication with heaven. Private prayer keeps up the trade of godliness. When private holiness is laid aside, a stab is given to the heart of piety.

3. A godly man is diligent in his calling

He takes care to provide for his family. The church must not exclude the shop. Mr. Perkins said: 'Though a man is endued with excellent gifts, hears the Word with reverence and receives the sacrament—yet if he does not practice the duties of his calling--all is sheer hypocrisy.' Piety never did grant a patent for idleness: 'We hear that some among you are idle. They are not busy; they are busybodies. Such people we command and urge in the Lord Jesus Christ to settle down and earn the bread they eat.' (2 Thess. 3:11,12). The bread that tastes most sweet--is obtained with most sweat. A godly man would rather fast--than eat the bread of idleness. Vain professing Christians talk of living by faith—but do not live in a calling. They are like the lilies of the field: 'they toil not, neither do they spin' (Matt. 6:28). An idle person is the devil's tennis ball, which he bandies up and down with temptation until at last the ball goes out of play.

4. A godly man sets bounds to himself in things lawful

He is moderate in matters of recreation and diet. He takes only so much as is needed for the restoration of health, and as may the better dispose him for God's service. Jerome lived abstemiously; his diet was a few dried figs and cold water. And Augustine in his 'Confessions' says: 'Lord, you have taught me to go to my food--as to a medicine.' If the bridle of reason checks the appetite, much more should the curbing-bit of grace do so. The life of a sinner is brutish; the glutton feeds 'without fear' (Jude 12), and the drunkard drinks without reason. Too much oil chokes the lamp, whereas a smaller quantity makes it burn more brightly. A godly man holds the golden bridle of temperance, and will not allow his table to be a snare.

5. A godly man is careful about moral righteousness

He makes conscience of equity as well as piety. The Scripture has linked both together: 'that we might serve him in holiness and righteousness' (Luke 1:74,75). Holiness: there is the first table of the law; righteousness: there is the second table of the law. Though a man may be morally righteous, and not godly — yet no one can be godly, unless he is morally righteous. This moral righteousness is seen in our dealings with men. A godly man observes that golden maxim, 'So in everything, do to others what you would have them do to you' (Matt. 7:12). There is a threefold injustice in business matters:

(1) Using false weights: 'the balances of deceit are in his hand' (Hos. 12:7). Men, by making their weights lighter, make their sin heavier. 'They make the ephah small' (Amos 8:5). The ephah was a measure they used in selling. They made the ephah small; they gave but scant measure. A godly man who takes the Bible in one hand, dare not use false weights in the other.

(2) Debasing a commodity: 'they sell the refuse of the wheat' (Amos 8:6). They would pick out the best grains of the wheat and sell the worst at the same price as they did the best. 'Your wine is mixed with water' (Isaiah 1:22). They adulterated their wine — yet made their customers believe it came from the pure grape.

(3) Taking a great deal more than the commodity is worth. 'If you sell anything unto your neighbor ... you shall not oppress one another' (Lev. 25:14). A godly man deals exactly but not exactingly. He will sell so as to help himself — but not to harm another. His motto is, 'a conscience void of offence toward God, and toward men' (Acts 24:16).

The hypocrite separates these two which God has joined together — righteousness and holiness. He pretends to be pure but is not just. It brings piety into contempt, when men hang out Christ's colors — yet will use fraudulent circumvention and, under a mask of piety, neglect morality. A godly man makes conscience of the second table of the law, as well as the first.

6. A godly man will forgive those who have wronged him

Revenge is sweet to nature. A gracious spirit passes by affronts, forgets injuries and counts it a greater victory to conquer an enemy by patience--than by power. It is truly heroic 'to overcome evil with good' (Romans 12:21). Though I would not trust an enemy — yet I would endeavor to love him. I would exclude him from my creed — but not from my prayer (Matt. 5:44).

Question: But does every godly man succeed in forgiving, yes, loving his enemies?

Answer: He does so in a gospel sense. That is:

(a) In so far as there is assent. He subscribes to it in his judgment as a thing which ought to be done: 'with my mind I serve the law of God' (Romans 7:25).

(b) In so far as there is grief. A godly man mourns that he can love his enemies no more: 'O wretched man that I am!' (Romans 7:24). 'Oh, this base cankered heart of mine, that has received so much mercy and can show so little! I have had millions forgiven me — yet I can hardly forgive pence!'

(c) In so far as there is prayer. A godly man prays that God will give him a heart to love his enemies. 'Lord, pluck this root of bitterness out of me, perfume my soul with love, make me a dove without gall.'

(d) In so far as there is effort. A godly man resolves and strives in the strength of Christ against all rancor and virulence of spirit. This is in a gospel sense to love our enemies. A wicked man cannot do this; his malice boils up to revenge.

7. A godly man lays to heart the miseries of the church

'We wept, when we remembered Zion' (Psalm 137:1). I have read of certain trees whose leaves, if cut or touched, the other leaves begin to contract and shrink, and for a time hang down their heads. Such a spiritual sympathy exists among Christians. When other parts of God's church suffer, they feel it themselves, as it were. Ambrose reports that when Theodosius was terminally ill, he was more troubled about the church of God than about his own sickness.

When the Lord strikes others, a godly heart is deeply affected: 'my affections shall sound like an harp' (Isaiah 16:11). Though things go well with a child of God in his own private life, and he lives in a house of cedar--he still grieves to see things go badly with the public. Queen Esther enjoyed the king's favor and all the delights of the court — yet when a warrant portending bloodshed was signed for the death of the Jews--she mourns and fasts, and ventures her own life to save theirs.

8. A godly man is content with his present condition

If provisions get low, his heart is tempered to his condition. A godly man puts a kind interpretation upon providence. When God brews him a bitter cup, he says, 'This is my medicine cup--it is to purge me and do my soul good.' Therefore he is most content (Phil. 4:11).

9. A godly man is fruitful in good works (Titus 2:7)

The Hebrew word for godly (chasid) signifies 'merciful', implying that to be godly and charitable are of equal force--one and the same. A good man feeds the hungry, clothes the naked. 'He is ever merciful' (Psalm 37:26). The more devout sort of the Jews to this day distribute the tenth part of their estate to the poor and they have a proverb among them, 'Give the tenth, and you will grow rich.' The hypocrite is all for faith, nothing for works; like the laurel which makes fine leaves--but bears no fruit.

10. A godly man will suffer persecution

He will be married to Christ, though he settles no other estate on him, than the cross. He suffers out of choice and with a spirit of gallantry (Heb. 11:35). Argerius wrote a letter to his friend, headed: 'From the pleasant gardens of the Leonine prison.' The blessed martyrs who put on the whole armor of God, blunted the edge of persecution by their courage. The juniper tree makes the coolest shadow--and the hottest coal. So persecution makes the coal of love hotter--and the shadow of death cooler.

Thus a godly man goes round the whole circle of pious duties and obeys God in whatever he commands.

Objection: But it is impossible for anyone to walk according to the full breadth of God's law, and to follow God fully!

Answer: There is a twofold obeying of God's law. The first is perfect, when all is done, which the law requires. This we cannot arrive at in this life. Secondly, there is an incomplete obedience which is accepted in Christ. This consists in four things:

(1) An approving of all God's commands: 'the commandment is holy and just and good ... I consent unto the law that it is good' (Romans 7:12, 16). There is both assent and consent.

(2) A sweet delight in God's commands: 'I will delight myself in your commandments, which I have loved' (Psalm 119:47).

(3) A cordial desire to walk in all God's commands: 'O that my ways were directed to keep your statutes' (Psalm 119:5).

(4) A real endeavor to tread in every path of the command: 'I turned my feet unto your testimonies' (Psalm 119:59).

This, God esteems perfect obedience--and is pleased to take it in good part. Zacharias had his failings; he hesitated through unbelief, for which he was struck dumb. Yet it is said that he 'walked in all the commands of the Lord blameless' (Luke 1:6), because he cordially endeavored to obey God in all things. Evangelical obedience is true in its essence, though not perfect in its degree; and where it comes short, Christ puts his merits into the scales--and then there is full weight.

23. A godly man walks with God

'Noah walked with God' (Gen. 6:9). The age in which Noah lived was very corrupt: 'the wickedness of man was great in the earth' (v.5). But the iniquity of the times, could not put Noah off his walk: 'Noah walked with God.' Noah is called a 'preacher of righteousness' (2 Peter 2:5):

1. Noah preached by doctrine

His preaching (say some of the rabbis) was in this vein: 'Turn from your evil ways, so that the waters of the flood will not come upon you and cut off the whole of Adam's race.'

2. Noah preached by his life

He preached by his humility, patience, sanctity. 'Noah walked with God.'

Question: What is it, to walk with God?

Answer: Walking with God imports five things:

1. Walking as under God's eye. Noah reverenced God. A godly man sets himself as in God's presence, knowing that his judge is looking on: 'I have set the Lord always before me' (Psalm 16:8). David's eyes were here.

2. The familiarity and intimacy which the soul has with God. Friends walk together and console themselves with one another. The godly make known their requests to God--and he makes known his love to them. There is a sweet fellowship between God and his people: 'Our fellowship (koinonia) is with the Father, and with his Son Jesus Christ' (1 John 1:3).

3. Walking above the earth. A godly man is elevated above all sublunary objects. The person who walks with God must ascend very high. A dwarf cannot walk among the stars, nor can a dwarfish, earthly soul walk with God.

4. Visible piety. Walking is a visible posture. Grace must be conspicuous to the onlookers. He who reveals something of God in his behavior, walks with God. He shines forth in biblical conduct.

5. Continued progress in grace. It is not only a step--but a walk. There is a going on towards maturity. A godly man does not sit down in the middle of the way--but goes on until he comes to the 'end of his faith' (1 Pet. 1:9). Though a good man may be out of the path, he is not out of the way. He may through infirmity step aside (as Peter did) — but he recovers by repentance and goes on in progressive holiness: 'The righteous will hold to their ways, and those with clean hands will grow stronger' (Job 17:9).

Use 1: See from this how improper it is to describe as godly, those who do not walk with God. They want to have Noah's crown — but they do not love Noah's walk. Most are found in the devil's black walk! 'Many walk, of whom I tell you weeping, that they are the enemies of the cross of Christ' (Phil. 3:18).

1. Some will commend walking with God, and say it is the rarest life in the world — but will not set one foot on the way. All who commend wine, do not pay the price. Many a father commends virtue to his child--but does not set him a pattern.

2. Others walk a few steps in the good old ways — but they retreat back again (Jer. 6:16). If the ways of God were not good, why did they enter them? If they were good, why did they forsake them? 'For it had been better for them not to have known the way of righteousness, than, after they have known it, to turn from the holy commandment' (2 Pet. 2:21).

3. Others slander walking with God as a melancholy walk. God accounts this as blasphemy: 'the way of truth shall be evil spoken of' (2 Pet. 2:2). In the Greek it is 'it shall be blasphemed.'

4. Others deride walking with God as if it were a way of foolish scrupulosity. 'What! Do you want to join the 'holy tribe'? Do you want to be wiser than others?' There are some people who, if it were in their power, would jeer holiness out of the world. The chair of the scornful, stands at the mouth of hell (Proverbs 19:29).

5. Others, instead of walking with God, walk according to the flesh (2 Pet. 2:10).

(1) They walk by fleshly opinions.

(2) They walk according to fleshly lusts.

(1) They walk by fleshly opinions. There are six of these:

(a) That it is best 'to do what most do, to steer after the course of the world — and to be in the world's mode.' They think it best--not to get a new heart — but to get into a new fashion.

(b) That reason is the highest judge and umpire in matters of piety. 'We must believe no further than we can see!' For a man to become a fool that he may be wise, to be saved purely by the righteousness of another, to keep all by losing all — this the natural man will by no means put in his creed.

(c) That a little religion will serve the turn. 'The lifeless form may in be kept up — but zeal is madness!' The world thinks that piety to be best which, like leaf-gold, is spread very thin.

(d) That the way which is exposed to affliction is not good. A stick, though it is straight, seems crooked under water. So piety, if it is under affliction, appears crooked to a carnal eye.

(e) That all a man's concern should be for the present world. As that profane cardinal said, he 'would leave his part in paradise to keep his cardinalship in Paris.'

(f) That sinning is better than suffering. It is greater concern to keep the skin whole--than the conscience pure.

These are such rules as the crooked serpent has found out — and whoever walks by them, shall neither know God, nor peace.'

(2) They walk according to fleshly lusts. 'For those who are after the flesh do mind the things of the flesh; but they that are after the Spirit the things of the Spirit.' Romans 8:5. 'For if you live after the flesh--you shall die: but if you through the Spirit do mortify the deeds of the body--you shall live.' Romans 8:13. They make provision (turn caterers) for the flesh (Romans 13:14). Such a person was the Emperor Heliogabalus. He so indulged the flesh that he never sat except among sweet flowers, mixed with amber and musk. He attired himself in purple, set with precious stones. He did not burn oil in his lamps — but a costly balsam brought from Arabia, very odoriferous. He bathed himself in perfumed water; he put his body to no other use — but to be a strainer for fine food and drink to run through.

The ungodly walk according to the flesh. If a drunken or unclean lust calls--they gratify it! They brand as cowards, all who dare not sin at the same rate as they do. These, instead of walking with God, walk contrary to him. Lust is the compass they sail by! Satan is their pilot--and hell the port they are bound for.

Use 2: Let us test whether we have this characteristic of the godly: Do we walk with God? That may be known:

1. By the way we walk in. It is a private, secluded way, in which only some few holy ones walk. Therefore it is called a 'pathway' to distinguish it from the common road: 'in the pathway thereof is no death' (Proverbs 12:28). 'Enter through the narrow gate. For wide is the gate and broad is the road that leads to destruction, and many enter through it. But small is the gate and narrow the road that leads to life, and only a few find it.' Matthew 7:13-14.

2. By a walk in the fear of God. 'Enoch walked with God' (Gen. 5:22). The Chaldean version renders it, 'he walked in the fear of the Lord.' The godly are fearful of that which may displease God. 'How then can I do this great wickedness--and sin against God!' (Gen. 39:9). This is not a base, servile fear — but:

(1) A fear springing from affection (Hos. 3:5). A child fears to offend his father out of the tender affection he has for him. This made holy Anselm say, 'If sin were on one side and hell on the other--I would rather leap into hell than willingly offend my God.'

(2) A fear joined with faith. 'By faith Noah, moved with fear' (Heb. 11:7). Faith and fear go hand in hand. When the soul looks at God's holiness, he fears. When he looks at God's promises, he believes. A godly man trembles — yet trusts. Fear preserves reverence, faith preserves cheerfulness. Fear keeps the soul from lightness, faith keeps it from sadness. By this we may know whether we walk with God, if we walk 'in the fear of God.' We are fearful of infringing his laws, and forfeiting his love. It is a brand set upon the ungodly: 'There is no fear of God before their eyes' (Romans 3:18). The godly fear--and do not offend (Psalm 4:4). The wicked offend--and do not fear (Jer. 5:23,24). Careless and dissolute walking will soon estrange God from us--and make him weary of our company: 'what communion has light with darkness?' (2 Cor. 6:14).

Use 3: Let me persuade all who wish to be accounted godly, to get into Noah's walk. When the truth of grace is in the heart--the beauty of grace is seen in the walk! 'Therefore, if anyone is in Christ, he is a new creation; the old has gone, the new has come!' 2 Corinthians 5:17

1. Walking with God is very pleasing to God. He who walks with God declares to the world, which company he loves most: 'His fellowship is with the Father' (1 John 1:3). He counts those the sweetest hours which are spent with God. This is very pleasing and acceptable to God: 'Enoch walked with God' (Gen. 5:24). And see how kindly God took this at Enoch's hand: 'he had this testimony, that he pleased God' (Heb. 11:5).

2. Close walking with God will be a good means to entice and allure others to walk with him. The apostle exhorts wives so to walk, that the husbands might be won by their conduct (1 Pet. 3:1). Justin Martyr confessed that he became a Christian by observing the holy and innocent lives of the early saints.

3. Close walking with God would put to silence the adversaries of the truth (1 Pet. 2:15). Careless behavior puts a sword into wicked men's hands to wound piety. What a sad thing it is when it is said of professing Christians--that they are as proud, as covetous and as unjust as others! Will this not expose the ways of God to contempt? But holy and close walking would stop the mouths of sinners, so that they should not be able to speak against God's people without giving themselves the lie. Satan came to Christ and 'found nothing in him' (John 14:30). What a confounding thing it will be to the wicked when holiness is the only thing they have to fasten on the godly as a crime. 'We will never find any basis for charges against this man Daniel unless it has something to do with the law of his God' (Dan. 6:5).

4. Walking with God is a pleasant walk. The ways of wisdom are called pleasantness (Proverbs 3:17). Is the light not pleasant? 'They shall walk, O Lord, in the light of your countenance' (Psalm 89:15). Walking with God is like walking among beds of spices, which send forth a fragrant perfume. This is what brings peace: 'walking in the fear of the Lord, and in the comfort of the Holy Spirit' (Acts 9:31). While we walk with God, what sweet music the bird of conscience makes in our breast! 'They shall sing in the ways of the Lord' (Psalm 138:5).

5. Walking with God is honorable. It is a credit for one of an inferior rank, to walk with a king. What greater dignity can be put upon a mortal man, than to converse with his Maker, and to walk with God every day?

6. Walking with God leads to rest: 'There remains therefore a rest to the people of God' (Heb. 4:9). Those who walk with their sins shall never have rest: 'they rest not day and night' (Rev. 4:8). But those who walk with God shall sit down in the kingdom of God (Luke 13:29); just as a weary traveler, when he comes home, sits down and rests. 'To him who overcomes, I will grant to sit with me in my throne' (Rev. 3:21). A throne denotes honor, and sitting denotes rest.

7. Walking with God is the safest walking. Walking in the ways of sin, is like walking on the banks of a river. The sinner treads on the precipice of the bottomless pit, and if death gives him a jog, he tumbles in. But it is safe going in God's way: 'Then shall you walk in your way safely' (Proverbs 3:23). He who walks with a guard walks safely. He who walks with God, shall have God's Spirit to guard him from sin, and God's angels to guard him from danger (Psalm 91:11).

8. Walking with God will make death sweet. It was Augustus' wish that he might have a euthanasia--a quiet, easy death without much pain. If anything makes our pillow easy at death it will be this, that we have walked with God in our lives. Do we think walking with God can do us any hurt? Did we ever hear any cry out on their deathbed--that they have been too holy, that they have prayed too much, or walked with God too much? No! That which has cut them to the heart has been this--that they have not walked more closely with God! They have wrung their hands, and torn their hair--to think that they have been so bewitched with the pleasures of the world. Close walking with God will make our enemy (death) be at peace with us. When King Ahasuerus could not sleep, he called for the book of records, and read it (Esther 6:1). So when the violence of sickness causes sleep to depart from our eyes, and we can call for conscience (that book of records) and find written in it, 'On such a day we humbled our souls by fasting; on such a day our hearts melted in prayer; on such a day we had sweet communion with God'—what a reviving this will be! How we may look death in the face with comfort and

say, 'Lord, now take us up to you in heaven. Where we have so often been by affection--let us now be by fruition.'

9. Walking with God is the best way to know the mind of God. Friends who walk together impart their secrets one to another: 'The secret of the Lord is with those who fear him' (Psalm 25:14). Noah walked with God--and the Lord revealed a great secret to him — destroying the old world and saving him in the ark. Abraham walked with God, and God made him one of his privy council (Gen. 24:40): 'Shall I hide from Abraham that thing which I do?' (Gen. 18:17). God sometimes sweetly unbosoms himself to the soul in prayer and in the holy supper, as Christ made himself known to the disciples in the breaking of bread (Luke 24:35).

10. They who walk with God shall never be wholly left by God. The Lord may withdraw for a time, to make his people cry after him the more — but he will not leave them altogether: 'I hid my face from you for a moment; but with everlasting kindness will I have mercy on you' (Isaiah 54:8). God will not cast off any of his old acquaintance; he will not part with one who has kept him company. 'Enoch walked with God: and he was not; for God took him' (Gen. 5:24). He took him up to heaven. As the Arabic renders it, 'Enoch was lodged in the bosom of divine love.'

Question: What may we do, to walk with God?

Answer 1: If you desire to walk with God--get off the old road of sin! He who would walk in a pleasant meadow--must turn off the road. The way of sin is full of travelers. There are so many travelers on this road, that hell, though it is of a great circumference, would gladly enlarge itself and make room for them (Isaiah 5:14). This way of sin seems pleasant--but the end is damnable. 'I have', says the harlot, 'perfumed my bed with myrrh, aloes and cinnamon' (Proverbs 7:17). See how with one sweet (the cinnamon) there were two bitters (myrrh and aloes). For that little sweet in sin at present there will be a far greater proportion of bitterness afterwards. Therefore get out of these briars. You cannot walk with God and sin: 'what fellowship has righteousness with unrighteousness?' (2 Cor. 6:14).

Answer 2: If you wish to walk with God--get acquainted with him. 'Acquaint now yourself with him' (Job 22:21). Know God in his attributes and promises. Strangers do not walk together.

Answer 3: If you desire to walk with God--get all differences removed. 'Can two walk together, except they are agreed?' (Amos 3:3). This agreement and reconciliation is made by faith: 'God presented him as a sacrifice of atonement, through faith in his blood' (Romans 3:25). When once we are friends, then we shall be called up to the top of the mount like Moses, and have this dignity conferred on us--to be the favorites of heaven and to forever walk with God.

Answer 4: If you desire to walk with God--get a liking for the ways of God. They are adorned with beauty (Proverbs 4:18);

they are sweetened with pleasure (Proverbs 3:17);

they are fenced with truth (Rev. 15:3);

they are accompanied with life (Acts 2:28);

they are lengthened with eternity (Hab. 3:6).

Be enamored with the way of piety--and you will soon walk in it.

Answer 5: If you desire to walk with God--take hold of his arm. Those who walk in their own strength will soon grow weary and tire. 'I will go in the strength of the Lord God' (Psalm 71:16). We cannot walk with God, without God. Let us press him with his promise: 'I will cause you to walk in my statutes' (Ezek. 36:27). If God takes us by the hand, then we shall 'walk, and not faint' (Isaiah 40:31).

24. A godly man strives to be an instrument for making others godly

He is not content to go to heaven alone, but wants to take others there. Spiders work only for themselves—but bees work for others. A godly man is both a diamond and a magnet—a diamond for the sparkling luster of grace, and a magnet for his attractiveness. He is always drawing others to embrace piety. Living things have a propagating virtue. Where piety lives in the heart, there will be an endeavor to propagate the life of grace in those we converse with: 'My son, Onesimus, whom I have begotten in my bonds' (Philem. 10). Though God is the fountain of grace—yet the saints are the pipes which transmit the living streams to others.

This great effort for the conversion of souls proceeds:

1. From the nature of godliness

Grace is like fire--which assimilates and turns everything into its own nature. Where there is the fire of grace in the heart, it will endeavor to inflame others. Grace is a holy leaven, which will be seasoning and leavening others with divine principles. Paul would gladly have converted Agrippa—how he courted him with rhetoric! 'King Agrippa, do you believe the prophets? I know you do' (Acts 26:27). His zeal and eloquence had almost captivated the king (v. 28). Then Agrippa said to Paul, 'Do you think that in such a short time you can persuade me to be a Christian?'

2. From a spirit of compassion

Grace makes the heart tender. A godly man pities those who are in the gall of bitterness. He sees what a deadly cup is brewing for the wicked! They must, without repentance, be bound over to God's wrath! The fire which rained on Sodom was but a painted fire in comparison with hell fire. This is a fire with a vengeance: 'Suffering the vengeance of eternal fire' (Jude 7). Now when a godly man sees Satan's captives ready to be damned, he strives to convert them from the error of their way: 'Knowing the terror of the Lord, we persuade men' (2 Cor. 5:11).

3. From a holy zeal he has for Christ's glory

The glory of Christ is as dear to him as his own salvation. Therefore, that this may be promoted--he strives with the greatest effort to bring souls to Christ.

It is a glory to Christ, when multitudes are born to him. Every star adds a luster to the sky; every convert is a member added to Christ's body, and a jewel adorning his crown. Though Christ's glory cannot be increased, as he is God—yet as he is Mediator, it may. The more that are saved, the more Christ is exalted. Why else should the angels rejoice at the conversion of a sinner—but because Christ's glory now shines the more? (Luke 15:10)

Use 1: This excludes those who are spiritual eunuchs from the number of the godly. They do not strive to promote the salvation of others. 'The one through whom no one else is born--is himself born unworthily.'

1. If men loved Christ, they would try to draw as many as they could to him. He who loves his captain will persuade others to come under his banner. This unmasks the hypocrite. Though a hypocrite may make a show of grace himself—yet he never bothers to procure grace in others. He is without compassion. I may allude to the verse: 'Let the dying die, and the perishing perish. Let those who are left eat one another's flesh' (Zech. 11:9). Let souls go to the devil, he cares not.

2. How far from being godly are those who instead of striving for grace in others, work to destroy all hopeful beginnings of grace in them! Instead of drawing them to Christ, they draw

them from Christ. Their work is to poison and harm souls. This harming of souls occurs in three ways:

(1) By bad edicts. So Jeroboam made Israel sin (1 Kings 16:26). He forced them to idolatry.

(2) By bad examples. Examples speak louder than precepts—but principally the examples of great men are influential. Men placed on high, are like the 'pillar of cloud.' When that went, Israel went. If great men live sinfully, others will follow them.

(3) By bad company. The breath of sinners is infectious. They are like the dragon which 'cast a flood out of his mouth' (Rev. 12:15). They cast a flood of oaths out of their mouths. Wicked tongues are set on fire by hell (Jas. 3:6). The sinner brings match and gunpowder--and the devil brings the fire! The wicked are forever setting snares and temptations before others, as the prophet speaks in another sense: 'I set pots full of wine, and cups, and I said unto them--Drink' (Jer . 35:5). So the wicked set pots of wine before others and make them drink, until reason is stupefied and lust inflamed. These who make men proselytes to the devil--are prodigiously wicked. How sad will be the doom of those who, besides their own sins, have the blood of others to answer for!

3. If it is the sign of a godly man to promote grace in others--then how much more ought he to promote it in his near relations. A godly man will be careful that his children should know God. He would be very sad if any of his family should burn in hell. He labors to see Christ formed in those who are himself in another edition. Augustine says that his mother Monica travailed with greater care and pain for his spiritual than for his natural birth.

The time of childhood is the fittest time to be sowing seeds of piety in our children. 'Who is it he is trying to teach? To whom is he explaining his message? To children weaned from their milk, to those just taken from the breast' (Isaiah 28:9). The wax, while it is soft and tender, will take any impression. Children, while they are young, will fear a reproof; when they are old, they will hate it.

(1) It is pleasing to God that our children should know him early in life. When you come into a garden, you love to pluck the young bud and smell it. God loves a saint in the bud. Of all the trees which the Lord could have chosen in a prophetic vision (Jer. 1:11), he chose the almond tree, which is one of the first of the trees to blossom. Such an almond tree is an early convert.

(2) By endeavoring to bring up our children in the fear of the Lord, we shall provide for God's glory when we are dead. A godly man should not only honor God while he lives—but do something that may promote God's glory when he is dead. If our children are seasoned with gracious principles, they will stand up in our place when we have gone, and will glorify God in their generation. A good piece of ground bears not only a fore-crop but an after-crop. He who is godly does not only bear God a good crop of obedience himself while he lives—but by training his child in the principles of piety, he bears God an after-crop when he is dead.

Use 2: Let all who have God's name placed on them, do what in them lies to advance piety in others. A knife touched with a magnet, will attract the needle. He whose heart is divinely touched with the magnet of God's Spirit, will endeavor to attract those who are near him to Christ. The heathen could say, 'We are not born for ourselves only.' The more excellent anything is, the more diffusive it is. In the body every member is diffusive: the eye conveys light; the head, spirits; the heart, blood. A Christian must not move altogether within his own circle—but seek the welfare of others. To be diffusively good makes us resemble God, whose sacred influence is universal.

And surely it will be no grief of heart, when conscience can witness for us that we have brought glory to God in this matter by working to fill heaven.

Not that this is in any way meritorious, or has any causal influence on our salvation. Christ's blood is the sole cause — but our promoting God's glory in the conversion of others--is a signal evidence of our salvation. As the rainbow is not a cause why God will not drown the world — but is a sign that he will not drown it; or as Rahab's scarlet thread hung out of the window (Joshua 2:18) was not a cause why she was exempted from destruction — but was a sign of her being exempted; just so, our building up others in the faith is not a cause why we are saved--but it is a symbol of our piety and a presage of our eternal felicity!

And thus I have shown the marks and characteristics of a godly man. If a person thus described is reputed a fanatic, then Abraham and Moses and David and Paul were fanatics, which I think none but atheists will dare to affirm!

Two Conclusions

Concerning the characteristic signs aforementioned, I shall lay down two conclusions:

1. These characteristics are a Christian's box of evidences

For as an impenitent sinner has the signs of reprobation on him, by which, as by so many spots and tokens, he may know he shall die, so whoever can show these happy signs of a godly man, may see the evidences of salvation in his soul, and may know he has 'passed from death unto life' (John 5:24). He is as sure to go to heaven as if he were in heaven already. Such a person is undoubtedly a member of Christ — and if he should perish, then a member of Christ might perish.

These blessed characteristics may comfort a Christian under all worldly dejection and diabolical suggestions. Satan tempts a child of God with this — that he is a hypocrite and has no title to the land of promise. A Christian may pull out these evidences and challenge the devil to prove that any wicked man or hypocrite ever had such a good certificate to show for heaven. Satan may sooner prove himself a liar, than the saint a hypocrite.

2. Whoever has one of these characteristics in truth, has everything in embryo

Whoever has one link of a chain has the whole chain.

Objection: But may a child of God say, 'Either I do not have all these characteristics or else they are so faintly stamped in me that I cannot discern them'?

Answer: To satisfy this scruple you must diligently observe the distinctions which the Scripture makes between Christians. It puts them into several classes and orders. Some are little children who have only recently begun breast-feeding on the gospel; others are young men who have grown up to more maturity of grace; others are fathers who are ready to take their degree of glory (1 John 2:12-14). Now, you who are only in the first rank or class may still have the vitals of godliness, as well as those who have arrived at a higher stature in Christ.

The Scripture speaks of the cedar and the bruised reed; the latter of which is as true a plant of the heavenly paradise, as the other. So the weakest ought not to be discouraged. Not all have these characteristics of godliness written in capital letters. If they are only faintly stamped on their souls, God can read the work of his Spirit there. Though the seal is only faintly set on the wax, it ratifies the will and gives a real conveyance of an estate. If there is found just some good thing towards the Lord (as it was said of Abijah), God will accept it (1 Kings 14:13).

An Exhortation to Godliness

Those who are still in their natural condition, who have never yet relished any sweetness in the things of God — let me beseech them, for the love of Christ, to strive to get these characteristics of the godly engraved on their hearts. Though godliness is the object of the world's scorn and hatred (as in Tertullian's days, the name of a Christian was a crime) — yet do not be ashamed to espouse godliness. Know that persecuted godliness is better than prosperous wickedness! What will all the world avail a man without godliness? To be learned and ungodly — is like a devil transformed into an angel of light; to be beautiful and ungodly — is like a lovely picture hung in an infected room; to be honorable in the world and ungodly — is like an ape in purple, or like that image which had a head of gold on feet of clay (Dan. 2:32,33). It is godliness which ennobles and consecrates the heart, making God and angels fall in love with it.

Strive for the reality of godliness. Do not rest in the common workings of God's Spirit. Do not think that it is enough to be intelligent and discursive. A man may discourse of piety to the admiration of others — yet not feel the sweetness of those things in his own soul. The lute gives a melodious sound to others — but does not at all feel the sound itself. Judas could make an elegant discourse about Christ — but did not feel virtue from him.

Do not rest in having your affections a little stirred. A hypocrite may have affections of sorrow like Ahab, or affections of desire like Balaam. These are slight and flashy, and do not amount to real godliness. Oh, strive to be like the king's daughter, 'all glorious within!' (Psalm 45:13)

In order that I may persuade men to become godly, I shall lay down some forcible motives and arguments, and may the Lord make them like nails fastened by his Spirit.

A. Let men seriously weigh their misery while they remain in a state of ungodliness

It may make them run out of this Sodom. The misery of ungodly men appears in nine particulars:

1. They are in a state of spiritual death

'Dead in trespasses' (Eph. 2:1). Dead they must surely be, who are cut off from Christ, the principle of life. For as the body without the soul is dead, so is the soul without Christ. This spiritual death is visible in the effect. It bereaves men of their senses. Sinners have no sense of God in them: 'Having lost all sensitivity' (Eph. 4:19). All their moral endowments, are only flowers strewn on a dead corpse, and what is hell but a sepulcher to bury the spiritually dead in?

2. Their offerings are polluted

Not only the ploughing of the wicked is sin, but the praying of the wicked is sin! 'The sacrifice of the wicked is an abomination to the Lord' (Proverbs 15:8; 21:4). If the water is foul in the well — it cannot be clean in the bucket. If the heart is full of sin — the duties cannot be pure. What straits every ungodly person is in, if he does not come to the ordinance. If he does not come — he despises it; if he does come — he defiles it.

3. Those who live and die ungodly, have no right to the covenant of grace

'At that time you were without Christ, strangers from the covenants of promise' (Eph. 2:12). And to be outside covenant, is to be like anyone in the old world outside the ark. The covenant is the gospel charter, which is enriched with many glorious privileges. But who may plead the benefit of this covenant? Surely only those whose hearts are inlaid with grace. Read the charter: 'A new heart also will I give you, and a new spirit will I put within you ... I will be your God' (Ezek. 36:26,28). A person dying in his ungodliness has no more to do with the new covenant, than a ploughman has to do with the privileges of a city corporation.

God's writing always comes before his seal. 'You are declared to be the epistle of Christ, written not with ink — but with the Spirit of the living God; not in tables of stone — but in fleshy tables of the heart' (2 Cor. 3:3). Here is a golden epistle: the writing is the work of faith; the tablet it is written on, is the heart; the finger that writes it is the Spirit. Now, after the Spirit's writing, comes the Spirit's sealing: 'after you believed, you were sealed with the Holy Spirit' (Eph. 1:13).

That is, you were sealed with an assurance of glory. What have ungodly men — those who have no writing — to do with the seal of the covenant?

4. The ungodly are spiritual fools

If a parent had a child who was very beautiful — but a fool, he would take little joy in him. The Scripture has dressed the sinner in a fool's coat and let me tell you — better be a fool void of reason, than a fool void of grace. This is the devil's fool, 'Fools make a mock at sin' (Proverbs 14:9). Is not that man a fool who refuses a rich share? God offers Christ and salvation — but the sinner refuses this share: 'Israel would not submit to me' (Psalm 81:11). Is not that man a fool who prefers a shiny penny before an inheritance? Is not that man a fool who tends his mortal part and neglects his angelic part, as if a man should paint the wall of his house and let the timber rot? Is not that man a fool who will feed the devil with his soul — like that emperor who fed his lion with pheasant? Is not that man a fool who lays a snare for himself (Proverbs 1:18); who consults his own shame (Hab. 2:10); who loves death (Proverbs 8:36)?

5. The ungodly are vile people

'I will make your grave; for you are vile' (Nah. 1:14). Sin makes men base; it blots their name; it taints their blood. 'They are all together become filthy' (Psalm 14:3). In the Hebrew it is 'they have become stinking.' If you call wicked men ever so bad, you cannot call them worse than their name deserves: they are swine (Matt. 7:6); vipers (Matt. 3:7); devils (John 6:70). The wicked are dross and refuse (Psalm 119:119), and heaven is too pure to have any dross mingled with it.

6. Their temporal mercies are continued in judgment

The wicked may have health and estate, yes, more than heart can wish (Psalm 73:7) — but 'their table is a snare' (Psalm 69:22). Sinners have their mercies with God's permission, but not with his love. The people of Israel would have been better without their quail, than to have had such sour sauce. The ungodly are usurpers; they lack a spiritual title to what they possess. Their good things are like cloth picked up at the draper's which is not paid for. Death will bring a sad reckoning at last.

7. Their temporal judgments are not removed in mercy

Pharaoh had ten arrows shot at him (ten plagues) and all those plagues were removed; but as his heart remained hard, those plagues were not removed in mercy. It was not a preservation — but a reservation. God reserved him as a signal monument of his justice, when he was drowned in the depths of the sea. God may reprieve men's lives, when he does not remit their sins. The wicked may have sparing mercy, but not saving mercy.

8. The ungodly, while they live, are exposed to the wrath of God

'He who believes not, the wrath of God abides on him' (John 3:36). Whoever lacks grace is like someone who lacks a pardon; every hour he is in fear of execution. How can a wicked man rejoice? Over his head hangs the sword of God's justice; and under him hell-fire burns.

9. The ungodly at death, must undergo God's fury and indignation

'The wicked shall be turned into hell' (Psalm 9:17). I have read of a lodestone in Ethiopia which has two corners. With one it attracts iron and with the other it repels it. So God has two hands: one of mercy and one of justice. With the one, he will draw the godly to heaven; with the other, he will thrust the sinner to hell.

And oh, how dreadful is that place! It is called a fiery lake (Rev. 20:15). That is, a lake to denote the many torments in hell; and a fiery lake to show the fierceness of the punishment. Strabo in his 'Geography' mentions a lake in Galilee of such a pestiferous nature that it scalds off the skin of whatever is thrown into it. But alas, that lake is cool, compared with this fiery lake into which the damned are thrown. To demonstrate that this fire is terrible, there are two most pernicious qualities in it:

(1) It is sulphurous; it is mixed with brimstone (Rev. 21:8), which is unsavory and suffocating.

(2) It is inextinguishable: the wicked shall be choked in the flames, though not consumed: 'And the devil was cast into the lake of fire and brimstone, where the beast and the false prophet are, and shall be tormented day and night forever and ever' (Rev. 20:10). See the deplorable condition of all ungodly people! In the eternal world, they shall have a life which always dies, and a death which always lives. May this not frighten men off their sins and make them become godly, unless they are resolved to feel how hot hell-fire is?

B. What rare people the godly are

'The righteous is more excellent than his neighbor' (Proverbs 12:26). Like the flower of the sun, like the wine of Lebanon, like the sparkling on Aaron's breastplate, such is the oriental splendor of a person embellished with godliness. The excellence of the godly appears in seven particulars:

1. The godly are precious

Therefore they are set apart for God: 'know that the Lord has set apart him who is godly for himself' (Psalm 4:3). We set apart things that are precious. The godly are set apart as God's peculiar treasure (Psalm 135:4); as his garden of delight (Cant 4:12); as his royal diadem (Isaiah 62:3). The godly are the excellent of the earth (Psalm 16:3), comparable to fine gold (Lam. 4:2); doubly refined (Zech. 13:9); they are the glory of creation (Isaiah 46:13.) Origen compares the saints to sapphires and crystal. God calls them his jewels (Mal. 3:17). They are jewels:

(1) For their value. Diamonds (says Pliny) were not known for a long time except among princes, and were hung on their diadems. God so values his people that he will give kingdoms for their ransom (Isaiah 43:3); He put his best Jewel (Christ) in pawn for them (John 3:16).

(2) For their luster. If one pearl of grace shines so brightly that it delights Christ's heart—'You have ravished my heart with one of your eyes' (Cant 4:9), that is, one of your graces—then how illustrious are all the graces together in a constellation!

2. The godly are honorable

'You have been honorable' (Isaiah 43:4). The godly are 'a crown of glory in the hand of the Lord' (Isaiah 62:3). They are 'plants of renown' (Ezek. 16:14). They are not only vessels of mercy but vessels of honor (2 Tim. 2:21). Aristotle calls honor the chief good thing. The godly are near akin to the blessed Trinity: they have the tutelage and guardianship of angels; they have 'God's name written upon them' (Rev. 3:12) and 'the Holy Spirit dwelling in them' (2 Tim. 1:14).

The godly are a sacred priesthood. The priesthood under the law was honorable. The king's daughter was wife to Jehoiada the priest (2 Chron. 22:11). It was a custom among the Egyptians to have their kings chosen from their priests. The saints are a divine priesthood to offer up spiritual sacrifices (1 Pet 2:9). They are co-heirs with Christ (Romans 8:17). They are kings (Rev. 1:6). Novarinus tells of an ancient king who invited a company of poor Christians and made them a great feast. On being asked why he showed so much respect to people of such poor birth and extraction, he told them, 'These I must honor as the children of the most high God. They will be kings and princes with me in the eternal world.'

The godly are in some sense higher than the angels. The angels are Christ's friends; these are his spouse. The angels are called morning stars (Job 38:7)—but the saints are clothed with the Sun of righteousness (Rev. 12:1). All men, says Chrysostom, are ambitious for honor. See, then, the honor of the godly! 'Wisdom is supreme; therefore get wisdom. Though it cost all you have, get understanding. Esteem her, and she will exalt you; embrace her, and she will honor you.' (Proverbs 4:7,8). The trophies of the saints' renown, will be erected in the eternal world.

3. The godly are loved by God

'The excellency of Jacob, whom he loved' (Psalm 47:4). A holy heart is the garden where God plants the flower of his love. God's love to his people is an ancient love, it dates from eternity (Eph. 1:4). He loves them with a choice, distinguishing love; they are the 'dearly beloved of his soul' (Jer. 12:7). The men of the world have bounty dropping from God's fingers—but the godly have love dropping from God's heart. He gives to one, a golden cup—to the other, a golden kiss. He loves the godly as he loves Christ (John 17:26). It is the same love in kind, though not in degree. Here the saints merely sip God's love; in heaven they shall drink of rivers of pleasure (Psalm 36:8). The love of God to His people is permanent. Death may take their life away from them—but not God's love: 'I have loved you with an everlasting love; I have drawn you with loving-kindness' (Jer. 31:3).

4. The godly are prudent people

They have good insight and foresight:

(1) They have good insight. 'He who is spiritual judges all things' (1 Cor. 2:15). The godly have insight into people and things. They have insight into people, because they have the anointing of God, and by a spirit of discerning they can see some differences between the precious and the vile (Jer. 15:19). God's people are not censorious—but they are judicious. They can see a foul heart—through a naked breast and a painted face. They can see a revengeful spirit—through a bitter tongue. They can guess at the tree—by the fruit (Matt. 12:33). They can see the plague tokens of sin appearing in the wicked, which makes them leave the tents of those sinners (Numb. 16:26).

The godly have insight into things mysterious. They can see much of the mystery of their own hearts. Take the greatest politician who understands the mysteries of state—he still does not understand the mystery of his own heart. You will sometimes hear him swear that his heart is good—but a child of God sees much heart corruption (1 Kings 8:38). Though some flowers of grace grow there, he still sees how fast the weeds of sin grow, and is therefore continually weeding his heart by repentance and mortification.

The godly can discern the mystery of the times: 'The children of Issachar were men who had understanding of the times' (1 Chron. 12:32). The godly can see when an age runs to seed— when God's name is dishonored, his messengers despised, his gospel eclipsed. The people of God strive to keep their garments pure (Rev. 16:15). Their care is that the times may not be the worse because of them; nor they the worse because of the times.

The godly understand the mystery of living by faith: 'The just shall live by faith' (Heb. 10:38). They can trust God's heart—where they cannot trace his hand. They can get comfort out of a promise, as Moses got water out of the rock (Exod. 17:6). 'Even though the fig trees have no blossoms, and there are no grapes on the vine; even though the olive crop fails, and the fields lie empty and barren; even though the flocks die in the fields, and the cattle barns are empty, yet I will rejoice in the Lord! I will be joyful in the God of my salvation' (Hab. 3:17,18).

(2) They have good foresight. They foresee the evil of a temptation: 'we are not ignorant of his devices' (2 Cor. 2:11). The wicked swallow temptations like pills, and when it is too late, feel these pills afflict their conscience. But the godly foresee a temptation, and will not come near. They see a snake under the beautiful flowers! They know that Satan's kindness—is craftiness!

The godly foresee temporal dangers: 'A prudent man foresees the evil, and hides himself' (Proverbs 22:3). The people of God see when the cloud of wrath is ready to drop on a nation, and they get into their rooms (Isaiah 26:20) – the attributes and promises of God; and into the clefts of the rocks – the bleeding wounds of Christ – and hide themselves. Well therefore, may they be baptized with the name of wise virgins.

5. The godly are the bulwark of a nation

The godly are the pillars to keep a city and nation from falling; they stave off judgment from a land. It was said of old, that so long as Hector lived, Troy could not be demolished. God could do nothing to Sodom – until Lot had gone out of it (Gen. 19:22). Golden Christians are bronze walls. The Lord would soon execute judgment in the world – were it not for the sake of a few pious people. Would God preserve the world only for drunkards and swearers? He would soon sink the ship – but for the fact that some of his elect are in it. Yet such is the indiscretion of men that they injure the saints and count as burdens, those who are the chief blessings (Isaiah 19:24).

6. The godly are of a brave, heroic spirit

'My servant Caleb, because he had another spirit' (Numb. 14:24). An excellent spirit was found in Daniel (Dan. 5:12). The godly hate that which is base and sordid. They will not enrich their purses by enslaving their consciences. They are noble and courageous in God's cause: 'the righteous are bold as a lion' (Proverbs 28.1). The saints live in accordance with their high birth: they yearn for God's love; they aspire to glory; they set their feet where worldly men set their heart; they display the banner of the gospel, lifting up Christ's name and interest in the world.

7. The godly are happy people

King Balak sent to curse the people of God – but the Lord would not allow it. 'God said unto Balaam, You shall not curse the people: for they are blessed' (Numb. 22:12). And Moses afterwards records it as a memorable thing that God turned the king's intended curse into a blessing: 'the Lord your God turned the curse into a blessing unto you' (Deut. 23:5). Those who are always on the strongest side must of necessity be happy: 'The Lord is on my side' (Psalm 118:6). They are happy – who have all conditions sanctified to them (Romans 8:28), who are crowned with peace while they live (Psalm 119:165) and with glory when they die (Psalm 73:24). And may this not tempt everyone to become godly? 'Happy are you, O Israel: a people saved by the Lord!' (Deut. 33:29).

C. To strive for godliness is most rational

1. It is the highest act of reason, to become a Christian

If, while he remains in nature's soil, he is poisoned with sin – no more actually fit for communion with God than a toad is fit to be made an angel – then it is very consonant to reason that he should strive for a change.

2. It is rational because this change is for the better

'Now are you light in the Lord' (Eph. 5:8). Will not anyone be willing to exchange a dark prison – for a king's palace? Will he not exchange his brass – for gold? You who become godly change for the better: you change your pride – for humility; you change your uncleanness – for holiness. You change a lust that will damn you – for a Christ who will save you. If men were not besotted, if their fall had not knocked their brains out – they would see that it is the most rational thing in the world to become godly.

D. The excellence of godliness

The excellence of godliness appears in several ways:

1. Godliness is our spiritual beauty

'The beauties of holiness' (Psalm 110:3). Godliness is to the soul, what the light is to the world — to illustrate and adorn it. It is not greatness which approves us in God's eye — but goodness. What is the beauty of the angels — but their sanctity? Godliness is the intricate embroidery and workmanship of the Holy Spirit. A soul furnished with godliness is filled with beauty, it is enameled with purity. This is the clothing of wrought gold which makes the King of heaven fall in love with us. Were there no excellence in holiness, the hypocrite would never try to paint it. Godliness sheds a glory and luster on the saints. What are the graces — but the golden feathers in which Christ's dove shines! (Psalm 68:13)

2. Godliness is our defense

Grace is called 'the armor of light' (Romans 13:12). It is light for beauty, and armor for defense. A Christian has armor of God's making, which cannot be shot through. He has the shield of faith, the helmet of hope, the breastplate of righteousness. This armor defends against the assaults of temptation, and the terror of hell.

3. Godliness breeds solid peace

'Great peace have those who love your law' (Psalm 119:165). Godliness composes the heart, making it quiet and calm like the upper region, where there are no winds and tempests. How can that heart be unquiet — where the Prince of Peace dwells? 'Christ in you' (Col. 1:27). A holy heart may be compared to the doors of Solomon's temple, which were made of olive tree, carved with open flowers (1 Kings 6:32). The olive of peace and the open flowers of joy are in that heart.

'I have spoken these things to you so that My joy may be in you and your joy may be complete.' John 15:11. Godliness does not destroy a Christian's joy — but refines it. His rose is without prickles, his wine without froth. He who is a favorite of heaven must of necessity be full of joy and peace. He may truly sing a sonnet to his soul and say, 'Soul, take your ease' (Luke 12:19). King Ptolemy asked someone how he might be at rest when he dreamed. He replied, 'Let piety be the scope of all your actions.' If anyone should ask me how he should be at rest when he is awake, I would return a similar answer: 'Let his soul be inlaid with godliness.'

4. Godliness is the best trade we can engage in

It brings profit. Wicked men say, 'It is vain to serve God; and what profit is it?' (Mal. 3:14). To be sure, there is no profit in sin: 'Treasures of wickedness profit nothing' (Proverbs 10:2). But godliness is profitable (1 Tim. 4:8). It is like digging in a gold mine, where there is gain, as well as toil. Godliness makes God himself our portion: 'The Lord is the portion of my inheritance' (Psalm 16:5). If God is our portion — all our estate lies in jewels! Where God gives himself, he gives everything else. Whoever has the castle, has all the royalties belonging to it. God is a portion that can be neither spent nor lost. 'God is the strength of my heart and my portion forever!' (Psalm 73:26). Thus we see that godliness is a thriving trade.

And as godliness brings profit with it, so it is profitable 'for all things' (1 Tim. 4:8). What else is profitable, besides godliness? Food will not give a man wisdom; gold will not give him health; honor will not give him beauty. But godliness is useful for all things: it fences off all troubles; it supplies all needs; it makes soul and body completely happy.

5. Godliness is an enduring substance

It knows no fall of the leaf. All worldly delights have a death's-head set on them. They are only shadows and they are fleeting. Earthly comforts are like Paul's friends, who took him to the ship and left him there (Acts 20:38). So these will bring a man to his grave and then take their farewell. But godliness is a possession we cannot be robbed of. It runs parallel with eternity. Force cannot weaken it; age cannot wither it. It outbraves sufferings; it outlives death (Proverbs 10:2). Death may pluck the stalk of the body — but the flower of grace is not hurt.

6. Godliness is so excellent that the worst men would like to have it, after they die

Though at present godliness is despised and under a cloud — yet at death all would like to be godly. A philosopher asked a young man whether he would like to be rich Croesus or virtuous Socrates. He answered that he would like to live with Croesus — and die with Socrates. So men would like to live with the wicked in pleasure — but die with the godly: 'Let me die the death of the righteous, and let my last end be like his!' (Numb. 23:10). If, then, godliness is so desirable at death, why should we not pursue it now?

E. There are only a few godly people

They are like the gleanings after vintage. Most receive the mark of the beast (Rev. 13:17). The devil keeps open house for all comers, and he is never without guests. This may prevail with us to be godly. If the number of the saints is so small, how we should strive to be found among these pearls! 'But a remnant shall be saved' (Romans 9:27). It is better to go to heaven with the few — than to hell in the crowd! Christ's flock is a little one. 'Don't be afraid, little flock, because your Father delights to give you the kingdom!' Luke 12:32

F. Consider how vain and contemptible other things are, which people void of godliness, busy themselves about

Men are taken up with the things of this life, and 'what profit has he who has labored for the wind?' (Eccles. 5:16). Can the wind fill? What is gold but dust (Amos 2:7), which will sooner choke than satisfy? Pull off the mask of the most beautiful thing under the sun — and look what is inside. There is care and vexation! And the greatest care is still to come — and that is to give account to God. Worldly joys are as fleeting as a bubble floating down the stream.

But godliness has real worth in it. If you speak of true honor, it is to be born of God; if of true valor, it is to fight the good fight of faith; if of true delight, it is to have joy in the Holy Spirit. Oh, then, espouse godliness! Here reality is to be had. Of other things we may say, 'They comfort in vain!' (Zech. 10:2)

Prescribing some helps to godliness

Question: But what shall we do, that we may be godly?

Answer: I shall briefly lay down some rules or helps to godliness.

1. Be diligent in the use of all means that may promote godliness. 'Strive to enter in at the strait gate' (Luke 13:24). What is purpose, without pursuit? When you have made your estimate of godliness, pursue those means which are most expedient for obtaining it.

2. Take heed of the world. It is hard for a clod of dust — to become a star. 'Love not the world' (1 John 2:15). Many would like to be godly — but the honors and profits of the world divert them. Where the world fills both head and heart — there is no room for Christ. He whose mind is rooted in the earth, is likely enough to deride godliness. When our Savior was preaching against sin, 'the Pharisees, who were covetous, derided him' (Luke 16:14). The world eats the heart out of godliness, as the ivy eats the heart out of the oak. The world kills with her golden darts!

3. Accustom yourselves to holy thoughts. Serious meditation represents everything in its true color. It shows the evil of sin, and the luster of grace. By holy thoughts, the head grows clearer and the heart better: 'I thought on my ways, and turned my feet unto your testimonies' (Psalm 119:59). If men would step aside a little out of the noise and hurry of business, and spend only

half-an-hour every day thinking about their souls and eternity, it would produce a wonderful alteration in them!

4. Watch your hearts. This was Christ's watchword to his disciples: 'Watch, therefore' (Matt. 24:42). The heart will incline us to sin, before we are aware. A subtle heart needs a watchful eye. Watch your thoughts, your affections. The heart has a thousand doors to run out from. Oh, keep close watch on your souls! Stand continually on your watch-towers (Hab. 2:1). When you have prayed against sin, watch against temptation. Most wickedness in the world is committed for lack of watchfulness. Watchfulness maintains godliness. It is the edging which keeps piety from fraying.

5. Make spending your time a matter of conscience. 'Redeeming the time' (Eph. 5:16). Many people fool away their time, some in idle visits, others in recreations and pleasures which secretly bewitch the heart and take it away from better things. What are our golden hours for — but to attend to our souls? Time misspent is not time lived — but time lost! Time is a precious commodity. A piece of wax in itself is not worth much — but when it is affixed to the label of a will and conveys an estate, it is of great value. Thus, time simply in itself is not so considerable — but as salvation is to be worked out in it, and a conveyance of heaven depends on using it well — it is of infinite concern!

6. Think of your short stay in the world. 'We are here for only a moment, visitors and strangers in the land as our ancestors were before us. Our days on earth are like a shadow, gone so soon without a trace!' (1 Chron. 29:15). There is only a span between the cradle and the grave. Solomon says there is a time to be born and a time to die (Eccles. 3:2) — but mentions no time of living — as if that were so short it was not worth naming! Time, when it has once gone, cannot be recalled. 'My life passes more swiftly than a runner. It flees away, filled with tragedy. It disappears like a swift boat, like an eagle that swoops down on its prey.' Job 9:25-26. This Scripture compares time to a flying eagle. Yet time differs from the eagle in this: the eagle flies forward and then back again--but time has wings only to fly forward --it never returns! 'Time flies irrevocably.'

The serious thoughts of our short stay here would be a great means of promoting godliness. What if death should come before we are ready? What if our life should breathe out before God's Spirit has breathed in? Whoever considers how flitting and winged his life is — will hasten his repentance!

7. Make this maxim your own — that godliness is the purpose of your creation. God never sent men into the world only to eat and drink and put on fine clothes — but that they might 'Serve him in holiness and righteousness' (Luke 1:74,75). God made the world only as a dressing room — to dress our souls in. He sent us here on the grand errand of godliness. Should nothing but the body (the brutish part) be looked after, this would be basely to degenerate, yes, to invert and frustrate the very purpose of our being!

8. Be often among the godly. They are the salt of the earth — and will help to season you. Their counsel may direct you; their prayers may enliven you. Such holy sparks may be thrown into your breasts as may kindle devotion in you. It is good to be among the saints, to learn the trade of godliness: 'He who walks with wise men shall be wise' (Proverbs 13:20).

An exhortation to persevere in godliness

Those who wear the mantle of godliness — and in the judgment of others are looked upon as godly — let me exhort you to persevere: 'Let us hold fast the profession of our faith' (Heb. 10:23). This is a seasonable exhortation in these times — when the devil's agents are abroad, whose whole work is to unsettle people and make them fall away from that former strictness in piety which they have professed.

1. It is much to be lamented – to see professing Christians wavering in religion. How many we see unresolved and unsteady, like Reuben, 'unstable as water' (Gen. 49:4). These the apostle rightly compares to 'waves of the sea ... and wandering stars' (Jude 13). They are not fixed in the principles of godliness. Beza writes of one Bolsechus, that 'his religion changed like the moon.' Such were the Ebionites, who kept both the Jewish and the Christian Sabbath. Many professors are like the river Euripus, ebbing and flowing in matters of piety. They are like reeds bending every way, either to the Mass or to the Koran. They are like the planet Mercury, which constantly varies, and is seldom constant in its motion. When men think of heaven and the recompense of reward, then they want to be godly – but when they think of persecution, then they are like the Jews who deserted Christ and 'walked no more with him' (John 6:66). If men's faces altered as fast as their opinions – we would not recognize them! To be thus vacillating and wavering in religion, argues lightness of thought. Feathers are blown in every direction, and so are feathery professors.

2. It is much to be lamented – to see professing Christians falling from that godliness which once they seemed to have. They have turned to worldliness and wantonness. The very mantle of their profession has fallen off; and indeed, if they were not fixed stars – it is no wonder to see them as falling stars. This spiritual epilepsy, or falling sickness, was never more rife.

It is a dreadful sin for men to fall from that godliness, which they once seemed to have. Chrysostom says, 'Apostates are worse than those who are openly wicked. They give godliness a bad name.' 'The apostate', says Tertullian, 'Seems to put God and Satan in the balance, and having weighed both their services, prefers the devil's service, and proclaims him to be the best master!' In that respect the apostate is said to put Christ to open shame (Heb. 6:6).

This will be bitter in the end (Heb. 10:38). What a worm, the apostate Spira felt in his conscience! In what horror of mind did the apostate Stephen Gardiner cry out upon his deathbed – that with Peter, he had denied his Master! But he had not repented with Peter!

That we may be steadfast in godliness and persevere, let us do two things:

1. Let us take heed of those things which will make us by degrees fall away from our profession. Let us:

(1) Beware of covetousness. 'Men shall be covetous ... having a form of godliness – but denying the power' (2 Tim. 3:2,5). One of Christ's own apostles was caught with this silver bait! Covetousness will make a man betray a good cause, and make shipwreck of a good conscience. I have read of some in the time of the Emperor Valens, who denied the Christian faith to prevent the confiscation of their goods.

(2) Beware of unbelief. 'Take heed, brethren, lest there be in any of you an evil heart of unbelief, in departing from the living God' (Heb. 3:12). There is no evil like an evil heart; no evil heart like an unbelieving heart. Why so? It makes men depart from the blessed God. He who does not believe God's mercy – will not dread his justice. Unbelief is the nurse of apostasy; therefore unbelieving and unstable go together: 'they believed not in God ... they turned back and tempted God' (Psalm 78:22,41).

(3) Take heed of cowardice. He who is afraid to be godly, must surely be evil: 'The fear of man brings a snare' (Proverbs 29:25). They who fear danger more than sin – will commit sin to avoid danger! Origen, out of fear of persecution, offered incense to the idol. Aristotle says, 'The reason why the chameleon turns so many colors, is through excessive fear.' Fear will make men change their religion, as often as the chameleon does her color! Christian, you who have made a

profession of godliness so long, and others have noted you for a saint in their calendar, why do you fear and begin to shrink back? The cause which you have embarked on is good; you are fighting against sin; you have a good Captain who is marching before you: Christ, 'the captain of your salvation' (Heb. 2:10).

What is it, that you fear? Is it loss of liberty? What is liberty worth, when conscience is in bonds? It is better to lose your liberty and keep your peace — than to lose your peace and keep your liberty. Is it loss of estate? Do you say, like Amaziah, 'What should I do about the silver I paid?' (2 Chron. 25:9) I would answer with the prophet, 'The Lord can give you much more than this' (v. 10). He has promised you 'an hundredfold' in this life — and if that is nothing, he will give you life everlasting (Matt. 19:29).

2. Let us use all means for perseverance

(1) Strive for a real work of grace in your soul. Grace is the best fortification: 'it is a good thing that the heart be established with grace' (Heb. 13:9).

Question: What is this real work of grace?

Answer: It consists in two things:

1. Grace lies in a heart-humbling work. The thorn of sin pricked Paul's conscience: 'Sin revived, and I died' (Romans 7:9). Though some are less humbled than others — as some bring forth children with less pangs — yet all have pangs.

2. Grace lies in a heart-changing work. 'But you are washed — but you are sanctified' (1 Cor. 6:11). A man is so changed as if another soul lived in the same body! If ever you would hold out in the ways of God, get this vital principle of grace. Why do men change their religion — but because their hearts were never changed? They do not fall away from grace — but for lack of grace.

(2) Be deliberate and judicious. Weigh things well in the balance: 'Who of you, wanting to build a tower, doesn't first sit down and calculate the cost to see if he has enough to complete it?' (Luke 14:28). Think to yourselves, what it will cost you to be godly. You must expect the hatred of the world (John 15:19). The wicked hate the godly for their piety. It is strange that they should do so. Do we hate a flower because it is sweet? The godly are hated for the perfume of their graces. Is a virgin hated for her beauty? The wicked hate the godly for the beauty of holiness which shines in them. Secret hatred will break forth into open violence (2 Tim. 3:12). Christians must count the cost before they build. Why are people so hasty in abandoning religion — if not because they were so hasty in taking it up?

(3) Get a clear, distinct knowledge of God. Know the love of the Father, the merit of the Son, the efficacy of the Holy Spirit. Those who do not know God aright, will by degrees renounce their profession. The Samaritans sometimes sided with the Jews, when they were in favor. Afterwards they disclaimed all kindred with the Jews, when they were persecuted by Antiochus. And no wonder they shuffled so in their religion, if you consider what Christ said of the Samaritans, 'You Samaritans worship what you do not know!' (John 4:22). They were enveloped by ignorance. Blind men are apt to fall, and so are those who are blinded in their minds.

(4) Enter on it purely out of choice. 'I have chosen the way of truth' (Psalm 119:30). Espouse godliness for its own worth. Whoever wishes to persevere must rather choose godliness with reproach — than sin with all its worldly pomp. Whoever takes up religion for fear — will lay it down again for fear. Whoever embraces godliness for gain — will desert it when the jewels of promotion are pulled off. Do not be godly from worldly design — but from pious choice.

(5) Strive for sincerity. This will be a golden pillar to support you. A tree that is hollow, must of necessity be blown down. The hypocrite sets up in the trade of religion – but he will soon break: 'their heart was not right with him, neither were they steadfast' (Psalm 78:37). Judas was first a sly hypocrite and then a traitor. If a piece of copper is gilded, the gilding will wash off. Nothing will hold out but sincerity: 'May integrity and honesty protect me, for I put my hope in you' (Psalm 25:21). How many storms was Job in! Not only Satan – but God himself set on him (Job 7:20), which was enough to have made him desist from being godly. Yet Job stood fast – because he stood upright: 'My righteousness I hold fast, and will not let it go; my heart shall not reproach me as long as I live' (Job 27:6). Those colors hold best, which are fixed in oils. If we wish to have our profession hold its color, it must be fixed in the oil of sincerity.

(6) Hold up the life and fervor of duty. 'Fervent in spirit, serving the Lord' (Romans 12:11). We put coals on the fire to keep it from going out. When Christians grow into a dull formality, they begin to be dispirited, and by degrees abate in their godliness. No one is so fit to make an apostate – as a lukewarm professing Christian.

(7) Exercise great self-denial. 'If anyone would come after me, he must deny himself and take up his cross daily and follow me. (Luke 9:23). Self-ease, self-ends, whatever comes in competition with (or stands in opposition to) Christ's glory and interest – must be denied! Self is the great snare; self-love undermines the power of godliness. The young man in the Gospel might have followed Christ – but something of self hindered (Matt. 19:20-22). Self-love is self-hatred. The man who cannot get beyond himself – will never get to heaven.

(8) Preserve a holy watchfulness over your hearts. The man who has gunpowder in his house, fears lest it should catch fire and explode. Sin in the heart is like gunpowder; it may make us fear lest a spark of temptation should fall on us and blow us up. There are two things which may make us always watchful of our hearts: the deceits of our hearts and the lusts of our hearts. When Peter was afraid that he should sink and cried to Christ, 'Lord, save me', then Christ took him by the hand and helped him (Matt. 14:30,31); but when Peter grew confident and thought he could stand alone, then Christ allowed him to fall. Oh, let us be suspicious of ourselves and in a holy sense 'clothe ourselves with trembling' (Ezek. 26:16).

(9) Strive for assurance. 'Give diligence to make your calling and election sure' (2 Pet. 1:10). The man who is sure that God is his God, is like a castle built on a rock – all the powers of hell cannot shake him. How can that man be constant in piety – who is at a loss about his spiritual estate, and does not know whether he has grace or not? It will be a difficult matter for a man to die for Christ, if he does not know that Christ has died for him. Assurance establishes a Christian in shaking times. He who has the Spirit of God bearing witness to his heart is the most likely to bear witness to the truth (Romans 8:16). Oh, give diligence! Be much in prayer, reading, holy conversation. These things are the oil, without which the lamp of assurance will not shine.

(10) Lay hold of God's strength. God is called the Strength of Israel (1 Sam. 15:29). It is in his strength that we stand, more than our own. The child is safest in the father's hands. It is not our holding God – but his holding us – which preserves us. A little boat tied fast to a rock is safe, and so are we, when we are tied to the 'rock of ages.'

Motives to Persevere in Godliness

So that I may encourage Christians to persevere in the profession of godliness, I shall propose these four considerations:

1. It is the glory and crown of a Christian to be grey-headed in godliness

'Mnason of Cyprus, an old disciple' (Acts 21:16). What an honor it is to see a Christian's garments red with blood—yet his conscience pure white and his graces green and flourishing!

2. How sinners persevere in their sins!

They are settled on their lees (Zeph. 1:12). The judgments of God will not deter or remove them. They say to their sin, as Ruth said to Naomi, 'Where you go, I will go ... the Lord do so to me, and more also, if anything but death parts you and me' (Ruth 1:16,17). So nothing shall part men from their sins. Oh, what a shame it is that the wicked should be fixed in evil—and we unfixed in good; that they should be more constant in the devil's service—than we are in Christ's service!

3. Our perseverance in godliness may be a means of confirming others

Cyprian's hearers followed him to the place of his suffering, and when they saw his steadfastness in the faith, they cried out, 'Let us also die with our holy pastor!' 'Many of the brethren, waxing confident by my bonds, are much more bold to speak the word' (Phil. 1:14). Paul's zeal and constancy animated the onlookers. His prison chains made converts in Nero's court—and two of those converts were afterwards martyrs, as history relates.

4. We shall lose nothing by our perseverance in godliness

There are eight glorious promises which God has entailed on the persevering saints:

(1) 'Be faithful, even to the point of death, and I will give you the crown of life.' (Rev. 2:10). Christian, you may lose the breath of life, but not the crown of life.

(2) 'To him who overcomes, I will give the right to eat from the tree of life, which is in the paradise of God' (Rev. 2:7). This tree of life is the Lord Jesus. This tree infuses life—and prevents death. The day we eat of this tree—our eyes shall indeed be opened to see God!

(3) 'To him who overcomes, I will give some of the hidden manna. I will also give him a white stone with a new name written on it, known only to him who receives it.' (Rev. 2:17). This promise consists of three branches:

(a) 'I will give to eat of the hidden manna.' This is mysterious. It signifies the love of God—which is manna for sweetness and hidden for its rarity.

(b) 'I will give him a white stone', that is, absolution. 'It may be called a precious stone,' says Jerome.

(c) 'And in the stone a new name', that is, adoption. He shall be reputed an heir of heaven, and no one can know it, except the one who has the privy seal of the Spirit to assure him of it.

(4) 'He who overcomes will, like them, be dressed in white. I will never blot out his name from the book of life, but will acknowledge his name before my Father and his angels' (Rev. 3:5). The persevering saint shall be clothed in white. This is an emblem of joy (Eccles. 9:8). He shall put off his mourning clothes, and be clothed in the white robe of glory.

'I will never blot out his name from the book of life.' God will blot a believer's sins out—but he will not blot his name out. The book of God's decree has no errata in it.

'But I will acknowledge his name.' If anyone has owned Christ on earth and worn his colors when it was death to wear them, Christ will not be ashamed of him—but will acknowledge his name before his Father and the holy angels. Oh, what a comfort and honor it will be to have a good look from Christ, at the last day! More—to have Christ own us by name and say, 'These were those who stood up for my truth and kept their garments pure, in a defiling age. These shall walk with me in white, for they are worthy.'

(5) 'Him who overcomes I will make a pillar in the temple of my God. Never again will he leave it. I will write on him the name of my God and the name of the city of my God, the new Jerusalem, which is coming down out of heaven from my God; and I will also write on him my new name.' (Rev. 3:12). There are many excellent things couched in this promise:

'I will make him a pillar in the temple of my God.' The hypocrite is a reed shaken by the wind — but the conquering saint shall be a glorious pillar, a pillar of strength and a pillar in the temple for sanctity.

'Never again will he leave it.' I understand this of a glorified state. 'Never again will he leave it,' that is, after he has overcome, he shall not go out to the wars any more. He shall never have any more sin or temptation to conflict with. No more noise of drum or cannon shall be heard — but having won the field, the believer shall now stay at home and divide the spoil.

'And I will write upon him the name of my God', that is, he shall be openly acknowledged as my child, just as the Son bears his Father's name. How honorable that saint must be, who has God's own name written on him!

'And I will write upon him the name of the city of my God', that is, he shall be enrolled as a citizen of the Jerusalem above. He shall be made free in the angelic society.

(6) 'To him who overcomes and does my will to the end, I will give authority over the nations' (Rev. 2:26). This may have a double mystery. Either it may be understood of the saints living on earth: they shall have power over the nations; their zeal and patience shall overpower the adversaries of truth (Acts 6:10); or, principally, it may be understood of the saints triumphing in heaven. They shall have power over the nations: they shall share with Christ in some of his power; they shall join with him in judging the world in the last days: 'the saints shall judge the world' (1 Cor. 6:2).

(7) 'To him who overcomes, I will give the right to sit with me on my throne' (Rev. 3:21):

(a) Here is, first, the saints' dignity: they shall sit upon the throne.

(b) Their safety: they shall sit with Christ. Christ holds them fast and no one shall pluck them off his throne. The saints may be turned out of their houses — but they cannot be turned out of Christ's throne! Men may as well pluck a star out of the sky — as a saint out of the throne!

(8) 'I will give him the morning star' (Rev. 2:28). Though the saints may be sullied with reproach in this life, though they may be termed factious and disloyal — Paul himself suffered trouble, in the opinion of some, as an evildoer (2 Tim. 2:9) — yet God will bring forth the saints' righteousness as the light, and they shall shine like the morning star, which is brighter than the rest. 'I will give him the morning star.' This morning star is meant of Christ, as if Christ had said, 'I will give the persevering saint some of my beauty; I will put some of my splendid rays on him; he shall have the nearest degree of glory to me, as the morning star is nearest the sun!

Oh, what soul-ravishing promises there are here! Who would not persevere in godliness! Whoever is not affected by these promises is either a stone or a brute.

Counsel for the Godly

Let me, in the next place, direct myself to those who have a real work of godliness in their hearts, and I would speak to them by way of:

1. Caution.

2. Counsel.

3. Comfort.

1. By way of caution

Do not blur these characteristics of grace in your souls. Though God's children cannot quite deface their graces — yet they may disfigure them. Too much carnal liberty may weaken their evidences, and so dim their luster that they cannot be read. These characteristics of the godly are precious things. Gold and diamonds cannot be compared with them. Oh, keep them well written in your hearts and they will be so many living comforts in a dying hour. It will not frighten a Christian to have all the signs of death in his body, when he can see all the signs of grace in his soul. He will say with Simeon, 'Lord, now let you your servant depart in peace' (Luke 2:29).

2. By way of counsel

You who are enriched with the treasures of godliness — bless God for it! This flower does not grow in nature's garden! You had enlisted yourselves under the devil and taken pay on his side, fighting against your own happiness — and then God came with converting grace and put forth a loving and gentle violence, causing you to espouse his cause against Satan! You had lain many years soaking in wickedness, as if you had been parboiled for hell — and then God laid you steeping in Christ's blood and breathed holiness into your heart! Oh, what cause you have to write yourselves down — as eternal debtors to free grace! He who does not give God the praise for his grace denies that God is its author. Oh, acknowledge the sovereign love of God! Admire distinguishing mercy! Set the crown of your praise — on the head of free grace! If we are to be thankful for the fruits of the earth, how much more for the fruits of the Spirit. It is good that there is an eternity coming, when the saints shall triumph in God and make his praise glorious!

3. By way of comfort

You who have only the least grain of godliness in sincerity, let me give you rich consolation: Jesus Christ will not discourage the weakest grace, but will nourish and preserve it to eternity. Grace which has only newly budded shall, by the beams of the Sun of righteousness, be prepared and ripened for glory. This I shall speak about more fully in the next chapter.

Comfort to the Godly

'A bruised reed he will not break, and a smoldering wick he will not snuff out, till he leads justice to victory.' Matthew 12:20

This text is spoken prophetically of Christ. He will not crow over the infirmities of his people; he will not crush grace in its infancy. I begin with the first, 'the bruised reed.'

Question: What is to be understood here by a reed?

Answer: It is not to be taken literally — but figuratively. It is a rational reed, the spiritual part of man, the soul, which may well be compared to a reed — because it is subject to imbecility and shaking in this life, until it grows up unto a firm cedar in heaven.

Question: What is meant by a bruised reed?

Answer: It is a soul humbled and bruised by the sense of sin. It weeps — but does not despair; it is tossed upon the waves of fear — yet not without the anchor of hope.

Question: What is meant by Christ's not breaking this reed?

Answer: The sense is that Christ will not discourage any mournful spirit who is in the pangs of the new birth. If the bruise of sin is felt, it shall not be mortal: 'A bruised reed shall he not break.' In the words there is an understatement; he will not break, that is, he will bind up the bruised reed, he will comfort it.

The result of the whole is to show Christ's compassion to a poor dejected sinner who smites on his breast and dare hardly lift up his eye for mercy. The heart of the Lord Jesus yearns for him; this bruised reed, he will not break.

In the text there are two parts:

(1) A supposition: a soul penitentially bruised.

(2) A proposition: it shall not be broken.

Doctrine: The bruised soul shall not be broken: 'He binds up their wounds' (Psalm 147:3). For this purpose Christ received both his mission and his unction, that he might bind up the bruised soul: 'the Lord has anointed me to bind up the broken-hearted' (Isaiah 61:1). But why will Christ not break a bruised reed?

1. Out of the sweetness of his nature. 'The Lord is full of compassion and mercy' (James 5:11). He begets compassion in other creatures and is therefore called 'the Father of mercies' (2 Cor. 1:3). And surely he himself is not without compassion. When a poor soul is afflicted in spirit, God will not exercise harshness towards it, lest he should be thought to lay aside his own tender disposition.

Hence it is, that the Lord has always been most solicitous for his bruised ones. As the mother is most careful of her children who are weak and sickly, 'He shall gather the lambs with his arm, and carry them in his bosom' (Isaiah 40:11). Those who have been spiritually bruised, who like lambs are weakly and tender, Christ will carry in the arms of free grace.

2. Because a contrite heart is his sacrifice. (Psalm 51:17). A bruised spirit sends forth tears which are like precious wine (Psalm 56:8). A bruised soul is big with holy desires, yes, is love-sick. Therefore, if a bruised reed has such virtue in it, Christ will not break it. No spices, when they are bruised, are so fragrant to us — as a contrite spirit is to God.

3. Because it so closely resembles Christ. Jesus Christ was once bruised on the cross: 'it pleased the Lord to bruise him' (Isaiah 53:10). His hands and feet were bruised with the nails; his side was bruised with the spear. A bruised reed resembles a bruised Savior. No, a bruised reed is a member of Christ; and though it is weak, Christ will not cut it off — but will cherish it so much the more.

(1) Will Christ not break the bruised reed? This tacitly implies that he will break unbruised reeds. Those who were never touched with trouble of spirit — but live and die in impenitence, are hard reeds or, rather, rocks. Christ will not break a bruised reed — but he will break a hard reed. Many do not know what it is to be bruised reeds. They are bruised outwardly by affliction — but they are not bruised for sin. They never knew what the pangs of the new birth meant. You will hear some thank God that they were always at peace, they never had any anxiety of spirit. These bless God for the greatest curse! Those who are not bruised penitentially — shall be broken judicially. Those whose hearts would not break for sin — shall break with despair. In hell there is nothing to be seen but a heap of stones and a hammer. A heap of stones — that is hard hearts; a hammer — that is God's power and justice, breaking them in pieces.

A bruised reed he will not break, and a smoldering wick he will not snuff out, till he leads justice to victory. Matthew 12:20

(2) Will Christ not break a bruised reed? See, then, the gracious disposition of Jesus Christ — he is full of mercy and sympathy. Though he may bruise the soul for sin, he will not break it. The surgeon may lance the body and make it bleed — but he will bind up the wound. As Christ has beams of majesty, so he has a heart of mercy. Christ has both the lion and the lamb in his

escutcheon: the lion, in respect of his fierceness to the wicked (Psalm 50:22), and the lamb, in respect of his mildness to his people. His name is Jesus, a Savior, and his office is a healer (Mal. 4:2). Christ made a plaster of his own blood — to heal a broken heart! Christ is the quintessence of love. Someone said, 'If the sweetness of all flowers were in one flower, how sweet that flower would be!' Christ is that flower. How full of mercy is Christ, in whom all mercy meets! Christ has a skillful hand and a tender heart. 'He will not break a bruised reed.'

Some are so full of harshness and cruelty, as to add affliction to affliction, which is to lay a greater burden on a dying man. But our Lord Jesus is a compassionate High Priest (Heb. 2:17). He is touched with the feeling of our infirmity. Every bruise of the soul goes to his heart! None refuse Christ — but such as do not know him. He is nothing but love incarnate! He himself was bruised to heal those who are bruised.

(3) Will Christ not break a bruised reed? See, then, what encouragement there is here for faith! Had Christ said that he would break the bruised reed, then indeed there would be ground for despair. But when Christ said that he will not break a bruised reed — this opens a door of hope for humble, bruised souls! If we can say that we have been bruised for sin, why do we not believe? Why do we droop under our fears and discouragements, as if there were no mercy for us? Christ says, 'He heals the broken in heart' (Psalm 147:3). 'No,' says unbelief, 'he will not heal me.' Christ says that he will cure the bruised soul. 'No,' says unbelief, 'he will kill it.' As unbelief makes our comforts void, so it tries to make the Word void, as if all God's promises were but forgeries. Has the Lord said that he will not break a bruised reed? Can truth lie? Oh, what a sin unbelief is! Some think it dreadful to be among the number of drunkards, swearers and whoremongers. Let me tell you, it is no less dreadful to be among the number of unbelievers (Rev. 21:8). Unbelief is worse than any other sin, because it brings God, his Word, and his promises into suspicion. It robs him of the richest jewel in his crown, which is his truth: 'He who believes not God, has made him a liar' (1 John 5:10).

Oh then, let all humbled sinners go to Jesus Christ. Christ was bruised with desertion, to heal those who are bruised with sin. If you can show Christ your sores and touch him by faith — you shall be healed of all your soul bruises! Will Christ not break you? Then do not undo yourself by despair.

Use 1: Will Jesus Christ not break a bruised reed? Then it reproves those who do what they can, to break the bruised reed. And they are such as try to hinder the work of conversion in others. When they see them wounded and troubled for sin, they dishearten them, telling them that piety is a sour, melancholy thing; and they had better return to their former pleasures. When an arrow of conviction is shot into their conscience, these pull it out again, and will not allow the work of conviction to go forward. Thus, when the soul is almost bruised, they hinder it from a thorough bruise. This is for men to be devils to others. If to shed the blood of another makes a man guilty, what is it to damn another's soul?

Use 2: This text is a spiritual honeycomb, dropping consolation into all bruised hearts. As we give stimulants to a body suffering from a fainting fit, so when sinners are bruised for their sins, I shall give some stimulant to revive them. This text is comforting to a poor soul who sits with Job among the ashes, and is dejected at the sense of its unworthiness. 'Ah!' says the soul, 'I am unworthy of mercy; what am I, that ever God should look on me? Those who have greater gifts and graces perhaps may obtain a look from God — but alas! I am unworthy.' Does your unworthiness trouble you? What more unworthy than a bruised reed? Yet there is a promise made to that condition: 'a bruised reed he will not break.' The promise is not made to the fig tree or olive tree, which are fertile plants — but to the bruised reed. Though you are despicable in your own eyes, a poor shattered reed — yet you may be glorious in the eyes of the Lord. Do

not let your unworthiness discourage you. If you see yourself as vile and Christ as precious —
this promise is yours! Christ will not break you — but will bind up your wounds.

Question: But how shall I know that I am savingly bruised?

Answer: Did God ever bring you to your knees? Has your proud heart been humbled? Did you
ever see yourself as a sinner and nothing but a sinner? Did you ever, with a weeping eye, look
on Christ? (Zech. 12:10) And did those tears drop from the eye of faith? (Mark 9:24) This is
gospel bruising. Can you say, 'Lord, though I do not see you — yet I love you; though I am in the
dark — yet I cast anchor on you!' This is to be a bruised reed.

Objection 1: But I fear I am not bruised enough.

Answer: It is hard to prescribe a just measure of humiliation. It is the same in the new birth as
in the natural. Some give birth with more pangs, and some with fewer. But would you like to
know when you are bruised enough? When your spirit is so troubled that you are willing to let
go those lusts which brought in the greatest income of pleasure and delight. When not only is
sin discarded but you are disgusted with it, then you have been bruised enough. The medicine
is strong enough when it has purged out the disease. The soul is bruised enough when the love
of sin is purged out.

Objection 2: But I fear I am not bruised as I should be. I find my heart so hard.

Answer 1: We must distinguish between hardness of heart and a hard heart. The best heart may
have some hardness — but though there is some hardness in it, it is not a hard heart. Names are
given according to the better part. If we come into a field that has tares and wheat in it, we do
not call it a field of tares, but a wheat field. So though there is hardness in the heart as well as
softness — yet God, who judges by that part which is more excellent, looks on it as a soft heart.

Answer 2: There is a great difference between the hardness in the wicked, and hardness in the
godly. The one is natural, the other is only accidental. The hardness in a wicked man is like the
hardness of a stone, which is an innate continued hardness. The hardness in a child of God, is
like the hardness of ice, which is soon melted by the sunbeams. Perhaps God has at present
withdrawn his Spirit, so the heart is congealed like ice. But let God's Spirit, like the sun, return
and shine on the heart, and then it has a gracious thaw on it and it melts in love.

Answer 3: Do you not grieve under your hardness? You sigh for lack of groans, you weep for
lack of tears. The hard reed cannot weep. If you were not a bruised reed, all this weeping could
not come from you.

Objection 3: But I am a barren reed; I bear no fruit; therefore I fear I shall be broken.

Answer: Gracious hearts are apt to overlook the good that is in them. They can spy the worm in
the leaf — but not the fruit. Why do you say you are barren? If you are a bruised reed, you are
not barren. The spiritual reed ingrafted into the true vine is fruitful. There is so much sap in
Christ that it makes all who are ingrafted into him bear fruit. Christ distills grace like drops of
dew on the soul: 'I will be as the dew unto Israel; he shall grow as the lily; his branches shall
spread, and his beauty shall be as the olive tree' (Hos. 14:5,6). The God who made the dry rod
blossom — will make the dry reed flourish.

So much for the first expression in the text. I proceed to the second: 'the smoking flax shall he
not quench.'

Question: What is meant by smoking?

Answer: By smoke is meant corruption. Smoke is offensive to the eye, so sin offends the pure
eye of God.

Question: What is meant by smoking flax?

Answer: It means grace mingled with corruption. As with a little fire there may be much smoke, so with a little grace there may be much corruption.

Question: What is meant by Christ's not quenching the smoking flax?

Answer: The meaning is that though there is only a spark of grace with much sin, Christ will not put out this spark. In the words there is a figure; 'he will not quench', that is, he will increase. Nothing is easier than to quench smoking flax; the least touch does it. But Christ will not quench it. He will not blow the spark of grace out — but will blow it up into a flame, he will make this smoking flax into a burning candle.

Doctrine: That a little grace mixed with much corruption shall not be quenched. For the illustrating of this I shall show you:

1. That a little grace is often mixed with much corruption.

2. That this little grace mixed with corruption shall not be quenched.

3. The reasons for the proposition.

1. Often in the godly, a little grace is mingled with much corruption

'Lord, I believe' — there was some faith; 'help my unbelief' (Mark 9:24) — there was corruption mixed with it. There are, in the best saints, inter-weavings of sin and grace: a dark side with the light; much pride mixed with humility; much earthliness with heavenliness. Grace in the godly smacks of an old crabtree stock.

No, in many of the regenerate there is more corruption than grace. So much smoke that you can scarcely discern any fire; so much distrust that you can hardly see any faith (1 Sam. 27:1); so much passion that you can hardly see any meekness. Jonah, a peevish prophet, quarrels with God, no, he justifies his passion: 'I do well to be angry, even unto death!' (Jonah 4:9). Here there was so much passion that it was hard to see any grace. A Christian in this life is like a glass that has more froth than wine, or like a diseased body that has more illness than vigor. It may humble the best to consider how much corruption is interlarded with their grace.

2. This little grace mixed with much corruption shall not be quenched

'The smoking flax he will not quench.' The disciples' faith was at first only small: 'they forsook Christ, and fled' (Matt. 26:56). Here there was smoking flax — but Christ did not quench that little grace but nourished and animated it. Their faith afterwards grew stronger and they openly confessed Christ (Acts 4:29,30). Here the flax was flaming.

3. The reasons why Christ will not quench the smoking flax

(1) Because this little spark which is in the smoking flax, is of divine production. It comes from the Father of lights, and the Lord will not quench the work of his own grace. Everything by the instinct of nature will preserve its own. The hen that hatches her young will preserve and nourish them; she will not destroy them as soon as they are hatched. God, who has put this tenderness into the creature to preserve its young, will much more nourish the work of his own Spirit in the heart. Will he light up the lamp of grace in the soul — and then put it out? This would be neither for his interest — nor for his honor.

(2) Christ will not quench the beginnings of grace, because a little grace is as precious as much grace. A small pearl is of value. Though the pearl of faith is little — yet if it is a true pearl, it shines gloriously in God's eyes. A goldsmith takes account of the least filings of gold, and will not throw them away. The pupil of the eye is only little — yet it is of great use; it can at once view a huge part of the heavens. A little faith can justify. A weak hand can tie the nuptial knot.

A weak faith can unite to Christ—as well as a strong faith. A little grace makes us like God. A silver penny bears the king's image on it, as well as a larger coin. The least grain of grace bears God's image on it—and will God destroy his own image? When the temples in Greece were demolished, Xerxes caused the temple of Diana to be preserved for the beauty of its structure. When God destroys all the glory of the world and sets it on fire—yet he will not destroy the least grace, because it bears a print of his own likeness on it. That little spark in the smoking flax, is a ray and beam of God's own glory.

(3) Christ will not quench the smoking flax, because this little light in the flax may grow into a flame. Grace is compared to a grain of mustard seed; it is the smallest of all seeds—but when it has grown, it is the largest of herbs, and becomes a tree (Matt. 13:31,32). The greatest grace was once little. The oak was once an acorn. The most renowned faith in the world, was once in its spiritual infancy. The greatest flame of zeal was once only smoking flax. Grace, like the waters of the sanctuary, rises higher (Ezek. 47:1-5). If, then, the smallest embryo and seed of holiness has a ripening and growing nature, the Lord will not allow it to be abortive.

(4) Christ will not quench the smoking flax, because when he preserves a little light in a great deal of smoke—here the glory of his power shines forth. The trembling soul thinks it will be swallowed up by sin. But God preserves a little quantity of grace in the heart—no, no, he makes that spark prevail over corruption, as the fire from heaven 'licked up the water in the trench' (1 Kings 18:38). So God gets himself a glorious name and carries away the trophies of honor: 'My strength is made perfect in weakness' (2 Cor. 12:9).

1. See the different dealings of God and men. Men, for a little smoke—will quench a great deal of light; God, for a great deal of smoke—will not quench a little light. It is the manner of the world, if they see a little failure in another, to pass by and quench a great deal of worth because of that failure. This is our nature, to aggravate a little fault and diminish a great deal of virtue; to see the infirmities and darken the excellences of others—as we take more notice of the twinkling of a star, than the shining of a star. We censure others for their passion—but do not admire them for their piety. Thus, because of a little smoke that we see in others, we quench much light.

God does not act like that. For a great deal of smoke, he will not quench a little light. He sees the sincerity—and overlooks many infirmities. The least sparks of grace he nourishes, and blows them gently with the breath of his Spirit until they break forth into a flame!

2. If Christ will not quench the smoking flax—then we must not quench the smoking flax in ourselves. If grace does not increase into so great a flame as we see in others, and we therefore conclude that we have no fire of the Spirit in us—that is to quench the smoking flax and to bear false witness against ourselves. As we must not credit false evidence, so neither must we deny true evidences of godliness. As fire may be hidden in the embers, so grace may be hidden under many disorders of soul. Some Christians are so skillful at this—accusing themselves for lack of grace—as if they had received a fee from Satan to plead for him against themselves.

It is a great mistake to argue from the weakness of grace—to its absence. It is one thing to be weak in faith—and another to lack faith. He whose eyesight is dim has defective sight—but he is not without sight. A little grace is grace, though it is smothered under much corruption.

3. If the least spark of grace shall not be quenched, then it follows as a great truth—that there is no falling from grace. If the least grain of grace should perish, then the smoking flax would be quenched. Grace may be shaken by fears and doubts—but not torn up by the roots. I grant that seeming grace may be lost; this wildfire may be blown out—but not the fire of the Spirit's kindling. Grace may be dormant in the soul—but not dead. As a man in a coma does not exert

vital energy, grace may be eclipsed, not extinct. A Christian may lose his comfort, like a tree in autumn which has shed its fruit—but there is still sap in the vine and 'the seed of God remains in him' (1 John 3:9). Grace is a flower of eternity.

This smoking flax cannot be quenched by affliction—but is like those trees of which Pliny writes—trees growing in the Red Sea, which though beaten by the waves, stand immovable, and though sometimes covered with water, flourish the more. Grace is like a true oriental diamond—which sparkles and cannot be broken.

I confess it is a matter of astonishment, that grace should not be wholly annihilated, especially if we consider two things:

(1) The malice of Satan. He is a malignant spirit and lays barriers in our way to heaven. The devil, with the wind of temptation, tries to blow out the spark of grace in our hearts. If this will not do, he stirs up wicked men and raises the militia of hell against us. What a wonder it is that this bright star of grace, should not be swept down by the tail of the dragon!

(2) The world of corruption in our hearts. Sin makes up the major part in a Christian. There are more dregs than grace in the holiest heart. The heart swarms with sin. What a great deal of pride and atheism there is in the soul! Now is it not astonishing that this lily of grace should be able to grow among so many thorns? It is as great a wonder that a little grace should be preserved in the midst of so much corruption—as to see a candle burning in the sea and not extinguished.

But though grace lives with so much difficulty, like the infant that struggles for breath—yet being born of God, it is immortal. Grace conflicting with corruption is like a ship tossed and beaten by the waves—yet it weathers the storm and at last gets to the desired haven. If grace should expire, how could this text be verified, 'The smoking flax he will not quench'?

Question: But how is it that grace, even the least degree of it, is not quenched?

Answer: It is from the mighty operation of the Holy Spirit. The Spirit of God, who is the source, continually excites and awakens grace in the heart. He is at work in a believer every day. He pours in oil, and keeps the lamp of grace burning. Grace is compared to a river of life (John 7:38). The river of grace can never be dried up, for the Spirit of God is the spring which feeds it.

Now it is evident from the covenant of grace, that the smoking flax cannot be quenched. 'The mountains shall depart, and the hills be removed; but the covenant of my peace shall not be removed, says the Lord' (Isaiah 54:10). If there is falling from grace, how is it an immovable covenant? If grace dies and the smoking flax is quenched, how is our state in Christ, better than it was in Adam? The covenant of grace is called 'a better covenant' (Heb. 7:22). How is it a better covenant than that which was made with Adam? Not only because it has a better Surety and contains better privileges—but because it has better conditions annexed to it: 'It is ordered in all things, and sure' (2 Sam. 23:5). Those who are taken into the covenant shall be like stars fixed in their orbit and shall never fall away. If grace might die and be quenched, then it would not be a better covenant.

Objection: But we are bidden not to quench the Spirit (1 Thess. 5:19), which implies that the grace of the Spirit may be lost and the smoking flax quenched.

Answer: We must distinguish between the common work of the Spirit and the sanctifying work. The one may be quenched, but not the other. The common work of the Spirit is like a picture drawn on the ice, which is soon defaced; the sanctifying work is like a statue carved in gold, which endures. The gifts of the Spirit may be quenched, but not the grace of the Spirit. There is the enlightening of the Spirit, and the anointing. The enlightening of the Spirit may fail — but the anointing of the Spirit abides: 'the anointing which you have received from him abides in you' (1 John 2:27). The hypocrite's blaze goes out, the true believer's spark lives and flourishes. The one is the light of a comet which wastes and evaporates (Matt. 25:8); the other is the light of a star which retains its luster.

From all that has been said, let a saint of the Lord be persuaded to do these two things:

1. To believe his privilege.

2. To pursue his duty.

1. To believe his privilege

It is the incomparable and unparalleled happiness of a saint, that his coal of grace shall not be quenched (2 Sam. 14:7). That grace in his soul which is weak and languid, shall not die — but recover its strength and increase. The Lord will make the smoking flax into a burning lamp. It would be very sad for a Christian to be continually chopping and changing: one day a member of Christ and the next day a limb of Satan; one day to have grace shine in his soul and the next day his light be put out in obscurity. This would spoil a Christian's comfort and break asunder the golden chain of salvation. But be assured, O Christian, that he who has begun a good work, will ripen it to perfection (Phil. 1:6). Christ will send forth judgment unto victory. He will make grace victorious over all opposing corruption. If grace should finally perish, what would become of the smoking flax? And how would that title properly be given to Christ, 'Finisher of the faith' (Heb. 12:2)?

Objection: There is no question that this is an undoubted privilege to those who are smoking flax and have the least beginnings of grace — but I fear I am not smoking flax; I cannot see the light of grace in myself.

Answer: So that I may comfort the smoking flax, why do you thus dispute against yourself? What makes you think you have no grace? I believe you have more than you would be willing to part with. You value grace above the gold of Ophir. How could you see the worth and luster of this jewel — if God's Spirit had not opened your eyes? You desire to believe and mourn — that you cannot believe. Are these tears not the beginnings of faith? You desire Christ and cannot be satisfied without him. This beating of the pulse evidences life. The iron could not move upwards if the loadstone did not draw it. The heart could not ascend in holy desires for God, if some heavenly loadstone had not been drawing it. Christian, can you say that sin is your burden, Christ is your delight and, as Peter once said, 'Lord, you know that I love you!' (John 21:17) This is smoking flax and the Lord will not quench it. Your grace shall flourish into glory. God will sooner extinguish the light of the sun than extinguish the dawning light of his Spirit in your heart.

2. To pursue his duty

There are two duties required of believers:

(1) Love. Will the Lord not quench the smoking flax — but make it at last victorious over all opposition? How the smoking flax should flame in love to God! 'Oh, love the Lord, all his saints' (Psalm 31:23). The saints owe much to God, and when they have nothing to pay, it is hard if they cannot love him. O you saints, it is God who carries on grace progressively in your souls. He is like a father who gives his son a small stock of money to begin with, and when he has traded a little, he adds more to the stock. So God adds continually to your stock. He drops oil into the lamp of your grace every day, and so keeps the lamp burning. This may inflame your love to God, who will not let the work of grace fail but will bring it to perfection: 'the

smoking flax he will not quench.' How God's people should long for heaven, when it will be their constant work to breathe out love and sound out praise!

(2) Labor. Some may think that if Christ will not quench the smoking flax — but make it burn brighter to the meridian of glory, then we need take no pains but leave God to do his own work. Take heed of drawing so bad a conclusion from such good premises. What I have spoken is to encourage faith — not to indulge sloth! Do not think God will do our work for us — while we sit still. As God will blow up the spark of grace by his Spirit — so we must be blowing it up by holy efforts. God will not bring us to heaven sleeping — but praying. The Lord told Paul that all in the ship would come safely to shore — but it must be by the use of means: 'Except these abide in the ship, you cannot be saved' (Acts 27:31). So the saints shall certainly arrive at salvation. They shall come to shore at last — but they must stay in the ship, in the use of ordinances, else they cannot be saved. Christ assures his disciples: 'None shall pluck them out of my hand' (John 10:28). But he still gives that counsel, 'Watch and pray, that you enter not into temptation' (Matt. 26:41). The seed of God shall not die — but we must water it with our tears. The smoking flax shall not be quenched — but we must blow it up with the breath of our effort.

The second comfort to the godly is that godliness promotes them to a close and glorious union with Jesus Christ. But I reserve this for the next chapter.

Mystical Union between Christ and His People

'My beloved is mine, and I am His.'

Canticles 2:16

In this Song of Songs, we see the love of Christ and his church running towards each other in a full torrent.

The text contains three general parts:

1. A symbol of affection: 'My beloved.'

2. A term of appropriation: 'is mine.'

3. A holy resignation: 'I am his.'

Doctrine: There is a marital union between Christ and believers. The apostle, having treated at large of marriage, winds up the whole chapter thus:

'This is a great mystery — but I speak concerning Christ and the church' (Eph. 5:32). What is closer than union? What sweeter? There is a twofold union with Christ:

1. A natural union. This all men have, Christ having taken their nature on him and not that of the angels (Heb. 2:16). But if there is no more than this natural union, it will give little comfort. Thousands are damned — though Christ is united to their nature.

2. A sacred union. By this we are mystically united to Christ. The union with Christ is not personal. If Christ's essence were transfused into the person of a believer, then it would follow that all that a believer does should be meritorious.

But the union between Christ and a saint is:

(a) Federal: 'My beloved is mine.' God the Father gives the bride; God the Son receives the bride; God the Holy Spirit ties the knot in marriage — he knits our wills to Christ and Christ's love to us.

(b) Effectual. Christ unites himself to his spouse by his graces and influences: 'of his fullness have all we received, and grace for grace' (John 1:16). Christ makes himself one with the spouse by conveying his image and stamping the impress of his own holiness upon her!

This union with Christ may well be called mystical. It is hard to describe the manner of it. It is hard to show how the soul is united to the body — and how Christ is united to the soul. But though this union is spiritual — it is real. Things in nature often work insensibly, yet really (Eccles. 11:5). We do not see the hand move on the sun-dial, yet it moves. The sun exhales and draws up the vapors of the earth insensibly yet really. So the union between Christ and the soul — though it is imperceptible to the eye of reason — is still real (1 Cor. 6:17).

Before this union with Christ there must be a separation. The heart must be separated from all other lovers, as in marriage there is a leaving of father and mother: 'Forget your own people, and your father's house.' (Psalm 45:10). So there must be a leaving of our former sins, a breaking off the old league with hell before we can be united to Christ. 'Ephraim shall say, What have I to do any more with idols?' (Hos. 14:8), or as it is in the Hebrew, 'with sorrows.' Those sins which were looked on before as lovers, are now sorrows. There must be a divorce, before a union.

The purpose of our marital union with Christ is twofold:

1. Co-habitation. This is one purpose of marriage, to live together: 'that Christ may dwell in your hearts' (Eph. 2:17). It is not enough to pay Christ a few complimentary visits in his ordinances — hypocrites may do so — but there must be a mutual associating. We must dwell upon the thoughts of Christ: 'he who abides in God' (I John 3:24). Married people should not live apart.

2. Fruit bearing: 'That you may be married to another; to Him who was raised from the dead — that we should bear fruit to God.' (Rom. 7:4). The spouse bears the fruits of the Spirit: love, joy, peace, patience, gentleness (Gal. 5:22). Barrenness is a shame in Christ's spouse!

This marriage union with Christ is the most noble and excellent union:

(a) Christ unites himself to many. In other marriages only one person is taken — but here millions are taken! Otherwise, poor souls might cry out, 'Alas! Christ has married So-and-so, but what is that to me? I am left out.' No, Christ marries thousands. It is a holy and chaste polygamy. Multitudes of people do not defile this marriage bed. Any poor sinner who brings a humble, believing heart may be married to Christ.

(b) There is a closer union in this holy marriage than there can be in any other. In other marriages, two make one flesh — but Christ and the believer make one spirit: 'But he who is joined to the Lord is one spirit with Him.' (I Cor. 6:17). Now as the soul is more excellent than the body, and admits of far greater joy, so this spiritual union brings in more astonishing delights and ravishments than any other marriage relationship is capable of. The joy that flows from the mystical union is unspeakable and full of glory (I Peter 1:8).

(c) This union with Christ never ceases. Other marriages are soon at an end. Death cuts asunder the marriage knot — but this marital union is eternal. You who are once Christ's spouse shall never again be a widow: 'I will betroth you to me forever' (Hosea 2:19). To speak properly, our marriage with Christ begins where other marriages end, at death.

In this life there is only the contract. The Jews had a time set between their engagement and marriage, sometimes a year or more. In this life there is only the engagement and contract; promises are made on both sides, and love passes secretly between Christ and the soul. He gives some smiles of his face, and the soul sends up her sighs and drops tears of love. But all this is only a preliminary work, and something leading up to the marriage. The glorious completing and solemnizing of the marriage is reserved for heaven. There, in heaven, is the marriage supper of the Lamb (Rev. 19:9) and the bed of glory perfumed with love where the souls of the elect shall be perpetually consoling themselves. 'Then shall we ever be with the Lord' (I Thess. 4:17). So death merely begins our marriage with Christ.

Use 1: If Christ is the head of the mystical body (Eph. 1:22), then this doctrine beheads the Pope, that man of sin who usurps this prerogative of being the head of the church, and so would defile Christ's marriage bed. What blasphemy this is! Two heads are monstrous. Christ is Head, as he is Husband. There is no vice-husband, no deputy in his place. The Pope is the beast in Revelation (Rev. 13:11). To make him head of the church, what would this be but to set the head of a beast upon the body of a man?

Use 2: If there is such a marital union, let us test whether we are united to Christ:

1. Have we chosen Christ to set our love upon, and is this choice founded on knowledge?

2. Have we consented to the match? It is not enough that Christ is willing to have us — but are we willing to have him? God does not so force salvation upon us that we shall have Christ whether we want to or not. We must consent to have him. Many approve of Christ — but do not give their consent. And this consent must be:

(a) Pure and genuine. We consent to have him for his own worth and excellence: 'You are fairer than the sons of men' (Psalm. 45:2).

(b) A present consent: 'now is the acceptable time' (2 Cor. 6:2). If we put Christ off with delays and excuses, perhaps he will stop coming. He will leave off wooing. 'His spirit shall no longer strive,' and then, poor sinner, what will you do? When God's wooing ends, your woes begin.

3. Have we taken Christ? Faith is the bond of the union. Christ is joined to us by his Spirit, and we are joined to him by faith. Faith ties the marriage knot.

4. Have we given ourselves up to Christ? Thus the spouse in the text says, 'I am his,' as if she had said, 'All I have is for the use and service of Christ.' Have

we made a surrender? Have we given up our name and will to Christ? When the

devil solicits by a temptation, do we say, 'We are not our own, we are Christ's; our tongues are his, we must not defile them with oaths; our bodies are his temple, we must not pollute them with sin?' If it is so, it is a sign that the Holy Spirit has produced this blessed union between Christ and us.

Use 3: Is there this mystical union? Then from that we may draw many inferences:

1. See the dignity of all true believers. They are joined in marriage with Christ! There is not only assimilation but union; they are not only like Christ but one with Christ. All the saints have this honor. When a king marries a beggar, by

virtue of the union she is ennobled and made of the blood royal. As wicked men are united to the prince of darkness, and he settles hell upon them as their inheritance, so the godly are divinely united to Christ, who is King of kings, and Lord of Lords (Rev. 19:16). By virtue of this sacred union the saints are dignified above the angels. Christ is the Lord of the angels — but not their husband.

2. See how happily all the saints are married. They are united to Christ, who is the best Husband, 'the Chief among ten thousand' (Cant 5:10). Christ is a Husband who cannot be paralleled:

(a) For tender care. The spouse cannot be as considerate of her own soul and credit as Christ is considerate of her: 'He cares for you' (I Pet. 5:7). Christ has a debate with himself, consulting and projecting how to carry on the work of our salvation. He transacts all our affairs, he attends to our business as his own. Indeed, he himself is concerned in it. He brings fresh supplies to his spouse. If she wanders out of the way, he guides her. If she stumbles, he holds her by the hand. If she falls, he raises her. If she is dull, he quickens her by his Spirit. If she is perverse, he draws her with cords of love. If she is sad, he comforts her with promises.

(b) For ardent affection. No husband loves like Christ. The Lord says to the people, 'I have loved you,' and they say, 'In what way have you loved us?' (Mal. 1:2). But we cannot say to Christ, 'In what way have you loved us?' Christ has given real demonstrations of his love to his spouse. He has sent her his Word, which is a love-letter, and he has given her his Spirit, which is a love token. Christ loves more than any other husband: Christ puts a richer robe on his bride: 'For He has clothed me with the garments of salvation, He has covered me with the robe of righteousness, as a bridegroom decks himself with ornaments, and as a bride adorns herself with her jewels.' (Isa. 61:10).

In this robe, God looks on us as if we had not sinned! This robe is as truly ours to justify us, as it is Christ's to bestow on us. This robe not only covers but adorns. Having on this robe, we are reputed righteous, not only as righteous as angels — but as righteous as Christ: 'that we might be made the righteousness of God in him' (2 Cor.5:21).

Christ gives his bride not only his golden garments but his image! He loves her into his own likeness. A husband may have a dear affection for his wife — but he cannot stamp his own image on her. If she is deformed, he may give her a veil to hide it — but he cannot put his beauty on her. But Christ imparts 'the beauty of holiness' to his spouse: 'Your fame went out among the nations because of your beauty, for it was perfect through My splendor which I had bestowed on you,' (Ezek. 16:14). When Christ marries a soul, he makes it lovely: 'You are all beautiful, my love' (Cant 4:7). Christ never thinks he has loved his spouse enough until he can see his own face in her.

Christ discharges those debts which no other husband can. Our sins are the worst debts we owe. If all the angels should contribute money, they could not pay one of these debts — but Christ frees us from these. He is both a Husband and a Surety. He says to justice what Paul said concerning Onesimus, 'But if he has wronged you or owes anything, put that on my account.' (Philem. 1:18).

Christ has suffered more for his spouse than ever any husband did for a wife. He suffered poverty and ignominy. He who crowned the heavens with stars was himself crowned with thorns. He was called a companion of sinners, so that we might be made companions of angels. He had no regard of his life; he leaped into the sea of his Father's wrath to save his spouse from drowning! Christ's love does not end with his life. He loves his spouse forever: 'I will betroth you to me forever' (Hos. 2:19). Well may the apostle call it 'a love which passes knowledge' (Eph. 3:19).

3. See how rich believers are. They have married into the crown of heaven, and by virtue of the marital union all Christ's riches go to believers: 'communion is founded in union.' Christ communicates his graces (John 1:16). As long as Christ has them, believers shall not be in need. And he communicates his privileges — justification, glorification. He settles a kingdom on his spouse as her inheritance (Heb. 12:28). This is a key to the apostle's riddle, 'as having nothing, and yet possessing all things' (2 Cor. 6:10). By virtue of the marriage union, the saints have an interest in all Christ's riches!

4. See how fearful a sin it is, to abuse the saints. It is an injury done to Christ, for believers are mystically one with him: 'Saul, Saul, why do you persecute me?' (Acts 9:4). When the body was wounded, the Head, being in heaven, cried out. In this sense, men crucify Christ afresh (Heb.

6:6), because what is done to his members is done to him. If Gideon was avenged upon those who slew his brethren, will not Christ much more be avenged on those that wrong his spouse (Judges 8:21)? Will a king tolerate having his treasure rifled, his crown thrown in the dust, his queen beheaded? Will Christ bear with the affronts and injuries done to his bride? The saints are the apple of Christ's eye (Zech. 2:8), and let those who strike at his eye answer for it. Isa 49:26 'I will feed those who oppress you with their own flesh, and they shall be drunk with their own blood as with sweet wine' (Isa.49:26).

5. See the reason why the saints so rejoice in the Word and sacrament, because here they meet with their Husband, Christ! The wife desires to be in the presence of her husband. The ordinances are the chariot in which Christ rides, the lattice through which he looks forth and shows his smiling face. Here Christ displays the banner of love (Cant 2:4). The Lord's Supper is nothing other than a pledge and security of that eternal communion which the saints shall have with Christ in heaven. Then he will take the spouse into his bosom. If Christ is so sweet in an ordinance, when we have only short glances and dark glimpses of him by faith, oh then, how delightful and ravishing will his presence be in heaven when we see him face to face and are forever in his loving embraces!

Use 4: This mystical union affords much comfort to believers in several cases:

1. In the case of the disrespect and unkindness of the world: 'in wrath they hate me' (Psalm. 55:3). But though we live in an unkind world, we have a kind Husband: 'As the Father has loved me, so have I loved you' (John 15:9). What angel can tell how God the Father loves Christ? Yet the Father's love to Christ is made the copy and pattern of Christ's love to his spouse! This love of Christ as far exceeds all created love as the sun outshines the light of a torch. And is not this a matter of comfort? Though the world hates me, Christ still loves me.

2. In the case of weakness of grace. The believer cannot lay hold on Christ, except with a trembling hand. There is a 'spirit of infirmity' on him. But oh, weak Christian, here is strong consolation: you have a marital union to Christ!

You are the spouse of Christ! Will he will bear with you as the weaker vessel? Will a husband divorce his wife because she is weak and sickly? No! he will be the more tender with her. Christ hates divorce—but he will pity infirmity. When the spouse is faint and ready to be discouraged, Christ puts his left hand under her head (Cant 2:6). This is the spouse's comfort when she is weak. Her Husband can infuse strength into her: 'My God shall be my strength' (Isa. 49:5).

3. In the case of death. When believers die—they go to their Husband! Who would not be willing to cross the gulf of death that they might meet with their Husband, Christ? 'I desire to loosen anchor' (Phil. 1:23), and be with Christ. What though the way is dirty? We are going to our friend. When a woman is engaged, she longs for the day of marriage. After the saints' funeral, their marriage begins. The body is a prison to the soul. Who would not desire to exchange a prison for a marriage bed? How glad Joseph was to go out of prison to the king's court! God is wise; he lets us meet with changes and troubles here, so that he may wean us from the world and make us long for death. When the soul is divorced from the body, it is married to Christ.

4. In the case of passing sentence at the day of judgment. There is a marriage union and, oh Christian, your Husband shall be your judge! A wife would not fear appearing at the bar if her husband was sitting as judge. What though the devil should bring in many indictments against you? Christ will expunge your sins in his blood. Could he possibly say, 'I shall condemn my spouse?' Oh, what a comfort this is! The Husband is judge! Christ cannot pass sentence against his spouse without passing it against himself. For Christ and believers are one.

5. In the case of the saints' suffering. The church of God is exposed in this life to many injuries—but she has a Husband in heaven who is mindful of her and will 'turn water into wine' for her. Now it is a time of mourning with the spouse because the Bridegroom is absent (Matt. 9:15). But shortly she shall put off her mourning. Christ will wipe the tears of blood off the cheeks of his spouse: 'He will swallow up death forever, and the Lord God will wipe away tears from all faces' (Isa. 25:8). Christ will comfort his spouse for as much time as she has been afflicted. He will solace her with his love; he will take away the cup of trembling and give her the cup of consolation. And now she shall forget all her sorrows, being called into the banqueting house of heaven and having the banner of Christ's love displayed over her.

Use 5: Let me press several duties upon those who have this marriage union with Christ:

1. Make use of this relationship in two cases:

(a) When the law brings in its indictments against you. The law says, 'Here there are so many debts to be paid!' and it demands satisfaction. Acknowledge the debt—but turn it all over to your Husband, Christ. It is a maxim in law that the suit must not go against the wife, as long as the husband is living. Tell Satan when he accuses you, 'It is true that the debt is mine—but go to my Husband, Christ! He will discharge it.' If we took this course, we might relieve ourselves of much trouble. By faith we turn over the debt to our Husband. Believers are not in a state of widowhood but of marriage. Satan will never go to Christ—he knows that justice is satisfied and the debt book cancelled—but he comes to us for the debt so that he may perplex us. We should send him to Christ and then all lawsuits would cease. This is a believer's triumph. When he is guilty in himself, he is worthy in Christ. When he is spotted in himself, he is pure in his Head.

(b) In the case of desertion. Christ may (for reasons best known to himself) step aside for a time: 'my beloved had withdrawn himself' (Cant 5:6). Do not say, therefore, that Christ has gone for good. It is a fruit of jealousy in a wife, when her husband has left her a while, to think that he has gone from her for good. Every time Christ removes himself out of sight, it is wrong for us to say, 'The Lord has forsaken me' (Isa. 49:14). This is jealousy, and it is a wrong done to the love of Christ and the sweetness of this marriage relationship. Christ may forsake his spouse in regards to comfort—but he will not forsake her in regard of union. A husband may be a thousand miles distant from his wife—but he is still a husband. Christ may leave his spouse—but the marriage knot still holds.

2. Rejoice in your Husband, Christ. Has Christ honored you by taking you into the marriage relationship and making you one with himself? This calls for joy. By virtue of the union, believers are sharers with Christ in his riches. It was a custom among the Romans, when the wife was brought home, for her to receive the keys of her husband's house, intimating that the treasure and custody of the house was now committed to her. When Christ brings his bride home to those glorious mansions which he has gone ahead to prepare for her (John 14:2), he will hand over the keys of his treasure to her, and she shall be as rich as heaven can make her! And shall not the spouse rejoice and sing aloud upon her bed (Psalm. 149:5)? Christians, let the times be ever so sad, you may rejoice in your spiritual espousals (Hab. 3:17,18). Let me tell you, it is a sin not to rejoice—you find fault with your Husband, Christ.

When a wife is always sighing and weeping, what will others say? 'This woman has a bad husband!' Is this the fruit of Christ's love to you, to reflect dishonor upon him? A melancholy spouse saddens Christ's heart. I do not deny that Christians should grieve for sins of daily occurrence—but to be always weeping (as if they mourned without hope) is dishonorable to the marriage relationship.

'Rejoice in the Lord always' (Phil. 4:4). Rejoicing brings credit to your husband. Christ loves a cheerful bride, and indeed the very purpose of God's making us sad is to make us rejoice. We sow in tears, so that we may reap in joy. The excessive sadness and contrition of the godly will make others afraid to embrace Christ. They will begin to question whether there is that satisfactory joy in religion which is claimed. Oh, you saints of God, do not forget consolation; let others see that you do not regret your choice. It is joy that puts liveliness and activity into a Christian: 'the joy of the Lord is your strength' (Neh. 8:10). The soul is swiftest in duty when it is carried on the wings of joy.

3. Adorn this marriage relationship, so that you may be a crown to your husband.

(a) Wear a veil. We read of the spouse's veil (Cant 5:7). This veil is humility.

(b) Put on your jewels. These are the graces which for their luster are compared to rows of pearl and chains of gold (Cant 1:10). These precious jewels distinguish Christ's bride from strangers.

(c) Behave as becomes Christ's spouse:

In chastity. Be chaste in your judgments; do not defile yourselves with error. Error adulterates the mind (1 Tim. 6:5). It is one of Satan's artifices — first to defile the judgment, then the conscience.

In sanctity. It is not for Christ's spouse to behave like harlots. A half-naked breast and a wanton tongue — do not befit a saint. Christ's bride must shine forth in gospel purity, so that she may make her husband fall in love with her. A woman was asked what dowry she brought her husband. She answered that she had no dowry — but she promised to keep herself chaste. So though we can bring Christ no dowry, yet he expects us to keep ourselves pure, not spotting the breasts of our virginity by contagious and scandalous sins.

4. Love your Husband, Christ (Cant 2:5). Love him though he is reproached and persecuted. A wife loves her husband when in prison. To inflame your love towards Christ, consider:

(a) Nothing else is fit for you to love. If Christ is your Husband, it is not fit to have other lovers who would make Christ grow jealous.

(b) He is worthy of your love. He is of unparalleled beauty: 'altogether lovely' (Cant 5:16).

(c) How fervent is Christ's love towards you! He loves you in your worst condition, he loves you in affliction. The goldsmith loves his gold in the furnace. Just so, Christ loves you notwithstanding your fears and blemishes. The saints' infirmities cannot wholly remove Christ's love from them (Jer. 3:1). Oh then, how the spouse should be endeared in her love to Christ! Perfect love to Christ, will be the excellence of heaven. Our love will then be like the sun in its full strength!

The Great Gain of Godliness

Introduction

Christian Reader,

'Of making many books there is no end, and much study wearies the body.' Ecclesiastes 12:12. Books are the 'children of the brain'. In this writing age, when they are brought forth ad nauseam, I intended that my pen should have been silent—but the variety and weightiness of this subject, as also the desire of some friends, did prevail with me to publish it. The main design of this excellent Scripture, is to encourage solid piety, and confute the atheists of the world, who imagine there is no gain in godliness. It was the speech of King Saul to his servants, 'Will the son of Jesse give every one of you fields and vineyards?' (1 Samuel 22:7). Will the world or men's lusts give them such noble recompenses of reward—as God bestows upon his followers! Surely, it is holiness which carries away the garland!

As for this treatise, it comes abroad in a plain dress: truth like a diamond—shines brightest in its native luster! Paul did not come to the Corinthians with excellency of speech, or the pride of oratory—his study was not to court—but convert. It is an unhappiness that, in these luxuriant times, religion should for the most part run either into notion or ceremony; the spirits of true religion are evaporated. When knowledge is turned into soul food and digested into practice— then it is saving. That God would accompany these few imperfect lines with the operation and benediction of his Holy Spirit, and make them edifying—is the prayer of him who is

Yours in all Christian service,

Thomas Watson, London, November 22, 1681

'Then those who feared the Lord talked with each other, and the Lord listened and heard. A scroll of remembrance was written in His presence concerning those who feared the Lord and thought upon His name. 'They will be mine,' says the Lord Almighty, 'in the day when I make up My jewels! I will spare them, just as in compassion a man spares his son who serves him. And you will again see the distinction between the righteous and the wicked, between those who serve God and those who do not.' Malachi 3:16-18

The 'scripture of truth' is the ground of faith. This portion of Scripture which now presents itself to our view, has its sacred elegancies, and is all glorious within. It was composed by Malachi, whose name means 'messenger'. He came as an ambassador from the God of heaven. This prophet was so famous that Origen and others injudiciously supposed him to be an angel. He lived after the building of the second temple and was contemporary with Haggai and Zechariah.

This blessed prophet lifted up his voice like a trumpet and told the Jewish nation of their sins. He was the last trumpet that sounded in the Old Testament. In the words of the text are these parts:

Part I. The character of the Godly

1. In general, they were fearers of God: 'those who feared the Lord.'

2. In particular—

a. They spoke often one to another.

b. They thought upon God's Name.

Part II. The Great Gain of their Godliness

1. The Lord regarded it—'the Lord listened and heard.'

2. The Lord recorded it—'a book of remembrance was written.

3. The Lord rewarded it. This reward consisted in three things:

a. God's owning them: 'They will be mine.'

b. God's honoring them: 'In the day when I make up my jewels.'

c. God's sparing them: 'I will spare them.'

Before I come to the several parts distinctly, note the connective word standing at the beginning of the text which may not be omitted, namely, the word THEN. 'Then those who feared the Lord talked with each other ...' Then, that is, after Israel's return from the Babylonian captivity; then, when the major part of the people grew corrupt, and came out of the furnace worse than they went in! In this bad juncture of time, then those who feared the Lord spoke often one to another.

Hence observe—that the profaneness of the times should not slacken our zeal—but heighten it. The looser others are—the stricter we should be. In those degenerate times when men were arrived at the peak and height of impudence, and dared to speak treason against heaven—then those who feared the Lord spoke often one to another. When others were plaintiffs—these were defendants; when others spoke against God—these spoke for God.

In Noah's days all flesh had corrupted itself (the old world was drowned in sin—before it was drowned in water). Now at this time, Noah was perfect in his generation, and Noah walked with God (Gen. 6:9). He was the phoenix of his age. Athanasius stood up in the defense of the truth when the world had turned Arian. The more outrageous others are in sin—the more courageous we should be for truth! When the atheists said, 'It is vain to serve God,' then those who feared the Lord spoke often one to another.

Why should we be holiest in evil times?

1. Because of the divine injunction. God charges us to be singular (Matt. 5:47), to be circumspect (Eph. 5:15), to be separate from idolaters (2 Cor. 6:17), to shine as lights in the dark world (Phil. 2:15). He forbids us to join together with sinners, or do as they do. The way to hell is a well-trodden road, and the Lord calls to us to turn out of the road: 'You shall not follow a multitude to do evil' (Exod. 23:2). This is sufficient reason to keep ourselves pure in a time of common infection. As God's Word is our rule—so his will is our warrant.

2. To be holiest in evil times, is an indication of the truth of grace. To profess religion when the times favor it, is no great matter. Almost all will court the Gospel Queen when she is hung with jewels. But to own the ways of God when they are decried and maligned, to love a persecuted truth—this evidences a vital principle of goodness. Dead fish swim down the stream—living fish swim against it. To swim against the common stream of evil, shows grace to be alive. The prophet Elijah continuing zealous for the Lord Almighty, when they had dug down God's altars—showed his heart and lips had been touched with a coal from the altar.

Use 1. See hence how unworthy they are of the name of Christians, who use sinful compliance, and cut the garment of their religion according to the mode and fashion of the times. They do not consult what is best—but what is safest. Complying spirits can truckle to the desires of others; they can bow either to the East or to the West; they prefer a whole skin before a pure conscience. They can, with the planet Mercury, vary their motion; they can, as the mariner, shift their sail with every wind and, as the mongrel Israelites, speak the language of both Canaan and Ashdod. These are like the Samaritans of whom Josephus says, when the Jews flourished they pretended to he akin to them—but when the Jews were persecuted, they disclaimed kindred with them. The old serpent has taught men crooked windings, and to be for that religion which does not have truth on its side – but worldly power.

Use 2. Let us keep up the vigor of our zeal, in degenerate times. We should by a holy contrariness – burn hotter in a frozen age. We live in the dregs of time; sin is grown common and impudent. It is excellent to walk contrary to the world, 'Do not conform any longer to the pattern of this world!' (Romans 12:2). Let us be as lilies and roses among the briars. Sin is never the better, because it is in fashion! Nor will this plea hold at the last day – that we did as the most did. God will say, 'Seeing you sinned with the multitude – you shall go to hell with the multitude!' Oh, let us keep pure among the dregs; let us be like fish that retain their freshness in salt waters; and as that lamp which shone in the smoking furnace (Gen. 15:17).

1. Consider – To be holy in times of general defection, is that with which God is greatly pleased. The Lord was much delighted with the holy conferences and dialogues of these saints in the text. When others were inveighing against God, that there should be a remnant of holy souls speaking of glory and the life to come – their words were music in God's ears!

2. Consider – To keep up a spirit in holiness in an adulterous generation is a Christian's honor. This was the glory of the church of Pergamum, that she held fast Christ's name – even where Satan's seat was (Rev. 2:13). The impiety of the times, is a foil to set off grace all the more, and give it a greater luster. Then a Christian is most lovely, when he is (as Ambrose says) like the cypress, which keeps its verdure and freshness in the winter season. 'Mark the perfect man, and behold the upright' (Psalm 37:37). An upright man is always worth beholding – but then he is most to be admired when like a bright star, he shines in the dark, and having lost all, he holds fast his integrity.

3. Consider – To be godly in a profligate age does much to animate weak beginners; it strengthens feeble knees (Isaiah 35:3) and shores up those temples of the Holy Spirit which are ready to fall. One man's zeal is a burning torch for others to catch fire at. How did the constancy of the martyrs inflame the love of many to the truth! Though only Christ's blood saves – yet the blood of martyrs may strengthen. Paul's prison chain made converts in Nero's court, two of whom were afterwards martyrs, as history relates. Mr. Bradford's holy advice and example, so confirmed Bishop Ferrar, that he would not touch the Roman pollution.

4. Consider – How sad will it be for professors to fall off from their former profession, and espouse a novel religion. Julian bathed himself in the blood of beasts offered in sacrifice to the heathen gods, and so as much as lay in him washed off his former baptism. In the time of Julius Caesar this astonishing thing happened: after a plentiful vintage, wild grapes appeared upon their vines, which was looked upon as an ominous sign. When men seemed to bring forth the fruits of righteousness, and afterwards bring forth the wild grapes of impiety – it is a sad omen and prognostic of their ruin! 'For it had been better for them not to have known the way of righteousness, than after they have known it, to turn from the holy commandment (2 Pet. 2:21). Let all this make us maintain the power of holiness in the worst times. Though others wonder we do not sin after the rate that they do – yet remember, it is better to go to heaven with a few than to hell in the crowd. 'Enter through the narrow gate. For wide is the gate and broad is the road that leads to destruction, and many enter through it. But small is the gate and narrow the road that leads to life, and only a few find it.' Matthew 7:13-14.

Question: How may we keep up the briskness and fervor of grace, in times of apostasy?

Answer 1. Let us beware of having our hearts too much linked to the world. The world damps zeal – as earth chokes the fire. We are bid to love our enemies; but the world is such an enemy as we must not love, 'Do not love the world or anything in the world.' (1 John 2:15). The world bewitches with her blandishments, and kills with her silver darts! He who is a Demas — will be a Judas! A lover of the world will, for a piece of money, betray a holy cause, and make shipwreck of a good conscience.

Answer 2. Let us be volunteers in piety; that is, choose God's service; 'I have chosen the way of truth' (Psalm 119:30). It is one thing to be good, with a holy end in view. Hypocrites are good only out of worldly design. They embrace the gospel for secular advantage, and these will in time, fall away. It is fabled that the Chelidonian stone keeps its virtue no longer than it is enclosed in gold; take it out of the gold, and it loses its virtue. False hearts are good no longer than they are enclosed in golden prosperity; take them out of the gold and they lose all their seeming goodness. But if we would retain our sanctity in backsliding times we must serve God purely out of choice. He who is godly out of choice, loves holiness for its beauty, and adheres to the gospel, when all the jewels of preferment are pulled off.

Answer 3. Let us be inlaid with sincerity. If a piece of timber begins to bend, it is because it is not sound. Why do any bend and comply against their conscience — but because their hearts are not sound. 'Their hearts were insincere toward Him, and they were unfaithful to His covenant.' (Psalm 78:37). Sincerity causes stability. When the apostle exhorts to stand fast in the evil day, among the rest of the Christian armor, he bids them put on the belt of truth, 'Stand firm then, with the belt of truth buckled around your waist.' (Eph. 6:14). The belt of truth is nothing else but sincerity.

Answer 4. Let us get love to Christ. Love is a holy fuel. It fires the affections, steels the courage, and carries a Christian above the love of life, and the fear of death. Many waters cannot quench love (Cant 8:7). Love made Christ suffer for us. If anyone asks what Christ died of, it may be answered, 'He died of love!' If we love Christ — we will own him in the worst times, and be like that virgin of whom Basil speaks who, not accepting deliverance upon sinful terms, cried out, 'Let life and money go! Welcome Christ!'

Answer 5. If we would keep up the sprightly vigor of grace in evil times, let us harden our hearts against the taunts and reproaches of the wicked. David was the song of the drunkards (Psalm 69:12). A Christian is never the worse for reproach. The stars are not the less glorious, though they have ugly names given them, the Bear, the Dragon, etc. Reproaches are but splinters of the cross. How will he endure the stake — who cannot bear a scoff? Reproaches for Christ, are ensigns of honor, and badges of adoption (1 Peter 4:14). Let Christians bind these reproaches, as a crown about their head. Better have men reproach you for being godly — than have God damn you for being wicked! Be not laughed out of your religion. If a lame man laughs at you for walking upright — will you therefore limp?

Answer 6. If we would keep up the vigor of devotion during evil times, let us beg God for confirming grace. Habitual grace may flag; Peter had habitual grace — yet was foiled; he lost a single battle, though not the victory. We need exciting, assisting, sustaining grace; not only grace in us — but grace with us (1 Cor. 15:10). Sustaining grace (which is a fresh gale of the Spirit) will carry us undauntedly through the world's blustering storms. Thus shall we be able to keep up our heroic zeal in corrupt times, and be as Mount Zion — which cannot be moved.

Part I. The character of the Godly

Having done with the frontispiece of the text, I begin, in the first place, with the character in general of the godly: they are fearers of God, 'Those who feared the Lord'. What fear is meant here? Considered negatively:

1. It is not meant of a natural fear, which is a tremor or palpitation of heart, occasioned by the approach of some imminent danger. 'They are afraid of dangers on the road' (Eccles. 12:5).

2. It is not meant of a sinful fear, which is twofold:

A superstitious fear. A black cat crossing the path, is by some more dreaded than a harlot lying in the bed.

A carnal fear. This is the fever of the soul which sets it a shaking. He who is timorous, will be treacherous; he will decoy his friend, and deny his God. Three times in one chapter Christ cautions us against the fear of men, (Matthew 10:26-31). Aristotle says that the reason why the chameleon turns into so many colors, is through excessive fear. Fear makes men change their religion as the chameleon does her colors!

A carnal fear is excruciating, 'fear has torment in it.' (1 John 4:18).The Greek word for torment is sometimes put for hell (Matt. 25:46). Fear has hell in it.

A carnal fear is pernicious. It indisposes for duty. The disciples, under the power of fear, were fitter to flee than to pray, (Matthew 26:56), and it puts men upon sinful means to save themselves: 'The fear of man brings a snare!' (Proverbs 29:25). What made Peter deny Christ, and Origen sprinkle incense before the idol — but fear?

Considered positively, the fear meant in the text is a divine fear, which is the reverencing and adoring of God's holiness, and the setting of ourselves always under his sacred inspection. The infinite distance between God and us causes this fear.

When God's glory began to shine out upon the Mount, Moses said, 'I exceedingly fear and quake!' (Heb. 12:21). Such as approach God's presence with light feathery hearts, and worship him in a crude, careless manner — have none of this fear.

'Those who feared the Lord'. In the words are two parts.

1. The Act — fear.

2. The Object — the Lord.

'Those who feared the Lord'. The fear of God is the sum of all true true religion. 'Now all has been heard; here is the conclusion of the matter: Fear God and keep his commandments, for this is the whole duty of man. (Ecclesiastes 12:13). Fear is the leading grace, the first seed which God sows in the heart. When a Christian can say little of faith, and perhaps nothing of assurance, yet he dares not deny that he fears God (Neh. 1:11). God is so great — that the Christian is afraid of displeasing him; and so good — that he is afraid of losing him.

Doctrine: It is an indispensable duty incumbent on Christians, to be fearers of God. 'Fear God!' (Eccles. 5:7). 'That you may fear the glorious and awesome name of the Lord your God!' (Deut. 28:58). This fear of God, is the very foundation of a saint. One can no more act as a Christian without the fear of God — than he can act as a man without reason. This holy fear is the fixed temper and complexion of the soul; this fear is not servile — but filial. There is a difference between fearing God, and being afraid of God. The godly fear God as a child does his father; the wicked are afraid of God as the prisoner is of the judge! This divine fear will appear admirable if you consider how it is mixed and interwoven with several of the graces.

1. The fear of God is mixed with love (Psalm 145:19, 20)

The chaste spouse fears to displease her husband, because she loves him. There is a necessity that fear and love should be in conjunction. Love is as the sails to make swift the soul's motion; and fear is as the ballast to keep it steady in true religion. Love will be apt to grow wanton, unless it is counter-balanced with fear.

2. The fear of God is mixed with faith. 'By faith Noah, moved with holy fear, prepared an ark' (Hebrews 11:7). When the soul looks either to God's holiness, or its own sinfulness — it fears.

But it is a fear mixed with faith in Christ's merits; the soul trembles — yet trusts. Like a ship which lies at anchor, though it shakes with the wind, yet it is fixed at anchor. God in great wisdom couples these two graces of faith and fear. Fear preserves seriousness, faith preserves cheerfulness. Fear is as lead to the net — to keep a Christian from floating in presumption; and faith is as cork to the net — to keep him from sinking in despair.

3. The fear of God is mixed with prudence. He who fears God has the serpent's eye in the dove's head. He foresees and avoids those rocks upon which others run. 'A prudent man sees danger and takes refuge, but the simple keep going and suffer for it.' (Proverbs 22:3). Though divine fear does not make a person cowardly — it makes him cautious.

4. The fear of God is mixed with hope. 'The eyes of the Lord are on those who fear him, on those whose hope is in his unfailing love' (Psalm 33:18). One would think that fear would destroy hope — but it nourishes it. Fear is to hope, as the oil to the lamp — it keeps it burning. The more we fear God's justice — the more we may hope in his mercy. Indeed, such as have no fear of God do sometimes hope — but it is not 'good hope through grace' (2 Thess. 5:26). Sinners pretend to have the 'helmet of hope' (1 Thess. 5:8) — but lack the 'breastplate of righteousness' (Eph. 6:14).

5. The fear of God is mixed with industry. 'Noah, moved with holy fear, prepared an ark' (Hebrews 11:7). There is a carnal fear, which represents God as a severe Judge. This takes the soul off from duty, 'I was afraid and went out and hid your talent in the ground' (Matthew 25:25).

But there is also a fear of diligence. A Christian fears — and prays; fears — and repents. Fear quickens industry. The spouse, fearing lest the bridegroom should come before she is dressed, hastens and puts on her jewels, that she may be ready to meet him. Fear causes a watchful eye — and a working hand. Fear banishes sloth out of its diocese. 'The greatest labor in true religion,' says holy fear, 'is far less than the least pain the damned feel in hell.' There is no greater spur in the heavenly race — than the fear of God.

The reasons enforcing this holy fear of God, include the following:

1. God's eye is always upon us. He who is under the eye of his earthly prince, will he careful of doing anything which would offend him. 'Does He not see my ways and number all my steps?' (Job 31:4). God sees in the dark: 'Even the darkness is not dark to You. The night shines like the day; darkness and light are alike to You' (Psalm 139:12). The night is no curtain, the clouds are no canopy — to hinder or intercept God's sight. God sees the heart. An earthly judge can judge of the fact — but God judges of the heart. 'I, the Lord, examine the mind, I test the heart!' (Jeremiah 17:10). He is like Ezekiel's wheels, 'full of eyes.' God is all eye! Should not this make us walk with fear and circumspection? We cannot sin — but our judge looks on!

2. God interprets our not fearing of Him — as a slighting of Him. As not to praise God is to wrong him — so not to fear God is to slight him. Of all things, a person can least endure to he slighted: 'Why has the wicked despised God?' (Psalm 10:13). For a worm to slight its Maker causes the fury to rise up in God's face! 'My fury will flare up!' (Ezekiel 38:18).

3. God has power to destroy us. 'Fear him who is able to destroy both soul and body in hell!' (Matthew 10:28). God can look us into our grave — and with a breath blow us into hell — and shall we not fear him! Is it easy to wrestle with flames? 'Who knows the power of his anger!' (Psalm 90:11). What engines or buckets can quench the infernal fire of hell? We are apt to fear men who may try to hurt us — but what is their power compared to God's power? They threaten a prison, God threatens hell. They threaten our life, God threatens our soul — and shall we not tremble before him! Oh, how dreadful, when the great fountains of God's wrath shall be broken

up, and all his bitter vials poured out! 'Can your heart endure, or can your hands be strong, in the day that I shall deal with you!' (Ezekiel 22:14)

Objection: But are not we bidden to serve God without fear? (Luke 1:74)

Answer. We must not fear God with such a fear, as the wicked do. They fear him as a Turkish slave does his master; they fear him in such a way as to hate him — and wish there were no God! We must not serve God with this hellish fear — but we must serve him with a sincere filial fear, sweetened with love.

Use 1. Refutation. This refutes the Papists who hold that a Christian cannot have assurance, because he is to serve God with fear. Assurance and fear are different — but not contrary. A child may have assurance of his father's love — yet a fear of offending him. Who was more fearful of sin than Paul? (1 Cor. 9:27) Yet who had more assurance? 'Christ, who loved me, and gave himself for me' (Gal. 2:20). Faith procures assurance (Eph. 1:13) fear preserves assurance.

Use 2. Instruction. It is a Christian duty to fear God. What strangers, then, are they to true religion — who are void of this holy fear! The godly fear — and sin not. The wicked sin — and fear not. They are like the Leviathan, who is 'made without fear' (Job 41:33). Lack of the fear of God is the innate cause of all wickedness: 'Whose mouth is full of cursing and bitterness, their feet are swift to shed blood' (Romans 3:14-15). Why was this? 'There is no fear of God before their eyes!' (verse 18).

Abraham surmised that the men of Gerar would stick at no sin. Why so? 'I thought, Surely the fear of God is not in this place' (Gen. 20:11). The judge in the Gospel is called an unjust judge (Luke 18:6); and no wonder, for he 'had no fear of God' (verse 2). There must be an excess of sin, where there the fear of God is lacking to restrain it. The water must overflow, where there are no banks to keep it out. We live in a godless age; would men dare to sin at the rate they do — if the fear of God were ruling in their hearts? Would they dare to swear, be immoral, use false weights, bear false witness, hate purity, deride God, forge plots, persecute Christ's body — if they had the fear of God before their eyes? These men proclaim to the world that they are atheists; they do not believe in the immortality of the soul. They are worse than brutish — a beast fears the fire — but these fear not hell-fire! They are worse than devils, for the devils 'believe and tremble' (James 2:19).

Use 3. Lamentation. Let us bewail the lack of the fear of God in our world. Why is it that so few fear God?

1. Men do not fear God — because they have not the knowledge of God. 'They hated knowledge, and did not choose the fear of the Lord' (Proverbs 1:29). Every sin is founded in ignorance of God. If only men knew God in his immense glory, they would be swallowed up with divine amazement. When the prophet Isaiah had a glimpse of God's glory, he was struck with holy consternation: 'Woe to me! I am ruined! For I am a man of unclean lips, and I live among a people of unclean lips, and my eyes have seen the King, the Lord Almighty!' (Isaiah 6:6). Ignorance of God, banishes the fear of God.

2. Men do not fear God — because they presume on his mercy. God is merciful, and they do not doubt of the virtue of this sovereign balm. But who is God's mercy for? 'His mercy extends to those who fear him' (Luke 1:50). Such as do not fear God's justice — shall not taste his mercy.

Let this be 'for a lamentation', that the fear of God is so vanished from our world. Why is it almost nowhere to be found? Some fear shame, others fear danger — but where is he who fears God?

And not only among the generality of people—but even among professing Christians, how few fear God in truth! Profession is often made a cloak to cover sin. Absalom palliated his treason with a religious vow (2 Samuel 15:7). The Pharisees made long prayer a cloak for oppression (Matt. 23:14). This is sordid—to carry on wicked designs—under a mask of piety. The snow covers many a dunghill. A snowy white profession covers many a foul heart! The sins of professors are more odious. Thistles are bad in a field—but worse in a garden. The sins of the wicked anger God—but the sins of professing Christians grieve him.

Use 4. Reproof.

1. This reproves jovial sinners, who are so far from fearing God, that they spend their time in mirth and wantonness! 'People were eating, drinking, marrying and being given in marriage up to the day Noah entered the ark. Then the flood came and destroyed them all!' (Luke 17:27). There is a place in Africa called Timbuktu, where the inhabitants spend all the day in playing and dancing. What sensual, jovial lives do the gallants of our age live! They spend their life in a frolic, as if God had made them to be like the leviathan who plays in the sea. 'They sing with tambourine and harp. They make merry to the sound of the flute.' (Job 21:12). They ride to hell upon the back of pleasure, and go merrily to damnation!

Does not God call us to trembling? Our sins presage evil. May not we fear that 'the glory is departing'? May not we fear the death of true religion before the birth of reformation? May not we fear that some momentous calamity should bring up the fear of former judgments? As the prophet Ezekiel says, 'Should we then make mirth?' (Ezekiel 21:10). But jovial spirits have banished the fear of God.

'How terrible it will be for you who sprawl on ivory beds surrounded with luxury, eating the meat of tender lambs and choice calves. You sing idle songs to the sound of the harp!' (Amos 6:4,5). Sinners whose hearts are hardened with soft pleasures, let them have their lusts—but farewell Christ and his gospel. 'They feast without fear' (Jude 12.). But they forget death will bring in the reckoning, and they must pay the reckoning in hell-fire! The Turkish sultan, when he intends the death of any of his minions, invites them to sumptuous feast, and then causes them to he taken away from the table and strangled. Just so, Satan gluts men with sinful pastimes and delights, and then strangles them! Foolish pleasure-lovers are like the fish that swim pleasantly through the silver streams of Jordan, until at last they fall into the Dead Sea. 'Those who want to be rich fall into temptation, a trap, and many foolish and harmful desires, which plunge people into ruin and destruction!' (1 Tim. 6:9).

2. This reproves secure sinners who have no fear of God. Like Laish of old, they are 'a secure people' (Judges 18:27). Those who are least safe—are most confident! Carnal security throws men into a deep sleep. Birds which roost in steeples, being used to the continual ringing of bells, the noise does not at all disturb them. So sinners who have been long used to the sound of Aaron's bells, though now and then they have a peal rung out against their sins yet, being used to it, they are not startled at all. A carnally secure sinner is known thus:

a. He lives as had as the worst, yet hopes to be saved as well as the best. 'I am safe, even though I am walking in my own stubborn way.' (Deut. 29:19). This is as if a man should drink poison—yet believe that he shall have his health. A secure sinner now lies in Delilah's lap—yet hopes to someday lie in Abraham's bosom!

b. A secure sinner thinks all is well, because all is in peace. He hears others speak of a 'spirit of bondage', and the terrors they have felt for sin—yet he thanks God that he never knew what trouble of spirit meant; he thinks his conscience is good, because it is quiet. When the devil keeps the palace—all is in peace' (Luke 11:12). Ungrounded peace presages an earthquake in the conscience.

c. A secure sinner is careless about his soul. The soul is the princely part, which is crowned with reason. A secure sinner provides for his body—but neglects his soul. He is like one who waters his flowers—but never minds his jewels. Behold here a secure person, who is in a spiritual lethargy; he has no sense of the life to come; he is destitute of the fear of God.

3. This reproves scoffers, who are the vilest of sinners. 'There shall come in the last days, scoffers' (2 Pet. 3:3). These Ishmaels jeer at holy living—and ridicule all true religion. They throw squibs of reproach at the saints. In the massacre at Paris, the Papists scoffed at the Protestants when they murdered them, 'Where is your God now? What has become of all your prayers now?' These are devils in the likeness of men! They are far from the fear of God! The scorner's chair stands at the mouth of hell!

Use 5. Exhortation. It exhorts us to get the fear of God planted in our hearts. 'Happy is he who fears always' (Proverbs 28:14). The fear of God would influence all our actions. It would make us godly in both tables of God's laws. It would make us holy towards God—and righteous towards men. We would be true in our promises—and just in our dealings (Matt. 7:12).

That I may press you to this holy fear—let me show you the dignity and excellency of fearing God:

1. The fear of God is the true badge and uniform of a saint. The saints of old were God-fearing men (Gen. 22:12; Acts 10:22); Obadiah feared the Lord greatly (I Kings 8:13). All the moral virtues in their highest elevation, do not make a saint. But here is the Christian's true character—he is one who fears God. Augustine said of himself, that he did knock at heaven-gate with a trembling hand. Christ calls his elect, 'his sheep' (John 10:27). Sheep are of a trembling nature. The saints are tremulous—they dare not take liberties as others do.

2. The fear of God is the beginning of true wisdom. (Proverbs 1:7). Wisdom is 'more precious than rubies' (Prov. 3:15). No jewel we wear so adorns us as wisdom. Now, the fear of Lord is our wisdom: 'The fear of the Lord—that is wisdom' (Job 28:28).

Wherein is the fear of God the true wisdom?

A. The fear of God is wisdom, in that it makes its careful about our spiritual accounts. Wisdom lies in nothing more than in keeping accounts exactly. The fear of God teaches a person to examine the state of his soul critically. 'O my soul, how is it with you?' Do you gain or lose? Is our faith in its infancy, being but newly laid to the breast of the promise? Or is it grown to some stature? How is it? Does grace or sin prevail? Thus the fear of God makes us wisely balance our accounts, and see how matters stand between God and our souls. 'I meditate in my heart, and my spirit made diligent search' (Psalm 77:6).

B. The fear of God is wisdom as it makes its understand divine secrets. 'The secret of the Lord is with those who fear him' (Psalm 21:14). He must he wise, who is acquainted with the secrets of heaven. A fearer of God is acquainted with the secret of election (1 Thess. 1:4), of God's love (Rev. 1:5), of the holy annointing (1 John 2:20). He knows God's mind: 'We have the mind of Christ (1 Cor. 2;16).

C. The fear of God is wisdom, in that it makes us consider. 'I considered my ways' (Psalm 119:59). A great part of wisdom lies in consideration. He who fears God considers how vain the world is—and therefore dares not love it. He who fears God considers how short time is—and therefore dares not lose it. He who fears God considers how precious salvation is—and therefore dares not neglect it.

D. The fear of God is wisdom, in that it makes its walk wisely. 'Walk in wisdom toward outsiders, making the most of the time' (Col. 4:5).

a. The fear of God makes us walk amiably: 'Abraham stood up and bowed himself to the children of Heth' (Gen. 2.3:7). Piety does not exclude courtesy.

b. The fear of God makes us walk inoffensively: it prevents not only scandals but indecencies. The veneration of God, causes circumcision of heart, and circumspection of life.

E. The fear of God is wisdom, as it preserves us from hell. It is wisdom to keep out of danger; fear makes us flee from the wrath to come.

3. The fear of God is the best certificate to show for heaven. Do you have knowledge? So has Satan. Do you have profession? So has Satan, he 'transforms himself into an angel of light' (2 Cor. 11:14). But do you have filial fear? In this you will excel him. The fear of God is, though not our plea for heaven — yet our evidence for heaven.

4. There is that in God, which may command fear:

1. 'He is clothed in awesome majesty!' (Job 37:22).

a. There is majesty in God's Name, Jehovah. It comes from a Hebrew root which speaks of God's absolute, eternal, and independent being.

b. There is majesty in God's looks. Job had but a glimpse of God, and he was even swallowed up with divine amazement: 'My ears had heard of you — but now my eyes have seen you. Therefore I despise myself and repent in dust and ashes!' (Job 42:5-6).

c. There is majesty in God's words. He speaks with majesty, as when he gave the law in thundering, insomuch that the people said, 'Let not God speak with us lest we die!' (Exodus 20:19).

d. There is majesty in God's attributes: his holiness, power, justice, which are the irradiations of the divine essence.

e. There is majesty in God's works: 'They will speak of the glorious splendor of your majesty, and I will meditate on your wonderful works. They will tell of the power of your awesome works, and I will proclaim your great deeds' (Psalm 145:5). Every creature sets forth God's majesty; we may see the majesty of God blazing in the sun, twinkling in the stars. God's majesty is discernable in those two wonders of nature, behemoth and leviathan (Job 40:18; 41:19).

In short, the majesty of God is seen in humbling the children of pride. He turned King Nebuchadnezzar out to pasture, and made him fellow-commoner with the beasts. Does not all this call for fear?

2. 'He is clothed in awesome majesty!' 'He is feared by the kings of the earth' (Psalm 76:12). There is a time coming when God will be dreadful to his enemies; when conscience is awake, when death strikes, when the last trumpet sounds. And shall we not fear this God? 'Do you not fear Me? Do you not tremble before Me?' (Jer. 5:22). Fearing God's justice — is the way not to feel it.

And let it not seem strange to you, if I tell you, that in respect of God's infinite majesty, there will be some of this blessed fear in heaven. Not a fear which has torment in it, for perfect love will cast out fear — but a holy, sweet, reverential fear. Though God has so much beauty in him as shall cause love, and joy, in heaven — yet this beauty is mixed with so much majesty, as shall cause a veneration in glorified saints.

5. The fear of God tends to life (Proverbs 19:23).

1. This is true in a temporal sense, 'The fear of the Lord prolongs life, but the years of the wicked are cut short' (Proverbs 10:27); in the original it is, 'adds days'. Long life is promised as a blessing, 'With long life will I satisfy him' (Psalm 91:16). The best way to come to 'a good old age', is the fear of God. Sin curtails the life: many a man's excess wastes his vital organs, enervates his strength, and cuts him short of those years which by the course of nature might be arrived at, 'Don't be excessively wicked, and don't be foolish. Why should you die before your time?' (Eccles. 7:17). You who desire to live long — live in the fear of God! 'The Lord commanded us to follow all these statutes and to fear the Lord our God for our prosperity always and for our preservation.' (Deut. 6:24).

2. This is true in a spiritual sense. 'The fear of the Lord tends to life' — namely, to 'life eternal'. Life is sweet, and eternal makes it sweeter. 'Eternal life is true life' (Augustine). The life of bliss has no term of years wherein it expires: 'Forever ...with the Lord!' The lamp of glory shines — but is never spent; so that divine fear tends to life; a life with God and angels forever.

6. The fear of God gives full satisfaction. 'He who has it, shall abide satisfied' (Prov. 19:23). Such as are destitute of God's fear, never meet with satisfaction. 'In the midst of his plenty, distress will overtake him; the full force of misery will come upon him' (Job 20:22). This is a riddle, to be full — yet not have enough. The meaning is there is still something lacking: he who fears not God, though his barns are full — yet his mind is not at rest. The sweet waters of pleasure do rather inflame the thirst — than satisfy it. 'I have run through all the delights and grandeurs of the world, and could never find full contentment', said the emperor Severus. But he who has the fear of the Lord 'shall abide satisfied'.

1. He shall be satisfied. His soul shall be filled with grace, his conscience with peace. A holy man said, when God had replenished him with inward joy, 'It is enough Lord, your servant is a full vessel, and can hold no more!'

2. He shall abide satisfied. This satisfaction shall not cease; it shall be a cordial in death, and a crown after death!

7. The fear of God makes a little to be sweet. 'Better is little with the fear of the Lord' (Prov. 15:16). Why is a little better? Because that little a believer has, he holds in his Head, Christ. That little is sweetened with the love of God. He has with that little a contented mind; and contentment turns Daniel's vegetables into choice meat (Dan. 1:12). Again, that little is a pledge of more; that little oil in the cruse — is but a pledge of that golden joy and bliss which the soul shall have in heaven. Thus a little with the fear of God, is better than all unsanctified riches. Lazarus' crumbs were better than the rich man's banquet!

8. The fear of God is a Christian's safety. He is invulnerable; nothing can hurt him. Plunder him of his money, he carries a treasure about him of which he cannot be robbed (Isaiah 33:6). Cast him into prison — his conscience is free; kill his body — it shall rise again. He who has on this breastplate of God's fear may be shot at — but can never be shot through.

9. The fear of God makes all things go well with us. 'How happy are those who fear the Lord — all who follow his ways! You will enjoy the fruit of your labor. How happy you will be! How rich your life!' (Psalm 128:1-2). Is it not well with that man who has all things working together for his good — and has nothing lacking which may do him good (Psalm 84:11)? If God sees health and riches good for him — he shall have them. Every providence shall center in his happiness. Oh, what an inducement is here to solid piety! Come whatever will, 'it shall be well with those who fear God' (Eccles. 8:12). When they die, they shall go to God; and while they live, everything in the world shall do them good.

10. The fear of God is a great cleanser. 'The fear of the Lord is clean' (Psalm 19:9). It is so:

1. In its own nature—it is a pure, crystal, orient grace.

2. In the effect of it—it cleanses the heart and life. As a spring works out the mud—so the fear of the Lord purges out the love of sin. The heart is the temple of God, and the fear of the Lord sweeps and cleanses this temple, that it may not be defiled.

11. The fear of God makes us accepted with God. 'In every nation he who fears him ... is accepted with him' (Acts 10:35). What was Paul so ambitious of? 'We labor that we may be accepted by him' (2 Cor. 5:9). Divine fear ingratiates us into divine favor. Such as are fearless of God, neither their persons nor offerings find acceptance: 'I despise your feast days, and I will not dwell in your solemn assemblies. Though you offer me burnt offerings ... I will not accept them' (Amos 5:21-22). Who will take a gift from one who has the plague!

12. The fear of God paves the way for spiritual joy. Some may think the fear of God breeds sadness; no, it is the inlet to joy! The fear of God is the morning star, which ushers in the sunlight of comfort: 'Walking in the fear of the Lord, and in the comfort of the Holy Spirit' (Acts 9:31). The fear of God has solid joy in it, though not frivolity. God mixes joy with holy fear, that fear may not seem slavish.

13. The fear of God drives out all base fear. Carnal fear is an enemy to true religion. The fear of God frightens fear away; it causes courage: 'Able men, such as fear God' (Exod. 18:21); some translations render it, 'men of courage'. When a dictator governed in Rome, all other offices ceased. Where the fear of God rules in the heart—it expels fleshly fear. When the empress Eudoxia threatened to banish Chrysostom, the preacher said, 'Tell her, I fear nothing but sin!' The fear of God swallows up all other fear, as Moses' rod swallowed up the magicians' rods.

14. To be void of God's fear, is folly. 'I said to the fools—do not deal foolishly' (Psalm 75:4).

1. Are not they fools who gratify their enemy? Those who lack the fear of God, do so. Satan baits his hook with pleasure and profit, and they swallow bait and hook and all! This pleases Satan; men's sins feast the devil. Who but a fool would please his enemy?

2. Is it not folly to prefer slavery before liberty? If a slave in the galley should have his freedom offered him—but says that he would rather tug at the oar and be a slave, than have his liberty—would he not be judged to be a fool? Such is the case of him who does not fear God. The gospel offers to free him from the miserable captivity of sin—but he chooses rather to be a slave to his lusts. He is like a servant under the law: 'I love my master—I will not go out free' (Exod. 21:5). The foolish sinner had rather have his ear bored to the devil's service, than be translated 'into the glorious liberty of the sons of God' (Rom. 8:21).

3. Is not he a fool who, having but one jewel, will venture the loss of it? The soul is the jewel, and the sinner is fearless of it, he will throw it away upon the world; as if one should throw pearls and diamonds into the river. He who pampers his body and neglects his soul, is like him who feasts his slave and starves his wife!

4. Is not he a fool who refuses a rich offer? If one should offer to adopt another and make him an heir of his vast estate, and he should refuse it, would not his discretion be called in question? God offers Christ to a sinner, and promises to entail all the riches of heaven upon him—but, lacking the fear of God, he refuses this great offer: 'Israel would have none of me' (Psalm 81:11). Is not this a prodigy of madness? Yay not the devil peg every sinner for a fool at the last day!

15. The fear of God is a sovereign antidote against apostasy. The devil was the first apostate. How rife is this sin! More shipwrecks are on land—than at sea; men make shipwreck of a good conscience. Apostates are said to put Christ to 'open shame' (Heb. 6:6). The fear of God is a preservative against apostasy: 'I will put my fear in their hearts—that they shall not depart

from me' (Jer. 32:40). I will so love them—that I will not depart from them; and they shall so fear me—that they shall not depart from me.

16. There are excellent promises made to those who fear God. 'Unto you who fear my name, shall the Sun of righteousness arise with healing in his wings' (Mat. 4:2). Here is a promise of Christ; he is a Sun for light and life-giving influence; and a Sun of righteousness, as he diffuses the golden beams of justification. And he has healing in his wings; the sun heals the air, dries up the cold moistures, exhales the vapors which would be pestilential. Just so, Christ has 'healing in his wings'; he heals the hardness and impurity of the soul. And the horizon in which this sun arises, is in hearts fearing God: 'To you who fear my name, shall the Sun of righteousness arise.'

And there is another great promise: 'He will bless those who fear the Lord, both small and great' (Psalm 115:13). God blesses such in their name, estate, souls. And this blessing can never be reversed! As Isaac said, 'I have blessed him—and he shall be blessed' (Gen. 27:37). Such as fear God are privileged people: none can take away from them—either their birthright or their blessing.

17. Fear is the admirable instrument in promoting salvation. 'Work out your salvation with fear' (Phil. 2:12). The fear of God, is that flaming sword which turns every way—to keep sin from entering (Prov. 16:6). The fear of God stands sentinel in the soul, and is ever upon its watchtower. Fear causes circumspection: he who walks in fear, treads warily. Fear gives birth to prayer, and prayer engages the help of heaven.

18. The Lord is much pleased with those who fear him. 'The Lord takes pleasure in those who fear him' (Psalm 147:1). In the Septuagint it is, 'The Lord bears good will towards those who fear him.' Some render it, 'The Lord delights in those who fear him.' Never did a suitor take such pleasure in a person he loved—as God does in those who fear him; they are his 'Hephzibah', which means, my delight is in her (Isaiah 61:4). He says of them as of Zion: 'This is my rest forever—here I will dwell' (Psalm 132:14). A sinner is 'a vessel in which is no pleasure' (Hos. 8:8). But fearers of God are his favorites.

19. Such as fear God are the only people that shall be saved. 'Salvation is near those who fear him' (Psalm 85:9). Salvation is said to be 'far from the wicked' (Psalm 119:155). They and salvation are so far apart—that they are likely never to meet. But God's salvation is near to those who fear him. What do we aspire after, but salvation? It is the end of all our prayers, tears, sufferings. Salvation is the crown of our desires, the flower of our joy. And who shall be enriched with salvation—only the fearers of God! 'His salvation is near those who fear him.'

Let these 19 powerful arguments persuade us to fear God.

Use 6. Trial. Let us put ourselves upon a strict scrutiny and trial, whether we have the fear of God planted in our hearts.

Question: How may we know whether we have the fear of God planted in our hearts?

Answer 1. The fear of God—will make a man fear SIN. 'How can I do this great wickedness— and sin against God?' (Gen. 39:9). Indeed, sin is the only evil thing; it is the evil of evils. Sin is the poison which the old serpent spat into our virgin nature! In sin there is both pollution and enmity. Sin is compared to a 'thick cloud' (Isaiah 44:22), which not only hides the light of God's face—but brings down showers of His wrath. Sin is worse than all evils. There is more evil in a drop of sin—than in a sea of affliction!

1. Sin is the cause of all affliction. Sin conjures up all the winds and storms in the world. The cause is worse than the effect. Out of this viperous womb come, 'evil thoughts, sexual

immorality, theft, murder, adultery, greed, wickedness, deceit, eagerness for lustful pleasure, envy, slander, pride, and foolishness.'

2. In affliction conscience may be quiet; the hail may beat upon the tiles, when there is music in the room. But sin terrifies the conscience. Nero, in the midst of feasts and Roman sports was full of horror of mind; the numbers of men he had killed troubled him. Cataline was frightened at every noise. Cain in killing Abel, stabbed half the world at one blow, yet he could not kill the worm in his own conscience!

Sin is the quintessence of evil—it puts a sting into death (1 Cor. 15:56). Sin is worse than hell:

a. Hell is a burden only to the sinner—but sin is a burden to God (Amos 2:13).

b. There is justice in hell—but sin is the most unjust thing. It would rob God of his glory, Christ of his purchase, the soul of its happiness. 'It is more bitter to sin against Christ, than to suffer the torments of hell', says Chrysostom. Is not sin then, to be feared? He who fears God is afraid of touching this forbidden fruit!

More particularly:

1. He who fears God—is afraid to do anything which he suspects may be sinful (Romans 14:23). He will not swallow oaths like pills, lest they should afterwards work in his conscience. He dares not mix anything in God's worship, which God has not appointed; he fears it is like offering strange fire. Where conscience is scrupulous, it is safer to forbear; for, 'what is not of faith is sin'.

2. He who fears God—fears the appearance of sin. 'Abstain from all appearance of evil' (1 Thes. 5:22). Some things have a bad look, and carry a show of evil in them. To go to the idol temple, though one does not join with them in worship, is an appearance of evil. He whose heart is ballasted with God's fear—flies from that which looks like sin. It was a good speech of Bernard to, 'By avoiding the act of sin we preserve our peace; by avoiding the appearance of it we preserve our fame.' The fear of God makes us shun the occasion of sin: the Nazarite under the law was not only to forbear wine—but he must not eat grapes, which might occasion intemperance. Joseph fled from his mistress' temptation; he would not be seen in her company.

The appearance of evil, though it does not defile one's own conscience, may offend another's conscience. And hear what the apostle says: When you 'wound their weak conscience, you sin against Christ!' (1 Cor. 8:12). Such as do not avoid the appearances and inlets to sin-make the truth of their grace to be suspected. How far are they from the fear of God who, forgetting their prayer, 'Lead us not into temptation', run themselves into the devil's mouth! They go to plays and theaters, which are the lures and inducements of filthiness! Others associate familiarly with the wicked, and are too often in their company: which is like going among those who have the plague! 'I wrote to you not to company with fornicators,' (1 Cor. 5:9). Business is one thing, keeping company is another. Polycarp would have no society with Marcion, the heretic. Twisting into a cord of friendship with sinners is an appearance of evil; it hardens them in sin, and wounds the credit of true religion.

Question: But did not Christ often converse with sinners?

Answer 1. Christ did sometimes go among the wicked; not that he approved of their sins—but as a physician goes among the diseased to heal them, so Christ intended to work a cure upon them (Mark 2:17). It was their conversion which he aimed at.

Answer 2. Though Jesus Christ did sometimes converse with sinners—yet he could receive no infection by them; his divine nature was a sufficient antidote against the contagion of sin. As the sun cannot be defiled with the thick vapors which are exhaled from the earth, and fly into the sky—so the black vapors of sin could not defile the Sun of righteousness. Christ was of such spotless purity, that he had no receptibility of evil. But the case is otherwise with us; we have a stock of corruption within. Therefore it is dangerous to mix with the wicked, lest we be defiled.

Such as revere the divine majesty of God, dare not go near the borders of sin. Those who went near the fiery furnace, though they did not go into it, were burned (Dan. 3:22).

3. He who fears God—dares not sin secretly. A hypocrite may forbear gross sin because of the shame—but not clandestine, secret sin. He is like one who shuts up his shop windows—but follows his trade within doors. But a man fearing God dares not sin, though he could walk invisibly, and no eye see him. 'You shall not curse the deaf, or put a stumbling block before the blind; but shall fear your God' (Lev. 19:14). If one should curse a deaf man, he cannot hear him. If one should lay a stumbling block in a blind man's way, he cannot see him. Yes—but the fear of God will make one avoid those sins—which can neither he heard or seen by men. God's seeing in secret, is a sufficient counter-poison against sin.

4. He who fears God—dares not commit sin, though it might bring him a profitable advantage. Gain is the golden bait with which Satan fishes for souls. This was the last temptation the devil used to Christ: 'All this will I give you' (Matt. 4:9). How many bow down to the golden image! Joshua who could stop the course of the sun—could not stop Achan in his pursuit after the wedge of gold! But he who fears God dares not sin to get preferment. David dared not touch the Lord's anointed, though he knew he was to reign next (1 Sam. 26:33). A godly man is assured that a full purse is but a poor recompense for a wounded conscience.

5. He who fears God—dares not gratify his own revengeful humor. Homer says that revenge is sweet as dropping honey; but grace makes a man rather bury an injury, than revenge it. He knows who has said, 'Vengeance is mine, I will repay' (Rom. 12:19). He who has the fear of God before his eyes, is so far from revenge, that he requites good for evil. Miriam murmured against Moses, and Moses prayed for her, that God would heal her of her leprosy (Num. 12:13). The prophet Elisha, instead of smiting his enemies, 'set bread and water before them' (2 Kings 6:22).

6. He who fears God—dares not do that which is of evil report, though possibly the thing in itself may be no sin. 'If any of you has a dispute with another, dare he take it before the ungodly for judgment?' (1 Cor. 6:1). Yes, some might say, what sin is it to have a just cause brought before unbelievers, that it may be decided? Oh but, might the apostle reply, though the thing in itself is lawful—yet because it sounds evil, and exposes your religion to the scorn and insult of unbelievers, you who fear God, should not dare to do it. It were better to decide it by a prudent arbitration. Everything is permissible for me—but not everything is beneficial' (1 Cor. 6:12).

7. He who fears God—is not only afraid of evil actions, but fears to offend God in his thoughts. 'Be careful not to harbor this wicked thought.' (Deut. 15:9). To think of sin with delight, is to act it over in the imagination. This is culpable. A man may think himself into hell! What were the apostate angels damned for—was it for any more than proud thoughts?

This is the first note of trial: He who reverences God—flees from sin. It is a saying of Anselm, 'If sin were on one side and hell on the other, I would rather leap into hell than willingly sin against God!'

Answer 2. He who fears God—walks by Scripture rule, rather than by the example of others. Example is, for the most part, corrupt. Examples of great men are influential. Pharaoh had taught Joseph to swear—but Joseph had not taught Pharaoh to pray. The examples of others cannot justify a thing which is intrinsically evil. A God-fearer directs the rudder of his life according to the compass of the Word. He looks to the sacred canon as the mariner to the compass, or Israel to the pillar of fire, to direct him. 'To the law and to the testimony!' (Isaiah 8:20).

Answer 3. He who fears God — keeps his commandments. 'Fear God and keep his commandments' (Eccles. 12:13) Luther said he had rather obey God, than work miracles. A gracious soul crosses his own will to fulfill God's. If the Lord bids him to crucify his favorite sin, or forgive his enemies — then he instantly obeys. A heathen exercising much cruelty to a Christian, asked him in scorn what great miracle his master Christ ever did? The Christian replied, 'This miracle, that though you treat me thus cruelly — I can forgive you.' A holy heart knows, that there is nothing lost by obedience. David swore to the Lord that he would not rest until he found a place for God (Psalm 132:4-5). And God swore back to David, that one of his offspring he would set one upon his throne (Psalm 132:11).

Answer 4. He who fears God — is alike godly in all companies. He diffuses the sweet savor of godliness wherever he goes. Hypocrites can change themselves into all shapes, and be as their company is; serious in one company and vain in another. He who reverences a Deity, is alike godly in all places. A steady pulse shows health: a steady walk shows grace. If a godly man is providentially placed among the wicked, he will not coalesce with them — but in his deportment displays a majesty of holiness.

Answer 5. He who fears God — is godly in the position where God has set him. Take an instance in Joseph: 'I fear God' (Gen. 42:18). And see a pattern of relative sanctity: he showed towards his master fidelity, towards his mistress purity, towards his father duty, towards his brethren generosity. A godly man makes his family, a training ground of piety (Psalm 102:1).

Answer 6. He who fears God, dares not neglect family or closet prayer. 'I give myself unto prayer' (Psalm 109:4). Prayer whispers in God's ears! Prayer is private conference with God. Why was Nymphas' house called a church (Col. 4:15). Because it was consecrated by prayer. A gracious soul puts forth fervent sighs in prayer (Rom. 8:26). And surely that prayer soonest pierces heaven — which pierces one's own heart.

If prayer be made the touchstone — then the number of those who fear God is but small. Are there not many prayerless families in this city and nation? 'You cast off fear, you restrain prayer' (Job 15:4). When men restrain prayer, they cast off the fear of God. It is the brand set upon reprobates, that 'they do not call on the Lord' (Psalm 14:4).

Answer 7. He who fears God will not oppress his neighbor. 'You shall not oppress one another; but you shall fear your God' (Lev. 25:17). How can he be holy — who is not just? A saint — yet an extortioner, is a contradiction. The fear of God would cure oppression. 'Will you even sell your brethren? Ought you not to walk in the fear of our God?' (Neh. 5:8-9). As if Nehemiah had said, If you had the fear of God, you would not be so wicked, you would not rise upon the ruins of others and — to wrong them, damn yourselves.

Answer 8. He who fears God — is given to works of mercy. The fear of God is always joined with love to our brethren. Grace may have a trembling hand — but it does not have a withered hand; it stretches itself out to relieve the needy, 'Pure and undefiled religion before our God and Father is this: to look after orphans and widows in their distress' (James 1:27). To visit them is not only to go to see them in affliction. Our Savior expounds what visiting is in Matthew 25:36, 'You visited me'; how was that? 'I was an hungry, and you gave me food' (verse 35). Good works are not the cause of our justification, but they are the evidence of our justification. How far are they from the fear of God, who are hard-hearted to Christ's poor! You may as well extract oil out of a flint — as the golden oil of charity out of their flinty hearts! The rich man denied Lazarus a crumb of bread — and he was denied a drop of water (Luke 16:21).

Answer 9. He who fears God—would rather displease man, than God. 'The midwives feared God, and did not as the king of Egypt commanded them—but saved the men children alive' (Exod. 1:17). What, not obey the king's command! How could this stand with their allegiance? Very well, because it was an unlawful command. The king had ordered them to put to death the Hebrew males—which they dared not do, for fear of incurring God's displeasure. King Nebuchadnezzar erected a golden image to be worshiped—but the three Hebrew children (or rather champions) said, 'Be it known unto you, O king, that we will not serve your gods—nor worship the golden image which you have set up!' (Dan. 3:18). They would rather burn—than bow! He who fears God, knows it is best to please God. He is the best Friend—but the worst Enemy!

Answer 10. The fear of God will make a man fear these six things:

1. Satan's snares

2. His own heart

3. Death

4. Judgment

5. Hell

6. Heaven

1. The fear of God will make a man afraid of Satan's snares. He has the eye of faith to see these snares, and the wing of fear to fly from them! Fear gives wings to the feet. 'We are not ignorant of his devices' (2 Cor. 2:11). The word means 'subtle stratagems'. Satan is called the 'old Serpent' (Rev. 12:9). Though he has lost his holiness, he has not lost his deceitfulness. His snares are so cunningly laid, that without the guidance of God's fear, we cannot escape them.

a. One subtle artifice of Satan—is to bait his hook with religion. He can change his flag, and hang out Christ's colors; here he transforms himself into an angel of light (2 Cor. 11:14). The devil tempts men to evil, 'that good may come' of it (Rom. 3:8). He whistles them into the snare of preferment, that hereby they may be in a capacity of doing God more service. The white devil is worst! Who would suspect Satan when he comes as a minister, and quoting Scripture?

b. Another snare of Satan—is to tempt to sin under a plea of necessity. Lot offered to expose his daughters to the lusts of the Sodomites, that he might preserve his angel-guests who were come into his house (Gen. 19:8). Did not Satan instigate him to this? Necessity will not excuse impiety.

c. Another snare of Satan—is to color over sin with the pretense of virtue. Alcibiades hung a finely embroidered curtain over a foul picture full of dragons and satyrs. Satan puts good names on sin, as physicians call that film in the eye which hinders the sight a 'pearl' in the eye. Satan colored over Jehu's ambition with the name of zeal (2 Kings 10:16). He makes men believe that revenge is valor, or that covetousness is frugality; as if one should write 'medicine' upon a bottle of poison!

d. Another snare of Satan—is to carry on his mischievous designs under a pretense of friendship. He puts off his lion's skin, and comes in sheep's clothing. Thus Satan came to Christ: 'Command that these stones be made bread' (Matt 4:3). As if he had said, 'I see you are hungry; I therefore out of pity, counsel you to get something to eat—turn these stones to bread, that your hunger may be satisfied.' But Christ spied the serpent in the temptation, and repulsed him. Thus Satan came to Eve in the guise of a friend. He said of the tree in the midst of the garden, 'You shall not surely die ... you shall be as gods' (Gen. 3:4-5). As if to say, 'I persuade you only to that which will put you into a better condition than now you are; eat of the tree of knowledge and it will make you omniscient!' What a kind devil was here! But Eve found a worm in the apple!

e. A fifth snare — if Satan cannot take a Christian off from duty, he will put him on too far in duty. Humiliation is a duty — but Satan suggests that the soul is not humbled enough: and indeed he never thinks it humbled enough, until it despairs. Satan comes thus to a man: 'Your sins have been great — so your sorrow should be proportionate. But is it so? Can you say you have been as great a mourner — as you have been a sinner? What is a drop of your sorrow — compared to a sea of your sin? This is laid only as a snare. The subtle enemy would have a Christian weep himself blind, and in a desperate plight, throw away the anchor of hope. And if Satan has such fallacies, and as a decoy draws so many millions into his snares, is there not cause of jealous fear lest we should be trapped? The fear of God — will make us fear hell's stratagems. Satan's snares are worse than his darts!

2. The fear of God will make a man afraid of his own heart. Luther used to say, that he feared his own heart more than the pope or cardinals! 'The heart is deceitful above all things' (Jer. 17:9).

It is 'deceitful'. The word signifies, it is a 'Jacob' or 'supplanter'. As Jacob supplanted his brother, and took away the blessing, so our hearts would supplant and beguile us.

'Above all things': there is deceit in weights, deceit in friends; but the heart has an art of deceiving beyond all. In the best hearts there is some fallaciousness. David was upright in all things, 'except in the affair concerning Uriah the Hittite' (1 Kings 15:5). A godly man, knowing there is a measure of this deceit in his heart, fears himself! The flesh is a bosom-traitor. No man can fathom what evil is in his heart. 'Is your servant a dog!' (2 Kings 8:13). Hazael could not believe his heart could give birth to such monsters. If one had come to Noah and said, 'You will be drunk shortly'; he would have said, 'Is your servant a dog?' No man knows the depth of evil which in his heart, or what scandal he may fall into — if God should leave him. Christ warns his own apostles to 'take heed of surfeiting and drunkenness' (Luke 21:34). A godly man therefore fears his heart with a fear of caution and jealousy.

The heart is not only stubborn — but subtle. Let us a little trace this impostor, and see if there is not cause to fear it. The heart shows its deceitfulness regarding sinful things — and sacred things.

The heart shows its deceitfulness regarding sinful things, this deceit is in the hiding of sin, as Rahab hid the spies in the flax (Josh. 2:6). So the heart hides sin. And how does it hide sin? Just as Adam hid himself under fig leaves — so the heart hides sin under the fig leaves of rationalization and excuses. 'It was done against my will; or done in a passion; or it was done along with others.' Aaron blamed his sin in the making of the golden calf, upon the people: 'The people are set on mischief' (Exod. 32:22). And Adam tacitly blamed his sin upon God himself: 'The woman You gave to be with me — she gave me some fruit from the tree, and I ate' (Gen. 3:12), as if to say, 'If You had not given me this tempting woman — I would not have eaten!'

The heart's deceit is seen in flattering us. It will make us believe we are not so bad as we are. The physician deceives the patient when he tells him that his disease is not so dangerous, when he is falling into the hands of death! The heart will tell a man that he is free from theft, when yet he robs others of their good name. The heart will tell a man that he is free from drunkenness when, though he will not be drunk with wine, he will be drunk with passion. Thus the heart is a flattering mirror to make one look better than he is! Is there not cause to suspect this impostor!

Secondly, the heart shows its deceitfulness regarding sacred things. It will be ready to put us off with counterfeit grace. Many have been deceived in taking false money; and many, it is to be feared, have been deceived in taking false grace.

The heart is ready to deceive with a false repentance. A sinner is troubled a little for sin, or rather the consequences of it, and perhaps sheds a few tears, and now his heart soothes him – and tells him that he is a true penitent. But every legal terror is not true repentance: 'They were pricked in their hearts' (Acts 2:37); yet after this, 'Peter said unto them repent' (verse 38). If every slight trouble for sin were true repentance – then Judas and Cain may be enrolled in the number of penitents. Evangelical repentance works a change of heart (1 Cor. 6:11). It produces sanctity. But the false penitent, though he has trouble of spirit – yet has no transformation or change of heart and life. He has a weeping eye – but an adulterous heart. Ahab fasts and puts on sackcloth – but after this, he puts the prophet Micah in prison (1 Kings 22:27).

The heart is apt to deceive with a false faith; it would put the dead child in the place of the living child. Those in the second chapter of John are said to believe; but Christ did not believe their faith (John 2:24). True faith, as it casts itself into Christ's arms to embrace him, so it casts itself at Christ's feet to serve him. But spurious faith, though it is forward to receive Christ's benefits – yet it plucks the crown from his head – and will not submit to his authority! (Isaiah 9:6). It would have him a Priest to save him – but not as a King upon his throne to rule him (Zech. 6:13).

Thus the heart is full of fallacies; he who fears God, fears his heart lest it should rob him of the blessing.

3. The fear of God – will make a man fear death. We should fear death, first, because it is such a serious thing, it is the inlet to eternity and puts us into an unalterable state!

Secondly, because of its proximity. It is nearer to us than we are aware; it may be within a few hours march of us! God may this night say, 'Give an account of your stewardship!' And what if death should come before we are ready?

Thirdly, because after death there is nothing to be done for our souls. There is no repenting in the grave: 'In the grave, where you are going, there is neither working nor planning' (Eccles. 9:10). So death is to be feared with a holy and pious fear.

Question: How far may a child of God fear death?

Answer 1. So far as the fear of death is a curb bit, to keep him from sin. A believer may lawfully make use of all means to deter him from sin. There is no stronger antidote against sin – than the fear of death. 'Am I sinning today – and tomorrow may be dying – and going to judgment!'

Answer 2. A child of God may so far fear death, as it makes him die to the world. The fear of death should sound a retreat and call us off from worldly vanities. What is the world? We must leave it shortly, and all we will then have, is our burying place (Gen. 49:30).

Answer 3. A child of God may so far fear death, as this fear fits him more for death. Jacob feared his brother Esau's coming against him, and he prepared to meet him, addressing himself to prayer (Gen. 32:7, 24). So when we fear death's coming, and we prepare to meet it – we set oh soul in order. This is a godly fear of death.

But this fear of death in the godly must he mixed with hope. The nature of death to a believer, is quite changed. Death is in itself a curse – but God has turned this curse into a blessing. To a child of God, death is not a destruction, but a deliverance. When the mantle of his flesh drops off, he ascends in a fiery chariot to heaven!

4. The fear of God—will make a man fear judgment. Anselm spent most of his thoughts upon the Day of Judgment; and Jerome thought he always heard that voice sounding in his ears, 'Arise you dead—and come to judgment!' That there shall be such a day is evident:

a. From God's veracity: he who is the Oracle of truth has asserted it: 'For he comes—for he comes to judge the earth' (Psalm 96:13). There is duplication here, firstly, to show the certainty: 'he comes, he comes'. It is an indubitable maxim. Secondly, to show the speediness, 'he comes, he comes', the time draws near—it is almost daybreak, and the judge is ready to take the bench! (James 5:9). God's decree cannot be reversed!

b. There shall he such a day for the vindication of God's justice. Things seem to be done in the world, very unequally: the godly suffer, the wicked prosper. Atheists are ready to think God has thrown aside the government of the world—and does not mind how things are transacted here below. Therefore there must he a judicial process, that God may undeceive the world and set all things right.

c. That there shall be such a day is evident by the principles engrafted in a natural conscience. When Paul reasoned of judgment to come, 'Felix trembled' (Acts 24:25). The prisoner at the bar—made the judge tremble! That a wicked man dying is so surprised with terrors—from where does this arise, but from a secret apprehension of ensuing judgment!

It will be a great judgment. Never was the like seen! We must all appear before the judgement seat! (2 Cor. 5:10). There is no fleeing, no absconding, no bribing, no appearing by a proxy—but all must make their personal appearance. Those who were above trial here, and the law could not reach them, must appear before the tribunal of heaven!

Who shall be the Judge? Jesus Christ (John 5:22.; Acts 17:31). 'He has appointed a day, in the which he will judge the world—by that man whom he has ordained.' Christ the Judge, is called man because he shall judge the world in a visible shape. He must be both God and man: he must be God, that he may see men's hearts—and he must be man, that he himself may be seen.

What a solemn day will this be, when Christ shall sit upon the bench of judicature! He will judge 'righteously' (Psalm 9:8). Though he himself was wronged, he will do no wrong. And he will judge thoroughly: 'Whose fan is in his hand and he will thoroughly purge his floor' (Matt. 3:12). He will see what is wheat—and what is chaff; who have his image upon them—and who the mark of the beast. Surely, the fear of God will cause a holy trembling at the thoughts of this day!

Question: In what sense should those who fear God—fear the Day of Judgment?

Answer: Not with a fear of dread or despondency, for the Day of Judgment will be a Jubilee—a blessed comfortable day to them! The thrush sings at the approach of rain—and so may believers at the approach of Judgment. Christ who is their Judge is also their Redeemer and Advocate. But,

a. The godly should so fear judgment as every day to renew their sorrow for sin. They have sins which creep upon them daily—and they must with Peter weep bitterly. They must steep their souls in the salty tears of repentance. It would be sad to be found at the last day, in any sin unrepented of.

b. The godly should so fear the Day of Judgment as to make them afraid of sins of omission. Not dressing a wound brings death. Not discharging duty may bring damnation. You may read the solemn process at the last day: 'I was hungry and you gave Me nothing to eat; I was thirsty and you gave Me nothing to drink; I was a stranger and you didn't take Me in; I was naked and you didn't clothe Me, sick and in prison and you didn't take care of Me' (Matt. 25:42). The charge here brought in, is for sins of omission. Christ does not say, 'You took away my food from me' — but 'You gave me nothing to eat'; He does not say, 'You put me in prison' — but 'You did not visit me.' The sins of omission condemned them. Not praying in the family, not attending the means of grace, not giving alms, will be the fatal indictment.

c. The godly should so far fear the Day of Judgment as to make them afraid of pretending in religion. For at that day, false hearts will be unmasked. Why did Paul walk with such integrity? 'You are witnesses and God also, how holily, and justly, and unblamably we behaved ourselves among you' (1 Thess. 2:10). What was the cause of this? Surely a fear of the approaching Judgment Day: 'For we must all appear before the judgement seat of Christ!' (2 Cor. 5:10). The word in the original means we must be made manifest, our hearts must be laid open before men and angels. Such is the witchcraft of hypocrisy, that it is hard in this life, to know who is a false professor, and who is sincere. But shortly there will be a full revealing. It is good for God's people so to fear judgment, as to make them strive against deceit and hypocrisy; for then the hypocrite will be found out.

5. The fear of God — makes a man fear hell. Hell is called the 'place of torment' (Luke 16:28). Not only notoriously wicked sinners — but such as fear God, ought to fear hell: 'I say unto you my friends, fear him who has power to cast into hell!' (Luke 12:4).

Question: How far should God's people fear hell?

Answer: Not so far, as to let go their hope. A mariner fears a storm — but not so as to throw away his anchor. Such as fear God — should fear hell in four ways.

a. Those who fear God ought to fear hell — as that which they have deserved. Their sins have merited hell. Woe to the holiest man alive — if God should weigh him in the balance of his justice!

b. Those who fear God ought to fear hell — insofar as this is a means to make them shake off spiritual sloth. This sleeping disease is apt to seize upon God's own people; 'the wise virgins slumbered' (Matt. 25:5). Now, so far as the fear of hell is an alarm or a warning-bell to awaken the godly out of security, and make them run faster to heaven, so far it is a godly and blessed fear.

c. The fear of hell is good in the godly — insofar as it makes them afraid of being in the number of those who shall go to hell. There are certain people who are in danger of hell:

First, those who have their heaven in this life: 'You who are given to pleasure' (Is. 47:8). Epicures swim in sensual delights; they would rather displease God — than deny the flesh. These shall take up their quarters in hell. 'The Lord, the Lord Almighty, called you on that day to weep and to wail, to tear out your hair and put on sackcloth. But see, there is joy and revelry, eating of meat and drinking of wine! 'Let us eat and drink,' you say, 'for tomorrow we die!' The Lord Almighty has revealed this in my hearing: 'Until your dying day this sin will not be atoned for,' says the Lord, the Lord Almighty!' (Isaiah 22:12-14) That is, this sin shall not be done away by any sacrifice.

Second, they are in danger to be cast into hell who live in the sin of adultery (Prov. 22:12). Those who burn in lust — shall burn in hell! 'Lord knows how to keep the unrighteous under punishment until the Day of Judgment, especially those who follow the polluting desires of the flesh.' (2 Pet. 2:9-10). See the corruption of man's nature! Instead of drinking water out of his own cistern, he loves stolen waters (Prov. 9:17). The same Latin word signifies a stable and a whore-house — both are for beasts!

Third, they are likely to go to hell who, by giving bad example, cause others to sin. Bad example, like the plague, is contagious. Great men are mirrors — by which the common people dress themselves. Such as give bad example, have not only their own sins, but the sins of others to answer for. That doubtless was the reason why the rich man entreated Abraham that one might go from the dead to preach to his brethren (Luke 16:27), and not that he had love to their souls, but because, while he was alive, he had occasioned his brethren's sins by his wicked example, and knew that their coming to hell would increase his torment!

Fourth, they are likely to go to hell who live and die in the contempt of God's Word. Ministers have preached until their lungs are exhausted — but men stop their ears and harden their hearts! 'They made their hearts as an adamant stone' (Zech. 7:12). Hardness of heart lies in the insensibility of the conscience (Eph. 4:19), and the inflexibility of the will (Jer. 44:16-17). Obdurate sinners shake out the arrow of conviction and scorn all godly reproof. When the prophet cried to the altar of stone, it broke apart (1 Kings 13:2). But sinners hearts do not break! These are likely to have the wrath of God flame about their ears! 'This will take place at the revelation of the Lord Jesus from heaven with His powerful angels, taking vengeance with flaming fire on those who don't know God and on those who don't obey the gospel of our Lord Jesus. These will pay the penalty of everlasting destruction, away from the Lord's presence and from His glorious strength!' (2 Thess. 1 :7-8).

Fifth, they shall go to hell who fall away (Mat. 13:6). Because they had no root — they withered. Flowers in a waterpot will keep green and fresh a while — but having no root, they wither. Demas made a fair show a while — but ended as the silkworm which, after all her fine spinning, at last becomes a common fly. 'If we deliberately keep on sinning after we have received the knowledge of the truth, no sacrifice for sins is left, but only a fearful expectation of judgment and of raging fire that will consume the enemies of God!' (Heb. 10:26-27).

Thus we see who are likely to be thrown into hell. Now it is good for the godly so to fear hell — as to fear to be in the number of those who shall go to hell.

d. The fear of hell is good in the godly — insofar as it is a fear mixed with rejoicing. 'Rejoice with trembling' (Psalm 2:11). A believer's fear of hell must he like the fear of the two Marys going from the sepulcher: 'They departed from the sepulcher with fear and great joy' (Matt. 28:8). With fear, because they had seen an angel; and with joy, because Christ was risen! So must the godly look on hell, with fear and joy. With fear, because of the fire; and with joy, because Christ has freed them from hell. A man who stands upon a high rock, fears when he looks down into the sea — yet rejoices that he is not there drowning in the waves. So a child of God, when he looks down into hell by contemplation, may fear because of the dreadfulness of the torment; yet this fear should be mingled with joy, to think he shall never come there! Jesus has delivered him 'from the wrath to come' (1 Thess. 1:10).

6. The fear of God will make a man fear Heaven. You may say, 'that is strange — we should rather hope for heaven.' No, a regenerate person is to fear heaven — lest he fall short of it. 'Therefore, while the promise remains of entering His rest, let us fear so that none of you should miss it!' (Heb. 4:1). It is a metaphor taken from athletes who, growing weary and lagging behind, come short of the prize. Who had more hope of heaven than Paul? Yet he was not without his fears: 'I discipline my body and bring it under strict control, so that after preaching to others, I myself will not be disqualified' (1 Cor. 9:27). And well may he who shall go to heaven, fear less he miss it, if you consider:

a. It is possible for many who make a splendid profession, to lose heaven. What do you think of the foolish virgins? They are called virgins because they were not tainted with any gross sin; yet these virgin-professors were shut out of heaven! (Matt. 25:10). Balaam, a prophet; and Judas, an apostle — were both shut out of heaven! We have seen some ships which had glorious names given them, the Good-speed, the Hope, the Safeguard — which were lost at sea.

b. It is possible to come near to heaven — yet fall short of it: 'You are not far from the kingdom of God' (Mark 12:34); yet he was not near enough! Men may commend the ministry of the Word, have their affections moved at an ordinance, and in outward show out-do the children of God (Num. 23:1-2); yet, not having the oil of sincerity in their vessels, they will fall short of eternal happiness. And how dismal is that — to lose God, to lose their souls, to lose their hopes! The millions of tears shed in hell — are not sufficient to bewail the loss of heaven! Well may such as have heaven in them, fear their coming short of it.

So much, then, for this sixth use, trial.

Question. How shall we arrive at this blessed fear?

Answer.

1. Let us set God ever in our eye — study his immensity! He is God Almighty (Gen. 17:1). He gives laws to the angels, binds the consciences of men, cuts off princes 'He breaks the spirit of rulers; he is feared by the kings of the earth.' (Psalm 76:12). The thoughts of God's incomprehensible greatness, should strike a holy awe in our hearts! Elijah wrapped his face in a mantle when God's glory passed by. The reason men do not fear God — is because they entertain slight thoughts of him! 'You thought that I was altogether like you!' (Psalm 50:21).

2. Let us pray for this fear of God, which is the root of all holiness, and the mother of all wisdom. 'Give me an undivided heart — that I may fear your name' (Psalm 86:11). The Lord has promised to put his fear in our heart (Jer. 32:40). Let us pray over this promise. While some pray for riches, and others for children — let us pray for a heart to fear God!

To conclude this, you who have this fear planted in your souls — bless God for it! 'You who fear the Lord — bless the Lord' (Psalm 135:20). God has done more for you than if he had made you kings and queens — and caused you to ride upon the high places of the earth! He has enriched you with that jewel which he bestows only upon the elect.

Oh, stand upon Mount Gerizim, blessing. The fear of God is an immortal seed springing up into glory! 'You who fear the Lord — praise him!' (Psalm 22:23). Begin the work of heaven now. Be spiritual choristers! Sound forth holy doxologies and triumphs! Say, as David, 'My mouth is full of praise and honor to You all day long!' (Psalm 71:8).

God has but little praise in the world. Who should thus pay that which is due to him — if not those who fear him?

Part 2: The Godly Should Speak of God

Having done with the character of the godly in general terms, I proceed next to their special characteristics: 'Then those who feared the Lord talked with each other'. When the wicked said, 'It is vain to serve God', then 'Then those who feared the Lord talked often with each other'. The meaning of this word, they 'talked often', is they discoursed piously together; their tongues were divinely tuned by the Holy Spirit.

Christians, when they meet together, should be much in 'holy conference'. This is not only an advice — but a charge: 'You must commit yourselves wholeheartedly to these commands I am giving you today. Repeat them again and again to your children. Talk about them when you are at home and when you are away on a journey, when you are lying down and when you are getting up again.' (Deut. 6:6). Indeed, where there is grace poured in — it will effuse out! Grace changes the language — and makes it spiritual. When the Holy Spirit came upon the apostles, they 'spoke with other tongues' (Acts 2:4). Grace makes Christian speak with other tongues. A godly Christian not only has the law of God in his heart (Psalm 37:31) — but in his tongue! (verse 30). The body is the temple of God (1 Cor. 6:19). The tongue is the organ in this temple, which sounds in holy discourse! 'The tongue of the just is as choice silver' (Prov. 10:20). He drops silver sentences, enriching others with spiritual knowledge! 'The good man brings good things out of the good stored up in him; and the evil man brings evil things out of the evil stored up in him. But I tell you that men will have to give account on the Day of Judgment for every careless word they have spoken. For by your words you will be acquitted, and by your words you will be condemned.' (Matt. 12:35-37). In the godly man's heart, there is a treasury of goodness, and this is not like a bag of hidden money — but he brings something out of the treasury within — to the enriching of others.

Grace is of the nature of fire, which will not be pent up. Like new wine, grace requires a vent (Acts 4:20). There is a principle within, which constrains to holy conference: 'I am full of words, and my spirit compels me to speak.' (Job 32:18).

The first use of this doctrine is for information. It shows the character and temper of true saints: they 'speak often one to another'; their lips drop as a honeycomb. The country to which a man belongs — is known by his language. He who belongs to the Jerusalem above — speaks the language of Canaan. None of God's children are dumb; their mouth is a 'wellspring of wisdom' (Prov. 18:4).

The second use is reproof. Here I may draw up a bill of indictment against five sorts of people.

1. Such as are silent in matters of true religion. They would be counted godly — but he must have good eyes, who can see it! I know not whether it is ignorance or timidity — which sets godly discourse aside. Many are as mute in piety — as if their tongues did cleave to the roof of their mouth! Had they any love to God, or had they ever tasted how sweet the Lord is — their mouth would 'talk of his righteousness' (Psalm 71:24).

Friends, what should concern us but salvation? What are the things of this world? They are neither real or lasting (Proverbs 23:5). Do we not see men heap up riches, and suddenly death, as God's sergeant, arrests them! What should we talk of — but the things pertaining to the kingdom of God? Let this cause blushing among Christians — that their meetings are so unprofitable, because they leave God out of their discourse!

Why is there no godly conference? Have you so much spiritual knowledge, that you need not have it increased? Have you so much faith, that you need not have it strengthened? Silence in piety — is a loud sin! We read of one who was possessed with a dumb devil (Mark 9:17). How many are spiritually possessed with a dumb devil!

2. It is a rebuke to such as, when they meet together, instead of speaking of heaven, have idle, frothy discourse! They talk — but do not say anything spiritually profitable. Their lips do not drop as a honeycomb. Their speaking is no more profitable, than an infant's mutterings. 'They speak vanity everyone with his neighbor' (Psalm 12:2). If Christ should ask some today, as he did the two disciples going to Emmaus, 'What are you discussing together as you walk along?' (Luke 24:17); they could not answer as those did, 'The things concerning Jesus the Nazarene!' No, perhaps they were talking about toys, or new fashions! If idle words must be accounted for (Matt. 12:36), Lord, what an account will some have to give!

3. It reproves the avaricious person who, instead of speaking of heaven, talks of nothing but the world. The farmer speaks of his plough and yoke of oxen; the tradesman of his wares and drugs; but not a word of God. 'The one who is from the earth belongs to the earth — and speaks as one from the earth.' (John 3:31). Many are like the fish in the gospel — which had money in its

mouth! (Matt. 17:27). They talk only of secular things, as if they imagined to fetch happiness out of that earth which God has cursed!

Seneca, being asked of what country he was, answered he was 'a citizen of this world'. We may know many to be citizens of this world — their speech betrays them! O souls bent towards the earth and empty of spiritual things!

4. It reproves those who do indeed speak often to one another — but with EVIL speech. 'The tongue also is a fire, a world of evil among the parts of the body. It corrupts the whole person, sets the whole course of his life on fire, and is itself set on fire by hell.' (James 3:6).

i. They speak one to another in harsh words. Their words should be like the 'waters of Shiloh — which go softly' (Isaiah 8:6). But too often they are fierce and biting. Water, when it is hot, soon boils over; when the heart is heated with anger — it soon boils over in furious speech!

Many curse in their anger. The tongue is made in the fashion of a sword — and it cuts like a sword! Angry words often harm the one who utters them. Rehoboam with one churlish word, lost ten tribes. A fiery spirit is unsuitable to the Master we serve — 'the Prince of Peace'; and to his message — 'the gospel of peace'. Such whose tongues are set on fire, let them take heed that they do not one day in hell, desire a drop of water to cool their tongue! (Luke 16:24).

ii. They speak one to another in a bad sense, who murmur and complain one to another. They do not complain of their sins — but their vain desires. Murmuring proceeds from unbelief: 'They did not believe his word: but murmured' (Psalm 106:24-25). When men distrust God's promises, they murmur at his providences. This is a sin God can hardly bear! 'How long shall I bear with this evil congregation, which murmurs against me?' (Num. 14:27). Israel's speeches were venomous, and God punished them with venomous serpents! (1 Cor: 10:10).

iii. They speak one to another in a bad sense who give vent to filthy, corrupt language. The heart is a cask full of wickedness, and the tongue is the tap which lets it flow out! When the face breaks out in sores and pimples — it shows that the blood is corrupt. When men break forth in filthy speech — it shows the heart is corrupt. We read that the lips of the leper were to be covered (Lev. 13:45). It would be a blessing — if we could cover the filthy lips of our spiritual lepers!

iv. They speak one to another in a bad sense who, instead of seasoning their words with grace, mix them with swearing. Swearers rend and tear God's name, and, like mad dogs — fly in the face of God! 'Because of swearing the land mourns' (Jer. 23:10). Some think it fine speech, to mix every sentence with an oath; as if they would go to hell genteelly. 'But', says one, 'it is my custom to swear.' Is this an excuse — or an aggravation of the sin? If a malefactor should he arraigned for robbery, and he should say to the judge, 'Spare me — for it is my custom to rob and steal', the judge would say, 'You shall all the more die!' For every oath that a man swears, God puts a drop of wrath into his vial!

v. It reproves those who, instead of speaking in a holy manner one to another, speak of others:

First, they speak of others in censuring. Some make it a part of their religion to talk about and criticize others. They do not imitate their graces — but speak upon their failings. God grant that professors may wash their hands of this! Were people's hearts more humble — their tongues would he more charitable! It is the sign of a hypocrite — to criticize others and commend himself.

Secondly, they speak of others in slandering. 'You slander your own mother's son!' (Psalm 50:20). Slandering is when we speak to the harm of another — and speak that which is not true. Worth is blasted by slander! Holiness itself is no shield from this sin. The lamb's innocency will not preserve it from the wolf! Job calls slandering 'the scourge of the tongue' (Job 5:21). You may smite a man—yet never touch him! A slanderer wounds another's reputation, and no physician can heal these wounds! The eye and the name—are two tender things. God takes it ill at our hands—to calumniate others, especially to slander those who help to keep up the credit of true religion: 'Were you not afraid to speak against my servant Moses?' (Num. 12:8). What, my servant, who has wrought so many miracles, whom I have spoken with face to face on the mount! Were you not afraid to speak against him!

The Greek word for slanderer signifies devil (1 Tim. 3:11). Slander is the devil's proper sin—he is 'the accuser of the brethren' (Rev. 12:10). The devil does not commit adultery—but he bears false witness. The slanderer may be indicted for clipping; he clips his neighbor's credit to make it weigh lighter. Our nature is prone to slander; but remember, it is just as much a sin in God's reckoning to break the Ninth Commandment, as the Eighth Commandment.

The third use is exhortation. Put this great duty into practice! Imitate these holy ones in the text, who 'spoke often one to another'. Jerome thinks they spoke something in defense of the providence of God; they vindicated God in his dealings, and exhorted one another not to be discouraged at the virulent speeches of the wicked—but still to hold on a course of piety. Thus, Christians, when you meet, give one another's souls a visit—impart your spiritual knowledge, impart your experiences to each other (Psalm 66:16). Samson having found honey, did not only eat of it himself—but carried it to his father and mother (Judges 14:9). Have you tasted the honey of the Word? Let others have a taste with you!

He who has been in a perfumer's shop does not only himself partake of those sweet fragrances—but some of the perfume sticks to his clothes, so that those who come near him partake of those perfumes. Just so, having ourselves partaken of the sweet savor of Christ's ointments, we should let others partake with us, and by our heavenly discourse, diffuse the perfume of piety to them. Let your words be seasoned with salt (Col. 4:6). Let grace be the salt which seasons your words and makes them savory. Christians should take all occasions for godly discourse, when they walk together, and sit at table together. This makes their eating and drinking to be 'to the glory of God' (1 Cor. 10:31). What makes it a communion of saints--but godly conversation?

But some may say they are barren of matter—and know not what to speak of. Have you walked so often through the field of Scripture—yet gathered no ears of corn? Have not you matter enough in the Word to furnish you with something to say? Let me suggest a few things to you. When you meet, speak one to another of the promises. No honey is so sweet—as that which drops from a promise! The promises are the support of faith, the springs of joy, and the saints royal charter. Are you citizens of heaven, and yet do not speak of your charter?

Speak of the preciousness of Christ. He is all beauty and love; he has laid down his blood as the price of your redemption. Have you a friend who has redeemed you—and yet you never speak of him?

Speak one to another of sin, what a deadly evil it is, how it has infected your virgin-nature, and turned it into a lesser hell.

Speak of the beauty of holiness, which is the souls embroidery, filling it with such orient splendor, as makes God and angels fall in love with it. The graces are the sacred characters of the divine nature.

Speak one to another of your souls: enquire whether they are in good health.

Speak about death and eternity: can you belong to heaven and not speak of your country?

Thus, you see, here is matter enough, for holy conference. Why then do you not maintain godly discourse? I believe that one main reason for the decay of the power of godliness, is a lack of Christian conference. People when they meet talk of vanities – but God and heaven are left out of their discourse! That I may persuade you in your conversations to put in a word about your souls – let me offer these few things for your consideration.

1. Holy conversation was the practice of the saints of old. Elijah and Elisha went on in godly discourse until the chariot of heaven came to part them (2 Kings 2:11). David's tongue was tuned to the language of Canaan, 'My tongue shall talk of your righteousness' (Psalm 71:24). The primitive Christians, into whatever company they came, spoke of a glorious kingdom they expected, so that some thought they were ambitious of worldly honor. But the kingdom they looked for, was not of this world but a kingdom with Christ in heaven. Jerome says that some of the Christian ladies spent much of their time in communing together, and would not let him alone – but continually asked him questions about their souls.

2. We are bidden to redeem the time (Eph. 5:16). The poets painted time with wings, because it flies so fast! Time lost must be redeemed, and is there any better way to redeem time, than to improve it in trading for heaven, and speaking of God and our souls?

3. Jesus Christ has left us a pattern. His words were perfumed with holiness, 'All bore him witness, and wondered at the gracious words which proceeded out of his mouth!' (Luke 4:22). Christ had grace poured into his lips (Psalm 45:2.). In all companies, he maintained godly discourse. When he sat on Jacob's well, he falls into an heavenly discourse with the woman of Samaria about the water of life (John 4:14). And so when Levi made him a feast (Luke 5:29), Christ feasts him in return – with heavenly discourse. And no sooner was Christ risen from the grave but he 'was speaking of the things pertaining to the kingdom of God' (Acts 1:3). The more spiritual we are in our speeches – the more we resemble Christ! Should not the members he like the Head? Christ will not be our Savior – unless we make him our pattern.

4. Godly discourse would prevent sinful discourse. Much sin passes in ordinary talk – as gravel and mud pass along with water. How many are guilty of tongue-sins! Godly discourse would prevent evil – as labor prevents idleness. If we accustomed our tongues to the heavenly dialect, the devil would not have so much power over us.

5. We may somewhat have a knowledge of men's hearts – by their common discourse. Words are the looking-glass of the mind. As you may judge of a face by the mirror, whether it be fair or foul; so by the words – we may judge of a man's heart. A lascivious tongue shows a lustful heart; an earthly tongue shows a covetous heart; a gracious tongue shows a gracious heart. The Ephraimites were known by their pronunciation, saying 'sibboleth' for 'shibboleth' (Judg. 12:6). So by the manner of our speech – it may be known to whom we belong. The tongue is the index of the heart! If you broach a cask, that which is within, will come out. By that which comes out of the mouth – you may guess what is within, in the heart! 'Of the abundance of the heart – the mouth speaks' (Luke 6:45).

6. Godly discourse is beneficial. 'The tongue of the wise brings healing.' (Proverbs 12:18) A word spoken in season may make such a powerful impression upon another's heart, which will do him good all his life. One single coal is apt to die – but many coals put together keep in the heat. Christians by their heavenly talk may 'blow up' one another's grace into a flame!

When the daughters of Jerusalem had conversed a while with the spouse, and had heard her describe Christ's admirable beauty, their affections began to be inflamed, and they would seek him with her. 'Where is your beloved gone, O fairest among women – that we may seek him with you?' (Cant. 6:1).

A Christian by divine discourse may enlighten another when he is ignorant; warm him when he is frozen; comfort him when he is sad; and confirm him when he is wavering. Latimer was much strengthened by discourse with Thomas Bilney in prison, and hearing his confession of faith. A godly life adorns true religion—a godly tongue propagates it! When the apostle would have us edify one another, what better way could he prescribe than this—to have such holy speeches proceed out of our mouths as might 'minister grace unto the hearers' (Eph. 4:29)?

7. We must be accountable to God for our speech. Words are judged light by men—but they weigh heavy in God's balance. By our words we shall be either saved or damned. 'For by your words you shall he justified, and by your words you shall be condemned' (Malt. 12:37). If our words have been seasoned with grace—then the acquitting sentence is likely to go on our side.

8. Godly discourse is a Christian's honor. The tongue is called our glory (Psalm 30:12), because it is the instrument of glorifying God. When our tongues are out of tune in murmuring, then they are not our glory; but when the organs sound in holy discourse, then our tongues are our glory.

9. Godly discourse will be a means to bring Christ into our company. While the two disciples were conferring about the death and sufferings of Christ, Jesus Christ himself came among them: 'While they communed together ... Jesus himself drew near, and went with them' (Luke 24:15). When bad discourse prevails—Satan draws near and makes one of the company; but when godly discourse is promoted—Jesus Christ draws near.

Let all that has been said excite us to godly discourse. Certainly, there is no better way than this to increase our stock of grace. Others by spending grow poor; but the more we spend ourselves in holy discourse, the richer we grow in grace; as the widow's oil, by pouring out, increased (2 Kings 4).

Question: How may godly conference be arrived at?

Answer 1. If you wish to discourse of true religion, get your minds well furnished with knowledge. Hereby, you will have a treasury to fetch from. 'I am pent up and full of words' (Job 32:18). Some are backward to speak of godly things for lack of matter. The empty vessel cannot run. If you would have your tongues run fluently in piety, they must be fed with a spring of knowledge. 'Let the word of Christ dwell in you richly' (Col. 3:16). In one of the miracles which Christ wrought, he first caused the water-pots to he filled with water, and then said, 'Now draw some out' (John 2:8). So we must first have our heads filled with knowledge, and then we shall be able to draw out to others in godly discourse.

Answer 2. If you would discourse readily in the things of God, make piety your delight. What men delight in—they will be speaking of. The sensualist speaks of his sports; the worldling of his rich purchase. Delight makes the tongue as the pen of a ready writer. The spouse, being delighted and enamored with Christ's beauty, could not conceal herself; she makes an elegant and passionate oration in the commendation of Christ. 'My beloved is white and ruddy, the chief among ten thousand! Yes—he is altogether lovely!' (Cant 5:10, 16).

Answer 3. Pray that God will both gift and grace you for Christian conference. 'O Lord, open my lips!' (Psalm 51:15). Satan has locked up men's lips. Pray that God will open them. Perhaps you pray that you may believe in Christ—but do you pray that you may commend him, and not be ashamed to speak of him before others? 'I will speak of your testimonies also before kings, and will not be ashamed' (Psalm 119:46). To end this, let me briefly insert two cautions:

Caution 1. I do not deny that it is lawful to confer of worldly business sometimes; communication requires conference. But with this proviso, that we should show more delight and earnestness in speaking of spiritual things than earthly things, remembering that the soul is far more valuable than the world.

Caution 2. When people speak of true religion, let it not be for any sinister, unworthy end, nor for ostentation — but for edification; and then, having your aim right, speak of the things of God, with life and affection, that others may perceive you feel those truths of which you speak.

A. The Godly Should Meditate on God's Name

The second special characteristic of the godly in the text is, 'they thought upon God's name.' These saints, when they were together — spoke of God; when they were alone — they thought of God. They 'thought upon his name'.

Question. What is meant by God's name?

Answer 1. By the name of God is meant his essence; God's name is put for God himself.

Answer 2. By the name of God is meant his glorious attributes, which are, as it were, the several letters of his name.

Answer 3. By the name of God is meant his worship and ordinances, where his name is called upon. 'Go to the place at Shiloh where I once put the Tabernacle to honor my name' (Jer. 7:12). That is, where I first set up my public worship.

Now this name of God, the saints in the text did contemplate, they thought upon his name. Thoughts are the first-born of the soul, the conceptions of the mind, the immediate fruit and outcome of a rational being. 'Thoughts are the representations of things in the imagination.' These devout souls in the text were chiefly busying their thoughts about God and heaven.

It is the inseparable sign of a godly man, to employ his chief thoughts about God: 'The thoughts of the righteous are right' (Proverbs 12:5); that is, they are set upon the right object. It is natural to think. Thoughts fly out of the mind — as sparks fly out of a furnace. The Hebrew word for a thought signifies the boughs of a tree, because thoughts shoot out from our minds as branches do from a tree. It is, I say, natural to think — but it is not natural to think of God; this is proper to a saint. His thoughts are sublime and seraphic — they fly to heaven.

The mind is a mint-house where thoughts are minted. David minted golden thoughts: 'I am still with you' (Psalm 139:18), that is, by divine contemplation. Thoughts are the travelers of the soul. David's thoughts kept on heavens road: 'I am continually with you' (Psalm 73:23). As the mariner's needle turns to the North Pole, so a saint's thoughts are still pointing towards God.

Question. Why is it, that the saints' thoughts mount up to God?

Answer 1. There will be this thinking on God — from those intrinsic perfections which are in him. The loveliness of the object, attracts the thoughts. God is the Supreme good. There is nothing but God, which is really worth thinking upon. 'You are my portion, O Lord' (Psalm 119:57). Will not a man's thoughts run upon his portion? A gracious soul has found pleasure in thinking on God (Psalm 63:5-6). He has had those transfigurations on the mount, those incomings of the Spirit, those enterings of God's love, those foretastes of glory — so that he cannot keep his thoughts off from God! To hinder him from thinking on God — is to bar him of all his pleasure.

Answer 2. There will be thinking on God — from the powerful operations of the Holy Spirit. We cannot of ourselves think a godly thought (2 Cor. 3:5) — but the Spirit elevates and fixes the heart on God: 'The Spirit lifted me up' (Ezek. 3:14). When you see the iron move upward — you know there has been some magnet drawing it. Just so, when the thoughts move upwards towards God, the Spirit has, as a divine magnet, drawn them!

First Use: Reproof.

Out of the quiver of this text I may draw several arrows of reproof:

1. It reproves those who do not think upon God's name. It is the brand-mark of a reprobate: 'God is not in all his thoughts' (Psalm 10:4). He endeavors to expunge and blot God out of his mind. Though he draws his breath from God—yet he does not think of him. His thoughts all shoot into the earth (Phil. 3:19). Had not sinners by their fall lost their head-piece, they would reason thus with themselves: 'Certainly God is best worth thinking on. Is there any excellency in the world? Then what excellency there is in God—who has made it! He gives the star its beauty, the flower its fragrance, food its pleasantness! If there is such deliciousness in the creature, what must there be in God! He must needs be better than all. O my soul, shall I admire the drop—and not the ocean? Shall I think of the workmanship, and not of him who made it?'

This forgetfulness of God, is the fruit of original sin—which has warped the soul, and taken it off from the right object.

2. It reproves such as indeed think of God—but who do not have RIGHT thoughts of him. As the Lord said to Eliphaz, 'You have not spoken of me what is right' (Job 42:7); so some think of God—but they do not think of him rightly.

1. They have low unworthy thoughts of God. They imagine God to be like themselves (Psalm 50:21). Men think that God is as short-sighted as they, and that he cannot see them through the thick canopy of the clouds. (He who makes a watch knows all the wheels and pins in it, and the spring which causes the motion.) God who is the inspector of the heart (Acts 1:24; 15:8) sees all the intrigues and private plots in the thoughts (Job 42:2; Amos 4:13). God knows the true motion of a false heart! 'I know, and am a witness—says the Lord' (Jer. 29:23).

2. Men have injurious thoughts of God.

First, they think that his ways are unjust. 'Yet you say—The way of the Lord is not just. Hear, O house of Israel—Is my way unjust? Is it not your ways that are unjust?' (Ezek. 18:25). Some call God's providence to the bar of reason, and judge his proceedings to be unjust. But God says, 'I will make justice the measuring line and righteousness the plumb line' (Isaiah 28:17). His ways are secret—but never unjust. God is most just in his way—when we think he is out of his way.

Secondly, they think that his ways are unprofitable. 'You have said—It is useless to serve God. What have we gained by keeping His requirements?' (Mal. 3:14). We cannot show our earnings. These are not right thoughts of God. Men think him to be a hard master; but God will be in no man's debt, he gives double pay: 'Neither do you kindle a fire on my altar for nothing' (Mal. 1:10).

3. It reproves such as, instead of thinking on God, have their minds wholly taken up with VAIN thoughts. Vain thoughts are the froth of the brain. 'How long shall your vain thoughts lodge within you?' (Jer. 4:14). I do not deny that vain thoughts may sometimes come into the best hearts—but they have a care to turn them out before night, that they do not lodge there. This denominates a wicked man. His thoughts dwell upon vanity; and well may his thoughts be said to be vain, because they do not turn to any profit! 'Vanity, and things wherein there is no profit' (Jer. 16:19). They are vain thoughts, which are about foolish things, and run all into straw. They are vain thoughts which do not better the heart, nor will give one drop of comfort at death, 'In that very day his thoughts perish' (Psalm 146:4). Vain thoughts are corrupt; they taint the heart and leave an evil tincture behind.

4. It reproves such as have, not only vain thoughts, but VILE thoughts.

Firstly, proud thoughts: while they view themselves in the mirror of self-love, they begin to take up venerable thoughts of themselves, and so pride fumes up into their head and makes them giddy! (Acts 5:36).

Secondly, impure thoughts. They think how to gratify their lusts — they 'make provision,' or as the word signifies, become 'caterers' for the flesh (Romans 13:14).

Sin begins in the thoughts. First men devise sin — then they act it (Mic. 2:1-2). For instance, if one seeks preferment, he thinks to himself by what ladder he may climb to honor. He will cringe and comply, and lay aside conscience, because he thinks that this is the way to rise. If a man would grow rich, he sets his thoughts to work how to obtain an estate. He will pull down his soul — to build up an estate. Would he wreak his malice on another? He frames a plan in his thoughts to harm him. As Jezebel (that painted harlot) when she would ruin Naboth, presently feigns a sham-plot and subtly thinks of a way how to dispatch him: 'She commanded: Call the citizens together for fasting and prayer and give Naboth a place of honor. Find two scoundrels who will accuse him of cursing God and the king. Then take him out and stone him to death!' (1 Kings 21:9-10).

Oh, the mischief of thoughts! A man may deny God in his thoughts: 'The fool has said in his heart — there is no God' (Psalm 14:1). He may commit adultery in his thoughts: 'Whoever looks on a woman to lust after her, has committed adultery with her in his heart' (Matt. 5:28). A man may murder another in his thoughts: 'Whoever hates his brother is a murderer' (1 John 3:15). O how much contemplative wickedness is in the world! Tremble at sinful thoughts. We startle at gross sin — but we are not troubled so much for sinful thoughts. Know firstly, that sin may be committed in the thoughts, though it never blossoms into outward act: 'The thought of foolishness is sin!' (Prov. 24:9). See this illustrated in two things:

Envy — the Jews envied Christ, for the fame of his miracles: 'Pilate knew that for envy they had delivered him' (Matt. 27:18). Here was sin committed in the thoughts. The Jews sinned by envying Christ, though they had never crucified him.

Discontentment--'The Lord accepted Abel and his offering, but he did not accept Cain and his offering. This made Cain very angry and dejected.' (Gen. 4:4-5). He maligned his brother, and his thoughts boiled up to discontentment. Here was sin committed in the thoughts. Cain sinned in being discontented, even if he had never murdered his brother.

Know that God will punish sinful thoughts. We say thoughts are free — and so they are in man's court; but God will punish for thoughts! It was set upon Herod's score, that he thought to destroy Christ under a pretense of worshiping him (Matt. 2:8).

Let us be humbled for the sins of our thoughts. 'If you have thought evil, lay your hand upon your mouth' (Proverbs 30:32); that is, humble and abase yourself before the Lord. The holiest people alive, need to be humbled for their thoughts:

First, for the instability of their thoughts. How do your thoughts dance up and down in prayer. It is hard to tie two godly thoughts together.

Secondly, for the impiety of their thoughts. In the fairest fruit, may be a worm — and in the best heart, evil thoughts may arise. Did men's hearts stand where their faces do, they would blush to look one upon another! Let us be deeply humbled for our thoughts. Let us look up to Christ, that he would stand between us and God justice, and that he would intercede for us, that the thoughts of our hearts may be forgiven.

Second use: Exhortation.

Let us think on God's Name; let us lock up ourselves with God every day; let our thoughts get wings and, with the birds of paradise, fly up towards heaven. Christians, look upon that day to be lost, in which you have not conversed with God in your thoughts; think of God in your closet, in your shop; trade above the moon. 'Isaac went out to meditate in the field' (Gen. 24:63). He walked in heaven by holy utterances. Our minds should be steeped in holy thoughts.

It is not enough to have a few transient thoughts of God — but there must be a fixing of our minds on God, until our hearts are warmed in love to him, and we can say, like those in Luke 24:32, 'Did not our heart burn within us!'

But what should the matter of our holy meditations be?

1. Think of God's immense being.

Adore his illustrious attributes, which are the beams by which the divine nature shines forth. Think of God's omniscience. He particularly and critically assesses all our actions, and notes them down in his book. Think of God's holiness, which is the most sparkling jewel of his crown (Exod. 15:11). Think of God's mercy: this makes all his other attributes sweet. Holiness without mercy, and justice without mercy, would be dreadful. Think of God's veracity: 'Abundant in truth' (Exod. 34:6); that is, God will be so far from coming short of his word, that he does more than he has said. He shoots beyond the promise, never short of it.

Think of the works of God: 'I will meditate also on all your works' (Psalm 77:12). God's works are bound up in three great volumes: Creation, Providence, Redemption. Here is sweet matter for our thoughts to expatiate upon.

To enforce the exhortation, let me propose some arguments and inducements to be frequent in the thoughts of God.

1. The reason why God has given us a thinking faculty, is that we may think on his Name. When our thoughts run out in vain things, we should think with ourselves thus: Did God give us this talent to misemploy? Did he give us thoughts that we should think of everything but him?

2. It we do not accustom ourselves to godly thoughts, we cannot be godly Christians. Thinking seriously on heavenly things — makes them stick in our minds, causes delight in them, and makes them nourish us. Musing on holy objects, is like digesting food, which turns it into nourishment. Without holy thoughts, there is no true religion. Can a man be pious and scarcely ever think of it?

3. We are deeply obliged to think on God. For, First, God is our Maker. 'It is he who has made us, and not we ourselves' (Psalm 100:3). Our bodies are God's fine needlework (Psalm 139:15). And as God has wrought the cabinet, so he has put a jewel in it — the precious soul. Has God made us — and shall not we think of him?

Secondly, God has sweetened our lives with various mercies. A city in Sicily is so finely situated, that the sun was never out of sight. Just so, God has so placed us by his providence, that the sunshine of his mercy is never out of sight. We are miraculously attended with his mercy! His mercy feeds us with the finest of the wheat — the bread of life; mercy guards us with a guard of angels; it makes the rock pour forth rivers of oil. Shall not the stream lead us to the fountain? Shall not we think of the God of our mercies? This is high ingratitude.

4. To have frequent and devout thoughts of God — evidences SINCERITY. No truer touchstone of sanctity exists, than the spirituality of the thoughts. What a man's thoughts are — that is the man! 'For as he thinks in his heart — so is he' (Proverbs 23:7). Thoughts are freer from hypocrisy, than words. One may speak well for applause, or to stand right in the opinion of others; but

when we are alone and think of God's Name, and admire his excellencies, this shows the heart to be right. Thoughts are freer from hypocrisy, than a man's external behavior. A man may be lovely in his outward behavior—yet have a covetous, revengeful mind! The acts of sin may be concealed, when the heart sits brooding upon sin. But to have the thoughts spiritualized and set upon God is a truer sign of sincerity—than a life free from vice.

What do your thoughts run upon? Where do they make their most frequent visits? Can you say, 'Lord, our hearts are still mounting up to heaven, our thoughts are lodged in paradise; though we do not see your face—yet we think on your Name!' This is a good evidence of sincerity. We judge men by their actions; God judges them by their thoughts!

5. Thinking much on God—would cure the love of the WORLD. Great things seem little—to him who stands high. To such as stand upon the top of the Alps, the great cities of Italy seem like little villages. For those who are mounted high in the contemplation of Christ and glory—how do the things of the world disappear, and even shrink into nothing! A soul elevated by faith above the visible planets, has the earth under his feet. A true saint intermeddles with secular affairs, more out of necessity than choice. Paul's thoughts are heavenly and sublime—he lived in the altitudes—and how he scorned the world! 'The world is crucified unto me!' (Gal. 6:14).

6. Thinking on God—would be expulsive of SIN. From whence is impiety—but from thoughtlessness? If only men carefully considered God's holiness and justice—would they dare sin at the rate they do! That which kept Joseph in check, was the thought of a sin-revenging God. When the delights of sin tickle us—let the thoughts of God come into men's minds, that he is both Spectator and Judge—and that after the golden crowns and women's hair—comes the lions teeth! (Rev. 9:8). This would put them into a cold sweat—and be as the angel's drawn sword! (Num. 22:31). It would scare them from sin!

7. Thinking on God, is an admirable means to increase our LOVE to God. As it was with David's meditations, 'As I was musing the fire burned' (Psalm 39:3); so it is with our musing on the Deity. While we are thinking on God—our hearts will kindle in love to him.

The reason our affections are so chilled and cold in religion—is that we do not warm them with thoughts of God. Hold a magnifying glass to the sun, and the glass burns that which is near to it. So when our thoughts are lifted up to Christ, the Sun of righteousness, our affections are set on fire. No sooner had the spouse been thinking upon her Savior's beauty—but she fell into love-sickness. (Cant. 5:8). O saints, do but let your thoughts dwell upon the love of Christ, who passed by angels and thought of you; who was wounded that, out of his wounds, the balm of Gilead might come to heal you; who leaped into the sea of his Father's wrath, to save you from drowning in the lake of fire! Think of this unparalleled love, which sets the angels wondering—and see if it will not affect your hearts and cause tears to flow forth!

8. Thinking on God, will by degrees transform us into his image. As Jacob's flock looking on the rods which had white streaks conceived and brought forth like them (Gen. 30:39), so by contemplating God's holiness, we are in some measure changed into his likeness! 'Beholding as in a mirror the glory of the Lord—we are changed into the same image' (2 Cor. 3:18). The contemplative sight of God was transforming; they had some print of God's holiness upon them; as Moses when he had been on the mount with God, his face shone! (Exod. 34:35). What is godliness, but God-likeness? And who are so like him—as those that think on his name?

9. Thinking on God is sweet. It ushers in a secret delight to the soul! 'My meditation of him shall be sweet' (Psalm 104:34). He whose head gets above the clouds—has his thoughts lifted high, has God in his eye, is full of divine raptures, and cries out as Peter in the transfiguration, 'Lord,

it is good for us to be here!' Holy thoughts are the dove we send out of the ark of our souls –
and they return with an olive branch of peace. Some complain that they have no joy in their
lives. It is no wonder, when they are such strangers to heavenly contemplation! Would you
have God give you joy and comfort – and never think of him? Indeed Israel had manna
dropped into their tents, and they never thought of it; but God will not drop down this manna
of heavenly joy on that soul which seldom or never thinks of him.

Would you have your spirits cheerful? Let your thoughts be heavenly! The higher the lark
flies – the sweeter it sings. Just so, the higher a soul ascends in the thoughts of God – the
sweeter joy it has!

10. Thoughts of God will turn to the best account. Thoughts spent on the world are often in
vain. Some spend thoughts about laying up a portion for a child; and perhaps either it dies, or
lives to be a severe trial to them. Others beat their brains how to rise in politics – when royal
favor has shone upon them, all of a sudden, an eclipse comes about, the king's smile is turned
into a frown, and then their thoughts are frustrated!

How oft do men build castles in the air! But the thoughts of God will turn to a good account,
they augment sanctification, and bring satisfaction: 'You satisfy me more than the richest of
foods. I will praise you with songs of joy. I lie awake thinking of you, meditating on you
through the night' (Psalm 63:5-6). The thoughts we have of God in the time of health, will be a
comfort to us in the time of sickness.

11. God thinks of us – and shall not we think of him? 'The Lord thinks upon me!' (Psalm 40:17).
God thinks on us every morning; his mercies are 'new every morning' (Lam. 3:23). He gives us
night-mercies, he rocks us asleep every night: 'So he gives his beloved sleep' (Psalm 127:2). And
if we awaken, he gives 'songs in the night' (Job 35:10). If God is thinking of us day and night,
shall not we think of his Name? How can we forget a friend – who is ever mindful of us? 'I
know the thoughts that I think toward you, with the Lord are thoughts of peace' (Jer 29:11).
Though God is out of our sight – we are not out of his thoughts!

12. God will one day reckon with us, for our thoughts. He will say, 'I gave you a mental faculty.
What have you done with it?' If God asks a covetous man, 'What have your thoughts been?
Which way have your thoughts run?' He will answer, 'To heap up riches!' If God asks princes
and emperors, 'How have you employed your thoughts?' They will say, 'By our scepter – to
beat down the power of godliness.' What a dreadful account will these people have to give at
last! Not only men's actions – but their thoughts will accuse them! 'Their consciences also
bearing witness, and their thoughts now accusing, now even defending them!' (Romans 2:15).

13. Our thoughts of God shall not be lost. God accepts the thought – for the deed. David had a
good thought come into his mind to build God a house, and God took it as kindly as if he had
done it! 'Forasmuch as it was in your heart to build an house for my name, you did well in that
it was in your heart' (2 Chron. 6:8). When Christians have thoughts of promoting God's glory –
that they would do such good acts if it were in their power – the Lord looks upon it as if they
had done it. So that our thoughts of God are not lost.

Let us think of God in a right manner. A good medicine may be spoiled in the making. So may a
good duty be spoiled in the doing. Thoughts may be good for the matter of them – yet may be
faulty in the manner. I shall show you, first, how thoughts of God may fail in their manner.
There is a right manner of thinking upon God.

1. How thoughts of God may fail in their manner.

First, a man may think good thoughts of God — yet not intend his glory. Jehu had good thoughts come into his mind, to destroy the Baal worshipers — but his intent was to advance himself unto the throne! Bad aims spoil good actions!

Secondly, a man may have good thoughts of God — but they are forced. When one bleeds under God's afflicting hand, he may think of God — yet have no love to him. 'When he slew them — then they remembered that God was their rock, and the most high God their Redeemer: nevertheless they only flattered him with their mouth' (Psalm 78:34-36). These were good thoughts — but it was to pay God a compliment in order to get rid of the affliction.

Thirdly, a man may have thoughts of God — out of a design to stop the mouth of conscience. Conscience lashes the profane sinner: 'What! Are you so wicked as never to think of God, who indulges you with so many favors!' Hereupon, he may have a few good thoughts; but they are irksome to him — this is not from a principle of conscience — but to quiet conscience.

Fourthly, a man may think of God with horror! He thinks of God's sovereignty, and dreads the thoughts of God. You see — one may think of God, yet the thoughts may become sinful.

2. The right manner of thinking on God.

First, our thoughts of God must be serious. Feathers float on the surface — but gold sinks into the water. Feathery spirits have some floating thoughts; but godly hearts sink deep in the thoughts of God!

Secondly, our thoughts of God must he spiritual. Take heed of framing any gross conceits of God in your minds, representing him by the likeness of the creature: 'You saw no form of any kind the day the Lord spoke to you at Horeb out of the fire' (Deut. 4:15). Conceive of God in Christ. We cannot see him any other way, as we cannot see the sun in the circle — but in the beams. The Godhead dwells in Christ's human nature (Col. 2:9). Think of God as a Spirit full of immense glory, propitious to us through a Mediator.

Thirdly, our thoughts of God must be delightful. With what delight does a child think of his father! A gracious soul counts them the sweetest hours, which are spent with God.

Fourthly, our thoughts of God must be operative and efficacious, leaving our hearts in a better tune. The thoughts of God's faithfulness must make us confide in him. The thoughts of God's holiness must make us conform to him. This is the right thinking on God — when it is influential, leaving us in a more heavenly frame.

Third use: Direction.

The text shows us how to have our thoughts frequently fixed upon God.

1. Begin the day with holy thoughts. 'When I awake, I am still with you' (Psalm 139:18). God should have the first buddings of our thoughts. In the law, the Lord would have the first fruits offered him. Give God your virgin thoughts in the morning. What the vessel is first seasoned with, it keeps the relish of, a long time after. The mind seasoned with godly thoughts in the morning, will keep the heart in a better state all the day long.

2. If you would think of God — take heed of hindrances.

1. Turn away your eyes from beholding vanity (Psalm 119:37). Vain objects poison the imagination; lascivious pictures and wanton talk leave bad impressions in the mind.

2. As far as you are able, call your thoughts off from the world. If worldly thoughts come crowding into our mind — godly thoughts will be lost in the crowd!

3. Get a love for God and his ways. One cannot but think — of that which he loves. 'Does a young woman forget her jewelry?' (Jer. 2:32). When she has not her jewel on her ear — she will

have it in her thoughts. A person deeply in love, cannot keep his thoughts off from the object he loves. The reason we think on God no more — is because we love him no more! Let there be but one spark of love to God — and it will fly upward in heavenly thoughts and prayers. By nature our hearts cannot be made to fix on God — but by love.

4. If you would think often on God, get a saving interest in him. 'This God is our God!' (Psalm 48:14). We think most — upon that which is our own. If a man rides by beautiful houses and gardens, he casts his eyes slightly upon them. But let him have a house of his own — and his thoughts dwell in it. Why do men think no more of God — but because they and God are strangers? Let a man's interest in God be cleared — and he will not be able to keep his thoughts off from God.

Part II. THE GREAT GAIN OF GODLINESS

'Then those who feared the Lord talked with each other, and the Lord hearkened and heard. A scroll of remembrance was written in his presence concerning those who feared the Lord and honored his name. 'They will be mine,' says the Lord Almighty, 'in the day when I make up my jewels. I will spare them, just as in compassion a man spares his son who serves him. And you will again see the distinction between the righteous and the wicked, between those who serve God and those who do not.' Malachi 3:16-18

A. The first of the good effects of the saints' piety — is that God REGARDED it. 'The Lord hearkened and heard.' These blessed ones in the text were speaking and thinking of God — and he did not turn away his ear from them, as if he had not minded them. But he hearkened and heard; which expression denotes both diligence and delight.

1. It notes the diligent heed God gave to these saints — he 'hearkened'. Here was attention of ear, and intentness of mind. Hearkening is the gesture of one who intently listens to what another says.

2. God's hearkening shows the delight he took in the holy dialogues of these saints. He was pleased with them; they were to him as a sweet melody.

God takes special notice of the good which he sees in his people. The children of God may perhaps think that God does not regard them: 'I cry unto you — and you do not hear me' (Job 30:20). The church complains that God shuts out her prayer (Lam. 3:8) — but though God is some times silent — he is not deaf! He takes notice of all the good services of his people: 'The Lord hearkened and heard.'

Why is it that God takes such notice of his people's services?

First, not from any merit in them — but the impulsive cause is his free grace! The best duties of the righteous, could not endure God's scales of justice — but God will display the trophies of his mercy. Free grace accepts — what stern justice would condemn!

Secondly, God's taking notice of the good in his people, is through Christ! 'He has made us accepted — in the beloved' (Eph. 1:6). Or, as Chrysostom renders it, he has made us 'favorites'. Through a red glass everything appears of a red color. Just so, through Christ's blood, both our persons and duties appear ruddy and beautiful in God's eyes!

Thirdly, God takes notice of the services of his people — because they flow from the principle of grace. God regards the voice of faith: 'O my dove ... let me hear your voice; for sweet is your voice' (Cant. 2:14). The services of the wicked are harsh and sour — but the godly give God the first-ripe cluster (Mic. 7:1), which grows from the sweet and pleasant root of grace.

First use: Information.

1. If God hearkens and hears, I infer from hence – God's OMNISCIENCE. How could he, being in heaven, hear what the saints speak and think – were he not omniscient? Through the bright mirror of his own essence he has a full knowlege of all things. He knows the intrigues of nations, and the stratagems of his enemies (Exod. 14:24). Future contingencies fall within his cognizance.

God's knowledge is foundational. He is the original, pattern, and prototype of all knowledge. God's knowledge is instantaneous. He knows all at once! Our knowledge is successive, we know one thing after another, and argue from the effect to the cause; but all things are in God's view – in one entire prospect. God's knowledge is infallible and not subject to mistake. Such is the infinity of his knowledge, that the apostle cries out in admiration, 'O the depth of the riches, both of the wisdom and knowledge of God!' (Romans 11:33). The world is to God as a beehive of glass, where you see the working of the bees and the framing of their honey-combs. All things are unveiled to the eye of Jehovah! 'Nothing in all creation is hidden from God's sight. Everything is uncovered and laid bare before the eyes of him to whom we must give account!' Hebrews 4:13

2. See God's goodness, who often passes by the failings of his people (Num. 23:21), and takes notice of the good in them.

'Sarah obeyed Abraham, calling him Lord' (1 Pet. 3:6). The Holy Spirit passes by Sarah's unbelief and laughing at the promise – and takes notice of her reverence to her husband; she called him Lord.

'You have heard of the patience of Job' (James 5:11). We have heard of his impatience, cursing his birthday – but the Lord does not upbraid him with that – but observes the good that was in him: 'You have heard of the patience of Job'. The painter who drew Alexander's picture, drew him with his finger upon his scar. Just so, God puts a finger of mercy upon the scars of his children! He sees their faith – and turns a blind eye to their failings!

3. See God's differing dealings towards the godly and the wicked. If the godly think on his name, he hearkens and hears; but if the wicked meddle with religious duties, he turns away his ear. 'He did not accept Cain and his offering' (Gen. 4:5). Suppose a man had a sweet breath – yet if he had the plague, nobody would come near him! Just so, though a sinner may give God many a sweet, elegant expression in prayer – yet, having the plague in his heart, God will not receive any offering from him! If God shuts men's prayers out of heaven, it is a sad prognostic that he will shut their persons out of heaven.

4. See the privilege of the godly – they have God's ear! 'The Lord hearkened and heard!' 'His ears are open unto their cry!' (Psalm 34:15). It would be counted a great happiness to have the king's ear. How astonishing is it to have God's ear! Believers have the Spirit of God breathing in them – and God cannot but hear the voice of his own Spirit.

5. See what an encouragement is here to be conversant in the duties of God's worship. God takes notice of the services of his people – he hearkens to them as to sweet music. Who would not come with their humble addresses to God – when he is so pleased with them (Prov. 15:8)

Objection 1 – But I deserve nothing.

Answer – God does not bestow his favors according to our desert – but according to his promise and grace.

Objection 2 – But I have prayed a long time and have no answer.

Answer – God may hear prayer when he does not answer. He may lend us his ear – when he does not show us his face! The text says, 'the Lord hearkened and heard.' It is not said he gave an answer—but he 'hearkened'. It befits suitors to wait. Faith waits upon God, patience waits for God. 'Like a servant's eyes on his master's hand—so our eyes are on the Lord our God until He shows us favor.' (Psalm 123:2).

6. See the difference between God and men. God takes notice of the good in his people; the wicked pass by the good in the godly—and take notice only of their failings. If they can spy any impropriety or blemish in them, they upbraid them with it; like those children who reproached Elisha for his baldness—but took no notice of the prophet's miracles (2 Kings 2:23).

7. From the words, 'the Lord hearkened and heard', take note of the folly of idolaters. They worship a God who can neither hearken nor hear! The Cretans pictured Jupiter without ears. Idol gods have ears—but hear not (Psalm 115:6). A lifeless god is good enough for a lifeless worship.

Second use: Exhortation.

1. Let the people of God stand and wonder:

a. Stand and wonder at God's condescension, that he who is so high in the praises and acclamations of the angels—should stoop so low as to listen to the lispings of his children. 'The Lord hearkened and heard!' Alas, God has no need of our services; he is infinitely blessed in reflecting upon the splendor of his own infinite being! We cannot add the least cubit to his essential glory: 'If you are righteous, what do you give Him, or what does He receive from your hand?' (Job 35:7). Yet such is his sweet condescension that he does as it were, stoop below himself, and take notice of his people's poor offerings.

b. Stand and wonder at God's love, that he should regard those services of his people, which are so mixed with corruption! 'Our righteousness is as filthy rags!' (Isaiah 64:6). The sacrifice of thanksgiving, which was the highest sacrifice, had some leaven mixed with it (Lev. 7:13). Our best duties have some leaven of imperfection mixed in them; yet such is God's love, that he receives and accepts them: 'I have eaten my honeycomb with my honey' (Cant. 5:1). Honey is sweet—but the honeycomb is harsh and bitter, and can hardly be eaten; yet such was Christ's love to his spouse, that he ate of her honeycomb, her services mixed with imperfection, and was pleased and delighted with them! Oh, the love of God, that he should have respect to our offerings, which are interlaced with sin! Our best duties, are sweet wine coming out of a sour cask.

2. If God hearkens to us when we speak—let us hearken to him when be speaks. In the Word, God speaks to us. He is said now to speak to us from heaven (Heb. 12:25), that is, by the Word. Does God hearken to us, and shall not we hearken to him? Be not like the deaf adder which stops her ear. This the Lord complains of: 'God does speak—now one way, now another—though man may not perceive it' (Job 33:14). If God's Word does not prevail with us—our prayers will not prevail with him.

B. The second good effect of the saints' piety—was that God recorded it. 'A book of remembrance was written before him'; the word in the original for 'book of remembrance' signifies 'a book of memorials' or 'monuments'. The words immediately foregoing recite God's hearkening and hearing; but lest any should say, though God does at the present hear the holy speech and thoughts of his children—yet may they not in time slip out of his mind? Therefore these words are added, 'a book of remembrance was written before him.' The Lord did not only hear the godly speeches of the saints—but recorded them, and wrote them down! 'A book of remembrance was written.'

This is spoken after the manner of men—not that God has any book of records by him. He does not need to write down anything for the help of his memory. He is not subject to forgetfulness.

Things done a thousand years ago are as fresh to him—as if they were done but yesterday: 'A thousand years in your sight are but as yesterday when it is past' (Psalm 90:4).

This 'book of remembrance', therefore, is a borrowed form of speech, taken from kings, who have their chronicles wherein they note memorable things. King Ahasuerus had his book of records, wherein were written the worthy deeds of Mordecai (Esther 6:1-2). Just so, God bears in mind, all the godly speeches and pious actions of his children. God's particular and critical assessment is a book of records, where nothing can be lost or torn out.

Doctrine: God eternally remembers all the good designs and pious endeavors of his people. 'God is not unjust; he will not forget your work and the love you have shown him, as you have helped his people and continue to help them.' (Heb. 6:10). There are eight things which God writes down in his book of remembrance:

1. The Lord writes down the names of his people. 'Whose names are written in the Book of Life' (Phil. 4:3). This book has no errata, 'I will never erase their names from the Book of Life!' (Rev. 3:5).

2. The Lord writes down the godly speech of his people. When Christians speak together of the mysteries of heaven (which is like music in concert), God is much delighted with it. When their tongues are going on earth—God's pen is going in heaven! 'Those who feared the Lord spoke often one to another, and a book of remembrance was written!'

3. The Lord writes down the tears of his people. Tears drop down to the earth—but they reach heaven! God has his bottle and his book: 'You keep track of all my sorrows. You have collected all my tears in your bottle. You have recorded each one in your book!' (Psalm 56:8). Tears drop from the saints—as water from the roses—they are fragrant to God—and he puts them in his bottle. And besides this, he has his book of remembrance, where he writes them down, 'You have recorded each one in your book!' Especially God writes down such tears as are shed for the sins of the times. 'There was another man among them, clothed in linen, with writing equipment at his side' (Ezek. 9:2). This was to write down the tears of the mourners, and to 'put a mark on the foreheads of the men who sigh and groan over all the abominations committed in the city' (verse 4).

4. God writes down the thoughts of his people. We can write down men's words—but we cannot write down their thoughts. It would perplex the angels—to write men's thoughts! But be assured, never a holy thought comes into our mind—but God writes it down! So in the text—a book of remembrance was written for those who thought upon his name. Two things are silent—yet have a voice:

1. Tears: 'the Lord has heard the voice of my weeping' (Psalm 6:8).

2. Thoughts: 'I know what they are thinking' (Isaiah 66:18).

5. God writes down the desires of his people. 'Lord, my every desire is known to You!' (Psalm 38:9); that is, 'It is set down in your book!' Desire is the spiritual appetite, or the soul's panting and breathing after God (Psalm 84:2). In this life we do rather desire God—than enjoy him. Can we say that we take our souls out of the quiver of our bodies, and shoot them into heaven? Do our affections sally forth towards Christ? Do we desire him superlatively and incessantly? Every such desire is put down in God's register book! Lord, my every desire is known to You!'

6. The Lord writes down the prayers of his people. (Jonah 2:7). Prayer, though it be not vocal, only mental, is recorded. 'Hannah spoke in her heart' (1 Sam. 1:13). That prayer, God wrote down and answered. God was better to her than her prayer; she prayed for a son—and God gave her a prophet! At times the heart is so full of grief, that it can only groan in prayer; yet a

groan is sometimes the best part of a prayer, and God writes it down: 'My groaning is not hidden from You!' (Psalm 38:9). If we cannot speak with elegance in prayer; if it is only lisping and chattering, God puts it in his book of remembrance: 'I chattered like a swallow, and then I moaned like a mourning dove. I am in trouble, Lord. Help me!' (Isaiah 38:14); yet that prayer was heard and registered, 'I have heard your prayer—I have seen your tears!' (verse 5).

7. God writes down the works of his people. Works of mercy must be done out of love to God. As Mary out of love brought her ointments and sweet spices, and anointed Christ's dead body—so out of pure love we must bring our ointments of charity to anoint the saints, which are Christ's living body. Such alms are not lost. With such sacrifices God is well pleased (Heb. 13:16). And that we should see how well the Lord is pleased with them, he writes them down thus: 'Your gifts to the poor have come up as a memorial offering before God.' (Acts 10:4).

8. God has a book of remembrance for the sufferings of his people. The saints' purgatory is in this life. But there are two things which may bear up their spirits:

First, every groan of theirs goes to God's heart: 'I have also heard the groaning of the children of Israel' (Exod. 6:5). In music when one string is touched—all the rest sound. When the saints are stricken—God's heart reverberates.

Secondly, God has a book of records, to write down his people's injuries. The wicked make wounds in the backs of the righteous, and then pour in vinegar. God writes down their cruelty: 'I remember what Amalek did to Israel' (1 Sam. 15:2). Amalek was Esau's grandchild (Gen. 36:12), a bitter enemy of Israel. The Amalekites showed their spite to Israel in two ways:

First, 'Remember what the Amalekites did to you along the way when you came out of Egypt. When you were weary and worn out, they met you on your journey and cut off all who were lagging behind; they had no fear of God.' (Deuteronomy 25:17-18)

Secondly, they openly gave battle to them, and would have hindered them from going into Canaan (Exod. 17:8). Now God took notice of Israel's sufferings by Amalek: 'I remember what Amalek did to Israel, and I have my book of remembrance; I write it down.' 'This is what the Lord Almighty says—I will punish the Amalekites for what they did to Israel when they waylaid them as they came up from Egypt. Now go, attack the Amalekites and totally destroy everything that belongs to them. Do not spare them; put to death men and women, children and infants, cattle and sheep, camels and donkeys.' (1 Sam. 15:2-3).

First use of the doctrine: Information.

I. This shows us that it is not in vain to serve God. The wicked who do not know God, think him to be a hard Master, and say, like those Job speaks of, 'What would we gain by praying to him?' (Job 21:15). But the text shows us that God records all the services of his people, 'a book of remembrance was written before him.' God's writing in his book is:

A. An honor to the saints. The Romans wrote the names of their senators in a book, and in token of honor they were called the 'chosen fathers' of the people. So God's book of remembrance shows his high esteem of his people and their services. He writes them down.

B. A mark of the special favor God bears to his people. He registers them and their services—with an intent to crown them! Tamerlane, wrote down all the memorable deeds of his soldiers, whom he afterwards advanced to places of dignity. God's service is most desirable; let us make Joshua's choice: 'As for me and my house—we will serve the Lord!' (Joshua 24:15).

If we should desert God's service, where shall we go? When Christ asked his disciples, Will you also go away? Peter said, 'Lord, to whom shall we go?' (John 6:68); as if to say, 'If we leave you, we do not know where to get help for ourselves.' Let us adhere to God; he has his book of memorials to record our allegiance. We may be losers for him – but we shall not be losers by him.

2. As God registers the good works of his people – so he has a book of remembrance to write down the sins of the wicked! 'Go now, write it on a tablet for them, inscribe it on a scroll, that for the days to come it may be an everlasting witness. These are rebellious people, deceitful children, children unwilling to listen to the Lord's instruction!' (Isaiah 30:8-9).

Men's sins are written in the book of conscience – and the book of God's omniscience. They think that because God does not speak to them by his loud judgments, therefore God does not know their sins. But though God does not speak – he writes: 'The sin of Judah is written with an iron stylus. With a diamond point it is engraved.' (Jer. 17:1). God writes down every act of oppression, bribery, and immorality. 'They never consider that I remember all their evil. Now their sins are all around them; they are right in front of My face!' (Hos. 7:2). King Belshazzar was carousing and drinking wine in bowls, and praising his gods of gold and silver; but while he was sinning – God was writing! 'At that very moment they saw the fingers of a human hand writing on the plaster wall of the king's palace. The king himself saw the hand as it wrote, and his face turned pale with fear. Such terror gripped him that his knees knocked together and his legs gave way beneath him!' (Dan. 5:5-6).

We read of God's book: 'The books were opened' (Rev. 20:12); and we also read of his bag: 'My transgression is sealed up in a bag' (Job 14:17). This seems to allude to law courts, where indictments against malefactors are sealed up in a bag, and produced at the trials. When God shall open his black book in which men's names are written, and his bag in which their sins are written – then their hearts will tremble, and their knees will knock together in terror! Every lie a sinner tells, every oath he swears, every drunken bout – God writes it down in his book of remembrance! And woe to him – if the book is not crossed out with the blood of Christ!

3. See the mercifulness of God to his children – who blots their sins out of his book of remembrance, and writes their good deeds in his book of remembrance. 'I, even I, am he who blots out your transgressions' (Isaiah 43:25). This is a metaphor borrowed from the case of a creditor who takes his pen and blots out the debt owing to him; so says God, I will 'blot out your transgressions'. Or as the Hebrew has it, 'I am blotting them out.'

God in forgiving sin, passes an act of oblivion or amnesty: 'I will remember their sin no more!' (Jer. 31:34). God will not upbraid his people with their former offences. We never read that when Peter repented, that Christ upbraided him for his denial of his Lord. Oh, the heavenly indulgence and kindness of God to his people! He remembers everything about them – but their sins! He writes down their good thoughts and speeches in a merciful book of remembrance; but their sins are as if they had never been – they are carried into the land of oblivion!

Second Use: Exhortation.

If God records our services – then let us record his mercies. Let us have our book of remembrance. A Christian should keep two books always beside him; one to write his sins in – that he may be humble; the other to write his mercies in – that he may be thankful. David had his book of remembrance: 'David appointed some of the Levites to be ministers before the ark of the Lord, to give thanks and praise to Him.' (1 Chron. 16:4). We should keep a book to record God's mercies – though I think it will be hard to get a book big enough to hold them! At such and such a time we were in straitened circumstances – and God supplied us; at another time under sadness of spirit – and God dropped in the oil of gladness; at another near death – and God miraculously restored us. If God is mindful of what we do for him – shall not we be mindful of what he does for us! God's mercies, like jewels, are too good to be lost! Get a book of remembrance!

Third Use: Comfort.

1. It is comfort to the godly — in the case of friends forgetting them. Joseph did Pharaoh's cupbearer a kindness — 'Yet the cupbearer did not remember Joseph; he forgot him.' (Gen. 40:23). It is only too usual to remember injuries — and forget kindnesses; but God has a book of remembrance where he writes down all his old friends. Near relations may sometimes be forgetful. The tender mother may forget her infant: 'Can a mother forget the baby at her breast and have no compassion on the child she has borne? Though she may forget, I will not forget you!' (Isa. 49:15). A mother may sooner forget her child — than God be forgetful. Christ our high priest, has the names of the saints written upon his breastplate, and all their good deeds written in his book of memorials! Let this be a remedy to revive the hearts of God's people; though friends may blot you out of their mind — yet God will not blot you out of his book!

2. This is consolation to the godly — the Lord keeps a book of remembrance for this end — that he may at the last day make a public and solemn mention of all the good which his saints have done. God will open his book of records and say, 'Then the King will say to those on His right — Come, you who are blessed by My Father, inherit the kingdom prepared for you from the foundation of the world. For I was hungry and you gave Me something to eat; I was thirsty and you gave Me something to drink; I was a stranger and you took Me in; I was naked and you clothed Me; I was sick and you took care of Me; I was in prison and you visited Me.' (Matt. 25:34-36).

God will make known all the memorable and pious actions of his people before men and angels! He will say, 'Here are those who have prayed and wept for sin; here are those who have been advocates for my truth; here are those who have laid to heart my dishonors, and have mourned for what they could not reform. These are my renowned ones, my Hephzibahs — in whom my soul delights!' (Isaiah 62:4).

What a glorious thing will this be — to have God express the high praise of his saints! When Alexander saw the sepulcher of Achilles, he cried out 'O happy Achilles, who had Homer to set forth your praise!' What an honor will it be to have the names and worthy deeds of the saints mentioned, and God himself to be the herald to proclaim their praises! (2 Cor. 4:5).

C. The third good effect of the saints' piety — was that God rewarded it. 'And they shall be mine, says the Lord Almighty, in that day when I make up my jewels!' (Mal. 3:17). The reward is threefold.

1. God's owning them: 'They shall he mine, says the Lord Almighty.'

2. God's honoring them: 'In that day when I make up my jewels.'

3. God's sparing them: 'I will spare them, as a man spares his own son that serves him.'

Note first, the Person speaking, 'the Lord Almighty'. This is too great a word to he passed by in silence. God is often in Scripture styled, 'the Lord Almighty' (Psalm 46:11; Isaiah 1:24); that is, he is the Supreme General, and Commander of all armies and forces, and gives victory to whom he will.

Question: Why is this name, 'the Lord Almighty', given to God?

Answer: Not because God needs any others to protect himself, or suppress his enemies. Earthly princes have armies to defend them from danger — but God needs none to help him: he can fight without an army. God puts strength into all armies. Other captains may give their soldiers armor; they cannot give them strength; but God does: 'You have girded me with strength for the battle' (Psalm 18:39). Why then is God said to have armies — if he needs them not?

Firstly, it is to set forth his sovereign power and grandeur; all armies and regiments are under his command.

Secondly, it is to show us that though God can effect all things by himself; yet in his wisdom he often uses the agency of the creature to bring to pass his will and purpose.

Question: What are these hosts or armies, of which God is the sovereign Lord?

Answer 1: God has an army in heaven — angels and archangels: 'I saw the Lord sitting on his throne with all the armies of heaven around him' (1 Kings 22:19). By the armies of heaven, is meant the angels; they, being spirits, are a powerful army: 'You his angels, which excel in strength' (Psalm 103:20). We read of one angel who destroyed in one night 'a hundred and eighty-five thousand men' (2 Kings 19:35). If one angel destroyed such a vast army, what can a whole legion of angels do? A legion consisted of six thousand, six hundred and sixty six. How many of these legions go to make up the heavenly host! (Dan. 7:10).

The stars are God's army too (Deut. 4:19). These were set in battalions and fought against God's enemies: 'The stars in their courses fought against Sisera' (Judg. 5:20). That is, the stars charged like an army, raising storms and tempests by their influences, and so destroying the whole army of Sisera.

Answer 2: God has armies upon earth, both rational and irrational. The rational are armies of men. These are under God's command and conduct. They do not stir without his warrant. The Lord has the managing of all military affairs. Not a stroke is struck — but God orders it! Not a bullet flies — but God directs it! As for the irrational armies, God can raise an army of flies, as he did against King Pharaoh (Exod. 8:24); an army of worms, as he did against King Herod (Acts 12:23). Oh, what a Lord is here — who has so many armies under his authority!

First use of the doctrine: Exhortation.

1. Let us dread this Lord Almighty! We fear men who are in power, and is not that God to be adored and feared, who does all thing at his good pleasure? 'All the peoples of the earth are regarded as nothing. He does as he pleases with the powers of heaven and the peoples of the earth. No one can hold back his hand or say to him — What have you done?' (Dan. 4:35).

His power is as large as his will. 'What his soul desires — that he does' (Job 23:13). God is a sovereign power over all. 'He pours contempt upon princes' (Job 12:21). He threw the proud angels to hell. God can with a word, unpin the wheels and break the axle of the creation. God's power is a glorious power (Col. 1:11). And in this it appears glorious — it is never consumed or exhausted. Men, while they exercise their strength, weaken it. 'Have you never heard or understood? Don't you know that the Lord is the everlasting God, the Creator of all the earth? He never grows faint or weary.' (Isaiah 40:28). 'I will use up My arrows against them.' (Deut. 32:23) Though God 'uses up his arrows' upon his enemies — yet he never exhausts his strength.

Oh, then tremble before this Lord Almighty! Remember, O hard-hearted sinner, how many ways God can be revenged on you! He can raise an army of diseases against you in your body. He can arm every creature against you, the dog, the boar, the elephant. He can arm conscience against you, as he did against Spira — making him a terror to himself. Oh, dread this Lord Almighty.

2. If God is the Lord Almighty — let us take heed of hardening our hearts against God. It was the saying of Pompey that with one stamp of his foot — he could raise all Italy up in arms. God can with a word — raise all the militia of heaven and earth against us, and shall we dare affront him!

'Who has hardened himself against him, and has prospered?' (Job 9:4). Such as live in the open breach of God's commandments, harden their hearts against God; they raise a war against heaven! 'He has stretched out his hand against God and has arrogantly opposed the Almighty!' (Job 15:25). Like warriors who muster up all the forces they can, to fight with their antagonists, so the sinner hardens and strengthens himself against Jehovah: 'He runs upon him, even on his neck, upon the thick bosses of his bucklers' (verse 26). Bucklers anciently had one great boss in the middle with a sharp spike in it to wound the adversary. The grossly wicked sinner encounters the God of heaven – and runs upon the thick bosses of his fury, which will wound mortally. Whoever hardened himself against God – and prospered? Will men go to measure arms with God! 'Do you have an arm like God's?' (Job 40:9).

God is almighty – and therefore can hurt his enemies; and he is invisible – therefore they cannot hurt him. Who can fight with a spirit? God will be too hard for his enemies in the long run: 'God will smash the heads of his enemies, crushing the skulls of those who love their guilty ways!' (Psalm 68:21).

How easily can God chastise rebels! 'The Lord looked down on the Egyptian forces from the pillar of fire and cloud, and threw them into confusion' (Exod. 14:24). It need cost God no more to destroy his proudest adversaries than a look – a cast of the eye! It is better to be prostrate at God's feet, and to meet him with tears in our eyes – rather than weapons in our hands! We overcome God, not by resistance – but by repentance!

3. If God is the Lord Almighty – let us be so wise as to engage him on our side. 'The Lord Almighty is with us!' (Psalm 46:11). Great is the privilege of having the Lord Almighty for us!

1. If the Lord Almighty is on our side, he can discover the subtle plots of enemies. Thus he detected the counsel of Ahithophel (2 Sam. 17:14). And did not the Lord discover the Popish conspirators of late, when they would have subverted true religion and, like Italian butchers, turned England into an Aceldama – a field of blood?

2. If the Lord Almighty is on our side, he can bridle his enemies and lay such a restraint upon their spirits that they shall not do the harm they intend. 'It is in the power of my hand to do you hurt (said Laban to Jacob) but the God of your father spoke unto me saying, Take heed that you speak not to Jacob either good or bad' (Gen. 31:29). Laban had power to do hurt – but no heart. When Balak called upon Balaam to curse Israel, God so dispirited Balaam that he could not discharge his thunderbolt: 'How shall I curse, those whom God has not cursed?' (Num. 23:8). He had a good mind to curse – but God held him back.

3. If the Lord Almighty is for us – he can help us, though means fail, and things seem to he given up for lost. When Gideon's army was small, and rendered despicable, then God crowned them with victory (Judges 7:2, 22). When the arm of flesh shrinks, then is the time for the arm of omnipotence to be put forth: 'The Lord will indeed vindicate His people and have compassion on His servants when He sees that their strength is gone' (Deut. 32:36). The less seen of man – the more of God.

4. If the Lord Almighty is on our side – he can save us in that very way, in which we think he will destroy us. Would not all have thought that the great fish's belly would have been Jonah's grave? But God made a fish to be a ship, in which he sailed safely to shore. Paul got to land by the breaking of the ship (Acts 27:44). God can make the adverse party do his work; he can cause divisions among the enemies, and turn their own weapons against themselves: 'I will set the Egyptians against the Egyptians' (Isaiah 19:22; Judges 7:22).

5. If the Lord Almighty is on our side – he can make the church's affliction – a means of her augmentation: 'The more they afflicted them – the more they multiplied' (Exod. 1:12). The

church of God is like that plant, which grows by cutting. Persecution propagates the church: the scattering of the apostles up and down was like scattering seed – it tended much to the spreading of the gospel (Acts 8:1, 4).

6. If the Lord Almighty is on our side – he can alter the scene and turn the balance of affairs whenever he pleases. 'He changes the times and the seasons' (Dan. 2:21). God can remove mountains which lie in the way, or leap over them. His power is without limit; he can bring harmony out of discord. He who brought Isaac out of a dead womb, and the Messiah out of a virgin's womb – what can he not do? The Lord Almighty can in an instant, alter the face of things. There are no impossibilities with God. If means fail, he can create. It is therefore, high prudence to get this Lord Almighty on our side. 'If God is for us – who can be against us?' (Rom. 8:31).

And if we would engage God to be on our side:

First, let us be earnest suitors to him – exercise eyes of faith, and knees of prayer (Jer. 14:9). And in prayer, let us use Joshua's argument, 'What will You do about Your great name?' (Josh. 7:9). Lord, if the cause of true religion loses ground, how will your name suffer!

Secondly, let us put away iniquity. (Job 11:14). Sin is not worth keeping. Who would keep a plague sore? Let us discard and abjure our sins (Jer. 7:3); and then the Lord Almighty will be on our side and, as a pledge of his favorable presence, he will entail the gospel, that crowning blessing, upon us and our posterity.

So much for the Person speaking, 'the Lord Almighty'.

A. God Rewards His People by Owning Them

I now come to the reward itself, the first part of which is – God's owning them, 'They shall be mine.' I take the sense of it to be, 'They shall be mine in covenant.' 'I entered into a covenant with you – and you became mine!' (Ezek. 16:8; Isa 43:1). This is no small blessing – to be in covenant with God. Therefore, when God told Abraham that he would enter into covenant with him, Abraham fell on his face (Gen. 17:3), as being amazed that the great God should bestow such a signal favor upon him. God never entered into covenant with the angels when they fell – but he proclaims himself God in covenant with believers, 'They shall be mine.' This covenant enriched with free grace, is a better covenant than that which was made with Adam in innocence, for:

1. The least failing would have made the first covenant null and void – but many failings do not invalidate the covenant of grace. I grant the least sin makes a trespass upon the covenant – but it does not cancel it. Every failing in the marital relation, does not break the marriage bond.

2. If the first covenant was violated, the sinner had no remedy; all doors of hope were shut. But the new covenant allows of a remedy. It provides a Surety, 'Jesus the mediator of the new covenant' (Heb. 12:24).

First use: Information.

See the amazing goodness of God to his people, to enter into covenant with them and say, 'You are mine!' 'He has made with me an everlasting covenant, ordered in all things and sure!' (2 Sam. 23:5). The first covenant stood upon the delicate foundation of works. Adam had no sooner a stock of original righteousness to trade with, then he broke the covenant. But this covenant of grace is confirmed with God's decree, and rests upon two mighty pillars – the oath of God, and the blood of God. That you may see how great a privilege it is to be owned by the Lord federally, consider:

1. If we are in covenant with God, and he says to us 'You are mine' – then all that is in God is ours! A person falling on hard times and then marrying a king, has a share in all the crown revenues. God having entered into a near relation with us and saying, 'You are mine' – we have a share in his rich revenues! The Lord says to every believer, as the King of Israel said to the King of Syria, 'I am yours, and all that I have is yours!' (1 Kings 20:4). My wisdom shall be yours to teach you, my holiness shall be yours to sanctify you, my mercy shall be yours to save you! What richer dowry – than Deity! God is a whole ocean of blessedness. If there is enough in him to fill the angels – then surely, he has enough to fill us!

2. If God says to us, 'You are mine' – then he will have a tender care for us. 'Cast all your care upon Him, because He cares for you!' (1 Pet. 5:7). God, to show his tender solicitude towards Israel, bore them 'on eagle's wings' (Exod. 19:4). The eagle carries her young ones upon her wing to defend them; the arrow must first shoot through the old eagle, before it can touch her young ones. A mother's care is seen in leading a child, so that it may not fall. Such is God's care: 'It was I who taught Israel how to walk, leading him along by the hand.' (Hos. 11:3). We may argue from the lesser to the greater, that if God takes care of the lowest insects and animals which creep upon the earth, much more will he take care of his covenant saints. He is still contriving and planning for their good. If they wander out of the way – he guides them; if they stumble – he holds them by the hand; if they fall – he raises them; if they become dull – he quickens them by his Spirit; if they are obstinate – he draws them with cords of love; if they are sad – he comforts them with his promises.

3. If God says to us, 'You are mine' – then he will entirely love us! 'I have loved you with an everlasting love' (Jer. 31:3). The Lord may give a man riches – and not love him; his prosperity may be as Israel's quails – sauced with God's wrath (Num. 11:32-33). But when God says, 'You are mine' – he cannot but love. Everyone loves his own. If God has any love better than another – his covenant people shall have it; he will extract the essence of his love for them; he loves them as he loves Christ! (John 17:23).

4. If God says to us, 'You are mine' – then he will not allow us to be in need. Believers are not only of God's family – but of Christ's body; and will the Head let the body starve? 'Truly you shall be fed' (Psalm 37:3). God has not promised dainties; he will not satisfy his people's lusts – but he will supply their needs. If the bill of fare should be restricted, what they lack in worldly comforts, they shall have in spiritual blessing: 'He shall bless your bread, and your water' (Exod. 23:25). God will rather work a miracle than that any of his children shall famish. The raven is so unnatural that she will hardly feed her young – yet she became a caterer and brought food to the prophet Elijah.

5. If God says to us, 'You are mine' – then we have great freedoms!

1. We are freed from the revenging wrath of God! We are not free from God's anger as a Father – but as a Judge. God will not pour his vindictive justice upon us. Christ has drunk the red wine of God's wrath upon the cross – that believers may not taste a drop of it!

2. We are freed from the predominant reign of sin. 'Sin shall not have dominion over you' (Romans 6:14). Though believers are not freed from the indwelling of sin, nor from combat with it – yet they are freed from its imperious command. As it it said of those beasts in Daniel, 'They had their dominion taken away – yet their lives were prolonged for a season' (Dan. 7:12), so sin lives in the regenerate, but its domination is taken away. And to be thus freed from the jurisdiction, power, and tyranny of sin – is no small blessing! A wicked man is at the command of sin, as the donkey at the command of the driver. The curse of Ham is upon him, 'a servant of

servants shall he be' (Gen. 9:25). He is a slave to his lusts, and a slave to Satan! Oh, what a privilege it is—to have one's neck out of the devil's yoke!

3. We are freed from the accusations of conscience. The worm of conscience is part of the torment of hell. But, God being our God, we are freed from the clamors of this hellish fury. Conscience sprinkled with Christ's blood speaks peace! A good conscience, like the bee, gives honey. It is like the golden pot which had manna in it (2 Cor. 1:12).

6. If God says to us, 'You are mine'—then we shall he his forever! 'This God is our God, forever and ever' (Psalm 48:14). You cannot say that you have health—and you shall have it forever. You cannot say that you have a child—and you shall have it forever. But if God is your God—you shall have him forever! The covenant of grace is a royal charter, and this is the happiness of it—it is made for eternity! Justification is never rescinded. The covenant between God and his people shall never be broken off. How false therefore is the opinion of falling from grace! Shall any whom God makes his own by federal union fall finally? Indeed if salvation has no better pillar to rest upon than man's will (as the Arminians hold) no wonder if there is falling away; but a Christian's stability in grace, is built upon a surer basis, namely, God's 'everlasting (or inviolable) covenant' (Isaiah 55:3). Once in Christ—forever in Christ. A star may sooner fall out of its place—than a true believer be plucked away from God! 'None of them is lost' (John 17:12). 'I give them eternal life, and they will never perish—ever! No one will snatch them out of My hand.' (John 10:28)

7. If God says to us, 'You are mine'—then he will take us up to himself at death! Death breaks the union between the body and the soul—but perfects the union between God and the soul. This is the emphasis of heaven's glory—to be forever with God. What is the joy of the blessed—but to have a clear, transparent sight of God, and to be in the sweet and soft embraces of his love forever! This has made the saints desire death, as the bride her wedding day! 'I have the desire to depart and be with Christ—which is far better!' (Phil. 1:23). 'Lead me, Lord, to that glory', said a holy man, 'a glimpse whereof I have seen as in a glass darkly.'

Second Use: Comfort.

Let this be for the consolation of the saints. There is a covenant union between God and them. God is theirs—and they are his! 'They shall be mine, says the Lord.' Here is a standing cordial for the godly. God looks upon them as having a propriety in them, 'They shall be mine!'

1. This is comfort, in respect of Satan's accusations. He accuses the saints first to God—then to themselves. But if God says, 'You are mine', this answers all of Satan's accusations. Christ will show the debt book, crossed out in his blood. It was a saying of Bucer, 'I am Christ's, and the devil has nothing to do with me.'

2. This is comfort, in respect of poverty. Believers are married to the King of heaven—and all that is in God is theirs! A philosopher comforted himself with this, that though he had no music or vine trees—yet he had the household gods with him. So we, though we have not the vine or fig tree—yet if God is ours and we are his—this creates joy in the most impoverished condition! And that which may raise the comfort of the godly higher, and cause a jubilation of spirit, is that shortly God will own his people before all the world, and say, 'These are mine!' At present the elect are not known: 'It does not yet appear what we shall be' (1 John 3:2). The saints are like kings in disguise; but how will their hearts leap for joy—when God shall pronounce that word, 'These are mine! The lot of free grace has fallen upon them! These shall lie forever in the bosom of my love!'

Third use: Exhortation.

To all who are yet strangers to God: labor to get into covenant with him, that he may say, 'You are mine!' Why does God woo and beseech you by his ambassadors, if he is not willing to be in covenant with you?

Question: What shall a poor forlorn creature do, to get into covenant with God?

Answer 1: If you would be in covenant with God--break off the covenant with sin! (1 Sam. 7:3). What king will be in league with a person who serves his enemy?

Answer 2: Labor for faith.

1. Faith in the mercy of God: 'I am merciful. I will not be angry with you forever' (Jer. 3:12). As the sea covers great rocks as well as little sands — so Gods mercy covers great sins! Manasseh, a bloody sinner, is held forth as a pattern of mercy. Some of the Jews who had a hand in crucifying Christ — yet had their sins forgiven!

2. Faith in the merit of Christ. Christ's blood is not only an atoning sacrifice to appease God — but a sacrifice to ingratiate us into God's favor, and make him look upon us with a smiling aspect (1 John 2:2).

B. God Rewards His People by Honoring Them

The second part of the saints reward — is God's honoring them: 'In that day when I make up my jewels'. Here are three propositions:

1. God greatly honors his people.

2. God's people are his jewels.

3. There is a day when God will make up his jewels.

1. God greatly honors his people. He speaks of them here with honor: 'In that day when I make up my jewels'. 'Since you were precious in my sight — you have been honorable' (Isaiah 43:4). Honor attends holiness. That the Lord highly honors those who fear him, is evident by four demonstrations.

1. In that he prefers them before others. He choose, them, and passes by the rest: 'Was not Esau Jacob's brother? Yet I have loved Jacob, but Esau I have hated!' (Mal. 1:2-3).

2. In that God gives them frequent love visits. It is counted an honor for a subject to have his prince visit him. 'Our fellowship is with the Father and with his Son, Jesus Christ' (1 John 1:3). The Rabbis say that Moses had one hundred and fifty conferences with God, and died with a kiss from God's mouth. What greater honor for a person — than to have God keep him company! (Exod. 33:11)?

3. In that God makes them rich heirs. We are 'joint-heirs with Christ' (Rom. 8:17). For a man to adopt another and make him heir to his estate — is no small honor done to him. The youngest believer is an heir, yes, and an heir of the crown! (1 Pet. 5:4). This crown he has in the promise (Rev. 2:10), and in the first fruits (Romans 8:23).

4. In that God sends his angels to be their servants. Such as are God's servants, have angels to be theirs: 'Are not all angels ministering spirits sent to serve those who will inherit salvation?' (Heb. 1:14).

First use: Who would not be fearers of God! This makes God have an honorable esteem of them. 'All men', says Chrysostom, 'are ambitious for honor.' True honor comes from God! (John 5:44).

Second use: If God so honors his people, let them honor him: 'Where is my honor?' (Mal. 1:6). Let the saints be God-exalters; let them lift up his name in the world, and make his praise glorious (Psalm 66:2). But I only glance at this.

2. God's people are his jewels. 'In that day when I make up my jewels!' Jewels are precious things; the Hebrew word for jewels signifies a treasure. A treasure is made up of costly things: gold, and diamonds, and rubies. Such a precious treasure, are the saints to God.

Question: In what sense are the saints, God's jewels?

Answer 1: They are jewels for their sparkling quality. Their holiness shines and sparkles in God's eyes! (Cant. 4:9), 'You have ravished my heart, with one of your eyes!' That is, with one of your graces.

Answer 2: The godly are jewels for their scarcity. Diamonds are not common. Just so, the godly are scarce and rare. There are but few of these to be found. There are many false professors (as there are paste diamonds) but few Israelites indeed. 'Few are chosen' (Matt. 20:16). Among the millions in Rome, there were but few senators. Just so, among the swarms of people in the world — there are but few true believers.

Answer 3: The godly are jewels for their price. Queen Cleopatra had two jewels which contained half the price of a kingdom. Thus the saints are jewels, for their value. God esteems them at a high rate; he parted with his best jewel for them. Christ's precious blood was shed to ransom these jewels!

Answer 4: The saints are jewels for their adorning quality. Jewels adorn those who wear them. The saints are jewels which adorn the world. Their piety mixed with prudence honors the gospel. Hypocrites eclipse true religion and make it badly spoken of. The saints as jewels render it illustrious, by their sanctity.

First use: Information.

1. See the worth of the godly — they are God's jewels — 'a royal diadem in the hand of your God' (Isaiah 62:3). That is, they are eminent above others, as a crown hung with jewels is a sign of the highest state and honor. The saints are God's glory (Isaiah 46:13), as if God's glory did lie in them.

2. See then that which may bring holiness into repute, and make us desire to be godly. It casts a splendor upon us, and makes God number us among his jewels! Some are loath to embrace godliness, for fear it will be a stain on their reputation, and bring them out of favor with great men. But you see how it raises a person's renown; it makes him precious in God's sight — he is a jewel! Believers, on account of their mystical union with Christ, have a preciousness above the angels! The angels are morning stars (Job 38:7). Believers are clothed with the sun of righteousness (Rev. 12:1).

3. See the different opinion which God has — of the godly and the wicked. The one he esteems precious, the other vile. 'You are vile' (Nahum 1:14). This is spoken of King Sennacherib; though he was by birth noble — yet he was by sin vile. The Hebrew word for vile signifies of base esteem. Though the wicked are high in dignity and worldly grandeur, yet God slights them. A dunghill may be higher than other ground — but it sends forth foul vapors: 'They have all together become filthy' (Psalm 14:3). In the original it is, 'They have become stinking.'

The wicked are compared to dogs and swine (2 Pet. 2:22) and to dross (Ezek. 22:19). Dross is the filth of the metal. Sinners are compared to chaff (Psalm 1:4). When a wicked man dies — there is only a little chaff blown away! A sinner is the most contemptible thing in the world; there is no worth in him while he lives — and no loss of him when he dies! A sinner is worse than a toad or serpent; a toad has nothing but what God has put into it — but a wicked man has that which the devil has put into him: 'Why has Satan filled your heart to lie to the Holy Spirit?' (Acts 5:3).

4. See what a high estimate we should set upon the godly; they are jewels, they are the glory of the creation. They are compared to stars for their beauty (Rev. 1:20), to spice trees for their perfume (Cant. 4:14). They are the excellent of the earth (Psalm 16:3). The Lord would soon destroy the earth—but that he has some of his jewels in it.

Prize the saints—though they are humbled with poverty. We esteem a diamond, though it lies in the dust. 'John's clothes were made of camel's hair, and he had a leather belt around his waist. His food was locusts and wild honey'—yet he was a jewel (Matt. 11:9). He was the morning star to usher in the Sun of righteousness into the world. The saints are precious—for they are God's lesser heaven! (Isaiah 57:15).

5. See the saints' safety: they are God's jewels, and he will take great care to preserve them. A man is careful that he does not lose his jewels. God often gives his people a temporal salvation. If a storm comes he knows how to hide his jewels. He hid a hundred prophets in a cave (1 Kings 18:4). The angel is commanded, before he poured his vial of curses on the earth, to seal the saints of God on their foreheads (Rev. 7:3), which was a mark of safety. God will ensure the spiritual safety of his jewels: 'None of them is lost!' (John 17:12). 'I give them eternal life, and they will never perish—ever! No one will snatch them out of My hand.' (John 10:28)

6. It the saints are God's jewels—then how incensed and enraged will God be, against those who have abused his jewels! Theodosius, counted them traitors who abused his statue. What will become of those who persecute God's saints, and tread upon his jewels! It goes near to God's heart—to see his jewels sprinkled with blood! What is done to them—the Lord takes as done to himself: 'Why do you persecute me!' (Acts 9:4). When the foot was trod on—the head cried out! The saints are God's royal diadem (Isaiah 62:3). Will a king endure to have his robes spat upon, or his crown-royal thrown in the dust! 'He reproved kings for their sakes!' (Psalm 105:14).

What monuments of God's vengeance were Nero, Diocletian, Gardiner, and the rest of that persecuting tribe! 'Shall not God avenge his own elect! I tell you—he will avenge them speedily!' (Luke 18:7-8). Persecutors stand in the place where all God's arrows fly! 'He ordains his arrows against the persecutors' (Psalm 7:13). That is a killing Scripture: 'The Lord will send a plague on all the nations that fought against Jerusalem. Their people will become like walking corpses, their flesh rotting away. Their eyes will shrivel in their sockets, and their tongues will decay in their mouths!' (Zech. 14:12).

Second use: Consolation.

Here is comfort to the people of God, in case of the world's disesteem of them—God values them as jewels! And his judgment is according to truth (Rom. 2:2). The wicked have low thoughts of the righteous. They beat down the price of these jewels as far as they can. They think them but refuse. They disdain them, and load them with slanders and invectives. The prophet Elijah was looked upon by Ahab as the 'troubler of Israel' (1 Kings 18:17), and Luther was called a 'trumpet of rebellion'. Paul was judged 'a pestilent fellow' (Acts 24:5). The wicked think that of all things in the world, the saints may be best exterminated: 'We have become the scum of the earth, the refuse of the world' (1 Cor. 4:13).

But this is a great consolation to believers that, low as is the esteem the reprobate world has of them—yet God has high thoughts of them; he numbers them among his jewels! They are compared for their preciousness, to gold and silver (Rev. 1:20). They are the coins and medals which bear God's own image! They are princes in all lands (Ps. 45:16). Christ engraves their names on his breast, as the names of the twelve tribes were engraved on precious stones upon Aaron's breastplate. God will give whole kingdoms to ransom his jewels (Isaiah 43:3). The wicked think the godly are not worthy to live in the world, 'Rid the earth of him! He's not fit to live!' (Acts 22:22) But God thinks the world is not worthy of them 'The world was not worthy of them.' (Heb. 11:38). Hence it is, that God takes away his jewels so fast, and places them in his heavenly treasury!

Third use: Exhortation.

1. To the people of God.

Are you one of God's jewels? I then beseech you to SHINE as jewels! Walk circumspectly and holily! 'That you may be blameless and pure, children of God who are faultless in a crooked and perverted generation, among whom you shine like stars in the world!' (Phil. 2:15). Such as are God's jewels, should let the world see, that they have worth in them. O Christians, let your lives be an imitation of the life of Christ! Such a jewel was Bradford, the martyr—so humble and innocent in his demeanor that, at his death, many of the Papists could not refrain from weeping!

Are you one of God's jewels? Do nothing that may eclipse or sully your luster! When professors are proud, envious or censorious; when they break their promises, or cheat their creditors—these do not look like saints! What will others say? These are the devil's dirt—not God's jewels. Oh, I beseech you who profess to be of a higher rank than others—honor that worthy name by which you are called; shine as earthly angels! 'You are a chosen race, a royal priesthood, a holy nation, a people for His possession—so that you may proclaim the praises of the One who called you out of darkness into His marvelous light!' (1 Pet. 2:9).

Alexander would have the Grecians known not only by their garments—but their virtues. God's people should he known by the sparkling of their graces! Shall there be no difference in behavior between the wicked and the godly—between a clod of earth and a diamond! Let it appear that you are heirs of heaven. You who are God's people, the Lord expects a holy life from you (Matt. 5:47). He looks that you should bring more glory to him—and by your exemplary piety--make proselytes to piety.

2. The godly should be thankful. God has taken you out of the rubbish of mankind—and made you his jewels! 'He raises up the poor out of the dust' (Psalm 113:7), that he may set him with princes. So God has raised you out of the dust of a natural estate, and ennobled you—that he may set you with angels, those princes above. Oh, admire God! Set the crown of your praises upon the head of free grace! A joyful, thankful frame of heart—is pleasing to God. If repentance is the joy of heaven, praise is the music of heaven! Bless God who has wrought such a change in you! From lumps of dirt and sin—he has made you into his jewels!

3. There is a time shortly coming when God will make up his jewels. 'In that day when I make up my jewels'.

Question 1: What is meant by God's making up his jewels?

Answer: There is a difference between God's making of jewels—and his making up of jewels. God's making of jewels is when he works grace in their hearts while on earth. What is God's making up of jewels? This implies two things.

Firstly, God's gathering his saints together. God's making up his jewels, implies his gathering his saints together. The godly in this life are like scattered diamonds, they are separated from one another, being dispersed all over the world. But there is a day coming when God will gather all his saints together, as one puts all his pearls together on a string. There must be such a collection or gathering together of God's scattered saints:

1. From the near relation they have to all the persons of the Trinity. God the Father has chosen these jewels and set them apart for himself (Psalm 4:3), and will he lose any of his elect? They

are related to Christ—he has bought these jewels with his blood, and will he lose his purchase? They are related to the Holy Spirit. He has sanctified them. When they were a lump of sin, he made them his jewels; and when he has bestowed cost on them, will he lose his cost? Will he not string these pearls, and put them in his celestial cabinet?

2. There must be a gathering together of God's scattered saints—from the prayer of Christ. It was Christ's prayer to his Father, that he would make up his jewels, that he would gather together his pearls, that they might be with him in heaven! 'That they may be with me—where I am!' (John 17:24). Christ will not be content—until all the elect jewels lie together in his bosom. He does not think himself complete—until all his saints are with him!

Use: Here is a sovereign comfort to the people of God in two cases.

1. In case of scattering. God's people are scattered up and down in the world; and, which is worse, these jewels lie among rubbish—they dwell among the wicked! 'Woe is me that I dwell in the tents of Kedar' (Psalm 120:5). Kedar was Ishmael's son. 'Woe is me', says David, 'that I live with an Ishmael-brood!' The wicked are still molesting the righteous. God's jewels lie scattered among the vile! But here is the comfort—that shortly God will gather his people from among the wicked—he will make up his jewels—and all his precious jewels shall lie with him in bliss!

2. It is comfort in case of dividing. God's people are now divided; their love for one another is very little. They often look suspiciously upon one another. These divisions are flaws in God's diamonds! Discord among Christians brings a reproach upon true religion, advances Satan's kingdom, and hinders the growth of grace! But this is comfort—God will shortly make up his jewels—he will so gather his saints together—that he will unite them together. They shall be all of one heart (Acts 2:46). What a happy time it will be—when the saints shall be as so many pearls upon one string—and shall accord together in a blessed unity!

Secondly, God's making up his jewels also implies his perfecting his saints. A thing is said to be made up—when it is perfected. You make up a garment, when you perfect it. You make up a watch, when you put all the wheels and pins in perfect order. So God's making up his jewels, signifies his perfecting them. The godly in this life are imperfect. They cast but a faint luster of holiness; they receive but 'the first fruits of the Spirit' (Rom. 8:23), that is, a small measure of grace. The first fruits under the law were but a handful, compared to the whole vintage.

The consideration of this may humble us. We are God's jewels—yet we are now imperfect. Our knowledge is chequered with ignorance (1 Cor 13:5). Our love to God is feeble. Behold here, flaws in the diamond. This may take down our topsail of pride—to consider how flawed and incomplete we are. But when God shall make up his jewels, and perfect his saints—it will be a glorious time! This brings me to the second question.

Question 2: What is that day—when God will make up his jewels?

Firstly, God makes up his jewels at the day of death. Then he makes the saints' graces, perfect. For this reason the departed saints are called 'just men made perfect' (Heb. 12:23). Sin so mixes with, and dwells within a Christian—that he cannot write a copy of holiness without blotting it. Grace, though it abates sin—yet it does not abolish corruption. But at death God makes up his jewels—he perfects the graces of his people. Will not that be a blessed time, never to have a vain thought again, never to be within the sight of a temptation, or the fear of a relapse?

This, I think, may make death desirable to the godly; then the Lord will complete the graces of His children! They shall be as holy as they desire to be, and as holy as God would have them to be! How will God's jewels sparkle--when they shall be without flaws! In that day of death when God makes up his jewels, the saints light will be clear, and their love will be perfect!

Their light will be clear. They shall be so divinely irradiated, that they shall know the 'deep things of God'. They shall in this sense be 'as the angels' (Matt. 22:30). Their faculty of thought shall be raised higher and made more capacious! Through the crystal glass of Christ's human nature, the saints shall have glorious transparent sights of God! They shall know as they are known (1 Cor. 13:12); a riddle too mysterious for us mortals, if not for angels, to expound!

In that day the saints love will be perfect. Love is the queen of the graces — it outlives all the other graces. In this life, our love to God is lukewarm and sometimes frozen. A believer weeps that he can love God no more. But at the day of death, when God makes up his jewels — then the saints' love shall be seraphic! The spark of love shall be blown up into a pure flame! The saints shall love God — as much as they desire! They shall love him superlatively and without defect — they shall be made up wholly of love. Oh, blessed day of death! When God shall make up his jewels, the saints graces shall shine forth in their meridian splendor!

Secondly, God makes up his jewels at the day of the Resurrection. Then he makes the saints bodies perfect. These, like sparkling diamonds, shall shine in glory! At the resurrection God is said to change the bodies of the saint, 'He will take these weak mortal bodies of ours and change them into glorious bodies like his own!' (Phil. 3:21). How will he change them? Not that they shall be other bodies than they were before. The substance of their bodies shall not be changed — but the qualities. As wool, when it is dyed into a purple color, is not altered in the substance — but in the quality, and is made more illustrious. Just so, God in making up his jewels, will cause a greater resplendency in the saints' bodies than before.

When God makes up the jewels of the saints' bodies at the resurrection, they shall be perfect in four ways:

1. In amiability or sweetness of beauty. Here the bodies of the righteous are often deformed. Leah has her weak eves, and Barzillai has his lameness; but at the resurrection the bodies of the saints shall be of unspotted loveliness. And no wonder, for they shall be made like Christ's glorious body (Phil. 3:21).

2. When God at the resurrection makes up the jewels of the saints' bodies, they shall have perfection of parts. Their bodies in this world may be maimed and disfigured; but in the day of the resurrection they shall have all the parts of their bodies restored (Acts 3:21). Such as have lost an eye, shall have their eye again; such as lack a leg or an arm, shall have their arm again.

3. When God makes up the jewels of the saints' bodies at the resurrection, they shall be swift and lively in their motion. Here on earth, the bodies of the saints move heavily — but then they shall be sprightly, and move rapidly from one place to another. Here the body is a weight; in heaven it shall be a wing!

4. When God makes up the jewels of the saints' bodies, they shall be immortal. The body once glorified, shall never be subject to death! 'For our perishable earthly bodies must be transformed into heavenly bodies that will never die!' (1 Cor. 15:53). Heaven is a healthy climate; no death-bell goes there. This mortal body shall put on immortality.

Let us labor to be in the number of God's jewels, that when the Lord shall make up his jewels, he may perfect our souls and bodies in glory

Question: How shall we know that we are in the number of God's jewels?

Answer: Have we holiness? 'But we are washed — but we are sanctified' (1 Cor. 6:11). We are not God's jewels by creation — but regeneration. If holiness sparkles in us — it is a sign we are God's jewels; and then when God comes to make up his jewels, he will put glory upon our souls and bodies forever!

C. God Rewards His People by Sparing Them

The third part of the saints reward is God's sparing them: 'I will spare them, just as in compassion a man spares his son who serves him.' The Hebrew word to spare signifies to use clemency. In this phrase, there is less said – and more intended. 'I will spare them', that is, 'I will deal with them as a father does with his son. The kind of tenderness that a father shows to his child, the same will I show to those that fear me.'

Doctrine: God will deal with those who fear him – as a compassionate father does with his dutiful son.

Two things are in this proposition:

1. That God is a Father. He is a father by creation. He has given us our being: 'Have not we all one father? Has not one God created us?' (Mal. 2:20). God is also a father by election: he has chosen out a certain number, to be his children (Eph. 1:4). And God is a father by special grace: he stamps his impress of holiness upon men (Col. 3:10). All God's children resemble him – though some are more like him than others.

2. That God will deal with those that fear him, as a compassionate father does with his dutiful son.

A. God will accept them, as a father does his son. If the child only lisps and can hardly speak plainly, the father takes all in good part. So God, as a father, will accept what his children do in sincerity: 'There will I require your offerings ... I will accept you with your sweet savor' (Ezek. 20:40-41).

B. To such as fear God, he will be full of pity to them, as a tender father is to his son. There are in God, affections of compassion and affections of delight.

Affections of compassion. A father feels for his child. God has great pity and tenderness towards his children. (Isaiah 63:15). The compassion of parents is steel and marble compared with God's – 'the tender mercy of our God' (Luke 1:78). In the Greek it is 'the affections of mercy'. These affections make God sympathize with his children in misery. He is touched in their wounds: 'As a father pities his children so the Lord pities those who fear him' (Psalm 103:13).

In God are also affections of delight. How dearly did Jacob love Benjamin! His life was bound up in him (Gen. 44:30). All the affections of parents come from God. They are but a drop of his ocean, a spark of his flame. God's love is a love that 'passes knowledge!' (Eph. 3:19). The saints cannot love their own souls, so entirely as God loves them. In particular,

a. God loves the persons of his children; they are the apple of his eye (Zech. 2:8). He engraves them upon the palms of his hands (Isaiah 49:16). This alludes to those who carry about them, engraved on the stone of their ring, the picture of some dear friend whom they entirely love.

b. God loves the places his children were born in, the better for their sakes: 'God loves the gates of Zion' (Psalm 87:2); 'This and that man was born in her' (verse 5); that is, 'this and that believer'. God loves the very ground his children walk upon. Why was Judea, the ancient seat of Israel, called 'a delightsome land' (Mal. 3:12)? Not so much delightful for the fruit growing in it – as for the saints living in it.

c. God so loves his children, that he charges the great ones of the world upon pain of death, not to hurt them. They are sacred to him. 'He allowed no one to oppress them; for their sake he rebuked kings: Do not touch my anointed ones; do my prophets no harm' (Psalm 105:14-15). By 'anointed' are meant such as have the anointing of the Spirit (1 John 2:20).

d. God delights in his children's company, he loves to see their faces, 'Let Me see your face, let Me hear your voice; for your voice is sweet, and your face is lovely.' (Cant. 2:14) If but two or three of God's children meet and pray together, God will he sure to make one of the company: 'There am I in the midst of them!' (Matt. 18:20).

e. God so loves his children that his eye is never off them: 'The eye of the Lord is upon those who fear him' (Psalm 33:18).

Question: But is this such a privilege—to have God's eye upon his children? God's eye is upon the wicked too.

Answer: it is one kind of eye that the Judge casts upon the malefactor; and another that the Prince casts upon his favorite. God's eye upon the wicked is an eye of vengeance—but his eye upon his children is an eye of benediction.

f. God sets a continual guard about his children, to preserve them from danger. He hides them in his pavilion (Psalm 27:5). He covers them with the golden feathers of his protection (Psalm 91:4). No prince goes so well guarded, as God's child, for he has a guard of angels about him. The angels are a numerous guard: 'The mountain was full of horses and chariots of fire' (2 Kings 6:17). Those horses and chariots of fire were the angels of God, gathered in the manner of a huge army to defend the prophet Elijah.

g. God clothes his children in rich garments: 'Her clothing is of wrought gold' (Psalm 45:13). Jacob loved his son Joseph and gave him a finer coat to wear than the rest of his brethren: 'He made him a coat of many colors' (Gen. 37:3). God loves his children and gives them a finer coat, more finely woven, a coat of diverse colors. It is partly made of Christ's righteousness, and partly of inherent holiness (Rev. 19:8).

h. Such is God's love that he thinks nothing too good for his children! He enriches them with the upper and lower springs; he gives them the finest of the wheat, and honey out of the rock; he makes them a feast of fat things (Isaiah 25:6). He gives them the body and blood of his Son, and delights to see his children spreading themselves as olive plants round about his table (Psalm 128:3).

3. God will receive the petitions of those who fear him—as a tender father receives his son's petitions. They may come boldly to the throne of grace (Heb. 4:16). If they come for pardon of sin, or strength against temptation, God will not deny them. Three things may cause boldness in prayer—the saints have a Father to pray to, the Spirit to help them to pray, and Jesus Christ as their Advocate to present their prayers.

4. On such as are fearers of God, God will bestow an inheritance, as a father does upon his son. This inheritance is no less than a kingdom! (Luke 12:32). In it are gates of pearl, rivers of pleasure; and (which is to be noted as a difference between God's settling an inheritance on his children, and an earthly father's settling an inheritance) a son cannot enjoy the inheritance until his father is dead; but every adopted child of God may at once enjoy both the inheritance and the father, because God is both father and inheritance! (Gen. 15).

5. With such as are fearers of God, God will pass by many infirmities. That is what is meant by this expression in the text, 'I will spare them as a man spares his own son.' What a wonder is this—that God did not spare the angels (2 Pct. 2:4)! No, he did not spare his natural Son (Rom. 8:32). Yet he will spare his adopted sons! 'I will spare, them, I will not use extremity as I might—but pass by many aberrations.'

Caution: It is not that the sins of God's children are hidden from him—but such is his paternal clemency that he is pleased to bear with many frailties in his children. He spares them as a father spares his son. How often do God's people grieve his Spirit by the neglect of spiritual watchfulness, or the loss of their first love; but God spares them! Israel provoked God with their murmurings—but he used fatherly indulgence towards them (Psalm 78:38; Neh. 9:17).

First Use: Information.

1. From this word, 'I will spare them as a man spares his son', take notice that even the best need sparing. 'If you, Lord, should mark iniquities—who shall stand?' (Psalm 130:3). The Papists speak of merits—but how can we merit—when our best services are so defective that we need sparing! How can these two stand together, our meriting and God's sparing? What will become of us without sparing mercy? We need to pray as Nehemiah, 'Remember me, O my God, concerning this also—and spare me according to the greatness of your mercy!' (Neh. 13:22). Let us fly to this asylum, 'Lord, spare us as a father spares his son!'

2. See God's different dealing with the godly and the wicked. The Lord will not spare the wicked: 'I will not pity, nor spare, nor have mercy—but destroy them!' (Jer. 13:14). It is sad when the prisoner begs of the judge to spare him—but the judge will show him no favor. God's cup of wrath is unmixed! (Rev. 14:10). Yet it is said to be mixed. The cup of wrath God gives the wicked is mixed with all sorts of punishments. But in this sense it is unmixed—it is without the least drop of mercy in it! (Psalm 78:45-51). God for a while reprieves men—but forbearance is not forgiveness. Though God spares his children—yet obdurate sinners shall feel the weight of his wrath!

3. If the Lord spares his people as a father does his son—then they should serve him as a son does his father.

1. They should serve him willingly. 'Serve Him with a whole heart and a willing mind, for the Lord searches every heart and understands the intention of every thought!' (1 Chron. 28:9). Cain's sacrifice was rejected, because he brought it grudgingly and against his will. It was rather the paying of a tax than a free-will offering. The best obedience is that which is voluntary, as that is the best honey which drops from the honeycomb. God sometimes accepts of willingness without the work (1 Kings 8:18)—but never of the work without willingness.

2. They should serve God universally. True obedience is universal; it observes one command as well as another; it fulfills difficult duties and dangerous duties. As the needle points the way that the magnet draws, so a gracious heart inclines to those things which the Word teaches (Luke 1:6). It is the note of a hypocrite to be partial in obedience; some sin he will indulge (2 Kings 5:18), some duty he will dispense with; his obedience is lame on one foot.

3. They should serve God swiftly. Beware of a dull temper of soul; the loveliness of obedience is in the liveliness of it. We read of two women, 'The wind was in their wings' (Zech. 5:9). Wings are swift—but wind in the wings denotes great swiftness. Such swiftness should be in our obedience to God. If God spares us as a father does his son, we should serve him as a son does his father.

Second Use: Exhortation.

If God spares us as a father does his son—let us imitate God. It is natural for children to imitate their parents; what the father does, the child is apt to learn the same.

Let us imitate God in this one thing—As God spares us, and passes by many failures—so let us be sparing in our censures of others; let us look upon the weaknesses and indiscretions of our brethren with a more tender compassionate eye.

Indeed, in cases of scandal we ought not to bear with others—but sharply reprove them. But if through inadvertence or passion they act wrongly—let us pity and pray for them. How much

God bears with us! He spares us, and shall not we be sparing to others? Perhaps they have been wronged, and false things may be said about them. Athanasius was falsely accused by the Arians of adultery; Basil was falsely accused of heresy. It is usual for the world to misrepresent the people of God; therefore let us be sparing in our censures. God spares us--and shall not we be sparing towards others?

Third use: Comfort.

Here is comfort to the children of God in case of failings. The Lord will not be severe to mark what they have done amiss — but will spare them. He passes by many infirmities: 'He will rest in his love' (2eph. 3:17); in the original it is, 'He will be silent in his love'. As if the prophet had said, though the church had her failings — yet God's love was such, that it would not allow him to mention them. God turns a blind eye to our many oversights: 'My eye spared them from destruction' (Ezek. 20:17).

I do not speak of presumptuous sins — but of failings such as vain thoughts, deadness in duty, sudden surprises by temptation. These being mourned for, God for Christ's sake will spare us as a father does his son.

This is one of the richest comforts in the Book of God. Who is he who lives — and sins not? How defective we are in our best duties! How full our lives are either of blanks or of blots! Were it not for God's sparing mercy — we would all go to hell. But this text is a choice cordial; if our hearts are sincere, God will spare us as a father does his son. 'I will not execute the fierceness of my anger' (Hos. 11:9).

I know not a greater rock of support, for a fainting Christian than this — God will abate the severity of the law. Though we come short in our duty, he will not fail of his mercy — but will spare us as a father spares his son.

The Difference Between Righteous and the Wicked

'Then you will again see the difference between the righteous and the wicked, between those who serve God and those who do not.' (Mal. 3:18).

Here follows the close of the chapter, which I shall little more than paraphrase. These words are spoken to the wicked, as learned expositors assert; for though the godly shall at last discern what a difference God makes between them and the wicked, how merciful he is to the one, and how severe to the other — yet this text is chiefly spoken to the wicked: 'You have said, It is vain to serve God!' (verse 14) 'From now on we will say, 'Blessed are the arrogant.' For those who do evil get rich, and those who dare God to punish them go free of harm.' (verse 15). Well, says God, though now you call the proud happy and the godly foolish — yet when I have made up my jewels — then you wicked ones shall see clearly what a difference I make between the righteous, and the wicked; between him who serves God — and him who does not serve him. Then, when it is too late, when the day of grace is past, and the drawbridge of mercy is pulled up — then shall you discern a difference between the holy and the profane!

Doctrine 1: The wicked at present have their eyes shut! 'To this day the Lord has not given you minds that understand, nor eyes that see, nor ears that hear!' (Deut. 29:4). Natural men have the sword upon their right eye, 'The sword will cut his arm and pierce his right eye! His arm will become useless, and his right eye completely blind!' (Zech. 11:17). They see no difference between the pious and the impious; they imagine that it fares as well with the wicked as with the righteous; nay, it seems to fare better with the wicked. The wicked flourish: 'These are the ungodly, who prosper in the world; they increase in riches' (Psalm 73: 12). Whereas those who pray and fast, are oppressed. The wicked bless themselves, and think they are now in a better condition than the righteous; the matter is not to be wondered at, for 'the god of this world has blinded the minds of sinners' (2 Cor. 4:4). But at last their eyes shall he opened; and that brings me to the second doctrine.

Doctrine 2: There is a time shortly coming when impious, grossly wicked sinners, shall SEE an obvious difference between the godly and the nicked. The tables will then be turned! 'Then you will again see the difference between the righteous and the wicked, between those who serve God and those who do not.'

Question: When is the time when the eyes of sinners shall he opened, and they shall see a difference between the righteous and the wicked?

Answer: There are two times when sinners shall see a manifest difference between the righteous and the wicked.

Firstly, at the Day of Judgment. That will be a day of manifest difference. Things will then appear in their proper colors; the difference will easily be seen between the godly and the wicked; the one being absolved—the other condemned!

Secondly, at the hour of separation, when God shall eternally separate the reprobate from the elect, as a winnowing fan separates the chaff from the wheat—and there shall be a visible discerning between the righteous and wicked. 'All the nations will be gathered in his presence, and he will separate them as a shepherd separates the sheep from the goats. He will place the sheep at his right hand and the goats at his left. And they will go away into eternal punishment, but the righteous will go into eternal life!' (Matt. 25:32-33, 46). Jesus Christ will take his saints up with him into glory—and will cast the wicked down to hell. He will make up the godly as jewels, and tie up the wicked in bundles to be burned! 'Bind them in bundles to burn them' (Matt. 13:30). Now sinners shall be convinced with a vengeance, that the state of the righteous and the wicked is different! They shall see the righteous advanced to a heavenly kingdom, and themselves cast into a fiery prison!

Oh, the dreadfulness of that place of torment! Could men lay their ears to the infernal lake, and but for one hour hear the groans and shrieks of the damned—they would tell us that they now see what before they would not believe—the infinite difference between the righteous and the wicked! In hell is torment upon torment, 'blackness of darkness' (Jude 13), 'chains of darkness' (2 Pet. 2:4). These chains are God's decree ordaining, and his power binding men under wrath! And that which accentuates and puts a sting into the torments of the wicked—is that they shall be always scorching in the fire of God's wrath! 'The smoke of their torment ascends up forever and ever' (Rev. 14:11).

Christ said of his suffering on the cross, 'It is finished!' But sinners shall never say of their sufferings in hell—that they are finished. No! if the damned had lain in hell as many thousand years as there are drops in the sea—eternity has yet to begin!

First use: Information.

This may inform all wicked men that, no matter how blind they are now—yet at last the veil shall be taken from their eyes! They now count themselves the only happy men, and look upon the people of God with derision. They load them with invectives and curse them with their slanders. Well, the time is not far off—when the wicked shall clearly discern who belong to Christ—and who belong to the devil. As Moses said to Korah and his company, 'Tomorrow the Lord will show who are his' (Num. 16:5), so at the Day of Judgment the Lord will show who are his—and who are not. Nay, sooner than that: at the day of death the wicked shall see how it will be with them for eternity!

Oh, that the eyes of sinners may be speedily opened — that they may see the difference of things, the beauty which is in holiness, and the astonishing madness that is in sin!

Second use: Consolation to the righteous.

Though at present they are slighted and have the odium of the world cast upon them — yet shortly God will make a visible difference between them and the wicked. As it was with Pharaoh's two officers, the butler and the baker; at first there seemed to be no difference between them — but in a short while there was difference made. The chief butler was advanced to honor — but the chief baker was executed (Gen. 40:21-22). So though now God's people are low and despised, and the wicked treat them with boastful insolence — yet when the critical day comes, there shall be a final separation made between the righteous and the wicked. The one shall be dignified — the other damned! 'And they will go away into eternal punishment, but the righteous will go into eternal life!' (Matt. 25:46).

Be encouraged therefore, saints of God — to persist in a course of holiness. Though now you seem to be lowermost — yet in the resurrection you shall be uppermost: 'The upright shall have dominion over them in the morning' (Psalm 49: 14). That is, they shall have dominion over the wicked in the morning of the resurrection. They shall then laugh the wicked to scorn (Psalm 52:6). 'Then you will see the difference between the righteous and the wicked, between those who serve God and those who do not.' Malachi 3:18

Finis

Made in United States
North Haven, CT
02 June 2024

53203183R00340